Arizona & New Mexico

W9-ARW-151

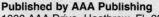

Published by AAA Publishing
1000 AAA Drive, Heathrow, FL 32746-5063
Copyright AAA 2011, All rights reserved

The publisher has made every effort to provide accurate, up-to-date information but accepts no responsibility for loss or injury sustained by any person using this book. TourBook® guides are published for the exclusive use of AAA members. Not for sale.

Advertising Rate and Circulation Information: (407) 444-8280

Printed in the USA by Quad/Graphics

This book is printed on paper certified by third-party standards for sustainably managed forestry and production.

Printed on recyclable paper.
Please recycle whenever possible.

Stock #4602

CONTENTS

Attractions, hotels, restaurants and other travel experience information are all grouped under the alphabetical listing of the city in which those experiences are physically located—or the nearest recognized city.

Arizona

New Mexico

Featured Information

AAA SHOWERS YOU WITH SAVINGS

Getting caught in a downpour isn't so bad when it's prices that are dropping all around you. AAA members who take advantage of Show Your Card & Save® member discounts know and love the feeling.

Your card is all you need. Go to **AAA.com/discounts** to search for deals. Remember to check **AAA.com/specialoffers** for even greater savings throughout the year.

AAA.com/discounts

AAA Travel Information
In Print, Online and On The Go

**Get AAA's reliable travel information
just the way you want it.**

- **TourBook® Guides** - Printed guidebooks available at AAA/CAA offices
- **Travel Guides** - Online destination content available at AAA.com and CAA.ca
- **eTourBook℠ Guides** - eReader travel guides available at AAA.com/ebooks

Create and save trips online with TripTik® Travel Planner and
use them on the go with the TripTik Mobile app.

- **TripTik Travel Planner** - Online trip planning at AAA.com and CAA.ca
- **TripTik Mobile** - Travel app details at AAA.com/mobile

Products and services are available through participating AAA and CAA clubs. Selections vary by location.
Mobile Services: Not all features may be available on all devices or in all areas.

Our New Look!

We've taken the travel series members use more than any other trip planning resource and made it even better, from the inside out.

Discover a colorful twist on your favorite features plus new additions that make the 2012 series our richest, most robust TourBook® edition yet.

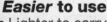

Easier to use
- Lighter to carry
- Improved readability
- Reorganized A to Z by city

Easier to navigate
- Mini tables of contents
- Page cross-referencing
- Quick-reference indexes

Easier to travel
- Navigable Atlas maps
- More destination photos
- Recommendations from AAA travel experts

Turn inside. It's a better guide — just for members.

A to Z City Listings

Cities and places are listed alphabetically within each state or province. Attractions, hotels and restaurants are listed once — under the city in which they are physically located.

Cities that are considered part of a larger destination city or area have an expanded city header. The header identifies the larger region and cross-references pages that contain shared trip planning resources:

- Destination map – outline map of the cities that comprise a destination city or area
- Attraction spotting map – regional street map marked with attraction locations
- Hotel/restaurant spotting map and index – regional street map numbered with hotel and restaurant locations identified in an accompanying index

Cities that are not considered part of a larger destination city or area but have a significant number of listings may have these resources within the individual city section:

- Attraction spotting map
- Hotel/restaurant spotting map and index

About Listed Establishments

AAA/CAA Approved attractions, hotels and restaurants are listed on the basis of merit alone after careful evaluation and approval by full-time, professionally trained AAA/CAA inspectors. An establishment's decision to advertise in the TourBook guide has no bearing on its evaluation or rating; nor does inclusion of advertising imply AAA endorsement of products and services.

Information in this guide was believed accurate at the time of publication. However, since changes inevitably occur between annual editions, please contact your AAA travel professional or visit AAA.com to confirm prices and schedules.

Location Abbreviations

Directions are from the center of town unless otherwise specified, using these highway abbreviations:

Bus. Rte.=business route
CR=county road
FM=farm to market

FR=forest road
Hwy.=Canadian highway
I=interstate highway
LR=legislative route
R.R.=rural route
SR/PR=state or provincial route
US=federal highway

Atlas Section

The Atlas Section provides navigable road maps from the AAA Road Atlas series. The overview map displays the entire coverage area. Corresponding, numbered detail maps offer a closer view for route planning and navigation.

Mobile Tags

Look for codes like this Microsoft Tag in the ads and restaurant listings to access special online offers, menus, videos and more.

To use Microsoft Tags:
- Download the free Tag Reader app to your smartphone at http://gettag.mobi.
- Start scanning Tags.
- Link to featured content.

Some advertisers use codes other than Microsoft Tags. In those cases, please note any accompanying text that indicates where to download the required reader.

Attraction Listings

> **ATTRACTION NAME,** 3 mi. n. off SR 20A (Main Ave.), consists of 250 acres with Olmsted-designed gardens, a 205-foot marble and coquina bell tower and a Mediterranean-style mansion. One of the state's oldest attractions, the tower and gardens were dedicated to the American people in 1929 by President Calvin Coolidge on behalf of their founder, a Dutch immigrant.
>
> Other features include daily concerts from the 60-bell carillon, a nature observatory and Nature Preserve Trail. The visitor center presents art exhibits, an orientation film and exhibits about the family legacy, the carillon and endangered plants and animals found on the property.
>
> **Hours:** Gardens daily 8-6. Last admission 1 hour before closing. Visitor center daily 9-5. Estate tours are given at noon and 2. Carillon concerts are given at 1 and 3. Phone ahead to confirm schedule. **Cost:** $10; $3 (ages 5-12). Gardens and estate $16; $8 (ages 5-12). **Phone:** (555) 555-5555.

AAA/CAA inspectors may designate an attraction of exceptional interest and quality as a GEM — a *Great Experience for Members*. See GEM Attraction Index (listed on CONTENTS page) for complete list of locations.

Adventure Travel

Activities such as air tours, hiking, skiing and white-water rafting are listed to provide member information and do not imply AAA/CAA endorsement. For your safety, be aware of inherent risks and adhere to all safety instructions.

Cost

Prices are quoted without sales tax in the local currency (U.S. or Canadian dollars). Children under the lowest age specified are admitted free when accompanied by an adult. Most establishments accept credit cards, but a small number require cash, so please call ahead to verify.

Icons

SAVE	Show Your Card & Save member discount
🅐	Camping facilities
🍴	Food on premises
🏊	Recreational activities
🐾	Pets on leash allowed
🅿	Picnicking allowed

District of Columbia only:

🚇	Metro station within 1 mile

Icon is followed by station name and AAA/CAA designated station number

Information-Only Attraction Listings

Bulleted listings, which include the following categories, are listed for informational purposes as a service to members:

- **Gambling establishments** (even if located in a AAA/CAA Approved hotel)
- **Participatory recreational activities** (those requiring physical exertion or special skills)
- **Wineries** that offer tours and tastings

Hotel and Restaurant Listings

1 Diamond Rating – AAA/CAA Approved hotels and restaurants are assigned a rating of one to five Diamonds. Red Diamonds distinguish establishments that participate in the AAA/CAA logo licensing program. For details, see p. 11 or AAA.com/Diamonds.

fyi indicates hotels and restaurants that are not AAA/CAA Approved and Diamond Rated but are listed to provide additional choices for members:

- **Hotels** may be unrated if they are: too new to rate, under construction, under major renovation, not evaluated, do not meet all AAA requirements. Hotels that do not meet all AAA requirements may be included if they offer member value or are the only option; details are noted in the listing.
- **Restaurants** may be unrated if they have not yet been evaluated by AAA.

2 Classification or Cuisine Type – noted immediately below the Diamond Rating

- **Hotel Classifications** indicate the style of operation, overall concept and service level. Subclassifications may also be added. (See p. 12 list.)
- **Restaurant Cuisine Types** identify the food concept from more than 100 categories. If applicable, a classification may also be added. (See p. 13 list.)

3 Dollar Amounts – Quoted without sales tax in the local currency (U.S. or Canadian dollars), rounded up to the nearest dollar. Most establishments accept credit cards, but a small number require cash, so please call ahead to verify.

- **Hotel Rates** indicate the publicly available two-person rate or rate range for a standard room, applicable all year unless effective dates are indicated.
- **Restaurant Prices** represent the minimum and maximum entree cost per person. Exceptions may include one-of-a-kind or special market priced items.

4 Spotting Symbol – Ovals containing numbers correspond with numbered location markings on hotel and restaurant spotting maps.

5 Parking – Unless otherwise noted, parking is free, on-site self parking.

6 Hotel Value Nationwide – Blue boxes highlight everyday member benefits available at all AAA/CAA Approved locations across a hotel chain. (See Just For Members section for details.)

7 Hotel Unit Limited Availability – Unit types, amenities and room features preceded by "some" are available on a limited basis, potentially as few as one.

8 Hotel Terms – Cancellation and minimum stay policies are listed. Unless otherwise noted, most properties offer a full deposit refund with cancellations received at least 48 hours before standard check-in. Properties that require advance payment may not refund the difference for early departures.

9 Hotel Check-in/Check-out – Unless otherwise noted, check-in is after 3 p.m. and check-out is before 10 a.m.

10 Restaurant Dress Code – Unless otherwise noted, dress is casual or dressy casual.

11 Restaurant Menu – Where indicated, menus may be viewed in a secure online environment at AAA.com or, if a mobile tag is provided, via the restaurant's website.

12 Hotel Icons – May be preceded by CALL, FEE and/or SOME UNITS.

Member Information:

SAVE Rate guarantee: discounted standard room rate or lowest public rate available at time of booking for dates of stay.

ECO Eco-certified by government or private organization. Visit AAA.com/eco for details.

☒ Smoke-free premises

Services:

🛜 Wireless Internet service on premises

✈ Airport transportation

🐾 Pets allowed (call property for restrictions and fees)

🍴 Restaurant on premises

🍴→ Restaurant off premises (walking distance)

🍽 Room service for 2 or more meals

HOTEL LISTING

HOTEL NAME

Phone: (555)555-5555   **50**

LOGO   **AAA Benefit:** Members save a minimum 5% off the best available rate.

Hotel
$109-$199

Address: 300 Main St 55555 **Location:** I-275 exit 31 southbound; exit 30 northbound. 1.6 mi w on SR 688 (Oak Rd). **Facility:** 149 units, some efficiencies. 3 stories, interior corridors. **Parking:** on-site (fee). **Terms:** check-in 4 pm, cancellation fee imposed. **Amenities:** video games. **Pool(s):** heated outdoor. **Activities:** whirlpool, exercise room. **Guest Services:** valet and coin laundry. **Free Special Amenities: newspaper and expanded continental breakfast.**

RESTAURANT LISTING

RESTAURANT NAME
Menu on AAA.com

Phone: 555/555-5555

Continental
$15-$35

AAA Inspector Notes: A romantic aura punctuates the modern and casual dining room, which is accented with floral arrangements and dramatic, freshly cut branches. The seasonal menu centers on Tuscan-American cuisine. The pastry chef's decadent creations are popular. Semi-formal attire. **Bar:** full bar. **Address:** 26 N Main St 55555 **Location:** SR A1A southbound, 2.7 mi so of jct SR 520.

Ⓛ Ⓓ

Ⓨ Full bar

🜨 Child care

BIZ Business services

&M Accessible features (Call property for available services and amenities.)

Activities:

🎲 Full-service casino

🏊 Pool

Health club on premises

Health club off premises

In-Room Amenities:

Pay movies

Refrigerator

Microwave

Coffee maker

No air conditioning

No TV

No cable TV

No telephones

13 Restaurant Icons

SAVE Show Your Card & Save member discount

No air conditioning

&M Accessible features (Call property for available services and amenities.)

Designated smoking section

B Breakfast

Ⓛ Lunch

Ⓓ Dinner

24 Open 24 hours

LATE Open after 11 p.m.

Maps. Directions. More.

TripTik® Travel Planner & TripTik Mobile App

Use AAA's complete online and on-the-go travel planning tools for your next trip.

- Find AAA Approved places to stay and dine
- Locate AAA recommended sights and activities
- Find nearby gas stations and get updated fuel prices
- Book hotels at low AAA member rates

Plan your trips online with TripTik Travel Planner. Use them on the go with the TripTik Mobile app.

Get TripTik Travel Planner at AAA.com/travel
Get TripTik Mobile app details at AAA.com/mobile

Just For Members

Understanding the Diamond Ratings

Hotel and restaurant evaluations are unscheduled to ensure our professionally trained inspectors encounter the same experience members do.

- When an establishment is Diamond Rated, it means members can expect a good fit with their needs. The inspector assigns a rating that indicates the type of experience to expect.
- While establishments at high levels must offer increasingly complex personalized services, establishments at every level are subject to the same basic requirements for cleanliness, comfort and hospitality. Learn more at AAA.com/Diamonds.

Hotels

Budget-oriented, offering basic comfort and hospitality.

Affordable, with modestly enhanced facilities, decor and amenities.

Distinguished, multi-faceted with enhanced physical attributes, amenities and guest comforts.

Refined, stylish with upscale physical attributes, extensive amenities and high degree of hospitality, service and attention to detail.

Ultimate luxury, sophistication and comfort with extraordinary physical attributes, meticulous personalized service, extensive amenities and impeccable standards of excellence.

Restaurants

Simple, familiar specialty food at an economical price. Often self-service, basic surroundings.

Familiar, family-oriented experience. Home-style foods and family favorites, often cooked to order, modestly enhanced and reasonably priced. Relaxed service, casual surroundings.

Fine dining, often adult-oriented. Latest cooking trends and/or traditional cuisine, expanded beverage offerings. Professional service staff and comfortable, well-coordinated ambience.

Distinctive fine-dining, typically expensive. Highly creative chefs, imaginative presentations and fresh, top-quality ingredients. Proficient service staff, upscale surroundings. Wine steward may offer menu-specific knowledge.

Luxurious and consistently world-class. Highly acclaimed chefs, artistic and imaginative menu selections using the finest ingredients. Maitre d' and unobtrusive, expert service staff.

What's the difference?

- Red Diamonds mark establishments that participate in the AAA/CAA logo licensing program for increased visibility to members.

- Black Diamonds identify all other AAA/CAA Approved and Diamond Rated establishments.

Hotel Classifications

Quality and comfort are usually consistent across each Diamond Rating level, but decor, facilities and service levels vary by classification.

1884 Paxton House Inn
Thomasville, GA

Bed & Breakfast – Typically small-scale, emphasizing personal touches. Individually decorated units may not include televisions, telephones or private bathrooms. Usually a common room and continental or full, hot breakfast.

Greenbrier Valley Resorts at Cobbly Nob, Gatlinburg, TN

Cabin – Vacation-oriented, typically small-scale, free-standing units with simple construction and basic decor. Often in wooded, rural or waterfront location. Cleaning supplies, utensils and bath linens provided. Check-in may be off site.

Camelot by the Sea
Myrtle Beach, SC

Condominium – Vacation-oriented, commonly for extended stays. Routinely rented through a management company. Generally one or more bedrooms, living room, full kitchen and eating area. Studio units combine sleeping and living areas. Cleaning supplies, utensils and linens provided. Check-in may be off site.

The Dunes on the Waterfront
Ogunquit, ME

Cottage – Vacation-oriented, typically small-scale, freestanding units with homey design and decor. Often in wooded, rural or waterfront location. Cleaning supplies, utensils and linens provided. Check-in may be off site.

The Lodge at Moosehead Lake, Greenville, ME

Country Inn – Similar to bed and breakfasts but larger scale with spacious public areas and dining facility that serves, at a minimum, breakfast and dinner.

The Grand America Hotel
Salt Lake City, UT

Hotel – Commonly multistory with interior room entrances. Unit styles vary. Public areas determined by overall theme, location and service level, but may include restaurant, shops, fitness center, spa, business center and meeting rooms.

Best Western Plus Sea Island Inn, Beaufort, SC

Motel – Commonly one- or two-story with exterior room entrances and drive-up parking. Typically one bedroom with bathroom. Limited public areas and facilities.

Lost Valley Ranch
Deckers, CO

Ranch – Typically a working ranch with rustic, Western theme, equestrian activities and various unit styles.

Indian Creek-Alexander Holiday Homes
Kissimmee, FL

Vacation Rental House – Commonly for extended stays. Typically large scale, freestanding and of varying design. Routinely rented through a management company. Often two or more bedrooms, living room, full kitchen, dining room and multiple bathrooms. Cleaning supplies, utensils and linens supplied. Check-in may be off site.

Hotel Subclassifications

These additional descriptives may be added to the classification for more information:

- **Boutique** – Often thematic and informal, highly personalized experience. May have fashionable, luxurious or quirky style.
- **Casino** – (Identified by listing icon) Extensive gambling facilities such as blackjack, craps, keno and slot machines.
- **Classic** – Landmark property, older than 50 years, renowned style and ambience.
- **Contemporary** – Design and theme reflective of current mainstream tastes and style.
- **Extended Stay** – Predominantly long-term units with full-service kitchens.
- **Historic** – Typically 75 years or older with historic architecture, design, furnishings, public record or acclaim and at least one of the following: maintains integrity of the historical nature, listed on the National Register of Historic Places, designated a National Historic Landmark or located in a National Register Historic District.
- **Resort** – Recreation-oriented, geared to a specific destination experience. Typically offer travel packages, meal plans, themed entertainment and social and recreational programs. Extensive recreational facilities may include spa treatments, golf, tennis,

skiing, fishing or water sports. Larger resorts may offer a variety of unit types.
- **Retro** – Contemporary design and theme that reinterpret styles of a bygone era.
- **Vacation Rental** – Typically a house, condo, cottage or cabin offering space, value and conveniences such as full kitchens and washers/dryers. Located in a resort or popular destination area near major points of interest. May require reservations and off-site check-in. Limited housekeeping services.
- **Vintage** – Design and theme reflective of a bygone era.

Restaurant Classifications

If applicable, in addition to the cuisine type noted under the Diamond Rating, restaurant listings may also include one or both classifications:

- **Classic** – Renowned and landmark operation in business for 25 plus years; unique style and ambience.
- **Historic** – Meets one of the following: Listed on National Register of Historic Places, designated a National Historic Landmark or located in a National Register Historic District.

Service Animals

Under the Americans with Disabilities Act (ADA), U.S. businesses that serve the public must allow people with disabilities to bring their service animals into all areas of the facility where customers are normally allowed to go.

Businesses may ask if an animal is a service animal and what tasks the animal has been trained to perform. Businesses may not ask about the person's disability, require special identification for the animal or request removal of the animal from the premises except in limited cases that require alternate assistance. Businesses may not charge extra fees for service animals, including standard pet fees, but may charge for damage caused by service animals if guests are normally charged for damage they cause.

Call the U.S. Department of Justice ADA Information Line: (800) 514-0301 or TTY (800) 514-0383, or visit ada.gov. Regulations may differ in Canada.

AAA/CAA Approved Hotels

For members, AAA/CAA Approved means quality assured.

- Only properties that meet basic requirements for cleanliness, comfort and hospitality pass inspection.
- Approved hotels receive a Diamond Rating that tells members the type of experience to expect.

Guest Safety

Inspectors view a sampling of rooms during evaluations and, therefore, AAA/CAA cannot guarantee the presence of working locks and operational fire safety equipment in every guest unit.

Member Rates

AAA/CAA members can generally expect to pay no more than the maximum TourBook listed rate for a standard room. Member discounts apply to rates quoted within the rate range and are applicable at the time of booking. Listed rates are usually based on last standard room availability. Within the range, rates may vary by season and room type. Obtain current AAA/CAA member rates and make reservations at AAA.com.

Exceptions

- Rates for properties operating as concessionaires for the U.S. National Park Service are not guaranteed due to governing regulations.
- Special advertised rates and short-term promotional rates below the rate range are not subject to additional member discounts.
- During special events, hotels may temporarily increase room rates, not recognize discounts or modify pricing policies. Special events may include Mardi Gras, the Kentucky Derby (including pre-Derby events), college football games, holidays, holiday periods and state fairs. Although some special events are listed in the TourBook guides and on AAA.com, it's always wise to check in advance with AAA travel professionals for specific dates.

If you are charged more than the maximum TourBook listed rate, question the additional charge. If an exception is not in effect and management refuses to adhere to the published rate, pay for the room and contact AAA/CAA. The amount paid above the stated maximum will be refunded if our investigation indicates an unjustified charge.

Reservations and Cancellations

When making your reservation, identify yourself as a AAA/CAA member and request written confirmation of your room type, rate, dates of stay, and cancellation and refund policies. At registration, show your membership card.

To cancel, contact the hotel or your AAA/CAA club office, depending on how you booked your reservation. Request a cancellation number or proof of cancellation.

If your room is not as specified and you have written confirmation of your reservation for a specific room type, you should be given the option of choosing a different room or receiving a refund. If management refuses to issue a refund, contact AAA/CAA.

Contacting AAA/CAA About Approved Properties

If your visit to a AAA/CAA Approved attraction, hotel or restaurant doesn't meet your expectations, please tell us about it — *during your visit or within 30 days*.

Use the easy online form at AAA.com/TourBookComments to send us the details, and save your receipts and other documentation for reference.

Or, send your written comments to us at: AAA Member Comments, 1000 AAA Dr., Heathrow, FL 32746.

AAA/CAA Preferred Hotels

All AAA/CAA Approved hotels are committed to providing quality, value and member service. In addition, those designated as AAA/CAA Preferred Hotels also offer these extra values at Approved locations nationwide. Valid AAA/CAA membership required.

- **Best AAA/CAA member rates for your dates of stay.**
- **Seasonal promotions and special member offers.** Visit AAA.com to view current offers.
- **Everyday member benefit.** Look for the blue boxes in the TourBook listings to find everyday values offered at all AAA/CAA Approved locations nationwide. Chains and offers valid at time of publication may change without notice.

- **Total satisfaction guarantee.** If you book your stay with AAA/CAA Travel and your stay fails to meet your expectations, you can apply for a full refund. Bring the complaint to the hotel's attention during the stay and request resolution; if the complaint is not resolved by the hotel, ask your AAA/CAA travel agent to request resolution through the AAA/CAA Assured Stay program.

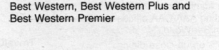

Preferred Hotels

	Best Western, Best Western Plus and Best Western Premier
HILTON WORLDWIDE	Conrad Hotels & Resorts, DoubleTree by Hilton, Embassy Suites, Hampton Inns & Suites, Hilton Hotels & Resorts, Hilton Garden Inns, Hilton Grand Vacations, Home2 Suites, Homewood Suites and Waldorf Astoria Collection
HYATT HOTELS & RESORTS	ANdAZ, Grand Hyatt, Hyatt Place, Hyatt Regency, Hyatt Summerfield Suites and Park Hyatt
Marriott HOTELS & RESORTS	Autograph Collection by Marriott, Courtyard, EDITION Hotels by Marriott, Fairfield Inn, JW Marriott, Marriott Hotels & Resorts, Renaissance Hotels, Residence Inn, Ritz-Carlton Hotels & Resorts, SpringHill Suites and TownePlace Suites
starwood Hotels and Resorts	Aloft, Element, Four Points, Le Meridien, Sheraton, St. Regis Hotels & Resorts, The Luxury Collection, Westin and W Hotels

Show Your Card & Save® Member Discounts

Visit AAA.com/Discounts to find local Show Your Card & Save discounts. Your AAA/CAA club may offer even greater discounts on theme park tickets. Amtrak, Gray Line and theme park discounts may be used for up to six tickets; restaurant savings may be used for up to six patrons. Other restrictions may apply.

ATTRACTIONS

SeaWorld, Busch Gardens, Sesame Place

SEAWORLD PARKS & ENTERTAINMENT

- Save on admission at the gate, participating AAA/CAA offices or AAA.com/SeaWorld.
- Save 10% on up-close dining; visit Guest Relations for details.

Six Flags

- Save on admission at the gate, participating AAA/CAA offices or AAA.com/SixFlags.

- Save 10% on merchandise of $15 or more at in-park stores.

Universal Orlando Resort and Universal Studios Hollywood

- Save on admission at the gate, participating AAA/CAA offices or AAA.com/Universal.

BE EXTRAORDINARY

- Save 10% at select food and merchandise venues in-park and at Universal CityWalk®.

The Entertainment Capital of L.A.™

DINING & SHOPPING

Hard Rock Cafe

- Save 10% on food, nonalcoholic beverages and merchandise at all U.S., Canadian and select international locations.

Landry's Seafood House, The Crab House, Chart House, Oceanaire, Saltgrass Steak House, Muer Seafood Restaurants and Aquarium Restaurants

LANDRY'S SEAFOOD · CHART HOUSE · THE CRAB HOUSE · AQUARIUM · SALTGRASS STEAK HOUSE

- Save 10% on food and nonalcoholic beverages at all of the above restaurants.
- Save 10% on merchandise at Aquarium and Downtown Aquarium restaurants.

Tanger Outlet Centers

- Save up to 20% on total purchase at select merchants with FREE coupon booklet available with registration at AAA customer service desk.

Tanger Outlets

- After first visit, get $5 gift card for each additional location visited in same calendar year.
- Location information: tangeroutlet.com.

TravelCenters of America/Petro Stopping Centers

- Save 10% at the more than 350 full-service and fast-food restaurants inside participating locations nationwide.

TRANSPORTATION & TOURS

Amtrak

- Save 10% on rail fare booked at least 3 days in advance of travel date at AAA.com/Amtrak.

Gray Line

- Save 10% on sightseeing tours of 1 day or less worldwide at AAA.com/GrayLine.

Hertz

- Save on daily, weekend, weekly and monthly rentals at AAA.com/hertz or 1-800-654-3080.

Get on the road to unlimited rewards

with the AAA Member Rewards Visa® credit card

2,500 BONUS POINTS
after first qualifying purchase*
Enough for your first reward!

- **TRIPLE POINTS** on all qualifying AAA purchases – including travel booked at AAA … or anywhere else!*
- **DOUBLE POINTS** for gas, grocery and drug store purchases*
- **1 POINT PER $1** spent on purchases everywhere else*
- **EXCLUSIVE REWARDS** including AAA vouchers good for travel, even car repairs … or choose merchandise, gift cards, or cash back

Scan this tag on your smartphone to apply.

Get the free mobile app at
http://gettag.mobi

Call: 1-866-665-3581 | Visit: AAA.com/CreditCard

Available at participating clubs only.

For information about rates, fees, other costs and benefits associated with the use of this credit card, please call the number or visit the website provided above.

*Earn 1 point per dollar of new net retail purchase transactions (qualifying purchases less credits, returns, and adjustments) ("Net Purchases") charged to the card each billing cycle. Earn 2 points per dollar (consisting of 1 base point and 1 bonus point) for Net Purchases made with the card at any eligible gas, grocery or pharmacy retail merchant categories as designated by us. Eligible merchants and their associated Merchant Category Codes ("MCC") are the following: (a) Gas Stations (MCC codes 5541 and 5542); (b) Grocery Stores (MCC codes 5411, 5422, 5441, 5451, 5462, and 5499); and (c) Pharmacy Stores (MCC codes 5122 and 5912). Purchases made at merchants that do not process transactions under these codes will not qualify to receive double points. Earn 3 points per dollar (consisting of 1 base point and 2 bonus points) for Net Purchases made with the card through any participating AAA Club, when AAA is the merchant of record, or at eligible retail travel merchant categories as designated by us. Eligible travel Merchant Category Codes ("MCC") are the following: (a) Airlines (MCC codes 3000-3299, and 4511); (b) Car Rental Agencies (MCC codes 3351-3441, and 7512); (c) Hotels, Motels, Inns and Resorts (MCC codes 3501-3999, and 7011); (d) Cruise Lines (MCC code 4411); and (e) Travel Agencies and Tour Operators (MCC Code 4722). Purchases made at merchants that do not process transactions under these codes will not qualify to receive triple points. You will qualify for 2,500 bonus points if you use your new account to make at least one purchase transaction that posts to your account within 90 days of the account open date. Limit (1) 2,500 bonus points credit per new account. Allow 8-12 weeks from qualifying for the bonus points to post to your account. Rewards begin at 2,500 points for merchandise, 5,000 points for cash and AAA reward vouchers and 15,000 points for air. Other restrictions apply. Complete details accompany new account materials.

This credit card program is issued and administered by FIA Card Services, N.A. Visa and Visa Signature are registered trademarks of Visa International Service Association and are used by the Issuer pursuant to license from Visa U.S.A. Inc. AAA is a trademark of American Automobile Association, Inc.

©2011 Bank of America Corporation

ARP5S5F2

Santa Rita Mountains, Coronado National Forest

Close your eyes and think about Arizona. Chances are the images that first come to mind are those of the Old West—cowboys, Indians, deserts, cacti—stuff straight out of TV Westerns.

Cowboys still do exist here, but they're more likely to be found assisting city slickers at modern guest ranches than lassoing cattle on a trail drive.

Native Americans, the first Arizonans, though a small percentage of today's population, are a major influence in everyday life. Reminders of their heritage are evident in national monuments, tribal parks and historic sites that preserve their ancient dwellings, customs and crafts.

As for the deserts, well, the sand and the intricate rock formations are still there, but their expanse is now broken by major metropolitan areas like Phoenix and Tucson and golf courses that seem strangely out of place. And rare species of cactus, such as

Arizona

the organ pipe and saguaro, are protected in their own preserves.

The Grand Canyon State

"Did the government build it?"

More than one flabbergasted visitor has asked this upon first seeing Arizona's Grand Canyon. Though it may sound preposterous, it's a question you'll find less naive after gazing at these myriad erosion-carved columns, arches and windows—a virtual cityscape of landforms that would make a Manhattanite feel at home.

No doubt Uncle Sam would love to claim responsibility for the Grand Canyon, but only Father Time can take credit for this natural wonder. Over millions of years geologic upheaval forced a former sea bottom into the sky, allowing wind and water to work their rock-sculpting magic. The result: a spectacle so awesome that some 5 million people from all over the world visit each year.

The South Rim area boasts many of the best vantage points from which to gape at the canyon in all its multihued glory. What's more, the tall pine trees here hide the great chasm from view until you are almost at its edge. Confronting this breathtaking scene as you emerge from the forest is an unforgettable experience.

In the early morning and late afternoon, colors dance along canyon walls in the rapidly changing sunlight. If a storm comes your

Tile Mural, Mission San Xavier del Bac

way, don't despair: Shadows of rain clouds can create striking patterns of darkness as they drift across the canyon's depths.

But even after visiting the Grand Canyon, don't think you've seen it all. An equally spectacular play of color and light awaits you at Monument Valley Navajo Tribal Park. Here you just might feel like you're walking through a Hollywood set, and with good reason: The valley, with its rose-tinted buttes and mesas, has served as backdrop for countless Westerns and car commercials.

Grand Canyon visitors frequently overlook another Arizona jewel—Sedona's Red Rock territory. Oak Creek Canyon has its own collection of buttes, spires and sheer rock walls that shimmer with shades of beige, ocher, salmon and scarlet. Beat the heat and go with Oak Creek's flow at Slide Rock State Park, where a waterslide—natural, not man-made—splashes from pool to pool.

"Married to the Ground"
Ancient cliff dwellings at Montezuma Castle, Canyon de Chelly and Navajo national monuments blend with their environs so well, they seem to have sprouted from the precipices they're perched upon.

Centuries after these towns in the sky were abandoned, architect Frank Lloyd Wright designed buildings—notably Taliesin West, his former home and studio in Scottsdale— according to his belief that they should harmoniously coexist with their surroundings.

Wright once encapsulated his design philosophy by saying his buildings were "married to the ground." It's easy to see why he chose Arizona as his studio's setting. Here the terrain seems a willing companion to man's handiwork: mesas rise from the desert like skyscrapers and pinnacles soar like church spires.

Recreation
Canyons. Mountains. Forests. Lakes. The extensive Colorado River. Arizona, derived from the Native American word meaning "little spring," is a veritable fountain of fun for outdoor types.

Hopefully you packed your putter. With more than 350 golf courses to choose from, people drive from all over the country to chip and putt. But watch out for hazards—Mesa, Phoenix, northern Scottsdale and Tucson are chock-full of challenging fairways.

Then there's *the* Canyon, the grandest of them all. For a bird's-eye view, try a helicopter or airplane tour; or capture that Old West spirit of adventure on a train ride from Williams. Peer off the edge while hiking along the South Rim Trail—the panorama will knock your socks off.

If you're more adventurous, follow Bright Angel Trail into the depths of the gorge. The South Kaibab and North Kaibab trails also are good treks on foot or on hoof: Mule rides are available for 2-day jaunts (advance reservations are required). Since it takes a full day to reach the canyon floor, camping is a popular option; contact Trip Planner, (928) 638-7888, for a backcountry permit.

Despite Arizona's arid landscape, there are plenty of places to find refreshment. Dip your toes, skis, jet ski, sailboard or speedboat into Glen Canyon National Recreation Area's Lake Powell or Lake Mead National Recreation Area's lakes Mead and Mojave. Why not explore the Colorado River on a peaceful float trip or an adrenaline-pumping ride through white-water rapids?

If fishing is your sport, head for the waters of the White Mountains, where you can hook all sorts of trout and bass. For information about hunting trophy elk or other game, contact the Arizona Game and Fish Department.

When it gets chilly, skiing at the Arizona Snowbowl, north of Flagstaff in the Coconino National Forest, is the cool thing to do. Other places to catch a chairlift are Sunrise Park, in Greer; Mount Lemmon, north of Tucson; and Elk Ridge Ski and Outdoor Recreation Area, in Williams.

Sabino Canyon, Coronado National Forest

Historic Timeline

1539	Franciscan friar Marcos de Niza searches unsuccessfully for the fabled Seven Cities of Cíbola throughout the Southwest.
1853	The Gadsden Purchase brings a portion of present-day southern Arizona and southern New Mexico under U.S. control.
1889	Phoenix is chosen as the territorial capital.
1911	The completion of the Roosevelt Dam on the Salt River delivers much-needed water to the area.
1912	Arizona enters the Union as the 48th state.
1919	Grand Canyon is designated a national park.
1966	The Miranda vs. Arizona ruling stipulates that arrested persons must be informed of their rights before any questioning occurs.
1973	Construction begins on the Central Arizona Project to bring Colorado River water to dry parts of the state.
1981	Arizonan Sandra Day O'Connor is appointed as the first woman member of the U.S. Supreme Court.
1991	Eight scientists researching ecosystem sustainability begin living in the glass-enclosed biomes of Biosphere 2 in Oracle.
2001	In just their fourth season, the Arizona Diamondbacks defeat the New York Yankees in the World Series.

What To Pack

Temperature Averages Maximum/Minimum	JANUARY	FEBRUARY	MARCH	APRIL	MAY	JUNE	JULY	AUGUST	SEPTEMBER	OCTOBER	NOVEMBER	DECEMBER
Flagstaff	41/14	44/17	48/20	57/27	67/33	76/40	81/50	78/49	74/41	63/31	51/22	43/16
Grand Canyon National Park	41/17	45/20	51/24	59/30	69/37	81/45	83/52	80/51	75/45	64/34	53/26	44/17
Kingman	57/31	61/34	66/37	75/42	82/49	94/57	97/67	96/65	90/57	79/47	67/38	56/31
Phoenix	65/38	69/41	74/45	84/52	93/60	101/68	105/77	102/76	98/70	88/57	75/45	66/38
Tucson	63/38	67/40	71/44	81/50	90/57	98/66	98/74	95/72	93/67	84/56	72/49	65/39
Yuma	68/43	73/46	78/50	86/57	93/64	101/71	106/81	104/81	100/74	90/62	76/50	68/44

From the records of The Weather Channel Interactive, Inc.

Good Facts To Know

ABOUT THE STATE

POPULATION: 6,392,017.

AREA: 113,909 square miles; ranks 6th.

CAPITAL: Phoenix.

HIGHEST POINT: 12,643 ft., Humphreys Peak.

LOWEST POINT: 70 ft., Colorado River.

TIME ZONE(S): Mountain. DST on Navajo Reservation only.

GAMBLING

MINIMUM AGE FOR GAMBLING: 21.

REGULATIONS

TEEN DRIVING LAWS: No more than one unrelated passenger under age 18 is permitted for the first six months unless accompanied by a parent or legal guardian. Driving is not permitted midnight-5 a.m. The minimum age for an unrestricted driver's license is 16 years, 6 months. Phone (800) 251-5866 for more information about Arizona driver's license regulations.

SEAT BELT/CHILD RESTRAINT LAWS: Seat belts required for driver and front-seat passengers ages 5 and older. Ages 5-16 are required to be in a child restraint or seat belt; child restraints are required for under age 5.

HELMETS FOR MOTORCYCLISTS: Required for riders under age 18.

RADAR DETECTORS: Permitted.

MOVE OVER LAW: Driver is required to slow down and vacate the lane nearest stopped police, fire and rescue vehicles using audible or flashing signals. The law also applies to recovery vehicles, such as tow trucks.

FIREARMS LAWS: Vary by state and/or county. Contact the Law Library of Arizona, 1700 W. Washington St., 3rd Floor, Phoenix, AZ 85007; phone (602) 926-3948.

HOLIDAYS

HOLIDAYS: Jan. 1 ■ Martin Luther King Jr. Day, Jan. (3rd Mon.) ■ Presidents Day, Feb. (3rd Mon.) ■ Memorial Day, May (last Mon.) ■ July 4 ■ Labor Day, Sept. (1st Mon.) ■ Columbus Day, Oct. (2nd Mon.) ■ Veterans Day, Nov. 11 ■ Thanksgiving, Nov. (4th Thurs.) ■ Christmas, Dec. 25.

MONEY

TAXES: Arizona's statewide sales tax is 6.6 percent, with local options to impose additional increments on goods and services, including lodgings.

VISITOR INFORMATION

INFORMATION CENTERS: State welcome centers provide details about Arizona attractions, accommodations, historic sites, parks and events. They are located in Lupton off I-40 westbound exit 359 ■ and in Phoenix at 125 N. Second St., Suite 120.

DAYLIGHT-SAVING TIME:
The Navajo Reservation is the only area in the state to observe daylight-saving time.

INDIAN RESERVATIONS:
Indian reservations are regarded as sovereign nations, making and enforcing laws pertaining to their land. The following rules are the most relevant to visitors to the reservations: Alcoholic beverages (including transportation and use) are prohibited; leaving established roadways and hiking cross-country is prohibited unless permission is obtained from the local tribal office; seat belts must be worn by motorists; and helmets must be worn by motorcyclists.

FURTHER INFORMATION FOR VISITORS:
Arizona Office of Tourism
1110 W. Washington St., Suite 155
Phoenix, AZ 85007
(602) 364-3700
(866) 275-5816

NATIONAL FOREST INFORMATION:
Southwestern Region
Public Affairs Office
333 Broadway Blvd. S.E.
Albuquerque, NM 87102
(505) 842-3292
(877) 444-6777 (reservations)

FISHING AND HUNTING REGULATIONS:
Arizona Game and Fish Department
5000 W. Carefree Hwy.
Phoenix, AZ 85086-5000
(602) 942-3000

RECREATION INFORMATION:
Arizona State Parks Board
1300 W. Washington St.
Phoenix, AZ 85007
(602) 542-4174
Arizona Public Lands Information Center
1 N. Central Ave., Suite 800
Phoenix, AZ 85004
(602) 417-9200

Arizona Annual Events
Please call ahead to confirm event details.

JANUARY	FEBRUARY	MARCH
■ Native American Art Festival--The Gathering Litchfield Park 623-695-9040 ■ Arizona National Horse Show / Scottsdale 602-258-8568 ■ Carefree Fine Art and Wine Festival / Carefree 480-837-5637	■ Matsuri: a Festival of Japan Phoenix 602-262-5071 ■ Cochise Cowboy Poetry and Music Gathering Sierra Vista 520-549-3868 ■ Gold Rush Days Wickenburg 928-684-5479	■ Heard Museum Guild Indian Fair and Market Phoenix 602-252-8840 ■ Arizona State Open Chili Championship Casa Grande 520-836-2125 ■ National Festival of the West / Scottsdale 602-996-4387
APRIL	**MAY**	**JUNE**
■ Glendale Jazz & Blues Festival / Glendale 623-930-2299 ■ Scottsdale Culinary Festival Scottsdale 480-945-7193 ■ Old West Founders Days Tombstone 888-457-3929	■ Queen Creek Peach Festival / Queen Creek 480-987-3100, ext. 1006 ■ Cinco de Mayo Celebration and Chihuahua Races Chandler 480-782-2735 ■ Wyatt Earp Days Tombstone 520-457-3291	■ Strawberry Festival / Pine 928-476-3655 ■ Arizona State HOG (Harley Owners Group) Rally Williams 928-955-2658 ■ Wool Festival / Flagstaff 928-774-6272
JULY	**AUGUST**	**SEPTEMBER**
■ Hopi Festival of Arts and Culture / Flagstaff 928-774-5213 ■ Fabulous Phoenix Fourth Phoenix 602-261-8645 ■ Tempe Town Lake Festival Tempe 480-350-5189	■ World's Oldest Continuous Rodeo / Payson 928-474-4515 ■ Eagar Daze / Eagar 928-333-4128, ext. 251 ■ Vigilante Days / Tombstone 520-457-3495	■ Navajo Nation Fair Window Rock 928-871-6703 ■ Oktoberfest / Sierra Vista 520-458-2065 ■ Brewery Gulch Daze Bisbee 520-432-5421
OCTOBER	**NOVEMBER**	**DECEMBER**
■ Helldorado Days Tombstone 520-378-5117 ■ Wild Western Festival Glendale 623-521-3856 ■ Arizona Exposition & State Fair / Phoenix 602-252-6771	■ Colorado River Crossing Balloon Festival / Yuma 928-343-1715 ■ Tucson Celtic Festival and Scottish Highland Games Tucson 520-743-9291 ■ Kobalt Tools 500 / Avondale 623-463-5400	■ Boat Parade of Lights Lake Havasu City 928-453-3444 ■ Pueblo Grande Museum Indian Market / Phoenix 602-495-0901 ■ Tempe Fall Festival of the Arts / Tempe 480-355-6069

Cactus, Saguaro National Park

Ceremonial Hopi Drum, Sedona

Chile Peppers, Barrio Histórico, Tucson

Paria Canyon, Vermilion Cliffs National Monument

Frank Lloyd Wright Window, Arizona Biltmore, A Waldorf Astoria Hotel, Phoenix

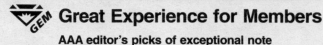 **Great Experience for Members**

AAA editor's picks of exceptional note

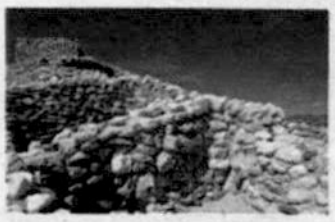

Tuzigoot National
Monument

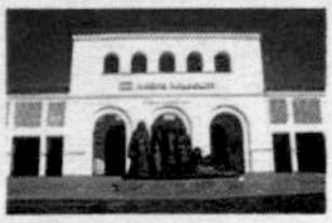

Heard Museum

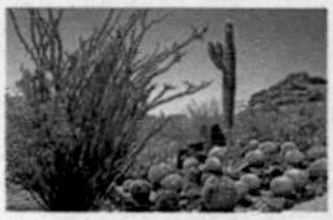

Desert Botanical
Garden

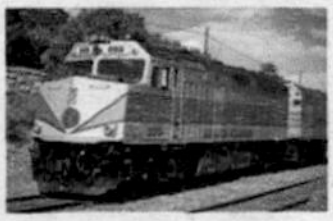

Grand Canyon
Railway

Arizona
Atlas Section

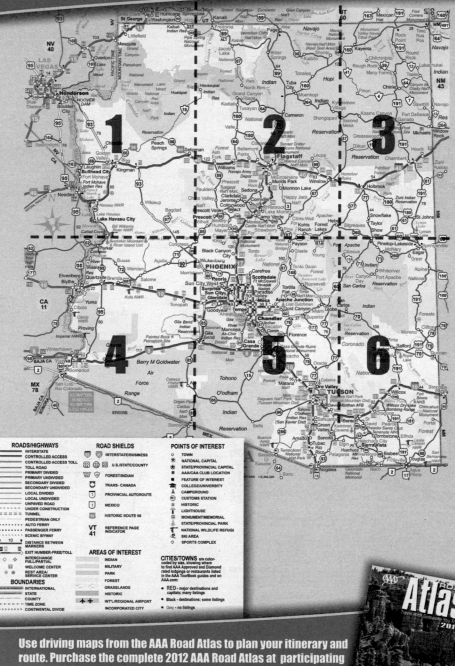

ROADS/HIGHWAYS
- INTERSTATE
- CONTROLLED ACCESS
- CONTROLLED ACCESS TOLL
- TOLL ROAD
- PRIMARY DIVIDED
- PRIMARY UNDIVIDED
- SECONDARY DIVIDED
- SECONDARY UNDIVIDED
- LOCAL DIVIDED
- LOCAL UNDIVIDED
- UNPAVED ROAD
- UNDER CONSTRUCTION
- TUNNEL
- PEDESTRIAN ONLY
- AUTO FERRY
- PASSENGER FERRY
- SCENIC BYWAY
- DISTANCE BETWEEN MARKERS
- EXIT NUMBER-FREE/TOLL
- INTERCHANGE FULL/PARTIAL
- WELCOME CENTER
- REST AREA/SERVICE CENTER

BOUNDARIES
- INTERNATIONAL
- STATE
- COUNTY
- TIME ZONE
- CONTINENTAL DIVIDE

ROAD SHIELDS
- INTERSTATE/BUSINESS
- U.S./STATE/COUNTY
- FOREST/INDIAN
- TRANS- CANADA
- PROVINCIAL AUTOROUTE
- MEXICO
- HISTORIC ROUTE 66
- VT 41 REFERENCE PAGE INDICATOR

AREAS OF INTEREST
- INDIAN
- MILITARY
- PARK
- FOREST
- GRASSLANDS
- HISTORIC
- INT'L/REGIONAL AIRPORT
- INCORPORATED CITY

POINTS OF INTEREST
- TOWN
- NATIONAL CAPITAL
- STATE/PROVINCIAL CAPITAL
- AAA/CAA CLUB LOCATION
- FEATURE OF INTEREST
- COLLEGE/UNIVERSITY
- CAMPGROUND
- CUSTOMS STATION
- HISTORIC
- LIGHTHOUSE
- MONUMENT/MEMORIAL
- STATE/PROVINCIAL PARK
- NATIONAL WILDLIFE REFUGE
- SKI AREA
- SPORTS COMPLEX

CITIES/TOWNS are color-coded by size, showing where to find AAA Approved and Diamond rated lodgings or restaurants listed in the AAA TourBook guides and on AAA.com:
- RED - major destinations and capitals; many listings
- Black - destinations; some listings
- Grey - no listings

Use driving maps from the AAA Road Atlas to plan your itinerary and route. Purchase the complete 2012 AAA Road Atlas at participating AAA/CAA offices, retail stores and online booksellers.

Atlas Road 2012

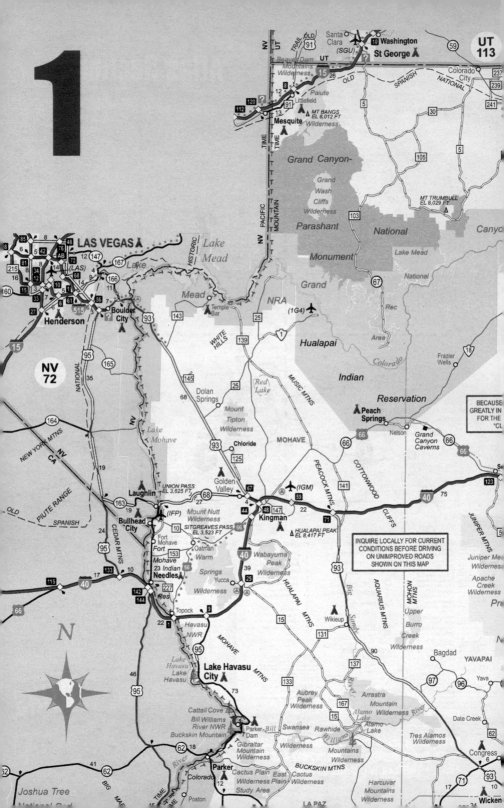

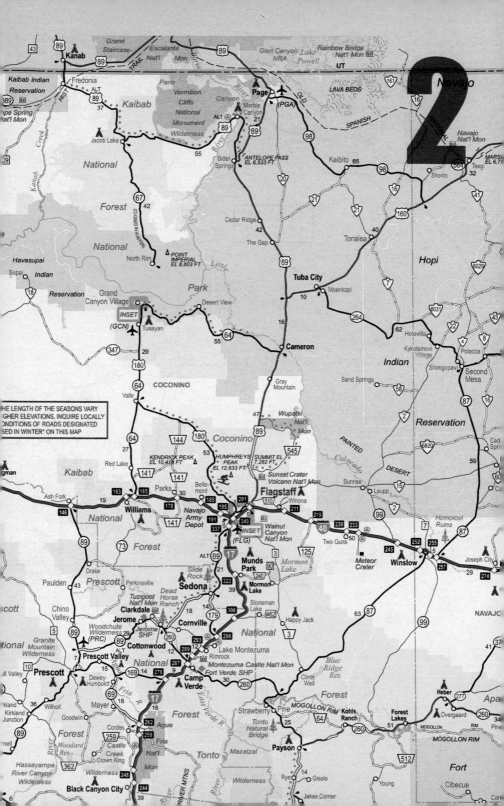

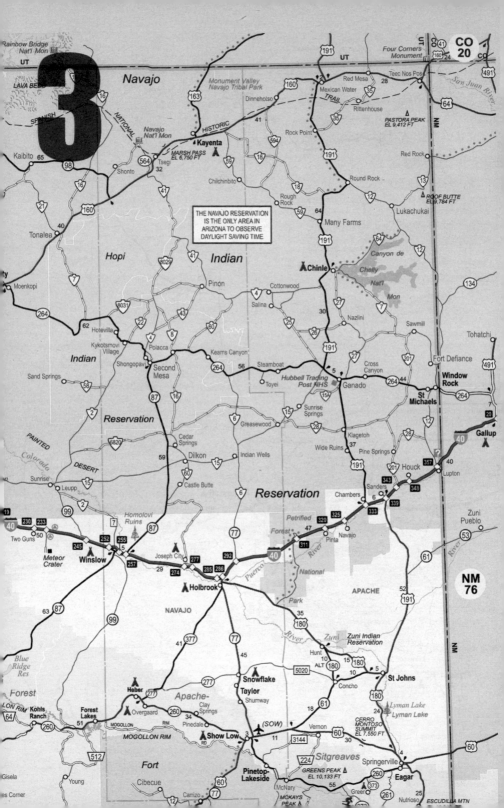

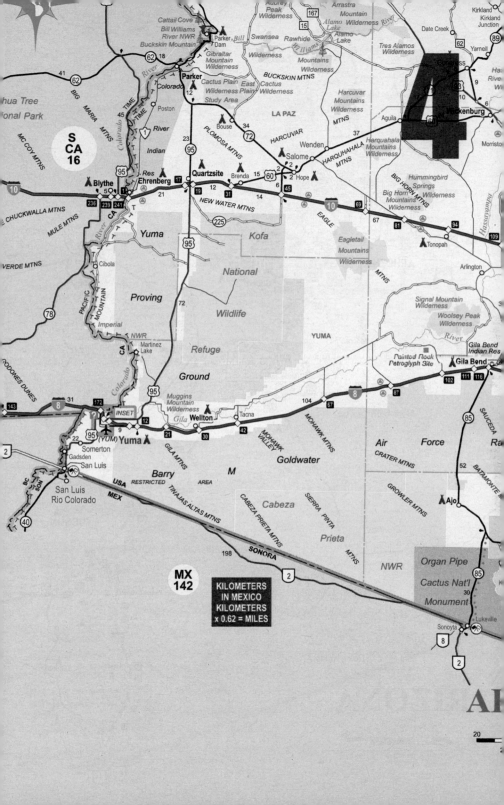

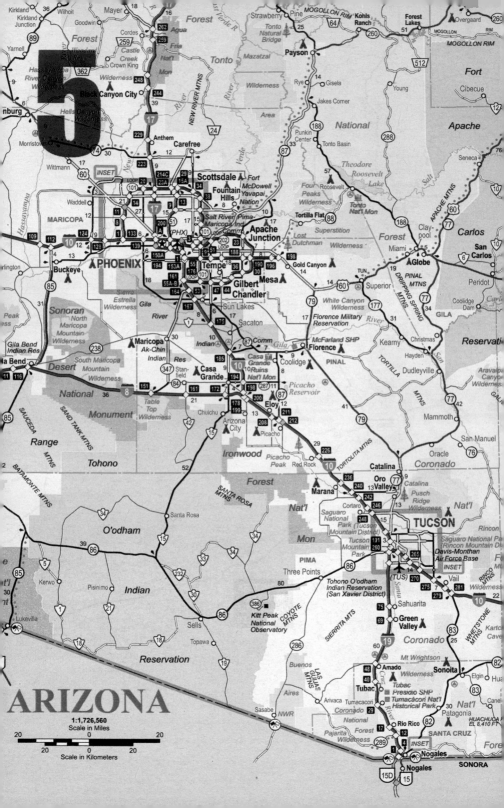

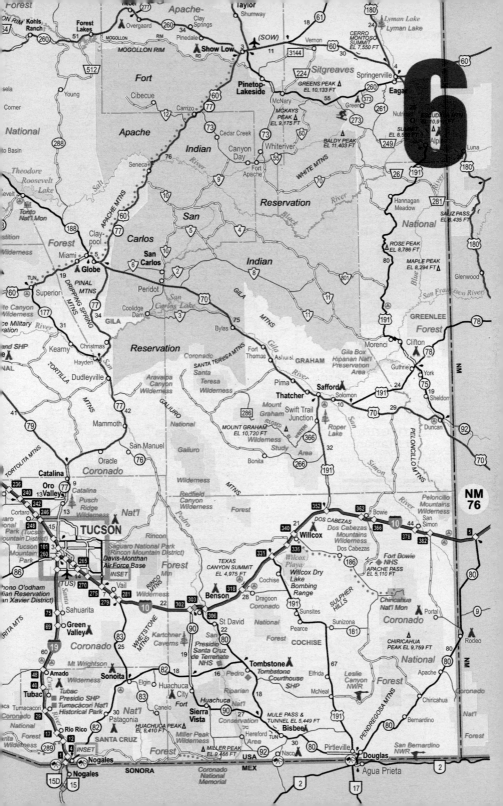

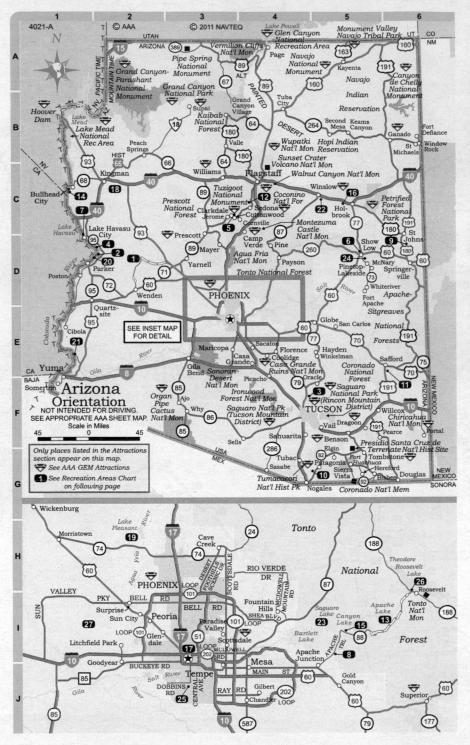

4021-A

© AAA   © 2011 NAVTEQ

Arizona Orientation

NOT INTENDED FOR DRIVING.
SEE APPROPRIATE AAA SHEET MAP.

Scale in Miles
45   0   45

Only places listed in the Attractions
section appear on this map.

▽ See AAA GEM Attractions

1 See Recreation Areas Chart
on following page

SEE INSET MAP
FOR DETAIL

Recreation Areas Chart

The map location numerals in column 2 show an area's location on the preceding map.

	MAP LOCATION	CAMPING	PICNICKING	HIKING TRAILS	BOATING	BOAT RAMP	BOAT RENTAL	FISHING	SWIMMING	PETS ON LEASH	BICYCLE TRAILS	WINTER SPORTS	VISITOR CENTER	LODGE/CABINS	FOOD SERVICE
NATIONAL PARKS *(See place listings.)*															
Grand Canyon (A-3) 1,218,376 acres.		•	•	•				•		•		•	•	•	•
Saguaro (F-5) 91,000 acres.		•	•	•						•		•	•		
NATIONAL FORESTS *(See place listings.)*															
Apache-Sitgreaves (D-6) 2.1 million acres. East-central Arizona. Horse rental.		•	•	•	•	•	•	•	•	•	•	•	•		•
Coconino (C-4) 1,821,495 acres. Northern Arizona.		•	•	•	•	•	•	•	•	•			•	•	•
Coronado (E-5) 1,780,196 acres. Southeastern Arizona.		•	•	•	•	•	•	•	•	•		•	•		•
Kaibab (B-3) 1.6 million acres. Northern Arizona.		•	•	•	•	•	•	•		•		•	•	•	•
Prescott (C-3) 1,238,154 acres. Central Arizona. Electric boat motors only. Horse rental.		•	•	•	•	•	•	•	•	•					•
Tonto (H-4) 2,900,000 acres. Central Arizona.		•	•	•	•	•	•	•	•	•				•	•
NATIONAL RECREATION AREAS *(See place listings.)*															
Glen Canyon (A-4) 1,250,000 acres.		•	•	•	•	•	•	•	•				•	•	•
Lake Mead (B-1) Southeastern Nevada. Scuba diving.		•	•	•	•	•	•	•	•	•			•	•	•
STATE															
Alamo Lake (D-2) 2,858 acres 38 mi. n. of US 60 via a paved road. *(See Wenden p. 314.)*	**1**	•	•		•	•		•		•			•		
Buckskin Mountain & River Island (D-2) 1,677 acres 11 mi. n. off SR 95. *(See Parker p. 127.)*	**2**	•	•	•	•	•		•	•	•			•		•
Catalina (F-5) 5,525 acres 9 mi. n. off SR 77. *(See Tucson p. 274.)*	**3**	•	•	•						•	•	•	•		
Cattail Cove (D-2) 2,375 acres off SR 95. *(See Lake Havasu City p. 105.)*	**4**	•	•	•	•	•		•	•	•			•		•
Dead Horse Ranch (C-3) 423 acres off 10th St. Bird-watching; horse trails. *(See Cottonwood p. 57.)*	**5**	•	•	•				•		•			•	•	
Fool Hollow Lake (D-5) 686 acres 2 mi. n. of US 60 off SR 260, then e. on Old Linden Rd. to 32nd Ave. *(See Show Low p. 249.)*	**6**	•	•	•	•	•		•		•			•		•
Lake Havasu (C-1) 928 acres n. of London Bridge off London Bridge Rd. *(See Lake Havasu City p. 105.)*	**7**	•	•	•	•	•	•	•	•	•			•		
Lost Dutchman (I-5) 320 acres 5 mi. n.e. off SR 88. *(See Apache Junction p. 37.)*	**8**	•	•	•						•	•	•	•		
Lyman Lake (D-6) 1,200 acres 14 mi. n. off US 60 onto US 180/191, then just off SR 81. *(See St. Johns p. 203.)*	**9**	•	•	•	•			•	•	•		•	•	•	
Patagonia Lake (G-5) 2,659 acres 7 mi. s.w. on SR 82, then 5 mi. w. following signs. *(See Patagonia p. 127.)*	**10**	•	•	•	•	•		•	•	•			•		•
Roper Lake (F-6) 339 acres .5 mi. s. off US 191. *(See Safford p. 202.)*	**11**	•	•	•	•			•	•	•			•		
Slide Rock (C-4) 55 acres 7 mi. n. off SR 89A within Oak Creek Canyon. *(See Sedona p. 231.)*	**12**		•	•					•	•			•	•	•
OTHER															
Apache Lake (I-5) 2,656 acres 30 mi. n.e. on SR 88. *(See Apache Junction p. 36.)*	**13**	•			•	•	•	•	•	•				•	•
Bullhead (C-1) 20 acres .25 mi. s. of Bullhead City. No tent camping.	**14**		•		•	•		•	•	•			•		
Canyon Lake (I-5) 950 acres 16 mi. n.e. on SR 88. *(See Apache Junction p. 36.)*	**15**	•	•	•	•	•	•	•	•	•					•
Cholla Lake (C-5) 360 acres 2 mi. e. of Joseph City on I-40. Water skiing.	**16**	•	•		•	•			•						

Recreation Areas Chart

The map location numerals in column 2 show an area's location on the preceding map.

	MAP LOCATION	CAMPING	PICNICKING	HIKING TRAILS	BOATING	BOAT RAMP	BOAT RENTAL	FISHING	SWIMMING	PETS ON LEASH	BICYCLE TRAILS	WINTER SPORTS	VISITOR CENTER	LODGE/CABINS	FOOD SERVICE
Encanto (I-3) 66 acres at 2605 N. 15th Ave. Golf (nine and 18 holes). *(See Phoenix p. 144.)*	17		•	•					•	•	•				•
Hualapai Mountain (C-2) 2,200 acres 12 mi. s.e. of Kingman. *(See Kingman p. 101.)*	18	•	•	•				•		•			•	•	
Lake Pleasant (H-2) 24,500 acres 29 mi. e. on SR 74, then 2 mi. n. off Castle Hot Springs Rd. *(See Morristown p. 117.)*	19	•	•		•	•	•	•	•	•					•
La Paz County (D-2) 165 acres 8 mi. n. of Parker via SR 95.	20	•	•			•	•	•	•	•			•		
Martinez Lake (E-1) 600 acres 25 mi. n. of Yuma. Water skiing.	21	•	•			•	•	•	•					•	•
McHood (C-5) 160 acres 5 mi. s.e. of Winslow off SR 99.	22		•			•		•	•	•					
Saguaro Lake (I-5) 1,280 acres 25 mi. n.e. of Mesa via US 60 and Bush Hwy. *(See Mesa p. 111.)*	23		•		•	•	•	•	•	•					•
Show Low Lake (D-5) 100 acres 5.5 mi. s.e. of Show Low via SR 260.	24	•	•	•	•			•	•	•					
South Mountain (J-3) 16,000 acres 8 mi. s. on S. Central Ave. Horse rental, playground. *(See Phoenix p. 146.)*	25		•	•						•	•		•		
Theodore Roosevelt Lake (H-6) 17,315 acres 29 mi. n.w. of Globe via SR 88. *(See Roosevelt p. 201.)*	26	•	•	•	•	•	•	•	•	•				•	•
White Tank Mountain (I-1) 26,337 acres 8 mi. s. of Surprise via SR 303, then 4 mi. w. on Olive Ave. Horse trails. *(See Surprise p. 255.)*	27	•	•	•						•	•				

Give as Good as You Get — Give AAA

You know how valuable your AAA card is. Now give this gift of security, value, and peace of mind. **Give AAA.**

To purchase a AAA Gift Membership, contact your local AAA office, visit AAA.com, or call 800-Join-AAA.

AGUA FRIA NATIONAL MONUMENT (D-4)

North of Phoenix off I-17 exit 259 to Bloody Basin Road or off exit 256 to Badger Springs, Agua Fria National Monument embraces 71,100 acres including the Agua Fria River canyon between Black Canyon City and Cordes Lake.

The river canyon, at an elevation of 2,150 feet above sea level, and Perry and Black mesas are the primary formations; elevations in the northern hills reach 4,500 feet. The monument preserves more than 450 prehistoric sites. Petroglyphs, terraced landscapes and pueblo ruins suggest the area was heavily populated A.D. 1250-1450 by an agrarian society skilled at growing food and sustaining life in the desert.

Semidesert grasslands and a riparian forest support abundant wildlife, including pronghorn, mountain lions, javelinas and white-tailed deer.

Camping, hiking and picnicking are permitted. There are no developed recreation sites or trails. Because the terrain is rugged and rocky, a high-clearance, four-wheel-drive vehicle is required. For further information contact the Monument Manager, Phoenix District, Bureau of Land Management, 21605 N. 7th Ave., Phoenix, AZ 85027; phone (623) 580-5500.

AJO (F-3) pop. 3,304, elev. 1,747'

The name Ajo comes either from the Tohono O'odham word for "paint" or the Spanish name for "garlic." Home to the first copper mine in the state, Ajo did not boom until ore-refining methods made the mining of low-grade ore profitable in the early 1900s.

In 1906 Col. John Greenway formed the New Cornelia Copper Co., which was eventually purchased by one of the nation's largest copper companies, Dodge Corp., in 1921. Visitors to the town can view the New Cornelia Open Pit Mine on Indian Village Road. The mine, which was shut down in 1984, is nearly 2 miles in diameter and 1,000 feet deep. Open October through May, its visitor center features a video and display of the mining operations as well as an observation area; phone (520) 387-7742.

Organ Pipe Cactus National Monument (see place listing p. 122), 32 miles south of Ajo, preserves a portion of the Sonoran Desert; its inhabitants include the statuesque organ pipe cactus as well as such desert foliage as saguaro, paloverde and ocotillo.

As in much of the southwest, the Spanish and American Indian influence can be seen in Ajo's Spanish Colonial Revival town square surrounded by a park, mission churches and Southwestern-style buildings. The Ajo Historical Museum, 160 W. Mission St., is housed in a mission church built in the 1930s; phone (520) 387-7105. Other historic buildings include the 1919 Curley School and the Greenway Mansion on Indian Village Road. A historic building tour takes place the third week in November; phone (520) 387-7742.

Ajo Chamber of Commerce: 400 Taladro St., Ajo, AZ 85321. **Phone:** (520) 387-7742.

CABEZA PRIETA NATIONAL WILDLIFE REFUGE is at 1611 N. Second Ave.; an entry permit must be obtained at the visitor center. Created in 1939 for the conservation and development of natural wildlife resources and to protect Sonoran Desert wildlife, the 860,000-acre refuge protects desert bighorn sheep and such endangered species as the Sonoran pronghorn, ferruginous pygmy-owl and lesser long-nosed bat. During spring and fall migration periods warblers, swallows, hawks, towhees and falcons can be seen. The Sonoran pronghorn fawning season takes place March 15 through July 15; three-fourths of the refuge is closed during this time.

Note: A four-wheel-drive vehicle is required on most of the refuge. Firearms are legal but must be unloaded; check with the refuge for regulations. Campfires are allowed at three designated campsites: Papago Well, Tule Well and Christmas Camp. At all other campsites, campers must use charcoal with a ground pan or a propane cookstove. **Hours:** Mon.-Fri. 8-4. **Cost:** Free. **Phone:** (520) 387-6483.

GUESTHOUSE INN   **Phone:** 520/387-6133

Historic Bed & Breakfast
$89-$99

Address: 700 W Guest House Rd 85321 **Location:** SR 85, 0.5 mi sw; from town plaza, take La Mina Ave and Hospital Dr. Located in a residential area. **Facility:** Built in 1925 as a home for visiting mine directors, this inn offers expansive rooms and two enclosed porches. 4 units. 1 story, interior corridors. **Terms:** office hours 9 am-8 pm, 3 day cancellation notice.

LA SIESTA MOTEL   **Phone:** 520/387-6569

Motel
Rates not provided

Address: 2561 N Ajo-Gila Bend Hwy 85321 **Location:** On SR 85, 1.8 mi n of town plaza. **Facility:** 32 units. 1 story, exterior corridors. **Terms:** office hours 8 am-9 pm. **Pool(s):** heated outdoor. **Activities:** whirlpool, tennis court, shuffleboard. **Guest Services:** coin laundry.

AMADO pop. 295
• Restaurants p. 36

AMADO TERRITORY INN   **Phone:** 520/398-8684

Bed & Breakfast
Rates not provided

Address: 3001 E Frontage Rd 85645 **Location:** I-19 exit 48, just e, then just s. Located on the grounds of Territory Ranch. **Facility:** A two-story-tall stone fireplace, a sunny breakfast room looking across a dry wash and a roadrunner that comes to visit create a charming environment. 15 units. 2 stories (no elevator), interior corridors. **Dining:** 2 restaurants. **Activities:** horseshoes.

WHERE TO EAT

AMADO TERRITORY STEAKHOUSE

Steak
$13-$32

Phone: 520/398-2651
AAA Inspector Notes: Located just off the interstate and adjacent to a pleasant B&B and a black opal site, this restaurant is a nice choice for a leisurely dinner. A desert garden setting provides a relaxing spot in which to enjoy grilled filet medallions with onion rings and hollandaise. Helpful staff members ensure a pleasant experience. **Bar:** full bar. **Address:** 3001 E Frontage Rd 85645 **Location:** I-19 exit 48, just e, then just s; adjacent to Amado Territory Inn. [D]

COW PALACE RESTAURANT & BAR

Steak
$6-$22

Phone: 520/398-1999
AAA Inspector Notes: Beyond grilled steaks, diners may order Mexican dishes, fresh salads, baby back ribs and grilled or fried fish. Established more than 50 years ago, the restaurant has been a frequent stop for travelers heading south from Tucson. **Bar:** full bar. **Address:** 28802 S Nogales Hwy 85645 **Location:** I-19 exit 48, just w, then just n. [B] [L] [D]

ANTHEM pop. 21,700

HAMPTON INN AT ANTHEM

Hotel
$79-$189

Phone: (623)465-7979
AAA Benefit:
Members save up to 10% everyday!

Address: 42415 N 41st Dr 85086 **Location:** I-17 exit 229 (Anthem Way), just w. **Facility:** 76 units. 3 stories, interior corridors. **Terms:** 1-7 night minimum stay, cancellation fee imposed. **Amenities:** high-speed Internet. **Pool(s):** heated outdoor. **Activities:** whirlpool, exercise room. **Guest Services:** coin laundry.

WHERE TO EAT

AFFINITO'S BISTRO

Indian
$10-$19

Phone: 623/465-0900
AAA Inspector Notes: Tandoor specialties and bread baked in a clay oven are at the centerpiece of a traditional menu of curried, lamb and vegetarian dishes. The upscale atmosphere features artwork and instrumental music. A weekday buffet draws a devoted lunch clientele. **Bar:** full bar. **Address:** 3655 W Anthem Way, Suite C-137 85086 **Location:** I-17 exit 229 (Anthem Way), 1 mi e; in Anthem Marketplace Shopping Center.

[L] [D] CALL &M

APACHE JUNCTION (J-5) pop. 35,840, elev. 1,715'
• Part of Phoenix area — see map p. 134

As its name implies, Apache Junction—the western terminus of the Apache Trail—is at the junction of US 60 and SR 88. The surrounding desert, lakes and mountains make Apache Junction a natural recreation site. Hiking, horseback riding, picnicking, rockhounding and water sports facilities are available.

At the junction of Old West Highway and SR 88 stands a monument to the memory of Jacob Waltz, purported discoverer of the Lost Dutchman Gold Mine, which is said to be in the nearby Superstition Mountains.

For eight consecutive weekends from the first Saturday in February through the last Sunday in March, the ☗ Arizona Renaissance Festival and Artisan Marketplace is held 7 miles east on US 60. Beginning at 10 a.m. and ending at 6 p.m., activities during this re-creation of a 16th-century European village at play during a market fair include jousting tournaments, wandering musicians, theatrical events and demonstrations of period crafts.

Apache Junction Chamber of Commerce: 567 W. Apache Tr., P.O. Box 1747, Apache Junction, AZ 85217. **Phone:** (480) 982-3141 or (800) 252-3141.

APACHE LAKE, 30 mi. n.e. on SR 88, is part of the Salt River chain of lakes. A popular recreation area, it is surrounded by the Tonto National Forest *(see place listing p. 264)*. To the south lies the Superstition Wilderness. *See Recreation Chart.* **Phone:** (928) 467-3200.

APACHE TRAIL (SR 88) starts at Apache Junction and proceeds for 39 mi., climbing past the famed Superstition Mountains, passing through Fish Creek Canyon and skirting the southern edges of Apache, Saguaro, Canyon and Roosevelt lakes, ending at Globe. The trail was created in 1905 to transport supplies from Phoenix and Globe to the construction site of Roosevelt Dam. The road parallels the ancient route of the Apaches through the canyons of the Salt River.

Note: The 25-mile portion of Apache Trail between Tortilla Flat and Roosevelt is a narrow, winding gravel road. It is not recommended during rainy weather, for inexperienced drivers or for vehicles more than 35 feet. West-to-east travel from Apache Junction to Globe will put you on the inside lane and grant all passengers the security of rock walls rather than the steep cliffs on the other side. **Phone:** (928) 467-3200.

Fish Creek Canyon is approximately 25 mi. n.e. of Apache Junction. The canyon is noted for massive, vividly colored walls rising as much as 2,000 feet above the highway. Formed by Fish Creek, which runs from the center of the Superstition Mountains northwest towards the Salt River, the canyon floor is lush with saguaro cacti, trees, bushes, reeds and waterfalls.

CANYON LAKE, 16 mi. n.e. on SR 88, is one of a series of lakes on the Salt River. Impounded by the Mormon Flat Dam, Canyon Lake twists for 10 miles through a magnificent gorge to Horse Mesa Dam. *See Recreation Chart.*

GOLDFIELD GHOST TOWN & MINE TOURS, 5 mi. n.e. on SR 88, passing Milepost 200 to 4650 E. Mammoth Mine Rd., offers mine tours, gold panning and specialty shops within view of the spectacular Superstition Mountains. Gunfights are performed

November through April. A museum features a large exhibit of antique mining equipment. A scenic narrow-gauge railroad also encompasses the town.

Hours: Daily 10-5. Gunfights Sat.-Sun. noon-4. Closed Christmas. **Cost:** Town free. Mine tour $7; $6 (ages 60+); $4 (ages 6-12). Train ride $6; $5 (ages 60+); $4 (ages 6-12). Museum $4; $3 (ages 60+); $1 (ages 6-12). **Phone:** (480) 983-0333. ⊓

Apache Trail Tours depart from Goldfield Ghost Town. Participants partake in 1- to 8-hour guided jeep tours of the Apache Trail, the Superstition Mountains and the Four Peaks Wilderness. Climate-controlled SUVs are available. Two-hour gold-panning experiences also are offered.

Hours: Tours daily by reservation. Closed Thanksgiving and Christmas. **Cost:** Two-hour tour $75; $60 (ages 3-13). Four-hour tour $100; $85 (ages 3-13). Phone for other tour rates. Two-hour tour requires a minimum of two people; 4-hour tour requires a minimum of four people. Reservations are required. **Phone:** (480) 982-7661.

LOST DUTCHMAN STATE PARK, 5 mi. n.e. off SR 88 to 6109 N. Apache Tr., offers 320 acres of hiking trails, camping and picnicking areas. Special moonlight hikes are offered monthly and guided hikes and campfire programs are offered weekly November through March. *See Recreation Chart.* **Hours:** Daily dawn-10 p.m. Office daily 8-4. **Cost:** $7 (per private vehicle, up to four passengers); $3 (per additional adult passenger in vehicle or individual arriving on foot or bicycle). Nonelectric camping $15 (per private vehicle). **Phone:** (480) 982-4485. 🅰 🐾 ⛲

SUPERSTITION MOUNTAIN MUSEUM, 4087 N. Apache Tr., contains exhibits and artifacts depicting local history and folklore. You'll find maps of the mythical Lost Dutchman Gold Mine; exhibits about Native Americans, geology and natural history; the Elvis Memorial Chapel and Apacheland Barn, featured in Western movies filmed at the Apacheland Movie Ranch; and reproductions of 19th-century buildings. Nature trails traverse the 12-acre grounds.

Time: Allow 1 hour minimum. **Hours:** Daily 9-4. Closed Jan. 1, Thanksgiving and Christmas. **Cost:** $5; $4 (ages 60+); $2 (students ages 17+ with ID); free (ages 0-16 with paying adult). **Phone:** (480) 983-4888. ⛲

SUPERSTITION MOUNTAINS, e. of town, were named for the many legends surrounding them. The fabled Lost Dutchman Gold Mine lies somewhere in these mountains. Whether the mine really exists is uncertain, but at least eight men were killed because of it and many others died searching for it. Monuments at Roosevelt Dam and Apache Junction commemorate Jacob Waltz, who allegedly discovered the mine.

APACHE JUNCTION MOTEL
Phone: 480/982-7702

◇
Motel
$49-$89

Address: 1680 W Apache Tr 85120 **Location:** US 60 exit 195, 2 mi n, then just w. **Facility:** 15 units. 1 story, exterior corridors. *Bath:* shower only. **Terms:** 3 day cancellation notice-fee imposed. **Free Special Amenities:** local telephone calls and high-speed Internet.

[SAVE] 🍴 📶 🔒 🖥 💻 / SOME UNITS FEE 🐕

BEST WESTERN APACHE JUNCTION INN
Phone: (480)982-9200

◇◇
Hotel
$80-$130

AAA Benefit: Members save up to 20%, plus 10% bonus points with Best Western Rewards®.

Address: 1101 W Apache Tr 85220 **Location:** US 60 exit 195, 2 mi n to W Apache Tr, then 0.4 mi e. **Facility:** 40 units. 2 stories (no elevator), interior/exterior corridors. **Terms:** 2 night minimum stay - seasonal. **Pool(s):** heated outdoor. **Activities:** whirlpool. **Guest Services:** coin laundry. **Free Special Amenities:** full breakfast and high-speed Internet. [SAVE] 🍴 🏊 📶 ✕ 🔒 🖥 💻

WHERE TO EAT

BARLEEN'S ARIZONA OPRY DINNER SHOW
Phone: 480/982-7991

◇◇
American
$30

AAA Inspector Notes: Three generations perform high-energy, country-style entertainment as diners feast on roast beef, mashed potatoes, corn, coleslaw, a roll and chocolate cake. **Bar:** beer only. **Reservations:** suggested. **Address:** 2275 Old West Hwy 85219 **Location:** US 60 exit Tomahawk Rd, 1 mi n, then 0.5 mi e. [D]

DIRTWATER SPRINGS
Phone: 480/983-3478

◇
Steak
$7-$24

AAA Inspector Notes: Steaks and ribs are favorites, but diners should not miss the classic Mexican-style dishes at this restaurant, owned and operated by friendly folks since 1987. Casual decor incorporates Western and hunting elements, including a few mounted animal heads. **Bar:** full bar. **Address:** 586 W Apache Tr 85220 **Location:** Center. [L] [D]

FEED BAG RESTAURANT
Phone: 480/983-3521

◇◇
American
$6-$12

AAA Inspector Notes: Fresh decor, ample portions of home-style food and smiling servers make this restaurant a popular place with locals. Breakfast includes the basics as well as tasty huevos rancheros, and half portions at lunch and dinner are great options for those with light appetites. **Address:** 300 S Phelps Dr 85220 **Location:** US 60 exit 196 (Idaho Rd/SR 88 E), 1.7 mi n to Old West Hwy, just w, then just s. [B] [L] [D]

HISTORIC MINING CAMP RESTAURANT & DUTCHMAN'S HIDE-OUT
Phone: 480/982-3181

◇◇
American
$10-$20

AAA Inspector Notes: Established in 1961, this restaurant sits at the base of the Superstition Mountains. At lunch, diners can choose from the a la carte menu featuring USDA Choice cuts of meat. All-you-can-eat dinners include roast chicken, baked ham and barbecue ribs served in the style of an early mining camp cook shanty. **Bar:** beer & wine. **Address:** 6100 E Mining Camp St 85219 **Location:** US 60 exit 196 (Idaho Rd/SR 88 E), 2.2 mi n to Apache Tr, 2.9 mi ne, then 1 mi e and n; via Nodak Rd and Mining Camp St, follow signs. [L] [D]

APACHE-SITGREAVES NATIONAL FORESTS (D-6)

Elevations in the forests range from 3,500 ft. in the Upper Sonoran Desert to 11,500 ft. at Mount Baldy. Refer to AAA maps for additional elevation information.

Along the south rim of the Colorado Plateau in east-central Arizona, the Apache-Sitgreaves national forests comprise nearly 2.1 million acres. They are named, respectively, for the Apaches and for Lt. Lorenzo Sitgreaves, who in 1851 led the first military topographical mapping expeditions across Arizona. The forests include the Mount Baldy, Bear Wallow and Escudilla wilderness areas and the Blue Range Primitive Area.

Hunting is permitted in season. Numerous lakes and streams offer trout fishing. Boats with motors larger than 8 horsepower are prohibited; on some lakes only electric motors are permitted. Trails are available for varying interests, including horseback riding, mountain biking, and hiking as well as for off-road vehicles. Picnic facilities are available in summer. Winter activities include cross-country skiing, snowmobiling, snowshoeing and ice fishing.

Visitor centers are at Big Lake and on the Mogollon Rim near Heber. Visitor information also is available in summer from attendants at developed campgrounds in the forests and district ranger offices.

The Coronado Trail Scenic Byway (US 191), 127 miles long and ranging from 3,500 to 9,000 feet high, connects the cities of Clifton/Morenci to Springerville/Eagar. The present Coronado Trail (US 191) commemorates portions of the historic route followed by Francisco Vázquez de Coronado when he sought the fabled Seven Cities of Cíbola in 1540. The road traverses areas that remain much as they were more than 450 years ago.

From Clifton the road climbs a corkscrew grade up Rose Peak to an elevation of 8,550 feet. Near this point a Forest Service lookout tower affords a magnificent panorama. Continuing northward, the trail rises to an elevation of 9,200 feet at Blue Vista. The steep, narrow road is not recommended for vehicles pulling trailers more than 20 feet long.

From the rim northward the road is noted for its spectacular autumn coloring. The named portion of the trail ends at Springerville, where US 191 joins US 60.

The White Mountains Scenic Byway is a series of connecting roads that forms a loop through the White Mountains of the Apache-Sitgreaves national forests. The 123-mile loop includes parts of SRs 73, 260, 273 and 373.

For more information contact the Forest Supervisor's Office, Apache-Sitgreaves National Forests, 30 S. Chiricahua Dr., P.O. Box 640, Springerville, AZ 85938; phone (928) 333-4301. *See Recreation Chart.*

AVONDALE pop. 76,238

- Hotels & Restaurants map & index p. 155
- Part of Phoenix area — see map p. 134

HILTON GARDEN INN PHOENIX/AVONDALE
Phone: (623)882-3351 **35**

Hotel
$119-$289

AAA Benefit:
Unparalleled hospitality at a special Member rate.

Address: 11460 W Hilton Way 85323 **Location:** I-10 exit 131 (Avondale Blvd), just s. **Facility:** 123 units. 4 stories, interior corridors. **Terms:** check-in 4 pm, 1-7 night minimum stay, cancellation fee imposed. **Amenities:** high-speed Internet. **Pool(s):** heated outdoor. **Activities:** whirlpool, exercise room. **Guest Services:** valet and coin laundry, area transportation-within 5 mi.

HOMEWOOD SUITES PHOENIX/AVONDALE
Phone: (623)882-3315 **36**

Extended Stay Hotel
$129-$289

AAA Benefit:
Contemporary luxury at a special Member rate.

Address: 11450 W Hilton Way 85323 **Location:** I-10 exit 131 (Avondale Blvd), just s. **Facility:** 123 efficiencies, some two bedrooms. 4 stories, interior corridors. **Terms:** check-in 4 pm, 1-7 night minimum stay, cancellation fee imposed. **Amenities:** high-speed Internet. **Pool(s):** heated outdoor. **Activities:** whirlpool, putting green, exercise room. **Guest Services:** valet and coin laundry, area transportation-within 5 mi.

BENSON (F-5) pop. 5,105, elev. 3,581'

On the Southern Pacific Railroad route, Benson grew as a distribution center for copper and silver mined in the San Pedro Valley. When railroad transportation began to decline in the 1920s, the town welcomed a new breed of traveler, fledgling motorists out to discover the Southwest. Benson's mining, ranching and railroad history is recalled at the San Pedro Valley Arts and Historical Society Museum; phone (520) 586-3070.

For a breed of a different kind, visit The Oasis Sanctuary at 5411 N. Teran Rd. Open by appointment only, the facility is an exotic bird sanctuary that permanently houses rescued psittacines (parrot-type) birds; phone (520) 212-4737.

Benson/San Pedro Valley Chamber of Commerce/Visitor Center: 249 E. 4th St., Benson, AZ 85602. **Phone:** (520) 586-2842.

KARTCHNER CAVERNS STATE PARK, 9 mi. s. of I-10 exit 302 off SR 90, contains one of the world's few living wet caves open for viewing. The guided Rotunda/Throne Room Tour takes visitors through rooms that contain more than 30 types of colorful formations growing for more than 200,000 years out of the limestone beneath the Whetstone Mountains. The guided Big Room Tour features striking calcite formations and giant boulders. Formations include stalactites, stalagmites, canopies, coral pipes, helictites and rimstone dams. Turnip shield and birdsnest quartz needle formations also may be found.

Discovered in 1974, the 7-acre cave system holds the world's second-longest soda straw formation and Kubla Khan, a 58-foot-high column. The skeleton of a Shasta ground sloth from the Pleistocene period is among the fossil finds. Within the 550-acre park are a discovery center with exhibits and interactive displays, an interpretive nature path and 5 miles of hiking trails.

Cameras are not permitted in the cave. **Time:** Allow 2 hours, 30 minutes minimum. **Hours:** Park open daily 7:30-6. Guided 1-hour Rotunda/Throne Room tours are given daily every 20 minutes 8:40-4:40. Guided 1.5-hour Big Room tours are given daily every 30 minutes 8:15-4:15, Oct. 15-Apr. 15. Closed Christmas.

Cost: $6 (per private vehicle, up to four passengers); $3 (per additional adult passenger in vehicle or individual arriving on foot or bicycle); free (with tour reservation). Rotunda/Throne Room tour $18.95; $9.95 (ages 7-13). Big Room tour $22.95; $12.95 (ages 7-13). Ages 0-6 are not permitted on Big Room tour. Rates may vary; phone ahead. Reservations are recommended. **Phone:** (520) 586-4100 for information, or (520) 586-2283 for tour reservations.

BEST WESTERN PLUS QUAIL HOLLOW INN
Phone: (520)586-3646

Hotel
$100-$130

AAA Benefit: Members save up to 20%, plus 10% bonus points with Best Western Rewards®.

Address: 699 N Ocotillo Rd 85602 **Location:** I-10 exit 304 (Ocotillo Rd), just s. **Facility:** 83 units. 1-2 stories (no elevator), exterior corridors. **Terms:** cancellation fee imposed. **Amenities:** Some: high-speed Internet. **Pool(s):** heated outdoor. **Activities:** whirlpool, exercise room. **Guest Services:** coin laundry. **Free Special Amenities:** full breakfast and high-speed Internet.

DESERT ROSE INN
Phone: 520/586-8800

Hotel
Rates not provided

Address: 630 S Village Loop 85602 **Location:** I-10 exit 302, just s. **Facility:** 62 units. 2 stories, interior corridors. **Amenities:** Some: high-speed Internet. **Pool(s):** heated outdoor. **Activities:** exercise room. **Guest Services:** coin laundry.

SUPER 8
Phone: (520)586-1530

Motel
$44-$80

Address: 855 N Ocotillo Rd 85602 **Location:** I-10 exit 304 (Ocotillo Rd), just n. **Facility:** 40 units. 2 stories (no elevator), exterior corridors. **Pool(s):** outdoor.

Enjoy great savings on hotel rates at AAA.com or CAA.ca

WHERE TO EAT

MAGALY'S MEXICAN RESTAURANT
Phone: 520/750-6530

Mexican
$7-$13

AAA Inspector Notes: Friendly staff serves economical and hearty Sonoran dishes prepared by the chef and owner. The neat and tidy room is decorated with Mexican handicrafts, which may be purchased. **Bar:** beer only. **Address:** 675 W 4th St 85602 **Location:** I-10 exit 304 (Ocotillo Rd), 0.5 mi s, then just w.

PALATIANO'S FAMILY RESTAURANT
Phone: 520/586-3523

American
$6-$18

AAA Inspector Notes: This popular local eatery serves a blend of classic Italian and American dishes including great burgers, seafood diavolo and a roast beef dinner. The special dessert is "my mother's bread pudding," served warm. **Bar:** wine only. **Address:** 601 W 4th St 85602 **Location:** I-10 exit 304 (Ocotillo Rd), 0.6 mi s; center.

BISBEE (G-5) pop. 5,575, elev. 5,300'
• Hotels p. 40 • Restaurants p. 40

Bisbee became internationally renowned during the 1880s mining rush, with the discovery of the Copper Queen Lode. Bisbee mines, nestled in the foothills of the Mule Mountains in southeast Arizona, have produced more than $2 billion in copper, gold, lead, silver and zinc. By 1900 Bisbee was the largest cosmopolitan center between St. Louis and San Francisco. Besides operating several stock exchanges, the town was a major venue for rodeos, circus, vaudeville, theater and lectures.

By the early 1970s most of the mines had closed, and artists' studios replaced the miners' shacks. Bisbee is now home to numerous art galleries and studios and serves as an enclave for more than 100 resident artists and artisans as well as actors, dancers, writers, musicians and photographers. Events and cultural activities are held throughout the year; contact the visitor center for further information.

Artifacts and period furnishings of early Bisbee are displayed at the Muheim Heritage House at 207 Youngblood Hill; phone (520) 432-7698. The house was completed in 1915 by a prominent local businessman. Another museum that preserves Bisbee's past through artifacts, clothing and memorabilia is the Bisbee Restoration Museum at 37 Main St.

Bisbee Visitor Center: #2 Copper Queen Plaza, Bisbee, P.O. Box 1642, AZ 85603. **Phone:** (520) 432-3554 or (866) 224-7233.

Shopping areas: The downtown section known as Old Bisbee has several specialty shops that sell antiques, assorted crafts, gifts, jewelry, turquoise and Western items.

BISBEE MINING AND HISTORICAL MUSEUM, 5 Copper Queen Plaza, jct. Main St. and Brewery Gulch, is in the building that served as the headquarters of the Copper Queen Consolidated Mining Company. An affiliate of the Smithsonian Institution, the museum examines local history and culture beginning in 1877. The exhibit Digging In tells the story of copper. The archival library contains photographs, manuscripts, documents and research books about state history and the copper mining era.

Hours: Daily 10-4. Closed Jan. 1, Thanksgiving and Christmas. **Cost:** $7.50; $6.50 (ages 60+); $3 (ages 3-16). **Phone:** (520) 432-7071.

QUEEN MINE, on SR 80 near The Lavender Pit mine, offers 1.25-hour tours by mine car into an underground copper mine. The tours are conducted by former miners. **Note:** Sweaters or jackets are recommended. **Hours:** Tours depart daily at 9, 10:30, noon, 2 and 3:30. Closed Thanksgiving and Christmas. **Cost:** $13; $5.50 (ages 4-12). Reservations are recommended. **Phone:** (520) 432-2071 or (866) 432-2071.

AMERICAS BEST VALUE INN & SUITES
Phone: (520)432-2293

Motel
$70-$360

Address: 1372 Hwy 92 85603 **Location:** 0.8 mi w of jct Naco Hwy; sw of downtown. **Facility:** 35 units, some two bedrooms and kitchens. 1-2 stories, exterior corridors. **Terms:** office hours 7 am-10 pm, cancellation fee imposed. **Guest Services:** coin laundry. **Free Special Amenities:** local telephone calls and high-speed Internet.

AUDREY'S INN
Phone: 520/227-6120

Condominium
$105-$125

Address: 20 Brewery Ave 85603 **Location:** Just nw of Main St; in historic district. **Facility:** Originally a gentleman's club in the early 1900s, this historic building now houses modern guest suites and two-level units, each with a full kitchen. 6 condominiums. 3 stories (no elevator), interior corridors. **Parking:** street only. **Terms:** cancellation fee imposed. **Guest Services:** coin laundry.

CANYON ROSE SUITES
Phone: 520/432-5098

Classic Historic Hotel
Rates not provided

Address: 27 Subway St 85603 **Location:** Corner of Shearer Ave; in historic district. **Facility:** This historic building, located just off Main Street, has been outfitted with attractive rooms and modern conveniences. 7 kitchen units. 2 stories (no elevator), interior corridors. **Parking:** street only. **Terms:** office hours 8 am-7 pm. **Guest Services:** coin laundry. **Free Special Amenities:** high-speed Internet and use of on-premises laundry facilities.

COPPER CITY INN
Phone: 520/432-1418

Bed & Breakfast
$120-$250

Address: 99 Main St 85603 **Location:** Center. **Facility:** The charming, well-appointed property with limited services is located in the historic district; registration is conducted by Internet. 4 units, some two bedrooms and kitchens. 2 stories (no elevator), interior corridors. **Guest Services:** complimentary laundry.

LETSON LOFT HOTEL
Phone: (520)432-3210

Historic Bed & Breakfast
$95-$195

Address: 26 Main St 85603 **Location:** Center; in historic district. **Facility:** The inn offers charming, individually decorated guest rooms as well as an art gallery. 8 units. 2 stories (no elevator), interior corridors. **Parking:** street only. **Terms:** office hours 8 am-6 pm, age restrictions may apply, cancellation fee imposed.

SAN JOSE LODGE
Phone: (520)432-5761

Motel
$60-$180

Address: 2102 Naco Hwy 85603 **Location:** SR 92 W, 1.5 mi s. **Facility:** 43 units, some kitchens. 1 story, exterior corridors. **Terms:** cancellation fee imposed. **Pool(s):** outdoor.

COPPER QUEEN HOTEL
Phone: 520/432-2216

[fyi] Not evaluated. **Address:** 11 Howell Ave 85603 **Location:** Corner of Brewery Ave; in historic district. Facilities, services, and decor characterize a midscale property.

WHERE TO EAT

BISBEE GRILLE
Phone: 520/432-6788

American
$8-$24

AAA Inspector Notes: Located in the center of the historic mining town, this grill is a popular casual lunch and dinner spot for both visitors and locals. Choose from grilled steaks, burgers, seafood and pasta dishes. **Bar:** full bar. **Reservations:** suggested. **Address:** 2 Copper Queen Plaza 85603 **Location:** Center; in Copper Queen Plaza. **Parking:** street only. L D

CAFE CORNUCOPIA
Phone: (520)432-4820

Deli
$6-$9

AAA Inspector Notes: The small space of this sidewalk delicatessen does not limit the big taste from soups and sandwiches. **Address:** 14 Main St 85603 **Location:** In historic district. **Parking:** street only. **Historic**

L

CAFE ROKA
Phone: 520/432-5153

New American
$14-$28

AAA Inspector Notes: This popular eatery is located in a restored 1907 building with a central oval bar. The chef/owner serves up New American cuisine excellently prepared using seasonal ingredients. **Bar:** full bar. **Reservations:** suggested. **Address:** 35 Main St 85603 **Location:** SR 80, just n; in historic downtown district. **Parking:** street only. D

HIGH DESERT MARKET & CAFE
Phone: 520/432-6775

American
$5-$10

AAA Inspector Notes: Tucked away on the high end of Main Street is this charming, casual eatery with sidewalk dining where diners can watch passersby while noshing on freshly made soups, organic salads and thick sandwiches. Evening dinners are available for take-out. Also available is a coffee and smoothie bar. **Address:** 203 Tombstone Canyon 85603 **Location:** 0.5 mi ne of jct SR 80 W and 80 E via Main St; across from courthouse.

B L D [AC]

POCO
Phone: 520/432-3733

Vegetarian
$7-$12

AAA Inspector Notes: This tiny space belies the big, bold flavors of fresh, Mexican vegan cuisine. Menu choices change daily, but may include such tasty items as black bean burgers with grilled poblano chiles, chorizo enchiladas and plantain fritters. There also is a nice selection of organic wines on tap. Make sure to save room for the delicious cupcakes. The outdoor patio is a nice option when weather permits. **Bar:** beer & wine. **Address:** 15 Main St 85603 **Location:** Center; in Peddler's Alley. **Parking:** street only. L D [AC]

SANTIAGO'S MEXICAN RESTAURANT
Phone: 520/432-1910

Regional Mexican
$3-$20

AAA Inspector Notes: At the city's main intersection, this bright and lively Mexican restaurant features fajitas sizzling on cast-iron plates, delicious fish tacos dressed with classic crumbly Mexican white cheese and a variety of fruit drinks and margaritas. **Bar:** full bar. **Address:** 1 Howell Ave 85603 **Location:** Corner of Brewery and Howell aves; center. **Parking:** street only. [L] [D]

SCREAMING BANSHEE PIZZA
Phone: 520/432-1300

Pizza
$8-$15

AAA Inspector Notes: Come join the fun at this eclectic and artsy bistro. Savor the specialty pizza, fired up in the pecan wood-burning oven. Locally grown, organic ingredients are used whenever possible. Wash it all down with a homemade sangria or margarita. **Bar:** full bar. **Address:** 200 Tombstone Canyon 85603 **Location:** 0.5 mi ne of jct SR 80 W and 80 E via Main St; next to courthouse. **Parking:** on-site and street. [L] [D]

BLACK CANYON CITY   pop. 2,837

KID CHILLEEN'S BBQ STEAKHOUSE
Phone: 623/374-5552

Steak
$6-$18

AAA Inspector Notes: Country barbecue, grilled steaks, roasted chicken and desserts are large enough to share at this casual spot. Live entertainment is featured on the weekends. **Bar:** full bar. **Address:** 33150 Coldwater Rd 85324 **Location:** I-17 exit 244, just e.

[L] [D]

BUCKEYE   pop. 50,876
• Part of Phoenix area — see map p. 134

DAYS INN-BUCKEYE
Phone: (623)386-5400

Hotel
$56-$158

Address: 25205 W Yuma Rd 85326 **Location:** I-10 exit 114 (Miller Rd), just sw. **Facility:** 60 units. 2 stories (no elevator), exterior corridors. **Terms:** cancellation fee imposed. **Amenities:** high-speed Internet. **Pool(s):** outdoor. **Activities:** whirlpool. **Guest Services:** coin laundry. **Free Special Amenities:** continental breakfast and high-speed Internet.

[SAVE] 🏊 📶 🔒 🖥 🍽 / SOME UNITS FEE 🐾

BULLHEAD CITY   (C-1) pop. 39,540, elev. 540'

Established originally as a supply and support base for builders of the Davis Dam, which impounds Lake Mojave in the Lake Mead National Recreation Area *(see place listing p. 108)*, Bullhead City has evolved into a vacation community. The city's accommodations industry thrives on the thousands of visitors drawn to the mild winter weather and the casinos across the river in Laughlin, Nev. Two bridges connect the towns, and a free river ferry is available.

Bullhead Area Chamber of Commerce: 1251 SR 95, Bullhead City, AZ 86429. **Phone:** (928) 754-4121 or (800) 987-7457.

COLORADO RIVER MUSEUM is at 2201 SR 68. Exhibits feature Mojave Indian artifacts, a Native American village display, the first telephone switchboard used in Bullhead City, a replica of 1885 Fort Mojave, a gold mine replica, minerals and gemstones, steamboat models and an 1859 Steinway

grand piano. Special activities also are offered; phone for details. **Time:** Allow 30 minutes minimum. **Hours:** Tues.-Sun. 10-4, Sept.-June. Closed Jan. 1, Easter, Thanksgiving and Christmas. **Cost:** $2; free (ages 0-12). **Phone:** (928) 754-3399.

BEST WESTERN BULLHEAD CITY INN
Phone: 928/754-3000

Hotel
Rates not provided

AAA Benefit: Members save up to 20%, plus 10% bonus points with Best Western Rewards®.

Address: 1126 Hwy 95 86429 **Location:** 1.8 mi s of Laughlin Bridge. **Facility:** 88 units. 2 stories (no elevator), exterior corridors. **Terms:** check-in 4 pm. **Amenities:** safes (fee). *Some:* high-speed Internet. **Pool(s):** outdoor. **Activities:** whirlpool. **Guest Services:** coin laundry. **Free Special Amenities:** local telephone calls and high-speed Internet.

[SAVE] [🍴] 🏊 [BIZ] 📶 🔒 🖥 🍽 / SOME UNITS FEE 🐾 🖥

LAKE MOHAVE RESORT MOTEL
Phone: 928/754-3245

Motel
Rates not provided

Address: 2690 E Katherine Spur Rd 86429 **Location:** Jct SR 95, 1.5 mi e on SR 68, 1 mi n, then 5.4 mi e; at Katherine Landing; in Lake Mead National Recreation area. **Facility:** 49 units, some efficiencies. 2 stories (no elevator), exterior corridors. **Activities:** rental boats, waterskiing, fishing. *Fee:* marina. [🍴] / SOME UNITS FEE 🐾 🔒 🖥 🍽

LODGE ON THE RIVER
Phone: (928)758-8080

Motel
$45-$125

Address: 1717 Hwy 95 86442 **Location:** 3.8 mi s of Laughlin Bridge. **Facility:** 64 units. 2 stories (no elevator), exterior corridors. **Terms:** 7 day cancellation notice-fee imposed. **Pool(s):** heated outdoor. **Guest Services:** coin laundry. **Free Special Amenities:** high-speed Internet.

[SAVE] [🍴] 🏊 📶 🔒 🖥 / SOME UNITS FEE 🐾 🍽

WHERE TO EAT

BLACK BEAR DINER
Phone: 928/763-2477

American
$7-$16

AAA Inspector Notes: A homey atmosphere characterizes this family-oriented restaurant. Familiar comfort foods, such as meatloaf with mashed potatoes, are at the heart of the menu and are served in generous portions. **Bar:** beer & wine. **Address:** 1751 W Hwy 95, Suite 25 86442 **Location:** 3.6 mi s of Laughlin Bridge. [B] [L] [D]

COLIANNO'S ITALIAN RESTAURANT
Phone: 928/758-7104

Italian
$9-$30

AAA Inspector Notes: The feeling here is decidedly Old World, complete with cozy checkered tablecloths. The menu lists steak, seafood and pasta dishes as well as specialty pizza. Carry-out service is available from the on-premises delicatessen. **Bar:** full bar. **Address:** 1884 Hwy 95 86442 **Location:** 4.1 mi s of Laughlin Bridge.

[L] [D]

EL PALACIO

Mexican
$5-$15

Phone: 928/763-2494

AAA Inspector Notes: In addition to assorted Mexican steak and seafood dishes, the menu lists more familiar burritos, enchiladas and tamales. The atmosphere is festive, with bright and colorful appointments. **Bar:** full bar.
Address: 1885 Hwy 95 86442 **Location:** 4.1 mi s of Laughlin Bridge. (L) (D) (🔀)

CAMERON pop. 885

CAMERON TRADING POST MOTEL, RESTAURANT & GIFT SHOP   **Phone:** 928/679-2231

Motel
$59-$109

Address: 466 N Hwy 89 86020 **Location:** 1 mi from east gate turn off. **Facility:** 66 units. 2-3 stories (no elevator), exterior corridors. **Terms:** check-in 4 pm. **Dining:** restaurant, see separate listing. **Activities:** hiking trails. **Free Special Amenities: local telephone calls and high-speed Internet.**
(See ad p. 91.)

[SAVE] [🍽] [📶] [✖] [💻]
/ SOME UNITS FEE [🐾] [🚻] [📷]

WHERE TO EAT

CAMERON TRADING POST RESTAURANT
                                 Phone: 928/679-2231

Southwestern
$6-$19

AAA Inspector Notes: Located at a busy intersection outside the Grand Canyon entrance, this restaurant is attached to a trading post and a motel, making it very convenient for travelers. Casual, friendly, helpful staff members deliver steaks, chicken and Mexican cuisine amid Native American decor. **Address:** 466 N Hwy 89 86020 **Location:** 1 mi from east gate turn off; in Cameron Trading Post Motel, Restaurant & Gift Shop.

(B) (L) (D)

CAMP VERDE (C-4) pop. 10,873, elev. 3,160'

Camp Verde was founded as Camp Lincoln in 1866 by Arizona Volunteers to defend pioneers from Apache raids. The fort was renamed Fort Verde a few years later by the U.S. Army. As the area became more peaceful, residents turned their energies toward cattle raising and farming, the two major industries in the broad Verde Valley. Native American ruins and cliff dwellings may be seen at nearby Montezuma Castle National Monument *(see place listing p. 117)* and Montezuma Well.

Camp Verde Chamber of Commerce: 385 S. Main St., Camp Verde, AZ 86322. **Phone:** (928) 567-9294.

FORT VERDE STATE HISTORIC PARK is 3 mi. e. of I-17. In one of the four restored structures of the old fort are Native American, pioneer and military artifacts. Officers' quarters, bachelor's housing and the doctor's quarters are furnished in period. **Time:** Allow 1 hour minimum. **Hours:** Thurs.-Mon. 9-5. Closed Christmas. **Cost:** $4; $2 (ages 7-13). **Phone:** (928) 567-3275.

[SAVE] **OUT OF AFRICA WILDLIFE PARK** is, from I-17 exit 287, 3 mi. w. on SR 260, following signs to park entrance. The Wildlife Preserve features a narrated tram or trolley tour; photography of predators from unobstructed platforms is permitted. Visitors may interact with giraffes and camels during the narrated African Bush Safari tour, attend a Predator Feed show, and watch caretakers activate the instinct of play at a Tiger Splash show. Special tour options include a 1-hour Unimog Bush Safari tour and a 3-hour Behind the Scenes VIP tour.

Time: Allow 1 hour minimum. **Hours:** Park open daily 9:30-5. Predator Feed Sun., Wed. and Fri. at 3. Tiger Splash daily at 1:15. Unimog Bush Safari tour departs daily at 11 and 2. Behind the Scenes VIP tour departs Wed.-Sun. at 10 and 1. Last admission 1 hour before closing. Closed July 4, Thanksgiving and Christmas. **Cost:** $36; $34 (ages 65+); $20 (ages 3-12). Unimog Bush Safari tour $15 (park admission not included). Behind the Scenes VIP tour $149; $125 (ages 3-12). Rates may vary; phone ahead. Behind the Scenes VIP tour reservations must be made 24 hours in advance. Reservations are required. **Phone:** (928) 567-2840. [🍽]

GAMBLING ESTABLISHMENTS

- **Cliff Castle Casino** is off I-17 exit 289 at 555 Middle Verde Rd. **Hours:** Daily 24 hours. **Phone:** (928) 567-7900 or (800) 381-7568.

RECREATIONAL ACTIVITIES
White-water Rafting

- **AAM's Mild to Wild Rafting & Jeep Tours Inc.** departs from Super 8 Motel at 1550 W. SR 260. Other activities are offered. **Hours:** Tours depart daily and at various times. **Phone:** (970) 529-4465 or (800) 567-6745.

CLIFF CASTLE CASINO HOTEL   **Phone:** 928/567-6611

Hotel
Rates not provided

Address: 333 Middle Verde Rd 86322 **Location:** I-17 exit 289, 0.4 mi se. **Facility:** Two miles south of Montezuma Castle National Monument, the hotel offers spacious but basic rooms. 80 units. 2 stories (no elevator), exterior corridors. **Terms:** check-in 4 pm. **Amenities:** high-speed Internet. **Dining:** The Gathering, see separate listing. **Activities:** whirlpool. **Guest Services:** area transportation-casino.

[SAVE] [♿] [🍽] [🍸] [📶] [✖] [💻]
/ SOME UNITS FEE [🐾] FEE [🚻]

COMFORT INN-CAMP VERDE   **Phone:** (928) 567-9000

Hotel
$59-$209

Address: 340 N Goswick Way 86322 **Location:** I-17 exit 287, just e, then just s. **Facility:** 85 units. 3 stories, interior corridors. **Terms:** cancellation fee imposed. **Pool(s):** heated outdoor. **Activities:** whirlpool. **Guest Services:** coin laundry. **Free Special Amenities: full breakfast and high-speed Internet.**

[SAVE] [🍽] [➡] [BIZ] [📶] [💻]
/ SOME UNITS FEE [🐾] FEE [🚻] FEE [📷]

SUPER 8-CAMP VERDE
◆ Motel
$56-$94

Phone: (928)567-2622
Address: 1550 W Hwy 260 86322
Location: I-17 exit 287, just e.
Facility: 44 units. 2 stories (no elevator), interior corridors. **Terms:** cancellation fee imposed. **Pool(s):** heated indoor. **Activities:** whirlpool.

WHERE TO EAT

THE GATHERING
◆◆
Regional American
$6-$24

Phone: 928/567-6611
AAA Inspector Notes: Patrons can relax in a quiet setting and benefit from friendly service while trying truly distinctive dishes. Crab and squash blossom cream puffs with chipotle ranch dipping sauce is representative of creative cuisine found here. The buffalo burger is popular, and the saguaro-glazed quail with chollo bud risotto scores a close second. **Bar:** full bar. **Address:** 333 Middle Verde Rd 86322 **Location:** I-17 exit 289, 0.4 mi se; in Cliff Castle Casino Hotel.

CANYON DE CHELLY NATIONAL MONUMENT (B-6)

In the Navajo Reservation 3 miles east of Chinle, Canyon de Chelly (d'-SHAY) National Monument is reached from Gallup or Shiprock, N.M., and Chambers, Holbrook, Winslow or Tuba City, Ariz. Five periods of Native American culture (Archaic, Basketmakers, early Pueblo, Hopi and Navajo), dating from 2500 B.C. to present, are represented within the 83,849-acre monument.

Archaic, Basketmakers and early Pueblo groups successively occupied the canyons until a reduction in population in A.D. 1350. During the 14th and 15th centuries the Hopis utilized the canyons. The Navajo arrived sometime in the 17th century and continue to live in the canyons, growing corn and peaches and herding livestock.

The 26-mile-long Canyon de Chelly is joined by the 25-mile-long Canyon del Muerto; red sandstone walls rise from 30 to 1,000 feet in a sheer, remarkably smooth ascent. Pictographs painted on the walls date from the earliest occupation to the Navajo era.

The principal area ruins are White House, Antelope House, Standing Cow and Mummy Cave. White House was first explored in 1848, and its architecture may indicate connections with Chaco Canyon. Antelope House is named for the large pictograph of running antelopes that appears there. Mummy Cave, in which some well-preserved human remains were discovered, has a three-story tower.

Authorized Navajo guides are available for canyon trips. The Thunderbird Lodge near the monument headquarters conducts trips into the canyon daily, depending on high water conditions, with six-wheel-drive vehicles. All-day tour (includes lunch) $82.95. Half-day tour $51.50; $39.95 (ages 0-11). Phone (928) 674-5841 or (800) 679-2473.

For individuals with their own four-wheel-drive vehicles, authorized guides are available at the visitor center for $15 per hour (3-hour minimum). Other regulations apply; *see Good Facts To Know*. Several private companies offer guided tours on horseback.

Except for a self-guiding trail from White House Overlook to the White House Ruin, all visitors within the canyons *must* be accompanied by a park ranger or an authorized guide.

Scenic drives traverse both sides of the canyon, affording views of most major ruins from overlooks. Allow 2 hours for each drive if stopping at all of the overlooks. Food and gas are available in Chinle. The visitor center is open daily 8-5; closed Christmas. The Navajo Reservation observes daylight-saving time, unlike the rest of the state; times listed reflect this when applicable. Monument admission free. For further information contact Canyon de Chelly National Monument, P.O. Box 588, Chinle, AZ 86503; phone (928) 674-5500 , ext. 222.

CAREFREE pop. 3,363
- Restaurants p. 44
- Part of Phoenix area — see map p. 134

THE BOULDERS, A WALDORF ASTORIA RESORT
Phone: (480)488-9009

◆◆◆
Resort Hotel
$249-$449 2/1-5/19
$149-$399 5/20-1/31

AAA Benefit: Unparalleled hospitality at a special Member rate.

Address: 34631 N Tom Darlington Dr 85377 **Location:** Scottsdale Rd, 11 mi n of Bell Rd. **Facility:** Nestled in the Sonora desert, this distinctive resort with its oversized casita rooms uses the natural topography of dramatic boulders in its design. 220 units, some kitchens and houses. 1-2 stories, exterior corridors. **Parking:** on-site and valet. **Terms:** 1-7 night minimum stay, cancellation fee imposed. **Amenities:** safes, honor bars. **Dining:** 6 restaurants, also, Latilla Dining Room, see separate listing. **Pool(s):** 4 heated outdoor. **Activities:** saunas, whirlpools, steamrooms, recreation programs, rental bicycles, hiking trails, jogging, spa. *Fee:* golf-36 holes, 8 tennis courts. **Guest Services:** valet laundry, area transportation-within resort.

CAREFREE RESORT & CONFERENCE CENTER
Phone: (480)488-5300

◆◆◆
Resort Hotel
$59-$870

Address: 37220 Mule Train Rd 85377 **Location:** SR 101 exit 36 (Pima Rd), 12.2 mi n to Cave Creek Rd, 1 mi w, then 0.4 mi n. **Facility:** Spacious rooms in the main building and expansive, well-appointed condominium units give this property appeal. 369 units, some kitchens and condominiums. 1-3 stories, interior/exterior corridors. **Parking:** on-site and valet. **Terms:** check-in 4 pm, 3 day cancellation notice-fee imposed. **Amenities:** *Some:* safes. **Pool(s):** 2 heated outdoor. **Activities:** whirlpools, 5 lighted tennis courts, recreation programs, rental bicycles, hiking trails, jogging, basketball, horseshoes, exercise room, spa. *Fee:* horseback riding. **Guest Services:** valet laundry, area transportation-within 5 mi.

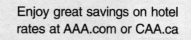

Enjoy great savings on hotel rates at AAA.com or CAA.ca

WHERE TO EAT

ENGLISH ROSE TEA ROOM   Phone: 480/488-4812

◆◆◆

Specialty
$8-$14

AAA Inspector Notes: The setting is tiny in space, but the charming decor is classic tea room. The friendly staff even offer a selection of hats guests may wear to make their luncheon or high tea a special experience. **Reservations:** required. **Address:** 201 Easy St, #103 85377 **Location:** From Tom Darlington Dr, just e on Wampum Way, then just n; center. **Parking:** street only. [L]

LATILLA DINING ROOM   Phone: 480/488-9009

◆◆◆ ◆◆◆

Regional American
$15-$40

AAA Inspector Notes: Highly imaginative and innovative preparations of regional favorites make up the menu. The sophisticated dining room is the renowned resort's premier place for enjoying upscale cuisine. **Bar:** full bar. **Reservations:** suggested. **Address:** 34631 N Tom Darlington Dr 85377 **Location:** Scottsdale Rd, 11 mi n of Bell Rd; in The Boulders, A Waldorf Astoria Resort. **Parking:** on-site and valet. [D]

CASA GRANDE (E-4) pop. 48,571, elev. 1,387'
• Restaurants p. 46

Casa Grande, founded in 1879, was named for the Hohokam Indian ruins *(see Casa Grande Ruins National Monument p. 46)* 20 miles northeast of town. Casa Grande, once dependent on agriculture and mining, is now a diversified community.

Greater Casa Grande Chamber of Commerce: 575 N. Marshall, Casa Grande, AZ 85122. **Phone:** (520) 836-2125 or (800) 916-1515.

CASA GRANDE VALLEY HISTORICAL SOCIETY AND MUSEUM, 110 W. Florence Blvd., has more than 16,000 items and 22,000 photos in its collection relating to life in the desert and regional history. Included are three period rooms, Native American artifacts, mining and agricultural exhibits, three antique fire engines, an antique doll house and a historical diorama. A barn and a restored 1935 one-room African-American grammar school are on the grounds.

Hours: Thurs.-Mon. noon-4, Sept. 15-May 15. Closed major holidays. **Cost:** $5; $4 (ages 60+); free (ages 0-16). **Phone:** (520) 836-2223.

BEST WESTERN PLUS CASA GRANDE
Phone: (520)836-1600

◆◆◆

Hotel
$70-$130

[Best Western PLUS logo]

AAA Benefit: Members save up to 20%, plus 10% bonus points with Best Western Rewards®.

Address: 665 N Via del Cielo Rd 85222 **Location:** I-10 exit 194 (SR 287), 1 mi w. Across from Regional Medical Center. **Facility:** 80 units. 2 stories (no elevator), exterior corridors. **Pool(s):** heated outdoor. **Activities:** whirlpool, exercise room. **Guest Services:** valet and coin laundry. **Free Special Amenities:** expanded continental breakfast and high-speed Internet.

[SAVE] [🍴] [🏊] [BIZ] [📶] [✕] [🔒] [📷] [📺]

COMFORT INN   Phone: (520)421-9878

◆◆◆

Hotel
$57-$119

Address: 2145 E Florence Blvd 85222 **Location:** I-10 exit 194 (SR 287), 0.5 mi w. **Facility:** 65 units. 2 stories (no elevator), interior corridors. **Terms:** cancellation fee imposed. **Amenities:** safes. **Pool(s):** heated outdoor. **Activities:** whirlpool, exercise room. **Guest Services:** coin laundry.

[SAVE] [🍴] [CALL] [&M] [🏊] [📶] [🔒] [📷] [📺]

Safety tip: Keep a current
AAA/CAA Road Atlas
in every vehicle

Moments that Last a Lifetime.

Save on Theme Park Tickets at AAA.com/Discounts.

Ask your local AAA office about additional savings. Valid membership card required.
Image compliments of SeaWorld Parks & Entertainment.

Show Your Card & Save

FRANCISCO GRANDE HOTEL & GOLF RESORT
Phone: (520)836-6444

Hotel
$79-$449

Address: 12684 W Gila Bend Hwy 85193 **Location:** I-8 exit 172 (Thornton Rd), 3.5 mi n, then 4.2 mi w. **Facility:** 64 units, some kitchens. 2-9 stories, exterior corridors. **Dining:** Legend's Restaurant, see separate listing. **Pool(s):** heated outdoor. **Activities:** whirlpool, exercise room. **Fee:** golf-18 holes, bicycles, massage. **Guest Services:** valet and coin laundry.

HOLIDAY INN EXPRESS & SUITES CASA GRANDE
Phone: (520)509-6333

Hotel
$85-$145

Address: 805 N Cacheries Ct 85122 **Location:** I-10 exit 194 (SR 287), 0.6 mi w. **Facility:** 77 units. 3 stories, interior corridors. **Amenities:** high-speed Internet. **Pool(s):** heated outdoor. **Activities:** whirlpool, exercise room. **Guest Services:** valet and coin laundry. **Free Special Amenities: full breakfast and high-speed Internet.**

HOLIDAY INN HOTEL CASA GRANDE
Phone: (520)426-3500

Hotel
$79-$199

Address: 777 N Pinal Ave 85122 **Location:** I-10 exit 194 (SR 287), 3.9 mi w. **Facility:** 176 units. 4 stories, interior corridors. **Terms:** 3 day cancellation notice-fee imposed. **Pool(s):** heated outdoor. **Activities:** whirlpool, exercise room. **Guest Services:** valet and coin laundry, area transportation-within 5 mi. **Free Special Amenities: high-speed Internet.**
(See ad this page.)

Visit AAA.com or CAA.ca
for one-stop travel
planning and reservations

Get pet travel tips
and enter the photo contest
at AAA.com/PetBook

▼ See AAA listing this page ▼

from: $79.99*

Midway Between Phoenix and Tucson

Holiday Inn

Hotel Features
- Award-Winning Cabo's Bar & Grill • Bar w/ Entertainment
- Room Service • Pool/Spa • Fitness Facility • Free Wi-Fi
- Upscale Bedding • Microwaves • Refrigerators • Business Services
- Meeting Space Available • Pet Friendly

AAA
Approved

Subject to availability. Higher rates may apply on some dates.

Holiday Inn Casa Grande
(877) 893-5944 • www.HolidayInncasagrande.com
777 N. Pinal Ave • Casa Grande, AZ 85122
From Phoenix: Take I-10E, exit #185. Go right at exit about 9 miles.
Hotel is on right side of Pinal Ave. & Florence Blvd.

Get the free mobile app at
http://gettag.mobi

MAINSTAY SUITES
Phone: (520)426-1177

◆◆ ◆◆
Extended Stay Hotel
$65-$130

Address: 851 N Henness Rd 85222 **Location:** I-10 exit 194 (SR 287), 1 mi w, then just n. **Facility:** 70 efficiencies. 2 stories (no elevator), interior corridors. **Terms:** cancellation fee imposed. **Activities:** exercise room. **Guest Services:** coin laundry.

SAVE ⊺⧾ ⟨⟩ ✕ ⊟ ⊡ ⊑

SUPER 8
Phone: (520)836-8800

◆◆ ◆◆
Hotel
$50-$81

Address: 2066 E Florence Blvd 85222 **Location:** I-10 exit 194 (SR 287), 0.6 mi w. **Facility:** 41 units. 2 stories (no elevator), interior corridors. **Pool(s):** outdoor. **Guest Services:** coin laundry. **Free Special Amenities: continental breakfast and high-speed Internet.**

SAVE ⊺⧾ ⊜ ⟨⟩ ⊑ / SOME UNITS FEE 🐕 ⊟ ⊡

WHERE TO EAT

BEDILLON'S CACTUS GARDEN RESTAURANT
Phone: 520/836-2045

◆◆ ◆◆
Southwestern
$8-$19

AAA Inspector Notes: This 80-year-old restored home enables visitors to visit a Western museum, walk through a cactus garden and devour a luscious meal. Creative sides such as jicama salad and fruit salsa enhance any sandwich, seafood or meat dish. **Bar:** full bar. **Reservations:** suggested. **Address:** 800 N Park Ave 85222 **Location:** I-10 exit 194 (SR 287), 3.8 mi w, then just n. ⓛ ⓓ

CAFÉ DE MANUEL
Phone: 520/421-3199

◆◆ ◆◆
Mexican
$6-$13

AAA Inspector Notes: This friendly, casual eatery serves fresh, traditional cuisine. Made-to-order dishes, such as enchilada salad, creamed chimichanga and carne asada, are worth the wait. Breakfasts include rellenos and eggs with machaca. **Bar:** full bar. **Address:** 1300 N Pinal Ave 85222 **Location:** Jct SR 84 and 287, 0.4 mi n on SR 387 (Pinal Ave). ⓑ ⓛ ⓓ

LEGEND'S RESTAURANT
Phone: 520/836-6444

◆◆ ◆◆
Western American
$11-$25

AAA Inspector Notes: This Southwest-style dining room and bar area serve up casual American favorites including seared Alaskan salmon, St. Louis barbecue ribs, lamb sirloin and crispy fish and chips. On nice days, diners can sit outside overlooking the expansive valley and distant mountains. **Bar:** full bar. **Address:** 2684 W Gila Bend Hwy 85293 **Location:** I-8 exit 172 (Thornton Rd), 3.5 mi n, then 4.2 mi w; in Francisco Grande Hotel & Golf Resort. ⓑ ⓛ ⓓ CALL ⧦Ⓜ

◆ CASA GRANDE RUINS NATIONAL MONUMENT (E-4)

Off SR 87/287, Casa Grande Ruins National Monument lies within the city limits of Coolidge (*see place listing p. 56*). The Casa Grande (Big House) was built by prehistoric peoples called Hohokam Ancestral Desert People prior to 1350 A.D. The four-story structure's ruins are constructed of layers of caliche mud and represent the height of Hohokam architecture. Around the main building are the remains of a walled village. A viewing platform overlooking a prehistoric ball court is behind the picnic area.

The Hohokam Ancestral Desert People lived in the area for many centuries prior to the construction of the Casa Grande. Sometime around 1450 Casa Grande was abandoned for unknown reasons after the Hohokam Ancestral Desert People had used it for only a century. The ruins were seen and named in 1694 by Father Eusebio Francisco Kino, a missionary who was led to the site by local Pima Indians.

The visitor center features a museum. Self-guiding tours and picnic facilities are available. Allow 1 hour minimum. Monument open daily 9-5; closed Thanksgiving and Christmas. Admission $5; free

AAA DISCOUNTS

Get the **AAA Discounts app** for iPhone and Android-compatible devices or the **CAA Savings app** for iPhone to find your way to thousands of nearby AAA/CAA member discounts. Save on shopping, dining, lodging and more. Get the best route there, plus driving directions and real-time tracking.

The app's Roadside Assistance feature enables members to send their GPS location when calling AAA/CAA for help.

AAA.com/mobile
CAA.ca/mobile

AAA CAA

(ages 0-15). For further information contact the Superintendent, Casa Grande Ruins National Monument, 1100 W. Ruins Dr., Coolidge, AZ 85128; phone (520) 723-3172.

CATALINA pop. 7,569
• Part of Tucson area — see map p. 268

BEST WESTERN CATALINA INN   **Phone:** (520)818-9500

Hotel
$69-$120

AAA Benefit: Members save up to 20%, plus 10% bonus points with Best Western Rewards®.

Address: 15691 N Oracle Rd 85739 **Location:** 4.6 mi n of Tangerine Rd. **Facility:** 49 units. 2 stories (no elevator), interior/exterior corridors. **Pool(s):** outdoor. **Activities:** exercise room. **Guest Services:** coin laundry. **Free Special Amenities: local telephone calls and high-speed Internet.**

MIRAVAL LIFE IN BALANCE RESORT
Phone: 520/825-4000

fyi   Not evaluated. **Address:** 5000 E Via Estancia Miraval 85739. Facilities, services, and decor characterize an upscale property.

WHERE TO EAT

MI TIERRA RESTAURANTE   **Phone:** 520/825-3040

Mexican
$7-$23

AAA Inspector Notes: The friendly staff, bright Mexican decor and traditional Sonoran dishes warm diners' hearts and satisfy their craving for a comfort meal. **Bar:** full bar. **Address:** 16238 N Oracle Rd 85739 **Location:** 5.3 mi n of Tangerine Rd. [L] [D]

CAVE CREEK (H-3) pop. 5,015, elev. 2,129'
• Part of Phoenix area — see map p. 134

Cave Creek was originally home to the Hohokam Ancestral Desert People, who irrigated their fields with water from Cave Creek. In 1870 a road was built to link the newly formed town of Cave Creek to Fort McDowell on the Verde River. The late 1800s saw the establishment of numerous mining camps in the surrounding mountains, and permanent settlers who followed took to ranching and farming.

Recreational activities abound in Cave Creek with the Tonto National Forest *(see place listing p. 264)* as its neighbor. Six lakes in the forest offer numerous opportunities for swimming, fishing and boating.

Carefree-Cave Creek Chamber of Commerce: 748 Easy St., Suite 9, P.O. Box 734, Carefree, AZ 85377. **Phone:** (480) 488-3381.

CAVE CREEK MUSEUM is at 6140 E. Skyline Dr. Exhibits depict archeological sites as well as what life was like for area pioneers, miners and ranchers. The museum features artifacts attributed to Ancestral Puebloan, Hohokam and Mogollon Indian cultures. A cabin from a tuberculosis sanitarium operating nearby in the 1920s is on the grounds as well as the first church in Cave Creek. **Time:** Allow 30 minutes minimum. **Hours:** Wed.-Thurs. and Sat.-Sun. 1-4:30, Fri. 10-4:30, Oct. 1-Memorial Day. **Cost:** $5; $3 (ages 55+ and students with ID); $2 (ages 0-12). **Phone:** (480) 488-2764.

BINKLEY'S RESTAURANT   **Phone:** 480/437-1072

New American
$40-$94

AAA Inspector Notes: Innovative, ambitious and exceptional cuisine is created by Chef Kevin Binkley and his team at this posh Cave Creek hideaway. It is worth the drive to sample the chef's tasting menu, which changes daily and features such exotic flavors as crispy seared foie gras, potato-crusted black cod, or Guinea hen with parsnip puree and black truffles. **Bar:** full bar. **Reservations:** suggested. **Address:** 6920 E Cave Creek Rd 85331 **Location:** Jct Scottsdale Rd, 0.5 mi e. [D]

EL ENCANTO MEXICAN RESTAURANT
Phone: 480/488-1752

Mexican
$7-$17

AAA Inspector Notes: An outdoor dining area features a mission-style garden with a pond and lots of shade trees. Southwestern, Mexican and Sonoran Mexican cuisine is featured in this relaxing oasis set in a scenic Western town. **Bar:** full bar. **Address:** 6248 E Cave Creek Rd 85331 **Location:** Center. [L] [D]

THE HORNY TOAD RESTAURANT   **Phone:** 480/488-9542

American
$7-$24

AAA Inspector Notes: Built like a Western-style barn, this restaurant has fun decor befitting its casual, friendly service. Guests can savor freshly prepared, mesquite-grilled meats and ample-size desserts. A patio is open when the weather cooperates. **Bar:** full bar. **Address:** 6738 E Cave Creek Rd 85331 **Location:** Jct Scottsdale Rd and Tom Darlington Dr, 0.8 mi w. [L] [D]

TONTO BAR & GRILL   **Phone:** 480/488-0698

American
$8-$29

AAA Inspector Notes: The casual setting, in an old dude ranch, and views of a golf course do not detract from the upscale, eclectic cuisine that award-winning chef Flatt prepares. The seasonally changing menu takes advantage of the freshest regional foods available. **Bar:** full bar. **Reservations:** suggested. **Address:** 5736 E Rancho Mañana Blvd 85331 **Location:** Jct Carefree Hwy, 2.4 mi n on Cave Creek Rd, just w; at Rancho Mañana Golf Resort. [L] [D]

CHANDLER (J-4) pop. 236,123
• Hotels p. 48 • Restaurants p. 52
• Hotels & Restaurants map & index p. 164
• Part of Phoenix area — see map p. 134

Chandler was founded by Dr. Alexander J. Chandler, a veterinary surgeon who bought 80 acres of land in the Salt River Valley in 1891 and created a series of canals. By 1900 his ranch covered 18,000 acres; in 1912, Chandler sold $50,000 worth of land to 300 speculators and the city was born. In the beginning, Chandler's chief industry was agriculture; alfalfa, cotton and grain were common crops. Today agriculture, while still in the picture, takes a back seat to manufacturing and electronics.

With their restored facades and colonnades, buildings in historic downtown Chandler add to the area's original character, giving it a distinct early-1900s ambience. A host of shopping and dining establishments as well as event opportunities are available to visitors year-round. Popular festivals include the Chandler Jazz Festival, offered the first

(See map & index p. 164.)

week of April; the Chandler 4th of July Fireworks Spectacular; and the Parade of Lights/Tumbleweed Tree Lighting Ceremony, held the first Saturday in December.

A return to the good old days of the West takes place at Rawhide Western Town & Steakhouse at Wild Horse Pass *(see attraction listing)* for 4 days in March during the National Festival of the West. Western music; a Western film festival; a cowboy trade show, featuring everything from horse gear to art to furniture; rodeo and shooting competitions; cowboy poetry; a mountain man encampment; a chuck wagon cook-off; special children's activities; and period costumes recall the glory days of early Western settlement.

HUHUGAM HERITAGE CENTER is at 4759 N. Maricopa Rd. Exhibits including art and archeological collections share the history and culture of the Gila River Indian Community. Educational classes and programs also are offered. **Time:** Allow 1 hour minimum. **Hours:** Wed.-Fri. 10-4. Closed major holidays. **Cost:** $5; $3 (ages 65+ and students with ID); free (ages 0-12 and Native Americans). **Phone:** (520) 796-3500.

[SAVE] **RAWHIDE WESTERN TOWN & STEAK-HOUSE AT WILD HORSE PASS,** 5700 W. North Loop Rd., is a replica of an 1880s frontier town. Craftsmen sell their wares in antique buildings and shops. The family-style entertainment includes stunt and comedy shows, sundown cookouts, burro rides, gold panning, and stagecoach and train rides.

Hours: Wed.-Sun. 5:30-9. Closed Christmas. Phone ahead to confirm schedule. **Cost:** Western town and parking free. Single-attraction tickets $5. One-day Town Pass unlimited use ticket $15. Prices may vary; phone ahead to confirm. **Phone:** (480) 502-5600. [TI]

Shopping areas: Downtown Chandler, south of Chandler Boulevard on Arizona Avenue, offers an eclectic mix of stores; from mouth-blown glassware made in China and handcrafted Indonesian furniture and accessories to a trendy clothing boutique and gift items from around the world, shoppers will be pleased. Just three miles west of downtown, Chandler Fashion Center features such name-brand stores as Eddie Bauer, J. Crew, Nordstrom and Victoria's Secret. A highlight in visiting the complex is Dancing Waters: a brilliant display of water, lights and music located in the Outdoor Village. Chandler Pavilions/Casa Paloma, an upscale shopping center east of US 10 on Ray Road, features several national stores including Ann Taylor, Banana Republic and Chico's.

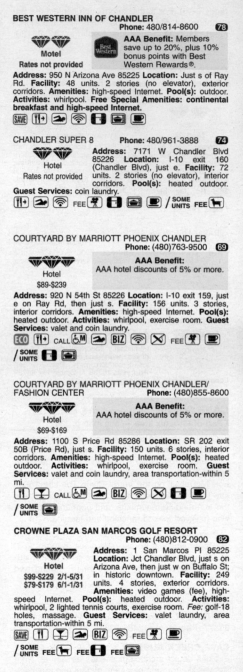

BEST WESTERN INN OF CHANDLER
                              Phone: 480/814-8600   [78]
Motel
Rates not provided
AAA Benefit: Members save up to 20%, plus 10% bonus points with Best Western Rewards®.
Address: 950 N Arizona Ave 85225 **Location:** Just s of Ray Rd. **Facility:** 48 units. 2 stories (no elevator), exterior corridors. **Amenities:** high-speed Internet. **Pool(s):** outdoor. **Activities:** whirlpool. **Free Special Amenities: continental breakfast and high-speed Internet.**

CHANDLER SUPER 8   Phone: 480/961-3888   [74]
Hotel
Rates not provided
Address: 7171 W Chandler Blvd 85226 **Location:** I-10 exit 160 (Chandler Blvd), just e. **Facility:** 72 units. 2 stories (no elevator), interior corridors. **Pool(s):** heated outdoor.
Guest Services: coin laundry.

COURTYARD BY MARRIOTT PHOENIX CHANDLER
                              Phone: (480)763-9500   [69]
Hotel
$89-$239
AAA Benefit: AAA hotel discounts of 5% or more.
Address: 920 N 54th St 85226 **Location:** I-10 exit 159, just e on Ray Rd, then just s. **Facility:** 156 units. 3 stories, interior corridors. **Amenities:** high-speed Internet. **Pool(s):** heated outdoor. **Activities:** whirlpool, exercise room. **Guest Services:** valet and coin laundry.

COURTYARD BY MARRIOTT PHOENIX CHANDLER/ FASHION CENTER   Phone: (480)855-8600
Hotel
$69-$169
AAA Benefit: AAA hotel discounts of 5% or more.
Address: 1100 S Price Rd 85286 **Location:** SR 202 exit 50B (Price Rd), just s. **Facility:** 150 units. 6 stories, interior corridors. **Amenities:** high-speed Internet. **Pool(s):** outdoor. **Activities:** whirlpool, exercise room. **Guest Services:** valet and coin laundry, area transportation-within 5 mi.

CROWNE PLAZA SAN MARCOS GOLF RESORT
                              Phone: (480)812-0900   [82]
Hotel
$99-$229 2/1-5/31
$79-$179 6/1-1/31
Address: 1 San Marcos Pl 85225 **Location:** Jct Chandler Blvd, just s on Arizona Ave, then just w on Buffalo St; in historic downtown. **Facility:** 249 units. 4 stories, exterior corridors. **Amenities:** video games (fee), high-speed Internet. **Pool(s):** heated outdoor. **Activities:** whirlpool, 2 lighted tennis courts, exercise room. *Fee:* golf-18 holes, massage. **Guest Services:** valet laundry, area transportation-within 5 mi.

Create complete trip routings and custom maps with the TripTik® Travel Planner on AAA.com or CAA.ca

(See map & index p. 164.)

FAIRFIELD INN & SUITES PHOENIX CHANDLER/ FASHION CENTER
Phone: (480)963-5300

Hotel
$59-$149

AAA Benefit: AAA hotel discounts of 5% or more.

Address: 1100 S Price Rd 85286 **Location:** SR 202 exit 50B (Price Rd), just s. **Facility:** 110 units. 6 stories, interior corridors. **Amenities:** high-speed Internet. **Pool(s):** heated outdoor. **Activities:** whirlpool, exercise room. **Guest Services:** valet and coin laundry, area transportation-within 5 mi.

FAIRFIELD INN BY MARRIOTT PHOENIX CHANDLER
Phone: (480)940-0099   **73**

Hotel
$59-$169

AAA Benefit: AAA hotel discounts of 5% or more.

Address: 7425 W Chandler Blvd 85226 **Location:** I-10 exit 160 (Chandler Blvd), just e, then s on Southgate Dr. **Facility:** 65 units. 3 stories, interior corridors. **Amenities:** high-speed Internet. **Pool(s):** heated outdoor. **Activities:** whirlpool. **Guest Services:** valet and coin laundry. **Free Special Amenities: expanded continental breakfast and high-speed Internet.**

HAMPTON INN & SUITES PHOENIX/CHANDLER FASHION CENTER
Phone: (480)917-9500

Hotel
$99-$199

AAA Benefit: Members save up to 10% everyday!

Address: 1231 S Spectrum Blvd 85286 **Location:** SR 202 exit 50B (Price Rd), just s. **Facility:** 153 units. 4 stories, interior corridors. **Terms:** 1-7 night minimum stay, cancellation fee imposed. **Amenities:** high-speed Internet. **Pool(s):** heated outdoor. **Activities:** whirlpool, exercise room. **Guest Services:** valet and coin laundry, area transportation-within 5 mi.

HAMPTON INN PHOENIX-CHANDLER
Phone: (480)753-5200   **71**

Hotel
$69-$169

AAA Benefit: Members save up to 10% everyday!

Address: 7333 W Detroit St 85226 **Location:** I-10 exit 160 (Chandler Blvd), just e, just n on 54th St, then just w. **Facility:** 101 units. 6 stories, interior corridors. **Terms:** 1-7 night minimum stay, cancellation fee imposed. **Amenities:** video games (fee). **Pool(s):** heated outdoor. **Activities:** whirlpool, exercise room. **Guest Services:** valet laundry.

HAWTHORN SUITES BY WYNDHAM-CHANDLER
Phone: (480)705-8881   **77**

Hotel
$79-$199

Address: 5858 W Chandler Blvd 85226 **Location:** I-10 exit 160 (Chandler Blvd), 1.5 mi e. **Facility:** 100 efficiencies, some two bedrooms. 2 stories (no elevator), interior corridors. **Pool(s):** heated outdoor, exercise room. **Guest Services:** valet and coin laundry. **Free Special Amenities: full breakfast and high-speed Internet.**

HILTON PHOENIX CHANDLER
Phone: (480)899-7400

Hotel
$109-$229

AAA Benefit: Members save 5% or more everyday!

Address: 2929 W Frye Rd 85224 **Location:** SR 202 exit 50B (Price Rd), 0.4 mi n, then just w. **Facility:** 197 units. 6 stories, interior corridors. **Terms:** 1-7 night minimum stay, cancellation fee imposed. **Amenities:** high-speed Internet (fee), safes. **Pool(s):** heated outdoor. **Activities:** whirlpool, exercise room. **Guest Services:** valet laundry, area transportation-within 5 mi.

HOLIDAY INN AT OCOTILLO
Phone: (480)203-2121

Hotel
$159-$299

Address: 1200 W Ocotillo Rd 85248 **Location:** I-10 exit 164 (Queen Creek Rd), 5.5 mi e, 1.1 mi s on Alma School Rd, then just w. **Facility:** 106 units. 4 stories, interior corridors. **Amenities:** high-speed Internet. **Pool(s):** heated outdoor. **Activities:** whirlpool, exercise room. **Guest Services:** valet and coin laundry, area transportation-within 5 mi.

HOMEWOOD SUITES BY HILTON PHOENIX-CHANDLER
Phone: (480)753-6200   **70**

Extended Stay Hotel
$99-$189

AAA Benefit: Contemporary luxury at a special Member rate.

Address: 7373 W Detroit St 85226 **Location:** I-10 exit 160 (Chandler Blvd), 0.4 mi e, n on 54th St, then just w. **Facility:** 83 efficiencies, some two bedrooms. 3 stories, interior corridors. **Terms:** 1-7 night minimum stay, cancellation fee imposed. **Amenities:** video games (fee). **Pool(s):** heated outdoor. **Activities:** whirlpool, exercise room. **Guest Services:** valet and coin laundry.

Share a New View on Travel at
AAATravelViews.com
Read stories, tips and trends from AAA insiders.
Post comments and get your questions answered by our travel experts.

(See map & index p. 164.)

HOMEWOOD SUITES BY HILTON-PHOENIX CHANDLER/FASHION CENTER

Phone: (480)963-5700

Extended Stay Hotel
$109-$219

AAA Benefit:
Contemporary luxury at a special Member rate.

Address: 1221 S Spectrum Blvd 85286 **Location:** SR 202 exit 50B (Price Rd), just s. **Facility:** 133 units, some two bedrooms and efficiencies. 4 stories, interior corridors. **Terms:** 1-7 night minimum stay, cancellation fee imposed. **Amenities:** high-speed Internet. **Pool(s):** heated outdoor. **Activities:** whirlpool, sports court, exercise room. **Guest Services:** valet and coin laundry, area transportation-within 5 mi.

QUALITY INN

Phone: (480)705-0922 **75**

Hotel
$59-$139

Address: 255 N Kyrene Rd 85226 **Location:** I-10 exit 160 (Chandler Blvd), 1.5 mi e, then just n. **Facility:** 70 units. 3 stories, interior corridors. **Terms:** cancellation fee imposed. **Amenities:** high-speed Internet. **Pool(s):** heated outdoor. **Guest Services:** coin laundry.

RADISSON PHOENIX-CHANDLER

Phone: (480)961-4444 **72**

Hotel
$109-$229

Address: 7475 W Chandler Blvd 85226 **Location:** I-10 exit 160 (Chandler Blvd), just e, then just s on Southgate Dr. Located in a commercial area. **Facility:** 159 units. 4 stories, interior corridors. **Terms:** cancellation fee imposed. **Amenities:** high-speed Internet. **Pool(s):** heated outdoor. **Activities:** whirlpool, exercise room. **Guest Services:** valet and coin laundry. **Free Special Amenities:** high-speed Internet and local transportation.

RED ROOF INN-CHANDLER

Phone: (480)857-4969 **76**

Hotel
$75-$135

Address: 7400 W Boston St 85226 **Location:** I-10 exit 160 (Chandler Blvd), just e, then s on Southgate Dr. **Facility:** 131 units. 4 stories, interior corridors. **Amenities:** Fee: video games, safes. **Pool(s):** heated outdoor. **Free Special Amenities:** local telephone calls and high-speed Internet.

RESIDENCE INN-CHANDLER FASHION CENTER

Phone: (480)782-1551 **80**

Extended Stay Hotel
$100-$190

AAA Benefit:
AAA hotel discounts of 5% or more.

Address: 200 N Federal St 85226 **Location:** I-10 exit 160 (Chandler Blvd), 4.2 mi e, just n on N Metro Blvd, then just e. Across from Chandler Fashion Center Mall. **Facility:** 102 units, some two bedrooms, efficiencies and kitchens. 3 stories, interior corridors. **Amenities:** Some: high-speed Internet. **Pool(s):** heated outdoor. **Activities:** whirlpool, sports court, exercise room. **Guest Services:** valet and coin laundry.

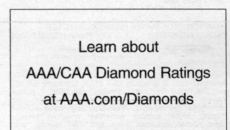

Learn about
AAA/CAA Diamond Ratings
at AAA.com/Diamonds

AAA/CAA HELPS MAKE
YOUR DISNEY
DREAMS COME TRUE.

With *AAA Vacations*® packages, you can create the Disney dream vacation that fits your family, your taste and your budget while enjoying great savings and benefits along the way!

Vacations®

©Disney WDWSALES-10-I8434

Contact your AAA/CAA Travel professional to get started today.   AAA.com

(See map & index p. 164.)

SHERATON WILD HORSE PASS RESORT & SPA
Phone: (602)225-0100

♦♦♦♦♦ ♦♦♦♦♦
Resort Hotel
$319-$969

Ⓢ **Sheraton** **AAA Benefit:** Members get up to 15% off, plus Starwood Preferred Guest® bonuses.

Address: 5594 W Wild Horse Pass Blvd 85226 **Location:** I-10 exit 162, 2.4 mi w. **Facility:** Wild horses roam the desert areas nearby, while the property's extensive grounds offer views of the golf course and mountains. 500 units. 4 stories, interior corridors. **Parking:** on-site and valet. **Terms:** check-in 4 pm, 7 day cancellation notice-fee imposed. **Amenities:** safes, honor bars. *Fee:* video games, high-speed Internet. **Dining:** 4 restaurants, also, Kai, see separate listing. **Pool(s):** 5 heated outdoor. **Activities:** saunas, whirlpools, steamrooms, waterslide, recreation programs, hiking trails, jogging, spa. *Fee:* golf-36 holes, 2 lighted tennis courts, horseback riding. **Guest Services:** valet laundry, area transportation-casino & golf course. **Free Special Amenities:** room upgrade (subject to availability with advance reservations). *(See ad this page.)*

SAVE ⊤⊤ 🚹 ⊻ 🏋 ➣ FEE✚ BIZ 🛜
✕ FEE🎥 💻 / SOME UNITS 🐾 FEE🛗

SPRINGHILL SUITES BY MARRIOTT-CHANDLER FASHION CENTER
Phone: (480)726-7666 **79**

♦♦♦♦♦
Hotel
$90-$180

AAA Benefit: AAA hotel discounts of 5% or more.

Address: 225 N Metro Blvd 85226 **Location:** I-10 exit 160 (Chandler Blvd), 4.2 mi e, then just n. Across from Chandler Fashion Center Mall. **Facility:** 101 units. 3 stories, interior corridors. **Amenities:** *Some:* high-speed Internet. **Pool(s):** heated outdoor. **Activities:** whirlpool, exercise room. **Guest Services:** valet and coin laundry.

⊤⊤ CALL 🛗 ➣ 🛜 ✕ 🛗 📷 💻

Complete Vacation Planning

AAA.com/Travel and **CAA.ca/Travel** – everything you need to plan and book your vacations, backed by the travel experts at local AAA/CAA offices.

▼ See AAA listing this page ▼

Life is Better when Shared

This unique resort features Native American culture, championship golf, Aji Spa, and AAA Five-Diamond dining at Kai. Enjoy stunning views from every guestroom, four sparkling pools, a 111-foot waterslide and family friendly activities and events. Enjoy horseback adventures and poolside movies.

Sheraton
Wild Horse Pass
RESORT & SPA

Scan to see our exclusive resort offers

Book at wildhorsepassresort.com or call 888-218-8989

Get the free mobile app at
http://gettag.mobi

spg.
Starwood Preferred Guest

Ⓐ *Four Diamond Award*

©2011 Starwood Hotels & Resorts Worldwide, Inc. All rights reserved. Valid only at participating hotels and resorts for stays booked through 2012. Sheraton, Preferred Guest, SPG and its logos are the trademarks of Starwood Hotels & Resorts Worldwide, Inc., or its affiliates.

(See map & index p. 164.)

WILD HORSE PASS HOTEL & CASINO
Phone: (520)796-7777

Contemporary Hotel
$59-$189

Address: 5040 Wild Horse Pass Blvd 85226 **Location:** I-10 exit 162, 2.4 mi w. **Facility:** This new luxury resort boasts many entertainment options including a theater and upscale dining. 242 units. 10 stories, interior corridors. **Parking:** on-site and valet. **Terms:** check-in 4 pm, cancellation fee imposed. **Amenities:** high-speed Internet, safes. **Dining:** 6 restaurants, also, Shula's America's Steak House, see separate listing, nightclub, entertainment. **Pool(s):** heated outdoor. **Activities:** whirlpool, exercise room. *Fee:* golf-36 holes. **Guest Services:** valet laundry, area transportation-within Indian community. **Free Special Amenities:** newspaper and high-speed Internet.
(See ad p. 185.)

WINDMILL SUITES OF CHANDLER
Phone: (480)812-9600 81

Hotel
$105-$155 2/1-4/30
$80-$105 5/1-1/31

Address: 3535 W Chandler Blvd 85226 **Location:** I-10 exit 160 (Chandler Blvd), 4 mi e. Located at Chandler Fashion Center Mall. **Facility:** 127 units. 3 stories, interior corridors. **Terms:** check-in 4 pm, cancellation fee imposed. **Pool(s):** heated outdoor. **Activities:** whirlpool, bicycles, limited exercise equipment. **Guest Services:** valet and coin laundry, area transportation-within 5 mi. **Free Special Amenities:** expanded continental breakfast and high-speed Internet.

WHERE TO EAT

ABUELO'S THE FLAVOR OF MEXICO
Phone: 480/855-0960

Regional Mexican
$7-$17

AAA Inspector Notes: The charming decor is reminiscent of a Mexican hacienda, with plants, folk art and statues. Representative of the upscale menu's distinctive combinations are mesquite-grilled, bacon-wrapped shrimp. Fresh herb flavors and ingredients enhance each menu item. **Bar:** full bar. **Reservations:** suggested. **Address:** 3440 W Chandler Blvd 85226 **Location:** SR 101 Expwy Loop exit 60 (Chandler Blvd), 0.4 mi w.
L D

BRUNCHIE'S
Phone: 480/899-5036 59

American
$5-$9

AAA Inspector Notes: A casual and homey spot in downtown Chandler's historic district, this eatery serves breakfast and lunch classics as well as Mexican specialties. **Address:** 17 E Boston St 85225 **Location:** Southeast corner of Arizona Ave and Boston St.
B L

C-FU GOURMET
Phone: 480/899-3888 49

Chinese
$5-$19

AAA Inspector Notes: Among favorite choices are moo goo gai pan and chicken lo mein, as well as the reasonably priced dim sum. Diners can choose live seafood from tanks and have it prepared in the style of their choice. **Bar:** full bar. **Address:** 2051 W Warner Rd 85224 **Location:** Southwest corner of Warner and Dobson rds.
L D

CORK RESTAURANT
Phone: 480/883-3773

New American
$14-$29

AAA Inspector Notes: Featuring dinner cuisine that is described as small-plates style, patrons are able to sample braised buffalo, tempura shrimp and duck confit all in one sitting. The menu items are artfully presented in an atmosphere that is equally sophisticated, and pairings are available from the award-winning wine list. **Bar:** full bar. **Reservations:** suggested. **Address:** 4991 Alma School Rd, Suite 1 85248 **Location:** SR 202 exit 48 (Alma School Rd), 4 mi s.
D

CYCLO VIETNAMESE CUISINE
Phone: 480/963-4490 56

Vietnamese
$10-$12

AAA Inspector Notes: In a small shopping plaza, this eatery has food bursting with flavor and freshness. Such dishes as chicken pineapple curry and jasmine tea-scented crème brûlée made without eggs are sure to please. Local chefs often visit to relax and enjoy the savory foods. **Address:** 1919 W Chandler Blvd, Suite 2 85224 **Location:** Just e of Dobson Rd.
L D

FOX'S PIZZA DEN
Phone: 480/899-3697 51

Pizza
$6-$19

AAA Inspector Notes: This pizzeria serves a wide selection of cooked-fresh pizzas, all prepared using a variety of ingredients. Try a wedgie, a thick double sandwich made of pizza crust filled with your choice of meats and cheese-it is crispy and delicious. **Address:** 2081 N Arizona Ave, Suite 125 85225 **Location:** US 60 exit 179 (Country Club Rd), 3 mi s; northeast corner of Warner Rd and Arizona Ave.
L D

KAI
Phone: 602/385-5726

Regional Southwestern
$35-$175

AAA Inspector Notes: Using Native American indigenous foods, this eatery's renowned chefs have created a seasonally changing tasting menu. Meats, game and seafood are enhanced by vegetable and herb sauces developed from native seeds. Sunset views against the mountain backdrop and wild horses roaming the area create a breathtaking scene. Semi-formal attire. **Bar:** full bar. **Reservations:** suggested. **Address:** 5594 W Wild Horse Pass Blvd 85226 **Location:** I-10 exit 162, 2.4 mi w; in Sheraton Wild Horse Pass Resort & Spa. **Parking:** on-site and valet.

(See ad p. 51.) D

KEEGAN'S GRILL
Phone: 480/814-0003

American
$8-$20

AAA Inspector Notes: A decor featuring witty quotes painted on the walls and huge wooden columns welcomes diners to this bistro. Friendly staff members serve dishes ranging from such comfort foods as meatloaf and barbecue ribs to more eclectic creations, including prosciutto-wrapped shrimp and Pacific Rim grilled chicken salad. **Bar:** full bar. **Address:** 1095 W Queen Creek Rd 85248 **Location:** I-10 exit 164 (Queen Creek Rd), 5.2 mi e.
L D

KONA GRILL
Phone: 480/792-1711 54

Pacific Rim
$9-$36

AAA Inspector Notes: The eclectic menu reflects Pacific influences. In addition to noodle dishes and sushi, it lists specialties of macadamia nut chicken and lemon grass-encrusted swordfish. The dining room has a large aquarium, a private area and a sushi bar. The patio opens during warm weather. **Bar:** full bar. **Address:** 3111 W Chandler Blvd 85226 **Location:** Just w of SR 101; in Chandler Fashion Center Mall.
L D CALL

(See map & index p. 164.)

LA STALLA   **Phone:** 480/855-9990

Italian
$7-$25

AAA Inspector Notes: This cozy, rustic kitchen offers a taste of Old World Italy in downtown Chandler. Pasta dishes, specialty pizzas and chicken, veal and seafood entrées line the menu. Sidewalk seating is an option in pleasant weather. **Bar:** full bar. **Reservations:** required. **Address:** 68 W Buffalo St 85225 **Location:** Jct Chandler Blvd, just s on Arizona Ave, then just w.

L D

PATSY GRIMALDI'S COAL BRICK-OVEN PIZZERIA
                                  Phone: 480/812-2100

Pizza
$4-$18

AAA Inspector Notes: Fresh ingredients and a coal-fired brick oven are the features at this New York style pizzeria. **Bar:** beer & wine. **Address:** 1035 W Queen Creek Rd 85248 **Location:** SR 202 exit 48 (Alma School Rd), 1.7 mi s, then just w. L D

P.F. CHANG'S CHINA BISTRO
                                  Phone: 480/899-0472   55

Chinese
$10-$21

AAA Inspector Notes: Trendy, upscale decor provides a pleasant backdrop for New Age Chinese dining. Appetizers, soups and salads are a meal by themselves. Vegetarian plates and sides, noodles, meins, chicken and meat dishes are created from exotic, fresh ingredients. **Bar:** full bar. **Address:** 3255 W Chandler Blvd 85226 **Location:** SR 101 exit Chandler Blvd, just e; across from Chandler Fashion Center Mall. L D CALL 🖩M

PITA JUNGLE   **Phone:** 480/855-3232   53

Mediterranean
$6-$15

AAA Inspector Notes: The atmosphere is casual in the dining area and on the lakeside patio of this eatery. The menu lists hot and cold pita wraps, pizza, falafel, spanakopita, salads and burgers, as well as healthful, natural vegetarian offerings. **Bar:** full bar. **Address:** 1949 W Ray Rd 85224 **Location:** Jct Dobson Rd; southeast corner. L D

RAWHIDE STEAKHOUSE   **Phone:** 480/502-5600

Steak
$8-$60

AAA Inspector Notes: Part of a Western town venue, this eatery offers hearty meals of mesquite-grilled steaks, ribs and chicken. Rich fruit or pecan pie desserts finish off your meal, and there is live entertainment nightly. **Bar:** full bar. **Address:** 5700 W North Loop Rd 85226 **Location:** I-10 exit 162, 0.8 mi w to 48th St, just s, then w. D

RUBIO'S FRESH MEXICAN GRILL

Mexican
$3-$7

For additional information, visit AAA.com

AAA Inspector Notes: Freshly prepared and healthful foods, bright decor and friendly staff are found in this upscale fast-food spot. A special treat, the salsa bar lines up four styles and flavors. **Bar:** beer only. L D

LOCATIONS:

Address: 5055 W Ray Rd 85226 **Location:** Jct Rural Rd; southwest corner. **Phone:** 480/753-0633

Address: 3111 W Chandler Blvd 85226 **Location:** SR 101 exit Chandler Blvd, just w; in Chandler Fashion Center Mall. **Phone:** 480/812-9460

SAIGON PHO & SEAFOOD   Phone: 480/786-8828   52

Vietnamese
$5-$13

AAA Inspector Notes: Dishes are prepared with fresh vegetables, herbs, beef, seafood, chicken and pork. From hot pot soups to fresh fish pulled from an on-site tank, this casual storefront eatery's offerings are infused with Eastern flavors. **Address:** 1381 N Alma School Rd 85224 **Location:** Jct Warner Rd, 0.5 mi s. L D

SERRANO'S MEXICAN RESTAURANT
                                  Phone: 480/899-3318

Regional Mexican
$6-$14

AAA Inspector Notes: A pleasant stop for lunch or dinner, the local chain is known for consistently good food and attractive, upscale Mexican-style décor. The warm bean dip starter stirs the appetite for traditional dishes such as chiles rellenos or seafood enchiladas prepared with fresh ingredients. Service is friendly. **Bar:** full bar. **Address:** 141 S Arizona Ave 85225 **Location:** 3 mi e on Chandler Blvd from jct SR 101, 0.3 mi s. L D

SHULA'S AMERICA'S STEAK HOUSE
                                  Phone: 520/796-1972

Steak
$25-$89

AAA Inspector Notes: Comfortable and club-like, the dining room is decorated with Dolphins football memorabilia. Finish off the 48-ounce porterhouse steak and be recognized on a plaque. The lamb chops and seafood are good, too, as is the to-die-for seven-layer chocolate cake. **Bar:** full bar. **Reservations:** suggested. **Address:** 5040 W Wild Horse Pass Blvd 85226 **Location:** I-10 exit 162, 2.4 mi w; in Wild Horse Pass Hotel & Casino. **Parking:** on-site and valet. D

TIEN WONG HOT POT   Phone: 480/802-2525   48

Asian
$5-$20

AAA Inspector Notes: Located in an unassuming shopping center in the heart of the valley's growing Asian community, the interior of this hot spot is trendy and fun. Choose from a list of a la carte ingredients including razor clams, Wagyu beef, quail eggs, dumplings and soba noodles; then the items are added to the broth and cooked in front of you, fondue style. There is no beer or wine served, but bringing your own is encouraged. **Address:** 2330 N Alma School Rd 85224 **Location:** US 60 exit 178 (Alma School Rd), 3.5 mi s. L D LATE

THE URBAN TEA LOFT   Phone: 480/786-9600   58

Coffee/Tea
$4-$14

AAA Inspector Notes: Tea is showcased at this cozy and stylish café, where tea pairings are available to complement the wide array of sandwiches, salads, homemade soups and delicious desserts. In the evenings, a more expansive dinner menu is featured. **Bar:** full bar. **Address:** 11 W Boston St, Suite 2 85225 **Location:** Just w of Arizona Ave; downtown. **Parking:** street only.

L D

Z'TEJAS SOUTHWESTERN GRILL
                                  Phone: 480/893-7550   50

Southwestern
$7-$25

AAA Inspector Notes: The young, friendly staff at this grill welcomes diners with smiles. Attractively presented entrées are prepared in a Southwestern style with influences from Texas, Louisiana and Arizona. Banana cream pie is among the show-stopping desserts. **Bar:** full bar. **Address:** 7221 W Ray Rd 85226 **Location:** I-10 exit 158, just e. L D

CHINLE pop. 4,518

BEST WESTERN CANYON DE CHELLY INN
Phone: (928)674-5875

Motel
$99-$109

AAA Benefit: Members save up to 20%, plus 10% bonus points with Best Western Rewards®.

Address: 100 Main St, Indian Rt 7 86503 **Location:** US 191, just e. **Facility:** 104 units. 2 stories (no elevator), exterior corridors. **Terms:** cancellation fee imposed. **Dining:** Junction Restaurant, see separate listing. **Pool(s):** heated indoor. **Activities:** sauna, whirlpool, exercise room. **Free Special Amenities:** local telephone calls and early check-in/late check-out.

HOLIDAY INN CANYON DE CHELLY
Phone: (928)674-5000

Hotel
$79-$139

Address: Indian Rt 7 86503 **Location:** US 191, 2.5 mi e; at entrance to Canyon de Chelly National Monument. **Facility:** 108 units. 2 stories (no elevator), interior corridors. **Terms:** cancellation fee imposed. **Dining:** Garcia's Restaurant, see separate listing. **Pool(s):** heated outdoor. **Activities:** exercise room. **Guest Services:** complimentary laundry.

THUNDERBIRD LODGE
Phone: (928)674-5841

Motel
$73-$143

Address: Indian Rt 7 86503 **Location:** US 191, 3.5 mi e; just e of visitor center. Located in Canyon de Chelly National Monument. **Facility:** 74 units. 1 story, exterior corridors. **Terms:** office hours 7 am-10 pm, cancellation fee imposed. **Dining:** Thunder Bird Cafeteria, see separate listing.

WHERE TO EAT

GARCIA'S RESTAURANT
Phone: 928/674-2511

American
$5-$22

AAA Inspector Notes: The menu at this restaurant includes a variety of American and Mexican dishes. **Address:** Indian Rt 7 86503 **Location:** US 191, 2.5 mi e; at entrance to Canyon de Chelly National Monument; in Holiday Inn Canyon de Chelly.

JUNCTION RESTAURANT
Phone: 928/674-8443

American
$5-$18

AAA Inspector Notes: Serving breakfast, lunch and dinner, the family restaurant lines up a good selection of beef, chicken and pork dishes, sandwiches and such Navajo favorites as mutton stew and fry bread. Local Native American arts and crafts are displayed. The dining patio opens seasonally. **Address:** 100 Main St, Rt 7 86503 **Location:** US 191, just e; in Best Western Canyon de Chelly Inn.

THUNDER BIRD CAFETERIA
Phone: 928/674-5841

American
$6-$20

AAA Inspector Notes: Among the cafeteria's comfort foods are some Mexican entrees and Navajo fry bread. Some steak and other dishes are prepared to order and delivered to the table. **Address:** Indian Rt 7 86503 **Location:** US 191, 3.5 mi e; just e of visitor center; in Thunderbird Lodge.

CHIRICAHUA NATIONAL MONUMENT (F-6)

Approximately 70 miles northeast of Douglas via US 191 and SR 181 or 36 miles southeast of Willcox via SR 186 and SR 181, Chiricahua (cheer-ee-KAH-wah) National Monument, also called the "Wonderland of Rocks," is in the Chiricahua Mountains at an elevation ranging from 5,180 to 7,310 feet. Nine miles of the 21-mile county road that runs south from Bowie across Apache Pass to SR 186 are unpaved and rough in places. Unseasoned mountain drivers and cars pulling trailers should avoid the narrow, winding route from Portal; it is closed in winter.

The 11,985-acre area encompasses lands once controlled by the Chiricahua Apaches under Cochise, who led the Native Americans' resistance to the white man during the 1860s.

The Chiricahua Mountains rise above the surrounding grasslands, providing shady forests and glens that harbor Mexican chickadees, raccoon-like coatimundis, javelinas and a number of other wildlife species. Among the monument's outstanding features are gigantic, erosion-sculptured monoliths of volcanic ash.

Current research indicates that about 27 million years ago violent eruptions from the nearby Turkey Creek caldera took place, covering the area with white-hot ash. After the ash fused and cooled into an almost 2,000-foot layer of rock, the forces of erosion sculpted it into the odd array of shapes that can be seen.

Formations include the Totem Pole, 137 feet high and only a yard thick at its narrowest point; the Mushroom; and Big Balanced Rock, weighing 1,000 tons and resting on a base about 4 feet thick. In some places canyon walls rise as much as 1,000 feet. Many areas can be reached only on foot.

Among the first pioneers to settle in the area were Ja Hu Stafford and Neil and Emma Erickson. By the 1920s one of the Erickson daughters, Lillian, and her husband, Ed Riggs, had turned the homestead into a guest ranch, built trails into the rocks and were the driving force in the creation of Chiricahua National Monument. Today Faraway Ranch is preserved as a historic site with tours offered *(see attraction listing).*

Picnicking, camping and parking areas are available near the visitor center in Bonita Canyon. Reached from the visitor center by 6 miles of paved mountain road, 6,780-foot Massai Point offers an overlook and an exhibit building. More than 17 miles of trails lead to all parts of the monument. Campground programs are conducted at designated times Friday through Saturday from April through May and September through October. Additional dates and times also may be available; contact the visitor center, (520) 824-3560, for an updated schedule.

Vehicles longer than 29 feet are not permitted beyond the visitor center. A hiker's shuttle departs to the high country daily at 8:30. Visitor center daily 8-4:30; closed Thanksgiving and Christmas. Park entrance fee $5 per person; free (ages 0-15). Shuttle free. Campers must register at the campground; a $12 per night fee is charged. Campgrounds will not accommodate travel trailers or motor homes more than 29 feet long.

For further information contact the Superintendent, Chiricahua National Monument, 12856 E. Rhyolite Creek Rd., Willcox, AZ 85643; phone (520) 824-3560, ext. 302.

FARAWAY RANCH, 1.5 mi. w. of the monument visitor center, is the homestead of pioneers Neil and Emma Erickson. The home was built in 1888 and additions were made through 1915. By the 1920s the Ericksons' daughter Lillian and her husband had turned the homestead into a working cattle and guest ranch.

Time: Allow 1 hour minimum. **Hours:** Homestead site accessible daily dawn-dusk. Guided tours of the home are given. Phone ahead to confirm schedule. **Cost:** Free. **Phone:** (520) 824-3560, ext. 302.

CHLORIDE pop. 271

SHEPS MINERS INN	Phone: (928)565-4251
◆◆◆ Motel $50-$75	**Address:** 9827 2nd St 86431 **Location:** Jct 2nd St and Elkhart Ave. **Facility:** 11 units. 1 story, exterior corridors. *Bath:* shower only. **Terms:** 7 day cancellation notice. **Dining:**

Yesterday's Restaurant, see separate listing. **Free Special Amenities: early check-in/late check-out and high-speed Internet.** [SAVE] 🍴 🛜 ✕ 🐢 📺 🐕

WHERE TO EAT

YESTERDAY'S RESTAURANT	Phone: 928/565-4251
◆ American $5-$25	**AAA Inspector Notes:** In a rustic setting off the beaten path, this three-meal restaurant presents a menu of varied sandwiches, soups and salads for lunch and several steak, seafood and pasta dishes for dinner. **Bar:** full

bar. **Address:** 9827 2nd St 86431 **Location:** Jct 2nd St and Elkhart Ave; in Sheps Miners Inn. [L] [D]

CIBOLA (E-1) pop. 250, elev. 240'

CIBOLA NATIONAL WILDLIFE REFUGE is 17 mi. s. on Neighbors Blvd., across the Cibola Bridge, then 3.5 mi. s. to 66600 Cibola Lake Rd. Home to many wildlife species including more than 288 species of birds as well as desert tortoises, mule deer and bobcats, the refuge has a visitor center with interpretive displays. A 1-mile nature trail winds through three native habitats: cottonwood, mesquite and willow.

From an elevated observation deck, winter visitors can view flocks of geese, ducks and sandhill cranes on a 20-acre pond. **Time:** Allow 30 minutes minimum. **Hours:** Refuge daily 8-4:30. Visitors center daily 8-4:30, Nov.-Feb.; Mon.-Fri. 8-1:30, rest of year. Wildlife is best viewed Dec.-Jan. Closed major holidays. **Cost:** Free. **Phone:** (928) 857-3253. 🏕

CLARKDALE (C-3) pop. 4,097, elev. 3,545'

Clarkdale was named after its founder, William Andrews Clark, who purchased the United Verde Copper Co. in Jerome in 1888. In 1911, the mine's smelter was relocated and Clarkdale was created to house the company's 7,000 employees. Clark controlled every detail of the town's construction and incorporated modern details including a sewer system and hardwood flooring in every home.

The town's proximity to Tuzigoot National Monument *(see place listing p. 313),* Prescott National Forest *(see place listing p. 200)* and Coconino National Forest allows for such outdoor activities as hiking and bird-watching.

Clarkdale Chamber of Commerce: 900 Main St., P.O. Box 161, Clarkdale, AZ 86324. **Phone:** (928) 634-9438.

VERDE CANYON RAILROAD, 300 N. Broadway, offers a 4-hour scenic ride through the Verde River Canyon, adjacent to the Sycamore Wilderness Area near Sedona. Visitors can see Sinagua Indian ruins and such desert fauna as American bald eagles, great blue herons, red-tailed hawks, javelinas and deer. The open-air viewing cars are available to all.

Hours: Most trains depart Wed.-Mon. at 1. Specialty rides are offered throughout the year; phone for details. Phone ahead to confirm schedule. **Cost:** First-class fare $79.95 (all ages). Coach fare $54.95; $49.95 (ages 65+); $34.95 (ages 2-12). Reservations are required. **Phone:** (928) 639-0010 or (877) 800-7326.

SU CASA OF CLARKDALE	Phone: 928/634-2771
◆◆◆ Mexican $7-$14	**AAA Inspector Notes:** Friendly service complements well-prepared dishes made to order from the freshest ingredients. The comfortable eatery is welcoming to families. **Bar:** full bar. **Address:** 1000 S Main St

86324 **Location:** Center. [L] [D]

COCONINO NATIONAL FOREST (C-4)

Elevations in the forest range from 2,600 ft. at Fossil Creek in the Verde Valley to 12,643 ft. at the San Francisco Peaks. Refer to AAA maps for additional elevation information.

Surrounding Flagstaff and Sedona, Coconino National Forest covers 1,821,495 acres. In the south the forest is cut by deep canyons; in the north the San Francisco Peaks attain the highest elevation in Arizona. These peaks, including Mount Humphreys, the state's highest point, and Mount Agassiz, are some of the places in Arizona where alpine conditions exist. Many roads provide scenic drives.

Outstanding features include the Mogollon Rim, at an altitude of 7,600 feet, and Oak Creek Canyon *(see Sedona p. 228).* Among the recreational facilities within the forest is the Arizona Snowbowl winter sports area *(see Flagstaff p. 62).* Lake Mary offers good fishing, boating and waterfowl hunting. Camping facilities are available in the area Memorial Day-Labor Day, with some facilities open throughout the year; an $8-$20 per night fee is charged. Campfire restrictions may be in effect.

For additional information contact the Forest Service, 1824 S. Thompson St., Flagstaff, AZ 86001; phone (928) 527-3600. *See Recreation Chart.*

COOLIDGE (E-4) pop. 11,825, elev. 1,430'

Coolidge is east of the entrance to Casa Grande Ruins National Monument *(see place listing p. 46)* and just west of Pinal Pioneer Parkway (SR 79), a scenic route south to Tucson.

GOLDEN ERA TOY AND AUTO MUSEUM, off SR 87 at 297 W. Central Ave., features a collection of antique toys, dolls and model trains as well as restored automobiles. **Hours:** Fri.-Sun. 11-5, Jan.-May. **Cost:** $6; $2 (ages 0-12). **Phone:** (480) 948-9570 or (520) 723-5044.

CORNVILLE (C-4) pop. 3,280, elev. 3,304'

PAGE SPRINGS FISH HATCHERY is 5 mi. n. on Page Springs Rd. Rainbow trout are raised here for release into the Verde River and Oak Creek. A walking tour of the facility, a nature trail and a visitors center are available. **Hours:** Daily 8-4. Closed Thanksgiving and Christmas. **Cost:** Free. **Phone:** (928) 634-4805.

THE MANZANITA RESTAURANT	Phone: 928/634-8851
▼▼ ▼▼ Continental $14-$23 Ⓛ Ⓓ	**AAA Inspector Notes:** This restaurant is popular and boasts a country setting. **Bar:** full bar. **Address:** 11425 E Cornville Rd 86325 **Location:** 4.5 mi e of jct SR 89A.

CORONADO NATIONAL FOREST (E-5)
• Attractions map p. 275

Elevations in the forest range from 3,000 ft. in the Santa Catalina Mountains to 10,720 ft. in the Pinaleno Mountains. Refer to AAA maps for additional elevation information.

In southeastern Arizona and southwestern New Mexico, Coronado National Forest's 12 widely scattered sections cover 1,780,000 acres. Named for Spanish explorer Francisco Vázquez de Coronado, who journeyed through southern Arizona in 1540, the forest's varied plant and animal life reflects the area's extremes of elevation: Flat deserts of cacti and paloverde give way to rugged, heavily forested mountains covered with oak, juniper, pine, fir and spruce, depending on the elevation.

Within the forest's boundaries are five fishing lakes. Mount Lemmon, northeast of Tucson, is one of the southernmost ski areas in the country. More than 1,100 miles of trails offer hiking opportunities.

Madera Canyon, nestled in the Santa Rita Mountains, is a popular bird-watching spot with more than 200 species, including hummingbirds, woodpeckers and swallows. Hiking trails, a nature trail, picnic areas and campgrounds complete the area.

Scenic drives include Swift Trail in the Pinaleno Mountains (Mount Graham), Ruby Road in the Tumacácori Mountains, Onion Saddle Road and Rucker Canyon Road in the Chiricahua Mountains and SRs 82 and 83. The winding 28-mile Sky Island Scenic Byway begins at Tanque Verde Road in the desert just outside the Tucson city limits and extends to the top of Mount Lemmon in the Santa Catalina Mountains. Pullouts provide opportunities to observe the contrasts of the lower and upper regions.

Legend has it that Cochise's grave is somewhere within the Cochise Stronghold Recreation Area in the Dragoon Mountains. A natural rock fortress, the stronghold is where the Chiricahua Apache leader hid from his enemies. Camping and picnicking are permitted, and interpretive trails are available.

Picnicking and camping fees range from $10-$20. Day pass $5. Further information can be obtained at district offices in Douglas, Nogales, Safford, Sierra Vista and Tucson, or contact the Supervisor, Coronado National Forest, Federal Building, 300 W. Congress St., Tucson, AZ 85701; phone (520) 388-8300. *See Recreation Chart.*

WHIPPLE OBSERVATORY is atop Mount Hopkins in the Santa Rita Mountains. The visitor center is accessible from I-19 exit 56 (Canoa Rd.); from Canoa Rd. turn e. to Frontage Rd., 3 mi. s. to Elephant Head Rd., 1 mi. e. to Mount Hopkins Rd., then 7 mi. s.e. The observatory houses one of the world's largest mirrored telescopes for conducting interstellar investigations. A visitor center has exhibits about astronomy, astrophysics and natural science as well as scenic views. A 6-hour guided tour of the observatory is available by appointment; phone for more information.

Hours: Visitor center open Mon.-Fri. 8:30-4:30. Tours depart Mon., Wed. and Fri. at 9, Mar.-Nov. Closed major holidays. **Cost:** Visitor center free. Observatory tour $7; $2.50 (ages 6-12). Ages 0-5 are not recommended. Reservations are required. **Phone:** (520) 670-5707.

CORONADO NATIONAL MEMORIAL (G-5)

Lying 22 miles south of Sierra Vista and 5 miles off SR 92, Coronado National Memorial was established to commemorate Francisco Vázquez de Coronado's exploration of the Southwest. The expedition, the first European venture across what is now the U.S.-Mexican border, began in February 1540 when the viceroy of Mexico sent young Coronado northward in search of gold from the fabled Seven Cities of Cíbola.

Coronado led an expedition of more than 1,400 soldiers and natives as well as 1,500 animals. Five months of hard travel brought the party not to the gold of the fabled cities but to the rock and adobe pueblos of the Zuni Indians near Zuni, N.M. After traveling as far east as central Kansas, the expedition gave up its search and retraced the route to Mexico in 1542.

Although they never found the city of gold, Coronado and his men found the Grand Canyon as well as many Hopi, Zuni and other villages. Besides paying tribute to Coronado's journey, the memorial's 4,750 acres provide a natural habitat for a variety of plants and animals.

The park, at the southern end of the Huachuca Mountains, is mostly oak woodland sprinkled with yucca, cholla and bear grass, which bloom from April to August. The mountains and canyons harbor wildlife ranging from bobcats to golden eagles. Three miles west of the visitor center, an overlook provides a sweeping view of the San Rafael Valley, the San Pedro Valley and the San Jose Peak in Mexico.

An alternative to driving to the pass is the 3-mile-long Joe's Canyon Trail, which begins near the visitor center. A half-mile hiking trail, with benches for resting, exhibits explaining the significance of Coronado's expedition, and markers bearing quotations from Coronado's journals, extends from the pass to Coronado Peak. The visitor center has a 14-foot-long window wall for viewing birds and wildlife. Picnic facilities are available dawn-dusk.

The visitor center is open daily 8-4; closed Thanksgiving and Christmas. Free. For further information write the Visitor Center, Coronado National Memorial, 4101 E. Montezuma Canyon Rd., Hereford, AZ 85615; phone (520) 366-5515.

CORONADO CAVE is accessible via a steep half-mile trail w. of the visitor center. The cave, which remains in its natural state with no lighting or guardrails, features two chambers connected by a narrow passageway. Several short tunnels branch from the main cavern and require some crawling. **Note:** Visitors must be equipped with one flashlight per person. Comfortable walking shoes and water also are recommended. **Hours:** Daily 8-4. **Cost:** Free. **Phone:** (520) 366-5515.

COTTONWOOD (C-3) pop. 11,265, elev. 3,314'
• Restaurants p. 58

One of two Arizona towns called Cottonwood, this Cottonwood is in the center of the 1,500-square-mile Verde Valley, which contributed to its development as a commerce center for the area. In 1874 soldiers from nearby Camp Verde were quartered in town. Settlers eventually arrived and named the community for a nearby stand of 16 large cottonwood trees. Cottonwood is about 2 miles southeast of Tuzigoot National Monument (see place listing p. 313).

Cottonwood Chamber of Commerce: 1010 S. Main St., Cottonwood, AZ 86326. **Phone:** (928) 634-7593.

BLAZIN' M RANCH is 1 mi. n. on 10th St. to 1875 Mabery Ranch Rd., following signs from Main St. Cowboy-style entertainment and a chuck wagon supper are offered in a re-created Western town with an art gallery and farm animals. There also are miniature train rides, a shooting gallery and a saloon.

Time: Allow 2 hours minimum. **Hours:** Performances are given Wed.-Sat. at 7:30 p.m. Gates open at 4, and the dinner bell rings at 6:30. **Cost:** $34.95; $32.95 (ages 65+); $24.95 (ages 2-12). Reservations are recommended. **Phone:** (928) 634-0334 or (800) 937-8643.

CLEMENCEAU HERITAGE MUSEUM is at jct. Willard St. and Mingus Ave. at 1 N. Willard St. The museum is housed in a former schoolhouse built 1923-24. Seven railroads that operated in the Verde Valley 1895-1953 are depicted in a working railroad diorama. The diorama also depicts farming and ranching. Exhibits on permanent display include a typical 1920s bedroom, kitchen and dining room as well as a schoolroom. **Time:** Allow 30 minutes minimum. **Hours:** Fri.-Sun. 11-3, Wed. 9-noon. **Cost:** Donations. **Phone:** (928) 634-2868.

DEAD HORSE RANCH STATE PARK is at 675 Dead Horse Ranch Rd. The Ireys family, who bought the ranch in the late 1940s, chose the name after finding a horse skeleton on the property. Once the stomping grounds of Native Americans and Spanish conquistadors, the park now features Quetta Seed Pine Orchard; three stocked fishing ponds; trails for hiking, biking and horseback riding; and picnic areas overlooking the Verde River. See Recreation Chart.

Cabins, camping and trail rides are available. Boating is permitted; as the park does not provide boats, visitors may bring nonmotorized personal watercraft. **Hours:** Park open daily 8-5. Ranger station 7:30-4:30; closed Christmas. **Cost:** $7 (per private vehicle, up to four passengers); $3 (per additional adult passenger in vehicle or individual arriving on foot or bicycle). Camping $15-$25 (per private vehicle). Cabins $55. Trail rides $64-$125 (per person). Reservations are required for cabins and group sites. **Phone:** (928) 634-5283. ▲ ⛺ ⊞

RECREATIONAL ACTIVITIES
Hot Air Ballooning
• **Sky High Balloon Adventures** departs from the Verde Valley. **Hours:** Tours depart daily at dawn (weather permitting). **Phone:** (800) 551-7597.

BEST WESTERN COTTONWOOD INN
Phone: (928)634-5575

Hotel
$90-$120

AAA Benefit: Members save up to 20%, plus 10% bonus points with Best Western Rewards®.

Address: 993 S Main St 86326 **Location:** On SR 89A, at SR 260. Across from a shopping center. **Facility:** 77 units. 1-2 stories (no elevator), exterior corridors. **Terms:** cancellation fee imposed. **Amenities:** Some: high-speed Internet. **Pool(s):** heated outdoor. **Activities:** whirlpool. **Guest Services:** coin laundry. **Free Special Amenities:** full breakfast and high-speed Internet.

SAVE ⊺⊹ ➔ FEE⊹ BIZ 🛜 ✕ ◻ ▯ / SOME UNITS FEE ⛺ ▯

LITTLE DAISY MOTEL Phone: 928/634-7865

Motel
Rates not provided

Address: 34 S Main St 86326 **Location:** On SR 89A, just n. **Facility:** 20 units, some efficiencies and cottages. 1 story, exterior corridors. **Terms:** office hours 7 am-10 pm.

🛎️ 🛜 📠 / SOME UNITS FEE 🐾 🍽️

MOTEL 6 Phone: (928)634-3678

Motel
$55-$149

Address: 1089 S SR 260 86326 **Location:** On SR 260, just e of jct SR 89A. **Facility:** 31 units. 2 stories (no elevator), exterior corridors. **Terms:** cancellation fee imposed. **Amenities:** high-speed Internet.

🛎️ 🛜 ❌ 📠 🖥️ / SOME UNITS 🐾

PINES MOTEL Phone: (928)634-9975

Motel
$59-$99

Address: 920 S Camino Real 86326 **Location:** Jct SR 260, just nw on SR 89A, then just s. **Facility:** 25 units, some efficiencies. 2 stories (no elevator), exterior corridors. **Terms:** office hours 8 am-10 pm. **Pool(s):** heated outdoor. **Guest Services:** coin laundry.

ECO 🛎️ 🏊 BIZ 🛜 ❌ 📠 🖥️ 🖥️ / SOME UNITS FEE 🐾

QUALITY INN Phone: (928)634-4207

Hotel
$90-$129

Address: 301 W SR 89A 86326 **Location:** On SR 89A, 1.8 mi s of jct SR 260. Across from Verde Valley Medical Center. **Facility:** 51 units. 2 stories (no elevator), exterior corridors. **Terms:** cancellation fee imposed. **Amenities:** safes (fee). **Pool(s):** outdoor. **Activities:** whirlpool. **Free Special Amenities:** continental breakfast and high-speed Internet. SAVE 🏊 BIZ 🛜 ❌ 📠 🖥️ 🖥️

SUPER 8 COTTONWOOD Phone: (928)639-1888

Hotel
$59-$85

Address: 800 S Main St 86326 **Location:** On SR 89A, 0.4 mi nw of jct SR 260. **Facility:** 52 units. 2 stories (no elevator), exterior corridors. **Terms:** cancellation fee imposed. **Pool(s):** outdoor. **Activities:** whirlpool.

SAVE 🛎️ 🏊 BIZ 🛜 🖥️ / SOME UNITS 📠 🖥️

THE VIEW MOTEL Phone: 928/634-7581

Motel
$59-$129

Address: 818 S Main St 86326 **Location:** On SR 89A, 0.4 mi nw of jct SR 260. **Facility:** 35 units, some three bedrooms and kitchens. 1 story, exterior corridors. **Pool(s):** heated outdoor. **Activities:** whirlpool. **Free Special Amenities:** local telephone calls and preferred room (subject to availability with advance reservations).

SAVE 🛎️ 🏊 🛜 📠 🖥️ / SOME UNITS FEE 🐾

WHERE TO EAT

MAI THAI ON MAIN Phone: 928/649-2999

Thai
$8-$15

AAA Inspector Notes: Dishes ranging from classic pad thai to choices of curry, including panang, red, mussamon and green, are served by friendly and helpful staff members who guide guests through the heat levels. Many vegetarian dishes are on the menu. **Bar:** full bar. **Address:** 157 S Main St 86326 **Location:** 1.1 mi nw of jct SR 260. L D

Get Involved and Keep Teens Safe

TeenDriving.AAA.com

Exploring the countryside or visiting a nearby city can be perfect opportunities for your teen to gain important driving experience. Visit TeenDriving.AAA.com for valuable learning-to-drive resources including teaching tools, safety tips, licensing information and a parent-teen driving agreement.

Plus, check out the free StartSmart teen driving program, developed by AAA and the National Institutes of Health.

Visit **TeenDriving.AAA.com** today. Get involved. Keep teens safe.

MURPHY'S GRILL-COTTONWOOD   Phone: 928/634-7272

▼▼▼ 💎💎

American
$8-$19

AAA Inspector Notes: For families and social meals, Murphy's casual atmosphere, friendly service and hearty portions cannot be beat. Try express lunches, like chicken stir-fry on pasta or pistachio chicken sweet potato salad. Thick steaks, burgers and grilled chicken are other popular choices. **Bar:** full bar. **Address:** 747 S Main St 86326 **Location:** On SR 89A, 0.4 mi nw of jct SR 260.

[L] [D]

NIC'S ITALIAN STEAK & CRAB HOUSE
Phone: 928/634-9626

▼▼▼ 💎💎

Steak
$11-$30

AAA Inspector Notes: Although the menu centers on steaks, patrons also will find a nice selection of traditional pasta dishes and fresh seafood. **Bar:** full bar. **Address:** 925 N Main St 86326 **Location:** Center.

[L] [D]

THE TAVERN GRILLE   Phone: 928/634-6669

▼▼ 💎💎

American
$9-$24

AAA Inspector Notes: This small restaurant is very popular and gets packed daily for the happy hour specials. The red brick walls are covered with flat-screen TVs making it a great place to enjoy the game. The menu serves upscale bar favorites such as ahi tuna sashimi, burgers, sandwiches, New York steak and pasta dishes. **Bar:** full bar. **Address:** 925 N Main St 86326 **Location:** Center. **Parking:** street only. [L] [D]

DOUGLAS (G-6) pop. 17,378, elev. 3,955'

Douglas, on the Mexican border, began as the site of annual roundups for surrounding ranches. The town was founded in 1901 by a copper-smelting company and is now a center for commerce, manufacturing, agriculture and tourism.

The Gadsden Hotel, 1046 G Ave., was built in 1906 and has a high-ceilinged lobby with a mural of Tiffany stained glass and a curving staircase. Of interest in the vicinity are many ghost towns and mining camps as well as shopping and sightseeing opportunities in nearby Agua Prieta, Mexico.

Douglas Visitors Center: 345 16th St., Douglas, AZ 85607. **Phone:** (520) 417-7344.

Self-guiding tours: Maps detailing self-guiding historical tours of Douglas are available at the visitor center.

SLAUGHTER RANCH MUSEUM (SAN BERNARDINO RANCH NATIONAL HISTORIC LANDMARK)
, 16 mi. e. on 15th St. (which turns into Geronimo Tr.), was the home of John Slaughter. The former Texas Ranger and sheriff of Cochise County developed the property he purchased in 1884 into a vast cattle ranch. Now restored, the opulent main house contains many original family photographs and furnishings. Also on the ranch are a car shed, granary, barn, icehouse and washhouse. Near the ranch is an early 1900s military outpost.

Time: Allow 2 hours minimum. **Hours:** Wed.-Sun. 10-3. Closed Jan. 1 and Christmas. **Cost:** $8; free (ages 0-15). **Phone:** (520) 558-2474. 🏛

BEST WESTERN DOUGLAS INN & SUITES
Phone: (520)364-5000

▼▼▼ 💎💎

Hotel
$90-$130

[Best Western logo]

AAA Benefit: Members save up to 20%, plus 10% bonus points with Best Western Rewards®.

Address: 199 E 7th St 85607 **Location:** Jct SR 80, 0.6 mi s on Pan American Ave. **Facility:** 69 units. 3 stories, interior corridors. **Amenities:** high-speed Internet. **Pool(s):** heated outdoor. **Activities:** whirlpool, exercise room. **Guest Services:** coin laundry. **Free Special Amenities:** local telephone calls and high-speed Internet.

[SAVE] [🍴] [🔲] [📶] [✕] [FEE🎬] [🔒] [🔲] [📺]

MOTEL 6 #305   Phone: (520)364-2457

▼▼ 💎

Motel
$51-$61 5/28-1/31
$45-$55 2/1-5/27

Address: 111 16th St (SR 80) 85607 **Location:** 1.2 mi e of jct SR 191. **Facility:** 98 units. 2 stories (no elevator), exterior corridors. **Bath:** shower only. **Pool(s):** outdoor. **Guest Services:** coin laundry.

[📶] [📶] [/SOME UNITS] [🔲] [🔒] [📺]

THE GADSDEN HOTEL   Phone: 520/364-4481

[fyi] Not evaluated. **Address:** 1046 G Ave 85607 **Location:** Center. Facilities, services, and decor characterize an economy property.

DRAGOON (F-5) pop. 209, elev. 4,615'

💎GEM **AMERIND FOUNDATION MUSEUM,** off Dragoon Rd. at 2100 N. Amerind Rd., is an extension of the Amerind (a contraction of American and Indian) Foundation's archeological research facility. Featured are artifacts, crafts, art and photographs documenting Native American cultures of the Southwest and Mexico. Items from Arctic and South American civilizations also are included.

An art gallery contains works with Western themes by such well-known artists as Carl Oscar Borg, William Leigh and Frederic Remington as well as a variety of paintings and furnishings dating from the 17th century. **Time:** Allow 1 hour, 30 minutes minimum. **Hours:** Tues.-Sun. 10-4. Closed major holidays. **Cost:** $8; $7 (ages 60+); $5 (ages 12-18 and students with ID). **Phone:** (520) 586-3666. 🏛

Plan. Map. Go.

TripTik® Travel Planner

Where premier mapping technology meets complete travel information. Only on AAA.com and CAA.ca.

EAGAR pop. 4,885

BEST WESTERN SUNRISE INN

Phone: (928)333-2540

Motel
$90-$123

AAA Benefit:
Members save up to 20%, plus 10% bonus points with Best Western Rewards®.

Address: 128 N Main St 85925 **Location:** Jct SR 260, just n; jct US 60, 1.5 mi s. **Facility:** 40 units. 2 stories (no elevator), exterior corridors. **Amenities:** Some: high-speed Internet. **Activities:** sauna, exercise room. **Guest Services:** coin laundry. **Free Special Amenities:** expanded continental breakfast and high-speed Internet.

SAVE ｜｜＋ BIZ 🛜 🔲 🖥 💻 / SOME UNITS FEE 🐾

Gateway to the White Mountains! Conveniently located next to Bashas Grocery & Trailriders Restaurant

EHRENBERG pop. 1,470

BEST WESTERN DESERT OASIS   Phone: 928/923-9711

Hotel
Rates not provided

AAA Benefit: Members save up to 20%, plus 10% bonus points with Best Western Rewards®.

Address: S Frontage Rd 85334 **Location:** I-10 exit 1, just s; 0.5 mi e of Colorado River. Located at Flying J Travel Plaza. **Facility:** 82 units. 2 stories (no elevator), interior corridors. **Amenities:** Some: high-speed Internet. **Pool(s):** outdoor. **Activities:** whirlpool, limited exercise equipment. **Guest Services:** coin laundry. **Free Special Amenities:** local telephone calls and high-speed Internet.

SAVE ｜｜＋ 🏊 🛜 🔲 🖥 💻 / SOME UNITS FEE 🐾

ELGIN (G-5) pop. 161, elev. 4,700'

WINERIES

• **Sonoita Vineyards,** 3 mi. s. on Elgin/Canelo Rd. **Hours:** Daily 10-4. Closed major holidays. **Phone:** (520) 455-5893.

ELOY pop. 16,631

MOTEL 6 - 1263

Motel
$51-$61 2/1-4/26
$45-$55 4/27-1/31

Phone: (520)836-3323

Address: 4965 S Sunland Gin Rd 85231 **Location:** I-10 exit 200, just w. **Facility:** 97 units. 2 stories (no elevator), exterior corridors. **Pool(s):** outdoor. **Guest Services:** coin laundry.

｜｜＋ 🏊 🛜 / SOME UNITS 🐾 FEE 🔲 FEE 🖥

FLAGSTAFF (C-4) pop. 65,870, elev. 6,905'

• **Hotels p. 65** • **Restaurants p. 71**
• **Hotels & Restaurants map & index p. 63**

Flagstaff rests on the Colorado Plateau under the gaze of the San Francisco Peaks amid ponderosa pine forests, high deserts and lakes. Dusted with snow in winter and wildflowers in summer, the mountains provide a scenic backdrop for what was once a mere rest stop.

The town's name was established by locals in 1881. It is believed that it refers to a ponderosa pine tree that was stripped of its branches and used as a flagstaff by members of an exploration party during Fourth of July celebrations in 1876. The flagstaff, visible from afar, remained in place to serve as a landmark for wagon trains bound for California; transients knew that they would find a good place to camp when they spotted the flagstaff.

Shepherd Thomas F. McMillan, said to be the town's first permanent resident, deemed the land perfect for raising sheep when he arrived in 1876. Early industry revolved around timber, sheep and cattle, but when the Atlantic and Pacific Railway Co. (now the Santa Fe) decided to merge with the Southern Pacific line, settlers again put out their welcome mats, providing water and supplies to the railroad crews. The railroad reached Flagstaff in 1882. The Flagstaff Railroad Depot, on SR 66 between S. San Francisco and S. Beaver streets, opened in 1926. Impressive with its Revival Tudor style, it now houses a visitor center and an Amtrak station.

Downtown Flagstaff, which grew up around the railroad depot, contains many historic buildings dating from the late 1800s to early 1900s. Plaques give insight to buildings' former functions.

The Northern Arizona Normal School, established in 1899, was renamed Northern Arizona University in 1966. The university contributes to Flagstaff's college town feel. NAU's north campus, which encompasses 140 acres, boasts numerous restored buildings constructed 1894-1935 of local sandstone. This area reputedly contains the largest number of restored sandstone buildings in the Southwest.

In the 1920s, Route 66 brought travelers through town; they stayed briefly yet contributed to the economy. Money from tourism helped Flagstaff become an incorporated city in 1928, and the route continues to attract visitors.

Another popular drive is the 54-mile scenic stretch of SR 89A that begins in Flagstaff, winds its way south through Oak Creek Canyon and ends in Jerome. (The steep, narrow road is not recommended for vehicles pulling trailers more than 40 feet long.)

The city remains a good home base for many day trips. Within the boundaries of Coconino County, the second largest in the country, visitors will find Grand Canyon National Park (see place listing p. 84), Meteor Crater (see attraction listing p. 322), Oak Creek Canyon (see Sedona p. 228), Sunset Crater Volcano National Monument (see place listing p. 254), Walnut Canyon National Monument (see place listing p. 313) and Wupatki National Monument (see place listing p. 323). The landscape varies from deep green woodlands to rugged, rocky escarpments and provides for nearly every recreational pursuit, from skiing and hiking to camping, hunting and fishing.

(See map & index p. 63.)

Flagstaff Convention & Visitors Bureau 323 W. Aspen Ave., Flagstaff, AZ 86001. **Phone:** (928) 779-7611 or (800) 217-2367. *(See ad this page.)*

Flagstaff Visitors Center: 1 E. Rte. 66, Historic Train Station, Flagstaff, AZ 86001. **Phone:** (928) 774-9541 or (800) 842-7293.

Self-guiding tours: A map outlining a walking tour of Flagstaff's historic downtown area is available at the Flagstaff Visitors Center in the historic train station on Route 66.

Shopping areas: Flagstaff Mall, 6 miles east at 4650 SR 89N, has more than 70 stores, including Dillard's, JCPenney and Sears. Flagstaff's downtown historic district also offers shopping opportunities.

THE ARBORETUM AT FLAGSTAFF, off SR 66 to Woody Mountain Rd., then 4 mi. s., highlights more than 2,500 regional plant species in natural settings. One of the country's largest collection of mountain wildflowers may be seen; peak season is July through August. A nature trail traverses meadows and a ponderosa pine forest. A guided garden tour is offered, and a presentation features animals native to the Southwest.

▼ *See AAA listing this page* ▼

The getaway not far away.
{ With easy access to everything grand.}

Plan your getaway to the cool, fresh air and pine-covered mountains of Flagstaff. With easy access to Sedona, the Grand Canyon and other world-famous attractions, it's the perfect hub to discovering beautiful northern Arizona.

Get the free mobile app at
http://gettag.mobi

Flagstaff The destination for all seasons
flagstaffarizona.org | 888.601.2340

(See map & index p. 63.)

Time: Allow 2 hours minimum. **Hours:** Daily 9-5, Apr.-Oct. Garden tour daily at 11, 1 and 3. Wildlife program Wed.-Sun. at noon and 2, May-Sept. **Cost:** $7; $6 (senior citizens); $3 (ages 6-17). **Phone:** (928) 774-1442.

ARIZONA HISTORICAL SOCIETY PIONEER MUSEUM is 2 mi. n.w. at 2340 N. Fort Valley Rd. (US 180). The museum is in a former hospital for the indigent built in 1908 and contains interpretive historical exhibits about livestock, medicine, domestic life and the lumbering industry in northern Arizona. A 1908 homesteader's cabin, a 1929 Baldwin articulated locomotive and a 1940s Santa Fe caboose are on the premises. Festivals take place throughout the year.

Time: Allow 1 hour minimum. **Hours:** Mon.-Sat. 9-5; closed Jan. 1, Martin Luther King Jr. Day, Presidents Day, Columbus Day, Veterans Day, Thanksgiving, Christmas and state employee furlough days. **Cost:** $5; free (ages 0-14). **Phone:** (928) 774-6272. 🏛

LOWELL OBSERVATORY is 1 mi. w. of downtown via Santa Fe Ave. to 1400 W. Mars Hill Rd., following signs. The observatory was founded in 1894 by Percival Lowell. Discoveries made here include Lowell's observations about the planet Mars, the basis for the theory of the expanding universe and the discovery of Pluto in 1930. Interactive exhibits are featured as well as the Pluto Walk, a model of the planets in sequential order. A guided tour begins with a multimedia presentation in the John Vickers McAllister Space Theatre. Research continues at the observatory with the operation of seven modern telescopes.

Hours: Daily 9 a.m.-10 p.m., June-Aug.; 9-5 (also Mon., Wed. and Fri.-Sat. 5:30-9:30), Sept.-Oct. and Mar.-May; noon-5 (also Mon., Wed. and Fri.-Sat. 5:30-9:30), rest of year. Closed major holidays. **Cost:** $10; $9 (ages 65+ and college students with ID); $4 (ages 5-17). **Phone:** (928) 233-3211 or (928) 774-3358.

MUSEUM OF NORTHERN ARIZONA is 3 mi. n. to 3101 N. Fort Valley Rd. (US 180). The museum contains displays about artistic traditions, native cultures and natural science, including exhibits about anthropology, biology and geology. A reproduction of a kiva—a meeting place and ceremonial room—also is featured. Recreation programs and festivals are offered in summer.

Hours: Daily 9-5. Closed Jan. 1, Thanksgiving and Christmas. **Cost:** $7; $6 (ages 65+); $5 (students with ID); $4 (Native Americans and ages 7-17). **Phone:** (928) 774-5213.

NORTHERN ARIZONA UNIVERSITY ART MUSEUM is at jct. McMullen Cir. and Knoles Dr., building #10 on campus. Three galleries offer oil paintings on canvas, sculptures and contemporary art. **Time:** Allow 30 minutes minimum. **Hours:** Tues.-Sat. noon-5. **Cost:** $2. **Phone:** (928) 523-3471.

◆ OAK CREEK CANYON— see Sedona p. 228.

RIORDAN MANSION STATE HISTORIC PARK is .5 mi. n. of jct. I-17 and I-40 (off Milton Rd.) at 409 W. Riordan Rd. Built in 1904, the 40-room mansion was home to prominent lumbermen Timothy and Michael Riordan and their families. The rustic exterior incorporates log-slab siding, volcanic stone arches and hand-split wood shingles. The lavish Arts and Crafts-style interior contains handcrafted and Stickley furniture, a Steinway piano, stained-glass windows and personal family items. The park's visitor center has exhibits and a children's "touch table."

Time: Allow 1 hour minimum. **Hours:** Grounds Thurs.-Mon. 9:30-5. Guided tours of the mansion are given on the hour 10-4. Closed Christmas. Phone ahead to confirm schedule. **Cost:** $7; $3 (ages 7-13). Reservations are recommended for guided tours. **Phone:** (928) 779-4395. 🏛

SCHULTZ PASS ROAD (FR 420) leads n. off US 180 and offers a scenic drive through Schultz Pass between the San Francisco Peaks and Elden Mountain. Travelers may also access the road via bicycle and horseback, often catching a glimpse of such resident animals as mule deer and elk.

Note: Portions of the road may be closed due to fire activity or inclement weather; snow closes the road during winter months. Passenger vehicles are not permitted during these conditions. **Phone:** (928) 526-0866 for current road condition updates from the Peaks Ranger Station.

RECREATIONAL ACTIVITIES
Skiing
• **Arizona Snowbowl,** in the San Francisco Peaks, is 7 mi. n. on Fort Valley Rd. (US 180), then 7 mi. n. on Snowbowl Rd. Other activities are offered. **Hours:** Skiing is available daily 9-4, mid-Dec. to mid-Apr. (weather permitting). Scenic sky ride Fri.-Sun. and holidays 10-4, Memorial Day-Labor Day. **Phone:** (928) 779-1951.

Simply Reliable

The Diamond Ratings in this TourBook guide are backed by our expert, in-person evaluations, whether the hotel or restaurant is no-frills, moderate or upscale.

Learn more at **AAA.com/Diamonds**

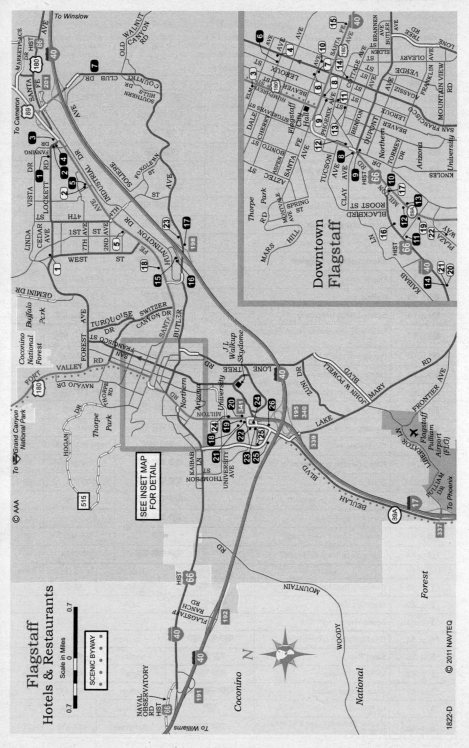

Flagstaff
Hotels & Restaurants

Downtown Flagstaff

Flagstaff

This index helps you "spot" where approved hotels and restaurants are located on the corresponding detailed maps. Hotel daily rate range is for comparison only and show the property's high season. Restaurant rate range is a combination of lunch and/or dinner. Turn to the listing page for more detailed rate information and consult display ads for special promotions.

FLAGSTAFF

Map Page	Hotels	Diamond Rated	High Season	Page
1 p. 63	Starlight Pines, A Bed & Breakfast	◆◆◆	$149-$189	71
2 p. 63	Hampton Inn East (See ad p. 66.)	◆◆◆	$79-$159	67
3 p. 63	Super 8 - Flagstaff Mall	◆◆	$45-$95 SAVE	71
4 p. 63	Days Inn & Suites (See ad p. 66.)	◆◆	$56-$138 SAVE	65
5 p. 63	Best Western Pony Soldier Inn & Suites	◆◆	$65-$150 SAVE	65
6 p. 63	The Inn at 410 Bed & Breakfast	◆◆◆	$160-$215	67
7 p. 63	Residence Inn by Marriott Flagstaff	◆◆◆	$98-$134 SAVE	71
8 p. 63	Highland Country Inn	◆◆	$59-$159 SAVE	67
9 p. 63	Drury Inn & Suites-Flagstaff	◆◆◆	$105-$234	67
10 p. 63	Embassy Suites-Flagstaff	◆◆◆	$129-$189 SAVE	67
11 p. 63	Travel Inn	◆	$59-$119 SAVE	71
12 p. 63	Budget Inn	◆◆	$59-$149 SAVE	65
13 p. 63	Econo Lodge-University	◆◆	$60-$130 SAVE	67
14 p. 63	Radisson Woodlands Hotel Flagstaff (See ad p. 70.)	◆◆◆	$89-$209 SAVE	70
15 p. 63	Ramada Inn-Lucky Lane	◆◆	$49-$199	70
16 p. 63	Holiday Inn Express	◆◆◆	$79-$159	67
17 p. 63	Little America Hotel (See ad p. 69.)	◆◆◆	$89-$199 SAVE	70
18 p. 63	La Quinta Inn & Suites Flagstaff	◆◆◆	$84-$192	68
19 p. 63	Fairfield Inn by Marriott	◆◆◆	$69-$149	67
20 p. 63	Quality Inn I-40/I-17	◆◆	$50-$140 SAVE	70
21 p. 63	Hilton Garden Inn (See ad p. 68.)	◆◆◆	$100-$185 SAVE	67
22 p. 63	Comfort Inn I-17/I-40	◆◆◆	$80-$200	65
23 p. 63	SpringHill Suites by Marriott	◆◆◆	$98-$157	71
24 p. 63	Hampton Inn & Suites	◆◆◆	$109-$159	67
25 p. 63	Motel 6-Flagstaff West #1000	◆	$55-$65	70
26 p. 63	Courtyard by Marriott-Flagstaff	◆◆◆	$98-$157	65

Map Page	Restaurants	Diamond Rated	Cuisine	Meal Range	Page
1 p. 63	Brandy's Restaurant & Bakery	◆◆	American	$5-$14	71
2 p. 63	Mamma Luisa	◆◆	Italian	$8-$17	73
3 p. 63	Josephine's	◆◆◆	American	$8-$30	72
4 p. 63	Brix Restaurant & Wine Bar	◆◆◆	American	$22-$31	71
5 p. 63	Salsa Brava	◆◆	Mexican	$5-$14	73
6 p. 63	Monsoon Downtown	◆◆	Asian	$8-$14	73
7 p. 63	Pasto Cucina Italiana	◆◆◆	Italian	$17-$27	73
8 p. 63	La Bellavia	◆	American	$5-$8	72
9 p. 63	Beaver Street Brewery & Whistle Stop Cafe	◆◆	American	$9-$13	71

Map Page	Restaurants (cont'd)	Diamond Rated	Cuisine	Meal Range	Page
⑩ p. 63	Swaddee Authentic Thai Cuisine	◆◆	Thai	$11-$16	73
⑪ p. 63	Macy's European Coffee House & Bakery	◆	Vegetarian	$5-$10	72
⑫ p. 63	**Granny's Closet Restaurant & Sports Grill**	◆◆	American	$6-$19	72
⑬ p. 63	Cottage Place Restaurant	◆◆◆	Continental	$20-$35	72
⑭ p. 63	Dara Thai Restaurant	◆	Thai	$9-$13	72
⑮ p. 63	Kachina Restaurant	◆	Mexican	$6-$18	72
⑯ p. 63	Galaxy Diner	◆◆	Comfort Food	$5-$12	72
⑰ p. 63	Bun Hugger's	◆	American	$5-$8	71
⑱ p. 63	China Star	◆	Chinese	$5-$8	72
⑲ p. 63	Little Thai Kitchen	◆	Thai	$6-$12	72
⑳ p. 63	**Woodlands Restaurant**	◆◆	American	$7-$24	73
㉑ p. 63	**Sakura Restaurant** *(See ad p. 70.)*	◆◆	Japanese	$5-$29	73
㉒ p. 63	Hiro's Sushi Bar & Japanese Restaurant	◆◆	Japanese	$5-$14	72
㉓ p. 63	**Black Bart's Steak House & Musical Revue**	◆◆	Steak	$12-$36	71
㉔ p. 63	Buster's	◆◆	American	$8-$29	71
㉕ p. 63	Delhi Palace	◆◆	Indian	$9-$17	72

BEST WESTERN PONY SOLDIER INN & SUITES
Phone: (928)526-2388 **5**

◆◆◆
Hotel
$65-$150

AAA Benefit: Members save up to 20%, plus 10% bonus points with Best Western Rewards®.

Address: 3030 E Route 66 86004 **Location:** I-40 exit 201, just n, then 1 mi w. Next to railroad tracks. **Facility:** 75 units, some two bedrooms. 2 stories (no elevator), interior corridors. **Amenities:** *Some:* high-speed Internet. **Pool(s):** heated indoor. **Activities:** whirlpool. **Free Special Amenities:** expanded continental breakfast and high-speed Internet.

BUDGET INN   Phone: (928)774-5038 **12**

◆◆
Motel
$59-$149 5/1-1/31
$49-$89 2/1-4/30

Address: 913 S Milton Rd 86001 **Location:** I-40 exit 195, 1.2 mi n. **Facility:** 38 units. 2 stories (no elevator), exterior corridors. **Terms:** 3 day cancellation notice-fee imposed. **Free Special Amenities:** local telephone calls and high-speed Internet.

COMFORT INN I-17/I-40   Phone: (928)774-2225 **22**

◆◆◆
Hotel
$80-$200

Address: 2355 S Beulah Blvd 86001 **Location:** I-40 exit 195, just n to Forest Meadows St, then 1 blk w. **Facility:** 85 units. 2 stories, interior corridors. **Terms:** cancellation fee imposed. **Pool(s):** heated outdoor. **Activities:** whirlpools, exercise room. **Guest Services:** valet and coin laundry.

COURTYARD BY MARRIOTT-FLAGSTAFF
Phone: (928)774-5800 **26**

◆◆◆
Hotel
$98-$157

AAA Benefit: AAA hotel discounts of 5% or more.

Address: 2650 S Beulah Blvd 86001 **Location:** I-40 exit 195, just n to Forest Meadows St, w to Beulah Rd, then just s. **Facility:** 164 units. 4 stories, interior corridors. **Amenities:** high-speed Internet. **Pool(s):** heated indoor. **Activities:** whirlpool, exercise room. **Guest Services:** valet and coin laundry, area transportation-Amtrak station.

DAYS INN & SUITES   Phone: (928)527-1477 **4**

◆◆◆
Hotel
$56-$138

Address: 3601 E Lockett Rd 86004 **Location:** I-40 business loop, then just n on Fanning Dr. **Facility:** 54 units. 3 stories, interior corridors. **Amenities:** high-speed Internet, safes. **Pool(s):** heated indoor. **Activities:** whirlpool. **Guest Services:** valet and coin laundry. **Free Special Amenities:** expanded continental breakfast and high-speed Internet. *(See ad p. 66.)*

Check out our travel blog at AAATravelViews.com

▼ See AAA listing p. 67 ▼

Hampton Inn Flagstaff East

Within a short drive of the Grand Canyon, NAU, and the Arizona Snowbowl!

Up to 10% off best available rate for AAA members!*

* = Based on availability.

Amenities include:
- Complimentary Hot Breakfast Bar
- Heated Indoor Pool and Spa Area
- Free Wireless High-Speed Internet
- Fitness Center
- Spacious Guest Rooms

Hampton Inn Flagstaff East • 3501 E Lockett Rd • Flagstaff, AZ 86004
Phone 800.317.9542 or 928.526.1885 • www.hamptoninnflagstaff.com

▼ See AAA listing p. 65 ▼

AAA Members mention this ad and

Save 20%
Off Published Rates*

Days Inn
The Best Value Under The Sun™

FREE Daybreak® Hot Breakfast

FREE Wireless Internet

EARN Wyndham Rewards® points for your stays**

PETS ACCEPTED for a fee.

SPACIOUS Family and Two-Room suites available

One of the **LARGEST** Indoor Pools & Spas in Flagstaff

Days Inn & Suites East Flagstaff
3601 E Lockett Road
Flagstaff, AZ 86004
928-527-1477

AAA
Approved

daysinn.com   1-800-Days-Inn®

*Certain restrictions apply. See daysinn.com for details. Rooms at this discount are limited and subject to availability at participating properties. Blackout dates and other restrictions may apply. Stay must be completed by 1/31/13. **A qualified stay is defined as a stay at a qualifying rate at one of the participating Wyndham Hotel Group properties. ©2011 Days Inns Worldwide, Inc. All Rights Reserved. All Days Inn hotels are independently owned and operated.

Explore the Travel Guides on AAA.com/Travel or CAA.ca/Travel

(See map & index p. 63.)

DRURY INN & SUITES-FLAGSTAFF
Phone: (928)773-4900 **9**

▼▼▼
Hotel
$105-$234

Address: 300 S Milton Rd 86001 **Location:** I-40 exit 195, 1.8 mi n on SR 89A (Milton Rd). **Facility:** 160 units, some two bedrooms. 6 stories, interior corridors. **Terms:** cancellation fee imposed. **Pool(s):** heated indoor. **Activities:** whirlpool, exercise room. **Guest Services:** valet and coin laundry.

ECO 🍴 CALL 🔊M 🛖 BIZ 🛜 ✕ FEE 📺 🖃
🖥 ⬛ / SOME UNITS 🐾

ECONO LODGE-UNIVERSITY
Phone: (928)774-7326 **13**

▼▼ ▼▼
Motel
$60-$130

Address: 914 S Milton Rd 86001 **Location:** I-40 exit 195, 1.2 mi n on SR 89A (Milton Rd). **Facility:** 66 units. 2 stories (no elevator), exterior corridors. **Terms:** cancellation fee imposed. **Pool(s):** heated outdoor. **Free Special Amenities: continental breakfast and high-speed Internet.**

SAVE 🍴 🛖 🛜 FEE 📺 ⬛
/ SOME UNITS FEE 🐾 🖃 🖥

EMBASSY SUITES-FLAGSTAFF
Phone: (928)774-4333 **10**

▼▼▼
Hotel
$129-$189 2/1-9/30
$119-$169 10/1-1/31

AAA Benefit: Members save 5% or more everyday!

Address: 706 S Milton Rd 86001 **Location:** I-40 exit 195, 1.5 mi n on SR 89A (Milton Rd). Adjacent to Northern Arizona University. **Facility:** 119 units, some two bedrooms. 3 stories, interior corridors. **Terms:** 1-7 night minimum stay, cancellation fee imposed. **Pool(s):** heated outdoor. **Activities:** whirlpool, exercise room. **Guest Services:** valet and coin laundry. **Free Special Amenities: full breakfast and newspaper.**

SAVE ECO 🍴 🛖 🍽 🛖 BIZ 🛜 FEE 📺 🖃
🖥 ⬛

FAIRFIELD INN BY MARRIOTT
Phone: (928)773-1300 **19**

▼▼▼
Hotel
$69-$149

AAA Benefit: AAA hotel discounts of 5% or more.

Address: 2005 S Milton Rd 86001 **Location:** I-40 exit 195, 0.5 mi n. **Facility:** 130 units. 3 stories, interior/exterior corridors. **Amenities:** high-speed Internet. **Pool(s):** heated outdoor. **Activities:** whirlpool, exercise room. **Guest Services:** valet laundry.

🍴 🛖 BIZ 🛜 ✕ ⬛ / SOME UNITS 🖃 🖥

HAMPTON INN & SUITES
Phone: (928)913-0900 **24**

▼▼▼
Hotel
$109-$159

AAA Benefit: Members save up to 10% everyday!

Address: 2400 S Beulah Blvd 86001 **Location:** I-40 exit 195, just n to Forest Meadows St, just w, then just s. **Facility:** 126 units, some efficiencies. 5 stories, interior corridors. **Terms:** 1-7 night minimum stay, cancellation fee imposed. **Amenities:** high-speed Internet. **Pool(s):** heated indoor. **Activities:** whirlpool, exercise room. **Guest Services:** valet and coin laundry.

🍴 CALL 🔊M 🛖 BIZ 🛜 ✕ ⬛
/ SOME UNITS 🖃 🖥

HAMPTON INN EAST
Phone: (928)526-1885 **2**

▼▼▼
Hotel
$79-$159

AAA Benefit: Members save up to 10% everyday!

Address: 3501 E Lockett Rd 86004 **Location:** I-40 exit 201, 0.5 mi w on I-40 business loop, then just n on Fanning Dr. **Facility:** 50 units. 3 stories, interior corridors. **Terms:** 1-7 night minimum stay, cancellation fee imposed. **Amenities:** Some: high-speed Internet. **Pool(s):** heated indoor. **Activities:** whirlpool, exercise room. **Guest Services:** valet laundry.

(See ad p. 66.)

🍴 CALL 🔊M 🛖 BIZ 🛜 ⬛ / SOME UNITS 🖃 🖥

HIGHLAND COUNTRY INN
Phone: (928)774-5041 **8**

▼▼ ▼▼
Motel
$59-$159 5/1-1/31
$49-$89 2/1-4/30

Address: 223 S Milton Rd 86001 **Location:** I-40 exit 195, 1.8 mi n on SR 89A (Milton Rd). **Facility:** 42 units. 2 stories (no elevator), exterior corridors. **Terms:** 3 day cancellation notice-fee imposed. **Guest Services:** coin laundry. **Free Special Amenities: local telephone calls and high-speed Internet.**

SAVE 🍴 🛜 FEE 📺 🖃 🖥

HILTON GARDEN INN
Phone: (928)226-8888 **21**

▼▼▼
Hotel
$100-$185

Hilton Garden Inn

AAA Benefit: Unparalleled hospitality at a special Member rate.

Address: 350 W Forest Meadows St 86001 **Location:** I-40 exit 195, 0.5 mi n on SR 89A (Milton Rd), then just w. **Facility:** 89 units. 3 stories, interior corridors. **Terms:** 1-7 night minimum stay, cancellation fee imposed. **Amenities:** high-speed Internet. **Pool(s):** heated indoor. **Activities:** sauna, whirlpool, exercise room. **Guest Services:** valet and coin laundry. **Free Special Amenities: full breakfast and high-speed Internet.**

(See ad p. 68.)

SAVE 🍴 CALL 🔊M 🛖 BIZ 🛜 FEE 📺 🖃 🖥
⬛

HOLIDAY INN EXPRESS
Phone: (928)714-1000 **16**

▼▼▼
Hotel
$79-$159

Address: 2320 E Lucky Ln 86004 **Location:** I-40 exit 198 (Butler Ave), just n, then just e. **Facility:** 155 units. 5 stories, interior corridors. **Pool(s):** heated indoor/outdoor. **Activities:** whirlpool, exercise room. Fee: game room. **Guest Services:** valet and coin laundry.

🍴 CALL 🔊M 🛖 🛜 ⬛ / SOME UNITS 🖃 🖥

THE INN AT 410 BED & BREAKFAST
Phone: (928)774-0088 **6**

▼▼▼
Bed & Breakfast
$160-$215

Address: 410 N Leroux St 86001 **Location:** Just n of Cherry Ave. **Facility:** A garden gazebo accents the grounds of this charming 1907 Craftsman home, which is comfortably furnished with antiques and southwestern touches. 9 units. 2 stories (no elevator), interior/exterior corridors. **Terms:** 2 night minimum stay - seasonal and/or weekends, 14 day cancellation notice-fee imposed. **Activities:** limited exercise equipment. **Guest Services:** complimentary laundry.

BIZ 🛜 ✕ 🛗 🖃 ⬛

(See map & index p. 63.)

LA QUINTA INN & SUITES FLAGSTAFF

Hotel

$84-$192

Phone: (928)556-8666 **18**

Address: 2015 S Beulah Blvd 86001 **Location:** I-40 exit 195, just n to Forest Meadows St, then just w. **Facility:** 128 units. 3-4 stories, interior corridors. **Amenities:** video games (fee). *Some:* high-speed Internet. **Pool(s):** heated outdoor. **Activities:** whirlpool, exercise room. **Guest Services:** valet and coin laundry.

Download eTourBook guides
for ereaders and smartphones
at AAA.com/ebooks

▼ *See AAA listing p. 67* ▼

WHEN TOMORROW'S A BIG DAY, STAY HGI TONIGHT.

Our hotel is located in Flagstaff Arizona. All rooms feature complimentary WiFi, a fridge, microwave, and coffee maker.

• Restaurant • Indoor Pool • 24/7 Pavilion Pantry®
• Guest laundry • Complimentary parking

Hilton Garden Inn®
Flagstaff

Hilton Garden Inn
350 West Forest Meadows St.
Flagstaff, AZ 86001
928-226-8888

HGI.com   1-877-STAY-HGI

Scan to book a room

Get the free mobile app at
http://gettag.mobi

©2011 Hilton Worldwide

▼ See AAA listing p. 70 ▼

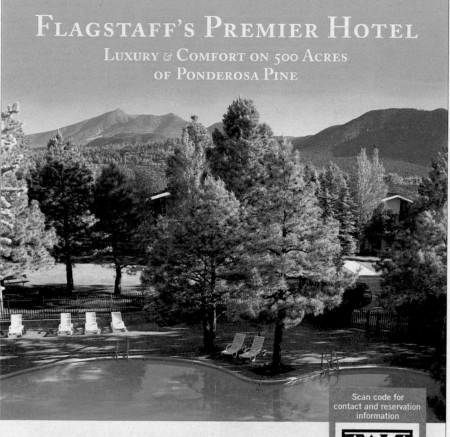

FLAGSTAFF'S PREMIER HOTEL
LUXURY & COMFORT ON 500 ACRES
OF PONDEROSA PINE

Scan code for
contact and reservation
information

get the free mobile app at
http://gettag.mobi

LITTLE
AMERICA
— Hotel —
F L A G S T A F F

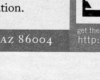

Visit our website at
FLAGSTAFF.LITTLEAMERICA.COM
or call 800.865.1403
for more information.

2515 EAST BUTLER AVENUE · FLAGSTAFF, AZ 86004

TourBook
Comments

Are we meeting your travel needs?

If your visit to an establishment listed in a AAA TourBook
guide doesn't meet your expectations, tell us about it.

Complete an easy online form at
AAA.com/TourBookComments.

(See map & index p. 63.)

LITTLE AMERICA HOTEL

◆◆◆◆ Hotel $89-$199

Phone: (928)779-7900   **17**

Address: 2515 E Butler Ave 86004 **Location:** I-40 exit 198 (Butler Ave), just s. **Facility:** 247 units, some two bedrooms and kitchens. 2 stories (no elevator), interior corridors. **Terms:** cancellation fee imposed. **Amenities:** video games (fee), high-speed Internet, safes. **Pool(s):** heated outdoor. **Activities:** whirlpool, hiking trails, playground, horseshoes, volleyball, exercise room. **Guest Services:** valet and coin laundry. **Free Special Amenities: high-speed Internet.** (See ad p. 69.)

[SAVE] [✈] [♦] [♦] [Y] [≈] [BIZ] [✈] [✗]
[FEE✖] [◧] [▢] / SOME UNITS [◫]

MOTEL 6-FLAGSTAFF WEST #1000

◆ Motel $55-$65 5/25-1/31 $45-$55 2/1-5/24

Phone: (928)779-3757   **25**

Address: 2745 S Woodlands Village Blvd 86001 **Location:** I-40 exit 195, just n to Forest Meadows St, w to Beulah Blvd, just s, then just w. **Facility:** 150 units. 3 stories, exterior corridors. *Bath:* shower only. **Pool(s):** heated outdoor. **Guest Services:** coin laundry.

[♦] CALL[▣] [≈] [✈] / SOME UNITS [▢] [◧] [◫]

QUALITY INN I-40/I-17

◆◆◆ Hotel $50-$140

Phone: (928)774-8771   **20**

Address: 2000 S Milton Rd 86001 **Location:** I-40 exit 195, just n to Forest Meadows St, then right. **Facility:** 96 units. 2 stories (no elevator), interior corridors. **Terms:** cancellation fee imposed. **Pool(s):** heated outdoor. **Free Special Amenities: expanded continental breakfast and high-speed Internet.**

[SAVE] [♦] [≈] [BIZ] [✈] [✗] [▢] / SOME UNITS FEE[✖]

RADISSON WOODLANDS HOTEL FLAGSTAFF

◆◆◆ Hotel $89-$209

Phone: (928)773-8888   **14**

Address: 1175 W Route 66 86001 **Location:** I-40 exit 195, 1.5 mi n on SR 89A (Milton Rd), then 0.5 mi w. **Facility:** 183 units. 3-4 stories, interior corridors. **Terms:** check-in 4 pm, 3 day cancellation notice-fee imposed. **Amenities:** video games (fee). *Some:* safes. **Dining:** Sakura Restaurant, Woodlands Restaurant, see separate listings. **Pool(s):** heated outdoor. **Activities:** sauna, whirlpools, exercise room. **Guest Services:** valet and coin laundry, area transportation-bus & train stations.

(See ad this page.)

[SAVE] [✈] [♦] [♦] [Y] [≈] [BIZ] [✈] [✗]
[FEE✖] [▢] / SOME UNITS [◧] [◫]

RAMADA INN-LUCKY LANE

◆◆ Hotel $49-$199

Phone: (928)779-3614   **15**

Address: 2350 E Lucky Ln 86004 **Location:** I-40 exit 198 (Butler Ave), just n, then just e. **Facility:** 100 units, some two bedrooms. 2-3 stories (no elevator), exterior corridors. **Terms:** cancellation fee imposed. **Pool(s):** heated outdoor. **Activities:** limited exercise equipment. **Guest Services:** coin laundry.

[♦] [≈] [✈] FEE[✖] [▢] / SOME UNITS FEE[✖] [◧] [◫]

Discover mobile travel solutions at AAA.com/mobile and CAA.ca/mobile

▼ See AAA listing this page ▼

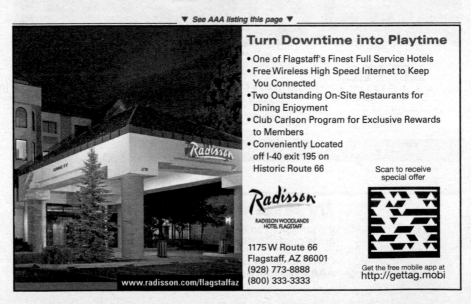

Turn Downtime into Playtime

- One of Flagstaff's Finest Full Service Hotels
- Free Wireless High Speed Internet to Keep You Connected
- Two Outstanding On-Site Restaurants for Dining Enjoyment
- Club Carlson Program for Exclusive Rewards to Members
- Conveniently Located off I-40 exit 195 on Historic Route 66

Scan to receive special offer

Radisson

RADISSON WOODLANDS HOTEL FLAGSTAFF

1175 W Route 66 Flagstaff, AZ 86001 (928) 773-8888 (800) 333-3333

www.radisson.com/flagstaffaz

Get the free mobile app at http://gettag.mobi

(See map & index p. 63.)

RESIDENCE INN BY MARRIOTT FLAGSTAFF
Phone: (928)526-5555 **7**

Extended Stay Hotel
$98-$134

AAA Benefit: AAA hotel discounts of 5% or more.

Address: 3440 N Country Club Dr 86004 **Location:** I-40 exit 201, 0.5 mi s. **Facility:** 102 units, some two bedrooms and kitchens. 2 stories (no elevator), interior/exterior corridors. **Terms:** check-in 4 pm. **Amenities:** high-speed Internet. **Pool(s):** heated outdoor. **Activities:** whirlpool, sports court, exercise room. **Guest Services:** valet and coin laundry. **Free Special Amenities: expanded continental breakfast and high-speed Internet.**

SPRINGHILL SUITES BY MARRIOTT
Phone: (928)774-8042 **23**

Contemporary Hotel
$98-$157

AAA Benefit: AAA hotel discounts of 5% or more.

Address: 2455 S Beulah Blvd 86001 **Location:** I-40 exit 195, just n to Forest Meadows St, then 1 blk w. **Facility:** 112 units. 5 stories, interior corridors. **Amenities:** Some: high-speed Internet. **Pool(s):** heated indoor. **Activities:** exercise room. **Guest Services:** coin laundry.

STARLIGHT PINES, A BED & BREAKFAST
Phone: (928)527-1912 **1**

Bed & Breakfast
$149-$189

Address: 3380 E Lockett Rd 86004 **Location:** I-40 exit 201, 0.5 mi w on I-40 business loop, then just n. **Facility:** Bathrooms in this stately Victorian-style home feature vintage claw-foot tubs as well as showers with handmade soap; rooms have a fireplace or porch. 4 units. 2 stories (no elevator), interior corridors. **Terms:** check-in 4 pm, 14 day cancellation notice-fee imposed. **Activities:** hiking trails.

SUPER 8 - FLAGSTAFF MALL
Phone: (928)526-0818 **3**

Motel
$45-$95

Address: 3725 N Kasper Ave 86004 **Location:** I-40 exit 201, just n, 0.5 mi w on I-40 business loop, then just n. Located on a busy commercial street. **Facility:** 89 units. 2 stories (no elevator), interior corridors. **Terms:** cancellation fee imposed. **Guest Services:** coin laundry. **Free Special Amenities: expanded continental breakfast and high-speed Internet.**

TRAVEL INN
Phone: (928)774-3381 **11**

Motel
$59-$119 5/1-1/31
$39-$99 2/1-4/30

Address: 801 W Route 66 86001 **Location:** I-40 exit 195, 1.2 mi n on SR 89A (Milton Rd), then just w. **Facility:** 48 units, some two bedrooms. 2 stories (no elevator), exterior corridors. **Terms:** 3 day cancellation notice. **Activities:** sauna, whirlpools. **Guest Services:** coin laundry. **Free Special Amenities: continental breakfast and high-speed Internet.**

WHERE TO EAT

BEAVER STREET BREWERY & WHISTLE STOP CAFE
Phone: 928/779-0079 **9**

American
$9-$13

AAA Inspector Notes: Among offerings at the casual restaurant are soups, fondues, salads, sandwiches and wood-fired pizza, as well as a selection of entrées at dinner. Several ales and beers are brewed on the premises. Patio dining is a nice option in pleasant weather. **Bar:** full bar. **Address:** 11 S Beaver St, #1 86001 **Location:** I-40 exit 195, 2 mi n to Santa Fe Ave, just e, then just s.

BLACK BART'S STEAK HOUSE & MUSICAL REVUE
Phone: 928/779-3142 **23**

Steak
$12-$36

AAA Inspector Notes: The staff doubles as entertainers providing the nightly musical revue at this rustic, casual restaurant. Oak-broiled steak, seafood, chicken and prime rib delight the palate. Full service is provided by an attentive staff casually attired fitting the theme of the restaurant. **Bar:** full bar. **Address:** 2760 E Butler Ave 86004 **Location:** I-40 exit 198 (Butler Ave), just se.

BRANDY'S RESTAURANT & BAKERY
Menu on AAA.com **Phone:** 928/779-2187 **1**

American
$5-$14

AAA Inspector Notes: Famous in these parts for breakfast and baked goods, this eatery also offers an extensive lunch menu and creative dinner options. Midday fare includes tuna melts, Reubens, hamburgers, grilled salmon and grilled portobello sandwiches, while dinner features mahi mahi, ahi tuna, steak, chicken, salmon, burgers and a few sandwiches. **Bar:** wine only. **Address:** 1500 E Cedar Ave, Suite 40 86004 **Location:** Route 66, 0.8 mi n on 4th St, then just w; in strip mall.

BRIX RESTAURANT & WINE BAR
Phone: 928/213-1021 **4**

American
$22-$31

AAA Inspector Notes: Contemporary American cuisine is served in an historic 1900s carriage house with a charming decor. The menu is created around fresh, local farmed and organic items including artisanal cheese, Manila clams, steak frites and seasonal fish. Guests also like to sit at the bar and enjoy the large wine selection. **Bar:** full bar. **Reservations:** suggested. **Address:** 413 N San Francisco St 86001 **Location:** 2 blks n of downtown.

BUN HUGGER'S
Phone: 928/779-3743 **17**

American
$5-$8

AAA Inspector Notes: This casual burger joint serves hearty burgers, chicken sandwiches and chili fries. After ordering be prepared for a wait before your name is called. **Bar:** beer only. **Address:** 901 S Milton Rd 86001 **Location:** I-40 exit 195, 1.5 mi n.

BUSTER'S
Phone: 928/774-5155 **24**

American
$8-$29

AAA Inspector Notes: For casual dining in a lively atmosphere, this restaurant is a favorite with students of nearby Northern Arizona University. Contemporary furnishings provide a selection of tables and booths with a view from large windows, perfect to enjoy the sunset. Salads and sandwiches are popular lunch offerings, while dinners typically revolve around steaks, chicken and a daily selection of fresh seafood. Portions are large, cooked to order and colorfully garnished. The staff is professional and cordial. **Bar:** full bar. **Address:** 1800 S Milton Rd 86001 **Location:** I-40 exit 195, 0.5 mi n; in Green Tree Village.

(See map & index p. 63.)

CHINA STAR
Phone: 928/774-8880 (18)

Chinese
$5-$8

AAA Inspector Notes: Two large, self-service tables display soups, salads, fruits and desserts, as well as a variety of chicken, beef and rice entrées, including moo goo gai pan. Parking is plentiful around the restaurant, which stands alone in front of a small shopping center. **Address:** 1802 E Route 66 86004 **Location:** I-40 exit 198 (Butler Ave), just w, just n on Enterprise Rd, then just e. ⓛ ⓓ

COTTAGE PLACE RESTAURANT
Phone: 928/774-8431 (13)

Continental
$20-$35

AAA Inspector Notes: Classical background music and contemporary decor highlight works by local artists in the cozy, restored 1909 bungalow set in an old downtown neighborhood. A cordial, formally attired staff presents a nice selection of international entrées as well as a prix fixe dinner with wine parings. **Bar:** beer & wine. **Reservations:** suggested. **Address:** 126 W Cottage Ave 86001 **Location:** Just s of downtown; just w of Beaver St. **Parking:** on-site and street. ⓓ

DARA THAI RESTAURANT
Phone: 928/774-8390 (14)

Thai
$9-$13

AAA Inspector Notes: Friendly staff serve a nice selection of Thai dishes in a relaxed, unpretentious setting. Spice levels are adjusted to suit each diner's taste. **Bar:** full bar. **Address:** 14 S San Francisco St 86001 **Location:** Corner of W Phoenix Ave and S San Francisco St; downtown. **Parking:** street only. ⓛ ⓓ

DELHI PALACE
Phone: 928/556-0019 (25)

Indian
$9-$17

AAA Inspector Notes: Located in a strip mall, this eatery serves such fresh traditional Indian cuisine as tandoori chicken, shish kebabs and a large assortment of breads. The service is casual and friendly, and the staff is eager to help guests understand Indian cuisine. Wash it all down with Indian tea or a mango milkshake. **Address:** 2700 S Woodlands Village Blvd 86001 **Location:** I-40 exit 195, just n to Forest Meadows St, w to Beulah Blvd, just s, then just w. ⓛ ⓓ

GALAXY DINER
Phone: 928/774-2466 (16)

Comfort Food
$5-$12

AAA Inspector Notes: On the west side of town on historic Route 66, this diner welcomes patrons with 1950s-era music and photographs of movie stars decorating the walls. On the menu are burgers, chicken-fried steak and roast beef. Shakes, malts and ice cream in a variety of flavors are among sweet choices. **Bar:** beer & wine. **Address:** 931 W Route 66 86001 **Location:** I-40 exit 195, 1.5 mi n on SR 89A (Milton Rd), then just w. ⓓ

GRANNY'S CLOSET RESTAURANT & SPORTS GRILL
Menu on AAA.com
Phone: 928/774-8331 (12)

American
$6-$19

AAA Inspector Notes: Since 1974, this casual eatery has served traditional Italian entrées, such as lasagna and spaghetti, as well as steaks, seafood, sandwiches and burgers. Lighter munchies, including wings, nachos and a host of other favorites, are popular in the sports bar. **Bar:** full bar. **Address:** 218 S Milton Rd 86001 **Location:** I-40 exit 195, 1.9 mi n on SR 89A (Milton Rd). ⓛ ⓓ

HIRO'S SUSHI BAR & JAPANESE RESTAURANT
Phone: 928/226-8030 (22)

Japanese
$5-$14

AAA Inspector Notes: Fresh sushi, tempura and other traditional dishes are served in a laid-back atmosphere. On the way out, be sure to peruse the small Japanese shop for distinctive gifts. **Bar:** wine only. **Address:** 1312 S Plaza Way 86001 **Location:** I-40 exit 195, 1 mi n on SR 89A (Milton Rd), then just sw. ⓛ ⓓ

HORSEMEN LODGE
Phone: 928/526-2655

American
$16-$27

AAA Inspector Notes: Decorated with saddles, tack room items and mounted game trophies, this Old West-style steakhouse is in a rural setting. It appeals to those seeking a glimpse and the taste of the Western past. Service is provided by a casually-clad staff, but you can help yourself to the soup and salad bar. **Bar:** full bar. **Address:** 8500 N Hwy 89 86002 **Location:** I-40 exit 201, 3.5 mi n. ⓓ

JOSEPHINE'S
Menu on AAA.com
Phone: 928/779-3400 (3)

American
$8-$30

AAA Inspector Notes: The eclectic menu is a showcase for steak, seafood, chicken, lamb and pork dishes prepared with European, Asian, Pan American and Southwestern influences. The renovated historic home and its outdoor seating area provide a casually comfortable setting. Reservations are highly recommended during the high season. **Bar:** full bar. **Reservations:** suggested. **Address:** 503 N Humphrey's St 86001 **Location:** Just n of jct Old Route 66. ⓛ ⓓ

KACHINA RESTAURANT
Phone: 928/779-1944 (15)

Mexican
$6-$18

AAA Inspector Notes: Sporting vintage decor, this popular restaurant prepares varied enchiladas, burritos, tamales and other traditional Mexican dishes, as well as tempting daily specials. Friendly servers are very attentive. **Bar:** full bar. **Address:** 522 E Route 66 86001 **Location:** Just e; downtown. ⓛ ⓓ

LA BELLAVIA
Phone: 928/774-8301 (8)

American
$5-$8

AAA Inspector Notes: Cozy, comfortable dining and daily specials are featured at this family-friendly restaurant. Try the house specialty, Swedish oat pancakes. **Address:** 18 S Beaver St 86001 **Location:** Just s of Old Route 66; downtown. **Parking:** street only. ⓑ ⓛ

LITTLE THAI KITCHEN
Phone: 928/226-9422 (19)

Thai
$6-$12

AAA Inspector Notes: As the name implies, this restaurant's size is limited. However, the delicious and fresh Thai dishes make it worth the wait for a table. **Address:** 1051 S Milton Rd 86001 **Location:** I-40 exit 195, 1.1 mi n. ⓛ ⓓ

MACY'S EUROPEAN COFFEE HOUSE & BAKERY
Phone: 928/774-2243 (11)

Vegetarian
$5-$10

AAA Inspector Notes: The perfect place to stop in for a quick bite or a specialty coffee, Macy's offers fresh vegetarian cuisine including sandwiches, soups and baked goods. **Address:** 14 S Beaver St 86001 **Location:** Just s of Route 66; in historic town center. **Parking:** street only. ⓑ ⓛ ⓓ

(See map & index p. 63.)

MAMMA LUISA
Phone: 928/526-6809 ②

Italian
$8-$17

AAA Inspector Notes: Just off historic Old Route 66, the small, cozy restaurant is conveniently located near lodging and shopping. Adorned in red-checkered tablecloths, its dining room appeals to those seeking a good Italian meal in an Old World atmosphere. Cordial, knowledgeable servers provide full service. **Bar:** full bar. **Reservations:** suggested. **Address:** 2710 N Steves Blvd 86004 **Location:** On US 180 and 89, just n of E Route 66; in Kachina Square Shopping Center. D

MONSOON DOWNTOWN
Phone: 928/226-8844 ⑥

Asian
$8-$14

AAA Inspector Notes: Located in the heart of downtown, this eatery offers a sushi bar and an open dining room with a flat-screen TV. The menu includes a variety of such Asian items as ahi tuna, pad thai noodles, kung pao chicken and honey lemon shrimp. The bar is popular and the service is casual and friendly. **Bar:** full bar. **Address:** 6 E Aspen Ave 86001 **Location:** Corner of Aspen Ave and Leroux St; downtown. **Parking:** street only. L D

PASTO CUCINA ITALIANA
Phone: 928/779-1937 ⑦

Italian
$17-$27

AAA Inspector Notes: This casual yet elegant bistro features fine Italian food that has won much local praise. The menu lists beef, seafood, chicken and pasta choices, all prepared with ingredients sourced from local farms. **Bar:** beer & wine. **Reservations:** suggested. **Address:** 19 E Aspen St 86001 **Location:** Route 66, just n on Leroux St, then just e; downtown. **Parking:** street only. L D

PICAZZO'S ORGANIC ITALIAN KITCHEN
Phone: 928/226-1000

Italian
$9-$20

AAA Inspector Notes: This upscale pizzeria, close to NAU, offers fresh pizza with homemade dough along with other casual Italian dishes. **Bar:** full bar. **Address:** 1300 S Milton Rd, Suite 101 86001 **Location:** I-40 exit 195, 0.8 mi n on SR 89A (Milton Rd). L D

SAKURA RESTAURANT
Phone: 928/773-9118 ㉑

Japanese
$5-$29

AAA Inspector Notes: Teppanyaki-style cooking is prepared in a traditional Japanese steakhouse atmosphere. A sushi bar also is offered. **Bar:** full bar. **Reservations:** suggested. **Address:** 1175 W Route 66 86001 **Location:** I-40 exit 195, 1.5 mi n on SR 89A (Milton Rd), then 0.5 mi w; in Radisson Woodlands Hotel Flagstaff. (See ad p. 70.) L D

SALSA BRAVA
Phone: 928/779-5293 ⑤

Mexican
$5-$14

AAA Inspector Notes: On historic Route 66, this restaurant serves a variety of Mexican dishes. Most folks order the Baja fish wraps, for which this place is known. **Bar:** full bar. **Address:** 2220 E Route 66 86001 **Location:** I-40 exit 201, 0.5 mi n, then 2.7 mi w. L D CALL ⌖M

Find valuable AAA/CAA
member savings
at AAA.com/discounts

SWADDEE AUTHENTIC THAI CUISINE
Phone: 928/773-1122 ⑩

Thai
$11-$16

AAA Inspector Notes: This small restaurant offers a variety of fresh Thai items such as pad thai, red curry, chicken satay and coconut ice cream. The service is casual along with the decor. **Bar:** beer & wine. **Address:** 115 E Aspen Ave 86001 **Location:** Jct N San Francisco St, just e; downtown. **Parking:** street only. L D

WOODLANDS RESTAURANT
Phone: 928/773-9118 ⑳

American
$7-$24

AAA Inspector Notes: A three meal menu is offered at this cafe with lunch dishes including salads, sandwiches, pasta, seafood and Mexican fare. Dinner has a larger selection including steak, seafood, pasta and Mexican entrees. **Bar:** full bar. **Address:** 1175 W Route 66 86001 **Location:** I-40 exit 195, 1.5 mi n on SR 89A (Milton Rd), then 0.5 mi w; in Radisson Woodlands Hotel Flagstaff. B L D CALL ⌖M

FLORENCE (E-4) pop. 25,536, elev. 1,493'
• Restaurants p. 74

One of Arizona's oldest towns and the seat of Pinal County, Florence was founded by Levi Ruggles in 1866. Many historic homes and buildings perpetuate its frontier atmosphere.

Scenic desert highways from Florence include Kelvin Highway, a county road running east to Kelvin, and the Pinal Pioneer Parkway, a part of SR 79 leading southeast to Oracle Junction. Markers along the parkway identify desert wildlife.

Florence Visitor Center: 24 W. Ruggles St., P.O. Box 2471, Florence, AZ 85132. **Phone:** (520) 868-4496.

PINAL COUNTY HISTORICAL MUSEUM, 715 S. Main St., displays Indian artifacts from the Southwest, blacksmith equipment, antique woodworking tools, cactus furniture and documents relating to the county's history. Farm machinery, an 1884 square piano, a collection of Tom Mix memorabilia and an Arizona state prison exhibit featuring hanging nooses also are offered.

Time: Allow 1 hour minimum. **Hours:** Tues.-Sat. 11-4, Sun. noon-4, Sept. 1-July 14. Closed major holidays. **Cost:** Donations. **Phone:** (520) 868-4382.

BLUE MIST MOTEL
Phone: (520)868-5875

Motel
$70-$85 2/1-4/15
$55-$75 4/16-1/31

Address: 40 S Pinal Pkwy 85132 **Location:** On SR 79, at SR 287. **Facility:** 22 units, some efficiencies. 1 story, exterior corridors. **Terms:** 3 day cancellation notice-fee imposed. **Pool(s):** outdoor. **Free Special Amenities:** local telephone calls and high-speed Internet.

SAVE ⏦ ⚯ 🛜 🔒 🖥 ▭

HOLIDAY INN EXPRESS & SUITES
Phone: (520)868-9900

Hotel
$99-$349 2/1-4/30
$69-$349 5/1-1/31

Address: 240 W Hwy 287 85132 **Location:** Just w of jct SR 79 and 287. **Facility:** 90 units. 3 stories, interior corridors. **Amenities:** high-speed Internet. **Pool(s):** heated outdoor. **Activities:** whirlpool, exercise room. **Guest Services:** coin laundry.

⏦ ⚯ BIZ 🛜 ✕ 🔒 🖥 ▭

RANCHO SONORA INN **Phone:** (520)868-8000

▼▼◆▼▼

Country Inn
$79-$225

Address: 9198 N Hwy 79 85232 **Location:** On SR 79, 5 mi s of SR 287. Located in a quiet desert area. **Facility:** In a quiet desert location, the inn's adobe-style buildings and casitas face a charming shaded patio with fountains and mature plantings. 8 units, some two bedrooms, kitchens and cottages. 1 story, exterior corridors. **Terms:** 3 day cancellation notice. **Pool(s):** heated outdoor. **Activities:** whirlpool, horseshoes. **Guest Services:** coin laundry.

🛗 �(🛜 ✕ 🗐
/ SOME UNITS FEE 🐾 🗷 🖨 🖵

WHERE TO EAT

MOUNT ATHOS RESTAURANT & CAFE
Phone: 520/868-0735

▼▼◆ ▼▼◆

Greek
$5-$18

AAA Inspector Notes: From breakfast to dinner, the busy restaurant's friendly staff pleases patrons with hearty portions of delicious Greek and Italian dishes. Gyros made with skewered beef and lamb are popular. A wide selection of crispy salads, sandwiches and pasta dishes means everyone will be satisfied. **Bar:** full bar. **Address:** 444 N Pinal Pkwy (SR 79) 85232 **Location:** Just s of jct SR 287 and 79.

Ⓑ Ⓛ Ⓓ

FOREST LAKES

FOREST LAKES LODGE **Phone:** (928)535-4727

▼

Motel
$54-$85

Address: 2823 SR 260 85931 **Location:** On SR 260; between MM 288 and 289. Located in a quiet area. **Facility:** 20 units. 2 stories (no elevator), exterior corridors. **Terms:** office hours 7 am-9 pm. **Activities:** hiking trails, volleyball. **Free Special Amenities:** expanded continental breakfast and high-speed Internet.

SAVE 🛜 🎇 🗐 🖨 / SOME UNITS FEE 🐾

FORT APACHE (D-5) pop. 143

FORT APACHE HISTORIC PARK, s. off SR 73, is a 288-acre site featuring 27 buildings dated 1870-1930, including officers' quarters, a guardhouse, stables, dormitories, the White Mountain Apache Cultural Center and Museum, a military cemetery, ancient petroglyphs and a re-created Apache village.

Tours: Guided tours are available. **Hours:** Park open daily 7 a.m.-dusk. **Cost:** (Includes White Mountain Apache Cultural Center and Museum) $5; $3 (ages 64+ and students with ID); free (ages 0-6). Reservations are recommended for guided tours. **Phone:** (928) 338-4625.

White Mountain Apache Cultural Center and Museum, s. off SR 73 to Indian Rte. 46, following signs, provides visitor orientation for Fort Apache Historic Park. The museum features two exhibits: The Fort Apache Legacy and Footprints of the Apache. Video presentations about the Apache creation story and cultural topics are available. Cultural and historical relics such as clothing, weapons and dolls are on display, as are works by local artists.

Time: Allow 1 hour minimum. **Hours:** Mon.-Sat. 8-5, Sun. 11-3, May-Sept.; Mon.-Fri. 8-5, rest of year. Closed major holidays. **Cost:** Included in Fort Apache Historic Park admission of $5; $3 (ages 64+ and students with ID); free (ages 0-6). **Phone:** (928) 338-4625. 🚻

FORT DEFIANCE (B-6) pop. 3,624, elev. 6,862'

Fort Defiance lies at the mouth of Canyon Bonito, or Blue Canyon, in the Navajo Reservation. In some places sheer walls overhang the canyon floor. Established in 1851, Fort Defiance saw action in the Navajo wars that occurred during the 1860s. For many years it has been the headquarters of the Bureau of Indian Affairs, Fort Defiance Agency.

Navajos on the reservation maintain much of their traditional way of life. They engage in agriculture, stock raising, employment on the reservation and seasonal off-reservation work. Many still dwell in hogans, circular log and earth huts. Distinctive Navajo blankets, rugs and silver and turquoise jewelry are crafted.

FORT HUACHUCA (G-5)

In southeastern Arizona, Fort Huachuca (wa-CHOO-ka) was founded in 1877 to combat raids by Native Americans and outlaws. In 1954 the fort became the site of the Army Electronic Proving Ground. The 73,272-acre fort is headquarters of the U.S. Army Information Systems Command, the U.S. Army Intelligence Center and various other military organizations. The Old Post retains many of the original buildings constructed in the late 19th century.

Note: Each visitor must be a U.S. citizen and present photo identification to gain admittance to the fort. Foreign nationals must be escorted by public affairs personnel. Proof of vehicle registration and insurance must be provided for each vehicle entering the premises.

FORT HUACHUCA MUSEUM is 3.6 mi. n.w. of Fort Huachuca's main gate in the Old Post area at Boyd and Grierson aves. Southwest history and the U.S. Army's activities in the area are depicted through exhibits in three buildings. **Hours:** Mon.-Fri. 9-4, Sat.-Sun. 1-4; closed Federal holidays. **Cost:** Donations. **Phone:** (520) 533-5736 or (520) 458-4716.

FOUNTAIN HILLS (I-4) pop. 22,489, elev. 1,600'
• Part of Phoenix area — see map p. 134

Fountain Hills is named for its rolling terrain and celebrated fountain. The community provides a number of recreation and vacation opportunities.

Fountain Hills Chamber of Commerce: 16837 E. Palisades Blvd., Fountain Hills, AZ 85268. **Phone:** (480) 837-1654.

THE FOUNTAIN is off Saguaro Blvd. in Fountain Park. Within a 28-acre lake, the 560-foot-tall white jet of water shoots above the town for 15 minutes daily on the hour 9-9. Wind gusts more than 12 mph may prevent operation. The surrounding 64-acre park is open daily dawn-11 p.m. **Cost:** Free. **Phone:** (480) 837-1654.

RIVER OF TIME MUSEUM, inside the library at 12901 N. La Montana Blvd., includes multimedia displays, historical and cultural programs, and activities educating visitors about the vital role of water in the Lower Verde Valley. Conditions in this part of the High Sonoran Desert forced such inhabitants as Native American tribes and early ranchers to invent ways to control water. Visitors learn about ancient canals and more recent dam projects as well as the area's developments in housing.

Tours: Guided tours are available. **Time:** Allow 30 minutes minimum. **Hours:** Tues.-Sat. 1-4, Sept.-May; Fri.-Sat. 1-4, rest of year. Closed major holidays. **Cost:** $3; $2 (ages 55+); $1 (ages 5-12). **Phone:** (480) 837-2612.

COMFORT INN   **Phone:** (480)837-5343
▼▼▼
Hotel
$100-$120
Address: 17105 E Shea Blvd 85268 **Location:** 0.5 mi w of SR 87 (Beeline Hwy). **Facility:** 48 units. 2 stories, interior corridors. **Terms:** 2 night minimum stay - seasonal and/or weekends, cancellation fee imposed. **Amenities:** Some: high-speed Internet. **Pool(s):** heated outdoor. **Activities:** whirlpool. **Guest Services:** coin laundry, area transportation-Mayo Clinic.

TOUCH, SEND, RELAX

Sprint

AAA

Roadside

AAA

Free app for your iPhone and Android

AAA.com/roadside

HOLIDAY INN HOTEL & SUITES-FOUNTAIN HILLS/MAYO CLINIC   **Phone:** (480)837-6565
▼▼▼▼
Hotel
$89-$159 2/1-4/30
$49-$159 5/1-1/31
Address: 12800 N Saguaro Blvd 85268 **Location:** Jct Shea Blvd, 2.2 mi n; center. Across from The Fountain. **Facility:** 104 units. 3 stories, interior corridors. **Terms:** 3 day cancellation notice-fee imposed.
Amenities: high-speed Internet. **Pool(s):** heated outdoor. **Activities:** whirlpool, putting green, exercise room. **Guest Services:** valet and coin laundry, area transportation-Mayo Clinic.

INN AT EAGLE MOUNTAIN   **Phone:** (480)816-3000
▼▼▼▼
Country Inn
$89-$279
Address: 9800 N Summer Hill Blvd 85268 **Location:** Loop 101 exit 41, 7.3 mi e on Shea Blvd, 0.3 mi e on Eagle Mountain Pkwy, then just w. **Facility:** Adjacent to a golf course and overlooking Phoenix Valley, the hotel's casitas and suites each include a fireplace and a two-person whirlpool. 42 units. 2 stories (no elevator), exterior corridors. **Terms:** 3 day cancellation notice. **Pool(s):** heated outdoor. **Activities:** whirlpool. *Fee:* golf-18 holes.

GANADO (B-6) pop. 1,210, elev. 6,386'

Ganado is one of the traditional meeting and trading centers of the Pueblo Colorado Valley. For centuries the valley has been a favored Native American gathering place, first for the Ancestral Puebloans and now for the Navajo. When John Hubbell bought the original trading post, he christened it Ganado to honor his Navajo friend Ganado Mucho and to distinguish the community from Pueblo, Colo.

Visitors to the reservation should be aware of certain travel restrictions; *see Good Facts To Know.*

HUBBELL TRADING POST NATIONAL HISTORIC SITE, .5 mi. w. via SR 264, is the oldest continuously operated trading post in the Navajo Nation. In 1878 John L. Hubbell bought the trading post and established himself as a leading trader. Hubbell's collection of Western art and Native American crafts is displayed in his furnished house on the site.

The trading post and the Hubbell home depict the role of trading in the history of the Southwest and the life of a trader's family. The trading post conducts business much as it did when the Hubbell family ran it. Members of the Navajo, Hopi, Zuni and other tribes sell and trade such crafts as handwoven rugs, jewelry, baskets and pottery. Ranger-led programs, guided house tours and weaving demonstrations are offered.

Time: Allow 1 hour minimum. **Hours:** Daily 8-6, May-Sept.; 8-5, rest of year. **Note:** In summer the reservation observes daylight-saving time, which is an hour later than outside the reservation. Closed Jan. 1, Thanksgiving and Christmas. **Cost:** Donations. Hubbell home tour $2. **Phone:** (928) 755-3475.

GILA BEND (E-3) pop. 1,922, elev. 735'

Gila Bend is the center for a prosperous stock-raising and farming region in the Gila River Valley. The first farms were established in 1699 by Jesuit missionary Father Eusebio Francisco Kino. Just west of town is the site of the infamous 1851 Oatman Massacre, where all but three children of a westward-bound family were killed by Apaches. Exhibits about area history are displayed in a museum at the information center.

Gila Bend Tourist Information Center and Chamber of Commerce: 644 W. Pima, P.O. Box A, Gila Bend, AZ 85337. **Phone:** (928) 683-2255.

AMERICA'S CHOICE INN & SUITES

♦♦ Motel $65

Phone: (928)683-6311

Address: 2888 Butterfield Tr 85337 **Location:** I-8 exit 119, just nw. **Facility:** 62 units. 3 stories (no elevator), interior corridors. **Terms:** cancellation fee imposed. **Pool(s):** outdoor.

BEST WESTERN SPACE AGE LODGE

Phone: (928)683-2273

♦♦ ♦♦ Motel $109-$189

AAA Benefit: Members save up to 20%, plus 10% bonus points with Best Western Rewards®.

Address: 401 E Pima St 85337 **Location:** Business Loop I-8; center. **Facility:** 41 units. 1 story, exterior corridors. **Amenities:** high-speed Internet. **Dining:** Space Age Restaurant, see separate listing. **Pool(s):** outdoor. **Activities:** whirlpool. **Free Special Amenities:** full breakfast and high-speed Internet. (See ad this page.)

Enjoy great savings on hotel rates at AAA.com or CAA.ca

▼ See AAA listing this page ▼

Scan this tag on your smartphone for more information

Get the free mobile app at http://gettag.mobi

BEST WESTERN Space Age Lodge
401 E. Pima Street, P.O. Box C
Gila Bend, AZ 85337
928-683-2273   866-683-7722
bestwesternspaceagelodge.com

· FREE BREAKFAST MEAL for our lodge guests, served at the SPACE AGE RESTAURANT
· Family style American and Mexican dining served all day, Gift Shop & Souvenirs
· All guest rooms are non smoking and include: 32" TV, Refrigerator, Coffee/Tea Maker, Iron & Board, Hair Dryer
· All Rooms have Pillow-top Mattresses, and Free High Speed Internet.
· Pet Friendly, Fee Required
· Business Center in Lobby provides Computer, Printer, Fax, Copier, and Internet Access for Guest Use
· Swimming Pool and Heated Spa
· Meeting Room-Seating up to 30 Persons

Each Best Western® branded hotel is independently owned and operated. Best Western and the Best Western marks are service marks or registered service marks of Best Western International, Inc. ©2012 Best Western International, Inc. All rights reserved. AAA and the AAA marks are service marks or registered service marks of the American Automobile Association.

AAA/CAA MEMBER DISCOUNTS AHEAD

Consider your AAA/CAA card as the smallest, lowest tech GPS navigator imaginable...it will take you right to the best deals in town, wherever "town" is for you. Go to **AAA.com/discounts** to find your way to the best deals.

AAA.com/discounts

WHERE TO EAT

SPACE AGE RESTAURANT   Phone: 928/683-2761

American
$5-$15

AAA Inspector Notes: Friendly servers dish up good food at this kitschy diner with a hard-to-miss spaceship design outside and a unique atmosphere inside. **Address:** 401 E Pima St 85337 **Location:** Business Loop I-8; center; in Best Western Space Age Lodge.

(B) (L) (D)

American/Mexican Dining-Original Space Murals-Gift Shop

GILBERT   (J-4) pop. 208,453
- Hotels & Restaurants map & index p. 164
- Part of Phoenix area — see map p. 134

GILBERT HISTORICAL MUSEUM, 10 S. Gilbert Rd., relates the history of the town. Housed in a 1913 school building, the museum has nine themed galleries. Highlights include a model train exhibit, a collection of military uniforms and a courtyard with antique farm and firefighting equipment. The museum also hosts quilting bees and an annual quilting show.

Tours: Guided tours are available. **Time:** Allow 1 hour minimum. **Hours:** Tues.-Sat. 9-4. Closed major holidays. **Cost:** $5; $4 (ages 60+); $3 (ages 5-12). **Phone:** (480) 926-1577. 🅰

THE RIPARIAN PRESERVE AT WATER RANCH is at 2757 E. Guadalupe Rd. The 110-acre preserve features interpretive exhibits, an observatory, a floating boardwalk and children's play areas. A great spot for bird-watching, the area is home to more than 200 species. Visitors can also fish (with a license) and camp on the grounds.

Ramadas can be rented by the hour. **Time:** Allow 1 hour minimum. **Hours:** Preserve daily dawn-dusk. Fishing lake daily dawn-10 p.m. Phone for observatory hours. **Cost:** Preserve free. Observatory $3. Camping $30-$40. Phone for other activity fees. Campsites must be reserved. Reservations are recommended. **Phone:** (480) 797-2019 or (480) 503-6200. 🔺 🗙 🅰

Safety tip: Keep a current

AAA/CAA Road Atlas

in every vehicle

HAMPTON INN & SUITES PHOENIX/GILBERT
Phone: (480)543-1500

Hotel
$69-$249

Hampton

AAA Benefit: Members save up to 10% everyday!

Address: 3265 S Market St 85297 **Location:** Loop 202 exit 42 (Val Vista Dr), just n, then just e. **Facility:** 96 units. 4 stories, interior corridors. **Terms:** 1-7 night minimum stay, cancellation fee imposed. **Amenities:** high-speed Internet. **Pool(s):** heated outdoor. **Activities:** whirlpool, exercise room. **Guest Services:** valet and coin laundry, area transportation-within 5 mi. **Free Special Amenities:** full breakfast and high-speed Internet.

[SAVE] [🍽] CALL [&M] [🏊] [BIZ] [📶] [🗙] [📶] [📷] [☕]

HYATT PLACE PHOENIX/GILBERT
Phone: (480)899-5900

Hotel
$79-$229

HYATT PLACE

AAA Benefit: Members save 10% or more everyday.

Address: 3275 S Market St 85297 **Location:** Loop 202 exit 42 (Val Vista Dr), just n, then just e. **Facility:** 127 units. 6 stories, interior corridors. **Terms:** cancellation fee imposed. **Pool(s):** heated outdoor. **Activities:** exercise room. **Guest Services:** valet laundry, area transportation-within 5 mi. **Free Special Amenities:** expanded continental breakfast and high-speed Internet.

[SAVE] [🍽] CALL [&M] [🏊] [BIZ] [📶] [🗙] FEE [📷] [📶]

[☕]

WHERE TO EAT

CANTINA LAREDO   Phone: 480/782-6777   (45)

Mexican
$8-$20

AAA Inspector Notes: Modern yet relaxed, this restaurant features creative Mexican fare. A great starter of top-shelf guacamole, which is prepared tableside, primes the palate for an entree of enchiladas, tacos, fajitas and chiles rellenos. **Bar:** full bar. **Address:** 2150 E Williams Field Rd 85295 **Location:** Loop 202 exit 40, 0.5 mi w. (L) (D)

Gourmet Mexican food, fresh-squeezed lime margaritas

FLANCER'S CAFE   Phone: 480/926-9077   (43)

Deli
$6-$24

AAA Inspector Notes: This café's incredible sandwiches are not made-they are created. Try the award-winning green chile turkey prepared with avocado slices, sizzling bacon and zippy green chile mayonnaise or the perfect prickly pear with a chicken breast baked in prickly pear glaze. Everything from the breads to the desserts is homemade and delicious. Pizza, pasta and salads also figure on the menu. **Bar:** beer & wine. **Address:** 610 N Gilbert Rd, Suite 300 85234 **Location:** US 60 (Superstition Frwy) exit 182 (Gilbert Rd), 1.6 mi s. (L) (D) (◥)

JOE'S REAL BBQ
Menu on AAA.com   Phone: 480/503-3805   (44)

Barbecue
$7-$18

AAA Inspector Notes: Pecan-grilled meats, barbecue beans, root beer made on site and fresh desserts are favorites at this family joint. The serve-yourself setting and optional patio seating lend to a fun atmosphere. **Address:** 301 N Gilbert Rd 85234 **Location:** US 60 (Superstition Frwy) exit 182 (Gilbert Rd), 2.1 mi s. **Parking:** street only. (L) (D)

(See map & index p. 164.)

PATSY GRIMALDI'S COAL BRICK-OVEN PIZZERIA
Phone: 480/814-7722

Pizza
$5-$18

AAA Inspector Notes: Fresh ingredients and a coal-fired brick oven are the features at this New York style pizzeria. **Bar:** beer & wine. **Address:** 2168 E Williams Field Rd 85295 **Location:** Loop 202 exit 40, 0.7 mi w; in San Tan Village. L D

SERRANO'S MEXICAN RESTAURANT
Phone: 480/507-5027

Mexican
$6-$18

AAA Inspector Notes: A pleasant stop for lunch or dinner, the local chain is known for consistently good food and attractive, upscale Mexican-style décor. The warm bean dip starter stirs the appetite for traditional dishes such as chiles rellenos or seafood enchiladas prepared with fresh ingredients. Service is friendly. **Bar:** full bar. **Address:** 959 N Val Vista Dr 85234 **Location:** US 60 (Superstition Hwy) exit 184 (Val Vista Dr), 1.4 mi s. L D

GLEN CANYON NATIONAL RECREATION AREA (A-4)

Along the Colorado River from Grand Canyon National Park in far north-central Arizona to Canyonlands National Park in southeastern Utah, Glen Canyon National Recreation Area is home to one of the highest dams in the United States. Part of the Colorado River storage project, the Glen Canyon Dam generates hydroelectric power that is distributed to cities and industries throughout the West; the dam's main purpose is water storage.

Reaching out to hidden canyons, sandy coves and inlets, and winding through towering red cliffs, 186-mile-long Lake Powell presents an ever-changing array of scenery and such recreational opportunities as water skiing, boating and fishing. Amenities include campsites, marinas, and boat rentals and tours. A copy of fishing regulations can be obtained at park ranger stations, the Carl Hayden Visitor Center, the Navajo Bridge Interpretive Center, the Bullfrog Visitor Center or at the administration offices in Page, Ariz.; phone (928) 355-2319.

The Bullfrog Visitor Center, at the Bullfrog Marina in Utah, exhibits the natural and cultural history of Glen Canyon and includes a life-size slot canyon model. The Navajo Bridge Interpretive Center, on US 89A near Lees Ferry, Ariz., features a historic pedestrian bridge over the Colorado River at Marble Canyon and outdoor exhibits highlighting the early river crossings. The interpretive center is open daily 9-5, Apr.-Oct., as staffing allows; phone (928) 355-2319 or (435) 684-7420.

Exhibits in the Carl Hayden Visitor Center, next to US 89, Glen Canyon Dam and Glen Canyon Bridge in Page illustrate the construction of the dam and bridge and include a relief model of the canyon country. Guided tours of the dam are available throughout the year. The center is open daily 8-6, Memorial Day-Labor Day; 8-5, Mar. 1-day before Memorial Day; 8:30-4:30, rest of year. Closed Jan. 1, Thanksgiving and Christmas. Phone (928) 608-6404.

Free evening programs are given at Wahweap campground, 7 miles northwest of Page off US 89, Memorial Day through Labor Day; phone or stop by the visitor center for a list of scheduled performance days and times.

Arrangements for boat tours on Lake Powell can be made at Wahweap Lodge and Marina; facilities, including public launching ramps, boat rentals, camping and boat and automobile fuel, are provided at Wahweap and at four other marinas on the lake. A boat ramp providing access to 15 miles of the Colorado River below Glen Canyon Dam is available at Lees Ferry, 5 miles north of Marble Canyon.

▼ See AAA listing p. 125 ▼

EXPLORE LAKE POWELL
• Scenic Boat Tours • Small Boat Rentals
• Lakeside Lodging • Fine Dining • At Wahweap Marina

888.272.3161
www.lakepowell.com

Lake Powell RESORTS & MARINAS
ARAMARK

Lake Powell Resorts & Marinas, managed by ARAMARK, is an authorized concessioner of the National Park Service, Glen Canyon National Recreation Area.

Boat excursions, which last from 4 to 6.5 hours, are available through Colorado River Discovery; phone (928) 645-9175 or (888) 522-6644. The tours begin near the Glen Canyon Dam and conclude at Lees Ferry. One-day raft trips on the Colorado River below the dam can be arranged in Page. Half-day and full-day trips are available to Rainbow Bridge National Monument, Utah, which is about 50 miles from Wahweap. Trips on the San Juan River leave from Mexican Hat and Bluff, Utah.

Park admission is $15 per private vehicle, or $7 per individual on foot or bicycle (both valid for up to 7 days). An annual pass is $30. An additional use fee of $16 is charged for one motorized water vessel (valid for up to 7 days); a use fee of $8 is charged for each additional water vessel on the same trailer.

For further information contact the Superintendent, Glen Canyon National Recreation Area, P.O. Box 1507, Page, AZ 86040; phone (928) 608-6404 or (928) 608-6200. *See Recreation Chart.*

GLENDALE (I-2) pop. 226,721, elev. 1,154'

- Restaurants p. 80
- Attractions map p. 142
- Hotels & Restaurants map & index p. 155
- Part of Phoenix area — see map p. 134

Established in 1892, Glendale retains much of its turn-of-the-20th-century charm. A tree-lined town square, red brick sidewalks and gaslights form an appropriate setting for the abundance of antique shops around shady Murphy Park in the city's historic downtown. Cerreta Candy Company, about half a mile east of Murphy Park at 5345 W. Glendale Ave., provides behind-the-scenes guided tours of its candy- and chocolate-making operations; phone (623) 930-9000.

In a more modern vein, Glendale also is home to Thunderbird, The American Graduate School of International Management and the jet fighter wing at Luke Air Force Base, purportedly the world's largest F-16 training base. Major League Baseball's Los Angeles Dodgers and Chicago White Sox play their spring training games at Camelback Ranch-Glendale, while the Arizona Cardinals football and Phoenix Coyotes hockey teams call the city home.

Glendale kicks off Arizona's calendar of events in early January with the ▽ Tostitos Fiesta Bowl, one of the nation's largest college bowl games. The game is played at The University of Phoenix Stadium, which also is the home stadium for the National Football League's Arizona Cardinals. In early February, chocoholics flock to Murphy Park for the ▽ Glendale Chocolate Affaire, which features chocolate purveyors from across the country.

Glendale Visitor Center: 5800 W. Glenn Dr., Suite 140, Glendale, AZ 85301. **Phone:** (623) 930-4500 or (877) 800-2601.

Shopping areas: Known as the Antique Capital of Arizona, more than 90 antique stores, specialty shops and restaurants are concentrated around

Glendale's town square, Murphy Park, at the intersection of Glendale and 58th avenues. Old Towne Glendale and the Historic Catlin Court Shops District specialize in arts, crafts, furniture, dolls, jewelry, period clothing and Western memorabilia. Arrowhead Towne Center contains 170 stores, including Dillard's and JCPenney.

SAHUARO RANCH PARK HISTORIC AREA is 2.5 mi. n. of Glendale Ave. to 9802 N. 59th Ave.; or take I-10 exit 138, then go n. 7.6 mi. on N. 59th Ave. Seventeen acres of a model fruit farm developed by William Henry Bartlett in 1885 feature seven original buildings, including an adobe house, a foreman's house, the main house and a fruit packing shed. A lavish rose garden planted in 1890, several citrus groves and free-roaming peacocks enhance the fenced grounds.

Tours: Guided tours are available. **Time:** Allow 1 hour minimum. **Hours:** Grounds daily 6 a.m.-dusk. Phone for guided tour schedule. Closed major holidays. Phone ahead to confirm schedule. **Cost:** Grounds free. Tours by donation. Admission is charged for special events. **Phone:** (623) 930-4200.

WET 'N' WILD PHOENIX, 4243 W. Pinnacle Peak Rd., features 20 acres of waterslides and wave pools, including the Maximum Velocity Dueling Water Coasters. The high-speed Constrictor raft ride sends riders down a tube slide with corkscrew turns. Changing rooms and showers are on the premises; lockers and tubes can be rented. **Hours:** Thurs.-Sat. 10-10, Sun.-Wed. 10-6, Memorial Day to mid-Sept.; schedule varies rest of year. Phone ahead to confirm schedule. **Cost:** $34.99; $27.99 (ages 65+ and under 42 inches tall). **Parking:** $7. **Phone:** (623) 201-2000. ▯

COMFORT SUITES GLENDALE
Phone: (623)271-9005 ⑫
Hotel
$89-$299
Address: 9824 W Camelback Rd 85305 **Location:** Loop 101 exit 5 (Camelback Rd), just w to 99th St, then just n. **Facility:** 100 units. 4 stories, interior corridors. **Terms:** cancellation fee imposed. **Amenities:** high-speed Internet. **Pool(s):** heated outdoor. **Activities:** whirlpool, exercise room. **Guest Services:** coin laundry, area transportation-within 7 mi. **Free Special Amenities:** full breakfast and high-speed Internet.

Free transport to Camelback Ranch & U of Phoenix Stadiums, Jobing.com Arena, Luke Air Force Base & more!

(See map & index p. 155.)

HAMPTON INN & SUITES GLENDALE/WESTGATE
Phone: (623)271-7771   **11**

Hotel
$109-$229

AAA Benefit:
Members save up to 10% everyday!

Address: 6630 N 95th Ave 85305 **Location:** Loop 101 exit 7 (Glendale Ave), just e, then 0.4 mi s. **Facility:** 149 units. 4 stories, interior corridors. **Terms:** 1-7 night minimum stay, cancellation fee imposed. **Amenities:** high-speed Internet. **Pool(s):** heated outdoor. **Activities:** whirlpool, exercise room. **Guest Services:** valet and coin laundry, area transportation-Westgate Center.

HOLIDAY INN EXPRESS HOTEL & SUITES
Phone: (623)939-8888   **9**

Hotel
$129-$209

Address: 9310 W Cabela Dr 85305 **Location:** Loop 101 exit 7 (Glendale Ave), 0.6 mi e to N Zanjero Blvd, then just n. **Facility:** 96 units. 3 stories, interior corridors. **Amenities:** high-speed Internet. **Pool(s):** heated outdoor. **Activities:** whirlpool, exercise room. **Guest Services:** valet laundry.

QUALITY INN & SUITES AT TALAVI
Phone: (602)896-8900   **5**

Hotel
$60-$130

Address: 5511 W Bell Rd 85308 **Location:** Loop 101 exit 14 (Bell Rd), 3.4 mi e. **Facility:** 74 units. 3 stories, interior corridors. **Terms:** cancellation fee imposed. **Pool(s):** outdoor. **Activities:** whirlpool. **Guest Services:** valet and coin laundry.

RENAISSANCE GLENDALE HOTEL & SPA
Phone: (623)937-3700   **10**

Hotel
$125-$269

AAA Benefit:
AAA hotel discounts of 5% or more.

Address: 9495 W Coyotes Blvd 85305 **Location:** Loop 101 exit 7 (Glendale Ave), just e to N 95th Ave, just n, then just e. **Facility:** A few steps from Glendale Stadium, this hotel offers well-decorated rooms and public areas with bright, desert colors and upscale amenities. 320 units. 11 stories, interior corridors. **Parking:** on-site and valet. **Amenities:** high-speed Internet (fee), safes. **Dining:** 2 restaurants, also, Soleil, see separate listing. **Pool(s):** heated outdoor, heated indoor. **Activities:** whirlpools, exercise room, spa. *Fee:* steamrooms. **Guest Services:** valet and coin laundry.

Visit AAA.com or CAA.ca

for one-stop travel

planning and reservations

RESIDENCE INN PHOENIX GLENDALE SPORTS & ENTERTAINMENT DISTRICT
Phone: (623)772-8900   **6**

Extended Stay Hotel
$97-$219

AAA Benefit:
AAA hotel discounts of 5% or more.

Address: 7350 W Zanjero Blvd 85305 **Location:** Loop 101 exit 7 (Glendale Ave), then e. **Facility:** 126 units, some two bedrooms, efficiencies and kitchens. 4 stories, interior corridors. **Amenities:** high-speed Internet. **Pool(s):** heated outdoor. **Activities:** whirlpool, putting green, exercise room. **Guest Services:** valet and coin laundry.

SPRINGHILL SUITES BY MARRIOTT
Phone: (623)878-6666   **4**

Hotel
$69-$199

AAA Benefit: AAA hotel discounts of 5% or more.

Address: 7810 W Bell Rd 85308 **Location:** Loop 101 exit 14 (Bell Rd), 0.3 mi e. Adjacent to Arrowhead Towne Center. **Facility:** 88 units. 4 stories, interior corridors. **Amenities:** high-speed Internet. **Pool(s):** heated outdoor. **Activities:** whirlpool, exercise room. **Guest Services:** valet and coin laundry. **Free Special Amenities: expanded continental breakfast and high-speed Internet.**

SPRINGHILL SUITES PHOENIX GLENDALE SPORTS & ENTERTAINMENT DISTRICT
Phone: (623)772-9200   **7**

Hotel
$67-$169

AAA Benefit:
AAA hotel discounts of 5% or more.

Address: 7370 N Zanjero Blvd 85305 **Location:** Loop 101 exit 7 (Glendale Ave), 0.6 mi e, then just n. **Facility:** 120 units. 4 stories, interior corridors. **Amenities:** high-speed Internet. **Pool(s):** heated outdoor. **Activities:** whirlpool, putting green, exercise room. **Guest Services:** valet and coin laundry.

STAYBRIDGE SUITES   **Phone:** (623)842-0000   **8**

Extended Stay Hotel
$129-$340 2/1-4/30
$79-$340 5/1-1/31

Address: 9340 W Cabela Dr 85305 **Location:** Loop 101 exit 7 (Glendale Ave), e on Zanjero Blvd, then left. **Facility:** 116 efficiencies, some two bedrooms. 4 stories, interior corridors. **Terms:** cancellation fee imposed. **Amenities:** high-speed Internet. **Pool(s):** heated outdoor. **Activities:** whirlpool, exercise room. **Guest Services:** valet and coin laundry.

WHERE TO EAT

CAMARONE'S RESTAURANT & CANTINA
Phone: 623/772 1110   **6**

Mexican
$10-$19

AAA Inspector Notes: This restaurant boasts arched ceilings, elegant draperies and a large outdoor patio bar. Wonderful menu offerings are made with fresh ingredients. Its huge lunch buffet is a tempting option. A friendly staff welcomes patrons to this spot, just a short walk from Glendale Stadium. **Bar:** full bar. **Address:** 6970 N 95th Ave 85305 **Location:** Loop 101 exit 7 (Glendale Rd), just e.

(See map & index p. 155.)

HAUS MURPHY'S   Phone: 623/939-2480   (8)

German
$7-$28

AAA Inspector Notes: As is the case in many favorite neighborhood pubs, the walls of this eatery are covered in photographs and memorabilia. The hearty food is freshly prepared and a selection of German beers are available to wash down the crispy schnitzels and plump sausages. **Bar:** full bar. **Reservations:** suggested. **Address:** 5739 W Glendale Ave 85301 **Location:** Just e of Grand Ave (US 60); center. **Parking:** street only. L D

MACAYO MEXICAN KITCHEN   Phone: 602/298-8080

Mexican
$8-$16

AAA Inspector Notes: The colorfully furnished Mexican-style eatery prepares Sonoran Mexican dishes. Friendly and efficient staffers serve traditional and lighter dishes flavored with this place's own chili peppers, which are grown near Tucson. **Bar:** full bar. **Address:** 6012 W Bell Rd 85308 **Location:** Just e of 59th Ave.

L D

NINFA'S MEXICAN KITCHEN

Phone: 623/561-9800   (4)

Mexican
$7-$16

AAA Inspector Notes: Known for their fajitas, this Texas based chain serves up delicious hearty fare in a fun and casual environment. **Bar:** full bar. **Reservations:** suggested. **Address:** 20004 N 67th Ave 85308 **Location:** Loop 101 exit 18 (67th Ave), just s. L D

RUBIO'S FRESH MEXICAN GRILL   Phone: 623/376-9868

Mexican
$3-$7

AAA Inspector Notes: Freshly prepared and healthful foods, bright decor and friendly staff are found in this upscale fast-food spot. A special treat, the salsa bar lines up four styles and flavors. **Bar:** beer only. **Address:** 20210 N 59th Ave 85308 **Location:** Loop 101 exit 19 (59th Ave), just n. L D

SOLEIL   Phone: 623/937-3700   (7)

Regional American
$11-$36

AAA Inspector Notes: A tempting range of mouthwatering selections are offered for breakfast, lunch and dinner at this upscale eatery. Beef, pork, chicken, fish and even antelope are prepared with a Southwestern flair. The menu is sure to please every palate. **Bar:** full bar. **Address:** 9495 W Coyotes Blvd 85305 **Location:** Loop 101 exit 7 (Glendale Ave), just e to N 95th Ave, just n, then just e; in Renaissance Glendale Hotel & Spa. **Parking:** on-site and valet. B L D CALL ❺M

THEE PITT'S "AGAIN"   Phone: 602/996-7488   (5)

Barbecue
$7-$18

AAA Inspector Notes: Diners can sample award-winning barbecue that has a distinct flavor. In addition to the standard Memphis-style pork, chicken, brisket and sausage pit-cooked over mesquite, the menu lists burgers, salads and sides, including coleslaw, potato salad, beans and corn on the cob. The diner displays colorful pig artwork. **Bar:** beer & wine. **Address:** 5558 W Bell Rd 85308 **Location:** Bell Rd, n on 55th Ave, then w; opposite Honeywell.

L D CALL ❺M

GLOBE (E-5) pop. 7,532, elev. 3,517'
• Hotels p. 82 • Restaurants p. 82

Named for a globe-shaped piece of almost pure silver reputedly found nearby, Globe has a colorful history punctuated by mining discoveries. It began as a mining community in 1876. The town's first boom was silver; the second was copper, which is still mined in large quantities. Globe also serves as a trading center for the San Carlos Apache Reservation (see San Carlos p. 204) 4 miles east.

Salt River Canyon, traversed by US 60 about 45 miles northeast, is 1,500 to 2,000 feet deep. About 5 miles wide at the top, the vertical-walled canyon winds for many miles with sedimentary rock layers visible from the road. At the foot of the canyon is a state roadside park. Running westward from Globe, scenic US 60 traverses Devil's Canyon before reaching Superior (see place listing p. 254).

Globe is the eastern terminus of yet another scenic highway, the Apache Trail (SR 88). The road runs northwest to Roosevelt and Theodore Roosevelt Lake Recreation Area (see Recreation Chart) before turning southwest toward Apache Junction (see attraction listing p. 36 for an advisory about driving this route).

Globe-Miami Regional Chamber of Commerce: 1360 N. Broad St., Globe, AZ 85501. **Phone:** (928) 425-4495 or (800) 804-5623.

BESH-BA-GOWAH ARCHAEOLOGICAL PARK, 1324 Jesse Hayes Rd., is a 300-room pueblo inhabited 1225-1400 by Salado Indians. Several rooms are restored and furnished in period. Artifacts from the ruins are displayed in the museum, and an ethnobotanical garden illustrating how native plants were used by the Salado is featured. A videotape presentation also is available. **Hours:** Daily 9-5. Closed Jan. 1, Thanksgiving and Christmas. **Cost:** $5; $4 (ages 65+); free (ages 0-11 with adult). **Phone:** (928) 425-0320.

COBRE VALLEY CENTER FOR THE ARTS, 101 N. Broad St., is housed in the 1906 Old Gila County Courthouse. The center presents sculptures, photography, paintings, ceramics, jewelry, quilts and other art forms created by local artists. A working stained-glass studio may be seen. The Copper City Community Players present live performance pieces in the center's theater; phone for schedule and admission information.

Time: Allow 30 minutes minimum. **Hours:** Mon.-Fri. 10-5, Sat.-Sun. 10-4. Closed major holidays. **Cost:** Donations. **Phone:** (928) 425-0884.

DEVIL'S CANYON, w. on US 60, is noted for its sharp ridges, rock strata and cathedral-like tower formations that illustrate the enormous geological pressures exerted on the region. The mineral wealth of the area is credited mainly to these forces. The Queen Creek Gorge, Bridge and Tunnel are on the drive through the canyon. **Phone:** (602) 225-5200 or (928) 402-6200.

THEODORE ROOSEVELT DAM AND LAKE— see Roosevelt p. 201.

RECREATIONAL ACTIVITIES
White-water Rafting
• **AAM's Mild to Wild Rafting & Jeep Tours Inc.** is 40 mi. n. off US 60/SR 77, following signs.

Hours: Daily late Feb.-late May. **Phone:** (970) 247-4789 or (800) 567-6745.

- **Arizona Rafting** is 45 mi. e. off US 60 at the bridge over the Salt River. **Hours:** Daily, Mar. 1-early May. **Phone:** (800) 462-7238.

QUALITY INN   **Phone:** 928/425-7575

Motel
Rates not provided

Address: 1515 South St 85501 **Location:** On US 60, 1 mi e of town. Adjacent to Round Mountain Park. **Facility:** 52 units. 2 stories (no elevator), exterior corridors. **Amenities:** safes. **Pool(s):** outdoor. **Activities:** whirlpool.

WHERE TO EAT

GUAYO'S ON THE TRAIL   **Phone:** 928/425-9969

Mexican
$6-$17

AAA Inspector Notes: For an array of traditional favorites-including menudo, crunchy salads and burritos-try this eatery with a friendly atmosphere. It's been serving locals for the past 40 years. **Bar:** full bar. **Address:** 14239 S Hwy 188 85501 **Location:** Jct US 60, 1.3 mi n.

GOLD CANYON (J-5) elev. 1,839'

RECREATIONAL ACTIVITIES
Horseback Riding

- **Donnelly's D-Spur Riding Stables** is e. on US 60 to Peralta Rd. (between Mileposts 204 and 205), 1 mi. n.e. to a gravel road, then 1 mi. e. to 15375 E. Peralta Rd. **Hours:** Daily year-round. Closed Christmas. **Phone:** (602) 810-7029.

BEST WESTERN GOLD CANYON INN & SUITES
     Phone: (480)671-6000

Hotel
$85-$135

AAA Benefit: Members save up to 20%, plus 10% bonus points with Best Western Rewards®.

Address: 8333 E Sunrise Sky Dr 85218 **Location:** US 60 exit Kings Ranch Rd, just n, then just e; 7 mi e of Apache Junction. **Facility:** 68 units. 2 stories, interior corridors. **Terms:** cancellation fee imposed. **Amenities:** high-speed Internet. **Pool(s):** heated outdoor. **Activities:** whirlpool, exercise room. **Guest Services:** valet and coin laundry. **Free Special Amenities:** full breakfast and high-speed Internet.

WHERE TO EAT

KOKOPELLI'S   **Phone:** 480/671-5517

American
$8-$33

AAA Inspector Notes: Views to the Superstition Mountains or over the adjacent golf course enhance the dining experience. The well-trained staff assists with choices of specialty steaks or preparations of chicken, seafood or veal. Gold Canyon mousse is a must for dessert. **Bar:** full bar. **Address:** 6100 S Kings Ranch Rd 85219 **Location:** US 60 exit Kings Ranch Rd, 1 mi n; in Gold Canyon Golf Resort. **Parking:** on-site and valet.

OPEN RANGE DELI & BBQ   **Phone:** 480/983-3020

Barbecue
$5-$24

AAA Inspector Notes: Cooked-to-order steaks, fresh seafood and a salad bar with fresh ingredients make this casual restaurant a good choice for dinner. Western decor characterizes the dining room. **Bar:** beer & wine. **Address:** 6030 S Kings Ranch Rd 85218 **Location:** US 60 exit Kings Ranch Rd, 1.1 mi n.

RED SAGE RESTAURANT   **Phone:** 480/671-0300

American
$6-$15

AAA Inspector Notes: For ample portions of family-style food served in a friendly manner, it is hard to beat this eatery, a popular drop-in spot for locals. **Bar:** full bar. **Address:** 8330 E Sunrise Sky Dr 85219 **Location:** US 60 exit Kings Ranch Rd, just n.

GOODYEAR (I-2) pop. 65,275, elev. 1,000'
- **Hotels & Restaurants map p. 155**
- **Part of Phoenix area — see map p. 134**

In the early 1900s Goodyear Tire & Rubber Company obtained tracts of land in the Salt River Valley, with the intent of growing Egyptian cotton, a component in tire cords. The small farms established on this land evolved into company towns, including one named for its originator. Just 14 miles west of Phoenix, the town is now a suburban residential community. Goodyear Ballpark, 1933 S. Ballpark Way, is the spring training center for Major League Baseball's Cleveland Indians and Cincinnati Reds.

Southwest Valley Chamber of Commerce: 289 N. Litchfield Rd., Goodyear, AZ 85338. **Phone:** (623) 932-2260.

ESTRELLA MOUNTAIN REGIONAL PARK, off I-10 Estrella Pkwy. S. exit, contains 19,840 acres of rugged desert terrain; more than 20 miles of trails for hiking, horseback riding and mountain biking; and an 18-hole golf course. Educational programs are offered; equestrian events are held throughout the year. **Hours:** Sun.-Thurs. 6 a.m.-8 p.m., Fri.-Sat. 6 a.m.-10 p.m. **Cost:** $6 (per private vehicle); $2 (per person arriving on foot, horseback or bicycle). Camping $10-$35. **Phone:** (623) 932-3811.

BEST WESTERN PLUS PHOENIX GOODYEAR INN
     Phone: (623)932-3210   52

Hotel
$80-$170

AAA Benefit: Members save up to 20%, plus 10% bonus points with Best Western Rewards®.

Address: 55 N Litchfield Rd 85338 **Location:** I-10 exit 128, 0.8 mi s. **Facility:** 85 units. 1-2 stories (no elevator), interior/exterior corridors. **Terms:** check-in 4 pm, cancellation fee imposed. **Amenities:** Some: high-speed Internet. **Pool(s):** heated outdoor. **Activities:** exercise room. **Guest Services:** valet and coin laundry, area transportation-within 3 mi. **Free Special Amenities:** expanded continental breakfast and high-speed Internet.

(See map & index p. 155.)

COMFORT SUITES GOODYEAR
Phone: 623/266-2884   **47**

Hotel
Rates not provided

Address: 15575 W Roosevelt St 85338 **Location:** I-10 exit 126, just s on Estrella Pkwy, then just w. **Facility:** 84 units. 3 stories, interior corridors. **Amenities:** high-speed Internet. **Pool(s):** heated outdoor. **Activities:** whirlpool, exercise room. **Guest Services:** valet and coin laundry.

Free full hot breakfast. Located 1 mile from Goodyear Ballpark and 7 miles from Luke Air Force Base

COMFORT SUITES

HAMPTON INN & SUITES   **Phone:** 623/536-1313   **46**

Hotel
Rates not provided

AAA Benefit:
Members save up to 10% everyday!

Address: 2000 N Litchfield Rd 85395 **Location:** I-10 exit 128, 0.5 mi n. **Facility:** 110 units, some efficiencies. 0 stories, interior corridors. **Terms:** check-in 4 pm. **Pool(s):** heated outdoor. **Activities:** whirlpool, sports court, exercise room. **Guest Services:** coin laundry.

HOLIDAY INN EXPRESS WEST PHOENIX/GOODYEAR
Phone: (623)535-1313   **48**

Hotel
$179-$199 2/1-5/1
$109-$149 5/2-1/31

Address: 1313 N Litchfield Rd 85395 **Location:** I-10 exit 128, just n. **Facility:** 90 units. 3 stories, interior corridors. **Terms:** check-in 4 pm. **Pool(s):** heated outdoor. **Activities:** whirlpool, exercise room. **Guest Services:** coin laundry.

HOLIDAY INN HOTEL & SUITES
Phone: (623)547-1313   **49**

Hotel
$165-$195 2/1-5/19
$159-$189 5/20-1/31

Address: 1188 N Dysart Rd 85395 **Location:** I-10 exit 129 (Dysart Rd), just n. **Facility:** 100 units. 4 stories, interior corridors. **Amenities:** video games (fee), high-speed Internet, safes. **Pool(s):** heated outdoor. **Activities:** whirlpool, exercise room. **Guest Services:** valet and coin laundry.

QUALITY INN & SUITES GOODYEAR
Phone: (623)932-9191   **50**

Hotel
$65-$180

Address: 950 N Dysart Rd 85338 **Location:** I-10 exit 129 (Dysart Rd), just s. **Facility:** 160 units. 2 stories (no elevator), exterior corridors. **Terms:** cancellation fee imposed. **Amenities:** safes. **Pool(s):** heated outdoor. **Activities:** whirlpool, exercise room. **Guest Services:** valet and coin laundry.

RESIDENCE INN BY MARRIOTT
Phone: (623)866-1313   **45**

Extended Stay Hotel
$82-$239

AAA Benefit:
AAA hotel discounts of 5% or more.

Address: 2020 N Litchfield Rd 85395 **Location:** I-10 exit 128, 0.6 mi n. **Facility:** 78 units, some two bedrooms and efficiencies. 3 stories, interior corridors. **Amenities:** high-speed Internet. **Pool(s):** heated outdoor. **Activities:** whirlpool, sports court, exercise room. **Guest Services:** coin laundry.

TOWNEPLACE SUITES BY MARRIOTT PHOENIX/GOODYEAR
Phone: (623)535-5009   **51**

Extended Stay Hotel
$74-$219

AAA Benefit:
AAA hotel discounts of 5% or more.

Address: 13971 W Fillmore St 85338 **Location:** I-10 exit 128, just s, then just w. **Facility:** 118 units, some two bedrooms, efficiencies and kitchens. 4 stories, interior corridors. **Terms:** check-in 4 pm. **Amenities:** high-speed Internet. **Pool(s):** heated outdoor. **Activities:** whirlpool, exercise room. **Guest Services:** valet and coin laundry.

WHERE TO EAT

BELLA LUNA RISTORANTE
Phone: 623/535-4642   **25**

Italian
$8-$25

AAA Inspector Notes: Enticing Italian dishes are freshly made and include shrimp and crab in a fra diavolo sauce over linguine and veal cutlets in a special white wine sauce with onions and peas. The light and delicate preparations are served by friendly staff in a modern setting. **Bar:** full bar. **Address:** 14175 W Indian School Rd, Suite A4 85338 **Location:** I-10 exit 128, 1.9 mi n.

BILL JOHNSON'S BIG APPLE RESTAURANT
Phone: 623/882-8288

Steak
$5-$28

AAA Inspector Notes: The locally popular barbecue and steak house offers a casual atmosphere, friendly service and hearty portions of the signature barbecue beef, chicken and pork. Save room for the fresh fruit pie, which is large enough to share. The casual Western atmosphere with helpful staff and a western barn setting make for a fun dining experience. **Bar:** full bar. **Address:** 1330 N Dysart Rd 85338 **Location:** I-10 exit 129 (Dysart Rd), just n.

MACAYO MEXICAN KITCHEN   **Phone:** 623/209-7000

Mexican
$6-$16

AAA Inspector Notes: The colorfully furnished Mexican-style eatery prepares Sonoran Mexican dishes. Friendly and efficient staffers serve traditional and lighter dishes flavored with this place's own chili peppers, which are grown near Tucson. **Bar:** full bar. **Address:** 1474 N Litchfield Rd 85338 **Location:** I-10 exit 128, just n.

(See map & index p. 155.)

TOMO JAPANESE CUISINE

Phone: 623/935-2031   26

Japanese
$8-$19

AAA Inspector Notes: This small and intimate shopping plaza sushi spot serves fresh fish and authentic Japanese favorites. **Bar:** full bar. **Address:** 1550 N Dysart Rd 85338 **Location:** I-10 exit 129 (Dysart Rd), 0.3 mi n; southwest corner of McDowell and Dysart rds.

L   D

GRAND CANYON NATIONAL PARK (A-3)

• Attractions map p. 86

> Elevations in the park range from 1,100 ft. in the lower part of the canyon to about 9,000 ft. at the North Rim. Refer to AAA maps for additional elevation information.

The Grand Canyon of the Colorado River is so magnificent, so humbling, you'll never forget the sensation you feel at first sight. And yes, if you visit in summer, the South Rim is so crowded you'll be griping about the crush of tourists for years to come. But this 277-mile-long canyon, sculpted by the mighty Colorado, is without question America's number one natural wonder.

Viewing aerial IMAX footage simply can't compare to finding a solitary spot somewhere, anywhere, in this mile-deep gorge, and silently watching a raven glide on the breeze above a vast panorama of pyramidal buttes, lonely mesas, rust-colored cliffs and shadowy side canyons.

Of course, not everyone who visits the canyon is compelled to wax poetic like a talking head in a Ken Burns documentary. In the early 19th century, James Ohio Pattie, the first American to lay eyes on the immense chasm, called it "horrid." Following an 1857 Army expedition, Lt. Joseph Ives deemed it a "profitless locality." If he could only witness the 5 million visitors a year who fill the hotels, ride the mules to Phantom Ranch, light up the gift shop cash registers and buzz over the canyon on helicopter tours.

As the hawk flies, it's 10 miles from the South Rim Village to the North Rim lodge. To grasp the canyon's geologic scope, a bit of textbook-speak is necessary. Eons of time are on display in the layer-cake-like strata of the canyon walls. Though scientists estimate the canyon is relatively young (5 to 6 million years old), the rock layers at the bottom, near the Colorado River, date back some 2 billion years. Put in perspective, the 270-million-year-old Permian Period layer (formed just prior to the age of the dinosaurs) is what you're standing on at the rim. No wonder they call the canyon "grand."

General Information and Activities

North Rim visitor services and facilities are open mid-May to mid-October; heavy snow closes the road to the North Rim during the winter (mid-November to mid-May). For road conditions and weather information phone (928) 638-7888.

South Rim visitor services and facilities are open all year. During the winter South Rim trails into the canyon are open; however, they can be dangerously icy from December through April. Trail conditions should be verified at the Backcountry Information Center or at Grand Canyon Visitor Center. Hikers are advised not to hike from the rim to the river and back in one day. Since nights are cool even in summer, pack warm clothing. However, be prepared for high daytime summer temperatures within the canyon.

The Guide, the park's visitor information newspaper, is handed out at all entrance stations. Inside you'll find everything from maps, shuttle schedules and trail descriptions to a complete roundup of ranger-led activities and programs.

Backpacking anywhere in the park or camping below the canyon rim requires a permit from the Backcountry Information Center, P.O. Box 129, Grand Canyon, AZ 86023. Permit requests and backcountry camping reservations are accepted by mail or in person up to 4 months in advance. For more information phone (928) 638-7875, Mon.-Fri. 1-5, or write the park directly to request a "Backcountry Trip Planner."

Several campgrounds are near both rims, just outside the park's boundaries. Reservations for National Park Service-operated campgrounds on the North and South rims can be made up to 6 months in advance by phoning (877) 444-6777 or TTY (877) 833-6777. *See Recreation Chart.*

Trans-Canyon Shuttle provides one-way and round-trip van transportation once daily to each of the canyon's rims from mid-May to mid-October. The 4.5-hour shuttle ride departs for the South Rim at 7 a.m. and begins its return to the North Rim at 1:30 p.m. The fare is $80 for a one-way ride; $150 for a round-trip ride. Reservations are required; phone (928) 638-2820 for information and reservations. **Note:** The shuttle is the only means of public transportation between the North and South rims.

Buses departing from Yavapai Lodge, Maswik Lodge and Bright Angel Lodge & Cabins take visitors on a variety of sightseeing tours. The 2-hour Hermits Rest Tour is $25; free (ages 0-16 with paying adult). The 3.75-hour Desert View Tour is $42; free (ages 0-16 with paying adult). The 90-minute Sunrise and Sunset tours are $20; free (ages 0-16 with paying adult). A Combination Tour ($57) and a Railway Express Tour ($65) also are available.

For bus tour information and advance reservations, contact Xanterra Parks & Resorts at (888) 297-2757. For same-day reservations, phone (928) 638-2631.

Flightseeing tours are offered from the South Rim and from several nearby cities, including Page, Phoenix, Sedona, Williams and Las Vegas, Nev.

Another way to glimpse the Grand Canyon from overlooks is on a four-wheel-drive tour. These back-road sightseeing trips through the Kaibab National Forest are led by guides well-versed in the ecology of the canyon, its history, wildlife and legends. Contact Grand Canyon Jeep Tours & Safaris at (928) 638-5337 or (800) 320-5337.

ADMISSION to the park, valid for both rims for up to 7 days, is $25 (per private vehicle); $12 (per person arriving by other means).

PETS are permitted in the park only if they are leashed, crated or otherwise physically restrained at all times. Pets are excluded entirely from backcountry areas and are not allowed below the rim. Kennels are available; reservations are recommended. Phone (928) 638-0534.

ADDRESS inquiries to the Superintendent, Grand Canyon National Park, P.O. Box 129, Grand Canyon, AZ 86023; phone (928) 638-7888. Information also is available from the Grand Canyon Chamber of Commerce, P.O. Box 3007, Grand Canyon, AZ 86023; phone (888) 472-2696 or (928) 638-2901.

GRAND CANYON NATIONAL PARK - SOUTH RIM
• Hotels p. 90 • Restaurants p. 95
• Attractions map p. 86

One superb canyon vista after another is what you'll see along the South Rim's paved roads. The 25-mile Desert View Drive (open year-round to private vehicles) connects the East Entrance Station with Grand Canyon Village, winding through a ponderosa pine forest and passing a half-dozen viewpoints (Grandview is a standout) along the way.

West of the village, Hermit Road leads to more overlooks (including the phenomenal Hopi Point) on its way to Hermit's Rest, where you'll find restrooms, a snack bar and a gift shop. The road is closed to private vehicles March through November but can be accessed by the park's free shuttle bus during these months.

In peak summer travel season, brace yourself for crowds. In most areas of Grand Canyon Village, parking is scarce. Free shuttles run year round at the village, and it's often wise to park at the visitor center and use the shuttle to get around. To avoid parking headaches all together, consider riding the free shuttle from Tusayan (the park's gateway town); service is available mid-May to mid-September.

If you're driving into the park through the South Entrance Station (near Tusayan), take note: The line of vehicles waiting to pay admission may be incredibly long. There are two express lanes for prepaid passes; paying admission outside the park at the National Geographic Visitor Center Grand Canyon *(see attraction listing)* is a smart move when traffic is heavy. Of course, the most obvious way to avoid possible delays is to get an early start.

Both helicopter and airplane tours of the canyon are available from the Grand Canyon National Park Airport in Tusayan, 5 miles south of the park headquarters. For information and reservations contact Air Grand Canyon, (800) 634-6801; Grand Canyon Airlines, (888) 635-7272; Grand Canyon Helicopters, (928) 638-2764; Maverick Helicopters, (888) 261-4414; or Papillon Grand Canyon Helicopters, (928) 638-7121 or (888) 635-7272.

BRIGHT ANGEL TRAIL starts just w. of Bright Angel Lodge & Cabins. Descending 4,460 feet to the Colorado River, the trail leads 9 miles to the river and Phantom Ranch. From Indian Garden, 4.4 miles below the trailhead, a branch trail leads 1.5 miles across the Tonto Platform to Plateau Point, offering a grand view of the Colorado River. To view the

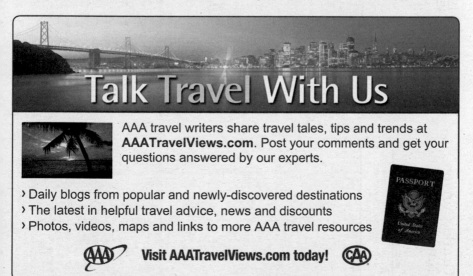

Talk Travel With Us

AAA travel writers share travel tales, tips and trends at **AAATravelViews.com**. Post your comments and get your questions answered by our experts.

> Daily blogs from popular and newly-discovered destinations
> The latest in helpful travel advice, news and discounts
> Photos, videos, maps and links to more AAA travel resources

AAA Visit AAATravelViews.com today! **CAA**

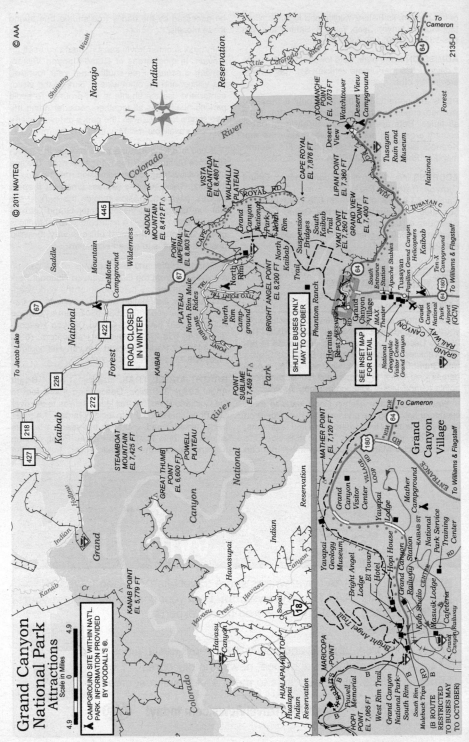

Grand Canyon National Park Attractions

Scale in Miles
4.9   0   4.9

X CAMPGROUND SITE WITHIN NAT'L. PARK. INFORMATION PROVIDED BY WOODALL'S ®.

ROAD CLOSED IN WINTER

SHUTTLE BUSES ONLY MAY TO OCTOBER

SEE INSET MAP FOR DETAIL

© AAA

© 2011 NAVTEQ

2135-D

To Cameron

Navajo Indian Reservation

Shinumo Wash

Little Colorado River

COMANCHE POINT EL 7,073 FT

Desert View Watchtower

Desert View Campground

Tusayan Ruin and Museum

National Forest

Colorado River

VISTA ENCANTADA EL 8,480 FT

WALHALLA PLATEAU

CAPE ROYAL EL 7,876 FT

SADDLE MOUNTAIN EL 8,412 FT

POINT IMPERIAL EL 8,803 FT

CAPE ROYAL RD.

Grand Canyon National Park North Rim

LIPAN POINT EL 7,360 FT

South Kaibab Trail

Suspension Bridges

YAKI POINT EL 7,260 FT

GRAND VIEW POINT EL 7,400 FT

North Rim

BRIGHT ANGEL POINT EL 8,200 FT

North Rim Mule Rides

PLATEAU

North Rim Campground

TIYO POINT TRL

Phantom Ranch

Kaibab Trail

Papillon Grand Canyon Helicopters

Ten-X Campground

Kaibab

South Entrance Station

Apache Stables

Tusayan

IMAX Theater

National Geographic Visitor Center Grand Canyon

Grand Canyon Village

HERMIT RD.

Hermits Rest

Grand Canyon National Park

Grand Canyon Airport (GCN)

To Williams & Flagstaff

TUSAYAN C

SADDLE MOUNTAIN WILDERNESS

Saddle Mountain

DeMotte Campground

POINT SUBLIME TRL

KAIBAB

KAIBAB NATIONAL FOREST

To Jacob Lake

POINT SUBLIME EL 7,459 FT

STEAMBOAT MOUNTAIN EL 7,425 FT

GREAT THUMB POINT EL 6,600 FT

POWELL PLATEAU

River

Grand Canyon National Park

KANAB POINT EL 5,779 FT

Kanab Cr

Havasupai Canyon

Havasu Creek

Supai

Indian Canyon

Reservation

Havasu

Indian Reservation

Colorado

Hualapai Indian Reservation

HUALAPAI HILLTOP

HOPI POINT EL 7,065 FT

445

67

422

272

226

218

427

18

Grand Canyon Village (inset)

To Cameron

MATHER POINT EL 7,120 FT

Grand Canyon Visitor Center

Mather Campground

Yavapai Geology Museum

Yavapai Lodge

Bright Angel Lodge

El Tovar Hotel

Hopi House

Grand Canyon Railway Station

Kolb Studio

Maswik Lodge

Cafeteria

National Park Service Training Center

Bright Angel Trail

MARICOPA POINT

Powell Memorial

West Rim Trail

Grand Canyon National Park South Rim

Grand Canyon Railway

RIM DR

64
180

ENTRANCE RD

VILLAGE LOOP RD

KAIBAB ST

CENTER RD

Grand Canyon Village

To Williams & Flagstaff

B ROUTE RESTRICTED TO BUSES MAY TO OCTOBER

64
180

64 163

B

depths from the rim, telescopes are available near Bright Angel Lodge & Cabins and at Desert View Watchtower.

Note: Hikers should check *The Guide,* the park's newsprint publication, for the latest information about the trail. Overnight hikers must obtain a camping permit. Water must be carried on all canyon trails.

GRAND CANYON CAVERNS—
see Peach Springs p. 129.

GEM GRAND CANYON RAILWAY—
see Williams p. 316.

GRAND CANYON SKYWALK—
see Peach Springs p. 129.

GRAND CANYON VISITOR CENTER is 5 mi. n. of the South Entrance Station near Mather Point. The center can be reached via a free shuttle bus from various locations in Grand Canyon Village. The visitor center is at an altitude of 6,950 feet and features indoor displays, a theater with a film, outdoor exhibits, an information center and views of the canyon from nearby observation points.

Note: Inquire at the center about local road conditions. **Hours:** Daily 8-6, Memorial Day Labor Day; 8-5, day after Labor Day-day before Memorial Day. Ranger programs are presented; phone for schedule. **Cost:** Free. **Phone:** (928) 638-7888.

GEM HAVASU CANYON—*see Supai p. 254.*

KOLB STUDIO, just w. of Bright Angel Lodge & Cabins, was built as a photography studio in 1904 for brothers Ellsworth and Emery Kolb, who took photos of tourists descending Bright Angel Trail *(see attraction listing)* on mules. The building now serves as both a bookstore and a gallery with changing Grand Canyon-related exhibits. Antique photographic equipment used by the Kolb brothers is on display, and you can snap your own photos from a small outdoor viewing area. **Time:** Allow 30 minutes minimum. **Hours:** Daily 8-6. **Cost:** Free. **Phone:** (928) 638-2481.

LIPAN POINT, along Desert View Dr., has an elevation of 7,250 feet and offers a fine view of the river, the Unkar Delta and the San Francisco Peaks.

NATIONAL GEOGRAPHIC VISITOR CENTER GRAND CANYON, 9 mi. s. of Grand Canyon Village at 450 SR 64 in Tusayan, features exhibits about Grand Canyon history, explorers, geology and wildlife. Visitors wishing to visit Grand Canyon National Park can obtain trip-planning information, purchase park passes and book tours. **Hours:** Daily 8 a.m.-10 p.m., Mar.-Oct.; 10-8, rest of year. **Cost:** Free. **Phone:** (928) 638-2468, (928) 638-0200 for tours or (866) 418-1208. *(See ad p. 88.)*

▼ See AAA listing p. 316 ▼

IT'S WILD.
JUST AS THE WEST ONCE WAS.

Drive thru our wild animal area, take a stroll in Fort Bearizona and don't miss our all-new bird show!

Get free mobile app at http://gettaf.mobi

BEARIZONA

A DRIVE-THRU WILDLIFE ADVENTURE AT THE GATEWAY TO THE GRAND CANYON
I-40, South of Exit 165 in historic Williams, AZ • www.bearizona.com • 928-635-2289 • www.facebook.com/bearizona

SAVE **IMAX Theater** is within the National Geographic Visitor Center Grand Canyon, 9 mi. s. of Grand Canyon Village at 450 SR 64 in Tusayan. Equipped with a seven-story screen and a six-track sound system, the theater presents the "Grand Canyon IMAX Movie," a film that depicts the history and captures the beauty of this geologic formation while showing parts of the canyon that can't be seen on tours.

Time: Allow 45 minutes minimum. **Hours:** The film is shown daily every hour on the half-hour 8:30-8:30, Mar.-Oct.; 10:30-6:30, rest of year. **Cost:** Film $12.50; $9.50 (ages 6-10). **Phone:** (928) 638-2468, (928) 638-0200 (for tours) or (866) 418-1208.

PHANTOM RANCH, at the bottom of the Grand Canyon, is reached by hiking *(see Bright Angel Trail)* or mule ride *(see South Rim Mule Trips).* The only lodging available below the rim, it provides dormitory accommodations, cabins and a dining room. Dormitories are available to hikers; cabin lodging is included with overnight mule trips. **Cost:** Dorm space $43.09. Reservations are required for lodging and meals and must be made well in advance, especially during summer and holidays. **Phone:** (303) 297-2757 or (888) 297-2757.

RIM TRAIL extends nearly 12 mi. along the rim of the canyon from Hermits Rest to Desert View Dr. (near Yaki Point). A paved section starting at Hermits Rest and extending east for about 1.5 miles accommodates wheelchairs and is suitable for walking and biking. Relatively flat, the paved 5-mile section from Maricopa Point to Pipe Creek Vista is better for children and casual hikers than the park's other more strenuous canyon trails. Pamphlets about the biology and geology of the canyon can be obtained from boxes along the trail.

SOUTH KAIBAB TRAIL begins near Yaki Point, 3.5 mi. e. of Grand Canyon Village. This is a steep, 7-mile trail to a Colorado River suspension bridge. Hikers can descend the trail and return by following the Colorado River .5 mile to the Bright Angel Trail which leads to Grand Canyon Village. A good 3-mile round-trip day hike leads from the head of South Kaibab Trail to Cedar Ridge, where beautiful views of the canyon may be seen.

Note: Visitors should not attempt to hike from the South Rim to the river and back in 1 day. The Kaibab Trail is strenuous and not recommended for hiking out of the canyon. The trip is recommended only for hardy individuals. Hikers should carry water (1 gallon per person per day), since none is available along the trail. The road to the trailhead is closed to private vehicles and may be reached by shuttle bus. **Hours:** Conducted hikes to Cedar Ridge are scheduled in summer.

SOUTH RIM MULE TRIPS depart from a point near the trailhead of the Bright Angel Trail. Offered through Xanterra Parks & Resorts, guided overnight mule trips take visitors along the Bright Angel Trail to Phantom Ranch in the bottom of the canyon. There also is a 3-hour ride through Kaibab Forest to the Abyss Overlook.

Note: For safety purposes, riders must be fluent in English, be taller than 4 feet 7 inches, and weigh less than 200 pounds when fully dressed (including equipment) for the Phantom Ranch ride or 225 pounds for the Abyss Overlook ride. The trips are strenuous and should be undertaken only by those in good physical condition; pregnant women are not permitted on the trips.

Hours: Trips depart daily year-round. **Cost:** Rates vary; phone ahead. Reservations are required and must be made well in advance, particularly during summer and holidays. **Phone:** (888) 297-2757.

TUSAYAN RUIN AND MUSEUM is 22 mi. e. of Grand Canyon Village on a short spur leading off Desert View Dr. The museum traces the development of the Native American culture at the canyon. Exhibits include a painting of the ruin, displays about modern tribes and such Ancestral Puebloan artifacts as pottery, twig figurines and rock drawings.

Tusayan Ruin is a U-shaped, prehistoric pueblo inhabited 1185-1225 by two generations of Ancestral Puebloans; it contains about 15 rooms and about 30

▼ See AAA listing p. 87 ▼

Explore Beyond the Rim

GRAND CANYON *Movie* IN **IMAX**

Available in 8 languages

• National Geographic Store & Exhibits
• Book Sightseeing Tours
• Visit with a National Park Ranger
• Purchase National Park Pass Here
• Condor Encounter Bird Show *(seasonal)*

Showing exclusively at the

NATIONAL GEOGRAPHIC

VISITOR CENTER

10% off IMAX® AAA DISCOUNT

Hwy. 64 at South Rim Park Entrance • (928) 638-2468 • explorethecanyon.com

It's how AAA members turn a drive into a journey.

AAA members get exclusive values on Hertz rentals in every car class ... ensuring ideal wheels for every trip!

For offers and complete terms,
visit AAA.com/hertz or Hertz.com.

Visit: Over 1,100 AAA Offices
Click: AAA.com/hertz
Call: 800-654-3080

people lived there. The Ancestral Puebloans are believed to be the ancestors of the Hopi as well as other Pueblo tribes.

An adjacent .1-mile paved trail runs around the pueblo. A self-guiding brochure is available at the trailhead. **Note:** Inclement weather may result in winter closures; phone ahead. **Tours:** Guided tours are available. **Hours:** Daily 9-5. Phone ahead to confirm schedule. **Cost:** Free. **Phone:** (928) 638-7888.

WATCHTOWER is 26 mi. e. of Grand Canyon Village at Desert View. Built in 1932, the 70-ft. tower built of stone and mortar was inspired by prehistoric towers found in the Four Corners region. From the brink of the canyon wall, the tower commands views of the river, the canyon, the Painted Desert and Kaibab National Forest *(see place listing p. 100)*; telescopes extend the view far into the Navajo Reservation and to the Colorado River.

Also at Desert View are food concessions, an information desk, a general store, a seasonal campground and a gas station. **Hours:** Daily 8-dusk, Memorial Day-Labor Day; 9-dusk, day after Labor Day-day before Memorial Day. **Cost:** Free.

YAVAPAI GEOLOGY MUSEUM, 1.5 mi. e. of Grand Canyon Village, offers exhibits and programs that explain the geologic history of the region. A panoramic view of the canyon is visible through the building's windows. **Hours:** Daily 8-8, June-Aug.; 8-6 in May and Sept.; 8-5, rest of year. **Cost:** Free.

RECREATIONAL ACTIVITIES

Bicycling
- **Bright Angel Bicycle Rentals** departs from the Grand Canyon Visitor Center. Tours and rentals are offered. **Hours:** Daily 8-6, May-Oct. **Phone:** (928) 814-8704.

Horseback Riding
- **Apache Stables** is 1 mi. n. of Tusayan off SR 64, then .25 mi. w. on FR 328/Moqui Dr. **Hours:** Daily, Mar.-Nov. (weather permitting). **Phone:** (928) 638-2891.

White-water Rafting
- **Raft Trips** is on the Colorado River. **Hours:** Trips operate Mar.-Oct. **Phone:** (928) 526-4575 or (800) 473-4576.

BEST WESTERN GRAND CANYON SQUIRE INN
Phone: (928)638-2681

Hotel
$101-$401

AAA Benefit: Members save up to 20%, plus 10% bonus points with Best Western Rewards®.

Address: 74 SR 64 86023 **Location:** On SR 64; 2 mi s of South Rim entrance. **Facility:** 250 units. 1-3 stories, interior/exterior corridors. **Terms:** check-in 4 pm, cancellation fee imposed. **Amenities:** safes (fee). *Some:* high-speed Internet. **Dining:** 2 restaurants, also, Coronado Room, see separate listing. **Pool(s):** heated outdoor. **Activities:** whirlpool, exercise room. *Fee:* game room. **Guest Services:** coin laundry. **Free Special Amenities:** expanded continental breakfast and high-speed Internet.

CANYON PLAZA RESORT GRAND CANYON
Phone: (928)638-2673

Hotel
$138-$268 3/15-1/31
$83-$178 2/1-3/14

Address: 406 Canyon Plaza Ln 86023 **Location:** On SR 64; 2 mi s of South Rim entrance. Located behind the Imax Theatre. **Facility:** 232 units. 3 stories, interior/exterior corridors. **Terms:** cancellation fee imposed. **Amenities:** video games (fee), high-speed Internet. **Pool(s):** heated outdoor. **Activities:** whirlpools. **Free Special Amenities:** high-speed Internet and use of on-premises laundry facilities.

7 min. from Grand Canyon National Park South Rim. Lush Indoor Garden Atrium, Buffet or Menu Dining.

EL TOVAR HOTEL
Phone: 303/297-2757

Historic Resort Hotel
$225-$475

Address: South Rim 86023 **Location:** At Grand Canyon Village South Rim. **Facility:** Built in 1905, this hotel along the canyon rim features a lodge-style lobby, updated rooms and a friendly staff. 78 units. 4 stories (no elevator), interior corridors. **Terms:** check-in 4 pm, cancellation fee imposed. **Amenities:** safes. **Dining:** restaurant, see separate listing.

THE GRAND HOTEL
Phone: (928)638-3333

Hotel
$119-$259

Address: Hwy 64 86023 **Location:** On SR 64; 2 mi s of South Rim entrance. **Facility:** 121 units. 3 stories, interior corridors. **Terms:** check-in 4 pm, 3 day cancellation notice-fee imposed. **Amenities:** safes. **Dining:** Canyon Star, see separate listing, entertainment. **Pool(s):** heated indoor. **Activities:** whirlpool, exercise room. *Fee:* game room. **Guest Services:** coin laundry. **Free Special Amenities:** children's activities.

Simply Reliable

The Diamond Ratings in this TourBook guide are backed by our expert, in-person evaluations, whether the hotel or restaurant is no-frills, moderate or upscale.

Learn more at **AAA.com/Diamonds**

▼ See AAA listing p. 42 ▼

LODGING NEAR

GRAND
CANYON

At the
HISTORIC

CAMERON
TRADING POST

Scan this tag on your smartphone!

Get the free mobile app at
http://gettag.mobi

30 MINUTES FROM GRAND CANYON
54 MILES N. OF FLAGSTAFF ON HWY 89
877-675-0614

Make Your Next Trip a Journey ...
With AAA and Hertz.

For reservations, **visit** your AAA/CAA travel
office, click on AAA.com/hertz or CAA.ca/
hertz, or **call** 800-654-3080 U.S./888-333-3120
Canada.

Show Your Card & Save®

HOLIDAY INN EXPRESS HOTEL & SUITES - GRAND CANYON
Phone: 928/638-3000

Hotel
Rates not provided

Address: 226 SR 64 86023 **Location:** On SR 64; 2 mi s of South Rim entrance. **Facility:** 196 units. 3 stories, interior corridors. **Terms:** check-in 4 pm. **Amenities:** high-speed Internet. **Pool(s):** heated indoor. **Activities:** whirlpools. *(See ad this page.)*

KACHINA LODGE
Phone: 303/297-2757

Hotel
$180-$190

Address: South Rim 86023 **Location:** At Grand Canyon Village South Rim. **Facility:** 49 units. 2 stories, interior corridors. **Terms:** open 4/15-1/31, check-in 4 pm, cancellation fee imposed. **Amenities:** safes.

MASWIK LODGE
Phone: 303/297-2757

Motel
$100-$185

Address: South Rim 86023 **Location:** At Grand Canyon Village South Rim. **Facility:** 278 units. 2 stories (no elevator), exterior corridors. **Terms:** check-in 4 pm, cancellation fee imposed. **Amenities:** *Some:* safes.

RED FEATHER LODGE
Phone: (928)638-2414

Hotel
$75-$250

Address: 300 SR 64 86023 **Location:** On SR 64; 2 mi s of South Rim entrance. **Facility:** 216 units, some kitchens. 2-3 stories, interior/exterior corridors. **Terms:** check-in 4 pm. **Amenities:** video games (fee). **Pool(s):** heated outdoor. **Activities:** whirlpool. **Guest Services:** coin laundry. **Free Special Amenities:** local telephone calls. *(See ad p. 93.)*

▼ See AAA listing this page ▼

Holiday Inn Express & Suites
GRAND CANYON

164 GUEST ROOMS
30 SUITES

- Indoor pool & spa
- Free Express Start® Breakfast
- Free in-room High Speed Internet
- 1 Bedroom suites available with refrigerator, coffeemaker, microwave, cable TV
- Walk to IMAX & local restaurants
- 2 Bedroom Kid's Suites with Video Games

Get the free mobile app at
http://gettag.mobi

1-888-473-2269 • www.gcanyon.com
LOCATED AT THE SOUTH RIM ENTRANCE

Share a New View on Travel at
AAATravelViews.com
Read stories, tips and trends from AAA insiders.
Post comments and get your questions answered by our travel experts.

THUNDERBIRD LODGE   Phone: 303/297-2757

Hotel
$180-$190

Address: South Rim 86023 **Location:** At Grand Canyon Village South Rim. **Facility:** 55 units. 2 stories (no elevator), interior/exterior corridors. **Terms:** open 4/15-1/31, check-in 4 pm, cancellation fee imposed. **Amenities:** safes.

YAVAPAI LODGE   Phone: 303/297-2757

Motel
$120-$170

Address: South Rim 86023 **Location:** 1 mi e of Grand Canyon Village South Rim. Located in a quiet area. **Facility:** 358 units. 1-2 stories (no elevator), interior/exterior corridors. **Terms:** open 3/7-11/4 & 11/21-1/2, check-in 4 pm, cancellation fee imposed. **Amenities:** *Some:* safes.

BRIGHT ANGEL LODGE & CABINS

Phone: 303/297-2757

fyi Not evaluated. **Address:** Hwy 64, South Rim 86023 **Location:** At Grand Canyon Village South Rim. Facilities, services, and decor characterize an economy property.

Get pet travel tips
and enter the photo contest
at AAA.com/PetBook

▼ See AAA listing p. 92 ▼

GRAND CANYON

Outdoor Pool and Spa (seasonal) • FREE High Speed Wireless Internet
Guest Laundry Facilities on Property • Pet Friendly (Motel)

RP's Stage Stop - Gifts, Coffee, Internet Café & Original Handcrafted Native American Jewelry

Scan for rates & availability

CONNECT WITH US

Red Feather Lodge

Get the free mobile app at http://gettag.mobi

LOCATED ONE MILE FROM
GRAND CANYON NATIONAL PARK'S SOUTH ENTRANCE
1-800-538-2345 • WWW.REDFEATHERLODGE.COM

10% DISCOUNT TO AAA MEMBERS

Reserve Your Room Now!
Toll Free:
800.644.8383

AAA Approved

Ask for the AAA Rate!
• Free made to order breakfast
• Free high-speed internet

On-site attractions:
• Hogan Espresso Coffee Shop
• Explore Navajo Interactive Museum
• Navajo Code Talkers Museum
• Historic Tuba City Trading Post

QUALITY INN
BY CHOICE HOTELS
Quality Inn
Navajo Nation

Explore Navajo.com
A Culture Like No Other!

10 N. Main Street,
Tuba City, AZ 86045
Tel: 928.283.4545
Toll Free: 800.644.8383

Great Rates!
Great Brands!
Great Guarantee!

AAA members get best available room rates with AAA preferred lodging partners.

Best Western International
Up to 20% Off the Best Rates
Best Western
Best Western Plus
Best Western Premier
The Hilton Family
5% or More Every Day
Conrad Hotels & Resorts,
DoubleTree by Hilton, Embassy Suites,
Hampton Inns & Suites, Hilton,
Hilton Garden Inns,
Hilton Grand Vacations,
Home2 Suites, Homewood Suites,
and Waldorf Astoria Collection
Hyatt Hotels & Resorts
10% Off Best Available Rates
ANdAZ, Grand Hyatt,
Hyatt Place, Hyatt Regency,
Hyatt Summerfield Suites,
and Park Hyatt

Marriott Hotels & Resorts
5% or More Every Day
Autograph Collection by Marriott,
Courtyard, EDITION Hotels by Marriott,
Fairfield Inn, JW Marriott,
Marriott Hotels & Resorts,
Renaissance Hotels, Residence Inn,
Ritz-Carlton Hotels, SpringHill Suites,
and TownePlace Suites
Starwood Hotels & Resorts
5-15% Off Best Available Rates
Aloft, Element, Four Points,
Le Meridien, Sheraton, St. Regis,
The Luxury Collection, Westin,
and W Hotels

Show Your Card & Save
Preferred Hotels

ASSURED STAY
Total Satisfaction Guarantee

Over 1 million rooms to fit your budget
100%
Satisfaction Guarantee
Exclusively for AAA Members!

Valid AAA Membership required. Not valid with other discounts or promotions. Good at participating locations only.
Other restrictions may apply. Offers subject to change without notice.

VISIT over 1,100 AAA Offices | **CLICK** AAA.com | **CALL** 1-866-AAA-SAVE (1-866-222-7283)

WHERE TO EAT

THE ARIZONA ROOM AT BRIGHT ANGEL LODGE
Phone: 928/638-2631

American
$8-$26

AAA Inspector Notes: The menu of this popular restaurant with windows looking toward the canyon features a selection of steak, barbecue, chicken and seafood. **Bar:** full bar. **Address:** 10 South Rim Ave 86023 **Location:** At Grand Canyon Village South Rim; between Bright Angel Lodge & Cabins and Thunderbird Lodge. [L] [D]

BRIGHT ANGEL RESTAURANT
Phone: 928/638-2631

American
$8-$26

AAA Inspector Notes: The restaurant presents an eclectic menu that lists everything from burgers and steak to fish tacos and lasagna. Service is fast. **Bar:** full bar. **Address:** South Rim 86023 **Location:** At Grand Canyon Village South Rim; in Bright Angel Lodge & Cabins.

[B] [L] [D] CALL 🖐M

CANYON STAR
Phone: 928/638-3333

American
$5-$45

AAA Inspector Notes: Featuring a Southwestern menu with steaks and a seasonal buffet, the restaurant also entertains guests with Native American dancers and singing cowboys. **Bar:** full bar. **Address:** Hwy 64 86023 **Location:** On SR 64; 2 mi s of South Rim entrance; in The Grand Hotel. [B] [L] [D]

CORONADO ROOM
Phone: 928/638-2681

Steak
$15-$30

AAA Inspector Notes: The menu features a nice selection of steaks, seafood, pastas and Mexican dishes. **Bar:** full bar. **Address:** 74 SR 64 86023 **Location:** On SR 64; 2 mi s of South Rim entrance; in Best Western Grand Canyon Squire Inn. [D]

EL TOVAR HOTEL DINING ROOM
Phone: 928/638-2631

Continental
$11-$35

AAA Inspector Notes: The very attractive dining room is the setting for a nice selection of veal, beef, seafood, chicken and vegetarian entrées. **Bar:** full bar. **Reservations:** suggested, for dinner. **Address:** South Rim 86023 **Location:** At Grand Canyon Village South Rim; in El Tovar Hotel. [B] [L] [D]

WE COOK PIZZA & PASTA
Phone: 928/638-2278

Italian
$7-$15

AAA Inspector Notes: After a long day exploring the canyon, locals and visitors congregate here for beer and pizza. Although specialty pizzas are the most popular choices, the menu also lists sandwiches, simple pasta dishes, calzones and a salad bar. **Bar:** wine only. **Address:** Hwy 64 86023 **Location:** On SR 64; 2 mi s of South Rim entrance. [L] [D]

 GRAND CANYON NATIONAL PARK - NORTH RIM

- Hotels p. 96
- Attractions map p. 86

Less visited than the South Rim, the North Rim is not as extensively developed. The views from the North and South rims differ considerably. Observers at Bright Angel Point on the North Rim can see the San Francisco Peaks, which are 80 miles south of the South Rim.

From Grand Canyon Village on the South Rim, it is 215 miles to Grand Canyon North Rim Lodge via SR 64 to Cameron, US 89 to its junction with US 89A at Bitter Springs, US 89A to Jacob Lake and scenic SR 67 to the North Rim Entrance Station. The 5-hour drive passes through the Navajo reservation, the Painted Desert and Kaibab National Forest.

A road runs 22 miles southeast from the Grand Canyon North Rim Lodge road to Point Imperial, Vista Encantada and Cape Royal. Point Imperial, at 8,803 feet, is the highest point on the canyon rim. These points all afford splendid views. Reservations for the North Rim Campground can be made up to 6 months in advance by phoning Reserve America at (877) 444-6777. *See Recreation Chart.*

GRAND CANYON CAVERNS—
see Peach Springs p. 129.

 GRAND CANYON RAILWAY—
see Williams p. 316.

GRAND CANYON SKYWALK—
see Peach Springs p. 129.

MARBLE CANYON, at the n.e. end of the park, is traversed by US 89A via the Navajo Bridge, which is 616 feet long and 467 feet high. The Colorado River lies in a 500-foot-deep gorge that cuts across the level plain on which the highway sits. A herd of bison inhabits House Rock Valley, about 22 miles west on a rough dirt road off US 89A.

NORTH KAIBAB TRAIL starts at the head of Roaring Springs Canyon. This 14.2-mile trail descends 5,850 feet to the river and Phantom Ranch, following Bright Angel Creek. **Note:** Only experienced hikers in good physical condition should use the trail. Check *The Guide,* the park's newsprint publication, for the latest information about the trail. Overnight hikers must obtain a camping permit and make camping reservations.

NORTH RIM MULE RIDES depart from a point near the trailhead of the North Kaibab Trail. Offered through Grand Canyon Trail Rides, half-day mule-back trips take visitors through the canyon to the Supai Tunnel. A 1-hour trip along the North Rim and a half-day trip to Uncle Jim's Point also are available. Trips do not go to the Colorado River.

Note: For safety purposes, riders must be fluent in English; they also must weigh less than 200 pounds when fully dressed (including equipment) for the half-day trip to the Supai Tunnel and less than 220 pounds when fully dressed for the 1-hour rim trip and the half-day trip to Uncle Jim's Point. The trips are strenuous and should be undertaken only by those in good physical condition; pregnant women are not permitted on the trips.

Hours: Half-day trips depart daily at 7:30 and 12:30, mid-May to mid-Oct. One-hour trips depart daily 8:30-1:30, mid-May to mid-Oct. **Cost:** Half-day trips $75. One-hour trip $40. Ages 0-9 are not permitted on half-day trips; ages 0-6 are not permitted on 1-hour trip. **Phone:** (435) 679-8665.

TUWEEP AREA is in the n.w. corner, via SR 389 and a 60-mile dirt road west of Fredonia.

Also known as Toroweap, the remote area embraces 40 miles of the Grand Canyon between Kanab Creek and the Uinkaret Mountains. Toroweap Overlook offers exceptional views of the Grand Canyon's inner gorge and of Lava Falls rapids. Vulcans Throne, a cinder cone, is on the Esplanade just west of Toroweap Overlook.

Note: Due to a lack of accommodations, the trip should not be attempted without adequate preparation and equipment. Water, gasoline and camping supplies are not available. Limited camping is offered south of the Tuweep Ranger Station; electricity and water are not available. The 60-mile dirt road is impassable when wet. A high-clearance, four-wheel-drive vehicle is recommended.

GRAND CANYON NORTH RIM LODGE
                                          Phone: 928/638-2611
[fyi]   Not evaluated. **Address:** North Rim 86052 **Location:** At Bright Angel Point. Facilities, services, and decor characterize a mid-scale property.

KAIBAB LODGE   **Phone:** 928/638-2389
[fyi]   Not evaluated. **Address:** SR 67 86003 **Location:** 26 mi s of jct SR 67 and Alternate Rt US 89. Facilities, services, and decor characterize a mid-scale property.

GRAND CANYON-PARASHANT NATIONAL MONUMENT (A-2)

In the northwestern corner of the state, Grand Canyon-Parashant National Monument comprises more than 1 million undeveloped acres bordered on the west by Nevada and on the south by Grand Canyon National Park *(see place listing p. 84).*

Exposed in the remote, unspoiled canyons and mesas are layers representing nearly 1.7 billion years of the earth's formation. Human occupation can be traced through such archeological finds as petroglyphs, pit houses and villages, with evidence pointing to habitation by hunter-gatherers as early as the Paleo-Indian and Archaic periods, and later by Puebloan and Southern Paiute cultures. Abandoned homesteads, ranches and mining camps are among the 19th- and 20th-century ruins preserved.

Wildlife is as diverse as the scenery. Two extreme ecological regions, the Mojave Desert and the Colorado Plateau, intersect within the boundaries of the monument, which is inhabited by bighorn sheep, coyotes, mule deer, turkeys and Kaibab squirrels as well as the endangered California condor.

Hiking, picnicking and primitive camping are permitted. There are no paved roads, services or developed recreation sites. Graded dirt roads are passable by two-wheel drive vehicles when dry but become impassable when wet. Use four-wheel drive vehicles with full-sized spare tires to travel alternative routes. Be prepared for adverse and isolated conditions; most of the monument has no cell phone coverage. For maps and further information contact the Arizona Strip District Field Office, Bureau of Land Management, 345 E. Riverside Dr., St. George, UT 84790; phone coverage. For maps and further information contact the Arizona Strip District Field Office, Bureau of Land Management, 345 E. Riverside Dr., St. George, UT 84790; phone (435) 688-3246.

Create complete trip routings and custom maps with the TripTik® Travel Planner on AAA.com or CAA.ca

Your Destination *Awaits*

AAA/CAA online travel information helps you pick the places you want to go. Get in-depth details for top destinations with **Travel Guides on AAA.com and CAA.ca**. Use **TripTik® Travel Planner** for maps, directions, hotel and restaurant information and much more.

AAA.com/travel and CAA.ca/travel
For complete trip planning resources

GREEN VALLEY pop. 21,391

- Hotels & Restaurants map & index p. 290
- Part of Tucson area — see map p. 268

COMFORT INN

Phone: (520)399-3736 **2**

Hotel
$110-$120

Address: 90 W Esperanza Blvd 85614 **Location:** I-19 exit 65, just w. **Facility:** 55 units. 2 stories, interior corridors. **Pool(s):** outdoor. **Activities:** whirlpool, exercise room. **Guest Services:** coin laundry. **Free Special Amenities: expanded continental breakfast and high-speed Internet.**

HOLIDAY INN EXPRESS

Phone: 520/625-0900 **1**

Hotel
Rates not provided

Address: 19200 S I-19 Frontage Rd 85614 **Location:** I-19 exit 69 (Duval Mine Rd), west side of interstate, then just s. **Facility:** 60 units. 3 stories, interior corridors. **Amenities:** high-speed Internet. **Pool(s):** heated indoor. **Activities:** whirlpool. **Guest Services:** coin laundry.

INN AT SAN IGNACIO CONDO HOTEL

Phone: (520)393-5700 **3**

Condominium
$79-$169 2/1-3/31
$69-$159 4/1-1/31

Address: 1861 W Demetrie Loop 85622 **Location:** I-19 exit 56 (Canoa Rd), 0.5 mi n on Frontage Rd, 0.3 mi w on Calle Tres, then just n on Camino Del Sol, follow signs. **Facility:** In a residential area, these units are large and well appointed, some with a washer and dryer. 84 condominiums. 1 story, exterior corridors. **Terms:** office hours 7 am-6 pm. **Pool(s):** heated outdoor. **Activities:** whirlpool. **Fee:** golf-36 holes. **Guest Services:** area transportation-within 5 mi. **Free Special Amenities: local telephone calls and high-speed Internet.**

Learn about
AAA/CAA Diamond Ratings
at AAA.com/Diamonds

WYNDHAM CANOA RANCH RESORT

Phone: (520)382-0450 **4**

Resort
Condominium
$79-$379

Address: 5775 S Camino Del Sol 85622 **Location:** I-19 exit 56 (Canoa Rd), just w, 0.5 mi n on Frontage Rd to Calle Tres, just w, then 1 mi s. **Facility:** Located across from the golf club, the well-appointed property offers lovely, spacious rooms. 90 condominiums. 3 stories, interior corridors. **Terms:** 3 day cancellation notice-fee imposed. **Amenities:** high-speed Internet. **Pool(s):** heated outdoor. **Activities:** whirlpool, exercise room. **Fee:** golf-36 holes, massage. **Free Special Amenities: newspaper.** *(See ad this page.)*

WHERE TO EAT

AGAVE AT DESERT DIAMOND CASINO

Phone: 520/342-2328 **1**

Regional American
$13-$25

AAA Inspector Notes: After a show or an evening in the casino, patrons can relax and enjoy friendly service and such dishes as Sea of Cortez cabrilla with cremini and green chiles. Chargrilled steaks are a specialty. **Bar:** full bar. **Reservations:** suggested. **Address:** 1100 W Pima Mine Rd 85629 **Location:** I-19 exit 80, just e; in Desert Diamond Casino. **Parking:** on-site and valet. L D

GRILL AT QUAIL CREEK

Phone: 520/393-5806 **2**

American
$8-$22

AAA Inspector Notes: Attractive contemporary decor surrounds this dining room, where guests eat overlooking the golf course. Friendly servers bring out freshly made and attractively presented beef, pork and seafood dishes. **Bar:** full bar. **Address:** 1490 N Quail Range Loop, #3 85614 **Location:** I-19 exit 63, 3.9 mi e, n on Continental Rd/Old Nogales Hwy, then 1.5 mi s. L D

▼ See AAA listing this page ▼

BE A FAMILY THAT TRAVELS, SWIMS, GOLFS AND HIKES TOGETHER. OR FIND YOUR OWN SEPARATE CORNERS OF PARADISE AND ENJOY A GOOD BOOK. AT WYNDHAM CANOA RANCH RESORT, FUN AND RELAXATION ARE AWAITING YOUR WHOLE FAMILY.

WATER BREAK

WYNDHAM
Hotels and Resorts

WYNDHAM CANOA RANCH RESORT
5775 S CAMINO DEL SOL
GREEN VALLEY, AZ 85622
CALL (520)382-0450
1-800-WYNDHAM OR VISIT
WWW.CANOARANCHGOLFRESORT.COM

Get the free mobile app at
http://gettag.mobi

All Wyndham® hotels are either franchised by the company or managed by Wyndham Hotel Management, Inc., one of its affiliates or through a joint-venture partner. ©2012 Wyndham Hotels and Resorts, LLC. All rights reserved.

(See map & index p. 290.)

GRILL ON THE GREEN AT CANOA RANCH GOLF CLUB
Phone: 520/393-1933   ④

▼▼▼
American
$8-$30

AAA Inspector Notes: Located in the Canoa Ranch Clubhouse, this casual spot offers great views across the putting green and valley to the Santa Rita Mountains. Feast on Australian grilled lamb with winter berry sauce or pistachio-crusted salmon. **Bar:** full bar. **Address:** 5800 S Camino del Sol 85614 **Location:** I-19 exit 56 (Canoa Rd), just w, 0.5 mi n on Frontage Rd, 0.3 mi w on Calle Tres, then 1 mi s. Ⓑ Ⓛ Ⓓ

LAVENDER   **Phone:** 520/648-0205   ③

▼▼▼
French
$8-$28

AAA Inspector Notes: A surprise is in store at this attractive bistro overlooking a golf course. The classically trained chef has adapted recipes using regional ingredients to create dishes that blend flavors and textures. Enjoyable dishes include rack of lamb with herbe de Provence crust and East Coast-style crab cakes. **Bar:** full bar. **Reservations:** suggested. **Address:** 77 E Paseo de Golf 85614 **Location:** I-19 exit 69, just e to Abrego Dr, then 2 mi s; in Country Club of Green Valley. Ⓛ Ⓓ

HAYDEN (E-5) pop. 662, elev. 2,062'

RAY MINE, off SR 177 at 27809 N. Mineral Creek Rd., is an open-pit copper mine. No tours of the mine are currently offered. **Hours:** An overlook is open daily 7-3. **Phone:** (520) 356-7811, ext. 2211.

HEBER

BEST WESTERN SAWMILL INN   **Phone:** (928)535-5053

◆◆
Motel
$60-$92

AAA Benefit: Members save up to 20%, plus 10% bonus points with Best Western Rewards®.

Address: 1877 Hwy 260 85928 **Location:** 0.5 mi e of center. **Facility:** 43 units. 2 stories (no elevator), exterior corridors. **Terms:** cancellation fee imposed. **Amenities:** *Some:* high-speed Internet. **Activities:** exercise room. **Guest Services:** coin laundry. **Free Special Amenities:** local telephone calls and high-speed Internet.

[SAVE] [ECO] [BIZ] 🛜 ▤ ▥ ▦ / SOME UNITS FEE 🐾

WHERE TO EAT

RED ONION LOUNGE   **Phone:** 928/535-4433

▼
American
$5-$18

AAA Inspector Notes: This restaurant's popular burgers are made from fresh USDA Choice ground chuck and cooked over an open flame. Great finger food appetizers, homemade soups, prime rib, baked ham steak, mesquite-grilled chicken and hand-cut fresh French-fried potatoes are among choices at the lively and laid-back sports bar, where NASCAR is central to the theme. **Bar:** full bar. **Address:** Hwy 260 85933 **Location:** SR 260, east of town. Ⓛ Ⓓ

HEREFORD (G-5) elev. 7,587'

THE NATURE CONSERVANCY'S RAMSEY CANYON PRESERVE is 5.9 mi. s. on SR 92 from jct. SR 90, then 3.5 mi. w. to 27 E. Ramsey Canyon Rd. The 380-acre preserve serves as a sanctuary for more than 400 species of plants; 170 species of birds, including hummingbirds and painted redstarts; various species of butterflies; and other wildlife, including black bears and Yarrow's spiny lizards. A natural history interpretive center is available.

Note: Parking is limited to 23 spaces. Picnicking is permitted only at the headquarters. Pets are not permitted. **Hours:** Daily 8-5, Mar.-Aug.; Thurs.-Mon. 8-5, rest of year. Guided 2-hour nature walks are offered Mon., Thurs. and Sat. at 9, Mar.-Oct. Closed Thanksgiving and Christmas. **Cost:** (Valid for 7 days) $5; free (ages 0-15 and first Sat. of the month). **Phone:** (520) 378-2785. 🏛

HOLBROOK (C-5) pop. 5,053, elev. 5,080'

Holbrook was founded in 1881 when the Atlantic and Pacific Railroad reached this point. Once called the "town too tough for women and churches," the community was named for Henry R. Holbrook, chief engineer of the railroad project. The seat of Navajo County, Holbrook is close to Petrified Forest National Park *(see place listing p. 168)* and several reservations.

The Little Colorado River's sweeping turns traverse westward through town, and the terrain consists of flat plains, rugged hills and small buttes. Official U.S. mail is delivered to Scottsdale in late January when the Pony Express rides from Holbrook.

The Navajo County Historic Courthouse, 100 E. Arizona St., hosts Native American dances Mon.-Fri. evenings, June-July. Phone the chamber of commerce to confirm schedule.

Holbrook Chamber of Commerce: 100 E. Arizona St., Holbrook, AZ 86025. **Phone:** (928) 524-6558 or (800) 524-2459.

Self-guiding tours: A self-guiding tour including the Navajo County Courthouse/Museum is available. Brochures can be obtained at the chamber of commerce.

Complete Vacation Planning

AAA.com/Travel and **CAA.ca/Travel** – everything you need to plan and book your vacations, backed by the travel experts at local AAA/CAA offices.

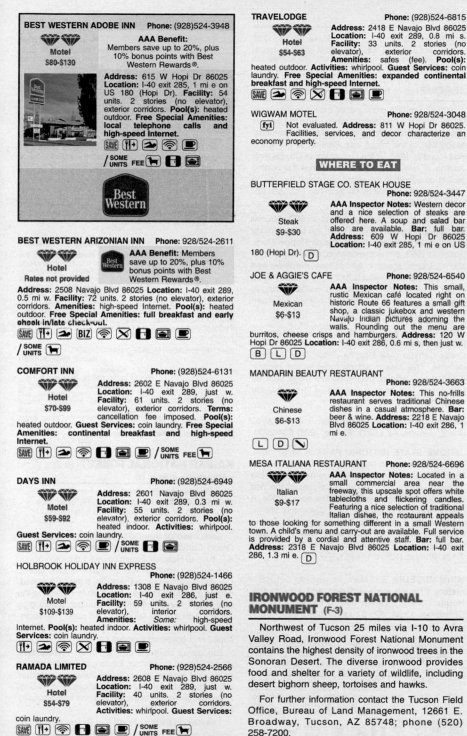

BEST WESTERN ADOBE INN   Phone: (928)524-3948

Motel
$80-$130

AAA Benefit: Members save up to 20%, plus 10% bonus points with Best Western Rewards®.

Address: 615 W Hopi Dr 86025 **Location:** I-40 exit 285, 1 mi e on US 180 (Hopi Dr). **Facility:** 54 units. 2 stories (no elevator), exterior corridors. **Pool(s):** heated outdoor. **Free Special Amenities: local telephone calls and high-speed Internet.**

BEST WESTERN ARIZONIAN INN   Phone: 928/524-2611

Hotel
Rates not provided

AAA Benefit: Members save up to 20%, plus 10% bonus points with Best Western Rewards®.

Address: 2508 Navajo Blvd 86025 **Location:** I-40 exit 289, 0.5 mi w. **Facility:** 72 units. 2 stories (no elevator), exterior corridors. **Amenities:** high-speed Internet. **Pool(s):** heated outdoor. **Free Special Amenities: full breakfast and early check in/late check-out.**

COMFORT INN   Phone: (928)524-6131

Hotel
$70-$99

Address: 2602 E Navajo Blvd 86025 **Location:** I-40 exit 289, just w. **Facility:** 61 units. 2 stories (no elevator), exterior corridors. **Terms:** cancellation fee imposed. **Pool(s):** heated outdoor. **Guest Services:** coin laundry. **Free Special Amenities: continental breakfast and high-speed Internet.**

DAYS INN   Phone: (928)524-6949

Motel
$59-$92

Address: 2601 Navajo Blvd 86025 **Location:** I-40 exit 289, 0.3 mi w. **Facility:** 55 units. 2 stories (no elevator), exterior corridors. **Pool(s):** heated indoor. **Activities:** whirlpool.

Guest Services: coin laundry.

HOLBROOK HOLIDAY INN EXPRESS   Phone: (928)524-1466

Motel
$109-$139

Address: 1308 E Navajo Blvd 86025 **Location:** I-40 exit 286, just e. **Facility:** 59 units. 2 stories (no elevator), interior corridors. **Amenities:** Some: high-speed Internet. **Pool(s):** heated indoor. **Activities:** whirlpool. **Guest Services:** coin laundry.

RAMADA LIMITED   Phone: (928)524-2566

Hotel
$54-$79

Address: 2608 E Navajo Blvd 86025 **Location:** I-40 exit 289, just w. **Facility:** 40 units. 2 stories (no elevator), exterior corridors. **Activities:** whirlpool. **Guest Services:** coin laundry.

TRAVELODGE   Phone: (928)524-6815

Hotel
$54-$63

Address: 2418 E Navajo Blvd 86025 **Location:** I-40 exit 289, 0.8 mi s. **Facility:** 33 units. 2 stories (no elevator), exterior corridors. **Amenities:** safes (fee). **Pool(s):** heated outdoor. **Activities:** whirlpool. **Guest Services:** coin laundry. **Free Special Amenities: expanded continental breakfast and high-speed Internet.**

WIGWAM MOTEL   Phone: 928/524-3048

fyi   Not evaluated. **Address:** 811 W Hopi Dr 86025. Facilities, services, and decor characterize an economy property.

WHERE TO EAT

BUTTERFIELD STAGE CO. STEAK HOUSE   Phone: 928/524-3447

Steak
$9-$30

AAA Inspector Notes: Western decor and a nice selection of steaks are offered here. A soup and salad bar also are available. **Bar:** full bar. **Address:** 609 W Hopi Dr 86025 **Location:** I-40 exit 285, 1 mi e on US 180 (Hopi Dr). D

JOE & AGGIE'S CAFE   Phone: 928/524-6540

Mexican
$6-$13

AAA Inspector Notes: This small, rustic Mexican café located right on historic Route 66 features a small gift shop, a classic jukebox and western Navajo Indian pictures adorning the walls. Rounding out the menu are burritos, cheese crisps and hamburgers. **Address:** 120 W Hopi Dr 86025 **Location:** I-40 exit 286, 0.6 mi s, then just w. B L D

MANDARIN BEAUTY RESTAURANT   Phone: 928/524-3663

Chinese
$6-$13

AAA Inspector Notes: This no-frills restaurant serves traditional Chinese dishes in a casual atmosphere. **Bar:** beer & wine. **Address:** 2218 E Navajo Blvd 86025 **Location:** I-40 exit 286, 1 mi e. L D

MESA ITALIANA RESTAURANT   Phone: 928/524-6696

Italian
$9-$17

AAA Inspector Notes: Located in a small commercial area near the freeway, this upscale spot offers white tablecloths and flickering candles. Featuring a nice selection of traditional Italian dishes, the restaurant appeals to those looking for something different in a small Western town. A child's menu and carry-out are available. Full service is provided by a cordial and attentive staff. **Bar:** full bar. **Address:** 2318 E Navajo Blvd 86025 **Location:** I-40 exit 286, 1.3 mi e. D

IRONWOOD FOREST NATIONAL MONUMENT (F-3)

Northwest of Tucson 25 miles via I-10 to Avra Valley Road, Ironwood Forest National Monument contains the highest density of ironwood trees in the Sonoran Desert. The diverse ironwood provides food and shelter for a variety of wildlife, including desert bighorn sheep, tortoises and hawks.

For further information contact the Tucson Field Office, Bureau of Land Management, 12661 E. Broadway, Tucson, AZ 85748; phone (520) 258-7200.

JACOB LAKE

JACOB LAKE INN   **Phone:** 928/643-7232
(fyi) Not evaluated. **Address:** Jct SR 89A & 67 86002. Facilities, services, and decor characterize an economy property.

JEROME (C-3) pop. 444, elev. 5,435'

In 1582 Spanish missionaries exploring the Verde Valley recorded that natives were using the copper mines near what is now Jerome. The missionaries' description of the mines was identical to the workings found in 1883 by the United Verde Co. Eugene Jerome of New York agreed to finance the mining project on condition the camp be named for him. In 1886 a smelter arrived by rail from Ash Fork and operations began in earnest.

Once a city with a population of 15,000, Jerome became a virtual ghost town when the United Verde Branch copper mines of the Phelps Dodge Corp. closed in 1953. Since then, shops, galleries, studios and museums, some housed in former brothels and saloons, have been established in the restored town which clings to Cleopatra Hill on the side of Mingus Mountain. Some of the restored homes are open during the Home Tour in May.

A 54-mile scenic stretch of SR 89A begins in Flagstaff and winds its way south through Oak Creek Canyon (see Sedona p. 228) and ends in Jerome. The steep, narrow road is not recommended for vehicles pulling trailers more than 40 feet long. The nearby mountains are ideal for camping, fishing and hunting.

Jerome Chamber of Commerce: 310 Hull Ave., Box K, Jerome, AZ 86331. **Phone:** (928) 634-2900.

JEROME STATE HISTORIC PARK is off SR 89A. The park museum in the 1916 adobe brick Douglas Mansion traces the history of local mining and the family of James S. Douglas, developer of the rich United Verde Extension Mine in the early 1900s. A movie highlighting the history of Jerome is shown continuously. **Time:** Allow 1 hour minimum. **Hours:** Park and museum Thurs.-Mon. 8:30-5. Closed Christmas. **Cost:** (Includes museum) $5; $2 (ages 7-13). **Phone:** (928) 634-5381. 🎫

MINE MUSEUM, 200 Main St., depicts Jerome's history through mine artifacts and equipment. **Hours:** Daily 9-5. Closed Jan. 1, Thanksgiving and Christmas. **Cost:** $2; $1 (ages 60+); free (ages 0-11). **Phone:** (928) 634-5477.

CONNOR HOTEL OF JEROME   Phone: (928)634-5006
◆◆◆◆◆   **Address:** 160 S Main St 86331
Historic Hotel   **Location:** Center. **Facility:** The
$95-$175   historic 1898 hotel offers charming renovated rooms filled with period pieces and modern tiled baths. 12 units. 2 stories (no elevator), interior corridors. **Parking:** street only. **Terms:** office hours 8 am-9 pm, 3 day cancellation notice. **Free Special Amenities:** newspaper and high-speed Internet.
[SAVE] 🛏️ 🍸 📶 🔌 🖨️ 💻 / SOME UNITS 🛏️

WHERE TO EAT

ALICE'S RESTAURANT   **Phone:** 928/634-2069
◆   **AAA Inspector Notes:** This small
Sandwiches   family-run restaurant concentrates on
$6-$12   fresh and organic soups, salads, sandwiches and breakfast items. It is very casual with freshly-made daily specials and popular outdoor seating.
Address: 403 Clark St, Suite B-8 86331 **Location:** Center. **Parking:** street only. [B] [L]

THE ASYLUM RESTAURANT   **Phone:** 928/639-3197
◆◆◆   **AAA Inspector Notes:** Billed as fun,
                       fine dining, the experience at this cozy
American   restaurant includes relaxed service
$10-$28   and spectacular views. The wide selection of wines, interesting sauces and creative combinations, such as roast maple leaf duck breast on green chili brown rice with plum serrano salsa, add up to fine dining. **Bar:** full bar. **Reservations:** suggested. **Address:** 200 Hill St 86331 **Location:** 0.3 mi s on SR 89A, just s on Cobblestone Rd; center; in Jerome Grand Hotel. [L] [D]

GRAPES   **Phone:** 928/639-8477
◆◆   **AAA Inspector Notes:** Although the
                       pizza is famous locally, other menu
Pizza   items-including hearty sandwiches,
$7-$14   entrée salads and full dinners-also are worth trying. A wine theme is carried through with different wines used in preparing the food and a selection of wine flights available for tasting. A nice outdoor dining patio makes a good rest stop. **Bar:** full bar. **Address:** 111 Main St 86331 **Location:** Center. **Parking:** street only. [L] [D]

JEROME PALACE/HAUNTED HAMBURGER
                              Phone: 928/634-0554
◆   **AAA Inspector Notes:** Patrons
                       should arrive before they are hungry,
American   as there is always a line waiting to
$5-$19   wolf down the great burgers and comfort food. In a historic house overlooking the valley, the restaurant is a good spot to rest and recuperate after the steep street walking tour. **Bar:** full bar. **Address:** 410 Clark St 86331 **Location:** Center. **Parking:** street only. [L] [D]

KAIBAB NATIONAL FOREST (B-3)
• Attractions map p. 86

Elevations in the forest range from 3,000 ft. to 10,418 ft. at Kendrick Peak. Refer to AAA maps for additional elevation information.

Comprised of three districts north and south of Grand Canyon National Park (see place listing p. 84), Kaibab National Forest covers 1.6 million acres. The portion north of the canyon includes Grand Canyon National Game Preserve, a thickly forested, domed limestone plateau. The Kaibab Plateau is the only known home of the Kaibab squirrel, a dark gray squirrel with a white tail and tufted ears. The southernmost of the three districts contains volcanic cones and scattered forested peaks.

Big game animals can be seen in roadside meadows and throughout the forest. Fishing can be enjoyed at several lakes. Recreational opportunities within the national forest include camping, hiking, mountain biking, horseback riding and cross-country skiing.

The Kaibab Plateau-North Rim Scenic Byway has been described as the most beautiful 42 miles in the

United States. The scenic parkway begins at Jacob Lake and winds through dense forests and alpine meadows to culminate at the North Rim of the Grand Canyon; the road is closed mid-October through May.

For further information contact the Kaibab Plateau Visitor Center, US 89A and SR 67, Jacob Lake, AZ 86022, phone (928) 643-7298; or the Williams and Forest Service Visitor Center, 200 W. Railroad Ave., Williams, AZ 86046; phone (928) 635-4061 or (800) 863-0546. *See Recreation Chart.*

KAYENTA (A-5) pop. 5,189, elev. 5,641'

Kayenta grew from a trading post that John Wetherill established in 1910. He first called it Oljeto, but eventually changed the name to Kayenta after a deep spring nearby. The area's uranium and coal deposits are important in the town's economy. Scenic US 163, beginning at US 160, passes through Kayenta before running 22 miles north to the Utah border and the entrance to Monument Valley Navajo Tribal Park *(see place listing p. 117).*

Crawley's Monument Valley Tours offers backcountry trips into areas of the park. For further information about the tours and the area contact Crawley's Monument Valley Tours, P.O. Box 187, Kayenta, AZ 86033; phone (928) 697-3463.

HAMPTON INN OF KAYENTA   Phone: 928/697-3170

◆◆◆
Hotel
Rates not provided

AAA Benefit: Members save up to 10% everyday!

Address: Hwy 160 86033 **Location:** Just w of US 163. **Facility:** 73 units. 3 stories, interior corridors. **Terms:** check-in 4 pm. **Dining:** Reuben Heflin Restaurant, see separate listing. **Pool(s):** heated outdoor. **Guest Services:** coin laundry.

WETHERILL INN   Phone: (928)697-3231

◆◆◆
Hotel
$85-$150

Address: US 163 86033 **Location:** 1 mi n of jct US 160. **Facility:** 54 units. 2 stories (no elevator), exterior corridors. **Terms:** cancellation fee imposed. **Amenities:** *Some:* high-speed Internet. **Pool(s):** heated indoor. **Guest Services:** coin laundry. **Free Special Amenities:** continental breakfast and high-speed Internet.

Wetherill Inn
Gateway to Monument Valley
FREE Continental Breakfast & High Speed Internet. Indoor Pool, Laundry.

Check out
our travel blog at
AAATravelViews.com

REUBEN HEFLIN RESTAURANT   Phone: 928/697-3170

◆◆
Regional American
$9-$24

AAA Inspector Notes: The decor is decidedly Southwestern, with an exposed beam ceiling and a warm fireplace. The menu centers on steak, seafood and Southwestern entrées. **Address:** Hwy 160 86033 **Location:** Just w of US 163; in Hampton Inn of Kayenta.

KEAMS CANYON (B-5) pop. 304, elev. 6,184'

Keams Canyon is within the Hopi Reservation that occupies a large tract in the center of the vast Navajo Reservation of northeastern Arizona. The reservation is crossed by SR 264, which runs between US 491, 8 miles north of Gallup, N.M., and US 160 at Tuba City. Noted for weaving, pottery and jewelry, the Hopi also farm and raise livestock. Information about Hopi ceremonies can be obtained from the Hopi Indian Agency in Keams Canyon, (928) 738-2228, or from the Hopi tribal headquarters in Kykotsmovi, (928) 734-3100.

Of particular interest are the villages of Old Oraibi and Walpi on First Mesa. High on a narrow, rocky mesa, Old Oraibi is possibly the oldest of the present Hopi villages; it is thought to be one of the oldest continuously inhabited cities in the country. A trading post and schools are in each village, and the main tribal headquarters is at nearby Kykotsmovi. Walpi occupies the end of a high mesa, where ancestors of the present inhabitants began building about 1680. You can learn about Hopi history and culture on a guided 1-hour walking tour of the First Mesa villages; for information phone Ponsi Hall Visitor Center, (928) 737-2262.

No photography, painting, recording or sketching are permitted while on the Hopi Reservation. Primitive campgrounds are at Second Mesa, next to the Hopi Cultural Center; phone (928) 734-2401.

KINGMAN (C-2) pop. 28,068, elev. 3,334'
• Hotels p. 102 • Restaurants p. 104

Kingman, the county seat of Mohave County, was established in the early 1880s with the arrival of the railroad.

Kingman's popularity is maintained as the main stop on the longest existing stretch of Historic Route 66—the first completely paved national highway in the country. Linking hundreds of towns and cities between Chicago and Los Angeles, Route 66 formed the main street of towns along its route, thus its nickname "Main Street of America." Today travelers can traverse some 140 miles of historic roadway beginning west of Ashfork, continuing from Seligman through Peach Springs to Kingman and through Oatman and Goldroad to Topock. For a self-guiding driving tour brochure contact the Historic Route 66 Association, 120 W. Andy Devine Ave., P.O. Box 66, Kingman, AZ 86402; phone (928) 753-5001.

Some 700 classic cars start their engines in Seligman and head 140 miles to Topock/Golden

Shores during the  Historic Route 66 Fun Run, held the first weekend in May. Communities along the route celebrate with food and entertainment.

At the junction of I-40 and US 93, Kingman is an access point to lakes Mead, Mohave and Havasu. Ghost towns surround this former gold-mining community. One such town is Oatman, a business and social center for surrounding mining camps during the early 20th century. With many of its original buildings still standing, Oatman draws both filmmakers and tourists. Visitors may even hand-feed the burros—descendants of those left behind by early-day miners—that roam the town's streets. From Kingman, Oatman is reached by SR 66 (Old Route 66).

Hualapai Mountain Park, 12 miles southeast, is named for the Native Americans who inhabited the mountains until the 1870s. Mountain elevations range from 5,000 to 8,500 feet. A variety of native wildlife lives here, including deer, eagles, elk, foxes, hawks, rabbits and squirrels. *See Recreation Chart.*

Kingman Powerhouse Visitor Center: 120 W. Andy Devine Ave., Kingman, AZ 86401. **Phone:** (928) 753-6106 or (866) 427-7866.

BONELLI HOUSE is e. off I-40 exit 48, then .2 mi. n. to 430 E. Spring St. Built in 1915, Bonelli House depicts the lifestyle of a prominent Arizona family in the early 20th century. It is outfitted with original furnishings and other period pieces similar to those used by the Bonelli family.

Features include a Victorian-style cupola where the children acted as sentries for their father's arrival from work, and a large wall clock that was once the only clock in town. **Time:** Allow 1 hour minimum. **Hours:** Mon.-Fri. 11-3. Closed major holidays. **Cost:** Donations. **Phone:** (928) 753-3195.

HISTORIC ROUTE 66 MUSEUM is at 120 W. Andy Devine Ave. Dioramas, murals and photos depict the history of historic Route 66 from its early use by Native Americans and pioneers to the travelers of the 1950s. A short film is presented; a reading room and archive are available. **Time:** Allow 30 minutes minimum. **Hours:** Daily 9-5. Closed Jan. 1, Easter, Thanksgiving and Christmas. **Cost:** $4; $3 (ages 61+); free (ages 0-12). Admission includes admittance to Bonelli House and Mohave Museum of History and Arts. **Phone:** (928) 753-9889.

MOHAVE MUSEUM OF HISTORY AND ARTS is off I-40 exit 48 .25 mi. s.e. to 400 W. Beale St. (US 93). Collections of turquoise, re-created Mohave and Hualapai dwellings and local artifacts and artwork depict the history of northwest Arizona. Other exhibits feature Andy Devine memorabilia, Lawrence Williams' portraits of presidents and first ladies and Mohave County ranching history. A re-created copper mine outfitted with original mining equipment depicts miners at work.

Hours: Mon.-Fri. 9-5, Sat. 1-5. Closed major holidays. **Cost:** (includes pass to Historic Route 66 Museum and Bonelli House) $4; $3 (ages 60+); free

(ages 0-11 with adult). **Phone:** (928) 753-3195.

BEST WESTERN PLUS A WAYFARER'S INN & SUITES   Phone: (928)753-6271

Hotel
$96-$128

AAA Benefit: Members save up to 20%, plus 10% bonus points with Best Western Rewards®.

Address: 2815 E Andy Devine Ave 86401 **Location:** I-40 exit 53, 0.5 mi w on Route 66. **Facility:** 101 units, some two bedrooms and efficiencies. 2 stories (no elevator), exterior corridors. **Amenities:** high-speed Internet. **Pool(s):** heated outdoor. **Activities:** whirlpool, exercise room. **Guest Services:** valet and coin laundry. Free Special Amenities: full breakfast and high-speed Internet. (See ad p. 103.)

BEST WESTERN PLUS KING'S INN & SUITES   Phone: (928)753-6101

Hotel
$94-$128

AAA Benefit: Members save up to 20%, plus 10% bonus points with Best Western Rewards®.

Address: 2930 E Andy Devine Ave 86401 **Location:** I-40 exit 53, just w on Route 66. **Facility:** 101 units, some two bedrooms and efficiencies. 2 stories (no elevator), exterior corridors. **Amenities:** high-speed Internet. **Pool(s):** heated outdoor. **Activities:** whirlpool, exercise room. **Guest Services:** valet and coin laundry. Free Special Amenities: full breakfast and high-speed Internet.

Best Western PLUS

The hospitality of "the mother road," with all the modern features, and a Free Hot Breakfast Buffet!

COMFORT INN   Phone: (928)718-1717

Motel
$95-$170

Address: 3129 E Andy Devine Ave 86401 **Location:** I-40 exit 53, just w on Route 66. **Facility:** 60 units. 3 stories, interior corridors. **Terms:** cancellation fee imposed. **Pool(s):** heated indoor. **Activities:** whirlpool, exercise room. **Guest Services:** coin laundry.

DAYS INN WEST   Phone: (928)753-7500

Motel
$44-$72

Address: 3023 E Andy Devine Ave 86401 **Location:** I-40 exit 53, just w on Route 66. **Facility:** 60 units. 2 stories (no elevator), exterior corridors. **Pool(s):** heated outdoor. **Activities:** whirlpool. **Guest Services:** coin laundry. Free Special Amenities: continental breakfast and high-speed Internet.

HAMPTON INN & SUITES   Phone: 928/692-0200

Hotel

AAA Benefit: Members save up to 10% everyday!

Rates not provided

Address: 1791 Sycamore Ave 86409 **Location:** I-40 exit 51, 0.3 mi n. **Facility:** 86 units. 4 stories, interior corridors. **Amenities:** video games (fee), high-speed Internet. **Pool(s):** heated indoor. **Activities:** whirlpool, exercise room. **Guest Services:** valet and coin laundry. **Free Special Amenities:** full breakfast and high-speed Internet.

SAVE 📶 CALL 🛗 🏊 BIZ 🛜 FEE 🎦 🖥 📺

📋

HOLIDAY INN EXPRESS HOTEL & SUITES   Phone: (928)718-4343

Hotel

$119-$219 4/17-1/31
$109-$199 2/1-4/16

Address: 3031 E Andy Devine Ave 86401 **Location:** I-40 exit 53, just w on Route 66. **Facility:** 75 units, some two bedrooms. 3 stories, interior corridors. **Terms:** cancellation fee imposed. **Amenities:** high-speed Internet. **Pool(s):** heated indoor. **Activities:** whirlpool, exercise room. **Guest Services:** valet and coin laundry. **Free Special Amenities:** full breakfast and high-speed Internet.

SAVE 📶 CALL 🛗 🏊 BIZ 🛜 🖥 📺 📋

/ SOME UNITS FEE 🐾

▼ See AAA listing p. 102 ▼

BEST WESTERN PLUS
A Wayfarer's Inn & Suites

AAA MEMBER DISCOUNT
20% Nov.-Feb.
15% Mar.-Oct.
Off Published Rates

Our most frequent guest comment is
"The best breakfast and cleanest hotel on our entire trip."

Easy access at I-40, Exit 53
2815 E. Andy Devine Rt. 66, Kingman, AZ 86401
www.bestwestern.com/awayfarersinn

For Reservations Call:
800-548-5695
928-753-6271

Get the free mobile app at
http://gettag.mobi

ALL ROOMS INCLUDE:

FREE FULL HOT BREAKFAST BUFFET

37" Flat Screen TVs, Free HBO
Free High-Speed Internet, Wired and Wireless
Granite Countertops in Newly Upgraded Baths
Refrigerators with Freezers & Microwaves

Select Queen Rooms, King Mini-Suites
Family or Executive Suites
Non-Smoking & a few smoking allowed rooms

Business Center
Fitness Center, Guest Laundry

Enclosed Heated Whirlpool
Seasonal Heated Exterior Swimming Pool

Located on the Quiet Side of the Highway

MOTEL 6 - 1114
Phone: (928)753-9222

Motel

$42-$52 5/28-1/31
$39-$49 2/1-5/27

Address: 424 W Beale St 86401 **Location:** I-40 exit 48, just se on Business Loop I-40/US 93. **Facility:** 80 units. 2 stories (no elevator), exterior corridors. **Pool(s):** heated outdoor. **Guest Services:** coin laundry.

SPRINGHILL SUITES BY MARRIOTT
Phone: (928)753-8766

Hotel

$98-$123

AAA Benefit: AAA hotel discounts of 5% or more.

Address: 3101 E Andy Devine Ave 86401 **Location:** I-40 exit 53, just w on Route 66. **Facility:** 73 units. 4 stories, interior corridors. **Amenities:** high-speed Internet. **Pool(s):** heated indoor. **Activities:** exercise room. **Guest Services:** valet and coin laundry. **Free Special Amenities:** full breakfast and high-speed Internet.

TRAVELODGE
Phone: (928)757-1188

Motel

$50-$59

Address: 3275 E Andy Devine Ave 86401 **Location:** I-40 exit 53, just e on Route 66. **Facility:** 65 units. 2 stories (no elevator), exterior corridors. **Amenities:** safes (fee). **Pool(s):** heated outdoor. **Guest Services:** coin laundry. **Free Special Amenities:** expanded continental breakfast and high-speed Internet.

WHERE TO EAT

ABC RESTAURANT
Phone: 928/753-6363

Chinese
$6-$15

AAA Inspector Notes: American and Chinese dishes can be ordered from the menu, and a Chinese buffet is available for both lunch and dinner. **Bar:** full bar. **Address:** 2890 E Andy Devine Ave 86401 **Location:** I-40 exit 53, just sw. L D

DAMBAR & STEAKHOUSE
Phone: 928/753-3523

Steak
$5-$21

AAA Inspector Notes: The menu incorporates a nice selection of steak, ribs, sandwiches and salads. The atmosphere is friendly. **Bar:** full bar. **Address:** 1960 E Andy Devine Ave 86401 **Location:** I-40 exit 53, 1.2 mi sw. L D

EL PALACIO
Phone: 928/718-0018

Mexican
$10-$21

AAA Inspector Notes: Located right on Route 66 in downtown Kingman in a building that is more than 100 years old, this family spot serves traditional fresh Mexican items. Menu highlights include chimichangas, burritos and marimba all served by casual and friendly staff. **Bar:** full bar. **Address:** 401 E Andy Devine Ave 86401 **Location:** Jct 4th St. **Parking:** on-site and street. L D

HUNAN CHINESE RESTAURANT
Phone: 928/692-8333

Chinese
$5-$10

AAA Inspector Notes: This family-run restaurant offers a reasonably priced lunch and dinner buffet in a traditionally decorated Asian-theme dining room. A regular menu offers several traditional Chinese cuisine. **Address:** 1851 Kino Ave 86409 **Location:** I-40 exit 51, 1 mi n, then just e. L D

KINGMAN CO. STEAKHOUSE
Phone: 928/718-2292

Steak
$6-$30

AAA Inspector Notes: Just off the interstate, this steakhouse is convenient for travelers. Casual, rustic decor incorporates antiques and stories of old settlers along the walls. The menu focuses on large cowboy-style steaks. **Bar:** full bar. **Address:** 3157 Stockton Hill Rd 86401 **Location:** I-40 exit 51, just s. L D

MATTINA'S RISTORANTE & STEAKHOUSE
Phone: 928/753-7504

Italian
$13-$25

AAA Inspector Notes: Located in an intimate yet casual cottage in historic downtown, this family-owned and operated bistro features aged premium steaks cut when ordered, as well as fresh seafood and Italian pasta dishes. The homemade tiramisu is a perennial favorite. Patio seating also is available. **Bar:** full bar. **Address:** 318 Oak St 86401 **Location:** Between 3rd and 4th sts; downtown. **Parking:** street only. D

MR. D'Z ROUTE 66 DINER
Phone: 928/718-0066

American
$5-$16

AAA Inspector Notes: Nestled along historic Route 66, patrons at this traditional 1950s-style diner can select seating at the counter or in pink and turquoise vinyl booths. Traditional diner fare is served such as burgers, chicken sandwich, chicken fried steak, all-day breakfast items and, of course, homemade desserts. **Address:** 105 E Andy Devine Ave 86401 **Location:** Jct Old Route 66 and 1st St; downtown. B L D

REDNECK'S SOUTHERN PIT BBQ
Phone: 928/757-8227

Southern Barbecue
$8-$18

AAA Inspector Notes: Located in the heart of Kingman, this spot offers Memphis-style barbecue in a fun cafeteria style decor. The family-owned and -operated restaurant is a perfect place for the family. **Address:** 420 E Beale St 86401 **Location:** Between 3rd and 4th sts; downtown. L D

KOHLS RANCH pop. 46

KOHL'S RANCH LODGE
Phone: 928/478-4211

Resort Condominium
Rates not provided

Address: 202 S Kohl's Ranch Lodge Rd 85541 **Location:** SR 87, 16.6 mi e on US 260, MM 238-239. **Facility:** Charming, attractively appointed lodge rooms and creekside cabins, ranging from cozy to spacious, await guests at this mountain resort. 66 condominiums. 1 story, interior/exterior corridors. **Terms:** check-in 4 pm. **Pool(s):** heated outdoor. **Activities:** saunas, whirlpool, fishing, putting green, tennis court, recreation programs in summer, hiking trails, playground, basketball, horseshoes, shuffleboard, volleyball, exercise room. **Fee:** horseback riding, game room. **Guest Services:** coin laundry.

LAKE HAVASU CITY (D-1) pop. 52,527, elev. 482'
• Restaurants p. 107

Lake Havasu City takes its name from the lake by which it lies. (Havasu is a Mohave Indian word meaning "blue-green water.") Formed by the impoundment of Parker Dam in 1938, Lake Havasu is fed by the Colorado River. The 45-mile-long lake has a maximum width of 3 miles and supplies water to Arizona, Los Angeles and intermediate cities.

Paved roads cross the lake at Topock on the north end and Parker Dam at the south end.

In 1963 industrialist Robert P. McCulloch Sr. purchased a 3,500-acre former Army Air Corps landing strip and rest camp on Pittsburg Point, a peninsula jutting into the Colorado River. After expanding the area by another 13,000 acres, McCulloch teamed up with Disneyland developer C.V. Wood to create a planned community and tourist destination.

The new town captured the world's attention in 1968 when McCulloch bought the London Bridge *(see attraction listing).* Originally built in 1831 by architect John Rennie, the multi-arch bridge resided over the Thames River until 1968, when it began to sink into the river. Dismantled stone by stone, the bridge was brought over from London and reconstructed on Pittsburg Point. A man-made canal (known today as Bridgewater Channel) was dug underneath, separating Pittsburg Point from the land and forming an island.

Nowadays the London Bridge is a center for boat tours of Lake Havasu and Topock Gorge. Operators offering a variety of excursions dock their boats under the celebrated span. Narrated cruises aboard various types of watercraft are offered through Blue Water Jet Boat Tours; phone (928) 855-7171 or (888) 855-7171.

Just over the bridge and along the island side of Bridgewater Channel, London Bridge Beach (1340 McCulloch Blvd.) has basketball and sand volleyball courts, playgrounds, picnicking facilities and a dog park. On the opposite side of the channel, Rotary Community Park Beach (1400 S. Smoketree Ave.) features volleyball and bocce courts, a skate park, playgrounds, picnicking facilities, a buoyed swimming area and a boardwalk.

Lake Havasu provides a setting for all types of water-related activities. Fishing is excellent, especially for striped and large-mouth bass, catfish and panfish; several public fishing docks and piers are available. Numerous companies rent canoes, kayaks, houseboats, pontoon boats, sailboats and other watercraft for use on the lake; contact the convention and visitors bureau for more information.

Believe it or not, lighthouses exist in landlocked Arizona. Twenty functioning one-third-scale replicas of famous U.S. lighthouses stand along the shoreline of Lake Havasu, providing navigational aid *and* a conversation piece.

In December a fleet of illuminated boats on the lake makes the 🚩 Boat Parade of Lights a dazzling sight spectators won't soon forget.

Lake Havasu City Convention and Visitors Bureau: 314 London Bridge Rd., Lake Havasu City, AZ 86403. **Phone:** (928) 453-3444 or (800) 242-8278.

Shopping areas: The English Village, Island Fashion Mall, Uptown District/Main Street and Shops at Lake Havasu all provide shopping opportunities in the London Bridge area.

CATTAIL COVE STATE PARK, 15 mi. s. off SR 95, is named after the numerous cattails in the park's cove. Water activities abound in the park. *See Recreation Chart.* Hiking and camping also are available. **Hours:** Daily 8-4:30. **Cost:** Mon.-Thurs. $10 (per private vehicle, up to four passengers); $3 (per additional adult passenger in vehicle or individual arriving on foot or bicycle). Fri.-Sun. $15 (per private vehicle). Camping $26 (per private vehicle). Boat-in campsites $20. Overnight trailer parking $15-$20. **Phone:** (928) 855-1223. 🅰 🍴 ⊗ 🏕 ⊞

HAVASU NATIONAL WILDLIFE REFUGE is off I-40 exit 1, following signs. The refuge consists of two areas: Topock Gorge, south of junction I-40 and the Colorado River, and Topock Marsh, north of I-40 on the Arizona side of the river. Topock Gorge includes the 18,000-acre Havasu Wilderness Area. The 37,515-acre refuge is home to the southwestern willow flycatcher, the Yuma clapper rail, migratory birds, beavers and bighorn sheep. The refuge headquarters is in Needles, Calif.

Note: The gorge is accessible only by boat. Hunting and fishing (in season) are permitted, as are boating and camping in designated areas. **Hours:** Refuge open daily 24 hours. Office open Mon.-Fri. 7:30-3:30. Closed major holidays. **Cost:** Free. **Phone:** (760) 326-3853.

LAKE HAVASU STATE PARK, n. of London Bridge off SR 95 and London Bridge Rd., stretches along the river. *See Recreation Chart.* Camping and hiking are available. **Hours:** Daily dawn-10 p.m. **Cost:** Day use fee Mon.-Thurs. $10 (per private vehicle, up to four passengers); $3 (per additional adult passenger in vehicle or individual arriving on foot or bicycle). Day use fee Fri.-Sun. $15 (per private vehicle). Camping $18 (per private vehicle). **Phone:** (928) 855-2784. 🅰 ⊗ 🏕 ⊞

LONDON BRIDGE, off US 95 along the Colorado River, was the famed span on the Thames River in London from 1831 to 1968, and now crosses a man-made channel of the Colorado River in the Arizona desert. The channel created an island that contains recreational facilities, including a golf course, marina and campground. Transported stone by stone from England and reassembled at this location in its original form, the bridge is a striking landmark in this community. **Tours:** Guided tours are available. **Phone:** (928) 453-3444, or (800) 242-8278 for the Lake Havasu Convention and Visitors Bureau.

DAYS INN LAKE HAVASU 　　　**Phone:** (928)855-7841
▽▽▽ ▽▽▽ 　　**Address:** 1700 McCulloch Blvd N
Motel 　　　86403 **Location:** Just ne of Lake
$40-$118 　　Havasu Ave; center. **Facility:** 89 units.
　　　　2 stories (no elevator), exterior corridors. **Amenities:** *Some:* high-speed Internet. **Pool(s):** heated outdoor. **Activities:** whirlpool. **Guest Services:** coin laundry.

HAMPTON INN LAKE HAVASU   Phone: (928)855-4071

Hotel
$119-$149

AAA Benefit: Members save up to 10% everyday!

Address: 245 London Bridge Rd 86403 **Location:** 0.5 mi n of London Bridge. **Facility:** 162 units. 4 stories, interior/exterior corridors. **Terms:** 1-7 night minimum stay, cancellation fee imposed. **Pool(s):** heated outdoor. **Activities:** whirlpool, bicycles, horseshoes, exercise room. **Guest Services:** coin laundry.

HAVASU TRAVELODGE   Phone: (928)680-9202

Motel
$57-$144

Address: 480 London Bridge Rd 86403 **Location:** 1 mi n of London Bridge. **Facility:** 41 units, some kitchens. 2 stories (no elevator), interior corridors. **Terms:** 3 day cancellation notice. **Amenities:** safes. **Activities:** whirlpool. **Free Special Amenities:** continental breakfast and high-speed Internet.

ISLAND INN HOTEL   Phone: 928/680-0606

Hotel
Rates not provided

Address: 1300 W McCulloch Blvd 86403 **Location:** 0.7 mi w of London Bridge/SR 95. **Facility:** 117 units. 4 stories, interior corridors. **Pool(s):** heated outdoor. **Activities:** whirlpool. **Guest Services:** valet and coin laundry.

ISLAND SUITES   Phone: 928/855-7333

Hotel
Rates not provided

Address: 236 S Lake Havasu Ave 86403 **Location:** Just s of jct McCulloch Blvd. **Facility:** 45 efficiencies. 2 stories (no elevator), interior corridors. **Pool(s):** heated outdoor. **Activities:** whirlpool, boat dock.

LAKE HAVASU CITY SUPER 8   Phone: (928)855-8844

Motel
$50-$89

Address: 305 London Bridge Rd 86403 **Location:** Just w of SR 95 exit Palo Verde Blvd; 0.5 mi n of London Bridge. **Facility:** 59 units. 3 stories (no elevator), interior corridors. **Terms:** cancellation fee imposed. **Pool(s):** outdoor. **Activities:** whirlpool.

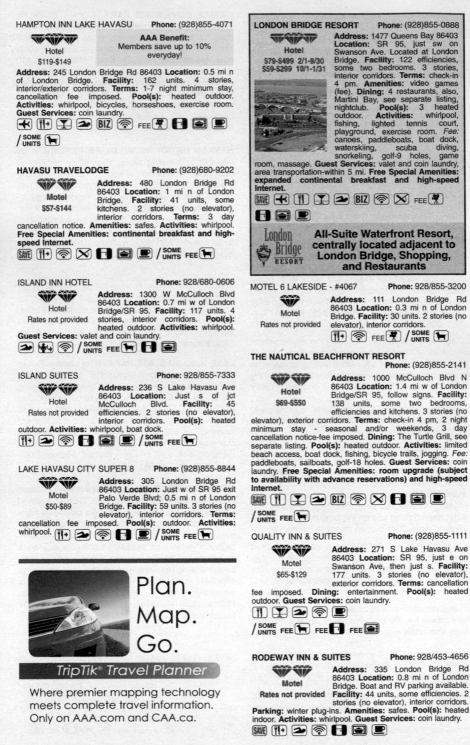

LONDON BRIDGE RESORT   Phone: (928)855-0888

Hotel
$79-$499 2/1-9/30
$59-$299 10/1-1/31

Address: 1477 Queens Bay 86403 **Location:** SR 95, just sw on Swanson Ave. Located at London Bridge. **Facility:** 122 efficiencies, some two bedrooms. 3 stories, interior corridors. **Terms:** check-in 4 pm. **Amenities:** video games (fee). **Dining:** 4 restaurants, also, Martini Bay, see separate listing, nightclub. **Pool(s):** 3 heated outdoor. **Activities:** whirlpool, fishing, lighted tennis court, playground, exercise room. *Fee:* canoes, paddleboats, boat dock, waterskiing, scuba diving, snorkeling, golf-9 holes, game room, massage. **Guest Services:** valet and coin laundry, area transportation-within 5 mi. **Free Special Amenities:** expanded continental breakfast and high-speed Internet.

London Bridge RESORT

All-Suite Waterfront Resort, centrally located adjacent to London Bridge, Shopping, and Restaurants

MOTEL 6 LAKESIDE - #4067   Phone: 928/855-3200

Motel
Rates not provided

Address: 111 London Bridge Rd 86403 **Location:** 0.3 mi n of London Bridge. **Facility:** 30 units. 2 stories (no elevator), interior corridors.

THE NAUTICAL BEACHFRONT RESORT
Phone: (928)855-2141

Hotel
$69-$550

Address: 1000 McCulloch Blvd N 86403 **Location:** 1.4 mi w of London Bridge/SR 95, follow signs. **Facility:** 138 units, some two bedrooms, efficiencies and kitchens. 3 stories (no elevator), exterior corridors. **Terms:** check-in 4 pm, 2 night minimum stay - seasonal and/or weekends, 3 day cancellation notice-fee imposed. **Dining:** The Turtle Grill, see separate listing. **Pool(s):** heated outdoor. **Activities:** limited beach access, boat dock, fishing, bicycle trails, jogging. *Fee:* paddleboats, sailboats, golf-18 holes. **Guest Services:** coin laundry. **Free Special Amenities:** room upgrade (subject to availability with advance reservations) and high-speed Internet.

QUALITY INN & SUITES   Phone: (928)855-1111

Motel
$65-$129

Address: 271 S Lake Havasu Ave 86403 **Location:** SR 95, just e on Swanson Ave, then just s. **Facility:** 177 units. 3 stories (no elevator), exterior corridors. **Terms:** cancellation fee imposed. **Dining:** entertainment. **Pool(s):** heated outdoor. **Guest Services:** coin laundry.

RODEWAY INN & SUITES   Phone: 928/453-4656

Motel
Rates not provided

Address: 335 London Bridge Rd 86403 **Location:** 0.8 mi n of London Bridge. Boat and RV parking available. **Facility:** 44 units, some efficiencies. 2 stories (no elevator), interior corridors. **Parking:** winter plug-ins. **Amenities:** safes. **Pool(s):** heated indoor. **Activities:** whirlpool. **Guest Services:** coin laundry.

Plan. Map. Go.

TripTik® Travel Planner

Where premier mapping technology meets complete travel information. Only on AAA.com and CAA.ca.

WHERE TO EAT

AMICI'S ITALIAN BAR & GRILL   Phone: 928/855-4413

Italian
$9-$22

AAA Inspector Notes: This family-run restaurant serves traditional-style Italian cuisine in an upscale decor. The service is friendly and the daily specials are great. **Bar:** full bar. **Address:** 42 S Smoketree Ave 86403 **Location:** Between Swenson St and McCulloch Blvd; uptown. L D

ANGELINA'S ITALIAN CUISINE   Phone: 928/680-3868

Italian
$10-$25

AAA Inspector Notes: This small family-run restaurant is busy and they do their best to make everyone feel comfortable. The menu consists of traditional fresh Italian items such as spaghetti, chicken parmigiana, fried calamari and gourmet pizza. Take out also is popular. **Bar:** beer & wine. **Address:** 2137 Acoma Blvd W 86403 **Location:** SR 95 exit Acoma Blvd W, 0.7 mi e. D

BARELY BROS. RESTAURANT & BREWERY   Phone: 928/505-7837

American
$11-$26

AAA Inspector Notes: Guests can enjoy a mixture of fun pub grub and gourmet cuisine at this brewery. This is a perfect spot to enjoy grand views of the London Bridge or watch a game on the many TVs. **Bar:** full bar. **Address:** 1425 N McCulloch Blvd 86403 **Location:** West side of London Bridge. L D

BBQ BILL'S BIG EASY BISTRO AND GATOR LOUNGE   Phone: 928/680-1100

American
$8-$18

AAA Inspector Notes: This casual bistro serves up slow-cooked barbecue items along with burgers, catfish and peach cobbler. The bar decor is fun as is the friendly staff. **Bar:** full bar. **Address:** 3557 Maricopa Ave 86406 **Location:** Jct McCulloch Blvd, just nw. B L D

CASA SERRANO   Phone: 928/854-5500

Mexican
$5-$13

AAA Inspector Notes: Friendly staffers welcome diners into a brightly colored dining room. Fresh ingredients in the wide variety of dishes will satisfy the most discriminating diner. **Bar:** full bar. **Address:** 150 Swanson Ave 86403 **Location:** Jct SR 95, just sw. L D

CHA' BONES   Phone: 928/854-5554

Steak
$7-$30

AAA Inspector Notes: Just north of London Bridge, this upscale eatery serves cooked-to-perfection steak and a wide range of tapas dishes for lighter meals. Tall fountains at the entry give an atmosphere of freshness to the attractive room. **Bar:** full bar. **Address:** 112 London Bridge Rd 86403 **Location:** Jct SR 95, 0.3 mi nw. L D

CHINA BUFFET   Phone: 928/854-9398

Asian
$5-$11

AAA Inspector Notes: This restaurant offers a large buffet that with such items as sushi, sweet and sour chicken, pizza, fresh fruit and large selection of desserts. Great for a quick lunch or dinner. **Address:** 91 London Bridge Rd, Suite 101 86403 **Location:** Just n of London Bridge. L D

FARRELL'S GOLDEN HORSESHOE STEAKHOUSE   Phone: 928/764-3800

Steak
$10-$25

AAA Inspector Notes: The Western theme is carried out in everything from buckets of peanuts on the table to such steak names as cowboy cut or cattle baron. Patrons can enjoy live entertainment while feasting on a choice of beef, seafood or pasta. Save room for the six-layer carrot cake. **Bar:** full bar. **Address:** 4501 N London Bridge Rd 86404 **Location:** SR 95, 6.1 mi n. L D

GALLAGHERS DINING & PUB   Phone: 928/855-8686

American
$7-$15

AAA Inspector Notes: Locals gather here at lunch for tasty sandwiches, wraps and hot dogs, and for hearty steaks, barbecue ribs and pasta dishes at dinner. A winning combination is a bowl of the chicken and white bean chili with a cold on-tap brew from the bar. From the multiple TVs to the piano and small stage for live performances, there always is something to keep patrons entertained. **Bar:** full bar. **Address:** 3524 McCulloch Blvd 86406 **Location:** 4.1 mi ne of London Bridge. B L D

JAVELINA CANTINA   Phone: 928/855-8226

Mexican
$6-$16

AAA Inspector Notes: Adding to this cantina's trendy decor are curved metal dividers, brightly colored tile walls and mounted plasma televisions so diners can watch sports while they eat. On a riverside patio, a misting system cools the summer heat while patrons enjoy classic, freshly prepared south-of-the-border cuisine. Wednesday nights feature $1 taco specials, and the place tends to get mobbed. **Bar:** full bar. **Address:** 1420 McCulloch Blvd 86403 **Location:** West side of London Bridge. L D

JUICY'S RIVER CAFE   Phone: 928/855-8429

American
$8-$15

AAA Inspector Notes: Serving hearty, homemade food for more than two decades, owner Mike Bradley even stops by guests' table to be sure they are satisfied. Breakfast dishes are popular with locals, and the award-winning café also offers a wide selection of sandwiches, salads and specials such as Pop's favorite meatloaf. **Bar:** beer & wine. **Address:** 25 N Acoma Blvd 86403 **Location:** Jct SR 95, 1.5 mi e on Mesquite Ave, then just s. B L D

KRYSTAL'S RESTAURANT   Phone: 928/453-2999

Steak
$12-$30

AAA Inspector Notes: Familiar selections of chicken, seafood and beef, including rib-eye, filet mignon and prime rib cuts are prepared in a simple, yet tasty, fashion. Chicken comes barbecued or broiled, while dominant seafood choices range from shrimp scampi to mahi mahi to the fisherman's platter-a must for those with hearty appetites. There are hints of formalized service. **Bar:** full bar. **Reservations:** suggested. **Address:** 460 El Camino Way 86403 **Location:** Just w of SR 95; 1.2 mi n of London Bridge. D

LO'S CHINESE RESTAURANT   Phone: 928/855-4800

Chinese
$6-$17

AAA Inspector Notes: The chef/owner offers sushi and classic dishes like sweet and sour pork and cashew chicken, full of chunky veggies and tender chicken slices. **Bar:** full bar. **Address:** 357 S Lake Havasu Ave 86403 **Location:** 0.7 mi s of McCulloch Blvd; center. L D

MARTINI BAY   Phone: 928/855-0888

♦♦♦
International
$10-$32

AAA Inspector Notes: High-gloss decor and fun music make this a happening place. Thankfully, the food is just as enjoyable as the surroundings. Mediterranean-inspired dishes include plates of freshly grilled steaks and seafood as well as cold, crisp salads. Plenty of hearty appetizers await, including marinated beef filet skewers to lighter options like smoked chicken quesadillas. **Bar:** full bar. **Address:** 1477 Queens Bay 86403 **Location:** SR 95, just sw on Swanson Ave; in London Bridge Resort.

(D)

MONTANA STEAK HOUSE   Phone: 928/855-3736

♦♦ ♦♦
Steak
$10-$25

AAA Inspector Notes: Western decor sets the stage at this casual family restaurant. Steaks, including filet mignon, New York strip and rib-eye, are the house specialty. Meals come with the usual accompaniments of soup or salad and a starch. **Bar:** full bar. **Address:** 3301 Maricopa Ave 86406 **Location:** 4.7 mi s of London Bridge; just off SR 95 on east side. (D)

MUDSHARK BREWING CO   Phone: 928/453-2981

♦♦ ♦♦
American
$9-$20

AAA Inspector Notes: This casual eatery offers tasty pub fare with a number of sandwiches, burgers, pizzas and pasta dishes. Don't forget to enjoy one of the brewmaster's handcrafted ales and lager, such as the dry heat hefeweizen or skyline stout. If guests would like to escape the ever-present sunshine, take a break in the outdoor shaded bier garden, which features cooling mists and sounds of a relaxing waterfall. **Bar:** full bar. **Address:** 210 Swanson Ave 86403 **Location:** Jct SR 95, just sw.

(L) (D)

THE RED ONION   Phone: 928/505-0302

♦♦ ♦♦
American
$6-$11

AAA Inspector Notes: This casual spot offers an open-air dining room. Serving up breakfast and lunch with such items as burgers and sandwiches, diners will find the service friendly and helpful. **Bar:** full bar. **Address:** 2013 McCulloch Blvd 86403 **Location:** Jct Smoketree Ave, just e; uptown. **Parking:** on-site and street.

(B) (L)

SCOTTY'S BROASTED CHICKEN & RIBS
    Phone: 928/680-4441

♦
Chicken
$5-$20

AAA Inspector Notes: This small restaurant specializes in broasted chicken and ribs. The service is very friendly and there is indoor and outdoor seating. **Address:** 410 El Camino Way 86403 **Location:** Just w of SR 95, 1.2 mi n of London Bridge. (L) (D)

SHUGRUE'S   Phone: 928/453-1400

♦♦ ♦♦
Steak
$8-$28

AAA Inspector Notes: Overlooking the channel to Lake Havasu and London Bridge, this restaurant bakes pastries and bread on the premises. Fresh seafood is offered daily, and Pacific Rim dishes are available Thursday evenings. **Bar:** full bar. **Reservations:** suggested. **Address:** 1425 McCulloch Blvd N 86403 **Location:** West side of London Bridge. (L) (D)

TACO HACIENDA   Phone: 928/855-8932

♦♦ ♦♦
Mexican
$4-$13

AAA Inspector Notes: High above the lake, this small eatery offers views from its outdoor patio and some indoor tables. Friendly owners set a pleasant tone for the staff, who serve classics along the lines of enchiladas with green chiles, seafood burritos and MJ's chicken and rice. **Bar:** full bar. **Address:** 2200 Mesquite Ave 86403 **Location:** Jct SR 95, 1.5 mi e. (L) (D)

THE TURTLE GRILL   Phone: 928/855-1897

♦♦ ♦♦
American
$8-$35

AAA Inspector Notes: Diners must choose between watching one of the 14 large TV screens and gazing at the lakefront views from this waterfront eatery. Island chicken penne, Caribbean Caesar and barbecue ribs are among choices that make mouths water. Create-your-own pizza gives guests a chance to unleash their creativity. **Bar:** full bar. **Address:** 1000 McCulloch Blvd N 86403 **Location:** 1.4 mi w of London Bridge/SR 95, follow signs; in The Nautical Beachfront Resort. (B) (L) (D)

LAKE MEAD NATIONAL RECREATION AREA (B-1)

Extending about 140 miles along the Colorado River from Grand Canyon National Park, Ariz., to Bullhead City, Ariz., Lake Mead National Recreation Area embraces 1.5 million acres in western Arizona and southern Nevada. Included are Lake Mohave and Lake Mead as well as an isolated pocket of land north of the lower portion of Grand Canyon National Park.

Three of America's four desert ecosystems—the Mojave, the Great Basin and the Sonoran deserts—meet in Lake Mead National Recreation Area. Therefore the area is home to numerous plants and animals, including bighorn sheep, mule deer, coyotes, foxes and bobcats as well as lizards and snakes. Threatened and endangered species such as the desert tortoise and peregrine falcon also live here.

Fishing is popular in both lakes all year; licenses are required. Largemouth bass, striped bass and catfish are the chief catches in Lake Mead, while rainbow trout and bass are plentiful in Lake Mohave. The recreation area can be enjoyed year-round and is a prime destination for swimming, boating, water skiing and fishing.

Area open daily 24 hours. The visitor center is open daily 8:30-4:30. Closed Jan. 1, Thanksgiving and Christmas. Food is available. Admission $10 per private vehicle or motorcycle (covers all passengers), $5 per pedestrian or bicyclist. Lake use fee $16 per boat. Passes are valid for up to 7 days. For further information contact the Lake Mead National Recreation Area Visitor Center, 601 Nevada Way, Boulder City, NV 89005; phone (702) 293-8990 or (702) 293-8906. *See Recreation Chart.*

HOOVER DAM, along US 93, stands 726 feet high and is one of the highest concrete dams ever constructed. Built 1931-35 in Black Canyon for flood control and water storage, it impounds Lake Mead, one of the largest man-made lakes in the United States.

The 45-minute self-guiding tour of the Hoover Dam Visitor Center includes a theater presentation depicting how irrigation from the Colorado River turned desert into farmland. The Power Plant Tour begins 530 feet underground and features a 30-minute guided tour of eight of the power plant's 17 generators. The Dam Tour includes a 1-hour guided tour of the generators, tunnels and inspection points. Both tours include a self-guiding tour of the visitor center and an exhibit gallery that highlights Hoover Dam's construction and importance.

The Mike O'Callaghan-Pat Tillman Memorial Bridge eliminates a longstanding traffic bottleneck by replacing the two-lane section of US 93 that crossed the Colorado River atop the concrete dam. The bridge has become something of an attraction itself: From its 6-foot-wide sidewalk pedestrians have a grand view of the dam 1,600 feet upstream, not to mention a jaw-dropping (and stomach-churning, for those afraid of heights) perspective of the turquoise Colorado River 890 feet below, wedged between the rock cliffs that form Black Canyon.

The 1,900-foot sidewalk running the length of the bypass bridge is accessible only from the Nevada side (it dead-ends at the Arizona side); take the exit for the old road to the dam. The parking lot for bridge visitors is about 2 miles down the road; use the parking garage at the Hoover Dam Visitor Center, another three-quarters of a mile down the road, if the bridge lot is full. The walk (and climb) to the sidewalk is lined with information panels detailing the bridge's construction.

Hours: Visitor center daily 9-6, Apr.-Sept.; 9-5, rest of year. Overlook closes at dusk. Last admission is 45 minutes before closing. Closed Thanksgiving and Christmas. **Cost:** Dam Tour $30. Power Plant Tour $11; $9 (ages 4-16, 62+ and military with ID); free (active military in uniform). Visitor center $8; free (ages 0-3). The Dam Tour is conducted on a first-come, first-served basis. Under 8 and the physically impaired are not permitted on the Dam Tour. **Parking:** $7. **Phone:** (702) 494-2517 or (866) 730-9097.

LAKE MEAD, extending behind Hoover Dam, is 110 miles long and averages 200 feet deep at normal capacity. The lake has a 550-mile shoreline.

Nevada recreational centers with marinas and launch facilities include Boulder Harbor, 4 miles northeast of Boulder City; Callville Bay, 22 miles east of North Las Vegas; and the Overton Beach and Echo Bay areas, both south of Overton. An additional Arizona center is about 80 miles north of Kingman at Temple Bar.

Films and exhibits about natural and cultural history are offered at the Alan Bible Visitor Center, 4 miles east of Boulder City at US 93 and Lakeshore Road, overlooking Lake Mead. A botanical and cactus garden surrounds the visitor center. *See Recreation Chart.*

Note: The Lake Mead reservoir dropped to a historic low point in November 2010 as the result of a 10-year drought. Although above-average spring snowmelt replenished the water level somewhat, phone ahead to verify the availability of launch ramps at recreational centers. **Hours:** Visitor center daily 8:30-4:30. Closed Jan. 1. **Cost:** $5 per private vehicle; $3 per person arriving by other means. Passes are valid for up to 5 days. Motorized boat $10. **Phone:** (702) 293-8990.

Lake Mead Cruises depart from the Lake Mead Cruises Landing at Hemenway Harbor on Lakeshore Rd. (SR 166). Excursion cruises on a paddlewheeler include a narration about area history and the construction of Hoover Dam. Brunch and dinner cruises also are available. **Hours:** Ninety-minute round-trip excursion cruises depart daily at noon and 2. **Cost:** Fare $24; $12 (ages 2-11). Reservations are recommended. **Phone:** (702) 293-6180.

LAKE MOHAVE extends 67 mi. s. from Hoover Dam to Davis Dam. Launching ramps, trailer sites, refreshment concessions, boat rentals and overnight accommodations are available at Katherine Landing, about 35 miles west of Kingman, Ariz., and at Cottonwood Cove, 14 miles east of Searchlight. Accommodations also are available a short distance away in Needles, Calif., and Bullhead City, Ariz. Willow Beach, 28 miles east of Boulder City on US 93, offers a launch ramp and concession facilities. Information about recreational facilities is available at all three sites.

LITCHFIELD PARK (I-2) pop. 5,476

WILDLIFE WORLD ZOO & AQUARIUM, 16501 W. Northern Ave., presents more than 500 rare and exotic species of animals including giraffes, lions, rhinoceroses, tigers, crocodiles, sharks, penguins, fish and tropical birds. Featured are lory parrot feeding, giraffe feeding, a safari train ride, a boat ride, a sky ride, a log-flume ride and wildlife encounter shows.

Hours: Zoo daily 9-6. Aquarium daily 9-9. **Cost:** Zoo and aquarium $27.50; $25.50 (ages 60+ on Tues.); $14.25 (ages 3-12). Aquarium after 5 p.m. $16.99; $14.99 (ages 60+ on Tues.); $8.99 (ages 3-12). Prices may vary; phone ahead. **Phone:** (623) 935-9453.

THE WIGWAM **Phone:** (623)935-3811 **39**

Historic Retro Hotel $99-$1800

Address: 300 Wigwam Blvd 85340 **Location:** I-10 exit 128 (Litchfield Rd), 2.4 mi n, then 0.4 mi e. **Facility:** Celebrating more than 75 years, this resort offers beautifully renovated public areas, a golf course by Robert Trent Jones Sr., lushly landscaped grounds and oversize rooms. 331 units, some two bedrooms. 1-2 stories (no elevator), exterior corridors. **Parking:** on-site and valet. **Terms:** check-in 4 pm, 3 day cancellation notice-fee imposed. **Amenities:** video games (fee), high-speed Internet, safes. **Dining:** 2 restaurants, also, Litchfield's, see separate listing. **Pool(s):** 3 heated outdoor. **Activities:** saunas, whirlpools, steamrooms, waterslide, recreation programs, jogging, playground, exercise room, spa. *Fee:* golf-54 holes, 9 lighted tennis courts, bicycles. **Guest Services:** valet laundry, area transportation (fee).

(See map & index p. 155.)

WHERE TO EAT

LITCHFIELD'S
◆◆ ◆◆
New American
$16-$29

Phone: 623/935-3811 (22)

AAA Inspector Notes: The menu at this upscale, casual dining room features many local, farm-to-table ingredients including Arizona trout with pecan sage butter, Double Check Ranch grass-fed tenderloin and Santa Fe lamb stew. If weather permits, enjoy a table outside overlooking the manicured grounds. **Bar:** full bar. **Reservations:** suggested. **Address:** 300 E Wigwam Blvd 85340 **Location:** I-10 exit 128 (Litchfield Rd), 2.4 mi n, then 0.4 mi e; in The Wigwam. **Parking:** on-site and valet.

[D] CALL [⌖M]

MARANA pop. 34,961
- Hotels & Restaurants map & index p. 282
- Part of Tucson area — see map p. 268

COMFORT INN & SUITES   **Phone:** (520)579-1099 (55)
◆◆ ◆◆
Hotel
$119-$209

Address: 8425 N Cracker Barrel Rd 85743 **Location:** I-10 exit 246 (Cortaro Rd), just w. **Facility:** 65 units. 3 stories, interior corridors. **Terms:** cancellation fee imposed. **Amenities:** high-speed Internet. **Pool(s):** outdoor. **Activities:** whirlpool, exercise room. **Guest Services:** coin laundry. **Free Special Amenities:** full breakfast and high-speed Internet.

[SAVE] [¶↑] [⊃] [⊚] [✕] [🛏] [🖬] [🖵]

COMFORT INN I-10 & INA   **Phone:** 520/579-7202 (60)
◆◆ ◆◆
Hotel
Rates not provided

Address: 4930 W Ina Rd 85743 **Location:** I-10 exit 248 (Ina Rd), just w. **Facility:** 60 units. 3 stories, interior corridors. **Amenities:** Some: high-speed Internet. **Pool(s):** outdoor. **Activities:** whirlpool, exercise room. **Guest Services:** coin laundry. [¶↑] [⊃] [⊚] [🛏] [🖬] [🖵]

DAYS INN & SUITES-TUCSON/MARANA
Phone: (520)744-6677 (57)
◆◆ ◆◆
Hotel
$45-$118

Address: 8370 N Cracker Barrel Rd 85743 **Location:** I-10 exit 246 (Cortaro Rd), just w. **Facility:** 62 units. 3 stories, interior corridors. **Amenities:** high-speed Internet. **Pool(s):** heated outdoor. **Activities:** whirlpool, exercise room. **Guest Services:** coin laundry. **Free Special Amenities:** expanded continental breakfast and high-speed Internet.

[SAVE] [¶↑] [⊃] [⊚] [🛏] [🖬] [🖵]

HOLIDAY INN EXPRESS   **Phone:** (520)572-4777 (58)
◆◆ ◆◆
Hotel
$149-$399 2/1-2/28
$99-$399 2/29-1/31

Address: 8373 N Cracker Barrel Rd 85743 **Location:** I-10 exit 246 (Cortaro Rd), just w, then just n. **Facility:** 83 units. 3 stories, interior corridors. **Terms:** 3 day cancellation notice. **Amenities:** high-speed Internet. **Pool(s):** heated outdoor. **Activities:** whirlpool, exercise room. **Guest Services:** valet and coin laundry.

[¶↑] CALL [⌖M] [⊃] [BIZ] [⊚] [🛏] [🖬] [🖵]

LA QUINTA INN & SUITES NW TUCSON MARANA
Phone: (520)572-4235 (56)
◆◆ ◆◆
Hotel
$139-$215

Address: 6020 W Hospitality Rd 85743 **Location:** I-10 exit 246 (Cortaro Rd), just w, then just n. **Facility:** 65 units, some efficiencies. 3 stories, interior corridors. **Amenities:** high-speed Internet. **Pool(s):** outdoor. **Activities:** whirlpool, exercise room. **Guest Services:** valet and coin laundry.

[¶↑] CALL [⌖M] [⊃] [BIZ] [⊚] [🛏] [🖬] [🖵]
/ SOME UNITS [🐕]

RED ROOF INN TUCSON NORTH
Phone: (520)744-8199 (59)
◆◆ ◆◆
Hotel
$41-$125

Address: 4940 W Ina Rd 85743 **Location:** I-10 exit 248 (Ina Rd), just w. **Facility:** 133 units. 4 stories, interior corridors. **Terms:** cancellation fee imposed. **Amenities:** safes (fee). **Pool(s):** heated outdoor. **Guest Services:** coin laundry. **Free Special Amenities:** local telephone calls and high-speed Internet.

[SAVE] [¶↑] [⊃] [⊚] FEE [📷🖥]
/ SOME UNITS [🐕] FEE [🛏] FEE [🖬]

THE RITZ-CARLTON, DOVE MOUNTAIN
Phone: (520)572-3000
◆◆ ◆◆
Resort Hotel
$179-$559

🦁 *The Ritz-Carlton*

AAA Benefit: Unequaled service at Special Member Savings.

Address: 15000 N Secret Springs Dr 85658 **Location:** I-10 exit 240 (Tangerine Rd), 5 mi e to Dove Mountain Dr, then 4.5 mi n, follow signs. **Facility:** Nestled in the Tortolita Mountains, this new resort features rooms with expansive views, luxurious baths and world-class golf facilities. 253 units. 1-5 stories, interior corridors. **Parking:** valet only. **Terms:** check-in 4 pm, cancellation fee imposed. **Amenities:** safes, honor bars. *Fee:* video games, high-speed Internet. **Dining:** 4 restaurants, also, Core Kitchen & Wine Bar, see separate listing. **Pool(s):** 3 heated outdoor. **Activities:** saunas, whirlpools, steamrooms, waterslide, 3 lighted tennis courts, recreation programs, hiking trails, spa. *Fee:* golf-18 holes, bicycles. **Guest Services:** valet laundry, area transportation-golf shop.

[SAVE] [¶↑] [🍴] CALL [⌖M] [⊃] [👨] [⊚] [✕]
FEE [📷🖥] [🖵] / SOME UNITS FEE [🐕] [🛏] [🖬]

WHERE TO EAT

CORE KITCHEN & WINE BAR   **Phone:** 520/572-3000
◆◆ ◆◆
Regional American
$25-$40

AAA Inspector Notes: Chef Joel Harrington creates unique, creative and memorable regional dishes at this elegant, yet casual eatery. Diners can sample such dishes as chili-lacquered New York strip with nopales relish, prickly pear barbecue quail and buffalo tenderloin with three chili aioli. **Bar:** full bar. **Reservations:** suggested. **Address:** 15000 N Secret Springs Dr 85658 **Location:** I-10 exit 240 (Tangerine Rd), 5 mi e to Dove Mountain Dr, then 4.5 mi n, follow signs; in The Ritz-Carlton, Dove Mountain. **Parking:** valet only. [D]

LA OLLA MEXICAN CAFE   **Phone:** 520/579-0950 (76)
◆◆ ◆◆
Mexican
$7-$15

AAA Inspector Notes: Fresh salsa and homemade guacamole will help start the meal while rich sauces and baked calabacitas, squash cooked with corn and tomatoes, enhance most entrées. Everything, from the chipotle shrimp and pork to the carne con chili rojo, is freshly made. Friendly staff will make this a comfortable dining experience. **Bar:** full bar. **Address:** 8553 N Silverbell Rd 85743 **Location:** I-10 exit 246 (Cortaro Rd), 0.9 mi w, then 1.4 mi n. [L] [D]

LI'L ABNER'S STEAKHOUSE
Phone: 520/744-2800 (77)
◆◆ ◆◆
Steak
$14-$34

AAA Inspector Notes: An area institution, this restaurant grills steaks, ribs and chicken on an outdoor pit. Young servers are energetic. The funky, Western-style building sports years of guest graffiti on the walls. **Bar:** full bar. **Reservations:** suggested. **Address:** 8500 N Silverbell Rd 85743 **Location:** I-10 exit 246 (Cortaro Rd), 0.9 mi w, then 1.3 mi n. [D]

MARICOPA (E-3) pop. 43,482, elev. 1,177'

Prevalent clear blue skies beckon fans of soaring to Maricopa. This area at the foot of the Sierra Estrella Mountains is noted for its thermal conditions. Arizona Soaring, (520) 568-2318, is at 22548 N. Sailport Way.

GAMBLING ESTABLISHMENTS

- **Harrah's Phoenix Ak-Chin Casino,** 1 mi. s. on SR 347 to 15406 Maricopa Rd. **Hours:** Daily 24 hours. **Phone:** (480) 802-5000 or (800) 427-7247.

HARRAH'S AK-CHIN CASINO RESORT

Phone: (480)802-5000

Hotel
$69-$399

Address: 15406 Maricopa Rd 85239 **Location:** Jct SR 238, 4.5 mi s on SR 347. **Facility:** Guests can lounge under palm trees in the courtyard or cool off in the pool, which features a swim-up cocktail bar. 148 units. 2 stories, interior/exterior corridors. **Terms:** check-in 4 pm, 3 day cancellation notice. **Amenities:** video games (fee), safes. **Dining:** 4 restaurants, entertainment. **Pool(s):** heated outdoor. **Activities:** whirlpool.

MAYER (D-3) pop. 1,497, elev. 4,402'

ARCOSANTI is off I-17 exit 262, then 2.5 mi. n.e. on a dirt road, following signs. The town is architect Paolo Soleri's prototype urban design based on his philosophy of arcology (architecture plus ecology). The town, which still is under construction, will be a pedestrian-oriented city with a goal of reducing urban sprawl and its impact on the environment. Educational workshops are held throughout the year. Monthly concerts take place in the Colly Soleri Music Center, except in winter; phone for schedule.

Hours: Visitor center daily 9-5. One-hour tours are conducted daily on the hour 10-11 and 1-4. Closed Jan. 1, Easter, Thanksgiving and Christmas. **Cost:** Tour $10; free (ages 0-11). Visitor center free. **Phone:** (928) 632-7135.

McNARY (D-5) pop. 528, elev. 7,309'

RECREATIONAL ACTIVITIES

Skiing

- **Sunrise Ski Area** is 15 mi. e. on SR 260, then 7 mi. s. on SR 273. Other activities are offered. **Hours:** Daily 9-4, Dec.-Apr. and Memorial Day-Labor Day (weather permitting). **Phone:** (928) 735-7669 or (800) 772-7669.

MESA (J-4) pop. 439,041, elev. 1,234'

Mesa (Spanish for "tabletop") is in the center of the Salt River Valley on a plateau. The area has long been inhabited by Native Americans, including the Hohokam Ancestral Desert People, or "the Departed Ones." The resourceful tribe realized the need for water for irrigation and dug some 125 miles of canals around 700 B.C. Some of these irrigation ditches are still in use and can be seen at the Park of the Canals and Mesa Grande Ruins.

In 1883 the founding Mormon community discovered the ancient canal system and used it to irrigate the thousands of fertile acres of farmland above the Salt River. Alfalfa, cotton, wheat and grapes were the major crops; citrus was introduced in 1897. Agriculture carried the town into the 20th century; today, the aviation, education and health care industries play a big role in Mesa's economy.

Recreation areas east and north of the city are easily accessible from Mesa. Rafting and other water sports on the Salt River are popular, as are varied activities available within the Apache Lake and Canyon Lake recreation areas *(see attraction listings p. 36)* and on Theodore Roosevelt Lake *(see attraction listing p. 201)* and Saguaro Lake. *See Recreation Chart.*

Mesa Convention and Visitors Bureau: 120 N. Center St., Mesa, AZ 85201. **Phone:** (480) 827-4700 or (800) 283-6372.

Shopping areas: The largest shopping centers in the city are Fiesta Mall, US 60 and Alma School Road, which offers Dillard's Clearance Center, Macy's and Sears; and Superstition Springs Center, at US 60 and Superstition Springs Boulevard, which offers Dillard's, JCPenney, Macy's and Sears.

Bargain hunters can find discounted name-brand merchandise at Power Square Mall, a half-mile south of US 60 at Power and Baseline roads. The Mesa Market Place and Swap Meet boasts more than 1,500 vendors offering new and used merchandise at its shaded facility at 10550 E. Baseline Rd.

ARIZONA MUSEUM FOR YOUTH, 35 N. Robson St., offers children the opportunity to view, create and explore various forms of art. Six new exhibitions are introduced each year, and workshops teach a variety of skills from cartooning to printmaking. ArtVille, a permanent gallery, highlights art activities for children ages 0-4. **Time:** Allow 1 hour minimum. **Hours:** Tues.-Sat. 10-4, Sun. noon-4. The main gallery is closed periodically for exhibit installation. Closed major holidays. Phone ahead to confirm schedule. **Cost:** $7; free (under 1). **Phone:** (480) 644-2467.

ARIZONA MUSEUM OF NATURAL HISTORY, 53 N. Macdonald St., covers the history of Arizona from the days of the dinosaurs to the 20th century. Permanent and temporary exhibits focus on Arizona's prehistoric life, featuring animated dinosaurs, dinosaur skeletons and other fossil specimens. Archeology displays highlight the life of Arizona's ancient Hohokam Ancestral Desert People, while reminders of old Mesa's past include territorial jail cells and the Lost Dutchman's Treasure Mine.

Time: Allow 1 hour minimum. **Hours:** Tues.-Fri. 10-5, Sat. 11-5, Sun. 1-5; closed state and major

(See map & index p. 164.)

holidays. **Cost:** $10; $9 (ages 65+); $8 (students with ID); $6 (ages 3-12). **Phone:** (480) 644-2230.

ARIZONA TEMPLE VISITOR CENTER is at 525 E. Main St. The center presents dioramas and an audiovisual program that explains the purpose of the temple and the history of the Mormon religion; paintings and statues are featured. Free guided tours of the visitor center end in a religious question-and-answer session. A pageant is presented during the two weeks before Easter, and a holiday lights display is featured late November through early January. **Time:** Allow 1 hour minimum. **Hours:** Daily 9-9. Guided tours are given daily. **Cost:** Free. **Phone:** (480) 964-7164.

COMMEMORATIVE AIR FORCE-ARIZONA WING, e. on SR 202 to jct. McKellips Rd. and Greenfield Rd. at 2017 N. Greenfield Rd. (adjoining Falcon Field), is dedicated to the preservation of World War II warplanes. Displays include such war artifacts as flight equipment and ration coupons. Of special interest is *Sentimental Journey,* a restored World War II B-17 bomber in flying condition.

Time: Allow 1 hour minimum. **Hours:** Daily 10-4, Oct.-May; Wed.-Sun. 9-3, rest of year. *Sentimental Journey* is on display late fall-early summer. Closed Thanksgiving and Christmas. **Cost:** $10; $9 (ages 62+); $3 (ages 5-12). **Phone:** (480) 924-1940.

GOLFLAND/SUNSPLASH, 155 W. Hampton Ave., is a 15-acre miniature golf and water park complex featuring three miniature golf courses, 10 waterslides including the Master Blaster and the Sidewinder, a wave pool, bumper boats, go-carts, a children's pool, a video arcade and a river for tubing.

Changing rooms and lockers are available. **Hours:** Sunsplash Sun.-Thurs. 11-7, Fri.-Sat. 11-8, June 1-Aug. 10; Sat.-Sun. 11-7, May 15-May 31; Sat. 11-8, Sun. 11-7, Aug. 11-Sept. 30. Golfland Mon.-Thurs. 11-11, Fri. 11 a.m.-midnight, Sat. 10 a.m.-midnight, Sun. 11-10, June-Aug.; Mon.-Thurs. 11-10, Fri. 11 a.m.-midnight, Sat. 10 a.m.-midnight, Sun. noon-10, Jan.-May; Mon.-Thurs. 11-10, Fri. 11 a.m.-midnight, Sat. 10 a.m.-midnight, Sun. 11-10, in Sept.; Mon.-Thurs. 11-10, Fri. 11 a.m.-12:30 a.m., Sat. 10 a.m.-12:30 a.m., Sun. noon-10, rest of year. Phone ahead to confirm schedule. **Cost:** Sunsplash $26.99; $19.99 (under 48 inches tall and after 4 p.m.); $2.78 (ages 0-2). Golfland free. Fees apply for golf, go-carts, bumper boats and other attractions. Prices may vary; phone ahead. **Phone:** (480) 834-8319. 🍴

MESA HISTORICAL MUSEUM is .9 mi. e. on Main St., then 3 mi. n. on Horne St. to 2345 N. Horne St. Antique farm equipment, furniture, clothing and other artifacts are housed in the main building, formerly a schoolhouse built in 1913. The museum features a replica 1882 adobe schoolhouse, changing exhibits and displays relating the history of Mesa from before it was founded to the present.

Time: Allow 30 minutes minimum. **Hours:** Thurs.-Sat. 10-4. Closed major holidays. **Cost:** $5; $4 (ages 65+); $3 (ages 3-12). **Phone:** (480) 835-7358. 🍴

ROCKIN' R RANCH, 6136 E. Baseline Rd., is a re-creation of a Western town where you can pan for gold. All-you-can-eat chuck wagon suppers are served cowboy style. A stage show has songs and humor of the Old West; a gunfight is staged after the show.

Hours: Meal preceding stage show begins at 6:30 Wed.-Sat., Dec.-Mar.; Fri.-Sat., Apr.-May and Sept. 26-Oct. 31; Sat., June 1-Sept. 25 and in Dec.; Thurs.-Sat., rest of year. Phone ahead to confirm schedule. **Cost:** $32; $22 (ages 3-12). Reservations are required. **Phone:** (480) 832-1539.

RECREATIONAL ACTIVITIES

Tubing

• **Salt River Tubing and Recreation** is 15 mi. n. of US 60 on Power Rd. **Hours:** Daily 9-4, May-Sept. (weather and water level permitting). **Phone:** (480) 984-3305.

ARIZONA GOLF RESORT & CONFERENCE CENTER
Phone: (480)832-3202 [58]

▼▼▼
Resort Hotel
$99-$209 10/1-1/31
$89-$209 2/1-9/30

Address: 425 S Power Rd 85206 **Location:** 1.3 mi n of US 60 (Superstition Frwy) exit 188 (Power Rd); southeast corner of Broadway and Power rds; entrance on Broadway Rd. **Facility:** This golf resort complex is surrounded by well-landscaped grounds and multiple buildings containing a variety of guest rooms and suites. 186 units, some efficiencies and kitchens. 2 stories (no elevator), exterior corridors. **Terms:** check-in 4 pm, cancellation fee imposed. **Amenities:** video games (fee), safes. **Dining:** 2 restaurants. **Pool(s):** 2 heated outdoor. **Activities:** whirlpools, basketball, volleyball, exercise room. *Fee:* golf-18 holes, massage. **Guest Services:** valet and coin laundry, area transportation-within 5 mi. **Free Special Amenities:** high-speed Internet and local transportation.

 / SOME UNITS FEE 🐕

BEST WESTERN LEGACY INN & SUITES
Phone: (480)457-8181 [66]

▼▼▼
Hotel
$85-$149

Best Western **AAA Benefit:** Members save up to 20%, plus 10% bonus points with Best Western Rewards®.

Address: 4470 S Power Rd 85212 **Location:** Santan Frwy (Loop 202) exit Power Rd, just n. **Facility:** 110 units. 3 stories, interior corridors. **Terms:** 7 day cancellation notice-fee imposed. **Amenities:** high-speed Internet. **Pool(s):** heated outdoor. **Activities:** whirlpool, exercise room. **Guest Services:** valet and coin laundry, area transportation-within 5 mi. **Free Special Amenities:** local telephone calls and high-speed Internet.

Explore the Travel Guides on AAA.com/Travel or CAA.ca/Travel

(See map & index p. 164.)

BEST WESTERN MEZONA INN
Phone: (480)834-9233 42

Hotel
$76-$175

AAA Benefit: Members save up to 20%, plus 10% bonus points with Best Western Rewards®.

Address: 250 W Main St 85201 **Location:** Just e of Country Club Dr; downtown. **Facility:** 128 units. 2 stories (no elevator), exterior corridors. **Amenities:** Some: high-speed Internet. **Pool(s):** heated outdoor. **Activities:** whirlpool. **Guest Services:** coin laundry. **Free Special Amenities:** expanded continental breakfast and high-speed Internet.

SAVE 📶 🏊 🛜 📠 🖥 🍴 / SOME UNITS FEE 🐾

BEST WESTERN SUPERSTITION SPRINGS
Phone: (480)641-1164 63

Hotel
$75-$176

AAA Benefit: Members save up to 20%, plus 10% bonus points with Best Western Rewards®.

Address: 1342 S Power Rd 85206 **Location:** Just n of US 60 (Superstition Frwy) exit 188 (Power Rd); northwest corner of Power Rd and Hampton Ave. Next to Superstition Springs Mall and Leisure World. **Facility:** 59 units, some kitchens. 2 stories (no elevator), exterior corridors. **Pool(s):** heated outdoor. **Activities:** whirlpool, exercise room. Guest Services: coin laundry. **Free Special Amenities:** continental breakfast and high-speed Internet.

SAVE 📶 🏊 🛜 📠 🖥 🍴 / SOME UNITS FEE 🐾

Next to a huge Shopping Center, 5 MI to Airport, Pets welcome, Home of Chicago Cubs Spring Training!

COMFORT INN & SUITES
Phone: (480)621-6375 43

Hotel
$66-$146

Address: 651 E Main St 85203 **Location:** US 60 (Superstition Frwy) exit 180 (Mesa Dr), 2 mi n, then 0.4 mi e. **Facility:** 48 units. 2 stories, interior corridors. **Terms:** cancellation fee imposed. **Amenities:** high-speed Internet, safes. **Pool(s):** heated outdoor. **Activities:** whirlpool. **Guest Services:** valet laundry. **Free Special Amenities:** expanded continental breakfast and high-speed Internet.

SAVE 📶 CALL 🐕 🏊 🛗 BIZ 🛜 ✕ 📠 🖥 🖥

COUNTRY INN & SUITES BY CARLSON
Phone: 480/641-8000 65

Hotel
Rates not provided

Address: 6650 E Superstition Springs Blvd 85206 **Location:** Just s of US 60 (Superstition Frwy) exit 188 (Power Rd), just sw. **Facility:** 126 units. 4 stories, interior corridors. **Amenities:** video games (fee), high-speed Internet. **Pool(s):** heated outdoor. **Activities:** whirlpool, exercise room. **Guest Services:** valet and coin laundry, area transportation-within 5 mi.

🛗 📶 CALL 🐕 🏊 BIZ 🛜 ✕ FEE 🎥 📠 🖥 🖥

COURTYARD BY MARRIOTT-MESA
Phone: (480)461-3000 48

Hotel
$62-$125

AAA Benefit: AAA hotel discounts of 5% or more.

Address: 1221 S Westwood Ave 85210 **Location:** US 60 (Superstition Frwy) exit 178 (Alma School Rd), 0.4 mi n, just e on Southern Ave, then just s. **Facility:** 149 units. 3 stories, interior corridors. **Amenities:** high-speed Internet. **Pool(s):** heated outdoor. **Activities:** whirlpool, exercise room. **Guest Services:** valet and coin laundry, area transportation-within 5 mi. **Free Special Amenities:** high-speed Internet.

SAVE ECO 📶 CALL 🐕 🏊 🛜 ✕ 🖥 / SOME UNITS 📠 🖥

DAYS HOTEL
Phone: (480)844-8900 59

Hotel
$50-$126

Address: 333 W Juanita Ave 85210 **Location:** US 60 (Superstition Frwy) exit 179 (Country Club Dr), just s, then just e. **Facility:** 120 units, some two bedrooms and kitchens. 3 stories, interior corridors. **Amenities:** safes (fee). Some: high-speed Internet. **Pool(s):** heated outdoor. **Activities:** whirlpool, exercise room. **Guest Services:** valet and coin laundry.

📶 🏊 BIZ 🛜 ✕ 📠 🖥 🖥 / SOME UNITS FEE 🐾

DAYS INN & SUITES MESA
Phone: (480)969-3600 44

Hotel
$40-$86

Address: 1750 E Main St 85203 **Location:** US 60 (Superstition Frwy) exit 182 (Gilbert Rd), 2.1 mi n, then 0.3 mi w. **Facility:** 63 units, some kitchens. 2 stories (no elevator), exterior corridors. **Pool(s):** outdoor. **Guest Services:** coin laundry. **Free Special Amenities:** continental breakfast and room upgrade (subject to availability with advance reservations).

SAVE 📶 🏊 🛜 📠 🖥 🖥 / SOME UNITS FEE 🐾

Kitchenette and Junior Suites available; Outdoor Patio with BBQ Grill

DAYS INN-EAST MESA
Phone: (480)981-8111 47

Hotel
$45-$99

Address: 5531 E Main St 85205 **Location:** 0.4 mi e of Higley Rd. **Facility:** 61 units. 2 stories (no elevator), exterior corridors. **Amenities:** Some: high-speed Internet. **Pool(s):** heated outdoor. **Activities:** whirlpool.

🛗 🏊 🛜 📠 🖥 🖥 / SOME UNITS FEE 🐾

DOBSON RANCH INN & RESORT
Phone: (480)831-7000 54

Hotel
$72-$165

Address: 1666 S Dobson Rd 85202 **Location:** Just s of US 60 (Superstition Frwy) exit 177 (Dobson Rd). **Facility:** 213 units. 2 stories, interior/exterior corridors. **Terms:** check-in 4 pm. **Amenities:** video games (fee), high-speed Internet. **Pool(s):** heated outdoor. **Activities:** whirlpools, exercise room. **Guest Services:** coin laundry. **Free Special Amenities:** full breakfast and high-speed Internet.

SAVE 📶 🏊 BIZ 🛜 ✕ FEE 🎥 📠 🖥 / SOME UNITS 🐾 🖥

(See map & index p. 164.)

EXTENDED STAYAMERICA-PHOENIX/MESA
Phone: (480)632-0201 **61**

Extended Stay Hotel

$75-$85 2/1-4/15
$60-$70 4/16-1/31

Address: 455 W Baseline Rd 85210 **Location:** US 60 (Superstition Frwy) exit 179 (Country Club Dr), 0.4 mi s on SR 87, then just w. **Facility:** 104 efficiencies. 3 stories, interior corridors. **Terms:** office hours 6:30 am-10:30 pm. **Guest Services:** coin laundry.

FAIRFIELD INN BY MARRIOTT PHOENIX MESA
Phone: (480)668-8000 **51**

Hotel
$49-$169

FAIRFIELD INN
Marriott

AAA Benefit: AAA hotel discounts of 5% or more.

Address: 1405 S Westwood Ave 85210 **Location:** Just n of US 60 (Superstition Frwy) exit 178 (Alma School Rd), just e on Grove St, then just s. **Facility:** 65 units. 3 stories, interior corridors. **Amenities:** high-speed Internet. **Pool(s):** heated outdoor. **Activities:** whirlpool. **Guest Services:** valet laundry. **Free Special Amenities: expanded continental breakfast and high-speed Internet.**

HAMPTON INN PHOENIX/MESA
Phone: (480)926-3600 **60**

Hotel
$89-$179 2/1-3/31
$59-$109 4/1-1/31

AAA Benefit: Members save up to 10% everyday!

Address: 1563 S Gilbert Rd 85204 **Location:** US 60 (Superstition Frwy) exit 182 (Gilbert Rd), just ne. **Facility:** 115 units. 4 stories, interior corridors. **Terms:** 1-7 night minimum stay, cancellation fee imposed. **Amenities:** video games (fee). **Pool(s):** heated outdoor. **Activities:** whirlpool, exercise room. **Guest Services:** valet and coin laundry.

HILTON PHOENIX EAST/MESA
Phone: (480)833-5555 **52**

Hotel
$129-$189 2/1-5/24
$79-$159 5/25-1/31

Hilton

AAA Benefit: Members save 5% or more everyday!

Address: 1011 W Holmes Ave 85210 **Location:** US 60 (Superstition Frwy) exit 178 (Alma School Rd), just n, then just e. Across from Fiesta Mall. **Facility:** 260 units. 8 stories, interior corridors. **Terms:** 1-7 night minimum stay, cancellation fee imposed. **Amenities:** video games (fee). Some: high-speed Internet (fee). **Pool(s):** heated outdoor. **Activities:** whirlpools, exercise room. **Guest Services:** valet laundry, area transportation-within 5 mi. **Free Special Amenities: local telephone calls and newspaper.**

HOLIDAY INN HOTEL & SUITES
Phone: (480)964-7000 **57**

Hotel
$99-$209 2/1-4/15
$79-$129 4/16-1/31

Address: 1600 S Country Club Dr 85210 **Location:** US 60 (Superstition Frwy) exit 179 (Country Club Dr), just s. **Facility:** 247 units, some two bedrooms. 6 stories, interior/exterior corridors. **Amenities:** video games (fee). **Pool(s):** heated outdoor. **Activities:** whirlpool, exercise room. **Guest Services:** valet and coin laundry.

HOMESTEAD STUDIO SUITES HOTEL PHOENIX-MESA
Phone: (480)752-2266 **56**

Extended Stay Hotel
$70-$80 2/1-4/15
$60-$70 4/16-1/31

Address: 1920 W Isabella Ave 85202 **Location:** Just s of US 60 (Superstition Frwy) exit 177 (Dobson Rd). **Facility:** 124 efficiencies. 2 stories (no elevator), exterior corridors. **Terms:** office hours 6 am-10 pm. **Guest Services:** coin laundry.

HOWARD JOHNSON INN MESA
Phone: (480)964-8000 **45**

Hotel
$50-$120

Address: 1625 E Main St 85203 **Location:** 2 mi n of US 60 (Superstition Frwy) exit Stapley Dr, 0.5 mi e. **Facility:** 96 units. 2 stories (no elevator), exterior corridors. **Terms:** cancellation fee imposed. **Amenities:** Some: high-speed Internet. **Pool(s):** heated outdoor. **Activities:** whirlpool. **Guest Services:** coin laundry.

HYATT PLACE PHOENIX/MESA
Phone: (480)969-8200 **40**

Hotel
$79-$299

HYATT PLACE

AAA Benefit: Members save 10% or more everyday.

Address: 1422 W Bass Pro Dr 85201 **Location:** Loop 202 exit 10 (Dobson Rd), just s, then just e. **Facility:** 152 units. 4 stories, interior corridors. **Terms:** cancellation fee imposed. **Amenities:** high-speed Internet. **Pool(s):** heated outdoor. **Activities:** putting green, exercise room. **Guest Services:** valet and coin laundry, area transportation-within 5 mi. **Free Special Amenities: expanded continental breakfast and high-speed Internet.**

LA QUINTA INN & SUITES PHOENIX MESA EAST
Phone: (480)654-1970 **64**

Hotel
$78-$192

Address: 6530 E Superstition Springs Blvd 85206 **Location:** US 60 (Superstition Frwy) exit 187 (Superstition Springs Blvd) eastbound, just se; exit 188 (Power Rd) westbound, just sw. **Facility:** 107 units. 6 stories, interior corridors. **Amenities:** video games (fee). **Pool(s):** heated outdoor. **Activities:** whirlpool, exercise room. **Guest Services:** valet and coin laundry, area transportation-within 5 mi.

LA QUINTA INN & SUITES PHOENIX MESA WEST
Phone: (480)844-8747 **49**

Hotel
$68-$170

Address: 902 W Grove Ave 85210 **Location:** US 60 (Superstition Frwy) exit 178 (Alma School Rd), just n, then just e. **Facility:** 125 units. 7 stories, interior corridors. **Amenities:** video games (fee). Some: high-speed Internet. **Pool(s):** heated outdoor. **Activities:** whirlpool, exercise room. **Guest Services:** valet and coin laundry.

MOTEL 6-MESA SOUTH #1030
Phone: (480)834-0066 **55**

Motel
$55-$65 2/1-4/18
$45-$55 4/19-1/31

Address: 1511 S Country Club Dr 85210 **Location:** US 60 (Superstition Frwy) exit 179 (Country Club Dr), northeast corner. Adjacent to Golf Land Amusement Park. **Facility:** 90 units. 2 stories (no elevator), exterior corridors. **Pool(s):** heated outdoor.

(See map & index p. 164.)

PHOENIX MARRIOTT MESA
Phone: (480)898-8300 **41**

 Marriott **AAA Benefit:** AAA
HOTELS & RESORTS hotel discounts of 5%
Hotel or more.
$79-$219

Address: 200 N Centennial Way 85201 **Location:** US 60 (Superstition Frwy) exit 180 (Mesa Dr), 2 mi n, just w on Main St, then just n. **Facility:** 275 units. 12 stories, interior corridors. **Terms:** check-in 4 pm. **Amenities:** high-speed Internet. **Pool(s):** heated outdoor. **Activities:** whirlpool, exercise room. **Guest Services:** valet and coin laundry. **Free Special Amenities: newspaper and high-speed Internet.**

QUALITY INN & SUITES MESA/PHOENIX
Phone: (480)964-2897 **53**

Address: 1410 S Country Club Dr 85210 **Location:** US 60 (Superstition Frwy) exit 179 (Country Club Dr), just n. Located in a commercial area. **Facility:** 117 units, some two bedrooms and efficiencies. 2 stories, exterior corridors. **Terms:** check-in 4 pm, cancellation fee imposed. **Pool(s):** heated outdoor. **Activities:** whirlpool, exercise room. **Guest Services:** coin laundry.

RESIDENCE INN BY MARRIOTT PHOENIX MESA
Phone: (480)610-0100 **50**

Extended Stay **AAA Benefit:**
Hotel AAA hotel discounts of 5% or more.
$79-$229

Address: 941 W Grove Ave 85210 **Location:** US 60 (Superstition Frwy) exit 178 (Alma School Rd), just n, then just e. **Facility:** 117 units, some two bedrooms, efficiencies and kitchens. 3 stories, interior corridors. **Amenities:** high-speed Internet. **Pool(s):** heated outdoor. **Activities:** whirlpool, sports court, exercise room. **Guest Services:** valet and coin laundry.

SLEEP INN OF MESA
Phone: (480)807-7760 **62**

Address: 6347 E Southern Ave 85206 **Location:** US 60 (Superstition Frwy) exit 188 (Power Rd), 0.8 mi n, then 0.4 mi w to mall entrance. Located at west end of Superstition Springs Mall. **Facility:** 84 units. 3 stories, interior corridors. **Terms:** cancellation fee imposed. **Pool(s):** heated outdoor. **Activities:** whirlpool, limited exercise equipment. **Guest Services:** coin laundry.

TRAVELODGE SUITES MESA
Phone: (480)832-5961 **46**

Address: 4244 E Main St 85205 **Location:** US 60 (Superstition Frwy) exit 185 (Greenfield Rd), 2 mi n, then just w. **Facility:** 76 units, some efficiencies. 2 stories (no elevator), exterior corridors. **Terms:** cancellation fee imposed. **Amenities:** safes. **Pool(s):** heated outdoor. **Activities:** whirlpool. **Guest Services:** coin laundry.

WESTGATE PAINTED MOUNTAIN GOLF RESORT
Phone: 480/654-3611

fyi Not evaluated. **Address:** 6302 E McKellips Rd 85215 **Location:** Loop 202 E exit 12 (McKellips Rd), 9.1 mi e; adjacent to golf course. Facilities, services, and decor characterize a mid-scale property.

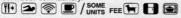
WHERE TO EAT

AMAZING JAKE'S
Phone: 480/926-7499 **38**

Specialty
$8-$10

AAA Inspector Notes: A party place for families with children, this eatery offers pizza, salad and pasta buffets, plus cake and ice cream for dessert. The kids will need the energy to partake in any number of games, including laser tag, bumper cars and a rock-climbing wall. All activities are indoors in a protected setting. **Bar:** beer & wine. **Address:** 1830 E Baseline Rd 85202 **Location:** US 60 (Superstition Frwy) exit 182 (Gilbert Rd), 0.4 mi s, then just w. **L** **D**

BILL JOHNSON'S BIG APPLE RESTAURANT
Phone: 480/969-6504

Steak
$6-$28

AAA Inspector Notes: The locally popular barbecue and steak house offers a casual atmosphere, friendly service and hearty portions of the signature barbecue beef, chicken and pork. Save room for the fresh fruit pie, which is large enough to share. The casual Western atmosphere with helpful staff and a western barn setting make for a fun dining experience. **Bar:** full bar. **Address:** 950 E Main St 85203 **Location:** US 60 (Superstition Frwy) exit 181 (Stapley Dr), 2 mi n, then just w. **B** **L** **D**

BLUE ADOBE GRILLE
Phone: 480/962-1000 **30**

Mexican
$7-$24

AAA Inspector Notes: Becoming a local favorite in the Southwestern dining scene, this restaurant prepares regional cuisine using red and green chiles from New Mexico. Bold flavors infuse the interesting and diverse dishes, including the honey pork tamale, pecan-roasted chicken quesadilla and tenderloin chiles rellenos. **Bar:** full bar. **Reservations:** suggested, Fri & Sat. **Address:** 144 N Country Club Dr 85201 **Location:** US 60 (Superstition Frwy) exit 179 (Country Club Dr), 2.1 mi n. **L** **D**

CULVER'S OF MESA
Phone: 480/733-5330 **36**

American
$3-$10

AAA Inspector Notes: This all-American fast food joint serves great burgers, sandwiches and desserts in a casual setting. **Address:** 1909 S Country Club Dr 85210 **Location:** US 60 (Superstition Frwy) exit 179 (Country Club Dr), 0.5 mi s. **L** **D**

FLANCER'S
Phone: 480/396-0077 **29**

Pizza
$6-$15

AAA Inspector Notes: Fun, friendly and casual best describe this East Valley pizza joint. Fresh, handmade New York-style pizza, calzones and pasta choices are some of the tasty items available. **Bar:** beer & wine. **Address:** 1902 N Higley Rd 85205 **Location:** SR 202 exit 21 (Higley Rd), 2.1 mi s. **L** **D**

THE LANDMARK RESTAURANT
Phone: 480/962-4652 **31**

American
$8-$27

AAA Inspector Notes: Dine in a restored church building amid Victorian decor. A varied menu and a large soup and salad bar are featured as well as an extensive display of Mesa historical photographs. **Bar:** full bar. **Address:** 809 W Main St 85201 **Location:** US 60 (Superstition Frwy) exit 179 (Country Club Dr), 2 mi n, then 0.5 mi w. **L** **D**

(See map & index p. 164.)

LITTLE MESA CAFE
Menu on AAA.com   Phone: 480/830-6201   (33)

American
$7-$17

AAA Inspector Notes: Some patrons might just start with the home-baked pies, which are as good as Grandma's, before digging into a fresh salad and such dishes as chicken-fried steak and center-cut pork chops. The casual decor and smiling servers put guests at ease. **Address:** 3929 E Main St 85205 **Location:** US 60 (Superstition Frwy) exit 184 (Val Vista Rd), 2 mi n, then just e. [B] [L] [D]

LOS DOS MOLINOS   Phone: 480/969-7475   (32)

Mexican
$6-$14

AAA Inspector Notes: This popular valley eatery has been serving delicious New Mexico-style Mexican food for nearly two decades. Specializing in spicy chili dishes, like shrimp Veracruz and carne adovada, there is good reason why their motto is "some like it hot.". **Bar:** full bar. **Address:** 260 S Alma School Rd 85210 **Location:** US 60 (Superstition Frwy) exit 178 (Alma School Rd), 1.7 mi n. [L] [D]

MACAYO MEXICAN KITCHEN   Phone: 480/820-0237

Mexican
$8-$16

AAA Inspector Notes: The colorfully furnished Mexican-style eatery prepares Sonoran Mexican dishes. Friendly and efficient staffers serve traditional and lighter dishes flavored with this place's own chili peppers, which are grown near Tucson. **Bar:** full bar. **Address:** 1920 S Dobson Rd 85202 **Location:** Baseline and Dobson rds; northwest corner. [L] [D]

MI AMIGOS MEXICAN GRILL   Phone: 480/892-6822   (35)

Mexican
$6-$15

AAA Inspector Notes: Bright and cheerful decor is welcoming at this casual grill, where the food is freshly prepared. Patrons savor the flavors in all the dishes, from tortilla soup to sizzling fajitas. **Bar:** full bar. **Address:** 1264 S Gilbert Rd 85204 **Location:** US 60 (Superstition Frwy) exit 182 (Gilbert Rd), 0.4 mi n. [L] [D]

MY BIG FAT GREEK RESTAURANT   Phone: 480/981-0010   (37)

Greek
$5-$21

AAA Inspector Notes: Employing friendly staff members, this eatery dishes up all the favorite Greek classics, like lamb souvlaki and moussaka, in large portions. An expanded menu pleases a wide range of patrons with such items as rib-eye, calzones and pizza. Baklava cheesecake and rich chocolate cake are tempting meal-enders. **Bar:** full bar. **Address:** 6447 E Southern Ave 85206 **Location:** 0.4 mi w of Power Rd. [L] [D]

ORGAN STOP PIZZA   Phone: 480/813-5700   (34)

Pizza
$6-$18

AAA Inspector Notes: Patrons enjoy a selection of freshly prepared pizza, spaghetti and such appetizers as fried zucchini or mushrooms while listening to nightly concerts given by the Mighty Wurlitzer organ. **Bar:** beer & wine. **Address:** 1149 E Southern Ave 85204 **Location:** US 60 (Superstition Frwy) exit 181 (Stapley Dr), 0.4 mi n, then just w. [D]

P.F. CHANG'S CHINA BISTRO
                    Phone: 480/218-4900   (40)

Chinese
$10-$21

AAA Inspector Notes: Trendy, upscale decor provides a pleasant backdrop for New Age Chinese dining. Appetizers, soups and salads are a meal by themselves. Vegetarian plates and sides, noodles, meins, chicken and meat dishes are created from exotic, fresh ingredients. **Bar:** full bar. **Address:** 6610 E Superstition Springs Blvd 85206 **Location:** US 60 (Superstition Frwy) exit 188 (Power Rd), just s, then just w. [L] [D]

PINK PEPPER THAI CUISINE
                    Phone: 480/839-9009   (39)

Thai
$7-$14

AAA Inspector Notes: Soft decor colors are a pleasant backdrop for the vivid flavors of the food. A wide selection of dishes-including the nicely spiced jumping shrimp with vegetables-demonstrates the chef's expertise. Somtum, a traditional Thai salad, blends green papaya, green beans and tomato along with dried shrimp and palm. Tempting dessert options include homemade ice creams and sticky rice with mango. **Bar:** full bar. **Address:** 1941 W Guadalupe Rd 85202 **Location:** US 60 (Superstition Frwy) exit 177 (Dobson Rd), 1.6 mi s. [L] [D]

RANCHO DE TIA ROSA   Phone: 480/659-8787   (28)

Mexican
$8-$20

AAA Inspector Notes: Four acres of grounds encompass the restaurant and greenhouses where organic produce is grown for the kitchen. A taqueria for take-out service is at the entrance, while the main building includes a front courtyard with seating, an indoor dining room and patio seating. **Bar:** full bar. **Address:** 3129 E McKellips Rd 85213 **Location:** 0.5 mi w of Val Vista Dr.
[L] [D] CALL [M]

RUBIO'S FRESH MEXICAN GRILL
               For additional information, visit AAA.com

Mexican
$3-$7

AAA Inspector Notes: Freshly prepared and healthful foods, bright decor and friendly staff are found in this upscale fast-food spot. A special treat, the salsa bar lines up four styles and flavors. **Bar:** beer only. [L] [D]

LOCATIONS:
Address: 6736 E Baseline Rd 85206 **Location:** US 60 (Superstition Frwy) exit 188 (Power Rd), just s. **Phone:** 480/830-2247

Address: 1649 S Stapley Rd 85204 **Location:** US 60 (Superstition Frwy) exit 181 (Stapley Rd), just s. **Phone:** 480/633-3119

Address: 884 W Warner Rd 85234 **Location:** Jct Cooper Rd; northwest corner. **Phone:** 480/539-8919

SERRANO'S MEXICAN RESTAURANT
               For additional information, visit AAA.com

Mexican
$6-$20

AAA Inspector Notes: A pleasant stop for lunch or dinner, the local chain is known for consistently good food and attractive, upscale Mexican-style décor. The warm bean dip starter stirs the appetite for traditional dishes such as chiles rellenos or seafood enchiladas prepared with fresh ingredients. Service is friendly. **Bar:** full bar. [L] [D]

LOCATIONS:
Address: 1955 W Guadalupe Rd 85202 **Location:** US 60 (Superstition Frwy) exit 177 (Dobson Rd), 1.6 mi s. **Phone:** 480/756-2992

Address: 1021 S Power Rd 85205 **Location:** Just n of Southern Blvd. **Phone:** 480/854-7455

Address: 1964 E McKellips Rd 85203 **Location:** Northeast corner of Gilbert and McKellips rds. **Phone:** 480/649-3503

MONTEZUMA CASTLE NATIONAL MONUMENT (C-4)

Off I-17 exit 289 on Montezuma Castle Hwy., Montezuma Castle National Monument contains ruins of an early cliff dwelling. Built in the 12th and 13th centuries, it is among the best preserved dwellings of its type. The foundation is in a vertical cliff 46 feet above the talus slope. The five-story castle, believed to be inhabited by Sinagua Indians, contains 20 rooms and was once accessible only by ladders. Other ruins dot the cliffs and hilltops around Beaver Creek.

As a preservative measure, tours into Montezuma Castle are not allowed, but a self-guiding trail offers good views of the castle and displays a scale model of its interior. The visitor center contains artifacts found in the area. Picnicking is permitted in designated areas. Allow 1 hour minimum. Visitor center and monument open daily 8-6, Memorial Day-Labor Day; 8-5, rest of year. Admission $5, free (ages 0-15). Phone (928) 567-3322.

MONTEZUMA WELL, about 11 mi. n.e., is a detached portion of the monument. The limestone sinkhole, 470 feet wide and 55 feet deep, is rimmed by pueblos and cliff dwellings. A source of water to the fields of ancient peoples, some of the ditches dug A.D. 1200-1300 are still visible. A self guiding trail is available. **Time:** Allow 1 hour minimum. **Hours:** Daily 8-6, Memorial Day-Labor Day; 8-5, rest of year. **Cost:** Free. **Phone:** (928) 567-3322, ext. 21.

MONUMENT VALLEY NAVAJO TRIBAL PARK (A-5)

Reached via scenic US 163 from Kayenta, Ariz., and from Gouldings and Mexican Hat, Utah, Monument Valley Navajo Tribal Park is a colorful region covering several thousand square miles within the Navajo Indian Reservation. The park contains Mystery Valley, where isolated monoliths of red sandstone tower as much as 1,000 feet above the valley floor.

The visitor center, 4 miles southeast of US 163, provides information about self-guiding tours. Guided tours from the center are offered daily; primitive camping and picnicking are permitted.

Horseback and four-wheel-drive trips through Monument Valley can be arranged through agencies in Arizona at Kayenta and in Utah at Bluff, Mexican Hat and Monument Valley. Overnight accommodations also are available in Gouldings, Kayenta and Mexican Hat; reservations are recommended.

Visitors should not photograph the Navajo people, their homes or their possessions without asking permission; a gratuity is usually requested. Other restrictions apply. For more information contact Monument Valley Navajo Tribal Park, P.O. Box 360289, Monument Valley, UT 84536.

The park is open daily 6 a.m.-8:30 p.m., May-Sept.; 8-5, rest of year (weather permitting). Closed Thanksgiving and Christmas. Last admission 30 minutes before closing. Recreational vehicles more than 25 feet long are not permitted on the self-guiding tour. Admission is $5; free (ages 0-9). Primitive camping fee is $10. Phone (435) 727-5870.

VISITOR CENTER, 4 mi. s.e. of US 163 near the Arizona/Utah border, offers an impressive panorama of the Mitten and Merrick buttes; exhibits about Native Americans; an auditorium; an outdoor amphitheater; a patio; a library; and a Navajo hogan, the traditional housing structure of the Navajo people.

Departing from the center are various guided tours led by Navajo tour operators, who take visitors down into the valley. Food is available in summer. **Time:** Allow 2 hours, 30 minutes minimum. **Hours:** Daily 6 a.m.-8 p.m., May-Sept.; 8-7, Mar.-Apr.; 8-5, rest of year. Closed Thanksgiving and Christmas. **Cost:** Visitor center $5; free (ages 0-9). **Phone:** (435) 727-5870 or (435) 727-5875.

MORMON LAKE

MORMON LAKE LODGE	Phone: 928/354-2227

[fyi] Not evaluated. **Address:** 1 Main St 86038 **Location:** I-17 exit 339, 30 mi s of Flagstaff via Lake Mary and Mormon Lake rds; follow brown signs. Facilities, services, and decor characterize an economy property.

WHERE TO EAT

MORMON LAKE LODGE STEAK HOUSE & SALOON
Phone: 928/354-2227

Steak
$5-$32

AAA Inspector Notes: Located in a remote location near a campground and lodge, the property sits in a wooded area near a small lake. Among offerings at the steakhouse are barbecue ribs, steak and chicken. The decor is rustic with a Western flair. **Bar:** full bar. **Reservations:** suggested. **Address:** 1 Main St 86038 **Location:** I-17 exit 339, 30 mi s of Flagstaff via Lake Mary and Mormon Lake rds; follow brown signs; in Mormon Lake Lodge. **Parking:** on-site and street.

[B] [L] [D]

Famed Open-pit Steakhouse serving up grilled fare

MORRISTOWN (H-1) elev. 1,971'

LAKE PLEASANT REGIONAL PARK, 12 mi. e. on SR 74, then 2 mi. n. off Castle Hot Springs Rd., encompasses more than 24,500 acres. A 10-lane boat ramp and a visitor center are available at the main entrance, and a four-lane ramp is at the north entrance. Books, brochures and exhibits about the Central Arizona Project, Waddell Dam and the lake are offered at the visitor center. *See Recreation Chart.*

Hours: Daily 24 hours. **Cost:** $6 (per private vehicle). Watercraft $2-$4 each. Camping $10-$35 (per private vehicle). **Phone:** (928) 501-1710 or (602) 372-7460.

Waddell Dam, at the southern end of Lake Pleasant, impounds Lake Pleasant. On the Agua Fria River, the earthen dam completed in 1992 is 4,700 feet long and 300 feet high.

MUNDS PARK pop. 631

MOTEL IN THE PINES	Phone: (928)286-9699
Motel $39-$89	Address: 80 W Pinewood Rd 86017
	Location: I-17 exit 322, just e.
	Facility: 22 units, some efficiencies. 2 stories (no elevator), exterior corridors.

SAVE / SOME UNITS FEE 🐕 🖥 📷 📱

NAVAJOLAND

Encompassing some 27,000 square miles, Navajoland includes parts of Arizona, Utah and New Mexico. Larger than the state of West Virginia, the sovereign nation is the largest Native American nation in the country.

From the stark monoliths of Monument Valley Navajo Tribal Park *(see place listing p. 117)* and the sheer walls of Canyon de Chelly National Monument *(see place listing p. 43)* to the ancient ruins of Navajo National Monument *(see place listing p. 119)*, Navajoland is home to more than a dozen national monuments. The area also contains the Petrified Forest National Park *(see place listing p. 168)*, 186-mile-long Lake Powell and various tribal parks and historic sites.

Heritage is important to the Navajo, and singing and dancing give the Navajo a chance to wear their traditional attire. Tribal dress includes knee-high moccasins, velvet vests, concho belts and silver and turquoise jewelry for both men and women. Powwows often are performed throughout the Navajo nation and visitors are invited to observe.

The Navajo, or Dineh, consider themselves an extension of Mother Earth and therefore treat nature with great respect. Not only rich in culture, the Navajo live in an area rich in minerals; oil, gas, coal and uranium lie beneath the arid desert. The discovery of oil in the 1920s prompted the Navajo to form their own tribal government to help handle the encroachment of mining companies.

Reorganized in 1991, the Navajo government consists of an elected president, vice president and 88 council delegates representing 110 local units of government. Council meetings take place four times a year in Window Rock *(see place listing p. 320)*; visitors are welcome.

Tradition also can be seen in the Navajo's arts and crafts, particularly the distinctive style of their vibrantly-colored rugs and blankets as well silver pieces, basketry and sand paintings. Visitors to the area can purchase Navajo wares at various shops throughout the area.

The following places in Navajoland are listed separately under their individual names: Fort Defiance, Ganado, Kayenta, Keams Canyon, Page,

▼ See AAA listing p. 321 ▼

Reserve Your Room Now! Toll Free: 800.662.6189

AAA Approved

Ask for the AAA Rate!
• Free made to order breakfast
• Free high-speed internet
• Free fitness center
• Free in-room coffee

Sample the local scenic attractions, history & culture of Window Rock. On-site restaurant & business center.

QUALITY INN
BY CHOICE HOTELS
Quality Inn
Navajo Nation Capital

Window Rock

ExploreNavajo.com
A Culture Like No Other!

48 West Highway 264,
Window Rock, AZ 86515
Tel: 928.871.4108
Toll Free: 800.662.6189

Second Mesa, Tuba City and Window Rock. Visitors should be aware of certain restrictions while in Navajoland; *see Good Facts To Know.*

Navajo Tourism Department-Navajoland: P.O. Box 663, Window Rock, AZ 86515. **Phone:** (928) 871-6436.

NAVAJO NATIONAL MONUMENT (A-4)

Reached via US 160 and a 9-mile paved road (SR 564), Navajo National Monument preserves some of the largest and most intact of Arizona's known cliff dwellings in perhaps the most awe-inspiring area in the Southwest. There are two areas that can be visited by ranger-guided tours, each of which contains a remarkable 13th-century Pueblo ruin.

The monument lies within the Navajo Indian Reservation. Traveling off paved roads is not permitted. Most of the unmarked dirt-surfaced roads on the reservation are private driveways; private Navajo property is not open to visitors. Visitors should be aware of certain restrictions; *see Good Facts To Know.*

Free year-round camping and picnicking are permitted near the monument headquarters. The 41 campsites are available on a first-come first-served basis and are usually filled by dusk during the summer; vehicles must be no longer than 30 feet in length. Accommodations are available at Kayenta; reservations are recommended. Gas and grocery services are not available in the park; the nearest services are 9 miles south at the junction of SR 564 and US 160.

Note: In summer the Navajo Reservation observes daylight-saving time, which is an hour later than outside the reservation.

At an elevation of approximately 7,300 feet, the visitor center at the monument headquarters offers exhibits of ancestral Native American artifacts, a 20-minute videotape tour of the Betatakin ruins, and a 25-minute videotape about the prehistoric culture. Check for fire restrictions at the campgrounds. Visitor center open daily 8-5, Memorial Day-Labor Day; 8-5, rest of year. Closed Jan. 1, Thanksgiving and Christmas. Free. Phone (928) 672-2700.

BETATAKIN AREA is 2.5 mi. from monument headquarters by way of a strenuous 5-mi. round-trip trail. This is the monument's most accessible area and is home to its headquarters. Ranger-guided tours depart daily at 8:15 a.m. and 10 a.m. from Memorial Day through Labor Day (weather permitting); tours depart daily at 10 a.m. the rest of the year. Hikers should arrive early to ensure a spot; this popular tour is limited to 25 people per day on a first-come, first-served basis. The cliff dwelling also can be viewed across the canyon from the end of the Sandal Trail year-round via a 1-mile round-trip self-guiding walk.

Note: Sturdy shoes and 2 quarts of water are recommended; the high altitude, heat and steep grade of the trail make good physical condition a requirement. Allow 3-5 hours for tour. **Hours:** Daily 8-5. **Cost:** Tour free. **Phone:** (928) 672-2700 for information and schedule updates.

KEET SEEL AREA is accessible by hiking a difficult 17-mi. round-trip trail. The area contains the largest and best-preserved cliff dwellings in the vicinity, which date 1250-1300. To protect these fragile ruins there is a daily limit of 20 people.

Note: This trip is not recommended for inexperienced hikers. Hikers are required to attend a trail briefing to receive a permit and are advised to bring sufficient bottled water. Primitive campgrounds are available for hikers. **Hours:** Trail open Memorial Day-Labor Day. Schedules for tours of the ruins vary. **Cost:** Free. Check with rangers at the visitor center for reservations; they can and should be made within 5 months of the date of the trip and be confirmed 1 week prior. Reservations are required. **Phone:** (928) 672-2700 for reservations, information and schedule updates.

NOGALES (G-4) pop. 20,837, elev. 3,865'
• Hotels p. 120 • Restaurants p. 120

Nogales (noh-GAH-lehs) is rich in Spanish history; Franciscan missionary Fray Marcos de Niza entered Santa Cruz County as early as 1539.

Mexico's Pacific Highway, a four-lane divided highway, starts in Nogales and continues through Guadalajara, Mexico, with connecting roads to Mexico City. Nogales is a popular port of entry for U.S. travelers as well as for more than 75 percent of winter fruits and vegetables shipped throughout the United States and Canada. Retail and wholesale trade with northern Mexico also is an important industry in the town.

Nogales-Santa Cruz County Chamber of Commerce and Visitor Center: 123 W. Kino Park Way, Nogales, AZ 85621. **Phone:** (520) 287-3685.

Simply Reliable

The Diamond Ratings in this TourBook guide are backed by our expert, in-person evaluations, whether the hotel or restaurant is no-frills, moderate or upscale.

Learn more at **AAA.com/Diamonds**

BEST WESTERN SONORA INN & SUITES
Phone: (520)375-6500

Hotel
$130-$150

AAA Benefit:
Members save up to 20%, plus 10% bonus points with Best Western Rewards®.

Address: 750 W Shell Rd 85621 **Location:** I-19 exit 4, just w to Frank Reed Rd, then just nw. **Facility:** 65 units. 3 stories, interior corridors. **Amenities:** high-speed Internet. **Pool(s):** heated outdoor. **Activities:** whirlpool, exercise room. **Guest Services:** valet and coin laundry. **Free Special Amenities: full breakfast and high-speed Internet.**

Free Hot Breakfast, Internet, Meeting Room, Coin Laundry, Heated Pool & Spa, Fitness Center, No Pets.

CANDLEWOOD SUITES
Phone: (520)281-1111

Extended Stay Hotel
$99-$149

Address: 875 N Frank Reed Rd 85621 **Location:** I-19 exit 4, just w to Frank Reed Rd, then just nw. **Facility:** 83 efficiencies. 3 stories, interior corridors. **Activities:** exercise room. **Guest Services:** valet and coin laundry.

HOLIDAY INN EXPRESS HOTEL NOGALES
Phone: (520)281-0123

Hotel
$99-$159

Address: 850 W Shell Rd 85621 **Location:** I-19 exit 4, just w to Frank Reed Rd, then just nw. **Facility:** 99 units. 3 stories, interior corridors. **Terms:** cancellation fee imposed. **Pool(s):** outdoor. **Activities:** whirlpool, exercise room. **Guest Services:** valet and coin laundry.

MOTEL 6 NOGALES #71
Phone: (520)281-2951

Motel
$51-$61 7/1-1/31
$45-$55 2/1-6/30

Address: 141 W Mariposa Rd 85621 **Location:** I-19 exit 4, 0.9 mi e. **Facility:** 79 units. 2 stories (no elevator), exterior corridors. **Pool(s):** outdoor. **Guest Services:** coin laundry.

Download eTourBook guides
for ereaders and smartphones
at AAA.com/ebooks

SIESTA MOTEL
Phone: (520)287-4671

Motel
$50-$60

Address: 673 N Grand Ave 85621 **Location:** On Business Loop I-19, 1 mi n of International border. Located in a business area. **Facility:** 46 units. 2 stories (no elevator), exterior corridors. **Terms:** cancellation fee imposed. **Amenities:** high-speed Internet. **Pool(s):** outdoor. **Activities:** whirlpool. **Free Special Amenities: continental breakfast and high-speed Internet.**

SIESTA MOTEL

Free Internet, Outdoor Pool Pets allowed with fee, Free Continental Breakfast.

WHERE TO EAT

MR. C'S RESTAURANT & SUPPER CLUB
Phone: 520/281-9000

Steak
$8-$46

AAA Inspector Notes: Views through tall windows in the hilltop eatery enhance meals that incorporate wonderfully tasty steaks, seafood and pasta along with a salad bar filled with crispy ingredients. The staff is pleasant. **Bar:** full bar. **Address:** 282 W View Point Dr 85621 **Location:** I-19 exit 4, 0.7 mi e to W Mastick Way, just s, then just w to top of hill. D

Visiting Mexico
Personal Safety

Thousands of Americans routinely cross the border into Mexico on a daily basis for business and personal reasons without incident, and crimes directed at tourists are unlikely. The possibility does exist, however, particularly in cities that are centers of activity for Mexican drug cartels. This violence grabs news headlines and adversely affects the daily lives of many Mexicans.

But for the casual visitor, safety almost always boils down to good old common sense. Stash traveler's checks and cash in different places; for example, in money belts and extra pockets sewn inside clothing. Keep photocopies of passports, credit cards and other documents in a separate place from the originals. Use parking lots or garages whenever possible. Legal parking is designated by a sign showing a red circle with a capital "E" inside; no-parking zones have signs with a diagonal red line through the "E."

Nearby Mexico

NOGALES, SONORA (B-2) pop. 220,292, elev. 3,674'

Note: For current information about safety/security issues in Nogales, go to the U.S. State Department website (travel.state.gov). For general safety-related information *see Personal Safety*.

The border city of Nogales (noh-GAH-lehs) is sometimes referred to as Ambos Nogales ("both Nogales") in recognition of the sister city of Nogales, Ariz. on the other side of the international boundary fence. Settlement of the area began shortly after present-day Arizona, New Mexico and California were ceded to the United States according to the terms of the Treaty of Guadalupe Hidalgo, which ended the Mexican-American War. It was not until 1882, however, that the town was officially established. It not only became—and continues to be—larger than its U.S. counterpart, but also has managed to retain a strong sense of Mexican identity.

Nogales is the gateway into northwestern mainland Mexico and points south, although many visitors just come for the day. Things heat up on weekends, when the underage Arizona crowd makes the hour pilgrimage south from Tucson to patronize the local bars and nightspots.

Mexican and U.S. Customs and Border Protection offices are open 24 hours daily. A tourist permit is not needed for in-town stays of less than 72 hours, but proof of citizenship is required. For southbound motorists, the official immigration checkpoint is 21 kilometers (13 miles) south of Nogales on Mex. 15. You can obtain a tourist permit here if you don't already have one, and must present a federal temporary vehicle importation permit or an "Only Sonora" temporary vehicle importation permit (if you intend to stay within the state of Sonora) and accompanying windshield sticker.

A vehicle permit is not required for travel to the following destinations in the state of Sonora: Rocky Point (Puerto Peñasco), Guaymas, San Carlos, Bahía Kino and other locations west of Mex. 15, as well as cities along Mex. 15 (Magdalena, Santa Ana, Hermosillo). An "Only Sonora" permit is required if driving within Sonora east of Mex. 15 as well as south of Empalme (about 350 miles south of the U.S. border). The permit can be obtained at Banjercito offices in Agua Prieta (opposite Douglas, Ariz.), Cananea (southwest of Agua Prieta on Mex. 2) and Empalme (on Mex. 15 at Km marker 98, just south of the Guaymas bypass).

From Tucson, I-19 south ends at Nogales, Ariz.; signs point the way to the border crossing. Mex. 15 begins at the border, but the downtown Nogales crossing passes through the most congested part of the city. Motorists intending to bypass Nogales for points south can save time by using the international truck crossing, known as the Mariposa crossing; take exit 4 off I-19, then proceed west on SR 189 (Mariposa Road), following signs that say "Border Truck Route" and "International Border." This route reconnects with Mex. 15 south of Nogales at the 21-kilometer (13-mile) immigration checkpoint. The charge at the toll booth approximately 6 miles south of the border is about $2 (U.S.).

If you're driving through downtown Nogales back to the United States, watch for the sign that says "Linea International"; follow the directions for the road that leads to the border crossing.

Since almost all of the tourist-oriented shopping is within easy walking distance of the border, it is recommended that day visitors park on the Arizona side and head into Mexico on foot. From the Nogales-Santa Cruz County Chamber of Commerce and Visitor Center, 123 W. Kino Park Way (just off the intersection of Grand Avenue and US 82) in Nogales, Ariz., it's about a 1.5-mile drive south to a series of guarded lots; all-day parking fees average about $8, and cash is expected. The turnstiles to Mexico are at the foot of the Port of Entry.

The shops and vendor stalls catering to tourists are concentrated within easy walking distance of the border along north-south Avenida Obregón. They sell pottery, baskets, fabrics, ceramics, leather goods, glassware, carved pine furniture, rugs, jewelry and more. Most business is conducted in English, bargaining is acceptable and even expected, and American currency is preferred. More exclusive establishments have fixed prices and carry crafts and gift items from all over Mexico. When buying at stalls or from street vendors, always check for quality.

Along with shopping, Nogales offers such standard tourist experiences as having your picture taken astride a donkey and listening to mariachi bands. And like other Mexican border cities, it's a place to get prescriptions filled at a cost that is often far less than stateside.

Nogales also has several good restaurants. La Roca Restaurant is just across the border on a side street off Avenida Ruiz Cortines (look for the large magnolia trees in front of the restaurant). Built into the base of a cliff, it has an elegant atmosphere, expert service by white-jacketed waiters and a menu emphasizing Sonoran specialties. Elvira's, close to the border on Avenida Obregón, has been a Nogales favorite since 1927. Diners come for signature dishes like tequila shrimp—and complimentary shots of tequila.

This ends the Nogales section and resumes the alphabetical city listings for Arizona.

ORACLE (F-5) pop. 3,686, elev. 4,513'
• **Part of Tucson area — see map p. 268**

Oracle is named for the ship which carried the town's founder, Albert Weldon, to the United States in the late 1800s. A local miner, Weldon built a brush camp where the town now stands. Originally a copper mining town, Oracle's present-day economy is based on tourism, electronics and arts and crafts. In the foothills of the Santa Catalina Mountains, 35 miles northeast of Tucson, Oracle's high altitude provides visitors a respite from the heat of the desert.

San Manuel/Mammoth/Oracle Tri-Community Chamber of Commerce: Write P.O. Box 416, San Manuel, AZ 85631. **Phone:** (520) 385-9322.

UNIVERSITY OF ARIZONA-BIOSPHERE 2, 5 mi. n.e. of jct. SRs 79 and 77 to 32540 S. Biosphere Rd., is a glass and steel structure that encompasses 3 acres and five biomes: rain forest, ocean, savanna, desert and marsh. The biosphere is a learning, teaching and research center for determining an ecosystem's ability to recycle air, water and nutrients in order to sustain human, plant and animal life.

The guided Under the Glass tour provides visitors a closer look at the interior of the facility, including its ocean, lung and technological systems. The tour begins with a film presentation at the visitor center and includes a .25-mile walking tour inside the Biosphere 2.

Note: The interior portion of the tour involves ascending and descending 150 steps and is not accessible by wheelchair or baby stroller. Comfortable walking shoes are recommended. **Time:** Allow 2 hours minimum. **Hours:** Daily 9-4. Tours are given daily. Closed Thanksgiving and Christmas. Phone ahead to confirm schedule. **Cost:** $20; $18 (ages 62+ and military with ID); $13 (ages 6-12). Reservations are recommended. **Phone:** (520) 838-6200.

ORGAN PIPE CACTUS NATIONAL MONUMENT (F-2)

In southwestern Arizona, Organ Pipe Cactus National Monument preserves a diverse and relatively undisturbed sample of the Sonoran Desert of particular interest to desert aficionados. The organ pipe cactus thrives within the United States primarily in this 516-square-mile preserve. The spectacular saguaro cacti, along with the paloverde, ironwood and ocotillo, also contribute to the desert landscape.

The monument contains a graded dirt park road: the 21-mile Ajo Mountain Drive. The scenic drive begins near the visitor center, and conditions are generally good for car travel. The drive is closed occasionally because of adverse weather conditions or construction; phone ahead. No trailers or recreational vehicles more than 25 feet are permitted on this park road.

The Kris Eggle Visitor Center, at Milepost 75 on scenic SR 85 (34 miles south of Ajo), is open daily 8-5; closed Thanksgiving and Christmas. Exhibits interpret the flora, fauna and cultural history of the monument. A 15-minute introductory slide program is shown upon request. Self-guiding interpretive trails are near the visitor center and the campground area ($12 per night).

Admission is by 7-day permit. The cost is $8 per private vehicle. For further information contact the Superintendent, Organ Pipe Cactus National Monument, 10 Organ Pipe Dr., Ajo, AZ 85321; phone (520) 387-6849.

ORO VALLEY pop. 41,011
• Hotels & Restaurants map & index p. 282
• Part of Tucson area — see map p. 268

FAIRFIELD INN & SUITES TUCSON NORTH/ORO VALLEY   Phone: (520)202-4000   64

Hotel
$109-$162

Address: 10150 N Oracle Rd 85737 **Location:** 3.9 mi n of jct Ina Rd. **Facility:** 89 units, some kitchens. 2 stories, interior corridors. **Amenities:** high-speed Internet. **Pool(s):** heated outdoor. **Activities:** whirlpool, exercise room. **Guest Services:** valet and coin laundry.

HILTON TUCSON EL CONQUISTADOR GOLF & TENNIS RESORT   Phone: 520/544-5000   65

Resort Hotel
Rates not provided

AAA Benefit: Members save 5% or more everyday!
Hilton

Address: 10000 N Oracle Rd 85704 **Location:** I-10 exit 248 (Ina Rd); jct Ina Rd, 4.4 mi n. Located in a quiet area. **Facility:** The large resort, located at the base of Catalina Mountains, has spacious rooms around a landscaped pool area. 428 units, some two bedrooms. 1-3 stories, interior/exterior corridors. **Parking:** on-site and valet. **Terms:** check-in 4 pm. **Amenities:** video games (fee), safes, honor bars. **Dining:** 3 restaurants, also, Dos Locos, see separate listing, entertainment. **Pool(s):** 3 heated outdoor. **Activities:** whirlpools, waterslide, basketball, horseshoes, volleyball. **Fee:** golf-45 holes, 31 lighted tennis courts, racquetball courts, horseback riding, massage. **Guest Services:** complimentary and valet laundry, area transportation-golf club.

ORO VALLEY HOTEL & SUITES   Phone: (520)544-2100   63

Hotel
$94-$147

Address: 11075 N Oracle Rd 85737 **Location:** 1.8 mi s of Tangerine Rd. **Facility:** 104 units. 3 stories, interior corridors. **Amenities:** high-speed Internet, safes. **Pool(s):** heated outdoor. **Activities:** whirlpool, exercise room. **Guest Services:** valet laundry.

THE CONDOS AT VISTOSO   Phone: 520/877-7924
fyi Not evaluated. **Address:** 655 W Vistoso Highlands Dr 85755 **Location:** Jct Tangerine Rd, 2.2 mi n on Rancho Vistoso Blvd, then just w. Facilities, services, and decor characterize a mid-scale property.

WHERE TO EAT

CAFFE TORINO RISTORANTE ITALIANO   Phone: 520/219-2994   82

Italian
$7-$15

AAA Inspector Notes: This popular spot allows guests to savor an omelet and coffee while enjoying mountain views from the front patio. Lunchtime choices include freshly made salads and hearty panini sandwiches that melt in the mouth. The dinner menu features Italian classics featuring such ingredients as veal, ravioli and gnocchi. **Bar:** full bar. **Address:** 10325 N La Canada Dr, Suite 151 85739 **Location:** Jct Lambert Ln. B L D

Discover mobile travel solutions at
AAA.com/mobile and CAA.ca/mobile

(See map & index p. 282.)

DOS LOCOS   Phone: 520/544-5000   (84)

Southwestern
$15-$28

AAA Inspector Notes: Diners experience Latin fusion foods that feature a wide selection of tapas, including roasted duck and mango quesadilla, along with chicken adobo and achiote-marinated beef medallions. Star-light dining on the patio is a nice option when the weather permits. **Bar:** full bar. **Reservations:** suggested. **Address:** 10000 N Oracle Rd I-10 exit 248 (Ina Rd); jct Ina Rd, 4.4 mi n; in Hilton Tucson El Conquistador Golf & Tennis Resort. **Parking:** on-site and valet. (D)

DRAGON VILLAGE RESTAURANT
                   Phone: 520/229-0388   (80)

Chinese
$7-$11

AAA Inspector Notes: This casual eatery serves freshly prepared classic meals and healthy foods. The sesame chicken is a local favorite, and soups are hearty and warm. Expect friendly service and large portions at this spot, voted one of the top 100 Chinese restaurants by a California trade publication. **Address:** 12152 N Rancho Vistoso Blvd, #180 85737 **Location:** Jct Tangerine Rd; northwest corner. (L) (D)

HARVEST   Phone: 520/731-1100   (81)

Regional American
$12-$25

AAA Inspector Notes: Sustainable, locally grown and seasonal are some of the words to describe the contemporary American fare at this upscale, modern yet comfortable dining spot. With a menu that changes seasonally, diners can expect fresh, organic offerings like the farmer's market medley of vegetables, empanadas made with local organic beef and tempting homemade desserts such as the chocolate truffle beignets. **Bar:** full bar. **Reservations:** suggested. **Address:** 10355 N La Canada Dr 85737 **Location:** Southwest corner of La Canada and Rancho Sonora drs. (D)

THE LOOP TASTE OF CHICAGO
                   Phone: 520/878-0222   (83)

Pizza
$6-$19

AAA Inspector Notes: Savor authentic deep-dish or thin-crust Chicago-style pizza, or many of the other delicious options at this lively and casual family-friendly restaurant. **Bar:** full bar. **Address:** 10180 N Oracle Rd 85704 **Location:** 3.9 mi n of jct Ina Rd. (L) (D)

RUBIO'S FRESH MEXICAN GRILL Phone: 520/297-9551

Mexican
$3-$8

AAA Inspector Notes: Freshly prepared and healthful foods, bright decor and friendly staff are found in this upscale fast-food spot. A special treat, the salsa bar lines up four styles and flavors. **Bar:** beer only. **Address:** 10509 N Oracle Rd 85739 **Location:** Jct N 1st Ave, just s. (L) (D)

Are we meeting your travel needs?

TourBook Comments

If your visit to an establishment listed in a AAA TourBook guide doesn't meet your expectations, tell us about it.

Complete an easy online form at **AAA.com/TourBookComments.**

PAGE (A-4) pop. 7,247, elev. 4,281'
• Hotels p. 124 • Restaurants p. 125

Established to provide housing and facilities for workers on the Glen Canyon Dam project, Page was named for John Chatfield Page, the commissioner of reclamation who devoted many years to the development of the upper Colorado River. The town is a center for outfitters who provide trips into the Glen Canyon National Recreation Area *(see place listing p. 78).*

Scenic flights over Lake Powell and the surrounding Navajo country as well as to the Grand Canyon depart from the Page airport. In early December, spectators gather near Lake Powell to watch the dazzling ◆ Festival of Lights Boat Parade.

Page-Lake Powell Chamber of Commerce: 34 S. Lake Powell Blvd., P.O. Box 727, Page, AZ 86040. **Phone:** (928) 645-2741.

ANTELOPE CANYON NAVAJO TRIBAL PARK, 1 mi. e. on SR 98, comprises two slot canyons with graceful, swirling red sandstone canyon walls carved by wind and rain over thousands of years. Visitors are driven 3.5 miles to the canyons and must tour the canyons with a licensed guide. Access to Lower Antelope Canyon requires a climb down ladders bolted to the canyon walls. On the Upper Antelope Canyon tour visitors walk right into the canyon.

Time: Allow 1 hour minimum. **Hours:** Entrance fee station daily 8-5, Apr.-Oct. Lower canyon daily 8-5, Apr.-Oct. Upper canyon daily 8-4, Apr.-Oct. Phone ahead to confirm schedule. **Cost:** Entrance fee $6; free (ages 0-7). Guided tour fees vary; phone ahead. **Phone:** (928) 698-2808.

GLEN CANYON NATIONAL RECREATION AREA—*see place listing p. 78.*

JOHN WESLEY POWELL MEMORIAL MUSEUM AND VISITOR INFORMATION CENTER, Lake Powell Blvd. and N. Navajo Dr., contains exhibits relating to area development, Native American culture, geology, paleontology, the Colorado River and John Wesley Powell, the river's first modern scientist-explorer. The museum staff can book Lake Powell, Colorado River and scenic air tours.

Nearby slot canyons may be viewed by guided tours only; tickets are available at the museum. **Hours:** Mon.-Fri. 9-5, mid-Feb. to mid-Dec. (also Sat. 9-5, mid-May to mid-Sept.). Closed major holidays. Phone ahead to confirm schedule. **Cost:** $5; $3 (ages 61+); $1 (ages 5-13). **Phone:** (928) 645-9496, or (888) 597-6873 to confirm hours or make bus reservations.

NAVAJO VILLAGE HERITAGE CENTER is at 1253 Coppermine Rd. Guests experience the Navajo culture and lifestyle in a traditional village. A variety of Navajo artisans, including silversmiths, rug weavers, potters and basket weavers, may be seen. The 2.5-hour Grand Tour includes an in-depth cultural presentation, dinner, Native American dances and campfire stories.

Hours: Tours Mon.-Sat. at 5, Mar.-May and Sept.-Oct.; at 6, June-Aug. **Cost:** Grand Tour $30; $20 (ages 11-17); $5 (ages 0-10). Tours require a minimum of 10 people. Reservations are required. **Phone:** (928) 660-0304.

AMERICAS BEST VALUE INN   Phone: (928)645-2858

Motel
$49-$149

Address: 75 S 7th Ave 86040 **Location:** 1 mi e of US 89 via Loop 89; just n of Lake Powell Blvd. **Facility:** 39 units. 2 stories (no elevator), exterior corridors. **Terms:** cancellation fee imposed. **Free Special Amenities: expanded continental breakfast and high-speed Internet.**

SAVE ꕤ BIZ 🛜 🖥 📥

BEST WESTERN ARIZONAINN   Phone: (928)645-2466

Hotel
$60-$140

AAA Benefit: Members save up to 20%, plus 10% bonus points with Best Western Rewards®.

Address: 716 Rimview Dr 86040 **Location:** 0.7 mi e of US 89 via Loop 89. **Facility:** 103 units. 3 stories, interior corridors. **Terms:** cancellation fee imposed. **Pool(s):** heated outdoor. **Activities:** whirlpool. **Guest Services:** coin laundry. **Free Special Amenities: local telephone calls and high-speed Internet.**

SAVE ꕤ 🛏 BIZ 🛜 🖂 🖥 / SOME UNITS 🖥 📥

BEST WESTERN PLUS AT LAKE POWELL
Phone: (928)645-5988

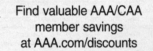

Hotel
$70-$220

AAA Benefit: Members save up to 20%, plus 10% bonus points with Best Western Rewards®.

Address: 208 N Lake Powell Blvd 86040 **Location:** 0.8 mi e of US 89 via Loop 89. **Facility:** 132 units. 4 stories, interior corridors. **Terms:** check-in 3:30 pm. **Pool(s):** heated outdoor. **Activities:** whirlpool, exercise room. **Free Special Amenities: local telephone calls and high-speed Internet.**
(See ad this page.)

SAVE ꕤ 🛏 BIZ 🛜 🖂 🖥 🖥 / SOME UNITS 📥

COURTYARD BY MARRIOTT   Phone: (928)645-5000

Hotel
$79-$299

AAA Benefit: AAA hotel discounts of 5% or more.

Address: 600 Clubhouse Dr 86040 **Location:** On Loop 89, jct US 89. **Facility:** 153 units. 2-4 stories, interior corridors. **Dining:** Pepper's, see separate listing. **Pool(s):** heated outdoor. **Activities:** whirlpool, exercise room. **Guest Services:** valet and coin laundry.

🍴 ꕤ 🛏 BIZ 🛜 🖂 🖥 📥

Find valuable AAA/CAA
member savings
at AAA.com/discounts

▼ *See AAA listing this page* ▼

BEST WESTERN PLUS AT LAKE POWELL
FOR RESERVATIONS CALL 888.794.2888
www.InnAtLakePowell.com   BwAtLakePowell@AOL.com

• **Senior Discount 15% off Published Rates**
• **Free Full Hot Breakfast Buffet**
• **Wi-Fi**
• **42" Flat Panel Cable Televisions**
• **Family Suites with 3 Beds**
• **Two Room Suites**
• **Fitness Room**
• **Convenient and Affordable**
• **Refrigerator and Microwave Available**

Get the free mobile app at
http://gettag.mobi

208 NORTH LAKE POWELL BLVD
PAGE/LAKE POWELL, AZ 86040
Tel: 928-645-5988
Each Best Western is independently owned and operated

HOLIDAY INN EXPRESS

Phone: 928/645-9000

Hotel
Rates not provided

Address: 751 S Navajo Dr 86040 **Location:** On Loop 89, 1.5 mi e of US 89. **Facility:** 74 units, some kitchens. 3 stories, interior corridors. **Pool(s):** outdoor. **Guest Services:** coin laundry.

LAKE POWELL DAYS INN & SUITES

Phone: (928)645-2800

Hotel
$50-$163

Address: 961 N Hwy 89 86040 **Location:** On US 89, just s. **Facility:** 82 units. 3 stories, interior corridors. **Amenities:** safes (fee). **Pool(s):** heated outdoor. **Activities:** whirlpool. **Guest Services:** coin laundry.

/ SOME UNITS FEE

LAKE POWELL RESORT AND MARINA

Phone: 928/645-2433

Resort Hotel
Rates not provided

Address: 100 Lakeshore Dr 86040 **Location:** 4 mi n of Glen Canyon Dam via US 89. **Facility:** Located in the Glen Canyon National Recreation Area, this hotel provides direct access to all sorts of water sports on Lake Powell. 350 units. 2 stories (no elevator), interior corridors. **Terms:** check-in 4 pm. **Dining:** Rainbow Room, see separate listing. **Pool(s):** 2 heated outdoor. **Activities:** sauna, whirlpool, rental boats, rental bicycles, exercise room. **Fee:** marina, waterskiing. **Guest Services:** coin laundry, area transportation-within 5 mi. **Free Special Amenities:** local telephone calls and early check-in/late check-out.
(See ad p. 78.)

SAVE / SOME UNITS FEE

WHERE TO EAT

BLUE BUDDHA SUSHI & TEPPANYAKI

Phone: 928/645-2161

Japanese
$8-$23

AAA Inspector Notes: From the outside, this restaurant does not scream modern or trendy. But once inside, its true colors shine. Patrons can sit back on couches to enjoy a fun Japanese menu with favorites like shrimp tempura, chicken teriyaki, pork dumplings, and, of course, fresh sushi. Traditional tables also are an option. **Bar:** full bar. **Address:** 644 N Navajo Dr, Suite G 86040 **Location:** 0.6 mi n of US 89 via Loop 89; in shopping center. D

BONKERS RESTAURANT

Phone: 928/645-2706

American
$8-$30

AAA Inspector Notes: Near downtown, this family-oriented restaurant prepares a variety of American favorites including burgers, ribs, pasta and chicken fingers. Several large murals depicting the area adorn the walls. Patio dining is a nice option in good weather. **Bar:** beer & wine. **Address:** 810 Navajo Dr 86040 **Location:** 1 mi s of US 89 via Loop 89, just ne of Lake Powell Blvd. D

THE DAM BAR & GRILLE

Phone: 928/645-2161

American
$7-$31

AAA Inspector Notes: On the menu at this casual, sports-bar restaurant is a nice selection of steak, chicken, seafood and pasta dishes, as well as an assortment of sandwiches. The staff at this conveniently located spot provides full service in a cordial and attentive fashion. **Bar:** full bar. **Address:** 644 N Navajo Dr, Suite C 86040 **Location:** 0.6 mi n of US 89 via Loop 89; in shopping center. L D

KEN'S OLD WEST RESTAURANT & LOUNGE

Phone: 928/645-5160

Steak
$10-$22

AAA Inspector Notes: This restaurant features a selection of cooked-to-order steak, seafood and prime rib entrées. Daily, live country and Western music lends an upbeat atmosphere to this rustic, downtown spot near Lake Powell and Glen Canyon National Park. A small salad bar welcomes self-service, and a cordial staff provides assistance. **Bar:** full bar. **Address:** 718 Vista Ave 86040 **Location:** 0.8 mi e of US 89 via Loop 89, then just n. D

MANDARIN GOURMET CHINESE CUISINE

Phone: 928/645-5516

Chinese
$6-$16

AAA Inspector Notes: The restaurant offers a variety of traditional Chinese dishes in a casual atmosphere. An extensive buffet is a good lunchtime option. **Address:** 683 S Lake Powell Blvd 86040 **Location:** Jct US 89. L D

PEPPER'S

Phone: 928/645-5000

Southwestern
$9-$32

AAA Inspector Notes: Enlivened by Southwestern decor, the comfortable hotel restaurant prepares a nice variety of Southwestern and American entrees. The lunch buffet is good for diners in a bit of a hurry. **Bar:** full bar. **Address:** 600 Clubhouse Dr 86040 **Location:** On Loop 89, jct US 89; in Courtyard by Marriott. B D

RAINBOW ROOM

Phone: 928/645-2433

American
$8-$30

AAA Inspector Notes: The dining room affords beautiful views of Lake Powell from every table. The lunch buffet lines up a selection of sandwiches, salads and entrées with a Southwestern flair, while the dinner menu centers on fresh fish and flame-broiled steaks. **Bar:** full bar. **Address:** 100 Lakeshore Dr 86040 **Location:** 4 mi n of Glen Canyon Dam via US 89; in Lake Powell Resort and Marina. B L D

RANCH HOUSE GRILLE

Phone: 928/645-1420

Breakfast
$5-$12

AAA Inspector Notes: Locals frequent this casual restaurant to satisfy cravings for hearty portions of comfort food. **Address:** 819 N Navajo Dr 86040 **Location:** Jct Loop 89, just n. B L

STROMBOLLI'S ITALIAN RESTAURANT & PIZZERIA

Phone: 928/645-2605

Italian
$9-$16

AAA Inspector Notes: Those in need of a break from enjoying the Page outdoors can slip into the casual, no-frills eatery for a quick repast of pizza or pasta. **Bar:** beer & wine. **Address:** 711 N Navajo Dr 86040 **Location:** 1 mi s of US 89 via Loop 89; just ne of Lake Powell Blvd. L D

PARADISE VALLEY (I-3) pop. 12,820, elev. 1,340'

- **Attractions map p. 142**
- **Hotels & Restaurants map & index p. 158**
- **Part of Phoenix area — see map p. 134**

COSANTI, 6433 E. Doubletree Ranch Rd., is the studio and workshop of architect-craftsman Paolo Soleri. Displays include sculptures, wind-bells and photographs of the Arcosanti project *(see Mayer p. 111)*, Soleri's prototype urban design based on his philosophy of arcology (architecture plus ecology). Most weekday mornings, visitors can watch bronze pours. **Time:** Allow 1 hour minimum. **Hours:** Mon.-Sat. 9-5, Sun. 11-5. Closed major holidays. **Cost:** Free. **Phone:** (480) 948-6145 or (800) 752-3187.

HERMOSA INN

Boutique Hotel
$199-$549

Phone: (602)955-8614 ⑥②
Address: 5532 N Palo Cristi Rd 85253 **Location:** 1 mi s of Lincoln Dr; corner of Stanford Dr. Located in a residential area. **Facility:** This historic home of cowboy artist Lon Megargee offers intimate lodging in adobe-style casitas, each with individually decorated rooms. 34 units. 1 story, exterior corridors. **Terms:** 7 day cancellation notice-fee imposed. **Amenities:** safes. *Some:* high-speed Internet. **Dining:** Lon's at the Hermosa, see separate listing. **Pool(s):** heated outdoor. **Activities:** whirlpools. *Fee:* massage. **Guest Services:** valet laundry.

MONTELUCIA RESORT & SPA

Resort Hotel
Rates not provided

Phone: 480/627-3200 ⑥①
Address: 4949 E Lincoln Dr 85253 **Location:** Southeast corner of Lincoln Dr and Tatum Blvd, enter from Lincoln Dr. **Facility:** This property is located on attractive and spacious grounds at the foot of the Camelback Mountains. A man-made cave and waterfall enhance the pool. 293 units, some two bedrooms and efficiencies. 1-3 stories, interior/exterior corridors. **Parking:** on-site and valet. **Terms:** check-in 4 pm. **Amenities:** high-speed Internet (fee), safes, honor bars. **Dining:** 3 restaurants, also, Prado, see separate listing, entertainment. **Pool(s):** 3 heated outdoor. **Activities:** saunas, whirlpools, steamrooms, bicycles, hiking trails, jogging, spa. **Guest Services:** valet laundry.

SANCTUARY ON CAMELBACK MOUNTAIN

Resort Hotel
$199-$849

Phone: (480)948-2100 ⑥③
Address: 5700 E McDonald Dr 85253 **Location:** SR 101 exit McDonald Dr, 3.9 mi w; 1.8 mi w of jct Scottsdale Rd. **Facility:** This quiet retreat offers luxurious rooms and amenities, some with fireplaces and panoramic views. 105 units, some efficiencies. 1 story, exterior corridors. **Parking:** on-site and valet. **Terms:** check-in 4 pm, 7 day cancellation notice-fee imposed. **Amenities:** high-speed Internet, safes, honor bars. **Dining:** Elements, see separate listing. **Pool(s):** 4 heated outdoor. **Activities:** whirlpools, steamrooms, 5 tennis courts, recreation programs, rental bicycles, hiking trails, jogging, spa. **Guest Services:** valet laundry, area transportation-within 5 mi. **Free Special Amenities:** newspaper and high-speed Internet. Affiliated with A Preferred Hotel.

Enjoy great savings on hotel rates at AAA.com or CAA.ca

WHERE TO EAT

EL CHORRO

Continental
$11-$47

Phone: 480/948-5170 ⑦②
AAA Inspector Notes: Serving the local area for more than 70 years, this small, charming restaurant has a nice selection of steaks, lamb and fresh seafood preparations. Complimentary sticky buns are a specialty. Outdoor seating is a pleasant option with a warming fireplace on chilly nights. **Bar:** full bar. **Reservations:** suggested. **Address:** 5550 E Lincoln Dr 85253 **Location:** 2 mi w of Scottsdale Rd; on north side of Lincoln Dr. **Parking:** on-site and valet.
Ⓛ Ⓓ

ELEMENTS

Fusion
$16-$45

Phone: 480/607-2300 ⑦④
AAA Inspector Notes: Using local farm-fresh organic vegetables and a wide selection of meat and seafood, chef Beau MacMillan creates Asian-inspired seasonal menus that satisfy the most discerning gourmet. Stunning views of the valley and sunsets enhance the experience. A private chef's tasting room is available. **Bar:** full bar. **Reservations:** suggested. **Address:** 5700 E McDonald Dr 85253 **Location:** SR 101 exit McDonald Dr, 3.9 mi w; 1.8 mi w of jct Scottsdale Rd; in Sanctuary on Camelback Mountain. **Parking:** valet only. Ⓑ Ⓛ Ⓓ

LON'S AT THE HERMOSA **Phone:** 602/955-7878 ⑦③

American
$10-$42

AAA Inspector Notes: Coming here for dinner is like returning to the "home ranch" in Arizona territorial days. The excellent menu selection centers on natural and organic foods, some grown on the premises. Choices include seafood, steak and fowl preparations, delivered with casual yet attentive service. **Bar:** full bar. **Reservations:** suggested. **Address:** 5532 N Palo Cristi Rd 85253 **Location:** 1 mi s of Lincoln Dr; corner of Stanford Dr; in Hermosa Inn. **Parking:** on-site and valet. Ⓑ Ⓛ Ⓓ

PRADO

Italian
$13-$30

Phone: 480/627-3004 ⑦①
AAA Inspector Notes: The restaurant's food and decor are inspired by traditional Andalusian cooking. Chef Claudio Urciuoli is an active member of the slow food movement, where savory, fresh ingredients are prepared simply over a wood-fired grill. **Bar:** full bar. **Reservations:** suggested. **Address:** 4949 E Lincoln Dr 85253 **Location:** Southeast corner of Lincoln Dr and Tatum Blvd, enter from Lincoln Dr; in Montelucia Resort & Spa. **Parking:** on-site and valet. Ⓓ CALL ⓈⓂ

PARKER (D-1) pop. 3,083, elev. 1,642'

Parker, founded in 1908, was named for Ely Parker, the first Native American commissioner for the U.S. government. The city originally was south of its current location but was moved to accommodate the Santa Fe Railroad. Parker is a trade center for the surrounding Native American communities and a water recreation destination attracting nearly 1 million visitors each year.

The Parker Dam and Power Plant, 17 miles north on SR 95, is considered the world's deepest because 65 percent of its structural height is below the riverbed. Overlooks on top of the dam provide views of Lake Havasu and the Colorado River. Just north of town on SR 95 is La Paz County Park *(see Recreation Chart)*.

Parker Area Chamber of Commerce: 1217 California Ave., Parker, AZ 85344. **Phone:** (928) 669-2174.

BILL WILLIAMS RIVER NATIONAL WILDLIFE REFUGE is off SR 95 (between Mileposts 160 and 161) at the delta of the Bill Williams River at its confluence with the Colorado River. A 9-mile corridor along the river encompasses desert riparian and upland habitat. Named after a trapper who explored the area in the 1800s, the 6,000-acre refuge preserves some of the last remaining riparian habitat in the Lower Colorado River Valley.

The refuge is home to beavers, bobcats, foxes, mule deer, bighorn sheep, raccoons and 360 species of birds. Fishing and limited hunting are permitted (in season). Camping is prohibited. **Hours:** Office open Mon.-Fri. 8-4. **Cost:** Free. **Phone:** (928) 667-4144.

BUCKSKIN MOUNTAIN STATE PARK & RIVER IS-LAND UNIT, 11 mi. n. off SR 95, is the state's "water playground" on the Colorado River. Activities include hiking, swimming, boating and fishing. The River Island Unit is 1 mile north of the park. *See Recreation Chart.* **Hours:** Daily 9-4:30. **Cost:** $10 (per private vehicle, up to four passengers); $3 (per additional adult passenger in vehicle or individual arriving on foot or bicycle). Camping $30 (per private vehicle). **Phone:** (928) 667-3231.

COLORADO RIVER INDIAN TRIBES MUSEUM is at 1007 Arizona Ave. The museum houses the Beebee Brown Basket Collection, excavations from the restoration of the nearby ghost town of La Paz, and historical and modern material about local tribes. **Time:** Allow 1 hour minimum. **Hours:** Mon.-Fri. 8-5. Closed major holidays. **Cost:** Free. **Phone:** (928) 669-8970.

GAMBLING ESTABLISHMENTS

- **Blue Water Resort and Casino,** 1 mi. n.e. on SR 95 to 11300 Resort Dr. **Hours:** Daily 24 hours. **Phone:** (928) 669-7000 or (888) 243-3360.

BEST WESTERN PARKER INN   Phone: (928)669-6060

Hotel
$69-$85

AAA Benefit: Members save up to 20%, plus 10% bonus points with Best Western Rewards®.

Address: 1012 Geronimo Ave 85344 **Location:** SR 95, just e. **Facility:** 45 units. 2 stories (no elevator), interior corridors. **Amenities:** *Some:* high-speed Internet. **Pool(s):** outdoor. **Guest Services:** coin laundry. **Free Special Amenities:** continental breakfast and high-speed Internet.

Safety tip: Keep a current
AAA/CAA Road Atlas
in every vehicle

BLUE WATER RESORT & CASINO

Phone: 928/669-7000

Resort Hotel
Rates not provided

Address: 11300 Resort Dr 85344 **Location:** Jct SR 62, 1.3 mi nw on SR 95. Located along the Colorado River. **Facility:** Attractive rooms with a balcony and views of a marina and the Colorado River make for a pleasant vacation or weekend getaway. 200 units. 5 stories, exterior corridors. **Parking:** on-site and valet. **Dining:** 3 restaurants, also, River Willow Fine Dining, see separate listing. **Pool(s):** 2 heated indoor. **Activities:** whirlpool, waterslide, limited beach access, fishing, exercise room. *Fee:* marina, miniature golf. **Guest Services:** valet laundry. **Free Special Amenities:** local telephone calls and high-speed Internet.

WHERE TO EAT

RIVER WILLOW FINE DINING   Phone: 928/669-7000

Continental
$18-$36

AAA Inspector Notes: Diners can enjoy a Prime steak, veal topped with crab meat and scallops with pasta all served in a casual yet upscale setting. **Bar:** full bar. **Reservations:** suggested. **Address:** 11300 Resort Dr 85344 **Location:** Jct SR 62, 1.3 mi nw on SR 95; in Blue Water Resort & Casino. **Parking:** on-site and valet.

PATAGONIA (G-5) pop. 913, elev. 4,057'

PATAGONIA LAKE STATE PARK, 7 mi. s.w. on SR 82, then 4 mi. w. following signs, is home to southeastern Arizona's largest lake. Bird-watching is a popular activity. Pontoon boat tours are available early October through April. Adjacent to the park is Sonoita Creek State Natural Area, which offers nature hikes and educational programs. *See Recreation Chart.*

Gas, boating, fishing and swimming are available. Jet boats and jet skis are prohibited. **Hours:** Daily 4 a.m.-10 p.m. Phone ahead to confirm schedule. **Cost:** $10 (per private vehicle, up to four passengers); $3 (per additional adult passenger in vehicle or individual arriving on foot or bicycle). Camping $17-$25 (per private vehicle). **Phone:** (520) 287-6965, or (520) 287-2791 for pontoon tour information.

PATAGONIA-SONOITA CREEK PRESERVE, w. off SR 82 onto 4th St., then 1.7 mi. s. on Pennsylvania Ave., is home to more than 300 species of birds as well as mountain lions, bobcats, deer, javelinas, coyotes, turtles and rattlesnakes. The preserve also protects the cottonwood-willow riparian forest containing some of the largest and oldest Fremont cottonwood trees in the world. A self-guiding nature trail and a visitor center are available.

Hours: Wed.-Sun. 6:30-4, Apr.-Sept.; 7:30-4, rest of year. Guided walks Sat. at 9. Closed Jan. 1, Thanksgiving and Christmas. **Cost:** $5; free (ages 0-15). **Phone:** (520) 394-2400.

PAYSON (D-4) pop. 15,301, elev. 4,887'

Known by such names as Green Valley, Long Valley, Big Valley and Union City, Payson was first settled by prospectors who came to the area seeking wealth. Payson's mines produced little, and cattle and lumber soon became the community's livelihood. With the help of Senator Payson of Chicago, the early residents helped establish a post office and named it and the town in his honor.

Surrounded by the lakes and dense woodlands of Tonto National Forest *(see place listing p. 264)* and the nearby Mogollon Rim, Payson has become a convenient getaway for visitors, with Phoenix only 90 minutes away.

Rim Country Regional Chamber of Commerce: 100 W. Main St., P.O. Box 1380, Payson, AZ 85547. **Phone:** (928) 474-4515 or (800) 672-9766.

RIM COUNTRY MUSEUM, 1 mi. w. on Main St. from jct. SR 87, then just n. to 700 Green Valley Pkwy., is comprised of several historic structures. A replica of the turn-of-the-20th-century Herron Hotel contains exhibits about the ancient cultures that developed around the Mogollon Rim as well as a 1908 kitchen, blacksmith shop and gold mine. Payson's original forest ranger's station and residence, built in 1907, depict the life of the forest ranger. Firefighting equipment also is featured. The 40-acre Green Valley Park neighbors the museum.

Time: Allow 30 minutes minimum. **Hours:** Wed.-Mon. 10-4. Closed Jan. 1, Thanksgiving and Christmas. **Cost:** (includes admittance to the Zane Grey Cabin) $5; $4 (ages 55+); $3 (ages 12-18). **Phone:** (928) 474-3483.

Zane Grey Cabin is at 700 Green Valley Pkwy. The replica cabin and the adjoining Rim Country Museum house the personal belongings and memorabilia of adventurer and "Riders of the Purple Sage" author Zane Grey. The original cabin was destroyed in the 1990 Dude Fire; exhibits in the museum focus on Grey's literary contributions and career achievements. Displays also document the history of the Payson community, which Grey frequented from 1918-29.

Hours: Wed.-Mon. 10-4. Closed Jan. 1, Thanksgiving and Christmas. **Cost:** (includes admittance to the Rim Country Museum) $5; $4 (ages 55+); $3 (ages 12-18). **Phone:** (928) 474-3483.

TONTO NATURAL BRIDGE STATE PARK, 10 mi. n.w. off SR 87, is bordered by Tonto National Forest. The bridge, among the world's largest natural travertine structures, reaches a height of 183 feet; the opening beneath is 150 feet wide and 400 feet long. A historic lodge (not available for overnight stays) is furnished with antiques that were lowered into the canyon using ropes and mules. There are four easily accessible viewpoints from which to see the bridge; the walk to each is less than a half-mile.

Note: Four trails lead into the canyon; all are steep and difficult for many persons to negotiate.

Pets are not permitted on canyon trails but are permitted at viewpoints. **Hours:** Daily 8-6, Memorial Day-Labor Day; Thurs.-Mon. 9-5, rest of year. Last admission 1 hour before closing. Closed Christmas. **Cost:** $5; $2 (ages 7-13). **Phone:** (928) 476-4202.

GAMBLING ESTABLISHMENTS

• **Mazatzal Casino,** .5 mi. s. on SR 87 (Beeline Hwy.) at Milepost 251. **Hours:** Daily 24 hours. **Phone:** (928) 474-6044 or (800) 777-7529.

AMERICAS BEST VALUE INN   **Phone:** (928)474-2283
♦ Motel
$50-$121
Address: 811 S Beeline Hwy 85541 **Location:** SR 87, 0.7 mi s of SR 260. **Facility:** 22 units. 1-2 stories (no elevator), interior/exterior corridors. **Free Special Amenities:** local telephone calls and high-speed Internet.

BEST WESTERN PAYSON INN   **Phone:** (928)474-3241
♦♦♦ Hotel
$60-$160
AAA Benefit: Members save up to 20%, plus 10% bonus points with Best Western Rewards®.
Address: 801 N Beeline Hwy 85541 **Location:** SR 87, 0.6 mi n of SR 260. **Facility:** 99 units, some two bedrooms. 2 stories (no elevator), exterior corridors. **Terms:** check-in 4 pm. **Amenities:** *Some:* high-speed Internet. **Pool(s):** heated outdoor. **Activities:** whirlpool, exercise room. **Guest Services:** coin laundry. **Free Special Amenities:** expanded continental breakfast and high-speed Internet.

COMFORT INN   **Phone:** 928/472-7484
♦♦♦ Hotel
Rates not provided
Address: 206 S Beeline Hwy 85541 **Location:** SR 87, just s of SR 260. **Facility:** 44 units. 3 stories, interior corridors. **Pool(s):** heated indoor. **Activities:** whirlpool. **Guest Services:** coin laundry. **Free Special Amenities:** expanded continental breakfast and high-speed Internet.

MAZATZAL HOTEL & CASINO   **Phone:** 928/474-6044
♦♦♦ Hotel
Rates not provided
Address: Hwy 87, MM 251 85547 **Location:** SR 87, 1.5 mi s of SR 260. **Facility:** The hotel offers well-appointed rooms with comfortable furnishings and spacious bathrooms with marble and granite accents. 40 units, some two bedrooms. 3 stories, interior corridors. **Pool(s):** heated indoor. **Activities:** whirlpool, exercise room. **Fee:** game room. **Guest Services:** area transportation-into town.

PAYSONGLO LODGE   **Phone:** (928)474-2382
♦♦ Motel
$59-$119 2/1-10/31
$49-$99 11/1-1/31
Address: 1005 S Beeline Hwy 85541 **Location:** SR 87, 0.9 mi s of SR 260. **Facility:** 47 units. 1-2 stories (no elevator), exterior corridors. **Terms:** cancellation fee imposed. **Pool(s):** outdoor. **Activities:** whirlpool. **Free Special Amenities:** continental breakfast and high-speed Internet.

SUPER 8 INN & SUITES OF PAYSON

Phone: (928)474-5241

🔷🔷 🔷🔷
Motel
$60-$130

Address: 809 E Hwy 260 85541 **Location:** 0.7 mi e of SR 87. **Facility:** 39 units. 2 stories (no elevator), exterior corridors. **Pool(s):** heated outdoor. **Activities:** whirlpool. **Free Special Amenities:** continental breakfast and high-speed Internet.

Central Payson Location off highway 260; Suites Available with fireplace and hot tub

WOODEN NICKEL CABINS   Phone: 928/478-4519

🔷🔷 🔷🔷
Cabin
Rates not provided

Address: 165 Hunter Creek Dr 85541 **Location:** SR 87, 22 mi e on SR 260, then 0.7 mi n; just w of MM 275, follow signs. **Facility:** 7 cabins, some efficiencies and kitchens. 1-2 stories (no elevator), exterior corridors. **Terms:** office hours 9 am-9 pm. **Activities:** hiking trails, playground, horseshoes.

WHERE TO EAT

CROSSWINDS RESTAURANT   Phone: 928/474-1613

🔷🔷 🔷🔷
American
$6-$12

AAA Inspector Notes: Reservations are suggested for the restaurant's popular breakfasts, but heartier burgers and fried chicken also satisfy. Patrons enjoy great views of small planes taking off and landing on the adjacent airstrip. **Address:** 800 W Airport Rd 85541 **Location:** Jct SR 260, 1.1 mi n on SR 87, then 0.9 mi w.

FARGO'S STEAKHOUSE   Phone: 928/474-7455

🔷🔷 🔷🔷
Steak
$8-$29

AAA Inspector Notes: The setting is much like a comfortable lakefront lodge, and the warm welcome from staff starts off a pleasant dining experience. Steaks and seafood may be combined for hearty meals. **Bar:** full bar. **Address:** 620 E Hwy 260 85541 **Location:** SR 260, 0.5 mi e of SR 87.

GERARDO'S FIREWOOD CAFE   Phone: 928/468-6500

🔷🔷 🔷🔷
Italian
$7-$24

AAA Inspector Notes: This pleasant trattoria-style restaurant serves rustic, homemade Italian food. Included on the menu are hand-tossed pizza cooked in wood-burning ovens, panini and traditional pasta preparations. Fish dishes are a local favorite. A salad buffet is offered at lunch. **Bar:** full bar. **Address:** 512 N Beeline Hwy 85541 **Location:** SR 87, 0.5 mi n of SR 260.

MACKY'S GRILL   Phone: 928/474-7411

🔷🔷 🔷🔷
American
$6-$15

AAA Inspector Notes: Diners will feel right at home in this friendly and casual eatery. Grab one of the specialty hamburgers such as the spicy fireside or savory guacamole burger. Relax afterwards and enjoy a slice of homemade pie or cheesecake while chatting with the locals. **Bar:** beer & wine. **Address:** 201 W Main St 85541 **Location:** Jct SR 87 and 260, 0.7 mi s, just w.

PEACH SPRINGS (B-2) pop. 1,090, elev. 4,788'

• Hotels p. 130 • Restaurants p. 130

Peach Springs is the trading center and headquarters for the Hualapai Indian Reservation, which covers nearly a million acres between the town and the Colorado River. The town also serves as the transportation corridor to the western parts of Grand Canyon National Park *(see place listing p. 84)*. Fishing is allowed on the river and at small ponds on the reservation. Primitive camping also is available.

GRAND CANYON CAVERNS, 12 mi. e. of Peach Springs at SR 66 Milepost 115, is reached by a 21-story elevator descent during the 45-minute standard tour or the 2-hour Explorers tour. The temperature is 56 degrees Fahrenheit throughout the year. Nearly a mile of lighted trails highlights colorful mineral formations. An abbreviated tour is available for the physically impaired.

Hours: Daily 9-5. Closed Christmas. **Cost:** Explorers tour $44.95. Standard tour $14.95; $9.95 (ages 5-12). Reservations for Explorers tour are required 72 hours in advance. **Phone:** (928) 422-3223.

GRAND CANYON SKYWALK is at the far western end of the Grand Canyon; from Peach Springs, take SR 66 w. about 44 mi. to CR 20, CR 20 n. about 39 mi. to CR 25, CR 25 n. about 7.3 mi. to CR 261 (Diamond Bar Rd.) and Diamond Bar Rd. 16.4 mi. n.e. to Grand Canyon West (the Hualapai Indian tribe's recreation area), an approximate 2.5-hour drive. Drivers should be aware that Diamond Bar Road—while maintained and almost always negotiable in a passenger car—is rough and unpaved.

Staunch environmentalists howled in protest when the Hualapai tribe built this horseshoe-shaped, glass-floored "sky bridge" on their reservation land in 2007. Extending 70 feet out from the canyon rim, the skywalk is suspended 4,000 feet above the canyon bottom and the Colorado River far, far below. Weighing 1.2 million pounds, it's unquestionably an architectural wonder and a unique engineering feat, and the views—as long as you don't suffer from acrophobia—are jaw-dropping. Grand Canyon National Park visitors should keep in mind that the location is remote, easily a 4.5-hour drive from the park's South Rim.

Note: To stroll on the skywalk you must first purchase a Grand Canyon West tour package; the fee includes bus transportation to the skywalk, a faux Native American village, a mock cowboy town and the Guano Point overlook. Personal items are not permitted on the skywalk (free lockers are available for storage). Cameras are strictly prohibited; you will be searched. Allow 2-4 hours minimum to view the skywalk and take the Grand Canyon West tour.

Hours: Daily 7-7, in summer; 8-5, rest of year (weather permitting). Last admission 2 hours before closing. **Cost:** Hualapai Legacy tour of Grand Canyon West (includes parking and permitting fee and hop-on, hop-off shuttle transportation to the Native American village, Hualapai Ranch and the

Guano Point overlook) $43.05; $39.85 (ages 55+); $35.03 (ages 3-11). Additional admission for skywalk $32.05; $28.85 (ages 55+); $24.03 (ages 3-11). **Phone:** (702) 220-8372. 〔¶〕

HUALAPAI LODGE   **Phone:** (928)769-2230
▼▼▼
Hotel
$100-$120

Address: 900 Historic Route 66 86434 **Location:** Center. Located near train tracks. **Facility:** 56 units. 2 stories, interior corridors. **Terms:** 3 day cancellation notice. **Dining:** Diamond Creek Restaurant, see separate listing. **Pool(s):** heated outdoor. **Activities:** whirlpool, exercise room. **Guest Services:** coin laundry. **Free Special Amenities: continental breakfast and high-speed Internet.**

[SAVE] [¶] CALL [M] [🛏] [BIZ] [📶] [💻]
/ SOME UNITS FEE[🐕] FEE[🛗] FEE[🍽]

WHERE TO EAT

DIAMOND CREEK RESTAURANT   **Phone:** 928/769-2800
▼▼▼
American
$6-$19

AAA Inspector Notes: Although this restaurant serves traditional American offerings, there are such Native American-influenced options as the Hualapai taco (a traditional taco served on fry bread), Hualapai stew and an Indian fry bread dessert. Equally loved are the half-pound charbroiled hamburgers, which can be built to specifications using several toppings. With pizza and homemade dessert on the menu, there is something for everyone. **Address:** 900 Route 66 86434 **Location:** Center; in Hualapai Lodge. [B] [L] [D]

PEARCE (F-5) elev. 4,400'

Pearce at the end of the 19th century was a booming mining town. Following the gold strike by John Pearce in 1894 people swarmed to the area, all but depopulating nearby Tombstone, whose mines were no longer productive. The Commonwealth Mine, Pearce's claim, maintained full operation until 1904, when an impeding water level and a cave-in reduced activities. It was worked sporadically until the late 1930s.

Pearce-Sunsites Chamber of Commerce and Visitors Center: 225 Frontage Rd., P.O. Box 536, Pearce, AZ 85625. **Phone:** (520) 826-3535.

PEORIA (I-2) pop. 154,065, elev. 1,138'
• Hotels & Restaurants map & index p. 155
• Part of Phoenix area — see map p. 134

[SAVE] **CHALLENGER SPACE CENTER** is 3.2 mi. n. on 91st Ave., 1 mi. e. on Lake Pleasant Blvd., then .3 mi. n. to 21170 N. 83rd Ave. An affiliate of the Smithsonian Institute, the center features permanent and temporary space exhibits as well as stargazing and planetarium programs. A highlight is the 2-hour simulated space mission, including launching and docking. The mission control room is based on the design of the Johnson Space Center; the spacecraft simulates a room on the International Space Station.

Time: Allow 1 hour minimum. **Hours:** Mon.-Fri. 9-4, Sat. 10-4. Phone for space mission schedule. Closed Jan. 1, Memorial Day, July 4, Labor Day, Thanksgiving and Christmas. **Cost:** $8; $7 (ages

55+ and military with ID); $5 (ages 4-18). Space mission $22.50; $19.50 (ages 4-18 and 55+). Third- and fourth-grade students must be with an adult on space mission. The space mission is not recommended for children ages 0-8. Reservations are required for space mission. **Phone:** (623) 322-2001.

COMFORT SUITES BY CHOICE HOTELS/PEORIA SPORTS COMPLEX   **Phone:** (623)334-3993 **24**
▼▼▼
Hotel
$59-$199

Address: 8473 W Paradise Ln 85382 **Location:** Loop 101 exit 14 (Bell Rd), just e to 83rd Ave, just s, then just w. **Facility:** 79 units. 3 stories, interior corridors. **Terms:** cancellation fee imposed. **Amenities:** safes (fee). **Pool(s):** heated outdoor. **Activities:** whirlpool. **Guest Services:** valet and coin laundry.

[📶+] [🛏] [♿+] [BIZ] [📶] [✕] FEE[🎬] [🛗] [🍽] [💻]
/ SOME UNITS FEE[🐕]

EXTENDED STAYAMERICA PHOENIX-PEORIA
   Phone: (623)487-0020 **28**
▼▼▼
Extended Stay Hotel
$70-$80 2/1-4/15
$60-$70 4/16-1/31

Address: 7345 W Bell Rd 85382 **Location:** Loop 101 exit 14 (Bell Rd), 1.2 mi e. **Facility:** 101 efficiencies. 3 stories, interior corridors. **Terms:** office hours 7 am-11 pm. **Guest Services:** coin laundry.

[📶+] [📶] [🛗] [🍽] [💻] / SOME UNITS FEE[🐕]

HAMPTON INN   **Phone:** (623)486-9918 **27**
▼▼▼
Hotel
$69-$199

AAA Benefit: Members save up to 10% everyday!

Address: 8408 W Paradise Ln 85382 **Location:** Loop 101 exit 14 (Bell Rd), just e to 83rd Ave, just s, then just w. Across from Peoria Sports Complex. **Facility:** 112 units. 5 stories, interior corridors. **Terms:** 1-7 night minimum stay, cancellation fee imposed. **Amenities:** video games (fee), high-speed Internet. **Pool(s):** heated outdoor. **Activities:** whirlpool, exercise room. **Guest Services:** valet and coin laundry.

[📶+] [🛏] [BIZ] [📶] FEE[🎬] [🛗] [🍽] [💻]
/ SOME UNITS [🐕]

HOLIDAY INN EXPRESS HOTEL & SUITES PEORIA NORTH/GLENDALE   **Phone:** (623)853-1313 **23**
▼▼▼
Hotel
$79-$229

Address: 16771 N 84th Ave 85382 **Location:** Loop 101 exit 14 (Bell Rd), just w, then just s. Located in a busy commercial area. **Facility:** 98 units. 4 stories, interior corridors. **Terms:** check-in 4 pm. **Amenities:** video games (fee). **Pool(s):** heated outdoor. **Activities:** limited exercise equipment. **Guest Services:** valet and coin laundry.

[📶+] CALL [M] [🛏] [BIZ] [📶] FEE[🎬] [💻]
/ SOME UNITS [🐕] [🛗] [🍽]

LA QUINTA INN & SUITES PHOENIX WEST PEORIA
   Phone: (623)487-1900 **25**
▼▼▼
Hotel
$78-$280

Address: 16321 N 83rd Ave 85382 **Location:** Loop 101 exit 14 (Bell Rd), just e, then just s. Adjacent to Peoria Sports Complex. **Facility:** 108 units. 3 stories, interior corridors. **Amenities:** video games (fee). **Pool(s):** heated outdoor. **Activities:** whirlpool, exercise room. **Guest Services:** valet and coin laundry.

[📶+] [🛏] [📶] [✕] FEE[🎬] [🛗] [🍽] [💻]
/ SOME UNITS [🐕]

(See map & index p. 155.)

RAMADA PEORIA CONVENTION CENTER
Phone: 623/979-7200   29

Hotel
Rates not provided

Address: 8955 W Grand Ave 85345 **Location:** Loop 101 N exit 11 (Grand Ave), 0.5 mi e. **Facility:** 101 units, some kitchens. 1-2 stories (no elevator), interior corridors. **Pool(s):** heated outdoor. **Activities:** exercise room. **Guest Services:** coin laundry.

/ SOME UNITS FEE

RESIDENCE INN BY MARRIOTT
Phone: (623)979-2074   26

Extended Stay Hotel
$95-$285

AAA Benefit:
AAA hotel discounts of 5% or more.

Address: 8435 W Paradise Ln 85382 **Location:** Loop 101 exit 14 (Bell Rd), just e, just s on 83rd Ave, then just w. Across from Peoria Sports Complex. **Facility:** 90 units, some two bedrooms and efficiencies. 3 stories, interior corridors. **Pool(s):** heated outdoor. **Activities:** whirlpool, sports court, exercise room. **Guest Services:** valet and coin laundry.

/ SOME UNITS FEE

WHERE TO EAT

ADUELO'S THE FLAVOR OF MEXICO
Phone: 623/878-8282

Mexican
$6-$20

AAA Inspector Notes: This charming setting is reminiscent of a Mexican hacienda, with statues, plants, folk art and full-size wall murals, as done by Diego Rivera. Representative of the upscale menu's distinctive choices is mesquite-grilled, bacon-wrapped shrimp. Fresh herb flavors and ingredients enhance each menu item. **Bar:** full bar. **Address:** 16092 N Arrowhead Fountains Center Dr 85382 **Location:** Loop 101 exit 14 (Bell Rd), just e to 83rd Ave, 0.4 mi s to Stadium Way, just w, then just s.

L D CALL

AH-SO STEAK & SUSHI
Phone: 623/487-8862   18

Japanese
$7-$35

AAA Inspector Notes: Guests can find it all here, from a fresh sushi bar to dining tables to teppan grill tables with chefs ready to put on a show. The menu lists the standard combinations of chicken, steak and seafood along with a large selection of rolls, sushi and sashimi. **Bar:** full bar. **Address:** 16610 N 75th Ave, Suite 104 85381 **Location:** Just s of Bell Rd.

L D

DILLON'S RESTAURANT
Phone: 623/979-5353   19

American
$7-$22

AAA Inspector Notes: The barbecue on this restaurant's menu is popular with local folks. Friendly, young servers bring out a selection of grilled meat, poultry and fish dishes along with homemade desserts large enough to share. The attractive decor has a country cottage feel. **Bar:** full bar. **Address:** 8706 W Thunderbird Rd 85381 **Location:** Loop 101 exit 12, just w.

L D

PATSY GRIMALDI'S COAL BRICK-OVEN PIZZERIA
Phone: 623/486-4455

Pizza
$4-$18

AAA Inspector Notes: Fresh ingredients and a coal-fired brick oven are the features at this New York style pizzeria. **Bar:** beer & wine. **Address:** 9788 W Northern Ave 85345 **Location:** Loop 101 N exit 8 (Northern Ave), 0.3 mi w; in Park West Shopping Center.

L D

P.F. CHANG'S CHINA BISTRO
Phone: 623/412-3335   17

Chinese
$10-$21

AAA Inspector Notes: Trendy, upscale decor provides a pleasant backdrop for New Age Chinese dining. Appetizers, soups and salads are a meal by themselves. Vegetarian plates and sides, noodles, meins, chicken and meat dishes are created from exotic, fresh ingredients. **Bar:** full bar. **Address:** 16170 N 83rd Ave 85382 **Location:** Just s of Bell Rd.

L D

RUBIO'S FRESH MEXICAN GRILL
Phone: 623/773-0998

Mexican
$3-$7

AAA Inspector Notes: Freshly prepared and healthful foods, bright decor and friendly staff are found in this upscale fast-food spot. A special treat, the salsa bar lines up four styles and flavors. **Bar:** beer only. **Address:** 7407 W Bell Rd 85345 **Location:** Jct 75th Ave; southeast corner.

L D

SATARA THAI CUISINE
Phone: 623/979-9696   16

Thai
$7-$12

AAA Inspector Notes: Authentic Thai cuisine is served in this modern and casual spot. Sample the curries, noodles and seafood specialties while sipping on an exotic cocktail. **Bar:** full bar. **Address:** 8350 W Paradise Ln 85382 **Location:** Loop 101 exit 14 (Bell Rd), just e, then just s on 83rd Ave.

L D

PETRIFIED FOREST NATIONAL PARK (C-6)

Elevations in the park range from 5,300 ft. at the Puerco River to 6,235 ft. at Pilot Rock. Refer to AAA maps for additional elevation information.

East of Holbrook, Petrified Forest National Park contains an abundance of petrified logs. Most of the brilliantly colored trees in the 221,621-acre park are prone, and many are in fragments. Early dinosaurs and other reptiles once roamed the area, and numerous fossil bones and fossil plants have been discovered in the park.

More than 200 million years ago trees clinging to eroding riverbanks fell into streams and were carried to this wet, swampy lowland. The trees were submerged in water and buried under river sediments that included volcanic ash rich in silica; a replacement process began to take place. Silica replaced the wood until the logs were virtually turned to stone. Iron oxide and other minerals stained the silica to produce rainbow colors.

Later the region was uplifted, and erosion exposed part of the logs; many remain buried to a depth of 300 feet. There are five areas with heavy concentrations of petrified wood in the park: Blue Mesa, Jasper Forest, Crystal Forest, Rainbow Forest (comprising Long Logs and Giant Logs near US 180) and Black Forest. The first four are accessible by the park road. Black Forest, in a designated wilderness area, can be reached from the parking lot at Kachina Point, down a switchback unimproved trail to the desert floor. The Rainbow Forest area contains the most colorful concentration of petrified wood.

General Information and Activities

The park is open daily 8-5; closed Christmas. Hours may be extended Mar.-Sept. Phone to confirm schedule.

The 28-mile drive through the park offers breathtaking views from Pintado Point and Kachina Point. Other scenic overlooks include Chinde, Nizhoni, Tawa, Tiponi and Whipple points.

Westbound motorists on I-40 should use the northern entrance to avoid backtracking. Visitors can view the Painted Desert (see attraction listing), ancient pueblos and petroglyphs, petrified log deposits and the Rainbow Forest Museum (see attraction listing). Motorists should exit on US 180 and continue west to Holbrook. Eastbound motorists can use the southern (Rainbow Forest) entrance off US 180, 19 miles from Holbrook, to see the same attractions in reverse order, then exit onto I-40 east. Allow 2 hours minimum.

Within the park it is unlawful to gather plants, sand, rocks or specimens of petrified wood of any size whatsoever; archeological material is likewise protected. Violations are punishable by heavy fines and imprisonment. Curio stores sell a variety of polished specimens collected from privately owned land outside the park.

There are no overnight accommodations in the park; backpack camping is allowed by permit only for hikers staying overnight in the Painted Desert wilderness area. Picnic sites are near the Rainbow Forest Museum and on the Painted Desert rim at Chinde Point. Gas, oil and food services are available next to the Painted Desert Visitor Center.

ADMISSION to the park is $10 per private vehicle, $5 per person arriving by other means.

PETS are permitted in the park only if they are leashed, crated or otherwise physically restricted at all times. With the exception of service animals, pets are not permitted in park buildings.

ADDRESS inquiries to the Superintendent, Petrified Forest National Park, P.O. Box 2217, Petrified Forest National Park, AZ 86028; phone (928) 524-6228.

AGATE BRIDGE, at a stopping point on the park road, is a petrified log that spans a 40-foot-wide ravine; 111 feet of the concrete-supported log are exposed.

NEWSPAPER ROCK, via a short side road 1 mi. s. of Puerco Pueblo, bears prehistoric petroglyphs that can be viewed through spotting scopes from an overlook.

PAINTED DESERT, partially contained in the northern part of the park, is an area of badlands that displays a variety of hues. Covered by a soft layer of earth, the desert's colorful erosion effects were created over the eons by mineralized water flows and mineral deposits. Overlooks with an especially scenic view include Chinde Point, Kachina Point, Pintado Point, Tawa Point and Tiponi Point. Every 30 minutes the Painted Desert Visitor Center offers a 20-minute film that explains how wood is petrified. **Hours:** Visitor center open daily 8-5. Hours may be extended Mar.-Sept. Closed Christmas. Phone ahead to confirm schedule. **Cost:** Free. **Phone:** (928) 524-6228.

PUERCO PUEBLO, s. of the Puerco River, is the remains of a Native American village that was abandoned more than 6 centuries ago. Petroglyphs can be seen along a short trail. During the Summer Solstice Celebration, held mid- to late June, a spiral petroglyph is interpreted by a park ranger; the solar marker interaction peaks at 9 a.m.

RAINBOW FOREST MUSEUM, near the s. entrance, contains polished petrified wood, fossils, fossil casts and exhibits telling the story of the early dinosaurs, giant reptiles and the petrified forest. A 20-minute film explains how wood is petrified. **Time:** Allow 30 minutes minimum. **Hours:** Daily 8-5. Hours may be extended Mar.-Sept. Phone ahead to confirm schedule. **Cost:** Free. **Phone:** (928) 524-6822 or (928) 524-6823.

Online & On the Go!

Travel smarter with **AAA/CAA Mobile Web** for your smartphone by visiting AAA.mobi or CAA.mobi.

Visit AAA.com/mobile or CAA.ca/mobile for more on-the-go solutions.

   AAA/CAA Mobile Web

Phoenix

Then & Now

In Phoenix, if you don't drink plenty of water, a golf stroke is promptly followed by heat stroke. Precious H20. Piped in from the Colorado, Salt and Verde rivers, it's what makes this ultrahot metropolis possible. Lush resorts, posh spas, superb museums and excellent restaurants surrounded by a starkly beautiful landscape, Phoenix is Arizona's big city-vacation oasis.

If your mental picture of Arizona is one of a Marlboro man riding merrily across the saguaro cactus-studded desert, that's here, too. Rising behind the downtown skyscrapers is Camelback Mountain, the go-to spot for desert-style hiking. East of the city, beyond the spill of cookie-cutter suburbs, are the rugged Superstition Mountains.

Of course, from late spring to late summer when daytime temps spike past the century mark for weeks on end, the only hiking you'll be doing is from Nordstrom to Neiman Marcus at the Scottsdale Fashion Square mall. Located about 10 miles northeast of downtown, Scottsdale—with its golf resorts, upscale eateries, hip nightlife and art galleries galore—is the state capital's tourist hot spot.

Downtown Phoenix, which has been spruced up over the past few decades, is where you can see the Arizona Diamondbacks turn double plays in their retractable-roofed stadium, listen to a Brahms concerto at Symphony Hall or watch a Phoenix Suns point guard hit an outside jump shot at US Airways Center.

The downtown core is loaded with restaurants and lively bars, especially in the streets surrounding the sports venues. But unless you get a charge out of staring up at modern glass-and-steel towers inhabited by the likes of Chase and U.S. Bank, this isn't exactly the stuff of walking tour brochures. A few exceptions include the 1929 Art Deco-style Luhrs Tower (at the corner of First Avenue and Jefferson Street) and Heritage Square, where the city's original Victorian brick buildings house small museums and a pair of popular restaurants.

Greater Phoenix, often maligned for its housing tracts full of stucco schlock, boasts many architectural jewels. Frank Lloyd Wright chose Scottsdale for the site of his gorgeous Taliesin West retreat. Wright also influenced the Mayan textile block design of the Arizona Biltmore, A Waldorf Astoria Hotel.

In the older neighborhoods surrounding the downtown core you'll drive down broad, sun-baked boulevards lined with ranch-style homes and aging strip malls. In these areas you'll find several outstanding Mexican eateries and a handful of small joints dishing up cheap and tasty Native American food.

Rosson House Museum, Heritage Square

(Continued on p. 135.)

Destination Phoenix

6033-A

This map shows cities in the Phoenix vicinity where you will find attractions, hotels and restaurants. Cities are listed alphabetically in this book on the following pages.

Fast Facts

ABOUT THE CITY

POP: 1,321,045 ▪ **ELEV:** 1,092 ft.

MONEY

SALES TAX: Arizona's statewide sales tax is 6.6 percent; an additional 2 percent is added in Phoenix and an additional 0.7 percent is added in Maricopa County. There is a hotel/motel tax of 13.27 percent. Rental cars incur a 15.1 percent tax, plus an 11.11 percent concession fee. There is a stadium tax of 3.25 percent. Parking at the airport includes a daily surcharge of 4.5 percent.

WHOM TO CALL

EMERGENCY: 911

POLICE (non-emergency): (602) 262-6151

HOSPITALS: Banner Good Samaritan Medical Center, (602) 839-2000 ▪ Maryvale Hospital, (623) 848-5000 ▪ St. Joseph's Hospital and Medical Center, (602) 406-3000.

WHERE TO LOOK AND LISTEN

NEWSPAPERS: The city's daily newspaper is *The Arizona Republic*, published in the morning.

RADIO: Phoenix radio station KTAR (92.3 FM) is a news/talk/traffic station ▪ KJZZ (91.5 FM) is a member of National Public Radio.

VISITOR INFORMATION

Greater Phoenix Convention and Visitors Bureau Downtown Visitor Information Center: 125 N. 2nd St., Suite 120, Phoenix, AZ 85004. **Phone:** (602) 254-6500 or (877) 225-5749.

The convention and visitors bureau distributes the helpful *Official Visitor Guide to Greater Phoenix* and *Greater Phoenix Dining Guide*.

TRANSPORTATION

AIR TRAVEL: Phoenix Sky Harbor International Airport (PHX), 4 miles southeast of downtown, is served by more than 20 major airlines. SuperShuttle is a 24-hour shared-ride service; phone (602) 244-9000 in metro Phoenix, or (800) 258-3826 outside Arizona. ExecuCar also is available from SuperShuttle; phone (602) 232-4600 or (800) 410-4444.

Airport limousine service, independent of the hotels, costs $40-$90. Some companies that serve the airport and certain downtown hotels are Arizona Limousines, (602) 267-7097 or (800) 678-0033; Carey Limousine, (602) 996-1955 or (800) 336-4646; and Desert Rose Limousine Service, (623) 780-0159 or (800) 716-8660. Cab service to downtown averages 20 minutes and costs an average of $20; traffic delays will increase the drive time and fare.

RENTAL CARS: Several rental car companies serve the Phoenix metropolitan area. At the airport, Hertz, (602) 267-8822 or (800) 654-3080, offers discounts to AAA members. Check the telephone directory for additional listings.

BUSES: Greyhound Lines Inc. has terminals at 2115 E. Buckeye Rd., (602) 389-4200, and 2647 W. Glendale Ave., (602) 246-4341, (800) 231-2222, or (800) 531-5332 (Spanish).

TAXIS: Taxi companies serving the greater Phoenix area include AAA Yellow Cab, (602) 252-5252 ▪ Discount Cab, (602) 200-2000 ▪ and VIP Taxi, (602) 300-3000.

PUBLIC TRANSPORTATION: METRO Light Rail connects downtown Phoenix to the neighboring communities of Tempe and Mesa. To reach Sky Harbor International Airport, get off at the station at 44th and Washington streets. From there, the free Phoenix Airport Shuttle bus offers service to all terminals.

Fares are $1.75 per ride or $3.50 for an all-day pass; self-serve ticket machines located at all stations accept cash and credit cards. The light rail operates 4:40 a.m.-11 p.m., with extended hours on Friday and Saturday. More information and printed route maps are available at downtown's Central Station (on Van Buren St. between Central and 1st avenues), or by phoning (602) 253-5000.

(Continued from p. 133.)

Hohokam Ancestral Desert People were the first people to settle in the Valley of the Sun (as the Phoenix area is known). They built a network of irrigation canals, farmed the beautiful wasteland and created a great city. But around the mid-1400s, the Hohokam mysteriously vanished. The 1860s saw a new frontier town begin to take shape atop the old Hohokam site. This rebirth, like the mythical Phoenix rising from the ashes, is what gives the city its name.

Now crisscrossed by a network of wide L.A.-style freeways, the greater metro area is home to some 4.3 million residents, making it the largest city in the desert Southwest.

One reason behind the explosive growth of the past 20 years is that the weather isn't always comparable to an oven set on broil. In the often warm, mild months of late fall, winter and early spring, when D.C. and NYC are bracing for the next "Snowmageddon," Phoenix residents are wearing shorts and reserving tee times.

Must Do: AAA Editor's Picks

- Touch scarlet cactus fruit, marvel at the iridescent wings of hummingbirds and watch butterflies touch down on wildflowers and giant saguaro cacti at the ☙ **Desert Botanical Garden,** where you'll find plenty of Sonoran Desert wonders to admire.

- **Hike** to the summit of **Camelback Mountain.** The double-humped peak soars above Paradise Valley and Arcadia. Climbing the vertical mile up the Summit (Echo Canyon) Trail, you'll know why it's called the "Scenic Stairmaster"—this is no casual amble (remember to bring water). At the top, scan the spectacular panorama of metropolitan Phoenix and the Sonoran Desert beyond.

- Pamper yourself in one of the **spa** capitals of the world. Walking through the tranquil lobby of the **Arizona Biltmore, A Waldorf Astoria Hotel**—with its architecture inspired by Frank Lloyd Wright—is a great way to begin your luxurious experience. At the spa, tie on a thick robe and delight in a rose quartz facial or a Sonoran stone massage.

- Go **power shopping** in Scottsdale. In the downtown **Arts District** you can browse art galleries galore. Nearby in **Old Town**—with its Wild West-themed wooden storefronts—you'll find touristy trinket emporiums and dealers of authentic Native American crafts. Funky clothing boutiques and one-of-a-kind shops line **5th Avenue.** And for those addicted to brand-name designer threads, there's the behemoth, three-story **Scottsdale Fashion Square** mall.

- Be a cowpoke for a day and **ride a horse** through Sonoran Desert country. In the foothills of **South Mountain Park,** you can trot and canter along more than 40 miles of trails. Hire horses and guides through Ponderosa Stables *(see Sports & Rec)*, or contact the Greater Phoenix Convention and Visitors Bureau.

- Take an **art walk** on **Roosevelt Street** just north of downtown on the first Friday of every month. Galleries and art studios stay open late, and the sidewalks are crowded with families, bohemian hipsters and street performers. This culture clash is a Phoenix rarity.

- "Batter up!" If it's late February or March, catch **spring training** with Major League Baseball's Cactus League. In the autumn, check out the Arizona Fall League, a proving ground for Major League farm teams. Phoenix is a hot place for sports—this is the hometown of the NBA **Suns,** NHL **Coyotes,** NFL **Cardinals** and MLB **Diamondbacks.**

- Hear bells at **Cosanti** in Paradise Valley. Paolo Soleri, an architect, sculptor and protégé of Frank Lloyd Wright, founded this site to further his organically inspired architecture. As you tour **Arcosanti,** observe the many spiraling, swooping edifices—there aren't any box-shaped buildings here. Sales from the foundation's renowned wind-bells support Soleri's structural experiments, and most weekday mornings you can watch foundry workers pour the bronze bells.

- Search for the fabled Lost Dutchman Gold Mine in the rugged **Superstition Mountains** east of the city. Even if you don't find the mine (no one has in more than 110 years), the scenery alone is a rich payoff. Stop at **Goldfield Ghost Town & Mine Tours** for some cheesy Wild West fun. Go **hiking** in nearby **Lost Dutchman State Park.** And then **drive** the windy but incredibly scenic **Apache Trail** road to **Canyon Lake** and beyond (the road is unpaved but suitable for passenger cars).

- Up, up and away—in a **hot air balloon.** From high in the clouds, marvel at the immensity of metro Phoenix and the stark beauty of its Sonoran Desert surroundings. The convention and visitors bureau can provide a list of ballooning companies.

Bells at Cosanti, Paradise Valley

Phoenix 1-day Itinerary

AAA editors suggest these activities for a great short vacation experience. Those staying in the area for a longer visit can access a 3-day itinerary at AAA.com/TravelGuide.

Morning

- Start your trip by communing with nature at the 🚩 **Desert Botanical Garden**, in 1,200-acre **Papago Park** on the east side of town. This is where visitors really come to understand the majesty of the Sonoran Desert and Phoenix's arid climate. You'll see native and exotic cacti, aloes and other plant species that thrive in desertlike conditions. Take the loop trail leading to the wildflower exhibits and find out what's in bloom. This area is lovely no matter what time of year you visit, but it's bursting with color in March and April.

- Next, drive south in Papago Park and enjoy the scenery—sandstone buttes dramatically jut skyward. Stop at the **Phoenix Zoo** and meet a Galapagos tortoise, a reticulated giraffe, a Grevy's zebra, a ring-tailed lemur and other heat-loving animals that live in replications of their own natural habitats. The zoo's grasslands and tropical jungles are so real that you might feel like you're on another continent.

Afternoon

- For lunch, head west toward downtown, where you'll spend the rest of the day. North of town, inhale a spicy barbecue sandwich or a slab of ribs at **Honey Bear's BBQ** on N. Central Avenue. If you'd rather do without sauce-caked chops and fingernails, grab some traditional eats with flair at the cozy, hip **Coronado Café**. This converted bungalow on N. 7th Street dishes up scrumptious salads, sandwiches, burgers and flatbreads in addition to heartier fare like juicy steaks, meatloaf and a seafood platter.

- Now duck indoors away from the desert heat at the 🚩 **Heard Museum**, 2301 N. Central Ave., and immerse yourself in Native American culture and arts. Stroll through the museum's 10 exhibit galleries and view baskets, drawings, paintings, photographs, pottery, jewelry, Kachina dolls, sculpture and textiles of the past and present. You can try your hand at bead looming, watch audiovisual presentations and unwind in the serene courtyards. Hit up the Heard Museum Shop on your way out if you're in the market for some authentic Native American arts and crafts.

- Also on N. Central Avenue, you can peruse the masters: Boucher, Rodin and Monet. Stop at 🚩 **Phoenix Art Museum** for some high art. You'll find more than 17,000 works from many art periods, ancient to contemporary. If you have a passion for high fashion, the Fashion Design collection is a must-see; if architecture and interior design interest you, you won't want to miss the Thorne Miniature Rooms exhibit. Even the kids will enjoy this place—there's a family-friendly, hands-on gallery, and elementary schoolers are given packs stuffed with puzzles and other activities that correspond with art displays.

- A visit to the 🚩 **Arizona Capitol Museum** on

Enjoy Ribs at Honey Bear's BBQ, N. Central Avenue

W. Washington Street, about 3 miles southwest of the N. Central Avenue museums, will definitely satisfy any history buff who wants to learn more about the state's fascinating beginnings. The museum is housed in the old state capitol building, built of tuff stone and granite and capped with a copper dome. Inside you'll explore former government officials' offices and the House and Senate chambers and view all sorts of historical and political memorabilia.

Evening

- For dinner in the area, check out **Pizzeria Bianco** on E. Adams Street. It may take awhile to be seated, but the wood-fired oven pizza is worth the wait. Pass the time with a glass of vino at Bar Bianco, the relaxed, chic wine bar next door. When it comes time to order your pie, opt for the Rosa, topped with Parmigiano-Reggiano cheese, red onion, rosemary and Arizona pistachios; or the Wiseguy, which has a tasty combination of fennel sausage, smoked mozzarella and roasted onion on top.

- If you have a hankering for "modern Mexican," head to **Barrio Cafe** on N. 16th Street. This offbeat joint's chef-owner puts an innovative spin on traditional Mexican dishes like *cochinita pibil* (slow-roasted pork), chicken in mole sauce, tacos and enchiladas. The guacamole, whipped up tableside with fresh avocados, spices and pomegranate seeds, is to die for. Wash it all down with a tequila-infused specialty drink—or, if you dare, *just* tequila. For dessert try the dangerously delectable *churros* (sugar-coated, tube-shaped fritters filled with *cajeta*, a sweet caramel flavoring made from goat's milk).

Arriving
By Car

Major highways make Phoenix readily accessible from all directions. The main route from Flagstaff and other points north is I-17, while the main route from the south and southeast is I-10. US 60, coming from the east, joins I-10 just north of Baseline Road.

In Phoenix I-10 intersects I-17 at 20th Street and leads west to Los Angeles. West of Phoenix, SR 85 intersects with I-10 and continues south to Gila Bend; I-8 can then be followed to Yuma and San Diego.

Getting Around
Street System

The streets in Phoenix form an orderly grid. Numbered streets run north and south, intersected by named streets going east and west. The axis is formed by Washington Street, which divides the city north and south, and Central Avenue, which determines the east and west sections. All avenues run west of Central; all streets, east.

Unless otherwise posted the speed limit on most streets is 25 mph. A right turn on red after a complete stop is legal unless otherwise posted. During rush hours the center turn lanes of 7th Avenue and 7th Street are reverse traffic flow lanes: morning rush hour one way into the city and evening rush hour one way out of the city. Try to avoid rush hours, 7-9 a.m. and 4-6 p.m.

Parking

Parking is regulated by meters. During business hours and in the downtown area certain one-way streets have restricted parking hours. Rates at public lots start at $1.50 per hour.

Shopping

If your monthly credit card statements read like shopping mall directories, this is your kinda town. The metro Phoenix phone book lists some two dozen major shopping malls.

At the high end is Biltmore Fashion Park, 2502 E. Camelback Rd., an open-air affair loaded with budget-busting names like Saks and Ralph Lauren. Desert Sky Mall, west of downtown at 7611 W. Thomas Rd., is more akin to the all-purpose suburban center you'll find back home (think Hot Topic, Sunglass Hut and Orange Julius).

The Outlets at Anthem, SR 17 and Anthem Way, are a good 30 minutes north of the city center, but if you're crazy for Ann Taylor and Calvin Klein at cutrate prices, it's worth the drive.

In the shadow of office buildings, downtown's open-air Arizona Center, at 400 E. Van Buren between 3rd and 5th streets, eschews the usual namebrand suspects in favor of independent clothing shops and a handful of tourist souvenir stores. Even if you keep the Visa card holstered, it's worth wandering around the nicely landscaped courtyards and fountains.

For authentic Native American arts and crafts, there's no topping the Heard Museum Shop, 2301 N. Central Ave. From high-quality jewelry and weavings to pottery and Kachina dolls, everything is purchased directly from Native American artists. The shop also stocks an extensive selection of books on the Southwest.

Vintage vinyl LPs are protected from the waxmelting Phoenix heat in the air-conditioned cocoon of Revolver Records, 918 N. 2nd St., at the corner of 2nd and Roosevelt streets. In addition to collectible punk, metal, jazz, blues and classic rock platters, you'll also find a wide selection of new and used CDs and DVDs.

The pedestrian-friendly Roosevelt Row, Roosevelt Street between 7th Street and Grand Avenue, is the heart of the Downtown Arts District. Once a rundown part of town, it's now home to several indie art galleries. If cutting-edge art is your thing, it's a must. If not, stick to Scottsdale (see p. 204), where you'll find galleries of all kinds, as well as the valley's best shopping in general.

Nightlife

You'll find most of the valley's nocturnal action in Scottsdale (see p. 204) and Tempe (see p. 256), but Phoenix proper is no slouch when it comes to live music, cocktail lounges and casual bars. Pick up the free weekly Phoenix New Times for a comprehensive roundup of club and concert listings.

The downtown streets are brimming with sports bars that get wild on big game nights. Located behind US Airways Center, and only a few blocks from Chase Field, Alice Cooper'stown (owned by the heavy metal shockmeister), 101 E. Jackson St., is

Browse Vintage Vinyl LPs at Revolver Records

loaded with flat-screen TVs, Cooper memorabilia and die-hard D-backs fans. Drinks are cheap and the pub grub menu features the 22-inch "Big Unit" hot dog. Welcome to your nightmare.

Everyone knows what to expect from SAVE Hard Rock Cafe, 3 S. 2nd St., and the Phoenix branch near US Airways Center holds no surprises. But it's still a fun spot to grab a pre- or post-game brew. Majerle's Sports Grill, 24 N. 2nd St., is owned by ex-Suns great Dan Majerle and draws big crowds during the NBA season.

If suds and ESPN SportsCenter aren't your scene, the city has several classy cocktail bars where you can sip a $12 appletini and chill in style. SoHo meets the Southwest at Mercbar, 2525 E. Camelback Rd., a dark, sexy lounge across the street from Biltmore Fashion Park. A few minutes northwest of downtown is Sidebar, 1514 N. 7th Ave., a snug watering hole with swank décor and bartenders who know their business.

Chivas Regal on the rocks is best enjoyed while gazing out at twinkling city lights. The upscale Jade Bar, 5700 E. McDonald Dr., obliges with outstanding nighttime views from its lofty locale at the Sanctuary on Camelback Mountain resort.

The Rhythm Room, 1019 E. Indian School Rd., is the place to catch live blues, roots rock and R&B. In the Downtown Arts District, the funky Paisley Violin Café, 1030 N.W. Grand Ave., hosts live jazz several nights a week. For country music and line dancing, you'll need to saddle up for Scottsdale (see p. 204).

Big Events

Right on the heels of the ⧸ Insight Bowl, Tempe starts the new year with the Fort McDowell Fiesta Bowl Parade, one of the country's largest parades. The ⧸ Tostitos Fiesta Bowl and all its pregame activities are on Glendale's agenda in early January.

Scottsdale's February highlights are the Parada del Sol and the Waste Management Phoenix Open golf tournament. Other top February events are the Arabian Horse Show, popular among equestrians, and the National Hot Rod Association (NHRA) Arizona Nationals.

March brings the Indian Fair and Market, held at the Heard Museum. The Maricopa County Fair happens in April. The Cinco de Mayo Festival and other Mexican celebrations occur in early May.

Various fall festivals take place in the Phoenix area from October into November. The Arizona Exposition & State Fair and the Cowboy Artists of America Exhibition in October draw crowds.

The Pueblo Grande Museum Auxiliary Indian Market is held the second weekend in December on the museum grounds, 4619 E. Washington St. The year's festivities conclude with *posadas,* Mexican neighborhood celebrations that take place during the 9 days preceding Christmas.

Sports & Rec

Phoenix's mild winters make it an all-year sports paradise. For spectators the winter months mean

"Intertribal Greeting" by Doug Hyde, Heard Museum

horse racing at Turf Paradise from October through early May; phone (602) 942-1101.

Note: Policies vary concerning admittance of children to pari-mutuel betting facilities. Phone for information.

During **baseball** season the Arizona Diamondbacks, 2001 World Series champs, play at the retractable-roofed Chase Field, 401 E. Jefferson St. in downtown Phoenix; phone (602) 462-6500. Both the Diamondbacks and the Colorado Rockies conduct spring training at Salt River Fields at Talking Stick in Scottsdale; phone (480) 270-5000.

Other teams with spring training sites in the Phoenix area include the Milwaukee Brewers at Maryvale Baseball Park in Phoenix, (800) 933-7890; the Oakland Athletics at Phoenix Municipal Stadium in Phoenix, (602) 495-7239; the Los Angeles Angels of Anaheim at Tempe Diablo Stadium in Tempe, (480) 350-5205; the Chicago Cubs at Hohokam Stadium in Mesa, (480) 644-6451; the Kansas City Royals and the Texas Rangers at Surprise Recreation Campus in Surprise, (623) 222-2222; the San Diego Padres and the Seattle Mariners at Peoria Sports Complex in Peoria, (623) 773-8700 or (623) 773-8720; the Los Angeles Dodgers and the Chicago White Sox at Camelback Ranch in Glendale, (623) 302-5000; the Cleveland Indians and the Cincinnati Reds at the Goodyear Ballpark in Goodyear, (623) 882-3120; and the San Francisco Giants at Scottsdale Stadium in Scottsdale, (480) 312-2580.

The US Airways Center, 201 E. Jefferson St., is the site of many of Phoenix's sporting events. It is the home court of the NBA Phoenix Suns **basketball** team November through April; phone (602) 379-7867. The WNBA's Phoenix Mercury take over the arena's court May through August; phone (602)

252-9622. April through August the arena also houses the Arizona Rattlers, Phoenix's professional **arena football** team; phone (480) 985-3292. September through April the Jobing.com Arena, 9400 W. Maryland Ave., is the home of the Phoenix Coyotes, the city's National **Hockey** League team; phone (480) 563-7825.

Professional **football** is played in Glendale, where the NFL Arizona Cardinals take the field at The University of Phoenix Stadium, 1 Cardinals Dr.; phone (602) 379-0102. The 🏈 Tostitos Fiesta Bowl football classic at the stadium is a January highlight.

National Hot Rod Association **drag racing** as well as **dragboat racing** are at Firebird Raceway, about 8 miles south of Phoenix at Maricopa Road and I-10; phone (602) 268-0200. Indy cars, NASCAR **stock cars and trucks,** and Grand Am sports cars race at Phoenix International Raceway; phone (623) 463-5400 *(see attraction listing p. 146).*

Licensed drivers can experience race car driving at Bob Bondurant School of High Performance Driving, I-10 and Maricopa Road; phone (480) 403-7600 or (800) 842-7223.

A round of **golf** in a panorama of mountain peaks and blue skies entices not only Arizona residents but visitors too. Golfing is a year-round activity in Arizona. There are more than 325 golf courses in the state, both public and private, appealing to all levels of proficiency. Phone (866) 865-4653 to reserve a tee time at any of the more than 120 Phoenix courses.

Phoenix courses include Club West, (480) 460-4400, 16400 S. 14th Ave.; Encanto, (602)

McCormick Ranch Golf Course, Scottsdale

253-3963, at 2745 N. 15th Ave.; The Foothills, (480) 460-4653, at 2201 E. Clubhouse Dr.; Maryvale, (623) 846-4022, at 5902 W. Indian School Rd.; Papago, (602) 275-8428, in Papago Park at 5595 E. Moreland St.; The Arizona Grand Golf Resort, (602) 431-6480, at 8000 S. Arizona Grand Pkwy.; Lookout Mountain Golf Club, (602) 866-6356, at 11111 N. 7th St.; and Stonecreek, (602) 953-9110, at 4435 E. Paradise Village Pkwy. S.

Golf courses in nearby Mesa include: Dobson Ranch, (480) 644-2291, at 2155 S. Dobson Rd.; Red Mountain Ranch, (480) 981-6501, at 6425 E. Teton Cir.; and Superstition Springs, (480) 985-5622, at 6542 E. Baseline Rd.

Courses in Scottsdale include: Marriott's Camelback, (480) 596-7050, at 7847 N. Mockingbird Ln.; Marriott's Mountain Shadows Resort, (480) 905-8999, at 5641 E. Lincoln Dr.; McCormick Ranch, (480) 948-0260, at 7505 E. McCormick Pkwy.; Starfire at Scottsdale Country Club, (480) 948-6000, at 11500 N. Hayden Rd.; TPC Scottsdale, (480) 585-4334, at 17020 N. Hayden Rd.; and Troon North, (480) 585-5300, at 10320 E. Dynamite Blvd.

Other area courses include: Gold Canyon, (480) 982-9090, at 6100 S. Kings Ranch Rd. in Apache Junction; Hillcrest, (623) 584-1500, at 20002 N. Star Ridge Dr. in Sun City West; The Legend at Arrowhead, (623) 561-1902, at 21027 N. 67th Ave. in Glendale; Ocotillo, (480) 917-6660, at 3751 S. Clubhouse Dr. in Chandler; We-Ko-Pa, (480) 836-9000, at 18200 East Toh Vee Cir. in Fort McDowell; and The Wigwam Resort, (623) 935-3811, at 300 E. Wigwam Blvd. in Litchfield Park. In Tempe are ASU-Karsten, (480) 921-8070, at 1125 E. Rio Salado Pkwy.; and Ken McDonald, (480) 350-5250, at 800 E. Divot Dr.

Tennis courts open to the public are plentiful at several high schools and park areas, including Encanto Park, 15th Avenue and Encanto Drive, and Granada Park, 6505 N. 20th St. The Phoenix Tennis Center, (602) 249-3712, at 6330 N. 21st Ave., has 22 lighted courts and reasonable rates; reservations are accepted.

The valley's beautiful desert country lends itself to **horseback riding.** Ponderosa Stables, (602) 268-1261, at 10215 S. Central Ave., offers trail rides.

Trails for **hiking** and **biking** are plentiful. A favorite hike is the 1-mile scenic trek to the summit of Piestewa Peak. Formerly known as Squaw Peak, the peak was renamed in honor of Lori Piestewa, an American servicewoman and Hopi who was killed in combat during Operation Iraqi Freedom in 2003. Hike In Phoenix, LLC *(see Scottsdale p. 207)* offers guided hiking trips along several mountain trails in Phoenix and Scottsdale; phone (877) 445-3749.

The Phoenix Parks and Recreation Department, (602) 534-6587, operates a number of parks; some have municipal **swimming** pools. Saguaro Lake and Canyon Lake*(see Recreation Chart)* offer **water skiing, boating** and **fishing.** The Salt River is popular with **tubing** enthusiasts. Salt River Tubing and Recreation *(see Mesa p. 112),* (480) 984-3305, rents tubes and also provides shuttle-bus service along the Salt River.

For the **shooting** enthusiast, the Ben Avery Shooting Range, (623) 582-8313, 25 miles north of Phoenix off I-17 exit 223, offers pistol, rifle and archery ranges and trap and skeet fields.

The suburb of Tempe boasts inland **surfing** at Big Surf *(see Tempe p. 257)*, (480) 994-2297; and **ice skating** at the Oceanside Ice Arena, (480) 941-0944, at 1520 N. McClintock Dr.

Hot air balloon rides over the metropolitan area and the Sonora Desert are available through several companies. Balloon rides average 1 hour and are usually followed by a champagne brunch. Many companies operate October through May, but some offer flights year-round. Prices range from $145 to $225 per person. Companies include: Aerogelic Ballooning, (480) 247-7813 or (866) 359-8329; Hot Air Expeditions, (480) 502-6999 or (800) 831-7610; and Unicorn Balloon Co., (480) 991-3666 or (800) 755-0935. **Soaring** is available at Turf Soaring School, (602) 439-3621, at 8700 W. Carefree Hwy. in Peoria.

Performing Arts

Phoenix's rapid growth has been cultural as well as industrial. The following theaters present a mix of classic and contemporary drama: Herberger Theater Center, (602) 254-7399, 222 E. Monroe; Phoenix Theatre, (602) 254-2151, 100 E. McDowell Rd.; Greasepaint Youtheatre, (602) 889-7609, 7020 E. 2nd St. in Scottsdale; and TheaterWorks, (623) 815-7930, at 8355 W. Peoria Ave. in Peoria. Arizona's professional state theater group, the Arizona Theater Co., (602) 256-6995, performs at the Herberger Theater Center during its October to June season.

The historic Orpheum Theatre, (602) 262-6225, at 203 W. Adams St., was originally built for vaudeville acts and movies in 1929. Scheduled to be condemned, the city bought the theater and in 1997 reopened it as a 1,400-seat performing arts center. Free guided tours of the Spanish Baroque Revival building are available; phone (602) 534-5600.

For music and dance lovers, the Arizona Opera, Ballet Arizona and Phoenix Symphony offer performances throughout the year. The symphony performs in the striking Symphony Hall, Phoenix Civic Plaza, 75 N. Second St.; phone (602) 262-7272.

Cabarets, special concerts, big-name entertainment, shows and lectures are presented at the Herberger Theater Center, (602) 254-7399, 222 E. Monroe; the Maricopa County Events Center, (623) 544-2888, 19403 R.H. Johnson Blvd. in Sun City West; and the ASU Gammage, (480) 965-3434, on the campus of Arizona State University at Mill Avenue and Apache Boulevard in Tempe.

Other special performance areas include US Airways Center, (602) 379-7800, 201 E. Jefferson St.; Arizona Veterans Memorial Coliseum, (602)

ASU Gammage, Tempe

252-6771, 1826 W. McDowell Rd.; Celebrity Theatre, (602) 267-1600, 440 N. 32nd St.; Cricket Pavilion, (602) 254-7200, 2121 N. 83rd Ave.; and the Comerica Theatre, (602) 379-2800, 400 W. Washington St. In Mesa are the Mesa Arts Center, (480) 644-6500, 1 E. Main St.; and the Mesa Amphitheater, (480) 644-2560, 263 N. Center St.

⚑ ATTRACTIONS

ARIZONA CAPITOL MUSEUM is in the Arizona Capitol building at 1700 W. Washington St. The Capitol is built of tuff stone from Kirkland Junction and granite from the Salt River Mountains. Opened in 1900, the four-story building served as the territorial capitol until statehood came in 1912; it then became the state capitol.

The restored wings feature artifacts and documents of early Arizona; political memorabilia; the offices of the governor, mine inspector and secretary of state; the House and Senate chambers; an exhibit about the USS *Arizona;* and a wax figure of the first governor of Arizona, George Hunt. How a bill becomes a law is explained in an exhibit called A Tale of Two Chambers. Behind the building is a 1974 structure containing executive branch offices. The legislative galleries adjoin the Capitol.

Hours: Mon.-Fri. 9-4; closed state holidays. Guided tours are given at 10 and 2. **Cost:** Free admission to museum and free parking at Wesley Bolin Park. **Phone:** (602) 926-3620 for information and tour reservations.

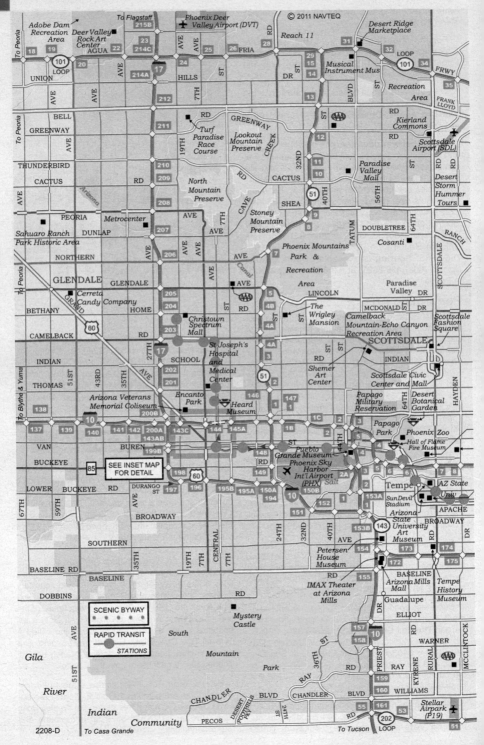

© 2011 NAVTEQ

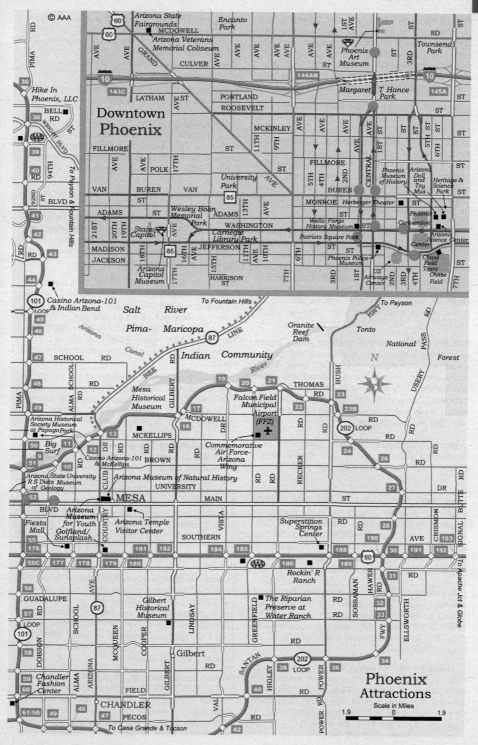

© AAA

Phoenix
Attractions

Scale in Miles

1.9   0   1.9

CHASE FIELD TOURS is at 401 E. Jefferson St. A 75-minute tour of the Arizona Diamondbacks ballpark encompasses the rotunda, a luxury suite, the dugout, and the visiting team's clubhouse or press box. **Hours:** Mon.-Sat. at 9:30, 11:00 and 12:30. **Cost:** $7; $5 (ages 7-12 and 56+); $3 (ages 4-6). **Phone:** (602) 514-8400 or (800) 821-7160.

SAVE **DEER VALLEY ROCK ART CENTER,** I-17 exit Deer Valley Road W., then 2 mi. w. to 3711 W. Deer Valley Rd., consists of a museum, archeological site and 47-acre nature preserve. Museum exhibits introduce visitors to rock art and the ancient Southwest Native American cultures that created it. A .25-mile trail provides a view of 1,500 hillside petroglyphs dating from 500 to more than 7,000 years old. The site is considered spiritual by Southwestern Native Americans.

Time: Allow 1 hour, 30 minutes minimum. **Hours:** Tues.-Sat. 9-5, Sun. noon-5, Oct.-Apr.; Tues.-Sun. 8-2, rest of year. Last trail admission 30 minutes prior to museum close. Guided tours are available by reservation Oct.-Apr. Closed Jan. 1, Easter, July 4, Thanksgiving, Christmas Eve and Christmas. **Cost:** $7; $4 (ages 62+ and students with ID); $3 (ages 6-12); free (ages 0-5). **Phone:** (623) 582-8007.

ENCANTO PARK, 2605 N. 15th Ave., has a lagoon and islands that serve as a waterfowl refuge; unusual trees and shrubs also can be seen. A children's amusement park with a carousel, train rides and bumper boats is on one of the islands. Tennis, basketball, racquetball and volleyball courts, boat rentals, a swimming pool and nature trails are available. *See Recreation Chart.*

Hours: Daily 5:30 a.m.-11 p.m. **Cost:** Park free. Amusement park ride prices vary; phone ahead. **Phone:** (602) 261-8993 or (602) 254-1200.

HALL OF FLAME FIRE MUSEUM, 6101 E. Van Buren St., houses one of the largest collections of firefighting equipment dating from 1725. A 10-minute videotape presentation introduces visitors to the museum's exhibits, which include hand- and horse-drawn pumpers, hook-and-ladder wagons and vehicles dating 1800-1969.

A wildland firefighting gallery explains the history and techniques of fighting wildfires. Other displays include fire marks, helmets, badges, patches, an interactive fire safety exhibit and play area for children, and artwork depicting major events in the history of fire service.

The National Firefighting Hall of Heroes recognizes firefighters who died in the line of duty and were decorated for bravery. **Time:** Allow 2 hours, 30 minutes minimum. **Hours:** Mon.-Sat. 9-5, Sun. noon-4. Closed Jan. 1, Thanksgiving and Christmas. **Cost:** $6; $5 (ages 62+); $4 (ages 6-17); $1.50 (ages 3-5). **Phone:** (602) 275-3473.

HEARD MUSEUM, 2301 N. Central Ave., is a museum of native cultures and art. Among the exhibits in its 11 galleries are contemporary, ethnological and historical materials of Southwestern Native Americans; Native American basketry, jewelry and pottery; and Kachina dolls.

Visitors are greeted with colorful images as they enter the exhibit area. The architecture, foods, culture and spirituality of more than 20 tribes from desert, uplands and the Colorado Plateau regions are examined. Interactive exhibits allow visitors to work on a bead loom and experience re-created geographic settings of Native Americans. Changing exhibits and audiovisual presentations also are featured.

Time: Allow 1 hour minimum. **Hours:** Mon.-Sat. 9:30-5, Sun. 11-5. Guided tours are given daily at noon, 1, 2 and 3. Closed Jan. 1, Easter, Memorial Day, July 4, Labor Day, Thanksgiving and Christmas. **Cost:** $15; $13.50 (ages 65+); $7.50 (ages 6-12); free (Native Americans). **Phone:** (602) 252-8848 or (602) 252-8840.

HERITAGE AND SCIENCE PARK is on Monroe St. between 5th and 7th sts. The park includes Heritage Square, comprised of eight late 19th-century structures that were part of the original site of Phoenix; they contain exhibits, museums and restaurants. The modern Lath House Pavilion serves as a community meeting area, botanical garden and festival site.

Validated parking is available in the garage at Fifth and Monroe sts. **Hours:** Buildings open Wed.-Sat. 10-4, Sun. noon-4; closed mid-Aug. through Labor Day. **Cost:** Parking: $2-$12. **Phone:** (602) 262-5029 or TTY (602) 262-6713.

Arizona Doll and Toy Museum, 7th and Monroe sts. at 602 E. Adams, exhibits antique dolls and toys from around the world. One exhibit is devoted to a late 19th-century schoolroom, featuring the dolls as students. **Time:** Allow 30 minutes minimum. **Hours:** Tues.-Sat. 10-4, Sun. noon-4, day after Labor Day-July 31. Closed major holidays. **Cost:** $3; $1 (ages 0-12). **Phone:** (602) 253-9337.

SAVE **Arizona Science Center,** 600 E. Washington St., offers more than 300 hands-on displays that allow visitors to explore such topics as biology, physics, psychology and digital communications in a fun and educational environment. Demonstrations, a rock-climbing wall, a SkyCycle ride, an IMAX theater and a planetarium also are featured. **Hours:** Daily 10-5. Closed Thanksgiving and Christmas. **Cost:** $12; $10 (ages 3-17 and 62+). Theater shows $8; $7 (ages 3-12). Rock wall and SkyCycle ride $5. **Phone:** (602) 716-2000.

Rosson House Museum, 7th and Monroe sts., was built in 1895 for Dr. Roland Lee Rosson, mayor of Phoenix 1895-96. The restored Victorian mansion, constructed in 6 months at a cost of $7,525, features lathe-worked posts on the veranda, pressed-tin ceilings, parquet floors, an elaborately carved staircase and period furnishings. Various events are presented throughout the year.

Hours: Guided tours are given Wed.-Sat. 10-4, Sun. noon-4, day after Labor Day to mid-Aug. Last tour begins 30 minutes before closing. Closed major holidays. **Cost:** $7.50; $6 (ages 63+); $4 (ages 6-12). **Phone:** (602) 262-5070.

MUSICAL INSTRUMENT MUSEUM is at 4725 E. Mayo Blvd. The museum boasts a collection of more than 14,000 musical instruments, some 5,000 of which are on display at any given time. Upon arrival you'll don a wireless headset that picks up signals transmitted from each exhibit; as you walk toward an exhibit you'll hear the sounds of the instruments displayed.

The ground-floor exhibit "Guitars. Many Forms, Many Countries" features two dozen wall-mounted guitars ranging from an 1800 English lute guitar to a 12-string Rickenbacker 360 (think The Beatles) to a 1978 Ibanez Iceman (think KISS). Just beyond the guitars is the Making Musical Instruments gallery, home to a sitar, a bass drum, an accordion and other instruments accompanied by identification plaques that explain each instrument's construction.

You can test your music-making skills in the Experience Gallery, admire instruments donated by or on loan from renowned musicians in the Artist Gallery (a highlight is the 1969 Steinway piano John Lennon used to compose "Imagine"), and view temporary exhibits in the Target Gallery.

Upstairs, six galleries are divided almost continentally: Africa and the Middle East, Asia, South America (including Mexico and the Caribbean), Oceania, North America (U.S. and Canada) and Europe. Each gallery has displays devoted to the music of individual countries. Asian *domburas* and *dutars* (long-necked lutes), Guatemalan *marimbas*, Tibetan *dungchen* (giant copper trumpets), and an enormous display of Fender guitars are among the many instruments you'll see.

Time: Allow 2 hours minimum. **Hours:** Mon.-Sat. 9-5 (also Thurs.-Fri. 5-9), Sun. 10-5. Closed Thanksgiving and Christmas. **Cost:** $15; $13 (ages 65+); $10 (ages 6-17). **Phone:** (480) 478-6000. 🍽

MYSTERY CASTLE, near South Mountain Park, is s. on Central Ave. then e. to 800 E. Mineral Rd. Built 1930-45 by Boyce Luther Gulley as his dream castle for his daughter, Mary Lou, the house is constructed of native stone. Gulley abandoned his family in 1930 upon learning of his illness; after his death his family discovered the castle and Mary Lou moved in. **Time:** Allow 30 minutes minimum. **Hours:** Thurs.-Sun. 11-4, Oct.-May. **Cost:** $5; $3 (ages 4-12). **Phone:** (602) 268-1581.

NORTH MOUNTAIN PARK, 9 mi. n. at 10600 N. 7th St., accesses more than 7,000 acres of the Phoenix Mountains Preserve. The park has various hiking trails, including the Penny Howe Barrier-Free Nature Trail, as well as picnic areas and a playground. **Hours:** Daily 5 a.m.-11 p.m. **Cost:** Free. **Phone:** (602) 495-5458.

PAPAGO PARK, jct. Galvin Pkwy. and Van Buren St., covers 1,200 acres and features fishing lagoons, bicycle paths, nature trails, picnic areas and a golf course. Hole-in-the-Rock is a sandstone rock formation used by the Hohokam Ancestral Desert People to mark the solstices and equinoxes. Hunt's Tomb, a white pyramid, is the burial place of Governor George Wiley Paul Hunt, Arizona's first governor. **Hours:** Daily 6 a.m.-7 p.m. **Cost:** Free. **Phone:** (602) 495-5458.

Desert Botanical Garden, 1201 N. Galvin Pkwy., covers more than 145 acres in Papago Park. The garden is devoted exclusively to arid land plants of the world. The paved Desert Discovery Trail leads visitors through the garden; other walkways include the Plants and People of the Sonoran Desert Trail, the Sonoran Desert Nature Trail and the Harriet K. Maxwell Desert Wildflower Trail.

The majority of the garden's plants are succulents and include cacti, aloes and century plants. The height of the wildflower blooming season is March through May. Special programs, including bird walks, flashlight tours and children's ecology camps, are offered. **Time:** Allow 2 hours minimum. **Hours:** Daily 7 a.m.-8 p.m., May-Sept.; 8-8, rest of year. **Cost:** $18; $15 (ages 60+); $10 (students with ID); $8 (ages 3-12). **Phone:** (480) 941-1225. 🍽

Phoenix Zoo, off N. Galvin Pkwy. in Papago Park, exhibits more than 1,300 mammals, birds and reptiles. The 125-acre zoo features four trails and is home to Southwestern animals; African meerkats, lions and a warthog; rain forest creatures; and a spectacled bear.

Other features include Harmony Farm, Monkey Village, the Tropical Flights Rain Forest and a Safari Train. Feel the Difference, an exhibit for the visually impaired, includes life-size sculptures of such animals as elephants, fish and insects. The displays are labeled in braille.

Time: Allow 2 hours minimum. **Hours:** Daily 9-5, Sept.-May; Mon.-Fri. 7-2, Sat.-Sun. 7-4, rest of year. Closed Christmas. **Cost:** $18; $13 (ages 60+); $9 (ages 3-12). **Phone:** (602) 273-1341. 🍽 🍴

PHOENIX ART MUSEUM, 1625 N. Central Ave., features more than 18,000 works of American, European, Asian, Latin American, Western American and contemporary art. Such renowned artists as Picasso, Rodin and Monet are represented within the various collections. Museum highlights include the Fashion Design collection, the Thorne Miniature Rooms exhibit, and photographs from the Center for Creative Photography. Traveling exhibitions are presented throughout the year.

Sculptures surround the main building and also are found within its courtyard. Families can enjoy PhxArtKids, an interactive gallery filled with hands-on exhibits. The museum also offers guests children's packs stuffed with puzzles and other activities corresponding with art displays to help those ages 6-10 understand and appreciate art.

Note: Restrictions apply to items that may be carried in; phone ahead for specific details. **Tours:** Guided tours are available. **Time:** Allow 1 hour minimum. **Hours:** Wed.-Sat. 10-5 (also Wed. 5-9), Sun. noon-5. Closed major holidays. **Cost:** $10; $8 (ages 65+ and full-time college students with ID); $4 (ages 6-17); free (Wed. 3-9). **Phone:** (602) 257-1222. 🍴

PHOENIX INTERNATIONAL RACEWAY is w. off I-10 to exit 131 (Avondale Blvd.), then 5.6 mi. s. to 7602 S. Avondale Blvd. Opened in 1964 at the foot of the Estrella Mountains, the raceway took off in 1988 with the arrival of the NASCAR Sprint Cup Series (formerly NASCAR Winston Cup Series).

Two annual NASCAR Sprint Cup Series weekends are the raceway's main draws. The facility has reserved seats for 76,000. With hillside and infield seating surrounding the 1-mile oval paved racetrack, the raceway can accommodate more than 100,000 fans.

Hours: Two major race weekends take place in Apr. and Nov. **Phone:** (623) 463-5400 for track information, (866) 408-7223, or TTY (866) 472-8725 for tickets.

PHOENIX POLICE MUSEUM is at 101 S. Central Ave., Suite 100. Exhibits include antique police cars, motorcycles, uniforms and badges. Highlights include 1880s and 1930s jail cells and a 1919 Ford Model T police car. A memorial room pays tribute to police officers killed in the line of duty. **Time:** Allow 30 minutes minimum. **Hours:** Mon., Wed., Fri. 9-3; closed city holidays. **Cost:** Donations. Reservations are recommended. **Phone:** (602) 534-7278.

PIONEER ARIZONA LIVING HISTORY MUSEUM is off I-17 exit 225 to 3901 W. Pioneer Rd. More than 26 original and reconstructed buildings, spread over 92 acres, replicate the territorial days of the Southwest 1863-1912. Costumed interpreters re-enact life in territorial Arizona during themed special events held monthly. **Time:** Allow 2 hours minimum. **Hours:** Wed.-Sun. 9-4, Sept.-May; 7-noon, rest of year (weather permitting). Closed Memorial Day, Labor Day, Thanksgiving and Christmas. **Cost:** $7; $6 (ages 60+); $5 (ages 5-17). **Phone:** (623) 465-1052.

PUEBLO GRANDE MUSEUM, 4619 E. Washington St., contains a prehistoric Hohokam village ruin that includes a platform mound, ball court and irrigation canals. Outdoor exhibits include full-size replicas of Hohokam pit houses and adobe compound houses. Interactive museum exhibits center on archeology and the life of the Hohokam. Changing exhibits and tours also are available. An Indian market is held in December.

Time: Allow 1 hour minimum. **Hours:** Mon.-Sat. 9-4:45, Sun. 1-4:45, Oct.-Apr.; Tues.-Sat. 9-4:45,

rest of year. Closed Memorial Day, July 4, Labor Day, Thanksgiving and Christmas. **Cost:** $6; $5 (ages 55+); $3 (ages 6-17). **Phone:** (602) 495-0901 or (877) 706-4408.

SHEMER ART CENTER, 5005 E. Camelback Rd., is in the first house built in the Arcadia section of Phoenix; the house was completed in early 1919. The restored Santa Fe Mission-style building with adobe walls contains changing exhibits of fine art; seasonal classes also are available.

A highlight is a Colonial mansion doll house. The landscaped grounds feature orchards and sculpture gardens. **Hours:** Tues.-Sat. 10-3 (also Thurs. 6:30-8:30 p.m.). Closed city and major holidays. Schedule varies seasonally; phone ahead. **Cost:** Donations. **Phone:** (602) 262-4727.

SOUTH MOUNTAIN PARK, 8 mi. s. at 10919 S. Central Ave., contains more than 16,000 acres of peaks, canyons and strange rock formations as well as native Arizona flora. There are some 50 miles of trails for hiking, horseback riding and mountain biking. Dobbins Lookout, accessible by road and trail, affords an excellent view; phone ahead for hours, as road closing times vary. A rock on Pima Canyon Road bears a Spanish inscription that reads: "Marcos de Niza; where he passed from Mexico to Aycos (Acoma) in the Year of Our Lord 1539." *See Recreation Chart.* **Hours:** Daily 5 a.m.-10 p.m. **Cost:** Free. **Phone:** (602) 495-5458. 🐎 🚴

WELLS FARGO HISTORY MUSEUM is at 145 W. Adams St. Exhibits portray Arizona stagecoach history beginning in the mid-1850s. An 1868 stagecoach and Western art by such artists as Frederic Remington and N.C. Wyeth are on display. **Time:** Allow 1 hour minimum. **Hours:** Mon.-Fri. 9-5. **Cost:** Free. **Phone:** (602) 378-1852.

THE WRIGLEY MANSION is at 2501 E. Talawa Tr. Completed in 1932, the Mediterranean-style mansion was built by chewing-gum magnate William Wrigley Jr. as a 50th wedding anniversary gift for his wife, Ada. Guided tours of the house provide a glimpse into the family's history. **Time:** Allow 1 hour minimum. **Hours:** Guided tours are given Tues.-Sat. at 10 and 3, Sept. 1 to mid-June. Closed Jan. 1 and Christmas. **Cost:** $15. Reservations are required. **Phone:** (602) 955-4079 or (888) 879-7201.

Sightseeing
Bus, Four-wheel-drive and Van Tours

A tour is the best way to get an overall view of the city, and a variety of tours are available. Several companies offer four-wheel-drive or van tours of the desert: Open Road Tours, (602) 997-6474 or (800) 766-7117; Vaughan's Southwest Custom Tours, (602) 971-1381 or (800) 513-1381; and Wayward Wind Tours Inc., (602) 867-7825 or (800) 804-0480.

Plane Tours

Westwind Air Service provides scenic tours of the Grand Canyon. For flight arrangements phone (480) 991-5557 or (888) 869-0866.

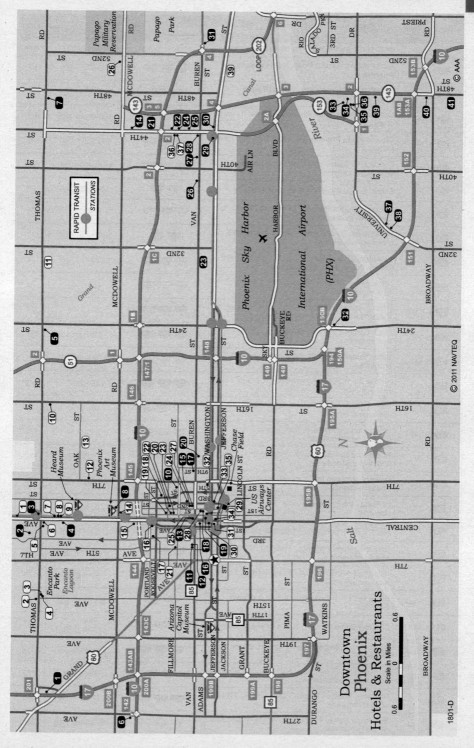

Downtown
Phoenix
Hotels & Restaurants

Scale in Miles

RAPID TRANSIT
STATIONS

© 2011 NAVTEQ

© AAA

1801-D

✈ Airport Accommodations

Map Page	PHOENIX SKY HARBOR INTERNATIONAL	Diamond Rated	High Season	Page
30 p. 147	**Aloft Phoenix Airport Hotel, just n of east entrance**	◆◆◆	$79-$229 (SAVE)	168
32 p. 147	**Best Western Airport Inn, 1 mi s of west entrance**	◆◆	$79-$149 (SAVE)	169
35 p. 147	**Courtyard by Marriott Phoenix Airport, 0.5 mi s of east entrance**	◆◆◆	$119-$249 (SAVE)	169
29 p. 147	**Crowne Plaza Phoenix Airport, 0.7 mi n of east entrance**	◆◆◆	$89-$169 (SAVE)	170
28 p. 147	**DoubleTree Suites by Hilton Hotel Phoenix, 1 mi n of east entrance**	◆◆◆	$149-$299 (SAVE)	170
23 p. 147	**Econo Lodge Airport, 1.5 mi w of entrance**	◆◆	$55-$65 (SAVE)	170
5 p. 147	**Embassy Suites Phoenix Airport at 24th St, 2.4 mi n of west entrance**	◆◆◆	$139-$209 (SAVE)	171
36 p. 147	**Fairfield Inn by Marriott Phoenix Airport, 0.5 mi s of east entrance**	◆◆	$69-$189 (SAVE)	171
40 p. 147	**Hampton Inn & Suites Phoenix Airport South/Tempe, 2.5 mi from east entrance**	◆◆◆	$59-$179 (SAVE)	171
24 p. 147	Hampton Inn Phoenix Airport North, 1.2 mi n of east entrance	◆◆◆	$59-$149	171
38 p. 147	Hilton Garden Inn Phoenix Airport, 1.5 mi se of west entrance	◆◆◆	$99-$169	171
26 p. 147	Hilton Garden Inn Phoenix Airport North, 2 mi n of east entrance	◆◆◆	$159-$199	171
33 p. 147	**Hilton Phoenix Airport, 0.5 mi s of east entrance**	◆◆◆	$109-$229 (SAVE)	172
39 p. 147	Holiday Inn & Suites Phoenix Airport, 1.5 mi s of east entrance	◆◆◆	$89-$189	172
14 p. 147	Holiday Inn & Suites Phoenix Airport North, 1.5 mi n of east entrance	◆◆◆	$99-$199	172
37 p. 147	Holiday Inn Express & Suites Phoenix Airport, 1.5 mi se of west entrance	◆◆◆	$79-$189	172
41 p. 147	Homewood Suites by Hilton Phoenix Airport South, 3 mi s of east entrance	◆◆◆	$109-$199	172
27 p. 147	**Howard Johnson Inn Airport Downtown, 1 mi n of east entrance**	◆◆	$49-$100 (SAVE)	172
7 p. 147	La Quinta Inn Phoenix-Arcadia, 2.3 mi n of east entrance	◆◆	$71-$134	173
21 p. 147	Marriott Phoenix Airport, 1.5 mi n of east entrance	◆◆◆	$100-$300	173
25 p. 147	**Radisson Hotel Phoenix Airport North, 1 mi n of east entrance**	◆◆◆	$69-$299 (SAVE)	173
22 p. 147	Residence Inn by Marriott Phoenix Airport, 1.3 mi n of east entrance	◆◆◆	$119-$239	173
34 p. 147	**Sleep Inn Phoenix Airport, 0.5 mi s of east entrance**	◆◆	$60-$150 (SAVE)	173
11 p. 164	**Comfort Suites Airport, 3 mi s of east entrance**	◆◆◆	Rates not provided (SAVE)	257
7 p. 164	**Hyatt Place Tempe/Phoenix Airport, 2.5 mi e of entrance**	◆◆◆	$89-$299 (SAVE)	259
8 p. 164	La Quinta Inn Phoenix Sky Harbor Airport South, 1 mi s of east entrance	◆◆	$54-$148	259
13 p. 164	**Sheraton Phoenix Airport Hotel-Tempe, 3 mi se of east entrance**	◆◆◆	$79-$359 (SAVE)	259
6 p. 164	**SpringHill Suites by Marriott Tempe Airport, 2.5 mi e of entrance**	◆◆◆	$69-$219 (SAVE)	259

Downtown Phoenix

This index helps you "spot" where approved hotels and restaurants are located on the corresponding detailed maps. Hotel daily rate range is for comparison only and show the property's high season. Restaurant rate range is a combination of lunch and/or dinner. Turn to the listing page for more detailed rate information and consult display ads for special promotions.

DOWNTOWN PHOENIX

Map Page	Hotels	Diamond Rated	High Season	Page
1 p. 147	La Quinta Inn Phoenix Thomas Road	◆◆	$52-$144	173
2 p. 147	Hampton Inn-Phoenix/Midtown (Downtown Area)	◆◆◆	$79-$199	171
3 p. 147	Hilton Suites-Phoenix	◆◆◆	$159-$269	172
4 p. 147	Fairfield Inn & Suites Phoenix Midtown	◆◆◆	$69-$189 SAVE	171
5 p. 147	Embassy Suites Phoenix Airport at 24th St	◆◆◆	$139-$209 SAVE	171
6 p. 147	Comfort Inn I-10 West/Central	◆◆	Rates not provided SAVE	169
7 p. 147	La Quinta Inn Phoenix-Arcadia	◆◆	$71-$134	173
8 p. 147	Quality Inn & Suites-Downtown	◆◆	$69-$169	173
10 p. 147	Holiday Inn Express Hotel & Suites - Ball Park	◆◆◆	$109-$199	172
11 p. 147	Americas Best Value Inn- Downtown Phoenix	◆◆	$55-$99 SAVE	168
12 p. 147	Budget Lodge Motel	◆◆	$45-$125 SAVE	169
13 p. 147	The Westin Phoenix Downtown	◆◆◆◆	$369-$589 SAVE	174
14 p. 147	Holiday Inn & Suites Phoenix Airport North	◆◆◆	$99-$199	172
15 p. 147	Sheraton Phoenix Downtown Hotel (See ad p. 174.)	◆◆◆◆	3299-3729 SAVE	173
16 p. 147	Hotel San Carlos	◆◆	$79-$199 SAVE	172
17 p. 147	SpringHill Suites by Marriott	◆◆◆	$79-$229 SAVE	173
18 p. 147	Hyatt Regency Phoenix	◆◆◆	$99-$499 SAVE	172
19 p. 147	Wyndham Phoenix Hotel	◆◆◆	$119-$479	174
20 p. 147	Super 8-Downtown Phoenix	◆◆	$45-$63 SAVE	174
21 p. 147	Marriott Phoenix Airport	◆◆◆	$100-$300	173
22 p. 147	Residence Inn by Marriott Phoenix Airport	◆◆◆	$119-$239	173
23 p. 147	Econo Lodge Airport	◆◆	$55-$65 SAVE	170
24 p. 147	Hampton Inn Phoenix Airport North	◆◆◆	$59-$149	171
25 p. 147	Radisson Hotel Phoenix Airport North	◆◆◆	$69-$299 SAVE	173
26 p. 147	Hilton Garden Inn Phoenix Airport North	◆◆◆	$159-$199	171
27 p. 147	Howard Johnson Inn Airport Downtown	◆◆	$49-$100 SAVE	172
28 p. 147	DoubleTree Suites by Hilton Hotel Phoenix	◆◆◆	$149-$299 SAVE	170
29 p. 147	Crowne Plaza Phoenix Airport (See ad p. 170.)	◆◆◆	$89-$169 SAVE	170
30 p. 147	Aloft Phoenix Airport Hotel	◆◆◆	$79-$229 SAVE	168
31 p. 147	Motel 6 Phoenix East #18	◆	$45-$55	173
32 p. 147	Best Western Airport Inn (See ad p. 169.)	◆◆	$79-$149 SAVE	169
33 p. 147	Hilton Phoenix Airport	◆◆◆	$109-$229 SAVE	172
34 p. 147	Sleep Inn Phoenix Airport	◆◆	$60-$150 SAVE	173
35 p. 147	Courtyard by Marriott Phoenix Airport	◆◆◆	$119-$249 SAVE	169
36 p. 147	Fairfield Inn by Marriott Phoenix Airport	◆◆	$69-$189 SAVE	171
37 p. 147	Holiday Inn Express & Suites Phoenix Airport	◆◆◆	$79-$189	172
38 p. 147	Hilton Garden Inn Phoenix Airport	◆◆◆	$99-$169	171
39 p. 147	Holiday Inn & Suites Phoenix Airport	◆◆◆	$89-$189	172
40 p. 147	Hampton Inn & Suites Phoenix Airport South/Tempe	◆◆◆	$59-$179 SAVE	171

DOWNTOWN PHOENIX (cont'd)

Map Page	Hotels (cont'd)	Diamond Rated	High Season	Page
41 p. 147	Homewood Suites by Hilton Phoenix Airport South	◇◇◇	$109-$199	172

Map Page	Restaurants	Diamond Rated	Cuisine	Meal Range	Page
1 p. 147	Duck and Decanter	◇	Deli	$6-$9	175
2 p. 147	Mu Shu Asian Grill	◇◇	Asian	$7-$16	176
3 p. 147	Persian Garden Cafe	◇◇	Middle Eastern	$10-$27	176
4 p. 147	The Original Hamburger Works	◇	American	$4-$7	176
5 p. 147	Pino's Pizza Al Centro	◇◇	Italian	$6-$17	176
6 p. 147	Honey Bear's BBQ	◇	Barbecue	$5-$18	176
7 p. 147	The Wild Thaiger	◇◇	Thai	$8-$17	177
8 p. 147	Durant's	◇◇◇	Steak	$9-$67	175
9 p. 147	Switch Restaurant & Wine Bar	◇◇◇	Comfort Food	$10-$25	177
10 p. 147	Barrio Cafe	◇◇	New Mexican	$10-$26	175
11 p. 147	Bacchanal Restaurant	◇◇	Greek	$15-$26	175
12 p. 147	Coronado Cafe	◇◇◇	American	$9-$29	175
13 p. 147	Tuck Shop	◇◇◇	Comfort Food	$16-$20	177
14 p. 147	Thai Hut	◇◇	Thai	$10-$15	177
15 p. 147	Cheuvront Restaurant & Wine Bar	◇◇◇	Continental	$10-$20	175
16 p. 147	Portland's	◇◇◇	American	$8-$29	177
17 p. 147	Lola Coffee	◇	Coffee/Tea	$2-$5	176
18 p. 147	Bliss	◇◇	American	$7-$15	175
19 p. 147	Matt's Big Breakfast	◇◇	American	$5-$15	176
20 p. 147	Moira Sushi Bar & Kitchen	◇◇◇	Japanese	$9-$15	176
21 p. 147	Cibo Urban Pizzeria Cafe	◇◇◇	Italian	$9-$15	175
22 p. 147	Sens Asian Tapas & Sake Bar	◇◇◇	Asian	$5-$12	177
23 p. 147	The Breadfruit Authentic Jamaican Grill	◇◇	Jamaican	$8-$15	175
24 p. 147	Sam's Cafe at the Arizona Center	◇◇	Southwestern	$10-$20	177
25 p. 147	Province	◇◇◇	American	$8-$32	177
26 p. 147	Indian Delhi Palace	◇◇	Indian	$9-$15	176
27 p. 147	District	◇◇◇	American	$9-$24	175
28 p. 147	Compass Restaurant	◇◇◇	American	$27-$40	175
29 p. 147	Matador Restaurant	◇◇	Mexican	$6-$25	176
30 p. 147	Duck and Decanter	◇	Deli	$5-$9	175
31 p. 147	Vitamin T	◇	Mexican	$5-$7	177
32 p. 147	Pizzeria Bianco	◇◇	Pizza	$10-$20	176
33 p. 147	Kincaid's Fish, Chop & Steak House	◇◇◇	Seafood	$16-$49	176
34 p. 147	The Arrogant Butcher	◇◇◇	American	$9-$35	175
35 p. 147	Hard Rock Cafe	◇◇	American	$9-$16 SAVE	176
36 p. 147	Lao Ching Hing Chinese Restaurant	◇◇	Chinese	$9-$13	176
37 p. 147	Szechwan Palace	◇◇	Chinese	$8-$19	177
39 p. 147	Stockyards Restaurant & 1889 Saloon	◇◇	Steak	$8-$40	177

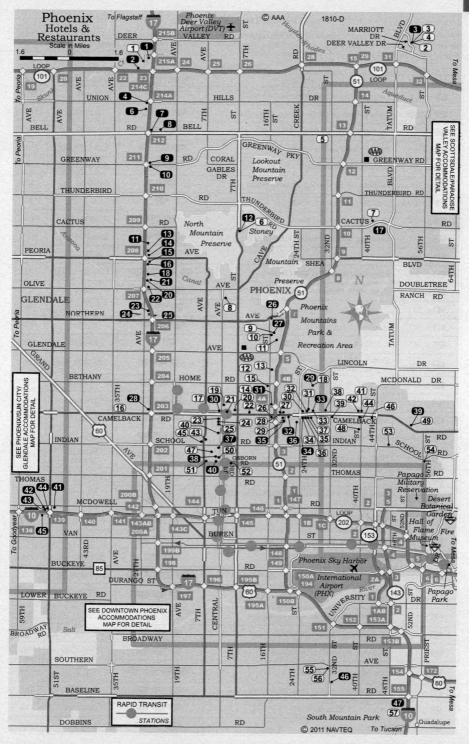

Phoenix Hotels & Restaurants

Phoenix

This index helps you "spot" where approved hotels and restaurants are located on the corresponding detailed maps. Hotel daily rate range is for comparison only and show the property's high season. Restaurant rate range is a combination of lunch and/or dinner. Turn to the listing page for more detailed rate information and consult display ads for special promotions.

PHOENIX

Map Page	Hotels	Diamond Rated	High Season	Page
① p. 151	Extended StayAmerica Phoenix-Deer Valley	◆◆	$65-$75	181
② p. 151	Country Inn & Suites By Carlson, Deer Valley	◆◆◆	$121-$229	179
③ p. 151	JW Marriott Desert Ridge Resort & Spa	◆◆◆◆	$134-$529 [SAVE]	183
④ p. 151	Comfort Inn-Phoenix North	◆◆◆	$59-$129 [SAVE]	179
⑤ p. 151	Sleep Inn Phoenix North	◆◆	$60-$130 [SAVE]	186
⑦ p. 151	Fairfield Inn by Marriott Phoenix North	◆◆	$49-$169 [SAVE]	182
⑧ p. 151	Motel 6 Phoenix-North #344	◆	$49-$59	184
⑨ p. 151	La Quinta Inn Phoenix North	◆◆	$48-$166	183
⑩ p. 151	Embassy Suites Phoenix North (See ad p. 181.)	◆◆◆	$99-$159 [SAVE]	180
⑪ p. 151	Candlewood Suites Phoenix	◆◆	$79-$139	178
⑫ p. 151	Pointe Hilton Tapatio Cliffs Resort	◆◆◆◆	$119-$219 [SAVE]	184
⑬ p. 151	Hyatt Place Phoenix-North	◆◆◆	$79-$209 [SAVE]	183
⑭ p. 151	Crowne Plaza Phoenix	◆◆◆	$99-$179	180
⑮ p. 151	Homewood Suites by Hilton Phoenix Metrocenter	◆◆◆	$99-$189	183
⑯ p. 151	Comfort Suites by Choice Hotels	◆◆	$59-$150	179
⑰ p. 151	Embassy Suites Phoenix-Scottsdale at Stonecreek Golf Club (See ad p. 181.)	◆◆◆	$89-$279 [SAVE]	180
⑱ p. 151	Courtyard by Marriott Phoenix North	◆◆◆	$71-$152	179
⑳ p. 151	TownePlace Suites Phoenix North	◆◆◆	$59-$149	186
㉑ p. 151	SpringHill Suites by Marriott-Metro Center	◆◆◆	$59-$149	186
㉒ p. 151	Sheraton Crescent Hotel	◆◆◆	$125-$635 [SAVE]	186
㉓ p. 151	Residence Inn by Marriott Phoenix	◆◆◆	Rates not provided	185
㉔ p. 151	Super 8 Phoenix Metro North	◆◆	$33-$71 [SAVE]	186
㉕ p. 151	Best Western Phoenix I-17 MetroCenter Inn (See ad p. 179.)	◆◆	Rates not provided [SAVE]	178
㉖ p. 151	Best Western Plus InnSuites Phoenix Hotel & Suites	◆◆◆	$75-$159 [SAVE]	178
㉗ p. 151	Pointe Hilton Squaw Peak Resort	◆◆◆	$119-$219 [SAVE]	184
㉘ p. 151	Quality Inn & Suites	◆◆	$55-$80 [SAVE]	184
㉙ p. 151	Arizona Biltmore, A Waldorf Astoria Hotel	◆◆◆◆	$109-$299 [SAVE]	178
㉚ p. 151	Maricopa Manor Bed & Breakfast Inn	◆◆◆	Rates not provided	184
㉛ p. 151	Extended Stay Deluxe Phoenix-Biltmore	◆◆	$95-$105	182
㉜ p. 151	Courtyard by Marriott-Camelback	◆◆◆	$71-$152	179
㉝ p. 151	Embassy Suites Phoenix-Biltmore	◆◆◆	$159-$299	180
㉞ p. 151	The Ritz-Carlton, Phoenix	◆◆◆◆	Rates not provided	185
㉟ p. 151	Homewood Suites by Hilton Phoenix-Biltmore	◆◆◆	$129-$159	182
㊱ p. 151	Hotel Highland at Biltmore	◆◆◆	$69-$189	183
㊲ p. 151	Hilton Garden Inn	◆◆◆	$129-$189	182

PHOENIX (cont'd)

Map Page	Hotels (cont'd)	Diamond Rated	High Season	Page
38 p. 151	Radisson Hotel Phoenix City Center	◆◆◆	$82-$189	184
39 p. 151	**Royal Palms Resort and Spa**	◆◆◆◆	$199-$599 SAVE	185
40 p. 151	Extended Stay Deluxe (Phoenix/Midtown)	◆◆	$85-$95	182
41 p. 151	La Quinta Inn & Suites Phoenix I-10 West	◆◆◆	$81-$179	183
42 p. 151	Motel 6 Phoenix West #696	◆	$49-$59	184
43 p. 151	**Red Roof Inn Phoenix West**	◆◆	$50-$126 SAVE	184
44 p. 151	Holiday Inn Phoenix West	◆◆◆	$129-$149	182
45 p. 151	Super 8-Phoenix West	◆◆	$45-$81	186
46 p. 151	**The Legacy Golf Resort**	◆◆◆	$99-$499 SAVE	183
47 p. 151	**Arizona Grand Resort**	◆◆◆◆	$199-$499 SAVE	178

Map Page	Restaurants	Diamond Rated	Cuisine	Meal Range	Page
1 p. 151	101 Asian Buffet	◆	Chinese	$4-$11	186
2 p. 151	**Ristorante Tuscany**	◆◆◆	Regional Italian	$14-$35	190
3 p. 151	Meritage Steakhouse	◆◆◆	American	$24-$55	189
4 p. 151	Roy's Desert Ridge	◆◆◆	Hawaiian	$20-$30	190
5 p. 151	India Palace	◆◆	Indian	$9-$14	188
6 p. 151	**Different Pointe of View**	◆◆◆◆	American	$29-$42	187
7 p. 151	Yasu Sushi Bistro	◆◆◆	Japanese	$12-$26	192
8 p. 151	Corbin's Bar & Grill	◆◆◆	American	$10-$21	187
9 p. 151	Rico's American Grill	◆◆◆	American	$11-$29	190
10 p. 151	Tutti Santi Ristorante	◆◆◆	Italian	$15-$25	191
11 p. 151	Aunt Chilada's Hideaway	◆◆	Mexican	$6-$18	186
12 p. 151	Christo's	◆◆	Italian	$13-$27	187
13 p. 151	The Rokerij	◆◆	Southwestern	$15-$29	190
14 p. 151	Fuego Bistro	◆◆	Latin American	$8-$26	187
15 p. 151	Phoenix City Grille	◆◆◆	American	$9-$31	190
16 p. 151	Great Wall Hong Kong Cuisine	◆◆	Chinese	$8-$15	188
17 p. 151	Hana Japanese Eatery	◆◆	Japanese	$9-$36	188
18 p. 151	**Wright's**	◆◆◆◆	American	$29-$39	192
19 p. 151	Windsor	◆◆	American	$9-$15	192
20 p. 151	Ticoz Resto-Bar	◆◆◆	Southwestern	$9-$20	191
21 p. 151	St. Francis	◆◆◆	New American	$12-$25	191
22 p. 151	Padres Modern Mexican Cuisine	◆◆	Mexican	$9-$20	190
23 p. 151	Maizie's Cafe & Bistro	◆◆	American	$8-$15	189
24 p. 151	Lola Coffee	◆	Coffee/Tea	$2-$5	189
25 p. 151	Hula's Modern Tiki	◆◆	Polynesian	$8-$24	188
26 p. 151	Duck and Decanter	◆	Deli	$6-$9	187
27 p. 151	The Parlor Pizzeria	◆◆	Pizza	$6-$16	190
28 p. 151	Greekfest	◆◆◆	Greek	$14-$24	188
29 p. 151	Miracle Mile Delicatessen	◆	Deli	$7-$13	189

Map Page	Restaurants (cont'd)	Diamond Rated	Cuisine	Meal Range	Page
30 p. 151	Christopher's Restaurant & Crush Lounge	◆◆◆	French	$9-$35	187
31 p. 151	The Capital Grille	◆◆◆	Steak	$11-$53	187
32 p. 151	Stingray Sushi	◆◆◆	Sushi	$6-$19	191
33 p. 151	Omaha Steakhouse	◆◆◆	American	$10-$32	189
34 p. 151	Bistro 24	◆◆◆	Continental	$16-$36	186
35 p. 151	Morton's The Steakhouse	◆◆◆	Steak	$29-$53	189
36 p. 151	Fuego Tacos	◆◆	Mexican	$8-$12	188
37 p. 151	McCormick & Schmick's	◆◆◆	Seafood	$14-$40	189
38 p. 151	**noca**	◆◆◆◆	New American	$22-$34	189
39 p. 151	Tarbell's	◆◆◆	American	$11-$35	191
40 p. 151	Pane Bianco	◆	Specialty	$8-$12	190
41 p. 151	Chelsea's Kitchen	◆◆◆	American	$10-$27	187
42 p. 151	Vincent on Camelback	◆◆◆	French	$26-$36	192
43 p. 151	Harley's Italian Bistro	◆◆	Italian	$8-$22	188
44 p. 151	The Grind	◆◆	American	$8-$17	188
45 p. 151	The Fry Bread House	◆	Regional Specialty	$3-$8	187
46 p. 151	Havana Cafe	◆◆	Cuban	$12-$29	188
47 p. 151	Gallo Blanco Cafe & Bar	◆◆	Mexican	$7-$16	188
48 p. 151	Postino Winecafe	◆◆	American	$9-$14	190
49 p. 151	**T. Cook's**	◆◆◆◆	Mediterranean	$16-$44	191
50 p. 151	Alexi's Grill	◆◆◆	Northern Italian	$9-$25	186
51 p. 151	Mi Patio Mexican Food	◆◆	Mexican	$5-$15	189
52 p. 151	China Chili	◆◆	Chinese	$7-$26	187
53 p. 151	Over Easy Cafe	◆◆	American	$5-$15	189
54 p. 151	Kitchen 56	◆◆◆	American	$15-$26	188
55 p. 151	**Quiessence**	◆◆◆◆	New American	$20-$30	190
56 p. 151	**Farm Kitchen at The Farm at South Mountain**	◆	American	$5-$10	187
57 p. 151	**Rustler's Rooste**	◆◆	Steak	$15-$31	191

Membership for Them = Peace of Mind for You

You always want the best for them. So give them the benefits of AAA membership.

To purchase a AAA Associate Membership, contact your local AAA office, visit AAA.com, or call 800-Join-AAA.

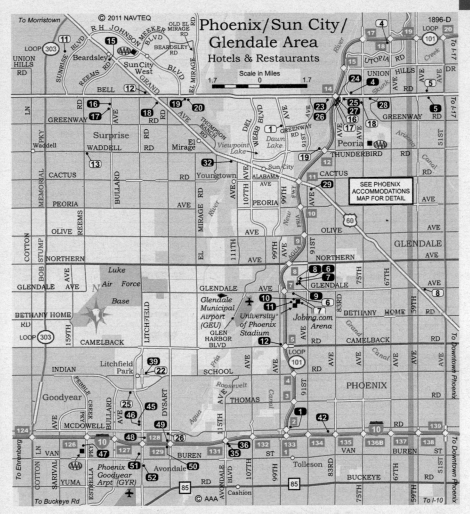

Phoenix/Sun City/Glendale Area

This index helps you "spot" where approved hotels and restaurants are located on the corresponding detailed maps. Hotel daily rate range is for comparison only and show the property's high season. Restaurant rate range is a combination of lunch and/or dinner. Turn to the listing page for more detailed rate information and consult display ads for special promotions.

PHOENIX

Map Page	Hotel	Diamond Rated	High Season	Page
1 this page	Courtyard by Marriott Phoenix West-Avondale	♦♦♦	$98-$188	180

GLENDALE

Map Page	Hotels	Diamond Rated	High Season	Page
4 this page	SpringHill Suites by Marriott	♦♦♦	$69-$199 SAVE	80
5 this page	Quality Inn & Suites at Talavi	♦♦♦	$60-$130 SAVE	80
6 this page	Residence Inn Phoenix Glendale Sports & Entertainment District	♦♦♦	$97-$219	80
7 this page	SpringHill Suites Phoenix Glendale Sports & Entertainment District	♦♦♦	$67-$169	80
8 this page	Staybridge Suites	♦♦♦	$129-$340	80

GLENDALE (cont'd)

Map Page	Hotels (cont'd)	Diamond Rated	High Season	Page
9 p. 155	Holiday Inn Express Hotel & Suites	◆◆◆	$129-$209	80
10 p. 155	Renaissance Glendale Hotel & Spa	◆◆◆◆	$125-$269	80
11 p. 155	Hampton Inn & Suites Glendale/Westgate	◆◆◆	$109-$229	80
12 p. 155	**Comfort Suites Glendale**	◆◆◆	$89-$299 (SAVE)	79

Map Page	Restaurants	Diamond Rated	Cuisine	Meal Range	Page
4 p. 155	Ninfa's Mexican Kitchen	◆◆	Mexican	$7-$16	81
5 p. 155	Thee Pitt's "Again"	◆◆	Barbecue	$7-$18	81
6 p. 155	Camarone's Restaurant & Cantina	◆◆	Mexican	$10-$19	80
7 p. 155	Soleil	◆◆◆	Regional American	$11-$36	81
8 p. 155	Haus Murphy's	◆◆	German	$7-$28	81

SURPRISE

Map Page	Hotels	Diamond Rated	High Season	Page
15 p. 155	**Hampton Inn & Suites Surprise**	◆◆◆	$125-$179 (SAVE)	255
16 p. 155	**Holiday Inn Express & Suites**	◆◆◆	$79-$249 (SAVE)	255
17 p. 155	**Residence Inn by Marriott Phoenix NW Surprise**	◆◆◆	$100-$120 (SAVE)	255
18 p. 155	**Comfort Inn & Suites of Surprise**	◆◆◆	$79-$139 (SAVE)	255
19 p. 155	**Windmill Suites in Surprise**	◆◆	Rates not provided (SAVE)	255
20 p. 155	Quality Inn & Suites	◆◆	$59-$169	255

Map Page	Restaurants	Diamond Rated	Cuisine	Meal Range	Page
11 p. 155	Dillon's Grand	◆◆	American	$7-$25	255
12 p. 155	My Greek Corner	◆◆	Greek	$6-$18	256
13 p. 155	Vogue Bistro	◆◆◆	New American	$9-$23	256

PEORIA

Map Page	Hotels	Diamond Rated	High Season	Page
23 p. 155	Holiday Inn Express Hotel & Suites Peoria North/Glendale	◆◆◆	$79-$229	130
24 p. 155	Comfort Suites by Choice Hotels/Peoria Sports Complex	◆◆	$59-$199	130
25 p. 155	La Quinta Inn & Suites Phoenix West Peoria	◆◆◆	$78-$280	130
26 p. 155	Residence Inn by Marriott	◆◆◆	$95-$285	131
27 p. 155	Hampton Inn	◆◆◆	$69-$199	130
28 p. 155	Extended StayAmerica Phoenix-Peoria	◆◆	$70-$80	130
29 p. 155	Ramada Peoria Convention Center	◆◆	Rates not provided	131

Map Page	Restaurants	Diamond Rated	Cuisine	Meal Range	Page
16 p. 155	Satara Thai Cuisine	◆◆	Thai	$7-$12	131
17 p. 155	P.F. Chang's China Bistro	◆◆◆	Chinese	$10-$21	131
18 p. 155	Ah-So Steak & Sushi	◆◆	Japanese	$7-$35	131
19 p. 155	Dillon's Restaurant	◆◆	American	$7-$22	131

YOUNGTOWN

Map Page	Hotel	Diamond Rated	High Season	Page
32 p. 155	**Best Western Inn & Suites of Sun City** (See ad p. 178.)	◆◆	$60-$130 (SAVE)	324

AVONDALE

Map Page	Hotels	Diamond Rated	High Season	Page
35 p. 155	Hilton Garden Inn Phoenix/Avondale	▽▽▽	$119-$289	38
36 p. 155	Homewood Suites Phoenix/Avondale	▽▽▽	$129-$289	38

LITCHFIELD PARK

Map Page	Hotel	Diamond Rated	High Season	Page
39 p. 155	**The Wigwam**	▽▽▽▽	$99-$1800 [SAVE]	109

Map Page	Restaurant	Diamond Rated	Cuisine	Meal Range	Page
22 p. 155	Litchfield's	▽▽▽	New American	$16-$29	110

TOLLESON

Map Page	Hotel	Diamond Rated	High Season	Page
42 p. 155	Premier Inns	▽▽	Rates not provided	262

GOODYEAR

Map Page	Hotels	Diamond Rated	High Season	Page
45 p. 155	Residence Inn by Marriott	▽▽▽	$82-$239	83
46 p. 155	Hampton Inn & Suites	▽▽▽	Rates not provided	83
47 p. 155	**Comfort Suites Goodyear**	▽▽▽	Rates not provided [SAVE]	83
48 p. 155	Holiday Inn Express West Phoenix/Goodyear	▽▽▽	$179-$199	83
49 p. 155	Holiday Inn Hotel & Suites	▽▽▽	$165-$195	83
50 p. 155	Quality Inn & Suites Goodyear	▽▽	$65-$100	83
51 p. 155	TownePlace Suites by Marriott Phoenix/Goodyear	▽▽▽	$74-$219	83
52 p. 155	**Best Western Plus Phoenix Goodyear Inn**	▽▽▽	$80-$170 [SAVE]	82

Map Page	Restaurants	Diamond Rated	Cuisine	Meal Range	Page
25 p. 155	Bella Luna Ristorante	▽▽▽	Italian	$8-$25	83
26 p. 155	Tomo Japanese Cuisine	▽▽	Japanese	$8-$19	84

SUN CITY

Map Page	Restaurant	Diamond Rated	Cuisine	Meal Range	Page
1 p. 155	Little Bite of Italy	▽▽	Italian	$9-$19	254

We Do Everything But Jump On The Beds

AAA backs the Diamond Ratings in this TourBook® guide with our expert, in-person evaluations – whether the hotel or restaurant is no-frills, moderate or upscale.

We welcome your feedback at AAA.com/TourBookComments.

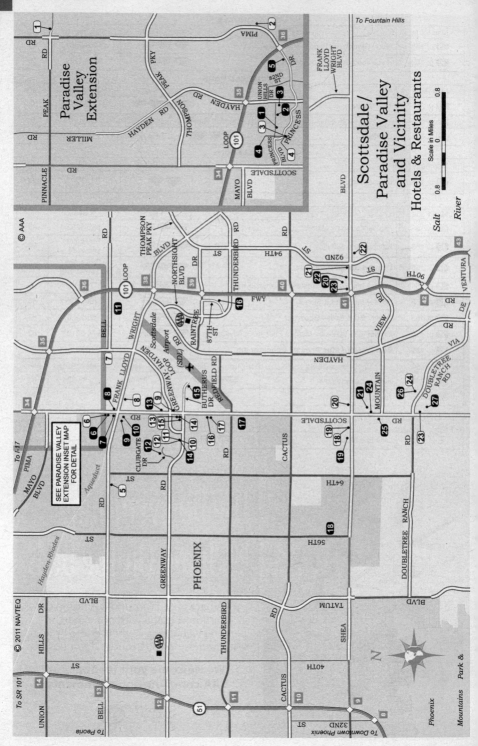

Scottsdale/
Paradise Valley
and Vicinity
Hotels & Restaurants

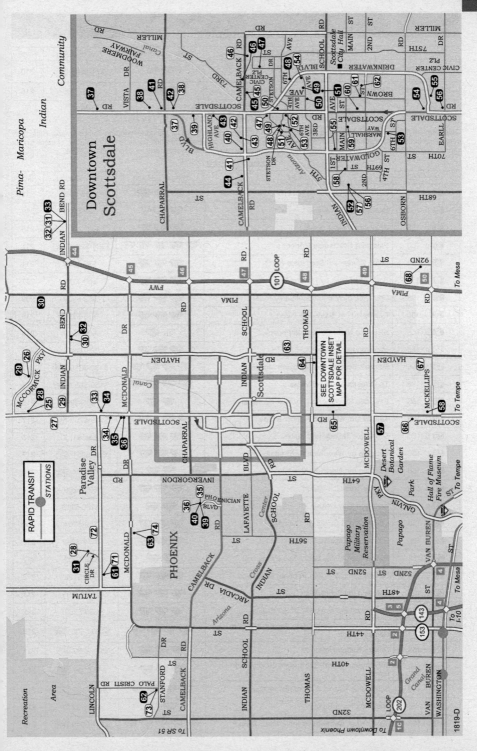

✈ Airport Accommodations

Map Page	SCOTTSDALE	Diamond Rated	High Season	Page
17 p. 158	Fairfield Inn North Scottsdale, 1.5 mi sw of airport	◇◇	$71-$194 SAVE	210
15 p. 158	Scottsdale Thunderbird Suites, at airport	◇◇◇	$59-$189	216

Scottsdale/Paradise Valley and Vicinity

This index helps you "spot" where approved hotels and restaurants are located on the corresponding detailed maps. Hotel daily rate range is for comparison only and show the property's high season. Restaurant rate range is a combination of lunch and/or dinner. Turn to the listing page for more detailed rate information and consult display ads for special promotions.

SCOTTSDALE

Map Page	Hotels	Diamond Rated	High Season	Page
1 p. 158	Xona Resort Suites, an Ascend Collection hotel	◇◇◇	$159-$399	219
2 p. 158	Scottsdale Villa Mirage	◇◇◇	$99-$359	216
3 p. 158	**Sheraton Desert Oasis**	◇◇◇	$99-$449 SAVE	216
4 p. 158	**Fairmont Scottsdale Princess**	◇◇◇◇◇	$134-$2699 SAVE	211
5 p. 158	Hilton Garden Inn Scottsdale North	◇◇◇	$79-$299	211
6 p. 158	SpringHill Suites by Marriott-Scottsdale North	◇◇◇	$59-$199	217
7 p. 158	Courtyard by Marriott/Scottsdale North	◇◇◇	$59-$209	209
8 p. 158	Residence Inn Scottsdale North	◇◇◇	$79-$257	215
9 p. 158	Sleep Inn North Scottsdale/Phoenix	◇◇	$69-$229	216
10 p. 158	Hampton Inn & Suites	◇◇◇	$79-$329	211
11 p. 158	**Marriott Scottsdale McDowell Mountain**	◇◇◇◇	$139-$379 SAVE	213
12 p. 158	**The Westin Kierland Villas**	◇◇◇◇	$159-$659 SAVE	217
13 p. 158	Extended StayAmerica-Phoenix-Scottsdale	◇◇	$85-$95	210
14 p. 158	**The Westin Kierland Resort & Spa**	◇◇◇◇	$139-$709 SAVE	217
15 p. 158	Scottsdale Thunderbird Suites	◇◇◇	$59-$189	216
16 p. 158	**Wingate by Wyndham Scottsdale**	◇◇◇	$80-$251 SAVE	217
17 p. 158	**Fairfield Inn North Scottsdale**	◇◇	$71-$194 SAVE	210
18 p. 158	Orange Tree Golf Resort	◇◇◇	$99-$200	214
19 p. 158	Extended Stay Deluxe Phoenix-Scottsdale	◇◇	$100-$110	210
20 p. 158	Country Inn & Suites By Carlson	◇◇◇	$59-$209	208
21 p. 158	Holiday Inn Express Scottsdale North	◇◇◇	$119-$249	212
22 p. 158	TownePlace Suites Scottsdale by Marriott	◇◇	$59-$209	217
23 p. 158	La Quinta Inn & Suites Phoenix Scottsdale	◇◇◇	$64-$192	213
24 p. 158	Hampton Inn Scottsdale	◇◇◇	$139-$199	211
25 p. 158	Homewood Suites by Hilton Scottsdale	◇◇◇	$69-$269	212
26 p. 158	**Hyatt Regency Scottsdale Resort & Spa at Gainey Ranch**	◇◇◇◇	$129-$605 SAVE	213
27 p. 158	**Gainey Suites Hotel**	◇◇◇	$99-$259 SAVE	211
28 p. 158	**Millennium Resort Scottsdale McCormick Ranch**	◇◇◇	$59-$339 SAVE	214
29 p. 158	**Scottsdale Resort & Conference Center**	◇◇◇◇	$79-$359 SAVE	216
30 p. 158	The Pima Inn & Suites	◇◇	$169-$219	215
31 p. 158	**JW Marriott Camelback Inn Resort & Spa**	◇◇◇◇◇	$134-$549 SAVE	213

SCOTTSDALE (cont'd)

Map Page	Hotels (cont'd)	Diamond Rated	High Season	Page
32 p. 158	Scottsdale Resort & Athletic Club	◈◈◈	$159-$609 SAVE	216
33 p. 158	Talking Stick Resort (See ad on insert, p. 218, inside back cover.)	◈◈◈◈	$109-$329 SAVE	217
34 p. 158	Hilton Scottsdale Resort & Villas	◈◈◈	$149-$249 SAVE	212
35 p. 158	Scottsdale Cottonwoods Resort	◈◈◈	Rates not provided SAVE	215
36 p. 158	Residence Inn by Marriott, Scottsdale/Paradise Valley	◈◈◈	$179-$269 SAVE	215
37 p. 158	DoubleTree Resort by Hilton Paradise Valley - Scottsdale	◈◈◈◈	$139-$239 SAVE	209
38 p. 158	Clarion Hotel Scottsdale	◈◈◈	$79-$119 SAVE	208
39 p. 158	The Phoenician (See ad p. 214.)	◈◈◈◈◈	$199-$2500 SAVE	215
40 p. 158	The Canyon Suites at The Phoenician (See ad p. 209.)	◈◈◈◈◈	$299-$2500 SAVE	207
41 p. 158	Chaparral Suites Scottsdale (See ad p. 210.)	◈◈◈	$99-$279 SAVE	208
42 p. 158	FireSky Resort & Spa, A Kimpton Hotel	◈◈◈	$115-$469 SAVE	211
43 p. 158	Days Inn Scottsdale Fashion Square	◈◈	$44-$144 SAVE	209
44 p. 158	Motel 6 Scottsdale #29	◈	$65-$85	214
45 p. 158	W Scottsdale	◈◈◈◈	$129-$699 SAVE	219
46 p. 158	Best Western Plus Sundial	◈◈◈	$100-$250 SAVE	207
47 p. 158	Hotel Indigo Scottsdale	◈◈◈	$139-$259 SAVE	212
48 p. 158	Hyatt Summerfield Suites Scottsdale/Old Town	◈◈◈	$79-$499 SAVE	213
49 p. 158	Hyatt Place Scottsdale/Old Town	◈◈◈	$89-$299 SAVE	213
50 p. 158	Marriott Scottsdale Suites Old Town	◈◈◈	$149-$349 SAVE	214
51 p. 158	Hilton Garden Inn Scottsdale Old Town	◈◈◈	$99-$209	212
52 p. 158	Hotel Valley Ho	◈◈◈◈	$129-$359 SAVE	213
53 p. 158	Homestead Studio Suites Hotel-Phoenix-Scottsdale	◈◈	$75-$85	212
54 p. 158	Scottsdale Old Town Courtyard by Marriott	◈◈◈	$129-$259 SAVE	216
55 p. 158	Comfort Suites by Choice Hotels-Old Town	◈◈	$70-$170	208
56 p. 158	Holiday Inn Express Hotel & Suites-Scottsdale	◈◈◈	$69-$229 SAVE	212
57 p. 158	Best Western Plus Papago Inn & Resort (See ad p. 208.)	◈◈◈	$60-$170 SAVE	207
58 p. 158	Hospitality Suite Resort	◈◈	$64-$144	212

Map Page	Restaurants	Diamond Rated	Cuisine	Meal Range	Page
1 p. 158	Mastro's Steakhouse	◈◈◈	Steak	$27-$78	222
2 p. 158	Lush Burger	◈◈	American	$8-$12	222
3 p. 158	Bourbon Steak	◈◈◈◈	Steak	$22-$175	219
4 p. 158	La Hacienda	◈◈◈	Mexican	$12-$31	222
5 p. 158	Havana Patio Cafe	◈◈	Cuban	$7-$25	221
6 p. 158	Persian Room	◈◈◈	Middle Eastern	$9-$35	223
7 p. 158	The Grill	◈◈◈	Steak	$11-$48	221
8 p. 158	Cantina Laredo	◈◈	Mexican	$8-$20	220
9 p. 158	Eddie V's Prime Seafood	◈◈◈	Seafood	$20-$40	221
10 p. 158	Brittlebush Bar & Grill	◈◈◈	American	$12-$14	220

Map Page	Restaurants (cont'd)	Diamond Rated	Cuisine	Meal Range	Page
⑪ p. 158	Nellie Cashman's Monday Club Cafe	▽▽▽	New American	$9-$28	222
⑫ p. 158	**Deseo**	▽▽▽▽	New Latin American	$24-$32	220
⑬ p. 158	Zinc Bistro	▽▽▽	French	$12-$34	225
⑭ p. 158	NoRTH	▽▽▽	New Italian	$8-$28	223
⑮ p. 158	P.F. Chang's China Bistro	▽▽▽	Chinese	$8-$25	224
⑯ p. 158	Jolta Java Coffeehouse & Sandwich Shoppe	▽	Coffee/Tea	$7-$10	222
⑰ p. 158	Sapporo	▽▽▽	Japanese	$15-$45	225
⑱ p. 158	Eli's American Grille	▽▽	American	$8-$31	221
⑲ p. 158	Sushi On Shea	▽▽	Japanese	$13-$38	225
⑳ p. 158	Pita Jungle	▽▽	Mediterranean	$6-$15	224
㉑ p. 158	Jade Palace Chinese Restaurant	▽▽	Chinese	$8-$20	221
㉒ p. 158	Renegade Canteen	▽▽▽	Western American	$15-$33	224
㉓ p. 158	Bloom	▽▽▽	American	$9-$29	219
㉔ p. 158	Alto Ristorante & Bar	▽▽▽	Italian	$18-$32	219
㉕ p. 158	Piñon Grill	▽▽▽	Southwestern	$15-$40	224
㉖ p. 158	**Palm Court**	▽▽▽▽	American	$12-$45	223
㉗ p. 158	Remington's	▽▽▽	American	$13-$30	224
㉘ p. 158	**BLT Steak**	▽▽▽▽	Steak	$26-$92	219
㉙ p. 158	Ruth's Chris Steak House	▽▽▽	Steak	$31-$40	224
㉚ p. 158	OC Seven Restaurant & Bar	▽▽	American	$8-$26	223
㉛ p. 158	Orange Sky	▽▽▽	Seafood	$24-$56	223
㉜ p. 158	Ocean Trail	▽▽	Creole	$13-$19	223
㉝ p. 158	Fleming's Prime Steakhouse & Wine Bar	▽▽▽	Steak	$19-$40	221
㉞ p. 158	Rancho Pinot	▽▽▽	American	$20-$31	224
㉟ p. 158	**Il Terrazzo**	▽▽▽▽	Italian	$18-$39	221
㊱ p. 158	**J & G Steakhouse**	▽▽▽▽	Steak	$16-$60	221
㊲ p. 158	Roaring Fork	▽▽▽	Western American	$13-$39	224
㊳ p. 158	Taggia	▽▽▽	Italian	$15-$32	225
㊴ p. 158	Posh Improvisational Cuisine	▽▽▽▽	International	$50-$140	224
㊵ p. 158	P.F. Chang's China Bistro	▽▽▽	Chinese	$10-$25	224
㊶ p. 158	Mastro's City Hall Steakhouse	▽▽▽	Steak	$27-$78	222
㊷ p. 158	Modern Steak	▽▽▽	Steak	$16-$78	222
㊸ p. 158	Kona Grill	▽▽▽	Pacific Rim	$9-$30	222
㊺ p. 158	Sushi Roku	▽▽▽	Japanese	$10-$35	225
㊻ p. 158	Don and Charlie's	▽▽	American	$11-$42	221
㊼ p. 158	The Breakfast Club	▽▽	Breakfast	$6-$15	220
㊽ p. 158	Cowboy Ciao	▽▽▽	American	$12-$35	220
㊾ p. 158	F n B Restaurant	▽▽▽	New American	$19-$27	221
㊿ p. 158	Bravo Bistro	▽▽	Italian	$9-$32	220

Map Page	Restaurants (cont'd)	Diamond Rated	Cuisine	Meal Range	Page
51 p. 158	Marcellino Ristorante	▽▽▽	Italian	$16-$47	222
52 p. 158	Stingray Sushi	▽▽▽	Sushi	$6-$18	225
53 p. 158	Citizen Public House	▽▽▽	American	$17-$32	220
54 p. 158	Pearl Sushi Lounge & Bomber Bar	▽▽	Sushi	$6-$14	223
55 p. 158	Arcadia Farms	▽▽	American	$11-$14	219
56 p. 158	Trader Vic's	▽▽▽	Pacific Rim	$16-$34	225
57 p. 158	Cafe Zu Zu	▽▽▽	American	$10-$30	220
58 p. 158	Old Town Tortilla Factory	▽▽	Mexican	$12-$33	223
59 p. 158	Malee's Thai On Main	▽▽	Regional Thai	$10-$21	222
60 p. 158	Iruna	▽▽▽	Small Plates	$8-$19	221
61 p. 158	The Mission	▽▽▽	Latin American	$23-$32	222
62 p. 158	Jewel of the Crown	▽▽	Indian	$7-$22	221
63 p. 158	Carlsbad Tavern	▽▽	Southwestern	$9-$25	220
64 p. 158	Tottie's Asian Fusion	▽▽	Asian	$8-$14	225
65 p. 158	Atlas Bistro	▽▽▽	International	$25-$35	219
66 p. 158	Los Sombreros	▽▽	Mexican	$15-$20	222
67 p. 158	The Salt Cellar Restaurant	▽▽▽	Seafood	$27-$50	225
68 p. 158	Cholla Prime Steakhouse	▽▽▽	Regional Steak	$20-$38	220

PARADISE VALLEY

Map Page	Hotels	Diamond Rated	High Season	Page
61 p. 158	**Montelucia Resort & Spa**	▽▽▽▽	Rates not provided SAVE	126
62 p. 158	Hermosa Inn	▽▽▽	$199-$549	126
63 p. 158	**Sanctuary on Camelback Mountain**	▽▽▽▽	$199-$849 SAVE	126

Map Page	Restaurants	Diamond Rated	Cuisine	Meal Range	Page
71 p. 158	**Prado**	▽▽▽▽	Italian	$13-$30	126
72 p. 158	El Chorro	▽▽▽	Continental	$11-$47	126
73 p. 158	**Lon's at the Hermosa**	▽▽▽▽	American	$10-$42	126
74 p. 158	**Elements**	▽▽▽▽	Fusion	$16-$45	126

Get Your Car Vacation Ready!

Before setting out on vacation, have your car checked out by a dependable AAA Approved Auto Repair facility.

AAA
Approved
Auto Repair

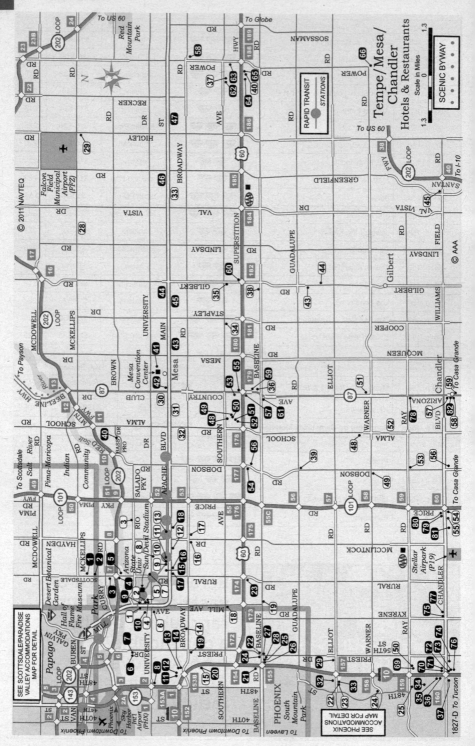

Tempe/Mesa/Chandler

This index helps you "spot" where approved hotels and restaurants are located on the corresponding detailed maps. Hotel daily rate range is for comparison only and show the property's high season. Restaurant rate range is a combination of lunch and/or dinner. Turn to the listing page for more detailed rate information and consult display ads for special promotions.

TEMPE

Map Page	Hotels	Diamond Rated	High Season	Page
1 p. 164	Quality Suites near Old Town Scottsdale	◆◆◆	$44-$79 SAVE	259
2 p. 164	Hampton Inn & Suites	◆◆◆	$109-$149	258
3 p. 164	Country Inn & Suites By Carlson, Phoenix Airport at Tempe	◆◆◆	$79-$209 SAVE	258
4 p. 164	Best Western Inn of Tempe	◆◆	$70-$140 SAVE	257
5 p. 164	Aloft Tempe	◆◆◆	$99-$279 SAVE	257
6 p. 164	SpringHill Suites by Marriott Tempe Airport	◆◆◆	$69-$219 SAVE	259
7 p. 164	Hyatt Place Tempe/Phoenix Airport	◆◆◆	$89-$299 SAVE	259
8 p. 164	La Quinta Inn Phoenix Sky Harbor Airport South	◆◆	$54-$148	259
9 p. 164	Tempe Mission Palms Hotel	◆◆◆◆	$99-$319 SAVE	260
10 p. 164	Courtyard by Marriott-Downtown Tempe	◆◆◆	$119-$269	258
11 p. 164	Homestead Studio Suites Hotel-Phoenix/Airport/Tempe	◆◆	$65-$75	258
12 p. 164	Red Roof Inn Phoenix Airport	◆◆	$49-$118 SAVE	259
13 p. 164	Sheraton Phoenix Airport Hotel Tempe	◆◆◆	$79-$359 SAVE	259
14 p. 164	Comfort Suites Airport	◆◆◆	Rates not provided SAVE	257
15 p. 164	Super 8 Tempe/ASU	◆◆	$53-$98 SAVE	260
16 p. 164	Tempe University Inn	◆◆	Rates not provided	260
17 p. 164	Four Points by Sheraton Tempe	◆◆◆	$75-$225 SAVE	258
18 p. 164	Ramada Limited Tempe-University	◆◆	$49-$119	259
19 p. 164	Fiesta Resort Conference Center	◆◆◆	$79-$159 SAVE	258
20 p. 164	Buttes, A Marriott Resort	◆◆◆	$99-$359	257
21 p. 164	Studio 6 Extended Stay #6031	◆◆	$53-$63	260
22 p. 164	Residence Inn by Marriott	◆◆◆	$104-$170	259
23 p. 164	Embassy Suites Phoenix-Tempe	◆◆◆	$109-$179	258
24 p. 164	Holiday Inn Express Hotel & Suites Tempe	◆◆◆	$119-$159	258
25 p. 164	Hotel Tempe InnSuites Airport @ the Mall	◆◆◆	$89-$199	259
26 p. 164	Ramada Inn - Arizona Mills Mall	◆◆	$59-$119	259
27 p. 164	SpringHill Suites Tempe at Arizona Mills Mall	◆◆◆	$62-$161	260
28 p. 164	Best Western Plus Tempe by the Mall	◆◆◆	$70-$140 SAVE	257
29 p. 164	Days Inn & Suites	◆◆	Rates not provided SAVE	258

Map Page	Restaurants	Diamond Rated	Cuisine	Meal Range	Page
1 p. 164	Gordon Biersch Brewery Restaurant	◆◆◆	American	$9-$30	261
2 p. 164	My Big Fat Greek Restaurant	◆◆	Greek	$5-$16	261
3 p. 164	Cadillac Ranch All-American Bar & Grill	◆◆	American	$10-$28	260
4 p. 164	La Bocca	◆◆	Pizza	$7-$16	261
5 p. 164	House of Tricks	◆◆◆	American	$7-$37	261

Map Page	Restaurants (cont'd)	Diamond Rated	Cuisine	Meal Range	Page
⑥ p. 164	Casey Moore's Oyster House	◆◆	American	$6-$25	260
⑦ p. 164	Sushi 101	◆◆	Sushi	$9-$24	262
⑧ p. 164	Republic Ramen	◆◆	Asian	$5-$7	261
⑨ p. 164	Pita Jungle	◆◆	Mediterranean	$5-$15	261
⑩ p. 164	Tasty Kabob	◆◆	Middle Eastern	$8-$21	262
⑪ p. 164	Cafe Istanbul & Market	◆◆	Middle Eastern	$6-$14	260
⑫ p. 164	Haji Baba Middle Eastern Food	◆◆	Middle Eastern	$6-$14	261
⑬ p. 164	**The Dhaba**	◆◆	Indian	$8-$14	261
⑭ p. 164	Lemon Grass Thai Cuisine	◆◆	Thai	$8-$13	261
⑮ p. 164	Top of the Rock Restaurant	◆◆◆	American	$24-$42	262
⑯ p. 164	Beaver Choice	◆◆	European	$9-$17	260
⑰ p. 164	Royal Taj	◆◆	Indian	$8-$18	261
⑱ p. 164	Byblos Restaurant	◆◆	Greek	$8-$19	260
⑲ p. 164	Tom's BBQ Chicago Style	◆	Barbecue	$6-$22	262

PHOENIX

Map Page	Hotels	Diamond Rated	High Season	Page
32 p. 164	**Clarion Hotel @ Phoenix Tech Center**	◆◆	$59-$189 [SAVE]	179
33 p. 164	Grace Inn Phoenix	◆◆	$69-$189	182
34 p. 164	Extended StayAmerica-Phoenix-Chandler	◆◆	$80-$90	180
35 p. 164	**Holiday Inn Express & Suites Phoenix-Chandler**	◆◆◆	$74-$139 [SAVE]	182
36 p. 164	La Quinta Inn & Suites Phoenix Chandler	◆◆◆	$58-$177	183
37 p. 164	Extended StayAmerica Phoenix-Chandler-E Chandler Blvd	◆◆	$80-$90	181

Map Page	Restaurants	Diamond Rated	Cuisine	Meal Range	Page
22 p. 164	Sakana Sushi and Grill	◆◆	Sushi	$8-$34	191
23 p. 164	Caffe Boa	◆◆◆	Italian	$7-$20	187
24 p. 164	Ruffino Italian Cuisine	◆◆◆	Italian	$8-$33	191
25 p. 164	RA Sushi Bar Restaurant	◆◆◆	Sushi	$8-$20	190

MESA

Map Page	Hotels	Diamond Rated	High Season	Page
40 p. 164	**Hyatt Place Phoenix/Mesa**	◆◆◆	$79-$299 [SAVE]	114
41 p. 164	**Phoenix Marriott Mesa**	◆◆◆	$79-$219 [SAVE]	115
42 p. 164	**Best Western Mezona Inn**	◆◆	$76-$175 [SAVE]	113
43 p. 164	**Comfort Inn & Suites**	◆◆◆	$66-$146 [SAVE]	113
44 p. 164	**Days Inn & Suites Mesa**	◆◆	$40-$86 [SAVE]	113
45 p. 164	Howard Johnson Inn Mesa	◆◆	$50-$120	114
46 p. 164	Travelodge Suites Mesa	◆	$50-$200	115
47 p. 164	Days Inn-East Mesa	◆◆	$45-$99	113
48 p. 164	**Courtyard by Marriott-Mesa**	◆◆◆	$62-$125 [SAVE]	113
49 p. 164	La Quinta Inn & Suites Phoenix Mesa West	◆◆◆	$68-$170	114
50 p. 164	Residence Inn by Marriott Phoenix Mesa	◆◆◆	$79-$229	115
51 p. 164	**Fairfield Inn by Marriott Phoenix Mesa**	◆◆	$49-$169 [SAVE]	114

MESA (cont'd)

Map Page	Hotels (cont'd)	Diamond Rated	High Season	Page
52 p. 164	**Hilton Phoenix East/Mesa**	◆◆◆	$129-$189 [SAVE]	114
53 p. 164	Quality Inn & Suites Mesa/Phoenix	◆◆	$49-$109	115
54 p. 164	**Dobson Ranch Inn & Resort**	◆◆◆	$72-$165 [SAVE]	113
55 p. 164	Motel 6-Mesa South #1030	◆	$55-$65	114
56 p. 164	Homestead Studio Suites Hotel Phoenix-Mesa	◆◆	$70-$80	114
57 p. 164	Holiday Inn Hotel & Suites	◆◆◆	$99-$209	114
58 p. 164	**Arizona Golf Resort & Conference Center**	◆◆◆	$99-$209 [SAVE]	112
59 p. 164	Days Hotel	◆◆◆	$50-$126	113
60 p. 164	Hampton Inn Phoenix/Mesa	◆◆◆	$89-$179	114
61 p. 164	Extended StayAmerica-Phoenix/Mesa	◆◆	$75-$85	114
62 p. 164	Sleep Inn of Mesa	◆◆	$50-$160	115
63 p. 164	**Best Western Superstition Springs**	◆◆	$75-$176 [SAVE]	113
64 p. 164	La Quinta Inn & Suites Phoenix Mesa East	◆◆◆	$78-$192	114
65 p. 164	Country Inn & Suites By Carlson	◆◆◆	Rates not provided	113
66 p. 164	**Best Western Legacy Inn & Suites**	◆◆◆	$85-$149 [SAVE]	112

Map Page	Restaurants	Diamond Rated	Cuisine	Meal Range	Page
28 p. 164	Rancho de Tia Rosa	◆◆	Mexican	$8-$20	116
29 p. 164	Flancer's	◆◆	Pizza	$6-$15	115
30 p. 164	Blue Adobe Grille	◆◆	Mexican	$7-$24	115
31 p. 164	The Landmark Restaurant	◆◆	American	$8-$27	115
32 p. 164	Los Dos Molinos	◆◆	Mexican	$6-$14	116
33 p. 164	**Little Mesa Cafe**	◆	American	$7-$17	116
34 p. 164	Organ Stop Pizza	◆	Pizza	$6-$18	116
35 p. 164	Mi Amigos Mexican Grill	◆◆	Mexican	$6-$15	116
36 p. 164	Culver's of Mesa	◆	American	$3-$10	115
37 p. 164	My Big Fat Greek Restaurant	◆◆	Greek	$5-$21	116
38 p. 164	Amazing Jake's	◆	Specialty	$8-$10	115
39 p. 164	Pink Pepper Thai Cuisine	◆◆	Thai	$7-$14	116
40 p. 164	P.F. Chang's China Bistro	◆◆◆	Chinese	$10-$21	116

CHANDLER

Map Page	Hotels	Diamond Rated	High Season	Page
69 p. 164	Courtyard by Marriott Phoenix Chandler	◆◆◆	$89-$239	48
70 p. 164	Homewood Suites by Hilton Phoenix-Chandler	◆◆◆	$99-$189	49
71 p. 164	Hampton Inn Phoenix-Chandler	◆◆◆	$69-$169	49
72 p. 164	**Radisson Phoenix-Chandler**	◆◆◆	$109-$229 [SAVE]	50
73 p. 164	**Fairfield Inn by Marriott Phoenix Chandler**	◆◆	$59-$169 [SAVE]	49
74 p. 164	Chandler Super 8	◆◆	Rates not provided	48
75 p. 164	**Quality Inn**	◆◆	$59-$139 [SAVE]	50
76 p. 164	**Red Roof Inn-Chandler**	◆◆	$75-$135 [SAVE]	50
77 p. 164	**Hawthorn Suites by Wyndham-Chandler**	◆◆◆	$79-$199 [SAVE]	49

CHANDLER (cont'd)

Map Page	Hotels (cont'd)	Diamond Rated	High Season	Page
78 p. 164	Best Western Inn of Chandler	◆◆	Rates not provided SAVE	48
79 p. 164	SpringHill Suites by Marriott-Chandler Fashion Center	◆◆◆	$90-$180	51
80 p. 164	Residence Inn-Chandler Fashion Center	◆◆◆	$100-$190	50
81 p. 164	Windmill Suites of Chandler	◆◆	$105-$155 SAVE	52
82 p. 164	Crowne Plaza San Marcos Golf Resort	◆◆◆	$99-$229 SAVE	48

Map Page	Restaurants	Diamond Rated	Cuisine	Meal Range	Page
48 p. 164	Tien Wong Hot Pot	◆◆	Asian	$5-$20	53
49 p. 164	C-Fu Gourmet	◆◆	Chinese	$5-$19	52
50 p. 164	Z'Tejas Southwestern Grill	◆◆◆	Southwestern	$7-$25	53
51 p. 164	Fox's Pizza Den	◆	Pizza	$6-$19	52
52 p. 164	Saigon Pho & Seafood	◆◆	Vietnamese	$5-$13	53
53 p. 164	Pita Jungle	◆◆	Mediterranean	$6-$15	53
54 p. 164	Kona Grill	◆◆◆	Pacific Rim	$9-$36	52
55 p. 164	P.F. Chang's China Bistro	◆◆◆	Chinese	$10-$21	53
56 p. 164	Cyclo Vietnamese Cuisine	◆◆	Vietnamese	$10-$12	52
57 p. 164	La Stalla	◆◆◆	Italian	$7-$25	53
58 p. 164	The Urban Tea Loft	◆◆	Coffee/Tea	$4-$14	53
59 p. 164	Brunchie's	◆◆	American	$5-$9	52

GILBERT

Map Page	Restaurants	Diamond Rated	Cuisine	Meal Range	Page
43 p. 164	Flancer's Cafe	◆◆	Deli	$6-$24	77
44 p. 164	Joe's Real BBQ	◆	Barbecue	$7-$18	77
45 p. 164	Cantina Laredo	◆◆	Mexican	$8-$20	77

DOWNTOWN PHOENIX
• **Restaurants p. 175**
• **Hotels & Restaurants map & index p. 147**

ALOFT PHOENIX AIRPORT HOTEL
Phone: (602)275-6300 **30**

Hotel
$79-$229

aloft A DESIGN BY W HOTELS

AAA Benefit: Enjoy the new twist, get up to 15% off + Starwood Preferred Guest® bonuses.

Address: 4450 E Washington St 85034 **Location:** SR 143 exit Washington St, just w. **Facility:** 143 units. 6 stories, interior corridors. *Bath:* shower only. **Terms:** cancellation fee imposed. **Amenities:** high-speed Internet, safes. **Pool(s):** heated outdoor. **Activities:** exercise room. **Guest Services:** valet and coin laundry, area transportation-within 5 mi. **Free Special Amenities: high-speed Internet and airport transportation.**

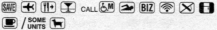

AMERICAS BEST VALUE INN- DOWNTOWN PHOENIX
Phone: (602)257-8331 **11**

Motel
$55-$99

Address: 424 W Van Buren St 85003 **Location:** Corner of 5th Ave; center. **Facility:** 37 units. (no elevator), exterior corridors. **Guest Services:** coin laundry. **Free Special Amenities: continental breakfast and high-speed Internet.**

Share a New View on Travel at
AAATravelViews.com

Read stories, tips and trends from AAA insiders. Post comments and get your questions answered by our travel experts.

(See map & index p. 147.)

BEST WESTERN AIRPORT INN
Phone: (602)273-7251

Hotel
$79-$149

 AAA Benefit: Members save up to 20%, plus 10% bonus points with Best Western Rewards®.

Address: 2425 S 24th St 85034 **Location:** I-10 exit 150B (24th St) westbound, just s; exit 151 (University Dr) eastbound, just n to I-10 westbound, 1 mi w to exit 150B (24th St), then just s. **Facility:** 117 units. 2 stories (no elevator), interior/exterior corridors. **Terms:** check-in 4 pm. **Amenities:** Some: safes. **Pool(s):** heated outdoor. **Activities:** saunas, whirlpool, exercise room. **Guest Services:** coin laundry, area transportation-bus depots. **Free Special Amenities:** high-speed Internet and airport transportation. *(See ad this page.)*

BUDGET LODGE MOTEL
Phone: (602)254-7247

Motel
$45-$125

Address: 402 W Van Buren St 85003 **Location:** Just w of Central Ave; center. **Facility:** 38 units. 2 stories (no elevator), interior/exterior corridors. **Terms:** cancellation fee imposed. **Amenities:** Some: high-speed Internet. **Free Special Amenities:** local telephone calls and high-speed Internet.

COMFORT INN I-10 WEST/CENTRAL
Phone: 602/415-1623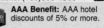

Hotel
Rates not provided

Address: 1344 N 27th Ave 85009 **Location:** I-10 exit 27th Ave eastbound, just n; exit 141 (35th Ave) westbound, just n, 1 mi e on McDowell Rd, then s. **Facility:** 65 units. 3 stories, interior corridors. **Amenities:** high-speed Internet. **Pool(s):** outdoor. **Activities:** whirlpool. **Guest Services:** coin laundry. **Free Special Amenities: continental breakfast and high-speed Internet.**

COURTYARD BY MARRIOTT PHOENIX AIRPORT
Phone: (480)966-4300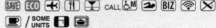

Hotel
$119-$249

 AAA Benefit: AAA hotel discounts of 5% or more.

Address: 2621 S 47th St 85034 **Location:** I-10 exit 151 (University Dr), 2 mi n, then just w. **Facility:** 145 units. 4 stories, interior corridors. **Amenities:** high-speed Internet. **Pool(s):** heated outdoor. **Activities:** whirlpool, exercise room. **Guest Services:** valet and coin laundry, area transportation-within 3 mi. **Free Special Amenities: high-speed Internet and airport transportation.**

▼ See AAA listing this page ▼

We've got comfortable rooms
at an equally comfortable value.

BEST WESTERN Airport Inn
2425 South 24th Street
Phoenix, AZ 85034
602-273-7251 | 800-528-8199
bwphoenixairportinn.com
bwphoenix.reservations@gmail.com

- 1 Mile South of Sky Harbor International Airport
- Free 24-Hour Airport Transportation
- Free Wireless High-Speed Internet
- Fitness Center/Business Center
- Rodehouse Restaurant & Lounge Located Next Door

Show Your Card & Save
Preferred Hotel

Each Best Western® branded hotel is independently owned and operated. Best Western and the Best Western marks are service marks or registered service marks of Best Western International, Inc. ©2012 Best Western International, Inc. All rights reserved. AAA and the AAA marks are service marks or registered service marks of the American Automobile Association.

Save Money in Your Sleep

Members get the best available room rates with AAA/CAA preferred lodging partners.

Visit over 1,100 AAA/CAA Offices   **Click** AAA.com/CAA.ca
Call 1-866-AAA-SAVE (222-7283)

Show Your Card & Save®
Preferred Hotels

(See map & index p. 147.)

CROWNE PLAZA PHOENIX AIRPORT
Phone: (602)273-7778 **29**

Hotel
$89-$169 2/1-5/13
$79-$169 5/14-1/31

Address: 4300 E Washington St 85034 **Location:** SR 202 exit 2 (44th St), 0.7 mi. s. **Facility:** 295 units. 10 stories, interior corridors. **Parking:** on-site and valet. **Terms:** cancellation fee imposed. **Amenities:** Some: safes. **Pool(s):** heated outdoor. **Activities:** whirlpool, exercise room. **Guest Services:** valet and coin laundry, area transportation-within 5 mi. **Free Special Amenities:** high-speed Internet and airport transportation.
(See ad this page.)

DOUBLETREE SUITES BY HILTON HOTEL PHOENIX
Phone: (602)225-0500 **28**

AAA Benefit: Members save 5% or more everyday!

Hotel
$149-$299 2/1-5/31
$109-$209 6/1-1/31

Address: 320 N 44th St 85008 **Location:** SR 202 exit 2 (44th St), 0.5 mi. s. **Facility:** 242 units. 6 stories, exterior corridors. **Terms:** 1-7 night minimum stay, cancellation fee imposed. **Amenities:** safes. Fee: video games, high-speed Internet. **Pool(s):** heated outdoor. **Activities:** whirlpool, exercise room. **Guest Services:** valet and coin laundry, area transportation-within 2 mi. **Free Special Amenities:** full breakfast and use of on-premises laundry facilities.

ECONO LODGE AIRPORT
Phone: (602)273-1601 **23**

Motel
$55-$65

Address: 3037 E Van Buren St 85008 **Location:** SR 202 exit 1C (32nd St), 0.6 mi. s, then just w. **Facility:** 95 units. 2 stories (no elevator), exterior corridors. **Terms:** cancellation fee imposed. **Pool(s):** heated outdoor. **Guest Services:** coin laundry. **Free Special Amenities:** continental breakfast and airport transportation.

Visit AAA.com or CAA.ca for one-stop travel planning and reservations

Get pet travel tips and enter the photo contest at AAA.com/PetBook

▼ See AAA listing this page ▼

SLEEP BETTER AT CROWNE PLAZA.®

Comfortable new bedding, just one feature of our Sleep Advantage.®

Welcome to the Crowne Plaza located in the heart of it all. We are one of the closest full service hotels to Sky Harbor Airport and the only one with a Light Rail stop at our front door. This places you 5 minutes from live sporting events downtown and Mill Avenue where you will find restaurants nightlife and shopping.

CROWNE PLAZA
HOTELS & RESORTS
crowneplaza.com
1.800.2CROWNE

Crowne Plaza Phoenix Airport
4300 East Washington St.
Phoenix, AZ 85034
602.273.7778
CPPhoenixAZ.com

Get the free mobile app at
http://gettag.mobi

©2011 InterContinental Hotels Group. All rights reserved. Most hotels are independently owned and operated.

(See map & index p. 147.)

EMBASSY SUITES PHOENIX AIRPORT AT 24TH ST
Phone: (602)957-1910 **5**

Hotel
$139-$209 2/1-5/24
$79-$199 5/25-1/31

AAA Benefit: Members save 5% or more everyday!

Address: 2333 E Thomas Rd 85016 **Location:** SR 51 exit 2 (44th St), just e. **Facility:** 182 units. 4 stories, exterior corridors. **Terms:** 1-7 night minimum stay, cancellation fee imposed. **Amenities:** Fee: video games, high-speed Internet. **Pool(s):** heated outdoor. **Activities:** whirlpool, exercise room. **Guest Services:** valet and coin laundry, area transportation-within 5 mi. **Free Special Amenities: full breakfast and manager's reception.**

FAIRFIELD INN & SUITES PHOENIX MIDTOWN
Phone: (602)716-9900 **4**

Hotel
$69-$189

AAA Benefit: AAA hotel discounts of 5% or more.

Address: 2520 N Central Ave 85004 **Location:** I-10 exit 145 (7th St), 0.8 mi n to Virginia Ave, 0.4 mi w, then 0.7 mi n. Located in a commercial area. **Facility:** 107 units. 4 stories, interior corridors. **Amenities:** video games (fee), high-speed Internet, safes. **Pool(s):** heated outdoor. **Activities:** whirlpool, exercise room. **Guest Services:** valet and coin laundry, area transportation-within 3 mi. **Free Special Amenities: full breakfast and airport transportation.**

FAIRFIELD INN BY MARRIOTT PHOENIX AIRPORT
Phone: (480)829-0700 **36**

Hotel
$69-$189

AAA Benefit: AAA hotel discounts of 5% or more.

Address: 4702 E University Dr 85034 **Location:** I-10 exit 151 (University Dr), 2 mi n, then e. **Facility:** 90 units. 3 stories, interior corridors. **Amenities:** high-speed Internet. **Pool(s):** heated outdoor. **Activities:** whirlpool, exercise room. **Guest Services:** valet and coin laundry, area transportation. **Free Special Amenities: expanded continental breakfast and high-speed Internet.**

HAMPTON INN & SUITES PHOENIX AIRPORT SOUTH/ TEMPE
Phone: (602)438-8688 **40**

Hotel
$59-$179

AAA Benefit: Members save up to 10% everyday!

Address: 4234 S 48th St 85040 **Location:** I-10 exit 153 (48th St/Broadway Rd), just s; exit 153B (52nd St/Broadway Rd) westbound, 0.4 mi w. **Facility:** 107 units. 4 stories, interior corridors. **Terms:** 1-7 night minimum stay, cancellation fee imposed. **Amenities:** video games (fee). Some: high-speed Internet. **Pool(s):** heated outdoor. **Activities:** whirlpool, exercise room. **Guest Services:** valet laundry, area transportation-within 5 mi. **Free Special Amenities: full breakfast and airport transportation.**

HAMPTON INN PHOENIX AIRPORT NORTH
Phone: (602)267-0606 **24**

Hotel
$59-$149

AAA Benefit: Members save up to 10% everyday!

Address: 601 N 44th St 85008 **Location:** SR 202 exit 2 (44th St), 0.3 mi s. Across from Chinese Cultural Center. **Facility:** 106 units. 4 stories, interior corridors. **Terms:** 1-7 night minimum stay, cancellation fee imposed. **Amenities:** video games (fee). **Pool(s):** heated outdoor. **Activities:** whirlpool, exercise room. **Guest Services:** valet and coin laundry, area transportation-within 5 mi.

HAMPTON INN-PHOENIX/MIDTOWN (DOWNTOWN AREA)
Phone: (602)200-0990 **2**

Hotel
$79-$199 6/1-1/31
$99-$109 2/1-5/31

AAA Benefit: Members save up to 10% everyday!

Address: 160 W Catalina Dr 85013 **Location:** Jct Thomas Rd, just n on Central Ave, then 0.3 mi w. Opposite St. Joseph's Hospital/Barrow Institute. **Facility:** 99 units. 4 stories, interior corridors. **Terms:** 1-7 night minimum stay, cancellation fee imposed. **Pool(s):** heated outdoor. **Activities:** whirlpool, exercise room. **Guest Services:** valet and coin laundry.

HILTON GARDEN INN PHOENIX AIRPORT
Phone: (602)470-0500 **38**

Hotel
$99-$169

AAA Benefit: Unparalleled hospitality at a special Member rate.

Address: 3422 E Elwood St 85040 **Location:** I-10 exit 151 (University Dr), just n. **Facility:** 93 units, some efficiencies. 3 stories, interior corridors. **Terms:** 1-7 night minimum stay, cancellation fee imposed. **Amenities:** video games (fee), high-speed Internet. Some: safes. **Pool(s):** heated outdoor. **Activities:** whirlpool, exercise room. **Guest Services:** valet and coin laundry, area transportation-within 5 mi.

HILTON GARDEN INN PHOENIX AIRPORT NORTH
Phone: (602)306-2323 **26**

Hotel
$159-$199 2/1-5/31
$99-$139 6/1-1/31

AAA Benefit: Unparalleled hospitality at a special Member rate.

Address: 3838 E Van Buren St 85008 **Location:** SR 202 exit 2 (40th St), 0.5 mi s, then just w. **Facility:** 192 units. 10 stories, interior corridors. **Terms:** 1-7 night minimum stay, cancellation fee imposed. **Amenities:** high-speed Internet, safes. **Pool(s):** heated outdoor. **Activities:** whirlpool, exercise room. **Guest Services:** valet and coin laundry, area transportation-within 5 mi.

Create complete trip routings and custom maps with the TripTik® Travel Planner on AAA.com or CAA.ca

(See map & index p. 147.)

HILTON PHOENIX AIRPORT
Phone: (480)894-1600 **33**

Hotel
$109-$229

AAA Benefit: Members save 5% or more everyday!
Hilton

Address: 2435 S 47th St 85034 **Location:** I-10 exit 151 (University Dr), 2 mi n, then just w. **Facility:** 257 units. 4 stories, interior corridors. **Terms:** 1-7 night minimum stay, cancellation fee imposed. **Amenities:** safes. *Fee:* video games, high-speed Internet. **Pool(s):** outdoor. **Activities:** whirlpool, exercise room. **Guest Services:** valet and coin laundry. **Free Special Amenities:** local telephone calls and early check-in/late check-out.

[icons] SAVE ... / SOME UNITS FEE ... FEE

HILTON SUITES-PHOENIX
Phone: (602)222-1111 **3**

Hotel
$159-$269 2/1-5/24
$79-$249 5/25-1/31

AAA Benefit: Members save 5% or more everyday!

Address: 10 E Thomas Rd 85012 **Location:** Just e of Central Ave; in Phoenix Plaza. **Facility:** 226 units. 11 stories, interior corridors. **Parking:** on-site (fee) and valet. **Terms:** 1-7 night minimum stay, cancellation fee imposed. **Amenities:** *Fee:* video games, high-speed Internet. **Pool(s):** heated indoor. **Activities:** whirlpool, exercise room. **Guest Services:** valet and coin laundry, area transportation-within 2 mi.

[icons] ... / SOME UNITS FEE

HOLIDAY INN & SUITES PHOENIX AIRPORT
Phone: (480)543-1700 **39**

Hotel
$89-$189 5/26-1/31
$119-$169 2/1-5/25

Address: 3220 S 48th St 85040 **Location:** SR 143 exit 2 (University Dr), just w, then just s. **Facility:** 114 units. 5 stories, interior corridors. **Terms:** cancellation fee imposed. **Amenities:** high-speed Internet. **Pool(s):** heated outdoor. **Activities:** whirlpool, exercise room. **Guest Services:** valet and coin laundry.

[icons]

HOLIDAY INN & SUITES PHOENIX AIRPORT NORTH
Phone: (602)244-8800 **14**

Hotel
$99-$199 2/1-5/31
$89-$159 6/1-1/31

Address: 1515 N 44th St 85008 **Location:** SR 202 exit 2 (44th St), 0.3 mi n. **Facility:** 228 units, some efficiencies. 4 stories, exterior corridors. **Amenities:** *Some:* high-speed Internet. **Pool(s):** heated outdoor. **Activities:** whirlpool, exercise room. **Guest Services:** valet and coin laundry, area transportation-within 5 mi.

[icons]

HOLIDAY INN EXPRESS & SUITES PHOENIX AIRPORT
Phone: (602)453-9900 **37**

Hotel
$79-$189

Address: 3401 E University Dr 85034 **Location:** I-10 exit 151 (University Dr), just n. **Facility:** 114 units. 4 stories, interior corridors. **Terms:** cancellation fee imposed. **Amenities:** high-speed Internet. **Pool(s):** heated outdoor. **Activities:** whirlpool, exercise room. **Guest Services:** valet and coin laundry, area transportation-within 5 mi.

[icons]

HOLIDAY INN EXPRESS HOTEL & SUITES - BALL PARK
Phone: (602)452-2020 **10**

Hotel
$109-$199 9/1-1/31
$89-$199 2/1-8/31

Address: 620 N 6th St 85004 **Location:** I-10 exit 145 (7th St), 0.5 mi s, then 1 blk w on Fillmore St. **Facility:** 90 units. 3 stories, interior corridors. **Amenities:** high-speed Internet. **Pool(s):** heated outdoor. **Activities:** whirlpool, sports court, exercise room. **Guest Services:** valet and coin laundry.

HOMEWOOD SUITES BY HILTON PHOENIX AIRPORT SOUTH
Phone: (602)470-2100 **41**

Extended Stay Hotel
$109-$199

AAA Benefit: Contemporary luxury at a special Member rate.

Address: 4750 E Cotton Center Blvd 85040 **Location:** I-10 exit 153 (48th St/Broadway Rd E), 0.4 mi s, then just w. **Facility:** 125 units, some two bedrooms and efficiencies. 4 stories, interior corridors. **Terms:** 1-7 night minimum stay, cancellation fee imposed. **Amenities:** high-speed Internet. **Pool(s):** heated outdoor. **Activities:** whirlpool, exercise room. **Guest Services:** valet and coin laundry, area transportation-within 5 mi.

[icons] CALL

HOTEL SAN CARLOS
Phone: (602)253-4121 **16**

Historic Hotel
$79-$199

Address: 202 N Central Ave 85004 **Location:** Just n of Washington St; center. **Facility:** Located along the light rail line, this charming historic hotel offers themed suites and attractive guest rooms. 128 units. 7 stories, interior corridors. **Parking:** on-site and valet. **Terms:** cancellation fee imposed. **Pool(s):** heated outdoor. **Guest Services:** valet laundry. **Free Special Amenities:** local telephone calls and high-speed Internet.

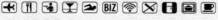

[icons] / SOME UNITS

HOWARD JOHNSON INN AIRPORT DOWNTOWN
Phone: (602)275-5746 **27**

Motel
$49-$100

Address: 4120 E Van Buren St 85008 **Location:** SR 202 exit 2 (44th St), 0.5 mi s, then just w. **Facility:** 47 units. 2 stories (no elevator), exterior corridors. **Amenities:** safes. **Pool(s):** outdoor. **Free Special Amenities:** high-speed Internet and airport transportation.

[icons] SAVE ... / SOME UNITS FEE

HYATT REGENCY PHOENIX
Phone: (602)252-1234 **18**

Hotel
$99-$499

AAA Benefit: Members save 10% or more everyday.

Address: 122 N 2nd St 85004 **Location:** Just n of Washington St; at Civic Plaza. **Facility:** 712 units, some two bedrooms and efficiencies. 24 stories, interior corridors. **Parking:** on-site and valet. **Terms:** cancellation fee imposed. **Amenities:** *Some:* high-speed Internet (fee), safes. **Dining:** 3 restaurants, also, Compass Restaurant, see separate listing. **Pool(s):** heated outdoor. **Activities:** whirlpool, exercise room. *Fee:* massage. **Guest Services:** valet laundry.

[icons] SAVE ECO ... CALL ... FEE ... / SOME UNITS

(See map & index p. 147.)

LA QUINTA INN PHOENIX-ARCADIA
Phone: (602)956-6500 **7**

Hotel
$71-$134

Address: 4727 E Thomas Rd 85018 **Location:** Just w of 48th St. **Facility:** 160 units. 2 stories, interior/exterior corridors. **Amenities:** safes. *Some:* high-speed Internet. **Pool(s):** heated outdoor. **Activities:** whirlpool, exercise room. **Guest Services:** coin laundry.

LA QUINTA INN PHOENIX THOMAS ROAD
Phone: (602)258-6271 **1**

Motel
$52-$144

Address: 2725 N Black Canyon Hwy 85009 **Location:** I-17 exit 201 (Thomas Rd), just e, then just s; on east side of freeway. **Facility:** 138 units. 2 stories (no elevator), exterior corridors. **Amenities:** video games (fee). **Pool(s):** outdoor. **Guest Services:** coin laundry.

MARRIOTT PHOENIX AIRPORT
Phone: (602)273-7373 **21**

Hotel
$100-$300

AAA Benefit: AAA hotel discounts of 5% or more.

Address: 1101 N 44th St 85008 **Location:** SR 202 exit 2 (44th St), just n. **Facility:** 345 units. 12 stories, interior corridors. **Amenities:** high-speed Internet (fee). **Pool(s):** heated outdoor. **Activities:** whirlpool, exercise room. **Guest Services:** valet and coin laundry.

MOTEL 6 PHOENIX EAST #18
Phone: (602)267-8555 **31**

Motel
$45-$55

Address: 5315 E Van Buren St 85008 **Location:** SR 202 E exit 4 (52nd St/Van Buren St), just s, then just e. **Facility:** 80 units. 2 stories (no elevator), exterior corridors. **Pool(s):** heated outdoor.

QUALITY INN & SUITES-DOWNTOWN
Phone: (602)528-9100 **8**

Hotel
$69-$169

Address: 202 E McDowell Rd 85004 **Location:** Just e of Central Ave. **Facility:** 48 units. 3 stories, interior corridors. **Terms:** cancellation fee imposed. **Pool(s):** heated outdoor. **Activities:** whirlpool. **Guest Services:** coin laundry, area transportation-within 2 mi.

RADISSON HOTEL PHOENIX AIRPORT NORTH
Phone: (602)220-4400 **25**

Hotel
$69-$299

Address: 427 N 44th St 85008 **Location:** SR 202 exit 2 (44th St), 0.5 mi s. **Facility:** 210 units. 7 stories, interior corridors. **Amenities:** high-speed Internet, safes. **Pool(s):** heated outdoor. **Activities:** whirlpool, exercise room. **Guest Services:** valet laundry, area transportation-within 5 mi. **Free Special Amenities: high-speed Internet and airport transportation.**

RESIDENCE INN BY MARRIOTT PHOENIX AIRPORT
Phone: (602)273-9220 **22**

Extended Stay Hotel
$119-$239

AAA Benefit: AAA hotel discounts of 5% or more.

Address: 801 N 44th St 85008 **Location:** SR 202 exit 2 (44th St), just s. **Facility:** 199 units, some two bedrooms and efficiencies. 4 stories, interior corridors. **Pool(s):** heated outdoor. **Activities:** whirlpool, sports court, exercise room. **Guest Services:** valet and coin laundry.

SHERATON PHOENIX DOWNTOWN HOTEL
Phone: (602)262-2500 **15**

Hotel
$299-$729

Sheraton STARWOOD
AAA Benefit: Members get up to 15% off, plus Starwood Preferred Guest® bonuses.

Address: 340 N 3rd St 85004 **Location:** I-10 exit 145A (7th St), 0.5 mi s to Fillmore St, just w, then just s. **Facility:** Stone used in the elegant hotel's lobby is from the same quarry as stone used for Jerusalem's Wailing Wall. 1000 units, some two bedrooms. 31 stories, interior corridors. **Parking:** on-site (fee) and valet. **Terms:** cancellation fee imposed. **Amenities:** safes. *Fee:* video games, high-speed Internet. **Dining:** 3 restaurants, also, District, see separate listing. **Pool(s):** heated outdoor. **Activities:** whirlpool, exercise room. *Fee:* massage. **Guest Services:** valet laundry, area transportation-within 1 mi. *(See ad p. 174.)*

SLEEP INN PHOENIX AIRPORT
Phone: (480)967-7100 **34**

Hotel
$60-$150

Address: 2621 S 47th Pl 85034 **Location:** I-10 exit 151 (University Dr), 2 mi n, then just w. **Facility:** 105 units. 3 stories, interior corridors. **Terms:** cancellation fee imposed. **Amenities:** *Some:* high-speed Internet. **Pool(s):** heated outdoor. **Activities:** whirlpool. **Guest Services:** valet and coin laundry, area transportation-within 2 mi. **Free Special Amenities: expanded continental breakfast and airport transportation.**

SPRINGHILL SUITES BY MARRIOTT
Phone: (602)307-9929 **17**

Hotel
$79-$229

SPRINGHILL SUITES Marriott
AAA Benefit: AAA hotel discounts of 5% or more.

Address: 802 E Van Buren St 85006 **Location:** I-10 exit 145 (7th St), just s, then just e. **Facility:** 122 units. 6 stories, interior corridors. **Amenities:** high-speed Internet. **Pool(s):** heated outdoor. **Activities:** whirlpool, exercise room. **Guest Services:** valet and coin laundry. **Free Special Amenities: full breakfast and airport transportation.**

(See map & index p. 147.)

SUPER 8-DOWNTOWN PHOENIX

Phone: (602)252-6823 **20**

Motel
$45-$63

Address: 965 E Van Buren St 85006 **Location:** I-10 exit 145 (7th St), just s, then just e. Located in a light-commercial area. **Facility:** 59 units. 2 stories (no elevator), exterior corridors. **Pool(s):** outdoor. **Guest Services:** coin laundry. **Free Special Amenities:** expanded continental breakfast and high-speed Internet.

Walking distance to Convention Center, Chase Field and US Airways Arena; Newly renovated 2010

Learn about
AAA/CAA Diamond Ratings
at AAA.com/Diamonds

THE WESTIN PHOENIX DOWNTOWN

Phone: (602)429-3500 **13**

Hotel
$369-$589 2/1-5/31
$369-$489 6/1-1/31

WESTIN HOTELS & RESORTS

AAA Benefit: Enjoy up to 15% off your next stay, plus Starwood Preferred Guest® bonuses.

Address: 333 N Central Ave 85004 **Location:** Northeast corner of Central Ave and Van Buren St. **Facility:** Spacious, modern and elegant guest rooms with sweeping views are the showcase of this new downtown property. 242 units. 26 stories, interior corridors. **Parking:** valet only. **Terms:** 3 day cancellation notice-fee imposed. **Amenities:** high-speed Internet (fee), safes. **Dining:** Province, see separate listing. **Pool(s):** heated outdoor. **Activities:** exercise room. **Fee:** massage. **Guest Services:** valet laundry. **Free Special Amenities:** newspaper.

WYNDHAM PHOENIX HOTEL

Phone: (602)333-0000 **19**

Hotel
$119-$479

Address: 50 E Adams St 85004 **Location:** Just w of 1st St; between 1st St and Central Ave. **Facility:** 520 units. 18 stories, interior corridors. **Parking:** on-site and valet. **Terms:** check-in 4 pm, 3 day cancellation notice-fee imposed. **Amenities:** high-speed Internet. **Dining:** 3 restaurants. **Pool(s):** heated outdoor. **Activities:** sauna, exercise room. **Guest Services:** valet laundry.

▼ See AAA listing p. 173 ▼

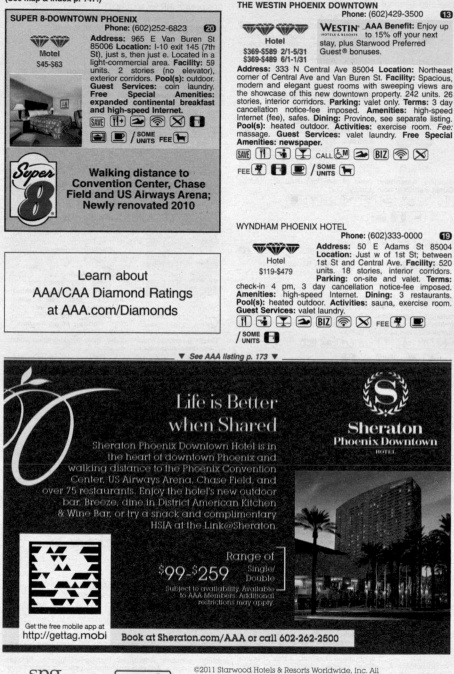

Life is Better when Shared

Sheraton Phoenix Downtown Hotel is in the heart of downtown Phoenix and walking distance to the Phoenix Convention Center, US Airways Arena, Chase Field, and over 75 restaurants. Enjoy the hotel's new outdoor bar, Breeze, dine in District American Kitchen & Wine Bar, or try a snack and complimentary HSIA at the Link@Sheraton.

Sheraton Phoenix Downtown HOTEL

Range of
$99-$259
Single/Double

Subject to availability. Available to AAA Members. Additional restrictions may apply.

Get the free mobile app at
http://gettag.mobi

Book at Sheraton.com/AAA or call 602-262-2500

spg.* Starwood Preferred Guest

AAA Show Your Card & Save

©2011 Starwood Hotels & Resorts Worldwide, Inc. All rights reserved. Valid only at participating hotels and resorts for stays booked through 2012. Sheraton, Preferred Guest, SPG and its logos are the trademarks of Starwood Hotels & Resorts Worldwide, Inc., or its affiliates.

(See map & index p. 147.)

WHERE TO EAT

THE ARROGANT BUTCHER
Phone: 602/324-8502 34

American
$9-$35

AAA Inspector Notes: Upscale comfort food meets hand-crafted specialty cocktails at this trendy downtown hot spot. Try the charcuterie for a mix of smoked meats and gourmet cheeses, or one of the daily specials including meatloaf and mashed potatoes, slow-roasted prime rib and Kurobuta baby back ribs. **Bar:** full bar. **Reservations:** suggested. **Address:** 2 E Jefferson St 85004 **Location:** Northwest corner of Jefferson and 1st sts; in CityScape. **Parking:** on-site (fee). L D

BACCHANAL RESTAURANT
Phone: 602/224-9377 11

Greek
$15-$26

AAA Inspector Notes: Named after the ancient Greek god of wine and celebration, this restaurant offers plenty of each. Live music and a belly dancer are featured Tuesday through Saturday nights. Well-prepared traditional Greek and Continental dishes are enjoyed while dinner guests join in the dancing. **Bar:** full bar. **Address:** 3015 E Thomas Rd 85016 **Location:** Jct 32nd St and E Thomas Rd, just w. D

BARRIO CAFE
Phone: 602/636-0240 10

New Mexican
$10-$26

AAA Inspector Notes: This neat cafe in the heart of town serves what the award-winning chef calls modern Mexican cuisine. Using creative blends of traditional sauces, she enhances such dishes as enchiladas with chicken or fish grilled in a banana leaf. Many vegetarian dishes also are offered. **Bar:** full bar. **Address:** 2814 N 16th St 85006 **Location:** Just s of Thomas Rd. L D

BLISS
Phone: 602/795-1792 18

American
$7-$15

AAA Inspector Notes: Hip and casual, this hot spot boasts a large outdoor bar and dining terrace overlooking downtown. Comfort food is served late, with such favorites as mama's pot roast, loaded macaroni and cheese and double-cut pork chops. **Bar:** full bar. **Address:** 901 N 4th St 85004 **Location:** Just s of Roosevelt St. **Parking:** street only. L D LATE

THE BREADFRUIT AUTHENTIC JAMAICAN GRILL
Phone: 602/267-1266 23

Jamaican
$8-$15

AAA Inspector Notes: This intimate modern storefront serves authentic Jamaican cuisine using fresh, organic ingredients. The jerk-rubbed chicken and escovitch tilapia are favorites. **Address:** 108 E Pierce St 85004 **Location:** Jct Central Ave, just e. **Parking:** street only.
L D

CHEUVRONT RESTAURANT & WINE BAR
Phone: 602/307-0022 15

Continental
$10-$20

AAA Inspector Notes: Located along the Central Corridor, this sophisticated spot features more than 40 artisan cheeses from around the world. Also on the menu are delicious gourmet pizza, upscale entrees and homemade desserts. **Bar:** full bar. **Address:** 1326 N Central Ave 85004 **Location:** Just s of McDowell Rd. L D

CIBO URBAN PIZZERIA CAFE
Phone: 602/441-2697 21

Italian
$9-$15

AAA Inspector Notes: Located downtown in an historic house, this intimate Italian cafe serves fresh made pizza, calzones, gourmet salads, and delicious nutella crepes for dessert. **Bar:** beer & wine. **Address:** 603 N 5th Ave 85003 **Location:** Corner of Fillmore St; center. **Parking:** on-site and street. L D

COMPASS RESTAURANT
Phone: 602/440-3166 28

American
$27-$40

AAA Inspector Notes: This revolving restaurant on the 24th floor offers panoramic views of the city. Innovative presentations of seafood, beef, lamb and chicken combine artistic color with tempting accompaniments to make a delightful meal. **Bar:** full bar. **Reservations:** suggested. **Address:** 122 N 2nd St 85004 **Location:** Just n of Washington St; at Civic Plaza; in Hyatt Regency Phoenix. **Parking:** on-site (fee). D CALL &M

CORONADO CAFE
Phone: 602/258-5149 12

American
$9-$29

AAA Inspector Notes: In a small converted house, this local favorite serves such trendy foods as grilled halibut tacos with chipotle slaw as well as warm, comfort foods like a tasty meatloaf sandwich with caramelized onions. The setting is casual and the waitstaff friendly. **Bar:** full bar. **Address:** 2201 N 7th St 85006 **Location:** Between E Oak St and E Monte Vista Rd. L D

DISTRICT
Phone: 602/817-5400 27

American
$9-$24

AAA Inspector Notes: Creative twists on American cuisine are attractively presented, and guests are even treated to cotton candy at the end of the meal. The spacious dining area has large windows overlooking the busy downtown street. There also is an energetic bar and lounge area with live entertainment on the weekends. **Bar:** full bar. **Reservations:** suggested. **Address:** 320 N 3rd St 85004 **Location:** I-10 exit 145A (7th St), 0.5 mi s to Fillmore St, just w, then just s; in Sheraton Phoenix Downtown Hotel. **Parking:** on-site (fee) and valet.
B L D LATE CALL &M

DUCK AND DECANTER
Phone: 602/234-3656 1

Deli
$6-$9

AAA Inspector Notes: This eatery cannot be beat for a quick, delicious lunch consisting of sandwiches and soups. Dinners may include wine, which can be selected from an excellent list. The baked goodies are excellent for dessert or to take home for an after-meal snack. **Bar:** wine only. **Address:** 3111 N Central Ave 85008 **Location:** Just n of Earll Dr. B L

DUCK AND DECANTER
Phone: 602/266-6637 30

Deli
$5-$9

AAA Inspector Notes: Located close to downtown attractions, this popular lunch spot is good for gourmet deli sandwiches and a nice selection of wines. **Bar:** beer & wine. **Address:** One N Central Ave, Suite 105 85004 **Location:** Corner of N 1st and E Washington sts. **Parking:** street only. B L CALL &M

DURANT'S
Menu on AAA.com
Phone: 602/264-5967 8

Steak
$9-$67

AAA Inspector Notes: For great steaks, a warm, friendly atmosphere and accomplished service, this restaurant fits the bill. A well-trained staff strives to provide a special dining experience. When entering from the parking area, diners may meet the grill chef as they walk through the kitchen. **Bar:** full bar. **Reservations:** suggested. **Address:** 2611 N Central Ave 85004 **Location:** 0.8 mi n of McDowell Rd. **Parking:** on-site and valet. L D

(See map & index p. 147.)

HARD ROCK CAFE   Phone: 602/261-7625   ③⑤

American
$9-$16

AAA Inspector Notes: Rock 'n' roll memorabilia decorates the walls of this popular theme restaurant. Live music on the weekends contributes to the bustling atmosphere. On the menu is a wide variety of American cuisine--from burgers and sandwiches to seafood, steaks and pasta. **Bar:** full bar. **Address:** 3 S 2nd St, Suite 117 85004 **Location:** At Jackson St; in Collier Center. **Parking:** street only. [SAVE] [L] [D]

HONEY BEAR'S BBQ   Phone: 602/279-7911   ⑥

Barbecue
$5-$18

AAA Inspector Notes: Barbecue sandwiches and ribs are slathered in a special, spicy tomato-based sauce at this popular eatery. **Bar:** beer & wine. **Address:** 2824 N Central Ave 85004 **Location:** Jct Central Ave and Thomas Rd, just s. [L] [D]

INDIAN DELHI PALACE   Phone: 602/244-8181   ㉖

Indian
$9-$15

AAA Inspector Notes: Classic Indian cuisine includes freshly made sauces, hot breads and spicy flavors. Local businesspeople favor the luncheon buffet. **Bar:** full bar. **Address:** 5104 E McDowell Rd 85008 **Location:** 0.5 mi e of SR 143. [L] [D]

KINCAID'S FISH, CHOP & STEAK HOUSE
Phone: 602/340-0000   ㉝

Seafood
$16-$49

AAA Inspector Notes: This popular restaurant has a bustling, warm ambience. The varied menu includes seafood, steak and excellent prime rib. Ample wine and dessert choices round out the meal. **Bar:** full bar. **Address:** Two S 3rd St 85004 **Location:** Southwest corner of 3rd and Washington sts; in Collier Center. **Parking:** on-site and street. [L] [D]

LAO CHING HING CHINESE RESTAURANT
Phone: 602/286-6168   ㊱

Chinese
$9-$13

AAA Inspector Notes: This comfortable restaurant features Shanghai-style cooking with more than 13 varieties of soup along with classic favorites including Peking duck and kung pao chicken. **Bar:** full bar. **Address:** 668 N 44th St 85008 **Location:** SR 202 exit 2 (44th St), just s; in Chinese Cultural Center. [L] [D]

LOLA COFFEE   Phone: 602/252-2265   ⑰

Coffee/Tea
$2-$5

AAA Inspector Notes: Delectable homemade pastries and savory quiche are the backdrops at this uptown chic coffee house. The real star is the fresh roasted coffee, where every espresso shot is hand-crafted from vintage machines. **Address:** 1001 N 3rd Ave 85003 **Location:** Corner of Roosevelt St. **Parking:** on-site and street. [B] [L] [D]

MATADOR RESTAURANT   Phone: 602/254-7563   ㉙

Mexican
$6-$25

AAA Inspector Notes: Offering fast service (especially at lunchtime), plenty of seating and tasty Mexican, American and Greek selections, this downtown eatery is popular with folks who work nearby. A full lounge is on site. The spacious dining area displays Mexican appointments. **Bar:** full bar. **Address:** 125 E Adams St 85004 **Location:** Jct E Adams and 1st sts. **Parking:** on-site (fee) and street. [B] [L] [D]

MATT'S BIG BREAKFAST   Phone: 602/254-1074   ⑲

American
$5-$15

AAA Inspector Notes: A very popular spot for breakfast, this tiny diner features fresh, local ingredients and such hearty favorites as the salami scramble or Belgian-style waffles with thick-cut bacon. Show up later on weekend mornings and be prepared for a wait. **Address:** 801 N 1st St 85004 **Location:** Northeast corner of McKinley and 1st sts. **Parking:** on-site and street. [B] [L]

MOIRA SUSHI BAR & KITCHEN
Phone: 602/254-5085   ⑳

Japanese
$9-$15

AAA Inspector Notes: An intimate, modern space welcomes diners who may choose from a blend of the traditional sushi and sashimi choices to more eclectic dishes such as intense red curry with kaffir lime leaves and pineapple. **Bar:** full bar. **Address:** 215 E McKinley St 85004 **Location:** Jct 3rd St, just w. **Parking:** street only. [L] [D]

MU SHU ASIAN GRILL   Phone: 602/277-9867   ②

Asian
$7-$16

AAA Inspector Notes: At this eatery, diners can choose from classic Szechuan-style dishes, a popular lunch buffet, or create-your-own stir-fry all served in a friendly and comfortable setting. **Bar:** beer & wine. **Address:** 1502 W Thomas Rd 85015 **Location:** Corner of 15th Ave and Thomas Rd. [L] [D]

THE ORIGINAL HAMBURGER WORKS
Phone: 602/263-8693   ④

American
$4-$7

AAA Inspector Notes: This is truly an original. Burgers are grilled under the careful eyes of patrons, and a salad cart stands waiting with fresh ingredients to accompany sandwiches. Diners also can opt for the crisply fried Arizona fries, zucchini or onion rings. **Bar:** full bar. **Address:** 2801 N 15th Ave 85013 **Location:** Just s of Thomas Rd. [L] [D]

PERSIAN GARDEN CAFE   Phone: 602/263-1915   ③

Middle Eastern
$10-$27

AAA Inspector Notes: Chef Jaafari creates meals from the freshest ingredients at this cafe. From the baba ghanoush or hummus to falafel, gyros, lamb or chicken kebabs and a number of vegetarian entrées, diners are sure to be satisfied with the flavors and portions at this café. Persian ice cream provides a decadent finish. **Address:** 1335 W Thomas Rd 85013 **Location:** Just e of 15th Ave. [L] [D]

PINO'S PIZZA AL CENTRO   Phone: 602/279-3237   ⑤

Italian
$6-$17

AAA Inspector Notes: It is all about the food at this casual, no frills midtown Italian bistro. The owner, Pino, is always in house and creates some of the most authentic Italian classic specialties west of the Mississippi. The meatballs, handmade pastas and calzones are outstanding, as is the tiramisu. At lunch, line up for delicious pizza available by the slice. **Bar:** beer & wine. **Address:** 139 W Thomas Rd 85013 **Location:** Just w of Central Ave. [L] [D]

PIZZERIA BIANCO   Phone: 602/258-8300   ㉜

Pizza
$10-$20

AAA Inspector Notes: Be prepared to wait for a table in order to sample what some critics have judged as the best pizza in the country. The freshly made, wood-fired pies come with a selection of fresh toppings. The dining room exudes casual energy, and the adjacent building provides a spot to wait and enjoy special wine and beer selections. **Bar:** beer & wine. **Address:** 623 E Adams St 85004 **Location:** I-10 exit 145 (7th St), 0.5 mi s, then just w. [D]

You'll believe it when you see it.
You'll love it when you live it.

TALKING STICK RESORT

(See map & index p. 147.)

PORTLAND'S
Phone: 602/795-7480   16
American
$8-$29

AAA Inspector Notes: Displaying upscale, trendy appointments, the convenient downtown restaurant nurtures a relaxed atmosphere. The chef/owners prepare flavorful food dubbed "New American" cuisine." Worth trying are rainbow trout stuffed with prosciutto and basil pesto or, a specialty, the Portland Champion white cheddar burger. **Bar:** full bar. **Address:** 105 W Portland St 85003 **Location:** Just w of Central Ave. **Parking:** street only.

L D

PROVINCE
Phone: 602/429-3600   25
American
$8-$32

AAA Inspector Notes: The cuisine at this modern, upscale dining spot is American with a distinct influence from South America and Spain. The menu changes seasonally and features farm-to-table, local ingredients. Try the homemade pasta, melted goat cheese fondue or the slow-roasted pork ropa vieja. **Bar:** full bar. **Reservations:** suggested. **Address:** 333 N Central Ave 85004 **Location:** Northeast corner of Central Ave and Van Buren St; in The Westin Phoenix Downtown. **Parking:** valet only.

B L D CALL ⚹M

SAM'S CAFE AT THE ARIZONA CENTER
Phone: 602/252-3545   24
Southwestern
$10-$20

AAA Inspector Notes: Those who are hungry after shopping, sports events or the theater will appreciate this restaurant's Southwestern fare. Applewood-smoked pecan salmon, adobo chicken pasta and steaming fajitas are sure to satisfy the hungriest patrons. **Bar:** full bar. **Reservations:** suggested. **Address:** 455 N 3rd St, #114 85004 **Location:** Northwest corner of Van Buren and 3rd sts. **Parking:** street only. L D

SENS ASIAN TAPAS & SAKE BAR
Phone: 602/340-9777   22
Asian
$5-$12

AAA Inspector Notes: The house DJ spins nightly at this downtown late-night hot spot. The menu features Asian-inspired tapas using innovative ingredients paired with unique cocktails and more than 60 types of sake. **Bar:** full bar. **Address:** 705 N 1st St, #120 85004 **Location:** Between McKinley and Pierce sts. **Parking:** street only. L D LATE

STOCKYARDS RESTAURANT & 1889 SALOON
Phone: 602/273-7378   39
Steak
$8-$40

AAA Inspector Notes: Since 1947, this restaurant has been serving nice selections of steak, prime rib and other entrees. Completely renovated in 2004, the warm and inviting decor features an attractive stone, dual-sided fireplace. **Bar:** full bar. **Address:** 5009 E Washington St 85034 **Location:** 0.5 mi e of 48th St. L D

SWITCH RESTAURANT & WINE BAR
Phone: 602/264-2295   9
Comfort Food
$10-$25

AAA Inspector Notes: Popular with the eclectic crowd for its specialty cocktails and late night dining, this urban hot spot feels like an intimate lounge. The menu ranges from galettes and crepes to such sophisticated entrées as blueberry duck breast and Provence chicken with risotto. **Bar:** full bar. **Address:** 2603 N Central Ave 85004 **Location:** Northeast corner of Central and Virginia aves. L D LATE

SZECHWAN PALACE
Phone: 602/685-0888   37
Chinese
$8-$19

AAA Inspector Notes: Located in the Chinese Cultural Center, this traditional establishment serves such favorites as kung pao chicken, Mongolian beef and shrimp in lobster sauce. **Bar:** beer & wine. **Address:** 668 N 44th St, Suite 108 85008 **Location:** Loop 202 exit 2 (44th St), just s; in Chinese Cultural Center. L D

THAI HUT
Phone: 602/253-8631   14
Thai
$10-$15

AAA Inspector Notes: Traditional Thai favorites and delicious desserts are available in a casual setting. **Bar:** beer & wine. **Address:** 101 E McDowell Rd 85004 **Location:** Jct Central Ave, just e.

L D

TUCK SHOP
Phone: 602/354-2980   13
Comfort Food
$16-$20

AAA Inspector Notes: Tucked in an historic neighborhood, this stylish bistro serves American classic comfort food with a fresh new twist. Menu items include citrus-brined fried chicken with white cheddar waffles, Medjool dates stuffed with chorizo and bananas Foster for dessert. **Bar:** full bar. **Address:** 2245 N 12th St 85006 **Location:** At Oak St. D CALL ⚹M

VITAMIN T
Phone: 602/688-8168   31
Mexican
$5-$7

AAA Inspector Notes: The "T" in this tiny, downtown spot's name is for tacos, and that is what one gets at this trendy eatery. Freshly prepared tacos and tortas come with such fillings as slow-roasted pork or brisket, grilled veggies and Oaxacan cheese. A local favorite, the Sonoran-dog always is a delicious choice. Homemade margaritas and shots of tequila keep the party going. **Bar:** full bar. **Address:** 1 E Washington St 85004 **Location:** Southwest corner of 1st and Washington sts. **Parking:** on-site (fee) and street.

L D

THE WILD THAIGER
Menu on AAA.com
Phone: 602/241-8995   7
Thai
$8-$17

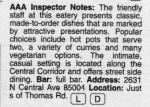

AAA Inspector Notes: The friendly staff at this eatery presents classic, made-to-order dishes that are marked by attractive presentations. Popular choices include hot pots that serve two, a variety of curries and many vegetarian options. The intimate, casual setting is located along the Central Corridor and offers street side dining. **Bar:** full bar. **Address:** 2631 N Central Ave 85004 **Location:** Just s of Thomas Rd. L D

Simply Reliable

The Diamond Ratings in this TourBook guide are backed by our expert, in-person evaluations, whether the hotel or restaurant is no-frills, moderate or upscale.

Learn more at **AAA.com/Diamonds**

PHOENIX

- Restaurants p. 186
- Hotels & Restaurants map & index p. 151, 155, 158, 164

ARIZONA BILTMORE, A WALDORF ASTORIA HOTEL
Phone: (602)955-6600 **29**

Historic Retro Hotel
$109-$299

AAA Benefit: Unparalleled hospitality at a special Member rate.

Address: 2400 E Missouri Ave 85016 **Location:** Jct Camelback Rd, 0.5 mi n on 24th St, then 0.4 mi e. Located in a residential area. **Facility:** This venerable valley resort is noted for its attentive staff, Frank Lloyd Wright-inspired design, elegant guest rooms and expansive grounds. 738 units, some kitchens. 2-4 stories, interior/exterior corridors. **Parking:** on-site and valet. **Terms:** check-in 4 pm, 1-7 night minimum stay, cancellation fee imposed. **Amenities:** video games (fee), high-speed Internet, safes, honor bars. **Dining:** 4 restaurants, also, Wright's, see separate listing. **Pool(s):** 8 heated outdoor. **Activities:** saunas, whirlpools, steamrooms, waterslide, recreation programs, rental bicycles, hiking trails, jogging, playground, basketball, spa. Fee: golf-36 holes, 7 lighted tennis courts. **Guest Services:** valet laundry, area transportation-Biltmore Fashion Park.

ARIZONA GRAND RESORT   Phone: (602)438-9000 **47**

Resort Hotel
$199-$499 2/1-5/22
$139-$499 5/23-1/31

Address: 8000 S Arizona Grand Pkwy 85044 **Location:** I-10 exit 155 (Baseline Rd), just w, then just s. **Facility:** Water plays a key role at this six-acre property, which features fountains, adult and children's pools, a waterslide and a simulated lazy river. 740 units, some kitchens. 2-5 stories, exterior corridors. **Parking:** on-site and valet. **Terms:** check-in 4 pm, 3 day cancellation notice-fee imposed. **Amenities:** safes, honor bars. Fee: video games, high-speed Internet. **Dining:** 3 restaurants, also, Rustler's Rooste, see separate listing, entertainment. **Pool(s):** 7 heated outdoor. **Activities:** whirlpools, steamrooms, waterslide, racquetball court, recreation programs, rental bicycles, hiking trails, jogging, basketball, spa. Fee: golf-18 holes. **Guest Services:** valet and coin laundry, area transportation-Arizona Mills Mall.

BEST WESTERN PHOENIX I-17 METROCENTER INN
Phone: 602/864-6233 **25**

Hotel
Rates not provided

AAA Benefit: Members save up to 20%, plus 10% bonus points with Best Western Rewards®.

Address: 8101 N Black Canyon Hwy 85021 **Location:** I-17 exit 206 (Northern Ave), just e, then just n; on east side of freeway. **Facility:** 147 units. 3 stories, exterior corridors. **Amenities:** safes. **Pool(s):** heated outdoor. **Activities:** whirlpool. **Guest Services:** valet and coin laundry. **Free Special Amenities:** full breakfast and high-speed Internet. (See ad p. 179.)

BEST WESTERN PLUS INNSUITES PHOENIX HOTEL & SUITES   Phone: (602)997-6285 **26**

Hotel
$75-$159

AAA Benefit: Members save up to 20%, plus 10% bonus points with Best Western Rewards®.

Address: 1615 E Northern Ave 85020 **Location:** SR 51 exit 7, 0.6 mi w. **Facility:** 111 units, some efficiencies. 2 stories (no elevator), exterior corridors. **Amenities:** high-speed Internet. **Pool(s):** heated outdoor. **Activities:** whirlpool, exercise room. **Guest Services:** valet and coin laundry. **Free Special Amenities:** local telephone calls and high-speed Internet.

CANDLEWOOD SUITES PHOENIX
Phone: (602)861-4900 **11**

Extended Stay Hotel
$79-$139

Address: 11411 N Black Canyon Hwy 85029 **Location:** I-17 exit 208 (Peoria Ave), just e, then 0.4 mi n. Adjacent to Saguaro Sports Park. **Facility:** 98 units, some efficiencies. 3 stories, interior corridors. **Terms:** office hours 7 am-11 pm. **Amenities:** high-speed Internet. **Pool(s):** heated outdoor. **Activities:** whirlpool, exercise room. **Guest Services:** complimentary laundry.

▼ See AAA listing p. 324 ▼

We've got comfortable rooms
at an equally comfortable value.

BEST WESTERN Inn & Suites of Sun City
11201 Grand Ave
Youngtown, AZ 85363
623-933-8211 800-253-2168
bestwestern.com/aaa

Show Your Card & Save

Scan this tag on your smartphone for moreinformation

Get the free mobile app at
http://gettag.mobi

Each Best Western® branded hotel is independently owned and operated. Best Western and the Best Western marks are service marks or registered service marks of Best Western International, Inc. ©2012 Best Western International, Inc. All rights reserved. AAA and the AAA marks are service marks or registered service marks of the American Automobile Association.

(See maps & indexes p. 151, 155, 158, 164.)

CLARION HOTEL @ PHOENIX TECH CENTER
Phone: (480)893-3900 **32**

Hotel
$59-$189

Address: 5121 E La Puenta Ave 85044 **Location:** I-10 exit 157 (Elliot Rd), just w, just n on 51st St, then just e. Located in a residential area. **Facility:** 188 units. 4 stories, exterior corridors. **Terms:** cancellation fee imposed. **Amenities:** high-speed Internet. **Pool(s):** heated outdoor. **Activities:** whirlpool, exercise room. **Guest Services:** valet and coin laundry, area transportation-within 5 mi. **Free Special Amenities:** full breakfast and manager's reception.

COMFORT INN-PHOENIX NORTH
Phone: (602)978-2222 **4**

Hotel
$59-$129

Address: 2641 W Union Hills Dr 85027 **Location:** I-17 exit 214A (Union Hills Dr), just w. **Facility:** 166 units. 2 stories, interior corridors. **Terms:** cancellation fee imposed. **Amenities:** *Some:* high-speed Internet. **Pool(s):** heated outdoor. **Activities:** whirlpool, exercise room. **Guest Services:** valet and coin laundry. **Free Special Amenities:** continental breakfast and high-speed Internet.

COMFORT SUITES BY CHOICE HOTELS
Phone: (602)861-3900 **16**

Hotel
$59-$150

Address: 10210 N 26th Dr 85021 **Location:** I-17 exit 208 (Peoria Ave), just e, just s on 25th Ave, then 0.3 mi w on W Beryl Ave. **Facility:** 60 units. 3 stories, interior corridors. **Terms:** cancellation fee imposed. **Amenities:** safes. **Pool(s):** heated indoor. **Activities:** whirlpool, exercise room. **Guest Services:** valet and coin laundry.

COUNTRY INN & SUITES BY CARLSON, DEER VALLEY
Phone: (623)879-9000 **2**

Hotel
$121-$229

Address: 20221 N 29th Ave 85027 **Location:** I-17 exit 215A (Rose Garden Ln), just w to 27th Ave, 0.4 mi s, then just w on Frontage Rd. **Facility:** 126 units. 4 stories, interior corridors. **Terms:** check-in 4 pm. **Amenities:** video games (fee), high-speed Internet. **Pool(s):** heated outdoor. **Activities:** whirlpool, exercise room. **Guest Services:** valet and coin laundry, area transportation-within 5 mi.

COURTYARD BY MARRIOTT-CAMELBACK
Phone: (602)955-5200 **32**

Hotel
$71-$152

AAA Benefit: AAA hotel discounts of 5% or more.

Address: 2101 E Camelback Rd 85016 **Location:** Jct 20th St and Camelback Rd. Located in Town and Country Shopping Center. **Facility:** 155 units. 4 stories, interior corridors. **Amenities:** high-speed Internet. **Pool(s):** heated outdoor. **Activities:** whirlpool, exercise room. **Guest Services:** valet and coin laundry.

COURTYARD BY MARRIOTT PHOENIX NORTH
Phone: (602)944-7373 **18**

Hotel
$71-$152

AAA Benefit: AAA hotel discounts of 5% or more.

Address: 9631 N Black Canyon Hwy 85021 **Location:** I-17 exit 207 (Dunlap Ave), just e, then 0.4 mi n. **Facility:** 146 units. 3 stories, interior corridors. **Amenities:** high-speed Internet. **Pool(s):** heated outdoor. **Activities:** whirlpool, exercise room. **Guest Services:** valet and coin laundry.

▼ See AAA listing p. 178 ▼

- Complimentary Full Hot Breakfast
- Complimentary Wi-Fi
- Business Center and ATM
- Outdoor Saltwater Pool & Spa (heated in Fall & Winter months)
- Offsite Partners with LA Fitness
- Meeting Room
- Restaurants and Shops within Walking Distance

BEST WESTERN METROCENTER INN PHOENIX I-17
8101 N Black Canyon Hwy
Phoenix, AZ 85021
TEL: (602) 864-6233
1-888-STAY206
(1-888-782-9206)
www.bestwesternmetrocenter.com

Get the free mobile app at
http://gettag.mobi

Check out our travel blog at AAATravelViews.com

(See maps & indexes p. 151, 155, 158, 164.)

COURTYARD BY MARRIOTT PHOENIX NORTH/HAPPY VALLEY
Phone: (623)580-8844

▼▼▼▼
Hotel
$69-$144

AAA Benefit:
AAA hotel discounts of 5% or more.

Address: 2029 W Whispering Wind Dr 85085 **Location:** I-17 exit 218 (Happy Valley Rd), 0.4 mi e to 23rd Ave, just s, then just e. **Facility:** 164 units. 5 stories, interior corridors. **Amenities:** high-speed Internet. **Pool(s):** heated outdoor. **Activities:** whirlpool, sports court, exercise room. **Guest Services:** valet and coin laundry, area transportation-within 5 mi.

🍽 🏊 BIZ 📶 ✕ 💻 / SOME UNITS 🔲 🔲

COURTYARD BY MARRIOTT PHOENIX WEST-AVONDALE
Phone: (623)271-7660 ❶

▼▼▼▼
Hotel
$98-$188

AAA Benefit:
AAA hotel discounts of 5% or more.

Address: 1650 N 95th Ln 85037 **Location:** I-10 exit 133 (99th Ave) eastbound, just n to McDowell Rd, 0.5 mi e, then just n; exit 134 (91st Ave) westbound, just n to McDowell Rd, just w, then just n. **Facility:** 127 units. 4 stories, interior corridors. **Amenities:** high-speed Internet. **Pool(s):** heated outdoor. **Activities:** whirlpool, exercise room. **Guest Services:** valet and coin laundry, area transportation-within 5 mi.

🍽 🍽 CALL 🏊 BIZ 📶 ✕ 🔲 💻 / SOME UNITS 🔲

CROWNE PLAZA PHOENIX
Phone: (602)943-2341 ❶❹

▼▼▼▼
Hotel
$99-$179

Address: 2532 W Peoria Ave 85029 **Location:** I-17 exit 208 (Peoria Ave), just e, then just n on 25th Ave. **Facility:** 248 units. 4 stories, interior corridors. **Terms:** cancellation fee imposed. **Amenities:** high-speed Internet. **Pool(s):** heated outdoor, heated indoor. **Activities:** whirlpools, exercise room. **Guest Services:** valet and coin laundry, area transportation-within 5 mi.

🍽 🍽 CALL 🏊 BIZ 📶 ✕ FEE 🔲 / SOME UNITS FEE 🐾

DRURY INN & SUITES PHOENIX PINNACLE PEAK
Phone: (623)879-8800

▼▼▼
Hotel
$85-$204

Address: 2335 W Pinnacle Peak Rd 85027 **Location:** I-17 exit 217 (Pinnacle Peak Rd), just e. **Facility:** 178 units. 7 stories, interior corridors. **Terms:** cancellation fee imposed. **Pool(s):** heated outdoor. **Activities:** whirlpool, exercise room. **Guest Services:** valet and coin laundry, area transportation-within 5 mi.

🍽 CALL 🏊 BIZ 📶 🔲 🔲 💻 / SOME UNITS 🐾

Explore the Travel Guides on AAA.com/Travel or CAA.ca/Travel

EMBASSY SUITES PHOENIX-BILTMORE
Phone: (602)955-3992 ❸❸

▼▼▼
Hotel
$159-$299 2/1-5/31
$99-$239 6/1-1/31

AAA Benefit:
Members save 5% or more everyday!

Address: 2630 E Camelback Rd 85016 **Location:** Just n of Camelback Rd, on 26th St. Adjacent to Biltmore Fashion Park. **Facility:** 232 units. 5 stories, interior corridors. **Terms:** 1-7 night minimum stay, cancellation fee imposed. **Amenities:** video games (fee). **Dining:** Omaha Steakhouse, see separate listing. **Pool(s):** heated outdoor. **Activities:** whirlpool, exercise room. **Guest Services:** valet and coin laundry, area transportation-within 3 mi.

🍽 🍽 🏊 BIZ 📶 FEE 🔲 🔲 🔲 💻 / SOME UNITS FEE 🐾

EMBASSY SUITES PHOENIX NORTH
Phone: (602)375-1777 ❶⓪

▼▼▼▼
Hotel
$99-$159 2/1-4/30
$59-$89 5/1-1/31

E
EMBASSY SUITES
HOTELS®

AAA Benefit:
Members save 5% or more everyday!

Address: 2577 W Greenway Rd 85023 **Location:** I-17 exit 211, just e. **Facility:** 314 units, some two bedrooms. 3 stories, exterior corridors. **Terms:** 1-7 night minimum stay, cancellation fee imposed. **Amenities:** high-speed Internet. **Pool(s):** heated outdoor. **Activities:** whirlpool, lighted tennis court, exercise room. **Guest Services:** valet and coin laundry, area transportation-within 5 mi. **Free Special Amenities:** full breakfast and manager's reception. (See ad p. 181.)

SAVE 🍽 🍽 🏊 BIZ 📶 FEE 🔲 🔲 🔲 💻 / SOME UNITS FEE 🐾

EMBASSY SUITES PHOENIX-SCOTTSDALE AT STONECREEK GOLF CLUB
Phone: (602)765-5800 ❶❼

▼▼▼▼
Hotel
$89-$279

E
EMBASSY SUITES
HOTELS®

AAA Benefit:
Members save 5% or more everyday!

Address: 4415 E Paradise Village Pkwy S 85032 **Location:** Just s of Cactus Rd; just w of Tatum Blvd. **Facility:** 270 units. 6 stories, interior corridors. **Terms:** 1-7 night minimum stay, cancellation fee imposed. **Amenities:** video games (fee), safes. *Some:* high-speed Internet (fee). **Pool(s):** heated outdoor. **Activities:** whirlpool, exercise room. **Fee:** golf-18 holes. **Guest Services:** valet and coin laundry, area transportation-within 5 mi. **Free Special Amenities:** full breakfast and manager's reception. (See ad p. 181.)

SAVE 🍽 🍽 🏊 BIZ 📶 FEE 🔲 🔲 🔲 💻

EXTENDED STAYAMERICA-PHOENIX-CHANDLER
Phone: (480)785-0464 ❸❹

▼▼▼
Extended Stay Hotel
$80-$90 2/1-4/15
$65-$75 4/16-1/31

Address: 14245 S 50th St 85044 **Location:** I-10 exit 159, just w on Ray Rd, just s, then just e. **Facility:** 101 efficiencies. 3 stories, interior corridors. **Guest Services:** coin laundry.

🍽 CALL 📶 🔲 🔲 💻 / SOME UNITS FEE 🐾

(See maps & indexes p. 151, 155, 158, 164.)

EXTENDED STAYAMERICA PHOENIX-CHANDLER-E
CHANDLER BLVD   Phone: (480)753-6700   37

◆◆ ◆◆
Extended Stay
Hotel
$80-$90 2/1-4/15
$65-$75 4/16-1/31
Guest Services: coin laundry.

Address: 5035 E Chandler Blvd
85048 **Location:** I-10 exit 160
(Chandler Blvd), just w. **Facility:** 129
efficiencies. 2 stories (no elevator),
exterior corridors. **Terms:** office hours
6:30 am-10:30 pm. **Pool(s):** heated
outdoor. **Activities:** exercise room.

EXTENDED STAYAMERICA PHOENIX-DEER VALLEY
Phone: (623)879-6609   1

◆◆ ◆◆
Extended Stay
Hotel
$65-$75 2/1-4/15
$50-$60 4/16-1/31
coin laundry.

Address: 20827 N 27th Ave 85027
Location: I-10 exit 215 (Rose Garden
Ln) northbound, just w; exit 215B
southbound, just w, then 0.4 mi s.
Facility: 104 efficiencies. 3 stories,
interior corridors. **Terms:** office hours
6:30 am-10:30 pm. **Guest Services:**

▼ See AAA listing p. 180 ▼

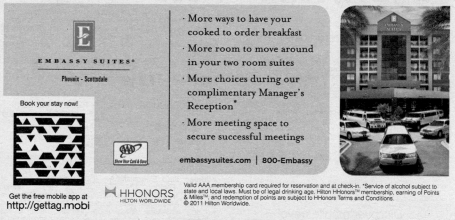

▼ See AAA listing p. 180 ▼

Download eTourBook guides for ereaders and smartphones at AAA.com/ebooks

(See maps & indexes p. 151, 155, 158, 164.)

EXTENDED STAY DELUXE PHOENIX-BILTMORE
Phone: (602)265-6800 **31**

Extended Stay Hotel
$95-$105 2/1-4/15
$75-$85 4/16-1/31

Address: 5235 N 16th St 85016 **Location:** Jct SR 51, just w on Camelback Rd, then just n. **Facility:** 111 efficiencies. 3 stories, interior corridors. **Terms:** office hours 6:30 am-10:30 pm. **Pool(s):** heated outdoor. **Activities:** whirlpool, exercise room. **Guest Services:** coin laundry.

EXTENDED STAY DELUXE (PHOENIX/MIDTOWN)
Phone: (602)279-9000 **40**

Extended Stay Hotel
$85-$95 2/1-4/15
$75-$85 4/16-1/31

Address: 217 W Osborn Rd 85013 **Location:** Just w of Central Ave; between Indian School and Thomas rds. **Facility:** 129 units, some efficiencies. 3 stories, interior corridors. **Pool(s):** heated outdoor. **Activities:** exercise room. **Guest Services:** coin laundry.

FAIRFIELD INN BY MARRIOTT PHOENIX NORTH
Phone: (602)548-8888 **7**

Hotel
$49-$169

AAA Benefit: AAA hotel discounts of 5% or more.

Address: 17017 N Black Canyon Hwy 85023 **Location:** I-17 exit 212, just e, then just n; on east side of freeway. **Facility:** 65 units. 3 stories, interior corridors. **Amenities:** high-speed Internet. **Pool(s):** heated outdoor. **Activities:** whirlpool. **Guest Services:** valet and coin laundry. **Free Special Amenities:** expanded continental breakfast and high-speed Internet.

GRACE INN PHOENIX
Phone: (480)893-3000 **33**

Hotel
$69-$189

Address: 10831 S 51st St 85044 **Location:** I-10 exit 157 (Elliot Rd), just w, then just s. **Facility:** 160 units, some efficiencies. 6 stories, interior corridors. **Terms:** cancellation fee imposed. **Amenities:** high-speed Internet. **Pool(s):** heated outdoor. **Activities:** whirlpool, lighted tennis court, shuffleboard. **Guest Services:** valet laundry.

HAMPTON INN & SUITES PHOENIX NORTH/HAPPY VALLEY
Phone: (623)516-9300

Hotel
$79-$199

AAA Benefit: Members save up to 10% everyday!

Address: 2550 W Charlotte Dr 85085 **Location:** I-17 exit 217 (Pinnacle Peak Rd), 0.6 mi n on Frontage Rd. **Facility:** 125 units. 4 stories, interior corridors. **Terms:** 1-7 night minimum stay, cancellation fee imposed. **Amenities:** high-speed Internet. **Pool(s):** heated outdoor. **Activities:** whirlpool, exercise room. **Guest Services:** valet and coin laundry, area transportation-within 5 mi.

Discover mobile travel solutions at AAA.com/mobile and CAA.ca/mobile

HILTON GARDEN INN
Phone: (602)279-9811 **37**

Hotel
$129-$189 2/1-5/31
$79-$139 6/1-1/31

AAA Benefit: Unparalleled hospitality at a special Member rate.

Address: 4000 N Central Ave 85012 **Location:** 0.3 mi s of Indian School Rd, just w on Clarendon Ave. Located in a commercial area. **Facility:** 156 units. 3-7 stories, interior corridors. **Terms:** 1-7 night minimum stay, cancellation fee imposed. **Amenities:** video games (fee), high-speed Internet. **Pool(s):** heated outdoor. **Activities:** whirlpool. **Guest Services:** valet and coin laundry, area transportation-within 5 mi.

HILTON GARDEN INN PHOENIX NORTH /HAPPY VALLEY
Phone: (623)434-5556

Hotel
$66-$160 2/1-8/31
$80-$152 9/1-1/31

AAA Benefit: Unparalleled hospitality at a special Member rate.

Address: 1940 W Pinnacle Peak Rd 85027 **Location:** I-17 exit 217 (Pinnacle Peak Rd), 0.8 mi e. **Facility:** 126 units. 4 stories, interior corridors. **Terms:** 1-7 night minimum stay, cancellation fee imposed. **Amenities:** high-speed Internet. **Pool(s):** heated outdoor. **Activities:** whirlpool, exercise room. **Guest Services:** area transportation-within 5 mi.

HOLIDAY INN EXPRESS & SUITES PHOENIX-CHANDLER
Phone: (480)785-8500 **35**

Hotel
$74-$139

Address: 15221 S 50th St 85044 **Location:** I-10 exit 160 (Chandler Blvd), just w, then just n. **Facility:** 125 units. 4 stories, interior corridors. **Terms:** cancellation fee imposed. **Pool(s):** heated outdoor. **Activities:** whirlpool, exercise room. **Guest Services:** valet and coin laundry. **Free Special Amenities:** full breakfast and high-speed Internet.

HOLIDAY INN PHOENIX WEST
Phone: (602)484-9009 **44**

Hotel
$129-$149 2/1-4/2
$89-$109 4/3-1/31

Address: 1500 N 51st Ave 85043 **Location:** I-10 exit 139 (51st Ave), just n. **Facility:** 144 units, some two bedrooms. 4 stories, interior corridors. **Terms:** check-in 4 pm. **Amenities:** high-speed Internet. **Pool(s):** heated outdoor. **Activities:** whirlpool, exercise room. **Guest Services:** valet laundry.

HOMEWOOD SUITES BY HILTON PHOENIX-BILTMORE
Phone: (602)508-0937 **35**

Extended Stay Hotel
$129-$159 2/1-4/30
$89-$129 5/1-1/31

AAA Benefit: Contemporary luxury at a special Member rate.

Address: 2001 E Highland Ave 85016 **Location:** Just e of 20th St. **Facility:** 124 efficiencies. 4 stories, interior corridors. **Terms:** 1-7 night minimum stay, cancellation fee imposed. **Amenities:** video games (fee). **Pool(s):** heated outdoor. **Activities:** sports court, exercise room. **Guest Services:** valet and coin laundry, area transportation-within 5 mi.

(See maps & indexes p. 151, 155, 158, 164.)

HOMEWOOD SUITES BY HILTON PHOENIX METROCENTER
Phone: (602)674-8900 **15**

Extended Stay Hotel

$99-$189 2/1-4/14
$72-$139 4/15-1/31

AAA Benefit: Contemporary luxury at a special Member rate.

Address: 2536 W Beryl Ave 85021 **Location:** I-17 exit 208 (Peoria Ave), just e, just s on 25th Ave, then just w. **Facility:** 126 efficiencies, some two bedrooms. 5 stories, interior corridors. **Terms:** 1-7 night minimum stay, cancellation fee imposed. **Amenities:** video games (fee). **Pool(s):** heated outdoor. **Activities:** sports court, exercise room. **Guest Services:** valet and coin laundry.

HOMEWOOD SUITES PHOENIX NORTH/HAPPY VALLEY
Phone: (623)580-1800

Extended Stay Hotel

$99-$199

AAA Benefit: Contemporary luxury at a special Member rate.

Address: 2470 W Charlotte Dr 85085 **Location:** I-17 exit 217 (Pinnacle Peak Rd), 0.6 mi n on Frontage Rd. **Facility:** 134 units, some two bedrooms and efficiencies. 4 stories, interior corridors. **Terms:** 1-7 night minimum stay, cancellation fee imposed. **Amenities:** high-speed Internet. **Pool(s):** heated outdoor. **Activities:** whirlpool, sports court, exercise room. **Guest Services:** valet and coin laundry, area transportation-within 5 mi.

HOTEL HIGHLAND AT BILTMORE
Phone: (602)956-5221 **36**

Hotel

$69-$189

Address: 2310 E Highland Ave 85016 **Location:** Just sw of Camelback Rd and 24th St. **Facility:** 119 units. 4 stories, interior corridors. **Pool(s):** heated outdoor. **Activities:** whirlpool, exercise room. **Guest Services:** valet laundry, area transportation-within 3 mi.

HYATT PLACE PHOENIX-NORTH
Phone: (602)997-8800 **13**

Hotel

$79-$209

AAA Benefit: Members save 10% or more everyday.

Address: 10838 N 25th Ave 85029 **Location:** I-17 exit 208 (Peoria Ave), just e, then 0.3 mi n. **Facility:** 127 units. 4 stories, interior corridors. **Terms:** cancellation fee imposed. **Amenities:** Some: high-speed Internet. **Pool(s):** heated outdoor. **Activities:** exercise room. **Guest Services:** valet laundry, area transportation-within 5 mi. **Free Special Amenities:** expanded continental breakfast and high-speed Internet.

JW MARRIOTT DESERT RIDGE RESORT & SPA
Phone: (480)293-5000 **3**

Resort Hotel

JW MARRIOTT

$134-$529

AAA Benefit: A deluxe level of comfort and a Member rate.

Address: 5350 E Marriott Dr 85054 **Location:** SR 101 exit 31 (Tatum Blvd), 0.4 mi n to Deer Valley Dr, then 0.5 mi e. **Facility:** This destination resort has activities for families or groups; a tri-level lobby opens to a courtyard with pools, water play areas and a flowing lazy river. 950 units. 6 stories, interior corridors. **Parking:** on-site (fee) and valet. **Terms:** check-in 4 pm, 3 day cancellation notice. **Amenities:** safes, honor bars. Fee: video games, high-speed Internet. **Dining:** 4 restaurants, also, Meritage Steakhouse, Ristorante Tuscany, Roy's Desert Ridge, see separate listings. **Pool(s):** 5 heated outdoor. **Activities:** saunas, whirlpools, steamrooms, waterslide, recreation programs, hiking trails, jogging, spa. Fee: golf-36 holes, 8 lighted tennis courts, bicycles. **Guest Services:** valet and coin laundry.

LA QUINTA INN & SUITES PHOENIX CHANDLER
Phone: (480)961-7700 **36**

Hotel

$58-$177

Address: 15241 S 50th St 85044 **Location:** I-10 exit 160 (Chandler Blvd), just w, then just n. Located in a light-commercial area. **Facility:** 117 units. 4 stories, interior corridors. **Amenities:** video games (fee). **Pool(s):** heated outdoor. **Activities:** whirlpool, exercise room. **Guest Services:** coin laundry.

LA QUINTA INN & SUITES PHOENIX I-10 WEST
Phone: (602)595-7601 **41**

Hotel

$81-$179

Address: 4929 W McDowell Rd 85035 **Location:** I-10 exit 139 (51st Ave), just n, then just e. **Facility:** 66 units, some two bedrooms and kitchens. 3 stories, interior corridors. **Amenities:** high-speed Internet. **Pool(s):** heated outdoor. **Activities:** whirlpool, exercise room. **Guest Services:** coin laundry.

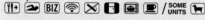

LA QUINTA INN PHOENIX NORTH
Phone: (602)993-0800 **9**

Hotel

$48-$166

Address: 2510 W Greenway Rd 85023 **Location:** I-17 exit 211, just e. **Facility:** 145 units. 2 stories (no elevator), exterior corridors. **Amenities:** video games. Some: high-speed Internet. **Pool(s):** heated outdoor. **Activities:** whirlpool, 2 lighted tennis courts, exercise room. **Guest Services:** valet and coin laundry.

THE LEGACY GOLF RESORT
Phone: (602)305-5500 **46**

Resort Condominium

$99-$499

Address: 6808 S 32nd St 85042 **Location:** I-10 exit 155 (Baseline Rd), 2.4 mi w, then 0.4 mi n. **Facility:** Elegant rooms and baths await you in the contemporary desert setting along with a golf course designed by Gary Panks. 328 condominiums. 2 stories (no elevator), exterior corridors. **Terms:** check-in 4 pm, cancellation fee imposed. **Amenities:** high-speed Internet, safes. **Pool(s):** heated outdoor. **Activities:** whirlpools, 2 lighted tennis courts, recreation programs, playground, shuffleboard, volleyball, exercise room. Fee: golf-18 holes, massage. **Guest Services:** complimentary laundry. **Free Special Amenities:** high-speed Internet and children's activities.

Find valuable AAA/CAA member savings at AAA.com/discounts

(See maps & indexes p. 151, 155, 158, 164.)

MARICOPA MANOR BED & BREAKFAST INN
Phone: 602/264-9200 **30**

Bed & Breakfast
Rates not provided

Address: 15 W Pasadena Ave 85013 **Location:** Just n of Camelback Rd; w of Central Ave. Located in a residential area. **Facility:** This 1928 Spanish mission home has elegantly decorated one- and two-bedroom patio suites, some with a gas or wood-burning fireplace. 6 units. 1 story, interior/exterior corridors. **Terms:** office hours 8 am-10 pm. **Amenities:** high-speed Internet. *Some:* safes, honor bars. **Pool(s):** outdoor. **Activities:** whirlpool.

MOTEL 6 PHOENIX-NORTH #344
Phone: (602)993-2353 **8**

Motel
$49-$59

Address: 2330 W Bell Rd 85023 **Location:** I-17 exit 212, just e. **Facility:** 139 units. 2 stories (no elevator), exterior corridors. **Terms:** office hours 7 am-10 pm. **Pool(s):** heated outdoor. **Guest Services:** coin laundry.

MOTEL 6 PHOENIX WEST #696
Phone: (602)272-0220 **42**

Motel
$49-$59

Address: 1530 N 52nd Dr 85043 **Location:** I-10 exit 139 (51st Ave), just n to McDowell Rd, just w, then just s. **Facility:** 147 units. 3 stories, exterior corridors. **Pool(s):** outdoor.

POINTE HILTON SQUAW PEAK RESORT
Phone: (602)997-2626 **27**

Resort Hotel
$119-$219 2/1-5/31
$89-$179 6/1-1/31

AAA Benefit: Members save 5% or more everyday!

Address: 7677 N 16th St 85020 **Location:** SR 51 exit Glendale Ave, 0.4 mi w, then 0.6 mi n. **Facility:** The resort's suites and large casitas are scattered throughout extensive grounds featuring shaded pool areas and courtyards with tiered fountains. 563 units, some houses. 3-4 stories, exterior corridors. **Terms:** check-in 4 pm, 1-7 night minimum stay, cancellation fee imposed. **Amenities:** safes. *Fee:* video games, high-speed Internet. **Dining:** 2 restaurants, also, Rico's American Grill, see separate listing. **Pool(s):** 8 heated outdoor. **Activities:** saunas, whirlpools, steamrooms, waterslide, recreation programs, hiking trails, playground, basketball, spa. *Fee:* miniature golf, 3 lighted tennis courts. **Guest Services:** valet and coin laundry, area transportation-Biltmore Shopping Center & Scottsdale Fashion Square.

Enjoy great savings
on hotel rates at
AAA.com or CAA.ca

POINTE HILTON TAPATIO CLIFFS RESORT
Phone: (602)866-7500 **12**

Resort Hotel
$119-$219 2/1-5/31
$89-$179 6/1-1/31

AAA Benefit: Members save 5% or more everyday!

Address: 11111 N 7th St 85020 **Location:** I-17 exit 207 (Dunlap Ave), 3 mi e, then 2 mi n. **Facility:** On extensive and nicely landscaped grounds, these one-bedroom suites are spread across several buildings, many with views across the valley. 584 units. 2-5 stories, exterior corridors. **Parking:** on-site and valet. **Terms:** check-in 4 pm, 1-7 night minimum stay, cancellation fee imposed. **Amenities:** honor bars. *Some:* high-speed Internet (fee), safes. **Dining:** 3 restaurants, also, Different Pointe of View, see separate listing, entertainment. **Pool(s):** 8 heated outdoor. **Activities:** sauna, whirlpools, steamroom, waterslide, recreation programs, hiking trails, jogging, basketball, spa. *Fee:* golf-18 holes, 2 lighted tennis courts, bicycles, exercise room. **Guest Services:** valet and coin laundry, area transportation (fee)-Paradise Valley Mall & Pointe Hilton Squaw Peak Resort.

QUALITY INN & SUITES
Phone: (602)242-8011 **28**

Hotel
$55-$80

Address: 5050 N Black Canyon Hwy 85017 **Location:** I-17 exit 203 (Camelback Rd), just w, then just n; on west side of freeway. **Facility:** 154 units. 3 stories, exterior corridors. **Terms:** cancellation fee imposed. **Amenities:** safes. **Pool(s):** heated outdoor. **Activities:** whirlpool. **Guest Services:** coin laundry.

We look forward to providing each guest with exceptional service and cozy accommodations.

RADISSON HOTEL PHOENIX CITY CENTER
Phone: (602)604-4900 **38**

Hotel
$82-$189

Address: 3600 N 2nd Ave 85013 **Location:** Just n of Osborn Rd, 0.5 mi s of Indian School Rd; downtown. **Facility:** 160 units. 6 stories, interior corridors. **Terms:** check-in 4 pm, 3 day cancellation notice-fee imposed. **Amenities:** video games (fee), high-speed Internet. **Pool(s):** outdoor, 2 heated outdoor. **Activities:** lighted tennis court, playground, volleyball, exercise room. **Guest Services:** valet and coin laundry, area transportation-within 3 mi.

RED ROOF INN PHOENIX WEST
Phone: (602)233-8004 **43**

Hotel
$50-$126

Address: 5215 W Willetta 85043 **Location:** I-10 exit 139 (51st Ave), just n, just e on McDowell Rd, then just s. **Facility:** 133 units. 4 stories, interior corridors. **Amenities:** video games (fee), safes. **Pool(s):** heated outdoor. **Free Special Amenities:** local telephone calls and high-speed Internet.

(See maps & indexes p. 151, 155, 158, 164.)

▼ See AAA listing p. 52 ▼

RESIDENCE INN BY MARRIOTT PHOENIX
Phone: 602/864-1900 **23**

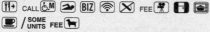
Extended Stay Hotel
Rates not provided

AAA Benefit:
AAA hotel discounts of 5% or more.

Address: 8242 N Black Canyon Hwy 85051 **Location:** I-17 exit 207 (Dunlap Ave), just w, then 0.8 mi s; on frontage road. **Facility:** 168 units, some two bedrooms and efficiencies. 2 stories (no elevator), interior/exterior corridors. **Amenities:** *Some:* high-speed Internet. **Pool(s):** heated outdoor. **Activities:** whirlpool, playground, sports court, limited exercise equipment. **Guest Services:** valet and coin laundry.

[icons] CALL / SOME UNITS FEE

RESIDENCE INN BY MARRIOTT PHOENIX NORTH/
HAPPY VALLEY **Phone:** (623)580-8833

Extended Stay Hotel
$79-$154

AAA Benefit:
AAA hotel discounts of 5% or more.

Address: 2035 W Whispering Wind Dr 85085 **Location:** I-17 exit 128 (Happy Valley Rd), 0.4 mi e to 23rd Ave, just s, then just e. **Facility:** 129 units, some two bedrooms, efficiencies and kitchens. 5 stories, interior corridors. **Amenities:** high-speed Internet. **Pool(s):** heated outdoor. **Activities:** whirlpool, sports court, exercise room. **Guest Services:** valet and coin laundry.

[icons] / SOME UNITS FEE

THE RITZ-CARLTON, PHOENIX
Phone: 602/468-0700 **34**

Hotel
Rates not provided

AAA Benefit:
Unequaled service at Special Member Savings.

Address: 2401 E Camelback Rd 85016 **Location:** Southeast corner of Camelback Rd and 24th St. Across from Biltmore Fashion Park. **Facility:** Catering to both business and leisure travelers, this elegant, service-oriented hotel has well-appointed guest rooms and large meeting spaces. 281 units, some two bedrooms and efficiencies. 11 stories, interior corridors. **Parking:** on-site (fee) and valet. **Amenities:** safes, honor bars. *Fee:* video games, high-speed Internet. **Dining:** Bistro 24, see separate listing, entertainment. **Pool(s):** heated outdoor. **Activities:** saunas, exercise room. *Fee:* massage. **Guest Services:** valet laundry.

[icons] FEE / SOME UNITS FEE

ROYAL PALMS RESORT AND SPA
Phone: (602)840-3610 **39**

Boutique Hotel
$199-$599 2/1-5/22
$179-$499 5/23-1/31

Address: 5200 E Camelback Rd 85018 **Location:** Just e of 52nd St. Located in a quiet residential area. **Facility:** Originally built as a private residence in the 1920s, this nine-acre hideaway nestled at the base of Camelback Mountain has Mediterranean-style guest units. 119 units, some kitchens. 1-2 stories, interior/exterior corridors. **Parking:** on-site and valet. **Terms:** check-in 4 pm, 7 day cancellation notice-fee imposed. **Amenities:** video games (fee), safes, honor bars. *Some:* high-speed Internet. **Dining:** T. Cook's, see separate listing. **Pool(s):** heated outdoor. **Activities:** whirlpools, steamrooms, exercise room, spa. **Guest Services:** valet laundry.

[icons] SAVE ECO / SOME UNITS FEE

ARE YOU READY TO RUN WILD?

A M E N I T I E S

• 242 Rooms & Suites
• 12,000 Sq. Ft. of meeting space
• 100,000 Sq. Ft. Vegas-style casino
• 8 Restaurants
• 4 Lounges

• 1,400-seat showroom
• Nightclub
• Outdoor pool with cabanas
• Free wireless internet
• Whirlwind Golf Club

Scan this tag on your smartphone to learn about our great rooms and suites.

Get the free mobile app at http://gettag.mobi

WILDHORSEPASS
HOTEL & CASINO

Owned and operated by the Gila River Indian Community
WinGilaRiver.com • 800-WIN-GILA

Like Us on [f] Sign up for [ ] at WinGilaRiver.com

Safety tip: Keep a current

AAA/CAA Road Atlas

in every vehicle

(See maps & indexes p. 151, 155, 158, 164.)

SHERATON CRESCENT HOTEL
Phone: (602)943-8200 **22**

Hotel
$125-$635

Sheraton STARWOOD MEMBER
AAA Benefit: Members get up to 15% off, plus Starwood Preferred Guest® bonuses.

Address: 2620 W Dunlap Ave 85021 **Location:** I-17 exit 207 (Dunlap Ave), just e. **Facility:** 342 units. 8 stories, interior corridors. **Parking:** on-site and valet. **Terms:** cancellation fee imposed. **Amenities:** video games (fee), safes. *Some:* high-speed Internet (fee). **Pool(s):** heated outdoor. **Activities:** saunas, whirlpool, waterslide, 2 lighted tennis courts, racquetball courts, playground, basketball, horseshoes, volleyball. **Guest Services:** valet laundry. **Free Special Amenities:** newspaper and local transportation.

[icons]

SLEEP INN PHOENIX NORTH
Phone: (602)504-1200 **6**

Hotel
$60-$130

Address: 18235 N 27th Ave 85053 **Location:** I-17 exit 214A (Union Hills Dr), just w, then just s. **Facility:** 61 units. 2 stories, interior corridors. *Bath:* shower only. **Terms:** cancellation fee imposed. **Amenities:** safes. *Some:* high-speed Internet. **Pool(s):** heated outdoor. **Activities:** whirlpool, exercise room. **Guest Services:** coin laundry. **Free Special Amenities:** expanded continental breakfast and high-speed Internet.

[icons]

**AAA Discount
All Interior Hotel
Deluxe Cont. Bkfst.
WIFI, Business & Fitness Ctrs
Pet Friendly, CableTV.**

SLEEP INN
BY CHOICE HOTELS

SPRINGHILL SUITES BY MARRIOTT-METRO CENTER
Phone: (602)943-0010 **21**

Hotel
$59-$149

AAA Benefit: AAA hotel discounts of 5% or more.

Address: 9425 N Black Canyon Frwy 85021 **Location:** I-17 exit 207 (Dunlap Ave), just e, then 0.3 mi n. **Facility:** 80 units. 3 stories, interior corridors. **Pool(s):** heated outdoor. **Activities:** whirlpool, exercise room. **Guest Services:** valet laundry.

[icons]

SUPER 8 PHOENIX METRO NORTH
Phone: (602)995-8451 **24**

Motel
$33-$71

Address: 8130 N Black Canyon Hwy 85051 **Location:** I-17 exit 206 (Northern Ave), just w, then just n on west side of freeway. **Facility:** 123 units. 2 stories (no elevator), exterior corridors. **Pool(s):** heated outdoor. **Activities:** whirlpool. **Guest Services:** coin laundry. **Free Special Amenities:** continental breakfast and high-speed Internet.

[icons]

Visit AAA.com or CAA.ca
for one-stop travel
planning and reservations

SUPER 8-PHOENIX WEST
Phone: (602)415-0888 **45**

Hotel
$45-$81

Address: 1242 N 53rd Ave 85043 **Location:** I-10 exit 139 (51st Ave), just s to Latham Rd, then just w. **Facility:** 67 units. 2 stories (no elevator), interior corridors. **Pool(s):** outdoor. **Guest Services:** coin laundry.

[icons]

TOWNEPLACE SUITES PHOENIX NORTH
Phone: (602)943-9510 **20**

Extended Stay Hotel
$59-$149

AAA Benefit: AAA hotel discounts of 5% or more.

Address: 9425 N Black Canyon Frwy 85021 **Location:** I-17 exit 207 (Dunlap Ave), just e, then 0.3 mi n. **Facility:** 94 units, some two bedrooms, efficiencies and kitchens. 3 stories, interior corridors. **Amenities:** high-speed Internet. **Pool(s):** heated outdoor. **Activities:** exercise room. **Guest Services:** valet and coin laundry.

[icons]

WHERE TO EAT

101 ASIAN BUFFET
Phone: 623/581-6888 **1**

Chinese
$4-$11

AAA Inspector Notes: A wide selection of Chinese and American favorites, fresh fruit and sushi are offered at this casual buffet. **Bar:** beer & wine. **Address:** 20440 N 27th Ave 85027 **Location:** I-17 exit 215A (Rose Ln), just w to 27th Ave, then just s. **L** **D**

ALEXI'S GRILL
Phone: 602/279-0982 **50**

Northern Italian
$9-$25

AAA Inspector Notes: Whether for a business lunch, a celebration or an intimate dinner, the friendly staff and eclectic foods prepared with a Mediterranean flair are sure to delight. The signature rack of lamb is highly recommended. **Bar:** full bar. **Reservations:** suggested. **Address:** 3550 N Central Ave 85012 **Location:** Just n of Osborn Rd. **L** **D**

AUNT CHILADA'S HIDEAWAY
Phone: 602/944-1286 **11**

Mexican
$6-$18

AAA Inspector Notes: Colorful decor, Mexican memorabilia and several patios, including one that is dog-friendly, enhance the rooms of this historic, hacienda-style building. Guests can select from traditional favorites such as chimichangas, enchiladas and fajitas (the house specialty). Live entertainment is on hand some evenings. **Bar:** full bar. **Address:** 7330 N Dreamy Draw Dr 85020 **Location:** SR 51 exit Glendale Ave, 0.4 mi w to 16th St, 0.6 mi to Morten Ave, then just e. **Parking:** on-site and street. **L** **D**

BISTRO 24
Phone: 602/952-2424 **34**

Continental
$16-$36

AAA Inspector Notes: A seasonally changing menu at this upscale bistro features the freshest ingredients. Highlights include crispy risotto croquettes or truffle pappardelle pasta. Expect attentive service from a friendly waitstaff. **Bar:** full bar. **Reservations:** suggested. **Address:** 2401 E Camelback Rd 85016 **Location:** Southeast corner of Camelback Rd and 24th St; in The Ritz-Carlton, Phoenix. **Parking:** valet only. **B** **L** **D**

(See maps & indexes p. 151, 155, 158, 164.)

CAFFE BOA   Phone: 480/893-3331   23

Italian
$7-$20

AAA Inspector Notes: Upscale presentations are a highlight here and include such rich, thick soups as shrimp bisque, plus grilled salmon with basmati rice. The menu lists pasta dishes including rigatoni puttanesca, as well as preparations of beef, chicken and seafood. Indoor and outdoor seating is available. **Bar:** full bar. **Address:** 5063 E Elliot Rd 85044 **Location:** I-10 exit 157 (Elliot Rd), 1 blk w; in Ahwatukee Shopping Center. L D

THE CAPITAL GRILLE   Phone: 602/952-8900   31

Steak
$11-$53

AAA Inspector Notes: Cherry wood and red leather assist in making this "clubby" dining room a beautiful spot to dine on excellent cuts of dry-aged beef. The staff is highly attentive and knowledgeable. **Bar:** full bar. **Address:** 2502 E Camelback Rd, Suite 199 85016 **Location:** Jct Camelback Rd and 26th St, just e; in Biltmore Fashion Park; on south side. L D

CARLOS O'BRIENS MEXICAN RESTAURANT
     Phone: 602/274-5881

Mexican
$6-$15

AAA Inspector Notes: This attractively decorated restaurant serves traditional northern Mexican fare in hearty portions. Both the food and the margaritas make this spot popular with the locals. **Bar:** full bar. **Address:** 1133 E Northern Ave 85020 **Location:** SR 51 exit Northern Ave, 1.4 mi w; sw of 12th St. L D LATE

CHELSEA'S KITCHEN   Phone: 602/957-2555   41

American
$10-$27

AAA Inspector Notes: A high-energy atmosphere, a helpful and knowledgeable waitstaff and cooked-to-order foods distinguish this upscale eatery in east Phoenix. Custom burgers include ahi tuna and veggie options. A nice selection of wines by the glass are offered. The fresh-made desserts are the perfect ending to the experience. Outdoor patio dining is offered. **Bar:** full bar. **Address:** 5040 N 40th St 85018 **Location:** Just n of Camelback Rd. L D

CHINA CHILI   Phone: 602/266-4463   52

Chinese
$7-$26

AAA Inspector Notes: This popular lunch spot features classic Chinese favorites served in a comfortable family-friendly setting. **Bar:** beer & wine. **Address:** 302 E Flower St 85012 **Location:** At 3rd St.

L D CALL

CHRISTOPHER'S RESTAURANT & CRUSH LOUNGE
     Phone: 602/522-2344   30

French
$9-$35

AAA Inspector Notes: This restaurant is located in an upscale modern space in the Biltmore Fashion Park. Diners will be delighted by regional American cuisine with classic French preparations. **Bar:** full bar. **Reservations:** suggested. **Address:** 2502 E Camelback Rd 85016 **Location:** Just e of 24th St; in Biltmore Fashion Park. L D

CHRISTO'S   Phone: 602/264-1784   12

Italian
$13-$27

AAA Inspector Notes: This popular restaurant in mid-town serves an excellent variety of traditional Italian dishes, including fettuccine monte casino, chicken Florentine and shrimp diavolo. The waitstaff, all dressed in tuxedo shirts, serve meals with casual and friendly commentary. **Bar:** full bar. **Address:** 6327 N 7th St 85014 **Location:** Just s of Maryland Ave. L D

CLAIM JUMPER   Phone: 623/581-8595

American
$8-$25

AAA Inspector Notes: Great menu variety makes this place a good stop for parties with diverse tastes. Choices include specialty appetizers, salads, rotisserie chicken and barbecue items, not to mention good comfort foods, such as traditional pot pie. Hearty portions satisfy big appetites. The atmosphere is fun and lively. **Bar:** full bar. **Address:** 3063 W Agua Fria Frwy 85027 **Location:** I-17 exit 214A (Yorkshire Dr), 0.4 mi w; in Deer Valley Plaza. L D

CORBIN'S BAR & GRILL   Phone: 602/466-3201   8

American
$10-$21

AAA Inspector Notes: Enjoy upscale casual dining in this lively and popular North Central spot. Specialties include barbecue pork ribs, thick-cut onion rings with chipotle-ranch dressing and bacon-wrapped scallops. **Bar:** full bar. **Address:** 8729 N Central Ave 85020 **Location:** Jct Dunlap and Central aves, 0.3 mi s. L D

DIFFERENT POINTE OF VIEW   Phone: 602/866-6350   6

American
$29-$42

AAA Inspector Notes: The panoramic views of the valley are truly spectacular at this mountain top restaurant, which offers indoor and outdoor dining areas. The menu reflects New American cuisine, incorporating some natural and organic ingredients. The restaurant boasts an award-winning, international wine list. **Bar:** full bar. **Reservations:** suggested. **Address:** 11111 N 7th St 85020 **Location:** I-17 exit 207 (Dunlap Rd), 3 mi e, then 2 mi n; in Pointe Hilton Tapatio Cliffs Resort. **Parking:** valet only. D

DUCK AND DECANTER   Phone: 602/274-5429   26

Deli
$6-$9

AAA Inspector Notes: This eatery cannot be beat for a quick, delicious lunch consisting of sandwiches, salads and soups. Dinners may include wine, which can be selected from an excellent list. Giftware featuring their duck logo as well as coffee beans are available for purchase. **Bar:** beer & wine. **Address:** 1651 E Camelback Rd 85016 **Location:** Just e of 16th St. B L

FARM KITCHEN AT THE FARM AT SOUTH MOUNTAIN
Menu on AAA.com   Phone: 602/276-6360   56

American
$5-$10

AAA Inspector Notes: Dining outdoors is a must, with meals in a basket given to patrons who can seek refuge under canvas awnings or shady trees. Picnic tables with checked cloths are on brick patios. Cool salads and warming soups share menu space with scrumptious pies, cookies and cakes. **Address:** 6106 S 32nd St 85042 **Location:** I-10 exit 151 (University Dr), 1.4 mi s, then just s of Southern Ave. L AC

THE FRY BREAD HOUSE   Phone: 602/351-2345   45

Regional Specialty
$3-$8

AAA Inspector Notes: For something unusual and a true Native American food, try the tasty fry-bread tacos with any of varied fillings. The honey-covered dessert fry bread is decadent. **Address:** 4140 N 7th Ave 85013 **Location:** Just n of Indian School Rd. B L D

FUEGO BISTRO   Phone: 602/277-1151   14

Latin American
$8-$26

AAA Inspector Notes: Patrons can feast upon authentic Cuban, Puerto Rican and Latin American favorites at this bistro including pernil asado, ropa vieja and arroz con gandules. The intimate dining room is complemented by a large outdoor patio featuring live entertainment on the weekends. **Bar:** full bar. **Reservations:** suggested. **Address:** 713 E Palo Verde Dr 85014 **Location:** Jct 7th St and Bethany Home Rd, just s, then just e. **Parking:** on-site and street. L D

(See maps & indexes p. 151, 155, 158, 164.)

FUEGO TACOS   Phone: 602/441-5728   36

Mexican
$8-$12

AAA Inspector Notes: Diners may choose from such gourmet tacos as short rib barbacoa, Baja fish or Pernil asado, served with homemade chips and salsa. Tasty churros satisfy dessert cravings. **Bar:** full bar. **Address:** 2501 E Camelback Rd 85022 **Location:** Southeast corner of Camelback Rd and 24th St; in Camelback Esplanade. L D

GALLO BLANCO CAFE & BAR   Phone: 602/274-4774   47

Mexican
$7-$16

AAA Inspector Notes: A fun and trendy spot set in the Clarendon Hotel, diners can nosh on such local favorites as carne asada tacos, tortas or the made-to-order-guacamole. **Bar:** full bar. **Address:** 401 W Clarendon Ave 85013 **Location:** Southwest corner of 4th and Clarendon aves; in The Clarendon Hotel. B L D

GREAT WALL HONG KONG CUISINE   Phone: 602/973-1112   16

Chinese
$8-$15

AAA Inspector Notes: Authentic dim sum is served daily during lunch hours in this large, unassuming dining room. Choose from a wide variety of small plates including delicious pork buns, siu mai and shrimp dumplings. An extensive a la carte menu also is available. **Bar:** full bar. **Address:** 3446 W Camelback Rd 85017 **Location:** Jct 35th Ave. L D

GREEKFEST   Phone: 602/265-2990   28

Greek
$14-$24

AAA Inspector Notes: Traditional Greek favorites are served in a taverna setting complete with whitewashed walls, arched windows and Greek music. The cheerful spot employs a polished staff. Choose from classic salads, souvlaki and moussaka, and follow your choice with baklava and strong Greek coffee. **Bar:** full bar. **Reservations:** suggested. **Address:** 1940 E Camelback Rd 85016 **Location:** Jct Camelback Rd and 20th St; northwest corner. L D

THE GRIND   Phone: 602/954-7463   44

American
$8-$17

AAA Inspector Notes: Modern and intimate, this gourmet burger joint is the latest addition to trendy eats in the neighborhood. The menu features organic and locally grown ingredients, all coal-fired in custom-made ovens. Try the sweet and spicy burger with candied jalapenos, followed by doughnuts with salted butterscotch. **Bar:** full bar. **Address:** 3961 E Camelback Rd 85018 **Location:** Southwest corner of 40th St and Camelback Rd. L D

HANA JAPANESE EATERY   Phone: 602/973-1238   17

Japanese
$9-$36

AAA Inspector Notes: This cozy spot serves traditional Japanese eats including bento and hibachi as well as fresh sushi. Save room for such desserts as mochi or tempura ice cream. **Address:** 5524 N 7th Ave 85013 **Location:** Jct 7th Ave and Camelback Rd, 0.6 mi n. **Parking:** on-site and street. L D

HARLEY'S ITALIAN BISTRO   Phone: 602/234-0333   43

Italian
$8-$22

AAA Inspector Notes: In a busy commercial area just north of downtown, this bistro presents a menu of such favorites as ravioli, spaghetti bolognese, fettuccine Alfredo, gnocchi and fresh seafood entrées, including sautéed salmon over penne in a light tomato sauce. In the evenings, a good option is New York-style, hand-tossed pizza baked in a brick oven. **Bar:** full bar. **Address:** 4221 N 7th Ave 85013 **Location:** I-10 exit 144, 2.2 mi n. L D

HAVANA CAFE   Phone: 602/952-1991   46

Cuban
$12-$29

AAA Inspector Notes: This small eatery presents a varied menu of Cuban, Spanish and South American dishes. The efficient waitstaff will gladly describe any and all foods. **Bar:** full bar. **Address:** 4225 E Camelback Rd 85018 **Location:** 0.5 mi w of 42nd St. L D

HULA'S MODERN TIKI   Phone: 602/265-8454   25

Polynesian
$8-$24

AAA Inspector Notes: Diners at this hip and fun Polynesian-style joint may start with the poke or the coconut shrimp rolls, then choose from the blackened ahi burger or Hawaiian jerk chicken or pork, and wash it all down with such signature cocktails as a mai tai or zombie. **Bar:** full bar. **Address:** 4700 N Central Ave 85012 **Location:** Jct Camelback Rd, just s. L D

INDIA PALACE   Phone: 602/942-4224   5

Indian
$9-$14

AAA Inspector Notes: Using fresh ingredients and spices, the eatery features such southern Indian foods as karahi chicken, beef or lamb rubbed with special spices and stir-fried with onion and bell pepper. A large selection of vegetarian dishes and tandoori breads are available. **Bar:** full bar. **Address:** 2941 W Bell Rd 85032 **Location:** I-17 exit 212, just w to Holmes Rd; southwest corner. L D

KEEGAN'S GRILL   Phone: 602/955-6616

American
$7-$17

AAA Inspector Notes: Patrons are treated like family in this neighborhood pub, which serves great sandwiches, freshly made soups and the house specialty: tender baby back ribs. **Bar:** full bar. **Address:** 3114 E Camelback Rd 85016 **Location:** Just w of 32nd St. L D

KEEGAN'S GRILL   Phone: 480/705-0505

American
$8-$20

AAA Inspector Notes: This restaurant and grill prepares great food, from soups and hearty sandwiches to barbecue ribs, seafood and steak. Save some room for the delicious desserts, such as the daily changing fruit cobbler. **Bar:** full bar. **Address:** 4723 E Ray Rd 85044 **Location:** I-10 exit 159 (Ray Rd), 0.5 mi w. L D

KITCHEN 56   Phone: 480/994-5656   54

American
$15-$26

AAA Inspector Notes: Casual American comfort food is on the menu at this gathering spot. Enjoy a wide variety of choices including charcuterie boards, pizza, pasta and such entrées as Cabernet-braised short ribs or ahi tuna with eggplant caponata-all while sipping hand-crafted cocktails and conversing with the locals. **Bar:** full bar. **Reservations:** suggested. **Address:** 3433 N 56th St 85018 **Location:** Southeast corner of 56th St and Indian School Rd. L D

(See maps & indexes p. 151, 155, 158, 164.)

LOLA COFFEE
Phone: 602/265-5652 (24)

Coffee/Tea
$2-$5

AAA Inspector Notes: Delectable homemade pastries and savory quiche are the backdrops at this uptown chic coffee house. The real star is the fresh roasted coffee, where every espresso shot is hand-crafted from vintage machines. **Address:** 4700 N Central Ave 85012 **Location:** Jct Camelback Rd, just s. B L D

MACAYO MEXICAN KITCHEN

Mexican
$8-$16

For additional information, visit AAA.com

AAA Inspector Notes: The colorfully furnished Mexican-style eatery prepares Sonoran Mexican dishes. Friendly and efficient staffers serve traditional and lighter dishes flavored with this place's own chili peppers, which are grown near Tucson. **Bar:** full bar. L D

LOCATIONS:
Address: 7829 W Thomas Rd 85033 **Location:** 0.5 mi w of 75th Ave; adjacent to Desert Sky Mall. **Phone:** 623/873-0313
Address: 4001 N Central Ave 85012 **Location:** Just n of Indian School Rd. **Phone:** 602/264-6141
Address: 1909 W Thunderbird Rd 85023 **Location:** I-17 exit 210, 0.5 mi e; jct 19th Ave; southwest corner.
Phone: 602/866-7034
Address: 12637 S 48th St 85044 **Location:** Just s of Warner Rd. **Phone:** 480/598-5101

MAIZIE'S CAFE & BISTRO
Phone: 602/274-2828 (23)

American
$8-$15

AAA Inspector Notes: This urban eatery is located in the uptown district steps from the light rail. The impressive wine list and unique signature cocktails complement eclectic salads, panini, gourmet pizzas and homemade desserts. The weekend brunch is very popular. **Bar:** full bar. **Address:** 4750 N Central Ave 85012 **Location:** Just s of Camelback Rd. L D

MCCORMICK & SCHMICK'S
Phone: 602/468-1200 (37)

Seafood
$14-$40

AAA Inspector Notes: This place is all about seafood, which is imported from all over the world. Among good choices are Washington state oysters, Maine clams, delicate Hawaiian escolar and tuna from Ecuador. The club-like decor is cozy and the staff is attentive. **Bar:** full bar. **Address:** 2575 E Camelback Rd 85016 **Location:** Southeast corner of 24th St and Camelback Rd; in Camelback Esplanade. **Parking:** on-site (fee) and valet. L D

MERITAGE STEAKHOUSE
Phone: 480/293-5000 (3)

American
$24-$55

AAA Inspector Notes: With classic style, the steaks and chops are grilled to perfection and the seafood is delicately sauced. Crisp salads and sides, such as sautéed asparagus and mushrooms, round out a meal served by attentive and courteous staff. **Bar:** full bar. **Reservations:** suggested. **Address:** 5350 E Marriott Dr 85054 **Location:** SR 101 exit 31 (Tatum Blvd), 0.4 mi n to Deer Valley Dr, then 0.5 mi e; in JW Marriott Desert Ridge Resort & Spa. **Parking:** on-site and valet. L D

MI PATIO MEXICAN FOOD
Phone: 602/277-4831 (51)

Mexican
$5-$15

AAA Inspector Notes: Fun and energetic identify the atmosphere at this eatery, while fresh and tasty describe the food. Try such interesting, creative dishes as green corn tamales or carne asada picado burrito with marinated fresh vegetables. **Bar:** full bar. **Address:** 3347 N 7th Ave 85013 **Location:** Southeast corner of Osborn Rd and 7th Ave. L D

MIRACLE MILE DELICATESSEN
Phone: 602/776-0992 (29)

Deli
$7-$13

AAA Inspector Notes: Since 1949, this New York-style deli has served delicious hot pastrami and corned beef sandwiches, along with other delicatessen favorites and daily entrée specials, including stuffed cabbage, homemade meatloaf and chicken noodle casserole. **Bar:** beer & wine. **Address:** 1949 E Camelback Rd 85016 **Location:** Just w of N 20th St; in Camelback Colonnade Shopping Center. L D

MORTON'S THE STEAKHOUSE
Phone: 602/955-9577 (35)

Steak
$29-$53

AAA Inspector Notes: Patrons should make sure to reserve ahead for the popular, well-known steakhouse. Large portions, including huge cuts of fine beef and plentiful seafood, are the norm. Even the vegetables are oversized, with baked potatoes big enough for sharing. **Bar:** full bar. **Reservations:** suggested. **Address:** 2501 E Camelback Rd 85016 **Location:** Southeast corner of Camelback Rd and 24th St. **Parking:** on-site (fee) and valet. D CALL &M

NOCA
Phone: 602/956-6622 (38)

New American
$22-$34

AAA Inspector Notes: Urban and sophisticated, this chic dining spot in the Camelback Corridor features innovative New American cuisine with a constantly changing menu. Specialties include duck confit with huckleberry waffles, and Japanese Wagyu cheesesteak. Homemade desserts are simple and amazing, including the trio of donuts with a malted milkshake. **Bar:** full bar. **Reservations:** suggested. **Address:** 3118 E Camelback Rd 85016 **Location:** Northwest corner of 32nd St and Camelback Rd. D CALL &M

OMAHA STEAKHOUSE
Phone: 602/553-8970 (33)

American
$10-$32

AAA Inspector Notes: This traditional steak house, with an upscale yet casual atmosphere, features certified Midwestern corn-fed beef. Also on the varied menu are pasta, seafood, lamb and pork dishes. After 10 meals, diners have their name engraved on a steak knife that sits in a display case to await their next meal. **Bar:** full bar. **Reservations:** suggested. **Address:** 2630 E Camelback Rd 85020 **Location:** Just n of Camelback Rd, on 26th St; in Embassy Suites Phoenix-Biltmore. L D

OREGANO'S PIZZA BISTRO
Phone: 602/241-0707

Pizza
$6-$23

AAA Inspector Notes: The high-energy eatery, with its young and attentive waitstaff, serves hearty, oversized portions of delicious pizza, salads, pasta and baked sandwiches. When the weather permits, the patio is a happening spot. **Bar:** full bar. **Address:** 1008 E Camelback Rd 85014 **Location:** Just e of 7th St. L D

OVER EASY CAFE
Phone: 602/468-3447 (53)

American
$5-$15

AAA Inspector Notes: On weekends, prepare to wait for a table at this very popular breakfast and lunch spot featuring such comfort foods as chicken fried steak, jalapeno cheddar biscuits with sausage gravy and homemade corned beef hash-all served up in a friendly, retro-style setting. **Address:** 4730 E Indian School Rd 85018 **Location:** Northwest corner of 48th St and Indian School Rd. B L

(See maps & indexes p. 151, 155, 158, 164.)

PADRES MODERN MEXICAN CUISINE **Phone:** 602/277-1749 ㉒

Mexican
$9-$20

AAA Inspector Notes: This intimate dining spot serves up such traditional favorites as enchiladas, tacos and burritos all with a modern twist. Try the mahi mahi tacos with guajillo honey glaze, or the chicken and poblano chiles rellenos, topped with caramelized onion, corn and goat cheese. Enjoy salsa dancing and live music on the weekends. **Bar:** full bar. **Reservations:** required. **Address:** 1044 E Camelback Rd 85014 **Location:** Jct 7th St and Camelback Rd; 0.4 mi e. L D

PANE BIANCO **Phone:** 602/234-2100 ㊵

Specialty
$8-$12

AAA Inspector Notes: This take-out spot offers just a few choices of sandwiches-such as tuna with red onion, gaeta olives and arugula on focaccia-but the quality is excellent. A complimentary mini-dessert is a custom caramel. Imported bottled beverages are available, and specialty food items such as gourmet olive oils and pasta also are available. **Address:** 4404 N Central Ave 85012 **Location:** 0.4 mi n of Indian School Rd.
L D CALL M

PAPPADEAUX SEAFOOD KITCHEN **Phone:** 602/331-3434

Regional Seafood
$12-$24

AAA Inspector Notes: A seafood lover's delight, the restaurant taps into a little bit of New Orleans with its Cajun dishes and elaborate menu selections. Patrons might start off with a creative choice of blackened oyster and shrimp fondeaux with crayfish and let the feast begin. While music plays in the background, patrons can dig into dirty rice or spicy gumbo loaded with seafood. Well-seasoned shrimp and fish are prepared in varied ways. **Bar:** full bar. **Address:** 11051 N Black Canyon Hwy 85029 **Location:** I-17 exit 208 (Peoria Ave), 0.6 mi n on Frontage Rd.
L D

THE PARLOR PIZZERIA **Phone:** 602/248-2480 ㉗

Pizza
$6-$16

AAA Inspector Notes: Housed in a former beauty parlor, this chic spot serves up delicious wood-fired pizza, gourmet salads and sandwiches. **Bar:** full bar. **Address:** 1916 E Camelback Rd 85016 **Location:** Just w of 20th St. L D

PHOENIX CITY GRILLE **Phone:** 602/266-3001 ⑮

American
$9-$31

AAA Inspector Notes: This friendly, comfortable neighborhood place employs capable servers who bring out traditional salads, sandwiches, pasta and chicken. Cedar-plank salmon is a favorite, and mesquite-smoked barbecue back pork ribs are lean and tasty. **Bar:** full bar. **Address:** 5816 N 16th St 85016 **Location:** 0.8 mi n of Camelback Rd. L D

POSTINO WINECAFE **Phone:** 602/852-3939 ㊽

American
$9-$14

AAA Inspector Notes: The light fare served in the recycled post office building incorporates Mediterranean blends and flavors. Including bruschetta toppings of roasted artichoke or ricotta with pistachios. The varied sandwich and salad menu continues through the evening. **Bar:** beer & wine. **Address:** 3939 E Campbell Ave 85018 **Location:** 0.5 mi n of Indian School Rd on 40th St, just w. **Parking:** on-site and valet. L D

QUIESSENCE **Phone:** 602/276-0601 (55)

New American
$20-$30

AAA Inspector Notes: Nestled into the backdrop of the Farm at South Mountain, the handcrafted New American cuisine served here is the real star. With a focus on local, market-fresh ingredients, the menu changes daily and never fails to impress. The farmer's feast is the signature chef's tasting menu and is an excellent way to sample the wide array of choices including handmade tarjine pasta with Florida shrimp, house-smoked meats and seafood, or milk braised ham with butternut mash and fruit compote. **Bar:** full bar. **Reservations:** suggested. **Address:** 6106 S 32nd St 85042 **Location:** I-10 exit 151 (University Dr/32nd St), 1.4 mi s; at Farm at South Mountain. D

RA SUSHI BAR RESTAURANT **Phone:** 480/940-1111 ㉕

Sushi
$8-$20

AAA Inspector Notes: Tucked in a busy shopping center, this upscale sushi bar offers a selection of innovatively designed seafood dishes served by a casual, efficient staff. Try the spinach gyoza to start. To end, the signature tempura cinnamon ice cream will serve three or four folks. **Bar:** full bar. **Address:** 4921 E Ray Rd 85044 **Location:** I-10 exit 159 (Ray Rd), just w.
L D LATE

RICO'S AMERICAN GRILL **Phone:** 602/997-5850 ⑨

American
$11-$29

AAA Inspector Notes: This popular and attractive restaurant offers seasonal patio dining, friendly staff and comfort foods prepared with Southwestern influences. Sharing space on the menu is a variety of fresh salads, seasonal soups, gourmet sandwiches and a variety of dinner entrées. **Bar:** full bar. **Address:** 7677 N 16th St 85020 **Location:** SR 51 exit Glendale Ave, 0.4 mi w, then 0.6 mi n; in Pointe Hilton Squaw Peak Resort.
B L D

RISTORANTE TUSCANY **Phone:** 480/293-3737 ②

Regional Italian
$14-$35

AAA Inspector Notes: Chef Brian Archibald brings a wonderful delicacy to hearty, country-style Tuscan dishes. Guests may sit with a view of the display kitchen during the meal or opt for a table overlooking a lake and distant mountains. **Bar:** full bar. **Reservations:** suggested. **Address:** 5350 E Marriott Dr 85054 **Location:** SR 101 exit 31 (Tatum Blvd), 0.4 mi n to Deer Valley Dr, then 0.5 mi e; in JW Marriott Desert Ridge Resort & Spa. **Parking:** on-site and valet. D CALL M

THE ROKERIJ **Phone:** 602/287-8900 ⑬

Southwestern
$15-$29

AAA Inspector Notes: The name of this eatery means smokehouse in Dutch, but diners can expect delicious grilled steaks, seafood and chicken dishes prepared with a flavorful Southwest flair. If a full meal is not needed, the downstairs grotto bar is a great place to unwind with a cocktail and small plates beside the cozy fireplace. **Bar:** full bar. **Address:** 6335 N 16th St 85016 **Location:** 0.8 mi n of Camelback Rd. L D

ROY'S DESERT RIDGE **Phone:** 480/419-7697 ④

Hawaiian
$20-$30

AAA Inspector Notes: An attractive setting and tropical motif blend well with friendly and attentive service. Widely varied seafood dishes, which change based on availability, are expertly prepared. Examples might include basil-seared ono, herb-crusted yellowtail and butterfish. Chocolate souffle is a house specialty. **Bar:** full bar. **Reservations:** suggested. **Address:** 5350 E Marriott Dr 85054 **Location:** SR 101 exit 31 (Tatum Blvd), 0.4 mi n to Deer Valley Dr, then 0.5 mi e; in JW Marriott Desert Ridge Resort & Spa. **Parking:** on-site and valet. D

(See maps & indexes p. 151, 155, 158, 164.)

RUBIO'S FRESH MEXICAN GRILL

For additional information, visit AAA.com

Mexican
$3-$9

AAA Inspector Notes: Freshly prepared and healthful foods, bright decor and friendly staff are found in this upscale fast-food spot. A special treat, the salsa bar lines up four styles and flavors. **Bar:** beer only. L D

LOCATIONS:
Address: 3009 W Agua Fria Frwy 85053 **Location:** I-17 exit 214A (Yorkshire Dr), 0.4 mi w; in Deer Valley. **Phone:** 623/580-4046

Address: 4340 E Indian School Rd, #1 85018 **Location:** Just w of 44th St. **Phone:** 602/508-1732

Address: 21001 N Tatum Blvd, #341130 85050 **Location:** Just n of SR 101; in Desert Ridge Marketplace. **Phone:** 480/473-9225

Address: 4747 E Bell Rd 85032 **Location:** Jct Tatum Blvd; northeast corner. **Phone:** 602/867-1454

Address: 4905 E Ray Rd 85044 **Location:** I-10 exit 159 (Ray Rd), 0.4 mi w to 48th St, then just s; southeast corner. **Phone:** 480/961-0621

RUFFINO ITALIAN CUISINE
Phone: 480/893-8544 　24

Italian
$8-$33

AAA Inspector Notes: A quiet and relaxing space in a busy city, this restaurant is known for its seafood specialties as well as more traditional dishes such as rigatoni bolognese and veal saltimbocca. **Bar:** full bar. **Reservations:** suggested. **Address:** 4902 E Warner Rd 85044 **Location:** I 10 exit 158, 0.6 mi w. L D

RUSTLER'S ROOSTE
Phone: 602/431-6474 　57

Steak
$15-$31

AAA Inspector Notes: Overlooking the city, this popular Western-style restaurant prepares a nice selection of steak, seafood and barbecue specialties. A band performs nightly. **Bar:** full bar. **Reservations:** suggested. **Address:** 8383 S 48th St 85044 **Location:** I-10 exit 155 (Baseline Rd), just w, then just s; in Arizona Grand Resort. D

ST. FRANCIS
Phone: 602/200-8111 　21

New American
$12-$25

AAA Inspector Notes: Seasonal American fare is served up in a modern chic setting. Patrons can choose from such wood-fired specialties as green chile pork stew and pork chop with fresh corn polenta, sweet peppers and whole grain mustard sauce. Homemade desserts include toffee pudding with sweet cream gelato. **Bar:** full bar. **Address:** 111 E Camelback Rd 85012 **Location:** Jct Central Ave, just e. **Parking:** on-site and valet. L D

SAKANA SUSHI AND GRILL
Phone: 480/598-0506 　22

Sushi
$8-$34

AAA Inspector Notes: One of four locations in the Valley, this restaurant is known for serving the freshest sushi in the area. The menu includes classic sushi and sashimi choices as well as Japanese favorites and full teppanyaki dinners. **Bar:** beer & wine. **Address:** 5061 E Elliot Rd 85044 **Location:** I-10 exit 157 (Elliot Rd), 0.3 mi w; in Ahwatukee Plaza. L D

SAUCE
Phone: 602/216-2400

Italian
$6-$11

AAA Inspector Notes: This restaurant's selections could be characterized as gourmet fast food. Among choices are sausage and caramelized onion or chicken and broccoli rabe pizza. Lasagna and fresh salads also are on the menu. A clean modern decor with indoor seating lends to a fun experience. **Bar:** beer & wine. **Address:** 742 E Glendale Ave 85020 **Location:** Jct 7th St; northeast corner. L D

STINGRAY SUSHI
Phone: 602/955-2008 　32

Sushi
$6-$19

AAA Inspector Notes: Bright colors and lively music set the stage at this sushi spot which attracts a younger, trendy crowd. Diners can enjoy a large selection of sushi, salads, bento and tasty main courses. Creative rolls, including the Godzilla and the lollipop are packed with fresh ingredients and topped with such creative glazes as sweet eel and unagi. **Bar:** full bar. **Address:** 2502 E Camelback Rd 85018 **Location:** Just e of 24th St; in Biltmore Fashion Park. **Parking:** on-site and valet. L D

TARBELL'S
Phone: 602/955-8100 　39

American
$11-$35

AAA Inspector Notes: This lively restaurant's monthly changing selection of creative dishes is complemented with 100 percent organic local produce and a variety of poultry, fish and beef. An open kitchen allows glimpses of the preparation process. The contemporary, simple design with abstract original art gracing the walls makes for a relaxed dining experience. Children are accommodated. The over-size desserts are fit to share with the bread pudding and Kentucky bourbon sauce being a sure winner. **Bar:** full bar. **Reservations:** suggested. **Address:** 3213 E Camelback Rd 85018 **Location:** Just e of 32nd Ave. **Parking:** on-site and valet. D

T-BONE STEAKHOUSE
Phone: 602/276-0945

Steak
$11-$36

AAA Inspector Notes: Friendly staff serves mesquite-broiled steaks and chicken. The dining room and outdoor patio afford panoramic views of the city skyline and Camelback Mountain. **Bar:** full bar. **Address:** 10037 S 19th Ave 85041 **Location:** 1.5 mi s of Baseline Rd. D

T. COOK'S
Phone: 602/808-0766 　49

Mediterranean
$16-$44

AAA Inspector Notes: Accomplished staffers serve a nice selection of Mediterranean entrees, including wood-burning rotisserie items, in elegant surroundings. Patio seating is an option. **Bar:** full bar. **Reservations:** suggested. **Address:** 5200 E Camelback Rd 85018 **Location:** Just e of 52nd St; in Royal Palms Resort and Spa. **Parking:** on-site and valet. B L D

TICOZ RESTO-BAR
Phone: 602/200-0160 　20

Southwestern
$9-$20

AAA Inspector Notes: Modern and lively, this uptown bistro serves a variety of comfort foods with a focus on Southwest flavors and festive cocktails in a casual contemporary setting. **Bar:** full bar. **Address:** 5114 N 7th St 85014 **Location:** Just n of Camelback Rd. L D LATE

TUTTI SANTI RISTORANTE
Phone: 602/216-0336 　10

Italian
$15-$25

AAA Inspector Notes: Vaulted ceilings, large, framed artwork and an outdoor terrace distinguish this family-operated local favorite serving fresh pasta. **Bar:** full bar. **Address:** 7575 N 16th St, Suite 5 85254 **Location:** SR 51 exit 5, just w on Glendale Ave, then 0.5 mi n; in Centre Pointe Shoppes. L D

(See maps & indexes p. 151, 155, 158, 164.)

VINCENT ON CAMELBACK

Phone: 602/224-0225 [42]

French
$26-$36

AAA Inspector Notes: Prepared with a French flair, the fresh seafood, lobster, duck confit, veal, rack of lamb, beef and Cornish hen all are attractively presented at this restaurant. Attentive, accomplished service is achieved in each of several intimate dining rooms, which are surrounded by fresh orchids. **Bar:** full bar. **Reservations:** suggested. **Address:** 3930 E Camelback Rd 85018 **Location:** Just w of 40th St, on north side of Camelback Rd. **Parking:** valet only. [D]

WINDSOR

Phone: 602/279-1111 [19]

American
$9-$15

AAA Inspector Notes: Upscale bar food and specialty cocktails delight the eclectic, lively crowd at this trendy North Central hot spot. Check out the fondue with pulled pork and sausage, the crab cake BLT and the Chicago-style tender belly hot dog. **Bar:** full bar. **Address:** 5223 N Central Ave 85012 **Location:** Jct Camelback Rd and Central Ave; 0.3 mi n. **Parking:** on-site and valet.

[L] [D] CALL

WRIGHT'S

Phone: 602/381-7668 [18]

American
$29-$39

AAA Inspector Notes: Elegant, attentive servers bring eye-pleasing and palate-satisfying dishes that take advantage of seasonally fresh ingredients. Menu selections range from the freshest seafood to aged steaks. The signature chocolate souffle is worth the wait. **Bar:** full bar. **Reservations:** suggested. **Address:** 2400 E Missouri Ave 85016 **Location:** Jct Camelback Rd, 0.5 mi n on 24th St, then 0.4 mi e; in Arizona Biltmore, A Waldorf Astoria Hotel. **Parking:** on-site and valet. [D]

YASU SUSHI BISTRO

Phone: 602/787-9181 [7]

Japanese
$12-$26

AAA Inspector Notes: Classic Japanese preparations at this bistro include abundant sushi selections, tempura and sumibiyaki for delicious grilled meats and seafood. Also, Chef Yasu creates such delectable small plates and entrees as creamy bacon wrapped scallops and homemade grilled chicken meatballs. **Bar:** full bar. **Reservations:** suggested. **Address:** 4316 E Cactus Rd 85032 **Location:** SR 51 exit 10 (Cactus Rd), 1.2 mi e. [D]

PICACHO (E-4) pop. 471, elev. 1,607'

PICACHO PEAK STATE PARK, .5 mi. s. off I-10 exit 219, is the site of Arizona's westernmost Civil War battle. In 1862 a dozen Union soldiers defeated 10 Confederate cavalrymen. The park is home to the 1,500-foot peak that was used as a landmark for settlers traveling between New Mexico and California. The Mormon Battalion constructed the road used by the forty-niners and the Butterfield Overland Stage.

Today trails meander throughout the park and to the top of the peak. A Civil War re-enactment is held each spring. **Hours:** Daily dawn-dusk. **Cost:** $7 (per private vehicle, up to four passengers); $3 (per individual arriving on foot or bicycle). Camping $15-$25. **Phone:** (520) 466-3183.

Senior Mobility Resources at Your Fingertips

AAASeniors.com

Measure Driving Fitness

Extend Safe Driving Years • Get Expert Advice

AAA is Dedicated to Keeping Seniors Driving as Long as Safely Possible

LIFELONG SAFE MOBILITY | AAASeniors.com is part of AAA's Lifelong Safe Mobility Campaign

PINE (D-4) pop. 1,963

PINE-STRAWBERRY MUSEUM is on SR 87 between Hardscrabble Rd. and Randall Dr. The museum houses artifacts from prehistoric Native American cultures and the Spanish, Anglo and Mormon pioneers who first settled the area. Exhibits include World War II memorabilia, farming implements, furnishings and clothing from the late 1800s. **Time:** Allow 1 hour minimum. **Hours:** Mon.-Thurs. 10-2, Fri.-Sat. 10-4, May 15-Oct. 15; Mon.-Sat. 10-2, rest of year. Closed Jan. 1, Easter, Thanksgiving and Christmas. Phone ahead to confirm schedule. **Cost:** Donations. **Phone:** (928) 476-3547.

PINETOP-LAKESIDE (D-5) pop. 4,282, elev. 6,960'
• Restaurants p. 194

Lakeside originally was named Fairview in 1880 by Mormon pioneers. Pinetop, also founded by Mormons, began in 1878 with a sawmill and ranching on the open range of the White Mountains. Before tourism, logging and ranching were the mainstays of the area. The twin towns were incorporated in 1984 as a resort area.

Pinetop-Lakeside, on the edge of the White Mountain Apache Reservation, is 10 miles southeast of Show Low on SR 260 on the edge of Mogollon Rim. The elevation makes the area cool in summer for trout fishing, camping and other activities. Winter sports such as snowmobiling, skiing and ice fishing are popular in the Apache-Sitgreaves National Forests *(see place listing p. 38)* and on the reservation. Fishing also is permitted by fee on the reservation.

Pinetop-Lakeside Chamber of Commerce: 102-C W. White Mountain Blvd. in Lakeside, P.O. Box 4220, Pinetop, AZ 85935. **Phone:** (928) 367-4290 or (800) 573-4031.

GAMBLING ESTABLISHMENTS
• **Hon-Dah Resort Casino and Conference Center,** 3 mi. e. at jct. SRs 260 and 73. **Hours:** Daily 24 hours. **Phone:** (928) 369-0299 or (800) 929-8744. *(See ad this page.)*

BEST WESTERN INN OF PINETOP

Phone: (928)367-6667

Motel $75-$139

AAA Benefit: Members save up to 20%, plus 10% bonus points with Best Western Rewards®.

Address: 404 E White Mountain Blvd 85935 **Location:** On SR 260. Located in Pinetop. **Facility:** 41 units. 2 stories (no elevator), exterior corridors. **Amenities:** *Some:* high-speed Internet. **Activities:** whirlpool. **Guest Services:** coin laundry. **Free Special Amenities: full breakfast and use of on-premises laundry facilities.**

Get pet travel tips and enter the photo contest at AAA.com/PetBook

▼ See AAA listing p. 194 ▼

Hon-Dah Resort Casino & Conference Center

Over 800 Slot Machines, Poker & Blackjack
Restaurant, Hotel, RV Park,
Convenience Store, Ski & Outdoor Shop

1-800-WAY-UP HI
928-369-7600
3 Miles South of Pinetop

FREE WI-FI

WHITE MOUNTAINS AZ

EXECUTIVE INN & SUITES　　Phone: 928/367-4146

Motel
$49-$89

Address: 1023 E White Mountain Blvd 85935 **Location:** On SR 260; east end of town. Located in Pinetop. **Facility:** 24 units. 2 stories (no elevator), exterior corridors. **Activities:** miniature golf.

HOLIDAY INN EXPRESS　　Phone: (928)367-6077

Hotel
$69-$159

Address: 431 E White Mountain Blvd 85935 **Location:** On SR 260. Located in Pinetop. **Facility:** 73 units. 2 stories, interior corridors. **Amenities:** *Some:* high-speed Internet. **Pool(s):** heated indoor. **Activities:** sauna, whirlpool, exercise room. **Guest Services:** coin laundry.

HON-DAH RESORT CASINO & CONFERENCE CENTER　　Phone: 928/369-0299

Hotel
$109-$200

Address: 777 Hwy 260 85935 **Location:** Jct SR 260 and 73; east end of town. Located in White Mountain Apache Reservation of Pinetop. **Facility:** The surrounding acres of wooded reservation, cool weather and outdoor sports are as enticing as the casino and large rooms at this mountain lodge. 128 units. 2 stories, interior corridors. **Terms:** check-in 4 pm. **Dining:** Indian Pine Restaurant, see separate listing, nightclub, entertainment. **Pool(s):** heated outdoor. **Activities:** sauna, whirlpool. *Fee:* game room. **Guest Services:** coin laundry. **Free Special Amenities:** newspaper and high-speed Internet.
(See ad p. 193.)

NORTHWOODS RESORT　　Phone: 928/367-2966

Cottage
Rates not provided

Address: 165 E White Mountain Blvd 85935 **Location:** On SR 260, MM 352. Located in Lakeside. **Facility:** 14 units, some houses and cottages. 1-2 stories, exterior corridors. **Terms:** office hours 9 am-10 pm, check-in 4 pm. **Activities:** whirlpool, hiking trails, playground, basketball, horseshoes, volleyball. **Guest Services:** coin laundry.

Are we meeting your travel needs?

If your visit to an establishment listed in a AAA TourBook guide doesn't meet your expectations, tell us about it.

Complete an easy online form at **AAA.com/TourBookComments.**

SUPER 8　　Phone: (928)367-3161

Hotel
$58-$99

Address: 1202 E White Mountain Blvd 85935 **Location:** On SR 260; east end of town. Located in Pinetop. **Facility:** 42 units. 2 stories (no elevator), interior corridors. **Terms:** cancellation fee imposed. **Pool(s):** heated indoor. **Activities:** whirlpool, limited exercise equipment. **Guest Services:** coin laundry. **Free Special Amenities:** continental breakfast and high-speed internet.

Convenient access to Sunrise Ski Resort, Hon-Dah Casino and the White Mountains.

TIMBERLODGE INN　　Phone: 928/367-4463

Motel
$45-$99

Address: 1078 E White Mountain Blvd 85935 **Location:** On SR 260; east end of town. Located in Pinetop. **Facility:** 29 units. 1-2 stories (no elevator), exterior corridors. **Terms:** office hours 8 am-11 pm, 2 night minimum stay, cancellation fee imposed. **Activities:** horseshoes, volleyball.

WOODLAND INN & SUITES　　Phone: (928)367-3636

Motel
$74-$169

Address: 458 E White Mountain Blvd 85935 **Location:** On SR 260; east end of town. Located in Pinetop. **Facility:** 42 units. 2 stories (no elevator), exterior corridors. **Terms:** 3 day cancellation notice-fee imposed. **Activities:** whirlpool. **Free Special Amenities:** full breakfast and high-speed Internet.

WHERE TO EAT

THE CHALET RESTAURANT & SHARKY'S SUSHI BAR　　Phone: 928/367-1514

American
$8-$23

AAA Inspector Notes: An attractive country decor welcomes guests at this casual restaurant, which appeals to both locals and travelers. The menu has a variety of steak, seafood and chicken selections, and a sushi bar, the only one in the county, is a big hit when open. A kind, efficient staff dons semi-formal, black-and-white uniforms. **Bar:** full bar. **Address:** 348 W White Mountain Blvd 85929 **Location:** On SR 260; in Lakeside. D

CHARLIE CLARK'S STEAK HOUSE　　Phone: 928/367-4900

Steak
$14-$32

AAA Inspector Notes: An informal, Western atmosphere characterizes the popular, long-established restaurant on the city's main thoroughfare. Saddles and chuckwagon-style utensils adorn the dining room, where patrons nosh on prime rib, seafood and mesquite-broiled steak. Lunch is served in the bar and on the patio by friendly staffers. **Bar:** full bar. **Address:** 1701 E White Mountain Blvd 85935 **Location:** On SR 260; east end of town; in Pinetop. L D

DARBI'S CAFE

American
$6-$17

Phone: 928/367-6556

AAA Inspector Notes: This roadside eatery serves specialty hot and cold sandwiches, salads, wraps, pasta plates, burgers, fish and chips, homemade chili con carne, salmon filet, steaks and homemade meatloaf. The friendly staff is a plus. **Address:** 237 E White Mountain Blvd 85935 **Location:** On SR 260; east end of town; in Pinetop. B L D

EL RANCHO RESTAURANT

Mexican
$8-$20

Phone: 928/367-4557

AAA Inspector Notes: The Chavez family recipes go back 60 years, but the friendly staff and owners of today contribute to a pleasant family dining experience. After noshing on traditional dishes, guests can savor flan or churros for dessert. **Bar:** full bar. **Address:** 1523 E White Mountain Blvd 85935 **Location:** On SR 260; in Pinetop. L D

GRUMPY JAKES BBQ & CATERING

Barbecue
$6-$18

Phone: 928/532-2266

AAA Inspector Notes: This small, family-run Western-style restaurant serves such traditional barbecue dishes as chicken, pulled pork and baby-back ribs. There is an all-you-can-eat fish fry every Friday. The service is casual and friendly. **Bar:** beer only. **Address:** 5647 White Mountain Blvd 85929 **Location:** Jct US 260, 4.6 mi s; in Pinetop. L D

INDIAN PINE RESTAURANT

American
$5-$18

Phone: 928/369-7422

AAA Inspector Notes: Located right off the casino floor, this restaurant offers a daily buffet and a full menu of American cuisine. The service is friendly yet very casual. **Bar:** full bar. **Address:** 777 Hwy 260 85935 **Location:** Jct SR 260 and 73; east end of town; in Hon-Dah Resort Casino & Conference Center. B L D

LOS CORRALES

Mexican
$5-$17

Phone: 928/367-5585

AAA Inspector Notes: The bright and lively family place is colorfully decorated in oranges, reds and yellows. Three-dimensional tabletops are sunny and fun. Otherwise ordinary Mexican dishes are alive with freshness and flavor and are presented by a well-groomed waitstaff. **Bar:** full bar. **Address:** 845 E White Mountain Blvd 85935 **Location:** On SR 260; in Pinetop. L D

LOTUS GARDEN

Asian
$5-$15

Phone: 928/367-2568

AAA Inspector Notes: Located in the center of town, this eatery offers a daily choice of a buffet or regular menu. The staff is friendly, helpful and casual. **Bar:** full bar. **Address:** 984 E White Mountain Blvd 85935 **Location:** On SR 260; east end of town; in Pinetop. L D

MOUNTAIN THAI RESTAURANT

Thai
$8-$15

Phone: 928/368-4166

AAA Inspector Notes: In a ramshackle little building not without its charms is this spot serving true Thai cuisine. Noi has brought back authentic recipes from her native Thailand, including delicious yom wun sen, a spicy dish of clear bean thread noodles with cucumbers and cabbage (which tastes better than it sounds!). Delicious soups are made with lemon grass and coconut milk. Everything is homemade, right down to the coconut ice cream. **Bar:** full bar. **Address:** 2741 Hwy 260 85929 **Location:** W on SR 260; in Lakeside. L D

THE PASTA HOUSE

Italian
$12-$23

Phone: 928/367-2782

AAA Inspector Notes: This intimate, cozy eatery features American Italian specialties such as chicken Jerusalem, sorrentino and piccata, scaloppine of veal and jumbo shrimp, linguine with clams in a white or red sauce, shrimp McAngelo with roasted pimentos, shallots and mushrooms and always a daily chef's special. Homemade desserts feature a variety of attractively presented cheesecakes, bananas foster and crème brûlée. A very good selection of wine fills the handsome wine racks. **Bar:** full bar. **Address:** 2188 E White Mountain Blvd 85935 **Location:** On SR 260; east end of town; in Pinetop. D

PIPE SPRING NATIONAL MONUMENT (A-3)

Off SR 389 15 miles west of Fredonia, Pipe Spring National Monument preserves a life-sustaining water source that Paiute Indians called Mu-tum-wa-va, or Dripping Rock. In the early 1870s, Mormon pioneers built a compound over the springs consisting of a sandstone fort and ranch house. Tours of the fort, named Winsor Castle, are offered. Pipe Spring has long served as a way station for weary travelers. The visitor center offers exhibits about Kaibab and pioneer culture and history.

Allow 1 hour minimum. Daily 7-5, June-Aug.; 8-4:30, rest of year. Closed Jan. 1, Thanksgiving and Christmas. Tours of Winsor Castle are given daily on the half-hour. Admission $5, free (ages 0-14). Phone (928) 643-7105.

PORTAL (F-6) elev. 4,773'

Portal received its name because it is at the entrance to Cave Creek Canyon. The town became a popular summer vacation spot for those seeking cool, high altitudes and such recreational pastimes as camping, fishing, hiking and hunting.

CAVE CREEK CANYON, s.w. via a paved road, displays brilliant colors and rugged towering cliffs of red rhyolite rising from the canyon floor. The Southwestern Research Station of the American Museum of Natural History in New York City is at the upper end of the canyon; its laboratories are closed to the public. Bird-watching and hiking opportunities are available. **Hours:** Visitor center open Fri.-Sun. 8:30-4, Memorial Day-Labor Day. **Phone:** (520) 558-2221 or (520) 364-6800.

POSTON (D-1) pop. 285, elev. 335'

The remains of a Japanese-American internment camp as well as a memorial may be found in Poston on Mohave Road. From May 1942 to November 1945, the 17,000-acre camp housed more than 17,000 Japanese-Americans, removed by executive order from California and southern Arizona during World War II.

The Poston Memorial Monument is a 30-foot concrete pillar representing unity of spirit; its hexagonal base represents a Japanese lantern. Twelve small pillars stand in a circle around the monument forming a working sundial. A kiosk, also in the shape of a lantern, holds plaques that relate the story of the camp.

PRESCOTT (C-3) pop. 39,843, elev. 5,346'
• Restaurants p. 198

The area around Prescott was first settled in 1864 by miners prospecting for gold. It was the presence of gold that prompted the cash-poor Union to designate Arizona as a territory in 1863. President Abraham Lincoln chose an area just north of Prescott as the first seat of government because the gold fields were nearby and because Southern sympathizers dominated Tucson. In 1867 the capitol was moved south to Tucson. However, Prescott briefly became capital again in 1877, a title it lost to Phoenix in 1889.

Named to honor historian William Hickling Prescott, the town was incorporated in 1883. Because of the surrounding pine forests, wooden structures rather than the typical adobe buildings were built. Fire devastated Prescott in 1900, but determined townsfolk rebuilt and developed a water system utilizing Del Rio Springs.

Surrounded by mountain ranges and nearly encircled by the Prescott National Forest, the town is now a resort community. Outdoor enthusiasts can indulge in camping, horseback riding, hiking, fishing, rockhounding and picnicking.

Yavapai Downs, 10401 SR 89A, offers Thoroughbred and quarterhorse races Saturday through Tuesday, Memorial Day weekend through Labor Day weekend; closed week of July 4. Phone (928) 775-8000.

Note: Policies concerning admittance of children to pari-mutuel betting facilities vary. Phone for information.

Prescott Chamber of Commerce and Visitor Information Center: 117 W. Goodwin St., Prescott, AZ 86303. **Phone:** (928) 445-2000 or (800) 266-7534.

Self-guiding tours: A leaflet outlining a self-guiding walking tour of Prescott's Victorian-era neighborhoods can be obtained at the chamber of commerce and visitor information center.

Shopping areas: Dillard's, JCPenney and Sears anchor the Prescott Gateway Mall, 3250 Gateway Blvd. near SR 69 and Lee Boulevard. Whiskey Row/Courthouse Square, downtown off SR 89 and Cortez Street, offers antique, souvenir and clothes shopping opportunities as well as several eateries.

BUCKY O'NEILL MONUMENT, on Courthouse Plaza, was created by Solon H. Borglum. It pays tribute to the First U.S. Volunteer Cavalry (Roosevelt's Rough Riders) and Capt. William O'Neill, the first volunteer in the Spanish-American War and organizer of the Rough Riders.

GRANITE BASIN, just inside Prescott National Forest about 12 mi. n.w., is a 7-acre lake lying at the foot of Granite Mountain. A recreation area offers hiking, horse trails and facilities, camping and fishing. **Cost:** Camping $18. **Parking:** Day use $5. **Phone:** (928) 443-8000.

GRANITE DELLS (Point of Rocks), 4 mi. n. on SR 89, is a summer playground on Watson Lake. Picnicking, rock climbing and fishing are popular activities. Granite formations line the highway for 2 miles. Recreational vehicle camping is permitted. **Cost:** Camping fee $28 (1-2 visitors); $3 per each additional visitor. **Phone:** (928) 445-9018.

HERITAGE PARK ZOOLOGICAL SANCTUARY, 6 mi. n. via SR 89, off Willow Creek Rd. in Heritage Park, presents exotic and native wild animals in their natural settings. Guided tours are available by appointment. **Hours:** Daily 9-5 (also Fri.-Sat. 5-8), May-Oct.; 10-4, rest of year. **Cost:** $8; $7 (ages 65+); $5 (ages 3-12). **Phone:** (928) 778-4242.

PHIPPEN MUSEUM—ART AND HERITAGE OF THE AMERICAN WEST, 6 mi. n.e. at 4701 N. SR 89, displays permanent and changing exhibitions by prominent Western artists, together with contemporary artwork depicting the American West. **Time:** Allow 30 minutes minimum. **Hours:** Tues.-Sat. 10-4, Sun. 1-4. **Cost:** $7; free (ages 0-11). **Phone:** (928) 778-1385.

SHARLOT HALL MUSEUM, downtown at 415 W. Gurley St., contains 3.5 acres of exhibits, historic buildings and gardens. The highlight is the Territorial Governor's Mansion, which had been restored by poet and historian Sharlot M. Hall. Hall filled the mansion with Native American and pioneer artifacts and opened it as a museum in 1928. Seven buildings built 1864-1937 and several exhibits trace the heritage of the area.

Also on the grounds are a theater that hosts plays during the summer; herb and rose gardens; and Fort Misery, the first log cabin built in Prescott. The museum contains a library and archives for research.

Time: Allow 1 hour minimum. **Hours:** Mon.-Sat. 10-5, Sun. noon-4, May-Sept.; Mon.-Sat. 10-4, Sun. noon-4, rest of year. Weekend events are held June-Oct.; phone ahead for information. Closed Jan. 1, Thanksgiving and Christmas. **Cost:** $5; free (ages 0-17). **Phone:** (928) 445-3122.

Governor's Mansion, part of the museum complex, was completed in 1864 for John N. Goodwin, Arizona's first territorial governor. The mansion's furnishings and artifacts depict the period 1864-67. The exhibit Behind Whiskey Row tells the story of Prescott's second-class citizens, including its Chinese workers, during the late 1800s.

John C. Frémont House, on the museum grounds, was built in 1875 and served as the home of the celebrated "Pathfinder" during his term as fifth territorial governor of Arizona. The furnishings and artifacts depict the period 1875-81.

William C. Bashford House, part of the museum complex, was built in 1877 and represents the late Victorian style. The home is furnished in period.

SMOKI MUSEUM, n. of Gurley St. at 147 N. Arizona Ave., is patterned after early Pueblo structures both in architecture and interior design. The museum contains art and artifacts pertaining to Native American pre-history, history and modern culture. Ceramics, baskets, beaded ornaments, clothing, jewelry and paintings are among the items displayed. **Hours:** Mon.-Sat. 10-4, Sun. 1-4. Closed Jan. 1-15, Easter, Thanksgiving, Christmas Eve and Christmas. **Cost:** $5; $4 (ages 56+); $3 (students with ID); free (ages 0-12 and Native Americans). **Phone:** (928) 445-1230.

THUMB BUTTE, 4 mi. w., is a rugged outcropping of granite. Extensive views are offered from the summit, which can be reached on foot. **Cost:** Free. **Parking:** $5. **Phone:** (928) 443-8000. 🎡

GAMBLING ESTABLISHMENTS

- **Bucky's Casino,** in the Prescott Resort at 1500 E. SR 69, just e. of jct. SR 89. **Hours:** Daily 24 hours. **Phone:** (928) 776-5695 or (800) 756-8744.

AMERICAS BEST VALUE INN   **Phone:** (928)776-1282

Motel
$60-$120

Address: 1105 E Sheldon St 86301 **Location:** 0.4 mi e of jct SR 89. **Facility:** 69 units. 2 stories (no elevator), interior corridors. **Amenities:** high-speed Internet, safes (fee). **Pool(s):** heated outdoor. **Guest Services:** coin laundry.

BEST WESTERN PRESCOTTONIAN
          Phone: (928)445-3096

Motel
$80-$130

AAA Benefit: Members save up to 20%, plus 10% bonus points with Best Western Rewards®.

Address: 1317 E Gurley St 86301 **Location:** On SR 89, just s of jct SR 69. **Facility:** 121 units, some two bedrooms. 2-3 stories (no elevator), exterior corridors. **Amenities:** Some: high-speed Internet. **Pool(s):** heated outdoor. **Activities:** whirlpool. **Guest Services:** valet and coin laundry. **Free Special Amenities: expanded continental breakfast and high-speed Internet.**

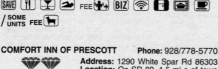

COMFORT INN OF PRESCOTT   **Phone:** 928/778-5770

Motel
Rates not provided

Address: 1290 White Spar Rd 86303 **Location:** On SR 89, 1.5 mi s of town center. **Facility:** 61 units, some efficiencies. 2 stories (no elevator), exterior corridors. **Amenities:** safes (fee). Some: high-speed Internet. **Activities:** whirlpool. **Guest Services:** coin laundry. **Free Special Amenities: full breakfast and high-speed Internet.**

Learn about
AAA/CAA Diamond Ratings
at AAA.com/Diamonds

FOREST VILLAS HOTEL   **Phone:** (928)717-1200

Hotel
$87-$109

Address: 3645 Lee Cir 86301 **Location:** Jct SR 69, just n on Lee Blvd, then just e. **Facility:** 62 units. 2 stories, interior corridors. **Amenities:** high-speed Internet. **Pool(s):** heated outdoor. **Activities:** whirlpool, exercise room. **Guest Services:** valet and coin laundry. **Free Special Amenities: full breakfast and high-speed Internet.**

HAMPTON INN PRESCOTT   **Phone:** (928)443-5500

Hotel
$89-$169

AAA Benefit: Members save up to 10% everyday!

Address: 3453 Ranch Dr 86303 **Location:** Jct SR 69 and Lee Blvd, just s. **Facility:** 76 units. 3 stories, interior corridors. **Terms:** 1-7 night minimum stay, cancellation fee imposed. **Pool(s):** heated indoor. **Activities:** whirlpool, hiking trails, exercise room. **Guest Services:** valet and coin laundry. **Free Special Amenities: full breakfast and high-speed Internet.**

HASSAYAMPA INN   **Phone:** (928)778-9434

Historic Hotel
$89-$219

Address: 122 E Gurley St 86301 **Location:** Jct Marina St; downtown. **Facility:** Guests enjoy the charm of yesteryear at this 1927 historic inn with its cozy rooms, beamed lobby ceiling and original manual elevator. 67 units. 3 stories, interior corridors. **Terms:** cancellation fee imposed. **Dining:** Peacock Room, see separate listing. **Activities:** exercise room. **Guest Services:** valet laundry.

HOLIDAY INN EXPRESS PRESCOTT
          Phone: (928)445-8900

Hotel
$79-$159

Address: 3454 Ranch Dr 86303 **Location:** Jct SR 69 and Lee Blvd, just s. **Facility:** 76 units. 3 stories, interior corridors. **Terms:** cancellation fee imposed. **Amenities:** Some: high-speed Internet. **Pool(s):** heated indoor. **Activities:** sauna, whirlpool, exercise room. **Guest Services:** valet and coin laundry.

HOTEL ST. MICHAEL   **Phone:** (928)776-1999

Historic Hotel
$79-$129

Address: 205 W Gurley St 86301 **Location:** Center; across from Courthouse Plaza. **Facility:** This historic building is filled with charm and offers pleasant guest rooms and modern baths. 72 units. 2 stories, interior corridors. **Terms:** 2 night minimum stay - seasonal and/or weekends. **Amenities:** Some: high-speed Internet. **Dining:** Bistro St. Michael, see separate listing.

HOTEL VENDOME   **Phone:** 928/776-0900

Historic Hotel
$69-$139

Address: 230 S Cortez St 86303 **Location:** S of Gurley St; downtown. **Facility:** This small 1880s historic hotel is a short distance from Courthouse Square and has two porches where guests can relax and watch passersby. 20 units. 2 stories (no elevator), interior corridors. **Terms:** office hours 7 am-10 pm, cancellation fee imposed.

MOTEL 6 #0166

Phone: (928)776-0160

▼◆▼
Motel
$55-$65 5/27-1/31
$45-$55 2/1-5/26

Address: 1111 E Sheldon St 86301 **Location:** 0.4 mi e of jct SR 89; center. **Facility:** 79 units. 2 stories (no elevator), exterior corridors. *Bath:* shower only. **Pool(s):** heated outdoor. **Guest Services:** coin laundry.

[icons]

PLEASANT STREET INN BED & BREAKFAST

Phone: 928/445-4774

▼◆▼◆▼
Bed & Breakfast
$130-$185

Address: 142 S Pleasant St 86303 **Location:** Just s of Gurley St; downtown. **Facility:** Built in 1906 and renovated in '91, the two-story Victorian house offers a pleasant stay just three blocks from Courthouse Plaza. 4 units. 2 stories (no elevator), interior corridors. **Parking:** street only. **Terms:** age restrictions may apply, 7 day cancellation notice-fee imposed.

[icons]

PRESCOTT CABIN RENTALS- LYNX CREEK FARM

Phone: 928/778-9573

▼◆▼
Cabin
$99-$219

Address: 5555 Onyx Dr 86303 **Location:** Jct SR 89, 5 mi e on SR 69, 0.4 mi s on dirt/gravel road. Located in a quiet rural area. **Facility:** 8 units, some kitchens and cottages. 1 story, exterior corridors. **Terms:** office hours 8 am-8 pm, off-site registration, check-in 4 pm, 2 night minimum stay - weekends, 31 day cancellation notice-fee imposed. **Activities:** hiking trails, playground, horseshoes.

[icons]

PRESCOTT PINES INN BED & BREAKFAST

Phone: 928/445-7270

▼◆▼
Bed & Breakfast
$100-$150

Address: 901 White Spar Rd 86303 **Location:** 1.3 mi s on Montezuma St. **Facility:** 11 units. 1 story, exterior corridors. **Terms:** 7 day cancellation notice-fee imposed.

[icons]

PRESCOTT RESORT & CONFERENCE CENTER

Phone: 928/776-1666

▼◆▼◆▼
Hotel
Rates not provided

Address: 1500 Hwy 69 86301 **Location:** Jct SR 69, just e. **Facility:** 160 units. 5 stories, interior corridors. **Amenities:** high-speed Internet, safes. **Dining:** 2 restaurants. **Pool(s):** heated indoor. **Activities:** sauna, whirlpool, exercise room, spa. **Guest Services:** valet laundry. **Free Special Amenities:** local telephone calls and high-speed Internet.

[icons]

RESIDENCE INN BY MARRIOTT

Phone: (928)775-2232

▼◆▼◆▼
Extended Stay Hotel
$99-$189

AAA Benefit:
AAA hotel discounts of 5% or more.

Address: 3599 Lee Cir 86301 **Location:** Jct SR 69, just n on Lee Blvd, then just e. **Facility:** 92 units, some two bedrooms, efficiencies and kitchens. 3 stories, interior corridors. **Amenities:** high-speed Internet. **Pool(s):** heated outdoor. **Activities:** whirlpools, sports court, exercise room. **Guest Services:** valet and coin laundry.

[icons]

SPRINGHILL SUITES BY MARRIOTT

Phone: (928)776-0998

▼◆▼◆▼
Hotel
$99-$189

AAA Benefit:
AAA hotel discounts of 5% or more.

Address: 200 E Sheldon St 86301 **Location:** On SR 89; at Marina St. **Facility:** 105 units. 3 stories, interior corridors. **Pool(s):** heated indoor. **Activities:** whirlpool, exercise room. **Guest Services:** valet and coin laundry.

[icons]

WYNDHAM GARDEN HOTEL PRESCOTT

Phone: 928/777-0770

▼◆▼◆▼
Hotel
Rates not provided

Address: 4499 E SR 69 86301 **Location:** On SR 69, 3.6 mi e of jct SR 89. **Facility:** 82 units. 2 stories, interior corridors. **Amenities:** high-speed Internet, safes. **Pool(s):** heated indoor. **Activities:** whirlpool, hiking trails, exercise room. **Guest Services:** valet and coin laundry.

[icons]

WHERE TO EAT

129 1/2 AN AMERICAN JAZZ GRILLE

Phone: 928/443-9292

▼◆▼◆▼
American
$8-$27

AAA Inspector Notes: The place for live jazz, this restaurant has some enticing specials such as chili shrimp and barbecue red snapper. Four sauce choices provide guests with creative options. **Bar:** full bar. **Address:** 129 1/2 N Cortez St 86301 **Location:** Just n of Gurley St. **Parking:** street only. [D]

BISTRO ST. MICHAEL

Phone: 928/776-1999

▼◆▼
American
$6-$15

AAA Inspector Notes: Contemporary American cuisine is served at this restored 1901 bistro. The service is friendly and a small bar offers gourmet coffee, beer and wine. **Bar:** beer & wine. **Address:** 205 W Gurley St 86301 **Location:** Center; across from Courthouse Plaza; in Hotel St. Michael. **Parking:** street only. **Historic**

[B] [L] [D]

EL GATO AZUL

Phone: 928/445-1070

▼◆▼
Mediterranean
$8-$20

AAA Inspector Notes: Enjoy leisurely lunches by the creek or cozy patio or terrace dining at this eatery. Rotating tapas and wine selections in late afternoon and nightly features are available. **Bar:** full bar. **Address:** 316 W Goodwin St 86303 **Location:** Just e of Granite St. **Parking:** street only. [L] [D]

FIREHOUSE KITCHEN

Phone: 928/776-4566

▼◆▼
American
$9-$24

AAA Inspector Notes: The small dining room of this eatery offers fun-favorites with such homemade items as St. Louis pork ribs, macaroni and cheese, cheese tortellini, buttermilk fried chicken, and a must have s'mores dessert. Guests also can enjoy a more casual feel in the upstairs bar area. **Bar:** full bar. **Address:** 218 W Goodwin St 86303 **Location:** Just w of Montezuma St. **Parking:** street only. [L] [D]

Check out
our travel blog at
AAATravelViews.com

GENOVESE'S   Phone: 928/541-9089

Italian
$7-$25

AAA Inspector Notes: Just around the corner from the park is a charmingly decorated Italian bistro where attentive staff members assist you through a meal that might include eggplant Milanese or chicken parmigiana. Hand-rolled pizza, calzones and panini attract those with a lighter appetite. **Bar:** full bar. **Address:** 217 W Gurley St 86301 **Location:** Just w of SR 89; center. **Parking:** street only. L D

GURLEY ST. GRILL   Phone: 928/445-3388

American
$7-$20

AAA Inspector Notes: Dine in the lively atmosphere of a restored, 1901 red brick building. Pizza, burgers, steak, pasta, seafood and spit-roasted chicken are menu highlights. **Bar:** full bar. **Address:** 230 W Gurley St 86301 **Location:** Just w of SR 89. **Parking:** street only.

L D

MACAYO MEXICAN KITCHEN   Phone: 928/776-7711

Mexican
$8-$16

AAA Inspector Notes: The colorfully furnished Mexican-style eatery prepares Sonoran Mexican dishes. Friendly and efficient staffers serve traditional and lighter dishes flavored with this place's own chili peppers, which are grown near Tucson. **Bar:** full bar. **Address:** 3250 Gateway Blvd, #516 86303 **Location:** In Prescott Gateway Mall. L D

MONK'S   Phone: 928/443-8587

Italian
$6-$15

AAA Inspector Notes: This contemporary restaurant serves casual and basic items such as sandwiches, calzones and pizza in a fun and loud atmosphere. The happy hour is very popular at the small bar open to the dining room. **Bar:** full bar. **Address:** 123 N Cortez St 86301 **Location:** Jct Gurley St, just n; downtown. **Parking:** street only. B L D

MURPHY'S RESTAURANT   Phone: 928/445-4044

American
$9-$46

AAA Inspector Notes: Restored to depict the era in which it was built, the historic 1890 mercantile now accommodates this restaurant, which serves mesquite-broiled seafood, steak and prime rib. Breads are baked daily on the premises. The pleasant waitstaff guide patrons through your casual dining experience. **Bar:** full bar. **Reservations:** suggested. **Address:** 201 N Cortez St 86301 **Location:** Downtown. **Parking:** street only. **Historic** L D

THE OFFICE RESTAURANT & BAR   Phone: 928/445-1211

Southwestern
$7-$16

AAA Inspector Notes: Patrons will not fool anyone by saying, "I'm going to the office," but they will find a nice selection of Southwestern dishes, including tortilla soup thick with chicken, and burgers with toppings from caramelized onions to green chiles. The warm cookie dessert is too tempting to share. **Bar:** full bar. **Address:** 128 N Cortez St 86301 **Location:** Just n of Gurley St; center. **Parking:** street only. L D

THE PALACE RESTAURANT AND SALOON   Phone: 928/541-1996

American
$8-$29

AAA Inspector Notes: Guests can enjoy casual, relaxed dining in Arizona's oldest bar and amid a restored 1880s decor. **Bar:** full bar. **Address:** 120 S Montezuma St 86301 **Location:** Just s of Gurley St; downtown. **Parking:** street only. **Historic** L D

PAPA'S ITALIAN RESTAURANT   Phone: 928/776-4880

Italian
$10-$15

AAA Inspector Notes: This family-run restaurant serves classic Italian favorites, many made from great family recipes. The dining room is small but comfortable and quaint. **Bar:** beer & wine. **Address:** 1124 White Spar Rd 86303 **Location:** On SR 89, 1.3 mi s of town center. D

PEACOCK ROOM   Phone: 928/778-9434

American
$8-$32

AAA Inspector Notes: Located in a historic 1927 hotel, this elegant dining room is named for what was once a brightly colored tile wall entry called Peacock Alley. The sophisticated menu lists pasta, steak, seafood and veal dishes, in addition to other specialties. **Bar:** full bar. **Reservations:** suggested. **Address:** 122 E Gurley St 86301 **Location:** Jct Marina St; downtown; in Hassayampa Inn. **Historic** B L D

PRESCOTT BREWING COMPANY   Phone: 928/771-2795

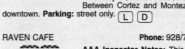

American
$7-$19

AAA Inspector Notes: An on-site brewery and in-house bakery are among offerings at this casual restaurant. **Bar:** full bar. **Address:** 130 W Gurley St, Suite A 86301 **Location:** Between Cortez and Montezuma sts; downtown. **Parking:** street only. L D

RAVEN CAFE   Phone: 928/717-0009

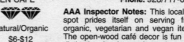

Natural/Organic
$6-$12

AAA Inspector Notes: This local hot spot prides itself on serving fresh organic, vegetarian and vegan items. The open-wood café decor is fun with distinctive local art along the walls. There are some self service aspects but the servers are very friendly and eager to please in this bustling atmosphere. **Bar:** beer & wine. **Address:** 142 N Cortez St 86301 **Location:** Jct Willis St; downtown. **Parking:** street only. B L D

THE ROSE RESTAURANT   Phone: 928/777-8308

Continental
$20-$38

AAA Inspector Notes: A restored, circa 1890s house is the setting for intimate dining. The home's original rooms now serve as dining spaces opening into one another; patio dining is available in season. The menu blends an excellent selection of beef, pasta, veal, chicken and vegetarian entrées with distinctive sauces and seasonings. **Bar:** full bar. **Reservations:** suggested. **Address:** 234 S Cortez St 86303 **Location:** Just s of Gurley St. **Historic** D

TAJ MAHAL   Phone: 928/445-5752

Northern Indian
$12-$19

AAA Inspector Notes: North Indian dishes, such as chicken tikka and lamb madras are on the menu, as well as tandoori, curry and other traditional selections. A vegan buffet is available on Wednesday evenings. Entertainment of live ethnic music and belly dancing often is scheduled. **Bar:** full bar. **Address:** 124 N Montezuma St 86301 **Location:** Jct Gurley St, just n; center. L D

ZEKE'S EATIN' PLACE   Phone: 928/776-4602

American
$5-$11

AAA Inspector Notes: A popular stop with locals for a hearty breakfast or lunch, this casual spot is known for its ample portions. The omelets and breakfast burritos will carry you through a long morning of work or touring. Its many movie posters feature famous Western actors. **Address:** 1781 E Hwy 69, #35 86301 **Location:** On SR 69, 1.2 mi e; in Frontier Village Center. B L

PRESCOTT NATIONAL FOREST (C-3)

Elevations in the forest range from 3,071 ft. in the Verde Valley to 7,971 ft. at Mount Union. Refer to AAA maps for additional elevation information.

Accessed via SR 89, SR 89A and SR 69 off I-17 in central Arizona, Prescott National Forest encompasses two long mountain ranges with varying elevations. In addition to its major access routes, other scenic but primitive roads not recommended for low-clearance vehicles penetrate the 1,238,154-acre forest. Phone ahead for current road condition updates.

Developed recreation areas are at Mingus Mountain and in Prescott Basin. Camping, picnicking, hiking and backpacking are popular recreational pursuits; many trails can be enjoyed year-round. Some popular day-use areas in Prescott have a $5 parking fee. Hunting is permitted in season with the appropriate state game license obtained from the Game and Fish Department; phone (928) 692-7700.

For further information contact Prescott National Forest, 344 S. Cortez St., Prescott, AZ 86303; phone (928) 443-8000 Mon.-Fri. 8-4:30. *See Recreation Chart.*

PRESCOTT VALLEY pop. 38,822

AMERICAS BEST VALUE INN   Phone: (928)772-2200

♦♦♦ ♦♦♦
Hotel
$59-$155

Address: 8383 E SR 69 86314 **Location:** On SR 69, just w of N Navajo Dr. **Facility:** 50 units. 2 stories (no elevator), interior corridors. **Pool(s):** heated indoor. **Activities:** whirlpool. **Guest Services:** coin laundry. **Free Special Amenities:** continental breakfast and high-speed Internet.

SAVE ⊇ BIZ 🛜 🔋 🖥 💻 / SOME UNITS FEE 🐾

COMFORT SUITES PRESCOTT VALLEY
Phone: (928)771-2100

♦♦♦ ♦♦♦
Hotel
$89-$150

Address: 2601 N Crownpointe Dr 86314 **Location:** Just w on SR 69, then n on Market St. **Facility:** 100 units. 4 stories, interior corridors. **Terms:** cancellation fee imposed. **Amenities:** high-speed Internet. **Pool(s):** heated outdoor. **Activities:** whirlpool, exercise room. **Guest Services:** valet and coin laundry. **Free Special Amenities: expanded continental breakfast and high-speed Internet.**

SAVE CALL 🄶M ⊇ BIZ 🛜 ✕ 🔋 🖥 💻 / SOME UNITS FEE 🐾

DAYS INN/PRESCOTT VALLEY   Phone: (928)772-8600

♦♦♦ ♦♦♦
Hotel
$45-$88

Address: 7875 E Hwy 69 86314 **Location:** On SR 69; corner of Windsong Rd. **Facility:** 78 units. 2 stories (no elevator), exterior corridors. **Pool(s):** heated outdoor. **Activities:** whirlpool. **Guest Services:** coin laundry.

🍽+ ⊇ BIZ 🛜 🔋 🖥 💻 / SOME UNITS 🐾

SUPER 8   Phone: (928)775-5888

♦♦♦ ♦♦♦
Hotel
$58-$108

Address: 7801 E SR 69 86314 **Location:** 0.4 mi w of Robert Rd. **Facility:** 54 units. 2 stories (no elevator), interior corridors. **Terms:** cancellation fee imposed. **Pool(s):** heated outdoor. **Guest Services:** coin laundry.

SAVE 🍽+ ⊇ BIZ 🛜 🔋 🖥 💻

WHERE TO EAT

GARCIA'S MEXICAN RESTAURANT
Phone: 928/759-9499

♦♦♦ ♦♦♦
Mexican
$7-$15

AAA Inspector Notes: The eatery serves classic preparations of all the favorites, including fajitas, burritos and tacos. The chicken enchilada with sour cream is excellent. Also on the menu are some lighter options. **Bar:** full bar. **Address:** 2992 Park Ave, Suite B 86314 **Location:** Jct SR 69, just n on Centre Ct, then just e; behind theater.

L D 🍸

TARA THAI 2 CUISINE   Phone: 928/772-3249

♦♦♦ ♦♦♦
Thai
$8-$17

AAA Inspector Notes: Fresh, cooked-to-order food makes up the menu at this modest eatery. Widely varied curries and specialties come with fragrantly scented rice and crispy vegetables. Homemade ice cream is a perfect end to the meal. **Bar:** beer & wine. **Address:** 6170 E State Rt 69, Suite 100 86314 **Location:** Just w of Prescott Hwy; west side of town. L D

ZEKE'S EATIN' PLACE   Phone: 928/775-9832

♦♦♦ ♦♦♦
American
$5-$25

AAA Inspector Notes: Given the ample portion sizes, guests must be mindful of how much of the entree they eat if they want to try the six-layer carrot or chocolate cakes. Such dishes as country-fried steak with mashed potatoes are sure to fill. **Bar:** full bar. **Address:** 2960 N Centre Ct 86314 **Location:** Jct SR 69, just n; across from movie theater. B L D

PRESIDIO SANTA CRUZ DE TERRENATE NATIONAL HISTORIC SITE (F-5)

Presidio Santa Cruz de Terrenate National Historic Site is 4 miles north of Tombstone on SR 80, 6 miles west on SR 82 to Fairbank, .75 miles west to In Balance Ranch Road, then 2 miles north in the San Pedro Riparian National Conservation Area. Established by the Spanish in 1776 on the banks of the San Pedro River, the presidio was built to protect the overland route east of Tucson. Because of the frequent Apache raids as well as the lack of proper supplies, Terrenate was abandoned less than 5 years after its establishment.

The site, once consisting of seven structures built around a central courtyard, contains signs showing what each of the structures originally looked like. Many of the adobe walls that surrounded the presidio are eroded and only a few remain. They were planned to be 15 feet tall, but were built to only 12 feet due to lack of funds. In addition, the bastion/gunpowder storehouse was never completed, and less than one-fourth of the planned barracks were never constructed because of insufficient funding.

The historic site is fragile, and visitors are instructed by signs to stay on the trails and not to touch the remaining structures. A 1.2-mile dirt trail leads from the parking lot to the presidio. Camping is permitted. Visitors should bring their own food and water as no facilities are available. Site admission free. Camping $2 per person per night. Phone (520) 439-6400.

QUARTZSITE (D-1) pop. 3,677, elev. 876'

A settler named Charles Tyson built a fort on this site in 1856 for protection against Native Americans. Because of a good water supply it soon became a stagecoach stop on the Ehrenburg-to-Prescott route. As the stage lines vanished, Fort Tyson, or Tyson's Wells (as it became known), was abandoned. A small mining boom in 1897 revitalized the area, and the settlement revived as Quartzsite.

The winter population of this desert town swells to 1 million during January and February because of the gem and mineral shows in the area. The Pow Wow Rock and Mineral Show began the rockhound winter migration to town in 1965; now eight major shows entice gem enthusiasts, collectors and jewelers to Quartzsite to buy and sell. In an event that has attained international scope, thousands of dealers offer raw and handcrafted merchandise throughout January and February.

Quartzsite Tourism Bureau: P.O. Box 85, Quartzsite, AZ 85346. **Phone:** (928) 916-1090.

HI JOLLY MEMORIAL, e. on I-10 in the old cemetery, honors Hadji Ali. Nicknamed Hi Jolly by soldiers and pioneers, the Arab came to Arizona in 1856 with an Army consignment of camels. The camels adapted well to their new environment but were never used successfully, partly because the sight of them caused horses, mules and cattle to stampede.

SUPER 8-QUARTZSITE   **Phone:** (928)927-8080

Motel
$72-$117

Address: 2050 Dome Rock Rd 85359 **Location:** I-10 exit 17, just s to Frontage Rd, then 0.6 mi w. **Facility:** 51 units. 2 stories (no elevator), interior corridors. **Terms:** 14 day cancellation notice-fee imposed. **Guest Services:** coin laundry.

QUEEN CREEK pop. 26,361

• Part of Phoenix area — see map p. 134

SERRANO'S MEXICAN RESTAURANT
    Phone: 480/987-0192

Mexican
$8-$15

AAA Inspector Notes: A pleasant stop for lunch or dinner, the local chain is known for consistently good food and attractive, upscale Mexican-style décor. The warm bean dip starter stirs the appetite for traditional dishes such as chiles rellenos or seafood enchiladas prepared with fresh ingredients. Service is friendly. **Address:** 22703 S Ellsworth Rd 85242 **Location:** SR 202 exit 36, s to E Ocotillo Rd, then just s. [L] [D]

RIO RICO pop. 18,962

ESPLENDOR RESORT AT RIO RICO
    Phone: (520)281-1901

Resort Hotel
$99-$249

Address: 1069 Camino Caralampi 85648 **Location:** I-19 exit 17 (Rio Rico Dr), just w to Camino Caralampi, then just s. Located in a quiet area. **Facility:** Overlooking the Santa Cruz River Valley, the resort blends old Southwest-style with modern conveniences. 179 units. 2-3 stories (no elevator), exterior corridors. **Amenities:** video games (fee). **Dining:** San Cayetano, see separate listing. **Pool(s):** heated outdoor. **Activities:** sauna, whirlpool, 4 lighted tennis courts, hiking trails, exercise room. **Fee:** golf-18 holes, massage. **Guest Services:** valet and coin laundry, area transportation-golf course. Affiliated with A Preferred Hotel.
(See ad p. 295.)

WHERE TO EAT

SAN CAYETANO   **Phone:** 520/281-1901

Regional American
$9-$25

AAA Inspector Notes: Diners appreciate the casual atmosphere and stunning views across the valley to the mountains beyond. Specialties include steaks, seafood, sandwiches and soups. **Bar:** full bar. **Reservations:** suggested. **Address:** 1069 Camino Caralampi 85648 **Location:** I-19 exit 17 (Rio Rico Dr), just w to Camino Caralampi, then just s; in Esplendor Resort at Rio Rico. [B] [L] [D]

ROOSEVELT (I-6) pop. 28, elev. 2,215'

THEODORE ROOSEVELT DAM AND LAKE is reached via SR 188 or SR 88 (the Apache Trail), a dirt road. Natives A.D. 1000 built 150 miles of stone-lined canals to irrigate their fields. Modern Arizona's reclamation of the Salt River Valley began with the completion of the Roosevelt Dam in 1911. Unlike other dams, the Roosevelt was made with thousands of hand-hewn stones.

As the first major federal reclamation project, the dam provides water and power to one of the state's richest agricultural regions. Many recreational opportunities are available on the lake. *See Recreation Chart.* **Cost:** $6 per motorized vehicle; $4 per boat. **Phone:** (928) 467-3200.

SACATON (E-4) pop. 2,672, elev. 1,127'

Sacaton, first visited by Spanish missionaries in 1696, was even then an ancient Pima Indian settlement; currently the town is the headquarters for the Pima Reservation. American pioneers noted the abundance of very tall grass, from which they derived the town name.

Japanese-American internment camp memorials and their sites may be found 9 miles west of Sacaton on Gila River Indian Tribal land. From July 1942 to November 1945, the 17,000-acre Gila River

Explore the Travel Guides
on AAA.com/Travel or
CAA.ca/Travel

Relocation Center housed more than 13,000 Japanese-Americans, removed by executive order from California during World War II. The center consisted of two camps named Butte and Canal. Today, memorial markers and concrete slab foundations are basically all that remain of the camps.

The Butte Camp markers are near a monument that lists the Japanese-American soldiers killed in World War II. The Canal Camp marker includes a map, photograph and descriptive information. Visitors must obtain a permit from the Gila River Indian Tribe to visit the sites.

SAFFORD (E-6) pop. 9,566, elev. 2,920'

The first American colony in the Gila Valley, Safford was founded in 1874 by farmers whose previous holdings had been washed away by the Gila River. From Safford the Swift Trail winds 36 miles to the top of 10,720-foot Mount Graham. En route the trail traverses five of the seven ecological zones in Western North America. Camping, hiking and picnicking are permitted. Gila Box Riparian National Conservation Area, 15 miles northeast, offers seasonal river floating opportunities.

The region south of Safford is known for its hot mineral water baths. Information about area spas is available from the chamber of commerce.

For seekers of fire agates and other semiprecious stones, there are two rockhound areas administered and maintained by the U.S. Bureau of Land Management. Black Hills Back Country Byway is a 21-mile scenic drive through the Black Hills. The drive is a graded dirt road with sharp turns and steep drops.

Round Mountain Rockhound Area, featuring chalcedony roses and fire agates, is 12 miles south of Duncan on US 70, west at Milepost 5.6, 7.1 miles to the BLM sign, then 2.5 miles south to the first collection area. A second collection area is 4.5 miles south using the left fork in the road. **Note:** The road is not maintained and is very rough. Because of the area's remote location, visitors should bring along plenty of water and gasoline. Phone ahead for road conditions. Information about these areas can be obtained by contacting the Bureau of Land Management, 711 14th Ave., Safford, AZ 85546; phone (928) 348-4400.

Graham County Chamber of Commerce: 1111 Thatcher Blvd., Safford, AZ 85546. **Phone:** (928) 428-2511 or (888) 837-1841.

EASTERN ARIZONA COLLEGE DISCOVERY PARK CAMPUS is at 1651 W. Discovery Park Blvd. Located at the base of Mount Graham, this site offers both nature and science enthusiasts an interactive experience. Trail paths with viewing areas feature diverse wildlife and ponds while the Gov Aker Observatory contains exhibits relating to time and space. **Note:** Rattlesnakes and Gila monsters roam the trails; use caution when walking. **Time:** Allow 30 minutes minimum. **Hours:** Mon.-Fri. 8-4.

Closed major holidays. **Cost:** Free. **Phone:** (928) 428-6260.

ROPER LAKE STATE PARK, 1 mi. s. off US 191, is at the base of Mount Graham. A great place to hike, camp, swim and picnic, this park features a rock-lined pool filled with water from the natural mineral hot springs. *See Recreation Chart.* **Hours:** Daily 6 a.m.-10 p.m. Phone ahead to confirm schedule. **Cost:** $7 (per private vehicle, up to four adult passengers); $3 (per additional adult passenger in vehicle or individual arriving on foot or bicycle). Camping $15-$23 (per private vehicle). Cabins $55. Reservations for camping are required 2 weeks in advance. **Phone:** (928) 428-6760.

BEST WESTERN DESERT INN   **Phone:** (928)428-0521

Motel
$75-$85

AAA Benefit: Members save up to 20%, plus 10% bonus points with Best Western Rewards®.

Address: 1391 W Thatcher Blvd 85546 **Location:** US 191, 1 mi w on US 70. **Facility:** 66 units, some efficiencies. 2 stories (no elevator), exterior corridors. **Pool(s):** outdoor. **Guest Services:** coin laundry. **Free Special Amenities:** full breakfast and high-speed Internet.

DAYS INN   **Phone:** (928)428-5000

Motel
$57-$109

Address: 520 E Hwy 70 85546 **Location:** US 191, 0.5 mi e. **Facility:** 43 units. 2 stories (no elevator), exterior corridors. **Amenities:** high-speed Internet. **Pool(s):** outdoor. **Activities:** whirlpool, limited exercise equipment. **Guest Services:** valet and coin laundry.

SUPER 8-SAFFORD   **Phone:** (928)428-5851

Motel
$68-$90

Address: 1578 W Thatcher Blvd 85546 **Location:** US 191, 1.3 mi w on US 70. **Facility:** 44 units. 2 stories (no elevator), exterior corridors. **Pool(s):** heated outdoor. **Guest Services:** valet laundry.

WHERE TO EAT

BRICK'S STEAKS & MORE   **Phone:** 928/348-8111

Steak
$5-$22

AAA Inspector Notes: This no-nonsense roadside restaurant features hearty portions, grilled steak and fruit cobblers that are popular with the locals. **Bar:** full bar. **Address:** 4367 S Hwy 191 85546 **Location:** 3.6 mi s of jct US 70 and 191. L D

CASA MAÑANA   **Phone:** 928/428-3170

Mexican
$5-$10

AAA Inspector Notes: Guests sit down amid simple, yet bright and cheerful decor while friendly staff members bring out a selection of salsa. Diners can peruse the menu for such classic dishes as homemade pork tamales, grilled chicken or beef fajitas. **Address:** 502 S 1st Ave 85546 **Location:** Jct US 70 and 191; center. L D

MANOR HOUSE   **Phone:** 928/428-7148

▼▼▼ ▼▼▼

American

$8-$25

AAA Inspector Notes: The family-style warmth offered by the staff reflects the owner's friendly manner. In addition to sandwiches, hearty dinners include Mexican, pasta, steaks and seafood dishes. A large gift shop is on the premises. **Bar:** full bar. **Address:** 415 E Hwy 70 85546 **Location:** US 191, 0.5 mi e. Ⓑ Ⓛ Ⓓ

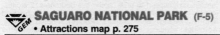

◆ **SAGUARO NATIONAL PARK** (F-5)
• Attractions map p. 275

Elevations in the park range from 2,500ft. on the desert floor along the loop roads to 8,666 ft. at Mica Mountain. Refer to AAA maps for additional elevation information.

Near Tucson, Saguaro National Park is divided into two districts: Rincon Mountain (Saguaro East) is about 15 miles east via Old Spanish Trail, and Tucson Mountain (Saguaro West) is 15 miles west via Speedway Boulevard. Both districts typify the Sonoran arboreal desert and contain stands of saguaro cacti, known for their sometimes humanlike shapes.

The saguaro grows only in southern Arizona, in California along the Colorado River and in the northern Mexican state of Sonora. It can live more than 200 years, attaining heights of 30 to 40 feet; a few exceptional ones exceed 50 feet. Its blossom, the state flower, appears in May and June. Native Americans use its fruit for food and as a beverage base.

In addition to protecting the saguaro and other desert vegetation of the Sonoran Desert, the park's Saguaro West district has rock formations decorated with Native American petroglyphs and designs.

At the park headquarters in Saguaro East a visitor center contains plant and animal exhibits and offers nature programs in the winter; phone (520) 733-5153. The 8-mile Cactus Forest Drive begins at the visitor center parking lot. Picnic facilities are available. Saguaro West's unpaved 5-mile Bajada Loop Drive winds through dense stands of saguaro cacti. A visitor center has exhibits, a slide show and interpretive programs; phone (520) 733-5158.

Saguaro East and Saguaro West are open daily 7 a.m.-dusk. Visitor centers open daily 9-5; closed Christmas. Admission to Saguaro East or Saguaro West is by 7-day or annual permit; 7-day permits cost $10 per private vehicle or $5 for persons arriving by other means. Backcountry backpacking is by permit only in Saguaro East; no drive-in camping permitted. **Cards:** AX, DS, MC, VI. For additional information contact the Superintendent, Saguaro National Park, 3693 S. Old Spanish Tr., Tucson, AZ 85730-5601; phone (520) 733-5153. *See Recreation Chart.*

SAHUARITA (F-4) pop. 25,259, elev. 2,702'
• Part of Tucson area — see map p. 268

ASARCO MINERAL DISCOVERY CENTER, off I-19 exit 80 to 1421 W. Pima Mine Rd., features hands-on exhibits about mining and minerals. A theater offers presentations about mining, mineral resources and reclamation. A 1-hour tour provides a look inside an operating open-pit copper mine.

Time: Allow 1 hour, 30 minutes minimum. **Hours:** Tues.-Sat. 9-5, Oct.-May; Tues.-Sat. 9-3 (also Sat. 3-5), rest of year. Guided tours are given Tues.-Sat. at 9:30, 11, 12:30, 2 and 3:30, Oct.-May; Sat. at 9:30, 11, 12:30, 2 and 3:30, rest of year. Closed major holidays. **Cost:** Center free. Mine tour $8; $6 (ages 62+); $5 (ages 5-12). **Phone:** (520) 625-8233 for tour reservations.

TITAN MISSILE MUSEUM, .75 mi. w. of I-19 exit 69 off Duval Mine Rd., is a formerly active Intercontinental Ballistic Missile (ICBM) complex preserved as a museum. Of the 54 Titan II ICBM sites in the U.S. weapon system, all except the missile museum have been destroyed.

Note: The tour includes descending/ascending 55 steps and may be cumbersome for the physically challenged or those with a heart condition. Arrangements may be made for the use of an elevator for the physically challenged. **Time:** Allow 1 hour minimum. **Hours:** Daily 8:45-5. Tours are given on the hour. Last admission 1 hour before closing. Closed Thanksgiving and Christmas. **Cost:** $9.50; $8.50 (ages 62+ and active military with ID); $6 (ages 7-12). **Phone:** (520) 625-7736.

GAMBLING ESTABLISHMENTS
• **Desert Diamond Casino,** 1100 W. Pima Mine Rd. **Hours:** Daily 24 hours. **Phone:** (520) 294-7777 or (866) 332-9467.

ST. JOHNS (C-6) pop. 3,480, elev. 5,650'
• Hotels p. 204

St. Johns Regional Chamber of Commerce: 180 W. Cleveland St., P.O. Box 929, St. Johns, AZ 85936. **Phone:** (928) 337-2000.

APACHE COUNTY HISTORICAL SOCIETY MUSEUM, .25 mi. w. of jct. US 191 and SR 61 at 180 W. Cleveland St., displays pioneer artifacts, mammoth bones, Native American artifacts, miniature replicas of early St. Johns homes, and antique guns and slot machines. **Time:** Allow 30 minutes minimum. **Hours:** Mon.-Fri. 9-4; other times by appointment. Closed major holidays. **Cost:** Donations. **Phone:** (928) 337-4737.

LYMAN LAKE STATE PARK is 14 mi. n. off US 60 onto US180/191, then just off SR 81, following signs. This 1,200-acre park is a great place for camping, hiking, swimming, fishing, water skiing and wildlife viewing. A marked trail leads to the ruins of Rattlesnake Point Pueblo, a village constructed and occupied by ancestors of the Hopi tribe during the 1300s. *See Recreation Chart.*

Cabins, yurts and group campsites are available by reservation. **Hours:** Daily 8-5, May-Sept. **Cost:** $7 (per private vehicle, up to four adult passengers);

$3 (per additional adult passenger in vehicle or individual arriving on foot or bicycle). Cabins $50. Yurts $35. Camping $15-$25 (two vehicles per site). **Phone:** (928) 337-4441. 🅰 ⊠ 🍴 🛖

DAYS INN

Phone: (928)337-4422

◇◇◇
Motel
$64-$99

Address: 125 E Commercial St 85936 **Location:** On US 191/SR 61; center. **Facility:** 39 units. 2 stories (no elevator), exterior corridors. **Guest Services:** coin laundry.

BIZ 📶 ⚡ 🖥 📺 / SOME UNITS FEE 🐾

ST. MICHAELS (B-6) pop. 1,443

ST. MICHAELS HISTORICAL MUSEUM, 24 Mission Rd. off SR 264 in the St. Michaels Mission complex, features permanent displays chronicling the work of the Franciscan Friars on the Navajo Nation. Temporary exhibits include examples of Navajo life and culture. The museum is housed in the original mission building, restored to its 1898 appearance. **Time:** Allow 30 minutes minimum. **Hours:** Mon.-Fri. 9-4, Memorial Day-Labor Day. **Cost:** Donations. **Phone:** (928) 871-4171.

NAVAJOLAND INN & SUITES

Phone: (928)871-5690

◇◇◇
Hotel
$70-$175

Address: 392 W Hwy 264 86511 **Location:** Jct SR 12, 1.5 mi w. **Facility:** 73 units. 2 stories (no elevator), exterior corridors. **Terms:** 14 day cancellation notice-fee imposed.
Pool(s): heated indoor. **Activities:** sauna, whirlpool, exercise room. **Guest Services:** coin laundry. **Free Special Amenities:** local telephone calls and high-speed Internet.

SAVE 🍴 ➤ 📶 🖥 / SOME UNITS FEE 🐾 ⚡ 🖥

SAN CARLOS (E-5) pop. 4,038, elev. 2,432'

San Carlos, north of Coolidge Dam, is a trading center and headquarters for the San Carlos Indian Agency. The Apaches operate one of the largest cattle ranches in this area. The San Carlos Apache Reservation offers some of the best trophy-hunting and fishing in the state; permits are required. For permit information contact the San Carlos Recreation and Wildlife Department, P.O. Box 97, San Carlos, AZ 85550; phone (928) 475-2343.

Coolidge Dam, about 9 miles southeast on the Gila River, impounds the waters that irrigate the Casa Grande Valley. Construction of the dam was delayed until a solution satisfactory to the Apache Indians was found concerning the disturbance of tribal burial grounds. Once it was agreed that a concrete slab would cover the cemetery, construction resumed.

Download eTourBook guides
for ereaders and smartphones
at AAA.com/ebooks

BEST WESTERN APACHE GOLD HOTEL

Phone: (928)475-7600

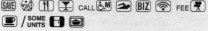

◇◇◇
Hotel
$89-$99

AAA Benefit: Members save up to 20%, plus 10% bonus points with Best Western Rewards®.

Address: US Hwy 70 85550 **Location:** Jct SR 77 S, 4.2 mi e. **Facility:** The many activities available, pleasant rooms and higher elevation make this a great place to visit for families or groups. 146 units, some two bedrooms. 2 stories, interior corridors. **Amenities:** video games (fee), high-speed Internet. **Dining:** entertainment. **Pool(s):** heated outdoor. **Activities:** whirlpool, exercise room. *Fee:* golf-18 holes. **Free Special Amenities:** local telephone calls and high-speed Internet.

SAVE 😊 🍴 ⍉ CALL 🅼 ➤ BIZ 📶 FEE 📺
🖥 / SOME UNITS ⚡ 🖥

SASABE (G-4) elev. 3,560'

BUENOS AIRES NATIONAL WILDLIFE REFUGE, 7 mi. n. on SR 286 at Milepost 8, is a 118,000-acre refuge established to preserve the endangered masked bobwhite quail and other grassland wildlife. The refuge contains extensive grasslands, seasonal streams and ponds. It is home to nearly 340 species of birds, including gray hawks, vermilion fly catchers and golden eagles. Other wildlife include coyotes, deer, foxes, javelinas, pronghorn antelope and bobcats. Trails are on the eastern side near the town of Arivaca.

Time: Allow 4 hours minimum. **Hours:** Refuge open daily 24 hours. Visitor center daily 7:30-4, mid-Aug. through May 31; Mon.-Fri. 7:30-4, rest of year. Visitor center closed Jan. 1, Thanksgiving and Christmas. Guided hikes in Brown Canyon are offered the second and fourth Sat. of the month, Nov.-Apr. **Cost:** Refuge free. Guided hikes $5. Reservations are required for guided hikes. **Phone:** (520) 823-4251, ext. 116.

SCOTTSDALE (I-3) pop. 217,385, elev. 1,259'

• Hotels p. 207 • Restaurants p. 219
• Hotels & Restaurants map & index p. 158
• Part of Phoenix area — see map p. 134

Scottsdale was named for Chaplain Winfield Scott, Civil War veteran and retired military man who in 1888 purchased some farmland near the center of present-day Scottsdale. The city's slogan, "The West's Most Western Town," certainly applies to the wooden storefronts and hitching posts of Old Town Scottsdale. But the rest of the city is better described as "South Beach meets the Sonoran Desert."

Chic and sophisticated, Scottsdale is home to more than 120 art galleries, an array of specialty stores, fine dining, hip nightlife, plush resorts and golf courses galore. In short, this is the Valley of the Sun's tourist hot spot.

Indian Bend Wash Greenbelt along Hayden Road offers 7 miles of trails for bicyclists and runners. McCormick-Stillman Railroad Park, 7301 E. Indian Bend Rd., (480) 312-2312, offers 1-mile rides on a scale train. Several full-size railroad cars, two train

(See map & index p. 158.)

depots, a 1907 locomotive, two Navajo hogans, playgrounds and an operating 1950s carousel are in the park. Picnic facilities are available.

The free Scottsdale trolley is a handy way to get around the downtown area. Following a route that includes stops at Old Town, the Arts District and Scottsdale Fashion Square, the trolley operates daily (except January 1, Memorial Day, July 4, Labor Day, Thanksgiving and Christmas) 11-6 (also Thurs. 6-9 p.m.) and runs every 15 minutes. For route maps and more information check hotel brochure racks, or phone (480) 421-1004.

Scottsdale Convention & Visitors Bureau: 4343 N. Scottsdale Rd., Suite 170, Scottsdale, AZ 85251. **Phone:** (480) 421-1004 or (800) 782-1117.

Self-guiding tours: Maps detailing self-guiding walking tours of Scottsdale's Old Town are available from the convention and visitors bureau. There's also a self-serve information kiosk loaded with maps and brochures at the corner of Main Street and Brown Avenue.

Shopping areas: Arizona's answer to Santa Fe, New Mexico, downtown Scottsdale is one of the biggest art gallery centers in the Southwest. Fine art collectors armed with high-limit plastic will want to head for the Arts District, along palm-lined Main Street (just w. of Scottsdale Rd.) and Marshall Way (between Main St. and 5th Ave.)

The Biltmore Gallery (7113 E. Main St.) specializes in works by big-name American West painters (think Charles Russell and Olaf Wieghorst). Obviously, this is museum-quality art that'll put a serious dent in your bank account. The Knox Artifacts Gallery (7056 E. Main St.) is a must for collectors of Pre-Columbian and Native American art.

If your taste leans more toward abstract squiggles on a huge white canvas, the Gebert Contemporary Art Gallery (7160 E. Main St.) deals in cutting-edge paintings and sculptures by established international artists. For modern art that's a bit more accessible to the masses, Xanadu Gallery (7039 E. Main St., #101) sells beautiful glass art, jewelry, paintings, photography and intriguing contemporary sculptures; some of it is surprisingly affordable.

The weekly Scottsdale ArtWalk (held Thursdays 7 p.m.-9 p.m.) is a fun way to get acquainted with the area. Many of the galleries stay open late for this "open house" event, which occasionally features live music and artist demonstrations.

If souvenirs are more your speed, Old Town Scottsdale (a four-block area bounded by Scottsdale Road, Indian School Road, Brown Avenue and 2nd Street) is loaded with trinket shops selling everything from fridge magnets to toy tomahawks. For authentic Native American crafts, try Bischoff's Shades of West (7247 E. Main St.) or Gilbert Ortega Galleries (3925 N. Scottsdale Rd.).

Old Town's wooden storefronts may very well put you in the mood to don Western duds. Saba's Famous Texas Boots (7254 Main St.) stocks brand names like Tony Lama and Nocona. Az-Tex Hats & Gifts (3903 N. Scottsdale Rd.) has a nice selection of quality cowboy hats and straw sun hats but, beware, prices are steep.

For clothes you might actually wear back home, head for the funky boutiques and shops lining 5th Avenue (between Scottsdale Rd. and Marshall Way). A relaxed shady lane, 5th also has jewelry stores, art galleries and a sprinkling of casual sidewalk cafes.

Just north of 5th Avenue is the Scottsdale Waterfront, a five-acre mixed-use development spread

▼ See AAA listing p. 360 ▼

RAINBOWRYDERS.
WWW.RAINBOWRYDERS.COM   877.771.0776

The Premier Balloon Ride Company of the Southwest

The Experience of a Lifetime...
Happening Right Now™

Experience Phoenix

Like Never Before.

(See map & index p. 158.)

along the banks of the Arizona Canal. The complex features a handful of mall stores (Sur La Table, Urban Outfitters), restaurants and the Fiesta Bowl Museum (7135 E. Camelback Rd., #190), a must-visit for college football fans; phone (480) 350-0900.

A massive three-story mall, Scottsdale Fashion Square (at the corner of Camelback and Scottsdale roads) has more than 250 stores, including upscale anchors like Barneys New York. At the Borgata of Scottsdale (just south of Lincoln Drive on Scottsdale Road), an elegant, open-air shopping complex modeled after a Tuscan village, you'll stroll cobblestone walkways past unique, high-end clothing boutiques and jewelers.

Shopping Tours: Spree! The Art of Shopping is an upscale shopping service and experience for those who want to channel their inner Carrie Bradshaw. Several round-trip tour packages are available and power shoppers have the choice of being picked up in either a limousine or luxury sedan. Tours run approximately 3 hours and advance reservations of at least 24 hours are required; phone (480) 661-1080 for more information or to make reservations.

Nightlife

Scottsdale lays claim to the valley's hottest dance club scene. You'll find the trendiest spots in the dozen-or-so city blocks southeast of the intersection of Scottsdale and Camelback roads. If you want to bump-n-grind alongside the valley's beautiful people, the 18,000-square-foot scenester-club Myst (7340 E. Shoeman Ln.) is a solid choice; phone (480) 970-5000.

For a good old Budweiser-fueled, boot-scootin' night on the town, head for Handlebar J (7116 E. Becker Ln.). A Scottsdale landmark since 1966, the club has live country music nightly, plus free country dance lessons every Wednesday, Thursday and Sunday night at 7; phone (480) 948-0110.

DESERT STORM HUMMER TOURS picks up passengers at the Rock Bottom Grille, jct. Shea Blvd. and SR 101 at 8668 E. Shea Blvd. Visitors explore the vast Sonoran Desert in an all-terrain H1 Hummer driven by an experienced guide.

The 4-hour Desert Adventure tour affords views of the desert's bouldered canyons, abundant plant life and rock formations and includes a nature walk. During the 3.5-hour Night Storm Adventure tour, visitors use high-tech stargazing and night-vision equipment.

Time: Allow 4 hours minimum. **Hours:** Desert Adventure tour departs daily at 8 and 1. Night Storm Adventure tour departs daily at 7 p.m. Phone ahead to confirm schedule. **Cost:** Desert Adventure tour $120; $100 (ages 5-16). Night Storm Adventure tour $125; $100 (ages 8-16). Reservations are required. **Phone:** (480) 922-0020.

HEARD MUSEUM NORTH is at 32633 N. Scottsdale Rd. Native American artwork from the Heard Museum's vast collection is shown here; exhibits change semiannually. The video Our Voices, Our Land presents Native Americans speaking about their culture. **Time:** Allow 30 minutes minimum. **Hours:** Mon.-Sat. 10-5, Sun. 11-5. Closed Jan. 1, Easter, Memorial Day, July 4, Labor Day, Thanksgiving and Christmas. **Cost:** $5; $4 (ages 65+); $2 (students with ID); free (ages 0-5 and second Sun. of the month). **Phone:** (480) 488-9817.

SCOTTSDALE CIVIC CENTER AND MALL, at Drinkwater Blvd. and 2nd St., includes a library, municipal buildings, a park, fountains, sculptures, a pond and landscaped lawns. Also on the mall is the Scottsdale Center for the Performing Arts, a forum for the visual and performing arts. **Cost:** Free. **Phone:** (480) 994-2787.

Scottsdale Historical Museum, 7333 E. Civic Center Mall, is housed in a 1909 red brick grammar school furnished in period. A replica of a barbershop, complete with a barber chair and tools, and an old-fashioned kitchen are featured. Other exhibits include a display of town memorabilia and a replica of a 1900 schoolroom. **Time:** Allow 30 minutes minimum. **Hours:** Wed.-Sun. 10-5, Oct.-May; Wed.-Sun. 10-2, in June and Sept. **Cost:** Donations. **Phone:** (480) 945-4499.

Scottsdale Museum of Contemporary Art, 7374 E. 2nd St., features works by contemporary artists from Arizona and around the world. Displays focusing on modern architecture and design also are offered. **Hours:** Tues.-Sat. 10-5 (also Thurs. 5-8), Sun. noon-5, day after Memorial Day-day before Labor Day; Wed.-Sat 10-5 (also Thurs. 5-8), Sun. noon-5, rest of year. Closed major holidays. **Cost:** $7; $5 (students with ID); free (ages 0-15 and on Thurs.). **Phone:** (480) 874-4666.

TALIESIN WEST, 12621 N. 114th St. (Frank Lloyd Wright Blvd.) at jct. Cactus Rd., was the winter home and studio of architect Frank Lloyd Wright. On nearly 600 acres of Sonoran Desert at the foothills of the McDowell Mountains, the complex of buildings is connected by gardens, terraces and walkways. Taliesin West is the international headquarters for the Frank Lloyd Wright Foundation.

Tours include a 1-hour Panorama Tour, a 90-minute Insights Tour, a 3-hour Behind the Scenes Tour, a 2-hour Desert Walk, and a 2-hour Night Lights on the Desert tour. The Panorama Tour provides a basic introduction to the complex and Wright's theories of architecture. The Insights Tour encompasses the famed Living Room and Wright's private living quarters. The Behind the Scenes Tour includes tea in the colorful dining room. The Desert Walk introduces visitors to the environment surrounding the complex and the Night Lights on the Desert tour affords you the opportunity to view the home at night. Other tours also are available.

(See map & index p. 158.)

Note: Tours may be canceled due to inclement weather; phone ahead to confirm. Walking shoes and sun protection are recommended. **Time:** Allow 1 hour minimum. **Hours:** Panorama Tour departs daily on the hour 10:15-3:15, Sept.-May; at 11 and 2, rest of year. Insights Tour departs every 30 minutes daily 9-4, Nov.-Apr.; every hour daily 9-4, rest of year. Behind the Scenes Tour departs Mon., Thurs. and Sat. at 9:15, Sept.-May; Mon. and Thurs. (also day before Thanksgiving and Christmas Eve) at 9:15, rest of year. Desert Walk departs daily at 11:15, Nov.-Apr. (weather permitting). Night Lights on the Desert Tour at 6:30, 7 and 7:30 p.m., May-Sept.; Fri. at 6, 6:30 and 7 p.m., Feb.-Apr.; Fri. at 6:30, 7 and 7:30 p.m., in Oct. Closed Easter, Thanksgiving and Christmas. Phone ahead to confirm schedule.

Cost: Panorama Tour $24; $20 (ages 60+ and active military and students with ID); $10 (ages 4-12). Insights Tour $32; $28 (ages 60+ and active military and students with ID); $17 (ages 4-12). Behind the Scenes Tour $60. Desert Walk $32. Night Lights on the Desert Tour $35; $30 (ages 60+ and active military and students with ID). Rates may vary and combination rates may be available; phone ahead. Tours not recommended for children ages 0-5, unless in strollers or parents' arms. Reservations are recommended for some tours. **Phone:** (855) 860-2700, ext. 494, or (480) 860-8810 for recorded tour information.

GAMBLING ESTABLISHMENTS

- **Casino Arizona—101 & Indian Bend,** Loop 101 and Indian Bend Rd. **Hours:** Daily 24 hours. **Phone:** (480) 850-7777 or (877) 724-4687.
- **Casino Arizona—101 & McKellips,** Loop 101 and McKellips Rd. **Hours:** Daily 24 hours. **Phone:** (480) 850-7777 or (877) 724-4687.

RECREATIONAL ACTIVITIES

Hiking

- **Hike In Phoenix, LLC** departs from various locations in Phoenix and Scottsdale; transportation to and from local hotels is offered. **Hours:** Daily 8-8. **Phone:** (877) 445-3749.

Hot Air Ballooning

- **Rainbow Ryders, Inc.** departs from various locations for flights over the Sonoran Desert. **Hours:** Daily at dawn and dusk (weather permitting). **Phone:** (877) 771-0776.

BEST WESTERN PLUS PAPAGO INN & RESORT
Phone: (480)947-7335 **57**

Hotel
$60-$170

AAA Benefit: Members save up to 20%, plus 10% bonus points with Best Western Rewards®.

Address: 7017 E McDowell Rd 85257 **Location:** From Scottsdale Rd, just w. Located in a busy commercial area. **Facility:** 58 units. 2 stories (no elevator), exterior corridors. **Terms:** 2 night minimum stay - seasonal, cancellation fee imposed. **Amenities:** Some: high-speed Internet. **Pool(s):** heated outdoor. **Activities:** exercise room. **Guest Services:** valet and coin laundry. **Free Special Amenities:** local telephone calls and high-speed Internet. (See ad p. 208.)

BEST WESTERN PLUS SUNDIAL
Phone: (480)994-4170 **46**

Hotel
$100-$250

AAA Benefit: Members save up to 20%, plus 10% bonus points with Best Western Rewards®.

Address: 7320 E Camelback Rd 85251 **Location:** Just e of Scottsdale Rd. **Facility:** 54 units. 3 stories, exterior corridors. **Amenities:** high-speed Internet. **Pool(s):** heated outdoor. **Activities:** whirlpool, limited exercise equipment. **Guest Services:** valet and coin laundry. **Free Special Amenities:** full breakfast and room upgrade (subject to availability with advance reservations).

THE CANYON SUITES AT THE PHOENICIAN
Phone: (480)423-2880 **40**

Resort Hotel
$299-$2500

THE LUXURY COLLECTION

AAA Benefit: Inspiring travels with your AAA Preferred rates.

Address: 6000 E Camelback Rd 85251 **Location:** 0.5 mi w of 64th St; in The Phoenician. **Facility:** A personal ambassador tends to every guests' needs such as a nightly wine tasting and a "tub turn down" with scented bath water. 60 units, some kitchens. 2 stories, interior corridors. **Parking:** on-site and valet. **Terms:** check-in 4 pm, 7 day cancellation notice-fee imposed. **Amenities:** high-speed Internet, safes, honor bars. **Pool(s):** heated outdoor. **Activities:** whirlpool, spa. **Guest Services:** valet laundry, area transportation Scottsdale Fashion Square. **Free Special Amenities:** high-speed Internet and manager's reception. (See ad p. 209.)

Make Your Next Trip a Journey ... With AAA and Hertz.

For reservations, **visit** your AAA/CAA travel office, **click** on AAA.com/hertz or CAA.ca/hertz, or **call** 800-654-3080 U.S./ 888-333-3120 Canada.

Show Your Card & Save

Hertz.

(See map & index p. 158.)

CHAPARRAL SUITES SCOTTSDALE
Phone: (480)949-1414 **41**

Hotel
$99-$279

Address: 5001 N Scottsdale Rd 85250 **Location:** At Chaparral Rd. **Facility:** 311 units, some two bedrooms. 4 stories, exterior corridors. **Terms:** cancellation fee imposed. **Amenities:** video games (fee), high-speed Internet, safes. **Pool(s):** 2 heated outdoor. **Activities:** whirlpools, lighted tennis court, exercise room. **Guest Services:** valet and coin laundry. *(See ad p. 210.)*

SAVE ✈ ▮▮ ▾ CALL 🅼
🐕 BIZ 🛜 FEE🎥 🍴
🖵 🖵 / SOME UNITS FEE🐕

CLARION HOTEL SCOTTSDALE
Phone: (480)945-4392 **38**

Hotel
$79-$119

Address: 5101 N Scottsdale Rd 85250 **Location:** Just n of Chaparral Rd. **Facility:** 211 units. 2 stories (no elevator), exterior corridors. **Terms:** cancellation fee imposed. **Amenities:** video games (fee). **Pool(s):** heated outdoor. **Activities:** whirlpool, exercise room. **Guest Services:** valet and coin laundry, area transportation-within 5 mi. **Free Special Amenities:** high-speed Internet and local transportation.

SAVE ▮▮ 🎥 ▾ CALL 🅼 🐕 BIZ 🛜 🗙
FEE🎥 🖵 / SOME UNITS FEE🐕 FEE🍴 FEE🍴 FEE🖵

COMFORT SUITES BY CHOICE HOTELS-OLD TOWN
Phone: (480)946-1111 **55**

Hotel
$70-$170

Address: 3275 N Drinkwater Blvd 85251 **Location:** N of Thomas Rd; just e of Scottsdale Rd. **Facility:** 60 units. 3 stories. **Terms:** cancellation fee imposed. **Amenities:** safes (fee). **Pool(s):** heated indoor. **Activities:** whirlpools, limited exercise equipment. **Guest Services:** valet and coin laundry.

🍴 CALL 🅼 🐕 🛜 🗙 🍴 🖵 🖵
/ SOME UNITS FEE🐕

COUNTRY INN & SUITES BY CARLSON
Phone: (480)314-1200 **20**

Hotel
$59-$209

Address: 10801 N 89th Pl 85260 **Location:** SR 101 exit 41, just e on Shea Blvd, then just n. **Facility:** 162 units. 3 stories, interior corridors. **Terms:** check-in 4 pm, 3 day cancellation notice-fee imposed. **Pool(s):** heated outdoor. **Activities:** whirlpool, exercise room. **Guest Services:** valet and coin laundry, area transportation-within 5 mi.

🍴 🐕 🛜 🗙 🍴 🖵 🖵 / SOME UNITS FEE🐕

Discover mobile travel solutions at AAA.com/mobile and CAA.ca/mobile

▼ See AAA listing p. 207 ▼

An Oasis in the Desert Best Western PLUS

Refresh, Relax & Experience the Beauty of Scottsdale

Located near Old Scottsdale, shopping, Desert Botanical Gardens, Phoenix Zoo, ASU, golfing, dining, Spring training facilities.

Heated pool in a lush tropical courtyard, soothing music, gazebo and a bird aviary.

On site coffee shop and lounge serving hot hors d'oeuvres. Business center, free high speed internet and WIFI.

BEST WESTERN PLUS
Papago Inn & Resort
7017 E McDowell Rd., Scottsdale, AZ 85257
480.947.7335 • 866-806-4400
Bestwestern.com/aaa

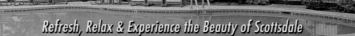

(See map & index p. 158.)

COURTYARD BY MARRIOTT/SCOTTSDALE NORTH
Phone: (480)922-8400 **7**

Hotel
$59-$209

AAA Benefit:
AAA hotel discounts of 5% or more.

Address: 17010 N Scottsdale Rd 85255 **Location:** Just n of Frank Lloyd Wright Blvd. **Facility:** 153 units. 3 stories, interior corridors. **Amenities:** safes. *Some:* high-speed Internet. **Pool(s):** heated outdoor. **Activities:** whirlpool, exercise room. **Guest Services:** valet and coin laundry, area transportation-within 5 mi.

COURTYARD SCOTTSDALE AT MAYO CLINIC
Phone: (480)860-4000

Hotel
$75-$195

AAA Benefit: AAA hotel discounts of 5% or more.

Address: 13444 E Shea Blvd 85259 **Location:** SR 101 exit 41, 5.8 mi e. Located at entrance to Mayo Clinic. **Facility:** 124 units. 2 stories, interior corridors. **Amenities:** high-speed Internet. **Pool(s):** heated outdoor. **Activities:** whirlpool, exercise room. **Guest Services:** valet and coin laundry, area transportation-Mayo Clinic. **Free Special Amenities:** newspaper and high-speed Internet.

DAYS INN SCOTTSDALE FASHION SQUARE
Phone: (480)947-5411 **43**

Motel
$44-$144

Address: 4710 N Scottsdale Rd 85251 **Location:** Just n of Camelback Rd. Located at north side of Scottsdale Fashion Square Shopping Center. **Facility:** 167 units. 2 stories (no elevator), exterior corridors. **Amenities:** safes. **Pool(s):** heated outdoor. **Activities:** whirlpool, volleyball. **Guest Services:** valet and coin laundry. **Free Special Amenities:** expanded continental breakfast and high-speed Internet.

DOUBLETREE RESORT BY HILTON PARADISE VALLEY - SCOTTSDALE
Phone: (480)947-5400 **37**

Hotel
$139-$239 2/1-5/19
$89-$189 5/20-1/31

DOUBLETREE
BY HILTON

AAA Benefit: Members save 5% or more everyday!

Address: 5401 N Scottsdale Rd 85250 **Location:** Just n of Chaparral Rd; on east side of Scottsdale Rd. **Facility:** Near restaurants and shops, the resort offers rooms with Sweet Dreams beds, custom pillows and high-quality sheets. Grounds are beautifully manicured. 378 units. 2 stories, exterior corridors. **Parking:** on-site and valet. **Terms:** check-in 4 pm, 1-7 night minimum stay, cancellation fee imposed. **Amenities:** safes, honor bars. *Fee:* video games, high-speed Internet. **Dining:** 2 restaurants. **Pool(s):** 2 heated outdoor. **Activities:** saunas, whirlpools, steamrooms, putting green, 2 lighted tennis courts, racquetball court, playground. *Fee:* massage. **Guest Services:** valet laundry, area transportation-within 2 mi.

▼ See AAA listing p. 207 ▼

THE CANYON SUITES
AT THE PHOENICIAN
A LUXURY COLLECTION RESORT
Scottsdale

You've Arrived

THE PHOENICIAN'S CANYON SUITES...
Raising the bar for service and luxury. An enchanting boutique resort within a world-class resort. A rare, unrivaled, sun-drenched destination set against legendary Camelback Mountain in the heart of Scottsdale.

- Personal Canyon Ambassador
- Chauffeured Mercedes
- Welcome Amenity and Wine Tasting
- Morning and Afternoon Refreshments
- Exclusive Canyon Suites Pool
- Complimentary Valet Parking, Health Club and High Speed Internet

RESERVATIONS: 800-955-7352
canyonsuites.com
6000 East Camelback Road, Scottsdale, Arizona 85251

Five Diamond Award

(See map & index p. 158.)

EXTENDED STAYAMERICA-PHOENIX-SCOTTSDALE
Phone: (480)607-3767   **13**

Extended Stay
Hotel
$85-$95 2/1-4/15
$70-$80 4/16-1/31

Address: 15501 N Scottsdale Rd 85254 **Location:** SR 101 exit Frank Lloyd Wright Blvd, 2 mi w, 0.5 mi s on Scottsdale Rd, then just e on Tierra Buena Ln. **Facility:** 120 efficiencies. 3 stories, exterior corridors. **Terms:** office hours 6:30 am-10:30 pm. **Guest Services:** coin laundry.

 / SOME UNITS FEE

EXTENDED STAY DELUXE PHOENIX-SCOTTSDALE
Phone: (480)483-1333   **19**

Extended Stay
Hotel
$100-$110 2/1-4/15
$75-$85 4/16-1/31

Address: 10660 N 69th St 85254 **Location:** Jct Scottsdale Rd, just w on Shea Blvd, then just n. Located in Agua Caliente Center. **Facility:** 106 efficiencies. 3 stories, interior corridors. **Terms:** office hours 6:30 am-10:30 pm. **Pool(s):** heated outdoor. **Activities:** whirlpool, exercise room. **Guest Services:** coin laundry.

 / SOME UNITS FEE

Find valuable AAA/CAA
member savings
at AAA.com/discounts

FAIRFIELD INN NORTH SCOTTSDALE
Phone: (480)483-0042   **17**

Hotel
$71-$194

AAA Benefit: AAA hotel discounts of 5% or more.

Address: 13440 N Scottsdale Rd 85254 **Location:** Just s of Thunderbird Rd; on west side of Scottsdale Rd. **Facility:** 132 units. 3 stories, interior/exterior corridors. **Amenities:** high-speed Internet. **Pool(s):** heated outdoor. **Activities:** whirlpool. **Guest Services:** valet and coin laundry. **Free Special Amenities:** expanded continental breakfast and high-speed Internet.

Share a New View on Travel at AAATravelViews.com

Read stories, tips and trends from AAA insiders. Post comments and get your questions answered by our travel experts.

▼ See AAA listing p. 208 ▼

The *amenities* will entice you. The *value* will convince you.®
Located in the heart of Scottsdale near fabulous shopping, fine dining and golf.

Chaparral Suites™
SCOTTSDALE

Complimentary amenities include:

- Cooked-to-order Breakfast daily (eggs, bacon, sausage, pancakes, etc.)
- Evening Reception Nightly 5:30-7:30pm
- Individual Airport Shuttle 6am – 10pm
- In-room Wired and Wireless Internet
- Tennis/Fitness Center   • USA Today
- Restaurant & Sports Bar On-Site

Up To 15% OFF* For the price of a room you get a two-room suite!

*10 to 15% discount off published rates, subject to availability. Not combinable with other promotions.

Reservations (800) 528-1456

(See map & index p. 158.)

FAIRMONT SCOTTSDALE PRINCESS
Phone: (480)585-4848   **4**

Resort Hotel
$134-$2699

Address: 7575 E Princess Dr 85255 **Location:** SR 101 exit 34 (Scottsdale Rd), 0.8 mi s, then just e; 0.6 mi n of Bell Rd. **Facility:** Site of PGA's Phoenix Open and the ATP tennis tournament, this 450-acre luxury resort features spacious units with balconies and terraces. 649 units. 1-4 stories, interior/exterior corridors. **Parking:** valet only. **Terms:** check-in 4 pm, 7 day cancellation notice. **Amenities:** safes, honor bars. *Fee:* video games, high-speed Internet. **Dining:** 3 restaurants, also, Bourbon Steak, The Grill, La Hacienda, see separate listings, entertainment. **Pool(s):** 5 heated outdoor. **Activities:** saunas, whirlpools, steamrooms, waterslide, fishing, recreation programs, rental bicycles, hiking trails, jogging, basketball, game room, volleyball, spa. *Fee:* golf-36 holes, 7 tennis courts (6 lighted). **Guest Services:** valet laundry, area transportation-within 5 mi.

Fairmont
SCOTTSDALE PRINCESS

Located in North Scottsdale overlooking the TPC Stadium, Golf Course and majestic McDowell Mountains

FIRESKY RESORT & SPA, A KIMPTON HOTEL
Phone: (480)945-7666   **42**

Hotel
$115-$469

Address: 4925 N Scottsdale Rd 85251 **Location:** Southeast corner of Scottsdale and Chaparral rds. **Facility:** Guest rooms at this intimate hotel feature marble showers and spa products; the pool and patio/bar both have an intriguing sand floor. 204 units. 2 stories (no elevator), interior corridors. **Parking:** on-site and valet. **Terms:** check-in 4 pm, 3 day cancellation notice-fee imposed. **Amenities:** safes, honor bars. **Dining:** Taggia, see separate listing. **Pool(s):** 2 heated outdoor. **Activities:** whirlpool, exercise room, spa. **Guest Services:** valet laundry, area transportation-within 3 mi. **Free Special Amenities:** high-speed Internet and manager's reception.

FOUR SEASONS RESORT SCOTTSDALE AT TROON NORTH
Phone: (480)515-5700

Resort Hotel
$129-$719

Address: 10600 E Crescent Moon Dr 85262 **Location:** SR 101 exit 36 (Pima Rd), 4.7 mi n, 2 mi e on Happy Valley Rd, then 1.5 mi n on Alma School Rd. **Facility:** Well-designed landscaping seamlessly blends with the desert surroundings, allowing for striking views from the territorial-style casitas. 210 units, some two and three bedrooms. 1-3 stories, exterior corridors. **Parking:** on-site (fee) and valet. **Terms:** check-in 4 pm, 7 day cancellation notice-fee imposed. **Amenities:** safes, honor bars. *Fee:* video games, high-speed Internet. **Dining:** 3 restaurants, also, Talavera, see separate listing. **Pool(s):** 3 heated outdoor. **Activities:** saunas, whirlpool, steamrooms, 2 lighted tennis courts, recreation programs, hiking trails, jogging, basketball, spa. *Fee:* golf-36 holes. **Guest Services:** valet and coin laundry. **Free Special Amenities:** children's activities and use of on-premises laundry facilities.

GAINEY SUITES HOTEL
Phone: (480)922-6969   **27**

Hotel
$99-$259 6/1-1/31
$179-$249 2/1-5/31

Address: 7300 E Gainey Suites Dr 85258 **Location:** Just e of Scottsdale Rd. **Facility:** 162 units, some two bedrooms and efficiencies. 2-3 stories, interior corridors. **Terms:** cancellation fee imposed. **Amenities:** video games (fee), high-speed Internet, safes. **Pool(s):** heated outdoor. **Activities:** whirlpool, exercise room. **Guest Services:** valet and coin laundry, area transportation-within 5 mi. **Free Special Amenities:** full breakfast and high-speed Internet.

HAMPTON INN & SUITES
Phone: (480)348-9280   **10**

Hotel
$79-$329

AAA Benefit:
Members save up to 10% everyday!

Address: 16620 N Scottsdale Rd 85254 **Location:** Just s of Bell Rd, then just w. **Facility:** 123 units, some efficiencies. 3 stories, interior/exterior corridors. **Terms:** 1-7 night minimum stay, cancellation fee imposed. **Amenities:** video games (fee). **Pool(s):** 2 heated outdoor. **Activities:** whirlpool, exercise room. **Guest Services:** valet and coin laundry, area transportation-within 5 mi.

HAMPTON INN SCOTTSDALE
Phone: (480)443-3233   **24**

Hotel
$139-$199 2/1-3/31
$59-$199 4/1-1/31

AAA Benefit:
Members save up to 10% everyday!

Address: 10101 N Scottsdale Rd 85253 **Location:** Just s of Shea Blvd. **Facility:** 130 units. 2 stories, interior corridors. **Terms:** 1-7 night minimum stay, cancellation fee imposed. **Amenities:** video games (fee). **Pool(s):** heated outdoor. **Activities:** whirlpool, exercise room. **Guest Services:** valet and coin laundry, area transportation-within 5 mi.

HILTON GARDEN INN SCOTTSDALE NORTH
Phone: (480)515-4944   **5**

Hotel
$79-$299

AAA Benefit:
Unparalleled hospitality at a special Member rate.

Address: 8550 E Princess Dr 85255 **Location:** SR 101 exit 36 (Pima Rd/Princess Dr), just w. **Facility:** 122 units. 3 stories, interior corridors. **Terms:** 1-7 night minimum stay, cancellation fee imposed. **Amenities:** video games (fee), high-speed Internet. **Pool(s):** heated outdoor. **Activities:** whirlpool, putting green, exercise room. **Guest Services:** valet and coin laundry, area transportation-within 5 mi.

Enjoy great savings on hotel rates at AAA.com or CAA.ca

(See map & index p. 158.)

HILTON GARDEN INN SCOTTSDALE OLD TOWN
Phone: (480)481-0400　**51**

Hotel
$99-$209 2/1-3/31
$69-$199 4/1-1/31

AAA Benefit:
Unparalleled hospitality at a special
Member rate.

Address: 7324 E Indian School Rd 85251 **Location:** Just e of Scottsdale Rd. **Facility:** 199 units. 7 stories, interior corridors. **Terms:** 1-7 night minimum stay, cancellation fee imposed. **Amenities:** video games (fee), high-speed Internet. **Pool(s):** heated outdoor. **Activities:** whirlpool, exercise room. **Guest Services:** valet and coin laundry.

HILTON SCOTTSDALE RESORT & VILLAS
Phone: (480)948-7750　**34**

Hotel
$149-$249 2/1-5/19
$99-$199 5/20-1/31

Hilton

AAA Benefit: Members save 5% or more everyday!

Address: 6333 N Scottsdale Rd 85250 **Location:** SR 101 exit 45, 2.1 mi w on McDonald Dr, then 0.3 mi s. **Facility:** Modern and sophisticated décor is highlighted in the lobby and framed by high ceilings and large windows; guest rooms overlook a tropical pool area. 235 units, some two bedrooms, efficiencies and kitchens. 2-3 stories, interior corridors. **Parking:** on-site and valet. **Terms:** check-in 4 pm, 1-7 night minimum stay, cancellation fee imposed. **Amenities:** video games (fee), safes. *Some:* honor bars. **Dining:** 3 restaurants. **Pool(s):** 2 heated outdoor. **Activities:** saunas, whirlpools, steamrooms. *Fee:* massage. **Guest Services:** valet laundry, area transportation-within 3 mi.

HOLIDAY INN EXPRESS HOTEL & SUITES-SCOTTSDALE
Phone: (480)675-7665　**56**

Hotel
$69-$229

Address: 3131 N Scottsdale Rd 85251 **Location:** Northeast corner of Scottsdale Rd and Earll Dr. **Facility:** 170 units, some efficiencies. 3 stories, interior corridors. **Terms:** check-in 4 pm, 3 day cancellation notice-fee imposed. **Amenities:** high-speed Internet. **Pool(s):** heated outdoor. **Activities:** whirlpool, exercise room. **Guest Services:** valet and coin laundry, area transportation-within 3 mi. **Free Special Amenities: full breakfast and local transportation.**

HOLIDAY INN EXPRESS SCOTTSDALE NORTH
Phone: (480)596-6559　**21**

Hotel
$119-$249 2/1-5/31
$119-$189 6/1-1/31

Address: 7350 E Gold Dust Ave 85258 **Location:** Just e of Scottsdale Rd; just s of Shea Blvd; on north side of Gold Dust Ave. Located in a light-commercial area. **Facility:** 122 units. 3 stories, interior corridors. **Terms:** 3 day cancellation notice-fee imposed. **Pool(s):** heated outdoor. **Activities:** whirlpool, exercise room. **Guest Services:** valet and coin laundry, area transportation-within 5 mi.

HOMESTEAD STUDIO SUITES HOTEL-PHOENIX-SCOTTSDALE
Phone: (480)994-0297　**53**

Extended Stay
Motel
$75-$85 2/1-4/15
$65-$75 4/16-1/31

Address: 3560 N Marshall Way 85251 **Location:** Just w of Scottsdale Rd on Goldwater, just s. **Facility:** 122 efficiencies. 2 stories (no elevator), exterior corridors. **Terms:** office hours 6:30 am-10:30 pm. **Pool(s):** heated outdoor. **Guest Services:** coin laundry.

HOMEWOOD SUITES BY HILTON SCOTTSDALE
Phone: (480)368-8705　**25**

Extended Stay
Hotel
$69-$269 2/1-5/31
$59-$189 6/1-1/31

AAA Benefit:
Contemporary luxury at a special
Member rate.

Address: 9880 N Scottsdale Rd 85253 **Location:** 0.5 mi s of Shea Blvd. **Facility:** 114 efficiencies, some two bedrooms. 3 stories, interior corridors. **Terms:** 1-7 night minimum stay, cancellation fee imposed. **Amenities:** video games (fee), high-speed Internet. **Pool(s):** heated outdoor. **Activities:** basketball, exercise room. **Guest Services:** valet and coin laundry, area transportation-within 5 mi, Mayo Clinic & Hospital.

HOSPITALITY SUITE RESORT
Phone: (480)949-5115　**58**

Hotel
$64-$144 2/1-5/31
$47-$109 6/1-1/31

Address: 409 N Scottsdale Rd 85257 **Location:** Just n of McKellips Rd; on east side of Scottsdale Rd. Located in a light-commercial and residential area. **Facility:** 210 units, some two bedrooms, efficiencies and kitchens. 2-3 stories, exterior corridors. **Amenities:** video games (fee). **Pool(s):** 3 heated outdoor. **Activities:** whirlpool, 2 lighted tennis courts, basketball, horseshoes, shuffleboard. **Guest Services:** valet and coin laundry, area transportation-within 3 mi.

HOTEL INDIGO SCOTTSDALE
Phone: (480)941-9400　**47**

Hotel
$139-$259 2/1-5/26
$99-$249 5/27-1/31

Address: 4415 N Civic Center Plaza 85251 **Location:** Scottsdale Rd, just e on Camelback Rd, just s on 75th St. **Facility:** 126 units. 5 stories, interior/exterior corridors. **Terms:** cancellation fee imposed. **Amenities:** video games (fee). **Pool(s):** heated outdoor. **Activities:** exercise room. **Guest Services:** valet laundry, area transportation-within 3 mi. **Free Special Amenities: local telephone calls and high-speed Internet.**

Safety tip: Keep a current AAA/CAA Road Atlas in every vehicle

(See map & index p. 158.)

HOTEL VALLEY HO
Phone: (480)248-2000 **52**

Boutique Contemporary Retro Hotel
$129-$359 2/1-6/1
$89-$289 6/2-1/31

Address: 6850 E Main St 85251 **Location:** 0.4 mi w of Scottsdale Rd, just s of Indian School Rd; on north side of Main St. **Facility:** Maintaining the flavor of the early 1950s, this hotel offers fully retro-fitted, trendy guest rooms with posh baths. 229 units. 2-6 stories, interior/exterior corridors. **Parking:** on-site and valet. **Terms:** check-in 4 pm, cancellation fee imposed. **Amenities:** high-speed Internet (fee), safes, honor bars. **Dining:** Cafe Zu Zu, Trader Vic's, see separate listings. **Pool(s):** heated outdoor. **Activities:** whirlpools, steamrooms, rental bicycles, exercise room, spa. **Guest Services:** valet laundry. Affiliated with A Preferred Hotel.

HYATT PLACE SCOTTSDALE/OLD TOWN
Phone: (480)423-9944 **49**

Hotel
$89-$299

AAA Benefit: Members save 10% or more everyday.

Address: 7300 E 3rd Ave 85251 **Location:** Just e of Scottsdale Rd. **Facility:** 127 units. 6 stories, interior corridors. **Terms:** cancellation fee imposed. **Amenities:** safes. *Some:* high-speed Internet. **Pool(s):** heated outdoor. **Activities:** exercise room. **Guest Services:** valet laundry. **Free Special Amenities: expanded continental breakfast and high-speed Internet.**

HYATT REGENCY SCOTTSDALE RESORT & SPA AT GAINEY RANCH
Phone: (480)444-1234 **26**

Resort Hotel
$129-$605

AAA Benefit: Members save 10% or more everyday.

Address: 7500 E Doubletree Ranch Rd 85258 **Location:** SR 101 exit 43, 2.6 mi w on Via de Ventura. **Facility:** The resort has a man-made beach, waterslide, spa and many family-friendly recreational activities; a Learning Center offers cultural programs. 493 units, some two bedrooms. 4 stories, interior/exterior corridors. **Parking:** on-site (fee) and valet. **Terms:** check-in 4 pm, 3 day cancellation notice-fee imposed. **Amenities:** high-speed Internet (fee), safes. **Dining:** 5 restaurants, also, Alto Ristorante & Bar, see separate listing, entertainment. **Pool(s):** 10 heated outdoor. **Activities:** saunas, whirlpools, steamrooms, waterslide, recreation programs, bicycles, playground, exercise room, spa. *Fee:* golf-27 holes, 4 lighted tennis courts. **Guest Services:** valet laundry, area transportation-shopping shuttle. **Free Special Amenities: newspaper.**

Visit AAA.com or CAA.ca
for one-stop travel
planning and reservations

HYATT SUMMERFIELD SUITES SCOTTSDALE/OLD TOWN
Phone: (480)946-7700 **48**

Extended Stay Hotel
$79-$499

AAA Benefit: Members save 10% or more everyday.

Address: 4245 N Drinkwater Blvd 85251 **Location:** 0.3 mi e of Scottsdale Rd. **Facility:** 164 units, some two bedrooms, efficiencies and kitchens. 3 stories (no elevator), exterior corridors. **Terms:** check-in 4 pm, cancellation fee imposed. **Amenities:** high-speed Internet. **Pool(s):** heated outdoor. **Activities:** whirlpool, exercise room. **Guest Services:** valet and coin laundry, area transportation-within 5 mi. **Free Special Amenities: full breakfast and high-speed Internet.**

JW MARRIOTT CAMELBACK INN RESORT & SPA
Phone: (480)948-1700 **31**

Contemporary Resort Hotel
$134-$549

AAA Benefit: A deluxe level of comfort and a Member rate.

Address: 5402 E Lincoln Dr 85253 **Location:** 0.5 mi e of Tatum Blvd; on north side of Lincoln Dr. **Facility:** A classic resort on 120 scenic acres, the hotel boasts elegant Southwestern décor with mountain views; seven units have a private pool. 453 units, some efficiencies. 1-2 stories, exterior corridors. **Parking:** on-site and valet. **Terms:** check-in 4 pm, 3 day cancellation notice. **Amenities:** safes, honor bars. *Fee:* video games, high-speed Internet. **Dining:** 6 restaurants, also, BLT Steak, see separate listing, entertainment. **Pool(s):** 2 heated outdoor. **Activities:** saunas, whirlpools, steamrooms, rental bicycles, hiking trails, playground, basketball, shuffleboard, spa. *Fee:* golf-36 holes, 6 lighted tennis courts. **Guest Services:** complimentary and valet laundry. **Free Special Amenities: newspaper.**

LA QUINTA INN & SUITES PHOENIX SCOTTSDALE
Phone: (480)614-5300 **23**

Hotel
$64-$192

Address: 8888 E Shea Blvd 85260 **Location:** SR 101 exit Shea Blvd; northeast corner. **Facility:** 140 units. 3 stories, interior corridors. **Amenities:** video games (fee), high-speed Internet. **Pool(s):** heated outdoor. **Activities:** whirlpool, exercise room. **Guest Services:** valet and coin laundry, area transportation-within 5 mi & Mayo Clinic.

MARRIOTT SCOTTSDALE MCDOWELL MOUNTAIN
Phone: (480)502-3836 **11**

Hotel
$139-$379

AAA Benefit: AAA hotel discounts of 5% or more.

Address: 16770 N Perimeter Dr 85260 **Location:** SR 101 exit 36 (Princess Dr), just w to N Perimeter Dr, then 0.6 mi s. **Facility:** This luxury hotel has a poolside bar area and is adjacent to the TPC Scottsdale Desert Golf Course. 270 units. 4 stories, interior corridors. **Parking:** on-site and valet. **Terms:** check-in 4 pm. **Amenities:** *Fee:* video games, high-speed Internet. **Pool(s):** heated outdoor. **Activities:** saunas, whirlpool, exercise room. **Guest Services:** valet and coin laundry, area transportation-within 10 mi.

(See map & index p. 158.)

MARRIOTT SCOTTSDALE SUITES OLD TOWN

Phone: (480)945-1550   **50**

Hotel
$149-$349

Marriott
HOTELS & RESORTS

AAA Benefit: AAA hotel discounts of 5% or more.

Address: 7325 E 3rd Ave 85251 **Location:** Just e of Scottsdale Rd. **Facility:** 243 units. 8 stories, interior corridors. **Parking:** on-site (fee) and valet. **Terms:** check-in 4 pm. **Amenities:** *Fee:* video games, high-speed Internet. **Pool(s):** heated outdoor. **Activities:** sauna, whirlpool, exercise room. **Guest Services:** valet and coin laundry.

MILLENNIUM RESORT SCOTTSDALE MCCORMICK RANCH

Phone: (480)948-5050   **28**

Hotel
$59-$339

Address: 7401 N Scottsdale Rd 85253 **Location:** 0.8 mi n of Indian Bend Rd. **Facility:** 176 units, some two bedrooms, three bedrooms and kitchens. 3 stories, interior corridors. **Terms:** check-in 4 pm, 3 day cancellation notice-fee imposed. **Amenities:** high-speed Internet. **Dining:** Piñon Grill, see separate listing. **Pool(s):** heated outdoor. **Activities:** canoeing, paddleboats, boat dock, fishing, lighted tennis court, bicycles, volleyball, exercise room. *Fee:* golf-36 holes. **Guest Services:** valet laundry, area transportation-golf & spa. **Free Special Amenities:** newspaper and room upgrade (subject to availability with advance reservations).

MOTEL 6 SCOTTSDALE #29

Phone: (480)946-2280   **44**

Motel
$65-$85 2/1-4/12
$51-$61 4/13-1/31

Address: 6848 E Camelback Rd 85251 **Location:** Just w of Scottsdale Rd. **Facility:** 122 units. 2 stories (no elevator), exterior corridors. **Pool(s):** heated outdoor. **Activities:** whirlpool. **Guest Services:** coin laundry.

ORANGE TREE GOLF RESORT

Phone: (480)948-6100   **18**

Hotel
$99-$200

Address: 10601 N 56th St 85254 **Location:** SR 101 exit 41 (Shea Blvd), 4.1 mi w, then just n. **Facility:** 160 units. 2 stories (no elevator), exterior corridors. **Terms:** check-in 4 pm, 3 day cancellation notice-fee imposed. **Amenities:** safes. **Pool(s):** heated outdoor. **Activities:** whirlpool, jogging, exercise room. *Fee:* golf-18 holes, massage. **Guest Services:** valet and coin laundry.

Get pet travel tips
and enter the photo contest
at AAA.com/PetBook

▼ See AAA listing p. 215 ▼

THE PHOENICIAN
A LUXURY COLLECTION RESORT
Scottsdale

You've Arrived

THE PHOENICIAN

Welcome to elegant accommodations, award-winning cuisine, a stunning golf course and a lavish spa. Located at the base of Camelback Mountain, The Phoenician is where lasting memories are made.

- 27 holes of Championship Golf
- 9 Sparkling Pools and 8 Restaurants
- Award-winning Centre for Well-Being Spa
- 11 Lighted Tennis Courts
- $25 million Art Collection

RESERVATIONS: 800-955-7352
thephoenician.com
6000 East Camelback Road, Scottsdale, Arizona 85251

AAA
Five Diamond
Award

(See map & index p. 158.)

THE PHOENICIAN

Phone: (480)941-8200 **39**

THE LUXURY COLLECTION

Resort Hotel
$199-$2500

AAA Benefit: Inspiring travels with your AAA Preferred rates.

Address: 6000 E Camelback Rd 85251 **Location:** 0.5 mi w of 64th St. **Facility:** Tucked at the base of Camelback Mountain, this resort features world-class dining and golf, a tropical lagoon and elegant rooms. 647 units, some two bedrooms and kitchens. 3-4 stories, interior/exterior corridors. **Parking:** valet and street only. **Terms:** check-in 4 pm, 7 day cancellation notice-fee imposed. **Amenities:** safes, honor bars. *Fee:* video games, high-speed Internet. **Dining:** 4 restaurants, also, Il Terrazzo, J & G Steakhouse, see separate listings, entertainment. **Pool(s):** 8 heated outdoor. **Activities:** saunas, whirlpools, steamrooms, waterslide, recreation programs, rental bicycles, hiking trails, jogging, playground, basketball, spa. *Fee:* golf-27 holes, 12 tennis courts (11 lighted). **Guest Services:** valet laundry, area transportation-within property. *(See ad p. 214.)*

THE PIMA INN & SUITES

Phone: (480)948-3800 **30**

Condominium
$169-$219 2/1-4/7
$79-$179 4/8-1/31

Address: 7330 N Pima Rd 85258 **Location:** 0.4 mi n of Indian Bend Rd; on west side of Pima Rd. **Facility:** 121 condominiums. 2 stories, interior/exterior corridors. **Terms:** cancellation fee imposed. **Amenities:** high-speed Internet. **Pool(s):** heated outdoor. **Activities:** sauna, whirlpool, bicycles, exercise room. **Guest Services:** valet and coin laundry, area transportation-within 5 mi.

RADISSON FORT MCDOWELL RESORT & CASINO

Phone: (480)789-5300

Resort Hotel
$79-$499

Address: 10438 N Ft. McDowell Rd 85264 **Location:** Jct Shea Blvd, 1.6 mi ne on SR 87. Located in a rural area with mountain views. **Facility:** Situated on the lands of Fort McDowell Yavapai Nation, this property boasts elegant guest rooms and baths reflecting Native American design. 246 units. 5 stories, interior corridors. **Parking:** on-site and valet. **Terms:** check-in 4 pm, cancellation fee imposed. **Amenities:** video games (fee), high-speed Internet, safes. **Dining:** Ahnala, see separate listing. **Pool(s):** 2 heated outdoor. **Activities:** whirlpools, exercise room, spa. *Fee:* golf-36 holes, horseback riding. **Guest Services:** valet laundry, area transportation-within 5 mi.

RESIDENCE INN BY MARRIOTT, SCOTTSDALE/PARADISE VALLEY

Phone: (480)948-8666 **36**

Extended Stay Hotel
$179-$269

Residence Inn Marriott

AAA Benefit: AAA hotel discounts of 5% or more.

Address: 6040 N Scottsdale Rd 85253 **Location:** Just n of McDonald Dr. **Facility:** 122 efficiencies, some two bedrooms. 2 stories (no elevator), interior/exterior corridors. **Amenities:** high-speed Internet. **Pool(s):** heated outdoor. **Activities:** whirlpool, sports court, exercise room. **Guest Services:** valet and coin laundry. **Free Special Amenities:** full breakfast and high-speed Internet.

RESIDENCE INN SCOTTSDALE NORTH

Phone: (480)563-4120 **8**

Extended Stay Hotel
$79-$257

AAA Benefit: AAA hotel discounts of 5% or more.

Address: 17011 N Scottsdale Rd 85255 **Location:** SR 101 exit 34 (Scottsdale Rd), 1.1 mi s; northeast corner of Frank Lloyd Wright Blvd and Scottsdale Rd. **Facility:** 120 units, some two bedrooms, efficiencies and kitchens. 3 stories, interior corridors. **Amenities:** video games (fee), high-speed Internet. **Pool(s):** heated outdoor. **Activities:** whirlpool, sports court, exercise room. **Guest Services:** valet and coin laundry, area transportation-within 5 mi.

SCOTTSDALE COTTONWOODS RESORT

Phone: (480)991-1414 **35**

Resort Hotel
Rates not provided

Address: 6160 N Scottsdale Rd 85253 **Location:** Just n of McDonald Dr. Adjacent to Borgata Shopping Village. **Facility:** Spread over 25 acres, the hotel's grounds are a combination of desert landscaping and wide, tree-shaded lawns. 171 units, some kitchens and houses. 1 story, exterior corridors. **Terms:** check-in 4 pm. **Amenities:** high-speed Internet (fee), safes. **Pool(s):** 2 heated outdoor. **Activities:** whirlpools, putting green, 4 tennis courts (2 lighted), jogging, shuffleboard, exercise room. *Fee:* massage. **Guest Services:** valet laundry, area transportation-within 5 mi. **Free Special Amenities:** early check-in/late check-out and preferred room (subject to availability with advance reservations).

Complete Vacation Planning

AAA.com/Travel and **CAA.ca/Travel** – everything you need to plan and book your vacations, backed by the travel experts at local AAA/CAA offices.

(See map & index p. 158.)

SCOTTSDALE OLD TOWN COURTYARD BY MARRIOTT
Phone: (480)429-7785 **54**

▼▼▼
Hotel
$129-$259

AAA Benefit: AAA hotel discounts of 5% or more.

Address: 3311 N Scottsdale Rd 85251 **Location:** Jct Drinkwater Blvd. **Facility:** 180 units. 5 stories, interior corridors. **Pool(s):** heated outdoor. **Activities:** whirlpool, exercise room. **Guest Services:** valet and coin laundry. **Free Special Amenities:** early check-in/late check-out and high-speed Internet.

SCOTTSDALE RESORT & ATHLETIC CLUB
Phone: (480)344-0600 **32**

▼▼▼
Hotel
$159-$609 2/1-4/15
$89-$259 4/16-1/31

Address: 8235 E Indian Bend Rd 85250 **Location:** 1.5 mi e of Scottsdale Rd. **Facility:** 85 units, some kitchens. 2 stories (no elevator), exterior corridors. **Terms:** cancellation fee imposed. **Amenities:** high-speed Internet. *Some:* safes. **Dining:** OC Seven Restaurant & Bar, see separate listing. **Pool(s):** 3 heated outdoor. **Activities:** saunas, whirlpools, 11 lighted tennis courts, spa. **Guest Services:** valet and coin laundry. **Free Special Amenities:** continental breakfast and high-speed Internet.

Scottsdale Resort & Athletic Club

Peaceful, prime location. Outstanding service, spacious suites and villas and an award-winning spa.

SCOTTSDALE RESORT & CONFERENCE CENTER
Phone: (480)991-9000 **29**

▼▼▼ ▼▼▼
Resort Hotel
$79-$359

Address: 7700 E McCormick Pkwy 85258 **Location:** Just w of Hayden Rd; 0.7 mi e of Scottsdale Rd. **Facility:** Highlights at the property include hacienda-style rooms, shaded courtyards and spacious public areas with gracious appointments. 326 units. 2-3 stories, interior/exterior corridors. **Parking:** on-site and valet. **Terms:** 3 day cancellation notice-fee imposed. **Amenities:** honor bars. *Fee:* video games, high-speed Internet. **Dining:** 3 restaurants, also, Palm Court, see separate listing. **Pool(s):** 2 heated outdoor. **Activities:** saunas, whirlpools, steamroom, rental bicycles, jogging, sports court, basketball, volleyball, exercise room, spa. *Fee:* 4 lighted tennis courts. **Guest Services:** valet laundry. **Free Special Amenities:** newspaper and high-speed Internet.

SCOTTSDALE THUNDERBIRD SUITES
Phone: (480)951-4000 **15**

▼▼▼
Hotel
$59-$189

Address: 7515 E Butherus Dr 85260 **Location:** 0.8 mi n of Thunderbird Rd; 0.5 mi e of Scottsdale Rd. Located at Scottsdale Municipal Airport. **Facility:** 120 units. 4 stories, interior/exterior corridors. **Terms:** cancellation fee imposed. **Pool(s):** heated outdoor. **Activities:** whirlpool, exercise room. **Guest Services:** valet and coin laundry, area transportation-within 5 mi.

SCOTTSDALE VILLA MIRAGE
Phone: (480)473-4000 **2**

▼▼▼
Condominium
$99-$359

Address: 7887 E Princess Blvd 85255 **Location:** SR 101 exit 34, 0.7 mi s on Scottsdale Rd, then 0.7 mi e. **Facility:** These garden-style condominiums are pleasantly appointed and convenient to shops, attractions and sports centers. 224 condominiums. 3 stories (no elevator), exterior corridors. **Terms:** check-in 4 pm, cancellation fee imposed. **Amenities:** *Some:* safes. **Pool(s):** heated outdoor. **Activities:** saunas, whirlpools, steamrooms, 2 lighted tennis courts, recreation programs, playground, volleyball, exercise room. *Fee:* massage. **Guest Services:** complimentary and valet laundry.

SHERATON DESERT OASIS
Phone: (480)515-5888 **3**

▼▼▼
Condominium
$99-$449

Sheraton **AAA Benefit:** Members get up to 15% off, plus Starwood Preferred Guest® bonuses.

Address: 17700 N Hayden Rd 85255 **Location:** SR 101 exit 35 (Hayden Rd), 0.5 mi s. **Facility:** Waterfalls spilling over boulders into pools, charming garden areas with tall palm trees and attractive, well-appointed rooms combine to create an oasis. 300 condominiums. 2-3 stories (no elevator), exterior corridors. **Terms:** check-in 4 pm, 3 day cancellation notice-fee imposed. **Amenities:** high-speed Internet, safes. **Pool(s):** 2 heated outdoor. **Activities:** whirlpool, recreation programs, playground, exercise room. **Guest Services:** complimentary laundry.

SLEEP INN NORTH SCOTTSDALE/PHOENIX
Phone: (480)998-9211 **9**

▼▼▼
Hotel
$69-$229

Address: 16630 N Scottsdale Rd 85254 **Location:** Just s of Bell Rd. **Facility:** 107 units. 3 stories, interior corridors. **Terms:** cancellation fee imposed. **Amenities:** video games (fee). **Pool(s):** heated outdoor. **Activities:** whirlpool, exercise room. **Guest Services:** valet and coin laundry, area transportation-within 5 mi.

Plan. Map. Go.

TripTik® Travel Planner

Where premier mapping technology meets complete travel information. Only on AAA.com and CAA.ca.

(See map & index p. 158.)

SPRINGHILL SUITES BY MARRIOTT-SCOTTSDALE NORTH   **Phone:** (480)922-8700 **6**

Hotel
$59-$199

AAA Benefit: AAA hotel discounts of 5% or more.

Address: 17020 N Scottsdale Rd 85255 **Location:** Just n of Frank Lloyd Wright Blvd. Located in a commercial area. **Facility:** 121 units. 4 stories, interior corridors. **Amenities:** Some: high-speed Internet, safes. **Pool(s):** heated outdoor. **Activities:** whirlpool, exercise room. **Guest Services:** valet and coin laundry, area transportation-within 5 mi.

TALKING STICK RESORT   **Phone:** (480)850-7777 **33**

Resort Hotel
$109-$329

Address: 9800 E Indian Bend Rd 85256 **Location:** SR 101 exit 44 (E Indian Bend Rd), just e. **Facility:** Reminiscent of a Vegas resort, this upscale property combines casino glitz with outstanding entertainment, fine dining and luxurious accommodations. 497 units. 15 stories, interior corridors. **Parking:** on-site and valet. **Terms:** 3 day cancellation notice-fee imposed. **Amenities:** high-speed Internet, safes. Some: honor bars. **Dining:** 3 restaurants, also, Ocean Trail, Orange Sky, see separate listings. nightclub, entertainment. **Pool(s):** 3 heated outdoor. **Activities:** whirlpools, steamrooms, exercise room. spa. Fee: golf-36 holes, game room. **Guest Services:** valet laundry. (See ad on insert, p. 218, inside back cover.)

TOWNEPLACE SUITES SCOTTSDALE BY MARRIOTT   **Phone:** (480)551-1100 **22**

Extended Stay Hotel
$59-$209

AAA Benefit: AAA hotel discounts of 5% or more.

Address: 10740 N 90th St 85260 **Location:** SR 101 exit Shea Blvd, just e to 90th St, then just n. **Facility:** 131 kitchen units, some two bedrooms. 3 stories, interior corridors. **Amenities:** high-speed Internet. **Pool(s):** heated outdoor. **Activities:** exercise room. **Guest Services:** valet and coin laundry, area transportation-within 5 mi.

THE WESTIN KIERLAND RESORT & SPA   **Phone:** (480)624-1000 **14**

Resort Hotel
$139-$709

WESTIN HOTELS & RESORTS **AAA Benefit:** Enjoy up to 15% off your next stay, plus Starwood Preferred Guest® bonuses.

Address: 6902 E Greenway Pkwy 85254 **Location:** 0.5 mi w of Scottsdale Rd. **Facility:** Located adjacent to an upscale shopping area in North Scottsdale, this upscale resort offers spectacular views across the lagoon to the golf course. 732 units. 11 stories, interior corridors. **Parking:** on-site and valet. **Terms:** check-in 4 pm, 7 day cancellation notice-fee imposed. **Amenities:** high-speed Internet (fee), safes, honor bars. **Dining:** 5 restaurants, also, Brittlebush Bar & Grill, Deseo, Nellie Cashman's Monday Club Cafe, see separate listings. **Pool(s):** 2 heated outdoor. **Activities:** saunas, whirlpools, steamrooms, waterslide, recreation programs, playground, basketball, exercise room, spa. Fee: golf-27 holes, 2 lighted tennis courts. **Guest Services:** valet laundry, area transportation-nearby shopping centers.

THE WESTIN KIERLAND VILLAS   **Phone:** (480)624-1700 **12**

Vacation Rental Condominium
$159-$659

WESTIN HOTELS & RESORTS **AAA Benefit:** Enjoy up to 15% off your next stay, plus Starwood Preferred Guest® bonuses.

Address: 15620 N Clubgate Dr 85254 **Location:** Jct Scottsdale Rd, 0.6 mi w on Greenway Pkwy, then just n. **Facility:** Elegant, attractively furnished rooms feature kitchens and balconies or patios, some overlooking the golf course. 298 condominiums. 3-4 stories, exterior corridors. **Terms:** check-in 4 pm, 3 day cancellation notice-fee imposed. **Amenities:** high-speed Internet, safes. **Pool(s):** 3 heated outdoor. **Activities:** sauna, whirlpools, steamroom, waterslide, recreation programs, playground, exercise room. Fee: golf-27 holes, 2 lighted tennis courts, massage. **Guest Services:** complimentary laundry, area transportation-within resort & shopping centers. **Free Special Amenities:** high-speed Internet.

WINGATE BY WYNDHAM SCOTTSDALE   **Phone:** (480)922-6500 **16**

Hotel
$80-$251

Address: 14255 N 87th St 85260 **Location:** SR 101 exit 39 (Raintree Dr), just w, then 0.3 mi s. **Facility:** 117 units, some two bedrooms and efficiencies. 4 stories, interior corridors. **Amenities:** video games (fee), high-speed Internet, safes. **Pool(s):** heated outdoor. **Activities:** whirlpool, putting green, exercise room. **Guest Services:** valet and coin laundry, area transportation-within 5 mi. **Free Special Amenities:** expanded continental breakfast and high-speed Internet.

AAA/CAA MEMBER DISCOUNTS AHEAD

Consider your AAA/CAA card as the smallest, lowest tech GPS navigator imaginable...it will take you right to the best deals in town, wherever "town" is for you. Go to **AAA.com/discounts** to find your way to the best deals.

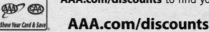
Show Your Card & Save

AAA.com/discounts

10% OFF BEST AVAILABLE RATES*
No daily resort fee

Winning makes a statement.

AAA
Four Diamond
Award

TALKING STICK RESORT

SCOTTSDALE | 877.563.1671 | TALKINGSTICKRESORT.COM

Proudly owned and operated by the Salt River Pima-Maricopa Indian Community.

*Must mention AAA at time of reservation to receive discount. Not valid for groups or with any other offer.

(See map & index p. 158.)

W SCOTTSDALE
Phone: (480)970-2100 **45**

▼▼▼
Hotel
$129-$699

W HOTELS

AAA Benefit: Special member room rates, plus Starwood Preferred Guest® bonuses.

Address: 7277 E Camelback Rd 85251 **Location:** Just e of Scottsdale Rd. **Facility:** This trendy hotel offers a zen garden as well as "whatever-whenever" service levels. Upscale rooms feature attractive bedding and spacious work areas. 224 units. 7 stories, interior corridors. **Parking:** on-site (fee) and valet. **Terms:** cancellation fee imposed. **Amenities:** safes, honor bars. *Fee:* video games, high-speed Internet. **Dining:** Sushi Roku, see separate listing. **Pool(s):** heated outdoor. **Activities:** exercise room, spa. **Guest Services:** valet laundry, area transportation-within 5 mi.

[SAVE] [🍴] [📶] [⅄] CALL [⌂M] [🛏] [BIZ] [📶] FEE[📺]
/ SOME UNITS FEE [🐾] [🔒] [🖥]

XONA RESORT SUITES, AN ASCEND COLLECTION HOTEL
Phone: (480)585-1234 **1**

▼▼▼
Hotel
$159-$399 2/1-5/15
$79-$349 5/16-1/31

Address: 7677 E Princess Blvd 85255 **Location:** SR 101 exit 34 (Scottsdale Rd), 0.8 mi s, then just e. **Facility:** 431 units, some two bedrooms and kitchens. 2-3 stories (no elevator), exterior corridors. **Terms:** cancellation fee imposed. **Pool(s):** 4 heated outdoor. **Activities:** whirlpools, recreation programs, jogging, exercise room. **Guest Services:** valet and coin laundry, area transportation-within 5 mi.

[🍴] [⅄] [🛏] [BIZ] [📶] [✕] FEE[📺] [🖥]
/ SOME UNITS FEE [🐾] [🔒] [🖥]

THE SCOTTSDALE PLAZA RESORT
Phone: 480/948-5000

[fyi] Not evaluated. **Address:** 7200 N Scottsdale Rd 85253 **Location:** Just n of Indian Bend Rd. Facilities, services, and decor characterize an upscale property.

WHERE TO EAT

AHNALA
Phone: 480/836-5305

▼▼▼
Regional Southwestern
$8-$37

AAA Inspector Notes: Attention is paid to presenting innovative dishes that showcase local ingredients, such as Idaho trout crusted with Fort McDowell pecans. Chef Ekberg enjoys chatting with diners as much as creating lush foods, such as Maine lobster empanadas. Ahnala (mesquite grilled) items feature wood obtained from the local Yavapai tribe. **Bar:** full bar. **Reservations:** suggested. **Address:** 10438 N Ft. McDowell Rd 85264 **Location:** Jct Shea Blvd, 1.6 mi ne on SR 87; in Radisson Fort McDowell Resort & Casino. **Parking:** on-site and valet. [B] [L] [D]

ALTO RISTORANTE & BAR
Phone: 480/444-1234 **24**

▼▼▼
Italian
$18-$32

AAA Inspector Notes: A modern, elegant space, friendly staff and excellent food attract patrons to this dining spot. Enjoy trying the delicate homemade pasta, including ravioli of mozzarella. Desserts range from delicate sorbets to hearty chocolate hazelnut mousse cake. **Bar:** full bar. **Address:** 7500 E Doubletree Ranch Rd 85258 **Location:** SR 101 exit 43, 2.6 mi w on Via de Ventura; in Hyatt Regency Scottsdale Resort & Spa at Gainey Ranch. **Parking:** on-site and valet. [D]

ARCADIA FARMS
Phone: 480/941-5665 **55**

▼▼ ▼▼
American
$11-$14

AAA Inspector Notes: The cheery garden decor delights diners' eyes in this popular eatery in mid-Scottsdale. Lush salads, thick sandwiches and desserts tempt any appetite. Patio seating is an option. **Bar:** beer & wine. **Reservations:** suggested. **Address:** 7014 E 1st Ave 85251 **Location:** Just w of Scottsdale Rd. **Parking:** valet and street only. [B] [L]

ATLAS BISTRO
Phone: 480/990-2433 **65**

▼▼▼
International
$25-$35

AAA Inspector Notes: Award-winning international cuisine is served in a simple, yet intimate setting. With an ever-changing menu, diners may see such exotic choices as crispy veal sweetbreads, California squab or Cape Cod skate. The cozy spot is BYOB (Bring Your Own Bottle), but is conveniently attached to a wine shop. **Reservations:** suggested. **Address:** 2515 N Scottsdale Rd 85257 **Location:** Jct Thomas Rd, 0.4 mi s. [D]

THE BAMBOO CLUB
Phone: 480/998-1287

▼▼▼
Pacific Rim
$9-$23

AAA Inspector Notes: The contemporary, upbeat and casual decor lends well to an atmosphere of conviviality. Friends and family get together over shared dishes from Thailand, China, Japan, Hawaii, Malaysia, Tahiti, Korea, Vietnam and other exotic Asian ports of call. The menu offers a wide selection of popular foods that are "sizzled, grilled, steamed, wokked or noodled" and includes choices ranging from finger foods to full entrees. **Bar:** full bar. **Reservations:** suggested. **Address:** 8624 E Shea Blvd 85260 **Location:** SR 101 exit 41, just w. [L] [D]

BLOOM
Phone: 480/922-5666 **23**

▼▼▼
American
$9-$29

AAA Inspector Notes: Such tasty dishes as marinated Chinese chicken salad and wood-grilled, center-cut pork chop with caramelized apples are beautifully presented. Sophisticated decor and attentive service add finishing touches to the dining experience. The eatery is completely non-smoking. **Bar:** full bar. **Reservations:** suggested. **Address:** 8877 N Scottsdale Rd, Suite 402 85253 **Location:** Just s of Doubletree Ranch Rd; in New Shops at Gainey Village. [L] [D]

BLT STEAK
Phone: 480/905-7979 **28**

▼▼▼ ▼▼
Steak
$26-$92

AAA Inspector Notes: Created by chef Laurent Tourondel, this sophisticated steakhouse combines Southwest flavors, outstanding cuts of beef including Kobe strip and wagyu rib-eye, seafood selections, and seasonings from the restaurant's own organic herb garden. The atmosphere is casual yet elegant, with sweeping views of the mountains. **Bar:** full bar. **Reservations:** suggested. **Address:** 5402 E Lincoln Dr 85253 **Location:** 0.5 mi e of Tatum Blvd; on north side of Lincoln Dr; JW Marriott Camelback Inn Resort & Spa. **Parking:** on-site and valet. [D]

BOURBON STEAK
Phone: 480/513-6002 **3**

▼▼▼ ▼▼
Steak
$22-$175

AAA Inspector Notes: Acclaimed chef Michael Mina's bourbon steak offers a diverse range of delectable menu selections. Along with the tender Kobe and all-natural USDA Prime beef, diners will find Colorado lamb, Kurobuta pork, Maine lobster, ahi tuna and Scottish salmon, to name a few. An incredible dining experience awaits. **Bar:** full bar. **Reservations:** suggested. **Address:** 7575 E Princess Dr 85255 **Location:** SR 101 exit 34 (Scottsdale Rd), 0.8 mi s, then just e; 0.6 mi n of Bell Rd; in Fairmont Scottsdale Princess. **Parking:** on-site and valet. [D] CALL [⌂M]

(See map & index p. 158.)

BRAVO BISTRO
Phone: 480/481-7614   50

Italian
$9-$32

AAA Inspector Notes: Near excellent shopping in Old Town Scottsdale, this intimate eatery serves both Italian and Mediterranean-inspired cuisine. Examples include penne with wild mushrooms, paella and Israeli couscous, along with prime grilled meats. **Bar:** full bar. **Reservations:** suggested. **Address:** 4327 N Scottsdale Rd 85251 **Location:** SR 101 exit 46 (Chaparral Rd), 2.1 mi w to Scottsdale Rd, then 0.8 mi s. **Parking:** on-site and valet.

D   LATE

THE BREAKFAST CLUB
Phone: 480/222-2582   47

Breakfast
$6-$15

AAA Inspector Notes: Breakfast choices will satisfy any sleepy patron wanting to jump-start the day. Friendly, wide-awake staffers quickly serve fresh coffee, eggs of any style, juices and homemade baked goods. Lunch salads and sandwiches are hearty. **Address:** 4400 N Scottsdale Rd 85251 **Location:** Northwest corner of Stetson Dr and Scottsdale Rd.   B   L

BRITTLEBUSH BAR & GRILL
Phone: 480/624-1000   10

American
$12-$14

AAA Inspector Notes: Dine while overlooking the golf greens at this relaxed eatery located at Westin Kierland Resort's golf shop. Friendly service, hearty salads and sandwiches with soups entice everyone. **Bar:** full bar. **Reservations:** suggested. **Address:** 6902 E Greenway Pkwy 85254 **Location:** 0.5 mi w of Scottsdale Rd; in The Westin Kierland Resort & Spa.   L   D

CAFE ZU ZU
Phone: 480/421-7997   57

American
$10-$30

AAA Inspector Notes: Chef Wiley delights the palate with delectable dishes such as orange-basted breast of duck or chicken picatta with lemon caper butter. Also on the menu are comfort foods including meatloaf and macaroni and cheese. The decor is reminiscent of a trendy, upscale version of a 1960s diner. **Bar:** full bar. **Address:** 6850 E Main St 85251 **Location:** 0.4 mi w of Scottsdale Rd, just s of Indian School Rd; on north side of Main St; in Hotel Valley Ho. **Parking:** on-site and valet.

B   L   D   CALL   M

CANTINA LAREDO
Phone: 480/951-3807   8

Mexican
$8-$20

AAA Inspector Notes: Modern yet relaxed, this restaurant features creative Mexican fare. A great starter of top-shelf guacamole, which is prepared tableside, primes the palate for an entree of enchiladas, tacos, fajitas and chiles rellenos. **Bar:** full bar. **Address:** 7361 E Frank Lloyd Wright Blvd 85260 **Location:** Just e of Scottsdale Rd.   L   D

Gourmet Mexican food, fresh-squeezed lime margaritas

CARLOS O'BRIENS MEXICAN RESTAURANT
Phone: 480/367-0469

Mexican
$6-$15

AAA Inspector Notes: This family restaurant serves all the classic Mexican favorites: fajitas, enchiladas and Spanish chicken. Attentive servers take guests through the meal, from chips and salsa to the sweet desserts, which are served in ample portions. **Bar:** full bar. **Address:** 7111 E Bell Rd 85254 **Location:** Just w of Scottsdale Rd.   L   D

CARLSBAD TAVERN
Phone: 480/970-8164   63

Southwestern
$9-$25

AAA Inspector Notes: There are no bats here. Instead, guests find great regional dishes served by a helpful staff. A newspaper menu offers horoscopes and fun reading, along with such choices as tequila shrimp and flan with prickly pear sauce. A pond and bridge highlight the outdoor patio area. **Bar:** full bar. **Address:** 3313 N Hayden Rd 85251 **Location:** Just s of Osborn Rd.

L   D   LATE

CHOLLA PRIME STEAKHOUSE
Phone: 480/850-7736   68

Regional Steak
$20-$38

AAA Inspector Notes: This fine-dining establishment has an elegant decor with Native American art adding sparks of color to the soft grays of the quiet room. Specialty items such as barbecue-spiced buffalo tenderloin join beef steaks, seafood and lamb on the menu. Fresh salads and tasty desserts complement any selection. **Bar:** full bar. **Reservations:** suggested. **Address:** 524 N 92nd St 85256 **Location:** SR 101 exit 50 (McKellips Rd), just ne; in Casino Arizona. **Parking:** on-site and valet.   D   CALL   M

CITIZEN PUBLIC HOUSE
Phone: 480/398-4208   53

American
$17-$32

AAA Inspector Notes: Enjoy the upscale and lively atmosphere of this gastro pub featuring an innovative menu with choices including fair trade coffee-charred short ribs and kilt-lifter fondue with hunter's sausage. Wash it all down with a hand-crafted classic cocktail. **Bar:** full bar. **Address:** 7111 E 5th Ave 85251 **Location:** Jct Scottsdale Rd, just w. **Parking:** street only.   D   LATE

CLAIM JUMPER
Phone: 480/951-6111

American
$10-$21

AAA Inspector Notes: Great menu variety makes this place a good stop for parties with diverse tastes. Choices include specialty appetizers, salads, rotisserie chicken and barbecue items, not to mention good comfort foods, such as traditional pot pie. Hearty portions satisfy big appetites. The atmosphere is fun and lively. **Bar:** full bar. **Address:** 7000 E Shea Blvd 85254 **Location:** Just w of jct N Scottsdale Rd and E Shea Blvd; in Scottsdale Promenade.

L   D   CALL   M

COWBOY CIAO
Phone: 480/946-3111   48

American
$12-$35

AAA Inspector Notes: Eclectic, artsy decor sets the stage for fun dining. Among "wine-friendly" dishes are peppercorn-seared sea bass with pan-fried penne and pig and pudding, a preparation of pulled pork in chipotle and balsamic barbecue sauce over chili grits. Try warm bread pudding or Mexican chocolate pot de creme for a satisfying meal-ender. **Bar:** full bar. **Reservations:** suggested. **Address:** 7133 E Stetson Dr 85251 **Location:** Just w of Scottsdale Rd; downtown. **Parking:** street only.

L   D

DESEO
Phone: 480/624-1202   12

New Latin American
$24-$32

AAA Inspector Notes: With influences spanning the Caribbean and South America, Chef Rodriguez prepares a savory selection of ceviche, creative seafood entrées and Kobe beef. The open kitchen allows for interaction among diners and chefs. Resident Cuban artist Nelson Miranda-Garcia demonstrates his talents five days a week in the dining room, and his work is on display. **Bar:** full bar. **Reservations:** suggested. **Address:** 6902 E Greenway Pkwy 85254 **Location:** 0.5 mi w of Scottsdale Rd; in The Westin Kierland Resort & Spa. **Parking:** on-site and valet.   D

(See map & index p. 158.)

DON AND CHARLIE'S
Phone: 480/990-0900 (46)

▼▼ ▼▼

American
$11-$42

AAA Inspector Notes: This restaurant appeals to the comfort zone-casual atmosphere, relaxed staff and a varied menu. Sports fans will enjoy perusing photographs of ball players, signed baseball bats and framed jerseys. I tried the specialty barbecue ribs-the sauce and preparation technique were delicious. Other menu items include broasted chicken and Momo's spaghetti marinara as well as an extensive steak list. Chocolate lovers will delight in the triple-layer cake, served with a gravy boat of chocolate sauce. **Bar:** full bar. **Address:** 7501 E Camelback Rd 85251 **Location:** Jct Scottsdale Rd, 0.3 mi e. **Parking:** on-site and valet. D

EDDIE V'S PRIME SEAFOOD
Phone: 480/538-8468 (9)

▼▼ ▼▼

Seafood
$20-$40

AAA Inspector Notes: Fresh seafood, steaks and tempting desserts will please any palate at this upscale dining spot. Seasonal fresh seafood selections might include Gulf snapper, swordfish, Jonah crab and West Australian lobster tails. A flaming butter cake topped with bananas Foster is a festive way to finish. **Bar:** full bar. **Reservations:** suggested. **Address:** 15323 N Scottsdale Rd 85254 **Location:** Jct Greenway Haven Loop; in Scottsdale Quarter. **Parking:** on-site and valet. D

ELI'S AMERICAN GRILLE
Phone: 480/948-9800 (18)

▼▼ ▼

American
$8-$31

AAA Inspector Notes: Large portions of sandwiches, steaks, chicken and some seafood dishes are served in this restaurant, where viewing sports is a main attraction. **Bar:** full bar. **Address:** 7000 E Shea Blvd, Suite 140 85254 **Location:** Jct Scottsdale Rd and E Shea Blvd, 2 blks w. L D LATE

FLEMING'S PRIME STEAKHOUSE & WINE BAR
Phone: 480/596-8265 (33)

▼▼ ▼

Steak
$19-$40

AAA Inspector Notes: The warm, clubby atmosphere is the ideal setting for perfectly grilled steaks and seafood. Side dishes come in hearty portions, and salads are fresh and crisp. More than 100 wine selections are available. **Bar:** full bar. **Reservations:** suggested. **Address:** 6333 N Scottsdale Rd 85250 **Location:** Loop 101 exit 45, 2.1 mi w on McDonald Dr, then 0.3 mi n; adjacent to Hilton Scottsdale Resort & Villas. **Parking:** on-site and valet. D

F N B RESTAURANT
Phone: 480/425-9463 (49)

▼▼ ▼

New American
$19-$27

AAA Inspector Notes: The focus at this tiny gem is on fresh, local, quality ingredients. Diners can watch the chef whip up delicious and eclectic comfort food from an ever-changing menu. Try the roasted Jidori chicken with spaetzle and blue lake green beans, or the grilled lamb tenderloin with eggplant, carrots and mint. The wine list features outstanding selections from local wineries. **Bar:** full bar. **Reservations:** suggested. **Address:** 7133 E Stetson Rd 85251 **Location:** Just w of Scottsdale Rd; downtown. **Parking:** street only. D

THE GRILL
Phone: 480/585-4848 (7)

▼▼ ▼

Steak
$11-$48

AAA Inspector Notes: Overlooking the TPC golf course, this upscale casual restaurant presents a menu of Prime, dry-aged steaks and fresh seafood. The well-trained staff delivers attentive, expert service. **Bar:** full bar. **Reservations:** suggested. **Address:** 7575 E Princess Dr 85253 **Location:** SR 101 exit 34 (Scottsdale Rd), 0.8 mi s, then just e; 0.6 mi n of Bell Rd; in Fairmont Scottsdale Princess. B L D

HAVANA PATIO CAFE
Phone: 480/991-1496 (5)

▼▼ ◆

Cuban
$7-$25

AAA Inspector Notes: Fresh Latin flavors and elements from Cuba and Spain infuse palate-pleasing dishes at this spot. The garden atmosphere is delightfully casual. A gluten-free menu is available upon request. **Bar:** full bar. **Address:** 6245 E Bell Rd 85254 **Location:** 1 mi w of Scottsdale Rd. L D

IL TERRAZZO
Phone: 480/423-2530 (35)

▼▼ ◆▼

Italian
$18-$39

AAA Inspector Notes: Upscale Italian dishes boast artisan cheeses, fresh organic vegetables and specially aged olive oil. The menu offers rich and creamy pasta with lobster, fresh porcini or lamb ragu, double-cut pork chops with black trumpet mushrooms, big eye tuna with Sicilian caponata and dry-aged, bone-in rib-eye. Guests can dine indoors with garden views or on a covered patio. The accomplished staff is friendly and knowledgeable. **Bar:** full bar. **Reservations:** suggested. **Address:** 6000 E Camelback Rd 85251 **Location:** 0.5 mi w of 64th St; in The Phoenician. **Parking:** on-site and valet. B L D CALL ♿M

IRUNA
Phone: 480/398-3020 (60)

◆▼◆

Small Plates
$8-$19

AAA Inspector Notes: The classy, yet casual decor of this spot features Joan Miro inspired artwork and barn-style rich wood ceilings. Fruity cocktails have the perfect amount of sweetness. The nicely balanced sugariness of the beets combined well with tart Spanish cheeses. The apple, fennel, walnut and grapefruit salad topped with Cabrales cheese crumbles is a refreshing twist. The calamari is crisp and soft, while the duck is pleasingly paired with pears and Marcona almonds. Service is friendly and enthusiastic. **Bar:** full bar. **Address:** 7217 E 1st St 85251 **Location:** Just e of jct Scottsdale Rd; in Old Town Scottsdale. **Parking:** street only. D

JADE PALACE CHINESE RESTAURANT
Phone: 480/391-0607 (21)

▼▼ ▼

Chinese
$8-$20

AAA Inspector Notes: In a strip mall across from the hospital, this restaurant is a friendly place to dine. On the menu are traditional favorites, as well as specialty dinners and healthy choices. Reasonably priced lunches include soup, crab puff, spring roll and fried rice. **Bar:** full bar. **Address:** 9160 E Shea Blvd 85260 **Location:** SR 101 exit Shea Blvd, 0.4 mi e. L D

J & G STEAKHOUSE
Phone: 480/214-8000 (36)

▼▼ ◆▼

Steak
$16-$60

AAA Inspector Notes: The first of many upscale steakhouses from Michelin starred chef Jean-Georges Vongerichten, this restaurant sits atop the Phoenician Resort and affords commanding views of the valley. Fresh, local ingredients combine with premium cuts of meat and global seafood selections to create a memorable experience. **Bar:** full bar. **Reservations:** suggested. **Address:** 6000 E Camelback Rd 85251 **Location:** 0.5 mi w of 64th St; in The Phoenician. **Parking:** on-site and valet. D CALL ♿M

JEWEL OF THE CROWN
Phone: 480/949-8000 (62)

▼▼ ▼▼

Indian
$7-$22

AAA Inspector Notes: Located in the Scottsdale Civic Center Mall in a garden setting, this colorfully decorated eatery offers specialties from Goa, India, including fiery vindaloo and a creamy spinach with yogurt sauce to drizzle over chicken or lamb. **Bar:** full bar. **Reservations:** required. **Address:** 7373 E Scottsdale Mall 85251 **Location:** Jct Scottsdale Rd, just e on 2nd St to Wells Fargo Ave, then just n to parking garage; in Scottsdale Civic Center Mall. **Parking:** street only. L D

(See map & index p. 158.)

JOLTA JAVA COFFEEHOUSE & SANDWICH SHOPPE
Phone: 480/607-7771 (16)

Coffee/Tea
$7-$10

AAA Inspector Notes: This charming coffeehouse serves tasty sandwiches, soups, salads and dessert in a laid-back setting featuring a lounge area and local artwork. **Address:** 14418 N Scottsdale Rd, Suite 185 85254 **Location:** Southwest corner of Acoma Dr and Scottsdale Rd. [B] [L] CALL &M

KONA GRILL
Phone: 480/429-1100 (43)

Pacific Rim
$9-$30

AAA Inspector Notes: The eclectic menu reflects Pacific influences. In addition to noodle dishes and sushi, lists specialties of macadamia nut chicken and lemon grass-encrusted swordfish. The dining room has a large aquarium, a private area and a sushi bar. The patio opens during warm weather. **Bar:** full bar. **Address:** 7014 E Camelback Rd 85251 **Location:** Just w of Scottsdale Rd; in Scottsdale Fashion Square Mall, ground level.

[L] [D] CALL &M

LA HACIENDA
Phone: 480/585-4848 (4)

Mexican
$12-$31

AAA Inspector Notes: Modern Mexican cuisine is served in an upscale, elegant setting at this eatery. Led by executive chef Richard Sandoval, the culinary team blends creative, bold flavors of the Southwest with traditional European cooking techniques. The Friday suckling pig roast is quite the feast. **Bar:** full bar. **Reservations:** suggested. **Address:** 7575 E Princess Dr 85255 **Location:** SR 101 exit 34 (Scottsdale Rd), 0.8 mi s, then just e; 0.6 mi n of Bell Rd; in Fairmont Scottsdale Princess. **Parking:** on-site and valet. [D]

LOS SOMBREROS
Phone: 480/994-1799 (66)

Mexican
$15-$20

AAA Inspector Notes: Located in a historic home, this small, colorful Mexican restaurant specializes in authentic Oaxacan cuisine with a French influence. **Bar:** full bar. **Address:** 2534 N Scottsdale Rd 85257 **Location:** Just s of Thomas St. [D]

LUSH BURGER
Phone: 480/686-8908 (2)

American
$8-$12

AAA Inspector Notes: Gourmet burgers, shakes and fresh salads are served in a hip, upscale diner setting. The large patio is perfect for warm weather days. **Bar:** beer & wine. **Address:** 18251 Pima Rd 85255 **Location:** SR 101 exit 36 (Princess Dr/Pima Rd), 0.5 mi e; in DC Ranch Crossing. [L] [D]

MACAYO MEXICAN KITCHEN
Phone: 480/596-1181

Mexican
$7-$16

AAA Inspector Notes: The colorfully furnished Mexican-style eatery prepares Sonoran Mexican dishes. Friendly and efficient staffers serve traditional and lighter dishes flavored with this place's own chili peppers, which are grown near Tucson. **Bar:** full bar. **Address:** 11107 N Scottsdale Rd 85254 **Location:** Just n of Shea Blvd.

[L] [D]

MALEE'S THAI ON MAIN
Phone: 480/947-6042 (59)

Regional Thai
$10-$21

AAA Inspector Notes: The food at this casual, popular restaurant is a showcase for interesting combinations of flavors and sauces. Yum woon sen blends chicken, shrimp, cilantro and lime. In the heart of the Old Scottsdale art district, this place also offers patio seating, weather permitting. Staff will happily make suggestions concerning good combinations and flavorful accents. **Reservations:** suggested. **Address:** 7131 E Main St 85251 **Location:** Just s of Indian School Rd; just w of Scottsdale Rd; on south side of Main St. **Parking:** street only.

[L] [D]

MARCELLINO RISTORANTE
Phone: 480/990-9500 (51)

Italian
$16-$47

AAA Inspector Notes: A sophisticated, warm ambience and a helpful, friendly staff create a welcoming atmosphere in which to enjoy wonderful homemade pasta dishes, including several with mussels, clams, shrimp or scallops. Veal, chicken, pork and beef round out classic selections that feature special taste twists. For example, the sauteed veal slices are drizzled with a tangy Gorgonzola sauce. **Bar:** full bar. **Reservations:** suggested. **Address:** 7114 E Stetson Dr 85251 **Location:** Just w of Scottsdale Rd; downtown. [L] [D]

MASTRO'S CITY HALL STEAKHOUSE
Phone: 480/941-4700 (41)

Steak
$27-$78

AAA Inspector Notes: For a purely sophisticated dining experience, it does not get much better than this special occasion steakhouse. Hand-cut USDA Prime steaks are served by an attentive staff that anticipates every need. Live entertainment and dancing create a festive scene in the lounge. **Bar:** full bar. **Reservations:** suggested. **Address:** 6991 E Camelback Rd 85251 **Location:** Corner of Goldwater Blvd. **Parking:** on-site and valet. [D]

MASTRO'S STEAKHOUSE
Phone: 480/585-9500 (1)

Steak
$27-$78

AAA Inspector Notes: For a purely sophisticated dining experience, it does not get much better than this steakhouse. Perfect for special occasions, this is where the well-heeled go to see and be seen. Hand-cut USDA Prime steaks are served by attentive staff that anticipates every need. Live entertainment provides the willing an opportunity to dance. **Bar:** full bar. **Reservations:** suggested. **Address:** 8852 E Pinnacle Peak Rd 85260 **Location:** SR 101 exit 36 (Pima Rd), 3.7 mi n; in La Mirada Shopping Center. **Parking:** on-site and valet. [D]

THE MISSION
Phone: 480/636-5005 (61)

Latin American
$23-$32

AAA Inspector Notes: Right in the heart of Old Town, this trendy, casual, and sophisticated hot spot serves modern Latin cuisine featuring such items as crispy cola pork and green chile duck confit. **Bar:** full bar. **Address:** 3815 N Brown Ave 85251 **Location:** In Old Town Scottsdale. [L] [D]

MODERN STEAK
Phone: 480/423-7000 (42)

Steak
$16-$78

AAA Inspector Notes: Expect a distinctive dining experience at this modern interpretation of a classic steakhouse. Glamorous surroundings combine with upscale presentations and attentive service. Signature dishes include the hot and cold wedge salad with blue cheese and bacon vinaigrette, Midwest prime beef filet and miso glazed Chilean sea bass with oyster mushrooms. **Bar:** full bar. **Reservations:** suggested. **Address:** 7014 E Camelback Rd 85251 **Location:** Jct Scottsdale Rd; in Scottsdale Fashion Square Mall. **Parking:** on-site and valet.   [L] [D]

NELLIE CASHMAN'S MONDAY CLUB CAFE
Phone: 480/624-1000 (11)

New American
$9-$28

AAA Inspector Notes: The namesake's history is worth reading at the comfortable cafe. Casually modern surroundings afford views to the courtyard, and artful dish presentations contribute to an enjoyable dining experience. **Bar:** full bar. **Address:** 6902 E Greenway Pkwy 85254 **Location:** 0.5 mi w of Scottsdale Rd; in The Westin Kierland Resort & Spa. **Parking:** on-site and valet. [B] [L] [D]

(See map & index p. 158.)

NORTH
Phone: 480/948-2055 ⑭

New Italian
$8-$28

AAA Inspector Notes: In the trendy Kierland shopping district, this upscale, modern eatery delights palates with fresh, innovative, Italian-based creations. Wood-fired pizza is a nice beginning. **Bar:** full bar. **Address:** 15024 N Scottsdale Rd, #160 85254 **Location:** Just w on Greenway Pkwy; in Kierland Commons. **Parking:** street only.

L D

OCEAN TRAIL
Phone: 480/850-7777 ㉜

Creole
$13-$19

AAA Inspector Notes: Traditional Creole-inspired dishes are made to order in the open air kitchen of this eatery. Diners can watch as chefs prepare spicy gumbo, hand-shucked oysters and other seafood specialties. Open to the casino floor, the atmosphere is loud and lively. **Bar:** full bar. **Address:** 9800 E Indian Bend Rd 85256 **Location:** SR 101 exit 44 (E Indian Bend Rd), just e; in Talking Stick Resort. **Parking:** on-site and valet.

L D 🗞

OC SEVEN RESTAURANT & BAR
Phone: 480/991-1571 ㉚

American
$8-$26

AAA Inspector Notes: For a casual meal between tennis matches or for an intimate dinner, this bistro offers upscale dishes with regional and Pacific Rim touches. Hearty soups, wrap sandwiches and grilled steaks are among the choices. **Bar:** full bar. **Address:** 8225 E Indian Bend Rd 85250 **Location:** 1.5 mi e of Scottsdale Rd; in Scottsdale Resort & Athletic Club. L D

OLD TOWN TORTILLA FACTORY
Phone: 480/945-4567 ㉘

Mexican
$12-$33

AAA Inspector Notes: Diners can enjoy the expansive outdoor dining patio with fountains and mature plantings at this eatery. Menu items range from traditional enchiladas and tamales to more refined steak and seafood dishes. This place prides itself on its varied margaritas and homemade tortillas. **Bar:** full bar. **Address:** 6910 E Main St 85251 **Location:** Just w of Goldwater Blvd.

D

ORANGE SKY
Phone: 480/850-7777 ㉛

Seafood
$24-$56

AAA Inspector Notes: Located on the 15th floor with panoramic views of the valley, this spacious restaurant boasts a modern, yet elegant, interior. Attentive service and a classic menu featuring steaks and seafood is offered. **Bar:** full bar. **Reservations:** suggested. **Address:** 9800 Indian Bend 85256 **Location:** SR 101 exit 44 (E Indian Bend Rd), just e; in Talking Stick Resort. **Parking:** on-site and valet. D

OREGANO'S PIZZA BISTRO
Phone: 480/348-0500

Pizza
$7-$23

AAA Inspector Notes: This high-energy eatery, with its young and attentive waitstaff, serves hearty, over-sized portions of delicious pizza, salads, pasta and baked sandwiches. The patio is the happening spot. **Bar:** wine only. **Address:** 7215 E Shea Blvd 85260 **Location:** Just e of Scottsdale Rd. L D

PALM COURT
Menu on AAA.com
Phone: 480/596-7700 ㉖

American
$12-$45

AAA Inspector Notes: The fine dining restaurant features a practiced staff that provides attentive, formal service. You'll find an eclectic selection of menu choices ranging from tableside-prepared salads to deftly prepared steaks. A perfect setting for a special occasion treat. **Bar:** full bar. **Reservations:** suggested. **Address:** 7700 E McCormick Pkwy 85258 **Location:** Just w of Hayden Rd; 0.7 mi e of Scottsdale Rd; in Scottsdale Resort & Conference Center. **Parking:** on-site and valet. D

PATSY GRIMALDI'S COAL BRICK-OVEN PIZZERIA
For additional information, visit AAA.com

Pizza
$9-$18

AAA Inspector Notes: Fresh ingredients and a coal-fired brick oven are the features at this New York-style pizzeria. Diners can enjoy pizza, salads and calzones all served in a lively atmosphere. **Bar:** beer & wine. L D

LOCATIONS:

Address: 4000 N Scottsdale Rd 85251 **Location:** Jct Indian School Rd, just s. **Phone:** 480/994-1100

Address: 20715 N Pima Rd 85255 **Location:** SR 101 exit 36 (Pima Rd), 2 mi n; in Village at Market Street. **Phone:** 480/515-5588

PEARL SUSHI LOUNGE & BOMBER BAR
Phone: 480/947-3275 ㊴

Sushi
$6-$14

AAA Inspector Notes: Situated in the heart of Old Town, this is the perfect spot for casual sushi and a specialty cocktail before hitting the nearby clubs. **Bar:** full bar. **Address:** 4252 N Drinkwater Blvd 85251 **Location:** Northwest corner of 3rd Ave and Drinkwater Blvd. **Parking:** on-site and valet. D LATE

PERSIAN ROOM
Phone: 480/614-1414 ⑥

Middle Eastern
$9-$35

AAA Inspector Notes: The owner's classic, traditionally prepared Persian dishes include marinated chicken shish kebab, koobideh kebab (ground beef) and dolma (stuffed grape leaves). Fragrant jasmine rice and crisp salads with the house yogurt dressing complete meals, which the owner puts together in classic presentations with large sprigs of fresh basil and mint along with slices of mild onion to cleanse the palate. Gilt-accented columns enhance the elegant dining room. **Bar:** full bar. **Address:** 17040 N Scottsdale Rd 85255 **Location:** Jct Bell Rd, just n.

L D

Simply Reliable

The Diamond Ratings in this TourBook guide are backed by our expert, in-person evaluations, whether the hotel or restaurant is no-frills, moderate or upscale.

Learn more at **AAA.com/Diamonds**

(See map & index p. 158.)

P.F. CHANG'S CHINA BISTRO

▼▼▼

Chinese
$10-$25

For additional information,
visit AAA.com

AAA Inspector Notes: Trendy, upscale decor provides a pleasant backdrop for New Age Chinese dining. Appetizers, soups and salads are a meal by themselves. Vegetarian plates and sides, noodles, meins, chicken and meat dishes are created from exotic, fresh ingredients. **Bar:** full bar. [L] [D]

LOCATIONS:
Address: 7135 E Camelback Rd 85251 **Location:** Southwest corner of Scottsdale Rd. **Phone:** 480/949-2610 (40)

Address: 7132 E Greenway Pkwy 85254 **Location:** 1 mi s of Bell Rd at Scottsdale Rd. **Phone:** 480/367-2999 (15)

PIÑON GRILL

▼▼▼

Southwestern
$15-$40

Phone: 480/948-5050 (25)

AAA Inspector Notes: Two seating options are offered at this grill: the intimate dining room or the patio, which affords a view over the lake to the golf course. Distinctive Southwestern Rim preparations of chicken, seafood, veal, steak and wild game are accompanied by succulent vegetables and sauces. A professional waitstaff team is attentive. **Bar:** full bar. **Reservations:** suggested. **Address:** 7401 N Scottsdale Rd 85253 **Location:** 0.8 mi n of Indian Bend Rd; in Millennium Resort Scottsdale McCormick Ranch. **Parking:** on-site and valet. [B] [L] [D]

PITA JUNGLE

▼▼

Mediterranean
$6-$15

Phone: 480/922-7482 (20)

AAA Inspector Notes: A casual atmosphere envelops the dining area and an entry patio at this "jungle." The menu offers a wide variety of hot and cold pita wraps, pizza, falafel, spanakopita, salads and burgers, as well as natural, healthful vegetarian offerings. The cilantro hummus is a great starter, with a light delicate flavor. **Bar:** full bar. **Address:** 7366 E Shea Blvd 85260 **Location:** Just e of jct Scottsdale Rd; in Shea Scottsdale East Plaza. [L] [D]

POSH IMPROVISATIONAL CUISINE

▼▼▼ ▼▼▼

International
$50-$140

Phone: 480/663-7674 (39)

AAA Inspector Notes: Diners will not see a menu at this chic dining spot, but what they will see is amazingly creative dishes, presented beautifully, in a modern and elegant setting. Chef Joshua Hebert creates improvisational tasting menus based on exotic, market-fresh ingredients tailored to the preferences of each patron. A sampling of dishes may include Kobe beef with pickled ramps, halibut cheeks with lemon aioli or mushroom braised veal. Desserts are equally impressive. **Bar:** full bar. **Reservations:** suggested. **Address:** 7167 E Rancho Vista Dr, Suite 111 85251 **Location:** Jct Scottsdale Rd, just w. **Parking:** on-site and valet. [D]

RANCHO PINOT

▼▼▼

American
$20-$31

Phone: 480/367-8030 (34)

AAA Inspector Notes: Taking advantage of seasonally fresh items, the menu changes frequently to bring diners an excellent variety of fresh meat, poultry and seafood. The high-energy dining room looks into the open kitchen, where chefs use mesquite-grill cooking for many dishes. The waitstaff are professional and accomplished in their tableside service. **Bar:** full bar. **Reservations:** suggested. **Address:** 6208 N Scottsdale Rd 85253 **Location:** Just s of Lincoln Dr; in Lincoln Plaza Shopping Center. [D]

RA SUSHI BAR RESTAURANT

▼▼

Sushi
$7-$20

Phone: 480/990-9256

AAA Inspector Notes: Fresh sushi creations are the specialty at this busy, bistro-style restaurant. Crunchy tempura is available for the less daring. Artful, tasty creations can be accented with seaweed, squid salad or rice. **Bar:** full bar. **Address:** 3815 N Scottsdale Rd 85251 **Location:** Corner of 1st St; in historic downtown. **Parking:** on-site and valet. [L] [D]

REMINGTON'S

▼▼▼

American
$13-$30

Phone: 480/951-5101 (27)

AAA Inspector Notes: Such New American cuisine lining this restaurant's menu include USDA Prime cuts of beef, mesquite-grilled chicken and braised veal osso buco. The well-trained staff assists patrons through any celebration or casual dinner. The patio opens when the weather permits. **Bar:** full bar. **Address:** 7200 N Scottsdale Rd 85253 **Location:** Just n of Indian Bend Rd; in The Scottsdale Plaza Resort. [L] [D]

RENEGADE CANTEEN

▼▼▼

Western American
$15-$33

Phone: 480/614-9400 (22)

AAA Inspector Notes: Chef Robert McGrath has once again created an innovative menu featuring Western-style comfort food including green chile pork stew, chicken hash with sage pesto and duck fajitas. The atmosphere is upscale yet casual, attracting a strong local following. **Bar:** full bar. **Address:** 9343 E Shea Blvd 85260 **Location:** Loop 101 exit 41 (Shea Blvd), 0.6 mi w. [L] [D]

ROARING FORK

▼▼▼

Western American
$13-$39

Phone: 480/947-0795 (37)

AAA Inspector Notes: Known for its excellent, award-winning food by chef McGrath, this restaurant is a repeated recipient of the notable James Beard award. Its spacious, upscale dining room is ideal for any special occasion. Service is consistently friendly and accomplished, and the salmon cooked campfire-style is among the signature dishes. **Bar:** full bar. **Reservations:** suggested. **Address:** 4800 N Scottsdale Rd, Suite 1700 85251 **Location:** Southwest corner of Chaparral and Scottsdale rds. [D]

RUBIO'S FRESH MEXICAN GRILL

▼▼

Mexican
$3-$7

For additional information,
visit AAA.com

AAA Inspector Notes: Freshly prepared and healthful foods, bright decor and friendly staff are found in this upscale fast-food spot. A special treat, the salsa bar lines up four styles and flavors. **Bar:** beer only. [L] [D]

LOCATIONS:
Address: 32415 N Scottsdale Rd 85262 **Location:** Just n of Asher Hills Rd; in Target Plaza. **Phone:** 480/575-7280

Address: 15704 N Pima Rd 85260 **Location:** SR 101 exit 38 (Frank Lloyd Wright Blvd), just w, then just s. **Phone:** 480/348-0195

RUTH'S CHRIS STEAK HOUSE

▼▼▼

Steak
$31-$40

Phone: 480/991-5988 (29)

AAA Inspector Notes: The main fare is steak, which is prepared from several cuts of prime beef and cooked to perfection, but the menu also lists lamb, chicken and seafood dishes. Guests should come hungry because the side dishes, which are among the a la carte offerings, could make a meal in themselves. **Bar:** full bar. **Reservations:** suggested. **Address:** 7001 N Scottsdale Rd 85253 **Location:** Northeast corner of Scottsdale and Indian Bend rds; in Seville Strip Center. [D]

(See map & index p. 158.)

THE SALT CELLAR RESTAURANT
Phone: 480/947-1963 〔67〕

Seafood
$27-$50

AAA Inspector Notes: Along a major thoroughfare in a not-so-hectic business area, this popular cellar restaurant flies in a large selection of fish and shellfish, as well as the "turf" to accompany it, daily from around the world. Dining areas display acid-etched glass-filled partitions and marine motif prints. Energetic servers ably describe all dishes and offer to crack crabs tableside. The restaurant has been in this location for 29 years. **Bar:** full bar. **Reservations:** suggested. **Address:** 550 N Hayden Rd 85257 **Location:** McDowell Rd, just s. 〔D〕

SAPPORO
Phone: 480/607-1114 〔17〕

Japanese
$15-$45

AAA Inspector Notes: Seated amid a trendy decor with waterfalls and jellyfish tanks, diners can indulge their whims for sushi and Pacific Rim foods. The knowledgeable waitstaff provides guidance through a large selection of fish and Kobe beef. **Bar:** full bar. **Reservations:** suggested. **Address:** 14344 N Scottsdale Rd 85254 **Location:** Just n of Thunderbird Rd. 〔D〕

SASSI RISTORANTE
Phone: 480/502-9095

Italian
$20-$40

AAA Inspector Notes: Set high in the desert foothills, this Tuscan-style villa is the perfect setting for any special occasion or romantic dinner. Take in the magnificent views while enjoying fresh and creative menu options inspired by Southern Italian cooking such as handmade ricotta gnocci with wild mushroom ragu and vanilla bean panna cotta with cherry reduction. **Bar:** full bar. **Reservations:** suggested. **Address:** 10455 E Pinnacle Peak Pkwy 85255 **Location:** SR 101 exit 36 (Pima Rd), 4.7 mi n, 2 mi e on Happy Valley Rd, 1 mi n on Alma School Rd, then just e. **Parking:** on-site and valet. 〔D〕

SAUCE
Phone: 480/321-8800

Pizza
$6-$10

AAA Inspector Notes: This restaurant's selections could be characterized as gourmet fast food. Among choices are sausage and caramelized onion or chicken and broccoli rabe pizza, as well as fresh salads and lasagna. Clean, modern decor makes for a fun dining experience. Diners can sit indoors or on a patio. **Bar:** beer & wine. **Address:** 14418 N Scottsdale Rd 85254 **Location:** Just n of Thunderbird Rd; in Thunderbird Square. 〔L〕 〔D〕

STINGRAY SUSHI
Phone: 480/941-4460 〔52〕

Sushi
$6-$18

AAA Inspector Notes: Bright colors and alternative music incite high energy at this sushi spot attracting a younger crowd, who nosh on a large selection of sushi, salads, bento and tasty main courses. In addition to all the favorite rolls, the choices include a few originals, like the Godzilla and lollipop, which are packed with fresh ingredients and topped with creative glazes (think sweet eel or unagi). **Bar:** full bar. **Address:** 4302 N Scottsdale Rd 85251 **Location:** Corner of 6th Ave; in historic downtown. **Parking:** street only. 〔L〕 〔D〕 〔LATE〕

SUSHI ON SHEA
Phone: 480/483-7799 〔19〕

Japanese
$13-$38

AAA Inspector Notes: This fun, casually elegant restaurant includes two saltwater aquariums and an expansive sushi bar. Patrons can enjoy fresh sushi, tempura, noodles and specialty dishes, such as sesame-crusted salmon or chicken katsu. **Bar:** full bar. **Address:** 7000 E Shea Blvd, #1510 85254 **Location:** Just w of Scottsdale Rd. 〔L〕 〔D〕

SUSHI ROKU
Phone: 480/970-2121 〔45〕

Japanese
$10-$35

AAA Inspector Notes: Seating is available in the chic, contemporary dining room or on the casual second-floor open poolside lounge area. The menu features a wide mix of skillfully prepared sushi as well as tempura, teriyaki and grilled meat selections. **Bar:** full bar. **Reservations:** suggested. **Address:** 7277 E Camelback Rd 85251 **Location:** Just e of Scottsdale Rd; in W Scottsdale. **Parking:** on-site (fee) and valet. 〔B〕 〔L〕 〔D〕

TAGGIA
Phone: 480/945-7666 〔38〕

Italian
$15-$32

AAA Inspector Notes: This bistro prepares coastal Italian food using the freshest seafood, local and organic vegetables and homemade pasta. Chef Volpe may circulate through the dining room to check on diners' meals. Innovative desserts include the trio of brûlée, with vanilla, chocolate and orange. **Bar:** full bar. **Reservations:** suggested. **Address:** 4925 N Scottsdale Rd 85251 **Location:** Southeast corner of Scottsdale and Chaparral rds; in FireSky Resort & Spa, A Kimpton Hotel. **Parking:** on-site and valet. 〔B〕 〔L〕 〔D〕

TALAVERA
Phone: 480/513-5086

American
$28-$72

AAA Inspector Notes: Chefs Mecinas and Goldstein have created a forum for dining that is exceptional. Using the freshest ingredients and specialty items, they offer Arizona grass-fed and Australian Wagyu beef prepared with regional flavors such as chorizo bread pudding and chipotle honeycomb polenta. Tasting menus change weekly. **Bar:** full bar. **Reservations:** suggested. **Address:** 10600 E Crescent Moon Dr 85262 **Location:** SR 101 exit 36 (Pima Rd), 4.7 mi n, 2 mi e on Happy Valley Rd, then 1.5 mi n on Alma School Rd; in Four Seasons Resort Scottsdale at Troon North. **Parking:** valet only. 〔D〕 CALL 〔&M〕

TOTTIE'S ASIAN FUSION
Phone: 480/970-0633 〔64〕

Asian
$8-$14

AAA Inspector Notes: Authentic Thai, Vietnamese, Laotian and Chinese styles of cooking can all be found at this casual and friendly eatery. In the evenings, the sushi bar adds another dimension to the already vast array of menu options. **Bar:** full bar. **Address:** 7901 E Thomas Rd 85251 **Location:** Southwest corner of Hayden and Thomas rds. 〔L〕 〔D〕

TRADER VIC'S
Phone: 480/421-7799 〔56〕

Pacific Rim
$16-$34

AAA Inspector Notes: Food inspired by Pacific Rim delicacies, and a decidedly fun and exotic Polynesian decor combine to make a memorable experience at this eatery. Start with their famous signature drink, the mai tai, and then choose from pupus, curries or dishes from the wood-fired Chinese oven. **Bar:** full bar. **Reservations:** suggested. **Address:** 6850 E Main St 85251 **Location:** 0.4 mi w of Scottsdale Rd, just s of Indian School Rd; on north side of Main St; in Hotel Valley Ho. **Parking:** on-site and valet. 〔D〕 〔LATE〕

ZINC BISTRO
Phone: 480/603-0922 〔13〕

French
$12-$34

AAA Inspector Notes: In Kierland Commons Shopping Mall, this French bistro prepares steak, roasted pork, lamb, chicken, seafood and some pasta dishes. A nice selection of salads and sandwiches appeals to those who want a lighter meal. **Bar:** full bar. **Address:** 15034 N Scottsdale Rd, Suite 140 85254 **Location:** Just w of jct N Scottsdale Rd and Greenway-Hayden Loop; in Kierland Commons. **Parking:** street only. 〔L〕 〔D〕

DU JOUR RESTAURANT
Phone: 480/603-1066

〔fyi〕 Not evaluated. The on-campus training facility for students of the Arizona Culinary Institute, the dining room overlooks the bakery kitchen where mouthwatering goodies are prepared. **Address:** 10585 N 114th St 85251 **Location:** Jct Shea Blvd, just s on 116th St.

L'ACADEMIE CAFE   Phone: 480/425-3025

[fyi]   Not evaluated. Prior to graduation, Scottsdale Culinary Institute's students put their talents to the test here. The friendly and accomplished staff offers guests a selection of sophisticated sandwiches and entrees, as well as pastry delights. **Address:** 4301 N Scottsdale Rd 85250 **Location:** East side of Scottsdale Rd, at 5th Ave; in The Galleria.

L'ECOLE RESTAURANT   Phone: 480/425-3018

[fyi]   Not evaluated. Diners can sample prix fixe lunches and sophisticated entrees at the original Scottsdale Culinary Institute student kitchen. The student staff is trained and affable. **Address:** 8100 E Camelback Rd 85251 **Location:** Just e of Hayden Rd.

SECOND MESA (B-5) pop. 962, elev. 5,680'

Second Mesa, near the junction of SRs 264 and 87, is within a Hopi Reservation that occupies a large tract in the center of the vast Navajo Reservation of northeastern Arizona. The mesa is home to three Hopi villages: Shungopavi, where most of the tribe's religious and ceremonial activities originated; Sipaulovi, the last village founded after the Pueblo Revolt of 1680; and Mishongnovi. Resident basketmakers specialize in coiled basketry, which involves wrapping, weaving and stitching colorful grasses and yucca together.

HOPI CULTURAL CENTER MUSEUM, 5 mi. w. of SR 87 on SR 264, displays basketry, weaving, jewelry and other artifacts depicting the history of the Hopi. Kachina dolls, representations of divine ancestral spirits, also are featured. **Time:** Allow 1 hour minimum. **Hours:** Mon.-Fri. 8-5, Sat.-Sun. 9-3. **Cost:** $3; $1 (ages 0-13). **Phone:** (928) 734-6650.

SEDONA (C-4) pop. 10,031, elev. 4,400'
• Hotels p. 235 • Restaurants p. 245
• Hotels & Restaurants map & index p. 232

Sedona is nestled between the massive, fire-hued rocks of Red Rock State Park and the lush gorges of Oak Creek Canyon *(see attraction listing p. 228).* The dusty, semi-arid topography is the base for giant, striped monoliths that take on shades from bright red to pale sand and seem to change color with each passing cloud or ray of sunshine. Since most of the rock is sedimentary, the portrait is constantly eroding and changing shape. Verdant Oak Creek Canyon, with juniper and cypress trees lining a clear stream, provides a sharp contrast.

So prominent are the buttes and pinnacles that locals have named them. Some of the more popular rock stars are Bell Rock, Cathedral Rock, Chimney Rock, Coffeepot Rock, Courthouse Butte and Snoopy Rock. Formations in the shape of a castle or merry-go-round also can be spotted. Conveniently, two nuns overlook a chapel. And close by, a submarine surfaces near a mushroom cap.

Sedona's rugged red rocks and canyons have even shared the screen with Hollywood movie stars. The area has served as a backdrop for dozens of Western movies. Some popular titles filmed here include "Angel and the Badman," "Broken Arrow," "Firecreek," "Midnight Run" and "The Quick and the Dead."

Mother Nature was kind to Sedona, blessing her with sharp light, bright blue skies, colorful terrain, picturesque sunsets and animated clouds. Inspired painters, sculptors and other creative souls flocked to Sedona and now call the area home. In 1965 the Cowboy Artists of America, a successful art organization, was founded in what is now Uptown; its goals remain to ensure accurate portrayal of Western scenes in art. An established art colony, Sedona boasts ubiquitous galleries and studios that display residents' artistic endeavors: Pottery, sculpture, paintings and jewelry embody a variety of styles, from Western and Southwestern to modern.

Tlaquepaque, on SR 179 just south of SR 89A, is a shopping village modeled after a small Mexican village. Notable for its architectural features alone, it houses a theater, a collection of galleries and restaurants as well as a chapel; musicians often perform in the courtyards.

Alongside artists live spiritualists, who embrace the energy set forth by such natural splendor. Sedona is purportedly home to several vortexes, specific fields that emit energy upward from the earth. First channeled and defined by Page Bryant in 1980, a vortex is said to emanate three types of energy: electrical (masculine), magnetic (feminine) or electromagnetic (neutral). Found at various locations, these natural power fields are thought to energize and inspire.

Sedona is said to contain a curiously high number of vortexes and is one of the few places in the world that possesses all three types of energy. Countless businesses in Sedona specialize in new age medicine, and many offer vortex or spiritual tours. Visitors may find vortexes at Bell Rock, Cathedral Rock and Boynton Canyon. At Airport Mesa, the attraction is twofold: Guests may locate an electric force as well as a great spot from which to view a spectacular sunset.

The town received its name in 1902 from T. Carl Schnebly, one of the first settlers in the area. Schnebly wanted to establish a post office, yet both names he submitted to the postmaster general—Schnebly Station and Oak Creek Crossing—were deemed too long for a cancellation stamp. At the suggestion of his brother, he suggested his wife's name, and it stuck.

The Schneblys weren't the first ones to reside in Sedona. Ancient cliff dwellings found in the area were constructed by the Southern Sinagua people (Spanish for "without water") around A.D. 1130-1300. Two of the largest cliff dwellings, Honanki and Palatki *(see attraction listings),* still retain a number of pictographs in the shapes of animals, people and various designs.

Sedona is the starting point for hikes and scenic drives through the Red Rock area. From the vista point on the Mogollon Rim to Sedona, Oak Creek Canyon Drive (SR 89A) winds through the canyon, offering a continuous display of natural beauty, including the area's signature colored rock formations as well as sudden changes in vegetation. Oak

(See map & index p. 232.)

Creek flows between 1,200-foot-tall canyon walls toward the red rocks of Sedona.

A Red Rock Pass is required for parking when visiting or hiking the many scenic areas in Sedona. Passes may be purchased at the Sedona Chamber of Commerce. A daily pass is $5; a weekly pass is $15. Passes are not valid in state parks or campgrounds.

Red Rock Country is just the spot for an exhilarating, hang-on-tight jeep adventure. Guided tours of the backcountry are offered by Red Rock Western Jeep Tours; phone (928) 282-6826 or (800) 848-7728.

Great West Adventure Co. provides transportation and tours to the Grand Canyon and the Hopi Reservation as well as scenic tours of Sedona via 14-passenger buses; Colorado River rafting trips also are available. Phone (928) 204-5506 or (877) 367-2383.

Sedona Chamber of Commerce: 331 Forest Rd., P.O. Box 478, Sedona, AZ 86336. **Phone:** (928) 282-7722 or (800) 288-7336.

Shopping areas: Art galleries and restaurants intermingle with specialty shops at Tlaquepaque, just south of Uptown on SR 179. Oakcreek Factory Outlets, 7 miles south on SR 179, offers more than 30 outlet stores. Other areas featuring galleries and shops are Hillside Sedona, Hozho Center and along SR 89A near the village of Oakcreek.

ARIZONA HELICOPTER ADVENTURES, departing from the Sedona Airport, offers a variety of in-flight, narrated sightseeing tours of Sedona and environs, including the Native American ruins of Boynton Canyon and the area's scenic red rock formations. **Hours:** Daily 9-5. Length of tours varies. Closed Christmas. **Cost:** $69-$159; $34.50-$79.50 (ages 3-11). Reservations are recommended. **Phone:** (928) 282-0904 or (800) 282-5141.

ARIZONA SAFARI JEEP TOURS, .3 mi. n. of jct. SRs 179 and 89A to 335 Jordan Rd., offers a variety of tours of Sedona, the Colorado Plateau and the Sonoran Desert. All tours include narration by educated guides with backgrounds in biology, geology and game and range management; hands-on animal demonstrations are featured. **Time:** Allow 2 hours minimum. **Hours:** Daily dawn-dusk. **Cost:** $39-$199; $33.75-$145 (ages 0-12). **Phone:** (928) 282-3012.

CHAPEL OF THE HOLY CROSS, .8 mi. s. off SR 179 on Chapel Rd., stands on a small mountain that provides scenic views. The contemporary Catholic shrine is constructed on the area's noted red rock. Built in 1956, the chapel is between two large red sandstone peaks with a ramp leading to the entrance. A 90-foot cross dominates the structure. **Time:** Allow 30 minutes minimum. **Hours:** Mon.-Sat. 9-5, Sun. 10-5. **Cost:** Free. **Phone:** (928) 282-4069.

A DAY IN THE WEST JEEP TOURS is at 252 N. SR 89A, .3 mi. n.e. from jct. SR 179. Comprehensive jeep tours of canyons, rock formations and trails are offered. Guides in old-fashioned cowboy garb dispense photography tips and provide information about local animals, geology, history and vegetation. Cowboy cookouts and horseback rides also are offered.

Note: Comfortable walking shoes are recommended. Inquire about weather policies. **Time:** Allow 1 hour minimum. **Hours:** Tours daily 8-dusk. **Cost:** $45-$169; $41-$152 (ages 55+); $35-$149 (ages 1-12); $34-$127 (retired military with ID); $23-$85 (active military with ID). Ages 0-18 months are not permitted. Reservations are recommended. **Phone:** (928) 282-4320 or (800) 973-3662. [TI]

GREAT VENTURE TOURS, with pickup from hotels in Sedona and Flagstaff, offers narrated coach tours along the east and south rims of the Grand Canyon. Highlights include the Painted Desert and the Navajo Indian Reservation. Colorado River float trips and white-water adventures also are offered; phone for information. **Hours:** Daily 8-6. **Cost:** $44-$549; $34-$549 (ages 3-15). Fares may vary; phone ahead to confirm. Reservations are required. **Phone:** (928) 282-4451 or (800) 578-2643.

HONANKI SOUTHERN SINAGUA CLIFF DWELLINGS, 9 mi. s.w. on SR 89A to Milepost 365, .5 mi. s. to FR 525, then 10.2 mi. n. via FR 525 (a dirt

▼ See AAA listing p. 237 ▼

SEDONA
ARIZONA

BEST WESTERN PLUS
INN of SEDONA

Best Western
PLUS

Unbeatable Views
of Sedona's Red Rocks!
• Terraced promenade decks
• Free deluxe continental breakfast
• Free wireless high speed internet access

800.292.6344
www.InnofSedona.com
1200 State Route 89A, Sedona, AZ 86336

Each Best Western® hotel is independently owned and operated. ©2011 Best Western International, Inc. All rights reserved.

(See map & index p. 232.)

road), is one of the largest ruins of Southern Sinagua cliff dwellings in the Red Rock area; occupation is estimated A.D. 1130-1280. The earliest pictographs on the rock walls predate Sinagua habitation.

Note: Phone the Red Rock Ranger District, (928) 203-7500, for information about road conditions prior to visiting the site. Hours: Daily 10-5:30, Memorial Day-Labor Day; 9:30-3:30, rest of year. Closed Jan. 1, Thanksgiving and Christmas. Cost: A Red Rock Pass (Day Pass $5, Weekly Pass $15 or Annual Pass $20) is required for admission. Phone: (928) 282-4119, or (928) 282-3854 to purchase a pass.

OAK CREEK CANYON, n. on SR 89A, is traversed by a scenic stretch of that road. About 16 miles long and rarely more than 1 mile wide, the canyon is known for its spectacularly colored white, yellow and red cliffs dotted with pine, cypress and juniper. Rocky gorges, unusual rock formations and buttes add interest to the drive.

Oak Creek is noted for trout fishing; throughout the canyon are Forest Service camping and picnicking grounds. Area maps are available from the chambers of commerce in Flagstaff and Sedona.

PALATKI RUINS AND RED CLIFFS ROCK ART SITE is 9 mi. s. on SR 89A, then 8 mi. n. via FRs 525 and 795 (dirt roads), following signs. Pictographs dating from the Archaic period of Native American culture are preserved in rock alcoves. It is believed that nearby cliff dwellings were occupied A.D. 650-1300 by the Southern Sinagua people.

Note: Sites are reached via walking trails; comfortable shoes are recommended. Parking is limited. Time: Allow 1 hour, 30 minutes minimum. Hours: Daily 9:30-3. Closed Jan. 1, Thanksgiving and Christmas. Cost: A Red Rock Pass (Day Pass $5, Weekly Pass $15 or Annual Pass $20) is required for admission. Reservations are required. Phone: (928) 282-4119, or (928) 282-3854 to purchase a pass.

[SAVE] PINK JEEP TOURS is at 204 N. SR 89A, .4 mi. n.e. from jct. SR 179. Passengers journey through the red-rock canyons, desert and forests of Sedona to 700-year-old Sinaguan cliff dwellings and Native American rock art sites. Well-trained guides share lore about local flora, fauna, geology and Native American history and legends. Other tours are available.

Time: Allow 1 hour, 30 minutes minimum. Hours: Departures require a minimum of 2 people. Tours daily 7-dusk. Closed Christmas. Cost: Fare $45-$155; $33.75-$145 (ages 0-12). Children ages 0-18 months are not permitted. Rates may vary; phone ahead. Phone: (928) 282-5000 or (800) 873-3662. *(See ad p. 229.)*

RED ROCK BI-PLANE, RED ROCK HELICOPTER AND SKY SAFARI TOURS AND CHARTERS, 1 mi. w. of SR 179 on SR 89A, then s. to 1225 Airport Rd.,

▼ *See AAA listing p. 231* ▼

Northern Light Balloon Expeditions, *Sedona*
(800) 230-6222

• Sedona Sunrise Balloon Flights
• In Business & FAA Certified since 1974
• Excellent Safety Record
• Complimentary Post Flight Picnic
• Free Pick-up at most Sedona Hotels
• 48 hour cancellation policy

We use exclusively the smaller seven passenger balloons, providing a more personalized service. One of only two balloon companies permitted by the Coconino National Forest to fly the Sedona Red Rock area. Northern Arizona's oldest, largest and most experienced company.

Get the free mobile app at
http://gettag.mobi

P.O. Box 1695, Sedona, AZ 86339 www.northernlightballoon.com
• (928) 282-2274 (Local) • (800) 230-6222 (Toll Free)

(See map & index p. 232.)
offers various aerial tours over Sedona as well as destination tours. Passengers can view from the air ancient Native American dwellings not accessible by foot or vehicle. **Hours:** Bi-plane and helicopter tours daily 9-5. Sky safari tours daily 8-5. **Cost:** Fare $70-$800. **Phone:** (928) 204-5939 or (888) 866-7433.

RED ROCK STATE PARK, 3 mi. s. off SR 89A on Lower Red Rock Loop Rd., features 286 acres of a riparian ecosystem. Oak Creek runs through the park creating a diverse riparian habitat that abounds with plants and wildlife. Displays in the visitor center highlight the ecology and conservation of Oak Creek. Nature hikes, bird walks, theater presentations and other planned activities are offered; phone for schedule.

Hours: Park open daily 8-5. Visitor center open daily 9-5. **Cost:** $10 (per private vehicle, up to four adult passengers); $3 (per additional adult passenger in vehicle or individual arriving on foot or bicycle); free (ages 0-13). **Phone:** (928) 282-6907.

REDSTONE TOURS, with pickup from Sedona and Flagstaff hotels, provides van tours led by naturalist guides. The 2.5-hour Sedona tour takes guests to such sites as the Airport overlook, Bell Rock, Tlaquepaque and the Sedona Heritage Museum.

▼ See AAA listing p. 228 ▼

Ask about our tour to the Grand Canyon... in Grand Style.

Pink Jeep Tours
SEDONA · ARIZONA · ESTABLISHED 1960

You gotta do it!
- Spectacular Off-Road Tours
- Magnificent Grand Canyon Tours
- Corporate & Team Building Events
- Group Outings & Special Events

Information & reservations:
800-873-3662 ▪ 928-282-5000 ▪ www.pinkjeep.com

Jeep® and the seven slot grille design are registered trademarks of Chrysler LLC, used under license. Tours permitted and conducted in Coconino National Forest.

(See map & index p. 232.)

The full-day Grand Canyon tour includes the South and East Rims; views of the Painted Desert; Ancestral Puebloan ruins and a Navajo Indian reservation; lunch is provided. A Colorado River float trip, a Grand Canyon tour with ruins and volcanoes, a Grand Canyon day hike, a Monument Valley tour and a trip to the Hopi reservation also are available.

Hours: Daily 8-6. **Cost:** Fare $38-$219; $32-$199 (ages 3-12). Reservations are required. **Phone:** (928) 203-0396 or (866) 473-3786.

SEDONA HERITAGE MUSEUM is .1 mi. n. of jct. SR 179 and SR 89A, then .6 mi. n. to 735 N. Jordan Rd. The museum features a restored one-room cabin built in 1930; additional rooms were added 1937-47. One exhibit is dedicated to more than 80 movies made in Sedona (mainly Westerns) and another depicts the lifestyle of the cowboy. A 1940 apple grading machine and a 1942 fire truck are on display. **Time:** Allow 1 hour minimum. **Hours:** Daily 11-3. Closed Jan. 1, Easter, Thanksgiving and Christmas. **Cost:** $5; free (ages 0-12). **Phone:** (928) 282-7038. ⚐

SEDONA OFFROAD ADVENTURES is at 336 SR 179, Suite F-103. Experienced guides take passengers on jeep excursions to Bear Wallow Canyon, the Red Rock Outback or Sedona vortexes. **Time:** Allow

▼ See AAA listing p. 231 ▼

Red Rock Balloons holds a permit from the Coconino National Forest. We join them in their efforts to preserve our lands for the enjoyment of future generations.

HOTEL PICKUP • CHAMPAGNE PICNIC
PERFECT FLYING RECORD • ONE FREE VIDEO PER RESERVATION

RED ROCK BALLOON ADVENTURES
1-800-258-3754
www.RedRockBalloons.com   Sedona, Arizona

(See map & index p. 232.)

1 hour minimum. **Hours:** Daily 9-dusk. **Cost:** $35-$99; $30-$57 (ages 1-12). **Phone:** (928) 204-1973 or (928) 282-6656.

SEDONA TROLLEY is at 276 N. SR 89A in uptown Sedona. Drivers provide sightseeing narration of the Sedona area. Two 55-minute tours are available. Tour A covers the south side of Sedona, including a stop at the Chapel of the Holy Cross. Tour B covers the west side of town into the Seven Canyons area and includes two stops for picture taking.

Time: Allow 1 hour minimum. **Hours:** Tour A departs daily at 10, noon, 2 and 4. Tour B departs daily at 9, 11, 1, 3 and 5. Closed Thanksgiving and Christmas. **Cost:** One tour $12; $6 (ages 0-12). Two tours $22; $11 (ages 0-12). **Phone:** (928) 282-4211.

SLIDE ROCK STATE PARK is 7 mi. n. on SR 89A to 6871 N. SR 89A, within Oak Creek Canyon. Developed around a natural 70-foot waterslide, the park is the site of the historic Pendley homestead and an apple orchard. Activities include swimming and picnicking. *See Recreation Chart.*

Note: Pets, glass containers and campfires are not permitted. **Hours:** Daily 8-7, Memorial Day-Labor Day; 8-6, May 1-day before Memorial Day and day after Labor Day-Sept. 30; 8-5, rest of year. Closed Christmas. Phone ahead to confirm schedule. **Cost:** $20 (per private vehicle, up to four passengers); $3 (each additional passenger ages 13+ and each individual arriving on foot or bicycle). Fees may vary; phone ahead. **Phone:** (928) 282-3034.

V-BAR-V RANCH PETROGLYPH SITE, 3 mi. e. off I-17 exit 298, following signs, contains 13 panels with more than 1,000 petroglyphs representing the Beaver Creek style of rock art. It is believed that the images of snakes, turtles, coyotes, stick-figured humans and palmlike trees were chiseled into the rock walls by the Sinagua people. **Tours:** Guided tours are available. **Time:** Allow 1 hour minimum. **Hours:** Fri.-Mon. 9:30-3. Closed Thanksgiving and Christmas. **Cost:** $5 per vehicle; free (Red Rock Pass holders). **Phone:** (928) 282-4119.

RECREATIONAL ACTIVITIES
Hot Air Ballooning
- **Northern Light Balloon Expeditions** provides transportation to the departure point. **Hours:** Tours depart daily at dawn (weather permitting). **Phone:** (928) 282-2274 or (800) 230-6222. *(See ad p. 228.)*
- **Red Rock Balloon Adventures** picks up from local hotels. **Hours:** Tours depart daily at dawn (weather permitting). **Phone:** (928) 284-0040 or (800) 258-3754. *(See ad p. 230.)*

Jeep Tours (Self-driving)
- **Barlow Jeep Rentals** is at 3009 W. SR 89A. **Hours:** Daily 8-6. Closed Christmas. **Phone:** (928) 282-8700 or (888) 920-5337.

More choices. Bigger savings.
Easier booking.

AAA.com

It all clicks at AAA.com/Travel

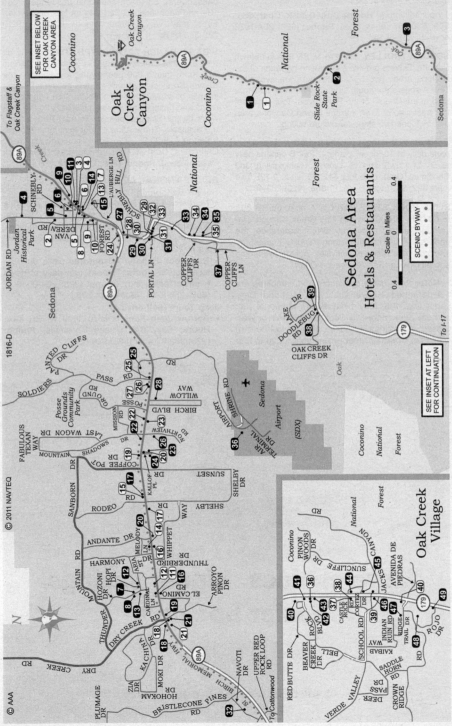

Sedona Area
Hotels & Restaurants

SCENIC BYWAY

Scale in Miles

Oak Creek
Canyon

SEE INSET BELOW
FOR OAK CREEK
CANYON AREA

SEE INSET AT LEFT
FOR CONTINUATION

Oak Creek
Village

© 2011 NAVTEQ

© AAA

1816-D

Sedona Area

This index helps you "spot" where approved hotels and restaurants are located on the corresponding detailed maps. Hotel daily rate range is for comparison only and show the property's high season. Restaurant rate range is a combination of lunch and/or dinner. Turn to the listing page for more detailed rate information and consult display ads for special promotions.

SEDONA

Map Page	Hotels	Diamond Rated	High Season	Page
1 p. 232	Junipine Resort	♦♦	$135-$400	241
2 p. 232	Slide Rock Lodge	♦	$99-$179	245
3 p. 232	Briar Patch Inn Bed & Breakfast	♦♦♦	$219-$395	237
4 p. 232	Apple Orchard Inn	♦♦♦	$115-$205	235
5 p. 232	**Rodeway Inn & Suites Iris Garden**	♦♦	Rates not provided (SAVE)	244
6 p. 232	Rose Tree Inn	♦♦	$109-$149	244
7 p. 232	Alma de Sedona Inn B&B	♦♦♦	Rates not provided	235
8 p. 232	**Casa Sedona Bed and Breakfast Inn** *(See ad p. 240.)*	♦♦♦♦	$139-$279 (SAVE)	237
9 p. 232	**Best Western Plus Arroyo Roble Hotel & Creekside Villas** *(See ad p. 238.)*	♦♦♦	$179-$399 (SAVE)	237
10 p. 232	**Matterhorn Inn** *(See ad p. 243.)*	♦♦♦	$99-$179 (SAVE)	242
11 p. 232	**Amara Hotel, Restaurant & Spa**	♦♦♦♦	$155-$295 (SAVE)	235
12 p. 232	Boots & Saddles Romantic Bed & Breakfast	♦♦♦	Rates not provided	237
13 p. 232	**Adobe Grand Villas**	♦♦♦	$399-$1200 (SAVE)	235
14 p. 232	**Orchards Inn of Sedona**	♦♦♦	Rates not provided (SAVE)	242
15 p. 232	**L'Auberge de Sedona Inn and Spa**	♦♦♦♦	$229-$725 (SAVE)	242
16 p. 232	**Days Inn Sedona**	♦♦	$50-$120 (SAVE)	237
17 p. 232	**Sedona Rouge Hotel & Spa**	♦♦♦♦	$229-$279 (SAVE)	244
18 p. 232	Southwest Inn at Sedona	♦♦♦	Rates not provided	245
19 p. 232	**Kokopelli Suites**	♦♦	$79-$239 (SAVE)	242
20 p. 232	Sedona Super 8	♦♦	$77-$126	245
21 p. 232	**Sedona Real Inn & Suites** *(See ad p. 236.)*	♦♦♦	$95-$340 (SAVE)	244
22 p. 232	Hampton Inn	♦♦♦	$129-$189	240
23 p. 232	**Villas of Sedona**	♦♦♦	$175-$250 (SAVE)	245
24 p. 232	The Lodge at Sedona	♦♦♦	$189-$349	242
25 p. 232	**Best Western Plus Inn of Sedona** *(See ad p. 239, p. 227.)*	♦♦♦	$109-$249 (SAVE)	237
26 p. 232	**Sedona Springs Resort**	♦♦♦	$125-$300 (SAVE)	244
27 p. 232	Cedars Resort	♦♦	$159	237
28 p. 232	Baby Quail Inn	♦♦	$70-$125	235
29 p. 232	**Sedona Motel**	♦♦	$90-$120 (SAVE)	244
30 p. 232	**El Portal Sedona Luxury Inn**	♦♦♦♦	$179-$399 (SAVE)	240
31 p. 232	Los Abrigados Resort & Spa	♦♦♦	Rates not provided	242
32 p. 232	Sedona Summit Resort	♦♦♦	$159-$599	245
33 p. 232	**The Inn on Oak Creek** *(See ad p. 241.)*	♦♦♦♦	$200-$295 (SAVE)	241
34 p. 232	King's Ransom Inn	♦♦	$85-$110	242

SEDONA (cont'd)

Map Page	Hotels (cont'd)	Diamond Rated	High Season	Page
35 p. 232	King's Ransom Sedona Hotel	◆◆	$99-$225	242
36 p. 232	Sky Ranch Lodge	◆◆	$80-$250	245
37 p. 232	Creekside Inn at Sedona	◆◆◆	$170-$279	237
38 p. 232	**Villas at Poco Diablo**	◆◆◆	$155-$195 (SAVE)	245
39 p. 232	**Poco Diablo Resort**	◆◆◆	Rates not provided (SAVE)	244
40 p. 232	**Canyon Villa Bed & Breakfast Inn of Sedona**	◆◆◆	$189-$349 (SAVE)	237
41 p. 232	**Wildflower Inn**	◆◆	$74-$169 (SAVE)	245
42 p. 232	Village Lodge	◆	$49-$89	245
43 p. 232	**La Quinta Inn Sedona / Village of Oak Creek**	◆◆	$89-$179 (SAVE)	242
44 p. 232	Kokopelli Inn	◆◆	Rates not provided	242
45 p. 232	**The Views Inn Sedona**	◆◆	$79-$149 (SAVE)	245
46 p. 232	**Desert Quail Inn**	◆◆	$69-$189 (SAVE)	237
47 p. 232	**Hilton Sedona Resort & Spa**	◆◆◆	$135-$269 (SAVE)	241
48 p. 232	Diamond Resorts International - The Ridge on Sedona Golf Resort	◆◆◆	Rates not provided	240
49 p. 232	Adobe Hacienda Bed & Breakfast	◆◆◆	$150-$299	235

Map Page	Restaurants	Diamond Rated	Cuisine	Meal Range	Page
1 p. 232	Junipine Cafe	◆◆	American	$8-$29	246
2 p. 232	Takashi Japanese Restaurant	◆◆	Japanese	$9-$22	248
3 p. 232	**Hundred Rox**	◆◆◆	Italian	$10-$38	246
4 p. 232	Open Range Grill & Tavern	◆◆	American	$12-$28	247
5 p. 232	Canyon Breeze	◆	Deli	$5-$10	245
6 p. 232	Oaxaca Restaurant	◆◆	Mexican	$10-$20	247
7 p. 232	The Orchards Bar & Grill	◆◆	Regional American	$9-$20	247
8 p. 232	Sally's BBQ	◆	Barbecue	$8-$15	248
9 p. 232	Thai Palace Uptown	◆◆	Thai	$8-$16	248
10 p. 232	Cowboy Club	◆◆	American	$8-$40	245
11 p. 232	Thai Spices	◆	Thai	$10-$17	248
12 p. 232	Nick's on the West Side	◆◆	American	$8-$21	247
13 p. 232	**L'Auberge Restaurant on Oak Creek**	◆◆◆◆	American	$18-$48	246
14 p. 232	Barking Frog Grille	◆◆◆	American	$8-$27	245
15 p. 232	**Red's**	◆◆◆	American	$8-$34	247
16 p. 232	Wild Orchid	◆◆	Asian	$9-$19	248
17 p. 232	Dahl & DiLuca Ristorante Italiano	◆◆◆	Italian	$13-$32	246
18 p. 232	Euro Deli	◆	Deli	$4-$9	246
19 p. 232	India Palace Cuisine	◆◆	Indian	$8-$17	246
20 p. 232	Troia's	◆◆	Italian	$13-$25	248
21 p. 232	Rainbow's End Relics	◆◆	Steak	$10-$28	247
22 p. 232	The Heartline Cafe	◆◆◆	American	$10-$30	246
23 p. 232	Red Planet Diner	◆◆	American	$8-$18	247

Map Page	Restaurants (cont'd)	Diamond Rated	Cuisine	Meal Range	Page
㉔ p. 232	Hiro's Sushi Bar & Japanese Restaurant	▽▽	Japanese	$7-$20	246
㉕ p. 232	Judi's Restaurant	▽▽	American	$9-$26	246
㉖ p. 232	New York Bagels and Deli	▽	Deli	$3-$8	247
㉗ p. 232	Szechuan Chinese Restaurant & Sushi Bar	▽▽	Asian	$10-$19	248
㉘ p. 232	**Red Rock BBQ**	▽▽	Barbecue	$7-$23	247
㉙ p. 232	El Rincon Restaurante Mexicano	▽▽	Mexican	$7-$10	246
㉚ p. 232	Oak Creek Brewery & Grill	▽▽	American	$10-$26	247
㉛ p. 232	Stakes & Sticks	▽▽	American	$10-$27	248
㉜ p. 232	**Rene At Tlaquepaque**	▽▽▽	Continental	$12-$45	248
㉝ p. 232	The Secret Garden Cafe	▽▽	American	$8-$16	248
㉞ p. 232	Shugrue's Hillside Grill	▽▽	Seafood	$15-$35	248
㉟ p. 232	Elote Cafe	▽▽	Mexican	$16-$25	246
㊱ p. 232	Tara Thai	▽▽	Thai	$8-$12	248
㊲ p. 232	Maria's Restaurant & Cantina	▽▽	Mexican	$8-$19	247
㊳ p. 232	Pago's Pizzeria & Italian Cuisine	▽▽	Italian	$5-$20	247
㊴ p. 232	Marketplace Cafe	▽▽	American	$8-$28	247
㊵ p. 232	**Cucina Rustica**	▽▽▽	Mediterranean	$13-$32	246

ADOBE GRAND VILLAS Phone: (928)203-7616 🔳13

▽▽▽ ▽▽▽
Boutique Bed & Breakfast
$399-$1200

Address: 35 Hozoni Dr 86336 **Location:** Jct SR 179, 2 mi w on SR 89A, just nw on Tortilla and Southwest drs, then just nw. Located in West Sedona residential area. **Facility:** This boutique-style B&B has spacious villas offering luxurious appointments; rooms have custom-designed furnishings and a private balcony or patio. 16 units, some two bedrooms and kitchens. 2 stories (no elevator), exterior corridors. **Terms:** office hours 8 am-6 pm, 2 night minimum stay - seasonal and/or weekends, 15 day cancellation notice-fee imposed. **Amenities:** high-speed Internet, safes. **Pool(s):** heated outdoor. **Activities:** whirlpool, steamroom, spa. **Guest Services:** valet laundry. **Free Special Amenities: full breakfast and high-speed Internet.**

ADOBE HACIENDA BED & BREAKFAST
Phone: (928)284-2020 🔳49

▽▽▽▽
Bed & Breakfast
$150-$299

Address: 10 Rojo Dr 86351 **Location:** Jct SR 89A, 7.5 mi s on SR 179. Located in Village of Oak Creek. **Facility:** Rooms in adobe-style buildings reflect varied southwest themes, and some overlook a flagstone patio and golf course. 5 units. 1 story, exterior corridors. **Terms:** office hours 8 am-9 pm, 2 night minimum stay - seasonal and/or weekends, age restrictions may apply, 14 day cancellation notice-fee imposed. **Activities:** Fee: golf-18 holes. **Guest Services:** complimentary laundry.

ALMA DE SEDONA INN B&B
Phone: 928/282-2737 🔳7

▽▽▽▽
Bed & Breakfast
Rates not provided

Address: 50 Hozoni Dr 86336 **Location:** Jct SR 179, 3 mi w on SR 89A, then 3 blks nw via Tortilla and Southwest drs. Located in a quiet residential area. **Facility:** Guest rooms at this pueblo-style inn are elegantly appointed and have a balcony or patio, some with views of the scenic red rocks. 12 units. 2 stories (no elevator), exterior corridors. **Terms:** office hours 8 am-6 pm, age restrictions may apply. **Pool(s):** heated outdoor.

AMARA HOTEL, RESTAURANT & SPA
Phone: (928)282-4828 🔳11

▽▽▽▽
Hotel
$155-$295

Address: 100 Amara Ln 86336 **Location:** Jct SR 179, 0.4 mi ne; center. **Facility:** This upscale property is nestled adjacent to Oak Creek. All units have a balcony or patio. 100 units. 2 stories, interior corridors. **Parking:** on-site and valet. **Terms:** check-in 4 pm, 3 day cancellation notice-fee imposed. **Amenities:** high-speed Internet, safes, honor bars. **Dining:** Hundred Rox, see separate listing, entertainment. **Pool(s):** heated outdoor. **Activities:** whirlpool, fishing, exercise room, spa. **Guest Services:** valet laundry, area transportation-within 5 mi.

APPLE ORCHARD INN Phone: (928)282-5328 🔳4

▽▽▽▽
Bed & Breakfast
$115-$205

Address: 656 Jordan Rd 86336 **Location:** Jct SR 179, just ne on SR 89A, then 0.5 mi n. Located in Uptown Sedona. **Facility:** In an idyllic setting against a backdrop of Wilson and Steamboat rock formations, the property features beautifully decorated units, two with a gas fireplace. 7 units. 2 stories (no elevator), interior corridors. **Terms:** office hours 8 am-6 pm, 2 night minimum stay - weekends, age restrictions may apply, 30 day cancellation notice-fee imposed. **Activities:** whirlpool, hiking trails. Fee: massage.

BABY QUAIL INN Phone: (928)282-2835 🔳28

▽▽▽▽
Motel
$70-$125

Address: 50 Willow Way 86336 **Location:** Jct SR 179, 1.4 mi w on SR 89A, just s. Located in a residential area. **Facility:** 11 units. 2 stories (no elevator), exterior corridors. **Terms:** office hours 8 am-8 pm, 2 night minimum stay - seasonal and/or weekends, 3 day cancellation notice-fee imposed. **Activities:** whirlpool.

▼ See AAA listing p. 244 ▼

Sedona Reāl
INN & SUITES

Your 10%
AAA Member
discount is
just the
beginning!

Comfort and Value in Sedona

From resort-like amenities to our signature concierge staff, Sedona Reāl will make your next trip to Sedona one you will never forget.

- Complimentary hot breakfast and WIFI
- Clean rooms and spacious suites
- Selected pet friendly rooms and suites
- Spectacular red rock patio view
- Oversized heated pool and spa
- Signature concierge service
- Resort amenities
- **Visit sedonareal.com/aaa for a full list of member benefits**

877.785.5489 | sedonareal.com

(See map & index p. 232.)

BEST WESTERN PLUS ARROYO ROBLE HOTEL & CREEKSIDE VILLAS
Phone: (928)282-4001 **9**

Hotel
$179-$399

AAA Benefit: Members save up to 20%, plus 10% bonus points with Best Western Rewards®.

Address: 400 N SR 89A 86336 **Location:** Jct SR 179, 0.5 mi ne. **Facility:** 65 units, some two bedrooms, kitchens and cottages. 5 stories, exterior corridors. **Amenities:** high-speed Internet, safes. **Pool(s):** 2 heated outdoor, heated indoor. **Activities:** sauna, whirlpools, steamroom, game room, exercise room. *Fee:* 2 lighted tennis courts, racquetball courts. **Guest Services:** coin laundry. **Free Special Amenities:** full breakfast and high-speed Internet. *(See ad p. 238.)*

BEST WESTERN PLUS INN OF SEDONA
Phone: (928)282-3072 **25**

Hotel
$109-$249

AAA Benefit: Members save up to 20%, plus 10% bonus points with Best Western Rewards®.

Address: 1200 W SR 89A 86336 **Location:** Jct SR 179, 1.2 mi w. **Facility:** 110 units. 1-3 stories (no elevator), exterior corridors. **Pool(s):** heated outdoor. **Activities:** whirlpool, exercise room. **Guest Services:** valet laundry, area transportation-within 5 mi. **Free Special Amenities:** expanded continental breakfast and local transportation. *(See ad p. 239, p. 227.)*

BOOTS & SADDLES ROMANTIC BED & BREAKFAST
Phone: 928/282-1944 **12**

Bed & Breakfast
Rates not provided

Address: 2900 Hopi Dr 86336 **Location:** Jct SR 179 W, 2.7 mi w on SR 89A, n on Tortilla Dr, 1 blk w on Southwest Dr, 1 blk n on Hozoni Dr, then just e. **Facility:** Casual, western décor lends a lively ambiance to its guest rooms, all of which have a gas fireplace and either a patio or balcony. 6 units. 2 stories (no elevator), interior/exterior corridors. **Terms:** office hours 7 am-9 pm.

BRIAR PATCH INN BED & BREAKFAST
Phone: (928)282-2342 **3**

Cottage
$219-$395

Address: 3190 N SR 89A 86336 **Location:** Jct SR 179, 3.4 mi ne. Located in Oak Creek Canyon. **Facility:** Classical music is performed six mornings a week at this inn on nine tree-shaded acres bordering Oak Creek. A massage gazebo is on the grounds. 19 units, some houses and cottages. 1 story, exterior corridors. **Terms:** office hours 8 am-8 pm, 2 night minimum stay - weekends, 14 day cancellation notice-fee imposed. **Activities:** *Fee:* fishing, massage.

Create complete trip routings and custom maps with the TripTik® Travel Planner on AAA.com or CAA.ca

CANYON VILLA BED & BREAKFAST INN OF SEDONA
Phone: (928)284-1226 **40**

Bed & Breakfast
$189-$349

Address: 40 Canyon Circle Dr 86351 **Location:** Jct SR 179, just w on Bell Rock Blvd, then just n. Located in Village of Oak Creek. **Facility:** A nearby desert provides outdoor interest at this upscale Spanish-Mission compound overlooking the red rocks. 11 units. 2 stories (no elevator), interior/exterior corridors. **Terms:** office hours 7:30 am-7 pm, age restrictions may apply, 14 day cancellation notice-fee imposed. **Pool(s):** outdoor. **Activities:** hiking trails. **Free Special Amenities:** full breakfast and high-speed Internet.

CASA SEDONA BED AND BREAKFAST INN
Phone: (928)282-2938 **8**

Bed & Breakfast
$139-$279

Address: 55 Hozoni Dr 86336 **Location:** Jct SR 179, 3 mi w on SR 89A, then 3 blks nw via Tortilla, Southwest and Hozoni drs. Located in a quiet residential area. **Facility:** Décor at the southwest-style inn includes unique, one-of-a-kind beds imported from around the world; all rooms feature a balcony, patio or terrace. 16 units. 2 stories (no elevator), interior/exterior corridors. **Terms:** office hours 8 am-6 pm, age restrictions may apply, 7 day cancellation notice-fee imposed. **Activities:** whirlpool, hiking trails.

Fee: massage. *(See ad p. 240.)*

CEDARS RESORT
Phone: (928)282-7010 **27**

Hotel
$159

Address: 20 W SR 89A 00000 **Location:** Jct SR 179, southeast corner. **Facility:** 38 units. 1-2 stories (no elevator), exterior corridors. **Terms:** office hours 6 am-10:30 pm, check-in 4 pm. **Pool(s):** heated outdoor. **Activities:** whirlpool, limited exercise equipment. *Fee:* fishing.

CREEKSIDE INN AT SEDONA
Phone: (928)282-4992 **37**

Bed & Breakfast
$170-$279

Address: 99 Copper Cliffs Dr 86336 **Location:** Jct SR 89A, 0.7 mi s on SR 179, then just w. Overlooks Oak Creek. **Facility:** The sights and sounds of Oak Creek, which runs along the property's border, creates a soothing ambiance. 6 units. 1 story, interior/exterior corridors. **Terms:** office hours 7 am-6 pm, 2 night minimum stay - weekends, age restrictions may apply, 14 day cancellation notice-fee imposed. **Activities:** fishing, hiking trails. *Fee:* massage.

DAYS INN SEDONA
Phone: (928)282-9166 **16**

Motel
$50-$120

Address: 2991 W Hwy 89A 86336 **Location:** Jct SR 179, 3 mi w. **Facility:** 66 units, some two bedrooms. 2 stories (no elevator), exterior corridors. **Amenities:** high-speed Internet. **Pool(s):** heated outdoor. **Activities:** whirlpool.

DESERT QUAIL INN
Phone: (928)284-1433 **46**

Hotel
$69-$189

Address: 6626 Hwy 179 86351 **Location:** Jct Bell Rock Blvd, 0.9 mi s. Across from factory outlet center. **Facility:** 41 units, some kitchens. 2 stories (no elevator), exterior corridors. **Terms:** office hours 7 am-10 pm, cancellation fee imposed. **Pool(s):** heated outdoor. **Guest Services:** coin laundry. **Free Special Amenities:** local telephone calls and high-speed Internet.

Best Western PLUS *Arroyo Roble* Hotel & Creekside Villas

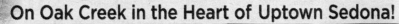

On Oak Creek in the Heart of Uptown Sedona!

Creekside Villas offer 2 bedrooms, 2½ baths, full kitchen, 2 fireplaces, patios & balconies . . . all located right on the banks of Oak Creek.

King and double queen rooms with magnificent red rock views from private balconies and/or patios.

Free use of fully equipped fitness room, in/outdoor pools & spas. New (2011) game room with air hockey, table shuffleboard, ping pong, Nintendo Wii™, and more!

Award Winning

- ◆ FREE full hot breakfast buffet
- ◆ Prime location next to shops & galleries
- ◆ Private balconies and/or patios
- ◆ Enjoy 600 feet of private frontage on Oak Creek
- ◆ Spectacular red rock views from 5 stories
- ◆ Luxurious Simmons pillowtop beds
- ◆ Fireplaces & whirlpool tubs available
- ◆ Free high-speed Internet in all rooms

SPECIAL OFFER

BOOK YOUR RESERVATION.

CALL TO RECEIVE SPECIAL PRICING FOR AAA MEMBERS

bestwesternsedona.com

For Reservations 1-800-773-3662

400 N. State Route 89A ◆ **Sedona, AZ 86336**

▼ See AAA listing p. 237 ▼

BEST WESTERN PLUS
INN of SEDONA

Best Western
PLUS

Unbeatable Views of Sedona's Red Rocks!

- Terraced promenade decks
- Free deluxe continental breakfast
- Free wireless high speed internet access
- Free "About Town" shuttle to local area
- Free concierge service

Scan this tag on your smartphone and start saving today!

Get the free mobile app at
http://gettag.mobi

800.292.6344 • www.InnofSedona.com
1200 State Route 89A, Sedona, AZ 86336

Photography courtesy of bcphotography.com

Each Best Western® hotel is independently owned and operated. ©2011 Best Western International, Inc. All rights reserved.

(See map & index p. 232.)

DIAMOND RESORTS INTERNATIONAL - THE RIDGE ON SEDONA GOLF RESORT   Phone: 928/284-1200

Condominium
Rates not provided

Address: 55 Sunridge Cir 86351 **Location:** Jct SR 89A, 7.4 mi s on SR 179, just w on Ridge Trail Dr, then just s. **Facility:** The resort's pueblo-style buildings offer attractively furnished suites and standard rooms; some units overlook the golf course, others offer red rock views. 236 condominiums. 2 stories (no elevator), exterior corridors. **Terms:** check-in 4 pm. **Amenities:** safes. **Pool(s):** 2 heated outdoor. **Activities:** whirlpools, recreation programs, exercise room. **Guest Services:** coin laundry.

ENCHANTMENT RESORT AND MII AMO SPA
Phone: (928)282-2900

Resort Hotel
$215-$450

Address: 525 Boynton Canyon Rd 86336 **Location:** Jct SR 179, 3.5 mi w on SR 89A, 5 mi n on Dry Creek Rd and FR 152C. Located in a quiet rural area. **Facility:** Tucked in Boynton Canyon under red rock cliffs, the property's adobe-style casitas range from studio units to one-, two- or three-bedroom suites, some with a private spa or pool. 234 units, some efficiencies and houses. 1 story, exterior corridors. **Terms:** check-in 4 pm, 7 day cancellation notice-fee imposed. **Amenities:** video games (fee), high-speed Internet, safes, honor bars. **Dining:** 2 restaurants, also, The Yavapai Restaurant, see separate listing. **Pool(s):** 5 heated outdoor, heated indoor. **Activities:** saunas, whirlpools, putting green, 6 tennis courts, recreation programs, bicycles, hiking trails, sports court, spa. **Guest Services:** complimentary and valet laundry, area transportation-Tlaquepaque & uptown. Affiliated with A Preferred Hotel.

EL PORTAL SEDONA LUXURY INN
Phone: (928)203-9405 30

Hotel
$179-$399

Address: 95 Portal Ln 86336 **Location:** Jct SR 89A, just s on SR 179, then just w. Adjacent to Tlaquepaque Plaza. **Facility:** Built to replicate early 1900s southwestern buildings, the hotel features elegantly appointed guest rooms that graciously surround a courtyard. 12 units. 2 stories (no elevator), interior/exterior corridors. **Terms:** 2 night minimum stay - weekends, 15 day cancellation notice-fee imposed. **Amenities:** high-speed Internet. **Activities:** *Fee:* massage. **Guest Services:** valet laundry, area transportation-within 5 mi. **Free Special Amenities:** local telephone calls and high-speed Internet.

HAMPTON INN   Phone: (928)282-4700 22

Hotel

AAA Benefit:
Members save up to 10% everyday!

$129-$189 2/1-10/31
$119-$179 11/1-1/31

Address: 1800 W Hwy 89A 86336 **Location:** Jct SR 179, 2 mi w. **Facility:** 55 units. 2 stories, interior corridors. **Terms:** 1-7 night minimum stay, cancellation fee imposed. **Amenities:** video games (fee). **Pool(s):** heated outdoor. **Activities:** whirlpool, exercise room. **Guest Services:** valet laundry.

▼ See AAA listing p. 237 ▼

Casa SED☀NA INN

Stay tonight for $169 dbl occ*
gourmet breakfast included

Get the free mobile app at
http://gettag.mobi

16 upscale rooms
www.casasedona.com

*first night

800-525-3756 - 55 Hozoni Dr Sedona, AZ 86336

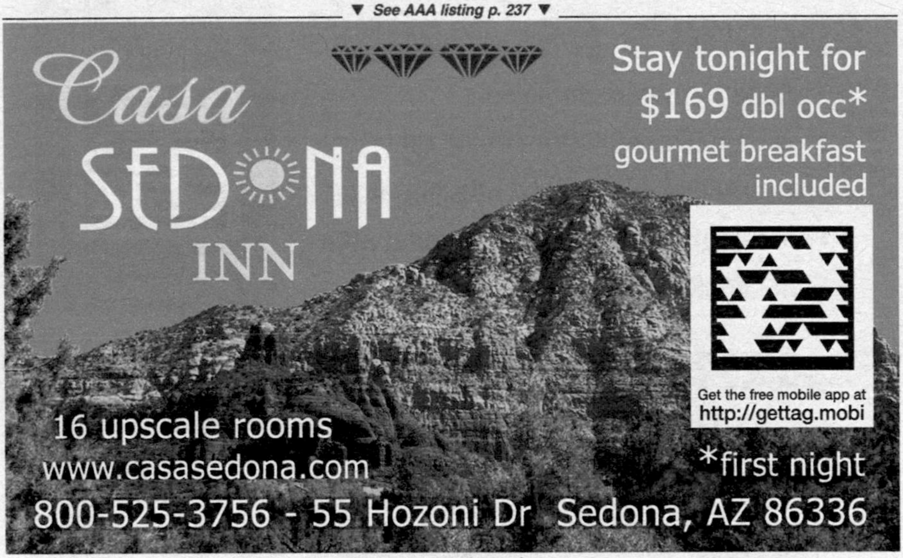

Are we meeting your travel needs?

If your visit to an establishment listed in a AAA TourBook guide doesn't meet your expectations, tell us about it.

Complete an easy online form at
AAA.com/TourBookComments.

(See map & index p. 232.)

HILTON SEDONA RESORT & SPA
Phone: (928)284-4040   **47**

Resort Hotel
$135-$269

AAA Benefit:
Members save 5% or more
everyday!

Address: 90 Ridge Trail Dr 86351
Location: Jct SR 89A, 7.3 mi s on
SR 179. Located in Village of Oak
Creek. **Facility:** Offering beautiful
red rock views, guest rooms
feature a patio and fireplace. One
pool's focal point is a
cactus-shaped fountain and
cascading waterfall. 219 units. 3
stories, interior corridors. **Terms:**
1-7 night minimum stay, cancellation fee imposed.
Amenities: high-speed Internet (fee), safes. **Dining:** 2
restaurants. **Pool(s):** 3 heated outdoor. **Activities:**
whirlpools, hiking trails, spa. *Fee:* golf-18 holes, 3 lighted
tennis courts. **Guest Services:** valet and coin laundry.

Northern AZ's resort
offering on-site golf and spa
in the heart of Sedona's
red rock country

THE INN ON OAK CREEK
Phone: (928)282-7896   **33**

Bed & Breakfast
$200-$295

Address: 556 SR 179 86336
Location: Jct SR 89A, 0.5 mi s.
Overlooks Oak Creek. **Facility:**
Located on Oak Creek and within
walking distance of shops and
galleries, the property's rooms
include a fireplace. Check-in is
available 3-6 pm. 11 units. 2 stories
(no elevator), interior corridors.
Terms: office hours 7:30 am-7 pm,
age restrictions may apply, 7 day
cancellation notice-fee imposed.
Activities: fishing. **Guest Services:**
valet laundry. **Free Special
Amenities:** early check-in/late
check-out and high-speed Internet.
(See ad this page.)

JUNIPINE RESORT
Phone: (928)282-3375   **1**

Condominium
$135-$400

Address: 8351 N SR 89A 86336
Location: Jct SR 179, 9 mi ne.
Located in a quiet area. **Facility:** 40
condominiums. 1-2 stories (no
elevator), exterior corridors. **Terms:** 7
day cancellation notice-fee imposed. **Dining:** Junipine Cafe,
see separate listing. **Activities:** hiking trails, basketball,
horseshoes. *Fee:* fishing. **Guest Services:** coin laundry.

▼ See AAA listing this page ▼

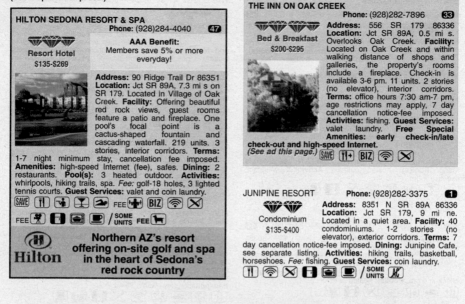

In the heart of Sedona, within its acclaimed gallery district, a premier bed-and-breakfast facility has been created with you—the guest—in mind. Gracefully suspended over Oak Creek, this unique inn features rooms with balconies and spectacular views of Sedona's majestic red rocks. This exceptional inn's cozy rooms all have private baths with spa tubs, gas fireplaces, TV's—and lots of privacy. Additional amenities include a full breakfast, afternoon refreshments, a private creekside park, and casually elegant rooms that evoke romance. The Inn On Oak Creek—come see what's in store for you.

Now Featuring!
THE ART OF COOKING
The Cooking School at
THE INN ON OAK CREEK
Sedona Arizona

556 Hwy. 179 · Sedona, AZ 86336 · www.innonoakcreek.com
(800) 499-7896 · (928) 282-7896 · FAX (928) 282-0696

Make Your Next Trip a Journey ... With AAA and Hertz.

For reservations, **visit** your AAA/CAA travel
office, **click** on AAA.com/hertz or
CAA.ca/hertz, or **call** 800-654-3080 U.S./
888-333-3120 Canada.

Show Your Card & Save

Hertz.

(See map & index p. 232.)

KING'S RANSOM INN
Phone: (928)282-3132 **34**

Hotel
$85-$110

Address: 725 Hwy 179 86336
Location: 0.7 mi s of jct SR 89A.
Facility: 53 units. 2 stories (no elevator), interior corridors. **Pool(s):** heated outdoor. **Activities:** whirlpool, hiking trails.

🍴➕ 🛏 BIZ 🛜 ✕ 💻 / SOME UNITS 🐾

KING'S RANSOM SEDONA HOTEL
Phone: (928)282-7151 **35**

Hotel
$99-$225

Address: 771 SR 179 86336
Location: 0.7 mi s of jct SR 89A.
Facility: 95 units. 2 stories (no elevator), interior/exterior corridors.
Terms: office hours 7 am-11 pm, cancellation fee imposed. **Dining:** Elote Cafe, see separate listing. **Pool(s):** heated outdoor. **Activities:** whirlpool, exercise room.

🍴 🍸 🛏 BIZ 🛜 ✕ 🛗 💻 / SOME UNITS FEE 🐾

KOKOPELLI INN
Phone: 928/284-1100 **44**

Hotel
Rates not provided

Address: 6465 Hwy 179 86351
Location: Jct Bell Rock Blvd, just s. Located in Village of Oak Creek. **Facility:** 42 units. 2 stories (no elevator), exterior corridors. **Terms:** check-in 4 pm. **Pool(s):** heated outdoor.

🍴➕ 🛏 BIZ 🛜 ✕ 🛗 💻

KOKOPELLI SUITES
Phone: (928)204-1146 **19**

Hotel
$79-$239

Address: 3119 W Hwy 89A 86336
Location: Jct SR 179, 3 mi w. Located in business section of West Sedona. **Facility:** 45 units, some kitchens. 2 stories (no elevator), exterior corridors. **Terms:** office hours 7 am-10 pm, 3 day cancellation notice-fee imposed. **Amenities:** safes. **Pool(s):** heated outdoor. **Activities:** whirlpool, limited exercise equipment. **Guest Services:** coin laundry. **Free Special Amenities: continental breakfast and high-speed Internet.**

SAVE 🛏 🛜 ✕ 🛗 🖨 💻 / SOME UNITS FEE 🐾

LA QUINTA INN SEDONA / VILLAGE OF OAK CREEK
Phone: (928)284-0711 **43**

Hotel
$89-$179

Address: 6176 SR 179 86351
Location: Jct Bell Rock Blvd, just s. Located in Village of Oak Creek. **Facility:** 100 units. 2 stories, interior corridors. **Pool(s):** heated outdoor.
Activities: whirlpool, exercise room. **Guest Services:** coin laundry. **Free Special Amenities: continental breakfast and high-speed Internet.**

SAVE 🍴➕ CALL 📶 🛏 BIZ 🛜 ✕ 💻 / SOME UNITS 🐾 🛗 🖨

L'AUBERGE DE SEDONA INN AND SPA
Phone: (928)282-1661 **15**

Hotel
$229-$725

Address: 301 L'Auberge Ln 86336
Location: Jct SR 179, just n on SR 89A, then ne; down the hill. Located in a secluded area. **Facility:** Lodge and individual cottages are nestled on several acres of landscaped, tree-shaded grounds along Oak Creek. The spa offers couples an open-air, creekside massage. 88 units, some two bedrooms and cottages. 1-2 stories (no elevator), interior/exterior corridors. **Parking:** valet only. **Terms:** 7 day cancellation notice-fee imposed. **Amenities:** safes. **Dining:** L'Auberge Restaurant on Oak Creek, see separate listing, entertainment. **Activities:** whirlpool, fishing, recreation programs, exercise room, spa. **Guest Services:** valet laundry.

SAVE 🍴 🍸 🛏 BIZ 🛜 ✕ FEE 🎿 🛗 💻 / SOME UNITS FEE 🐾 🖨

THE LODGE AT SEDONA
Phone: (928)204-1942 **24**

Bed & Breakfast
$189-$349

Address: 125 Kallof Pl 86336
Location: Jct SR 89A 1.8 mi w on SR 89A, then just s. Located in a secluded area. **Facility:** The elegant Mission-style inn sits on three acres and features warmly decorated public areas. Many units include a gas fireplace and private deck; one unit has an outdoor shower. 14 units. 1-2 stories (no elevator), interior/exterior corridors. **Terms:** office hours 7 am-7 pm, 2 night minimum stay - seasonal, age restrictions may apply, 14 day cancellation notice-fee imposed. **Activities:** sports court, horseshoes.

🍴➕ 🛗➕ BIZ 🛜 ✕ FEE 🎿 ☎ / SOME UNITS FEE 🐾 📺 🛗

LOS ABRIGADOS RESORT & SPA
Phone: 928/282-1777 **31**

Resort
Condominium
Rates not provided

Address: 160 Portal Ln 86336
Location: Jct SR 89A, just s on SR 179, then just w. Adjacent to Tlaquepaque Arts & Crafts Village. **Facility:** Surrounded by 22 acres along Oak Creek, the property offers many recreation options. Some of the property's attractive suites include a fireplace and outdoor spa. 196 efficiencies. 2 stories (no elevator), exterior corridors. **Terms:** check-in 4 pm. **Amenities:** Some: safes. **Dining:** Stakes & Sticks, see separate listing. **Pool(s):** 2 heated outdoor. **Activities:** saunas, whirlpools, steamrooms, 2 lighted tennis courts, recreation programs in summer, playground, sports court, basketball, horseshoes, volleyball, exercise room, spa. Fee: miniature golf. **Guest Services:** valet and coin laundry, area transportation (fee)-within 15 mi.

🍴 🍸 🛏 BIZ 🛜 ✕ 🛗 🖨 💻 / SOME UNITS FEE 🐾

MATTERHORN INN
Phone: (928)282-7176 **10**

Motel
$99-$179

Address: 230 Apple Ave 86336
Location: Jct SR 179, just ne on SR 89A; uptown. Located in a central shopping district. **Facility:** 23 units. 2 stories (no elevator), exterior corridors. **Terms:** office hours 8 am-10 pm. **Pool(s):** heated outdoor. **Activities:** whirlpool. **Free Special Amenities: local telephone calls and high-speed Internet.**
(See ad p. 243.)

SAVE 🍴➕ 🛏 🛜 ✕ FEE 🎿 🛗 💻 / SOME UNITS FEE 🐾

ORCHARDS INN OF SEDONA
Phone: 928/282-2405 **14**

Hotel
Rates not provided

Address: 254 N SR 89A 86336
Location: Jct SR 179, just ne on SR 89A. Located in Uptown Sedona shopping area. **Facility:** 69 units. 2-3 stories (no elevator), exterior corridors.
Dining: The Orchards Bar & Grill, see separate listing. **Pool(s):** heated outdoor. **Activities:** whirlpool. **Guest Services:** coin laundry.

SAVE 🍴 🍸 🛏 BIZ 🛜 ✕ FEE 🎿 🛗 🖨 💻 / SOME UNITS FEE 🐾

Create complete trip routings and custom maps with the TripTik® Travel Planner on AAA.com or CAA.ca

▼ See AAA listing p. 242 ▼

Located in the center of Sedona's famous uptown district.
Just steps away from shops, galleries, and restaurants.

※ Spectacular views from your room's private deck.

※ 23 large, classically appointed guest rooms furnished with coffee makers, hair dryers, refrigerators and irons with boards.

※ Free in room high-speed wireless internet access and voice mail.

※ Relax in our heated pool (seasonal) and open air hot tub.

※ Winter Vacation Special: Stay one night at full price, get the second night half price or stay two nights full price, and get the third night free. Sun. - Thurs. only. Dec. 1 - Feb. 28, Holiday periods excluded. No other discounts apply.

For reservations, call:
1-800-372-8207 Tel: (928) 282-7176
Email: info@ matterhorninn.com
www. matterhorninn.com

Share a New View on Travel at
AAATravelViews.com

Read stories, tips and trends from AAA insiders.
Post comments and get your questions answered by our travel experts.

(See map & index p. 232.)

POCO DIABLO RESORT

Phone: 928/282-7333 `39`

Resort Hotel
Rates not provided

Address: 1752 State Route 179 86336 **Location:** Jct SR 179, 2 mi s of SR 89A. **Facility:** Buildings are spread across several acres containing gardens and a courtyard pool. Guest rooms, some with a fireplace, are spacious and feature either a patio or balcony. 137 units. 2 stories (no elevator), exterior corridors. **Terms:** check-in 4 pm. **Amenities:** video games (fee), high-speed Internet. **Pool(s):** heated outdoor. **Activities:** whirlpools, 4 tennis courts (2 lighted), hiking trails, playground, exercise room. *Fee:* golf-9 holes, massage. **Guest Services:** valet and coin laundry.

SAVE ⟨icons⟩ / SOME UNITS FEE ⟨icon⟩

POCO DIABLO RESORT

Buildings on several acres with gardens & courtyard. Pet friendly. Spacious rooms with balcony or patio

RODEWAY INN & SUITES IRIS GARDEN

Phone: 928/282-2223 `5`

Motel
Rates not provided

Address: 390 Jordan Rd 86336 **Location:** Jct SR 179, 0.3 mi ne on SR 89A, just n. Located in Uptown Sedona. **Facility:** 15 units, some two bedrooms and kitchens. 1-2 stories, exterior corridors. **Terms:** office hours 6 am-11 pm. **Activities:** whirlpool. **Guest Services:** coin laundry. **Free Special Amenities:** continental breakfast and high-speed Internet.

SAVE ⟨icons⟩ / SOME UNITS

ROSE TREE INN

Phone: (928)282-2065 `6`

Motel
$109-$149

Address: 376 Cedar St 86336 **Location:** Jct SR 179, 0.4 mi ne on SR 89A, just nw on Apple, then just ne. Located in a quiet area. **Facility:** 5 units, some kitchens. 1 story, exterior corridors. **Terms:** office hours 8 am-10 pm, 2 night minimum stay - seasonal and/or weekends, cancellation fee imposed. **Guest Services:** complimentary laundry.

⟨icons⟩

SEDONA MOTEL

Phone: (928)282-7187 `29`

Motel
$90-$120

Address: 218 SR 179 86336 **Location:** Jct SR 89A, just s. Located in a busy area. **Facility:** 16 units. 1 story, exterior corridors. **Terms:** office hours 8:30 am-9 pm, 2 night minimum stay - seasonal and/or weekends, cancellation fee imposed. **Amenities:** safes. **Free Special Amenities:** local telephone calls and early check-in/late check-out.

SAVE ⟨icons⟩

SEDONA REAL INN & SUITES

Phone: (928)282-1414 `21`

Hotel
$95-$340

Address: 95 Arroyo Piñon Dr 86336 **Location:** Jct SR 179, 3.4 mi w on SR 89A, just sw. Located in West Sedona. **Facility:** 89 units, some kitchens. 2 stories (no elevator), exterior corridors. **Terms:** office hours 6 am-midnight, 2-3 night minimum stay - seasonal and/or weekends, cancellation fee imposed. **Amenities:** high-speed Internet. **Pool(s):** heated outdoor. **Activities:** whirlpool, exercise room. **Guest Services:** valet and coin laundry. **Free Special Amenities:** expanded continental breakfast and high-speed Internet.
(See ad p. 236.)

SAVE ⟨icons⟩ / SOME UNITS FEE ⟨icon⟩

SEDONA ROUGE HOTEL & SPA

Phone: (928)203-4111 `17`

Hotel
$229-$279 2/29-1/31
$209-$249 2/1-2/28

Address: 2250 W Hwy 89A 86336 **Location:** Jct SR 179, 2 mi w. **Facility:** The North African- and Andalusian-style hotel includes a rooftop patio, spa, restaurant/nightclub and a meditation area with lighted columns. 77 units. 2-3 stories, interior/exterior corridors. **Terms:** 2 night minimum stay - seasonal and/or weekends, 3 day cancellation notice-fee imposed. **Amenities:** high-speed Internet. **Dining:** Red's, see separate listing. **Pool(s):** heated outdoor. **Activities:** whirlpools, steamrooms, exercise room. *Fee:* massage. **Guest Services:** valet laundry. **Free Special Amenities:** local telephone calls and newspaper.

SAVE ECO ⟨icons⟩ / SOME UNITS FEE ⟨icon⟩

SEDONA ROUGE

Boutique Hotel in convenient West Sedona location.

SEDONA SPRINGS RESORT

Phone: (928)204-3400 `26`

Condominium
$125-$300

Address: 55 Northview Rd 86336 **Location:** Jct SR 179, 1.6 mi w on SR 89A, then just e. Located in West Sedona. **Facility:** In an apartment-style complex surrounding a central courtyard with pools, many of these spacious units have garden-style whirlpool baths and showers. 40 condominiums. 2 stories (no elevator), exterior corridors. **Terms:** office hours 7 am-10 pm, check-in 4 pm, 14 day cancellation notice-fee imposed. **Amenities:** safes. **Pool(s):** heated outdoor. **Activities:** whirlpools, putting green, exercise room. **Guest Services:** coin laundry.

SAVE ⟨icons⟩

Complete Vacation Planning

AAA.com/Travel and **CAA.ca/Travel** – everything you need to plan and book your vacations, backed by the travel experts at local AAA/CAA offices.

(See map & index p. 232.)

SEDONA SUMMIT RESORT
Phone: (928)204-3100   **32**

Condominium
$159-$599

Address: 4055 Navoti Dr 86336 **Location:** Jct SR 179, 3.8 mi w on SR 89A, then just n on Bristlecone Pine Dr. **Facility:** The Santa Fe-style buildings offer some red rock views. Lodgings include spacious suites or standard rooms in a garden setting with a lush courtyard. 417 condominiums. 1-2 stories (no elevator), exterior corridors. **Terms:** check-in 4 pm, cancellation fee imposed. **Amenities:** safes. **Pool(s):** 4 heated outdoor. **Activities:** whirlpools, recreation programs, game room, exercise room. **Guest Services:** complimentary and valet laundry.

SEDONA SUPER 8
Phone: (928)282-1533   **20**

Hotel
$77-$126

Address: 2545 W Hwy 89A 86336 **Location:** Jct SR 179, 2.4 mi w. **Facility:** 66 units. 3 stories, interior corridors. **Terms:** cancellation fee imposed. **Pool(s):** heated outdoor. **Guest Services:** coin laundry.

SKY RANCH LODGE
Phone: (928)282-6400   **36**

Motel
$80-$250

Address: 1105 Airport Rd 86336 **Location:** Jct SR 179, 1 mi w on SR 89A, then 1 mi s. **Facility:** 94 units, some cottages. 2 stories (no elevator), exterior corridors. **Terms:** office hours 7 am-10 pm, check-in 4 pm, 2 night minimum stay - weekends. **Pool(s):** heated outdoor. **Activities:** whirlpool, hiking trails. **Guest Services:** coin laundry.

SLIDE ROCK LODGE
Phone: (928)282-3531   **2**

Motel
$99-$179

Address: 6401 N SR 89A 86336 **Location:** Jct SR 179, 6.6 mi n. **Facility:** 18 units. 1 story, exterior corridors. *Bath:* shower only. **Terms:** office hours 8 am-8 pm, 2 night minimum stay - seasonal and/or weekends, 7 day cancellation notice-fee imposed. **Activities:** fishing, hiking trails.

SOUTHWEST INN AT SEDONA
Phone: 928/282-3344   **18**

Hotel
Rates not provided

Address: 3250 W Hwy 89A 86336 **Location:** Jct SR 179, 3.5 mi w. Located in West Sedona. **Facility:** 28 units. 2 stories (no elevator), exterior corridors. **Terms:** office hours 7 am-9 pm. **Pool(s):** heated outdoor. **Activities:** whirlpool, exercise room.

THE VIEWS INN SEDONA
Phone: (928)284-2487   **45**

Hotel
$79-$149

Address: 65 E Cortez Dr 86351 **Location:** Jct Bell Rock Blvd, 0.9 mi s on SR 179, just e. Located in Village of Oak Creek. **Facility:** 39 units. 2 stories (no elevator), exterior corridors. **Terms:** office hours 7 am-11 pm, 2 night minimum stay - weekends. **Pool(s):** outdoor. **Activities:** whirlpool. **Guest Services:** coin laundry. **Free Special Amenities:** continental breakfast and high-speed Internet.

VILLAGE LODGE
Phone: 928/284-3626   **42**

Motel
$49-$89

Address: 105 Bell Rock Plaza 86351 **Location:** Jct SR 179, just w. Located in Village of Oak Creek. **Facility:** 17 units. 2 stories (no elevator), interior/exterior corridors. **Terms:** office hours 8 am-8 pm, 2 night minimum stay - weekends, 3 day cancellation notice-fee imposed.

VILLAS AT POCO DIABLO
Phone: (928)204-3300   **38**

Condominium
$155-$195

Address: 1752 S Hwy 179 86336 **Location:** On SR 179, 2 mi s of jct SR 89A. Located in a quiet area. **Facility:** Nestled above a rocky creek and a resort golf course, the spacious villas offer welcoming views and a shady retreat from the desert heat. 33 condominiums. 1 story, exterior corridors. **Terms:** office hours 7:30 am-4:30 pm, check-in 4 pm, 14 day cancellation notice-fee imposed. **Pool(s):** heated outdoor. **Activities:** whirlpool, basketball. **Guest Services:** coin laundry.

VILLAS OF SEDONA
Phone: (928)204-3400   **23**

Condominium
$175-$250

Address: 120 Kallof Place Rd 86336 **Location:** Jct SR 179, 1.6 mi w on SR 89A, then just s. Located in West Sedona. **Facility:** The apartment-style complex surrounds a central courtyard with a pool. Most of the spacious townhome units have a private, outdoor whirlpool. 40 condominiums. 2 stories (no elevator), exterior corridors. **Terms:** office hours 7 am-10 pm, check-in 4 pm, 14 day cancellation notice-fee imposed. **Amenities:** safes. **Pool(s):** heated outdoor, heated indoor. **Activities:** sauna, whirlpool, putting green, playground. *Fee:* game room. **Guest Services:** coin laundry.

WILDFLOWER INN
Phone: (928)284-3937   **41**

Hotel
$74-$169

Address: 6086 Hwy 179 86351 **Location:** Jct SR 179 and Bell Rock Blvd. Located in Village of Oak Creek. **Facility:** 29 units. 2 stories (no elevator), exterior corridors. **Terms:** office hours 7 am-10 pm, cancellation fee imposed. **Activities:** sauna, exercise room. **Guest Services:** coin laundry. **Free Special Amenities:** continental breakfast and high-speed Internet.

WHERE TO EAT

BARKING FROG GRILLE
Phone: 928/204-2000   **14**

American
$8-$27

AAA Inspector Notes: Enjoy an upbeat atmosphere at this lovely Southwestern-style restaurant with its brick and stucco walls adorned with colorful rugs, pottery and pictures. Several dining sections including attractive patios, some enhanced with a fireplace. The menu is extensive with items ranging from ribs, steaks, rotisserie chicken and pork, to blackened halibut tacos, plantain-encrusted swordfish and caramelized scallops. A lighter menu with sandwiches, burgers and French dip also is available. **Bar:** full bar. **Address:** 2620 W Hwy 89A 86336 **Location:** Jct SR 179, 2.4 mi w. L   D

CANYON BREEZE
Phone: 928/282-2112   **5**

Deli
$5-$10

AAA Inspector Notes: Catering to foot traffic, this large cafeteria-style deli serves quick bites such as pizza, panini, coffee and ice cream. There is a full bar that overlooks the beautiful red rocks. **Bar:** full bar. **Address:** 300 N Hwy 89A 86336 **Location:** Jct SR 179, just ne on SR 89A; uptown. **Parking:** street only. B   L   D

COWBOY CLUB
Phone: 928/282-4200   **10**

American
$8-$40

AAA Inspector Notes: One of the more popular restaurants in Sedona, the menu at this eatery revolves around buffalo meat. There are buffalo burgers, flank steak, tenderloin and soup. Try the buffalo flank steak, a super tender meat served in an amazing sweet-brown sauce. There also are more traditional items such as burgers, cedar plank salmon and beef steaks for the non-adventurous. The casual country decor is fun with lively servers. A long wooden bar is fully stocked and serves locally-brewed beer. **Bar:** full bar. **Address:** 241 N Hwy 89A 86336 **Location:** SR 179, 0.5 mi n. L   D

(See map & index p. 232.)

CUCINA RUSTICA
Menu on AAA.com
◆◆◆
Mediterranean
$13-$32
Phone: 928/284-3010　㊵
AAA Inspector Notes: Boasting a decor akin to that of an elegant seaside villa, this eatery prepares such hearty dishes as marinated and grilled pork loin and roast chicken in lemon-garlic sauce. **Bar:** full bar. **Reservations:** suggested. **Address:** 7000 Hwy 179, Suite 126A 86351 **Location:** Just s of Bell Rock Blvd. D

DAHL & DILUCA RISTORANTE ITALIANO
Phone: 928/282-5219　⑰
◆◆◆
Italian
$13-$32
AAA Inspector Notes: Located in West Sedona, this refined dining spot features delicious seafood, steak, veal and chicken dishes with creative touches using creamy and wine sauces dashed with lemon, basil, garlic, capers or other herbs. Examples of the traditional entrées include piatto Milanese and linguine carbonara. Servers are professional, yet offer a casual style to service. Quiet tones present a feeling of an outdoor garden. Entertainment is offered nightly. **Bar:** full bar. **Reservations:** suggested. **Address:** 2321 W Hwy 89A 86336 **Location:** Jct SR 179, 3 mi w; in West Sedona. D

ELOTE CAFE
Phone: 928/203-0105　㉟
◆◆◆
Mexican
$16-$25
AAA Inspector Notes: Many homemade Mexican items are served in the small casual atmosphere at this cafe. The popular restaurant does not take reservations for parties less than five, so be prepared to wait. **Bar:** full bar. **Address:** 771 SR 179 86336 **Location:** 0.7 mi s of jct SR 89A; in King's Ransom Sedona Hotel. D

EL RINCON RESTAURANTE MEXICANO
Phone: 928/282-4648　㉙
◆◆
Mexican
$7-$10
AAA Inspector Notes: The casual eatery serves freshly prepared classics and specialty chimichangas that are robust meals for hungry art shoppers. Patio dining also is available. **Bar:** full bar. **Reservations:** suggested. **Address:** Hwy 179 at the Bridge 86336 **Location:** Just s of jct SR 179 and 89A; in Tlaquepaque Plaza. L D

EURO DELI
Phone: 928/282-4798　⑱
◆
Deli
$4-$9
AAA Inspector Notes: This eatery is a casual deli that serves European style sandwiches for breakfast and lunch. While guest wait they can shop for European style foods. **Address:** 3190 W Hwy 89A 86336 **Location:** Jct SR 179, 3 mi w. B L

THE HEARTLINE CAFE
Phone: 928/282-0785　㉒
◆◆◆
American
$10-$30
AAA Inspector Notes: The warm, intimate interior and pleasant waitstaff at this eatery complement the imaginative selection of Southwestern cuisine. The wine list is extensive. **Bar:** full bar. **Reservations:** suggested. **Address:** 1610 W Hwy 89A 86336 **Location:** On SR 89A, 1.5 mi s of jct SR 179. D

HIRO'S SUSHI BAR & JAPANESE RESTAURANT
Phone: 928/282-0992　㉔
◆◆◆
Japanese
$7-$20
AAA Inspector Notes: This upscale restaurant is located atop a large cliff giving guests a panoramic view of the city. Fresh sushi items along with Japanese favorites are served including shrimp tempura, ahi tuna salad, salmon teriyaki and specialty rolls. **Bar:** full bar. **Address:** 101 SR 89A, #F-29 86336 **Location:** Jct SR 179; in The Piñon Pointe Plaza. L D

HUNDRED ROX
Phone: 928/282-4828　③
◆◆◆
Italian
$10-$38
AAA Inspector Notes: Set amidst Sedona's famed Red Rock and alongside beautiful Oak Creek, this restaurant offers a creative selection of California-inspired Northern Italian and Mediterranean dishes. From the smoked provolone eggplant and chicken parmigiana duet to the truffle-grilled filet mignon, to the fresh seasonal fish, the staff delights in creating delectable dishes with a unique flair. **Bar:** full bar. **Address:** 100 Amara Ln 86336 **Location:** Jct SR 179, 0.4 mi ne; center; in Amara Hotel, Restaurant & Spa. B D CALL ⬥M

INDIA PALACE CUISINE
Phone: 928/204-2300　⑲
◆◆◆
Indian
$8-$17
AAA Inspector Notes: Competent and friendly waitstaff serve an extensive offering ranging from various tandoori entrées to seafood, chicken, lamb and vegetable dishes. The daily lunch buffet is filling. **Bar:** full bar. **Address:** 1910 W SR 89A, Suite 102 86336 **Location:** Jct SR 179, 1.8 mi w. L D

JAVELINA CANTINA
Phone: 928/282-1313
◆◆◆
Mexican
$10-$16
AAA Inspector Notes: In a popular and upscale shopping area with art galleries and shops nearby, the relaxed eatery affords spectacular views of the Red Rock from inside or on the covered patio. Large portions of fresh food are served in a festive setting punctuated by bright glass lamps, punched-tin sconces and tall windows. The energetic staff is quick to meet service needs. **Bar:** full bar. **Address:** 671 Hwy 179 86336 **Location:** SR 89A, 0.8 mi s; in Hillside Courtyard and Marketplace, Bldg F, ground level. L D

JUDI'S RESTAURANT
Phone: 928/282-4449　㉕
◆◆◆
American
$9-$26
AAA Inspector Notes: Antiques and beamed ceilings contribute to the comfortable, cozy atmosphere. The menu centers on chicken, pasta, seafood and steak dishes. A favorite choice is barbecue baby back ribs. A shady courtyard offers additional seating. **Reservations:** suggested. **Address:** 40 Soldier's Pass Rd 86336 **Location:** Jct SR 179, 1 mi w on SR 89A; northeast corner. L D

JUNIPINE CAFE
Phone: 928/282-7406　①
◆◆◆
American
$8-$29
AAA Inspector Notes: Located north of Sedona along Oak Creek Canyon, this cozy eatery serves a nice variety of beef, chicken and pasta dishes. The dining room sports simple, rustic decor, highlighted by locally created paintings and photographs, all of which are for sale. Outdoor dining is an option in good weather. **Bar:** full bar. **Reservations:** suggested. **Address:** 8351 N SR 89A 86336 **Location:** Jct SR 179, 9 mi ne; in Junipine Resort. B L D

L'AUBERGE RESTAURANT ON OAK CREEK
Phone: 928/282-1661　⑬
◆◆◆◆
American
$18-$48
AAA Inspector Notes: Enjoy dining on the shady banks of Oak Creek, where every seat at this eatery offers a creek-side view. Contemporary American cuisine with French influences is served for breakfast, lunch and dinner. An outdoor wine bar is available, weather permitting. **Bar:** full bar. **Reservations:** suggested. **Address:** 301 L'Auberge Ln 86336 **Location:** Jct SR 179, just n on SR 89A, then ne; down the hill; in L'Auberge de Sedona Inn and Spa. **Parking:** valet only. B L D

(See map & index p. 232.)

MARIA'S RESTAURANT & CANTINA
Phone: 928/284-3739 (37)

Mexican
$8-$19

AAA Inspector Notes: This eatery offers classic Mexican dishes along with specialty appetizers such as rattlesnake eggs, which are cheese-stuffed jalapeños that test your tongue for pepper-hot heat. **Bar:** full bar. **Address:** 6446 Hwy 179 86351 **Location:** 0.5 mi s of Bell Rock Blvd. B L D

MARKETPLACE CAFE
Phone: 928/284-5478 (39)

American
$8-$28

AAA Inspector Notes: This spacious restaurant is decorated in Hollywood memorabilia offering booth and table seating, seasonal patio dining and a vast array of menu options. Food is very well prepared and portions are ample. The intriguing cocktail list is a crowd pleaser. **Bar:** full bar. **Address:** 6645 SR 179 86351 **Location:** On SR 179; in Village of Oak Creek Outlet Mall Shopping Complex. L D

NEW YORK BAGELS AND DELI
Phone: 928/204-1242 (26)

Deli
$3-$8

AAA Inspector Notes: This small deli is family run by native New Yorkers. Bagels are the specialty but it is a full deli and pizza is served for dinner. **Address:** 1650 W SR 89A 86336 **Location:** Jct SR 179, 1.3 mi w. B L D

NICK'S ON THE WEST SIDE
Phone: 928/204-2088 (12)

American
$8-$21

AAA Inspector Notes: Locally popular for breakfast, this restaurant draws in folks for its eggs Judi dish, which outsells its French toast. For lunch or dinner, barbecue and Mexican dishes are hearty options. **Bar:** full bar. **Address:** 2920 W Hwy 89A 86336 **Location:** On SR 89A, 2.7 mi w of jct SR 179. B L D

OAK CREEK BREWERY & GRILL
Phone: 928/282-3300 (30)

American
$10-$26

AAA Inspector Notes: The microbrewery's owner, who trained in Germany, designs the prize-winning, freshly brewed beers. Accompaniments include crisp salads, hearty sandwiches, pizza, steaks and ribs. Desserts are awesome. **Bar:** full bar. **Address:** 336 Hwy 179, Suite D201 86336 **Location:** Jct SR 89A, 0.3 mi s; in Tlaquepaque Arts & Crafts Village. L D

OAXACA RESTAURANT
Phone: 928/282-4179 (6)

Mexican
$10-$20

AAA Inspector Notes: This family-friendly place serves dishes from the Mexican region of the same name. For more than 20 years, the family has prepared foods, being conscious of dietary concerns, using vegetable oils and no additives. **Bar:** full bar. **Address:** 321 N SR 89A 86336 **Location:** Jct Apple Rd and SR 89A. L D

OPEN RANGE GRILL & TAVERN
Phone: 928/282-0002 (4)

American
$12-$28

AAA Inspector Notes: The large two-story windows display panoramic views of the red rocks for which Sedona is known. The casual dining room offers an open kitchen and minimal decorations. The menu offers fresh Southwestern American cuisine-the blackened salmon is great. The service is friendly. **Bar:** full bar. **Address:** 320 SR 89A 86336 **Location:** Jct SR 179, just ne. **Parking:** street only. L D

THE ORCHARDS BAR & GRILL
Phone: 928/282-2405 (7)

Regional American
$9-$20

AAA Inspector Notes: From the day's start to the finish, this popular eatery provides such well-cooked dishes as eggs Benedict, hearty burgers and sandwiches as well as Mexican regional dishes. The staff is friendly. **Bar:** full bar. **Address:** 254 N Hwy 89A 86336 **Location:** Jct SR 179, just ne on SR 89A; in Orchards Inn of Sedona. B L D

PAGO'S PIZZERIA & ITALIAN CUISINE
Phone: 928/284-1939 (38)

Italian
$5-$20

AAA Inspector Notes: This small family-owned-and-operated restaurant features traditional fresh Italian cuisine including pizza, chicken parmigiana, veal Marsala, spaghetti and other favorites. **Address:** 6446 SR 179, #221 86351 **Location:** Jct Bell Rock Blvd, just s; in Village of Oak Creek. L D

PICAZZO'S ORGANIC ITALIAN KITCHEN
Phone: 928/282-4140

Italian
$9-$20

AAA Inspector Notes: This eatery is an upscale pizzeria in the North side of town offering fresh pizza with homemade dough along with other casual Italian dishes. **Bar:** full bar. **Address:** 1855 W Hwy 89A 86336 **Location:** Jct SR 179, 2 mi w. L D

RAINBOW'S END RELICS
Phone: 928/282-1593 (21)

Steak
$10-$28

AAA Inspector Notes: A former homestead from the early 1900s and the oldest restaurant in Sedona, the spot is filled with antiques and memorabilia. The eatery is known for prime steaks, barbecue and seafood as well as its pleasant staff. **Bar:** full bar. **Address:** 3235 W SR 89A 86336 **Location:** Jct SR 179, 3.1 mi w. L D

RED PLANET DINER
Phone: 928/282-6070 (23)

American
$8-$18

AAA Inspector Notes: Earthlings are welcomed at this family-friendly, cosmic café. The menu lists burgers, salads, sandwiches and diner fare, such as chicken-fried steak and moonloaf with brown gravy. Patio seating is a nice option. **Bar:** full bar. **Address:** 1655 W Hwy 89A 86336 **Location:** Jct SR 179, 1.7 mi w. L D

RED ROCK BBQ
Phone: 928/204-5975 (28)

Barbecue
$7-$23

AAA Inspector Notes: This casual restaurant serves great barbecue along with other casual items including hot wings, Chicago hot dogs and Philly cheesesteaks. The dining room is bright with a fun Southwest decor and some flat-screen TVs. **Bar:** full bar. **Address:** 150 Hwy 179 #1 86336 **Location:** Jct SR 89A, just s. L D

RED'S
Phone: 928/340-5321 (15)

American
$8-$34

AAA Inspector Notes: Trendy California-style decor fits well in this red rock town. Attentive staffers watch over tables to assist patrons through a memorable dining experience. Chef Ron Moler creates his own delectable version of meatloaf, grilled seafood and salads such as grilled endive with pear and honey-spiced pecans, which simply delights. Live entertainment is scheduled Tuesday through Saturday. **Bar:** full bar. **Reservations:** suggested. **Address:** 2250 W Hwy 89A 86336 **Location:** Jct SR 179, 2 mi w; in Sedona Rouge Hotel & Spa. B L D

(See map & index p. 232.)

RENE AT TLAQUEPAQUE   Phone: 928/282-9225   32

Continental
$12-$45

AAA Inspector Notes: Tucked into the upscale, art-filled Tlaquepaque Mall, this quietly elegant dining room is where diners are treated to attentive service and Continental and American favorites. Entertainers perform on weekends. The efficient staff work as a team to quietly meet your dining needs. **Bar:** full bar. **Reservations:** suggested. **Address:** 336 Hwy 179, B-118 86336 **Location:** SR 89A, 0.3 mi s on SR 179; in Tlaquepaque Arts & Crafts Village.
L D

SALLY'S BBQ   Phone: 928/300-3701   8

Barbecue
$8-$15

AAA Inspector Notes: This small, self-service restaurant is located in the rear of East Sedona Shopping Area. Slow-smoked barbecue items are offered including pulled pork, ribs and beef brisket. **Bar:** beer only. **Address:** 250 Jordan Rd, #9 86336 **Location:** SR 179, 0.6 mi n. **Parking:** on-site and street. L D

THE SECRET GARDEN CAFE   Phone: 928/203-9564   33

American
$8-$16

AAA Inspector Notes: Just off the Tlaquepaque courtyard, this casual eatery serves fresh salads, homemade soups and such innovative sandwiches as the ahi tuna wrap. The dessert showcase holds mile-high carrot or chocolate cakes, pies and other delicacies that will tempt even a staunch dieter. **Bar:** full bar. **Address:** 336 Hwy 179, Suite F101 86336 **Location:** Jct SR 89A, 0.3 mi s; at north end of Tlaquepaque Arts & Crafts Village.
B L

SHUGRUE'S HILLSIDE GRILL   Phone: 928/282-5300   34

Seafood
$15-$35

AAA Inspector Notes: The hillside location of this grill features large picture windows looking toward the mountains as well as an inviting seasonal deck. The specialty is seafood although the menu also includes selections of beef, lamb and chicken. **Bar:** full bar. **Address:** 671 Hwy 179 86336 **Location:** Jct SR 89A, 0.8 mi s; in Hillside Courtyard and Marketplace, Building D, upper level. L D

STAKES & STICKS   Phone: 928/204-7849   31

American
$10-$27

AAA Inspector Notes: Upscale decor characterizes the warm interior of this popular sports bar. The menu varies from simple pub grub to filet mignon, offering something for everyone. The attentive staff serves guests with smiles and ease as the many TVs broadcast sporting events. **Bar:** full bar. **Address:** 160 Portal Ln 86336 **Location:** Jct SR 89A, just s on SR 179, then just w; in Los Abrigados Resort & Spa. B D

SZECHUAN CHINESE RESTAURANT & SUSHI BAR   Phone: 928/282-9288   27

Asian
$10-$19

AAA Inspector Notes: This casual restaurant serves such traditional Chinese cuisine as orange chicken and Mongolian beef along with fresh sushi. The staff is casual and friendly. **Bar:** full bar. **Address:** 1350 W Hwy 89A 86336 **Location:** Jct SR 179, 1.3 mi w. L D

TAKASHI JAPANESE RESTAURANT   Phone: 928/282-2334   2

Japanese
$9-$22

AAA Inspector Notes: This restaurant offers an excellent selection of Japanese appetizers, entrées and sushi in a dining room with attractive decor. Sake and Japanese beer are available. Outdoor dining is offered, weather permitting. **Bar:** full bar. **Reservations:** suggested. **Address:** 465 Jordan Rd 86336 **Location:** SR 89A, 0.4 mi n; in north Uptown Sedona area. D

TARA THAI   Phone: 928/284-9167   36

Thai
$8-$12

AAA Inspector Notes: This local favorite serves authentic, made-to-order Thai dishes spiced to diners' preference. The small restaurant has a very casual atmosphere and friendly service. **Bar:** beer & wine. **Address:** 34 Bell Rock Plaza 86351 **Location:** Jct Bell Rock Blvd, just s; in Bell Rock Plaza Village. L D

THAI PALACE UPTOWN   Phone: 928/282-8424   9

Thai
$8-$16

AAA Inspector Notes: This small and upscale restaurant serves very fresh Thai favorites such as a pad thai, fried rice and coconut soup. The servers exude a proud demeanor and promote the fresh ingredients. **Address:** 260 Van Deren Rd 86336 **Location:** Jct SR 89A, just nw on Jordan Rd, then just e. **Parking:** on-site and street.
L D

THAI SPICES   Phone: 928/282-0599   11

Thai
$10-$17

AAA Inspector Notes: This small eatery serves fresh Thai favorites and pride themselves on serving organic vegetables. Very casual and a perfect place for a care-free lunch or dinner. **Address:** 2986 W SR 89A 86336 **Location:** Jct SR 179, 3 mi w. L D

TROIA'S   Phone: 928/282-0123   20

Italian
$13-$25

AAA Inspector Notes: Since 1997, this casual eatery has prepared pizza, pasta, and traditional favorites, including veal piccata, chicken Marsala, four-cheese lasagna and a selection of seafood entrées. Guests can opt for patio seating. **Bar:** full bar. **Address:** 1885 W Hwy 89A 86336 **Location:** Jct SR 179, 1.8 mi w. D

WILD ORCHID   Phone: 928/282-4422   16

Asian
$9-$19

AAA Inspector Notes: This small intimate restaurant serves bright and vibrant Asian-inspired cuisine such as strawberry shrimp rolls, tropical fried rice and pad thai. The service is casual and very friendly. The small bar broadcasts sporting events on the TV. **Bar:** full bar. **Address:** 2611 W SR 89A 86336 **Location:** Jct SR 179, 2.5 mi w. L D

THE YAVAPAI RESTAURANT   Phone: 928/204-6000

American
$15-$46

AAA Inspector Notes: While taking in stunning views of Boynton Canyon, diners can savor such dishes as sesame-crusted and grilled ahi tuna and cold-smoked buffalo tenderloin. The elegant service and decor complete a truly distinguished dining experience. The exceptional Sunday champagne brunch includes a variety of traditional and Southwestern dishes. **Bar:** full bar. **Reservations:** suggested. **Address:** 525 Boynton Canyon Rd 86336 **Location:** Jct SR 179, 3.5 mi w on SR 89A, 5 mi n on Dry Creek Rd and FR 152C; in Enchantment Resort and Mii amo Spa. B L D

SELIGMAN   pop. 445

CANYON LODGE
Phone: 928/422-3255

Motel
Rates not provided

Address: 22340 Old Hwy 66 86337
Location: I-40 exit 121, 1 mi n, then 0.7
mi e. **Facility:** 16 units, some kitchens.
2 stories (no elevator), exterior
corridors. **Free Special Amenities:**
continental breakfast and high-speed Internet.

SAVE CALL &M ⊗ ✕ FEE 🐾 🔋 🖼 💻
/ SOME UNITS FEE 🐕

DELUXE INN MOTEL
Phone: (928)422-3244

Motel
$48-$57

Address: 22295 Old Hwy 66 86337
Location: I-40 exit 121 eastbound, 1
mi n, then 0.7 mi e; exit 123
westbound, just ne on I-40 business
loop, then 2.4 mi w. **Facility:** 15 units.
1 story, exterior corridors. **Terms:** cancellation fee imposed.
Free Special Amenities: local telephone calls and high-speed Internet.

SAVE 📶 ⊗ FEE 🐾 🔋 / SOME UNITS 🐕 🖼

HISTORIC ROUTE 66 MOTEL
Phone: 928/422-3204

Motel
$62-$82

Address: 22750 W Old Hwy 66 86337
Location: I-40 exit 121, 1 mi n, then
just e. **Facility:** 16 units. 1 story,
exterior corridors. *Bath:* shower only.
Terms: 3 day cancellation notice.

SAVE 📶 ⊗ ✕ 🔋 🖼

SUPAI MOTEL
Phone: (928)422-4153

Motel
$52-$62

Address: 22450 Old Hwy 66 86337
Location: I-40 exit 121, 1 mi n, then
0.7 mi e. **Facility:** 15 units. 1 story,
exterior corridors. **Terms:** cancellation
fee imposed. **Amenities:** high-speed
Internet. **Free Special Amenities: early check-in/late
check-out and high-speed Internet.**

SAVE 📶 ⊗ ✕ FEE 🐾 / SOME UNITS 🔋 🖼

WHERE TO EAT

DELGADILLOS SNOW CAP DRIVE-IN
Phone: 928/422-3291

fyi   Not evaluated. Located on Route 66, this eatery
offers an enjoyable experience for all. After chowing
down a burger and fries, diners can view old cars, trucks and
antiques in the courtyard. Patrons should be alert for the
staff's pranks and humor. Make sure you order mustard, a
small drink with a straw and an ice cream cone-but be
prepared. **Address:** 301 W Chino Ave 86337

SELLS   (F-4) pop. 2,495, elev. 2,379'

Originally known as Indian Oasis, Sells was renamed in 1918 in honor of Indian commissioner
Cato Sells. The dependable water supply made the
area a popular stop for travelers, even in prehistoric
times.

Sells is the headquarters of the Tohono O'odham
Indian Reservation. In addition to this vast reservation west of Tucson, a smaller tract is south of
Tucson at the site of Mission San Xavier del Bac
(see Tucson p. 276). Mainly farmers and ranchers,
the Tohono O'odham are known for their hand-
crafted baskets and pottery.

KITT PEAK NATIONAL OBSERVATORY is 20 mi.
e. on SR 86, then 12 mi. s. on SR 386, within the
Tohono O'odham reservation in the Quinlan Mountains. The facility conducts astronomical research
and contains 27 telescopes, including the world's

largest solar telescope and the Mayall 4-meter telescope. Exhibits and a nightly stargazing program
are featured.

Travelers are advised to check on weather and
road conditions. **Tours:** Guided tours are available.
Hours: Visitor center daily 9-4. Guided tours of the
facility are offered at 10, 11:30 and 1:30. Night observation program begins at dusk, Sept. to mid-July.
Closed Jan. 1, Thanksgiving and Christmas.

Cost: Visitor center free. Guided tours Nov.-May
$7.75; $4 (ages 7-12). Guided tours rest of year
$5.75; $3 (ages 7-12). All-day pass Nov.-May $9.75;
$4.25 (ages 7-12). All-day pass rest of year $7.75;
$3.25 (ages 7-12). Night observation program $48;
$44 (ages 62+ and students with ID). Reservations
are required for night observation program and
should be made 1 month in advance. **Phone:** (520)
318-8726. 🎫

SHOW LOW   (D-5) pop. 10,660, elev. 6,347'
• Hotels p. 250 • Restaurants p. 250

Show Low took its name from the winning hand in
a poker game between Native American scout Col.
Croyden E. Cooley and his friend Marion Clark. The
town's main street, Deuce of Clubs, was named
after the winning card.

On the edge of the Mogollon Rim, the town offers
numerous recreational pursuits, including fishing,
camping, hiking and horseback riding.

Show Low Chamber of Commerce: 81 E. Deuce
of Clubs, Show Low, AZ 85901. **Phone:** (928)
537-2326 or (888) 746-9569.

FOOL HOLLOW LAKE RECREATION AREA, 2 mi.
n. of US 60 off SR 260, then e. on Old Linden Rd. to
park entrance, offers fishing and boating in a lake
covering the old town site of Adair. Camping among
the 100-foot-tall pine trees also is available. *See
Recreation Chart.* **Hours:** Park daily 5 a.m.-10 p.m.
Office daily 8-4:30. **Cost:** Mar. 15-Oct. 15 $7 (per
private vehicle, up to four passengers); $3 (per ad-
ditional adult passenger in vehicle or individual arriving on foot or bicycle). Rest of year $3 (per private
vehicle). Camping Mar. 15-Oct. 15 $17-$30 (per private vehicle). Camping rest of year $15-$25 (per private vehicle). **Phone:** (928) 537-3680.
🏕 ⊗ 🐕 🎫

SHOW LOW HISTORICAL SOCIETY MUSEUM is
at 561 E. Deuce of Clubs. The 16-room museum is
housed in Show Low's former city hall, police department and jail building. You'll see an original jail
cell, a railroad display, a quilt room, a kitchen filled
with items from the 1800s and early 1900s, and
photos of the town and its well-known residents and
visitors. **Time:** Allow 30 minutes minimum. **Hours:**
Wed.-Sat. 10-3 (weather permitting). Closed major
holidays. **Cost:** Donations. **Phone:** (928) 532-7115.

BEST WESTERN PAINT PONY LODGE
Phone: (928)537-5773

◆◆ Motel $80-$120

Best Western **AAA Benefit:** Members save up to 20%, plus 10% bonus points with Best Western Rewards®.

Address: 581 W Deuce of Clubs Ave 85901 **Location:** On US 60 and SR 260. **Facility:** 50 units. 2 stories (no elevator), exterior corridors. **Amenities:** *Some:* high-speed Internet. **Guest Services:** coin laundry. **Free Special Amenities:** full breakfast and high-speed Internet.

🟦 🍽 🐾 BIZ 📶 FEE 📹 🛗 🖥 💻
/ SOME UNITS FEE 🐕

DAYS INN
Phone: (928)537-4356

◆◆ Motel $44-$140

Address: 480 W Deuce of Clubs Ave 85901 **Location:** On US 60 and SR 260. **Facility:** 122 units. 2 stories (no elevator), interior/exterior corridors. **Terms:** 3 day cancellation notice. **Pool(s):** heated outdoor. **Guest Services:** coin laundry.

🍽 🍸 🏊 BIZ 📶 FEE 📹 🛗 🖥
/ SOME UNITS FEE 🐕

HAMPTON INN & SUITES (SHOW LOW/PINETOP)
Phone: (928)532-4444

◆◆◆ Hotel $124-$164 5/31-1/31 $119-$154 2/1-5/30

AAA Benefit: Members save up to 10% everyday!

Address: 1501 E Woolford Rd 85902 **Location:** On SR 260, 1.5 mi s of US 60. **Facility:** 73 units. 3 stories, interior corridors. **Terms:** 1-7 night minimum stay, cancellation fee imposed. **Amenities:** high-speed Internet. **Pool(s):** heated indoor. **Activities:** whirlpool, exercise room. **Guest Services:** coin laundry.

🏊 BIZ 📶 ✕ 🛗 🖥 💻

HOLIDAY INN EXPRESS
Phone: (928)537-5115

◆◆◆ Hotel $105-$188 2/1-10/21 $98-$188 10/22-1/31

Address: 151 W Deuce of Clubs Ave 85901 **Location:** On US 60 and SR 260. **Facility:** 71 units. 3 stories, interior corridors. **Pool(s):** heated indoor. **Activities:** whirlpool, exercise room. **Guest Services:** coin laundry.

🍽 CALL 📞 🏊 BIZ 📶 ✕ FEE 📹 🛗 💻
/ SOME UNITS 🖥

K C MOTEL
Phone: (928)537-4433

◆◆ Motel Rates not provided

Address: 60 W Deuce of Clubs Ave 85901 **Location:** On US 60 and SR 260. **Facility:** 35 units. 1-2 stories (no elevator), exterior corridors. **Terms:** office hours 6 am-10:30 pm. **Amenities:** high-speed Internet. **Free Special Amenities:** expanded continental breakfast and high-speed Internet.

🟦 🍽 📶 FEE 📹 🛗 🖥 💻

KIVA MOTEL
Phone: (928)537-4542

◆ Motel $58-$68

Address: 261 E Deuce of Clubs Ave 85901 **Location:** On US 60 and SR 260; center. **Facility:** 20 units. 1 story, exterior corridors. **Terms:** office hours 7:30 am-10:30 pm, 3 day cancellation notice. **Activities:** sauna, whirlpool. **Free Special Amenities:** local telephone calls and high-speed Internet.

🟦 🍽 📶 FEE 📹 🛗 🖥 💻 / SOME UNITS FEE 🐕

SLEEP INN
Phone: 928/532-7323

◆◆◆ Hotel Rates not provided

Address: 1751 W Deuce of Clubs Ave 85901 **Location:** 2 mi w of jct US 60 and SR 260, south side. **Facility:** 70 units. 3 stories, interior corridors. *Bath:* shower only. **Amenities:** *Some:* high-speed Internet. **Pool(s):** heated indoor. **Activities:** whirlpool. **Guest Services:** coin laundry.

CALL 📞 🏊 BIZ 📶 FEE 📹 🛗 💻
/ SOME UNITS FEE 🐕 🖥

WHERE TO EAT

BRANDING IRON STEAKHOUSE
Phone: 928/537-5151

◆◆ Steak $7-$30

AAA Inspector Notes: A wide selection of broiled beef cuts, along with lobster and fish dishes, gives everyone a favorite choice. Freshly baked bread is served warm, and fixings from the fresh salad bar complete the meal. **Bar:** full bar. **Address:** 1261 E Deuce of Clubs Ave 85901 **Location:** Jct US 60 and SR 260.

B L D 🍸

CAPT'N RON'S SEAFOOD SHACK
Phone: 928/532-1005

◆ Fish & Chips $5-$15

AAA Inspector Notes: This stainless steel shack is family friendly and very casual. The menu revolves around fish and chips but also serves other basic items such as chicken fingers, fried scallops and several grilled fish options. The owners are very hands on serving guests and making sure everyone is happy. **Address:** 1650 E Deuce of Clubs Ave 85901 **Location:** On US 60 and SR 260.

L D

LICANO'S MEXICAN FOOD & STEAK HOUSE
Phone: 928/537-8220

◆◆ Mexican $6-$28

AAA Inspector Notes: The attractive dining room resembles that of a stylish steakhouse. Seafood and steak entrées include Alaskan salmon grilled in a lemon butter sauce, slow-roasted prime rib and bacon-wrapped filet mignon, but the classic dishes of Mexico are what are warm and filling here. Guests can count on pleasant service with a friendly smile. **Bar:** full bar. **Address:** 573 W Deuce of Clubs Ave 85902 **Location:** US 60 and SR 260; center.

L D

SIERRA VISTA (G-5) pop. 43,888, elev. 4,600'
• Restaurants p. 252

Sierra Vista has been built upon the historic past of Fort Huachuca *(see place listing p. 74)*, established in 1877. The fort is now the largest single employer in southern Arizona, and most of its personnel live in the area. The scenery makes Sierra Vista special: The city is nestled on the eastern slopes of the Huachuca Mountains and overlooks the San Pedro River Valley. Nature lovers are attracted to nearby Coronado National Memorial *(see place listing p. 56)*, San Pedro Riparian National Conservation Area (6 miles east) and Ramsey Canyon Preserve.

Sierra Vista Visitor Center: 3020 E. Tacoma St., Sierra Vista, AZ 85635. **Phone:** (520) 417-6960 or (800) 288-3861.

FORT HUACHUCA MUSEUM—
see Fort Huachuca p. 74.

AMERICAS BEST VALUE INN
Phone: 520/459-5380

Motel
Rates not provided

Address: 100 Fab Ave 85635 **Location:** Jct Business SR 90 and Fry Blvd, then just e of main gate to Fort Huachuca. **Facility:** 52 units. 2 stories (no elevator), exterior corridors. **Amenities:** high-speed Internet, safes. **Pool(s):** outdoor. **Guest Services:** coin laundry. **Free Special Amenities: continental breakfast and early check-in/late check-out.**

SAVE ⁜ ⛵ 📶 🛗 🖥 🖨 / SOME UNITS FEE 🐾

BEST WESTERN MISSION INN
Phone: (520)458-8500

Hotel
$79-$129

AAA Benefit:
Members save up to 20%, plus 10% bonus points with Best Western Rewards®.

Address: 3460 E Fry Blvd 85635 **Location:** Just w of jct SR 90 and 92. **Facility:** 40 units. 2 stories (no elevator), exterior corridors. **Amenities:** high-speed Internet. **Pool(s):** heated outdoor. **Guest Services:** coin laundry. **Free Special Amenities: full breakfast and high-speed Internet.**

SAVE ⁜ CALL 🅜 ⛵ 📶
❌ 🛗 🖥 🖨 🖥 / SOME UNITS FEE 🐾

Best Western

Free Hot Breakfast, Heated Pool, Pets with deposit, Military discount, Free WIFI, Cable, HBO, Laundry.

CANDLEWOOD SUITES
Phone: (520)439-8200

Extended Stay Hotel
$119-$152

Address: 1904 S Hwy 92 85635 **Location:** Jct SR 90 and 92, 1.4 mi s. **Facility:** 71 efficiencies. 3 stories, interior corridors. **Amenities:** high-speed Internet. **Pool(s):** heated outdoor. **Activities:** whirlpool, exercise room. **Guest Services:** valet and coin laundry.

⁜ ⛵ BIZ 📶 ❌ 🛗 🖥 🖨
/ SOME UNITS FEE 🐾

COMFORT INN & SUITES
Phone: 520/459-0515

Hotel
Rates not provided

Address: 3500 E Fry Blvd 85635 **Location:** Just w of jct SR 90 and 92. **Facility:** 65 units. 3 stories, interior corridors. **Amenities:** high-speed Internet. **Pool(s):** heated outdoor. **Activities:** whirlpool, exercise room. **Guest Services:** coin laundry.

⁜ CALL 🅜 ⛵ 📶 ❌ 🛗 🖥 🖨

FAIRFIELD INN & SUITES BY MARRIOTT
Phone: (520)439-5900

Hotel
$80-$134

AAA Benefit:
AAA hotel discounts of 5% or more.

Address: 3855 El Mercado Loop 85635 **Location:** Jct SR 90, 1.5 mi s on SR 92. Located at Sierra Vista Mall. **Facility:** 67 units. 3 stories, interior corridors. **Amenities:** high-speed Internet. **Pool(s):** heated outdoor. **Activities:** whirlpool, exercise room. **Guest Services:** valet and coin laundry.

⁜ ⛵ BIZ 📶 ❌ 🛗 🖥 🖨

Learn about AAA/CAA Diamond Ratings at AAA.com/Diamonds

GARDEN PLACE SUITES
Phone: 520/439-3300

Hotel
$139-$149

Address: 100 N Garden Ave 85635 **Location:** Just n of Fry Blvd. **Facility:** 96 efficiencies. 3 stories, interior corridors. **Amenities:** high-speed Internet. **Pool(s):** heated outdoor. **Activities:** whirlpool, exercise room. **Guest Services:** valet and coin laundry.

⁜ ⛵ BIZ 📶 ❌ FEE 📹 🛗 🖥 🖨

GATEWAY STUDIO SUITES
Phone: (520)458-5555

Hotel
$129

Address: 203 S Garden Ave 85635 **Location:** Just s of Fry Blvd; se of Main. **Facility:** 83 efficiencies. 3 stories, interior corridors. **Amenities:** high-speed Internet. **Pool(s):** heated outdoor. **Activities:** whirlpool, exercise room. **Guest Services:** valet and coin laundry.

⁜ ⛵ BIZ 📶 ❌ 🛗 🖥 🖨

HAMPTON INN SIERRA VISTA
Phone: (520)439-5400

Hotel
$99-$199

Hampton

AAA Benefit: Members save up to 10% everyday!

Address: 4100 Snyder Blvd 85635 **Location:** On SR 92, 1 mi s of SR 90. **Facility:** 58 units. 3 stories, interior corridors. **Terms:** 1-7 night minimum stay, cancellation fee imposed. **Amenities:** high-speed Internet. **Pool(s):** heated indoor. **Activities:** whirlpool, bicycle trails, exercise room. **Guest Services:** valet and coin laundry. **Free Special Amenities: expanded continental breakfast and high-speed Internet.**

SAVE ⁜ ⛵ BIZ 📶 ❌ 🖥 / SOME UNITS 🛗 🖨

HOLIDAY INN EXPRESS
Phone: (520)439-8800

Hotel
$99-$119

Address: 1902 S Hwy 92 85635 **Location:** Jct SR 90 and 92, 1.4 mi s. **Facility:** 77 units. 3 stories, interior corridors. **Amenities:** high-speed Internet. **Pool(s):** heated outdoor. **Activities:** whirlpool, exercise room. **Guest Services:** valet and coin laundry.

⛵ BIZ 📶 FEE 📹 🛗 🖥 🖨 / SOME UNITS FEE 🐾

QUALITY INN
Phone: (520)458-7900

Hotel
$61-$67

Address: 1631 S Hwy 92 85635 **Location:** On SR 92, 1 mi s of jct SR 90. **Facility:** 103 units. 2 stories (no elevator), interior corridors. **Terms:** cancellation fee imposed. **Amenities:** high-speed Internet. **Pool(s):** outdoor. **Activities:** whirlpool, exercise room. **Guest Services:** valet and coin laundry. **Free Special Amenities: expanded continental breakfast and room upgrade (subject to availability with advance reservations).**

SAVE ⁜ ⛵ BIZ 📶 🛗 🖥 🖨 / SOME UNITS FEE 🐾

RODEWAY INN & SUITES
Phone: 520/459-7110

Extended Stay Motel
Rates not provided

Address: 250 Carroll Dr 85635 **Location:** Just n of Fry Blvd; just e of main gate to Fort Huachuca. **Facility:** 55 kitchen units. 1-2 stories (no elevator), exterior corridors. **Terms:** office hours 8 am-10 pm. **Amenities:** high-speed Internet. **Pool(s):** heated outdoor. **Activities:** whirlpool, game room, limited exercise equipment. **Guest Services:** coin laundry.

⁜ ⛵ 📶 🛗 🖥 🖨

SIERRA SUITES
Phone: (520)459-4221

Hotel
$85-$119

Address: 391 E Fry Blvd 85635 **Location:** Jct SR 90 and 92, 2.2 mi w. **Facility:** 100 units. 2 stories (no elevator), exterior corridors. **Terms:** cancellation fee imposed. **Amenities:** Some: high-speed Internet. **Pool(s):** heated outdoor. **Activities:** whirlpool. **Guest Services:** valet and coin laundry. **Free Special Amenities:** full breakfast and high-speed Internet. (See ad this page.)

▼ See AAA listing this page ▼

Sierra Suites

10% off
Published Rates

Close to Tombstone, Bisbee, Kartchner Caverns & Ft. Huachuca

391 E. Fry Blvd, Sierra Vista, AZ 85635
520.459.4221
www.sierravistasuites.com

* free deluxe breakfast including a variety of hot and cold items
* free wifi and hardwired internet
* upgraded and expanded fitness room
* flatscreen HD TVs
* large outdoor heated pool, jacuzzi & patio
* all rooms include refrigerator, microwave and free local calls
* guest laundry

Not affiliated with the Sierra Suites™ Hotel Chain

Exclusive AAA Offers
Get the free mobile app at http://gettag.mobi

SUN CANYON INN
Phone: (520)459-0610

Hotel
$93-$104

Address: 260 N Garden Ave 85635 **Location:** Just n of Fry Blvd; just e of main gate to Fort Huachuca. **Facility:** 80 units. 4 stories, interior corridors. **Terms:** 3 day cancellation notice-fee imposed. **Amenities:** high-speed Internet, safes. **Pool(s):** heated outdoor. **Activities:** whirlpool, exercise room. **Guest Services:** valet and coin laundry. **Free Special Amenities:** full breakfast and high-speed Internet.

TOWNEPLACE SUITES BY MARRIOTT
Phone: (520)515-9900

Extended Stay Hotel
$107-$170

AAA Benefit:
AAA hotel discounts of 5% or more.

Address: 3399 Rodeo Dr 85635 **Location:** Jct SR 90, 1.5 mi s on SR 92, just w on Avenida Cochise, just s on Oakmont Dr, then just e. **Facility:** 71 efficiencies, some two bedrooms. 3 stories, interior corridors. **Amenities:** high-speed Internet. **Pool(s):** heated outdoor. **Activities:** exercise room. **Guest Services:** coin laundry.

THE WESTERN MOTEL
Phone: 520/458-4303

Motel
$45-$55

Address: 43 W Fry Blvd 85635 **Location:** 0.4 mi e of main gate to Fort Huachuca. **Facility:** 25 units, some efficiencies. 1 story, exterior corridors. **Terms:** 3 day cancellation notice. **Amenities:** high-speed Internet. **Free Special Amenities: local telephone calls and high-speed Internet.**

WINDEMERE HOTEL & CONFERENCE CENTER
Phone: (520)459-5900

Hotel
$99-$159

Address: 2047 S Hwy 92 85635 **Location:** 1.5 mi s of jct SR 90. **Facility:** 151 units. 3 stories, interior corridors. **Terms:** check-in 4 pm, cancellation fee imposed. **Amenities:** video games (fee). **Dining:** Maestro's Restaurant, see separate listing. **Pool(s):** outdoor. **Activities:** whirlpool, exercise room. **Guest Services:** valet and coin laundry.

WHERE TO EAT

THE BREAD BASKET
Phone: 520/458-8580

Breads/Pastries
$4-$9

AAA Inspector Notes: This small bakery serves a Continental breakfast, in addition to warm, hearty lunches from 11 am to 2 pm. **Address:** 355 W Wilcox Dr 85635 **Location:** Jct Fry Blvd, just s on Business Rt SR 90 (Buffalo Soldier Tr), just e. [B] [L]

COUNTRY HOUSE FAMILY RESTAURANT
Phone: 520/378-4400

American
$7-$14

AAA Inspector Notes: The warm cottage atmosphere is charming, and the friendly staff welcomes diners as family. Classic foods-such as hearty burgers, grilled pork chops and country-fried steak-can be enjoyed. The owners have been here since 1996. **Bar:** full bar. **Address:** 4373 S Hwy 92 85650 **Location:** Jct SR 90, 4.5 mi s. [B] [L] [D]

DELIO'S ITALIAN RESTAURANT   Phone: 520/378-1066

Italian
$5-$22

AAA Inspector Notes: A longtime local favorite, Delio's offers traditional Italian dishes in a festive, upbeat atmosphere. In addition to daily specials, the ample menu features toasted ravioli, crab cakes, a variety of pastas and build-your-own pizza. **Bar:** full bar. **Address:** 3637 S Hwy 92 85650 **Location:** Jct SR 90 and 92, 4.8 mi s. L D

HANA TOKYO JAPANESE RESTAURANT
Phone: 520/458-1993

Japanese
$10-$30

AAA Inspector Notes: This bright and modern eatery has teppan tables and a sushi bar. **Bar:** full bar. **Address:** 1633 S Hwy 92 85635 **Location:** Jct SR 90 and 92, 1.1 mi s.

L D CALL M

LA CASITA MEXICAN RESTAURANT & CANTINA
Phone: 520/458-2376

Mexican
$7-$19

AAA Inspector Notes: Cheerful Mexican decor pleases the eye, and hearty, traditional dishes satisfy any appetite at this popular spot. **Bar:** full bar. **Address:** 465 E Fry Blvd 85635 **Location:** 2.1 mi w of jct SR 90 and 92. L D

MAESTRO'S RESTAURANT   Phone: 520/459-5900

Continental
$7-$25

AAA Inspector Notes: Select from a wide variety of continental favorites at this restaurant, including seafood paella, grilled steaks and fettuccine Alfredo. **Bar:** full bar. **Reservations:** suggested. **Address:** 2047 S Hwy 92 85635 **Location:** 1.5 mi s of jct SR 90; in Windemere Hotel & Conference Center. D L D

THE MESQUITE TREE RESTAURANT
Phone: 520/378-2758

American
$10-$25

AAA Inspector Notes: This casual restaurant presents a diverse menu of steaks, prime rib, barbecue foods and seafood, chicken and pasta dishes. When the weather is nice, guests can request a seat on the patio. **Bar:** full bar. **Reservations:** suggested. **Address:** 6398 S Hwy 92 85615 **Location:** 7 mi s of jct SR 90 and 92. D

TANUKI JAPANESE RESTAURANT & SUSHI BAR
Phone: 520/459-6853

Japanese
$6-$18

AAA Inspector Notes: A nice selection of fresh sushi and sashimi can be found at this restaurant. Patrons can choose from teriyaki, tempura or yakitora classics. **Bar:** full bar. **Address:** 1221 E Fry Blvd 85635 **Location:** Jct SR 90, 1.7 mi w. L D

SNOWFLAKE pop. 5,590

COMFORT INN   Phone: (928)536-3888

Hotel
$60-$130

Address: 2055 S Main St 85937 **Location:** SR 77, just s of town. **Facility:** 64 units. 2 stories (no elevator), interior corridors. **Terms:** cancellation fee imposed. **Pool(s):** heated indoor. **Activities:** whirlpool, exercise room. **Guest Services:** coin laundry.

BIZ / SOME UNITS FEE

SOMERTON (F-1) pop. 14,287, elev. 103'

GAMBLING ESTABLISHMENTS
• **Cocopah Casino,** jct. US 95 (Ave. B) and 15th St. at 15318 S. Ave. B. **Hours:** Daily 24 hours. **Phone:** (928) 726-8066 or (800) 237-5687.

SONOITA pop. 818

SONOITA INN   Phone: 520/455-5935

fyi   Not evaluated. **Address:** 3243 Hwy 82 85637 **Location:** Center. Facilities, services, and decor characterize a mid-scale property.

SONORAN DESERT NATIONAL MONUMENT (E-3)

South of Phoenix in south-central Arizona, Sonoran Desert National Monument comprises mountain ranges, wide valleys and several saguaro cactus forests on 486,000 acres. The functioning desert ecosystem is a habitat for an array of wildlife, including desert bighorn sheep, mule deer, bobcats, desert tortoises, raptors, owls and bats.

It is believed that ancestors of the O'odham, Quechan, Cocopah and other tribes occupied villages in the area, which contains archeological and historical sites. Remnants of historic trails used by Juan de Anza, the Mormons and the Overland Stage can be found along a well-worn 20-mile corridor. A high-clearance vehicle is required. For further information contact the Bureau of Land Management, Phoenix District, 21605 N. 7th Ave., Phoenix, AZ 85027; phone (623) 580-5500 or (602) 417-9200.

SPRINGERVILLE (D-6) pop. 1,961, elev. 6,862'

Springerville is in a cattle-ranching area of eastern Arizona. Created by shield volcanoes, the town neighbors the White Mountains, where visitors can enjoy outdoor activities year-round. In a wing of the Latter-day Saints Church on Apache Street is a collection of European artworks and furniture dating from the Renaissance to the early 20th century. The Renee Cushman Art collection, 418 E. Main St., is shown by appointment; phone (928) 333-2123.

Springerville-Eagar Regional Chamber of Commerce: 418 E. Main St. (in the Casa Malpais visitor center), P.O. Box 31, Springerville, AZ 85938. **Phone:** (928) 333-2123 or (866) 733-2123.

CASA MALPAIS PUEBLO, 418 E. Main St., is a 15-acre restoration project of Mogollon and ancient pueblo ruins occupied 1250-1400. Pottery, artifacts and baskets unearthed at the project are displayed in the museum. After watching an orientation film, visitors drive to the site for a guided walking tour (self-guiding tours are not permitted).

Time: Allow 1 hour, 30 minutes minimum. **Hours:** Museum Tues.-Sat. 8-4. Site tours depart at 9, 11 and 2 (weather permitting). Closed Jan. 1, Thanksgiving and Christmas. **Cost:** $8; $6 (ages 60+); $5 (children and students with ID); free (ages 0-3). **Phone:** (928) 333-5375.

Check out
our travel blog at
AAATravelViews.com

SUN CITY (I-2) pop. 37,499, elev. 1,140'
• Hotels & Restaurants map & index p. 155
• Part of Phoenix area — see map p. 134

Twelve miles northwest of Phoenix but part of the metropolitan area of the capital city, Sun City is one of the largest and most popular retirement communities in the country. By 1978 it had reached its population goal of more than 40,000, with most residential property in use. Sun City West, 2.5 miles west via Grand Avenue, offers a similar array of golf courses, stores, restaurants, recreation areas and other services.

Sun City Visitors Center: 16824 N. 99th Ave., Sun City, AZ 85351. **Phone:** (623) 977-5000 or (800) 437-8146.

LITTLE BITE OF ITALY   **Phone:** 623/972-3311   ①

▼▼   **AAA Inspector Notes:** This casual neighborhood eatery features classic
Italian   Italian favorites. **Bar:** full bar.
$9-$19   **Address:** 15456 N 99th Ave 85351
            Location: Jct Greenway Rd.

Ⓛ Ⓓ CALL 🅼

SUNSET CRATER VOLCANO NATIONAL MONUMENT (B-4)

Lying approximately 12 miles north of Flagstaff via US 89, then 2 miles east on Sunset Crater-Wupatki Loop Road, the 1,000-foot-high cinder cone of Sunset Crater Volcano dominates the surrounding fields of cinders, lava flows and spatter cones. The bright-reddish hues of the decomposed, water-stained sulfuric rock at the summit are in stark contrast with the black basalt of the adjacent rocks. From a distance the mountain appears to be on fire.

Dark at the base, the volcano also has shades of red, orange and yellow leading to the summit and takes on a rosy tint during the hour before sunset. In 1892 John Wesley Powell noted the phenomenon and purportedly gave the cone its name.

Sunset Crater Volcano first erupted A.D. 1064-65 and was active intermittently for nearly 200 years. A self-guiding trail leads over the Bonito lava flow; sturdy walking shoes are recommended. A paved road crosses the lava flow and connects the monument with Wupatki National Monument *(see place listing p. 323)*. Picnicking is permitted.

Fire restrictions may apply. Allow 30 minutes minimum. Visitor center daily 8-5, May-Oct.; 9-5, rest of year. Closed Christmas. Admission $5 per person (includes Wupatki National Monument); free (ages 0-15). Phone (928) 526-0502.

SUPAI (B-3) pop. 208, elev. 3,195'

HAVASU CANYON is accessible from Hualapai Hilltop, which is reached from SR 66 via a turnoff 5 miles e. of Peach Springs. There are no services after the turnoff. Most of the 65-mile road from Peach Springs is in good condition.

Havasu Canyon is home to the village of Supai, which serves as the governmental center of the

Havasupai Indian Reservation. Automobiles must be left at Hualapai Hilltop; the 8-mile journey to the canyon floor and Havasu Falls can be covered on horseback, helicopter or on foot down a precipitous trail.

Note: The trail is only recommended for experienced hikers in good physical condition. The return climb out of the canyon is very arduous. Summer temperatures may prohibit daytime trips; phone ahead to confirm. Hikers must carry at least one gallon of water. Camping is permitted; no open fires are allowed. Swimming is permitted. Horse rental is available.

Hours: Office hours daily 5:30 a.m.-7 p.m., Apr.-Oct.; 9-3, rest of year. **Cost:** Entrance fee $35 (per person). Camping $17 (per person). Helicopter fee $85 (per person). Reservations for horses and campgrounds are required. Helicopter tours have limited availability; reservations are not accepted. **Phone:** (928) 448-2141, or (928) 448-2180 for general information and reservations.

SUPERIOR (J-6) pop. 2,837, elev. 2,730'

Although it began as a silver-mining town, Superior owes its existence to its proximity to some of the deepest and richest copper lodes in the country. Near Superior is Apache Leap Cliff, where, according to legend, 75 Apache warriors leaped to their deaths rather than be captured by the cavalry. The town also is near the southern terminus of US 60 (Gila/Pinal Scenic Drive), which travels northward through Tonto National Forest, Salt River Canyon and the Fort Apache Indian Reservation.

Superior Chamber of Commerce: 20 N. Magma, P.O. Box 95, Superior, AZ 85273. **Phone:** (520) 689-0200.

BOYCE THOMPSON ARBORETUM STATE PARK, 3 mi. w. on US 60 at Milepost 223, has more than 300 acres of desert plants collected from all over the world; 50 acres are accessible for viewing. Founded in the 1920s by mining magnate Col. William Boyce Thompson, the arboretum has nature paths leading past towering trees, cacti, mountain cliffs, a streamside forest, a desert lake, hidden canyon and panoramic views.

Two miles of developed trails are available for hiking. An interpretive center has educational displays and two greenhouses housing cacti and succulents. **Time:** Allow 1 hour minimum. **Hours:** Daily 8-5, Oct.-Apr.; 6-3, rest of year. Seasonal tours are available. Closed Christmas. Phone ahead to confirm schedule. **Cost:** $9; $4.50 (ages 5-12). **Phone:** (520) 689-2811 or (520) 689-2723. 🎟 🎡

Explore the Travel Guides
on AAA.com/Travel or
CAA.ca/Travel

SURPRISE (I-2) pop. 117,517, elev. 1,178'
• Hotels & Restaurants map & index p. 155
• Part of Phoenix area — see map p. 134

In the Sonoran desert, Surprise was founded in 1937 by Homer C. Ludden, a state legislator who named the town after his hometown in Nebraska. Surprise Stadium is the spring training center for the Kansas City Royals and the Texas Rangers. Eight miles southwest is White Tank Mountain Regional Park *(see Recreation Chart)*, which offers 22 miles of trails for hiking, horseback riding and mountain biking. Hohokam petroglyphs and such wildlife as the cactus wren, the official state bird, may be seen.

Surprise Regional Chamber of Commerce: 16126 N. Civic Center, Surprise, AZ 85374. **Phone:** (623) 583-0692.

COMFORT INN & SUITES OF SURPRISE
Phone: (623)544-6874　**18**

Hotel
$79-$139

Address: 13337 W Grand Ave 85374 **Location:** Jct Bell Rd, 0.4 mi se. **Facility:** 86 units. 3 stories, interior corridors. **Amenities:** high-speed Internet. **Pool(s):** heated outdoor. **Activities:** whirlpool, exercise room. **Guest Services:** valet and coin laundry. **Free Special Amenities: full breakfast and high-speed internet.**

HAMPTON INN & SUITES SURPRISE
Phone: (623)537-9122　**15**

Hotel
$125-$179 2/1-4/30
$80-$170 5/1-1/31

AAA Benefit: Members save up to 10% everyday!

Address: 14783 W Grand Ave 85374 **Location:** Jct Bell Rd, 2 mi nw. **Facility:** 100 units. 4 stories, interior corridors. **Terms:** 1-7 night minimum stay, cancellation fee imposed. **Amenities:** high-speed Internet. **Pool(s):** heated outdoor. **Activities:** whirlpool, exercise room. **Guest Services:** valet and coin laundry. **Free Special Amenities: expanded continental breakfast and high-speed Internet.**

HOLIDAY INN EXPRESS & SUITES
Phone: (623)975-5540　**16**

Hotel
$79-$249

Address: 16540 N Bullard Ave 85374 **Location:** Jct US 60 (Grand Ave), 1.4 mi w on Bell Rd, then just s. **Facility:** 115 units. 4 stories, interior corridors. **Amenities:** high-speed Internet. **Pool(s):** heated outdoor. **Activities:** whirlpool, exercise room. **Guest Services:** valet and coin laundry. **Free Special Amenities: expanded continental breakfast and high-speed Internet.**

QUALITY INN & SUITES
Phone: (623)583-3500　**20**

Hotel
$59-$169

Address: 16741 N Greasewood St 85374 **Location:** US 60 (Grand Ave), 1.1 mi e on Bell Rd, then just s. **Facility:** 69 units. 3 stories, interior corridors. **Terms:** cancellation fee imposed. **Amenities:** safes. **Pool(s):** heated indoor. **Activities:** whirlpool, exercise room. **Guest Services:** coin laundry.

RESIDENCE INN BY MARRIOTT PHOENIX NW SURPRISE
Phone: (623)249-6333　**17**

Extended Stay Hotel
$100-$120

AAA Benefit: AAA hotel discounts of 5% or more.

Address: 16418 N Bullard Ave 85374 **Location:** Jct US 60 (Grand Ave), 1.4 mi w on Bell Rd, then just s. **Facility:** 116 units, some two bedrooms, efficiencies and kitchens. Interior corridors. **Amenities:** high-speed Internet. **Pool(s):** heated outdoor. **Activities:** whirlpool, sports court, exercise room. **Guest Services:** valet and coin laundry. **Free Special Amenities: full breakfast and high-speed Internet.**

WINDMILL SUITES IN SURPRISE
Phone: 623/583-0133　**19**

Hotel
Rates not provided

Address: 12545 W Bell Rd 85374 **Location:** US 60 (Grand Ave), 1 mi e. **Facility:** 126 units. 3 stories, interior corridors. **Terms:** check-in 4 pm. **Pool(s):** heated outdoor. **Activities:** whirlpool, bicycles, limited exercise equipment. **Guest Services:** valet and coin laundry. **Free Special Amenities: expanded continental breakfast and high-speed Internet.**

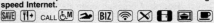
WHERE TO EAT

DILLON'S GRAND
Phone: 623/584-8494　**11**

American
$7-$25

AAA Inspector Notes: The barbecue at this eatery is popular with local folks. Friendly, young servers bring out a selection of grilled meat, poultry and fish dishes, along with hearty desserts to share. The attractive dining room overlooks a golf course and pools with waterfalls. **Bar:** full bar. **Address:** 19900 N Remington Dr 85374 **Location:** Jct Bell Rd, 3 mi nw on Grand Ave, 1 mi sw on Sunrise Blvd, then 0.4 mi nw. L D

MACAYO MEXICAN KITCHEN
Phone: 623/975-9570

Mexican
$8-$16

AAA Inspector Notes: The colorfully furnished Mexican-style eatery prepares Sonoran Mexican dishes. Friendly and efficient staffers serve traditional and lighter dishes flavored with this place's own chili peppers, which are grown near Tucson. **Bar:** full bar. **Address:** 15565 W Bell Rd 85379 **Location:** Jct Reems Rd; southwest corner. L D

Plan. Map. Go.
TripTik® Travel Planner

Where premier mapping technology meets complete travel information. Only on AAA.com and CAA.ca.

(See map & index p. 155.)

MY GREEK CORNER **Phone:** 623/544-4040 ⑫

♦♦♦
Greek
$6-$18

AAA Inspector Notes: The food is fresh at this fast, casual eatery serving classic Greek favorites as well as burgers, soups and salads. **Bar:** beer & wine. **Address:** 13746 W Bell Rd 85374 **Location:** Jct Grand Ave, just

w. Ⓛ Ⓓ

VOGUE BISTRO **Phone:** 623/544-9109 ⑬

♦♦♦
New American
$9-$23

AAA Inspector Notes: This casual, yet stylish, bistro serves up contemporary American cuisine with a French influence. Try the Tuscan flatbread for starters, followed up by steamed mussels or the hearty meatloaf. **Bar:** full bar. **Address:** 15411 W Waddell Rd 85379 **Location:** Jct US 60, 4.5 mi w; in Marley Park Plaza Shopping Center. Ⓛ Ⓓ

TAYLOR pop. 4,112

RODEWAY INN - SILVER CREEK INN
Phone: 928/536-2600

♦♦♦
Motel
Rates not provided

Address: 825 N Main St 85939 **Location:** On SR 77. **Facility:** 42 units. 2 stories (no elevator), exterior corridors. **Guest Services:** coin laundry. **Free Special Amenities:** full breakfast and high-speed Internet.

[SAVE] 🛜 🔌 🖥 💻 / SOME UNITS FEE 🐾

TEMPE (J-3) pop. 161,719, elev. 1,159'
• Restaurants p. 260
• Attractions map p. 142
• Hotels & Restaurants map & index p. 164
• Part of Phoenix area — see map p. 134

Founded as Hayden's Ferry in 1872, Tempe originally was named for Charles Trumbull Hayden, who owned a flour mill and operated a ferry across the Salt River. The town was renamed Tempe (Tem-PEE) in 1879 for the area's alleged resemblance to the Vale of Tempe in ancient Greece.

In 1886 the dusty cow town became the home of the Arizona Territorial Normal School, later to become Arizona State University *(see attraction listing)*. Downtown Tempe has a laid-back college town feel.

The ASU Gammage, one of the last major buildings designed by Frank Lloyd Wright, is a performing arts center on the campus of Arizona State University. Phone (480) 965-6912 for information about free guided tours of the center.

In early December, crowds head downtown for the 🎭 Tempe Fall Festival of the Arts, which features a live entertainment stage, street performers and hundreds of vendor booths. Sun Devil Stadium hosts the popular 🎭 Insight Bowl in late December.

Tempe Convention and Visitors Bureau: 51 W. Third St., Suite 105, Tempe, AZ 85281. **Phone:** (480) 305-1365 or (800) 283-6734.

Shopping areas: Specialty shops are scattered throughout downtown Tempe, the five-block segment of Mill Avenue between 3rd Street and University Drive. Arizona Mills Mall, I-10 and Baseline Road, is one of the state's largest shopping and entertainment complexes. Tempe Marketplace, at McClintock Drive and Rio Salado Parkway, is a popular outdoor shopping and entertainment destination.

Nightlife

Beer swilling frat boys inhale chicken wings as they root on ASU in the sports bars on shady Mill Avenue. Gordon Biersch Brewery (420 S. Mill Ave., #201) pours tasty brew and has a second floor terrace overlooking the street action below; phone (480) 736-0033. The Tavern on Mill (404 S. Mill Ave.) boasts nearly 40 flat-screen HDTVs and is usually packed on big game nights; phone (480) 967-5887.

If you're up for cheesy good fun, try the Big Bang (501 S. Mill Ave., #B-101), an underground dueling pianos bar. The pianists put on a high-energy, audience participation show sure to embarrass you; phone (480) 557-5595.

ARIZONA HISTORICAL SOCIETY MUSEUM AT PAPAGO PARK, 1300 N. College Ave., portrays the history of 20th-century central Arizona through hands-on exhibits and multimedia displays. Galleries feature exhibits about the history of transportation in the state; Arizona's roles in World War II; the rise of a thriving metropolis in the desert; the storied history of Major League Baseball spring training; and Arizona native and former U.S. Supreme Court justice Sandra Day O'Connor. Children's activities, tours and educational programs are offered throughout the year.

Hours: Tues.-Sat. 10-4, Sun. noon-4; closed Jan. 1, July 4, Veterans Day, Thanksgiving, Christmas and state employee furlough days. **Cost:** $5; $4 (ages 12-18 and 60+); free (first Sat. of the month). Ages 0-16 must be accompanied by an adult. **Phone:** (480) 929-9499. 🎟

ARIZONA STATE UNIVERSITY is at University Dr. and Mill Ave. The university's main campus includes the distinctive ASU Gammage, a concert hall designed by Frank Lloyd Wright that is one of his last completed nonresidential designs. The Arboretum at ASU encompasses the entire campus. Self-guiding walking tour brochures are available at the Information Center in the Memorial Union and the Visitors Center. **Hours:** Arboretum open daily dawn-dusk. **Phone:** (480) 965-9011.

Arizona State University Art Museum is housed in the Nelson Fine Arts Center at 51 E. 10th St. The museum's primary focus is on contemporary art in interactive formats that emphasize new ideas and media. Across the street, the Ceramics Research Center features more than 4,500 pieces reflecting the world's social, cultural and historical aspects. Changing exhibitions and special events also are presented. **Hours:** Museum and ceramic research

(See map & index p. 164.)

center Tues.-Sat. 11-5 (also Tues. 5-8 during academic year). Closed major holidays. **Cost:** Free. **Phone:** (480) 965-2787.

BIG SURF, 1500 N. McClintock Rd., provides man-made waves in a wave pool and beaches. There also are 18 waterslides, several volleyball courts and three activity pools. **Hours:** Daily 10-6, Memorial Day-Labor Day. **Cost:** $26; $19.50 (ages 55+ and under 48 inches tall); $3 (ages 0-2). After 3 p.m. $15. **Phone:** (480) 994-2297.

IMAX THEATER AT ARIZONA MILLS, off I-10 Baseline Rd. exit at the mall, presents films that are based on both IMAX and IMAX 3D technology. IMAX 3D films require the use of 3D headsets. The lifelike images are projected on a screen that is six stories high. Hollywood feature films are shown. **Hours:** IMAX, IMAX 3D and feature-length films are shown daily. Phone ahead to confirm schedule. **Cost:** $15; $12 (ages 60+); $11 (ages 3-13). **Phone:** (480) 897-4629.

TEMPE HISTORY MUSEUM is off US 60 exit 174 (Rural Rd.), then .4 mi. n. to 809 E. Southern Ave. The museum has four themed areas: College Town, Building Our Community, Living Together and Surviving in the Desert. Reading and computer stations as well as a children's gallery filled with hands-on activities provide educational opportunities. **Hours:** Tues.-Sat. 10-5, Sun. 1-5. Closed major holidays. **Cost:** Donations. **Phone:** (480) 350-5100.

ALOFT TEMPE   Phone: (480)621-3300   5

Hotel
$99-$279

AAA Benefit: Enjoy the new twist, get up to 15% off + Starwood Preferred Guest® bonuses.

Address: 951 E Playa Del Norte Dr 85281 **Location:** SR 202 Loop (Red Mountain Frwy) exit 7 (Rural Rd), just s on Scottsdale Rd, then just e. **Facility:** 136 units. 5 stories, interior corridors. **Bath:** shower only. **Terms:** cancellation fee imposed. **Amenities:** video games (fee), high-speed Internet, safes. **Pool(s):** heated outdoor. **Activities:** exercise room. **Fee:** bicycles. **Guest Services:** valet and coin laundry. **Free Special Amenities: continental breakfast and high-speed Internet.**

BEST WESTERN INN OF TEMPE
                          Phone: (480)784-2233   4

Hotel
$70-$140

AAA Benefit: Members save up to 20%, plus 10% bonus points with Best Western Rewards®.

Address: 670 N Scottsdale Rd 85281 **Location:** SR 202 Loop (Red Mountain Frwy) exit 7 (Rural Rd S), just s. **Facility:** 103 units. 4 stories, interior corridors. **Amenities:** Some: high-speed Internet. **Activities:** whirlpools, exercise room. **Guest Services:** valet laundry, area transportation-within 3 mi. **Free Special Amenities: expanded continental breakfast and airport transportation.**

BEST WESTERN PLUS TEMPE BY THE MALL
                          Phone: (480)820-7500   28

Hotel
$70-$140

AAA Benefit: Members save up to 20%, plus 10% bonus points with Best Western Rewards®.

Address: 5300 S Priest Dr 85283 **Location:** I-10 exit 155 (Baseline Rd), 0.4 mi e, then just s. **Facility:** 158 units. 4 stories, interior corridors. **Terms:** cancellation fee imposed. **Amenities:** high-speed Internet. **Pool(s):** heated outdoor. **Activities:** whirlpool, exercise room. **Guest Services:** valet and coin laundry, area transportation-within 5 mi. **Free Special Amenities: full breakfast and airport transportation.**

BUTTES, A MARRIOTT RESORT
                          Phone: (602)225-9000   20

Resort Hotel
$99-$359

AAA Benefit: AAA hotel discounts of 5% or more.

Address: 2000 Westcourt Way 85282 **Location:** I-10 exit 153 (Broadway Rd) westbound, 0.8 mi w to 48th St, then 0.3 mi s; exit 48th St eastbound, 0.5 mi s. **Facility:** Ensconced on the side of a mountain, the beautiful resort is enhanced by extensive desert landscaping and sweeping city views. 353 units. 4 stories, interior corridors. **Parking:** on-site and valet. **Amenities:** high-speed Internet (fee), safes, honor bars. **Dining:** 2 restaurants, also, Top of the Rock Restaurant, see separate listing. **Pool(s):** 2 heated outdoor. **Activities:** saunas, whirlpools, waterslide, 4 lighted tennis courts, recreation programs in winter, hiking trails, jogging, horseshoes, volleyball, exercise room, spa. **Guest Services:** valet laundry. **Free Special Amenities: preferred room (subject to availability with advance reservations).**

COMFORT SUITES AIRPORT
                          Phone: 480/446-9500   14

Hotel
Rates not provided

Address: 1625 S 52nd St 85281 **Location:** I-10 exit 153B (Broadway Rd). **Facility:** 92 units. 3 stories, interior corridors. **Amenities:** Some: high-speed Internet. **Pool(s):** heated outdoor. **Activities:** whirlpool, exercise room. **Guest Services:** valet and coin laundry. **Free Special Amenities: full breakfast and manager's reception.**

COMFORT SUITES

**100% Non-smoking Suites
Free Airport Shuttle from
Sky Harbor Int'l Airport**

Download eTourBook guides
for ereaders and smartphones
at AAA.com/ebooks

(See map & index p. 164.)

COUNTRY INN & SUITES BY CARLSON, PHOENIX AIRPORT AT TEMPE
Phone: (480)858-9898 **3**

Hotel
$79-$209

Address: 808 N Scottsdale Rd 85281 **Location:** SR 202 Loop (Red Mountain Frwy) exit 7 (Rural Rd S), just n. **Facility:** 83 units. 4 stories, interior corridors. **Terms:** cancellation fee imposed. **Amenities:** high-speed Internet. **Pool(s):** heated outdoor. **Activities:** whirlpool, exercise room. **Guest Services:** valet and coin laundry, area transportation-within 5 mi. **Free Special Amenities: full breakfast and airport transportation.**

SAVE ⊀ ⁑♦ CALL ⎮M ⊇ 🛜 ✕ FEE 🎥 🗎
🖼 💻 / SOME UNITS FEE 🐾

COURTYARD BY MARRIOTT-DOWNTOWN TEMPE
Phone: (480)966-2800 **10**

Hotel
$119-$269

AAA Benefit:
AAA hotel discounts of 5% or more.

Address: 601 S Ash Ave 85281 **Location:** SR 143 (Hohokam Expwy) exit University Dr, 2.2 mi e, then 0.3 mi n. **Facility:** 160 units. 3 stories, interior corridors. **Amenities:** high-speed Internet. **Pool(s):** heated outdoor. **Activities:** whirlpool, exercise room. **Guest Services:** valet and coin laundry, area transportation-within 5 mi.

ECO ⊀ ⁑♦ ⊇ 🛜 ✕ 💻
/ SOME UNITS 🗎 🖼

DAYS INN & SUITES
Phone: 480/345-8585 **29**

Hotel
Rates not provided

Address: 1660 W Elliot Rd 85284 **Location:** I-10 exit 157, just e. **Facility:** 139 units, some efficiencies. 3 stories, exterior corridors. **Pool(s):** 2 heated outdoor. **Activities:** whirlpool. **Guest Services:** valet and coin laundry. **Free Special Amenities: expanded continental breakfast and high-speed Internet.**

SAVE ⁑♦ ⊇ 🛜 🗎 🖼 💻 / SOME UNITS FEE 🐾

EMBASSY SUITES PHOENIX-TEMPE
Phone: (480)897-7444 **23**

Hotel
$109-$179 2/1-5/15
$79-$159 5/16-1/31

AAA Benefit:
Members save 5% or more everyday!

Address: 4400 S Rural Rd 85282 **Location:** US 60 (Superstition Frwy) exit 174 (Rural Rd), just s. **Facility:** 224 units. 2-3 stories, exterior corridors. **Terms:** 1-7 night minimum stay, cancellation fee imposed. **Amenities:** Fee: video games, high-speed Internet. **Pool(s):** heated outdoor. **Activities:** whirlpool, exercise room. **Guest Services:** valet and coin laundry, area transportation-within 3 mi.

⊀ ⁑ ⊻ ⊇ BIZ 🛜 FEE 🎥 🗎 🖼 💻

FIESTA RESORT CONFERENCE CENTER
Phone: (480)967-1441 **19**

Hotel
$79-$159

Address: 2100 S Priest Dr 85282 **Location:** I-10 exit 153 (Broadway Rd), 0.5 mi e. **Facility:** 270 units. 3 stories, exterior corridors. **Terms:** cancellation fee imposed. **Pool(s):** heated outdoor. **Activities:** whirlpool, exercise room, spa. **Guest Services:** valet laundry, area transportation-within 5 mi. **Free Special Amenities: local telephone calls and high-speed Internet.**

SAVE ⊀ ⁑ ⊻ ⊇ BIZ 🛜 ✕ FEE 🎥 🗎
💻 / SOME UNITS FEE 🐾

FOUR POINTS BY SHERATON TEMPE
Phone: (480)968-3451 **17**

Hotel
$75-$225

FOUR POINTS BY SHERATON **AAA Benefit:** Members get up to 15% off, plus Starwood Preferred Guest® bonuses.

Address: 1333 S Rural Rd 85281 **Location:** US 60 (Superstition Frwy) exit 174 (Rural Rd), 2 mi n. Located at southeast area of Arizona State University campus. **Facility:** 187 units. 4 stories, interior corridors. **Terms:** cancellation fee imposed. **Pool(s):** heated outdoor. **Activities:** exercise room. **Guest Services:** valet laundry, area transportation-within 5 mi. **Free Special Amenities: newspaper and airport transportation.**

SAVE ⊀ ⁑ ⊻ CALL ⎮M ⊇ BIZ 🛜 ✕
FEE 🎥 💻 / SOME UNITS FEE 🐾 FEE 🗎 FEE 🖼

HAMPTON INN & SUITES
Phone: (480)675-9799 **2**

Hotel
$109-$149 2/1-4/15
$69-$109 4/16-1/31

AAA Benefit:
Members save up to 10% everyday!

Address: 1429 N Scottsdale Rd 85281 **Location:** SR 202 Loop (Red Mountain Frwy) exit 7 (Rural Rd S), 0.5 mi n. **Facility:** 162 units, some two bedrooms and efficiencies. 1-3 stories, exterior corridors. **Terms:** 1-7 night minimum stay, cancellation fee imposed. **Pool(s):** 2 heated outdoor. **Activities:** whirlpool, putting green, lighted tennis court, exercise room. **Guest Services:** valet and coin laundry, area transportation-within 5 mi.

⊀ ⁑♦ ⊇ BIZ 🛜 ✕ 💻
/ SOME UNITS 🐾 🗎 🖼

HOLIDAY INN EXPRESS HOTEL & SUITES TEMPE
Phone: (480)831-9800 **24**

Hotel
$119-$159 2/1-4/1
$109-$129 4/2-1/31

Address: 1520 W Baseline Rd 85283 **Location:** I-10 exit 155 (Baseline Rd), 0.4 mi e. Adjacent to Arizona Mills Mall. **Facility:** 128 units. 6 stories, interior corridors. **Terms:** cancellation fee imposed. **Amenities:** high-speed Internet. **Pool(s):** heated outdoor. **Activities:** whirlpool, exercise room. **Guest Services:** valet and coin laundry.

⁑♦ CALL ⎮M ⊇ BIZ 🛜 ✕ 🗎 💻
/ SOME UNITS 🖼

HOMESTEAD STUDIO SUITES HOTEL-PHOENIX/AIRPORT/TEMPE
Phone: (480)557-8880 **11**

Extended Stay Hotel
$65-$75 2/1-4/15
$55-$65 4/16-1/31

Address: 2165 W 15th St 85281 **Location:** I-10 exit 153 (Broadway Rd), 0.3 mi ne, just nw on S 52nd St, then just w. **Facility:** 95 units, some efficiencies. 3 stories, interior corridors. **Terms:** office hours 6:30 am-10:30 pm. **Pool(s):** heated outdoor. **Activities:** exercise room. **Guest Services:** coin laundry.

⁑♦ ⊇ 🛜 🗎 🖼 💻 / SOME UNITS FEE 🐾

Discover mobile travel solutions at AAA.com/mobile and CAA.ca/mobile

(See map & index p. 164.)

HOTEL TEMPE INNSUITES AIRPORT @ THE MALL
Phone: (480)897-7900   **25**

Hotel
$89-$199 2/1-4/30
$69-$139 5/1-1/31

Address: 1651 W Baseline Rd 85283 **Location:** I-10 exit 155 (Baseline Rd), just e. **Facility:** 160 units, some efficiencies. 2 stories (no elevator), exterior corridors. **Terms:** cancellation fee imposed. **Amenities:** high-speed Internet. **Pool(s):** heated outdoor. **Activities:** whirlpool, putting green, 2 lighted tennis courts, playground, basketball, exercise room. **Guest Services:** valet and coin laundry, area transportation-within 5 mi.

HYATT PLACE TEMPE/PHOENIX AIRPORT
Phone: (480)804-9544   **7**

Hotel
$89-$299

HYATT PLACE

AAA Benefit: Members save 10% or more everyday.

Address: 1413 W Rio Salado Pkwy 85281 **Location:** Just w of Priest Dr. **Facility:** 123 units. 6 stories, interior corridors. **Terms:** cancellation fee imposed. **Amenities:** video games (fee), safes. *Some:* high-speed Internet. **Pool(s):** heated outdoor. **Activities:** exercise room. **Guest Services:** valet laundry, area transportation-within 5 mi. **Free Special Amenities: expanded continental breakfast and high-speed Internet.**

LA QUINTA INN PHOENIX SKY HARBOR AIRPORT SOUTH
Phone: (480)967-4465   **8**

Hotel
$54-$148

Address: 911 S 48th St 85281 **Location:** I-10 exit 153 (Broadway Rd) eastbound; exit 153A (University Dr) westbound, 0.8 mi n; on south side of University Dr; east side of SR 143 (Hohokam Expwy). **Facility:** 128 units. 3 stories, interior/exterior corridors. **Amenities:** video games (fee). *Some:* high-speed Internet. **Pool(s):** heated outdoor. **Activities:** exercise room. **Guest Services:** coin laundry.

QUALITY SUITES NEAR OLD TOWN SCOTTSDALE
Phone: (480)947-3711   **1**

Extended Stay Hotel
$44-$79

Address: 1635 N Scottsdale Rd 85281 **Location:** SR 202 Loop (Red Mountain Frwy) exit 7, 0.6 mi n. **Facility:** 140 units, some efficiencies. 2-3 stories (no elevator), exterior corridors. **Terms:** cancellation fee imposed. **Amenities:** safes. *Some:* high-speed Internet. **Pool(s):** heated outdoor. **Activities:** whirlpool, putting green, exercise room. **Guest Services:** valet and coin laundry. **Free Special Amenities: local telephone calls and high-speed Internet.**

RAMADA INN - ARIZONA MILLS MALL
Phone: (480)413-1188   **26**

Hotel
$59-$119

Address: 1701 W Baseline Rd 85283 **Location:** I-10 exit 155 (Baseline Rd), just e. **Facility:** 119 units. 3 stories, exterior corridors. **Pool(s):** heated outdoor. **Activities:** whirlpool, exercise room. **Guest Services:** coin laundry.

RAMADA LIMITED TEMPE-UNIVERSITY
Phone: (480)736-1700   **18**

Motel
$49-$119

Address: 1915 E Apache Blvd 85281 **Location:** US 60 (Superstition Frwy) exit 175, 1.9 mi n on McClintock Dr, then 0.3 mi e. **Facility:** 56 units. 2 stories (no elevator), exterior corridors. **Amenities:** safes. **Pool(s):** heated outdoor. **Activities:** whirlpool. **Guest Services:** valet laundry.

RED ROOF INN PHOENIX AIRPORT
Phone: (480)449-3205   **12**

Hotel
$49-$118

Address: 2135 W 15th St 85281 **Location:** I-10 exit 153 (Broadway Rd), just nw on S 52nd St, then just w. **Facility:** 125 units. 3 stories, interior corridors. **Amenities:** video games (fee). **Pool(s):** heated outdoor. **Free Special Amenities: local telephone calls and high-speed Internet.**

RESIDENCE INN BY MARRIOTT
Phone: (480)756-2122   **22**

Extended Stay Hotel
$104-$170

AAA Benefit: AAA hotel discounts of 5% or more.

Address: 5075 S Priest Dr 85282 **Location:** I-10 exit 155 (Baseline Rd), 0.4 mi e, then just n. Across from Arizona Mills Mall. **Facility:** 126 units, some two bedrooms and kitchens. 2 stories (no elevator), interior/exterior corridors. **Amenities:** high-speed Internet. **Pool(s):** heated outdoor. **Activities:** whirlpool, sports court, exercise room. **Guest Services:** valet and coin laundry.

SHERATON PHOENIX AIRPORT HOTEL-TEMPE
Phone: (480)967-6600   **13**

Hotel
$79-$359

Sheraton

AAA Benefit: Members get up to 15% off, plus Starwood Preferred Guest® bonuses.

Address: 1600 S 52nd St 85281 **Location:** I-10 exit 153B (Broadway Rd) westbound; exit 153A (48th St) eastbound, 0.3 mi ne. Located in a business and industrial park area. **Facility:** 210 units. 4 stories, interior corridors. **Terms:** 3 day cancellation notice-fee imposed. **Amenities:** *Some:* high-speed Internet (fee). **Pool(s):** heated outdoor. **Activities:** whirlpool, exercise room. **Guest Services:** valet laundry, area transportation-within 3 mi.

SPRINGHILL SUITES BY MARRIOTT TEMPE AIRPORT
Phone: (480)968-8222   **6**

Hotel
$69-$219

SPRINGHILL SUITES

AAA Benefit: AAA hotel discounts of 5% or more.

Address: 1601 W Rio Salado Pkwy 85281 **Location:** Just w of Priest Dr. **Facility:** 130 units. 6 stories, interior corridors. **Amenities:** *Some:* high-speed Internet. **Pool(s):** heated outdoor. **Activities:** whirlpool, exercise room. **Guest Services:** valet and coin laundry. **Free Special Amenities: high-speed Internet.**

(See map & index p. 164.)

SPRINGHILL SUITES TEMPE AT ARIZONA MILLS MALL
Phone: (480)752-7979　**27**

▼▼▼
Hotel
$62-$161

AAA Benefit:
AAA hotel discounts of 5% or more.

Address: 5211 S Priest Dr 85283 **Location:** I-10 exit 155 (Baseline Rd); southeast corner of Baseline Rd and Priest Dr. Across from Arizona Mills Mall. **Facility:** 121 units. 3 stories, interior corridors. **Amenities:** *Some:* high-speed Internet. **Pool(s):** heated outdoor. **Activities:** whirlpool, exercise room. **Guest Services:** valet and coin laundry, area transportation-within 5 mi.

🛫 🛏️ 🏊 BIZ 📶 ✕ 🏧 🖨️ 🖥️
/ SOME UNITS FEE 🐕

STUDIO 6 EXTENDED STAY #6031
Phone: (602)414-4470　**21**

▼▼▼
Extended Stay Motel
$53-$63

Address: 4909 S Wendler Dr 85282 **Location:** I-10 exit 155 (Baseline Rd), just w, then 0.4 mi n. **Facility:** 149 efficiencies. 2 stories (no elevator), exterior corridors. **Terms:** office hours 7 am-8 pm. **Pool(s):** heated outdoor.

Guest Services: coin laundry.

🛏️ 🏊 📶 🏧 🖨️ 🖥️ / SOME UNITS FEE 🐕

SUPER 8 TEMPE/ASU
Phone: (480)967-8891　**15**

▼▼
Motel
$53-$98

Address: 1020 E Apache Blvd 85281 **Location:** Just e of Rural Rd; just e of ASU main campus. **Facility:** 55 units. 2 stories (no elevator), exterior corridors. **Terms:** cancellation fee imposed. **Pool(s):** heated outdoor. **Activities:** whirlpool. **Free Special Amenities: expanded continental breakfast and high-speed Internet.**

SAVE 🛏️ 🏊 📶 🏧 🖨️ 🖥️ / SOME UNITS FEE 🐕

TEMPE MISSION PALMS HOTEL
Phone: (480)894-1400　**9**

▼▼▼▼
Hotel
$99-$319 5/22-1/31
$159-$299 2/1-5/21

Address: 60 E 5th St 85281 **Location:** Jct University Dr, just n on Mill Ave, then just e; downtown. **Facility:** In the downtown area surrounded by shops and restaurants, the hotel offers newly renovated and upscale rooms and baths. 303 units. 4 stories, interior corridors. **Parking:** on-site and valet. **Terms:** cancellation fee imposed. **Amenities:** safes. **Pool(s):** heated outdoor. **Activities:** whirlpools, exercise room. *Fee:* massage. **Guest Services:** valet laundry, area transportation-within 5 mi. **Free Special Amenities: local telephone calls and preferred room (subject to availability with advance reservations).**

SAVE ECO 🛫 🍽️ 🛋️ 🍸 🏊 BIZ 📶 ✕
FEE 🐾 🏧 🖨️ 🖥️ / SOME UNITS FEE 🐕

TEMPE MISSION PALMS

Adjacent to Mill Avenue, Arizona State University and just 4.5 miles from Phoenix Sky Harbor Airport

TEMPE UNIVERSITY INN
Phone: 480/966-7202　**16**

▼▼▼
Hotel
Rates not provided

Address: 1031 E Apache Blvd 85281 **Location:** SR 202 Loop (Red Mountain Frwy) exit 7 (Rural Rd S) 1.5 mi s, then just e. **Facility:** 72 units, some kitchens. 3 stories, interior corridors. **Pool(s):** heated outdoor. **Activities:** sauna, whirlpool, exercise room. **Guest Services:** valet and coin laundry, area transportation-within 5 mi.

🛫 🛏️ 🏊 BIZ 📶 ✕ 🖥️
/ SOME UNITS FEE 🐕 🏧 🖨️

WHERE TO EAT

BEAVER CHOICE
Phone: 480/921-3137　**16**

▼▼▼
European
$9-$17

AAA Inspector Notes: Delicious, homemade Scandinavian and European influenced dishes await at this family-owned, casual storefront eatery. The chicken schnitzel cordon bleu is a crowd favorite, as is the Quebec poutine. **Address:** 1743 E Broadway Rd 85282 **Location:** Southwest corner of Broadway Rd and McClintock Dr. L D CALL 🦽M

BYBLOS RESTAURANT
Phone: 480/894-1945　**18**

▼▼
Greek
$8-$19

AAA Inspector Notes: In business for more than 25 years, this casual Greek spot serves delicious homemade favorites including moussaka, kebabs and the chef's favorite-an oven-roasted lamb platter. Save room for the homemade desserts. **Bar:** full bar. **Address:** 3332 S Mill Ave 85282 **Location:** Just s of Southern Ave.
L D

CADILLAC RANCH ALL-AMERICAN BAR & GRILL
Phone: 480/894-1111　**3**

▼▼
American
$10-$28

AAA Inspector Notes: Located upstairs in the Tempe Marketplace Mall, this energetic eatery has all the great American classics like hot wings, burgers, cold sandwiches and steaks. You can ride the bucking bull under the red, white and blue canopy, if you feel particularly brave. **Bar:** full bar. **Address:** 2000 E Rio Salado Pkwy, Suite 2105 85281 **Location:** SR 101 exit 52, continue n to Rio Salado Pkwy, 0.5 mi w; in Tempe Marketplace Mall. L D

CAFE ISTANBUL & MARKET
Phone: 480/731-9499　**11**

▼▼
Middle Eastern
$6-$14

AAA Inspector Notes: The café's appetizers-including stuffed grape leaves, Lebanese lamb sausage and fava beans seasoned with garlic and lemon-are great lead-ins to marinated meats and poultry, which are gently grilled and served with homemade garlic sauce. Belly dancing enhances the atmosphere on weekends. **Address:** 1310 E Apache Blvd 85281 **Location:** 0.5 mi e of Rural Rd. L D

CASEY MOORE'S OYSTER HOUSE
Phone: 480/968-9935　**6**

▼▼
American
$6-$25

AAA Inspector Notes: This historic 1910 house, rumored to be haunted by a trio of ghosts, is a showcase for a casual eatery that serves more than seafood. On the menu are such salads as spinach berry, a selection of classic sandwiches and Creole- and Southwestern-influenced dishes, including chipotle chicken and Cajun-style shrimp. **Bar:** full bar. **Reservations:** suggested. **Address:** 850 S Ash Ave 85281 **Location:** Jct Mill Ave, just w on University Dr, then just s. **Historic** L D

(See map & index p. 164.)

CLAIM JUMPER
Phone: 480/831-8200

American
$8-$24

AAA Inspector Notes: Great menu variety makes this place a good stop for parties with diverse tastes. Choices include specialty appetizers, salads, rotisserie chicken and barbecue items, not to mention good comfort foods, such as traditional pot pie. Hearty portions satisfy big appetites. The atmosphere is fun and lively. **Bar:** full bar. **Address:** 1530 W Baseline Rd 85283 **Location:** I-10 exit 160 (Baseline Rd), just e. L D

THE DHABA
Phone: 480/446-2824 (13)

Indian
$8-$14

AAA Inspector Notes: Savor authentic Indian cuisine while sampling such favorites as tikka masala, paneer with tamarind chutney and freshly baked naan. **Bar:** beer & wine. **Address:** 1874 E Apache Blvd 85281 **Location:** SR 101 exit 53 northbound (Apache Blvd); exit 52 southbound (Rio Salado Pkwy toward Apache Blvd), 0.8 mi w. L D

GORDON BIERSCH BREWERY RESTAURANT
Phone: 480/736-0033 (1)

American
$9-$30

AAA Inspector Notes: As the name implies this restaurant features fresh, brewed-on-site beer which is crafted in a German tradition. What may not be evident is the wide variety of foods like meal-sized salads, burgers and sandwiches, pizza, pastas, steaks and seafood that is also a huge draw for an upscale, casual dining experience. **Bar:** full bar. **Address:** 420 S Mill Ave 85281 **Location:** Northwest corner of 5th St and S Mill Ave. **Parking:** street only. L D

HAJI BABA MIDDLE EASTERN FOOD
Phone: 480/894-1905 (12)

Middle Eastern
$6-$14

AAA Inspector Notes: Enjoy authentic Middle Eastern favorites in this no-frills dining room attached to a market. **Address:** 1513 E Apache Blvd 85281 **Location:** Jct Rural Rd, 0.7 mi e. L D

HOUSE OF TRICKS
Phone: 480/968-1114 (5)

American
$7-$37

AAA Inspector Notes: Guests to the "house" can dine on a pleasant shaded patio or inside the quaint bungalow. Offerings include freshly prepared salads, hearty sandwiches and grilled rib-eye or seafood. **Bar:** full bar. **Reservations:** suggested. **Address:** 114 E 7th St 85281 **Location:** Just e of Mill Ave. **Parking:** on-site and street. L D

LA BOCCA
Phone: 480/967-5244 (4)

Pizza
$7-$16

AAA Inspector Notes: This stylish and sophisticated pizzeria and wine bar hosts a lively happy hour every day. Sit outside along bustling Mill Avenue and take in the sights and sounds while dining on gourmet pizza and listening to live music. **Bar:** full bar. **Address:** 699 S Mill Ave, Suite 115 85281 **Location:** Jct Mill Ave and 7th St. **Parking:** street only. L D

LEMON GRASS THAI CUISINE
Phone: 480/967-9121 (14)

Thai
$8-$13

AAA Inspector Notes: Patrons enjoy freshly cooked foods, including dishes like pad thai, eggplant and garlic and chicken or seafood combinations cooked in low to spicy red curry sauce. A neatly kept dining room has charming wooden carvings and Thai cottage roof details. **Address:** 818 W Broadway Rd, Suite 108 85282 **Location:** Just e of Priest Rd. L D

MACAYO MEXICAN KITCHEN
Phone: 480/966-6677

Mexican
$8-$16

AAA Inspector Notes: The colorfully furnished Mexican-style eatery prepares Sonoran Mexican dishes. Friendly and efficient staffers serve traditional and lighter dishes flavored with this place's own chili peppers, which are grown near Tucson. **Bar:** full bar. **Address:** 300 S Ash Ave 85281 **Location:** I-10 exit 153 (Broadway Rd), 2 mi e on Broadway Rd, 1.5 mi n on Mill Ave, just w on Fifth St, then just n. L D

MY BIG FAT GREEK RESTAURANT
Phone: 480/966-5883 (2)

Greek
$5-$16

AAA Inspector Notes: Named after the hit film, this restaurant prepares fun, creative Greek dishes that are sure to entice. **Bar:** full bar. **Address:** 525 S Mill Ave 85281 **Location:** Downtown. **Parking:** on-site and street. L D LATE

PITA JUNGLE
Phone: 480/804-0234 (9)

Mediterranean
$5-$15

AAA Inspector Notes: The atmosphere is super-casual in the dining area and on the patio. On the menu is a wide variety of hot and cold pita wraps, pizza, falafel, spanakopita, salads and burgers as well as natural, healthful vegetarian offerings. **Bar:** beer & wine. **Address:** 1250 E Apache Blvd, Suite 113 85282 **Location:** 0.4 mi e of jct Rural Rd and Apache Blvd. L D

REPUBLIC RAMEN
Phone: 480/388-3685 (8)

Asian
$5-$7

AAA Inspector Notes: Friendly staff at this quick serve will guide you through the Asian noodle-style soup menu, with a choice of different broths and toppings. A full menu of boba, or bubble-teas, also are available. **Bar:** beer & wine. **Address:** 1301 E University Dr 85281 **Location:** SR 202 Loop exit 7 (Rural Rd), 1 mi s, then 0.5 mi e. L D

ROYAL TAJ
Phone: 480/967-5234 (17)

Indian
$8-$18

AAA Inspector Notes: Traditional specialties encompass a variety of vegetarian dishes including spinach, eggplant and peas in spiced sauces. The chicken korma is luscious and includes nuts and a spicy cream sauce. **Bar:** full bar. **Address:** 1845 E Broadway Rd 85282 **Location:** Just e of McClintock Dr. L D

RUBIO'S FRESH MEXICAN GRILL
Phone: 480/897-3884

Mexican
$3-$8

AAA Inspector Notes: Freshly prepared and healthful foods, bright decor and friendly staff are found in this upscale fast-food spot. A special treat, the salsa bar lines up four styles and flavors. **Bar:** beer only. **Address:** 1712 E Guadalupe Rd, Suite 107 85281 **Location:** Jct McClintock Dr; northwest corner. L D

SERRANO'S MEXICAN RESTAURANT
Phone: 480/345-0044

Regional Mexican
$6-$14

AAA Inspector Notes: A pleasant stop for lunch or dinner, the local chain is known for consistently good food and attractive, upscale Mexican-style décor. The warm bean dip starter stirs the appetite for traditional dishes such as chiles rellenos or seafood enchiladas prepared with fresh ingredients. Service is friendly. **Bar:** full bar. **Address:** 6440 S Rural Rd 85283 **Location:** Just s of Guadalupe Rd; west side. L D

(See map & index p. 164.)

SUSHI 101
Phone: 480/317-0101   (7)

▽▲▽ ▽▲▽
Sushi
$9-$24

AAA Inspector Notes: A fun, family-owned business offering happy hour all week. Select from classic and inventive rolls, as well as fresh nigiri and sashimi and lunch bento boxes. **Bar:** full bar. **Address:** 920 E University Dr 85281 **Location:** Northeast corner of Rural Rd and University Dr. L D LATE

TASTY KABOB
Phone: 480/966-0260   (10)

▽▲▽ ▽▲▽
Middle Eastern
$8-$21

AAA Inspector Notes: This small eatery is an excellent choice for Persian foods. The owner not only works as the friendly hostess but also prepares the delectable desserts. Diners can choose from varied kebabs or try walnuts in pomegranate sauce with chicken or beef. **Bar:** full bar. **Address:** 1250 E Apache Blvd, #116 85281 **Location:** 0.4 mi e of Rural Rd. L D CALL 🅜

TOM'S BBQ CHICAGO STYLE
Phone: 480/820-0728   (19)

▽▲▽
Barbecue
$6-$22

AAA Inspector Notes: This unpretentious strip-mall eatery displays Chicago memorabilia and serves barbecue beef brisket, pulled pork, smoked chicken, rib tips and side dishes. **Bar:** beer only. **Address:** 115 E Baseline Rd 85283 **Location:** I-10 exit 155, just e of Mill Ave. L D

TOP OF THE ROCK RESTAURANT
Phone: 602/431-2370   (15)

▽▲▽ ▽▲▽ ▽▲▽
American
$24-$42

AAA Inspector Notes: This fine-dining establishment treats guests to mountain-top panoramic views. Solid rock juts up and around the casually elegant dining room. An open kitchen affords a hint of what culinary delights lie in store. **Bar:** full bar. **Reservations:** suggested. **Address:** 2000 Westcourt Way 85282 **Location:** I-10 exit 153 (Broadway Rd) westbound, 0.8 mi w to 48th St, then 0.3 mi s; exit 48th St eastbound, 0.5 mi s; in The Buttes, A Marriott Resort. **Parking:** on-site and valet. D

THATCHER pop. 4,865

SPRINGHILL SUITES BY MARRIOTT THATCHER
Phone: (928)428-6900

▽▲▽ ▽▲▽ ▽▲▽
Hotel
$94-$104

AAA Benefit: AAA hotel discounts of 5% or more.

Address: 2855 W Hwy 70 85552 **Location:** US 191, 2.5 mi w. **Facility:** 71 units. 3 stories, interior corridors. **Amenities:** high-speed Internet. **Pool(s):** heated outdoor. **Activities:** exercise room. **Guest Services:** valet and coin laundry.

 🛗 CALL 🅜 ⊠ 📶 ✕ 🖥 ⊟ ▭

TOLLESON pop. 6,545
• Hotels & Restaurants map & index p. 155
• Part of Phoenix area — see map p. 134

PREMIER INNS
Phone: 623/533-4660   (42)

▽▲▽ ▽▲▽
Hotel
Rates not provided

Address: 8399 W Lynwood St 85353 **Location:** I-10 exit 135 (83rd Ave), just n, then just w. **Facility:** 132 units. 2 stories (no elevator), exterior corridors. **Pool(s):** outdoor. **Activities:** whirlpool. **Guest Services:** coin laundry.

🛗 ⊠ 📶 🖥 / SOME UNITS 🐾

◤GEM◥ TOMBSTONE (G-5) pop. 1,380, elev. 4,540'
• Restaurants p. 264

"The town too tough to die," Tombstone was perhaps the most renowned of Arizona's old mining camps. When Ed Schieffelin came to Camp Huachuca with a party of soldiers and left the fort to prospect, his comrades told him that he would find his tombstone rather than silver. Thus, in 1877 Schieffelin named his first claim Tombstone, and rumors of rich strikes made a boomtown of the settlement that adopted this name.

Over the course of 7 years the mines produced millions of dollars in silver and gold before rising underground waters forced suspension of operations.

Days of lawlessness and violence in Tombstone climaxed with the infamous battle between Wyatt Earp and his brothers against the Clanton brothers, fought at the rear entrance to the O.K. Corral.

Many of Tombstone's historic buildings are within an area bounded by Fremont, 6th, Toughnut and 3rd streets. Among them are St. Paul's Episcopal Church, built in 1882; the Crystal Palace, one of the most luxurious saloons in the West; and the Tombstone Epitaph building, where the oldest continuously published paper in Arizona is still being printed. Western printing history exhibits in the front office are free to the public.

Tombstone Chamber of Commerce: 109 S. 4th St., P.O. Box 995, Tombstone, AZ 85638. **Phone:** (520) 457-9317 or (888) 457-3929.

BIRD CAGE THEATRE, 6th and Allen sts., was built in 1881 and remains virtually unchanged, with the original fixtures, furnishings and interior still intact. A combination theater, saloon and dance hall, the theater was known in its heyday as the bawdiest nightspot between Basin Street and the Barbary Coast. The refrain from the song "Only a Bird in a Gilded Cage" was inspired by this opera house saloon. **Time:** Allow 1 hour minimum. **Hours:** Daily 8-6. Closed Christmas. **Cost:** $10; $9 (ages 60+ and military with ID); $8 (ages 8-18); $28 (family). **Phone:** (520) 457-3421 or (800) 457-3423.

BOOTHILL GRAVEYARD, at the w. city limits off SR 80, contains 300 marked graves of early citizens as well as graves of some of the town's famous and infamous residents. This is reportedly the first cemetery to be called "Boot Hill." **Time:** Allow 1 hour minimum. **Hours:** Daily 7:30-6. Closed Jan. 1 and Christmas. **Cost:** Donations. **Phone:** (520) 457-3300.

HISTORAMA is next to the main entrance of the O.K. Corral. A 25-minute multimedia presentation narrated by actor Vincent Price offers a look at Tombstone's history. This is a good starting point for a tour of the town. **Hours:** Shows run every 30 minutes daily 10-4:30. Closed Thanksgiving and Christmas. **Cost:** $6; free (ages 0-5). Combination ticket with O.K. Corral (includes gunfight reenactment) $10; free (ages 0-5). **Phone:** (520) 457-3456.

O.K. CORRAL, between 3rd and 4th sts. on Allen St., includes the site where the Gunfight at the O.K. Corral took place on Oct. 26, 1881. A re-enactment of the gunfight takes place daily at 2 p.m. **Time:** Allow 30 minutes minimum. **Hours:** Daily 9-5. Closed Thanksgiving and Christmas. **Cost:** Combination ticket with Historama (includes gunfight reenactment) $10; free (ages 0-5). **Phone:** (520) 457-3456.

Camillus Fly Studio is between 3rd and 4th sts. on Fremont St., entered through the O.K. Corral. This is the re-created studio and boardinghouse of the pioneer photographer. Photographs of early Tombstone and its personalities are displayed. **Time:** Allow 30 minutes minimum. **Hours:** Daily 9-5. Closed Thanksgiving and Christmas. **Cost:** Admission included with O.K. Corral. **Phone:** (520) 457-3456.

ROSE TREE MUSEUM AND BOOKSTORE, 116 S. 4th St. at the corner of 4th and Toughnut sts., features the world's largest rosebush, which now covers more than 8,700 square feet; the size of the bush is verified by "The Guinness Book of World Records" yearly. The white-blossomed shrub was planted as a cutting sent from Scotland about 1885. Rose slips may be purchased. Exhibits include antique furniture brought to Tombstone by covered wagon in 1880.

   Time: Allow 30 minutes minimum. **Hours:** Daily 9-5. Closed Thanksgiving and Christmas. **Cost:** $5; $4 (military with ID); free (ages 0-13 with adult). **Phone:** (520) 457-3326.

SCHIEFFELIN HALL is at 4th and Fremont sts. Early Tombstone's theatrical and civic center, Schieffelin Hall is one of the largest adobe structures in the West. **Hours:** closed to the public.

TOMBSTONE COURTHOUSE STATE HISTORIC PARK, 223 E. Toughnut St., was built in 1882. The building contains displays pertaining to the history of Tombstone and Cochise County, using antiques and artifacts to present the lives of former citizens. **Time:** Allow 1 hour minimum. **Hours:** Daily 9-5. Closed Christmas. **Cost:** $5; $2 (ages 7-13). **Phone:** (520) 457-3311.

APACHE SPIRIT RANCH   Phone: (520)457-7299

Ranch
$370-$480

Address: 895 W Monument Rd 85638 **Location:** 2.5 mi nw of center. **Facility:** On the outskirts of town on more than 250 acres, this unique ranch features a replica of an old western town and a Native American camp. 17 units, some two bedrooms. 1 story, exterior corridors. **Terms:** cancellation fee imposed. **Pool(s):** heated outdoor. **Activities:** whirlpool, recreation programs, hiking trails, jogging, horseback riding, horseshoes. **Guest Services:** area transportation.

BEST WESTERN LOOKOUT LODGE
          Phone: (520)457-2223

Hotel
$108-$130

AAA Benefit: Members save up to 20%, plus 10% bonus points with Best Western Rewards®.

Address: 781 N Hwy 80 85638 **Location:** On CR 80, 1 mi n. Located in a quiet area. **Facility:** 40 units. 2 stories (no elevator), exterior corridors. **Pool(s):** outdoor. **Free Special Amenities:** local telephone calls and high-speed Internet. *(See ad this page.)*

▼ *See AAA listing this page* ▼

BEST WESTERN Lookout Lodge 🅰🅰🅰
          Approved

• Free Complimentary Hot Breakfast at Ranch22 Rest.

• Easy Walk to Historic Downtown Tombstone

• Free PC use, Wireless Internet, Seasonal Outdoor Heated Pool, Natural Trail, Gardens, Patio Waterfall and Fire Pits

• Newly Renovated Rooms feature spectacular views of the Dragoon Mountains

• AAA and Senior Discounts. Pet Friendly

BEST WESTERN Lookout Lodge
781 N. Hwy. 80, Tombstone AZ 85638
520.457.2223 | 877.652.6772
www.bestwesterntombstone.com

Best Western

Each Best Western® Hotel is independently owned and operated. Best Western and the Best Western marks are service marks or registered service marks of Best Western International, Inc. ©2010 Best Western International, Inc. All rights reserved.

Get the free mobile app at
http://gettag.mobi

HOLIDAY INN EXPRESS TOMBSTONE
                    Phone: (520)457-9507

Hotel

$99-$129 2/1-5/31
$94-$119 6/1-1/31

Address: 580 W Randolph Way 85638 **Location:** Jct SR 82 and 80, 2 mi s, then just w; 1 mi n of center. **Facility:** 60 units. 2 stories (no elevator), interior corridors. **Terms:** cancellation fee imposed. **Amenities:** high-speed Internet. **Pool(s):** heated outdoor. **Activities:** whirlpool. **Guest Services:** coin laundry. **Free Special Amenities: expanded continental breakfast and high-speed Internet.**

THE LONGHORN RESTAURANT   **Phone:** 520/457-3405

American
$7-$20

AAA Inspector Notes: This historic district corner eatery, popular with locals and tourists, serves a good selection of steak, sandwiches and Mexican entrées in an Old West decor. Desserts, such as deep-dish apple pie and the death by chocolate, are served large enough to share. **Bar:** beer & wine. **Address:** 501 E Allen St 85638 **Location:** Corner of 5th St; in historic district. **Parking:** street only. B L D

O.K. CAFE   **Phone:** 520/457-3980

American
$6-$10

AAA Inspector Notes: The popular eatery can be crowded during breakfast and lunch. Foods are prepared from scratch, and the coffee is said to be the best in town. Hefty buffalo burgers are the specialty. **Address:** 220 E Allen St 85638 **Location:** Northeast corner of 3rd and Allen sts; center. **Parking:** street only. B L

TONTO NATIONAL FOREST (H-4)

Elevations in the forest range from 1,300 ft. at Apache Junction to 7,900 ft. at the Mogollon Rim in the Payson District. Refer to AAA maps for additional elevation information.

Stretching some 90 miles south from the scenic Mogollon Rim to the city of Scottsdale, the Tonto National Forest encompasses 2.9 million acres of spectacular pine, brush and cactus country, making it one of the largest national forests. Elevations range from 1,300 feet to almost 7,900 feet in the northern pine country. Eight regions have been designated as wilderness areas; the entire forest offers more than 860 miles of trails for backpacking, hiking and horse travel.

Scenic roadways in the area include the Apache Trail (SR 88) *(see Apache Junction p. 36)*, Beeline Highway (SR 87) and Young Highway (SR 288). Some unpaved roads are very rough, so phone ahead for current road condition updates. **Note:** The Apache Trail (SR 88) is a winding road and is not suitable for motor homes or vehicle-towing; nearly 22 miles of the road is unpaved.

Six lakes allow boating, swimming and fishing; Saguaro, Bartlett, Canyon, Apache and Theodore Roosevelt lakes have marina facilities. Tubing is a popular pastime in the summer on the lower Salt River. Campgrounds, picnic sites and other recreational opportunities also are available throughout

the forest. A map showing roads, recreation sites and tourist services can be obtained from the local Forest Service office for $9.

For further information contact the Forest Supervisor's Office, Tonto National Forest, 2324 E. McDowell Rd., Phoenix, AZ 85006; phone (602) 225-5200. *See Recreation Chart.*

TONTO NATIONAL MONUMENT (I-6)

Four miles east of Roosevelt Dam on SR 188, Tonto National Monument preserves the most accessible of south-central Arizona's prehistoric cliff dwellings. The remains of a two-story pueblo built in a natural cave are visible from the headquarters parking area. A half-mile paved foot trail ascends 350 feet and leads to cliff dwellings that were occupied by the Salado culture in the 13th and 14th centuries. Summer temperatures are high; wear a hat and suitable shoes and carry sufficient water.

Ranger-conducted, 3-hour tours to the less accessible 40-room Upper Cliff Dwelling are available November through April. The tour is limited to 15 people per day; reservations are required. Phone (928) 467-2241 for reservations.

A visitor center and museum contain artifacts from the Salado culture, including examples of the pottery and woven textiles for which they are noted. Allow 1 hour, 30 minutes minimum. Park and visitor center open daily 8-5; closed Christmas. Trail to the Lower Cliff Dwelling closes 1 hour before park closing. Picnic area 8-4:45. Admission $3; free (ages 0-15). Phone (928) 467-2241.

TORTILLA FLAT

TORTILLA FLAT   **Phone:** 480/984-1776

American
$5-$11

AAA Inspector Notes: Representative of robust fare are half-pound burgers and varied Mexican dishes, such as enchiladas and killer chili served in a sourdough bowl. The saloon awaits drivers who make the picturesque trip up SR 88 from Apache Junction. **Bar:** beer & wine. **Address:** 1 Main St (SR 88) 85290 **Location:** Center. **Parking:** on-site and street. B L D

TUBAC (G-4) pop. 1,191, elev. 3,200'

Tubac, meaning "sinking water," was a Pima village when Jesuit Eusebio Francisco Kino visited the area in 1691. A presidio and mission were established in 1752 (the first military base in Arizona) shortly after the Pima revolted against Spanish encroachment. Between 1752 and 1856 some 500 people lived at Tubac, but in 1776 the presidio was moved to help fortify the strategically important Tucson. With the Gadsden Purchase in 1853, the town became a part of the United States.

The Mexican War, the California gold rush of 1849 and the raiding Apaches depopulated the town throughout much of the 19th century. However, in 1859 Arizona's first newspaper was printed by a local mining company who revived the town. By 1860 Tubac was the largest town in Arizona, but the Civil War left the town unprotected, and it was deserted once again. Once the Apaches ceded control of the area in the late 1800s, Tubac began to grow, but it never regained its earlier importance.

Next to the old presidio, modern Tubac is a small community of writers and artists. Many of the shops and galleries in town sell the local art.

Tubac Chamber of Commerce: 50 Bridge Rd., Room B-8 (at the Tubac Community Center), P.O. Box 1866, Tubac, AZ 85646. **Phone:** (520) 398-2704.

TUBAC PRESIDIO STATE HISTORIC PARK is off I-19 at 1 Burruel St. Arizona's first state park encompasses the Spanish military site that made Tubac Arizona's first European settlement in 1752. An underground archeological exhibit reveals portions of the captain's house. The museum contains Native American, Spanish, Mexican and American territorial artifacts and the working hand press that printed Arizona's first newspaper in 1859.

Historical buildings include a restored 1885 schoolhouse, a furnished Mexican row house, and Otero Hall, which displays 16 William Ahrendt paintings depicting Arizona history. A living-history program portraying life in Tubac is offered; phone for information. **Time:** Allow 1 hour minimum. **Hours:** Daily 9-5. Closed Christmas. **Cost:** $4; $2 (ages 7-13); free (ages 0-6). **Phone:** (520) 398-2252.

TUBAC GOLF RESORT & SPA   Phone: (520)398-2211

Historic Retro Hotel
$129-$289

Address: 1 Otero Rd 85646 **Location:** I-19 exit 40 (Chavez Siding Rd), on east side, then 2 mi s. Located in a quiet area. **Facility:** Set on several acres of landscaped grounds, some of the hotel's well furnished rooms and suites include a fireplace. 98 units, some two bedrooms and efficiencies. 1 story, exterior corridors. **Terms:** check-in 4 pm, 3 day cancellation notice-fee imposed. **Amenities:** safes. **Dining:** 2 restaurants, also, Stables Dining Room, see separate listing. **Pool(s):** heated outdoor. **Activities:** saunas, whirlpools, steamrooms, tennis court, hiking trails, exercise room, spa. Fee: golf-27 holes, bicycles. **Guest Services:** valet and coin laundry. **Free Special Amenities:** local telephone calls and high-speed Internet.

[SAVE] [ECO] [⚑] [🛎] [Y] [🛏] [BIZ] [🛜] [✕] [🔋] [▯]
/ SOME UNITS FEE [🐕]

WHERE TO EAT

SHELBY'S BISTRO   Phone: 520/398-8075

Regional American
$10-$22

AAA Inspector Notes: Tucked in a courtyard, the brightly decorated bistro serves fresh salads, hearty sandwiches, a selection of steaks and pasta as well as yummy desserts. Patio seating overlooks a fountain. **Bar:** full bar. **Address:** 19 Tubac Rd-Mercado de Baca 85646 **Location:** I-19 exit 34, just e to Frontage Rd, just n to Plaza Rd, then just e. [L] [D]

STABLES DINING ROOM   Phone: 520/398-2678

American
$9-$35

AAA Inspector Notes: Built in the original Otero Ranch stables, this attractive dining room is bedecked in ranch decor and boasts a view of the golf course. Varied Southwestern and traditional American dishes include chimichangas, Australian lamb chops and the house specialty, prime rib, which is served on weekends. **Bar:** full bar. **Reservations:** suggested. **Address:** 1 Otero Rd 85646 **Location:** I-19 exit 40 (Chavez Siding Rd), on east side, then 2 mi s; in Tubac Golf Resort & Spa. **Historic**
[B] [L] [D]

We Keep You
on the go

AAA Mobile Battery Service is your passport to a happy vacation before, during and after your trip!

800-AAA-HELP (800-222-4357)   AAA.com

TUBA CITY (B-4) pop. 8,611, elev. 4,936'

Tuba City was named after Tuve, a Hopi leader. Natural springs attracted generations of Hopi, Navajo and Paiute Indians to the area. In 1875 the city was laid out and settled by Mormons, who used blocks of dressed stone from nearby prehistoric sites to build structures, some of which still stand.

The town lies on US 160, 10 miles east of US 89 within Arizona's northeastern Indian country, which encompasses the Navajo and Hopi Indian reservations. A variety of Native American crafts are produced, including baskets, pottery and silver products.

QUALITY INN NAVAJO NATION

Hotel
$89-$119

Phone: (928)283-4545
Address: 10 N Main St 86045
Location: 1 mi n of US 160. Adjacent to historic Tuba Trading Post. **Facility:** 80 units. 2 stories (no elevator), interior corridors. **Terms:** cancellation fee imposed. **Dining:** Hogan Restaurant, see separate listing. **Activities:** exercise room. **Guest Services:** coin laundry. **Free Special Amenities: full breakfast and high-speed Internet.**
(See ad p. 94.)

MOENKOPI LEGACY INN AND SUITES

Hotel
$89-$229

Phone: (928)283-4500
Address: US 160 & SR 264 86045
Location: Jct US 160 and SR 264. **Facility:** 100 units, some two bedrooms. 3 stories, interior corridors. **Terms:** check-in 4 pm, cancellation fee imposed. **Pool(s):** heated outdoor. **Activities:** whirlpool, exercise room. **Free Special Amenities: continental breakfast and high-speed Internet.**
(See ad this page.)

WHERE TO EAT

HOGAN RESTAURANT

Southwestern
$8-$22

Phone: 928/283-4545
AAA Inspector Notes: This casual restaurant draws a big breakfast crowd from the hotel next door. The service is very basic and slow at times. The menu consist of a mix between Navajo specialties, Mexican and American cuisine. **Address:** 10 N Main St 86045 **Location:** 1 mi n of US 160; in Quality Inn Navajo Nation.

▼ See AAA listing this page ▼

EXPERIENCE HOPI
Moenkopi Legacy Inn & Suites

Scan code for special AAA information

Get the free mobile app at
http://gettag.mobi

Adjacent to Tuba City, AZ

A PLACE WHERE ART, CULTURE, & TRADITION COME ALIVE!

Tour the Hopi Mesa's with a guide
Connect with Hopi artists
Hotel Experience Hopi Programs

Denny's 24 hour service

Plan your Trip to Hopi Now by Visiting www.Experiencehopi.com — 928-283-4500

AAA/CAA MEMBER DISCOUNTS AHEAD

Consider your AAA/CAA card as the smallest, lowest tech GPS navigator imaginable...it will take you right to the best deals in town, wherever "town" is for you. Go to **AAA.com/discounts** to find your way to the best deals.

AAA.com/discounts

Tucson

Then & Now

Tucson is a culturally-rich city that enjoys a starkly beautiful Sonoran Desert setting and reliably warm weather. It's this tourism trifecta that today draws droves of golfers, hikers, shopaholics, Mexican-food lovers and leisure-wear resort lizards to Arizona's second largest city.

With a population just shy of the half-million mark, Tucson has seen some unfortunate stucco-and-strip-mall suburban sprawl. But make no mistake, this is no homogenized Phoenix Junior. With the lovely Santa Catalina Mountains as a backdrop and the towering cacti of Saguaro National Park *(see place listing p. 203)* at its doorstep, Tucson feels connected to its surroundings.

A compact cluster of modest high-rise buildings shades the downtown core. Many of the city's historical adobes were bulldozed back in the 1960s. However, a good number of the low-slung Spanish and Mexican-era structures re-

main, especially in the Barrio Histórico neighborhood (just south of downtown) and the central El Presidio Historic District.

When the summer sun isn't blazing, the latter is a nice area for a leisurely stroll, shopping at the Old Town Artisans market *(see Shopping p. 270)* and perhaps a happy hour Cadillac margarita at El Charro Café, the city's oldest restaurant.

Downtown's Stone Avenue is home to two of the city's most important houses of worship. The baroque St. Augustine Cathedral looks like it's been plucked straight out of a colonial Mexican town. The historic 1910 Stone Avenue Temple now houses the Jewish History Museum, 564 S. Stone Ave. One of Arizona's first synagogues, it features a mix of neo-classic, Romanesque and Moorish styles; phone (520) 670-9073.

While the downtown core boasts some beautiful public murals and buildings (including the mosaic-tile domed Pima County Courthouse) and the excellent Tucson Museum of Art and Historic Block *(see attraction listing p. 277)* in addition to a pair of historic neighborhoods, some tourists complain there's little else to entertain a non-history buff for more than a few hours.

Enter the Rio Nuevo revitalization project, designed to draw more visitors downtown. Approved more than a decade ago, development plans include a convention center expansion and a new luxury hotel next door. Locals often use the phrase "a total mess" to describe the project's ongoing stalled status.

On the east side of downtown is the lively Congress Street district. Tourists, Tucson scenesters and young hippie-hobos amble down sidewalks lined with early 20th-century buildings. Amtrak trains rumble into the lovingly restored

Pima County Courthouse through a Viewing Panel

(Continued on p. 269.)

Destination Tucson

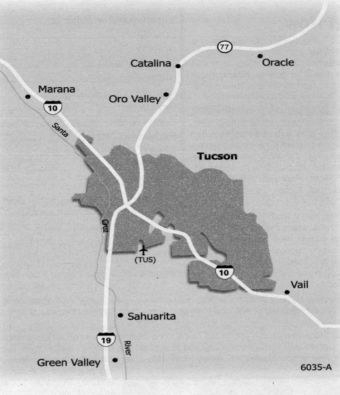

This map shows cities in the Tucson vicinity where you will find attractions, hotels and restaurants. Cities are listed alphabetically in this book on the following pages.

Fast Facts

ABOUT THE CITY

POP: 486,699 ▪ **ELEV:** 2,389 ft.

MONEY

SALES TAX: Arizona's statewide sales tax is 6.6 percent; an additional 2 percent is levied in Tucson. The tax on a hotel room in Pima County is 12.05 percent, plus an additional $2 per room per night in Tucson. There is a combined state and county rental car tax of 10 percent, plus a Pima County rental car fee of $3.50 per rental; a concession fee of 11.1 percent is added if the car is picked up at the airport, and an additional 2 percent tax is added if the car is picked up off airport property but within the Tucson city limits.

WHOM TO CALL

EMERGENCY: 911

POLICE (non-emergency): (520) 791-4444

HOSPITALS: Carondelet St. Joseph's Hospital, (520) 873-3000 ▪ Carondelet St. Mary's Hospital, (520) 872-3000 ▪ Northwest Medical Center, (520) 742-9000 ▪ University Medical Center, (520) 694-0111.

WHERE TO LOOK AND LISTEN

NEWSPAPERS: The major newspaper is the *Arizona Daily Star*, published every morning. The city's free independent paper is *The Tucson Weekly*, published on Thursdays.

RADIO: Tucson radio stations KNST (790 AM) and KVOI (690 AM) are news/talk radio stations ▪ KUAZ (89.1 FM and 1550 AM) is a member of National Public Radio.

VISITOR INFORMATION

Metropolitan Tucson Convention & Visitors Bureau: 100 S. Church Ave., Suite 7199, Tucson, AZ 85701. **Phone:** (520) 624-1817 or (800) 638-8350.

The bureau, in La Placita plaza, can provide a variety of information, including the *Visit Tucson Official Destination Guide*. The bureau's visitor center is open Mon.-Fri. 9-5, Sat.-Sun. 9-4; closed major holidays.

TRANSPORTATION

AIR TRAVEL: Ten miles south of downtown, Tucson International Airport (TUS), (520) 573-8100, is served by many major passenger airlines. Short-term airport parking costs $1 per half-hour up to $12 per day; long-term parking costs $9 for 24 hours ($2 for the first hour, then $1.50 per half-hour up to $9 per day).

The Arizona Stage Coach, (520) 889-1000, provides van service throughout the Tucson area; prices range from $5-$61. Sunset Limousine, (520) 573-9418, provides limousine service throughout the Tucson area; prices range from $55-$125 per hour. Cab service to downtown averages 20 minutes and costs $27-$30.

RENTAL CARS: Hertz, (520) 573-5201 or (800) 654-3131, offers discounts to AAA members. Check the telephone directory for listings of other agencies.

RAIL SERVICE: The Amtrak station, 400 N. Toole, accommodates Amtrak rail lines. For advance ticket and schedule information phone (800) 872-7245. Tickets may also be purchased at the station.

BUSES: The terminal for Greyhound Lines Inc. is at 471 W. Congress St.; phone (520) 792-3475 or (800) 231-2222.

TAXIS: There are many independent taxi companies in Tucson. Rates are not regulated by the city. One company that serves the area is Yellow Cab, (520) 624-6611.

PUBLIC TRANSPORTATION: Sun Tran, (520) 792-9222, operates a fleet of modern buses throughout the metropolitan area. The Ronstadt Transit Center, on 6th Avenue between Congress and Pennington streets, is the main downtown bus station. The fare to all points is $1.50; 50c (ages 65+ with valid ID and the physically impaired); free (ages 0-5). Fares can be paid to the bus driver or at self-serve ticket machines (cash only).

More useful to visitors is the Old Pueblo Trolley, (502) 792-1802. Vintage, fully restored electric street cars travel from the Congress Street area to the University of Arizona via 4th Avenue and University Boulevard. The trolley runs Friday 6 p.m.-10 p.m., Saturday noon to midnight and Sunday noon to 6 p.m. The one-way fare is $1.25; 75c (ages 6-12). On Sunday the fare is 25c for all. You can board the trolley at any of the "Car stops here" signs along the route.

(Continued from p. 267.)

Railroad Depot. After dark, indie rock fans line up under the historic Rialto Theatre's electric pink-and-purple neon marquee for a sold-out gig. It's also here you'll find the 1919 Hotel Congress.

Spanish, Mexican and Western heritage play big parts the in city's cultural pageant. But the constant parade of Arizona Wildcats T-shirts you'll see on the street reminds you this is a college town as well.

The University of Arizona campus sits a few miles northeast of downtown. Linking UofA with the Congress Street district is Tucson's offbeat shopping and dining strip, 4th Avenue *(see Shopping p. 270)*.

Golf and spa resorts, McMansions and modern shopping centers are ubiquitous in the foothill neighborhoods on the tony north side of town. Climbing further into the Catalina Mountains you can hit the slopes at the country's southernmost ski area.

Arriving
By Car

Tucson's major approach and through-route is I-10, the nation's southernmost transcontinental highway. Primarily an east-west route, it angles into the city from the southeast and the northwest. Northbound, I-10 intersects with I-19 in south Tucson and then continues along the west side of the city, providing access to the downtown area. Once I-10 leaves the city, it proceeds northwest to Phoenix, 120 miles away.

A major approach from the west is I-8, which originates in San Diego and joins with I-10 about midway between Phoenix and Tucson. Because both I-10 and I-8 traverse desert country, some of their sections are subject to dust storms, particularly in spring and early summer. Local radio stations broadcast advisories during these fluctuating weather conditions, and interstate signs with changeable messages warn motorists.

A well-known route reaching Tucson from the north is SR 77. One of the area's oldest two-lane routes, it is especially scenic. South of Tucson, I-19 leads to the Mexican border at Nogales.

Getting Around
Street System

Tucson is laid out in a grid pattern. Numbered streets run east-west to the south of Speedway Boulevard, and numbered avenues run north-south to the west of Euclid Avenue. Address numbers start at the intersection of Broadway, the north-south divider, and Stone, the east-west divider. Unless otherwise posted the speed limit on most streets is 25 to 40 mph.

Hopi Indian Carved Kachina Doll

Parking

Metered parking is available on many downtown streets, but be sure to check signs and meters for restricted times and limits. There also are a number of commercial garages and lots. Rates average around $2 per hour or $5 per day.

Shopping

If you've come to Tucson itchin' to buy turquoise, Kachina dolls and dream catchers, the world is your oyster. But Southwestern art and crafts are only part of the city's shopping picture. You can also overstuff your carry-on bag or car trunk with goods from funky boutiques, cutting-edge art galleries and high-end shopping malls.

Downtown in the El Presidio district, Old Town Artisans, 201 N. Court Ave., is housed in an 1850s adobe building that sits on an entire city block. The half dozen shops and galleries deal mainly in traditional Native and Latin American crafts (pottery, carvings, blankets), but you'll also find some contemporary jewelry and art here.

The Tucson Museum of Art and Historic Block's excellent Museum Store, 140 N. Main Ave., carries a nice selection of works by some of the state's best artists (read: expensive), as well as art books and affordable gift items.

On the east side of downtown you'll find a sprinkling of modern art galleries in the Congress Street district; there are more galleries a few blocks north in the Warehouse Arts District (at the corner of 6th Avenue and 6th Street). Platform Gallery, 439 N. 6th Ave., sells visually striking paintings and sculpture by contemporary Southwest artists. For more information on galleries, check hotel brochure racks for the Tucson Gallery Association's Downtown Art & Lunch guide map, or phone (520) 629-9759.

Without question, downtown's most eclectic shopping and dining area is 4th Avenue (between 9th Street and University Boulevard). With the exception of a prehistoric Dairy Queen, you won't see a single chain store or restaurant (not even a Starbucks) on the entire strip, which is exactly how Tucson hipsters like it.

This is a college town, so books are big. Antigone Books, 411 N. 4th Ave., has a feminist bent. If you need a copy of "Eat Pray Love," there's no danger Antigone is sold out. In addition to chick lit and other off-beat titles, there's a selection of cute gift items. One musty whiff of The Book Stop, 214 N. 4th Ave., and you know you've ascended to used-book heaven.

Fashionistas will find two of the street's best clothing boutiques near University Boulevard. The styles at Zoe Boutique, 735 N. 4th Ave., range from trendy to funky-casual. Inside an old pale green bungalow home, Desert Vintage & Costume, 636 N. 4th Ave., is the place to hunt for 1920s flapper dresses, bellbottoms and poodle skirts.

Tucson's Map & Flag Center, 3239 N. First Ave., is a bit off the beaten path, but a must for back-country adventurers. The store carries topographic maps for the entire state, plus travel guidebooks and detailed road maps.

As for malls, Tucson isn't in league with Phoenix, but it's no slouch, either. Tucson Mall, 4500 N. Oracle Rd., is the city's biggest center. Outlet fanatics can bargain hunt at the Foothills Mall, 7401 N. La Cholla Blvd. Tucson's newest mall is the open-air La Encantada, 2905 E. Skyline Dr. In addition to more than 50 restaurants and high-end shops (think Brooks Brothers and Louis Vuitton), there's an Apple Store in case your iPod's on the fritz.

For a shopping courtyard filled with unique specialty boutiques, try the hacienda-style St. Philip's Plaza, at the southeast corner of Campbell Avenue and River Road. The plaza's Grey Dog Trading Company specializes in Native American art and crafts. On Sundays the plaza hosts a farmers market.

Nightlife

Tucson's nightlife is mainly concentrated in the downtown area. Whether you choose to catch a live band, sip designer cocktails or guzzle beer alongside UofA students, many spots are within walking distance of one another.

Club Congress, 311 E. Congress St., has been called one of the country's best live music clubs by *Esquire* magazine. Just off the lobby of the historic Hotel Congress, the venue books mostly local and regional alt-rock bands. The stage, backed with red velvet drapes and framed by gothic-style metalwork, overlooks a dance floor that's shoulder-to-shoulder on weekends; phone (520) 622-8848.

If you'd rather skip the club and its surprisingly high cover charge, yet still be able to hear the music, opt for the Hotel Congress Lobby Bar. The décor is classic Southwest Deco, the scene is laid-back and there's a casual patio out back as well.

Across the street is the Rialto Theatre, 318 E. Congress St., a restored 1920 vaudeville and movie palace that now hosts mid-level touring acts (think George Clinton, Lucinda Williams and Franz Ferdinand); phone (520) 740-1000.

The miraculously rehabilitated Fox Tucson Theatre, 17 W. Congress St., screens classic movies just as it did back in its 1930s and '40s heyday. Also equipped with a stage, the Fox books some live music acts and ballet performances; phone (520) 547-3040.

If your taste in flicks leans more toward cult movies and indie films, the tiny Screening Room, 127 E. Congress St., shows kung fu double features, Herschell Gordon Lewis splatter fests and the like; phone (520) 882-0204. Even better is The Loft Cinema, 3233 E. Speedway Blvd. (a few minutes east of the UofA campus), which has two screens and theme nights like "Mondo Mondays" and "Scream-o-rama"; phone (520) 795-7777.

Fourth Avenue is loaded with casual bars and pubs popular with UofA students. On the upscale side is Sky Bar, 536 N. 4th Ave., a sleek space that's a chill-out cafe by day and a hip bar by night. DJs

Fox Tucson Theatre

spin techno and house beats on weekends; there's live jazz on Thursdays. Every night, flat-screen TVs show astronomical images taken from the bar's very own telescope; phone (520) 622-4300.

If it's live music you're after, PLUSH, 340 E. 6th St. (corner of 4th Ave. and 6th St.) is the neighborhood's best bet. The majority of acts playing this funky club/bar are local indie rock bands, but a quick scan of the schedule will turn up some folk, bluegrass and acoustic singer-songwriter acts as well; phone (520) 798-1298.

For country music you'll need to gas up the F-150 and head to east Tucson. Opened in 1962, The Maverick Live Country Club, 6622 E. Tanque Verde Rd., offers live music Tuesday through Saturday; phone (520) 298-0430.

Romantics in the mood to clink wine glasses, hear a jazz pianist and gaze out at the twinkling city lights should head for the hilltop Hacienda del Sol Guest Ranch Resort, 5501 N. Hacienda del Sol Rd. Both the elegant Terraza Lounge and the comfy Joesler Room are classy spots for a tête-á-tête; phone (520) 299-1501.

Big Events

The Southern Arizona Square and Round Dance Festival begins the year's activities in January. In February the city boasts another superlative: the world's largest gem and mineral show. During the ♦ Tucson Gem and Mineral Show the Tucson Convention Center is filled with some 250 dealers selling to the public.

If you like horses and cowboys, Tucson is the place to be in late February during ♦ La Fiesta de los Vaqueros, held at the rodeo grounds. This classic professional rodeo event features a parade with people on foot, on horseback and in every size and shape of horse-drawn vehicle. The 8-day-long fiesta ends with the rodeo finals, in which some of the best riders and ropers on the circuit compete.

The Yaqui Easter Lenten Ceremony combines old Yaqui traditions with Christian beliefs in a weeklong celebration. In March and again in December Tucson's 4th Avenue holds a huge street fair filled with artisans selling and demonstrating their crafts. Enhanced by music and food vendor booths, these weekends attract visitors and residents alike. The Annual International Mariachi Conference comes to town in April. Mid-month brings the Pima County Fair.

Tucson's fall activities begin in late September and early October as Mount Lemmon Ski Valley plays host to Oktoberfest. Luminaria Nights are held for 3 nights in December at the Tucson Botanical Gardens.

Sports & Rec

Tucson's city parks and Pima County parks offer facilities for almost any activity. A number of **swimming** pools and **tennis, racquetball** and **handball** courts are available as well as picnic areas, playgrounds, and **soccer** and ball fields. For information about facilities and reservations for their use contact the Pima County Parks and Recreation office at 3500 W. River Rd., (520) 877-6000, or Tucson Parks and Recreation at 900 S. Randolph, (520) 791-4873.

Tucson's climate is made to order for **golf** addicts. More than 40 courses are in the vicinity—everything from world-renowned resorts to public

Watch a Rodeo at La Fiesta de los Vaqueros

access courses. Some were designed by Robert Cupp, Tom Fazio, Arthur Hill, Robert Trent Jones, Jack Nicklaus and other noted architects.

Among the courses in Tucson are: Hilton Tucson El Conquistador Golf and Tennis Resort, Pusch Ridge Golf Course, (520) 544-5000 or (520) 544-1900, 10000 N. Oracle Rd. and 10555 N. La Cañada Dr.; Omni Tucson National, (520) 297-2271, 2727 W. Club Dr.; Randolph Municipal, (520) 791-4161, 600 S. Alvernon Way; Santa Rita, (520) 762-5620, 16461 S. Houghton Rd.; and Ventana Canyon, (520) 577-4061, 6200 N. Clubhouse Ln. Also in the area is Canoa Hills, (520) 648-1880, at 1401 W. Calle Urbano in Green Valley.

Hiking is probably the best way to get up close and personal with the flora and fauna of the Sonoran Desert. Tucson Mountain Park is laced with hiking trails. The Santa Catalina Mountains offer many areas of unspoiled beauty as well. Hiking permits are required for some areas. Empty vehicles will be fined or towed if a permit is not displayed.

For more information about permits and National Forest fee areas, contact the Coronado National Forest office in Tucson; phone (520) 388-8300. Catalina State Park *(see attraction listing p. 274 and Recreation Chart)*, (520) 628-5798, has trails that can challenge the experienced hiker but not intimidate the novice; two longer trails begin at the end of the park's paved road. For more information about hiking phone the county's recreation office at (520) 877-6000.

Another great way to see the countryside is on a trail ride. Several stables offer half-day, full-day and overnight **horseback riding** trips into the mountains and desert. Check hotel brochure racks for stables. **Skiing** is available at Mount Lemmon Ski Valley, a scenic 30-mile drive northeast from Tucson. The southernmost ski area in the nation, Mount Lemmon offers both downhill and cross-country skiing. A scenic sky ride on the ski lift is offered during the off-season. Phone (520) 576-1400 for snow condition updates.

The University of Arizona's Wildcats excite crowds during the **football** and **basketball** seasons. Home football games are played at Arizona Stadium, and basketball teams tip off at McKale Memorial Center.

Greyhound racing happens at Tucson Greyhound Park, (520) 884-7576, 2601 S. 3rd Ave. at 36th Street. The dogs race Monday through Saturday, year-round.

Note: Policies concerning admittance of children to pari-mutuel betting facilities vary. Phone for information.

Performing Arts

When it comes to theater, Tucson offers many choices. Top billing is given to the Arizona Theatre Company, Arizona's professional state theater. This premier company performs six plays during its September through May season at the Temple of Music

Gila Woodpecker, Arizona-Sonora Desert Museum

and Art, (520) 622-2823, 330 S. Scott Ave. A forum for experimental theater is The Invisible Theatre, (520) 882-9721, 1400 N. 1st Ave., which stages six plays between September and June.

Entertainment for the entire family is available at the Gaslight Theatre, (520) 886-9428, 7010 E. Broadway, where melodramas, comedies and musicals encourage audience participation; reservations are required. The University of Arizona adds to Tucson's theater offerings. The school's resident company, (520) 621-7008, 1025 N. Olive St., presents its offerings of musicals and serious drama in spring, summer and fall, while the UA Presents series brings national touring companies to Centennial Hall, (520) 621-3341, 1020 E. University Blvd.

No bit players, Tucson's opera company plays a major part in the performing arts arena. Accompanied by a full orchestra in the Tucson Convention Center from October through April, members of the Arizona Opera, (520) 293-4336, present five operas.

Completing the cultural scene are the city's orchestras. The Tucson Symphony Orchestra, (520) 882-8585, plays both classical and pop music in the Tucson Music Hall at the Tucson Convention Center September to May. Under the desert skies at the DeMeester Outdoor Performance Center in Reid Park, the Tucson Pops Orchestra, (520) 722-5853, entertains audiences in the spring and fall. From September through May the University of Arizona's Centennial Hall resounds with sounds from Broadway shows to jazz to chamber music performed by guest artists and musicians.

ATTRACTIONS

ARIZONA HISTORICAL SOCIETY/ARIZONA HISTORY MUSEUM, 949 E. 2nd St., features exhibits about 1870s Native American, Mexican and Anglo families; the life of Apache warrior Geronimo; and various modes of 19th- and early 20th-century transportation. Museum highlights include a full-size replica of a 100-year-old underground copper mine and a hands-on exhibit that describes Tucson's history, land use and environment along the Santa Cruz River. A research library is available.

Time: Allow 1 hour minimum. **Hours:** Museum Mon.-Sat. 10-4. Closed Jan. 1, Martin Luther King Jr. Day, Presidents Day, Memorial Day, July 4, Labor Day, Columbus Day, Veterans Day, Thanksgiving, Christmas and state employee furlough days. Library hours vary; phone ahead. **Cost:** $5; $4 (ages 12-18 and 60+); free (first Sat. of the month). Validated parking is available in the garage at E. 2nd Street and N. Euclid Avenue. **Phone:** (520) 628-5774.

Arizona Historical Society/Downtown History Museum, 140 N. Stone Ave., depicts downtown Tucson's history from its origins as a Spanish presidio in 1775 to modern times. Visitors may visit a 19th-century hotel lobby and an old-time barbershop. Explore the history of downtown's police force, firefighters, schools, libraries, businesses and theaters. An exhibit about the 1934 capture of John Dillinger and his gang includes his bulletproof vest.

Time: Allow 30 minutes minimum. **Hours:** Tues.-Fri. 10-4. Closed Jan. 1, July 4, Veterans Day, Thanksgiving, Christmas and state employee furlough days. **Cost:** $3; $2 (ages 12-18 and 60+); free (first Fri. of the month). Validated parking is available on lower level of Wells Fargo Bank garage on E. Alameda Street. **Phone:** (520) 770-1473.

ARIZONA HISTORICAL SOCIETY/FORT LOWELL MUSEUM, jct. Fort Lowell and Craycroft rds. at 2900 N. Craycroft Rd. in Fort Lowell Park, features a reconstructed officer's quarters from a military post active 1873-91. Learn about the history of the fort, its soldiers and their families as well as the story of the Apache Indian Wars. Military and horse equipment, uniforms, period furniture and photographs of army life are on display.

Time: Allow 1 hour minimum. **Hours:** Fri.-Sat. 10-4. Closed Jan. 1, July 4, Veterans Day, Thanksgiving, Christmas and state employee furlough days. **Cost:** $3; $2 (ages 12-18 and 60+); free (first Sat. of the month). **Phone:** (520) 885-3832.

ARIZONA-SONORA DESERT MUSEUM, 14 mi. w. in Tucson Mountain Park at 2021 N. Kinney Rd., exhibits more than 300 live animal species, including mountain lions, prairie dogs, Gila monsters, hawks, bighorn sheep and hummingbirds in natural habitats. Almost 2 miles of paths lead visitors through landscapes containing more than 1,300

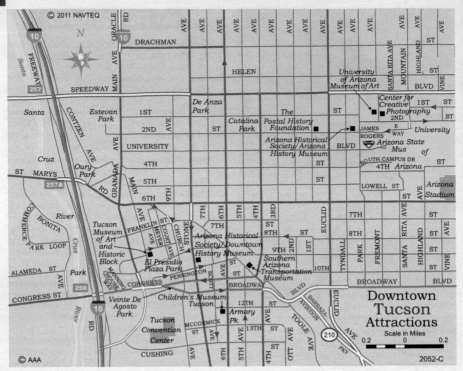

© 2011 NAVTEQ

Downtown
Tucson
Attractions

Scale in Miles
0.2   0   0.2

© AAA

2052-C

species of plants indigenous to the Sonoran Desert region; included are desert grasslands, cactus and desert gardens.

A pollination gardens complex shows interactions between insects, birds, bats and plants, and a fenceless enclosure allows javelinas to explore hillsides and take mud baths.

A simulated walk-through limestone cave features a collection of regional gems and minerals. A display about how the planet has evolved with explanations of erosion, volcanic and seismic activity and plate tectonics also is featured. **Time:** Allow 2 hours minimum. **Hours:** Daily 7:30-5, Mar.-May; 7-4:30, June-Sept. (also Sat. 4:30-10, June-Aug.); 8:30-5, rest of year. Last admission 45 minutes before closing. **Cost:** Sept.-May $14.50; $4.50 (ages 6-12). Rest of year $12; $3 (ages 6-12). **Phone:** (520) 883-2702 or (520) 883-1380. [🍴]

ARIZONA STATE MUSEUM is at 1013 E. University Blvd. on the University of Arizona campus. Reputedly the region's oldest and largest anthropology museum, it preserves material objects and interprets the history of Southwestern cultures, from prehistoric mammoth hunters to present-day Native Americans and northern Mexico natives.

The Paths of Life: American Indians of the Southwest exhibit highlights the origin, history and contemporary life of Apache, Hopi, Navajo, Tohono O'odham, Southern Paiute and other indigenous groups. There's a mix of prehistoric artifacts, historical objects, commissioned artwork, videotape interviews and dioramas.

Southwest Native American pottery from the museum's more than 20,000-piece collection spanning 2,000 years is showcased. The library and archives contain more than 40,000 volumes as well as photographs and archeological excavation reports.

Tours: Guided tours are available. **Time:** Allow 1 hour minimum. **Hours:** Museum Mon.-Sat. 10-5. Library and archives Mon.-Thurs. 10-3. Closed major holidays. **Cost:** $5; free (ages 0-17 and students with ID). **Phone:** (520) 621-6302, or (520) 621-4695 for the library and archives.

CATALINA STATE PARK, 9 mi. n. off SR 77 Milepost 81 to 11570 N. Oracle Rd., is home to 5,525 acres of desert plants. At the base of the Santa Catalina Mountains, the park's activities include birdwatching, hiking, camping and horseback riding. A .75-mile interpretive trail winds around the Romero Ruins, the site of a Hohokam village occupied 500-1450. *See Recreation Chart.*

Hours: Park open daily 5 a.m.-10 p.m. Ranger station daily 8-5. **Cost:** $7 (per private vehicle, up to four passengers); $3 (per additional adult passenger in vehicle or individual arriving on foot or bicycle). Camping $15-$25 (per private vehicle). **Phone:** (520) 628-5798. [🏕][🐎][🏞]

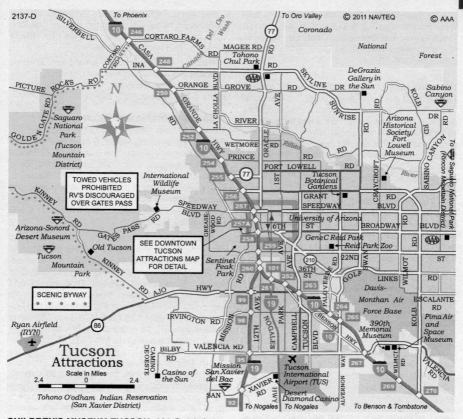

2137-D

Tucson Attractions
Scale in Miles
2.4 0 2.4

Tohono O'odham Indian Reservation
(San Xavier District)

TOWED VEHICLES PROHIBITED RV'S DISCOURAGED OVER GATES PASS

SEE DOWNTOWN TUCSON ATTRACTIONS MAP FOR DETAIL

SCENIC BYWAY

© 2011 NAVTEQ   © AAA

CHILDREN'S MUSEUM TUCSON, 200 S. 6th Ave., encourages learning through hands-on exhibits and programs geared toward children ages 2-10. Museum highlights include the Public Safety, Ocean Discovery Center, Build It and Enchanted Rainforest exhibits. **Hours:** Mon.-Fri. 9-8, Sat.-Sun. 10-5, Memorial Day-Labor Day; Tues.-Fri. 9-5, Sat.-Sun. 10-5, rest of year. Holiday hours may vary; phone ahead. Last admission 30 minutes before closing. Closed Easter, Thanksgiving and Christmas. **Cost:** $8; $6 (ages 2-18 and 61+). **Phone:** (520) 792-9985.

CORONADO NATIONAL FOREST—
see place listing p. 56.

DEGRAZIA GALLERY IN THE SUN is in the foothills of the Santa Catalina Mountains, 1 mi. n. of Sunrise Dr. at 6300 N. Swan Rd. More than 15,000 ceramics, paintings and sculptures created by Southwestern artist Ettore "Ted" DeGrazia are featured in permanent and rotating exhibits. Mission in the Sun, an open-air adobe chapel built in the 1950s by DeGrazia and his Native American friends, adjoins the gallery on the 10-acre National Historic site. The artist's final resting place is marked beside the chapel.

Hours: Daily 10-4. Closed Jan. 1, Easter, Thanksgiving and Christmas. **Cost:** Donations. **Phone:** (520) 299-9191 or (800) 545-2185.

GENE C. REID PARK, 22nd St. and Country Club Rd., is a 160-acre park offering picnic areas, tennis courts, an outdoor performance center, a rose garden and Hi Corbett Field. **Hours:** Park open daily 6:30 a.m.-11 p.m. **Cost:** Free. **Phone:** (520) 791-4873.

Reid Park Zoo, off 22nd St. just w. of Alvernon Rd. in Gene C. Reid Park, houses more than 550 animals representing 150 species, including baboons, bears, giraffes, ostriches and zebras. Each habitat and species is fully described. Guests may feed and interact with giraffes at Giraffe Encounter, travel the perimeter of the zoo in a train in Reid Park and cool off in Kenya Get Wet, a water playground. **Time:** Allow 2 hours minimum. **Hours:** Daily 9-4, Sept.-May; 8-3, rest of year. Giraffe Encounter daily at 10. Closed Thanksgiving and Christmas. **Cost:** $7; $5 (ages 62+); $3 (ages 2-14). Giraffe Encounter $2. Train rides $2. **Phone:** (520) 791-4022 or (520) 791-4760.

INTERNATIONAL WILDLIFE MUSEUM is 5 mi. w. of I-10 on Speedway Blvd. to 4800 W. Gates Pass Rd. Tucson's interactive natural history museum contains dioramas depicting more than 400 species of mammals, insects, birds and prehistoric animals from around the world. Hands-on exhibits and interactive displays are found throughout the 40,000-square-foot museum.

A 98-seat theater offers hourly natural history films. **Hours:** Mon.-Fri. 9-5, Sat.-Sun. 9-6. Closed Thanksgiving and Christmas. **Cost:** $8; $6 (ages 62+ and military with ID); $3 (ages 4-12). **Phone:** (520) 629-0100. 🍴

THE MINI-TIME MACHINE MUSEUM OF MINIATURES is at 4455 E. Camp Lowell Dr., just w. of Swan Rd. The entry rotunda has a domed ceiling painted to look like the night sky; lining the walls are information panels explaining how miniatures are made. You'll watch a narrated introductory film in the Magic Theater before exploring the museum's three main areas: The History Gallery, Exploring the World and Enchanted Realm.

In The History Gallery you'll find miniature exhibits from the 1700s through the mid-1900s (think cutaways of English mansions and old New England homes). Exploring the World has everything from British pubs to Southwest adobes to Japanese farmhouses to train depots.

The Enchanted Realm's miniature miscellanea includes haunted mansions, medieval castles, dragons, pirate dioramas and a Christmas-themed exhibit. In the center of the gallery is the Enchanted Tree, a massive sculpture of a tree with eyes, a nose and a mouth.

Note: Flash photography is not permitted. **Time:** Allow 1 hour minimum. **Hours:** Tues.-Sat. 9-4. Closed major holidays. **Cost:** $7; $6 (ages 65+ and military with ID); $5 (ages 4-17). **Phone:** (520) 881-0606.

MISSION SAN XAVIER DEL BAC is 9 mi. s. off I-19 exit 92, on San Xavier Rd. in the Tohono O'odham Indian Reservation. Though founded by Jesuit Father Eusebio Francisco Kino before 1700, the present structure was built 1783-97 by the Franciscans. The missionaries were forced to leave San Xavier in 1828 but returned in 1911, and since that time have maintained old San Xavier as the main church and school of the Tohono O'odham.

This is the only Kino mission in the nation still active in preaching to the Tohono O'odham. Called the "White Dove of the Desert," the structure is an impressive example of Spanish mission architecture. The domes, carvings, arches and flying buttresses distinguish it from other missions. The interior murals and the altar are especially noteworthy.

A continuous video presentation is shown in the museum, and a self-guiding tour is available. **Hours:** Mission daily 7-5. Museum daily 8-4:30. **Cost:** Donations. **Phone:** (520) 294-2624.

OLD TUCSON is 12 mi. w. via Speedway Blvd. or Ajo Way in Tucson Mountain Park; follow signs. Erected in 1939, this replica of 1860s Tucson was the location for the movies "Arizona" and "Tombstone." More than 350 films and TV shows have been filmed here.

Highlights include a Native American village, stagecoach rides, live gunfights, stunt demonstrations, Western musical revues and the Film History Museum. Trail rides are offered.

Hours: Fri.-Sun. 10-6, June-Sept. Closed Thanksgiving, Christmas Eve and Christmas. Phone ahead to confirm schedule. **Cost:** $16.95; $10.95 (ages 4-11). **Phone:** (520) 883-0100. 🍴

PIMA AIR AND SPACE MUSEUM is at 6000 E. Valencia Rd.; from I-10 take exit 267. Displayed are 300 aircraft, including the DC-6 used by Presidents John F. Kennedy and Lyndon B. Johnson. Additional aircraft in hangars and along pathways include a replica 1903 Wright Flyer and a SR-71 Blackbird. One-hour bus tours of the Aircraft Maintenance and Regeneration Group (AMARG) facility on Davis-Monthan Air Force Base feature more than 4,400 U.S. military aircraft.

Note: Government-issued photo ID is required to enter the base, and visitors are not permitted to leave the bus. **Hours:** Museum daily 9-5. Last admission 1 hour before closing. Bus tour schedule varies; phone ahead. Closed Thanksgiving and Christmas. **Cost:** Museum Nov.-May $15.50; $12.75 (ages 62+ and military with ID); $9 (ages 7-12). Museum rest of year $13.75; $11.75 (ages 62+ and military with ID); $8 (ages 7-12). Bus tours $7; $4 (ages 7-12). **Phone:** (520) 574-0462. 🍴

390th Memorial Museum is at 6000 E. Valencia Rd. The museum honors the men of the 390th Bombardment Group, many of whom died while flying B-17 bombers in World War II. Exhibits include a B-17 (also known as the "Flying Fortress"), aircraft models, flight gear, guns, photos, a Quonset hut and other memorabilia. A 54-minute video presentation includes interviews with surviving members and actual film clips from the war.

Tours: Guided tours are available. **Time:** Allow 30 minutes minimum. **Hours:** Daily 10-4:30. Closed Thanksgiving and Christmas. **Cost:** Free with paid admission to Pima Air and Space Museum. **Phone:** (520) 574-0287.

THE POSTAL HISTORY FOUNDATION, 920 N. First Ave., features stamps, postmarks and books tracing the history of the U.S. Postal Service and caters to serious philatelists and postal historians as well as casual collectors. Original equipment from the Naco post office as well as antique file cabinets and post office memorabilia are on display.

An adjacent building houses a research library of philatelic literature and a collection of Civil War memorabilia, books and documents. **Tours:** Guided tours are available. **Time:** Allow 30 minutes minimum. **Hours:** Mon.-Fri. 8-3, Sat. 10-2. Closed major holidays. **Cost:** Donations. **Phone:** (520) 623-6652.

SABINO CANYON is at 5900 N. Sabino Canyon Rd., 17 mi. e. via Tanque Verde and Sabino Canyon rds. Part of the Coronado National

Forest *(see place listing p. 56)*, this desert oasis in the Santa Catalina Mountains offers spectacular panoramic views and a wide range of recreational activities. Visitors can hike along a network of trails; go horseback riding; take a dip in a swimming hole or waterfall; and observe javelinas, roadrunners, white-tailed deer and other native wildlife.

Sabino Canyon Tours offers narrated excursions into the canyon aboard shuttle buses. A shuttle also transports hikers to the Bear Canyon trailhead.

Note: Beware of mountain lions and rattlesnakes within the canyon. Pets are not permitted. **Time:** Allow 1 hour minimum. **Hours:** Visitor reception area daily 8:30-4:30. Phone ahead to confirm schedule. **Cost:** $5 (per private vehicle); free (interagency pass holders and those arriving on foot or bicycle). Sabino Canyon tour $8; $4 (ages 3-12). Bear Canyon shuttle $3; $1 (ages 3-12). Cash only. **Parking:** $5. **Phone:** (520) 749-8700. ⛲

SAGUARO NATIONAL PARK—
see place listing p. 203.

SENTINEL PEAK PARK, off Broadway w. of I-10 on Sentinel Peak Rd., contains the peak more popularly known as "A" Mountain because of the big "A" annually whitewashed on it by University of Arizona freshmen. It affords an excellent view of Tucson and surrounding mountains. At night the city's lights are particularly captivating from this vantage point. **Hours:** Mon.-Sat. 8-8, Sun. 8-6. **Phone:** (520) 791-5909.

SOUTHERN ARIZONA TRANSPORTATION MUSEUM is at 414 N. Toole Ave. Exhibits at this museum and interpretive center include artifacts and memorabilia relating to the history of the railroad and transportation in southern Arizona. The former Southern Pacific Railroad Depot has been restored to its 1941 design and includes a train depot. A historic 1900 steam locomotive is on display; visitors may see it close-up on Saturdays.

Tours: Guided tours are available. **Time:** Allow 30 minutes minimum. **Hours:** Tues.-Thurs. and Sun. 11-3, Fri.-Sat. 10-4. Locomotive access Sat. 10-1. Phone ahead for guided tour schedule. **Cost:** Donations. Guided tours $5. **Phone:** (520) 623-2223.

TOHONO CHUL PARK is at 7366 N. Paseo del Norte. Tohono O'odham for "desert corner," Tohono Chul Park is a 49-acre desert preserve set amid a rapidly growing urban area. The park features nature trails, a Geology Wall, a Children's Garden, a greenhouse and changing art exhibits. Displays educate visitors about water conservation, arid lands and the traditions and cultures of the Southwest. Guided and self-guiding tours are available.

Hours: Park open daily 8-5, Aug.-May; 7-3, rest of year. Exhibit building open daily 9-5. **Cost:** $8; $5 (ages 62+ and active military with ID); $3 (students with ID); $2 (ages 5-12). **Phone:** (520) 742-6455. 🍴

TUCSON BOTANICAL GARDENS, 2150 N. Alvernon Way, covers 5.5 acres and features Zen, children's, herb, historical, iris, sensory, bird-watching and xeriscape gardens as well as a Native American crop garden. Exhibits include a seasonal tropical butterfly house. Special events are held throughout the year.

Tours: Guided tours are available. **Hours:** Daily 8:30-4:30. Closed Jan. 1, July 4, Thanksgiving, Christmas Eve and Christmas. **Cost:** $8; $4 (ages 4-12). **Phone:** (520) 326-9686. 🍴

TUCSON MOUNTAIN PARK, 8 mi. w. on Speedway Blvd. and Kinney Rd., encompasses approximately 20,000 acres of the Tucson Mountains and adjoining mesa land and embraces one of the largest areas of saguaro and natural desert growth in the Southwest. Camping is available at the Gilbert Ray Campground. Trails for hiking and horseback riding are available.

Hours: Park open daily dawn-dusk. **Cost:** Park free. Camping $10-$20 per night. **Phone:** (520) 877-6000, or (520) 883-4200 for campground information. ⛲

TUCSON MUSEUM OF ART AND HISTORIC BLOCK is at 140 N. Main Ave. Visitors can view collections of Latin American, Western, Asian, modern and contemporary art. The museum also comprises five homes built 1850-1907 in the El Presidio Historic District, including adobe structures housing Western and Latin American collections; the J. Knox Corbett House, a Mission Revival bungalow with Arts and Crafts *objets d'art* (open October through April); and La Casa Cordova, a Mexican-style adobe home (open November through April). A library and changing art exhibits are featured, and art lectures and classes are offered.

Tours: Guided tours are available. **Hours:** Museum Tues.-Sat. 10-6, Sun. noon-6. Closed major holidays. **Cost:** Museum $8; $6 (ages 60+ and veterans with ID); $3 (students with ID); free (ages 0-12, active military with ID and on first Sun. of the month). Guided tours free with paid admission. **Phone:** (520) 624-2333.

UNIVERSITY OF ARIZONA, bounded by Euclid Ave., E. Helen St., Campbell Ave. and E. 7th St., was founded in 1885 as the state's first institution of higher learning. Today the campus encompasses 353 acres and is one of the nation's top research universities. A 1.5-hour guided walking tour of the campus is available; tours depart from the main lobby of the old varsity building. **Hours:** Walking tour Mon.-Fri. at 10 and 2, Sat. at 2, Sept.-May; Mon., Wed. and Fri.-Sat. at 9, rest of year. **Cost:** Free. **Phone:** (520) 621-3641.

Center for Creative Photography is at 1030 N. Olive Rd., n. of 2nd St. The center houses more than 60,000 photographs representing the work of about 1,400 photographers, one of the most comprehensive collections in the world. Temporary exhibitions are on display.

The center's library contains more than 10,000 monographs, catalogs, books and periodicals. Videotaped interviews and lectures and the archives of major photographers are available for viewing. **Hours:** Building and gallery Mon.-Fri. 9-5, Sat.-Sun. 1-4. Library Mon.-Fri. 11-3. PrintViewing room Mon.-Fri. 2-4, Sept.-Apr.; Mon., Wed. and Fri. 2-4, rest of year. Closed major holidays. Phone ahead to confirm schedule.

Cost: Donations. Reservations are recommended for the PrintViewing room. Metered public parking is available in the visitor section of the Park Avenue Garage, just n. of Speedway Blvd., with direct pedestrian access to the center's front door. **Phone:** (520) 621-7968.

Mineral Museum, on the lower level of UA Science: Flandrau at 1601 E. University Blvd., displays fine gems, meteorites and mineral specimens from around the world. The museum specializes in minerals from Arizona and Mexico. Visitors can use a microscope to see micro-size specimens. **Hours:** Mon.-Thurs. 10-3 (also Thurs. 6-9 p.m.), Fri.-Sat. 10-7 and 8-11, Sun. noon-5. Closed major holidays. Phone ahead to confirm schedule. **Cost:** (Includes UA Science: Flandrau) $7.50; $5 (ages 4-15). **Phone:** (520) 621-4227.

UA Science: Flandrau, 1601 E. University Blvd., is filled with hands-on, interactive exhibits geared toward school-aged kids. You can view a slide show of astronomy photos on a high-definition flat-screen TV and pose in front of a camera that projects an infrared image of you on a big wall-mounted screen.

Must-sees include an Apollo display featuring a model of the Saturn V rocket; a raised-relief wall map of the Martian surface; and a zoetrope (a drum-shaped object that, when spun, makes a series of static pictures appear to move) exhibit. A planetarium presents astronomy and laser-light shows, and a 16-inch telescope is available for night viewing in the observatory.

Time: Allow 1 hour minimum. **Hours:** Mon.-Fri. 10-3 (also Thurs.-Fri. 6-9 p.m.), Sat. 10-9, Sun. 1-4. Observatory Wed.-Sat. 7-10 p.m. (weather permitting). Phone for planetarium show options and schedule. Closed major holidays. **Cost:** (Includes Mineral Museum) $7.50; $5 (ages 4-15). Phone for laser-light show prices. **Phone:** (520) 621-7827.

University of Arizona Museum of Art, s.e. corner of Park Ave. and Speedway Blvd. in the Fine Arts Complex, features the Samuel H. Kress Collection, with more than 60 European paintings, sculptures and decorative objects from the 14th through the 19th centuries. Among the museum's 20th-century paintings and sculptures are works by Mark Rothko, Jackson Pollock and Helen Frankenthaler. A collection of models and sculptures by Jacques Lipchitz

may be seen. Six galleries of changing exhibits also are offered.

Time: Allow 1 hour minimum. **Hours:** Tues.-Fri. 9-5, Sat.-Sun. noon-4. Closed major holidays. **Cost:** $5; free (ages 0-18 and students and military with ID). Hourly-rate parking is available. **Phone:** (520) 621-7567.

UNIVERSITY OF ARIZONA-BIOSPHERE 2—
see Oracle p. 122.
GAMBLING ESTABLISHMENTS
• **Casino of the Sun,** I-19 Valencia exit, 4.5 mi. w., then .5 mi. s. to 7474 S. Camino de Oeste. **Hours:** Daily 24 hours. **Phone:** (520) 879-5405 or (800) 344-9435.
• **Desert Diamond Casino,** I-19 Valencia exit, 1 mi. e., then 1 mi. s. to 7350 S. Nogales Hwy. **Hours:** Daily 24 hours. **Phone:** (520) 294-7777 or (866) 332-9467.

Sightseeing
Bus Tours
[SAVE] Gray Line, (520) 622-8811 or (800) 276-1528, offers sightseeing tours to Tucson's major sites as well as trips to Tombstone and the Grand Canyon. Overnight and multiple-day tours are available.

Walking Tours
For those who prefer to explore the city and its environs on their own, the *Visit Tucson Official Destination Guide,* distributed by the Metropolitan Tucson Convention and Visitors Bureau, 100 S. Church Ave., contains walking tour information; phone (520) 624-1817 or (800) 638-8350 to have a free copy mailed to you before your trip. Visitors may also pick up a destination guide at the Tucson Visitor Center at 110 S. Church Ave., Suite 7199 (in La Placita plaza), Mon.-Fri. 9-5, Sat.-Sun. 9-4.

While you're there ask for the free Presidio Trail Historical Walking Tour brochure, which includes a map of the Presidio Trail, a bright turquoise stripe painted on the sidewalks that wind through the heart of downtown Tucson. The 2.5-mile trail begins at the intersection of Church and Washington streets and passes more than 20 numbered historical sites, including the Pima County Courthouse and the Tucson Museum of Art and Historic Block *(see attraction listings).* If you follow the trail without the walking tour brochure and its written descriptions, don't worry; most sites on the tour are marked by plaques.

Find valuable AAA/CAA

member savings

at AAA.com/discounts

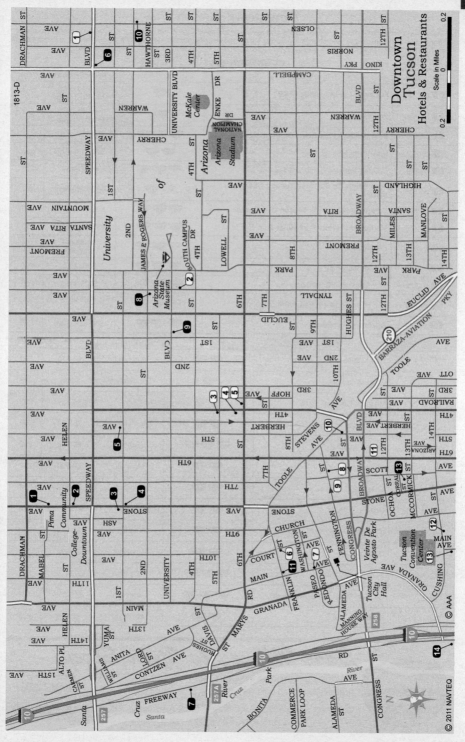

Downtown
Tucson
Hotels & Restaurants

Scale in Miles

© 2011 NAVTEQ

© AAA

Downtown Tucson

This index helps you "spot" where approved hotels and restaurants are located on the corresponding detailed maps. Hotel daily rate range is for comparison only and show the property's high season. Restaurant rate range is a combination of lunch and/or dinner. Turn to the listing page for more detailed rate information and consult display ads for special promotions.

DOWNTOWN TUCSON

Map Page	Hotels	Diamond Rated	High Season	Page
1 p. 279	Rodeway Inn-University of AZ	▽	Rates not provided (SAVE)	291
2 p. 279	Econo Lodge	▽	Rates not provided (SAVE)	291
3 p. 279	Best Western Plus Royal Sun Inn & Suites	▽ ▽ ▽	$70-$170 (SAVE)	291
4 p. 279	University Inn	▽ ▽	$49-$139 (SAVE)	292
5 p. 279	Catalina Park Inn Bed and Breakfast	▽ ▽ ▽	$139-$189	291
6 p. 279	Four Points by Sheraton Tucson University Plaza	▽ ▽	$60-$260 (SAVE)	291
7 p. 279	Country Inn & Suites Tucson City Center	▽ ▽ ▽	$99-$199 (SAVE)	291
8 p. 279	Marriott University Park Hotel	▽ ▽ ▽	$99-$180 (SAVE)	291
9 p. 279	Peppertrees Inn	▽ ▽ ▽	Rates not provided	291
10 p. 279	Adobe Rose Inn	▽ ▽ ▽	$90-$230	290
11 p. 279	El Presidio Bed & Breakfast Inn	▽ ▽ ▽	$125-$155	291
13 p. 279	The Royal Elizabeth Bed & Breakfast Inn	▽ ▽ ▽	Rates not provided	292
14 p. 279	Arizona Riverpark Inn	▽ ▽ ▽	$89-$299 (SAVE)	290

Map Page	Restaurants	Diamond Rated	Cuisine	Meal Range	Page
① p. 279	Trident Grill	▽ ▽	American	$7-$15	293
② p. 279	Silver Mine Subs	▽	Sandwiches	$5-$8	293
③ p. 279	Magpie's Gourmet Pizza	▽ ▽	Pizza	$5-$24	293
④ p. 279	Delectables	▽ ▽	International	$8-$20	292
⑤ p. 279	Athens on 4th Ave	▽ ▽ ▽	Greek	$9-$25	292
⑥ p. 279	El Charro Cafe	▽ ▽	Mexican	$9-$20	292
⑦ p. 279	Café a la C'Art	▽ ▽	American	$8-$12	292
⑧ p. 279	Cafe Poca Cosa	▽ ▽	Mexican	$13-$25	292
⑨ p. 279	47 Scott	▽ ▽	American	$9-$19	292
⑩ p. 279	Cup Cafe	▽ ▽	American	$8-$22	292
⑪ p. 279	DOWNTOWN Kitchen + Cocktails	▽ ▽ ▽	American	$12-$32	292
⑫ p. 279	Cushing Street Bar & Restaurant	▽ ▽ ▽	American	$12-$19	292
⑬ p. 279	El Minuto Cafe	▽ ▽	Mexican	$7-$14	293

Save Money in Your Sleep

Members get the best available room rates with AAA/CAA preferred lodging partners.

Visit over 1,100 AAA/CAA Offices   **Click** AAA.com/CAA.ca
Call 1-866-AAA-SAVE (222-7283)

Show Your Card & Save
Preferred Hotels

Don't Take A Vacation From Your Car Seat

Vacations should be fun and hassle-free. Hertz provides free use of a child seat with every vehicle rental for AAA members! Contact your AAA travel counselor or visit us at AAA.com/hertz for reservations.

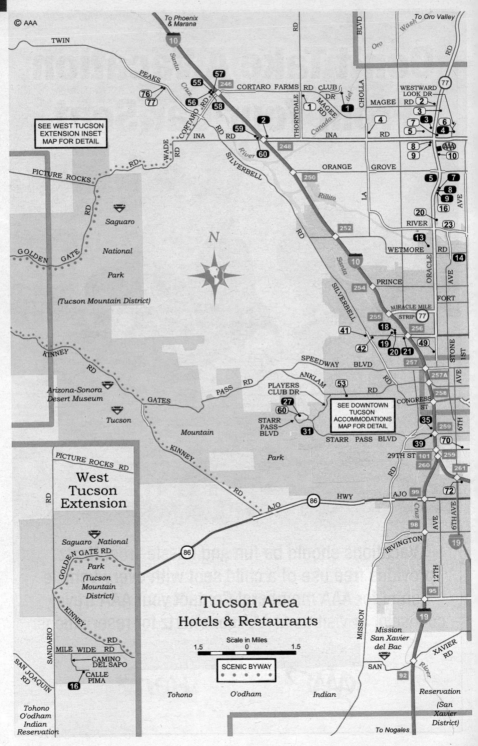

© AAA

Tucson Area
Hotels & Restaurants

Scale in Miles
1.5   0   1.5

SCENIC BYWAY
• • • • • • •

West
Tucson
Extension

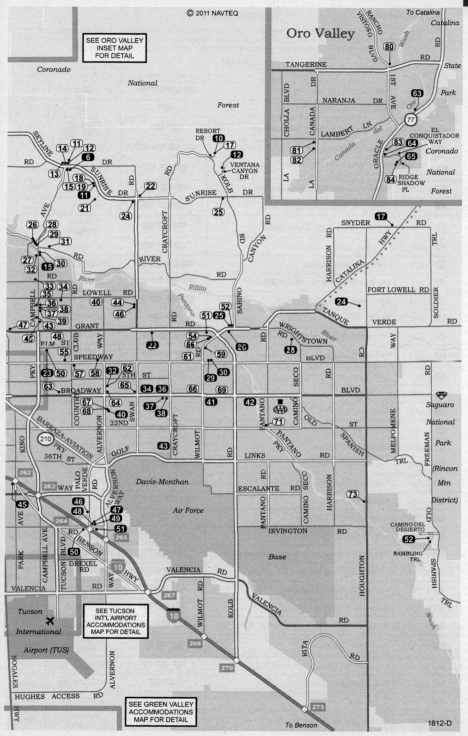

© 2011 NAVTEQ

Oro Valley

1812-D

Tucson Area

This index helps you "spot" where approved hotels and restaurants are located on the corresponding detailed maps. Hotel daily rate range is for comparison only and show the property's high season. Restaurant rate range is a combination of lunch and/or dinner. Turn to the listing page for more detailed rate information and consult display ads for special promotions.

TUCSON

Map Page	Hotels	Diamond Rated	High Season	Page
1 p. 282	**Omni Tucson National Resort**	▼▼▼▼	$109-$459 (SAVE)	301
2 p. 282	Motel 6 Tucson North #1127	▼	$51-$61	301
3 p. 282	**Oracle Foothills Quality Inn & Suites**	▼▼	Rates not provided (SAVE)	301
4 p. 282	**Westward Look Resort** *(See ad p. 305.)*	▼▼▼▼	$149-$449 (SAVE)	305
5 p. 282	**Best Western Plus InnSuites Tucson Foothills Hotel & Suites**	▼▼▼	$79-$169 (SAVE)	293
6 p. 282	**Embassy Suites Tucson-Paloma Village**	▼▼▼	$99-$289 (SAVE)	296
7 p. 282	TownePlace Suites by Marriott	▼▼▼	$99-$199	304
8 p. 282	Hampton Inn & Suites Tucson Mall	▼▼▼	Rates not provided	297
9 p. 282	La Posada Lodge & Casitas	▼▼▼	$105-$172	300
10 p. 282	**Loews Ventana Canyon**	▼▼▼▼	$149-$449 (SAVE)	301
11 p. 282	**The Westin La Paloma Resort & Spa**	▼▼▼▼	$99-$539 (SAVE)	305
12 p. 282	**The Lodge @ Ventana Canyon**	▼▼▼▼	$149-$799 (SAVE)	301
13 p. 282	Comfort Suites at Tucson Mall	▼▼	$100-$220	294
14 p. 282	Holiday Inn Express Hotel & Suites-Tucson Mall	▼▼▼	$139-$299	298
15 p. 282	**Windmill Suites at St. Philip's Plaza**	▼▼▼	Rates not provided (SAVE)	305
16 p. 282	Casa Tierra Adobe B&B Inn	▼▼▼	$165-$285	293
17 p. 282	Jeremiah Inn Bed & Breakfast	▼▼▼	$120-$150	300
18 p. 282	Super 8-Tucson	▼▼	$49-$99	304
19 p. 282	Holiday Inn Express Inn & Suites-Grant Rd	▼▼▼	$79-$149	298
20 p. 282	Comfort Inn-Grant Rd	▼▼	$60-$120	294
21 p. 282	Hampton Inn Tucson North	▼▼▼	$89-$159	297
22 p. 282	Extended StayAmerica-Tucson-Grant Rd	▼▼	$70-$80	296
23 p. 282	**Arizona Inn**	▼▼▼▼	$329-$579 (SAVE)	293
24 p. 282	Indian Hill Bed & Breakfast	▼▼▼	$120-$175	299
25 p. 282	Comfort Suites at Sabino Canyon	▼▼	$89-$139	294
26 p. 282	**Ramada Foothills Inn & Suites** *(See ad p. 303.)*	▼▼▼	$64-$169 (SAVE)	301
27 p. 282	JW Marriott Starr Pass Resort & Spa	▼▼▼▼	$299-$351	300
28 p. 282	The Inns at El Rancho Merlita	▼▼▼	$99-$295	299
29 p. 282	Residence Inn by Marriott-Tucson	▼▼▼	$99-$209	303
30 p. 282	**Radisson Suites Tucson** *(See ad p. 302.)*	▼▼▼	$76-$269 (SAVE)	301
31 p. 282	**Starr Pass Golf Suites**	▼▼▼	Rates not provided (SAVE)	304
32 p. 282	**Lodge on the Desert** *(See ad p. 300.)*	▼▼▼	$109-$429 (SAVE)	300
34 p. 282	**Viscount Suite Hotel**	▼▼	$79-$225 (SAVE)	304
35 p. 282	**Travelodge**	▼	$29-$81 (SAVE)	304
36 p. 282	Embassy Suites Tucson-Williams Center	▼▼▼	Rates not provided	296

TUCSON (cont'd)

Map Page	Hotels (cont'd)	Diamond Rated	High Season	Page
37 p. 282	Courtyard by Marriott-Tucson Williams Centre	◆◆◆	$84-$193	294
38 p. 282	Residence Inn by Marriott Williams Centre	◆◆◆	$98-$359	304
39 p. 282	**Super 8 Downtown Tucson Convention Area**	◆◆	$49-$117 (SAVE)	304
40 p. 282	**DoubleTree by Hilton Tucson - Reid Park**	◆◆◆	$179-$299 (SAVE)	296
41 p. 282	La Quinta Inn Tucson East	◆◆	$58-$144	300
42 p. 282	**Hilton Tucson East** *(See ad p. 299.)*	◆◆◆	$139-$159 (SAVE)	298
43 p. 282	**Super 8 Central East**	◆	$36-$80 (SAVE)	304
45 p. 282	**Americas Best Value Inn-Tucson**	◆◆	$44-$160 (SAVE)	293
46 p. 282	Holiday Inn Hotel & Suites-Tucson Airport North	◆◆◆	$59-$189	298
47 p. 282	Crossland Economy Studios-Tucson-Butterfield Dr	◆	$60-$70	295
48 p. 282	**Days Inn Airport**	◆◆	$41-$85 (SAVE)	295
49 p. 282	Fairfield Inn Tucson I-10 by Marriott	◆◆	$77-$113	296
50 p. 282	Studio 6 Extended Stay #6002	◆◆	$53-$63	304
51 p. 282	**Red Roof Inn-Tucson South**	◆	$39-$120 (SAVE)	302
52 p. 282	Hacienda del Desierto	◆◆◆	$129-$279	296

Map Page	Restaurants	Diamond Rated	Cuisine	Meal Range	Page
1 p. 282	Colt's Taste of Texas	◆◆	Steak	$8-$26	307
2 p. 282	Michelangelo Ristorante Italiano	◆◆◆	Italian	$9-$29	310
3 p. 282	Metropolitan Grill	◆◆◆	American	$6-$21	310
4 p. 282	Mosaic Cafe Dos	◆◆	Mexican	$8-$16	310
5 p. 282	Tohono Chul Park Tea Room	◆◆	American	$8-$16	312
6 p. 282	**Gold** *(See ad p. 305.)*	◆◆◆◆	American	$12-$29	308
7 p. 282	Jax Kitchen	◆◆◆	American	$13-$24	308
8 p. 282	Bluefin Seafood Bistro	◆◆◆	Seafood	$9-$29	306
9 p. 282	Wildflower Tucson	◆◆◆	American	$10-$29	312
10 p. 282	Hi Falutin Western Grill	◆◆◆	American	$9-$25	308
11 p. 282	**Anthony's In The Catalinas**	◆◆◆◆	Continental	$30-$55	306
12 p. 282	Acacia	◆◆◆	New American	$18-$29	306
13 p. 282	Firebirds Wood Fired Grill	◆◆◆	American	$8-$35	307
14 p. 282	NoRTH	◆◆◆	New Italian	$9-$28	310
15 p. 282	Fleming's Prime Steakhouse & Wine Bar	◆◆◆	Steak	$19-$50	308
16 p. 282	Miguel's at La Posada	◆◆◆	Latin American	$9-$29	310
17 p. 282	Flying V Bar & Grill	◆◆◆	Regional Southwestern	$15-$26	308
18 p. 282	**Janos**	◆◆◆◆	French	$28-$50	308
19 p. 282	J Bar-A Latin Grill	◆◆◆	Caribbean	$13-$28	308
20 p. 282	Chantilly Tea Room	◆◆	Specialty	$6-$27	306
21 p. 282	**The Grill at Hacienda del Sol**	◆◆◆◆	Southwestern	$24-$38	308
22 p. 282	Bazil's	◆◆◆	Regional Italian	$15-$40	306

Map Page	Restaurants (cont'd)	Diamond Rated	Cuisine	Meal Range	Page
㉓ p. 282	Zona 78	◆◆	Italian	$9-$16	312
㉔ p. 282	Trattoria Pina	◆◆	Italian	$8-$35	312
㉕ p. 282	Risky Business	◆◆	American	$8-$23	311
㉖ p. 282	Om Modern Asian Kitchen	◆◆◆	Asian	$8-$24	310
㉗ p. 282	Sullivan's Steakhouse	◆◆◆	Steak	$20-$65	312
㉘ p. 282	P.F. Chang's China Bistro	◆◆◆	Chinese	$8-$21	311
㉙ p. 282	Zinburger	◆◆	Specialty	$8-$14	312
㉚ p. 282	Vivace Restaurant	◆◆◆	Italian	$12-$33	312
㉛ p. 282	El Corral Steakhouse	◆◆	American	$10-$20	307
㉜ p. 282	Choice Greens	◆◆	Specialty	$5-$10	306
㉝ p. 282	Ghinis French Caffe	◆◆	French	$6-$13	308
㉞ p. 282	Cody's Beef 'n Beans	◆◆	Steak	$7-$20	307
㉟ p. 282	Pastiche Modern Eatery	◆◆◆	American	$8-$25	311
㊱ p. 282	Beyond Bread	◆◆	American	$7-$11	306
㊲ p. 282	Opa! Greek Cuisine & Fun	◆◆	Greek	$9-$14	310
㊳ p. 282	Lovin' Spoonfuls	◆◆	Vegetarian	$6-$12	309
㊴ p. 282	elle wine bistro	◆◆◆	American	$12-$30	307
㊵ p. 282	Le Rendez-vous	◆◆◆	French	$10-$50	309
㊶ p. 282	Teresa's Mosaic Cafe	◆◆	Mexican	$8-$16	312
㊷ p. 282	Rusty's Family Restaurant & Sports Grille	◆◆	American	$6-$17	311
㊸ p. 282	India Oven	◆◆	Indian	$10-$15	308
㊹ p. 282	Chad's Steakhouse & Saloon	◆◆	Steak	$8-$24	306
㊺ p. 282	Blue Willow Restaurant Bakery	◆◆	American	$8-$13	306
㊻ p. 282	McMahon's Steakhouse	◆◆◆	Steak	$8-$60	310
㊼ p. 282	Sher-E-Punjab	◆◆	Indian	$8-$14	311
㊽ p. 282	Kingfisher	◆◆◆	Regional American	$8-$26	309
㊾ p. 282	La Fuente Restaurant	◆◆	Mexican	$8-$19	309
㊿ p. 282	Main Dining Room at the Arizona Inn	◆◆◆◆	Continental	$12-$40	309
51 p. 282	Montana Avenue	◆◆◆	Regional American	$14-$25	310
52 p. 282	The Eclectic Cafe	◆◆	American	$6-$14	307
53 p. 282	Daisy Mae's Steakhouse	◆◆	Steak	$15-$31	307
54 p. 282	Dakota Cafe & Catering Company	◆◆◆	American	$9-$30	307
55 p. 282	Choice Greens	◆◆	Specialty	$7-$9	306
56 p. 282	Pinnacle Peak Restaurant	◆	Steak	$9-$23	311
57 p. 282	The Dish Bistro Bar	◆◆◆	American	$19-$34	307
58 p. 282	Feast	◆◆	American	$9-$18	307

Map Page	Restaurants (cont'd)	Diamond Rated	Cuisine	Meal Range	Page
59 p. 282	Jonathan's Cork	▽▽▽	Southwestern	$15-$38	308
60 p. 282	**Primo**	▽▽▽▽	Regional Italian	$26-$42	311
61 p. 282	Lotus Garden	▽▽	Chinese	$7-$23	309
62 p. 282	Lodge on the Desert	▽▽▽	American	$11-$32	309
63 p. 282	Zemam's	▽▽	Ethiopian	$7-$13	312
64 p. 282	Old Pueblo Grill	▽▽▽	Regional American	$10-$20	310
65 p. 282	The Hungry Fox Restaurant and Country Store	▽▽	American	$5-$10	308
66 p. 282	Neo of Melaka	▽▽	Asian	$7-$29	310
67 p. 282	Cactus Rose Steakhouse	▽▽	Steak	$14-$35	306
68 p. 282	Javelina Cantina	▽▽	Southwestern	$12-$23	308
69 p. 282	Delhi Palace	▽▽	Indian	$8-$16	307
70 p. 282	Mi Nidito Family Restaurant	▽▽	Mexican	$5-$13	310
71 p. 282	Casa del Rio	▽▽	Mexican	$5-$12	306
72 p. 282	Silver Saddle Steakhouse	▽▽	Steak	$6-$55	311
73 p. 282	Tucson McGraw's Original Cantina	▽▽	American	$6-$24	312

MARANA

Map Page	Hotels	Diamond Rated	High Season	Page
55 p. 282	**Comfort Inn & Suites**	▽▽	$119-$209 SAVE	110
56 p. 282	La Quinta Inn & Suites NW Tucson Marana	▽▽▽	$139-$215	110
57 p. 282	**Days Inn & Suites-Tucson/Marana**	▽▽	$45-$118 SAVE	110
58 p. 282	Holiday Inn Express	▽▽▽	$149-$399	110
59 p. 282	**Red Roof Inn Tucson North**	▽▽	$41-$125 SAVE	110
60 p. 282	Comfort Inn I-10 & Ina	▽▽	Rates not provided	110

Map Page	Restaurants	Diamond Rated	Cuisine	Meal Range	Page
76 p. 282	La Olla Mexican Cafe	▽▽	Mexican	$7-$15	110
77 p. 282	Li'l Abner's Steakhouse	▽▽	Steak	$14-$34	110

ORO VALLEY

Map Page	Hotels	Diamond Rated	High Season	Page
63 p. 282	Oro Valley Hotel & Suites	▽▽▽	$94-$147	122
64 p. 282	Fairfield Inn & Suites Tucson North/Oro Valley	▽▽▽	$109-$162	122
65 p. 282	**Hilton Tucson El Conquistador Golf & Tennis Resort**	▽▽▽▽	Rates not provided SAVE	122

Map Page	Restaurants	Diamond Rated	Cuisine	Meal Range	Page
80 p. 282	Dragon Village Restaurant	▽▽	Chinese	$7-$11	123
81 p. 282	Harvest	▽▽▽	Regional American	$12-$25	123
82 p. 282	Caffe Torino Ristorante Italiano	▽▽	Italian	$7-$15	122
83 p. 282	The Loop Taste of Chicago	▽▽	Pizza	$6-$19	123
84 p. 282	Dos Locos	▽▽▽	Southwestern	$15-$28	123

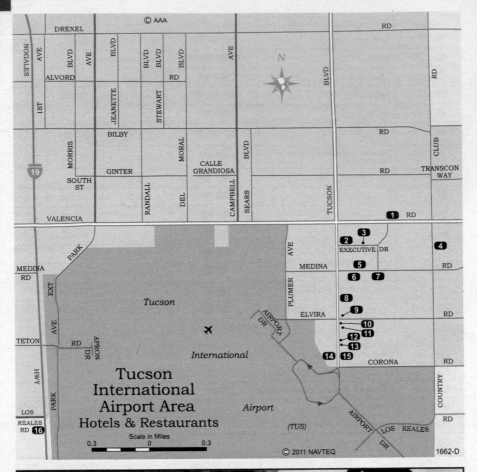

Tucson International Airport Area
Hotels & Restaurants

Scale in Miles

© 2011 NAVTEQ

1662-D

Are we meeting your travel needs?

Are we meeting your travel needs?
Contact us at: www.AAA.com/TourBookComments
or
Member Comments
1000 AAA Drive - Box 61, Heathrow, FL 32746-5063

If your visit to a listed property doesn't meet your expectations, now you can tell us about it immediately, instead of waiting until you're home.

Visit **AAA.com/TourBookComments** to complete an easy online form

✈ Airport Accommodations

Map Page	TUCSON INTERNATIONAL	Diamond Rated	High Season	Page
8 p. 288	Clarion Hotel Tucson Airport, just n of entrance	♦♦♦	$55-$102	294
10 p. 288	**Comfort Suites Tucson Airport, just n of entrance**	♦♦	$79-$169 SAVE	294
5 p. 288	**Country Inn & Suites By Carlson, Tucson-Airport, 0.4 mi n of entrance**	♦♦♦	$79-$169 SAVE	294
2 p. 288	Courtyard by Marriott-Tucson Airport, 0.6 mi n of entrance	♦♦♦	$71-$175	294
11 p. 288	**Fairfield Inn by Marriott at Tucson Airport, just n of entrance**	♦♦♦	$66-$132 SAVE	296
14 p. 288	**Four Points by Sheraton Tucson Airport, at terminal entrance**	♦♦♦	$79-$219 SAVE	296
12 p. 288	Hampton Inn Tucson Airport, just n of entrance	♦♦♦	$79-$209	297
4 p. 288	Hilton Garden Inn Tucson Airport, 0.4 mi ne of entrance	♦♦♦	$119-$169	297
6 p. 288	**Holiday Inn Express Tucson Airport, 0.5 mi n of entrance**	♦♦♦	$169-$189 SAVE	298
9 p. 288	**Hyatt Place Tucson Airport, just n of entrance**	♦♦♦	$79-$249 SAVE	298
13 p. 288	La Quinta Inn & Suites Tucson Airport, just n of entrance	♦♦♦	$68-$159	300
1 p. 288	**Quality Inn at Tucson Airport, 1 mi ne of entrance**	♦♦	$59-$139 SAVE	301
15 p. 288	Radisson Suites Hotel Tucson Airport, at entrance	♦♦♦	$89-$189	301
7 p. 288	Residence Inn Tucson Airport, 0.5 mi n of entrance	♦♦♦	$89-$249	304
3 p. 200	Staybridge Suites Tucson Airport, 0.7 mi n of entrance	♦♦♦	$109-$249	304

Tucson International Airport

This index helps you "spot" where approved hotels and restaurants are located on the corresponding detailed maps. Hotel daily rate range is for comparison only and show the property's high season. Restaurant rate range is a combination of lunch and/or dinner. Turn to the listing page for more detailed rate information and consult display ads for special promotions.

TUCSON

Map Page	Hotels	Diamond Rated	High Season	Page
1 p. 288	**Quality Inn at Tucson Airport**	♦♦	$59-$139 SAVE	301
2 p. 288	Courtyard by Marriott-Tucson Airport	♦♦♦	$71-$175	294
3 p. 288	Staybridge Suites Tucson Airport	♦♦♦	$109-$249	304
4 p. 288	Hilton Garden Inn Tucson Airport	♦♦♦	$119-$169	297
5 p. 288	**Country Inn & Suites By Carlson, Tucson-Airport**	♦♦♦	$79-$169 SAVE	294
6 p. 288	**Holiday Inn Express Tucson Airport**	♦♦♦	$169-$189 SAVE	298
7 p. 288	Residence Inn Tucson Airport	♦♦♦	$89-$249	304
8 p. 288	Clarion Hotel Tucson Airport	♦♦♦	$55-$102	294
9 p. 288	**Hyatt Place Tucson Airport**	♦♦♦	$79-$249 SAVE	298
10 p. 288	**Comfort Suites Tucson Airport**	♦♦	$79-$169 SAVE	294
11 p. 288	**Fairfield Inn by Marriott at Tucson Airport**	♦♦♦	$66-$132 SAVE	296
12 p. 288	Hampton Inn Tucson Airport (See ad p. 298.)	♦♦♦	$79-$209	297
13 p. 288	La Quinta Inn & Suites Tucson Airport	♦♦♦	$68-$159	300
14 p. 288	**Four Points by Sheraton Tucson Airport (See ad p. 297.)**	♦♦♦	$79-$219 SAVE	296
15 p. 288	Radisson Suites Hotel Tucson Airport	♦♦♦	$89-$189	301
16 p. 288	**Desert Diamond Hotel & Casino**	♦♦♦	$99-$209 SAVE	296

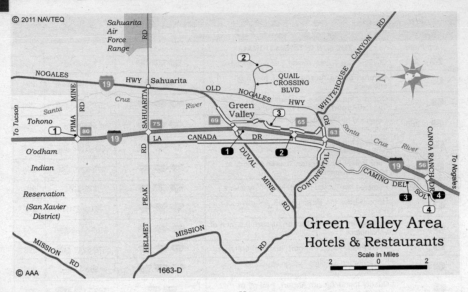

© 2011 NAVTEQ

Green Valley Area
Hotels & Restaurants

Scale in Miles

© AAA   1663-D

Green Valley Area

This index helps you "spot" where approved hotels and restaurants are located on the corresponding detailed maps. Hotel daily rate range is for comparison only and show the property's high season. Restaurant rate range is a combination of lunch and/or dinner. Turn to the listing page for more detailed rate information and consult display ads for special promotions.

GREEN VALLEY

Map Page	Hotels	Diamond Rated	High Season	Page
1 this page	Holiday Inn Express	◆◆	Rates not provided	97
2 this page	**Comfort Inn**	◆◆◆	$110-$120 SAVE	97
3 this page	**Inn at San Ignacio Condo Hotel**	◆◆◆	$79-$169 SAVE	97
4 this page	**Wyndham Canoa Ranch Resort** *(See ad p. 97.)*	◆◆◆	$79-$379 SAVE	97

Map Page	Restaurants	Diamond Rated	Cuisine	Meal Range	Page
1 this page	Agave at Desert Diamond Casino	◆◆	Regional American	$13-$25	97
2 this page	Grill at Quail Creek	◆◆◆	American	$8-$22	97
3 this page	Lavender	◆◆◆	French	$8-$28	98
4 this page	Grill on the Green at Canoa Ranch Golf Club	◆◆◆	American	$8-$30	98

DOWNTOWN TUCSON

- Restaurants p. 292
- Hotels & Restaurants map & index p. 279

ADOBE ROSE INN

◆◆◆
Bed & Breakfast
$90-$230

Phone: (520)318-4644 **10**

Address: 940 N Olsen Ave 85719 **Location:** I-10 exit 257 (Speedway Blvd), 2.5 mi e, then just s. Located in a quiet residential area. **Facility:** Built in 1933, this adobe home located in a residential area has a charming, brick-faced courtyard shaded by tall trees. Some rooms feature a cozy fireplace. 6 units, some kitchens. 1-2 stories (no elevator), interior/exterior corridors. **Terms:** check-in 4 pm, age restrictions may apply, 14 day cancellation notice-fee imposed. **Pool(s):** outdoor. **Activities:** whirlpool. *Fee:* massage. **Guest Services:** complimentary laundry.

ARIZONA RIVERPARK INN

◆◆◆
Hotel
$89-$299 2/1-4/30
$69-$249 5/1-1/31

Phone: (520)239-2300 **14**

Address: 350 S Freeway 85745 **Location:** I-10 exit 258 (Broadway Blvd/Congress St), just w, then 0.4 mi s. **Facility:** 174 units. 2 stories (no elevator), interior/exterior corridors. **Terms:** 3 day cancellation notice-fee imposed. **Amenities:** high-speed Internet, safes. **Pool(s):** heated outdoor. **Activities:** whirlpool, lighted tennis court, hiking trails, shuffleboard, exercise room. **Guest Services:** valet and coin laundry. **Free Special Amenities:** full breakfast and high-speed Internet.

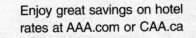

Enjoy great savings on hotel rates at AAA.com or CAA.ca

(See map & index p. 279.)

BEST WESTERN PLUS ROYAL SUN INN & SUITES
Phone: (520)622-8871   **3**

▼▼▼▼
Hotel
$70-$170

AAA Benefit: Members save up to 20%, plus 10% bonus points with Best Western Rewards®.

Address: 1015 N Stone Ave 85705 **Location:** I-10 exit 257 (Speedway Blvd), 0.8 mi e, then just s. **Facility:** 79 units. 2 stories (no elevator), exterior corridors. **Amenities:** high-speed Internet. **Pool(s):** heated outdoor. **Activities:** whirlpool, exercise room. **Free Special Amenities:** full breakfast and high-speed Internet.

SAVE ECO [icons] / SOME UNITS FEE [icon]

CATALINA PARK INN BED AND BREAKFAST
Phone: 520/792-4541   **5**

▼▼▼▼
Bed & Breakfast
$139-$189

Address: 309 E 1st St 85705 **Location:** I-10 exit 257 (Speedway Blvd), 1 mi e to 5th Ave, just s, then just e. Located in West University Historic District. **Facility:** This 1927 Spanish Mission-style home in the historic district has attractively appointed rooms. Lush gardens, a porch and arbors surround the house. 5 units. 1-2 stories (no elevator), interior/exterior corridors. **Parking:** street only. **Terms:** open 2/1-6/15 & 9/15-1/31, office hours 8 am-9 pm, check-in 4 pm, 2 night minimum stay - seasonal and/or weekends, age restrictions may apply, 14 day cancellation notice-fee imposed. [icons] / SOME UNITS [icon]

COUNTRY INN & SUITES TUCSON CITY CENTER
Phone: (520)867-6200   **7**

▼▼▼▼
Hotel
$99-$199 2/1-4/30
$69-$149 5/1-1/31

Address: 705 N Freeway 85745 **Location:** I-10 exit 257 (St. Mary's Rd/Speedway Blvd), just w, then just s. **Facility:** 79 units. 3 stories, interior corridors. **Amenities:** high-speed Internet. **Pool(s):** heated outdoor. **Activities:** whirlpool, exercise room. **Guest Services:** valet and coin laundry, area transportation-within 3 mi. **Free Special Amenities:** full breakfast and high-speed Internet.

SAVE [icons] / SOME UNITS FEE [icon]

Free Hot Breakfast Buffet and High Speed Internet
Club Carlson Rewards

COUNTRY INN & SUITES
BY CARLSON
I love this Country.

ECONO LODGE
Phone: 520/622-6714   **2**

▼▼▼
Motel
Rates not provided

Address: 1136 N Stone Ave 85705 **Location:** I-10 exit 257 (Speedway Blvd) eastbound, just e, then just n. **Facility:** 48 units. 3 stories (no elevator), exterior corridors. **Terms:** office hours 6 am-10 pm. **Pool(s):** outdoor. **Free Special Amenities:** continental breakfast and high-speed Internet.

SAVE [icons] / SOME UNITS FEE [icons]

Safety tip: Keep a current AAA/CAA Road Atlas in every vehicle

EL PRESIDIO BED & BREAKFAST INN
Phone: 520/623-6151   **11**

▼▼▼
Classic Historic Bed & Breakfast
$125-$155

Address: 297 N Main Ave 85701 **Location:** I-10 exit 258 (Broadway Blvd/Congress St), 0.3 mi e, 0.3 mi n on Granada Ave, then just e on Franklin St. Located in El Presidio Historic District. **Facility:** This 1886 Victorian adobe is located within a charming historic pocket that is walking distance from museums and the art district. Nicely decorated rooms surround quiet courtyard gardens. 4 units, some efficiencies. 1 story, interior/exterior corridors. **Parking:** street only. **Terms:** check-in 4 pm, 2 night minimum stay - seasonal and/or weekends, age restrictions may apply, 14 day cancellation notice.

[icons] / SOME UNITS [icons]

FOUR POINTS BY SHERATON TUCSON UNIVERSITY PLAZA
Phone: (520)327-7341   **6**

▼▼▼
Hotel
$60-$260

FOUR POINTS BY SHERATON **AAA Benefit:** Members get up to 15% off, plus Starwood Preferred Guest® bonuses.

Address: 1900 E Speedway Blvd 85719 **Location:** Southeast corner of Speedway Blvd and Campbell Ave. **Facility:** 150 units, some efficiencies. 7 stories, interior corridors. **Terms:** cancellation fee imposed. **Amenities:** video games (fee), high-speed Internet. **Pool(s):** heated outdoor. **Activities:** exercise room. **Guest Services:** valet and coin laundry. **Free Special Amenities:** newspaper and high-speed Internet.

SAVE [icons] CALL [icons] FEE [icons] / SOME UNITS FEE [icons]

MARRIOTT UNIVERSITY PARK HOTEL
Phone: (520)792-4100   **8**

▼▼▼
Hotel
$99-$180

Marriott HOTELS & RESORTS **AAA Benefit:** AAA hotel discounts of 5% or more.

Address: 880 E 2nd St 85719 **Location:** I-10 exit 257 (Speedway Blvd), 1.2 mi e to Euclid Ave, then just s. **Facility:** 250 units. 9 stories, interior corridors. **Amenities:** Some: high-speed Internet (fee). **Pool(s):** heated outdoor. **Activities:** whirlpool, exercise room. **Guest Services:** valet laundry.

SAVE [icons] CALL [icons] BIZ [icons] FEE [icons] / SOME UNITS FEE [icon] FEE [icon]

PEPPERTREES INN
Phone: 520/622-7167   **9**

▼▼▼
Bed & Breakfast
Rates not provided

Address: 724 E University Blvd 85719 **Location:** I-10 exit 257 (Speedway Blvd), 1.5 mi e, 0.3 mi s on Euclid Ave, then just w. **Facility:** Southwestern guest houses and two territorial homes dating from 1905 surround a flagstone patio and blue-tiled fountain; special diet meals are available. 6 units, some two bedrooms, kitchens and cottages. 1-2 stories (no elevator), interior/exterior corridors. **Bath:** shower only. **Terms:** office hours 8 am-8 pm. **Amenities:** high-speed Internet. **Activities:** Fee: massage.

[icons]

RODEWAY INN-UNIVERSITY OF AZ
Phone: 520/622-6446   **1**

▼▼▼
Motel
Rates not provided

Address: 1248 N Stone Ave 85705 **Location:** I-10 exit 257 (Speedway Blvd) eastbound, just e, then just n. **Facility:** 40 units. 2 stories (no elevator), exterior corridors. **Pool(s):** outdoor. **Free Special Amenities:** continental breakfast and high-speed Internet.

SAVE [icons] / SOME UNITS FEE [icon]

(See map & index p. 279.)

THE ROYAL ELIZABETH BED & BREAKFAST INN
Phone: 520/670-9022 13

Historic Bed & Breakfast
Rates not provided

Address: 204 S Scott Ave 85701 **Location:** I-10 exit 258 (Broadway Blvd/Congress St); 1 mi e to Scott Ave, then just s. **Facility:** Built in 1878, this Victorian adobe home has been beautifully restored and features large rooms, antiques and walled patios. Check-in is by appointment. 6 units. 1 story, interior corridors. **Amenities:** safes. **Pool(s):** heated outdoor. **Activities:** whirlpool. **Guest Services:** valet laundry.

UNIVERSITY INN
Phone: (520)791-7503 4

Motel
$49-$139

Address: 950 N Stone Ave 85705 **Location:** Jct Stone Ave and 1st St, 1 blk s of Speedway Blvd. **Facility:** 38 units. 2 stories (no elevator), exterior corridors. **Terms:** 3 day cancellation notice-fee imposed. **Amenities:** *Some:* high-speed Internet. **Pool(s):** outdoor. **Guest Services:** coin laundry. **Free Special Amenities: continental breakfast and high-speed Internet.** SAVE

HOTEL CONGRESS
Phone: 520/622-8848

fyi Not evaluated. **Address:** 311 E Congress St 85701 **Location:** I-10 exit 258 (Broadway Blvd/Congress St), 0.7 mi e to 5th Ave, then just n. Facilities, services, and decor characterize an economy property.

WHERE TO EAT

47 SCOTT
Phone: 520/624-4747 9

American
$9-$19

AAA Inspector Notes: This hip downtown pub serves modern American comfort food in a lively and casual setting. Try the catfish macaroni and cheese or the pork belly with braised apples and cabbage. Wash it all down with one of the hand-crafted cocktails or carefully selected wine choices. **Bar:** full bar. **Reservations:** suggested. **Address:** 47 N Scott Ave 85701 **Location:** I-10 exit 258 (Broadway Blvd/Congress St), 0.6 mi e to Scott Ave, then just n. **Parking:** street only. L D

ATHENS ON 4TH AVE
Phone: 520/624-6886 5

Greek
$9-$25

AAA Inspector Notes: Located not far from the University campus, in an area of interesting boutique shops and coffee houses, this eatery offers a simple decor reminiscent of Greek cafes. Chef-owner Andreas Delfakis thoughtfully prepares traditional Greek dishes, including moussaka, dolmades (stuffed grape leaves), spanakopita (spinach pie) and chicken souvlaki. Classic desserts include baklava and rice pudding. An outdoor patio offers al fresco dining and a young staff is knowledgeable and helpful. **Bar:** full bar. **Address:** 500 N 4th Ave, Suite 6 85705 **Location:** Northeast corner of 6th St and 4th Ave; center. D

CAFÉ A LA C'ART
Phone: 520/628-8533 7

American
$8-$12

AAA Inspector Notes: Tucked into the side garden of the museum is this delightful luncheon café, which is open only for lunch on weekdays. The chef-owner prepares creative salads and sandwiches, such as grilled salmon on focaccia with chipotle sauce. Desserts are not to be missed. **Address:** 150 N Main Ave 85701 **Location:** Broadway Blvd/Congress St, just n on Granada Ave, just e on Paseo Redondo, just n on Main Ave to Washington St, then just e; on grounds of Tucson Art Museum. B L D

CAFE POCA COSA
Phone: 520/622-6400 8

Mexican
$13-$25

AAA Inspector Notes: This café's location has an upscale and trendy look. A helpful staff serves an interesting and creative variety of regional Mexican cuisine. The blackboard menu changes twice daily. **Bar:** full bar. **Reservations:** suggested. **Address:** 110 E Pennington St 85701 **Location:** I-10 exit 258 (Broadway Blvd/Congress St), 0.6 mi e to Scott Ave, then just n. **Parking:** on-site (fee) and street. L D

CUP CAFE
Phone: 520/798-1618 10

American
$8-$22

AAA Inspector Notes: Located in the historic Hotel Congress, this café is a popular place for breakfast, but crispy salads, hearty sandwiches and steak dinners have their own following with the lunch and dinner crowds. Homemade desserts spinning in a display case tantalize taste buds. **Bar:** full bar. **Address:** 311 E Congress St 85701 **Location:** I-10 exit 258 (Broadway Blvd/Congress St), 0.7 mi e to 5th Ave, then just n; in Hotel Congress. **Classic** B L D

CUSHING STREET BAR & RESTAURANT
Phone: 520/622-7984 12

American
$12-$19

AAA Inspector Notes: This historic house now is an upscale eatery with an eclectic and casual decor featuring items from a French mansion in Mexico City. Southwestern flavors enhance such traditional offerings as roasted pork loin and shrimp quesadillas. Patio seating is available. **Bar:** full bar. **Address:** 198 W Cushing St 85701 **Location:** I-10 exit 258 (Broadway Blvd/Congress St), 0.5 mi e to Church Ave, just s, then just w. D

DELECTABLES
Phone: 520/884-9289 4

International
$8-$20

AAA Inspector Notes: Lively at lunch, this eatery presents a menu of casual, European, gourmet-style dishes. In addition to salads and sandwiches, choices include many vegetarian creations. **Bar:** full bar. **Address:** 533 N 4th Ave 85705 **Location:** Just n of 6th St. L D

DOWNTOWN KITCHEN + COCKTAILS
Phone: 520/623-7700 11

American
$12-$32

AAA Inspector Notes: Local celebrity chef Janos Wilder has created his latest dining destination in the heart of downtown. The stylish eatery features contemporary American cuisine with a Southwestern flair. The varied menu includes nightly specials including beef cheeks with creamy potato puree, buttermilk fried chicken with cheesy grits and seafood gumbo. Try the dark chocolate jalapeno sundae for a distinctive ending. **Bar:** full bar. **Reservations:** suggested. **Address:** 135 S 6th Ave 85701 **Location:** I-10 exit 258 (Broadway Blvd/Congress St), 0.8 mi e, then just s. L D CALL

EL CHARRO CAFE
Phone: 520/622-1922 6

Mexican
$9-$20

AAA Inspector Notes: This busy, popular restaurant has been operated by the same family since 1922. Several small dining areas and an outdoor cantina add to the charm. **Bar:** full bar. **Address:** 311 N Court Ave 85701 **Location:** I-10 exit 257A (St. Mary's Rd), 0.7 mi e, then just s; in El Presidio Historic District. **Parking:** street only. L D

(See map & index p. 279.)

EL MINUTO CAFE
Phone: 520/882-4145   13

◆◆ ◆◆
Mexican
$7-$14

AAA Inspector Notes: A short distance from the convention center, this family-owned eatery serves such traditional dishes as chicken and beef enchiladas. The cheese crisps with toppings of carne seca and green chiles are popular. **Bar:** full bar. **Address:** 354 S Main Ave 85701 **Location:** I-10 exit 258 (Broadway Blvd/Congress St), 0.4 mi e on Broadway Blvd, just s on Church Ave, then just w on Cushing St. L D

MAGPIE'S GOURMET PIZZA
Phone: 520/628-1661   3

◆◆ ◆◆
Pizza
$5-$24

AAA Inspector Notes: Mouthwatering pizza is made fresh to order at this eatery, and guests can choose from a variety of toppings to create their own gourmet pie. The lunch option of salad and a slice is ample for most appetites. An outdoor patio allows casual dining while watching the street activity. **Bar:** beer & wine. **Address:** 605 N 4th Ave 85705 **Location:** Just n of 6th St. **Parking:** street only. L D

PATSY GRIMALDI'S COAL BRICK-OVEN PIZZERIA
Phone: 520/882-6100

◆◆ ◆◆
Pizza
$4-$18

AAA Inspector Notes: Fresh ingredients and a coal-fired brick oven are the features at this New York style pizzeria. **Bar:** beer & wine. **Address:** 446 N Campbell Ave 85719 **Location:** Southeast corner of 6th St and Campbell Ave. L D

SILVER MINE SUBS
Phone: 520/620-6400   2

◆◆
Sandwiches
$5-$8

AAA Inspector Notes: The cold or warm and toasty sandwiches at this casual eatery hit the spot for hungry folks. Choose from chicken, turkey, tuna, roast beef and meatball subs. The chili, thick with meat and beans, is awesome. Delivery is available until 3 am for campus students studying hard. **Address:** 760 N Tyndall Ave 85719 **Location:** Jct University Blvd. L D LATE

TRIDENT GRILL
Phone: 520/795-5755   1

◆◆ ◆◆
American
$7-$15

AAA Inspector Notes: A nautical theme, a pool table and warm, friendly servers lend to the atmosphere found here. These aspects combine with good sandwiches and salads, such as the applewood BLT and Trident cobb, to make the eatery popular with area college students. **Bar:** full bar. **Address:** 2033 E Speedway Blvd 85719 **Location:** Just e of Campbell Ave. L D LATE

TUCSON
- Restaurants p. 306
- Hotels & Restaurants map & index p. 282, 288

AMERICAS BEST VALUE INN-TUCSON
Phone: (520)884-5800   45

◆◆ ◆◆
Hotel
$44-$160

Address: 810 E Benson Hwy 85713 **Location:** I-10 exit 262, just s. **Facility:** 99 units. 2 stories (no elevator), exterior corridors. **Pool(s):** heated outdoor. **Guest Services:** coin laundry. **Free Special Amenities:** continental breakfast and early check-in/late check-out.

SAVE (T+) CALL M ⊃ 📶 ⊞ / SOME UNITS ⊠

ARIZONA INN
Phone: (520)325-1541   23

◆◆ ◆◆ ◆
Historic Hotel
$329-$579 2/1-4/15
$139-$399 4/16-1/31

Address: 2200 E Elm St 85719 **Location:** I-10 exit 257 (Speedway Blvd), 2.5 mi e, 0.5 mi n on Campbell Ave, then just e. Located in a quiet residential area. **Facility:** The historic property has kept the integrity of the early 1900s-style rooms but with elegant appointments. Lush, expansive gardens surround the hotel. 97 units, some two bedrooms and houses. 1-2 stories (no elevator), exterior corridors. **Parking:** on-site and valet. **Terms:** 14 day cancellation notice-fee imposed. **Amenities:** high-speed Internet, safes. **Dining:** 2 restaurants, also, Main Dining Room at the Arizona Inn, see separate listing, entertainment. **Pool(s):** heated outdoor. **Activities:** saunas, 2 lighted tennis courts, bicycles, exercise room. **Fee:** massage. **Guest Services:** valet laundry. **Free Special Amenities:** local telephone calls and high-speed Internet.

SAVE FEE (T+) (TI+) ⊃ Y ⊃ BIZ 📶 ⊠
⊞ ⊡ / SOME UNITS ⊟

ARIZONA INN
Close to the University of Arizona and the University Medical Center.

BEST WESTERN PLUS INNSUITES TUCSON FOOTHILLS HOTEL & SUITES
Phone: (520)297-8111   5

◆◆ ◆◆
Hotel
$70-$160

Best Western PLUS

AAA Benefit: Members save up to 20%, plus 10% bonus points with Best Western Rewards®.

Address: 6201 N Oracle Rd 85704 **Location:** I-10 exit 250 (Orange Grove Rd), 4 mi e, then just s. **Facility:** 159 units, some efficiencies. 2 stories (no elevator), exterior corridors. **Terms:** cancellation fee imposed. **Amenities:** high-speed Internet. **Pool(s):** heated outdoor. **Activities:** whirlpool, 2 lighted tennis courts, exercise room. **Guest Services:** valet and coin laundry. **Free Special Amenities:** full breakfast and manager's reception.

SAVE (TI+) ⊃ 📶 ⊞ ⊡ ⊡ / SOME UNITS FEE ⊠

CASA TIERRA ADOBE B&B INN
Phone: (520)578-3058   16

◆◆ ◆◆
Bed & Breakfast
$165-$285

Address: 11155 W Calle Pima 85743 **Location:** I-10 exit 257 (Speedway Blvd), 9.5 mi w, 3.8 mi nw on Kinney Rd, 1.4 mi w on Mile Wide Rd, then 0.7 mi s on Camino Del Sapo, follow signs. Located in a quiet, secluded desert area. **Facility:** Built in 1989, this charming adobe home is situated in a isolated desert setting with a central interior courtyard and views across Avra Valley. 4 units, some two bedrooms. 1 story, exterior corridors. **Terms:** open 2/1-6/15 & 8/15-1/31, office hours 9 am-7 pm, check-in 4 pm, 2 night minimum stay, 14 day cancellation notice-fee imposed. **Activities:** whirlpools, exercise room. 📶 ⊠ W ⊞ ⊡

CASINO DEL SOL RESORT, SPA AND CONFERENCE CENTER
Phone: 520/324-9000

fyi
Resort Hotel
Rates not provided

Too new to rate, opening scheduled for November 2011. **Address:** 5655 W Valencia Rd 85757 **Location:** I-19 exit 95 (Valencia Rd), 5.8 mi w. **Amenities:** 215 units, restaurant, coffeemakers, microwaves, refrigerators, pool, exercise facility.

Visit AAA.com or CAA.ca for one-stop travel planning and reservations

(See maps & indexes p. 282, 288.)

CLARION HOTEL TUCSON AIRPORT
Phone: (520)746-3932 **8**

Hotel
$55-$102

Address: 6801 S Tucson Blvd 85756 **Location:** Just n of Tucson International Airport. **Facility:** 188 units. 2 stories (no elevator), interior corridors. **Amenities:** safes. *Some:* high-speed Internet. **Pool(s):** heated outdoor. **Activities:** whirlpool, exercise room. **Guest Services:** valet and coin laundry, area transportation-within 5 mi.

COMFORT INN-GRANT RD
Phone: (520)547-1755 **20**

Hotel
$60-$120

Address: 1560 W Grant Rd 85745 **Location:** I-10 exit 256 (Grant Rd), just w. **Facility:** 67 units. 3 stories, interior corridors. **Terms:** cancellation fee imposed. **Amenities:** high-speed Internet. **Pool(s):** outdoor. **Activities:** whirlpool, exercise room. **Guest Services:** valet and coin laundry.

COMFORT SUITES AT SABINO CANYON
Phone: (520)298-2300 **25**

Hotel
$89-$139

Address: 7007 E Tanque Verde Rd 85715 **Location:** Jct Grand Rd, 0.4 mi ne. **Facility:** 90 units. 2 stories, exterior corridors. **Terms:** cancellation fee imposed. **Pool(s):** heated outdoor. **Activities:** whirlpool. **Guest Services:** coin laundry.

We've got your next set of wheels...

AAA

Find your style with ease using AAA AutoMaker® on AAA.com

Whether you are just starting a family, traveling with pets, are an all-terrain adventurist or just escape in the family fun mobile, we've got your next set of wheels.

Find your style with AAA AutoMaker on AAA.com

COMFORT SUITES AT TUCSON MALL
Phone: (520)888-6676 **13**

Hotel
$100-$220

Address: 515 W Auto Mall Dr 85705 **Location:** I-10 exit 254 (Prince Rd), 1.9 mi e, then 1.2 mi n. **Facility:** 87 units. 3 stories, interior corridors. **Terms:** cancellation fee imposed. **Amenities:** safes (fee). **Pool(s):** heated outdoor. **Activities:** whirlpool, exercise room. **Guest Services:** valet and coin laundry.

COMFORT SUITES TUCSON AIRPORT
Phone: (520)295-4400 **10**

Hotel
$79-$169

Address: 6935 S Tucson Blvd 85756 **Location:** Just n of Tucson International Airport. **Facility:** 82 units. 3 stories, interior corridors. **Terms:** cancellation fee imposed. **Amenities:** high-speed Internet. **Pool(s):** heated outdoor. **Activities:** whirlpool, exercise room. **Guest Services:** coin laundry, area transportation-within 2 mi. **Free Special Amenities: full breakfast and airport transportation.**

COUNTRY INN & SUITES BY CARLSON, TUCSON-AIRPORT
Phone: (520)741-9000 **5**

Hotel
$79-$169

Address: 6681 S Tucson Blvd 85756 **Location:** 0.4 mi n of Tucson International Airport entrance. **Facility:** 83 units. 3 stories, interior corridors. **Terms:** cancellation fee imposed. **Amenities:** *Some:* high-speed Internet. **Pool(s):** heated outdoor. **Activities:** whirlpool, exercise room. **Guest Services:** valet and coin laundry. **Free Special Amenities: full breakfast and high-speed Internet.**

COURTYARD BY MARRIOTT-TUCSON AIRPORT
Phone: (520)573-0000 **2**

Hotel
$71-$175

AAA Benefit:
AAA hotel discounts of 5% or more.

Address: 2505 E Executive Dr 85756 **Location:** On Tucson Blvd, 0.7 mi n of Tucson International Airport entrance. **Facility:** 149 units. 3 stories, interior corridors. **Amenities:** high-speed Internet. **Pool(s):** heated outdoor. **Activities:** whirlpool, exercise room. **Guest Services:** valet and coin laundry, area transportation-within 5 mi.

COURTYARD BY MARRIOTT-TUCSON WILLIAMS CENTRE
Phone: (520)745-6000 **37**

Hotel
$84-$193

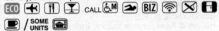

AAA Benefit:
AAA hotel discounts of 5% or more.

Address: 201 S Williams Blvd 85711 **Location:** Jct Campbell Ave, 3.8 mi e on Broadway Blvd, then just s. **Facility:** 153 units. 3 stories, interior corridors. **Pool(s):** heated outdoor. **Activities:** whirlpool, exercise room. **Guest Services:** valet and coin laundry.

(See maps & indexes p. 282, 288.)

CROSSLAND ECONOMY STUDIOS-TUCSON-BUTTERFIELD DR
Phone: (520)745-3612 [47]

Extended Stay Hotel
$60-$70 2/1-4/15
$55-$65 4/16-1/31

Address: 4800 S Butterfield Dr 85714 **Location:** I-10 exit 264B eastbound, just n to Irvington Rd, just e to Hotel Dr, then just n; exit 264 westbound, just n. **Facility:** 117 units, some efficiencies. 3 stories, exterior corridors. *Bath:* shower only. **Terms:** office hours 6:30 am-10:30 pm. **Guest Services:** coin laundry.

DAYS INN AIRPORT
Phone: (520)747-8988 [48]

Hotel
$41-$85

Address: 4855 S Palo Verde Blvd 85714 **Location:** I-10 exit 264 westbound; exit 264B eastbound, just n. **Facility:** 65 units. 2 stories (no elevator), exterior corridors. **Amenities:** high-speed Internet. **Pool(s):** outdoor. **Activities:** whirlpool. **Guest Services:** coin laundry.

▼ See AAA listing p. 201 ▼

A SHORT DRIVE CAN BE EXCEPTIONAL
JUST 30 MINUTES SOUTH OF TUCSON

SPECTACULAR SETTING IN THE HEART OF THE OLD WEST

Esplendor
RESORT at RIO RICO

AAA SPECIAL RATES STARTING AT $99*

800-288-4746 ~ WWW.ESPLENDOR-RESORT.COM
1069 CAMINO CARALAMPI, RIO RICO, AZ
A ROBERT TRENT JONES SR. DESIGNED GOLF COURSE
*BASED ON DOUBLE OCCUPANCY

Get the free mobile app at
http://gettag.mobi

Get pet travel tips and enter the photo contest at AAA.com/PetBook

(See maps & indexes p. 282, 288.)

DESERT DIAMOND HOTEL & CASINO
Phone: (520)342-3100 **16**

Hotel
$99-$209

Address: 7350 S Nogales Hwy 85756 **Location:** I-19 exit 95 (Valencia Rd), 1.4 mi e, then 1 mi s. **Facility:** The property boasts upscale guest rooms. A fire pit near the pool offers a cozy spot to unwind. 148 units. 4 stories, interior corridors. **Terms:** cancellation fee imposed. **Amenities:** high-speed Internet, safes. **Dining:** 4 restaurants. **Pool(s):** heated outdoor. **Activities:** whirlpool, exercise room. **Guest Services:** valet laundry. **Free Special Amenities: continental breakfast and high-speed Internet.**

DOUBLETREE BY HILTON TUCSON - REID PARK
Phone: (520)881-4200 **40**

Hotel
$179-$299 2/1-4/30
$109-$229 5/1-1/31

AAA Benefit: Members save 5% or more everyday!

Address: 445 S Alvernon Way 85711 **Location:** I-10 exit 259 (22nd St), 4 mi e, then just n. **Facility:** 287 units. 2-9 stories, interior/exterior corridors. **Terms:** 1-7 night minimum stay, cancellation fee imposed. **Amenities:** high-speed Internet (fee). **Dining:** Cactus Rose Steakhouse, Javelina Cantina, see separate listings. **Pool(s):** heated outdoor. **Activities:** whirlpool, 3 lighted tennis courts, exercise room. *Fee:* massage. **Guest Services:** valet laundry, area transportation-within 3 mi. **Free Special Amenities: local telephone calls and newspaper.**

EMBASSY SUITES TUCSON-PALOMA VILLAGE
Phone: (520)352-4000 **6**

Hotel
$99-$289

AAA Benefit: Members save 5% or more everyday!

Address: 3110 E Skyline Dr 85718 **Location:** Jct Sunrise and Skyline drs; southeast corner. **Facility:** 119 units. 2-3 stories, interior corridors. **Terms:** check-in 4 pm, 1-7 night minimum stay, cancellation fee imposed. **Amenities:** *Fee:* video games, high-speed Internet. **Pool(s):** heated outdoor. **Activities:** whirlpool, exercise room. **Guest Services:** valet and coin laundry, area transportation-within 5 mi. **Free Special Amenities: full breakfast and manager's reception.**

EMBASSY SUITES TUCSON-WILLIAMS CENTER
Phone: 520/745-2700 **36**

Hotel
Rates not provided

AAA Benefit: Members save 5% or more everyday!

Address: 5335 E Broadway Blvd 85711 **Location:** Jct Campbell Ave, 3.9 mi e. **Facility:** 142 units. 3 stories, exterior corridors. **Amenities:** *Fee:* video games, high-speed Internet. **Pool(s):** heated outdoor. **Activities:** whirlpool, exercise room. **Guest Services:** valet and coin laundry, area transportation-within 5 mi.

Create complete trip routings and custom maps with the TripTik® Travel Planner on AAA.com or CAA.ca

EXTENDED STAYAMERICA-TUCSON-GRANT RD
Phone: (520)795-9510 **22**

Extended Stay Hotel
$70-$80 2/1-4/15
$60-$70 4/16-1/31

Address: 5050 E Grant Rd 85712 **Location:** 0.5 mi e of Swan Rd. Located near hospital. **Facility:** 120 efficiencies. 3 stories, exterior corridors. **Terms:** office hours 6:30 am-10:30 pm. **Guest Services:** coin laundry.

FAIRFIELD INN BY MARRIOTT AT TUCSON AIRPORT
Phone: (520)295-8800 **11**

Hotel
$66-$132

AAA Benefit: AAA hotel discounts of 5% or more.

Address: 6955 S Tucson Blvd 85706 **Location:** Just n of Tucson International Airport. **Facility:** 85 units. 3 stories, interior corridors. **Pool(s):** heated outdoor. **Activities:** whirlpool, exercise room. **Guest Services:** valet and coin laundry. **Free Special Amenities: expanded continental breakfast and high-speed Internet.**

FAIRFIELD INN TUCSON I-10 BY MARRIOTT
Phone: (520)747-7474 **49**

Hotel
$77-$113

AAA Benefit: AAA hotel discounts of 5% or more.

Address: 4850 S Hotel Dr 85714 **Location:** I-10 exit 264 westbound; exit 264B eastbound, just n. **Facility:** 65 units. 3 stories, interior corridors. **Amenities:** high-speed Internet. **Pool(s):** heated outdoor. **Activities:** whirlpool, limited exercise equipment. **Guest Services:** coin laundry.

FOUR POINTS BY SHERATON TUCSON AIRPORT
Phone: (520)746-0271 **14**

Hotel
$79-$219

FOUR POINTS BY SHERATON **AAA Benefit:** Members get up to 15% off, plus Starwood Preferred Guest® bonuses.

Address: 7060 S Tucson Blvd 85756 **Location:** At entrance to Tucson International Airport. **Facility:** 150 units. 2-3 stories, interior corridors. **Amenities:** *Some:* high-speed Internet. **Pool(s):** heated outdoor. **Activities:** whirlpool, exercise room. **Guest Services:** valet laundry. **Free Special Amenities: high-speed Internet and airport transportation.** *(See ad p. 297.)*

HACIENDA DEL DESIERTO
Phone: (520)298-1764 **52**

Bed & Breakfast
$129-$279

Address: 11770 E Rambling Tr 85747 **Location:** Jct Houghton Rd, 2 mi e on Escalante Rd, 1.3 mi s on Old Spanish Tr, then just w on Camino del Desierto Rd, through security gates. **Facility:** Near Saguaro National Park, guests can lounge on the porch or patio and spy small desert creatures roaming the grounds at this B&B. 4 units, some two bedrooms, efficiencies and kitchens. 1 story, exterior corridors. **Terms:** check-in 4 pm, 2 night minimum stay - seasonal, 7 day cancellation notice-fee imposed. **Activities:** whirlpool, hiking trails. *Fee:* massage.

(See maps & indexes p. 282, 288.)

HAMPTON INN & SUITES TUCSON MALL
Phone: 520/618-8000

Hotel
Rates not provided

Address: 5950 N Oracle Rd 85704 **Location:** I-10 exit 250 (Orange Grove Rd), 4 mi e, then 0.5 mi s. **Facility:** 109 units, some efficiencies. 3 stories, interior corridors. **Pool(s):** heated outdoor. **Activities:** whirlpool, exercise room. **Guest Services:** valet and coin laundry, area transportation (fee)-within 5 mi.

AAA Benefit:
Members save up to 10% everyday!

FEE 🚭 🍴 CALL 📶 🏊 BIZ 📶 💻 / SOME UNITS 🛏 🖥

HAMPTON INN TUCSON AIRPORT
Phone: (520)918-9000 🅛

Hotel
$79-$209

AAA Benefit:
Members save up to 10% everyday!

Address: 6971 S Tucson Blvd 85756 **Location:** Just n of Tucson International Airport. **Facility:** 126 units. 4 stories, interior corridors. **Terms:** 1-7 night minimum stay, cancellation fee imposed. **Amenities:** video games (fee). **Pool(s):** heated outdoor. **Activities:** whirlpool, exercise room. **Guest Services:** valet and coin laundry, area transportation-within 5 mi. *(See ad p. 298.)*

🚭 🍴 🏊 📶 🗙 FEE 📹 🛏 🖥 💻

HAMPTON INN TUCSON NORTH
Phone: (520)206-0602 🅛

Hotel
$89-$159

AAA Benefit:
Members save up to 10% everyday!

Address: 1375 W Grant Rd 85745 **Location:** I-10 exit 256 (Grant Rd), just w. **Facility:** 92 units. 5 stories, interior corridors. **Terms:** 1-7 night minimum stay, cancellation fee imposed. **Amenities:** video games (fee). **Pool(s):** heated outdoor. **Activities:** whirlpool, exercise room. **Guest Services:** valet and coin laundry.

🍴 CALL 📶 🏊 BIZ 📶 🗙 FEE 📹 🛏 🖥 💻 / SOME UNITS 🐕

HILTON GARDEN INN TUCSON AIRPORT
Phone: (520)741-0505 🄬

Hotel
$119-$169 2/1-5/31
$89-$109 6/1-1/31

AAA Benefit:
Unparalleled hospitality at a special Member rate.

Address: 6575 S Country Club Rd 85706 **Location:** Jct Tucson Blvd, 0.4 mi e on Valencia Rd, just s. **Facility:** 125 units. 3 stories, interior corridors. **Terms:** 1-7 night minimum stay, cancellation fee imposed. **Amenities:** video games (fee), high-speed Internet. **Pool(s):** heated outdoor. **Activities:** whirlpool, exercise room. **Guest Services:** valet and coin laundry, area transportation-within 5 mi.

🚭 🍴 🍽 CALL 📶 🏊 BIZ 📶 🗙 FEE 📹 🛏 🖥 💻

▼ See AAA listing p. 296 ▼

FOUR POINTS BY SHERATON

EXCLUSIVE OFFERS FOR AAA MEMBERS

Choose from two great offers at Four Points by Sheraton Tucson Airport - free breakfast for two or up to 30% off. And with SPG® member benefits you get even more. With stylish rooms, free Internet access and free bottled water, find everything you need to travel the way you like.

BOOK NOW AT WWW.FOURPOINTSTUCSONAIRPORT.COM
OR CALL 520 746 0271

spg® Starwood Preferred Guest

©2011 Starwood Hotels & Resorts Worldwide, Inc. Offer expires 01/31/2013. All Rights Reserved. For full terms and conditions, visit starwoodhotels.com/AAA

Simply Reliable

The Diamond Ratings in this TourBook guide are backed by our expert, in-person evaluations, whether the hotel or restaurant is no-frills, moderate or upscale.

Learn more at **AAA.com/Diamonds**

(See maps & indexes p. 282, 288.)

HILTON TUCSON EAST
Phone: (520)721-5600 **42**

Hotel
$139-S159 2/1-4/30
$79-S99 5/1-1/31

AAA Benefit: Members save 5% or more everyday!

Address: 7600 E Broadway Blvd 85710 **Location:** 0.5 mi e of Kolb Rd. **Facility:** 232 units. 7 stories, interior corridors. **Terms:** 1-7 night minimum stay, cancellation fee imposed. **Amenities:** video games (fee). **Pool(s):** heated outdoor. **Activities:** whirlpool, exercise room. **Guest Services:** valet laundry, area transportation-within 3 mi. **Free Special Amenities:** early check-in/late check-out and high-speed Internet. *(See ad p. 299.)*

HOLIDAY INN EXPRESS HOTEL & SUITES-TUCSON MALL
Phone: (520)202-5000 **14**

Hotel
$139-$299 2/1-3/31
$99-$139 4/1-1/31

Address: 620 E Wetmore Rd 85705 **Location:** Just w of N 1st Ave. **Facility:** 105 units, some efficiencies. 3 stories, interior corridors. **Terms:** 3 day cancellation notice. **Amenities:** video games (fee), high-speed Internet, safes. **Pool(s):** heated outdoor. **Activities:** whirlpool, exercise room. **Guest Services:** valet and coin laundry.

HOLIDAY INN EXPRESS INN & SUITES-GRANT RD
Phone: (520)624-3200 **19**

Hotel
$79-$149

Address: 1564 W Grant Rd 85745 **Location:** I-10 exit 256 (Grant Rd), just w. **Facility:** 92 units. 3 stories, interior corridors. **Amenities:** high-speed Internet. **Pool(s):** heated outdoor. **Activities:** whirlpool, exercise room. **Guest Services:** valet and coin laundry.

HOLIDAY INN EXPRESS TUCSON AIRPORT
Phone: (520)889-6600 **6**

Hotel
$169-$189 2/1-4/30
$109-$129 5/1-1/31

Address: 2548 E Medina Rd 85756 **Location:** 0.5 mi n of Tucson International Airport entrance. **Facility:** 98 units. 3 stories, interior corridors. **Amenities:** high-speed Internet. **Pool(s):** heated outdoor. **Activities:** whirlpool, exercise room. **Guest Services:** valet and coin laundry, area transportation-within 5 mi.

HOLIDAY INN HOTEL & SUITES-TUCSON AIRPORT NORTH
Phone: (520)746-1161 **46**

Hotel
$59-$189

Address: 4550 S Palo Verde Blvd 85714 **Location:** I-10 exit 264 westbound; exit 264B eastbound, 0.5 mi n. **Facility:** 301 units. 3-6 stories, interior/exterior corridors. **Terms:** cancellation fee imposed. **Amenities:** *Some:* high-speed Internet. **Pool(s):** heated outdoor. **Activities:** whirlpool, exercise room. **Guest Services:** valet and coin laundry, area transportation-within 5 mi.

HYATT PLACE TUCSON AIRPORT
Phone: (520)295-0405 **9**

Hotel
$79-$249

HYATT PLACE

AAA Benefit: Members save 10% or more everyday.

Address: 6885 S Tucson Blvd 85756 **Location:** Just n of Tucson International Airport. **Facility:** 120 units. 5 stories, interior corridors. **Terms:** cancellation fee imposed. **Amenities:** safes. *Some:* high-speed Internet. **Pool(s):** heated outdoor. **Activities:** exercise room. **Guest Services:** valet laundry, area transportation-within 5 mi. **Free Special Amenities:** expanded continental breakfast and high-speed Internet.

▼ *See AAA listing p. 297* ▼

located at the intersection of good savings and great value.

No matter where you travel, there is always a clean and cozy Hampton in town. Our strong partnership with AAA allows us to offer special rates* to all AAA members.

FREE hot breakfast

clean and fresh Hampton bed™

FREE high-speed internet access

friendly service

show your card and save

Hampton Inn Tucson Airport
6971 S. Tucson Blvd., Tucson, AZ 85756
520-918-9000 | 520-889-4002

© 2011 Hilton Worldwide. *Valid for current AAA members only. Subject to availability at participating Hampton hotels. Valid for stays booked and completed between January 1, 2012 and December 31, 2012. Enter your AAA number and promotion code "AAA" at time of booking. Must present your current and valid AAA card at check-in. The discount rate relates to the hotel's Best Available Rate. Best Available Rate is a specific rate type that varies depending on time of purchase, is unrestricted, non-qualified, and excludes discount or negotiated rates not available to the general public, including but not limited to: membership, corporate, government, promotional, group, packages, unpublished or rates only available on auction websites. Additional restrictions may apply.

(See maps & indexes p. 282, 288.)

INDIAN HILL BED & BREAKFAST
Phone: 520/760-4200 [24]

Bed & Breakfast
$120-$175

Address: 2955 N Tomahawk Tr 85749 **Location:** Jct Speedway Blvd, 1.2 mi n on Houghton Rd, just w on Tanque Verde Rd, then 0.7 mi n. **Facility:** Sweeping views of the mountains surround this modern home, where large rooms have patios and fully-equipped baths. The suite has a barbecue grill. 4 units. 1 story, interior/exterior corridors. *Bath:* shower only. **Terms:** 2 night minimum stay - seasonal and/or weekends, 3 day cancellation notice-fee imposed. **Pool(s):** outdoor. **Activities:** rental bicycles. *Fee:* massage.

THE INNS AT EL RANCHO MERLITA
Phone: 888/218-8418 [28]

Bed & Breakfast
$99-$295

Address: 1924 N Corte El Rancho Merlita 85715 **Location:** Jct Speedway and Pantano, 1 mi n to Wrightstown, then 0.8 mi e, just right, follow signs. **Facility:** Once the winter home of Merle Norman, this tranquil retreat offers beautifully decorated guest rooms surrounded by desert landscaping, nature trails and mountain vistas. 8 units. 1 story, interior/exterior corridors. **Terms:** office hours 8 am-6 pm, 2 night minimum stay - seasonal and/or weekends, age restrictions may apply, 14 day cancellation notice-fee imposed. **Amenities:** safes. *Some:* high-speed Internet. **Pool(s):** outdoor. **Activities:** whirlpool, game room, horseshoes. *Fee:* massage.

▼ See AAA listing p. 298 ▼

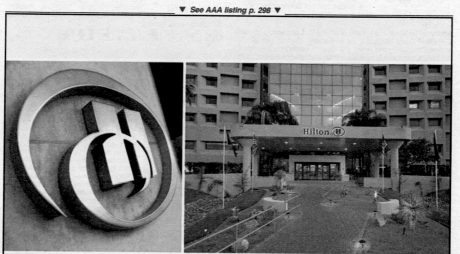

Hilton Tucson East is Ready to Welcome You

If you're looking for a relaxing getaway, Hilton Tucson East is the perfect place to stay. Enjoy world-renowned hospitality and service, a convenient location and all the amenities you'd expect from a Hilton Hotel.

Plan a romantic weekend, a week with your family or simply take some time for yourself. Get away from the everyday at Hilton Tucson East.

7600 E. Broadway Blvd., Tucson, AZ 85710
1-800-916-2221 | www.hiltontucsoneast.com

Approved

Hilton
Tucson East
©2010 Hilton Worldwide

HHONORS
HILTON WORLDWIDE

(See maps & indexes p. 282, 288.)

JEREMIAH INN BED & BREAKFAST
Phone: (520)749-3072 **17**

Bed & Breakfast
$120-$150

Address: 10921 E Snyder Rd 85749 **Location:** Jct Grant Rd, 3.6 mi ne on Tanque Verde Rd, 3.7 mi ne on Catalina Hwy, then just w. Located in a quiet residential area. **Facility:** The contemporary home with southwestern architecture is located in a peaceful desert setting at the foothills of the Santa Catalina Mountains. 4 units, some two bedrooms. 1 story, interior corridors. **Terms:** 7 day cancellation notice. **Pool(s):** outdoor. **Activities:** whirlpool. **Guest Services:** complimentary laundry.

JW MARRIOTT STARR PASS RESORT & SPA
Phone: (520)792-3500 **27**

Resort Hotel
$299-$351

AAA Benefit:
A deluxe level of comfort and a Member rate.

Address: 3800 W Starr Pass Blvd 85745 **Location:** I-10 exit 259 (Starr Pass Blvd), 4.8 mi w. **Facility:** Carved out of the hillside overlooking the valley, the elegant setting complements the hotel's comfortable upscale rooms and spacious baths. 575 units. 6 stories, interior corridors. **Parking:** valet and street only. **Terms:** check-in 4 pm. **Amenities:** high-speed Internet (fee), safes, honor bars. **Dining:** 5 restaurants, also, Primo, see separate listing. **Pool(s):** 2 heated outdoor. **Activities:** whirlpools, steamrooms, waterslide, 2 lighted tennis courts, recreation programs, rental bicycles, hiking trails, basketball, exercise room, spa. **Fee:** golf-27 holes. **Guest Services:** valet and coin laundry.

LA POSADA LODGE & CASITAS
Phone: (520)887-4800 **9**

Hotel
$105-$172

Address: 5900 N Oracle Rd 85704 **Location:** 0.5 mi s of Orange Grove Rd. **Facility:** 72 units. 3 stories, exterior corridors. **Amenities:** high-speed Internet. **Dining:** Miguel's at La Posada, see separate listing. **Pool(s):** heated outdoor. **Activities:** whirlpool, exercise room. **Guest Services:** area transportation (fee)-within 5 mi.

LA QUINTA INN & SUITES TUCSON AIRPORT
Phone: (520)573-3333 **13**

Hotel
$68-$159

Address: 7001 S Tucson Blvd 85706 **Location:** Just n of Tucson International Airport. **Facility:** 143 units. 4 stories, interior corridors. **Amenities:** video games (fee). *Some:* high-speed Internet. **Pool(s):** heated outdoor. **Activities:** whirlpool, exercise room. **Guest Services:** valet and coin laundry.

LA QUINTA INN TUCSON EAST
Phone: (520)747-1414 **41**

Hotel
$58-$144

Address: 6404 E Broadway Blvd 85710 **Location:** Just e of Wilmot Rd. **Facility:** 140 units. 2 stories (no elevator), exterior corridors. **Pool(s):** outdoor. **Activities:** whirlpool. **Guest Services:** coin laundry.

LODGE ON THE DESERT
Phone: (520)320-2000 **32**

Hotel
$109-$429

Address: 306 N Alvernon Way 85711 **Location:** I-10 exit 258 (Broadway Blvd/Congress St), 4 mi e, then just n. **Facility:** 103 units, some two bedrooms. 1-2 stories (no elevator), exterior corridors. **Terms:** 3 day cancellation notice-fee imposed. **Amenities:** safes. *Some:* high-speed Internet. **Dining:** restaurant, see separate listing. **Pool(s):** heated outdoor. **Activities:** whirlpool. **Guest Services:** valet laundry. **Free Special Amenities:** local telephone calls and high-speed Internet.

(See ad this page.)

▼ See AAA listing this page ▼

Member Savings Up to *20% OFF* Published Rates

scan this tag on your smartphone and start saving today!

get the free mobile app at
http://gettag.mobi

• 103 rooms
• restaurant & bar
• heated pool
• pet-friendly
• close to The U of A

LODGE ON THE DESERT
Authentic Arizona.

Tucson, AZ
LodgeOnTheDesert.com
877.498.6776

(See maps & indexes p. 282, 288.)

THE LODGE @ VENTANA CANYON
Phone: (520)577-1400 **12**

Resort Hotel
$149-$799 2/1-4/30
$99-$799 5/1-1/31

Address: 6200 N Clubhouse Ln 85750 **Location:** I-10 exit 256 (Grant Rd), 8.6 mi e, 0.6 mi e on Tanque Verde Rd, 2 mi n on Sabino Canyon Rd, then 3.2 mi n on Kolb Rd. Located in a residential resort area. **Facility:** This boutique-style resort, set at the foot of Catalina Mountains, has spacious rooms and baths, all provided in an intimate setting. 50 efficiencies, some two bedrooms. 2 stories, interior/exterior corridors. **Parking:** on-site and valet. **Terms:** check-in 4 pm, 21 day cancellation notice-fee imposed. **Amenities:** safes. **Pool(s):** heated outdoor. **Activities:** saunas, whirlpools, steamrooms, hiking trails, jogging, exercise room, spa. *Fee:* golf-36 holes, 12 lighted tennis courts. **Guest Services:** valet and coin laundry, area transportation-within 2 mi. **Free Special Amenities: newspaper and high-speed Internet.**

LOEWS VENTANA CANYON
Phone: (520)299-2020 **10**

Resort Hotel
$149-$449

Address: 7000 N Resort Dr 85750 **Location:** I-10 exit 256 (Grant Rd), 8.6 mi e, 0.6 mi ne on Tanque Verde Rd, 2 mi n on Sabino Canyon Rd, then 3.5 mi n on Kolb Rd. Located in a quiet area. **Facility:** The elegant building, reminiscent of a Frank Lloyd Wright design, sits at the base of Catalina Mountains and is surrounded by full resort facilities. 398 units. 3-4 stories, interior/exterior corridors. **Parking:** on-site and valet. **Terms:** check-in 4 pm, 3 day cancellation notice-fee imposed. **Amenities:** safes. **Dining:** 3 restaurants, also, Flying V Bar & Grill, see separate listing, entertainment. **Pool(s):** 2 heated outdoor. **Activities:** saunas, whirlpools, steamrooms, recreation programs, rental bicycles, hiking trails, jogging, playground, basketball, spa. *Fee:* golf-36 holes, 4 lighted tennis courts. **Guest Services:** valet laundry, area transportation-within 2 mi.

MOTEL 6 TUCSON NORTH #1127
Phone: (520)744-9300 **2**

Hotel
$51-$61 2/1-4/7
$45-$55 4/8-1/31

Address: 4630 W Ina Rd 85741 **Location:** I-10 exit 248 (Ina Rd), just e to Camino de Oeste, then just n. **Facility:** 118 units. 2 stories, interior corridors. **Pool(s):** outdoor. **Guest Services:** coin laundry.

OMNI TUCSON NATIONAL RESORT
Phone: (520)297-2271 **1**

Resort Hotel
$109-$459

Address: 2727 W Club Dr 85742 **Location:** I-10 exit 246 (Cortaro Rd), 3.5 mi e, then n on Shannon Rd. **Facility:** Set on several manicured acres, the resort's guest rooms, suites and haciendas overlook a golf course. An extensive health spa is on site. 128 units, some kitchens. 1-2 stories (no elevator), exterior corridors. **Parking:** on-site and valet. **Terms:** 3 day cancellation notice-fee imposed. **Amenities:** safes, honor bars. *Some:* high-speed Internet. **Dining:** 3 restaurants. **Pool(s):** 2 heated outdoor. **Activities:** saunas, whirlpools, steamrooms, 4 lighted tennis courts, recreation programs, hiking trails, shuffleboard, volleyball, spa. *Fee:* golf-36 holes. **Guest Services:** valet laundry.

ORACLE FOOTHILLS QUALITY INN & SUITES
Phone: 520/575-9255 **3**

Hotel
Rates not provided

Address: 7411 N Oracle Rd 85704 **Location:** SR 77 (Oracle Rd), just n of Ina Rd. **Facility:** 155 units, some kitchens. 2-3 stories, exterior corridors. **Pool(s):** heated outdoor. **Activities:** whirlpool, putting green. **Guest Services:** valet and coin laundry, area transportation-within 3 mi. **Free Special Amenities: expanded continental breakfast and newspaper.**

QUALITY INN AT TUCSON AIRPORT
Phone: (520)294-2500 **1**

Hotel
$59-$139

Address: 2803 E Valencia Rd 85706 **Location:** 1 mi ne of Tucson International Airport; just e of Tucson Blvd. **Facility:** 98 units. 3 stories, interior/exterior corridors. **Terms:** cancellation fee imposed. **Amenities:** high-speed Internet, safes (fee). **Pool(s):** outdoor. **Activities:** whirlpool. **Guest Services:** coin laundry.

RADISSON SUITES HOTEL TUCSON AIRPORT
Phone: (520)225-0800 **15**

Hotel
$89-$189

Address: 7051 S Tucson Blvd 85756 **Location:** At entrance to Tucson International Airport. **Facility:** 204 units. 3 stories, exterior corridors. **Terms:** cancellation fee imposed. **Amenities:** video games (fee). **Pool(s):** heated outdoor. **Activities:** whirlpool, exercise room. **Guest Services:** valet and coin laundry.

RADISSON SUITES TUCSON
Phone: (520)721-7100 **30**

Hotel
$76-$269

Address: 6555 E Speedway Blvd 85710 **Location:** Just e of Wilmot Rd. **Facility:** 299 units. 5 stories, exterior corridors. **Terms:** cancellation fee imposed. **Amenities:** *Some:* high-speed Internet. **Pool(s):** heated outdoor. **Activities:** whirlpool, game room, exercise room. **Guest Services:** valet and coin laundry, area transportation-within 3 mi. *(See ad p. 302.)*

RAMADA FOOTHILLS INN & SUITES
Phone: (520)886-9595 **26**

Hotel
$64-$169

Address: 6944 E Tanque Verde Rd 85715 **Location:** Jct Campbell Ave, 5.5 mi e on Grant Rd, then jne. **Facility:** 115 units. 2 stories, exterior corridors. **Amenities:** safes (fee). *Some:* high-speed Internet. **Pool(s):** heated outdoor. **Activities:** whirlpool. **Guest Services:** valet and coin laundry. **Free Special Amenities: expanded continental breakfast and high-speed Internet.** *(See ad p. 303.)*

(See maps & indexes p. 282, 288.)

RED ROOF INN-TUCSON SOUTH

Phone: (520)571-1400 **51**

Hotel
$39-$120

Address: 3704 E Irvington Rd 85714
Location: I-10 exit 264 westbound; exit 264B eastbound. **Facility:** 118 units. 2 stories, exterior corridors.
Terms: cancellation fee imposed.
Amenities: safes. **Pool(s):** heated outdoor. **Free Special Amenities:** local telephone calls and high-speed Internet.

Learn about

AAA/CAA Diamond Ratings

at AAA.com/Diamonds

▼ See AAA listing p. 301 ▼

RELAX. REFRESH. REJUVENATE.

UP TO 20% OFF BEST AVAILABLE RATE.

FULL HOT AMERICAN BREAKFAST BUFFET INCLUDED.

• Centrally located near Tucson's renowned shopping & attractions.

• Oversized pool set in a lush courtyard oasis.

• Complimentary high-speed Internet access.

• Breeze Patio Bar and Grill.

Radisson
Suites Tucson

Radisson Suites Tucson P: 520. 721.7100 TF: 1.800.333.3333 W: RadissonTucson.com

(See maps & indexes p. 282, 288.)

RESIDENCE INN BY MARRIOTT-TUCSON
Phone: (520)721-0991    29

Extended Stay
Hotel
$99-$209

AAA Benefit:
AAA hotel discounts of 5% or more.

Address: 6477 E Speedway Blvd 85710 **Location:** Just e of Wilmot Rd. **Facility:** 128 units, some efficiencies and kitchens. 2 stories (no elevator), exterior corridors. **Terms:** check-in 4 pm. **Amenities:** *Some:* high-speed Internet. **Pool(s):** heated outdoor. **Activities:** whirlpool, sports court, exercise room. **Guest Services:** valet and coin laundry, area transportation-within 2 mi.

/ SOME UNITS   FEE

Check out
our travel blog at
AAATravelViews.com

▼ *See AAA listing p. 301* ▼

enjoy
your stay

leave the rest to us℠
rates from
15% Off*
All Published Rates "TourBook Special"

Key property features
- Beautiful tropical courtyard
- Free Hot Breakfast Buffet/social happy hours Daily
- Fridge, coffee makers, micro in all rooms
- Free High Speed Internet and wired secured Internet available
- Convenient store RAMADA MART open 24 hours

- Special Rates all year long
- Heated Pool & Hot Spa are open for longer hours

Get the free mobile app at
http://gettag.mobi

Ramada Foothills Inn & Suites Resort
1-888-666-7934 – www.ramadafoothillstucson.com
6944 E Tanque Verde Rd
Tucson, AZ 85715
520-886-9595 From Mexico 01-800-681-1817
ramada.com
1-800-2Ramada

RAMADA
SERVICE & SATISFACTION IS OUR BUSINESS

* Rates are subject to availability. Blackout dates and other restrictions may apply. Single/Double occupancy. Cannot be combined with any offers or special rates. This hotel is independently owned and operated under a license agreement with Ramada Worldwide Inc. © 2012 Ramada Worldwide Inc.

(See maps & indexes p. 282, 288.)

RESIDENCE INN BY MARRIOTT WILLIAMS CENTRE
Phone: (520)790-6100 **38**

Extended Stay
Hotel
$98-$359

AAA Benefit:
AAA hotel discounts of 5% or more.

Address: 5400 E Williams Cir 85711 **Location:** Jct Campbell Ave, 3.8 mi e on Broadway Blvd, then just s and just e on Williams Blvd. **Facility:** 120 units, some two bedrooms and efficiencies. 4 stories, interior corridors. **Amenities:** *Some:* high-speed Internet. **Pool(s):** heated outdoor. **Activities:** whirlpool, sports court, exercise room. **Guest Services:** valet and coin laundry, area transportation-within 5 mi.

RESIDENCE INN TUCSON AIRPORT
Phone: (520)294-5522 **7**

Extended Stay
Hotel
$89-$249

AAA Benefit:
AAA hotel discounts of 5% or more.

Address: 2660 E Medina Rd 85756 **Location:** 0.5 mi n of airport entrance on Tucson Blvd, just e. **Facility:** 124 efficiencies. 3 stories, interior corridors. **Amenities:** high-speed Internet. **Pool(s):** heated outdoor. **Activities:** whirlpool, sports court, exercise room. **Guest Services:** valet and coin laundry.

STARR PASS GOLF SUITES Phone: 520/670-0500 **31**

Condominium
Rates not provided

Address: 3645 W Starr Pass Blvd 85745 **Location:** I-10 exit 259 (Starr Pass Blvd), 3.8 mi w. **Facility:** Surrounded by mountains and golf course fairways, the property's spacious suites offer every amenity desired for a long-term stay. 80 condominiums. 1 story, exterior corridors. **Terms:** office hours 6 am-midnight, check-in 4 pm. **Amenities:** high-speed Internet. **Pool(s):** heated outdoor. **Activities:** whirlpool, 2 tennis courts, hiking trails, basketball, exercise room. **Fee:** golf-27 holes. **Guest Services:** complimentary and valet laundry.

STAYBRIDGE SUITES TUCSON AIRPORT
Phone: (520)807-1004 **3**

Extended Stay
Hotel
$109-$249 2/1-5/31
$109-$159 6/1-1/31

Address: 2705 E Executive Dr 85756 **Location:** 0.7 mi n of Tucson International Airport. **Facility:** 97 efficiencies, some two bedrooms. 3 stories, interior corridors. **Amenities:** high-speed Internet. **Pool(s):** heated outdoor. **Activities:** whirlpool, exercise room. **Guest Services:** valet and coin laundry.

STUDIO 6 EXTENDED STAY #6002
Phone: (520)746-0030 **50**

Extended Stay
Motel
$53-$63 2/1-3/31
$49-$59 4/1-1/31

Address: 4950 S Outlet Center Dr 85706 **Location:** I-10 exit 264A eastbound; exit 264B westbound, just s, then just nw on Julian Dr. **Facility:** 120 efficiencies. 2 stories (no elevator), exterior corridors. **Terms:** office hours 7 am-9 pm. **Pool(s):** heated outdoor. **Guest Services:** coin laundry.

SUPER 8 CENTRAL EAST Phone: (520)790-6021 **43**

Motel
$36-$80

Address: 1990 S Craycroft Rd 85711 **Location:** I-10 exit 265 (Alvernon Way), 4.4 mi ne on Alvernon Way Golflinks Rd, then 0.4 mi n. **Facility:** 40 units. 2 stories (no elevator), exterior corridors. **Terms:** 3 day cancellation notice-fee imposed. **Pool(s):** outdoor. **Guest Services:** coin laundry. **Free Special Amenities: continental breakfast and high-speed Internet.**

SUPER 8 DOWNTOWN TUCSON CONVENTION AREA
Phone: (520)791-9282 **39**

Motel
$49-$117

Address: 715 W Starr Pass Blvd 85713 **Location:** I-10 exit 259 (22nd St/Starr Pass Blvd), just w. **Facility:** 68 units. 2 stories (no elevator), exterior corridors. **Amenities:** high-speed Internet. **Pool(s):** outdoor. **Activities:** whirlpool. **Guest Services:** coin laundry. **Free Special Amenities: continental breakfast and high-speed Internet.**

SUPER 8-TUCSON Phone: (520)620-6500 **18**

Motel
$49-$99

Address: 1550 W Grant Rd 85745 **Location:** I-10 exit 256 (Grant Rd), just w. **Facility:** 65 units. 2 stories (no elevator), exterior corridors. **Pool(s):** outdoor. **Activities:** whirlpool. **Guest Services:** coin laundry.

TOWNEPLACE SUITES BY MARRIOTT
Phone: (520)292-9697 **7**

Extended Stay
Hotel
$99-$199

AAA Benefit:
AAA hotel discounts of 5% or more.

Address: 405 W Rudasill Rd 85704 **Location:** Jct Orange Grove Rd, 0.5 mi s on Oracle Rd, then just w. **Facility:** 76 units, some two bedrooms and kitchens. 3 stories, interior corridors. **Amenities:** high-speed Internet. **Pool(s):** heated outdoor. **Activities:** exercise room. **Guest Services:** valet and coin laundry.

TRAVELODGE Phone: (520)622-8089 **35**

Motel
$29-$81

Address: 1000 S Freeway 85745 **Location:** I-10 exit 259 (22nd St/Starr Pass Blvd), just w, then just n. **Facility:** 42 units. 2 stories (no elevator), interior corridors. **Amenities:** *Some:* safes. **Guest Services:** coin laundry.

VISCOUNT SUITE HOTEL Phone: (520)745-6500 **34**

Hotel
$79-$225

Address: 4855 E Broadway Blvd 85711 **Location:** Just e of Swan Rd. **Facility:** 216 units, some two bedrooms. 4 stories, interior corridors. **Terms:** 10 day cancellation notice-fee imposed. **Amenities:** video games (fee). *Some:* high-speed Internet, safes. **Pool(s):** heated outdoor. **Activities:** whirlpool, exercise room. **Guest Services:** valet and coin laundry. **Free Special Amenities: full breakfast and high-speed Internet.**

(See maps & indexes p. 282, 288.)

THE WESTIN LA PALOMA RESORT & SPA
Phone: (520)742-6000   **11**

Resort Hotel
$99-$539

WESTIN HOTELS & RESORTS   **AAA Benefit:** Enjoy up to 15% off your next stay, plus Starwood Preferred Guest® bonuses.

Address: 3800 E Sunrise Dr 85718 **Location:** SR 77 (Oracle Rd), 4.6 mi e on Ina Rd via Skyline and Sunrise drs, then just s on Via Palomita. **Facility:** In an attractive desert setting, the resort features large rooms with balconies or patios. Guests will enjoy the beautiful pool area with a waterfall, pond, swim-up bar and waterslide. 487 units. 3 stories, exterior corridors. **Parking:** on-site and valet. **Terms:** check-in 4 pm, 7 day cancellation notice-fee imposed. **Amenities:** safes. **Dining:** 4 restaurants, also, Janos, J Bar-A Latin Grill, see separate listings. **Pool(s):** 5 heated outdoor. **Activities:** saunas, whirlpools, steamrooms, waterslide, recreation programs, hiking trails, jogging, playground, spa. *Fee:* golf-27 holes, 10 tennis courts (8 lighted), racquetball court. **Guest Services:** valet laundry, area transportation-within 3 mi. **Free Special Amenities: newspaper and children's activities.**

[icons: SAVE ECO FEE ... BIZ ... FEE ... / SOME UNITS ...]

WESTWARD LOOK RESORT
Phone: (520)297-1151   **4**

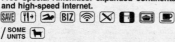
Resort Hotel
$149-$449

Address: 245 E Ina Rd 85704 **Location:** I-10 exit 248 (Ina Rd), 6 mi e, then just n on Westward Look Dr. Located in a quiet area. **Facility:** Nestled on 80 acres, this full-service resort boasts fabulous views of the Catalina Mountains and features pools surrounded by flowers and trees. 244 units. 1-2 stories (no elevator), exterior corridors. **Parking:** on-site and valet. **Terms:** check-in 4 pm, 7 day cancellation notice-fee imposed. **Amenities:** safes. **Dining:** Gold, see separate listing. **Pool(s):** 3 heated outdoor. **Activities:** whirlpools, recreation programs, hiking trails, jogging, sports court, basketball, horseshoes, shuffleboard, volleyball, exercise room, spa. *Fee:* 8 tennis courts (5 lighted), bicycles, horseback riding. **Guest Services:** valet laundry. **Free Special Amenities: local telephone calls and newspaper.**
(See ad this page.)

[icons: SAVE ECO ... BIZ ... FEE ... / SOME UNITS FEE ...]

WINDMILL SUITES AT ST. PHILIP'S PLAZA
Phone: 520/577-0007   **15**

Hotel
Rates not provided

Address: 4250 N Campbell Ave 85718 **Location:** I-10 exit 254 (Prince Rd), 4 mi e, then 1 mi n. **Facility:** 122 units. 3 stories, interior corridors. **Terms:** check-in 4 pm. **Pool(s):** heated outdoor. **Activities:** whirlpool, bicycles, limited exercise equipment. **Guest Services:** valet and coin laundry. **Free Special Amenities: expanded continental breakfast and high-speed Internet.**

[icons: SAVE ... BIZ ... / SOME UNITS ...]

**Explore the Travel Guides
on AAA.com/Travel or
CAA.ca/Travel**

CANYON RANCH
Phone: 520/749-9000

[fyi] Not evaluated. **Address:** 8600 E Rockcliff Rd 85749. Facilities, services, and decor characterize an upscale property.

HACIENDA DEL SOL GUEST RANCH RESORT
Phone: 520/299-1501

[fyi] Not evaluated. **Address:** 5601 N Hacienda del Sol Rd 85718 **Location:** Jct SR 77 (Oracle Rd), 5.4 mi e on Ina Rd/Skyline and Sunrise drs, 0.6 mi s to Via Alcalde, then just nw. Facilities, services, and decor characterize a mid-scale property.

TANQUE VERDE RANCH
Phone: 520/296-6275

[fyi] Not evaluated. **Address:** 14301 E Speedway Blvd 85748. Facilities, services, and decor characterize an upscale property.

▼ *See AAA listing this page* ▼

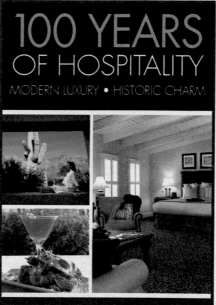

100 YEARS
OF HOSPITALITY
MODERN LUXURY • HISTORIC CHARM

Westward Look Resort and Arizona are turning 100! Discover a Tucson treasure boasting a beautiful fusion of modern luxury and historic charm, spacious rooms, award-winning dining and a soothing spa.

WESTWARD LOOK RESORT
1912 *The Soul of the Southwest* 2012
CELEBRATING 100 YEARS

www.westwardlook.com
Tucson, AZ • 800.722.2500

(See maps & indexes p. 282, 288.)

WHERE TO EAT

ACACIA
Phone: 520/232-0101 (12)

New American
$18-$29

AAA Inspector Notes: Chef Albert Hall has opened a charming facility with such creative dishes as sustainable salmon with tomato-kiwi salsa. The modern dining room features sweeping views across the city. **Bar:** full bar. **Reservations:** suggested. **Address:** 3001 E Skyline Dr 85718 **Location:** Northeast corner of Skyline Dr and Campbell Ave. (L) (D)

ANTHONY'S IN THE CATALINAS
Phone: 520/299-1771 (11)

Continental
$30-$55

AAA Inspector Notes: In a desert setting with city and mountain views, this pleasant dining room becomes a window to the world. A comprehensive selection of wines complements well-presented dishes offered with accomplished service. **Bar:** full bar. **Reservations:** suggested. **Address:** 6440 N Campbell Ave 85718 **Location:** I-10 exit 250 (Orange Grove Rd), 7 mi e to Skyline Dr, 0.5 mi e, then just n. **Parking:** on-site and valet. (D)

THE BAMBOO CLUB
Phone: 520/514-9665

Pacific Rim
$10-$26

AAA Inspector Notes: The contemporary, upbeat and casual decor lends well to an atmosphere of conviviality. Friends and family get together over shared dishes from Thailand, China, Japan, Hawaii, Malaysia, Tahiti, Korea, Vietnam and other exotic Asian ports of call. The menu offers a wide selection of popular foods that are "sizzled, grilled, steamed, wokked or noodled" and includes choices ranging from finger foods to full entrees. **Bar:** full bar. **Reservations:** suggested. **Address:** 5870 E Broadway Blvd, #524 85711 **Location:** Just w of Wilmot Rd; in Park Place Mall. **Parking:** on-site and valet. (L) (D)

BAZIL'S
Phone: 520/577-3322 (22)

Regional Italian
$15-$40

AAA Inspector Notes: Family members pride themselves on their years of friendly service, and the warm ambience of the dining room is a perfect setting. Wonderful traditional dishes, such as chicken rollatini or veal piccata, are popular choices. **Bar:** full bar. **Reservations:** suggested. **Address:** 4777 E Sunrise Dr, Suite 119 85718 **Location:** Northeast corner of Sunrise Dr and Swan Rd. (D)

BEYOND BREAD
Phone: 520/322-9965 (36)

American
$7-$11

AAA Inspector Notes: This popular place prepares hearty breakfasts, homemade soup and luncheon sandwiches to please any taste. The eatery features upscale decor that allows for a friendly display of breads and pastries. **Address:** 3026 N Campbell Ave 85719 **Location:** Just s of Ft Lowell Rd. (B) (L) (D)

BLUEFIN SEAFOOD BISTRO
Phone: 520/531-8500 (8)

Seafood
$9-$29

AAA Inspector Notes: Diners may sit upstairs to overlook the courtyard or downstairs near the bar at this bistro. Delightful selections of fresh fish range from wild salmon to ahi tuna to a variety of shellfish, prepared with various toppings and cooking styles. **Bar:** full bar. **Address:** 7053 N Oracle Rd 85718 **Location:** Just s of Ina Rd; in Casas Adobes. (L) (D)

BLUE WILLOW RESTAURANT BAKERY
Phone: 520/327-7577 (45)

American
$8-$13

AAA Inspector Notes: Known for its breakfasts--including a variety of omelets and fresh breads--this restaurant also treats guests to relaxed dinners, daily specials and friendly, helpful service. Romance blooms on the charming patio in the evening. **Bar:** beer & wine. **Address:** 2616 N Campbell Ave 85719 **Location:** Just n of Glenn. (B) (L) (D)

CACTUS ROSE STEAKHOUSE
Phone: 520/323-5220 (67)

Steak
$14-$35

AAA Inspector Notes: An intimate atmosphere greets diners who may choose from a menu of prime steaks, seafood and pasta. Sunday brunch is very popular. **Bar:** full bar. **Address:** 445 S Alvernon Way 85711 **Location:** I-10 exit 259 (22nd St), 4 mi e, then just n; in DoubleTree by Hilton Tucson - Reid Park. (B) (L) (D)

CASA DEL RIO
Phone: 520/296-2309 (71)

Mexican
$5-$12

AAA Inspector Notes: This casual east side eatery has been serving up traditional Sonoran-style favorites since 1979. Specialties include chimichangas, fajitas and red or green chili con carne. **Bar:** full bar. **Address:** 1060 S Pantano Rd 85710 **Location:** Jct E 22nd St, just n. (L) (D)

CHAD'S STEAKHOUSE & SALOON
Phone: 520/881-1802 (44)

Steak
$8-$24

AAA Inspector Notes: Western-style decor sets the stage for hearty dishes including Chicago baby back ribs and the Arizona tumbleweed-a fresh, whole, fried onion served with dipping sauce. **Bar:** full bar. **Address:** 3001 N Swan Rd 85712 **Location:** Jct Swan and Ft Lowell rds; northwest corner. (L) (D)

CHANTILLY TEA ROOM
Phone: 520/622-3303 (20)

Specialty
$6-$27

AAA Inspector Notes: Elegant duchess tea service, with tiered trays of delectable morsels, is one option at this popular luncheon spot. Salads, quiche, soup and sandwiches round out the menu. **Reservations:** suggested. **Address:** 5185 N Genematas Dr 85704 **Location:** Jct River Rd, just n on Oracle Rd, then just e. (B) (L)

CHOICE GREENS
Phone: 520/319-2467 (55)

Specialty
$7-$9

AAA Inspector Notes: Freshly made salads with a choice of greens, protein, taste-enhancing extra choppings and nearly two dozen dressings make for a perfect, fast meal. Panini and hearty cold sandwiches also are among the casual restaurant's offerings. **Bar:** wine only. **Address:** 2829 E Speedway Blvd 85716 **Location:** Just w of Country Club Rd. (L) (D) CALL

CHOICE GREENS
Phone: 520/319-2467 (32)

Specialty
$5-$10

AAA Inspector Notes: Patrons can create their own made-to-order salads from a vast array of greens, protein, toppings and nearly two dozen dressings. Hearty soups, sandwiches and desserts also are offered. **Bar:** beer & wine. **Address:** 4205 N Campbell Ave 85718 **Location:** Jct River Rd, just s. (L) (D)

(See maps & indexes p. 282, 288.)

CLAIM JUMPER   Phase: 520/795-2900

American
$8-$25

AAA Inspector Notes: Great menu variety makes this place a good stop for parties with diverse tastes. Choices include specialty appetizers, salads, rotisserie chicken and barbecue items, not to mention good comfort foods, such as traditional pot pie. Hearty portions satisfy big appetites. The atmosphere is fun and lively. **Bar:** full bar. **Address:** 3761 E Broadway Blvd 85716 **Location:** 0.7 mi e of Country Club Rd. [L] [D]

CODY'S BEEF 'N BEANS   Phone: 520/322-9475   (34)

Steak
$7-$20

AAA Inspector Notes: The Cody burger gets raves from the locals but the tender grilled steaks at this eatery are mouthwatering and flavorful. Side dishes, including everything from onion rings and coleslaw, complete the satisfying meal in this small eatery with its Western bunkhouse decor. **Bar:** beer & wine. **Address:** 2708 E Ft Lowell Rd 85716 **Location:** Just w of Country Club Rd. [L] [D]

COLT'S TASTE OF TEXAS   Phone: 520/572-5968   (1)

Steak
$8-$26

AAA Inspector Notes: This Northwest Tucson steakhouse is known for its down-home, country-style cooking. On the menu are large cuts of cooked-to-order meats, barbecue, ribs, seafood and enormous desserts sure to satisfy the heartiest appetite. **Bar:** full bar. **Reservations:** suggested. **Address:** 8310 N Thornydale Rd 85741 **Location:** I-10 exit 246 (Cortaro Rd), 2.6 mi e [L] [D]

DAISY MAE'S STEAKHOUSE
Phone: 520/792-8888   (53)

Steak
$15-$31

AAA Inspector Notes: Steaks are cooked just as patrons prefer in this casual eatery. Many folks lend to the decor by signing $1 bills and having them hung on the wall. **Bar:** full bar. **Address:** 2735 W Anklam Rd 85745 **Location:** I-10 exit 257A (St. Mary's Rd), 2 mi w. [D]

DAKOTA CAFE & CATERING COMPANY
Phone: 520/298-7188   (54)

American
$9-$30

AAA Inspector Notes: Located in Trail Dust Town, the casually decorated dining room and patio seating are pleasant backdrops for exciting meals. Chef Carl Hendrick takes seriously his heart-healthy dishes, vegetarian choices and daily fresh fish items. Using cooking styles and food elements from around the world, he blends interesting ingredients in such dishes as tempura-coconut shrimp with mango chutney and pork tenderloin filled with poblano chiles, spinach and white cheddar cheese. **Bar:** full bar. **Reservations:** suggested. **Address:** 6541 E Tanque Verde Rd 85715 **Location:** Jct Campbell Ave, 5.6 mi e on Grant Rd, then just s. [L] [D]

DELHI PALACE   Phone: 520/296-8585   (69)

Indian
$8-$16

AAA Inspector Notes: Local business people come to this eatery for the popular lunch buffet; well-presented evening dinners are every bit as good. Food choices center on traditional preparations of tandoori, curry, seafood and vegetarian ingredients. Desserts are made on the premises, and kulfi is excellent. **Bar:** full bar. **Address:** 6751 E Broadway Blvd 85710 **Location:** Jct Wilmot Rd, 0.5 mi e. [L] [D]

THE DISH BISTRO BAR   Phone: 520-326-1714   (57)

American
$19-$34

AAA Inspector Notes: This intimate dining space does not intimidate the chef, who serves big-time flavors; one option is grilled salmon with sweet corn beurre blanc. The attentive staff assists with meal choices and may offer tastes of wines. **Bar:** beer & wine. **Address:** 3131 E 1st St 85716 **Location:** I-10 exit 257 (Speedway Blvd), 3.2 mi e; at RumRunner. [D]

THE ECLECTIC CAFE   Phone: 520/885-2842   (52)

American
$6-$14

AAA Inspector Notes: This storefront eatery has pizazz. On the menu are innovative foods ranging from warm salads made with spicy or cooked meats and cool veggies to hearty sandwiches and a good selection of Mexican classics. **Bar:** wine only. **Address:** 7053 E Tanque Verde Rd 85715 **Location:** Jct Grant Rd, 0.5 mi ne. [L] [D]

EL CORRAL STEAKHOUSE
Phone: 520/299-6092   (31)

American
$10-$20

AAA Inspector Notes: Built in the late 1800s, the historic adobe ranch house is a nice spot for casual dining. Reservations are not accepted. **Bar:** full bar. **Address:** 2201 E River Rd 85718 **Location:** I-10 exit 254 (Prince Rd), 0.4 mi e, 1 mi n on Campbell Ave, then just e. **Historic** [D]

ELLE WINE BISTRO   Phone: 520/327-0500   (39)

American
$12-$30

AAA Inspector Notes: Attentive service accompanies an eclectic menu, including a selection of pasta, seafood and such dishes as pork medallions with a sweet peach glaze. The imaginative wine list features an excellent by-the-glass selection. **Bar:** full bar. **Reservations:** suggested. **Address:** 2970 N Campbell Ave 85719 **Location:** Just s of Fort Lowell Rd; in Campbell Plaza Shopping Center. [L] [D]

FEAST   Phone: 520/326-9363   (58)

American
$9-$18

AAA Inspector Notes: Although take-out is a segment of the business, the dine-in option offers friendly staff who see to patrons' every need. The menu centers on such upscale dishes as cream of asparagus soup, a salad that includes curried chicken, and vegetarian offerings. An extensive wine list is offered. **Bar:** full bar. **Reservations:** suggested. **Address:** 3719 E Speedway Blvd 85712 **Location:** Just w of Alvernon Way. [L] [D]

FIREBIRDS WOOD FIRED GRILL
Phone: 520/577-0747   (13)

American
$8-$35

AAA Inspector Notes: The restaurant re-creates the atmosphere of a mountain lodge. Hand-cut steaks and seafood dominate the menu, which also lists a few pork and chicken entrees, as well as elk tenderloin medallions and buffalo meatloaf. The kitchen uses wood grilling, and pizzas bake in a wood-burning oven. Flavorful food, enhanced presentations and a skilled, knowledgeable and attentive staff, together with distinctive physical elements, make this place appealing. **Bar:** full bar. **Address:** 2985 E Skyline Dr 85718 **Location:** Jct Campbell Ave; northwest corner; in La Encantada Plaza. [L] [D]

(See maps & indexes p. 282, 288.)

FLEMING'S PRIME STEAKHOUSE & WINE BAR
Phone: 520/529-5017   15

Steak
$19-$50

AAA Inspector Notes: The warm, clubby atmosphere is the ideal setting for perfectly grilled steaks and seafood. Side dishes come in hearty portions, and salads are fresh and crisp. More than 100 wine selections are available. **Bar:** full bar. **Reservations:** suggested. **Address:** 6360 N Campbell Ave 85718 **Location:** Southeast corner of Skyline Dr and Campbell Ave. **Parking:** on-site and valet. D

FLYING V BAR & GRILL   Phone: 520/299-2020   17

Regional
Southwestern
$15-$26

AAA Inspector Notes: Dry-aged, New York strip steak is one of the 12 signature features at this lakeside dining spot where seafood and meats are custom grilled to meet diners' expectations. The house guacamole, made tableside, garners rave reviews from the local clientele. **Bar:** full bar. **Reservations:** suggested. **Address:** 7000 N Resort Dr 85750 **Location:** I-10 exit 256 (Grant Rd), 8.6 mi e, 0.6 mi ne on Tanque Verde Rd, 2 mi n on Sabino Canyon Rd, then 3.5 mi n on Kolb Rd; in Loews Ventana Canyon Resort. D

GHINIS FRENCH CAFFE   Phone: 520/326-9095   33

French
$6-$13

AAA Inspector Notes: This busy bistro's breakfast omelets and luncheon salads are prepared in the French country style. Menu offerings are treats either for a celebration or a relaxed meal with friends. The full-service French bakery allows for take-home goodies. **Bar:** beer & wine. **Address:** 1803 E Prince Rd 85719 **Location:** Just w of Campbell Ave. B L

GOLD   Phone: 520/917-2930   6

American
$12-$29

AAA Inspector Notes: The view over the valley below, which is particularly breathtaking at night, complements the fine-dining experience at this sophisticated restaurant. Sonoran Desert spices and flavors infuse classic and contemporary cuisine. Among desserts prepared on site are a poached pear stuffed with pistachio mousse and the delectable ancho chili chocolate bombe. **Bar:** full bar. **Reservations:** suggested. **Address:** 245 E Ina Rd 85704 **Location:** I-10 exit 248 (Ina Rd), 6 mi e, then just n on Westward Look Rd; in Westward Look Resort. **Parking:** on-site and valet. *(See ad p. 305.)* B L D

THE GRILL AT HACIENDA DEL SOL
Phone: 520/529-3500   21

Southwestern
$24-$38

AAA Inspector Notes: Both in the main dining room and on the patio, this charming ambience of old Tucson is apparent in the decor. Seasonal menu offerings are prepared with the freshest ingredients and show innovative flavor combinations. **Bar:** full bar. **Reservations:** suggested. **Address:** 5601 N Hacienda del Sol Rd 85718 **Location:** Jct SR 77 (Oracle Rd), 5.4 mi e on Ina Rd/Skyline and Sunrise drs, 0.6 mi s to Via Alcalde, then just nw; in Hacienda del Sol Guest Ranch Resort. **Parking:** on-site and valet. D

HI FALUTIN WESTERN GRILL
Phone: 520/297-0518   10

American
$9-$25

AAA Inspector Notes: The charming Western decor is bright and fun. Hearty and pleasing eats range from cattle boss pot roast to flat-iron rib-eye. Stetson-clad servers are friendly and helpful. **Bar:** full bar. **Address:** 6780 N Oracle Rd 85704 **Location:** Jct Ina Rd, 0.5 mi s.
L D

THE HUNGRY FOX RESTAURANT AND COUNTRY STORE
Phone: 520/326-2835   65

American
$5-$10

AAA Inspector Notes: Friendly staffers know the booth preferences of regulars in the popular breakfast and lunch eatery serving hearty portions. Homemade soups and oversized cinnamon buns are top choices. **Address:** 4637 E Broadway Blvd 85711 **Location:** Jct Swan Rd and Broadway Blvd; northwest corner. B L

INDIA OVEN   Phone: 520/326-8635   43

Indian
$10-$15

AAA Inspector Notes: The menu lists all the classic dishes one might expect, like crisp tandoori chicken, lamb tikka and shrimp masala. Locals pack the daily lunch buffet, and the friendly owner often strolls the open, colorful dining room. **Bar:** full bar. **Address:** 2727 N Campbell Ave 85719 **Location:** Just s of Glenn St.
L D

JANOS   Phone: 520/615-6100   18

French
$28-$50

AAA Inspector Notes: Although Janos is noted for its innovative French-inspired Southwestern cuisine, the accomplished service adds a special element to the dining experience. The chef-owner often chats with guests. **Bar:** full bar. **Reservations:** suggested. **Address:** 3770 E Sunrise Dr 85718 **Location:** SR 77 (Oracle Rd), 4.6 mi e on Ina Rd via Skyline and Sunrise drs, then just s on Via Palomita; in The Westin La Paloma Resort & Spa. **Parking:** on-site and valet. D

JAVELINA CANTINA   Phone: 520/881-4200   68

Southwestern
$12-$23

AAA Inspector Notes: A lively atmosphere and happy hour specials greet the after-work crowd at this cantina. **Bar:** full bar. **Address:** 445 S Alvernon Way 85711 **Location:** I-10 exit 259 (22nd St), 4 mi e, then just n; in DoubleTree by Hilton Tucson - Reid Park. D

JAX KITCHEN   Phone: 520/219-1235   7

American
$13-$24

AAA Inspector Notes: Located in a strip mall on the north side, this simple yet sophisticated dining spot features a menu that changes seasonally. Comprised of such items as steamed mussels with chorizo, duck leg confit salad and a decadent red velvet cake, it is best described as modern comfort food. **Bar:** full bar. **Reservations:** suggested. **Address:** 7286 N Oracle Rd 85704 **Location:** Jct Ina Rd, just n. D

J BAR-A LATIN GRILL   Phone: 520/615-6100   19

Caribbean
$13-$28

AAA Inspector Notes: This is the place to meet and greet in town. The chef's high-energy, delectable food makes this spot popular with both locals and visitors. Indulge in such rich dishes as Dos Equis-marinated carne asada or achiote rock shrimp soft tacos. **Bar:** full bar. **Address:** 3770 E Sunrise Dr 85718 **Location:** SR 77 (Oracle Rd), 4.6 mi e on Ina Rd via Skyline and Sunrise drs, then just s on Via Palomita; in The Westin La Paloma Resort & Spa. **Parking:** on-site and valet. D

JONATHAN'S CORK   Phone: 520/296-1631   59

Southwestern
$15-$38

AAA Inspector Notes: Chef Landeen flavors his dishes with a Southwestern flair and then may stop by tables with a greeting and to ask about the meal. The dining room is appointed in a casual ranch-style decor. **Bar:** full bar. **Reservations:** suggested. **Address:** 6320 E Tanque Verde Rd 85715 **Location:** Jct Speedway Blvd, 0.5 mi ne. D LATE

(See maps & indexes p. 282, 288.)

KINGFISHER
Phone: 520/323-7739 (48)

Regional American
$8-$26

AAA Inspector Notes: Diners can expect a large selection of fresh fish and shellfish as well as pasta, beef and chicken selections. A summer menu centers on regional cuisine. Live entertainment is a draw on Saturday and Monday evenings. **Bar:** full bar. **Reservations:** suggested. **Address:** 2564 E Grant Rd 85716 **Location:** I-10 exit 256 (Grant Rd), 3.5 mi e. L D

LA FUENTE RESTAURANT
Phone: 520/623-8659 (49)

Mexican
$8-$19

AAA Inspector Notes: Hanging plants and weekend jazz or mariachi music lend to the colorful atmosphere at this laid-back restaurant with attentive service, which has served the area for more than 40 years. The Mexican fare is tasty, and the Sunday champagne brunch from 11 am to 2 pm is a treat. **Bar:** full bar. **Address:** 1749 N Oracle Rd 85705 **Location:** I-10 exit 256 (Grant Rd), 0.9 mi e, then 0.5 mi s. L D

LA PARRILLA SUIZA
Phone: 520/624-4300

Mexican
$8-$19

AAA Inspector Notes: The casual atmosphere and friendly, efficient waitstaff contribute to a pleasant outing at this locally popular eatery. Styled as Mexico City cuisine, traditional dishes are prepared with a Continental flair. **Bar:** full bar. **Address:** 2720 N Oracle Rd 85705 **Location:** 0.5 mi s of Fort Lowell Rd. L D

LA PARRILLA SUIZA
Phone: 520/572-7200

Mexican
$8-$15

AAA Inspector Notes: Bright decor with a high-peaked ceiling and open bar lends to a fresh setting in which to savor central Mexican cuisine. Pleasant servers assist patrons through the meal. During the winter, mariachi music enlivens the place on weekends. **Bar:** full bar. **Address:** 4250 W Ina Rd 85741 **Location:** I-10 exit 248 (Ina Rd), 0.5 mi e. L D

LE RENDEZ-VOUS
Phone: 520/323-7373 (40)

French
$10-$50

AAA Inspector Notes: Patrons of this small, charming restaurant are served elegantly prepared French dishes by attentive and well-trained waitstaff. **Bar:** full bar. **Address:** 3844 E Fort Lowell Rd 85716 **Location:** Jct Oracle Rd, 4 mi e. L D

LODGE ON THE DESERT
Phone: 520/325-3366 (62)

American
$11-$32

AAA Inspector Notes: The brightly appointed Southwestern dining room and covered patio are highlights at this casual yet sophisticated restaurant. The seasonal menu prepared by the executive chef includes creative dishes, including citrus-rosemary-glazed chicken. **Bar:** full bar. **Reservations:** suggested. **Address:** 306 N Alvernon Way 85711 **Location:** I-10 exit 258 (Broadway Blvd/Congress St), 4 mi e, then just n. B L D

LOTUS GARDEN
Phone: 520/298-3351 (61)

Chinese
$7-$23

AAA Inspector Notes: Although this restaurant's focus is on preparing Cantonese and Szechuan cuisine, the owners also offer monthly wine tastings with special foods. The rose-and-gray decor is refreshing, and a small patio allows for al fresco dining. Popular with area professionals, the luncheon special includes soup, an egg roll and a choice of more than a dozen entrées. Mongolian beef and kung pao chicken are among dinner favorites. **Bar:** full bar. **Reservations:** suggested. **Address:** 5975 E Speedway Blvd 85712 **Location:** Just w of Wilmot Rd. L D

LOVIN' SPOONFULS
Phone: 520/325-7766 (38)

Vegetarian
$6-$12

AAA Inspector Notes: Folks do not miss the animal products at this enjoyable vegetarian eatery. Hearty breakfasts, big "bacon" cheeseburgers, and "chicken" salad made with tofu will have you fooled. The clean, modern dining room passes the comfort test. **Bar:** beer & wine. **Address:** 2990 N Campbell Ave 85719 **Location:** Just s of Fort Lowell Rd. B L D

MACAYO MEXICAN KITCHEN
Phone: 520/722-8090

Mexican
$8-$16

AAA Inspector Notes: The colorfully furnished Mexican-style eatery prepares Sonoran Mexican dishes. Friendly and efficient staffers serve traditional and lighter dishes flavored with this place's own chili peppers, which are grown near Tucson. **Bar:** full bar. **Address:** 7040 E Broadway Rd 85710 **Location:** Just w of Kolb Rd. L D

MAIN DINING ROOM AT THE ARIZONA INN
Phone: 520/325-1541 (50)

Continental
$12-$40

AAA Inspector Notes: Decorated as it might have been when the inn opened some 80 years ago, this restaurant is a nice spot for refined dining. Tall windows overlook a landscaped courtyard, and mirrors and soft lighting create a soothing atmosphere. Diners savor preparations of seafood, beef and lamb or select from the ever-changing chef's tasting menu. After the meal, it is worth the splurge to try such desserts as homemade ginger cappuccino ice cream. **Bar:** full bar. **Reservations:** suggested. **Address:** 2200 E Elm St 85719 **Location:** I-10 exit 257 (Speedway Blvd), 2.5 mi e, 0.5 mi n on Campbell Ave, then just e; in Arizona Inn. **Parking:** on-site and valet. B L D

MAMA'S FAMOUS PIZZA & HEROS
Phone: 520/751-4600

Pizza
$6-$38

AAA Inspector Notes: With four Tucson locations, this popular eatery has been serving New York-style pizza, pasta dishes and sandwiches for nearly three decades. **Bar:** beer & wine. **Address:** 50 S Houghton Rd 85748 **Location:** Southwest corner of Broadway Blvd and Houghton Rd. L D

MAMA'S FAMOUS PIZZA & HEROS
Phone: 520/750-1919

Pizza
$6-$38

AAA Inspector Notes: With four Tucson locations, this popular eatery has been serving New York-style pizza, pasta dishes and sandwiches for nearly three decades. **Bar:** beer & wine. **Address:** 6996 E 22nd St 85710 **Location:** Southwest corner of 22nd St and Kolb Rd. L D

MAMA'S FAMOUS PIZZA & HEROS
Phone: 520/297-3993

Pizza
$6-$38

AAA Inspector Notes: With four Tucson locations, this popular eatery has been serving New York-style pizza, pasta dishes and sandwiches for nearly three decades. **Bar:** beer & wine. **Address:** 7965 N Oracle Rd 85704 **Location:** Southwest corner of Oracle and Magee rds. L D

MAMA'S FAMOUS PIZZA & HEROS
Phone: 520/319-8856

Pizza
$6-$38

AAA Inspector Notes: With four Tucson locations, this popular eatery has been serving New York-style pizza, pasta dishes and sandwiches for nearly three decades. **Bar:** beer & wine. **Address:** 4500 E Speedway Blvd 85712 **Location:** Just w of Swan Rd. L D

(See maps & indexes p. 282, 288.)

MCMAHON'S STEAKHOUSE
Phone: 520/327-7463 46

Steak
$8-$60

AAA Inspector Notes: An elegant, curving wine cellar and original Western art mark very upscale decor at this eatery set outside of downtown. Such starters as fire-roasted chiles and Caesar salad complement top-notch beef and prime seafood entrées. Steak Christiani or Gugino's veal scaloppine are popular choices, and the champagne strawberries are a special treat. Marinated berries are dipped in a coating and quickly fried for a decadent dessert. Expect smooth, accomplished service from a team-oriented waitstaff. **Bar:** full bar. **Reservations:** suggested. **Address:** 2959 N Swan Rd 85712 **Location:** I-10 exit 256 (Grant Rd), 5.6 mi e, then 0.7 mi n. **Parking:** valet only. L D CALL &M

METROPOLITAN GRILL
Phone: 520/531-1212 3

American
$6-$21

AAA Inspector Notes: Popular with locals and families, this high-energy, upscale eatery presents a wide selection of pizza and entrées cooked over a wood fire. Easy to find in a corner strip mall, the restaurant employs a very friendly, attentive waitstaff. **Bar:** full bar. **Reservations:** suggested. **Address:** 7892 N Oracle Rd 85704 **Location:** I-10 exit 248 (Ina Rd), 5 mi e, then 1 mi n; in Plaza Escondida Shopping Center. L D

MICHELANGELO RISTORANTE ITALIANO
Phone: 520/297-5775 2

Italian
$9-$29

AAA Inspector Notes: This family-owned and -operated restaurant serves a large selection of classic dishes from veal Marsala to chicken Toscanini served with artichokes and mushrooms over cheese tortellini. Homemade desserts are too tempting to miss. Patio seating is available. **Bar:** full bar. **Address:** 420 W Magee Rd 85704 **Location:** I-10 exit 248 (Ina Rd), 5.5 mi e, then 1 mi n on SR 77 (Oracle Rd). L D

MIGUEL'S AT LA POSADA
Phone: 520/887-3777 16

Latin American
$9-$29

AAA Inspector Notes: Lovely Latin flavors, a wide range of tequilas and martinis, friendly service and a quietly elegant room all combine to make a meal at this fine dining spot memorable. From simmered pork loin on a banana leaf boat to chicken and wild mushroom enchiladas, each dish awakens the senses. **Bar:** full bar. **Address:** 5900 N Oracle Rd 85704 **Location:** 0.5 mi s of Orange Grove Rd; in La Posada Lodge & Casitas. L D

MI NIDITO FAMILY RESTAURANT
Phone: 520/622-5081 70

Mexican
$5-$13

AAA Inspector Notes: Mi Nidito means little nest, and guests will be cozy in this one. Hearty portions are served in the bright, welcoming dining room. In the Clinton booth, patrons can taste a dish named after the former president during his visit in 1999. **Bar:** beer & wine. **Address:** 1813 S 4th Ave 85713 **Location:** I-10 exit 259 (Starr Pass Blvd), 0.8 mi e on 22nd St, then 0.6 mi s; northeast corner of 29th St and 4th Ave. L D

MONTANA AVENUE
Phone: 520/298-2020 51

Regional American
$14-$25

AAA Inspector Notes: Fresh, modern decor greets guests at this eatery serving such comfort dishes as roasted chicken with macaroni and cheese as well as more adventurous items such as braised lamb shank or rainbow trout grilled to perfection. **Bar:** full bar. **Address:** 6390 E Grant Rd 85715 **Location:** Just w of Wilmot Rd. L D

MOSAIC CAFE DOS
Phone: 520/297-8470 4

Mexican
$8-$16

AAA Inspector Notes: Diners come to this café for delicious, freshly cooked food, as well as the friendly and helpful staff. An added bonus is the patting out and cooking of tortillas right before their eyes. **Bar:** full bar. **Address:** 7350 N La Cholla Blvd 85741 **Location:** Just n of Ina Rd. L D

NEO OF MELAKA
Phone: 520/747-7811 66

Asian
$7-$29

AAA Inspector Notes: The casual eatery offers a diverse and flavorful blend of Malaysian and Chinese foods, from spicy satay skewers of chicken or beef to sambal, a hot, spicy toasted pepper sauce served with seafood, beef, tofu or chicken. **Bar:** full bar. **Address:** 6133 E Broadway Blvd 85711 **Location:** Just w of Wilmot Rd. L D

NORTH
Phone: 520/299-1600 14

New Italian
$9-$28

AAA Inspector Notes: Robust Northern Italian foods and attentive servers are hallmarks at this restaurant. Huge windows afford views across the valley. Diners can choose from a wide selection of wines and martinis. **Bar:** full bar. **Address:** 2995 E Skyline Dr 85718 **Location:** Jct Campbell Ave; northwest corner; in La Encantada Plaza. L D

OLD PUEBLO GRILL
Phone: 520/326-6000 64

Regional American
$10-$20

AAA Inspector Notes: Whether on the outside walled patio or inside among large cactus plants, diners can enjoy innovative foods with Southwestern flair served by bright young staff. **Bar:** full bar. **Address:** 60 N Alvernon Way 85711 **Location:** Just n of Broadway Blvd. L D

OM MODERN ASIAN KITCHEN
Phone: 520/299-7815 26

Asian
$8-$24

AAA Inspector Notes: Trendy decor and attractive food can be found at this casual eatery. Menu highlights include chicken or shrimp lemak made with lemongrass and coconut milk. Spice levels can be adjusted to guests' preferences. A variety of sorbets, like lychee or mango, will cool the palate at the end of the meal. **Bar:** full bar. **Reservations:** suggested. **Address:** 1765 E River Rd 85718 **Location:** Jct Campbell Rd, just w. L D

OPA! GREEK CUISINE & FUN
Phone: 520/327-2841 37

Greek
$9-$14

AAA Inspector Notes: Get moderately priced Greek favorites at this busy eatery. The menu lists hearty appetizers like hummus, a crisp, classic Greek salad, moussaka, chicken or beef kebabs and souvlaki. Dine al fresco when the weather permits. **Bar:** wine only. **Address:** 2990 N Campbell Ave, #130 85719 **Location:** Just s of Fort Lowell Rd. L D CALL &M

OREGANO'S PIZZA BISTRO
Phone: 520/327-8955

Italian
$7-$22

AAA Inspector Notes: This high-energy bistro employs a young and attentive waitstaff that serves hearty, oversized portions of delicious food. Offerings range from pizza and salads to pasta and baked sandwiches. The patio can be the happening place. **Bar:** full bar. **Address:** 4900 E Speedway Blvd 85712 **Location:** 0.6 mi w of Craycroft Rd. L D

(See maps & indexes p. 282, 288.)

PASTICHE MODERN EATERY
Phone: 520/325-3333 (35)

American
$8-$25

AAA Inspector Notes: The decor, featuring interesting modern art, sets a backdrop for quiet dining. Local products figure significantly in classic, yet creative, dishes that entice guests to try new flavors. Find Guinness steak topped with pepper bacon, porter cheddar and fried egg on grilled sourdough; thyme-crusted sea bass with smoked tomato-caper beurre blanc and champagne cream sauce; and chipotle salmon cakes with corn topped with dill aioli. A wine shop offers more than 800 selections. **Bar:** full bar. **Reservations:** suggested. **Address:** 3025 N Campbell Ave 85719 **Location:** Just s of Fort Lowell Rd. [L] [D]

P.F. CHANG'S CHINA BISTRO
Phone: 520/615-8788 (28)

Chinese
$8-$21

AAA Inspector Notes: Trendy, upscale decor provides a pleasant backdrop for New Age Chinese dining. Appetizers, soups and salads are a meal by themselves. Vegetarian plates and sides, noodles, meins, chicken and meat dishes are created from exotic, fresh ingredients. **Bar:** full bar. **Address:** 1805 E River Rd 85718 **Location:** Just w of jct Campbell Ave. [D]

PINNACLE PEAK RESTAURANT
Phone: 520/296-0911 (56)

Steak
$9-$23

AAA Inspector Notes: In a Western town with a small town square, shops and an opera house, this popular restaurant continues the Western theme in its decor and menu. Diners can count on reliable, down-home fare. Reservations are not accepted. **Bar:** full bar. **Address:** 6541 E Tanque Verde Rd 85715 **Location:** Jct Campbell Ave, 5.6 mi e on Grant Rd, then just s. [D]

PRIMO
Phone: 520/792-3500 (60)

Regional Italian
$26-$42

AAA Inspector Notes: Chef Melissa Kelly brings a fresh approach to Italian cuisine from such delicate side dishes as grilled white and green asparagus with quail egg to the whole roast Mediterranean sea bass with steamed cockles. Luscious desserts vie to being your attention back to the table from the Southern views over the distant valley. **Bar:** full bar. **Reservations:** suggested. **Address:** 3800 W Starr Pass Blvd 85745 **Location:** I-10 exit 259 (Starr Pass Blvd), 4.8 mi w; in JW Marriott Starr Pass Resort & Spa. **Parking:** on-site and valet. [D] CALL

RA SUSHI BAR RESTAURANT
Phone: 520/615-3970

Sushi
$9-$22

AAA Inspector Notes: This hip meet-and-greet place prepares fresh and innovative sushi and a selection of bento box meals that make lunch a treat. The gyoza are spicy and delicious, and any of the tempura selections will be sure to please. **Bar:** full bar. **Address:** 2905 E Skyline Dr, Suite 289 85718 **Location:** Jct Campbell Ave; northwest corner; in La Encantada Plaza. [L] [D]

RISKY BUSINESS
Phone: 520/577-0021 (25)

American
$8-$23

AAA Inspector Notes: This northeast location is full of brightly colored walls, mountain views and such tasty dishes as peppered roast beef sandwich, down-home meatloaf, Greek pasta salad and build-your-own pizza. **Bar:** full bar. **Address:** 6866 E Sunrise Dr 85750 **Location:** Southwest corner of Kolb Rd and E Sunrise Dr. [L] [D]

RUBIO'S FRESH MEXICAN GRILL

For additional information, visit AAA.com

Mexican
$3-$7

AAA Inspector Notes: Freshly prepared and healthful foods, bright decor and friendly staff are found in this upscale fast-food spot. A special treat, the salsa bar lines up four styles and flavors. **Bar:** beer only. [L] [D]

LOCATIONS:
Address: 5870 E Broadway Blvd, #532 85711 **Location:** Just w of Wilmot Rd; in Park Place Mall.
Phone: 520/514-9166
Address: 2906 N Campbell Ave 85719 **Location:** Jct Glenn St, just n. **Phone:** 520/319-9881

RUSTY'S FAMILY RESTAURANT & SPORTS GRILLE
Phone: 520/623-3363 (42)

American
$6-$17

AAA Inspector Notes: Depending on the patron's mood, the front sports bar with banners and 50 TVs is a good place for sandwiches or burgers, while the larger dining room welcomes families and groups. Both offer friendly service. **Bar:** full bar. **Address:** 2075 W Grant Rd 85745 **Location:** I-10 exit 256 (Grant Rd), 1.1 mi w. [L] [D]

SAUCE
Phone: 520/297-8575

Italian
$7-$11

AAA Inspector Notes: This restaurant's selections could be characterized as gourmet fast food. Among choices are sausage and caramelized onion or chicken and broccoli rabe pizza. Lasagna and fresh salads also are on the menu. A clean modern decor with patio or indoor seating adds to a fun dining experience. **Bar:** wine only. **Address:** 7117 N Oracle Rd 85718 **Location:** Just s of Ina Rd. [L] [D]

SAUCE
Phone: 520/514-1122

Italian
$6-$11

AAA Inspector Notes: This restaurant's selections could be characterized as gourmet fast food. Interesting pizzas include chicken Caesar with Parmesan, roasted eggplant and hummus varieties. Lasagna, panini and fresh salads also appear on the menu. A clean, modern decor with patio and indoor seating adds to the fun dining experience. **Bar:** wine only. **Address:** 5285 E Broadway Blvd, Suite 101 85711 **Location:** Just w of Craycroft Rd. [L] [D]

SHER-E-PUNJAB
Phone: 520/624-9393 (47)

Indian
$8-$14

AAA Inspector Notes: The storefront of this eatery is simple, but the neat, tidy decor welcomes guests to experience the home-style cuisine of India. Try crisp samosa appetizers full of meat or vegetables. Fragrant curries include chicken, lamb, seafood and beef. **Bar:** full bar. **Address:** 853 E Grant Rd 85719 **Location:** Just e of 1st Ave. [L] [D]

SILVER SADDLE STEAKHOUSE
Phone: 520/622-6253 (72)

Steak
$6-$55

AAA Inspector Notes: Mesquite wood not only imparts a delicate flavor to meats but also plays a key role in the eatery's decor. The popular grill's bar top is the huge trunk of a mesquite tree that came from Trincheros, Mexico. The friendly staff keeps beverages filled and lets patrons in on all the extras, from sandwiches to vaquero grande, a 1.5-pound T-bone. **Bar:** full bar. **Reservations:** suggested. **Address:** 310 E Benson Hwy 85713 **Location:** I-10 exit 261, south side on Frontage Rd, then just e of 6th Ave. [L] [D]

(See maps & indexes p. 282, 288.)

SULLIVAN'S STEAKHOUSE

Phone: 520/299-4275 (27)

Steak
$20-$65

AAA Inspector Notes: Named for John L. Sullivan, heavyweight champion of the world in the 1880s, the upscale steak house prepares a wide selection of steaks, chops and seafood. Decorated with black-and-white photographs of Sullivan, Jack Dempsey and other boxing legends. Bar: full bar. Reservations: suggested. Address: 1785 E River Rd 85718 Location: Just w of Campbell Ave. Parking: on-site and valet. (L) (D)

TERESA'S MOSAIC CAFE

Phone: 520/624-4512 (41)

Mexican
$8-$16

AAA Inspector Notes: Atop a hill, the friendly spot serves freshly made tortillas that diners may watch being made as they enjoy one of the many classic Mexican dishes. Bar: full bar. Reservations: suggested. Address: 2456 N Silver Mosaic Dr 85745 Location: I-10 exit 256 (Grant Rd), 1 mi w; northwest corner of Silver Bell and Grant rds. (B) (L) (D)

TOHONO CHUL PARK TEA ROOM

Phone: 520/797-1222 (5)

American
$8-$16

AAA Inspector Notes: Surrounded by Tohono Chul Park, this refreshing stopping place affords desert garden views. Breakfasts and luncheons are locally popular, and afternoon tea, complete with scones, is served daily. Bar: full bar. Address: 7366 N Paseo Del Norte 85704 Location: Jct Oracle Rd, just w on Ina Rd, then just n.

(B) (L)

TRATTORIA PINA

Phone: 520/577-6992 (24)

Italian
$8-$35

AAA Inspector Notes: Near the base of the Catalina Mountains, the intimate eatery has a charming patio and display kitchen. On the menu are hearty pasta dishes, wood-fired oven pizzas and a wide variety of veal, lamb, beef and seafood preparations. Bar: full bar. Address: 5541 N Swan Rd 85718 Location: Just s of Sunrise Dr.

(L) (D)

TUCSON MCGRAW'S ORIGINAL CANTINA

Phone: 520/885-3088 (73)

American
$6-$24

AAA Inspector Notes: Perched on a hill overlooking the valley south of the city is a casual eatery with see forever views. Representative of good home-style cooking are mesquite-barbecue dishes, which locals have enjoyed for 20 years. Servers are friendly. Bar: full bar. Address: 4110 S Houghton Rd 85730 Location: 0.6 mi n of jct Irvington Rd.

 (L) (D)

VIVACE RESTAURANT

Phone: 520/795-7221 (30)

Italian
$12-$33

AAA Inspector Notes: In popular St. Philip's Plaza, the restaurant employs accomplished staffers who assist diners through a meal that might include classic osso buco or a more contemporary dish such as crab-filled breaded chicken breast. Selections are prepared with the freshest mix of ingredients. Patio seating is a nice option in good weather. Bar: full bar. Reservations: suggested. Address: 4310 N Campbell Ave 85718 Location: I-10 exit 254 (Prince Rd), 4.2 mi e, then 1.2 mi n. (L) (D)

WILDFLOWER TUCSON

Phone: 520/219-4230 (9)

American
$10-$29

AAA Inspector Notes: In keeping with the restaurant's name, the modern, trendy decor includes oversized photographs of brightly colored flowers, as well as flowers incorporated into some plate presentations. Delectable meat and seafood dishes are prepared in a synthesis of Asian, French and New American cooking styles. Bar: full bar. Reservations: suggested. Address: 7037 N Oracle Rd 85718 Location: Just s of Ina Rd. (L) (D)

ZEMAM'S

Phone: 520/323-9928 (63)

Ethiopian
$7-$13

AAA Inspector Notes: Spicy Ethiopian dishes are served in a casual atmosphere with leisurely service. Forks are offered, but the traditional style of eating with fingers is always acceptable. Address: 2731 E Broadway Blvd 85716 Location: Just e of Tucson Blvd. (L) (D)

ZINBURGER

Phone: 520/299-7799 (29)

Specialty
$8-$14

AAA Inspector Notes: Popular with locals, this high-energy bistro serves a selection of gourmet burgers-from Kobe beef to Clint's almost famous veggie option-plus salads, floats and shakes. Bar: full bar. Address: 1865 E River Rd 85718 Location: Just w of jct Campbell Ave. Parking: on-site and valet. (L) (D)

ZONA 78

Phone: 520/888-7878 (23)

Italian
$9-$16

AAA Inspector Notes: Innovative pizza with passion, as the chef says, is prepared in stone-fired ovens at this eatery and share menu space with yummy salads, pasta, steaks and such seafood as cedar-plank salmon. A large wine list features ample Italian selections. Bar: full bar. Address: 78 W River Rd 85718 Location: Just w of jct Stone Ave; northwest corner. (L) (D)

 ## TUMACÁCORI NATIONAL HISTORICAL PARK (G-4)

Approximately 19 miles north of Nogales off I-19 exit 29, Tumacácori National Historical Park preserves the abandoned Mission San Jose de Tumacácori. Once a Pima Indian village, Tumacácori was visited by Jesuit Eusebio Francisco Kino in 1691. In 1767 the Jesuits were expelled from Tumacácori by the King of Spain and replaced by Franciscans. The Franciscans began building the present massive adobe church about 1800, but it was never completed. Apache raids, neglect and a terrible winter contributed to its abandonment in 1848, yet afterward people continued to visit the site.

Anglo-Americans first visited the site in 1849, but Apache raids forced the settlers to leave. The area became a national monument in 1908. The 1990 addition of two Spanish mission sites, Guevavi and Calabazas, increased the total acreage to 47. Guevavi and Calabazas can be visited by reservation only. A historic museum distinguished by architectural features of the Sonora missions unfolds local history and describes mission life.

A self-guiding tour includes the church and cemetery, mortuary chapel, portions of the convent area, a patio garden and a visitor center/museum. Picnic facilities are available. Allow 1 hour minimum. Daily 9-5; closed Thanksgiving and Christmas. Admission $3; free (ages 0-15). Admission is valid for 7 days. Phone (520) 398-2341.

 TUZIGOOT NATIONAL MONUMENT (C-3)

About 2 miles northwest of Cottonwood via Main Street to Tuzigoot Road, Tuzigoot National Monument preserves the remains of a pueblo that was occupied by the Sinagua Indians from about A.D. 1000 until the tribe's 1425 migration from the area. From more than 110 rooms archeologists have recovered stone and bone tools, textiles, pottery, shell beads and bracelets, which are displayed in the visitor center.

Allow 1 hour minimum. Daily 8-6, Memorial Day-Labor Day; 8-5, rest of year. Admission $5; free (ages 0-15). Phone (928) 634-5564.

VAIL (F-5) pop. 10,208, elev. 3,225'
• Part of Tucson area — see map p. 268

COLOSSAL CAVE MOUNTAIN PARK, off I-10 exit 279, then 7 mi. n. on Colossal Cave Rd. to 16721 E. Old Spanish Trail, is a 2,200-acre park with what is considered by some to be the world's largest dry cavern. Only partially explored, the cave has chambers and lighted passageways. The park also includes two museums, a butterfly garden and a gemstone sluice as well as wagon rides and hiking and horse trails. Guided 45-minute cave tours are offered; extended tours are available. Guided trail rides also are available.

Hours: Daily 8-5, mid-Mar. to mid-Sept.; 9-5, rest of year. **Cost:** $5 (per private vehicle, up to six passengers); $1 (per additional passenger). Cave tours $13; $11 (military with ID); $6.50 (ages 5-12). **Phone:** (520) 647-7275.

VALLE (B-3) pop. 832

PLANES OF FAME AIR MUSEUM is at the Valle Airport near jct. SR 64 and US 180 at 755 Mustang Way. Covering aviation history from World War I through the supersonic jet age, the museum's collection includes Gen. Douglas MacArthur's personal transport plane *Bataan*, a Lockheed C-121A Constellation. Other aircraft include a Grumman F-11F Tiger formerly used by the Navy's Blue Angels and a 1944 Messerschmitt BF109G-10. A flyby is held in June.

Time: Allow 1 hour minimum. **Hours:** Daily 9-5. Closed Thanksgiving and Christmas. **Cost:** $6.95; $1.95 (ages 5-11); free (active military with ID). Constellation tour $3. **Phone:** (928) 635-1000.

VERMILION CLIFFS NATIONAL MONUMENT (A-3)

Bounded on the east by Glen Canyon National Recreation Area, on the west by Kaibab National Forest, to the north by the Utah border and to the south by SR 89, remote Vermilion Cliffs National Monument contains 293,000 acres of unspoiled plateaus, canyons and cliffs. Elevations range from 3,100 to 7,100 feet.

Ancestral Puebloan villages and geologic formations can be found on the monument lands, which were traversed by Spanish explorers, Mormon missionaries and Mexican traders. Animal inhabitants include desert bighorn sheep, mule deer, pronghorn and mountain lions. For further information contact the Arizona Strip Field Office, Bureau of Land Management; 345 E. Riverside Dr., St. George, UT 84790; phone (435) 688-3200.

 WALNUT CANYON NATIONAL MONUMENT (C-4)

Off I-40 exit 204, 7.5 miles east of Flagstaff, Walnut Canyon National Monument preserves the remains of more than 300 pre-Columbian dwellings built on a series of ledges in the 400-foot-deep gorge. Inhabited by the Walnut Canyon community (archeologists are uncertain of what these inhabitants called themselves) about 1000-1200, the single-family dwellings are visible from the visitor center on the canyon rim.

The self-guiding Island Trail, which descends 185 feet over the course of a half mile, is an interesting but arduous paved path that leads past 25 of the cliff dwelling rooms. The Rim Trail, a pleasant .75-mile round trip, features two overlooks into the canyon as well as access to a small pueblo and pit house. Snow and ice might close both trails at times in winter and spring.

Interpretive programs are available by reservation from Memorial Day through Labor Day. A museum and picnic facilities are available; however, food is not available. Pets are not allowed on park trails, in buildings or tied to fixed objects.

Note: The Island Trail includes descending/ascending 240 steps and might be cumbersome for the physically challenged and those with heart conditions.

Allow 1 hour, 30 minutes minimum. Daily 8-5, May-Oct.; 9-5, rest of year. Closed Christmas. Last admittance to main trail is 1 hour before closing. Admission $5 per person; free (ages 0-15). For further information contact the Superintendent, Walnut Canyon National Monument, 6400 N. SR 89, Flagstaff, AZ 86004; phone (928) 526-3367.

WELLTON pop. 2,882

MICROTEL INN & SUITES AT COYOTE WASH
Phone: (928)785-3777
Hotel
$53-$69
Address: 28784 Commerce Way 85356 **Location:** I-8 exit 30, just s. **Facility:** 93 units. 3 stories, interior corridors. **Amenities:** high-speed Internet. **Pool(s):** outdoor. **Activities:** whirlpool. **Guest Services:** coin laundry.

WENDEN (D-2) pop. 728, elev. 1,869'

ALAMO LAKE STATE PARK, 38 mi. n. of US 60 via a paved road, offers views of the Buckskin and Rawhide mountains from its site on the Bill Williams River. Activities include fishing, camping, boating and hiking. *See Recreation Chart.* **Hours:** Park open daily 24 hours. Visitor center open daily 8-5. Visitor center hours may vary; phone ahead. **Cost:** $7 (per private vehicle, up to four passengers); $3 (per additional adult passenger in vehicle or individual arriving on foot or bicycle). Camping $13-$25 (per private vehicle). **Phone:** (928) 669-2088.

WHITERIVER (D-5) pop. 4,104

Center of the Fort Apache Reservation fishing, camping and recreation area, Whiteriver also is the administrative headquarters of the 1,664,874-acre reservation. Four miles south is Fort Apache *(see place listing p. 74),* an active scout post during the Indian Wars. The fort remained a military post until the early 1920s and is now the site of the Theodore Roosevelt Indian School.

Seven miles west of town via a dirt road are the Kinishba Ruins, a partially restored Pueblo village inhabited 1050-1350; phone (928) 338-4625 to confirm road and weather conditions. Visitors are welcome at both the Alchesay National Fish Hatchery, (928) 338-4901, 4.3 miles north via SR 73, and the Williams Creek Hatchery, (928) 338-4902, 8 miles n. via SR 73 following signs.

WHY (F-3)

GAMBLING ESTABLISHMENTS
• **Golden Hasañ Casino,** SR 86 Milepost 55. **Hours:** Daily 10 a.m.-midnight. **Phone:** (520) 547-4306 or (866) 332-9467.

WICKENBURG (G-1) pop. 6,363, elev. 2,071'

Nineteen miles southwest of Wickenburg is the Vulture Gold Mine, which yielded more than $20 million in gold during the hectic period following its discovery by Henry Wickenburg in 1863. Allegedly Wickenburg found the gold in one of the rocks he was hurling at his escaping mule.

The gold rush that ensued reached such proportions that by 1866 Wickenburg was the third largest city in Arizona and missed becoming the territorial capital by only two votes. Still standing in the center of town is the old mesquite jail tree to which lawmen chained their prisoners during the early boom years; no one wanted to take time from mining to build a proper jail.

The Hassayampa River, running through town, was called "the river which flows upside down" by Native Americans because its main flow is 20 feet below the surface. It is one of the last and greatest natural riparian areas in the state.

Wickenburg, known for its Old West atmosphere and many dude ranches, brings the past to life in February during Gold Rush Days and again in August, when the Desert Caballeros ride into the Bradshaw Mountains to spend several days under the stars; the whole town gathers to bid the horsemen farewell as they ride off into the mountains.

Wickenburg Chamber of Commerce: 216 N. Frontier St., Wickenburg, AZ 85390. **Phone:** (928) 684-5479 or (800) 942-5242.

DESERT CABALLEROS WESTERN MUSEUM, 21 N. Frontier St., contains dioramas depicting the town's history, a re-creation of an early Wickenburg street scene, ancient native artifacts and collections of gems and minerals. A gallery displays some 600 pieces of cowboy gear, including saddles, spurs and chaps, along with works by such noted Western artists as Frederic Remington and Charles Russell.

Time: Allow 1 hour minimum. **Hours:** Mon.-Sat. 10-5, Sun. noon-4, Sept.-May; Tues.-Sat. 10-5, Sun. noon-4, rest of year. Closed Jan. 1, Easter, July 4, Thanksgiving and Christmas. **Cost:** $7.50; $6 (senior citizens); free (ages 0-16, and active military with guest). **Phone:** (928) 684-2272.

BEST WESTERN RANCHO GRANDE
Phone: 928/684-5445

Hotel
Rates not provided

AAA Benefit: Members save up to 20%, plus 10% bonus points with Best Western Rewards®.

Address: 293 E Wickenburg Way 85390 **Location:** On US 60; center. **Facility:** 78 units, some efficiencies and kitchens. 1-2 stories (no elevator), exterior corridors. **Amenities:** *Some:* high-speed Internet. **Pool(s):** heated outdoor. **Activities:** whirlpool, horseshoes, volleyball. **Guest Services:** valet laundry. **Free Special Amenities:** local telephone calls and high-speed Internet.

LOS VIAJEROS INN
Phone: (928)684-7099

Hotel
$75-$120

Address: 1000 N Tegner Rd 85390 **Location:** 1 mi n of jct US 60 and 93. **Facility:** 57 units. 2 stories (no elevator), exterior corridors. **Pool(s):** heated outdoor. **Activities:** whirlpool.

Guest Services: valet laundry.

Are we meeting your travel needs?

TourBook Comments

If your visit to an establishment listed in a AAA TourBook guide doesn't meet your expectations, tell us about it.

Complete an easy online form at **AAA.com/TourBookComments.**

SUPER 8 WICKENBURG   Phone: (928)684-0808
Motel
$58-$126
Address: 1021 N Tegner St 85390 **Location:** 1 mi n of US 60 and 93. **Facility:** 41 units. 2 stories (no elevator), interior/exterior corridors. **Terms:** cancellation fee imposed. **Guest Services:** coin laundry. **Free Special Amenities:** expanded continental breakfast and high-speed Internet.

/SOME UNITS FEE

Great Value! Conveniently located across from Denny's Restaurant and historic downtown Wickenburg.

WICKENBURG INN   Phone: (928)684-5461
Hotel
$69-$95
Address: 850 E Wickenburg Way 85390 **Location:** 1.3 mi se on US 60. **Facility:** 29 units. 2 stories (no elevator), interior corridors. **Terms:** 5 day cancellation notice. **Pool(s):** outdoor. **Activities:** whirlpool. **Guest Services:** valet and coin laundry.

/SOME UNITS FEE

WHERE TO EAT

ANITA'S COCINA   Phone: 928/684-5777
Mexican
$7-$16
AAA Inspector Notes: Popular with the locals, this casual eatery serves hearty portions of such classic dishes as cheese enchiladas with rice and beans and chiles rellenos. **Bar:** full bar. **Address:** 57 N Valentine St 85390 **Location:** Just n of US 60; center. **Parking:** street only. B L D

GOLD NUGGET RESTAURANT   Phone: 928/684-0648
American
$7-$33
AAA Inspector Notes: A pleasant staff serves beef, chicken and fish entrees in the historical landmark's dining rooms, which are appointed with turn-of-the-20th-century furnishings. Guests can enjoy an early breakfast in the coffee shop. **Bar:** full bar. **Address:** 222 E Wickenburg Way 85390 **Location:** On US 60, just se of jct US 60 and 93; center. B L D

WILLCOX (F-5) pop. 3,757, elev. 4,156'
• Hotels p. 316 • Restaurants p. 316

Willcox grew from a small cow town into one of the country's major cattle-shipping centers. In days past the large cattle ranches in the surrounding hills and valleys were notorious as refuges for fugitive gunslingers, who often brought their business to town: Wyatt Earp's brother Warren was killed at Headquarters Saloon in 1900. Saloons and other buildings from the late 1800s can be seen in or near the historic district, bounded by Railroad and Haskell avenues and Maley and Stewart streets.

Rex Allen was born and raised in Willcox. Tributes to the cowboy actor include the Rex Allen Arizona Cowboy Museum *(see attraction listing)* on Railroad

Avenue and a bronze statue in a park across from the museum. A bronze heart imbedded in the statue at Allen's request represents his enduring love for his hometown.

Cattle raising is still important, but added to the contemporary economic mix are ostrich farming and the cultivation of apples, peaches, pistachios, onions and tomatoes. At a variety of "U-pick" farms northwest via Fort Grant Road, visitors can pluck fresh produce straight from the orchards and fields July through October.

Birding is a popular diversion in Sulphur Springs Valley, a mecca for migrating waterfowl and shorebirds as well as wintering raptors. Sandhill cranes arrive in October and stay through February.

Southeast of town at Apache Pass is the isolated Old Fort Bowie National Historic Site. The fort was built in 1862 to guard the Butterfield Overland Trail and to protect pioneers from Apache raids and skirmishes with Native Americans led by Cochise and Geronimo. The site can only be reached by traveling the last 1.5 miles on foot. The high elevation and temperature extremes might make this hike unsuitable for some. Water is available at the fort, but hikers should bring their own canteen. Beware of flash floods, mountain lions and rattlesnakes. All historic items and natural features are strictly protected; metal detectors, digging tools, guns and hunting are prohibited.

Willcox Regional Visitor Center and Chamber of Commerce: 1500 N. Circle I Rd., Willcox, AZ 85643. **Phone:** (520) 384-2272 or (800) 200-2272.

Self-guiding tours: Brochures for a self-guiding walking tour of the historic district are available from the visitor center.

CHIRICAHUA REGIONAL MUSEUM is at 127 E. Maley St. History exhibits cover such topics as the railroad, Butterfield Stage Line, U.S. Cavalry, Apache Indians and development of farming, ranching and mining. The museum is housed in a turn-of-the-20th-century hardware store featuring original wooden floors and a pressed tin ceiling. **Time:** Allow 30 minutes minimum. **Hours:** Mon.-Sat. 10-4. Closed major holidays. **Cost:** Donations. **Phone:** (520) 384-3971.

REX ALLEN ARIZONA COWBOY MUSEUM AND COWBOY HALL OF FAME, 150 N. Railroad Ave., honors the career of Western star Rex Allen, who was born in Willcox in 1920. Allen's life is depicted from his ranching and homesteading years through his radio, television and film career. Through photographs, storyboards, clothing and ranch implements the museum also highlights the pioneers and ranchers who shaped the West. Rex Allen Days take place the first weekend in October.

Hours: Daily 10-4. Closed Jan. 1, Thanksgiving and Christmas. **Cost:** $3 (per couple); $2 (per person); $5 (family); free (military with ID). **Phone:** (520) 384-4583 or (877) 234-4111.

DAYS INN

◆◆◆ ◆◆◆
Motel
$43-$75

Phone: (520)384-4222
Address: 724 N Bisbee Ave 85643 **Location:** I-10 exit 340, just s. Adjacent to shopping center. **Facility:** 73 units. 2 stories (no elevator), exterior corridors. **Amenities:** high-speed Internet. **Pool(s):** outdoor. **Guest Services:** coin laundry. **Free Special Amenities:** continental breakfast and high-speed Internet.

HOLIDAY INN EXPRESS & SUITES WILLCOX

◆◆◆ ◆◆◆
Hotel
$89-$129 2/1-5/31
$84-$119 6/1-1/31

Phone: (520)384-3333
Address: 1251 N Virginia Ave 85643 **Location:** I-10 exit 340, just n. **Facility:** 100 units. 3 stories. interior corridors. **Amenities:** high-speed Internet. **Pool(s):** heated outdoor. **Activities:** exercise room. **Guest Services:** coin laundry.

QUALITY INN

◆◆◆
Hotel
Rates not provided

Phone: 520/384-3556
Address: 1100 W Rex Allen Dr 85643 **Location:** I-10 exit 340, just s. **Facility:** 91 units. 2 stories (no elevator), exterior corridors. **Pool(s):** heated outdoor. **Guest Services:** coin laundry.

SUPER 8

◆◆◆
Hotel
$43-$58

Phone: (520)384-0888
Address: 1500 W Ft. Grant Rd 85643 **Location:** I-10 exit 340, just n. **Facility:** 50 units. 2 stories (no elevator), interior corridors. **Pool(s):** heated indoor. **Activities:** whirlpool. **Guest Services:** coin laundry.

WHERE TO EAT

BIG TEX BAR-B-QUE

◆◆◆ ◆◆◆
Barbecue
$6-$20

Phone: 520/384-4423
AAA Inspector Notes: This old railroad dining car across from the train tracks serves as an interesting spot for sitting down to a hearty lunch or dinner. Outstanding barbecue, including sandwiches served on homemade buns, pairs perfectly with freshly baked fruit pies. **Bar:** beer & wine. **Address:** 130 E Maley St 85643 **Location:** Just se of Business Loop I-10; center. **Parking:** street only. L D

SALSA FIESTA

◆◆◆ ◆◆◆
Mexican
$7-$13

Phone: 520/384-4233
AAA Inspector Notes: Bright, cheerful decor with Mexican artifacts matches the friendly service at this small eatery that serves big taste in the traditional dishes of northern Mexico. It is fun to choose your level of spiciness from mild to chipotle verde (pretty hot). **Bar:** full bar. **Address:** 1201 W Rex Allen Dr 85643 **Location:** I-10 exit 340, just s. L D

WILLIAMS (C-3) pop. 3,023, elev. 6,752'
• Restaurants p. 320

Williams was named after William (Bill) Shirley Williams, the early mountain man who guided trapping parties and expeditions through the wilderness.

Primarily a resort town, Williams marks the beginning of the major entrance route to Grand Canyon National Park *(see place listing p. 84)*. The town is at the base of Bill Williams Mountain, which boasts an 18-hole golf course and a ski area offering both downhill and cross-country skiing. In the surrounding Kaibab National Forest *(see place listing p. 100)*, cross-country skiing and hiking are popular. Cataract, Kaibab Dog Trail and White Horse lakes offer camping, picnicking and fishing.

Williams and Forest Service Visitor Center: 200 West Railroad Ave., Williams, AZ 86046. **Phone:** (928) 635-4061 or (800) 863-0546.

BEARIZONA, off I-40 exit 165 at 1500 E. SR 64, is a drive-through wildlife park set in a 160-acre forest. During the 2.5-mile drive you'll see bison, black bears, American burros, bighorn and Dall sheep, wolves and other animals in naturalistic habitats. Afterward, you can park the car and walk through Fort Bearizona, an area that's home to young foxes, black bears, bobcats and javelinas. A birds of prey show is presented three times daily.

Cars are available for visitors arriving on foot or by motorcycle. A shuttle is available in Fort Bearizona for the physically impaired. **Time:** Allow 1 hour minimum. **Hours:** Daily 8-6, May-Aug.; 9-4:30, Mar.-Apr. and Sept.-Dec. **Cost:** $18.25; $16.25 (ages 65+); $9 (ages 4-12). Maximum per private vehicle $90.25. **Phone:** (928) 635-2289. *(See ad p. 87.)*

GRAND CANYON DEER FARM, 6769 E. Deer Farm Rd. off I-40, has several varieties of deer and such other animals as peacocks, reindeer, llamas and antelope. Visitors are permitted to walk among the deer and feed them. **Hours:** Daily 9-6, mid-Mar. to mid-Oct.; 10-5, rest of year. Closed Thanksgiving and Christmas. **Cost:** $9.95; $8.50 (ages 62+); $5.95 (ages 3-13). **Phone:** (928) 635-4073 or (800) 926-3337.

GRAND CANYON RAILWAY, .5 mi. s. of I-40 exit 163 (Grand Canyon Blvd.), offers round-trip excursions through grassy plains and pine forests to the South Rim of the Grand Canyon aboard vintage 1950s-era passenger cars powered by vintage diesel locomotives. Strolling musicians, Western characters and a mock train robbery provide entertainment during the ride.

Passengers arrive at the 1910 Grand Canyon Depot, in the historic district at the South Rim; the depot is the only working log depot in the country. A Wild West show takes place daily at 9. Four classes of train service are available. For an additional fee, bus tours of the South Rim with lunch are available.

Refreshments are available. **Hours:** Train departs daily at 9:30 and returns at 5:45 with a 3.5-hour stopover at the canyon. Closed Christmas Eve and Christmas. Phone ahead to confirm schedule.

Cost: Round-trip coach fare $70; $40 (ages 0-16). One-way fare available; upgraded seats are available for an additional fee. Fare does not include admission to Grand Canyon National Park. Fares may vary; phone ahead. Reservations are recommended. **Phone:** (800) 843-8724.

BEST WESTERN PLUS INN OF WILLIAMS
Phone: (928)635-4400

Hotel
$79-$199

AAA Benefit:
Members save up to 20%, plus 10% bonus points with Best Western Rewards®.

Address: 2600 W Route 66 86046 **Location:** I-40 exit 161, just e. **Facility:** 80 units, some two bedrooms and kitchens. 2 stories (no elevator), interior corridors. **Amenities:** high-speed Internet. **Dining:** Western View Steakhouse, see separate listing, entertainment. **Pool(s):** heated outdoor. **Activities:** whirlpool. **Guest Services:** coin laundry. **Free Special Amenities: expanded continental breakfast and high-speed Internet.**

SAVE [icons] FEE [icons] / SOME UNITS FEE [icon]

Best Western PLUS

Ideal location between two world destinations Grand Canyon 50 miles North and Sedona 50 miles South

---

CANYON COUNTRY INN   Phone: (928)635-2349

Motel
$69-$109

Address: 442 W Route 66 86046 **Location:** I-40 exit 163, 0.5 mi s, then just w on Railroad Ave (Business Loop 40). **Facility:** 14 units. 2 stories (no elevator), interior/exterior corridors. **Terms:** open 3/1-12/31. **Free Special Amenities: expanded continental breakfast and high-speed Internet.**

SAVE [icons]

COMFORT INN NEAR GRAND CANYON
Phone: 928/635-4045

Hotel
Rates not provided

Address: 911 W Route 66 86046 **Location:** I-40 exit 161, 1 mi e. **Facility:** 74 units. 2 stories, interior corridors. **Pool(s):** heated indoor. **Activities:** whirlpool. **Guest Services:** coin laundry.

[icons] / SOME UNITS [icons]

DAYS INN OF WILLIAMS   Phone: (928)635-4051

Motel
$50-$118

Address: 2488 W Route 66 86046 **Location:** I-40 exit 161, just e. **Facility:** 72 units. 2 stories (no elevator), interior corridors. **Amenities:** safes. **Pool(s):** heated indoor. **Activities:** whirlpool. **Guest Services:** coin laundry.

[icons] / SOME UNITS FEE [icons]

ECONO LODGE   Phone: (928)635-4085

Motel
$70-$150

Address: 302 E Route 66 86046 **Location:** I-40 exit 163, 0.5 mi s, then just e. **Facility:** 39 units. 2 stories (no elevator), exterior corridors. **Terms:** cancellation fee imposed. **Free Special Amenities: expanded continental breakfast and high-speed Internet.**

SAVE [icons] / SOME UNITS [icons]

GRAND CANYON RAILWAY HOTEL
Phone: (928)635-4010

Hotel
$109-$349

Address: 235 N Grand Canyon Blvd 86046 **Location:** I-40 exit 163, 0.5 mi s. Located at historic Williams Depot. **Facility:** 298 units. 2 stories, interior corridors. **Terms:** 3 day cancellation notice. **Dining:** 2 restaurants. **Pool(s):** heated indoor. **Activities:** whirlpool, playground, basketball, volleyball, exercise room. **Fee:** game room. **Guest Services:** coin laundry. **Free Special Amenities: high-speed Internet.**

SAVE [icons] / SOME UNITS [icons]

Find more than 13,000 pet-friendly AAA/CAA Approved hotels and campgrounds.

Purchase The AAA PetBook® at participating AAA/CAA club offices, online at bn.com and in fine book stores.

Traveling with Your Pet
The AAA PetBook

To enter the annual AAA PetBook Photo Contest, visit AAA.com/PetBook.

GRAND LIVING BED & BREAKFAST

Phone: 928/635-4171

Bed & Breakfast
$140-$290

Address: 701 Quarter Horse Rd 86046 **Location:** I-40 exit 165 (Williams/Grand Canyon), 1 mi s on Business Loop 40, then just w on Rodeo Rd. Located in a residential area. **Facility:** This beautifully decorated log cabin-style residence provides comfortable rooms and public areas; three rooms feature a fireplace. 6 units. 1 story, interior/exterior corridors. **Terms:** check-in 4 pm, age restrictions may apply, 11 day cancellation notice-fee imposed.

HIGHLANDER MOTEL

Phone: (928)635-2541

Motel
$45-$75

Address: 533 W Route 66 86046 **Location:** I-40 exit 161, 1.3 mi e. **Facility:** 11 units, some efficiencies. 1 story, exterior corridors. **Terms:** 2 night minimum stay - seasonal, cancellation fee imposed. **Free Special Amenities:** full breakfast and high-speed Internet.

HOLIDAY INN WILLIAMS

Phone: (928)635-4114

Hotel
$119-$159 3/1-1/31
$109-$139 2/1-2/29

Address: 950 N Grand Canyon Blvd 86046 **Location:** I-40 exit 163, just s. **Facility:** 120 units, some two bedrooms. 2 stories (no elevator), interior corridors. **Terms:** cancellation fee imposed. **Dining:** Doc Holliday Steak House, see separate listing. **Pool(s):** heated indoor. **Activities:** whirlpool, exercise room. **Guest Services:** coin laundry.

HOWARD JOHNSON EXPRESS INN

Phone: (928)635-9561

Hotel
$63-$144

Address: 511 N Grand Canyon Blvd 86046 **Location:** I-40 exit 163, just s. **Facility:** 56 units. 2 stories (no elevator), interior corridors. **Terms:** cancellation fee imposed. **Amenities:** safes (fee). **Pool(s):** heated indoor. **Activities:** whirlpool. **Free Special Amenities:** continental breakfast and high-speed Internet. (See ad this page.)

KNIGHTS INN

Phone: (928)635-1412

Motel
$45-$72

Address: 750 N Grand Canyon Blvd 86046 **Location:** I-40 exit 163, just s. **Facility:** 19 units, some two bedrooms. 2 stories (no elevator), interior corridors. **Terms:** cancellation fee imposed. **Free Special Amenities:** continental breakfast and high-speed Internet.

Closest town to Grand Canyon, 1 mile from Historic Route 66. Hair dryer, Iron & Board. Free parking,

▼ *See AAA listing this page* ▼

Howard Johnson®
Express Inn

**511 N. Grand Canyon Blvd.
Williams, AZ 86046**

- free rise & dine® breakfast†
- free high speed internet
- earn wyndham rewards® points!
- indoor heated pool and spa
- walking distance to the grand canyon railway depot
- close to the grand canyon national park

AAA members 15% off published rates*

hojo.com
1·800·I·GO·HOJO

*Advanced reservations required. Rooms at this discount are limited and subject to availability at participating properties. Blackout dates and other restrictions apply. Cannot be combined with any other special offers or discounts. See hojo.com for full details and requirements. †Rise & Dine® Breakfast available at most locations. All Howard Johnson Hotels are independently owned and operated. ©2012 Howard Johnson International, Inc. All Rights Reserved.

THE LODGE ON ROUTE 66

Motel
$90-$230

Phone: 928/635-4534
Address: 200 E Route 66 86046 **Location:** I-40 exit 163, 0.5 mi s, then just e. **Facility:** 19 units. 1 story, exterior corridors. **Terms:** office hours 8 am-10 pm, check-in 4 pm. **Free Special Amenities:** expanded continental breakfast and high-speed Internet. *(See ad this page.)*

SAVE ✦ 🛜 ✕ ✉ 💻 / SOME UNITS 🅱 🗄

QUALITY INN

Hotel
Rates not provided

Phone: 928/635-9888
Address: 1029 N Grand Canyon Blvd 86046 **Location:** I-40 exit 163, just n. **Facility:** 79 units. 2 stories (no elevator), interior corridors. **Pool(s):** heated outdoor. **Activities:** whirlpool.

✦ CALL 🅴🅼 🛎 🛜 ✕ 💻

QUALITY INN MOUNTAIN RANCH RESORT

Hotel
$79-$169

Phone: (928)635-2693
Address: 6701 E Mountain Ranch Rd 86046 **Location:** I-40 exit 171 (Deer Farm Rd), just s. Located in a scenic country area. **Facility:** 73 units. 2 stories (no elevator), exterior corridors. **Terms:** cancellation fee imposed. **Dining:** The Ranch Bar & Grill, see separate listing. **Pool(s):** heated outdoor. **Activities:** whirlpool, putting green, 2 tennis courts, basketball, horseshoes. *Fee:* horseback riding, exercise room.

SAVE ✦ 🍸 🛎 BIZ 🛜 ✕ 💻
/ SOME UNITS FEE 🐾 🅱 🗄

**In the Heart of N. AZ
Full Service Hotel Resort,
Full Service Restaurant
on Premises.**

QUALITY INN

RODEWAY INN & SUITES DOWNTOWNER MOTEL

Motel
Rates not provided

Phone: 928/635-4041
Address: 201 E Route 66 86046 **Location:** I-40 exit 163, 0.5 mi s, then just e. **Facility:** 16 units. 1 story, exterior corridors. **Terms:** office hours 8 am-10 pm, check-in 4 pm.

✦ 🛜 ✕ ✉ 💻 / SOME UNITS 🅱 🗄

TRAVELODGE WILLIAMS

Motel
$36-$144

Phone: (928)635-2651
Address: 430 E Route 66 86046 **Location:** I-40 exit 163, 0.5 mi s, then just e. **Facility:** 41 units, some two bedrooms. 2 stories (no elevator), exterior corridors. **Pool(s):** heated outdoor. **Activities:** whirlpool. **Guest Services:** coin laundry. **Free Special Amenities:** expanded continental breakfast and high-speed Internet.

SAVE ✦ 🛎 BIZ 🛜 🅱
💻 / SOME UNITS FEE 🐾 🗄

Travelodge

FREE Bear Bites Breakfast at newly renovated hotel. Kids 12 and under stay free. Free parking.

CANYON MOTEL & RV PARK   Phone: 928/635-9371
🅵🆈🅻   Not evaluated. **Address:** 1900 E Rodeo Rd/Route 66 86046 **Location:** I-40 exit 165 (Grand Canyon), 1 mi s on Business Loop 40, then just w. Facilities, services, and decor characterize an economy property.

Share a New View on Travel at

AAATravelViews.com

Read stories, tips and trends from AAA insiders. Post comments and get your questions answered by our travel experts.

▼ See AAA listing this page ▼

"Gateway to the Grand Canyon"
Williams, AZ

The Lodge on Route 66 convenient to:
• Grand Canyon Railroad Station
• Shopping, Dining, and, Entertainment
Williams, AZ centrally located to:
• The Grand Canyon, Painted Desert, Petrified Forest, Sedona, Jerome, Winter recreation and sports

$89.99 - $229.99
Double Occupancy
Discounts available
Winter Rates, Jan. – Feb. may be lower.

THE LODGE
AAA

www.thelodgeonroute66.com

928-635-4534

WHERE TO EAT

CRUISER'S ROUTE 66 BAR & GRILL
Phone: 928/635-2445

American
$8-$21

AAA Inspector Notes: Located in historic downtown, this pleasant family restaurant prepares a variety of Mexican, steak and chicken dishes in a setting reminiscent of the 1950s. Cordial staff members deliver sizzling fajitas, the house specialty. **Bar:** full bar. **Address:** 233 W Route 66 86046 **Location:** Jct Route 66 and 3rd St. **Parking:** street only. [L] [D]

DARA THAI CAFE
Phone: 928/635-2201

Thai
$6-$12

AAA Inspector Notes: This small casual restaurant offers traditional Thai cuisine with casual service. The dining room is small so do not be surprised if there is a wait. **Address:** 145 W Route 66 86046 **Location:** Center. **Parking:** street only. [L] [D]

DOC HOLIDAY STEAK HOUSE
Phone: 928/635-4114

Steak
$7-$26

AAA Inspector Notes: Enjoy breakfast or dinner in an Old West atmosphere. Specializing in prime rib and hand-cut steaks diners also can enjoy fresh seafood or pasta. A salad bar is available as well as a breakfast buffet on many days. **Bar:** full bar. **Address:** 950 N Grand Canyon Blvd 86046 **Location:** I-40 exit 163, just s; in Holiday Inn Williams. [B] [D] CALL [&M]

PANCHO MCGILLICUDDY'S
Phone: 928/635-4150

Mexican
$6-$13

AAA Inspector Notes: On the National Register of Historic Places and renovated in 1993, the downtown building once was a boisterous spot along Saloon Row. Railroad workers, cowboys, loggers and rowdy locals came to visit the saloons, gambling houses and houses of ill repute. Now a casual family restaurant, the historic property features attractive Western decor and an authentic Mexican menu with fajitas, enchiladas and chiles rellenos. Expect cordial service from a waitstaff in casual attire. **Bar:** full bar. **Address:** 141 Railroad Ave 86046 **Location:** I-40 exit 163, 0.5 mi s. [L] [D] [✕] [◥]

PINE COUNTRY RESTAURANT
Phone: 928/635-9718

American
$5-$22

AAA Inspector Notes: Home-style cooking is at the heart of a menu that including entrées, soups and salads. No meal, however, is complete without a piece of one of the delicious, homemade pies. This small storefront is in historic downtown Williams, and its relaxed dining room projects a homelike feel thanks to a number of craft items displayed. Full service is provided by a casually attired, polite staff. **Address:** 107 N Grand Canyon Blvd 86046 **Location:** Cross street Route 66; downtown. **Parking:** on-site and street. [B] [L] [D]

THE RANCH BAR & GRILL
Phone: 928/635-2693

American
$9-$26

AAA Inspector Notes: Only a few minutes from the historic town of Williams, this casual restaurant employs cordial and knowledgeable servers. Menu offerings include steak, seafood and pasta dishes. **Bar:** full bar. **Address:** 6701 E Mountain Ranch Rd 86046 **Location:** I-40 exit 171 (Deer Farm Rd), just s; in Quality Inn Mountain Ranch Resort. [D]

RED RAVEN RESTAURANT
Phone: 928/635-4980

American
$6-$22

AAA Inspector Notes: This small, upscale restaurant surprises visitors to the old downtown area of this old Route 66 town. Among contemporary dishes on the varied dinner menu are tempura shrimp, flat-iron steak, Baja tacos, soufflés and creme brûlée. During lunch, the menu scales down a bit, with such choices as Philadelphia cheese steaks, club sandwiches and Reubens. **Bar:** full bar. **Address:** 135 W Route 66 86046 **Location:** I-40 exit 163, 0.5 mi s, then just e. **Parking:** street only. [L] [D]

ROD'S STEAK HOUSE
Menu on AAA.com
Phone: 928/635-2671

Steak
$6-$25

AAA Inspector Notes: Serving travelers along historic Route 66, the restaurant has served its specialty steaks-as well as seafood and chicken dishes-since 1946. A must-try is the sugar-dipped charred steak, a surprising delight. **Bar:** full bar. **Address:** 301 E Route 66 86046 **Location:** Center. [L] [D]

ROSA'S CANTINA
Phone: 928/635-0708

Mexican
$6-$18

AAA Inspector Notes: Friendly servers bring out good Mexican food, including enchiladas, tamales and rellenos. Large portions mean no one goes away hungry. The decor is modest, and outdoor seating also is an option. **Bar:** full bar. **Address:** 411 N Grand Canyon Blvd 86046 **Location:** I-40 exit 163, 0.5 mi s. [L] [D]

WESTERN VIEW STEAKHOUSE
Phone: 928/635-4400

Steak
$15-$31

AAA Inspector Notes: This small restaurant is located off the lobby of the hotel and offers an upscale menu of such items as filet mignon, halibut and shrimp scampi. **Bar:** full bar. **Address:** 2600 W Route 66 86046 **Location:** I-40 exit 161, just e; in Best Western Plus Inn of Williams. [D] CALL [&M]

Relaxed dining with forest views and a specialty menu

WINDOW ROCK (B-6) pop. 2,712

Window Rock is the capital of the Navajo nation and seat of its tribal government. The elected tribal council meets in the council house at least four times a year. Window Rock also contains the U.S. government's Bureau of Indian Affairs, Navajo Area Office. The headquarters of the Navajo Arts and Crafts Enterprises is just east of the junction of SR 264 and Navajo Route 12.

Navajo Tourism Department-Window Rock: Write P.O. Box 663, Window Rock, AZ 86515. **Phone:** (928) 871-6436.

NAVAJO NATION MUSEUM, at jct. SR 264 and Loop Rd., contains photographs, jewelry, textiles and other items relating to the history and culture of the Navajo people. One exhibit describes the arduous 1864 ordeal known as the "Long Walk," in which the Navajo were removed from tribal lands and marched some 300 miles to a Fort Sumner, N.M., prison camp. **Hours:** Mon.-Sat. 9-5 (also Thurs.-Fri. 5-7). **Cost:** Donations. Cash only. **Phone:** (928) 871-7941. [Ⅱ]

QUALITY INN NAVAJO NATION CAPITAL

Phone: (928)871-4108

▼▼ ▼▼
Hotel
$81-$101

Address: 48 W Hwy 264 86515 **Location:** Center. **Facility:** 56 units. 2 stories (no elevator), exterior corridors. **Terms:** cancellation fee imposed. **Dining:** Dine' Restaurant, see separate listing. **Free Special Amenities:** full breakfast and high-speed Internet. *(See ad p. 118.)*

[SAVE] [🍴] [BIZ] [📶] [🔌] [🍽]
[☕] / SOME UNITS FEE [🐕]

WHERE TO EAT

DINE' RESTAURANT

Phone: 928/871-4108

▼▼ ▼▼
Regional American
$10-$20

AAA Inspector Notes: Near the center of town and a museum, the family-centered hotel restaurant offers three meals daily. On the dinner menu is a variety of selections, including steak and seafood, Mexican entrees, Navajo mutton stew and fry bread. **Address:** 48 W Hwy 264 86515 **Location:** Center; in Quality Inn Navajo Nation Capital. [B] [L] [D]

WINKELMAN (E-5) pop. 353, elev. 1,928'

A mining and agricultural center, Winkelman is near the 8.5-mile Aravaipa Canyon, a wilderness retreat that was once the headquarters of the Apache Indians. The canyon's abundant vegetation, nourished by the year-round flow of Aravaipa Creek, contrasts with the surrounding desert terrain.

Off SR 77, then 13 miles east on a paved and gravel road, the canyon is within the 4,044-acre Aravaipa Canyon Primitive Area. Permits are required to enter the area; contact the Bureau of Land Management's District Office in Safford; phone (928) 348-4400. Visitation to the area is limited; reservations are required.

WINSLOW (C-5) pop. 9,655, elev. 4,856'
• Hotels p. 323 • Restaurants p. 323

Winslow was named after Gen. Edward Francis Winslow, a president of the Atlantic and Pacific Railroad. This railroad center is an important shipping and trading site. A two-story mural and bronze statue at Standin' on the Corner Park in downtown Winslow illustrate the Eagles' song "Take It Easy" and its well-known reference to the town. The Apache-Sitgreaves National Forests *(see place listing p. 38)* lie south of town.

Winslow Chamber of Commerce: 523 W. Second St., Winslow, AZ 86047. **Phone:** (928) 289-2434.

HOMOLOVI STATE PARK, 2 mi n. of I-40 on SR 87, preserves structures and cultural artifacts from the late migration period of the Hopi (1200s-1300s). On the grounds are a visitor center, a museum, various

You KNOW the dangers
Chatting on the phone...
Texting while driving...

STAY FOCUSED
Keep Your Mind on the Road

Be a Better Driver

AAA   CAA

trails and a campground. **Hours:** Daily dawn-10 p.m. Office daily 8-5. Closed Christmas. **Cost:** $7 (per private vehicle, up to four adult passengers); $3 (each additional adult passenger and individuals arriving by bicycle or on foot). Camping $25 (two vehicles per site). **Phone:** (928) 289-4106.

LA POSADA is off I-40 exit 253, then 1 mi. s. to Second St., just e. to 303 E. Second St. (Rte. 66). Designed by Mary Elizabeth Jane Colter and considered her masterpiece, La Posada attracted such luminaries as Howard Hughes, Albert Einstein and Bob Hope. Constructed in 1929 in the style of an 1869 Spanish hacienda, the building has stone and tile floors, glass murals, original furnishings and gardens. Antiques and art from around the globe decorate this working hotel.

Time: Allow 1 hour, 30 minutes minimum. **Hours:** Daily 7 a.m.-10 p.m. **Cost:** Free. **Phone:** (928) 289-4366.

METEOR CRATER, 22 mi. w. on I-40, then 6 mi. s. off exit 233, was formed nearly 50,000 years ago by a meteorite; the crater is 550 feet deep, 2.4 miles in circumference and nearly 1 mile across.

The meteor, estimated to have been 150 feet across and traveling 26,000 mph, slammed into the rocky plain and left a crater that was originally 700 feet deep and more than 4,000 feet across. Because the terrain of the crater is very similar to that of the moon, NASA once trained Apollo astronauts here.

The Discovery Center relays information about the formation of the crater and features interactive displays about meteorites and asteroids. A large-screen theater presents "Collisions and Impacts."

Visitors can view the crater from numerous locations on the rim. Also included are an Astronaut Wall of Fame and an Apollo test capsule.

Guided rim tours of the crater are offered. **Note:** Closed-toe footgear is required for rim tours. Inquire about weather policies. **Time:** Allow 2 hours minimum. **Hours:** Daily 7-7, Memorial Day-Labor Day; 8-5, rest of year. Guided rim tours depart daily on the hour 9:15-2:15 (weather permitting). Closed Christmas. **Cost:** $15; $14 (ages 60+); $8 (ages 6-17). **Phone:** (928) 289-5898 or (800) 289-5898. *(See ad this page.)*

ROCK ART RANCH is off I-40 exit 286, 1.5 mi. s. on SR 77 to McLaws Rd., 10.7 mi. w. to Territorial Rd., 7.5 mi. w. to Rock Art Ranch Rd., then 2.2 mi. s.w. to ranch entrance. The working cattle ranch consists of more than 7,000 acres. The restored bunkhouse of the Hashknife Cattle Company, a large 19th-century ranching operation, is featured. Ancestral Puebloan and Hohokam artifacts and pots, some dating to 7,500 years old, are displayed in a barn-like building. Visitors may drive 2 miles with a guide to Chevelon Canyon and examine more than 3,000 petroglyphs, many more than 6,000 years old, on canyon walls.

Note: A descent into a 50-foot-deep canyon is required to view the petroglyphs; appropriate attire and footwear are strongly recommended. The climb and descent are not recommended for the physically impaired, elderly guests and small children. **Time:** Allow 2 hours, 30 minutes minimum. **Hours:** Mon.-Sat. 9-3. Closed major holidays. **Cost:** Fee $20-$30. Additional fees apply for other activities. Reservations for all activities are recommended 2 to 3 days in advance. **Phone:** (928) 288-3260.

▼ *See AAA listing this page* ▼

Experience The *BEST* Preserved Meteorite Impact Site on Earth!

See our listing under Winslow

Scan tag with a smartphone and...
EXPERIENCE THE
IMPACT!

OPEN YEAR ROUND
meteorcrater.com • 800.289.5898
20 miles west of Winslow on I-40

Get the free mobile app at
http://gettag.mobi

Discount on admission to AAA Members

BEST WESTERN PLUS WINSLOW INN

Phone: (928)289-2960

Hotel
$70-$140

AAA Benefit: Members save up to 20%, plus 10% bonus points with Best Western Rewards®.

Address: 816 Transcon Ln 86047 **Location:** I-40 exit 255, just n. **Facility:** 54 units. 2 stories (no elevator), interior corridors. **Pool(s):** heated indoor. **Activities:** whirlpool, exercise room. **Guest Services:** coin laundry. **Free Special Amenities:** full breakfast and high-speed Internet.

ECONO LODGE AT I-40

Phone: (928)289-4687

Motel
$54-$63

Address: 1706 N Park Dr 86047 **Location:** I-40 exit 253, just s. **Facility:** 72 units. 2 stories (no elevator), exterior corridors. **Terms:** cancellation fee imposed. **Pool(s):** outdoor. **Guest Services:** coin laundry. **Free Special Amenities:** continental breakfast and high-speed Internet. *(See ad this page.)*

LA POSADA HOTEL

Phone: (928)289-4366

Historic Hotel
$109-$169

Address: 303 E 2nd St 86047 **Location:** I-40 exit 253, 1 mi s to Route 66 (2nd St), then just e; in historic downtown. **Facility:** This restored historic hotel, built to resemble a fabulous Spanish hacienda, is tastefully decorated and sits on eight well-tended acres. 45 units. 2 stories (no elevator), interior corridors. **Terms:** 7 day cancellation notice-fee imposed. **Dining:** The Turquoise Room, see separate listing.

WHERE TO EAT

MOJO CAFE

Phone: 928/289-6656

Coffee/Tea
$3-$7

AAA Inspector Notes: Billboards on either side of Interstate 40 will guide you to this unexpected oasis in the desert featuring burritos, salads, muffins, scones, cheesecake, gourmet cinnamon rolls, bagels, espresso, hot and iced coffee and smoothies with nutritional extras including cool treats for the kids. The wireless Internet, relaxed and comfortable ambience and upbeat music are sure to please. **Address:** 1700 N Park Dr 86047 **Location:** I-40 exit 253, just s. B L

THE TURQUOISE ROOM

Phone: 928/289-2888

Southwestern
$8-$34

AAA Inspector Notes: Eight hand-painted glass and tin chandeliers grace the restaurant's high beamed ceilings. Elk, quail, salmon, beef, lamb and pork, flavored with home-grown herbs, are always on the menu. Boxed lunches is another option, which include fresh grilled and chilled salmon, herb-roasted chicken breast and fresh breads. **Bar:** full bar. **Reservations:** suggested. **Address:** 303 E 2nd St 86047 **Location:** I-40 exit 253, 1 mi s to Route 66 (2nd St), then just e; in historic downtown; in La Posada Hotel. B L D

WUPATKI NATIONAL MONUMENT (B-4)

Lying about 33 mi. n. of Flagstaff and reached via US 89, 35,253-acre Wupatki National Monument contains more than 2,600 archeological sites, including some 1,000 structures. Thanks to increased rainfall and the water-retaining layer of ash and cinders covering the ground after the late 11th-century eruption of Sunset Crater Volcano (south of the monument), farming became productive enough that at one time the region may have been one of the more densely populated sections of northern Arizona. The original inhabitants of Wupatki are believed to have been ancestors of the Hopi Indians.

▼ *See AAA listing this page* ▼

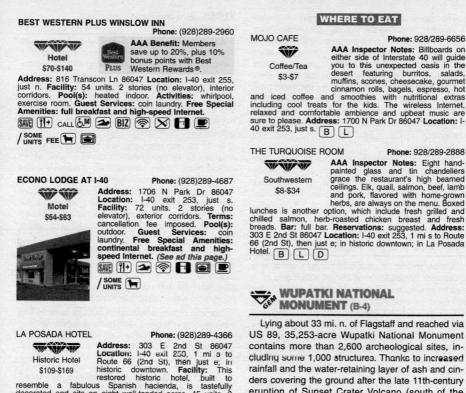

Vacation Convenience & Home Comforts

EconoLodge
BY CHOICE HOTELS

WINSLOW

•Continental Breakfast •Free Wi-Fi Internet
•Seasonal Outdoor Pool •Pets Welcome

928-289-4687

I-40 at Exit 253
1706 North Park Dr • Winslow, AZ

The largest and one of the most impressive sites is Wupatki, or "Long-cut House," containing more than 100 rooms. Nearby are a ceremonial amphitheater, ball court and "blow hole." Other important ruins are the Citadel, Nalakihu, Lomaki and the three-story Wukoki, all reachable by short, self-guiding trails. Most of the ruins were inhabited from about 1100-1225. Picnicking is available. Visitors must stay on the trails; the backcountry is closed to unguided travel in order to protect the cultural resources.

Allow 1 hour minimum. Visitor center open daily 9-5; closed Christmas. Ruins and trails open daily dawn-dusk. Admission $5 per person; free ages 0-15. Admission includes Sunset Crater Volcano National Monument *(see place listing p. 254)*. Phone (928) 679-2365.

YARNELL (D-3) pop. 649, elev. 4,800'

Yarnell sprang up as a gold-mining town after a prospector named Harrison Yarnell struck gold on a nearby mountain peak in 1863. Some active mines still produce silver, gold and copper; however, the area's primary industries are cattle raising and tourism. Many vacationers visit Yarnell in the summer to escape the desert heat and to enjoy the many recreational pursuits the area offers.

Yarnell/Peeples Valley Chamber of Commerce: Write P.O. Box 275, Yarnell, AZ 85362. **Phone:** (928) 427-6582.

SHRINE OF ST. JOSEPH OF THE MOUNTAINS, .5 mi. w. off SR 89, is an open-air mountainside shrine with statues that depict scenes of The Last Supper, Garden of Gethsemane, The Way of the Cross and the Risen Christ. Information is available at the shrine or by writing P.O. Box 267, Yarnell, AZ 85362. **Hours:** Open daily 24 hours. **Cost:** Donations. **Phone:** (928) 778-5229.

YOUNGTOWN pop. 6,156
- Hotels & Restaurants map & index p. 155
- Part of Phoenix area — see map p. 134

BEST WESTERN INN & SUITES OF SUN CITY
Phone: (623)933-8211 **32**

Hotel
$60-$130

AAA Benefit: Members save up to 20%, plus 10% bonus points with Best Western Rewards®.

Address: 11201 Grand Ave 85363 **Location:** On US 60, just se of 113th Ave. **Facility:** 96 units, some efficiencies. 2 stories (no elevator), interior/exterior corridors. **Amenities:** *Some:* high-speed Internet. **Pool(s):** heated outdoor. **Guest Services:** coin laundry. **Free Special Amenities:** full breakfast and high-speed Internet.

(See ad p. 178.)

SAVE [icons] / SOME UNITS

YUMA (E-1) pop. 93,064, elev. 200'
- Restaurants p. 329

Although he was not the first white man to visit the area, Father Eusebio Francisco Kino was the first to recognize the Yuma Crossing as the gateway to California. Yet Kino's discovery would not be used for almost a century until Juan Bautista de Anza, presidial captain of Tubac, arrived in search of an overland route to California through Yuma. The Anza expedition reached Mission San Gabriel, near present-day Los Angeles.

In 1779 two missions were founded at the crossing by Father Francisco Garcés, who, along with all the colonists, was later killed during the last major uprising of the Quechan Indians. With the destruction of the colony the crossing again faded from memory. Fifty years passed before it was rediscovered, this time by Kit Carson. It finally became a permanent settlement during the California gold rush of 1849.

Lutes Casino on Main Street, the oldest continuous pool hall and domino parlor in the state, began as a grocery store in 1901. Today visitors can play dominos and pool or just browse around the room filled with eclectic memorabilia.

Yuma is host to a number of outdoor events. The city becomes flooded with hunters when hunting season opens over Labor Day weekend. Golf is a popular pastime with 13 lush golf courses from which to choose.

Yuma Visitors Bureau: 201 N. 4th Ave., Yuma, AZ 85364. **Phone:** (928) 783-0071 or (800) 293-0071.

Self-guiding tours: The Colorado River crossing in Yuma is the site of several historical and cultural buildings, most of which are open to the public. Brochures about self-guiding tours are available from the visitors bureau.

Shopping areas: Yuma Palms Regional Center, 1463 S. Yuma Palms Pkwy., is anchored by Dillard's and JCPenney.

ARIZONA HISTORICAL SOCIETY/SANGUINETTI HOUSE MUSEUM AND GARDENS, 240 S. Madison Ave., was the home of pioneer merchant E.F. Sanguinetti. The house contains late-19th-century period rooms and exhibits about the history of Yuma and the lower Colorado River region. The colorful early-1900s-style aviaries and gardens combine exotic and local birds and plants. The adjacent Adobe Annex, once the home of steamboat captain Jack Mellon, houses the museum library.

Hours: Tues.-Sat. 10-4; closed Jan. 1, July 4, Veterans Day, Thanksgiving, Christmas and state employee furlough days. **Cost:** $3; $2 (ages 12-18 and 60+); free (first Sat. of the month). **Phone:** (928) 782-1841.

IMPERIAL NATIONAL WILDLIFE REFUGE encompasses 25,125 acres along the lower Colorado River. The Arizona section of the refuge is 40 mi. n. off US 95 via Martinez Lake Rd., following signs.

The remainder of the refuge can be reached best by boat or four-wheel-drive vehicle. Canada geese, ducks, egrets and eagles gather at the refuge. Hiking, hunting, fishing and boating are permitted in designated areas. Maps and public-use regulations are available upon request.

Hours: Daily dawn-dusk. Visitor center open Mon.-Fri. 7:30-4, Sat.-Sun. 9-4, Nov. 15-Mar. 31; Mon.-Fri. 7:30-4, rest of year. Closed major holidays. **Cost:** Free. **Phone:** (928) 783-3371.

KOFA NATIONAL WILDLIFE REFUGE is at 9300 E. 28th St. Encompassing the Kofa and Castle Dome mountains, the refuge preserves the habitat of the desert bighorn sheep.

Remote Palm Canyon is 18 miles south of Quartzsite on US 95, then 7 miles east on a maintained gravel road. It is one of the few places in Arizona where native palms grow. They can be seen from a point 200 yards away via a half-mile hike up a moderately steep trail.

Note: The last 200 yards to the palms present a strenuous climb. Refuge roads are rough and are best navigated by four-wheel-drive and high-clearance vehicles. Entering abandoned mines is prohibited. **Hours:** Refuge and canyon accessible daily 24 hours. **Cost:** Free. **Phone:** (928) 783-7861.

YUMA QUARTERMASTER DEPOT STATE HISTORIC PARK, I-8 4th Ave. exit to 201 N. 4th Ave., is on a 20-acre site on the s. side of the Colorado River. The park salutes 5 centuries of transportation across the Colorado River. From 1864 through 1883 the U.S. Army Quartermaster Depot stored and distributed supplies for military posts throughout the Southwest. Five restored buildings stand on the site that once comprised the depot. The depot office was built in 1872. **Hours:** Daily 9-4:30, Oct.-May; Tues.-Sun. 9-4:30, rest of year. Closed Christmas. **Cost:** Free. **Phone:** (928) 783-0071.

YUMA TERRITORIAL PRISON STATE HISTORIC PARK is off I-8 exit 1 (Giss Pkwy.), on a bluff on the s. side of the Colorado River "meander" (where the river bends). Erected in 1876, the building was a prison until 1909. The adobe walls, which no longer stand, were 8 feet thick at the base and 5 feet thick at the top, and at full capacity confined 400 prisoners. Of interest are the cellblocks, the "dark cell"

and a museum. Interpretive programs are offered. **Hours:** Daily 8-5. Closed Christmas. **Cost:** $4; $1 (ages 7-13). **Phone:** (928) 783-4771.

BEST WESTERN PLUS INNSUITES YUMA MALL HOTEL & SUITES   **Phone:** (928)783-8341

(fyi)
Hotel
$79-$129

AAA Benefit: Members save up to 20%, plus 10% bonus points with Best Western Rewards®.

Under major renovation, scheduled to be completed October 2011. **Last Rated:** ▼▼▼ **Address:** 1450 Castle Dome Ave 85365 **Location:** I-8 exit 2 (16th St/US 95), just e to Yuma Palms Pkwy, just n, then just w. **Facility:** 166 units, some efficiencies. 2-3 stories (no elevator), exterior corridors. **Amenities:** high-speed Internet. **Pool(s):** heated outdoor. **Activities:** whirlpool, exercise room. **Guest Services:** valet and coin laundry, area transportation-within city limits. **Free Special Amenities:** full breakfast and manager's reception.

SAVE 🚫 ⛔ 👤 🍽 🛳 🛜 🛄 🖥 💻 / SOME UNITS FEE 🐕

CANDLEWOOD SUITES   **Phone:** (928)726-2800

▼▼▼
Extended Stay Hotel
$90-$189

Address: 2036 S Ave 3 E 85365 **Location:** I-8 exit 3, just n, then just w on Frontage Rd. **Facility:** 95 efficiencies. 4 stories, interior corridors. **Terms:** cancellation fee imposed. **Amenities:** high-speed Internet. **Activities:** basketball, exercise room. **Guest Services:** complimentary and valet laundry, area transportation-within 3 mi.

🚫 🍴 CALL 🛗M BIZ 🛜 ✕ 🛄 🖥 💻 / SOME UNITS FEE 🐕

CLARION SUITES   **Phone:** (928)726-4830

▼▼▼
Hotel
$79-$152

Address: 2600 S 4th Ave 85364 **Location:** I-8 exit 2 (16th St/US 95) eastbound, 1 mi w, then 1.3 mi s; exit 3 (SR 280) westbound, 0.5 mi s, then 2 mi w. **Facility:** 163 units. 3 stories, exterior corridors. **Terms:** cancellation fee imposed. **Amenities:** video games (fee). Some: high-speed Internet. **Pool(s):** heated outdoor. **Activities:** whirlpool, exercise room. **Guest Services:** valet and coin laundry, area transportation-within 5 mi.

🚫 🍴 🛳 BIZ 🛜 ✕ FEE 🦮 🛄 🖥 💻 / SOME UNITS FEE 🐕

COMFORT INN   **Phone:** (928)782-1200

▼▼▼
Hotel
$69-$99

Address: 1691 S Riley Ave 85365 **Location:** I-8 exit 2 (16th St/US 95), just w. **Facility:** 81 units. 3 stories, interior corridors. **Amenities:** Some: high-speed Internet. **Pool(s):** heated outdoor. **Activities:** whirlpool, exercise room. **Guest Services:** valet and coin laundry.

🍴 CALL 🛗M 🛳 🛜 🛄 🖥 💻 / SOME UNITS FEE 🐕

Complete Vacation Planning

AAA.com/Travel and **CAA.ca/Travel** – everything you need to plan and book your vacations, backed by the travel experts at local AAA/CAA offices.

DAYS INN
Phone: (928)329-7790

Motel
$50-$85

Address: 1671 E 16th St 85365 **Location:** I-8 exit 2 (16th St/US 95), just e. **Facility:** 64 units. 2 stories (no elevator), exterior corridors. **Terms:** 2 night minimum stay - seasonal. **Pool(s):** outdoor. **Activities:** whirlpool. **Guest Services:** valet and coin laundry. **Free Special Amenities: continental breakfast and high-speed Internet.**

FAIRFIELD INN BY MARRIOTT
Phone: (928)345-1800

Hotel
$107-$120

AAA Benefit:
AAA hotel discounts of 5% or more.

Address: 1801 S Sunridge Dr 85365 **Location:** I-8 exit 2 (16th St/US 95), e to Sunridge Dr, then just s. **Facility:** 64 units. 3 stories, interior corridors. **Amenities:** high-speed Internet. **Pool(s):** heated outdoor. **Activities:** whirlpool, exercise room. **Guest Services:** valet and coin laundry, area transportation-within 5 mi.

HAMPTON INN & SUITES
Phone: (928)329-5600

Hotel
$109-$149

AAA Benefit:
Members save up to 10% everyday!

Address: 1600 E 16th St 85365 **Location:** I-8 exit 2 (16th St/US 95), just e, then just n. Adjacent to large mall. **Facility:** 90 units. 4 stories, interior corridors. **Terms:** 1-7 night minimum stay, cancellation fee imposed. **Amenities:** high-speed Internet. **Pool(s):** heated outdoor. **Activities:** whirlpool, exercise room. **Guest Services:** valet and coin laundry.

HILTON GARDEN INN YUMA
Phone: (928)783-1500

Hotel
$89-$109

Hilton Garden Inn **AAA Benefit:** Unparalleled hospitality at a special Member rate.

Address: 310 N Madison Ave 85364 **Location:** I-8 exit 1 (Harold C. Giss Pkwy), w to rotary, then 0.4 mi n. **Facility:** 150 units. 4 stories, interior corridors. **Terms:** 1-7 night minimum stay, cancellation fee imposed. **Amenities:** high-speed Internet. **Pool(s):** heated outdoor. **Activities:** whirlpool, exercise room. **Guest Services:** valet and coin laundry. **Free Special Amenities: high-speed Internet.**

HOLIDAY INN
Phone: (928)782-9300

Hotel
$109-$169 2/1-5/31
$99-$169 6/1-1/31

Address: 1901 E 18th St 85365 **Location:** I-8 exit 2 (16th St/US 95), 0.4 mi e on 16th St, just s on Pacific Ave, then just w. **Facility:** 121 units. 4 stories, interior corridors. **Terms:** cancellation fee imposed. **Amenities:** high-speed Internet. **Pool(s):** heated outdoor. **Activities:** whirlpool, exercise room. **Guest Services:** valet and coin laundry, area transportation-within 3 mi.

HOLIDAY INN EXPRESS
Phone: (928)317-1400

Hotel
$89-$169

Address: 2044 S Ave 3 E 85365 **Location:** I-8 exit 3, just n, then just w on Frontage Rd. **Facility:** 120 units. 4 stories, interior corridors. **Terms:** cancellation fee imposed. **Amenities:** high-speed Internet. **Pool(s):** heated outdoor. **Activities:** whirlpool, exercise room. **Guest Services:** valet and coin laundry, area transportation-within 3 mi.

HOMEWOOD SUITES BY HILTON
Phone: (928)782-4100

Extended Stay Hotel
$109-$309

AAA Benefit:
Contemporary luxury at a special Member rate.

Address: 1955 E 16th St 85365 **Location:** I-8 exit 2 (16th St/US 95), 0.4 mi e. **Facility:** 108 kitchen units. 4 stories, interior corridors. **Terms:** 1-7 night minimum stay, cancellation fee imposed. **Amenities:** high-speed Internet. **Pool(s):** heated outdoor. **Activities:** whirlpool, putting green, exercise room. **Guest Services:** valet and coin laundry, area transportation-within 5 mi.

HOWARD JOHNSON INN
Phone: (928)344-1420

Hotel
$56-$122

Address: 3181 S 4th Ave 85364 **Location:** I-8 exit 3E (SR 280 S), 1 mi s to 32nd St, then 2 mi w. Across from shopping centers. **Facility:** 120 units. 2 stories (no elevator), exterior corridors. **Pool(s):** outdoor. **Activities:** whirlpool. **Guest Services:** valet and coin laundry.

LA FUENTE INN & SUITES
Phone: (928)329-1814

Hotel
$80-$179

Address: 1513 S 4th St 85365 **Location:** I-8 exit 2 (16th St/US 95), just e. **Facility:** 96 units. 2 stories (no elevator), exterior corridors. **Terms:** cancellation fee imposed. **Amenities:** high-speed Internet. **Pool(s):** heated outdoor. **Activities:** whirlpool, exercise room. **Guest Services:** coin laundry. **Free Special Amenities: full breakfast and high-speed Internet.** (See ad p. 327.)

MICROTEL INN & SUITES
Phone: (928)345-1777

Hotel
$69-$74

Address: 11274 S Fortuna Rd 85367 **Location:** I-8 exit 12 (Fortuna Rd), just s, then w on frontage road. **Facility:** 109 units, some efficiencies. 3 stories, interior corridors. **Terms:** check-in 4 pm. **Amenities:** high-speed Internet. **Pool(s):** heated outdoor. **Activities:** whirlpool, exercise room. **Guest Services:** coin laundry.

Plan. Map. Go.
TripTik® Travel Planner

Where premier mapping technology meets complete travel information. Only on AAA.com and CAA.ca.

OAK TREE INN

Hotel
$69-$99

Phone: (928)539-9000
Address: 1731 Sunridge Dr 85365
Location: I-8 exit 2 (16th St/US 95), just e, then just s. Located in a commercial area. **Facility:** 119 units. 2 stories (no elevator), interior corridors. **Terms:** 3 day cancellation notice-fee imposed. **Pool(s):** heated outdoor. **Activities:** exercise room. **Guest Services:** coin laundry. **Free Special Amenities: full breakfast and high-speed Internet.**

RADISSON HOTEL YUMA

Hotel
$99-$180

Phone: (928)783-8000
Address: 1501 S Redondo Center Dr 85365 **Location:** I-8 exit 2 (16th St/US 95), just w, then just n. **Facility:** 154 units. 4 stories, interior corridors. **Amenities:** high-speed Internet. *Some:* safes. **Dining:** Market Wine Bar Bistro, see separate listing. **Pool(s):** heated outdoor, heated indoor. **Activities:** whirlpools, exercise room. **Guest Services:** complimentary and valet laundry.

▼ See AAA listing p. 326 ▼

LA FUENTE INN & SUITES

1513 EAST 16TH ST. YUMA, AZ 85365

1-800-841-1814

lafuenteinn.com

$69*

AAA TOURBOOK INTRODUCTORY SPECIAL □

Complimentary Hot Breakfast Buffet 5am-9am

Complimentary Cocktails 5pm-7pm w/ appetizers Mon-Thurs

Free High Speed Internet & USA Today

In House Fitness Center and use of World Gym Fitness Center

Extra Large Pool & Spa with 4 BBQ's and lush Courtyard

Airport Shuttle Service

In-Room Refrigerator, Microwave & Coffee

AAA Approved

* Intro Spec- Must call hotel direct for reservation and present Tourbook at check-in to receive one time use per member, 7 night maximum, introductory special rate. Applies to Jr. Suite - King bed; 2/1-5/31 add $15; Two room suites add $10. Restrictions & Blackout Periods Apply - Call for Details.

Download eTourBook guides for ereaders and smartphones at AAA.com/ebooks

▼ See AAA listing p. 329 ▼

www.yumacabana.com

Independent by design.
Savings you deserve.

AAA Approved

- All Rooms 100% Smoke-Free
- Free Continental Breakfast
- Eco-Friendly Saltwater Pool & BBQ Area
- Free High Speed Wireless & Free Local Calls
- Free STARZ (5 Channels), ESPN 1 & 2
- La-Z-Boys, Microwaves, Refrigerators, Hair Dryers
- Suites & Equipped Kitchens Available
- Balconies & Patios Available
- Guest Laundry, Business & Fax Services
- Unmatched Personalized & Friendly Service
- Award-winning Customer Service

Yuma Cabana Motel
2151 S. 4th Avenue
Yuma, Arizona 85364
(800) 874-0811

Reserve Now! Scan with your smart phone

▼ See AAA listing p. 329 ▼

Shilo INN

FREE HIGH SPEED INTERNET
KIDS 12 & UNDER STAY FREE
COMPLIMENTARY BREAKFAST

AAA MEMBERS GET 10% OFF USE CODE "AAA11"

888-390-8222 SHILOINNS.COM
1550 S. Castle Dome Ave., Yuma, AZ 85365

Discover mobile travel solutions at
AAA.com/mobile and CAA.ca/mobile

SHILO INN HOTEL & SUITES-YUMA
Phone: (928)782-9511

◆◆◆
Hotel
$70-$170

Address: 1550 S Castle Dome Ave 85365 **Location:** I-8 exit 2 (16th St/US 95), just e to Yuma Palms Pkwy, just n, then just w. **Facility:** 135 units, some kitchens. 4 stories, interior corridors. **Terms:** check-in 4 pm, cancellation fee imposed. **Amenities:** video games (fee). *Some:* high-speed Internet. **Pool(s):** heated outdoor. **Activities:** sauna, whirlpool, steamroom, exercise room. **Guest Services:** valet and coin laundry. **Free Special Amenities:** expanded continental breakfast and high-speed Internet.

(See ad p. 328.)

[SAVE] [✈] [↟↟↟] CALL [△M] [⇌] [✈] [✕] FEE [🎦] [🔒]
[⊟] [▭] / SOME UNITS FEE [🐾]

SPRINGHILL SUITES BY MARRIOTT
Phone: (928)783-7853

◆◆◆
Hotel
$94-$134

AAA Benefit:
AAA hotel discounts of 5% or more.

Address: 1825 E 18th St 85365 **Location:** I-8 exit 2 (16th St/US 95), 0.5 mi e to Sunridge Dr, 0.3 mi s, then just e. **Facility:** 82 units. 3 stories, interior corridors. **Amenities:** high-speed Internet. **Pool(s):** heated outdoor. **Activities:** whirlpool, exercise room. **Guest Services:** valet and coin laundry. [✈] [↟↟↟] [⇌] [✈] [✕] [🔒] [⊟] [▭]

TOWNEPLACE SUITES BY MARRIOTT
Phone: (928)783-6900

◆◆◆
Extended Stay Hotel
$107-$134

AAA Benefit:
AAA hotel discounts of 5% or more.

Address: 1726 S Sunridge Dr 85365 **Location:** I-8 exit 2 (16th St/US 95), just e to Sunridge Dr, then just s. **Facility:** 81 units, some two bedrooms, efficiencies and kitchens. 4 stories, interior corridors. **Amenities:** high-speed Internet. **Pool(s):** heated outdoor. **Activities:** exercise room. **Guest Services:** valet and coin laundry, area transportation-within 5 mi.

[✈] [↟↟↟] CALL [△M] [⇌] [BIZ] [✈] [✕] [🔒] [⊟] [▭]
/ SOME UNITS FEE [🐾]

WINGATE BY WYNDHAM
Phone: (928)783-1400

◆◆◆
Hotel
$85-$95

Address: 1760 S Sunridge Dr 85365 **Location:** I-8 exit 2 (16th St/US 95), just e to Sunridge Dr, then just s. **Facility:** 76 units. 3 stories, interior corridors. **Terms:** cancellation fee imposed. **Amenities:** high-speed Internet, safes. **Pool(s):** outdoor. **Activities:** whirlpool, exercise room. **Guest Services:** coin laundry. **Free Special Amenities:** expanded continental breakfast and high-speed Internet.

[SAVE] [↟↟↟] CALL [△M] [⇌] [BIZ] [✈] [✕] [CTV] [🔒] [⊟]
[▭]

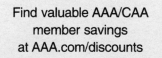

Find valuable AAA/CAA member savings at AAA.com/discounts

YUMA CABANA MOTEL
Phone: (928)783-8311

◆◆◆
Motel
$75-$130 2/1-3/31
$46-$130 4/1-1/31

Address: 2151 S 4th Ave 85364 **Location:** I-8 exit 2 (16th St/US 95), 1 mi w, then 0.5 mi s. **Facility:** 63 units, some efficiencies. 2 stories (no elevator), interior corridors. *Bath:* shower only. **Terms:** 3 day cancellation notice-fee imposed. **Amenities:** high-speed Internet. **Pool(s):** heated outdoor. **Activities:** shuffleboard. **Guest Services:** coin laundry. **Free Special Amenities:** continental breakfast and high-speed Internet.
(See ad p. 328.)

[SAVE] [↟↟↟] [⇌] [✈] [✕] [🔒]
[⊟] / SOME UNITS FEE [🐾] [▭]

WHERE TO EAT

AH-SO SUSHI & STEAK RESTAURANT
Phone: 928/329-7442

◆◆
Japanese
$5-$36

AAA Inspector Notes: An upbeat eatery with dynamic teppan grill tables, the chefs put on a show for diners. The range of sushi covers ahi tuna to yellowtail. **Bar:** full bar. **Address:** 1325 S Yuma Palms Pkwy, Suite B5 85365 **Location:** I-8 exit 2 (16th St/US 95), just e, then just n; adjacent to movie theater. [L] [D]

BURGERS & BEER
Phone: 928/783-3987

◆◆
American
$5-$14

AAA Inspector Notes: Hence the name, this casual sports bar restaurant offers a large variety of gourmet burgers along with American and Mexican favorites. This is a perfect place the watch the game due to the many large flat screen TVs. **Bar:** beer & wine. **Address:** 321 W 20th St 85364 **Location:** I-8 exit 2 (16th St/US 95), 1 mi w, 0.4 mi s on 4th Ave, then just e. [B] [L] [D]

CIAO BELLA
Phone: 928/783-3900

◆◆◆
Italian
$8-$28

AAA Inspector Notes: Diners at this eatery can expect classic antipasti, such as mussels in marinara sauce, lush pasta and other Italian dishes, including osso buco with potato dumplings and grilled shrimp with basil pesto and capellini. Bouquets of dried flowers and art lights contribute to the charming decor of the great special-occasion spot. There is limited parking available. **Bar:** full bar. **Reservations:** suggested. **Address:** 2255 S 4th Ave 85364 **Location:** I-8 exit 2 (16th St/US 95), 1 mi w, then 0.7 mi s. [D]

THE CROSSING RESTAURANT
Phone: 928/726-5551

◆◆
American
$8-$18

AAA Inspector Notes: The owners of this local institution use the freshest ingredients for their hearty, family-style meals. Flame-broiled chicken and the open-faced hot prime rib sandwich are popular choices. **Bar:** full bar. **Address:** 2690 S 4th Ave 85364 **Location:** I-8 exit 2 (16th St/US 95), 1 mi w, then 1.5 mi s. [L] [D]

DON QUIJOTE-MEXICAN & AMERICAN FOOD
Phone: 928/342-3313

◆◆
Mexican
$5-$20

AAA Inspector Notes: Head here for fun dining in a brightly decorated spot with ample portions and a friendly staff. The casual, family-focused restaurant's menu includes a wide selection of Mexican and American dishes. **Bar:** full bar. **Address:** 11411 S Fortuna Rd, #214 85367 **Location:** I-8 exit 12 (Fortuna Rd), 0.4 mi s. [L] [D]

Jump-start your vacation savings with AAA.

AAA members get access to member-only CD and IRA CD rates that have consistently beat the national average.† And you'll enjoy easy account opening and management. You know AAA delivers discounts and valuable roadside assistance. Now find out how we can boost your savings, too. Open your account at **AAA.com/Deposits** or call **1-800-347-7054** for 24/7 customer service.

CDs   IRA CDs   MONEY MARKET ACCOUNTS   ONLINE SAVINGS

Deposit accounts offered through Discover Bank, Member FDIC.
† National Average APYs based on rates of top 50 U.S. banks by deposit provided by Informa Research Services, Inc. as of 2/2/11.

EL PAPPAGALLO MEXICAN RESTAURANT
Phone: 928/343-9451

◆◆ (2 diamonds)

Mexican
$8-$15

AAA Inspector Notes: Family recipes are used in the food preparation at this small, casual restaurant. Staff is friendly and eager to help with suggestions. **Bar:** full bar. **Address:** 1401 S Ave B 85364 **Location:** I-8 exit 2 (16th St/US 95), 2.5 mi w, then just n. L D

THE GARDEN CAFE
Phone: 928/783-1491

◆◆ (2 diamonds)

American
$8-$11

AAA Inspector Notes: Relax in a true garden setting, with trees overhead for shade, terraced areas for dining, a charming gazebo and cages of singing birds. The menu offers freshly prepared salads, soups and sandwiches, including a tri-tip sandwich, perfect for heartier appetites, along with Virginia ham and chicken selections. **Reservations:** suggested. **Address:** 250 S Madison Ave 85364 **Location:** I-8 exit 1 (Harold C. Giss Pkwy), 0.4 mi w, then just n. **Parking:** street only. B L

GRAND CHINA
Phone: 928/344-2805

◆◆ (2 diamonds)

Chinese
$7-$27

AAA Inspector Notes: Mandarin and Szechuan cuisine dominates the offerings at this eatery, but a limited selection of American dishes is available. A lunch buffet is set up weekdays from 11 am to 2 pm, and a steak and seafood dinner buffet lures patrons on Friday and Saturday. On the business loop of the interstate, the restaurant is near the airport. A large, lower-level lounge serves as a popular gathering place. The attentive staff provides quiet and sure service. **Bar:** full bar. **Address:** 350 E 32nd St 85364 **Location:** I-8 exit 2 (16th St/US 95) southbound, 0.5 mi w, then 2 mi s on Arizona Ave; exit 3 northbound, 1 mi s, then 2 mi w on I-8 business loop. L D

HUNTER STEAKHOUSE
Phone: 928/783-1166

◆◆◆ (3 diamonds)

Steak
$19-$40

AAA Inspector Notes: A local institution for more than 40 years, the dark wood masculine interior sets the stage for hearty cuts of steak, ribs, lamb chops, chicken and seafood specialties, all served by a friendly and attentive staff. **Bar:** full bar. **Reservations:** suggested. **Address:** 2355 S 4th Ave 85364 **Location:** I-8 exit 2 (16th St/US 95), 1 mi w, then 0.8 mi s. L D

JULIEANNA'S PATIO CAFE
Phone: 928/317-1961

◆◆◆ (3 diamonds)

American
$9-$29

AAA Inspector Notes: Located near a major medical center with some buildings housing physician's offices nearby, this café has an artfully decorated dining room with colorful fabric patterns and bright paintings, as well as a large, outdoor patio with brightly painted, wrought-iron furnishings and metal sculptures. A young and friendly waitstaff are watchful that guests lack for nothing. **Bar:** full bar. **Address:** 1951 W 25th St 85364 **Location:** I-8 exit 3 (SR 280), jct 24th St and 19th Ave, then just s; at Picacho Mountain Medical Center. L D

KNEADERS BAKERY & CAFE
Phone: 928/783-4099

◆ (1 diamond)

Deli
$5-$8

AAA Inspector Notes: Fresh kneaded and baked bread is prepared on-site along with pastries, salads and soups-all served in a comfortable country decor. **Address:** 1651 E Castle Dome Ave 85364 **Location:** I-8 exit 2 (16th St/US 95), just e. B L D

LA FONDA TORTILLA FACTORY
Phone: 928/783-6902

◆◆ (2 diamonds)

Mexican
$6-$10

AAA Inspector Notes: This casual restaurant serves authentic Mexican cuisine which makes it one of the most popular in Yuma. **Bar:** beer & wine. **Address:** 1095 S 3rd Ave 85364 **Location:** Jct W 11th St. **Parking:** on-site and street. B L D

LUTES CASINO
Phone: 928/782-2192

◆ (1 diamond)

American
$4-$6

AAA Inspector Notes: Not really a casino, this is the oldest pool hall in Arizona, now serving dogs and burgers with all the fixings. There still are some tables where patrons can practice billiards amid movie poster-clad walls and pictures (some a bit risqué), game machines and such ceiling art as a large model helicopter and a full-size Schwinn bike. **Bar:** full bar. **Address:** 221 Main St 85364 **Location:** Just n of Harold C. Giss Pkwy; center. L D

MANDARIN GARDEN
Phone: 928/342-6336

◆◆ (2 diamonds)

Chinese
$6-$18

AAA Inspector Notes: This eatery's popular buffet covers a full spectrum of Mandarin and other Chinese dishes. The friendly staff and servers make any meal special. **Bar:** full bar. **Address:** 12415 S Frontage Rd 85367 **Location:** I-8 exit 14 (Foothills), just s, then 0.6 mi w. L D

MARKET WINE BAR BISTRO
Phone: 928/783-8000

◆◆◆ (3 diamonds)

American
$10-$25

AAA Inspector Notes: This bright and vibrant restaurant offers a popular lounge and wine bar. The menu include items such as fresh fish, filet mignon, scallops, lamb and calamari. **Bar:** full bar. **Reservations:** suggested. **Address:** 1501 S Redondo Center Dr 85365 **Location:** I-8 exit 2 (16th St/US 95), just w, then just n; in Radisson Hotel Yuma. L D

MOSTLY MUFFINS BAKERY & CAFE
Phone: 928/783-7484

◆ (1 diamond)

Specialty
$4-$8

AAA Inspector Notes: In the wee hours of the morning, the kitchen staff is busy making special treats for breakfast and hearty sandwiches and soups for lunch. A casual atmosphere, good coffee and low-fat to decadent muffins help diners start their day. **Address:** 2451 W 16th St 85365 **Location:** I-8 exit 2 (16th St/US 95), 2.4 mi w. B L

NINJA SUSHI
Phone: 928/782-4000

◆◆ (2 diamonds)

Sushi
$10-$30

AAA Inspector Notes: Diners can find fresh, tasty sushi in the middle of the desert, as this fun and popular spot proves. Other Japanese favorites such as teriyaki, udon and tempura also are available. **Bar:** full bar. **Address:** 1400 E 16th St 85365 **Location:** I-8 exit 2 (16th St/US 95), just e. L D

RIVER CITY GRILL
Phone: 928/782-7988

◆◆◆ (3 diamonds)

Seafood
$17-$28

AAA Inspector Notes: Bright, eclectic decor sets a tone for excitement. Fresh fish are sent from the Northwest. Try wild salmon with polenta blueberry jus or mustard-crusted halibut, but do not get so full that you do not leave room for dessert, such as chocolate bread pudding. **Bar:** full bar. **Reservations:** suggested. **Address:** 600 W 3rd St 85364 **Location:** I-8 exit 1 (Harold C. Giss Pkwy), 1 mi w. L D

YUMA LANDING BAR & GRILL
Phone: 928/782-7427

◆◆◆ (3 diamonds)

American
$5-$18

AAA Inspector Notes: On the historic site of the first plane landing in Arizona in 1911, this restaurant displays early city memorabilia throughout its dining rooms. Representative of the diverse selection of American, Mexican and Italian entrées are barbecue ribs, beef fritters and liver and onions. **Bar:** full bar. **Address:** 195 S 4th Ave 85364 **Location:** I-8 exit 172 (4th Ave) eastbound, 0.5 mi s; exit 1 (Harold C. Giss Pkwy) westbound, 1 mi w; in Best Western Coronado Motor Hotel. **Historic** B L D

Salinas Pueblo Missions National Monument, near Mountainair

New Mexico

Welcome to New Mexico, deemed the home of the world's finest chile peppers, where you can fire up your taste buds with 10-plus varieties—most in the "extra hot" category.

Ristras, colorful strings of sun-dried chile peppers, drape café entryways and residential doorways. They're said to ward off evil, welcome visitors and alert guests to the fiery delicacies served there.

But chile isn't the only thing that heats things up. The radiant symbol that has come to represent New Mexico (found on its license plate and flag) is the Zia Pueblo sign for sun. Four rays extend from the center, signifying directions, seasons, periods of the day and stages of life.

Hundreds of rainbow-colored gentle giants fill the sunny sky with hot air during balloon festivals held statewide. The selection is anything but ordinary at the Albuquerque International Balloon Fiesta: It's common to see such diverse shapes as a castle, parrot,

Feather Display, New Mexico State Fair, Albuquerque

spare tire, cola can, corncob and yes, even Dumbo, everyone's favorite flying elephant.

From the basket of a balloon you can glimpse centuries-old, flat-roofed houses and cliff dwellings constructed of adobe—sun-dried bricks of earth, sand, charcoal and grass. This mixture served as the primary building material for pueblos, communal settlements established by the Spanish in the 16th century.

Working pueblos remain at Taos and elsewhere in north-central New Mexico. Each retains an independent government, social order and religious practice. Artisans produce traditional art individual to their own pueblo: Turquoise jewelry, storyteller dolls, pottery, drums, carvings, Navajo rugs and weavings are coveted by visitors and collectors alike.

Some pueblos welcome guests to experience their heritage at annual festivals held in honor of the pueblo's patron saint. Corn, deer or buffalo dances are executed according to strict standards, culminating in a flamboyant display of colorful costumes.

While native traditions at the pueblos continue, only stark stone and adobe walls remain at the uninhabited Chaco Culture National Historical Park, and at Aztec Ruins and Bandelier national monuments. Explore what were once thriving Ancestral Puebloan communities: multistory cliff dwellings with remnants of hundreds of rooms, kivas (ceremonial meeting halls) and petroglyphs offer a warm welcome into the state's rich cultural past.

Sizzling Secrets

Southeastern New Mexico was a hotbed of controversy when, in 1947, a farmer discovered exotic metal debris on a sheep ranch. Some say it was the wreckage of a flying saucer, while others believe it to be the result of tests performed by the U.S. Air Force.

The mysteries surrounding what was dubbed the "Roswell Incident" make the International UFO Museum & Research Center in Roswell all the more intriguing. Don't miss the annual Roswell UFO Festival—held in July—where aliens are the hot ticket.

Or you can learn more about another top-secret scientific development—the Manhattan Project. Los Alamos was chosen as the hot spot for a weapons laboratory that developed and tested the atomic bomb during World War II. Visit the Bradbury Science Museum and peruse artifacts from the project.

If you can't stand the heat, pack a jacket and head for the cool solace of Carlsbad Caverns. At 830 feet below ground, the three-level Big Room begs exploration. Arguably one of the world's biggest underground chambers, it encompasses 8 acres—and at 56 F, it's definitely cool.

Recreation

From snow-clad mountains and sandy desert lowlands to rusty looking canyons and verdant timbered forests, the New Mexico landscape is a tapestry of colors and shapes that can be enjoyed in any season.

North-central New Mexico is *the* place for snow skiing. Sandia Peak Ski Area, just east of Albuquerque in the Cibola National Forest, packs a variety of trails, bowls and catwalks into a wedge of mountain.

Santa Fe Ski Area, north of Santa Fe, attracts families and first-timers to its groomed slopes for downhill skiing. With runs for beginning, intermediate and advanced skiers as well as freestyle areas for both snowboarding and skiing, Angel Fire Resort, east of Taos, is another family favorite.

Alpine skiing is the winter sport of choice at Taos Ski Valley, where snowfall averages more than 300 inches per year—the most in the state—and the vertical drop exceeds 2,600 feet.

Enchanted Forest, east of Red River; Sugarite Canyon State Park, on the Colorado border near Raton; and Manzano Mountain State Park, southeast of Albuquerque, welcome cross-country skiers.

When the snow melts, shift gears and explore the state by bicycle. Trails in southern New Mexico are as varied as the terrain. Fresnal Canyon Loop traverses the Sacramento Mountains foothills, just northeast of Alamogordo, passing through villages and orchards. Race the jackrabbits on a 4.5-mile loop around Tortugas Mountain, 1 mile southeast of Las Cruces. This desertlike area's riding surface comes in three textures: rocky, sandy and smooth.

Bicycling on paved surfaces can be a family event at Chaco Culture National Historical Park, in the northwest. An easy 9-mile circle tour begins at the visitor center and offers stops at several archeological ruins. The king of the road-rides may well be a 70-mile round-trip excursion via state and forest roads from Carlsbad to Sitting Bull Falls, in Lincoln National Forest.

With some 1,500 miles of trails, Gila National Forest, in the southwest, invites camping, hiking and backpacking. State parks, too, cater to this trinity of outdoor activities. Strike camp beside Elephant Butte Lake in that state park; walk among the aspens in Hyde Memorial; or press deep into primitive Morphy Lake State Park's backwoods.

The spring thaw creates a flood of whitewater rafting opportunities in northern New Mexico, especially on the Rio Grande and Rio Chama.

Aliens, Roswell UFO Festival

Historic Timeline

1598	Conquistador Juan de Oñate takes possession of New Mexico for Spain.
1680	The victorious Pueblo Rebellion expels Spanish rule.
1850	New Mexico becomes a U.S. territory.
1862	Key Civil War battles are waged at Glorieta Pass and Valverde.
1864	Col. Kit Carson forces more than 8,000 Navajos to make the 300-mile Long Walk to Bosque Redondo.
1912	New Mexico is admitted to the Union as the 47th state.
1916	The United States invades Mexico after Pancho Villa attacks Columbus.
1945	The United States tests the first atomic bomb at Trinity Site.
1947	Reports of a crashed UFO spark media interest in Roswell.
1986	The United States' deepest limestone cave is discovered in Carlsbad Caverns National Park.
2006	Founded in 1706, Albuquerque celebrates its 300th anniversary.

What To Pack

Temperature Averages Maximum/Minimum	JANUARY	FEBRUARY	MARCH	APRIL	MAY	JUNE	JULY	AUGUST	SEPTEMBER	OCTOBER	NOVEMBER	DECEMBER
Albuquerque	47/23	53/27	59/32	70/41	80/51	89/60	92/65	90/63	83/58	72/45	57/32	47/25
Carlsbad	61/27	65/31	73/38	81/46	88/54	95/63	95/66	94/65	89/59	79/47	69/35	59/27
Clayton	47/19	50/22	55/25	66/36	74/46	83/55	87/60	86/60	80/51	69/40	60/28	49/21
Las Cruces	57/28	64/31	70/37	79/45	88/53	96/61	97/67	95/66	91/59	82/47	67/33	59/29
Roswell	55/21	61/25	68/31	78/42	86/50	94/60	95/64	93/62	86/54	77/42	69/29	57/22
Santa Fe	40/19	43/23	51/29	59/35	68/43	78/52	80/57	79/56	73/49	62/39	50/28	41/20

From the records of The Weather Channel Interactive, Inc.

Good Facts To Know

ABOUT THE STATE

POPULATION: 2,059,179.

AREA: 121,599 square miles; ranks 5th.

CAPITAL: Santa Fe.

HIGHEST POINT: 13,161 ft., Wheeler Peak.

LOWEST POINT: 2,842 ft., Red Bluff Reservoir.

TIME ZONE(S): Mountain. DST.

GAMBLING

MINIMUM AGE FOR GAMBLING: 21.

REGULATIONS

TEEN DRIVING LAWS: No more than one passenger under the age of 21 is permitted (family members exempt). Driving is not permitted midnight-5 a.m. The minimum age for an unrestricted driver's license is 16 years, 6 months. Phone (888) 683-4636 for more information about New Mexico's driver's license regulations.

SEAT BELT/CHILD RESTRAINT LAWS: Seat belts required for driver and front-seat passengers 18 and older. Children ages 7 until 18 must use child restraints or seat belts; child restraints required for under 7 years or under 60 pounds.

HELMETS FOR MOTORCYCLISTS: Required for riders under 18.

RADAR DETECTORS: Permitted.

MOVE OVER LAW: Driver is required to slow down and vacate the lane nearest stopped police, fire and rescue vehicles using audible or flashing signals.

FIREARMS LAWS: Vary by state or county. Contact New Mexico Department of Public Safety, 6301 Indian School Rd. N.E., Suite 310, Albuquerque, NM 87110; phone (505) 841-8053.

HOLIDAYS

HOLIDAYS: Jan. 1 ■ Martin Luther King Jr. Day, Jan. (3rd Mon.) ■ Memorial Day, May (last Mon.) ■ July 4 ■ Labor Day, Sept. (1st Mon.) ■ Columbus Day, Oct. (2nd Mon.) ■ Veterans Day, Nov. 11 ■ Thanksgiving, Nov. (4th Thurs.) ■ Presidents Day (observed day after Thanksgiving) ■ Christmas, Dec. 25.

MONEY

TAXES: New Mexico has a 5.13 percent gross receipts tax, with local option for additional increments of up to 3 percent.

VISITOR INFORMATION

INFORMATION CENTERS: State welcome centers that provide maps, weather information, brochures and information about attractions, accommodations, historic sites, parks and events are at I-10W near Anthony ■ US 64/84 at Chama ■ I-40 exit 22 at Gallup ■ I-40W near Glenrio ■ I-10E exit 20 at Lordsburg ■ I-25 exit 451 near Raton ■ I-25 mile marker 268, 17 miles south of Santa Fe, near the Santo Domingo Indian Reservation ■ at 491 Old Santa Fe Tr. in downtown Santa Fe ■ and at US 60/70/84 near Texico.

ROAD CONDITIONS:
The State Department of Transportation provides current information about road closures and conditions; phone (800) 432-4269.

SPECIAL NOTE: Plague bacilli, a condition promoted by fleas, is endemic to New Mexico. Pet owners are advised to provide flea protection for their animals.

FURTHER INFORMATION FOR VISITORS:
New Mexico Department of Tourism
Lamy Building
491 Old Santa Fe Tr.
Santa Fe, NM 87501-2753
(505) 827-7400
(800) 545-2070

NATIONAL FOREST INFORMATION:
Southwestern Region
333 Broadway Blvd. S.E.
Albuquerque, NM 87102
(505) 842-3292
(877) 444-6777
TTY (505) 842-3198 (reservations)

FISHING AND HUNTING REGULATIONS:
Department of Game and Fish
1 Wildlife Way
P.O. Box 25112
Santa Fe, NM 87504
(505) 476-8000

RECREATION INFORMATION:
State Parks Division
1220 S. St. Francis Dr.
P.O. Box 1147
Santa Fe, NM 87504
(505) 476-3355
(888) 667-2757

New Mexico Annual Events
Please call ahead to confirm event details.

JANUARY	FEBRUARY	MARCH
▪ Casper Baca Bares, Broncs and Bulls Spectacular Rodeo / Farmington 505-287-9534 ▪ Souper Bowl / Albuquerque 505-247-2052, ext. 222 ▪ Mesilla Valley Balloon Rally Las Cruces 505-382-5465	▪ For the Love of Art Month Las Cruces 575-527-0020 ▪ Mount Taylor Winter Quadrathlon / Grants 800-748-2142 ▪ ARTFeast / Santa Fe 505-982-1648	▪ Cowboy Days / Las Cruces 575-522-4100 ▪ National Fiery Foods and Barbecue Show Albuquerque 505-873-8680 ▪ Rockhound Roundup Deming 575-267-4399

APRIL	MAY	JUNE
▪ Park 'N the Park Car Show Rio Rancho 505-891-4737 ▪ White Sands International Film Festival / Las Cruces 877-345-6973 ▪ Gathering of Nations Powwow / Albuquerque 505-836-2810	▪ Blessing of the Field Las Cruces 505-522-4100 ▪ Northern New Mexico Fine Arts and Crafts Guild Cathedral Park Show Santa Fe 505-473-5590 ▪ Truth Or Consequences Renaissance Fiesta Truth Or Consequences 505-894-6600	▪ New Mexico Arts and Crafts Fair / Albuquerque 505-884-9043 ▪ Rodeo de Santa Fe Santa Fe 505-471-4300 ▪ Fine Art and Wine Festival Red River 575-754-2366

JULY	AUGUST	SEPTEMBER
▪ Fiestas de Taos / Taos 800-732-8267 ▪ Santa Fe International Folk Art Market / Santa Fe 505-476-1197 ▪ Freedom Days / Farmington 800-448-1240	▪ Hot Chili Days, Cool Mountain Nights / Red River 877-754-1708 ▪ Angel Fire Balloon Rally Angel Fire 575-377-6555 ▪ Inter-Tribal Indian Ceremonial / Gallup 888-685-2564	▪ The Whole Enchilada Fiesta / Las Cruces 505-541-2444 ▪ New Mexico Wine Festival Bernalillo 505-867-8687 ▪ New Mexico State Fair Albuquerque 505-265-1791

OCTOBER	NOVEMBER	DECEMBER
▪ Harvest Festival / Santa Fe 505-471-2261 ▪ Albuquerque International Balloon Fiesta Albuquerque 505-821-1000 ▪ Lincoln County Cowboy Symposium Ruidoso Downs 505-378-4142	▪ Las Cruces International Mariachi Concerts and Festival / Las Cruces 575-525-1735 ▪ Weems International Artfest Albuquerque 505-293-6133 ▪ Renaissance ArtsFaire Las Cruces 505-523-6403	▪ Red Rock Balloon Rally Gallup 505-863-3841 ▪ WinterFest / Los Alamos 505-661-4844 ▪ Old-Fashioned Christmas Truth Or Consequences 575-740-3902

Chile Peppers

Albuquerque International
Balloon Fiesta

Pueblo Bonito, Chaco
Culture National Historical
Park

Traditional New Mexico Home

New Mexico State Fair, Albuquerque

Great Experience for Members

AAA editor's picks of exceptional note

Cumbres & Toltec
Scenic Railroad

Vietnam Veterans
Memorial State Park

San Miguel Mission
Church

Carlsbad Caverns
National Park

Abiquiu (E-3)
Chimney Rock *(See p. 350.)*

Acoma Pueblo (G-2)
Acoma Pueblo (Sky City) *(See p. 351.)*

Alamogordo (I-4)
New Mexico Museum of Space History
(See p. 352.)

Albuquerque (F-3)
ABQ BioPark Zoo *(See p. 357.)*
Anderson-Abruzzo Albuquerque International
Balloon Museum *(See p. 357.)*
Explora! *(See p. 357.)*
New Mexico Museum of Natural History &
Science *(See p. 358.)*
Old Town *(See p. 358.)*
Sandia Peak Aerial Tramway *(See p. 359.)*

Angel Fire (E-4)
Vietnam Veterans Memorial State Park
(See p. 388.)

Aztec Ruins National Monument (D-2)
Aztec Ruins National Monument *(See p. 390.)*

Bandelier National Monument (B-3)
Bandelier National Monument *(See p. 390.)*

**Capulin Volcano National
Monument (D-5)**
Capulin Volcano National Monument
(See p. 392.)

Carlsbad Caverns National Park (I-4)
Carlsbad Caverns National Park *(See p. 394.)*

**Chaco Culture National Historical
Park (E-2)**
Chaco Culture National Historical Park
(See p. 396.)

Chama (D-3)
Cumbres & Toltec Scenic Railroad
(See p. 397.)

Cochití Pueblo (C-3)
Kasha-Katuwe Tent Rocks National
Monument *(See p. 403.)*

**Gila Cliff Dwellings National
Monument (H-2)**
Gila Cliff Dwellings National Monument
(See p. 414.)

Las Cruces (I-3)
New Mexico Farm & Ranch Heritage Museum
(See p. 420.)

Los Alamos (A-3)
Bradbury Science Museum *(See p. 428.)*

Roswell (H-5)
Roswell Museum and Art Center *(See p. 438.)*

Santa Fe (F-4)
Museum of International Folk Art *(See p. 451.)*
San Miguel Mission Church *(See p. 452.)*

Santa Teresa (J-3)
War Eagles Air Museum *(See p. 473.)*

Tucumcari (F-5)
Mesalands Dinosaur Museum *(See p. 487.)*

White Sands Missile Range (D-3)
White Sands Missile Range Museum
(See p. 488.)

White Sands National Monument (I-3)
White Sands National Monument *(See p. 488.)*

Save Money in Your Sleep

Members get the best available room rates with AAA/CAA
preferred lodging partners.

Visit over 1,100 AAA/CAA Offices   **Click** AAA.com/CAA.ca
Call 1-866-AAA-SAVE (222-7283)

Show Your Card & Save
Preferred Hotels

New Mexico
Atlas Section

ROADS/HIGHWAYS
- INTERSTATE
- CONTROLLED ACCESS
- CONTROLLED ACCESS TOLL
- TOLL ROAD
- PRIMARY DIVIDED
- PRIMARY UNDIVIDED
- SECONDARY DIVIDED
- SECONDARY UNDIVIDED
- LOCAL DIVIDED
- LOCAL UNDIVIDED
- UNPAVED ROAD
- UNDER CONSTRUCTION
- TUNNEL
- PEDESTRIAN ONLY
- AUTO FERRY
- PASSENGER FERRY
- SCENIC BYWAY
- DISTANCE BETWEEN MARKERS
- EXIT NUMBER-FREE/TOLL
- INTERCHANGE FULL/PARTIAL
- WELCOME CENTER
- REST AREA/ SERVICE CENTER

ROAD SHIELDS
- INTERSTATE/BUSINESS
- U.S./STATE/COUNTY
- FOREST/INDIAN
- TRANS-CANADA
- PROVINCIAL AUTOROUTE
- MEXICO
- HISTORIC ROUTE 66
- REFERENCE PAGE INDICATOR

POINTS OF INTEREST
- TOWN
- NATIONAL CAPITAL
- STATE/PROVINCIAL CAPITAL
- AAA/CAA CLUB LOCATION
- FEATURE OF INTEREST
- COLLEGE/UNIVERSITY
- CAMPGROUND
- CUSTOMS STATION
- HISTORIC
- LIGHTHOUSE
- MONUMENT/MEMORIAL
- STATE/PROVINCIAL PARK
- NATIONAL WILDLIFE REFUGE
- SKI AREA
- SPORTS COMPLEX

AREAS OF INTEREST
- INDIAN
- MILITARY
- PARK
- FOREST
- GRASSLANDS
- HISTORIC
- INT'L/REGIONAL AIRPORT
- INCORPORATED CITY

CITIES/TOWNS are color-coded by size, showing where to find AAA Approved and Diamond rated lodgings or restaurants listed in the AAA TourBook guides and on AAA.com.
- RED - major destinations and capitals; many listings
- Black - destinations; some listings
- Gray - no listings

BOUNDARIES
- INTERNATIONAL
- STATE
- COUNTY
- TIME ZONE
- CONTINENTAL DIVIDE

Use driving maps from the AAA Road Atlas to plan your itinerary and route. Purchase the complete 2012 AAA Road Atlas at participating AAA/CAA offices, retail stores and online booksellers.

Atlas ROAD
Travel With Someone You Trust
2012

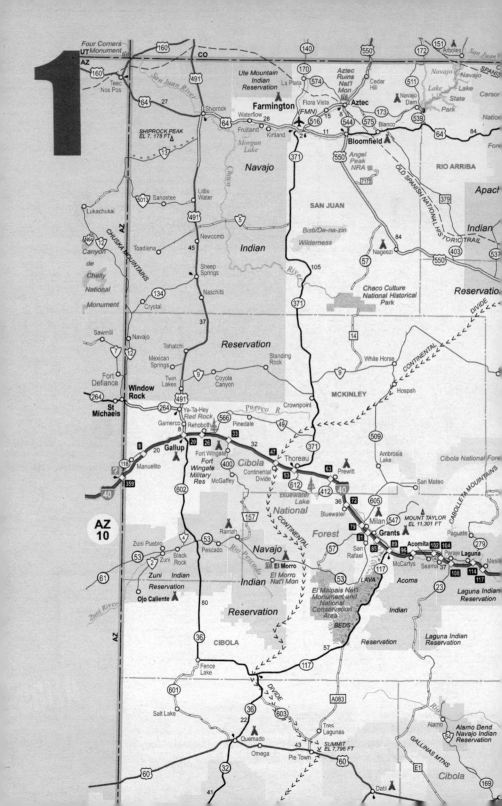

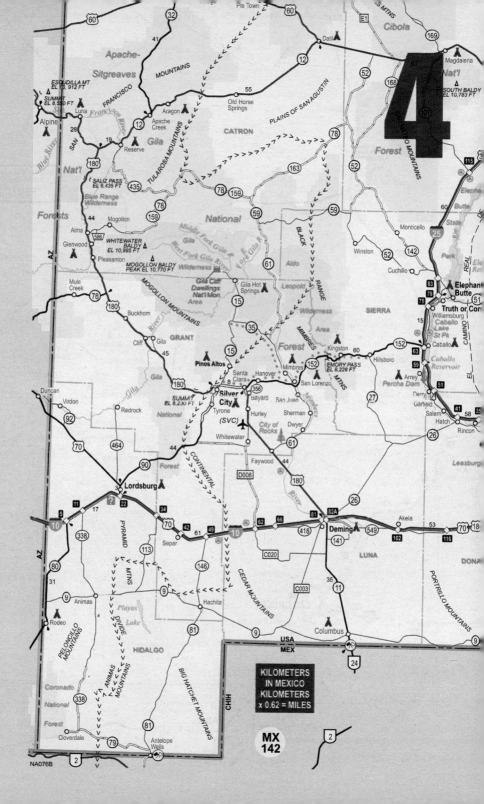

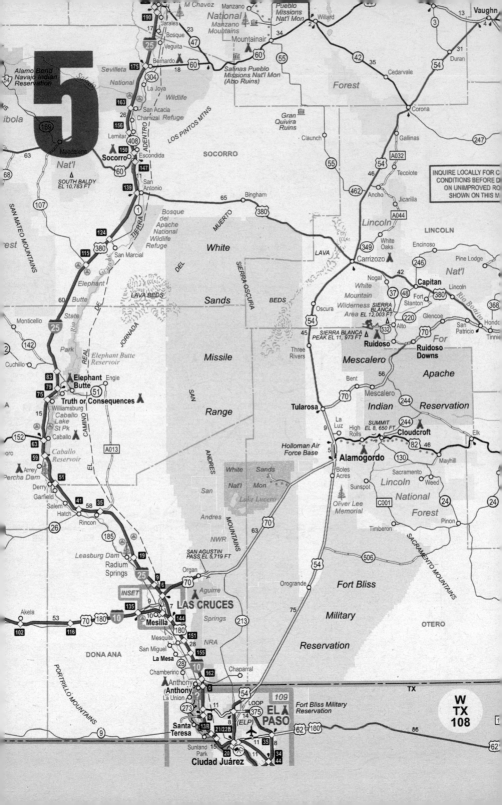

NEW MEXICO

1:1,647,360
Scale in Miles
Scale in Kilometers

AAA/CAA TRIPTIK® MOBILE
Navigation · Gas Prices · Hotels

Free app for your iPhone or Android* device featuring:

· Maps and directions · Updated fuel prices*
· Hotel reservations function · Voice guidance for next maneuver
· AAA inspector notes for lodgings and restaurants
· Location identification for member AAA/CAA roadside assistance

Download it FREE Today
From the iTunes Store or Android Market*

**AAA.com/mobile or
CAA.ca/mobile**

U.S. users: scan this
tag to download the
app to your iPhone
or Android device

Get the free mobile app at
http://gettag.mobi

Android version and fuel prices/locations available for U.S. users only.

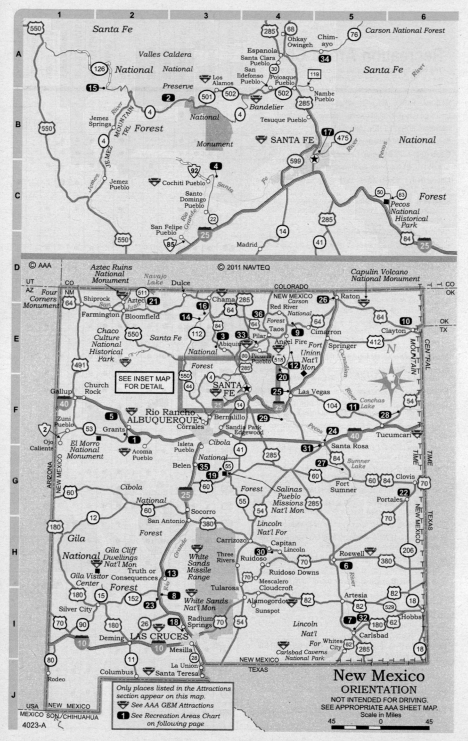

New Mexico

ORIENTATION

NOT INTENDED FOR DRIVING.
SEE APPROPRIATE AAA SHEET MAP.
Scale in Miles

Only places listed in the Attractions section appear on this map.
▲ See AAA GEM Attractions
❶ See Recreation Areas Chart on following page

© 2011 NAVTEQ

© AAA

4023-A

Recreation Areas Chart

The map location numerals in column 2 show an area's location on the preceding map.

	MAP LOCATION	CAMPING	PICNICKING	HIKING TRAILS	BOATING	BOAT RAMP	BOAT RENTAL	FISHING	SWIMMING	PETS ON LEASH	BICYCLE TRAILS	WINTER SPORTS	VISITOR CENTER	LODGE/CABINS	FOOD SERVICE
NATIONAL PARKS *(See place listings.)*															
Chaco Culture (E-2) 33,974 acres. Northwest New Mexico.		•	•	•						•	•		•		
NATIONAL FORESTS *(See place listings.)*															
Carson (D-4) 1,500,000 acres. North-central New Mexico.		•	•	•				•		•	•	•	•		
Cibola (G-2) 1,625,542 acres. Central New Mexico.		•	•	•				•	•	•			•		
Gila (H-1) 3,321,000 acres. Southwestern New Mexico.		•	•	•	•	•		•	•	•			•		
Lincoln (H-4) 1,103,441 acres. South-central New Mexico. Horse rental.		•	•	•				•		•	•	•	•		•
Santa Fe (A-5) 1,600,000 acres. North-central New Mexico between the San Pedro Mountains and the Sangre de Cristo Mountains.		•	•	•				•		•	•	•	•		
NATIONAL CONSERVATION AREAS															
El Malpais (F-2) 376,000 acres 23 mi. s. of I-40 via SRs 53 and 117. *(See Grants p. 415.)*	❶	•	•	•						•	•		•		
Valles Caldera (B-2) 89,000 acres 18 mi. w. of Los Alamos off SR 4. *(See Los Alamos p. 428.)*	❷		•	•				•					•		
ARMY CORPS OF ENGINEERS															
Abiquiu Lake (E-3) 4,015 acres 7 mi. n.w. of Abiquiu via US 84. Water skiing. *(See Abiquiu p. 350.)*	❸	•	•		•	•		•	•	•			•		
Cochiti Lake (C-3) 1,200 acres 5 mi. n. of Pea Blanca on SR 22. Golfing, sailing, windsurfing. *(See Cochiti Pueblo p. 403.)*	❹	•	•	•	•	•	•	•	•	•			•		
STATE															
Bluewater Lake (F-2) 3,000 acres 28 mi. n.w. of Grants off I-40.	❺	•	•		•	•		•	•	•		•	•		
Bottomless Lakes (H-5) 1,400 acres 12 mi. s.e. of Roswell via US 380, then 3 mi. s. on SR 409. *(See Roswell p. 437.)*	❻	•	•	•	•		•	•	•	•			•		
Brantley Lake (I-5) 3,000 acres 12 mi. n. of Carlsbad off US 285.	❼	•	•		•	•		•		•			•		
Caballo Lake (I-3) 11,610 acres 16 mi. s. of Truth or Consequences off I-25. *(See Truth or Consequences p. 486.)*	❽	•	•		•	•		•	•	•			•		
Cimarron Canyon (E-4) 33,000 acres 12 mi. w. of Cimarron via US 64. *(See Cimarron p. 399.)*	❾	•	•	•				•		•			•		
Clayton Lake (E-6) 471 acres 12 mi. n. of Clayton on SR 370. *(See Clayton p. 400.)*	❿	•	•	•	•	•		•		•	•		•		
Conchas Lake (F-5) 290 acres 34 mi. n.w. of Tucumcari via SR 104. *(See Tucumcari p. 487.)*	⓫	•	•		•	•	•	•	•	•			•	•	•
Coyote Creek (E-4) 80 acres 17 mi. n.e. of Mora on SR 434.	⓬	•	•	•				•		•			•		
Elephant Butte Lake (H-3) 40,056 acres 5 mi. n. of Truth or Consequences off I-25. *(See Truth or Consequences p. 486.)*	⓭	•	•		•	•	•	•	•	•			•	•	•
El Vado Lake (E-3) 1,730 acres 4 mi. n.e. of El Vado off SR 112.	⓮	•	•	•	•	•		•	•	•			•	•	
Fenton Lake (A-1) 700 acres 38 mi. w. of Los Alamos via SRs 4 and 126. Canoeing, cross-country skiing.	⓯	•	•		•	•		•		•		•	•		
Heron Lake (E-3) 4,107 acres 11 mi. w. of Tierra Amarilla via US 84 and SR 95.	⓰	•	•	•	•	•		•	•	•			•		
Hyde Memorial (B-5) 350 acres 8 mi. n.e. of Santa Fe on Hyde Park Rd.	⓱	•	•	•						•		•	•		•
Leasburg Dam (I-3) 240 acres 15 mi. n.w. of Las Cruces via I-25 and SR 157. Canoeing; playground.	⓲	•	•		•	•	•	•		•			•		
Manzano Mountains (G-3) 160 acres 16 mi. n.w. of Mountainair via SR 55.	⓳	•	•	•						•	•	•	•		
Morphy Lake (F-4) 30 acres 25 mi. n. of Las Vegas off SR 518. *(See Las Vegas p. 425.)*	⓴	•	•	•	•	•		•		•					
Navajo Lake (D-2) 21,000 acres 23 mi. n.e. of Bloomfield on SR 511. *(See Bloomfield p. 391.)*	㉑	•	•	•	•	•	•	•	•	•			•	•	
Oasis (G-6) 193 acres 6.5 mi. n. of Portales off SR 467. *(See Portales p. 434.)*	㉒	•	•	•				•		•			•		
Percha Dam (I-2) 84 acres 21 mi. s. of Truth or Consequences via I-25. Playground.	㉓	•	•					•	•	•			•		

Recreation Areas Chart

The map location numerals in column 2 show an area's location on the preceding map.

	MAP LOCATION	CAMPING	PICNICKING	HIKING TRAILS	BOATING	BOAT RAMP	BOAT RENTAL	FISHING	SWIMMING	PETS ON LEASH	BICYCLE TRAILS	WINTER SPORTS	VISITOR CENTER	LODGE/CABINS	FOOD SERVICE
Santa Rosa Lake (F-5) 500 acres 7 mi. n. of Santa Rosa via SR 91. Water skiing; nature trail. *(See Santa Rosa p. 472.)*	24	•	•	•	•	•		•	•	•	•		•		
Storrie Lake (F-4) 83 acres 4 mi. n. of Las Vegas off SR 518. Windsurfing. *(See Las Vegas p. 425.)*	25	•	•	•	•	•		•	•	•				•	
Sugarite Canyon (D-5) 3,600 acres 10 mi. n.e. of Raton via SR 72. Historic. Canoeing, cross-country skiing, mountain climbing, snowmobiling. *(See Raton p. 434.)*	26	•	•	•	•	•		•		•	•		•		
Sumner Lake (G-5) 6,700 acres 16 mi. n.w. of Fort Sumner on US 84.	27	•	•	•	•	•		•	•	•	•		•		
Ute Lake (F-6) 1,500 acres 2 mi. s.w. of Logan on SR 540. *(See Tucumcari p. 487.)*	28	•	•	•	•	•		•	•	•	•		•		
Villanueva (F-4) 1,679 acres 31 mi. s.w. of Las Vegas via I-25 and SR 3.	29	•	•	•				•	•	•			•		
OTHER															
Fort Stanton (H-4) 24,000 acres 7.7 mi. w. of Lincoln on US 380, then 1 mi. s. on SR 220. Caving; horse trails. *(See Lincoln p. 427)*	30	•	•	•									•		
Janes-Wallace Memorial (G-4) 1 mi. s. of Santa Rosa on SR 91. *(See Santa Rosa p. 472.)*	31	•	•						•				•		
Lake Carlsbad (I-5) In Carlsbad on Park Dr. Water skiing. *(See Carlsbad p. 393.)*	32	•			•	•		•	•	•			•		
Orilla Verde (E-4) 2,840 acres 6 mi. n of Pilar on SR 570.	33	•	•	•				•			•	•		•	
Santa Cruz Lake (A-5) 2,543 acres 14 mi. e. of Española via SRs 76 and 4. Mountain biking.	34	•	•	•		•		•		•	•				
Sen. Willie M. Chavez (G-3) 150 acres on the Rio Grande at Belen.	35	•	•					•		•	•				
Wild Rivers (E-4) 20,300 acres 5 mi. w. of Questa off SR 378.	36	•	•	•	•	•		•		•	•		•		

Available at participating AAA/CAA offices. Selections vary by location.

Get Travel-Ready!
Your AAA/CAA Travel Store has great member values on:
- Luggage
- Travel Accessories
- Atlases • Travel Guides

TRAVEL STORE
GREAT MEMBER VALUES

ABIQUIU (E-3) pop. 231, elev. 6,063'

In the mid-18th century Abiquiu (AH-be-cue) was one of several settlements the Spanish government provided for *Genízaros,* people of mixed blood who were either the Spaniards' own prisoners or captives ransomed from the Comanches or Apaches and later released from slavery. By 1778 the community was a stop on the Old Spanish Trail, which led westward to an infant coastal hamlet called Los Angeles.

Abiquiu was the birthplace of Padre Antonio José Martínez, the priest credited with the establishment of the Southwest's first coeducational school. His lifelong crusade to educate his people took him to Taos in 1826, then into politics.

The area is known for its colorful, rugged rock formations and other scenic features. Abiquiu Lake *(see Recreation Chart),* 7 miles northwest via US 84, provides opportunities for water sports while controlling downstream flooding and sedimentation. The Carson and Santa Fe national forests *(see place listings p. 396 and 472)* surround the lake.

As anyone who has seen her landscapes would suspect, artist Georgia O'Keeffe spent winters and springs in Abiquiu and summers and autumns at nearby Ghost Ranch. Along US 84 are some of the views O'Keeffe captured in her work. Guided tours of the Georgia O'Keeffe Home and Studio are available only by reservation mid-March through November. Tours, which accommodate 12 people, require advanced payment and depart from the nearby Abiquiu Inn; phone (505) 685-4539. The artist's ashes were scattered at Pedernal, the flat-topped mountain to the south of Ghost Ranch.

GHOST RANCH is 12 mi. n.w. on US 84. Georgia O'Keeffe owned a summerhouse and painted familiar scenes at this 21,000-acre ranch, now a Presbyterian education and retreat center. The facility includes hiking trails, a meditation labyrinth and two museums. Horseback rides are offered from mid-March through Thanksgiving weekend; phone for reservations. Georgia O'Keeffe at Ghost Ranch landscape tours are offered seasonally. **Hours:** Daily 8-5. Landscape tours Tues. and Thurs.-Sat. at 1:30, mid-Mar. to mid-Nov. **Cost:** Grounds and hiking trails free. Landscape tour $25. Horseback riding $45. **Phone:** (505) 685-4333 or (877) 804-4678. ⟦Ⅱ⟧ ⟦A⟧

Chimney Rock is 12 mi. n.w. on US 84. The trailhead is located at the arroyo behind the Ghost Ranch museums and past the Corral Block complex.

This is the most popular of several hiking trails at Ghost Ranch, and deservedly so; it's an absolute stunner. The well-marked trail ascends a ridge to the top of a red rock mesa that is within striking distance of Chimney Rock, a tall, spire-shaped rock. Along the way you'll see drought-tolerant vegetation like cholla, prickly pear cactus, saltbush and piñon pine.

After reaching the top of the mesa hikers approach Chimney Rock from behind, getting close enough for a dizzying look at the valley floor below. Spectacular 360-degree vistas take in the Piedra Lumbre basin, Mt. Pedernal on the western horizon and an array of multicolored sandstone and gypsum formations. The views as the trail climbs from 6,500 to 7,100 feet are splendid.

Note: The round-trip distance is 3 miles. Hikers should check in at the conference center office before and after hiking. Wear hiking boots or non-slip athletic shoes and a hat (there's no shade), and bring water. Stay on the marked trail and do not attempt to climb any of the rock formations. **Time:** Allow 2 hours minimum. **Hours:** Daily 8-5. **Cost:** Free. **Phone:** (505) 685-4333 or (877) 804-4678.

Florence Hawley Ellis Museum of Anthropology is 12 mi. n.w. on US 84. Part of the Ghost Ranch Education and Retreat Center, the museum features exhibits depicting 12,000 years of civilization within the Chama-Rio Grande region. Contemporary Southwestern art also is displayed. **Time:** Allow 30 minutes minimum. **Hours:** Mon.-Sat. 9-5, Sun. 1-5. **Cost:** Donations. **Phone:** (505) 685-4333 or (877) 804-4678.

Ruth Hall Museum of Paleontology is 12 mi. n.w. on US 84. The museum at the Ghost Ranch Education and Retreat Center documents the area's rich fossil record, including the 1947 discovery of a small, predatory dinosaur named *Coelophysis.* **Time:** Allow 30 minutes minimum. **Hours:** Mon.-Sat. 9-5, Sun. 1-5. **Cost:** Donations. **Phone:** (505) 685-4333 or (877) 804-4678.

THE ABIQUIU INN   **Phone:** 505/685-4378
⟦fyi⟧ Not evaluated. **Address:** 21120 Hwy 84 87510 **Location:** On US 84, 3 mi n of jct SR 554. Facilities, services, and decor characterize a mid-scale property.

GHOST RANCH B&B   **Phone:** 505/685-4333
⟦fyi⟧ Not evaluated. **Address:** HC 77, Box 11 87510 **Location:** On US 84, 12 mi n; between MM 224 and 225, then 1 mi e on Private Dr 1708, follow signs. Facilities, services, and decor characterize an economy property.

WHERE TO EAT

CAFE ABIQUIU   **Phone:** 505/685-4378
◆◆ ◆◆   **AAA Inspector Notes:** This charming restaurant has a creative menu that
Southwestern   includes selections from
$10-$21   Mediterranean pizza to trout tacos. The dessert tray presentation will tempt with luscious creations but the summer berry pudding is a must-try. **Address:** 21120 Hwy 84 87510 **Location:** On US 84, 3 mi n of jct SR 554.
⟦B⟧ ⟦L⟧ ⟦D⟧

Enjoy great savings on hotel rates at AAA.com or CAA.ca

ACOMA PUEBLO (G-2) elev. 6,550'

One of the oldest continuously inhabited settlements in the country—evidence dates it from A.D. 1150—Acoma was well established when Francisco Vázquez de Coronado explored New Mexico in 1540. Inhabitants of Sky City, as the pueblo was known, worked fields on the plains 357 feet below their village and climbed back atop the mesa each night. Acoma afforded protection through decades of warfare, but the numerical superiority of the Spaniards proved too much. A final battle in 1599 vanquished the community.

Today only a few dozen Acomans live year-round on the mesa top; others live in nearby villages but return to Sky City for cultural observances. Visitors must register at the Sky City Cultural Center and Haak'u Museum (see attraction listings below.) at the base of the mesa, where permits and guided tours are available.

About 3 miles northeast is Enchanted Mesa, which looms 430 feet above the surrounding plain. According to Acoma tribal folklore, this was an ancestral settlement, but access to it was wiped out by a violent storm, leaving several Acoma women and children to starve on the mesa top.

ACOMA PUEBLO (SKY CITY) is off I-40 exit 102, then 15 mi. s. on R.R. 30/32 to the Sky City Mesa. Occupied by the Acomans since the second century, this 367-foot-high mesa is topped by one of the largest adobe structures in North America, the 1629 Spanish mission San Esteban del Rey. Building materials, including great log beams hand cut on Mount Taylor some 30 miles north, were manually carried to the summit by Acoman laborers.

More than 15 Acoma families live on the mesa in dwellings without running water or electricity while observing the customs and traditions of their ancestors. Pottery makers showcasing their works for sale outside their homes are observed on guided walking tours featuring the pueblo, the plaza and the mission church, with its ecclesiastic art, tapestries and hand-carved woodwork.

Visitors to the mesa must arrange for a guide at the Sky City Cultural Center and Haak'u Museum, located at the base of the pueblo. Videotaping is not allowed on the mesa; a permit for still photography may be acquired at the cultural center. **Time:** Allow 3 hours minimum. **Hours:** Daily 9-6, Apr.-Oct. Last tour departs 1 hour before closing. Closed short periods in June, July and Oct., and other days without notice. **Cost:** Guided tours $20; $17 (senior citizens, military and college students with ID); $12 (ages 6-17); $55 (family, two adults and two children). Still-camera photography fee without tour $10. **Phone:** (505) 552-7860, or (800) 747-0181 for information about guided tours. 🍴

Sky City Cultural Center and Haak'u Museum, off I-40 exit 108, then 12 mi. s. to the Sky City Mesa, features two galleries with temporary displays.

Note: Revealing clothing, video cameras and cell phones are not permitted. **Time:** Allow 1 hour minimum. **Hours:** Daily 9-5, Apr.-Oct.; Fri.-Sun. 10-5, late Nov.-early Mar. Last tour departs 1 hour before closing, Apr.-Oct.; 2 hours before closing, late Nov.-early Mar. Schedule varies during week of Dec. 25; phone ahead. Closed short periods in June, July and Oct., and other days without notice. **Cost:** Guided tours $20; $17 (senior citizens, military and college students with ID); $12 (ages 6-17); $55 (family, two adults and two children). Still-camera photography fee without tour $10. **Phone:** (505) 552-7860, or (800) 747-0181 for information about guided tours. 🍴

ACOMITA

SKY CITY CASINO HOTEL   Phone: 505/552-6123
♦♦♦♦♦
Hotel
Rates not provided

Address: I-40 exit 102 87034
Location: I-40 exit 102, just n.
Facility: 134 units. 3 stories, interior corridors. **Terms:** check-in 4 pm.
Amenities: video games (fee).
Pool(s): heated outdoor. **Activities:** whirlpool, exercise room. **Guest Services:** coin laundry. **Free Special Amenities:** full breakfast and high-speed Internet.

SAVE 🍴 CALL 🅼 🛏 📶 FEE 📷 💻
/ SOME UNITS 🚻 🖼

ALAMOGORDO (I-4) pop. 30,403, elev. 4,335'
• Hotels p. 352 • Restaurants p. 353

A ready water supply from the looming Sacramento Mountains prompted the town's founding as a railroad terminal in 1898. Alamogordo—Spanish for "fat cottonwood"—grew quickly as ranching, lumber production, farming and tourism were added to its assets. Nevertheless, modern development has been due primarily to the Holloman Air Force Base. Diversified industry, much of it related to space, also contributes to the economy.

The Air Force Missile Development Center conducts rocket and allied research at the base, while the National Solar Observatory in Sunspot (see attraction listing p. 477) works to advance knowledge of the sun. The nearby White Sands Missile Range (see place listing p. 488) administers the testing, evaluating, researching and assessing of military systems and commercial products.

Tularosa Basin Historical Society Museum, 1301 N. White Sands Blvd., focuses on local and regional history; phone (575) 434-4438. Leading eastward to Cloudcroft (see place listing p. 401), US 82 passes through the state's only highway tunnel.

In July, Alamogordo hosts the Southern New Mexico Festival of Quilts.

Alamogordo Chamber of Commerce and Aubrey Dunn Sr. Visitor Center: 1301 N. White Sands Blvd., Alamogordo, NM 88310. **Phone:** (575) 437-6120 or (800) 826-0294.

ALAMEDA PARK AND ZOO is at 1321 N. White Sands Blvd., jct. US 54 and 10th St. The 7-acre zoo is home to 90 species of American and exotic wild-life including herd animals, cougars, bears, wolves and birds. Shaded lawns, recreation facilities and a playground are offered. **Hours:** Daily 9-5. Closed Jan. 1 and Christmas. **Cost:** $2.50; $1.50 (ages 3-11 and 60+). **Phone:** (575) 439-4290.

NEW MEXICO MUSEUM OF SPACE HISTORY is 2 mi. e. of US 54/70 at jct. Indian Wells Rd. and Scenic Dr. This large complex includes the museum, Stapp Air and Space Park, Astronaut Memorial Garden, International Space Hall of Fame and New Mexico Space Academy. Exhibits honor pioneers from many nations and include international space program items. A special display chronicles the pivotal role that New Mexico plays in the ongoing race to space. The museum also serves as the repository and archive for Spaceport America.

At the Clyde W. Tombaugh IMAX Dome Theater and Planetarium, films are projected on a 40-foot wraparound dome screen. An outdoor display features launch vehicles and spacecraft.

Time: Allow 2 hours minimum. **Hours:** Daily 9-5; closed Thanksgiving and Dec. 25. IMAX films are shown daily on the hour 11-5, Memorial Day-Labor Day; schedule varies rest of year. **Cost:** Museum $6; $5 (ages 60+ and military with ID); $4 (ages 4-12). IMAX admission $6; $5.50 (ages 60+ and military with ID); $4.50 (ages 4-12). Prices may be higher for certain movies. **Phone:** (575) 437-2840 or (877) 333-6589.

OLIVER LEE MEMORIAL STATE PARK is 12 mi. s. on US 54. A green oasis flourishes here around the springs of Dog Canyon, a deep ravine on the west-facing flank of the Sacramento Mountains. The park features historical exhibits and the restored 19th-century house of rancher Oliver Milton Lee. **Hours:** Park daily 24 hours. Visitor center daily 9-4. One-hour ranch house tours are given Sat.-Sun. at 3. **Cost:** $5 per private vehicle. **Phone:** (575) 437-8284.

TOY TRAIN DEPOT is 1 mi. n. on US 70/54 to 1991 N. White Sands Blvd. Hundreds of models and toy train displays are housed in an old depot. Built in 1898, a narrow-gauge train ride runs outdoors through neighboring Alameda Park. **Time:** Allow 30 minutes minimum. **Hours:** Wed.-Sun. noon-4:30. Last train departs 30 minutes before closing. **Cost:** $4. Train $4. Combination ticket $6. **Phone:** (575) 437-2855 or (888) 207-3564.

BEST WESTERN DESERT AIRE INN
Phone: (575)437-2110

Motel
$79-$126

AAA Benefit:
Members save up to 20%, plus 10% bonus points with Best Western Rewards®.

Address: 1021 S White Sands Blvd 88310 **Location:** 1.6 mi s of jct US 82/70 and 54. **Facility:** 92 units, some kitchens. 2 stories (no elevator), exterior corridors. **Amenities:** Some: high-speed Internet. **Pool(s):** heated outdoor. **Activities:** sauna, exercise room. Fee: game room. **Guest Services:** valet and coin laundry. Free **Special Amenities:** local telephone calls and high-speed Internet.

Best Western

Welcome to your home away from home!
Free WI-FI! Pets w/fee, Microfridges, Fitness room. Great Staff!

COMFORT INN & SUITES   **Phone:** (575)434-4200

Hotel
$86-$95

Address: 1020 S White Sands Blvd 88310 **Location:** 1.6 mi e of jct US 54 and 70. **Facility:** 91 units, some efficiencies and kitchens. 2 stories, exterior corridors. **Terms:** cancellation fee imposed. **Amenities:** high-speed Internet. **Pool(s):** heated outdoor. **Activities:** whirlpool, exercise room. **Guest Services:** valet and coin laundry.

DAYS INN   **Phone:** (575)437-5090

Motel
$54-$67

Address: 907 S White Sands Blvd 88310 **Location:** 1.6 mi s of jct US 82/70 and 54. **Facility:** 40 units. 2 stories (no elevator), exterior corridors. **Parking:** winter plug-ins. **Pool(s):** outdoor. **Guest Services:** coin laundry. Free **Special Amenities:** continental breakfast and high-speed Internet.

Find your way:
AAA/CAA Road Atlases.
Available in standard and Easy Reading formats.
Purchase at participating AAA/CAA club offices, online at bn.com and in fine book stores.

FAIRFIELD INN & SUITES ALAMOGORDO
Phone: (575)437-4000

Hotel
$107-$131

AAA Benefit: AAA hotel discounts of 5% or more.

Address: 300 Panorama Blvd 88310 **Location:** 1.6 mi s of jct US 82/70 and 54, just e. **Facility:** 73 units, some efficiencies. 4 stories, interior corridors. **Amenities:** high-speed Internet. **Pool(s):** heated indoor. **Activities:** whirlpool, exercise room. **Guest Services:** valet and coin laundry. **Free Special Amenities: continental breakfast and high-speed Internet.**

HAMPTON INN
Phone: (575)439-1782

Hotel
$119-$149

AAA Benefit:
Members save up to 10% everyday!

Address: 1295 Hamilton Rd 88310 **Location:** 1.6 mi s of jct US 82/70 and 54, just e on Panorama Blvd, then just s. **Facility:** 70 units. 3 stories, interior corridors. **Terms:** 1-7 night minimum stay, cancellation fee imposed. **Amenities:** video games (fee), high-speed Internet. **Pool(s):** heated indoor. **Activities:** whirlpool, exercise room. **Guest Services:** valet and coin laundry.

HOLIDAY INN EXPRESS HOTEL & SUITES
Phone: (575)434-9773

Hotel
$111-$124

Address: 100 Kerry Ave 88310 **Location:** 1.6 mi s of jct US 54 and 70, just e on Panorama Blvd, then just s. **Facility:** 80 units. 3 stories, interior corridors. **Terms:** cancellation fee imposed. **Amenities:** high-speed Internet. **Pool(s):** heated indoor. **Activities:** whirlpool, exercise room. **Guest Services:** valet and coin laundry.

SUPER 8-ALAMOGORDO
Phone: (575)434-4205

Hotel
$54-$63

Address: 3204 N White Sands Blvd 88310 **Location:** Just s of jct US 54/70 and 82. Across from mall and adjacent to fairgrounds. **Facility:** 54 units. 2 stories (no elevator), interior corridors. **Amenities:** *Some:* high-speed Internet. **Guest Services:** coin laundry. **Free Special Amenities: continental breakfast and high-speed Internet.**

WHITE SANDS MOTEL
Phone: 575/437-2922

Motel
$59-$99

Address: 1101 S White Sands Blvd 88310 **Location:** 1.6 mi s of jct US 54/70 and 82. **Facility:** 25 units. 1 story, exterior corridors. **Free Special Amenities: continental breakfast and high-speed Internet.**

WHERE TO EAT

MARGO'S MEXICAN FOOD
Phone: 575/434-0689

Regional Mexican
$6-$15

AAA Inspector Notes: This long-time restaurant serves heaping plates of fresh-made, traditional New Mexican favorites. **Bar:** beer & wine. **Address:** 501 1st St 88310 **Location:** Just e of White Sands Blvd; downtown.

MEMORIES RESTAURANT
Phone: 575/437-0077

American
$5-$27

AAA Inspector Notes: Set in a historic turn-of-the-twentieth-century Victorian home, this restaurant offers traditional American favorites served in a cozy atmosphere. The extensive menu includes homemade soups, salads, sandwiches and a variety of beef, chicken and fish entrées. Save room for the luscious lemon meringue pie. **Bar:** beer & wine. **Address:** 1223 New York Ave 88310 **Location:** In historic downtown. **Parking:** on-site and street.

PEPPER'S GRILL
Phone: 575/437-9717

Steak
$6-$30

AAA Inspector Notes: One of the city's finer restaurants, this grill prepares great steaks. Try the white cap: filet mignon topped with a portobello mushroom and a spectacular sauce. The setting is almost one of fine dining, and service, provided by staff members attired in black and white, is cheerful. While it is still mainly a steakhouse, this place has the feel of a special-occasion spot at night. **Bar:** beer & wine. **Address:** 3200 N White Sands Blvd 88310 **Location:** On US 54/70; north end of town.

SUNSET RUN
Phone: 575/434-9000

Barbecue
$8-$18

AAA Inspector Notes: Set in a rural farm setting, this restaurant overlooks a lush green pasture with grazing cows, goats and donkey Odie. Generous portions of meat are smoked over apple wood and slathered with original Jack Daniels sauce. The down-home menu lists such favorites as homemade potato chips, served with green chile dipping sauce, and corn pudding, prepared with moist cornbread, green chile and beans. Save room for one of the decadent desserts, including bread pudding with bourbon and butter sauce. **Bar:** beer & wine. **Address:** 54 McDonald Rd 88310 **Location:** Just w of jct 10th St and US 54.

ALBUQUERQUE (F-3) pop. 545,852, elev. 4,957'

The Duke City. Burque. ABQ. They're all nicknames for New Mexico's largest city, and etymologically speaking, you wonder if it isn't because the full name (pronounced "AL-buh-kur-kee") isn't a bit of a tongue twister. While Burque and ABQ are simply shorter versions, the Duke City is a tribute to Don Francisco Fernández de la Cueva, the 8th Duke of Alburquerque of Spain—and somewhere along the way the first "r" got dropped.

Albuquerque was founded in 1706 as a Spanish colonial outpost and farming community along the Rio Grande. The town was laid out in traditional Spanish fashion: a central plaza bordered by a church on one side and government buildings on the other. Following the Mexican-American War in 1846-47 the U.S. government established a federal garrison to protect American settlers during the period of westward expansion, and the town became a major supply depot.

The arrival of the Atchison, Topeka and Santa Fe Railroad in 1880 ushered in a more modern era. The plaza, however, was bypassed; the rail yards were built 2 miles to the east. The area languished, but

(See map & index p. 362.)

fortunately for the benefit of future visitors it didn't lose its trademark Spanish character; today Old Town *(see attraction listing p. 358)* is a tourist hot spot.

The city fills a wide valley between the Sandia Mountains to the east and the sweeping plateau country paralleling the north-south flowing Rio Grande to the west. It's a big city that doesn't look like one. The modest downtown skyline is no match for the twin summits of the Sandias (10,678-foot Sandia Crest and 9,702-foot South Sandia Peak). This small mountain range—running about 17 miles north to south and 4 to 8 miles east to west—is nevertheless steep and rugged, and gives Albuquerque a prominent backdrop. *Sandia* is the Spanish word for watermelon, and dramatic Southwestern sunsets often cast a pinkish hue over the mountains. The ponderosa pines growing along the top of the range even suggest (if you have an active imagination) a watermelon's green rind.

Adding a great deal more color are the fanciful shapes of hot-air balloons. Balloonists from all over the world come here to fly, especially during the 9-day ▼ Albuquerque International Balloon Fiesta in the first half of October. Not only are morning temperatures cool at this time of year, but an atmospheric effect known as the "Albuquerque Box" makes precision flying possible. The "box" is a set of predictable wind patterns that balloon navigators can take advantage of to change direction by varying their altitude, thus staying within a confined area.

The most dramatic sight at this major annual event is the mass ascensions, hundreds of spherical, brilliantly hued balloons taking to the air at once in coordinated flights. The spectacle is a photographer's dream. Also popular is the Special Shape Rodeo, when cows, pigs, soft drink cans and other nontraditional balloon shapes have their turn aloft. During evening Balloon Glows, pilots fire up their propane burners and masses of balloons are illuminated from within. The Anderson-Abruzzo Albuquerque International Balloon Museum in Balloon Fiesta Park *(see attraction listing p. 357)* is a great place to learn more about hot-air ballooning.

The high desert landscape in and around Albuquerque is a study in shades of brown. This region averages a meager 9 inches of rain a year, so the predominant vegetation is drought-tolerant sagebrush, which forms distinctive silvery-green clumps. Desert plants like yucca and juniper thrive. The sunlight is piercing, the sky huge. The wind often blows. But it's hardly desolate. Wildlife abounds in the wetlands bordering the Rio Grande, as do cottonwood trees, which form a green ribbon along the river's course. Cottonwoods like water; their presence was a welcome sight to 19th-century pioneers traveling across the Great Plains, since a grove of cottonwoods meant shade, wood and a water supply.

Mexican heritage is evident in the prevalence of terra cotta and turquoise; the two colors even adorn concrete abutments along I-25. But New Mexican cuisine is more of a state affair. It's not Tex-Mex, and it's not California-style Mexican. The chief difference boils down to chile peppers. New Mexico chiles come in two varieties, green and red (the color depends on the stage of ripeness when picked). They're served roasted or chopped, but usually as a sauce—and at many restaurants in town you're more likely to be asked "Green or red?" than "Sweet or unsweet tea?" If you want both, the proper response is "Christmas." A green chile-slathered cheeseburger is a local delicacy, along with blue corn enchiladas and sopaipillas, puffy pieces of fried bread that should be drizzled liberally with honey.

East-west Central Avenue navigates downtown Albuquerque, passes the University of New Mexico and runs through the funky Nob Hill district. The avenue is better known to out-of-towners as Historic Route 66, an icon for American auto travel. During its golden era in the 1930s and '40s a slew of whimsically designed motels, diners and service stations opened along Route 66, beckoning motorists to stop. The completion of I-40 in 1959 was a blow, allowing drivers to zip along without being bogged down by stop signs and traffic lights. Most of the roadside architecture is gone, although you'll still see the occasional pueblo-inspired building and Art Deco storefront, reminders of the Duke City's good old days.

Albuquerque Convention and Visitors Bureau: 20 First Plaza N.W., Suite 601, P.O. Box 26866, Albuquerque, NM 87125. **Phone:** (505) 842-9918 or (800) 284-2282.

Self-guiding tours: Brochures of driving tours through Albuquerque and nearby communities are available from the convention and visitors bureau.

Shopping areas: The most interesting shopping isn't in chain stores; it's at places where you can immerse yourself in the distinctive culture of the Southwest. And there's no better place to start than Old Town's enticing collection of shops, galleries and artist studios.

You'll find Native American pottery, weavings, turquoise and silver jewelry, *retablos* (religious paintings), tinwork, custom-made furniture and more. The Aceves Old Town Basket & Rug Shop (301 Romero St. in Plaza Don Luis) is a treasure trove of ceramic figures, decorative tiles, knickknacks and handwoven textiles; items are literally packed to the rafters here. Southwestern Handcrafts & Gifts (1919 Old Town Rd. in Plaza Hacienda) is a general store that carries everything from stoneware, Kachina dolls and decorated vases to Route 66 and Roswell alien souvenirs.

For fine-quality items like Mata Ortiz and Cochiti Pueblo pottery, gourd masks and miniature clay figures, visit the Ancient Traditions Gallery (400-A San Felipe St.). The Penfield Gallery of Indian Art (2043 S. Plaza) has Navajo rugs, sand paintings, and fetish and storyteller figures. Oaxacan wood carvings and finely crafted turquoise earrings are on display

(See map & index p. 362.)

at the Tanner Chaney Gallery (323 Romero St. in Plazuela Sombra).

In addition to T-shirts, beads and the ubiquitous *ristras* (strings of dried red chiles), search out the unusual. For Mexican folk art (think *calavera* skeleton figures, tin ornaments and all things Frida Kahlo), check out Hispaniae (410 Romero St.). And no shopping trip to Old Town is complete without a stop at The Candy Lady (524 Romero St. at Mountain Road). Chile brittle, homemade fudge, a wall devoted to black licorice—it's all here, including sugar-free chocolate truffles for those feeling a bit guilty.

Nob Hill-Highland is another area with an offbeat selection of shops lining Central Avenue (Route 66). Antiques and collectibles dealers display their wares at the Antique Specialty Mall (4516 Central Ave.). Old World Imports (3019 Central Ave.) sells textiles, antique jewelry and Oriental carpets.

As the name implies, Cowboys and Indians Antiques (4000 Central Ave.) features Indian baskets, Zuni fetishes, spurs, horse figure clocks and turquoise jewelry. Lilly Barrack (3205 Central Ave.) specializes in contemporary silver jewelry, often in designs paired with uncut gemstones.

Astro-Zombies (3100 Central Ave.) has a huge collection of comics (DC, Marvel, Dark Horse, Japanese manga), graphic novels and collectible toys from Star Wars characters to Godzilla. Next door is Masks Y Mas (Masks and More), where much of the merchandise revolves around Mexico's Day of the Dead celebration—skeleton figures, bizarre-looking masks and lots of original art. Even if you don't buy anything, the wildly colorful wall murals at both of these establishments are worth a look.

In downtown Albuquerque, TrendBenderz (311-B Gold Ave.) is a funky little boutique with vintage clothing, handmade jewelry and art created by New Mexico artists. There's more art (paintings, painted furniture, pet portraits), plus unusual jewelry and decorative home and office accessories, at Patrician Design (216 Gold Ave.).

A block north, Skip Maisel's Indian Jewelry & Crafts (510 Central Ave.) is in a historic building complete with a neon Indian chief sign. This large emporium is crammed with pottery, rugs, Hopi dolls, opal jewelry and cool items like the feather-bedecked charms called dream catchers. You also can observe Native American crafters at work in the store.

Another one-stop destination for quality arts and crafts is the Bien Mur Indian Market Center at Sandia Pueblo (I-25 to exit 234, then east on Tramway Road to Rainbow Road). The circular building's kiva-shaped showroom displays authentic Native American items like war bonnets, moccasins, musical instruments (flutes, rattles, drums), Zuni fetishes, Hopi and Navajo jewelry, Kachina carvings, rugs and pottery. An added attraction is the 107-acre buffalo preserve established by the pueblo—a section of which borders the parking lot—where you can observe these magnificent beasts in a natural setting.

Albuquerque's mall of choice is ABQ Uptown (Louisiana Boulevard and Indian School Road), an outdoor mix of retailers and restaurants that includes the usual suspects (Eddie Bauer, Talbots, Ann Taylor and Williams-Sonoma). Nearby at Louisiana and Menaul boulevards is the Coronado Center, with anchors JCPenney, Macy's and Sears as well as some 130 additional stores and eateries.

Nightlife: The KiMo Theatre (423 Central Ave. at 5th Street) opened in 1927 as a movie palace, boasting an architectural style dubbed "Pueblo Deco." This is one of only a handful of theaters in the country that incorporate Native American design motifs (ceiling beams that resemble logs, rows of buffalo skulls with glowing eyes), all carefully restored since the theater was rescued from the brink of demolition in the 1970s. Performances run the gamut from music to film showings to special events; for event information phone (505) 768-3522.

Downtown nightspots include Burt's Tiki Lounge (313 Gold St.), a small club with faux-tropical decor, a pool table and a no-cover-charge policy that brings in a variety of local bands from rock and punk to hip-hop and alt-country. DJs spin tunes on Wednesdays and Thursdays; it's closed on Sunday. Next door is the Atomic Cantina, a laid-back bar with punk, rock, indie and rockabilly bands several nights a week, plus karaoke on Wednesdays and DJ sets on Thursdays. Phone (505) 247-2878.

Shows at the Launchpad, 618 Central Ave. (look for the silver sputnik above the door) lean toward punk, hardcore and metal, with occasional appearances by national bands; phone (505) 764-8887. Blues, blues-rock and country-rock musicians take the stage for shows at Low Spirits, 2823 2nd St. (two blocks north of Menaul Boulevard in the Near North Valley neighborhood). The bar has an open mic happy hour weekdays from 4-8. For ticket information phone (505) 886-1251.

Q Bar, in the Hotel Albuquerque at Old Town (800 Rio Grande Blvd.), is a swanky lounge with a piano bar, plush seating areas and a billiards room. The cocktails here are pricey but expertly made. There's live music—mostly jazz—Wednesday through Saturday evenings; for table reservations phone (505) 222-8718. More casual is O'Niell's Irish Pub (4310 Central Ave.) in Nob Hill, where local musicians play on weekends: blues, jazz and rock on Saturday (10 p.m.-1 a.m.) and Celtic, folk and bluegrass on Sunday (4-7). Phone (505) 255-6782.

Vernon's Jazz Club is an intimate lounge that seats just 50 and aims to replicate the speakeasies of the Prohibition era, at least in ambience (subdued lighting, black walls, red stage curtains). It's the kind of atmosphere that will appeal to serious jazz fans. There's a cover charge of $10 and a one-drink minimum per set. The club is inside Vernon's Hidden Valley Steakhouse, 6855 4th St. (in the northern suburb of Los Ranchos). Patrons are urged to

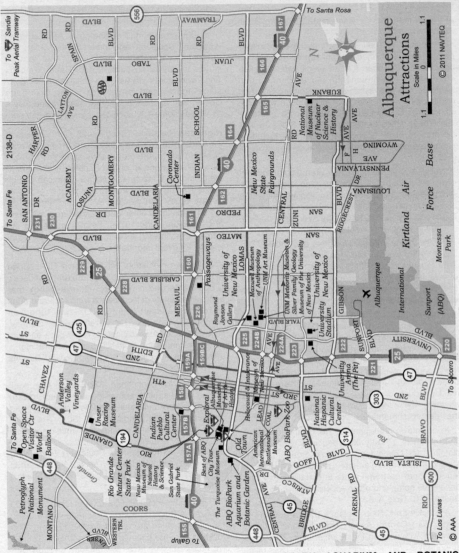

Albuquerque Attractions

Scale in Miles

© 2011 NAVTEQ

To Santa Rosa

To Sandia Peak Aerial Tramway

To Santa Fe

To Santa Fe

To Gallup

To Los Lunas

To Socorro

National Museum of Nuclear Science & History

Kirtland Air Force Base

Albuquerque International Sunport (ABQ)

Montessa Park

New Mexico State Fairgrounds

University of New Mexico

Maxwell Museum of Anthropology — UNM Art Museum

UNM Meteorite Museum & Silver Family Geology Museum of the University of New Mexico

University Arena (The Pit)

University Stadium

National Hispanic Cultural Center

Raymond Jonson Gallery

Passageways

Anderson Valley Vineyards

Unser Racing Museum

Indian Pueblo Cultural Center

Explora!

Albuquerque Museum of Art & History

Holocaust & Intolerance Museum of New Mexico

Turquoise Museum

Best of ABQ City Tour

Old Town

American International Rattlesnake Museum

ABQ BioPark Zoo

ABQ BioPark Aquarium and Botanic Garden

New Mexico Museum of Natural History & Science

San Gabriel State Park

Rio Grande Nature Center State Park

Open Space Visitor Ctr

World Balloon

Petroglyph National Monument

(See map & index p. 362.)

"dress well." Reservations are recommended; phone (505) 341-0831.

Sandia Resort & Casino (north on I-25 to exit 234, then east a quarter mile on Tramway Road) provides the necessary sparkle for a glitzy evening out. This expansive resort sits on Sandia Pueblo land and has outstanding views of the Sandia Mountains. The casino features more than 2,100 slots, a bevy of table games (blackjack, craps, roulette, mini baccarat), live keno and a nonsmoking poker room. Big-name concerts take place at the resort's outdoor amphitheater from late May to mid-September; for ticket and schedule information phone (800) 745-3000.

ABQ BIOPARK AQUARIUM AND BOTANIC GARDEN are at 2601 Central Ave. N.W. Marine habitats of the Gulf of Mexico and other ecosystems are presented at the aquarium. Tanks contain stingrays, jellyfish, eels, sharks and other aquatic life. The botanic garden features Mediterranean and desert conservatories, a children's fantasy garden, water and plant exhibits, demonstration gardens, the PNM Butterfly Pavilion, a butterfly-hummingbird garden, the Rio Grande Heritage Farm and the Sasebo Japanese Garden.

Time: Allow 1 hour, 30 minutes minimum. **Hours:** Daily 9-5 (also Sat.-Sun. 5-6, Memorial Day-Labor Day). Last admission 30 minutes before closing. Closed Jan. 1, Thanksgiving and Christmas. **Cost:**

(See map & index p. 362.)

$7; $3 (ages 3-12 and 65+). Combination ticket (not sold Mon.) with ABQ BioPark Zoo $12; $5 (ages 3-12 and 65+). **Phone:** (505) 768-2000. 🍴

ABQ BIOPARK ZOO is at 903 Tenth St. S.W. The zoo houses more than 1,000 animals representing some 250 species in a variety of naturalistic habitats. Popular residents include chimpanzees, gorillas, elephants, polar bears, giraffes, hippos, mountain lions, jaguars and zebras. Tropical America features toucans, spider monkeys, tamarins, tarantulas and colorful bromeliads. The 6-acre Africa Exhibit is home to warthogs, cheetahs, spotted hyenas and Marabou storks. Seal and sea lion feedings take place daily in a 350,000-gallon tank.

Hours: Daily 9-5 (also Sat.-Sun. 5-6, Memorial Day-Labor Day). Last admission 30 minutes before closing. Closed Jan. 1, Thanksgiving and Christmas. **Cost:** $7; $3 (ages 3-12 and 65+). Combination ticket (not sold Mon.) with ABQ BioPark Aquarium and Botanic Garden $12; $5 (ages 3-12 and 65+). Ages 0-12 must be with an adult. **Phone:** (505) 768-2000. 🍴

THE ALBUQUERQUE MUSEUM OF ART & HISTORY is at 2000 Mountain Rd. N.W. The museum features national and international exhibits and art of the Southwest and explores 400 years of Albuquerque history through permanent displays, exhibitions and guided walking tours of Old Town. The collection includes works from major New Mexican artists from the early 20th century to the present. A sculpture garden also is featured.

Tours: Guided tours are available. **Time:** Allow 2 hours minimum. **Hours:** Tues.-Sun. 9-5. Thirty-minute gallery tours depart Tues.-Sun. at 2. Sculpture garden tours depart Tues.-Sat. at 10, Apr.-Nov. Old Town walking tours depart Tues.-Sun. at 11, mid-Mar. to mid-Dec. Closed Jan. 1, Thanksgiving and Christmas. **Cost:** $4; $2 (ages 65+); $1 (ages 4-12); free (Sun. 9-1 and first Wed. of the month). **Phone:** (505) 243-7255.

AMERICAN INTERNATIONAL RATTLESNAKE MUSEUM is at 202 San Felipe St. N.W. More than 30 species of live rattlesnakes are displayed at the museum, which offers films and information about snakes and other reptiles. Artwork featuring snakes, herpetological fossils and skeletons, and other items also are featured. **Time:** Allow 30 minutes minimum. **Hours:** Mon.-Sat. 10-6, Sun. 1-5, June-Aug., Mon.-Fri. 11:30-5:30, Sat. 10-6, Sun. 1-5, rest of year. **Cost:** $5; $4 (ages 60+ and students and military with ID); $3 (ages 3-12). **Phone:** (505) 242-6569.

ANDERSON-ABRUZZO ALBUQUERQUE INTERNATIONAL BALLOON MUSEUM is at 9201 Balloon Museum Dr. N.E. Embrace the spirit of adventure through interactive exhibits about balloon flight, which dates to the early 1700s. In addition to highlighting the history of ballooning, exhibits

also reveal the many uses of balloons in the scientific realm, from weather forecasting to the development of Project Strato-Lab, a U.S. Navy program designed to gather data about human physiology in the stratosphere and a precursor to space exploration.

Other exhibit topics include recreational ballooning and lighter-than-air craft used in conflicts ranging from the Civil War to World War II. Colorful balloons of all shapes and sizes are suspended throughout the two-story grand hall, and some can be viewed up close from a catwalk. Collections include gondolas, balloon systems, books, ephemera and decorative arts.

The museum is named after pioneering balloonists and Albuquerque natives Maxie Anderson and Ben Abruzzo, who, along with a third pilot, were the first to cross the Atlantic Ocean in a gas balloon.

Tours: Guided tours are available. **Time:** Allow 1 hour minimum. **Hours:** Tues.-Sun. 9-5. Closed Jan. 1, Thanksgiving, Dec. 25 and Mon. holidays. **Cost:** $4; $2 (ages 65+); $1 (ages 4-12). Free (Sun. 9-1 and first Fri. of the month). **Phone:** (505) 768-6020.

BEST OF ABQ CITY TOUR departs from just outside Old Town's Plaza Don Luis at 303 Romero St. Narrated 76-minute tours on a distinctively Southwestern trolley include such sights as Old Town, Route 66, historic neighborhoods, Museum Row, the Railyards, the University of New Mexico and the ABQ BioPark Zoo.

Note: Sunscreen or a light jacket may be necessary in some months. **Time:** Allow 1 hour, 30 minutes minimum. **Hours:** Tours depart Tues.-Fri. at 11 and 1, Sat. at 11, 1 and 3, Sun. at 1 and 3. Hours vary seasonally and on holidays. Phone ahead to confirm schedule. **Cost:** $25; $22 (ages 65+ and students with ID); $12 (ages 0-12). **Phone:** (505) 240-8000.

EXPLORA! is at 1701 Mountain Rd. N.W. Visitors wander through a maze of personal learning centers at this innovative museum featuring more than 250 hands-on science, technology and art exhibits. Giant bubbles, hair-raising demonstrations of static electricity and a laminar-flow fountain entertain children and adults alike while encouraging independent thinking, exploration and experimentation. **Time:** Allow 1 hour minimum. **Hours:** Mon.-Sat. 10-6, Sun. noon-6. Closed Jan. 1, July 4, week after Labor Day, Thanksgiving and Christmas. **Cost:** $8; $5 (ages 65+); $4 (ages 1-11). **Phone:** (505) 224-8300.

HOLOCAUST & INTOLERANCE MUSEUM OF NEW MEXICO is at 616 Central Ave. S.W. Dedicated to combating hate and intolerance and promoting understanding through education, the museum's documents, photographs and artifacts illustrate how ethnic intolerance engenders global conflict. Exhibits depict the Holocaust, Native American persecution, slavery in America and the

(See map & index p. 362.)

Rwandan, Armenian and Greek genocides. **Tours:** Guided tours are available. **Time:** Allow 1 hour minimum. **Hours:** Tues.-Sat. 11-3:30. Closed major holidays. **Cost:** Donations. **Phone:** (505) 247-0606.

INDIAN PUEBLO CULTURAL CENTER is at 2401 12th St. N.W. The center depicts the history, art and culture of New Mexico's 19 American Indian pueblos. The main museum features an extensive collection of artifacts, and an intergenerational learning classroom and programs offer hands-on learning about the Pueblo people. Traditional dances take place weekly. An exhibit gallery highlights the work of traditional and contemporary artists.

Time: Allow 30 minutes minimum. **Hours:** Daily 9-5. Closed Jan. 1, Memorial Day, July 4, Labor Day, Thanksgiving and Christmas. **Cost:** $6; $5.50 (ages 62+); $3 (ages 5-17 and college students with ID). **Phone:** (505) 843-7270. [↑]

NATIONAL HISPANIC CULTURAL CENTER is at 1701 Fourth St. S.W. Mayan temples, Spanish haciendas and adobe pueblos influenced the architecture of this 51-acre site, which features an art museum, a theater complex, a library and a genealogy center. Cultural programs and activities are offered throughout the year, many accompanied by children's events. **Time:** Allow 30 minutes minimum. **Hours:** Museum open Tues.-Sun. 10-5. Library open Tues.-Sat. 10-5. Closed Jan. 1, Thanksgiving and Christmas. **Cost:** Museum $3; $2 (ages 60+); free (ages 0-15 and to all Sun.). **Phone:** (505) 246-2261. [↑]

NATIONAL MUSEUM OF NUCLEAR SCIENCE & HISTORY is at 601 Eubank Blvd. S.E. The nation's official museum for the history and science of the Nuclear Age features replicas of the world's first two atomic weapons, Little Boy and Fat Man. Exhibits cover such topics as atomic theory, the Cold War, pioneers in nuclear science, uranium processing, radiation facts and the testing of the first atomic bomb. A hands-on physics lab for children also is available. The outdoor Heritage Park has numerous airplanes and other large artifacts. History films are shown daily.

Time: Allow 2 hours minimum. **Hours:** Daily 9-5. Closed Jan. 1, Easter, Thanksgiving and Christmas. **Cost:** $8; $7 (ages 6-17 and 60+). **Phone:** (505) 245-2137.

◥◣ **NEW MEXICO MUSEUM OF NATURAL** ▼GEM **HISTORY & SCIENCE** is .5 mi. s. of I-40 on Rio Grande Blvd., then 2 blks. e. to 1801 Mountain Rd. N.W. The origins and geological history of the Southwest are explored through full-scale dinosaur models, a walk-through volcano model, an ice age cave replica, a time machine and a fossil preparation area. A saltwater tide pool, a hands-on naturalist center, botanical exhibits and planetarium shows

also are offered. The Lockheed Martin DynaTheater presents giant-screen film adventures to exotic locales.

Time: Allow 1 hour minimum. **Hours:** Daily 9-5. DynaTheater films are shown on the hour 10-5; other show schedules vary. Closed Jan. 1, Thanksgiving and Christmas. **Cost:** Museum or planetarium show $7; $6 (ages 60+); $4 (ages 3-12). DynaTheater $10; $8 (ages 60+); $6 (ages 3-12). Combination tickets are available. **Phone:** (505) 841-2800.

◥◣ **OLD TOWN** is .5 mi. s. of I-40 exit 157A via ▼GEM Rio Grande Blvd. Albuquerque began where Old Town stands today, and the focal point of community life in the city's beginnings remains a place where people come to meet, sightsee and above all, shop. It doesn't look much like it did some 3 centuries ago, but Old Town's narrow streets, winding brick walkways, hidden patios and wrought-iron benches do invite visitors to relax and stay awhile.

The focal point of this village-like setting is a tree-shaded plaza with a gazebo, the scene of frequent impromptu musical performances. Standing on the plaza's north side is the San Felipe de Neri Church, founded in 1706 by Fray Manuel Moreno, a Franciscan priest. The original church building collapsed during the very rainy summer of 1792; the present adobe structure, in the shape of a cross and with walls 5 feet thick, dates from 1793. The church's rose garden is a lovely, quiet spot to relax.

Surrounding the plaza is a pedestrian-only district (bounded north/south by Mountain Road and Central Avenue and east/west by Rio Grande Boulevard and 19th Street) containing more than 150 shops, boutiques, galleries and artist studios. Browsers will find all things Southwestern, of course, but Old Town shops offer everything from handmade Native American jewelry, Oaxacan woodcarvings and Mata Ortiz pottery to painted ponies, Christmas ornaments and Route 66 memorabilia. Across from the plaza's east side, in the 200 block of San Felipe Road, vendors and local artists display their wares on blankets under the building *portal* (porch). And it's a sure bet that before you leave you'll see a couple of *ristras*, those hanging strings of dried red chile peppers that all but shout out "New Mexico."

Pick up a free Old Town map at the information center in Plaza Don Luis (303 Romero St.). **Hours:** Guided 75-minute walking tours depart from the information center Fri.-Wed. at 10, noon, 2 and 4 (weather permitting). **Cost:** Tour (includes museum admission) $10; $9 (ages 55+); $8 (ages 13-17); $5 (ages 0-12). **Phone:** (505) 246-8687 or (505) 243-3215. [↑]

OPEN SPACE VISITOR CENTER is at 6500 Coors Blvd., N.W. The center offers information and resources about Albuquerque's Open Space Program with exhibits interpreting the natural and cultural resources protected by city-wide program. An art gallery, agricultural fields that draw a variety of wildlife and beautiful views of the Sandia Mountains are offered. Comfortable indoor and outdoor viewing

(See map & index p. 362.)

areas are available to watch sandhill cranes and other migratory birds during their fall and winter migratory season. There are 3 miles of walking trails through the river bosque accessible from the visitor center. **Time:** Allow 1 hour minimum. **Hours:** Tues.-Sun. 9-5. Closed major holidays. Phone ahead to confirm schedule. **Cost:** Free. **Phone:** (505) 897-8831.

PETROGLYPH NATIONAL MONUMENT is at 4001 Unser Blvd. Boca Negra Canyon, Rinconada Canyon and Piedras Marcadas Canyon all afford opportunities for viewing petroglyphs by way of self-guiding trails. A visitor center offers trail guides and park information. **Time:** Allow 1 hour minimum. **Hours:** Daily 8-5. Closed Jan. 1, Thanksgiving and Christmas. **Cost:** Free. **Parking:** Mon.-Fri. $1; Sat.-Sun. $2 at Boca Negra Canyon. **Phone:** (505) 899-0205, ext. 335.

RIO GRANDE NATURE CENTER STATE PARK is at 2901 Candelaria Rd. N.W. On the central Rio Grande flyway, the park provides a winter refuge for migrating sandhill cranes and other waterfowl. Trails along the Rio Grande, classrooms, a library and visitor center exhibits are offered. **Time:** Allow 30 minutes minimum. **Hours:** Park daily 8-5. Visitor center daily 10-5. Closed Jan. 1, Thanksgiving and Christmas. **Cost:** $3 (per private vehicle), $15 (vehicles with eight or more people). Exact change is required. **Phone:** (505) 344-7240.

SANDIA CREST—
see Cibola National Forest p. 399.

SANDIA PEAK AERIAL TRAMWAY is off I-25 exit 234, then 6 mi. e. on Tramway Rd. The 2.7-mile tramway, one of the world's longest, transports visitors above the deep canyons and spectacular terrain of the western Sandia Mountains in the Cibola National Forest. A Forest Service visitor center is in the upper tram terminal. Restaurants operate at the base and summit.

Sandia Peak is a popular recreation spot. Skiers frequent the 10,378-foot peak from mid-December to mid-March. In summer 24 miles of trails are available for mountain biking. Bicycle rentals are available weekends and holidays, Memorial Day weekend through Labor Day, and in October during the Albuquerque International Balloon Fiesta.

Hours: Trams depart every 20-30 minutes daily 9-9, Memorial Day-Labor Day and during the Albuquerque International Balloon Fiesta; Wed.-Mon. and holidays 9-8, Tues. 5-8, rest of year. The tram is closed for 10 days in Apr. and Nov. for maintenance. **Cost:** Round-trip tram fare $20; $17 (ages 13-20, ages 62+ and military with ID); $12 (ages 5-12). **Phone:** (505) 856-7325 or (505) 856-6419.

THE TURQUOISE MUSEUM is at 2107 Central Ave. N.W. A mine tunnel provides entrance to this museum, which features rare turquoise specimens from around the world. Interactive silversmith and lapidary demonstrations are offered. **Hours:** Mon.-Fri. 9:30-5, Sat. 9:30-4. Last admission 1 hour before closing. Closed major holidays. **Cost:** $4; $3 (ages 0-17 and 55+). **Phone:** (505) 247-8650.

UNIVERSITY OF NEW MEXICO is 2 mi. e. on Central Ave./US 66. The university occupies a 640-acre campus and enrolls approximately 27,000 students. College buildings feature Pueblo Revival architecture, and the grounds are designated as a National College Arboretum. Of particular interest are several museums and libraries as well as Popejoy Hall, home to ballet, musicals, lectures and the New Mexico Symphony Orchestra.

Some 3,000 Native American dancers and singers participate in the 🎗 Gathering of Nations Powwow, held at University Arena in April. In December University Stadium hosts the 🎗 New Mexico Bowl, in which teams representing the Mountain West and Western Athletic conferences compete for a 20-inch Zia Pueblo pottery trophy. **Phone:** (505) 277-1989.

Maxwell Museum of Anthropology is on Redondo Dr. just e. of University Blvd. on the University of New Mexico campus. The museum explores the cultures of the world with a special emphasis on the heritage of the Southwest. Permanent exhibits include People of the Southwest and Ancestors.

Traveling with Your Pet
The AAA PetBook

FRANCE

ROAD Atlas

AAA CAA

Discover AAA Travel Publications
Purchase at participating AAA/CAA club offices, online at bn.com and in fine book stores.

(See map & index p. 362.)

Changing exhibits also are presented. **Hours:** Tues.-Sat. 10-4. Closed major holidays. **Cost:** Donations. **Phone:** (505) 277-4405.

Silver Family Geology Museum of the University of New Mexico is at 200 Yale Blvd. (Northrop Hall) in the Earth and Planetary Sciences Building. Various types of minerals, the geology of the Earth and New Mexico fossils are depicted in more than 20 exhibits. Guided tours are offered by appointment. **Time:** Allow 30 minutes minimum. **Hours:** Mon.-Fri. 8-noon and 1-4:30. Closed major holidays. **Cost:** Donations. **Phone:** (505) 277-4204.

UNM Art Museum is at Cornell St. and Redondo Dr. N.E. on the University of New Mexico campus, inside the Center for the Arts. The permanent collection includes some 30,000 pieces of rotating photography, prints and paintings spanning the 18th through the 20th centuries. **Time:** Allow 1 hour minimum. **Hours:** Tues.-Sun. 10-4. Closed major holidays. **Cost:** Donations. **Phone:** (505) 277-4001.

UNM Meteorite Museum, part of the Institute of Meteoritics, is on the first floor of the Earth and Planetary Sciences Building, 200 Yale Blvd. (Northrop Hall) on the University of New Mexico campus. The institute is a center for the teaching and research of space and planetary sciences, and is the home of one of the world's largest collections of meteorites. Hundreds of meteorites discovered throughout the world are displayed, including the 1,000 kg Norton County stony meteorite. **Time:** Allow 30 minutes minimum. **Hours:** Mon.-Fri. 9-4. Closed major and university holidays. **Cost:** Free. **Phone:** (505) 277-4204.

UNSER RACING MUSEUM is at 1776 Montano N.W. The museum traces the history of the Unser family in racing from the early 1900s to the present. Exhibits—some interactive—include antique cars, trophies and uniforms. The Indy simulator is sure to get your engine going. Changing exhibits also are offered. **Time:** Allow 1 hour minimum. **Hours:** Daily 10-4. **Cost:** $10; $6 (ages 60+ and military with ID); free (ages 0-16 with adult). **Phone:** (505) 341-1776.

RECREATIONAL ACTIVITIES

Hot Air Ballooning

- **Rainbow Ryders, Inc.** departs from various locations for flights over the Rio Grande Valley. **Hours:** Daily at dawn. **Phone:** (505) 823-1111 or (800) 725-2477. *(See ad this page, p. 205.)*
- **World Balloon** meets at 6390 Coors Blvd. N.W. **Hours:** Departures daily beginning at dawn (weather permitting). Office hours daily 8-8. Closed Jan. 1, Thanksgiving and Christmas. **Phone:** (505) 293-6800.

White-water Rafting

- **Passageways** departs El Vado Ranch at the base of El Vado Dam and Lower Chama Canyon. **Hours:** Daily July-Aug. **Phone:** (505) 265-4542.

GAMBLING ESTABLISHMENTS

- **Hard Rock Hotel & Casino Albuquerque** is at 11000 Broadway S.E. **Hours:** Mon.-Thurs. 9 a.m.-5 a.m., Fri.-Sun. and holidays 24 hours. **Phone:** (505) 724-3800 or (877) 747-5382.
- **Sandia Resort & Casino** is at 30 Rainbow Rd. N.E. **Hours:** Sun.-Wed. 8 a.m.-4 a.m., Thurs.-Sat. 24 hours. **Phone:** (505) 796-7500 or (800) 526-9366.

▼ *See AAA listing this page* ▼

RAINBOWRYDERS®
WWW.RAINBOWRYDERS.COM 800.725.2477
The Premier Balloon Ride Company of the Southwest
The Experience of a Lifetime... Happening Right Now™
Experience Albuquerque
Like Never Before.

No Street Signs?
No Mile Markers?
No Problem.

AAA members have another reason to feel safer on the road. If you need roadside assistance and call from your GPS-enabled mobile phone, AAA will rescue you – even if you aren't sure where you are.

Activate the **FREE** AAA FindMe[SM] service today by going to AAA.com/AAAFindMe.

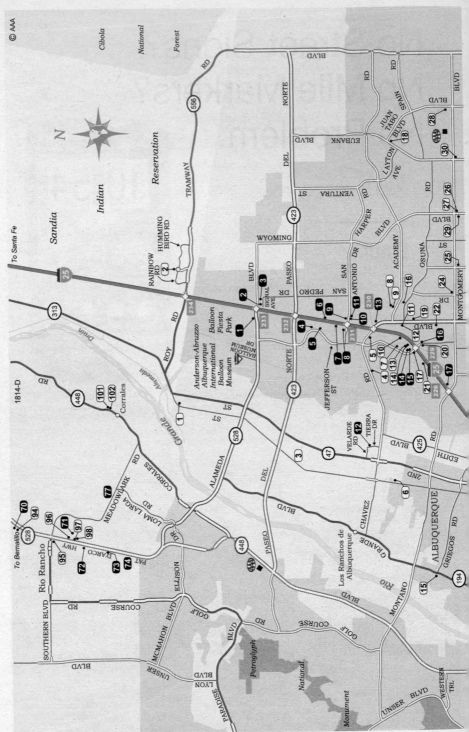

© AAA

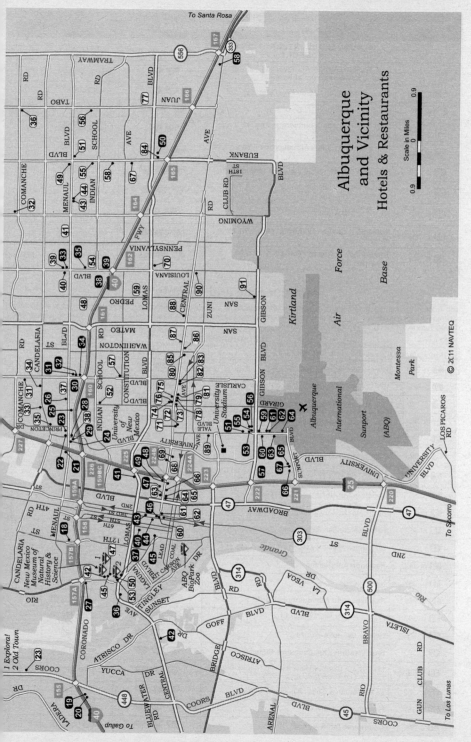

Albuquerque
and Vicinity

Hotels & Restaurants

Scale in Miles
0.9   0   0.9

© 2011 NAVTEQ

✈ Airport Accommodations

Map Page	ALBUQUERQUE INTERNATIONAL SUNPORT	Diamond Rated	High Season	Page
62 p. 362	Best Western Airport Albuquerque InnSuites Hotel & Suites, just nw of terminal	◆◆	$69-$169 SAVE	369
61 p. 362	Comfort Inn-Airport, 0.5 mi nw of terminal	◆◆	$67-$135	370
53 p. 362	Courtyard by Marriott (Airport), 1 mi nw of terminal	◆◆◆	$85-$159	371
54 p. 362	Days Inn & Suites Albuquerque Airport, 1 mi n of terminal	◆◆	$54-$108 SAVE	372
55 p. 362	Fairfield Inn & Suites Albuquerque Airport, 1 mi n of terminal	◆◆◆	$63-$109 SAVE	372
60 p. 362	Hampton Inn-Airport, 0.7 mi s of terminal	◆◆◆	$79-$159 SAVE	373
65 p. 362	Holiday Inn & Suites Albuquerque Airport - University, 1 mi w of terminal	◆◆◆	$99-$159	374
59 p. 362	La Quinta Inn Albuquerque Airport, 1 mi nw of terminal	◆◆	$68-$133	377
64 p. 362	Sheraton Albuquerque Airport Hotel, 0.3 mi w of terminal	◆◆◆	$89-$219 SAVE	380
56 p. 362	TownePlace Suites by Marriott, 1 mi n of terminal	◆◆◆	$69-$109 SAVE	380

Albuquerque and Vicinity

This index helps you "spot" where approved hotels and restaurants are located on the corresponding detailed maps. Hotel daily rate range is for comparison only and show the property's high season. Restaurant rate range is a combination of lunch and/or dinner. Turn to the listing page for more detailed rate information and consult display ads for special promotions.

ALBUQUERQUE

Map Page	Hotels	Diamond Rated	High Season	Page
1 p. 362	Holiday Inn Express Hotel & Suites	◆◆◆	$99-$169	374
2 p. 362	Comfort Inn & Suites by Choice Hotels	◆◆	$63-$180	370
3 p. 362	Staybridge Suites Albuquerque North	◆◆◆	$89-$359 SAVE	380
4 p. 362	Courtyard by Marriott Journal Center	◆◆◆	$89-$219	371
5 p. 362	Albuquerque Marriott Pyramid North	◆◆◆	$105-$189	369
6 p. 362	Clarion Hotel Albuquerque	◆◆◆	$59-$175	370
7 p. 362	La Quinta Inn & Suites Albuquerque Journal Ctr NW	◆◆◆	$62-$122	377
8 p. 362	Hampton Inn-North	◆◆◆	$76-$89 SAVE	373
9 p. 362	La Quinta Inn Albuquerque Northeast	◆◆	$64-$126	377
10 p. 362	Hilton Garden Inn Albuquerque Journal Center	◆◆◆	$89-$139	374
11 p. 362	Homewood Suites by Hilton-Journal Center	◆◆◆	$117-$143	374
12 p. 362	Hacienda Antigua Inn	◆◆◆	$149-$209 SAVE	372
13 p. 362	Nativo Lodge	◆◆◆	$89-$159	378
14 p. 362	Residence Inn Albuquerque- North	◆◆◆	$109-$139 SAVE	378
15 p. 362	Drury Inn & Suites-Albuquerque	◆◆◆	$95-$184	372
16 p. 362	Holiday Inn Hotel & Suites	◆◆◆	$99-$199	374
17 p. 362	Best Western Plus Executive Suites	◆◆◆	$70-$160 SAVE	370
18 p. 362	Holiday Inn Express Hotel & Suites Albuquerque Historic Old Town (See ad p. 375.)	◆◆◆	$109-$259	374
19 p. 362	La Quinta Inn & Suites Albuquerque West	◆◆◆	$74-$144	377
20 p. 362	Hampton Inn & Suites	◆◆◆	$69-$129	373
21 p. 362	ClubHouse Inn & Suites	◆◆◆	$89-$129 SAVE	370

ALBUQUERQUE (cont'd)

Map Page	Hotels (cont'd)	Diamond Rated	High Season	Page
22 p. 362	**Super 8 of Albuquerque**	◆◆	$39-$80 (SAVE)	380
23 p. 362	La Quinta Inn & Suites Albuquerque Midtown *(See ad p. 377.)*	◆◆◆	$107-$214	377
24 p. 362	Fairfield Inn Albuquerque-University Area	◆◆	$84-$159	372
25 p. 362	**Holiday Inn Express Albuquerque Midtown**	◆◆◆	$79-$129 (SAVE)	374
26 p. 362	Candlewood Suites	◆◆◆	$79-$149	370
27 p. 362	**Best Western Plus Rio Grande Inn** *(See ad p. 371.)*	◆◆◆	$99-$169 (SAVE)	370
28 p. 362	MCM Elegante Hotel *(See ad p. 378.)*	◆◆◆	Rates not provided	377
29 p. 362	Hilton Albuquerque	◆◆◆	Rates not provided	373
30 p. 362	Suburban Extended Stay Hotels	◆◆	$60-$100	380
31 p. 362	**Park Inn by Radisson** *(See ad p. 379.)*	◆◆◆	$99-$239 (SAVE)	378
32 p. 362	**Econo Lodge Midtown**	◆	Rates not provided (SAVE)	372
33 p. 362	**Albuquerque Sheraton Uptown Hotel** *(See ad p. 369.)*	◆◆◆	$99-$229 (SAVE)	369
34 p. 362	Hampton Inn University-Midtown	◆◆◆	$69-$129	373
35 p. 362	**Hyatt Place Albuquerque Uptown**	◆◆◆	$89-$189 (SAVE)	376
36 p. 362	**Monterey Non-Smokers Motel-Old Town**	◆◆	$64-$100 (SAVE)	378
37 p. 362	Bottger Mansion Bed and Breakfast	◆◆◆	$119-$189	370
38 p. 362	Hilton Garden Inn Albuquerque Uptown	◆◆◆	$119-$175	374
39 p. 362	**The Albuquerque Marriott Hotel**	◆◆◆	$104-$200 (SAVE)	369
40 p. 362	**Brittania & W E Mauger Estate Bed & Breakfast**	◆◆◆	$99-$204 (SAVE)	370
41 p. 362	Embassy Suites Albuquerque Hotel & Spa	◆◆◆	$111-$227	372
42 p. 362	Sandia Peak Inn	◆◆	Rates not provided	380
43 p. 362	DoubleTree by Hilton Hotel Albuquerque	◆◆◆	$85-$155	372
44 p. 362	**Hyatt Regency Albuquerque**	◆◆◆	$89-$240 (SAVE)	377
45 p. 362	The Hotel Blue	◆◆	Rates not provided	375
46 p. 362	**Hotel Andaluz** *(See ad p. 376.)*	◆◆◆◆	$139-$329 (SAVE)	375
47 p. 362	**Albuquerque Downtown Historic Bed & Breakfast**	◆◆◆	$89-$209 (SAVE)	369
48 p. 362	**Econo Lodge Downtown**	◆◆	$50 (SAVE)	372
49 p. 362	**Hotel Parq Central**	◆◆◆◆	$140-$420 (SAVE)	375
50 p. 362	**Holiday Inn Express**	◆◆◆	$82-$92 (SAVE)	374
51 p. 362	Residence Inn by Marriott Albuquerque Airport	◆◆◆	$94-$169	379
53 p. 362	Courtyard by Marriott (Airport)	◆◆◆	$85-$159	371
54 p. 362	**Days Inn & Suites Albuquerque Airport**	◆◆	$54-$108 (SAVE)	372
55 p. 362	**Fairfield Inn & Suites Albuquerque Airport**	◆◆◆	$63-$109 (SAVE)	372
56 p. 362	**TownePlace Suites by Marriott**	◆◆◆	$69-$109 (SAVE)	380
57 p. 362	Country Inn & Suites Albuquerque Airport	◆◆◆	Rates not provided	370
58 p. 362	**Econo Lodge East**	◆	$45-$55 (SAVE)	372
59 p. 362	La Quinta Inn Albuquerque Airport	◆◆	$68-$133	377

ALBUQUERQUE (cont'd)

Map Page	Hotels (cont'd)	Diamond Rated	High Season	Page
60 p. 362	Hampton Inn-Airport *(See ad p. 373.)*	▽▽▽	$79-$159 SAVE	373
61 p. 362	Comfort Inn-Airport	▽▽	$67-$135	370
62 p. 362	Best Western Airport Albuquerque InnSuites Hotel & Suites	▽▽	$69-$169 SAVE	369
63 p. 362	Hilton Garden Inn Albuquerque Airport	▽▽▽	$85-$160	374
64 p. 362	Sheraton Albuquerque Airport Hotel	▽▽▽	$89-$219 SAVE	380
65 p. 362	Holiday Inn & Suites Albuquerque Airport - University	▽▽▽	$99-$159	374
66 p. 362	Staybridge Suites Albuquerque Airport	▽▽▽	$109-$159	380
67 p. 362	Hyatt Place Albuquerque Airport	▽▽▽	$79-$169 SAVE	375

Map Page	Restaurants	Diamond Rated	Cuisine	Meal Range	Page
1 p. 362	El Pinto	▽▽	Mexican	$8-$23	382
2 p. 362	Bien Shur Restaurant	▽▽▽	International	$25-$34	381
3 p. 362	Casa de Benavidez New Mexican Restaurant	▽▽	Mexican	$8-$21	381
4 p. 362	Vic's Daily Cafe	▽▽	American	$7-$10	387
5 p. 362	Cajun Kitchen	▽▽	Cajun	$9-$18	381
6 p. 362	Sadie's Dining Room	▽▽	Mexican	$2-$16	386
7 p. 362	Fox and Hound Pub & Grill	▽▽	American	$6-$15	382
8 p. 362	Trombino's Bistro Italiano	▽▽▽	Italian	$8-$23	387
9 p. 362	Scarpa's	▽▽	Italian	$7-$11	387
10 p. 362	P.F. Chang's China Bistro	▽▽▽	Chinese	$10-$25	386
11 p. 362	Perennials Restaurant	▽▽	Breakfast	$9-$12	385
12 p. 362	Saigon Restaurant	▽▽	Vietnamese	$7-$20	386
13 p. 362	Pars Cuisine	▽▽▽	Mediterranean	$6-$18	385
14 p. 362	Jersey Jack's Eatery	▽	Regional Deli	$5-$8	383
15 p. 362	Johndhis BBQ	▽	American	$6-$17	383
16 p. 362	Monroe's Restaurant	▽▽	Mexican	$7-$17	384
17 p. 362	Nick & Jimmy's Restaurant & Bar	▽▽▽	Mediterranean	$13-$28	385
18 p. 362	Mykonos Cafe & Taverna	▽▽	Greek	$10-$20	385
19 p. 362	Siam Cafe	▽▽	Thai	$8-$11	387
20 p. 362	Landry's Seafood House	▽▽	Seafood	$8-$28 SAVE	384
21 p. 362	Chama River Brewing Company	▽▽	American	$9-$28	381
22 p. 362	Azuma	▽▽	Japanese	$7-$30	381
23 p. 362	Mimmo's Ristorante & Pizzeria	▽	Italian	$8-$18	384
24 p. 362	Chez Axel	▽▽	French	$6-$23	381
25 p. 362	Weck's	▽▽	American	$5-$9	388
26 p. 362	India Palace	▽▽	Indian	$8-$20	383
27 p. 362	Yen Ching Restaurant	▽	Chinese	$6-$25	388
28 p. 362	Flying Star Cafe	▽▽	American	$7-$13	382
29 p. 362	The Range Cafe	▽▽	American	$8-$18	386
30 p. 362	Scarpa's Brick Oven Pizza	▽▽	Italian	$6-$11	387

Map Page	Restaurants (cont'd)	Diamond Rated	Cuisine	Meal Range	Page
③① p. 362	East Ocean Chinese Seafood Restaurant	◆◆	Chinese	$5-$12	382
③② p. 362	Ortega's Mexican Restaurant & Grill	◆◆	Regional Mexican	$7-$11	385
③③ p. 362	Panza Llena Cafe	◆◆	American	$5-$8	385
③④ p. 362	Hello Deli	◆◆	American	$5-$8	383
③⑤ p. 362	Milly's Restaurant	◆	American	$5-$10	384
③⑥ p. 362	Garcia's Kitchen	◆◆	Mexican	$4-$10	382
③⑦ p. 362	Richard's Mexican Restaurant	◆◆	Mexican	$6-$10	386
③⑧ p. 362	**Rancher's Club of New Mexico**	◆◆◆	American	$21-$78	386
③⑨ p. 362	ABQ Grill	◆◆	American	$9-$23	380
④⓪ p. 362	Cheese & Coffee Gourmet Deli	◆◆	Deli	$7-$10	381
④① p. 362	Krung Thai	◆◆	Thai	$7-$12	383
④② p. 362	Seasons Rotisserie & Grill	◆◆	American	$8-$32	387
④③ p. 362	Ho-Lo-Ma Chinese Restaurant	◆◆	Chinese	$6-$12	383
④④ p. 362	Los Cuates del Norte	◆◆	Mexican	$5-$11	384
④⑤ p. 362	**Church Street Cafe**	◆◆	Mexican	$8-$16	381
④⑦ p. 362	La Crepe Michel	◆◆◆	French	$6-$14	383
④⑧ p. 362	Mario's Pizzeria & Ristorante	◆◆	Italian	$7-$15	384
④⑨ p. 362	Taco Sal	◆◆	Mexican	$6-$10	387
⑤⓪ p. 362	La Placita on the Plaza	◆◆	Mexican	$5-$15	384
⑤① p. 362	Papa Felipe's	◆◆	Mexican	$3-$12	385
⑤② p. 362	Padilla's Mexican Kitchen	◆◆	Mexican	$2-$8	385
⑤③ p. 362	Antiquity Restaurant	◆◆◆	Continental	$20-$30	380
⑤④ p. 362	**Marcello's Chophouse**	◆◆◆	Steak	$9-$49	384
⑤⑤ p. 362	Paisano's Italian Restaurant	◆◆	Italian	$7-$26	385
⑤⑥ p. 362	A Taste of Italy	◆	International	$4-$8	381
⑤⑦ p. 362	**Taj Mahal Cuisine of India**	◆◆	Indian	$9-$17	387
⑤⑧ p. 362	Ming Dynasty	◆◆	Chinese	$6-$10	384
⑤⑨ p. 362	Christy Mae's	◆	American	$7-$12	381
⑥⓪ p. 362	JC's New York Pizza Department	◆	Italian	$6-$17	383
⑥① p. 362	Tucanos Brazilian Grill	◆◆◆	Brazilian	$11-$21	387
⑥② p. 362	Gold Street Caffé	◆◆	American	$6-$14	383
⑥③ p. 362	The Artichoke Cafe	◆◆◆	American	$10-$35	381
⑥④ p. 362	**Standard Diner**	◆◆	American	$8-$14	387
⑥⑤ p. 362	Fresh Choices	◆	Italian	$7	382
⑥⑥ p. 362	The Grove Cafe & Market	◆◆	American	$7-$11	383
⑥⑦ p. 362	La Salita	◆◆	Mexican	$3-$15	384
⑥⑧ p. 362	66 Diner	◆◆	Burgers	$6-$10	380
⑥⑨ p. 362	The Copper Lounge	◆◆	American	$8-$18	382
⑦⓪ p. 362	The Cooperage	◆◆	American	$8-$36	382
⑦① p. 362	Frontier Restaurant	◆	American	$5-$11	382

Map Page	Restaurants (cont'd)	Diamond Rated	Cuisine	Meal Range	Page
72 p. 362	Gyros Mediterranean	◆	Greek	$9-$11	383
73 p. 362	Mannie's Family Restaurant	◆	American	$6-$9	384
74 p. 362	La Provence Brasserie	◆◆	French	$7-$25	384
75 p. 362	Yanni's Mediterranean Grill & Opa Bar	◆◆◆	Mediterranean	$8-$35	388
76 p. 362	Zinc Wine Bar & Bistro	◆◆◆	American	$8-$28	388
77 p. 362	Paul's Monterey Inn	◆◆	American	$7-$24	385
78 p. 362	Nob Hill Bar & Grill	◆◆◆	American	$10-$25	385
79 p. 362	Vivace	◆◆	Italian	$6-$20	387
80 p. 362	Ragin' Shrimp	◆◆	Cajun	$9-$18	386
81 p. 362	Kelly's Brewery & Restaurant	◆◆	American	$3-$12	383
82 p. 362	Gecko's Bar & Tapas	◆◆	American	$6-$14	382
83 p. 362	Scalo Northern Italian Grill	◆◆◆	Northern Italian	$10-$29	387
84 p. 362	The Owl Cafe	◆◆	American	$5-$10	385
85 p. 362	Orchid Thai Cuisine	◆◆	Thai	$5-$16	385
86 p. 362	Loyola's Family Restaurant	◆◆	Mexican	$4-$9	384
87 p. 362	El Taco Tote	◆	Mexican	$5-$9	382
88 p. 362	Cafe Dalat	◆◆	Vietnamese	$6-$13	381
89 p. 362	Quarters Bar-B-Que	◆◆	Barbecue	$4-$45	386
90 p. 362	May Cafe	◆◆	Vietnamese	$6-$15	384
91 p. 362	**Cervantes Restaurant & Lounge**	◆◆	Regional Mexican	$8-$23	381

RIO RANCHO

Map Page	Hotels	Diamond Rated	High Season	Page
70 p. 362	**Days Inn Rio Rancho**	◆◆	$55-$117 SAVE	436
71 p. 362	Rio Rancho Super 8	◆◆	$40-$85	437
72 p. 362	**Inn at Rio Rancho Hotel and Conference Center**	◆◆	$59-$119 SAVE	437
73 p. 362	Hilton Garden Inn Albuquerque North/Rio Rancho	◆◆◆	$89-$159	437
74 p. 362	Extended StayAmerica Albuquerque-Rio Rancho	◆◆	$64-$99	437

Map Page	Restaurants	Diamond Rated	Cuisine	Meal Range	Page
94 p. 362	Banana Leaf Asian Cuisine	◆◆	Asian	$7-$15	437
95 p. 362	O'Hare's Grille & Pub	◆◆	American	$7-$30	437
96 p. 362	Smokehouse BBQ	◆	Barbecue	$5-$12	437
97 p. 362	Hot Tamales	◆◆	New Mexican	$6-$14	437
98 p. 362	Federico's Mexican Food	◆	Mexican	$5-$10	437

CORRALES

Map Page	Hotel	Diamond Rated	High Season	Page
77 p. 362	The Chocolate Turtle Bed & Breakfast	◆◆◆	$119-$149	404

Map Page	Restaurants	Diamond Rated	Cuisine	Meal Range	Page
101 p. 362	Indigo Crow Cafe	◆◆◆	American	$7-$30	404
102 p. 362	Hannah & Nate's Market Cafe	◆◆	American	$7-$9	404

(See map & index p. 362.)

ALBUQUERQUE DOWNTOWN HISTORIC BED & BREAKFAST
Phone: 505/842-0223 **47**

Historic Bed & Breakfast
$89-$209

Address: 207 & 209 High St NE 87102 **Location:** I-25 exit 224A northbound; exit 224B southbound, just w, then n. **Facility:** Comprised of two restored historic homes, the beautifully renovated B&B is nestled downtown and offers comfortable accommodations. 9 units, some kitchens. 1-2 stories (no elevator), interior corridors. *Bath:* some shared. **Parking:** on-site and street. **Terms:** check-in 4 pm, 7 day cancellation notice-fee imposed. **Activities:** whirlpool. **Guest Services:** valet laundry. **Free Special Amenities:** full breakfast and high-speed Internet.

THE ALBUQUERQUE MARRIOTT HOTEL
Phone: (505)881-6800 **39**

Hotel
$104-$200

Marriott HOTELS & RESORTS **AAA Benefit:** AAA hotel discounts of 5% or more.

Address: 2101 Louisiana Blvd NE 87110 **Location:** I-40 exit 162 westbound; exit 162B eastbound, just n. Located in Northeast Heights. **Facility:** 411 units. 17 stories, interior corridors. **Amenities:** *Fee:* video games, high-speed Internet. **Pool(s):** heated indoor/outdoor. **Activities:** saunas, whirlpool, exercise room. **Guest Services:** valet and coin laundry. **Free Special Amenities:** newspaper and local transportation.

ALBUQUERQUE MARRIOTT PYRAMID NORTH
Phone: (505)821-3333 **5**

Hotel
$105-$189

AAA Benefit: AAA hotel discounts of 5% or more.

Address: 5151 San Francisco Rd NE 87109 **Location:** I-25 exit 232, just w, then 1 mi s on Pan American Frwy NE. **Facility:** 310 units. 10 stories, interior corridors. **Amenities:** high-speed Internet (fee). **Pool(s):** heated indoor/outdoor. **Activities:** whirlpools, game room, exercise room. *Fee:* massage. **Guest Services:** valet and coin laundry.

ALBUQUERQUE SHERATON UPTOWN HOTEL
Phone: (505)881-0000 **33**

Hotel
$99-$229

Sheraton HOTELS & RESORTS **AAA Benefit:** Members get up to 15% off, plus Starwood Preferred Guest® bonuses.

Address: 2600 Louisiana Blvd NE 87110 **Location:** I-40 exit 162, 0.8 mi n. Located in Northeast Heights. **Facility:** 295 units. 8 stories, interior corridors. **Terms:** cancellation fee imposed. **Amenities:** high-speed Internet (fee), safes. **Dining:** ABQ Grill, see separate listing. **Pool(s):** heated indoor. **Activities:** whirlpool, exercise room. **Guest Services:** valet laundry, area transportation-within 2 mi. **Free Special Amenities:** newspaper and local transportation. (See ad this page.)

▼ See AAA listing this page ▼

rise in style

Sheraton Albuquerque UPTOWN

The Sheraton Uptown is Albuquerque's premier hotel located in the heart of the dining and shopping district

Scan this tag on your smartphone and start saving today!

1-800-252-7772
2600 Louisiana Blvd NE
Albuquerque, NM 87110
www.sheraton.com/albuquerqueuptown

GET THE FREE MOBILE APP AT
http://gettag.mobi

BEST WESTERN AIRPORT ALBUQUERQUE INNSUITES HOTEL & SUITES
Phone: (505)242-7022 **62**

Hotel
$69-$169

Best Western **AAA Benefit:** Members save up to 20%, plus 10% bonus points with Best Western Rewards®.

Address: 2400 Yale Blvd SE 87106 **Location:** I-25 exit 222 (Gibson Blvd) northbound; exit 222A southbound, 1 mi e, then just s. **Facility:** 101 units. 2 stories (no elevator), interior corridors. **Amenities:** high-speed Internet. **Pool(s):** heated outdoor. **Activities:** whirlpool, limited exercise equipment. **Guest Services:** valet and coin laundry, area transportation-within 5 mi. **Free Special Amenities:** full breakfast and high-speed Internet.

(See map & index p. 362.)

BEST WESTERN PLUS EXECUTIVE SUITES
Phone: (505)830-0900 **17**

Hotel
$70-$160

AAA Benefit: Members save up to 20%, plus 10% bonus points with Best Western Rewards®.

Address: 4630 Pan American Frwy NE 87109 **Location:** I-25 exit 228, just e. **Facility:** 88 units. 3 stories, interior corridors. **Amenities:** high-speed Internet. **Pool(s):** heated indoor. **Activities:** whirlpool, exercise room. **Guest Services:** valet and coin laundry. **Free Special Amenities:** local telephone calls and high-speed Internet.

BEST WESTERN PLUS RIO GRANDE INN
Phone: (505)843-9500 **27**

Hotel
$99-$169

AAA Benefit: Members save up to 20%, plus 10% bonus points with Best Western Rewards®.

Address: 1015 Rio Grande Blvd NW 87104 **Location:** I-40 exit 157A (Rio Grande Blvd), just s. **Facility:** 173 units. 4 stories, interior corridors. **Terms:** cancellation fee imposed. **Amenities:** high-speed Internet. **Pool(s):** heated outdoor. **Activities:** whirlpool, exercise room. **Guest Services:** valet and coin laundry. **Free Special Amenities:** local telephone calls and high-speed Internet. *(See ad p. 371.)*

BOTTGER MANSION BED AND BREAKFAST
Phone: (505)243-3639 **37**

Historic Bed & Breakfast
$119-$189

Address: 110 San Felipe NW 87104 **Location:** I-40 exit 157A (Rio Grande Blvd), 1.5 mi s, then just e; off Central Ave. **Facility:** Located in the historic Old Town area, the classic Victorian home features period furnishings and artifacts. A hearty breakfast is served daily. 7 units. 2 stories (no elevator), interior corridors. **Terms:** office hours 7 am-7 pm, 14 day cancellation notice-fee imposed.

BRITTANIA & W E MAUGER ESTATE BED & BREAKFAST
Phone: (505)242-8755 **40**

Historic Bed & Breakfast
$99-$204

Address: 701 Roma Ave NW 87102 **Location:** I-25 exit 225, 1 mi w, then just s on 7th Ave. **Facility:** Centrally located in the downtown area, the restored Queen Anne-style residence features rooms with high ceilings and gorgeous wood work. 8 units. 3 stories (no elevator), interior corridors. *Bath:* shower only. **Terms:** check-in 4 pm, 10 day cancellation notice-fee imposed. **Free Special Amenities:** full breakfast.

CANDLEWOOD SUITES
Phone: (505)888-3424 **26**

Extended Stay Hotel
$79-$149

Address: 3025 Menaul Blvd NE 87107 **Location:** I-40 exit 160, just n to Menaul Blvd, then 0.5 mi w. **Facility:** 123 efficiencies. 3 stories, interior corridors. **Terms:** 3 day cancellation notice. **Amenities:** high-speed Internet. **Activities:** exercise room. **Guest Services:** complimentary laundry.

CLARION HOTEL ALBUQUERQUE
Phone: (505)823-1300 **6**

Hotel
$59-$175

Address: 7620 Pan American Frwy NE 87109 **Location:** I-25 exit 231 (San Antonio Dr), 0.8 mi n on frontage road. **Facility:** 168 units. 3 stories, interior corridors. **Terms:** cancellation fee imposed. **Pool(s):** heated outdoor. **Activities:** exercise room. **Guest Services:** valet and coin laundry, area transportation.

CLUBHOUSE INN & SUITES
Phone: (505)345-0010 **21**

Hotel
$89-$129

Address: 1315 Menaul Blvd NE 87107 **Location:** I-25 exit 227A southbound, 1.5 mi to Menaul Blvd, then just w; exit 225 northbound, 1.8 mi, then just w. **Facility:** 137 units. 2 stories (no elevator), interior corridors. **Amenities:** high-speed Internet. **Pool(s):** heated outdoor. **Activities:** whirlpool. **Guest Services:** valet and coin laundry, area transportation-within 5 mi. **Free Special Amenities:** full breakfast and manager's reception.

COMFORT INN-AIRPORT Phone: (505)243-2244 **61**

Hotel
$67-$135

Address: 2300 Yale Blvd SE 87106 **Location:** I-25 exit 222A southbound; exit 222 (Gibson Blvd) northbound, 1 mi n, then just s. **Facility:** 118 units. 3 stories, interior/exterior corridors. **Terms:** cancellation fee imposed. **Amenities:** high-speed Internet. *Fee:* video games, safes. **Pool(s):** heated outdoor. **Activities:** whirlpool. **Guest Services:** valet laundry.

COMFORT INN & SUITES BY CHOICE HOTELS
Phone: (505)822-1090 **2**

Hotel
$63-$180

Address: 5811 Signal Ave NE 87113 **Location:** I-25 exit 233, just e via Alameda Blvd. **Facility:** 68 units. 3 stories, interior corridors. **Terms:** cancellation fee imposed. **Amenities:** safes (fee). **Pool(s):** heated indoor. **Activities:** whirlpool. **Guest Services:** valet and coin laundry.

COUNTRY INN & SUITES ALBUQUERQUE AIRPORT
Phone: 505/246-9600 **57**

Hotel
Rates not provided

Address: 2601 Mulberry SE 87106 **Location:** I-25 exit 222 (Gibson Blvd), just e. **Facility:** 80 units. 3 stories, interior corridors. **Amenities:** video games (fee). **Pool(s):** heated outdoor. **Activities:** exercise room. **Guest Services:** valet and coin laundry, area transportation (fee)-surrounding area.

(See map & index p. 362.)

COURTYARD BY MARRIOTT (AIRPORT)
Phone: (505)843-6600   **53**

Hotel
$85-$159

AAA Benefit:
AAA hotel discounts of 5% or more.

Address: 1920 Yale Blvd SE 87106 **Location:** I-25 exit 222 (Gibson Blvd) northbound; exit 222A southbound, 1 mi e, then just n. **Facility:** 150 units. 4 stories, interior corridors. **Amenities:** high-speed Internet. **Pool(s):** heated indoor. **Activities:** whirlpool, exercise room. **Guest Services:** valet and coin laundry.

COURTYARD BY MARRIOTT JOURNAL CENTER
Phone: (505)823-1919   **4**

Hotel
$89-$219

AAA Benefit:
AAA hotel discounts of 5% or more.

Address: 5151 Journal Center Blvd NE 87109 **Location:** I-25 exit 232, just s on Pan American Frwy NE. **Facility:** 150 units. 1-4 stories, interior corridors. **Pool(s):** heated indoor. **Activities:** whirlpool, exercise room. **Guest Services:** valet and coin laundry.

▼ See AAA listing p. 370 ▼

OLD TOWN CHARM

Enjoy your Albuquerque experience at our ideal location, within walking distance of Old Town Plaza, five museums, and dozens of restaurants, shops, and galleries. Just minutes away are the Albuquerque Zoo, and Bio Park, Indian Pueblo Cultural Center and Downtown Business District. Exit 157A off I-40 at Rio Grande Blvd.

BEST WESTERN PLUS
RIO GRANDE INN

1015 Rio Grande Blvd NW
Albuquerque, New Mexico 87104
505.843.9500
Reservations:
800.959.4726
www.riograndeinn.com

Savor Southwest cuisine in the Albuquerque Bar and Grill. Our pool and spa are open year round. We have free wireless Internet and a business center.

Get the free mobile app at
http://gettag.mobi

AAA
Approved

(See map & index p. 362.)

DAYS INN & SUITES ALBUQUERQUE AIRPORT
Phone: (505)247-1500 **54**

Hotel
$54-$108

Address: 2331 Centre Ave SE 87106 **Location:** I-25 exit 222A, 1 mi e to Yale Blvd, just n, then just e. **Facility:** 57 units. 3 stories, interior corridors. **Pool(s):** heated indoor. **Activities:** whirlpool, exercise room. **Guest Services:** valet and coin laundry. **Free Special Amenities: expanded continental breakfast and airport transportation.**

DOUBLETREE BY HILTON HOTEL ALBUQUERQUE
Phone: (505)247-3344 **43**

Hotel
$85-$155

AAA Benefit: Members save 5% or more everyday!

Address: 201 Marquette Ave NW 87102 **Location:** I-25 exit 224B, 0.8 mi w to 2nd St, then just n; downtown. Adjacent to Albuquerque Convention Center. **Facility:** 295 units. 15 stories, interior corridors. **Parking:** on-site (fee). **Terms:** 1-7 night minimum stay, cancellation fee imposed. **Amenities:** video games (fee). **Pool(s):** heated outdoor. **Activities:** exercise room. **Guest Services:** valet laundry, area transportation-within 2 mi.

DRURY INN & SUITES-ALBUQUERQUE
Phone: (505)341-3600 **15**

Hotel
$95-$184

Address: 4310 The 25 Way NE 87109 **Location:** I-25 exit Jefferson St NE; northwest quadrant of exchange. **Facility:** 164 units. 6 stories, interior corridors. **Terms:** cancellation fee imposed. **Amenities:** high-speed Internet. **Pool(s):** heated outdoor. **Activities:** whirlpool, exercise room. **Guest Services:** valet and coin laundry.

ECONO LODGE DOWNTOWN
Phone: (505)243-1321 **48**

Motel
$50

Address: 817 Central Ave NE 87102 **Location:** I-25 exit 224A northbound; exit 224B southbound, just w. **Facility:** 44 units. 2 stories (no elevator), exterior corridors. **Terms:** cancellation fee imposed. **Pool(s):** heated outdoor.

Close to all major hospitals and airport. Also close to the University of New Mexico.

EconoLodge
BY CHOICE HOTELS

ECONO LODGE EAST
Phone: (505)292-7600 **58**

Hotel
$45-$55

Address: 13211 Central Ave NE 87123 **Location:** I-40 exit 167 (Central Ave), just w. **Facility:** 58 units. 3 stories (no elevator), exterior corridors. **Terms:** cancellation fee imposed.

ECONO LODGE MIDTOWN
Phone: 505/880-0080 **32**

Hotel
Rates not provided

Address: 2412 Carlisle Blvd NE 87110 **Location:** I-40 exit 160, just n. **Facility:** 38 units. 2 stories (no elevator), exterior corridors. **Free Special Amenities: continental breakfast and high-speed Internet.**

EMBASSY SUITES ALBUQUERQUE HOTEL & SPA
Phone: (505)245-7100 **41**

Hotel
$111-$227

AAA Benefit: Members save 5% or more everyday!

Address: 1000 Woodward Pl NE 87102 **Location:** I-25 exit 224B, just w. **Facility:** 261 units. 9 stories, interior corridors. **Terms:** 1-7 night minimum stay, cancellation fee imposed. **Amenities:** safes. *Fee:* video games, high-speed Internet. **Pool(s):** heated indoor. **Activities:** whirlpool, exercise room, spa. *Fee:* game room. **Guest Services:** valet and coin laundry.

FAIRFIELD INN ALBUQUERQUE-UNIVERSITY AREA
Phone: (505)889-4000 **24**

Hotel
$84-$159

AAA Benefit: AAA hotel discounts of 5% or more.

Address: 1760 Menaul Blvd NE 87102 **Location:** I-40 exit 160, just n to Menaul Blvd, then 1 mi w. **Facility:** 188 units. 3 stories, interior corridors. **Pool(s):** heated indoor. **Activities:** sauna, whirlpool, exercise room. **Guest Services:** valet and coin laundry.

FAIRFIELD INN & SUITES ALBUQUERQUE AIRPORT
Phone: (505)247-1621 **55**

Hotel
$63-$109

FAIRFIELD INN
AAA Benefit: AAA hotel discounts of 5% or more.

Address: 2300 Centre Ave SE 87106 **Location:** I-25 exit 222 (Gibson Blvd) northbound; exit 222A southbound, 1 mi e to Yale Blvd; northeast jct Gibson and Yale blvds. **Facility:** 118 units. 4 stories, interior corridors. **Amenities:** high-speed Internet. **Pool(s):** heated outdoor. **Activities:** whirlpool, exercise room. **Guest Services:** valet and coin laundry. **Free Special Amenities: full breakfast and airport transportation.**

HACIENDA ANTIGUA INN
Phone: (505)345-5399 **12**

Historic Bed & Breakfast
$149-$209 2/1-10/31
$139-$179 11/1-1/31

Address: 6708 Tierra Dr NW 87107 **Location:** I-25 exit 230 (Osuna Dr), 2 mi w, then just n. **Facility:** This adobe hacienda dating to the 1700s features several rooms with a fireplace or a wood-burning stove as well as attractive brick floors. 8 units. 1 story, interior/exterior corridors. **Terms:** check-in 4 pm, 10 day cancellation notice-fee imposed. **Pool(s):** outdoor. **Activities:** whirlpool.

Safety tip: Keep a current AAA/CAA Road Atlas in every vehicle

(See map & index p. 362.)

HAMPTON INN-AIRPORT Phone: (505)246-2255 [60]

Hotel
$79-$159

AAA Benefit: Members save up to 10% everyday!

Address: 2231 Yale Blvd SE 87106 **Location:** I-25 exit 222A southbound; exit 222 (Gibson Blvd) northbound, 1 mi e, then just n. **Facility:** 62 units. 3 stories, exterior corridors. **Terms:** 1-7 night minimum stay, cancellation fee imposed. **Amenities:** high-speed Internet. **Pool(s):** heated indoor. **Activities:** sauna, whirlpool, exercise room. **Guest Services:** valet laundry.

(See ad this page.)

HAMPTON INN & SUITES Phone: (505)833-3700 [20]

Hotel
$69-$129

AAA Benefit: Members save up to 10% everyday!

Address: 6150 Iliff Rd NW 87121 **Location:** I-40 exit 155, 0.6 mi s, then just w. **Facility:** 88 units. 4 stories, interior corridors. **Terms:** 1-7 night minimum stay, cancellation fee imposed. **Amenities:** high-speed Internet. **Pool(s):** heated indoor. **Activities:** whirlpool, exercise room. **Guest Services:** valet and coin laundry.

HAMPTON INN-NORTH Phone: (505)344-1555 [8]

Hotel
$76-$89

AAA Benefit: Members save up to 10% everyday!

Address: 5101 Ellison NE 87109 **Location:** I-25 exit 231 (San Antonio Dr), just w. **Facility:** 123 units. 3 stories, exterior corridors. **Terms:** 1-7 night minimum stay, cancellation fee imposed. **Amenities:** video games (fee). **Pool(s):** heated outdoor. **Activities:** exercise room. **Guest Services:** valet laundry. **Free Special Amenities:** full breakfast and high-speed Internet.

HAMPTON INN UNIVERSITY-MIDTOWN Phone: (505)837-9300 [34]

Hotel
$69-$129

AAA Benefit: Members save up to 10% everyday!

Address: 2300 Carlisle Blvd NE 87110 **Location:** I-40 exit 160, just w, then just n. **Facility:** 130 units. 4 stories, interior corridors. **Terms:** 1-7 night minimum stay, cancellation fee imposed. **Pool(s):** heated outdoor. **Activities:** whirlpool, exercise room. **Guest Services:** valet and coin laundry.

HARD ROCK HOTEL & CASINO ALBUQUERQUE Phone: (505)724-3800

Resort Hotel
$119-$800

Address: 11000 Broadway SE 87105 **Location:** I-25 exit 215, 0.5 mi s of Isleta Pueblo. **Facility:** This resort has everything needed for a relaxing, fun-filled stay. 201 units. 6 stories, interior corridors. **Parking:** on-site and valet. **Terms:** cancellation fee imposed. **Amenities:** high-speed Internet, safes. **Dining:** 7 restaurants, nightclub, entertainment. **Pool(s):** indoor/outdoor. **Activities:** golf-27 holes, basketball, horseshoes, volleyball, exercise room, spa. **Fee:** saunas, whirlpools, steamrooms, fishing, game room. **Guest Services:** valet laundry, area transportation-Railrunner station. **Free Special Amenities:** high-speed Internet and airport transportation.

HILTON ALBUQUERQUE Phone: 505/884-2500 [29]

Hotel
Rates not provided

AAA Benefit: Members save 5% or more everyday!

Address: 1901 University Blvd NE 87102 **Location:** I-40 exit 160, just n to Menaul Blvd, then 1.1 mi w. **Facility:** 261 units. 2-12 stories, interior corridors. **Parking:** on-site (fee) and valet. **Amenities:** high-speed Internet. **Dining:** 3 restaurants, also, Rancher's Club of New Mexico, see separate listing, entertainment. **Pool(s):** heated outdoor. **Activities:** whirlpool, exercise room. **Guest Services:** valet laundry.

▼ See AAA listing this page ▼

located at the intersection of good savings and great value.

No matter where you travel, there is always a clean and cozy Hampton in town. Our strong partnership with AAA allows us to offer special rates* to all AAA members.

Hampton Inn - Airport
2231 Yale Blvd SE Albuquerque, NM 87106
(505) 246-2255

© 2011 Hilton Worldwide. *Valid for current AAA members only. Subject to availability at participating Hampton hotels. Valid for stays booked and completed between January 1, 2012 and December 31, 2012. Enter your AAA number and promotion code "AAA" at time of booking. Must present your current and valid AAA card at check-in. The discount rate relates to the hotel's Best Available Rate. Best Available Rate is a specific rate type that varies depending on time of purchase, is unrestricted, non-qualified, and excludes discount or negotiated rates not available to the general public, including but not limited to: membership, corporate, government, promotional, group, packages, unpublished or rates only available on auction websites. Additional restrictions may apply.

Visit AAA.com or CAA.ca for one-stop travel planning and reservations

(See map & index p. 362.)

HILTON GARDEN INN ALBUQUERQUE AIRPORT
Phone: (505)765-1000 **63**

Hotel
$85-$160

AAA Benefit:
Unparalleled hospitality at a special Member rate.

Address: 2601 Yale Blvd SE 87106 **Location:** I-25 exit 222 (Gibson Blvd), 1 mi e, then just s. **Facility:** 107 units. 4 stories, interior corridors. **Terms:** 1-7 night minimum stay, cancellation fee imposed. **Amenities:** high-speed Internet. *Fee:* video games, safes. **Pool(s):** heated indoor. **Activities:** whirlpool, exercise room. **Guest Services:** valet and coin laundry, area transportation-within 5 mi.

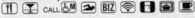

HILTON GARDEN INN ALBUQUERQUE JOURNAL CENTER
Phone: (505)314-0800 **10**

Hotel
$89-$139

AAA Benefit:
Unparalleled hospitality at a special Member rate.

Address: 5320 San Antonio Dr NE 87109 **Location:** I-25 exit 231 (San Antonio Dr), just e. **Facility:** 94 units. 4 stories, interior corridors. **Terms:** 1-7 night minimum stay, cancellation fee imposed. **Amenities:** video games (fee), high-speed Internet, safes. **Pool(s):** heated indoor. **Activities:** whirlpool, exercise room. **Guest Services:** valet and coin laundry.

HILTON GARDEN INN ALBUQUERQUE UPTOWN
Phone: (505)944-0300 **38**

Hotel
$119-$175

AAA Benefit:
Unparalleled hospitality at a special Member rate.

Address: 6510 Americas Pkwy 87110 **Location:** I-40 exit 162, just n, then just w; in Northeast Heights. **Facility:** 149 units. 7 stories, interior corridors. **Terms:** 1-7 night minimum stay, cancellation fee imposed. **Amenities:** video games (fee), high-speed Internet, safes. **Pool(s):** heated indoor. **Activities:** whirlpool, waterslide, exercise room. **Guest Services:** valet and coin laundry.

HOLIDAY INN & SUITES ALBUQUERQUE AIRPORT - UNIVERSITY
Phone: (505)944-2255 **65**

Hotel
$99-$159

Address: 1501 Sunport Pl SE 87106 **Location:** I-25 exit 221, 0.5 mi e to University Blvd, then just n. **Facility:** 121 units. 4 stories, interior corridors. **Amenities:** high-speed Internet, safes (fee). **Pool(s):** heated indoor. **Activities:** sauna, whirlpool, exercise room. **Guest Services:** valet and coin laundry.

HOLIDAY INN EXPRESS
Phone: (505)275-8900 **50**

Hotel
$82-$92

Address: 10330 Hotel Ave NE 87123 **Location:** I-40 exit 165 (Eubank Blvd), just e. **Facility:** 104 units. 2 stories (no elevator), exterior corridors. **Amenities:** safes. **Pool(s):** heated indoor. **Activities:** sauna, whirlpool, game room, exercise room. **Guest Services:** valet and coin laundry. **Free Special Amenities:** full breakfast and high-speed Internet.

HOLIDAY INN EXPRESS ALBUQUERQUE MIDTOWN
Phone: (505)881-0544 **25**

Hotel
$79-$129

Address: 2500 Menaul Blvd NE 87107 **Location:** I-40 exit 160, just n to Menaul Blvd, then 0.6 mi w. **Facility:** 122 units. 6 stories, interior corridors. **Terms:** cancellation fee imposed. **Amenities:** video games (fee). *Some:* high-speed Internet. **Pool(s):** heated outdoor. **Activities:** exercise room. **Guest Services:** valet and coin laundry, area transportation-within 5 mi. **Free Special Amenities:** full breakfast and high-speed Internet.

HOLIDAY INN EXPRESS HOTEL & SUITES
Phone: (505)797-2291 **1**

Hotel
$99-$169

Address: 5401 Alameda Blvd NE 87113 **Location:** I-25 exit 233, just w. **Facility:** 62 units. 3 stories, interior corridors. **Amenities:** high-speed Internet, safes. **Pool(s):** heated indoor. **Activities:** whirlpool, exercise room. **Guest Services:** valet and coin laundry.

HOLIDAY INN EXPRESS HOTEL & SUITES ALBUQUERQUE HISTORIC OLD TOWN
Phone: (505)842-5000 **18**

Hotel
$109-$259

Address: 2300 12th St NW 87104 **Location:** I-40 exit 157B eastbound; exit 158 westbound; s of jct Menaul Blvd. **Facility:** 108 units. 4 stories, interior corridors. **Amenities:** high-speed Internet. **Pool(s):** heated indoor. **Activities:** whirlpool, exercise room. **Guest Services:** valet and coin laundry. *(See ad p. 375.)*

HOLIDAY INN HOTEL & SUITES
Phone: (505)944-2222 **16**

Hotel
$99-$199

Address: 5050 Jefferson St NE 87109 **Location:** I-25 exit 229 northbound, just n on east frontage road, then just s; exit 229 southbound, s on west frontage road to Jefferson St, then just e. **Facility:** 122 units. 6 stories, interior corridors. **Amenities:** high-speed Internet, safes. **Pool(s):** heated indoor. **Activities:** whirlpool, waterslide, exercise room. **Guest Services:** valet and coin laundry.

HOMEWOOD SUITES BY HILTON-JOURNAL CENTER
Phone: (505)998-4663 **11**

Extended Stay Hotel
$117-$143

AAA Benefit:
Contemporary luxury at a special Member rate.

Address: 5400 San Antonio Dr NE 87109 **Location:** I-25 exit 231 (San Antonio Dr), just e. **Facility:** 63 efficiencies. 3 stories, interior corridors. **Terms:** 1-7 night minimum stay, cancellation fee imposed. **Amenities:** high-speed Internet. **Pool(s):** heated indoor. **Activities:** whirlpool, exercise room. **Guest Services:** valet and coin laundry.

Get pet travel tips and enter the photo contest at AAA.com/PetBook

(See map & index p. 362.)

HOTEL ANDALUZ
▼▼▼ ▼▼▼
Historic Hotel
$139-$329

Phone: (505)242-9090 **46**
Address: 125 2nd St NW St NW 87102 **Location:** I-25 exit 224A northbound; exit 224B southbound, jct Copper Ave and 2nd St; downtown. Located in a commercial area. **Facility:** The property showcases "green" technology and is the only historic hotel in the country with LEED certification. 107 units. 10 stories, interior corridors. **Parking:** on-site (fee) and valet. **Terms:** cancellation fee imposed. **Amenities:** high-speed Internet, safes, honor bars. **Dining:** entertainment. **Guest Services:** valet laundry. **Free Special Amenities: high-speed Internet.**
(See ad p. 376.)

SAVE ⊞ ⊡ ⊞ ⊞ ⊞ BIZ 📶 ✕
/ SOME UNITS FEE ⊡

THE HOTEL BLUE
▼▼▼
Hotel
Rates not provided

Phone: 505/924-2400 **45**
Address: 717 Central Ave NW 87102 **Location:** 8th St and Central Ave; downtown. **Facility:** 139 units. 6 stories, exterior corridors. **Amenities:** high-speed Internet. **Pool(s):** outdoor. **Activities:** limited exercise equipment. **Guest Services:** valet laundry, area transportation-local attractions.

⊞ ⊡ ⊞ BIZ 📶 ⊞ ⊞ ⊞
/ SOME UNITS FEE ⊡

HOTEL PARQ CENTRAL
▼▼▼ ▼▼▼
Boutique Vintage Hotel
$140-$420

Phone: (505)242-0040 **49**
Address: 806 Central Ave SE 87102 **Location:** I-25 exit 224A northbound; exit 224B southbound, just w. **Facility:** This renovated 1926 hotel reflects a blend of historic elegance and contemporary comfort with chic stylish décor. 74 units. 4 stories, interior corridors. **Terms:** cancellation fee imposed. **Amenities:** high-speed Internet, safes. **Activities:** whirlpool, exercise room. *Fee:* massage. **Guest Services:** valet and coin laundry, area transportation-within 3 mi. **Free Special Amenities: expanded continental breakfast and airport transportation.**

SAVE ⊞ ⊡ ⊞ ⊞ BIZ 📶 ✕ ⊡
/ SOME UNITS FEE ⊡

HYATT PLACE ALBUQUERQUE AIRPORT
Phone: (505)242-9300 **67**
▼▼▼
Hotel
$79-$169

HYATT PLACE

AAA Benefit: Members save 10% or more everyday.

Address: 1400 Sunport Blvd SE 87106 **Location:** I-25 exit 221, 0.3 mi e to University Blvd exit, then just n to Woodward Rd. **Facility:** 127 units. 6 stories, interior corridors. **Terms:** cancellation fee imposed. **Amenities:** *Some:* video games (fee), high-speed Internet, safes. **Pool(s):** heated outdoor. **Activities:** exercise room. **Guest Services:** valet laundry, area transportation-within 5 mi. **Free Special Amenities: expanded continental breakfast and high-speed Internet.**

SAVE ⊞ ⊡ ⊞ CALL ⊞ 🏊 BIZ 📶 ✕
/ SOME UNITS ⊞ ⊞

▼ See AAA listing p. 374 ▼

STAY IMPRESSED.

Holiday Inn Express Hotel & Suites
Albuquerque Historic Old Town
2300 12th St NW
Albuquerque, NM 87104
(505)842-5000
holidayinnexpress.com/albuquerquenw

Get the free mobile app at
http://gettag.mobi

STAY YOU.™

Stay You.™ is a registered trademark of Six Continents Hotels, Inc. ©2011 InterContinental Hotels Group. All Rights Reserved. Most hotels are independently owned and/or operated.

Simply Reliable

The Diamond Ratings in this TourBook guide are backed by our expert, in-person evaluations, whether the hotel or restaurant is no-frills, moderate or upscale.

Learn more at **AAA.com/Diamonds**

(See map & index p. 362.)

HYATT PLACE ALBUQUERQUE UPTOWN

Phone: (505)872-9000 [35]

Hotel
$89-$189

HYATT PLACE

AAA Benefit: Members save 10% or more everyday.

Address: 6901 Arvada Ave NE 87110 **Location:** I-40 exit 162, 0.7 mi n. **Facility:** 126 units. 6 stories, interior corridors. **Terms:** cancellation fee imposed. **Amenities:** video games (fee), safes. *Some:* high-speed Internet. **Pool(s):** heated outdoor. **Activities:** exercise room. **Guest Services:** valet laundry. **Free Special Amenities:** expanded continental breakfast and high-speed Internet.

SAVE CALL &M BIZ X

Create complete trip routings and custom maps with the TripTik® Travel Planner on AAA.com or CAA.ca

▼ See AAA listing p. 375 ▼

DISCOVER HOTEL ANDALUZ

SAVE UP TO
20% OFF
CONTACT US
OR SCAN BELOW

Get the free mobile app at
http://gettag.mobi

AAA
Four Diamond
Award

Experience true luxury in an iconic Albuquerque hotel. Our pet-friendly, luxury boutique hotel offers AAA Four Diamond accommodations, exquisite dining in Lucia, a scenic rooftop bar Ibiza and is an ideal venue for special events, meetings & weddings.

ANDALUZ

125 SECOND STREET NW
DOWNTOWN ALBUQUERQUE, NM
HOTELANDALUZ.COM

FOR RESERVATIONS:
877.987.9090
505.242.9090

(See map & index p. 362.)

HYATT REGENCY ALBUQUERQUE
Phone: (505)842-1234 **44**

Hotel
$89-$240

HYATT
HOTELS & RESORTS.

AAA Benefit: Members save 10% or more every day.

Address: 330 Tijeras Ave NW 87102 **Location:** I-25 exit 224B, 0.5 mi w; downtown. **Facility:** 395 units. 20 stories, interior corridors. **Parking:** on-site (fee) and valet. **Terms:** cancellation fee imposed. **Amenities:** video games (fee). *Some:* safes. **Dining:** 2 restaurants. **Pool(s):** heated outdoor. **Activities:** saunas, whirlpools, exercise room. *Fee:* massage. **Guest Services:** valet laundry. **Free Special Amenities:** early check-in/late check-out and high-speed Internet.

SAVE ECO [icons] CALL &M [icons] BIZ [icon]
/ SOME UNITS FEE [icons]

LA QUINTA INN ALBUQUERQUE AIRPORT
Phone: (505)243-5500 **59**

Hotel
$68-$133

Address: 2116 Yale Blvd SE 87106 **Location:** I-25 exit 222 (Gibson Blvd) northbound; exit 222A southbound, 1 mi e. **Facility:** 105 units. 3 stories, exterior corridors. **Amenities:** video games (fee), high-speed Internet. **Pool(s):** heated outdoor. **Activities:** exercise room. **Guest Services:** valet and coin laundry, area transportation-within 5 mi.

[icons] CALL &M [icons]
/ SOME UNITS [icons]

LA QUINTA INN ALBUQUERQUE NORTHEAST
Phone: (505)821-9000 **9**

Motel
$64-$126

Address: 5241 San Antonio Dr NE 87109 **Location:** I-25 exit 231 (San Antonio Dr), just e. **Facility:** 130 units. 2 stories (no elevator), exterior corridors. **Amenities:** video games (fee). *Some:* high-speed Internet. **Pool(s):** heated outdoor. **Guest Services:** coin laundry.

[icons] CALL &M [icons] / SOME UNITS [icons]

LA QUINTA INN & SUITES ALBUQUERQUE JOURNAL CTR NW
Phone: (505)345-7500 **7**

Hotel
$62-$122

Address: 7439 Pan American Frwy NE 87109 **Location:** I-25 exit 231 (San Antonio Dr), just w. **Facility:** 97 units. 3 stories, interior corridors. **Pool(s):** heated outdoor. **Activities:** exercise room. **Guest Services:** valet and coin laundry.

[icons] / SOME UNITS [icons]

LA QUINTA INN & SUITES ALBUQUERQUE MIDTOWN
Phone: (505)761-5600 **23**

Hotel
$107-$214

Address: 2011 Menaul Blvd 87107 **Location:** Jct University and Menaul blvds, just e. **Facility:** 72 units. 3 stories, interior corridors. **Amenities:** high-speed Internet. **Pool(s):** heated indoor. **Activities:** whirlpool, limited exercise equipment. **Guest Services:** valet and coin laundry.
(See ad this page.)

[icons] CALL &M [icons] BIZ [icons]
[icons] / SOME UNITS [icons]

LA QUINTA INN & SUITES ALBUQUERQUE WEST
Phone: (505)839-1744 **19**

Hotel
$74-$144

Address: 6101 Iliff Rd NW 87121 **Location:** I-40 exit 155, just sw. **Facility:** 118 units. 5 stories, interior corridors. **Amenities:** video games (fee). **Pool(s):** heated outdoor. **Activities:** whirlpool, exercise room. **Guest Services:** valet and coin laundry.

[icons] CALL &M [icons] BIZ [icons]
/ SOME UNITS [icons]

MCM ELEGANTE HOTEL
Phone: 505/884-2511 **28**

Hotel
Rates not provided

Address: 2020 Menaul Blvd NE 87107 **Location:** I-40 exit 160, 0.3 mi n to Menaul Blvd, then 1 mi w. **Facility:** 341 units. 2-5 stories, interior corridors. **Amenities:** video games (fee). **Pool(s):** heated indoor. **Activities:** whirlpool, exercise room. **Guest Services:** valet and coin laundry, area transportation-Old Town, hospitals & mall. *(See ad p. 378.)*

[icons] [icons] CALL &M [icons] BIZ [icons]
/ SOME UNITS [icons]

▼ See AAA listing this page ▼

Your Travel Dollars Go Further With Great Rates Plus:

- Free Bright Side Breakfast®, Plus Hot Items
- Free high-speed Internet
- Comfy Pillowtop Beds
- Free Fitness Center

- Meeting Room
- Pets Welcome
- Indoor Pool & Hot Tub
- Conveniently located near I-40 & I-25

For Reservations, call 505-761-5600
2011 Menual Blvd.
Albuquerque, NM 87107

800-SLEEPLQ | **LQ.com**
(753-3757)

LA QUINTA
INNS & SUITES
wake up on the bright side®

(See map & index p. 362.)

MONTEREY NON-SMOKERS MOTEL-OLD TOWN
Phone: (505)243-3554 **36**

Motel
$64-$100 2/1-10/31
$58-$68 11/1-1/31

Address: 2402 Central Ave SW 87104 **Location:** I-40 exit 157A, 0.5 mi s on Rio Grande Blvd, then 0.3 mi w. **Facility:** 15 units. 1 story, exterior corridors. **Pool(s):** heated outdoor. **Guest Services:** coin laundry. **Free Special Amenities:** local telephone calls and high-speed Internet.

2 Blks: Old Town, Restaurants, Museums, Shops. 1 Blk: Aquarium, Botanic Garden, Zoo. 2 mi Downtown.

NATIVO LODGE
Phone: (505)798-4300 **13**

Hotel
$89-$159

Address: 6000 Pan American Frwy NE 87109 **Location:** I-25 exit 230, just e. **Facility:** 146 units. 5 stories, interior corridors. **Terms:** cancellation fee imposed. **Pool(s):** heated indoor/outdoor. **Activities:** sauna, whirlpool, exercise room. **Guest Services:** valet and coin laundry. Affiliated with A Preferred Hotel.

PARK INN BY RADISSON
Phone: (505)888-3311 **31**

Hotel
$99-$239

Address: 2500 Carlisle Blvd NE 87110 **Location:** I-40 exit 160, just n. **Facility:** 314 units. 2-4 stories, interior/exterior corridors. **Terms:** check-in 4 pm, cancellation fee imposed. **Pool(s):** heated indoor. **Activities:** whirlpool, waterslide. **Guest Services:** valet and coin laundry. **Free Special Amenities:** high-speed Internet and airport transportation.
(See ad p. 379.)

RESIDENCE INN ALBUQUERQUE- NORTH
Phone: (505)761-0200 **14**

Extended Stay Hotel
$109-$139

AAA Benefit: AAA hotel discounts of 5% or more.

Address: 4331 The Lane at 25 NE 87109 **Location:** I-25 exit 229 (Jefferson St), just w, just n to The Lane at 25 NE, then just e. **Facility:** 90 units, some two bedrooms, efficiencies and kitchens. 3 stories, interior corridors. **Amenities:** *Some:* high-speed Internet. **Pool(s):** heated outdoor. **Activities:** whirlpool, exercise room. **Guest Services:** valet and coin laundry. **Free Special Amenities:** full breakfast and high-speed Internet.

▼ *See AAA listing p. 377* ▼

MCM Elegante ★★★★

2020 Menaul Blvd, NE Albuquerque, NM
(505) 884-2511 • Toll Free: (888) 897-9644
www.mcmelegante.com

Scan this tag on your smartphone for more info

Luxurious and Comfortable Beds
Free Hot Breakfast with Eggs Cooked to Order • Free Happy Hour

Learn about AAA/CAA Diamond Ratings

at AAA.com/Diamonds

(See map & index p. 362.)

RESIDENCE INN BY MARRIOTT ALBUQUERQUE AIRPORT   Phone: (505)242-2844 **51**

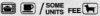

Extended Stay Hotel
$94-$169

AAA Benefit:
AAA hotel discounts of 5% or more.

Address: 2301 International Dr SE 87106 **Location:** I-25 exit 222 northbound; exit 222A southbound, 1 mi e of jct Yale Blvd SE, then just n. **Facility:** 110 units, some two bedrooms, efficiencies and kitchens. 4 stories, interior corridors. **Amenities:** high-speed Internet. **Pool(s):** heated indoor. **Activities:** whirlpool, sports court, exercise room. **Guest Services:** valet and coin laundry.

▼ See AAA listing p. 378 ▼

ROUTE 66 CASINO HOTEL   Phone: 505/352-7866

Hotel
$70-$100

Address: 14500 Central Ave 87121 **Location:** I-40 exit 140, just w. **Facility:** This casino property sports a fun Route 66 décor throughout. 154 units. 6 stories, interior corridors. **Parking:** on-site and valet. **Terms:** check-in 4 pm. **Amenities:** high-speed Internet, safes. **Dining:** 4 restaurants, nightclub, entertainment. **Pool(s):** heated indoor. **Activities:** whirlpool, game room, exercise room. **Guest Services:** coin laundry.
(See ad this page.)

New Mexico's Only Indoor Water Park

- Minutes from Airport, ABQ Uptown, Old Town, UNM and Kirtland Air Force Base
- On Site Restaurant and Lounge
- Free in room Wi-Fi and a 24 hour business Center
- Full Service Fitness Center, Indoor Pool & Whirlpool
- 30,000 Sq Ft water park with slides, activity pools, dual wave riders, lazy river & indoor outdoor Whirlpool
- Ask for 15% AAA discount

park inn
by Radisson

800-670-7275
parkinn.com

2500 Carlisle Blvd NE • Albuquerque, NM 87110 • 505-888-3311

▼ See AAA listing this page ▼

ESCAPE

Scan this code with your Smartphone.
Get the free mobile app at http://gettag.mobi

*AAA Discount

$89 SUN - THUR | $119 FRI & SAT
$70* SUN - THUR | $99* FRI & SAT

ROUTE 66 Casino Hotel
Get Your Kicks!

I-40 EXIT 140 ♥ 1.866.711.STAY(7829) ♥ RT66CASINO.COM

(See map & index p. 362.)

SANDIA PEAK INN
Phone: 505/831-5036 [42]

Hotel
Rates not provided

Address: 4614 Central Ave SW 87105 **Location:** I-40 exit 157A (Rio Grande Blvd), just s, then 2 mi w. **Facility:** 41 units. 2 stories (no elevator), exterior corridors. **Pool(s):** heated indoor. **Guest Services:** coin laundry.

SHERATON ALBUQUERQUE AIRPORT HOTEL
Phone: (505)843-7000 [64]

Hotel
$89-$219

(S) Sheraton
AAA Benefit: Members get up to 15% off, plus Starwood Preferred Guest® bonuses.

Address: 2910 Yale Blvd SE 87106 **Location:** I-25 exit 225 northbound; exit 222A southbound, 1 mi e on Gibson Blvd, then 0.5 mi s. **Facility:** 276 units. 15 stories, interior corridors. **Amenities:** video games (fee). *Some:* high-speed Internet (fee). **Pool(s):** outdoor. **Activities:** exercise room. **Guest Services:** valet laundry. **Free Special Amenities:** local telephone calls and high-speed Internet.

STAYBRIDGE SUITES ALBUQUERQUE AIRPORT
Phone: (505)338-3900 [66]

Extended Stay Hotel
$109-$159 2/1-10/14
$99-$149 10/15-1/31

Address: 1350 Sunport Pl SE 87106 **Location:** I-25 exit 221, 0.3 mi e to University Blvd exit, then just n to Woodward Rd. **Facility:** 100 efficiencies, some two bedrooms. 4 stories, interior corridors. **Amenities:** high-speed Internet. **Pool(s):** heated outdoor. **Activities:** whirlpool, putting green, exercise room. **Guest Services:** valet and coin laundry, area transportation-within 3 mi.

STAYBRIDGE SUITES ALBUQUERQUE NORTH
Phone: (505)266-7829 [3]

Extended Stay Hotel
$89-$359

Address: 5817 Signal Ave NE 87113 **Location:** I-25 exit 233 (Alameda Blvd), just e; jct Alameda Blvd and Signal Ave. **Facility:** 90 units, some two bedrooms and efficiencies. 3 stories, interior corridors. **Terms:** 3 day cancellation notice. **Amenities:** high-speed Internet. **Pool(s):** heated indoor. **Activities:** whirlpool, putting green, exercise room. **Guest Services:** valet and coin laundry, area transportation-within 5 mi. **Free Special Amenities:** full breakfast and high-speed Internet.

SUBURBAN EXTENDED STAY HOTELS
Phone: (505)883-8888 [30]

Extended Stay Motel
$60-$100

Address: 2401 Wellesley Dr NE 87107 **Location:** I-40 exit 160, just n to Menaul Blvd, just w, then just s. Located in Northeast Heights. **Facility:** 134 efficiencies. 2 stories (no elevator), exterior corridors. **Terms:** office hours 7 am-11 pm, cancellation fee imposed. **Guest Services:** valet and coin laundry.

SUPER 8 OF ALBUQUERQUE
Phone: (505)888-4884 [22]

Hotel
$39-$80

Address: 2500 University Blvd NE 87107 **Location:** I-25 exit 225 northbound, 1.9 mi n on frontage road to Menaul Blvd, then just e; exit 227 (Comanche Rd) southbound, 0.9 mi s to Menaul Blvd, then just e. **Facility:** 149 units. 3 stories, interior corridors. **Guest Services:** coin laundry, area transportation-hospitals, bus & train depot. **Free Special Amenities:** continental breakfast and high-speed Internet.

TOWNEPLACE SUITES BY MARRIOTT
Phone: (505)232-5800 [56]

Extended Stay Hotel
$69-$109

TownePlace SUITES MARRIOTT
AAA Benefit: AAA hotel discounts of 5% or more.

Address: 2400 Centre Ave SE 87106 **Location:** I-25 exit 222 (Gibson Blvd) northbound; exit 222A southbound, 1 mi e to Yale Blvd, at northeast jct Gibson and Yale blvds, then just e. **Facility:** 107 units, some two bedrooms and kitchens. 4 stories, interior corridors. **Amenities:** high-speed Internet. **Pool(s):** heated outdoor. **Activities:** whirlpool, exercise room. **Guest Services:** valet and coin laundry. **Free Special Amenities:** expanded continental breakfast and airport transportation.

SANDIA RESORT & CASINO
Phone: 505/796-7500

[fyi]   Not evaluated. **Address:** 30 Rainbow Rd NE 87113 **Location:** I-25 exit 234, just e. Facilities, services, and decor characterize an upscale property.

WHERE TO EAT

66 DINER
Phone: 505/247-1421 [68]

Burgers
$6-$10

AAA Inspector Notes: Patrons can return to the 1950s for some of the best burgers and American comfort food in town. Delicious desserts will please as well. **Address:** 1405 Central Ave NE 87106 **Location:** Jct Central Ave and University Blvd, just w. [B] [L] [D]

ABQ GRILL
Phone: 505/881-0000 [39]

American
$9-$23

AAA Inspector Notes: This locally popular restaurant has a warm and inviting atmosphere that is enhanced by rich dark woods and decorative architecture. Creative artwork intensifies its appeal. **Bar:** full bar. **Reservations:** suggested. **Address:** 2600 Louisiana Blvd NE 87110 **Location:** I-40 exit 162, 0.8 mi n; in Sheraton Albuquerque Uptown. [B] [L]

ANTIQUITY RESTAURANT   Phone: 505/247-3545 [53]

Continental
$20-$30

AAA Inspector Notes: This cozy, intimate restaurant specializes in steak dishes and is perfect for that special occasion or a romantic dinner for two. A fine selection of wines suits the most discriminating palate. This place is popular with the tourists who frequent Old Town, as well as local steak connoisseurs. **Bar:** beer & wine. **Reservations:** suggested. **Address:** 112 Romero St NW 87104 **Location:** I-40 exit 157A, 0.5 mi s to Romero St, just n of Central Ave; just s of Old Town Plaza; in Old Town. **Parking:** street only. [D]

(See map & index p. 362.)

THE ARTICHOKE CAFE   Phone: 505/243-0200   63

American
$10-$35

AAA Inspector Notes: The fine-dining establishment features New American cuisine prepared with a Southwestern flair. Creativity marks the appetizers, salads and entrees. Diners will find a sophisticated selection of wines and luscious desserts, particularly the lavender panna cotta. **Bar:** beer & wine. **Reservations:** suggested. **Address:** 424 Central Ave SE 87102 **Location:** I-25 exit 224B, s to Central Ave, then w. L D

A TASTE OF ITALY   Phone: 505/275-8334   56

International
$4-$8

AAA Inspector Notes: This modest café serves mostly Italian fare: pizza, submarine sandwiches and pasta dishes. Also sharing menu space are some Greek selections, such as gyros, souvlaki and spanakopita. The luncheon buffet is marvelous and filling. **Address:** 1945 Juan Tabo Blvd NE 87112 **Location:** Jct Menaul Blvd, just s; jct Brentwood Hills. L D

AZUMA   Phone: 505/880-9800   22

Japanese
$7-$30

AAA Inspector Notes: A tasty meal, this restaurant's dragon roll has artistic appeal. The presentation of appetizers and entrées shows careful attention to visual detail. **Bar:** beer & wine. **Address:** 4701 San Mateo Blvd NE 87109 **Location:** Jct Montgomery and San Mateo blvds, just n. L D CALL M

BIEN SHUR RESTAURANT   Phone: 505/796-7500   2

International
$25-$34

AAA Inspector Notes: At the top of the Sandia Resort, the tasteful restaurant and bar offers spectacular views of the Sandia Mountains and golf course to the east or the city of Albuquerque to the west. Outdoor seating is available on the ninth-floor terrace. The creative menu offers a variety of fish, poultry, fowl, game and steaks. The excellent dessert cart presentation is difficult to resist. **Bar:** full bar. **Reservations:** suggested. **Address:** 30 Rainbow Rd NE 87113 **Location:** I-25 exit 234, just e; in Sandia Resort & Casino. D CALL M

CAFE DALAT   Phone: 505/266-5559   88

Vietnamese
$6-$13

AAA Inspector Notes: Named for the owner's hometown in Vietnam, this modest-looking restaurant presents an extensive menu of vegetarian, chicken and seafood dishes. Giant bowls of soup are among favorite choices. **Bar:** beer & wine. **Address:** 5615 Central Ave NE 87108 **Location:** Jct Central Ave and San Mateo Blvd, just e. L D

CAJUN KITCHEN   Phone: 505/344-5355   5

Cajun
$9-$18

AAA Inspector Notes: The jambalaya is spicy, and these folks sure know how to cook shrimp, crawfish etouffee and catfish. The gumbo and po' boy sandwiches also are a great choice. **Bar:** beer & wine. **Address:** 4500 Osuna Rd NE, Suite 155 87109 **Location:** Jct Osuna Rd and Jefferson St, just e. L D CALL M

CASA DE BENAVIDEZ NEW MEXICAN RESTAURANT
Phone: 505/898-3311   3

Mexican
$8-$21

AAA Inspector Notes: The garden patio setting, with a pond and lush foliage, is ideal for relaxing with a margarita and generous portions of New Mexican specialties. Although the red chile salsa gets most of the buzz, the green chile also is great. **Bar:** full bar. **Reservations:** required. **Address:** 8032 4th St NW 87114 **Location:** Jct 4th St and El Pueblo Rd, just s. B L D

CERVANTES RESTAURANT & LOUNGE
Phone: 505/262-2253   91

Regional Mexican
$8-$23

AAA Inspector Notes: Well-prepared New Mexican dishes-including excellent carne adovada, chiles rellenos and homemade tamales-are featured at this locally popular restaurant. Served as an appetizer with tortilla chips, salsa commands real authority. This place is near Kirtland Air Force Base. **Bar:** full bar. **Address:** 5801 Gibson Rd SE 87108 **Location:** Jct San Pedro Dr. L D

CHAMA RIVER BREWING COMPANY
Phone: 505/342-1800   21

American
$9-$28

AAA Inspector Notes: A Santa Fe atmosphere, along with Northern New Mexico cuisine, give this impressive restaurant and brewery its personality. The menu lists a good selection of sandwiches. **Bar:** full bar. **Address:** 4939 Pan American Frwy NE 87109 **Location:** I-25 exit 229, just w. L D

CHEESE & COFFEE GOURMET DELI
Phone: 505/883-1226   40

Deli
$7-$10

AAA Inspector Notes: Those who visit this family spot might think they are in deli heaven. The selection of sandwiches is legion, service is quick and friendly and the staff is generous with the coffee. **Address:** 2679 Louisiana Blvd NE 87110 **Location:** Jct Menaul and Louisiana blvds, just n; in Encantada Square. L

CHEZ AXEL   Phone: 505/881-8104   24

French
$6-$23

AAA Inspector Notes: The aromas of France-olive oil, warm breads, anchovies, fresh seafood, tomatoes and herbs-waft through the small, simply decorated dining area. Tempting accompaniments include crunchy French bread and a good selection of pastries and desserts. **Bar:** beer & wine. **Reservations:** required. **Address:** 6209 Montgomery Blvd NE 87109 **Location:** Corner of Montgomery Blvd and San Pedro Dr, just e. L D

CHRISTY MAE'S   Phone: 505/255-4740   59

American
$7-$12

AAA Inspector Notes: This unpretentious family operation prepares home-style cooking, including a good selection of soups, salads, sandwiches and pot pies. Breads and desserts, such as carrot cake, are prepared in house. **Address:** 1400 San Pedro Dr NE 87110 **Location:** I-40 exit 162 westbound; exit 162A eastbound, 0.5 mi s on Louisiana Blvd to Lomas Blvd, 0.5 mi w to San Pedro Dr, then just n; corner of Mountain and San Pedro drs. B L D

CHURCH STREET CAFE   Phone: 505/247-8522   45

Mexican
$8-$16

AAA Inspector Notes: This 1706 adobe house also contains an art gallery. Tasty Mexican dishes, such as tamales, chiles rellenos and burritos, as well as a selection of sandwiches, are served in the dining room and on the patio. **Bar:** beer & wine. **Address:** 2111 Church St NW 87104 **Location:** I-40 exit 157A, 0.5 mi s to Mountain Rd, then just e; in Old Town. **Parking:** street only. B L D

(See map & index p. 362.)

THE COOPERAGE   **Phone:** 505/255-1657   70

American
$8-$36

AAA Inspector Notes: Known for its steaks, prime rib and well-stocked salad bar, this restaurant is a longtime favorite in Northeast Heights. The exterior design resembles a giant wine barrel, and the rustic interior is circular as well. Comfortable decor makes it a relaxing place in which to enjoy a fine meal. **Bar:** full bar. **Address:** 7220 Lomas Blvd NE 87110 **Location:** Jct Lomas and Louisiana blvds, just e. L D

THE COPPER LOUNGE   **Phone:** 505/242-7490   69

American
$8-$18

AAA Inspector Notes: A recent addition between downtown and the University of New Mexico, this popular restaurant serves a grand selection of scrumptious sandwiches, burgers, salads and Mexican favorites. A lively lounge is on site. Portions are plentiful. **Bar:** full bar. **Address:** 1504 Central Ave SE 87106 **Location:** I-25 exit 224B, s to Central Ave, then just e. L D LATE

EAST OCEAN CHINESE SEAFOOD RESTAURANT
   Phone: 505/889-9315   31

Chinese
$5-$12

AAA Inspector Notes: A favorite dining spot of the local Asian community, this restaurant prepares delicately flavored seafood dishes, as well as fiery Szechuan selections. Live Dungeness crab, in season, is prepared using traditional recipes. The restaurant is also known for its economical luncheon menu. **Bar:** beer & wine. **Address:** 3601 Carlisle Blvd NE 87110 **Location:** Jct Candelaria Rd, just n. L D

EL PINTO   **Phone:** 505/898-1771   1

Mexican
$8-$23

AAA Inspector Notes: Southwestern decor, fireplaces and indoor waterfalls add visual interest to the many rooms of the local favorite established in 1962. The roomy patio, which seats 600, is believed to be the state's largest. The menu focuses on basic New Mexican fare, including enchiladas, burritos and carne adovada. The flavorful assortment of salsas are available in jars for purchase. **Bar:** full bar. **Address:** 10500 4th St NW 87114 **Location:** I-25 exit 234 (Tramway Blvd), 1.5 mi w to SR 556 (which becomes 4th St), then just s. L D CALL

EL TACO TOTE   **Phone:** 505/265-5188   87

Mexican
$5-$9

AAA Inspector Notes: This first U.S. location of the famous Mexico chain is where patrons can build tacos the way they like them, with a great selection of sauces and toppings that take the basic taco to a culinary work of art. **Bar:** beer only. **Address:** 4701 Central Ave NE 87108 **Location:** Jct Central Ave and Washington St, just e. B L

FLYING STAR CAFE   **Phone:** 505/275-8311   28

American
$7-$13

AAA Inspector Notes: This eatery has a trendy coffee-shop setting with an area for reading magazines while enjoying quiche, pizza, salad, stir-fry, sandwiches, baguettes and dessert. Sustainable, local and organic products are featured. They have a good range of coffees and Italian soda, and seating on the outside deck. **Bar:** beer & wine. **Address:** 4501 Juan Tabo Blvd NE 87111 **Location:** Just n of jct Montgomery Blvd. B L D

FOX AND HOUND PUB & GRILL
   Phone: 505/344-9430   7

American
$6-$15

AAA Inspector Notes: The combination sports bar and restaurant is popular with locals who work in the area. Pub food, salads and steaks are house specialties. **Bar:** full bar. **Reservations:** suggested. **Address:** 4301 The Lane at 25 NE 87109 **Location:** I-25 exit 229, just w, then just n. L D LATE CALL

FRESH CHOICES   **Phone:** 505/242-6447   65

Italian
$7

AAA Inspector Notes: Brick walls and hardwood floors lend to this restaurant's quaint bistro atmosphere. The buffet offers such items as salads, pizza, Italian meatballs, beef stroganoff, herb chicken, muffins, pudding and fresh pies and cakes. **Bar:** beer & wine. **Address:** 402 Central Ave SW 87102 **Location:** I-25 exit 224B, 1 mi w; downtown. **Parking:** street only. L D

FRONTIER RESTAURANT   **Phone:** 505/266-0550   71

American
$5-$11

AAA Inspector Notes: Across the street from the University of New Mexico campus, this well-known dining spot prepares jumbo homemade sweet rolls and a large selection of Southwestern dishes, burgers and sandwiches. Students love this place, which has been in business more than 30 years. **Address:** 2400 Central Ave SE 87106 **Location:** Corner of Central and Harvard aves, just e. B L D LATE

GARCIA'S KITCHEN   **Phone:** 505/275-5812   36

Mexican
$4-$10

AAA Inspector Notes: Green chile and carne adovada addictions have been born at this casual spot. And many tortilla worshipers make pilgrimage here on a regular basis. This bright and flashy restaurant serves breakfast all day long. **Bar:** beer & wine. **Address:** 3601 Juan Tabo Blvd NE 87111 **Location:** Southwest corner of Juan Tabo Blvd and Comanche Rd. B L D

GARDUNO'S OF MEXICO RESTAURANT & CANTINA
   Phone: 505/880-0055

Mexican
$6-$15

AAA Inspector Notes: Enjoy a margarita and hearty servings of creative regional favorites in a casual and fun atmosphere. **Bar:** full bar. **Address:** 2100 Louisiana 87110 **Location:** I-40 exit 162 westbound; exit 162B eastbound, just n; next to Winrock Mall. L D CALL

GARDUNO'S OF MEXICO RESTAURANT & CANTINA
   Phone: 505/890-7000

Mexican
$8-$19

AAA Inspector Notes: Enjoy a margarita and hearty servings of creative regional favorites at this casual and fun cantina. **Bar:** full bar. **Address:** 10031 Coors Blvd 87113 **Location:** 0.5 mi s of jct Alameda Blvd NW; near Cottonwood Mall. L D

GECKO'S BAR & TAPAS   **Phone:** 505/262-1848   82

American
$6-$14

AAA Inspector Notes: This friendly neighborhood lounge serves pub fare, such as hot wings, burgers and nachos, as well as a wide selection of creative tapas. In the Nob Hill area, this place is a favorite with University of New Mexico students. **Bar:** full bar. **Address:** 3500 Central Ave SE 87106 **Location:** Jct Central Ave and Carlisle Blvd; southwest corner; in Nob Hill Center. L D

(See map & index p. 362.)

GOLD STREET CAFFÉ   Phone: 505/765-1633   62

American
$6-$14

AAA Inspector Notes: A popular spot for morning coffee drinkers, this cozy café also serves imaginative daily luncheon specials. Delicious pastries are popular with folks from nearby downtown offices and businesses. Bar: beer & wine. Address: 218 Gold Ave SW 87102 Location: I-25 exit 224B, 1 mi w, just s, then just w. Parking: on-site (fee). B L

THE GROVE CAFE & MARKET   Phone: 505/248-9800   66

American
$7-$11

AAA Inspector Notes: This popular bustling café recently was voted Albuquerque's best breakfast and brunch spot. The highest quality seasonal ingredients are used including local and organic produce, fresh baked breads, artisanal cheese plus preservative-free meats. The market features high-quality gourmet items and foodie gifts. Address: 600 Central Ave SE 87102 Location: I-25 exit 224A northbound; exit 224B southbound, just w. B L

GYROS MEDITERRANEAN   Phone: 505/255-4401   72

Greek
$9-$11

AAA Inspector Notes: Across from the university and frequented by students and faculty alike, the restaurant prepares tasty Greek salad and good souvlaki. The baklava is a good meal-ender. Address: 106 Cornell Dr SE, #A 87106 Location: I-25 exit 224B, e to Harvard Ave, then just s. Parking: on-site (fee). L D

HELLO DELI   Phone: 505/889-3354   34

American
$5-$8

AAA Inspector Notes: This popular quick-service eatery specializes in breakfast and lunch. In addition to a fine selection of salads, sandwiches and burgers, guests can order hearty breakfast items anytime. Address: 3401 Candelaria Rd NE, #G 87107 Location: Jct Carlisle Blvd and Candelaria Rd, just w. B L

HIGH FINANCE   Phone: 505/243-9742

American
$9-$32

AAA Inspector Notes: Patrons enjoy a great view of the city from the restaurant's vantage point atop the 10,378-foot Sandia Peak. Ticket prices to ride the aerial tramway, the only way to access this place, are reduced for those who make reservations. It is wise to be prepared for a time-consuming meal. Bar: full bar. Reservations: suggested. Address: 40 Tramway Rd 87122 Location: I-25 exit 234 (Tramway Rd), 5.5 mi e to Sandia Peak Tramway base terminal. Parking: on-site (fee). L D

HO-LO-MA CHINESE RESTAURANT   Phone: 505/296-1271   43

Chinese
$6-$12

AAA Inspector Notes: Generous portions of traditional, moderately priced Chinese fare-such as sweet and sour pork, chow mein and egg foo yong-are the order of the day. Bar: beer & wine. Address: 8624 Menaul Blvd NE 87112 Location: Jct Wyoming and Menaul blvds, just e. L D

IL VICINO WOOD OVEN PIZZA   Phone: 505/271-0882

Pizza
$6-$10

AAA Inspector Notes: Wood-oven pizza is the signature dish, but great sandwiches and salads also are served. Wine complements the meal. Bar: beer & wine. Address: 11225 Montgomery Blvd NE 87111 Location: Jct Montgomery and Juan Tabo blvds. L D CALL M

INDIA PALACE   Phone: 505/271-5009   26

Indian
$8-$20

AAA Inspector Notes: A daily luncheon buffet lines up exotic East Indian dishes such as tandoori and makhani chicken, saag paneer and the lentil soup called "dal." Dinner is more formal with elaborate seafood and lamb specialties. Bar: beer & wine. Reservations: suggested. Address: 4410 Wyoming Blvd NE, Suite Q 87111 Location: Jct Montgomery and Wyoming blvds, just s. L D

JC'S NEW YORK PIZZA DEPARTMENT   Phone: 505/766-6973   60

Italian
$6-$17

AAA Inspector Notes: This downtown restaurant's patio affords a good view of busy Central Avenue. A good selection of pizza can be prepared with all the expected toppings. Also on the menu are salads and pasta dishes, as well as beer and wine. Bar: beer & wine. Address: 215 Central Ave NW, Suite 1B 87102 Location: Jct 2nd St, just w. Parking: street only. L D

JERSEY JACK'S EATERY   Phone: 505/268-1130   14

Regional Deli
$5-$8

AAA Inspector Notes: Popular with the folks who work in nearby offices, this eatery prepares interesting sandwich selections, salads and yummy desserts. Patrons also find a good selection of beer and soft drinks. Service is efficient and friendly. Bar: beer & wine. Address: 4320 The 25 Way, #650 87109 Location: I-25 exit 229 (Jefferson St), just e. B L D CALL M

JOHNDHIS BBQ   Phone: 505/345-3354   15

American
$6-$17

AAA Inspector Notes: In a converted home, this lively North Valley eatery presents a menu that incorporates choices such as New Mexican-style green chile stew, barbecue brisket, steaks and salads. Bar: beer & wine. Address: 3851 Rio Grande Blvd NW 87107 Location: I-40 exit 157A, 2.3 mi n; southwest corner of Rio Grande Blvd and Griegos Rd. L D

KELLY'S BREWERY & RESTAURANT   Phone: 505/262-2739   81

American
$3-$12

AAA Inspector Notes: A sunny street side patio area greets guests at this pleasant setting, the perfect spot for drinks or dining with friends. Pub-style food is served with a grand selection of microbrewed beers. Bar: full bar. Address: 3222 Central Ave SE 87106 Location: Jct Central and Wellesley aves. Parking: street only. L D

KRUNG THAI   Phone: 505/292-9319   41

Thai
$7-$12

AAA Inspector Notes: Well-prepared traditional Thai cuisine can be ordered as spicy or mild as desired. Thai iced tea is a popular beverage. Address: 7923 Menaul Blvd NE 87110 Location: Jct Wyoming and Menaul blvds, just w. L D

LA CREPE MICHEL   Phone: 505/242-1251   47

French
$6-$14

AAA Inspector Notes: Off the beaten path, this well-known Old Town café serves fine French cuisine. The crepes are fabulous. Bar: beer & wine. Address: 400 San Felipe St NW, #C-2 87104 Location: Jct San Felipe St and Central Ave, just n; in Old Town. Parking: street only. L D

(See map & index p. 362.)

LANDRY'S SEAFOOD HOUSE
Phone: 505/875-0101 (20)

Seafood
$8-$28

AAA Inspector Notes: An ideal spot for healthy seafood dinners and special occasions, the restaurant produces a wonderful clam chowder. Menu selections come from all the world's oceans. **Bar:** full bar. **Address:** 5001 Jefferson St NE 87109 **Location:** I-25 exit 229 (Jefferson St), just e. SAVE L D CALL M

LA PLACITA ON THE PLAZA
Phone: 505/247-2204 (50)

Mexican
$5-$15

AAA Inspector Notes: New Mexican food is the specialty at this local favorite on The Plaza in Old Town. The Navajo taco is made with Indian fry bread, covered with a wonderful, creamy red chile sauce and topped with melted cheese and shredded lettuce. **Bar:** full bar. **Address:** 306 1/2 San Felipe St NW 87104 **Location:** I-40 exit 157A (Rio Grande Blvd), 0.5 mi s to Romero St, then just e on The Plaza. **Parking:** street only. L D

LA PROVENCE BRASSERIE
Phone: 505/254-7644 (74)

French
$7-$25

AAA Inspector Notes: This lively bistro with classic French country cuisine offers an extensive wine list. **Bar:** beer & wine. **Reservations:** suggested. **Address:** 3001 Central Ave NE 87106 **Location:** In University and Nob Hill area. **Parking:** street only.

B L D

LA SALITA
Phone: 505/299-9968 (67)

Mexican
$3-$15

AAA Inspector Notes: A longtime favorite Northeast Heights dining spot, this restaurant serves generous portions of freshly prepared Mexican favorites, including stuffed sopaipillas, enchiladas and burritos. Dinners are humongous and colorfully decorated with chopped lettuce, diced tomatoes and melted cheese. The chile salsa is superlative. **Address:** 1217 Eubank Blvd NE 87112 **Location:** Jct Lomas and Eubank blvds, just n.

L D

LOS CUATES DEL NORTE
Phone: 505/237-2800 (44)

Mexican
$5-$11

AAA Inspector Notes: Waits are commonplace at this large and locally popular restaurant, where New Mexican specialties include fajitas, dark red and spicy salsa, hefty burger-filled burritos, chicken enchiladas on corn tortillas and refried beans and rice. **Bar:** full bar. **Address:** 8700 Menaul Blvd NE 87112 **Location:** Jct Menaul and Wyoming blvds, just w. L D

LOYOLA'S FAMILY RESTAURANT
Phone: 505/268-6478 (86)

Mexican
$4-$9

AAA Inspector Notes: Patrons can dine on both American and New Mexican fare. Reasonable prices, generous portions and exceptional red chile are hallmarks of this neighborhood eatery. **Address:** 4500 Central Ave SE 87108 **Location:** Jct Central and Adams aves. B L

MANNIE'S FAMILY RESTAURANT
Phone: 505/265-1669 (73)

American
$6-$9

AAA Inspector Notes: This long-time favorite has been serving folks in the University of New Mexico area for more than 30 years. Moderately priced American and New Mexican food is plated in generous portions. Service is fast. **Bar:** beer & wine. **Address:** 2900 Central Ave SE 87106 **Location:** Jct Central and Girard Blvd.

B L D

MARCELLO'S CHOPHOUSE
Phone: 505/837-2467 (54)

Steak
$9-$49

AAA Inspector Notes: Attentive service at this upscale steakhouse makes for an enjoyable dining experience. The freshest steaks and chops plus excellent fish and shellfish top the menu. A creative twist on comfort sides include truffled macaroni and cheese and green chile mashed potatoes. The hot chocolate cake is a definite treat. **Bar:** full bar. **Reservations:** suggested, for dinner. **Address:** 2201 Q St NE, Suite 9B 87110 **Location:** I-40 exit 162, 0.5 mi n; in Uptown Center.

L D CALL M

MARIO'S PIZZERIA & RISTORANTE
Phone: 505/883-4414 (48)

Italian
$7-$15

AAA Inspector Notes: This popular neighborhood dining spot has established a loyal following. On the menu are plentiful portions of fine pizza, calzones and pasta dishes. **Bar:** beer & wine. **Address:** 2401 San Pedro Blvd NE 87110 **Location:** I-40 exit 162, 0.5 mi n to Indian School Rd, 1 mi w, then just n; in Butterfield Plaza.

L D

MAY CAFE
Phone: 505/265-4448 (90)

Vietnamese
$6-$15

AAA Inspector Notes: Excellent lemon grass chicken is one of many well-prepared entrées at this ethnically decorated restaurant. **Bar:** beer & wine. **Address:** 111 Louisiana Blvd SE 87108 **Location:** Jct Central Ave and Louisiana Blvd, just s. L D

MILLY'S RESTAURANT
Phone: 505/884-0707 (35)

American
$5-$10

AAA Inspector Notes: Hearty breakfasts and lunches are priced moderately at this family spot. Enticing daily specials such as meatloaf are served with mashed potatoes, gravy and a vegetable. The sandwich selection is substantial. Brownies make a great dessert. **Address:** 2100 Candelaria Rd NE 87107 **Location:** Jct Candelaria Rd and Princeton Ave. B L

MIMMO'S RISTORANTE & PIZZERIA
Phone: 505/831-4191 (23)

Italian
$8-$18

AAA Inspector Notes: This restaurant sets up a daily luncheon buffet with an array of tasty choices, including lasagna and pizza. The menu offers a wide selection of Italian specialties. **Bar:** beer & wine. **Address:** 3301 Coors Blvd NW 87120 **Location:** I-40 exit 155, just n; in Ladera Shopping Center. L D

MING DYNASTY
Phone: 505/296-0298 (58)

Chinese
$6-$10

AAA Inspector Notes: The traditional American-style Chinese restaurant is complete with a dim sum lunch and a comfortable, ethnically decorated dining room. **Bar:** beer & wine. **Address:** 1551 Eubank Blvd NE 87112 **Location:** Jct Eubank Blvd and Indian School Rd, just s. L D

MONROE'S RESTAURANT
Phone: 505/881-4224 (16)

Mexican
$7-$17

AAA Inspector Notes: Long a popular dining spot for those who enjoy New Mexican food, this restaurant produces local favorites, as well as some seafood dishes popular along the Mexican coast. **Bar:** beer & wine. **Address:** 6051 Osuna Rd NE 87109 **Location:** I-25 exit 230 (San Mateo Blvd), 0.4 mi s, then just e.

B L D

(See map & index p. 362.)

MYKONOS CAFE & TAVERNA

Phone: 505/291-1116 ⑱

Greek
$10-$20

AAA Inspector Notes: This popular, family-operated restaurant features traditional Greek dishes, such as moussaka, pastitsio and spanakopita. Deftly prepared from an old family recipe, the avgolemono soup, with its lemony flavor and interesting texture, is particularly pleasing. **Bar:** full bar. **Reservations:** suggested. **Address:** 5900 Eubank Blvd NE, Suite E-18 87111 **Location:** S of jct Eubank and Juan Tabo blvds; in Mountain Run Shopping Center.
L D

NICK & JIMMY'S RESTAURANT & BAR

Phone: 505/344-9169 ⑰

Mediterranean
$13-$28

AAA Inspector Notes: This bustling restaurant, popular with local business clientele, offers a professional and attentive staff. Plentiful servings of Mediterranean favorites are featured along with Prime steak and seafood. **Bar:** full bar. **Reservations:** suggested. **Address:** 5021 S Pan American Frwy NE 87109 **Location:** I-25 exit 229 (Jefferson St) southbound, just s; exit northbound, just w, then just s. L D LATE

NOB HILL BAR & GRILL **Phone:** 505/266-4455 (78)

American
$10-$25

AAA Inspector Notes: An upscale joint is the theme of this trendy and hip hangout. The lively atmosphere is where the in-crowd is to be seen enjoying great food and cocktails. **Bar:** full bar. **Address:** 3128 Central Ave SE 87106 **Location:** Jct southwest corner of Girard Blvd. **Parking:** street only. L D

ORCHID THAI CUISINE **Phone:** 505/265-4047 (85)

Thai
$5-$16

AAA Inspector Notes: Traditional menu offerings range from delicately flavored dishes to fiery hot renditions. Guests can be sure what they order will be colorful, flavorful and exotic. Try the Thai iced tea. **Bar:** beer & wine. **Address:** 4300 Central Ave SE 87108 **Location:** Jct Central Ave and Graceland Dr; southeast corner. L D

ORTEGA'S MEXICAN RESTAURANT & GRILL

Phone: 505/298-0223 ㉜

Regional Mexican
$7-$11

AAA Inspector Notes: This neighborhood restaurant builds its menu on Mexican favorites, including chiles rellenos, enchiladas, burritos, tamales, tacos and fajitas. The Navajo taco with either red or green chili is especially good. **Bar:** beer & wine. **Address:** 3617 Wyoming Blvd NE 87111 **Location:** Jct Comanche Rd and Wyoming Blvd, just n. L D

THE OWL CAFE **Phone:** 505/291-4900 (84)

American
$5-$10

AAA Inspector Notes: The café delivers its distinctive green-chile cheeseburgers in a '50s diner setting complete with tableside jukeboxes and soda-jerk malts. It also offers a wide-ranging menu of stir-fried veggies, chicken-fried steak and red-chili pork tamales. **Bar:** beer & wine. **Address:** 800 Eubank Blvd NE 87123 **Location:** I-40 exit 165 (Eubank Blvd), just n. B L D

PADILLA'S MEXICAN KITCHEN

Phone: 505/262-0115 (52)

Mexican
$2-$8

AAA Inspector Notes: New Mexican favorites-such as carne adovada, tamales and green chile enchiladas stuffed with chicken or beef-are among dishes prepared at this popular eatery, a neighborhood fixture for many years. **Bar:** beer & wine. **Address:** 1510 Girard Ave NE 87106 **Location:** Corner of Indian School Rd and Girard Ave NE, just s. L D

PAISANO'S ITALIAN RESTAURANT

Phone: 505/298-7541 (55)

Italian
$7-$26

AAA Inspector Notes: Patrons can unwind in the cozy dining room or on the romantic patio to nosh on colorful traditional dishes, such as eggplant parmigiana accented by tasty red marinara sauce. The wine selection is good and homemade desserts are luscious. **Bar:** beer & wine. **Address:** 1935 Eubank Blvd NE 87112 **Location:** I-40 exit 165 (Eubank Blvd), 1.4 mi n. L D

PANZA LLENA CAFE **Phone:** 505/884-1199 ㉝

American
$5-$8

AAA Inspector Notes: Patrons should arrive early for lunch at this popular yet unpretentious eatery, as the daily specials sell out quickly. Fried chicken served on Thursday is worth the wait. Also worthwhile are the scrumptious, freshly prepared desserts. **Address:** 3225 Girard Blvd NE 87107 **Location:** Corner of Candelaria Rd and Girard Blvd, just n. B L

PAPA FELIPE'S **Phone:** 505/292-8877 (51)

Mexican
$3-$12

AAA Inspector Notes: A welcoming cantina lounge and pleasant, ethnic look are combined with well-prepared food and efficient service at this long-popular dining spot. Try the fresh sopaipillas, and save room for flan. **Bar:** full bar. **Address:** 9800 Menaul Blvd NE 87112 **Location:** Jct Eubank and Menaul blvds, just e.
L D

PAPPADEAUX SEAFOOD KITCHEN

Phone: 505/345-0240

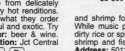

Regional Seafood
$8-$50

AAA Inspector Notes: A seafood lover's delight, the restaurant taps into a little bit of New Orleans with its Cajun dishes and elaborate menu selections. Patrons might start off with a creative choice of blackened oyster and shrimp fondeaux with crayfish and let the feast begin. While music plays in the background, patrons can dig into dirty rice or spicy gumbo loaded with seafood. Well-seasoned shrimp and fish are prepared in varied ways. **Bar:** full bar. **Address:** 5011 Pan American Frwy NE 87109 **Location:** I-25 exit 229 (Jefferson St), just s. L D

PARS CUISINE **Phone:** 505/345-5156 ⑬

Mediterranean
$6-$18

AAA Inspector Notes: This popular restaurant's exotic decor evokes a typical Middle Eastern villa. Persian and Greek dishes include chelo-kebab barg and lamb souvlaki, prepared in the traditional manner. **Bar:** beer & wine. **Address:** 4320 The 25 Way, Suite 100 87109 **Location:** I-25 exit 229 (Jefferson St), just e. L D

PAUL'S MONTEREY INN **Phone:** 505/294-1461 (77)

American
$7-$24

AAA Inspector Notes: Thick and juicy steaks, prime rib, surf and turf, ribs and shrimp-all served in ample portions-keeps this casual spot a local favorite. The setting, with dark upholstery and wall coverings, evokes a 1960s-era lounge. **Bar:** full bar. **Reservations:** suggested. **Address:** 1000 Juan Tabo Blvd NE 87112 **Location:** Just n of jct Lomas Blvd. L D

PERENNIALS RESTAURANT

Phone: 505/888-5800 ⑪

Breakfast
$9-$12

AAA Inspector Notes: A pleasant, light and bright dining room and diet-conscious menu are focuses at this eatery. The menu comprises tasty soups, salads and sandwiches, such as the Colonel Chris burger made with Angus beef. There also is a nice selection of wines. **Bar:** beer & wine. **Address:** 7636 Arroyo Del Oso Ave NE 87109 **Location:** Jct San Mateo and Osuna blvds; northwest corner; in Fiesta del Norte Center. B L

(See map & index p. 362.)

P.F. CHANG'S CHINA BISTRO
Phone: 505/344-8282 (10)

Chinese
$10-$25

AAA Inspector Notes: Trendy, upscale decor provides a pleasant backdrop for New Age Chinese dining. Appetizers, soups and salads are a meal by themselves. Vegetarian plates and sides, noodles, meins, chicken and meat dishes are created from exotic, fresh ingredients. **Bar:** full bar. **Reservations:** suggested. **Address:** 4440 The 25 Way NE 87109 **Location:** I-25 exit 230, just w. [L] [D]

QUARTERS BAR-B-QUE
Phone: 505/299-9864

Barbecue
$8-$32

AAA Inspector Notes: A homey, rustic look is what diners find at this popular eatery. Widely known for barbecue spare ribs, beef and hot links, don't pass up the chance to try the Alaskan king crab legs. Plan to save room for dessert-especially tempting to those with a sweet tooth are the mud pie and cheesecake. **Bar:** full bar. **Address:** 4516 Wyoming Blvd NE Blvd NE 87111 **Location:** I-40 exit 164 eastbound, 3 mi n; exit 164C westbound, 0.5 mi w on Lomas Blvd, then 3.3 mi n. [L] [D]

QUARTERS BAR-B-QUE
Phone: 505/897-3341

Barbecue
$7-$24

AAA Inspector Notes: Known for its barbecue, this west side location features a lively lounge area. **Bar:** full bar. **Address:** 3700 Ellison Dr NW 87114 **Location:** Jct McMahon Blvd NW and Ellison Dr, just e; near Cottonwood Mall. [L] [D]

QUARTERS BAR-B-QUE
Phone: 505/843-7505 (89)

Barbecue
$4-$45

AAA Inspector Notes: The original location of this popular local restaurant chain is near the airport and features a lively lounge scene as well as the barbecue for which they are famous. **Bar:** full bar. **Address:** 801 Yale Blvd SE 87106 **Location:** I-25 exit 223, 1 mi e on Avenida Cesar Chavez, jct Yale Blvd, just n. [L] [D]

RAGIN' SHRIMP
Phone: 505/254-1544 (80)

Cajun
$9-$18

AAA Inspector Notes: Near the University of New Mexico, this small and trendy Nob Hill eatery specializes in huge Gulf shrimp served over rice or angel hair pasta with a choice of several sauces. Also delicious are the jambalaya, chicken breast, pork tenderloin, pasta dishes and French bread. Ragin' dipping sauce complements the entrées. Retro decor and a young waitstaff attired in Gen X finery lends to this place's lively atmosphere. **Bar:** beer & wine. **Address:** 3624 Central Ave NE 87108 **Location:** I-40 exit 160, 1.7 mi s on Carlisle Blvd, then just e at Copper Ave; in Nob Hill. [L] [D]

RANCHER'S CLUB OF NEW MEXICO
Menu on AAA.com **Phone:** 505/889-8071 (38)

American
$21-$78

AAA Inspector Notes: A fine dining restaurant with an elegant lounge and dining room that, at the same time, reflects a ranch motif yet displays a cultivated, upscale ambience. The house specializes in the finest steak and seafood available, grilled over exotic woods and served by a professional staff that is well known for polished and refined service. **Bar:** full bar. **Reservations:** required. **Address:** 1901 University Blvd NE 87102 **Location:** I-40 exit 160, just n to Menaul Blvd, then 1.1 mi w; in Hilton Albuquerque. **Parking:** on-site and valet. [D]

THE RANGE CAFE
Phone: 505/293-2633 (29)

American
$8-$18

AAA Inspector Notes: This colorful café features some of the best dishes of two cultures. In addition to spicy New Mexican food, such as green chile enchiladas, the menu lists good ole American food and sandwiches. **Bar:** beer & wine. **Address:** 4401 Wyoming Blvd NE 87111 **Location:** Jct Montgomery and Wyoming blvds, just s. [B] [L] [D] CALL [M]

RICHARD'S MEXICAN RESTAURANT
Phone: 505/881-1039 (37)

Mexican
$6-$10

AAA Inspector Notes: Heart-healthful New Mexican cuisine is the specialty, and traditional favorites are prepared to be low in cholesterol and fat but high on flavor and taste. Try the delicious green chile chicken enchiladas. **Bar:** beer & wine. **Address:** 3301 Menaul Blvd NE, Suite 1 87107 **Location:** Jct Carlisle Blvd, just w; in American Square. [B] [L]

RUDY'S COUNTRY STORE AND BAR-B-QUE

Barbecue
$7-$16

For additional information, visit AAA.com

AAA Inspector Notes: This small, informal barbecue chain has a twist: The tasty food is ordered by the pound. Guests can mix and match and order three-quarters of a pound of beef with a half-pound of turkey or pork, for example. Desserts and coleslaw are prepackaged, and precooked beans accompany the meat. A drive-through window is available at most locations. **Bar:** beer only. [L] [D]

LOCATIONS:
Address: 2321 Carlisle Blvd NE 87110 **Location:** I-40 exit 160, just n. **Phone:** 505/884-4000
Address: 10136 Coors Blvd NW 87114 **Location:** Just s of jct Alameda Blvd NW. **Phone:** 505/890-7113

SADIE'S DINING ROOM
Phone: 505/345-5339 (6)

Mexican
$2-$16

AAA Inspector Notes: This popular restaurant dishes up some of the hottest New Mexican food you'll find, so expect a wait to be seated. The chicken enchilada on corn shell is wonderful. The interior is decorated in the traditional Southwestern pink and turquoise. **Bar:** full bar. **Address:** 6230 4th St NW 87107 **Location:** 0.5 mi s of jct Osuna Rd. [L] [D]

SAIGON RESTAURANT
Phone: 505/884-0706 (12)

Vietnamese
$7-$20

AAA Inspector Notes: Patrons experience the subtle, exotic flavors of Vietnam at the family-owned café, where traditional menu offerings are served in generous portions. **Bar:** beer & wine. **Address:** 6001 San Mateo Blvd NE, #D4 87109 **Location:** I-25 exit 230 (San Mateo Blvd), 0.4 mi s; jct San Mateo Blvd and Osuna Rd; in Fiesta Norte Center. [L] [D]

SANDIAGO'S MEXICAN GRILL AT THE TRAM
Phone: 505/856-6692

Mexican
$10-$26

AAA Inspector Notes: Dazzling evening city views are available from either the patio or dining room. The fish specialties are prepared in an authentic Mexican style; try the plantain-wrapped halibut for a little bit of Mexico. Save room for the heavenly chocolate flan. **Bar:** full bar. **Address:** 40 Tramway Rd NE 87122 **Location:** At eastern end of tramway access road; in same building as tram departure point. [L] [D]

(See map & index p. 362.)

SCALO NORTHERN ITALIAN GRILL
Phone: 505/255-8782 (83)

Northern Italian
$10-$29

AAA Inspector Notes: This lively restaurant's bustling kitchen makes its pasta in house and also turns out tasty salads; plenty of beef, lamb and veal creations; and fabulous desserts. Refined yet simple decor, accented by crisp white tablecloths, lends to an inviting atmosphere. Patio seating is available. This place is popular with the local business community, tourists and the students and staff of the nearby University of New Mexico. **Bar:** full bar. **Reservations:** suggested. **Address:** 3500 Central Ave SE 87106 **Location:** I-25 exit 167 (Central Ave), 2 mi e; in Nob Hill Shopping Center. L D

SCARPA'S
Phone: 505/821-1885 (9)

Italian
$7-$11

AAA Inspector Notes: Popular with the folks who work in nearby office complexes and stores, this restaurant is known for its imaginative jumbo salad and personal-size pizza. Adventurous pizza meld exotic ingredients, such as shiitake mushrooms, caramelized onions and Alaskan salmon. **Bar:** beer & wine. **Address:** 5500 Academy Rd NE 87109 **Location:** Just e of jct San Mateo Blvd. L D

SCARPA'S BRICK OVEN PIZZA
Phone: 505/323-0222 (30)

Italian
$6-$11

AAA Inspector Notes: Options for topping your thin, crispy pie range from old faves like pepperoni and fresh basil to artichoke hearts and oak-grilled chicken in the popular pizzeria, where the busy buzz is from the locals, who also drop by for beer on tap, pasta and gourmet salads. **Bar:** beer & wine. **Address:** 9700 Montgomery Blvd NE 87111 **Location:** Jct Montgomery and Eubank blvds; southeast corner. L D

SEASONS ROTISSERIE & GRILL
Phone: 505/766-5100 (42)

American
$8-$32

AAA Inspector Notes: The young, affluent clientele comes to this trendy, contemporary spot to see and be seen. Inspired by the changing seasons, the menu features imaginative culinary creations and fine wines chosen to complement them. Sunset views are spectacular from rooftop outdoor tables. **Bar:** full bar. **Reservations:** suggested. **Address:** 2031 Mountain Rd NW 87104 **Location:** Just n of Old Town; in San Felipe Plaza. L D

SIAM CAFE
Phone: 505/883-7334 (19)

Thai
$8-$11

AAA Inspector Notes: The speedy lunch buffet appeals to those with limited time. Others might prefer to order from the menu to sample the subtle or spicy flavors of Thai cuisine. In either case, the Thai iced tea is a must. **Address:** 5500 San Mateo Blvd NE, #101 87109 **Location:** I-25 exit 230, 0.6 mi s; jct Osuna Rd and San Mateo Blvd, just s. L D

STANDARD DINER
Phone: 505/243-1440 (64)

American
$8-$14

AAA Inspector Notes: Flashback in time at this upscale retro diner with a modern creative twist on comfort food favorites. The standard mac and cheese and finer loaf are house specialties along with country fried tuna with wasabi guacamole and mouthwatering fish tacos. Also on the menu are creative salads, sandwiches and burgers. **Bar:** beer & wine. **Address:** 320 Central Ave SE 87102 **Location:** I-25 exit 224A northbound; exit 224B southbound, just w; jct Central Ave and Arno St. **Parking:** on-site and street. L D

TACO SAL
Phone: 505/298-2210 (49)

Mexican
$6-$10

AAA Inspector Notes: This well-known neighborhood eatery has been on the scene for more than 40 years. Red or green chile tops off flavorful Northern New Mexican specialties. **Bar:** beer & wine. **Address:** 9621 Menaul Blvd NE 87112 **Location:** Jct Eubank and Menaul blvds; northwest corner. L D

TAJ MAHAL CUISINE OF INDIA
Menu on AAA.com **Phone:** 505/255-1994 (57)

Indian
$9-$17

AAA Inspector Notes: On the menu at this eatery are such traditional dishes as curries, tandoori, masalas, kormas and saegs. **Bar:** beer & wine. **Address:** 1430 Carlisle Blvd NE 87110 **Location:** I-40 exit 160, 0.5 mi s. L D

TEXAS LAND AND CATTLE STEAKHOUSE
Phone: 505/343-9800

Steak
$7-$25

AAA Inspector Notes: A variety of large prime steaks, delicious salads and scrumptious desserts await you at the friendly Texas ranch-style restaurant. Try the signature slow-smoked sirloin, which never fails to please, or the Caesar salad, another favorite. A Texas steakhouse means everything is bigger, from large cuts and oversize salads to potatoes and side dishes. Those not in the mood for beef can opt for chicken, quail or seafood. Dessert is an occasion. **Bar:** full bar. **Address:** 4949 Pan American Frwy NE 87109 **Location:** I-25 exit 229 (Jefferson St), just s on frontage road. L D

TROMBINO'S BISTRO ITALIANO
Phone: 505/821-5974 (8)

Italian
$8-$23

AAA Inspector Notes: Well-prepared and delicious entrées-including pasta, veal, poultry, seafood and aged steaks-are served in this locally popular restaurant's Mediterranean atmosphere. Fresh ingredients, tasty homemade breads, sauces, pizza and tempting desserts complete the menu. **Bar:** full bar. **Address:** 5415 Academy Rd NE 87109 **Location:** I-25 exit 230 (Osuna Rd), just s on San Mateo Blvd to Academy Rd, then just e. L D

TUCANOS BRAZILIAN GRILL
Phone: 505/246-9900 (61)

Brazilian
$11-$21

AAA Inspector Notes: This downtown restaurant caters to meat lovers. Casually attired servers bring multiple courses consisting of freshly cooked beef, pork, chicken and sausage to the table on long, swordlike skewers. The extensive salad bar adds to this place's popularity. **Bar:** full bar. **Address:** 110 Central Ave SW 87102 **Location:** Jct 1st St. **Parking:** on-site and street. L D

VIC'S DAILY CAFE
Phone: 505/341-9710 (4)

American
$7-$10

AAA Inspector Notes: The cafe is well known for its green chile sauce, which can be had with breakfast or lunch choices and is a particularly nice accompaniment to the chicken enchiladas. For those who prefer an American entrée, blue ribbon meatloaf is sure to please. **Address:** 3600 Osuna Rd NE, #105 87109 **Location:** I-25 exit 230 (Osuna Rd), 0.5 mi w. B L

VIVACE
Phone: 505/268-5965 (79)

Italian
$6-$20

AAA Inspector Notes: This is a small, nicely appointed trattoria offering a bounty of pasta, panini and grilled beef and chicken. Or diners may want to sample the robust bistecca Fiorentina, spaghetti carbonara, grilled yellowfin tuna or mussels steamed in Pernod. **Bar:** beer & wine. **Address:** 3118 Central Ave SE 87106 **Location:** Just e of jct Richmond Dr; in Nob Hill area. **Parking:** street only. L D

(See map & index p. 362.)

WECK'S
▼◆▼ ▼◆▼
American
$5-$9
Phone: 505/881-0019 (25)

AAA Inspector Notes: Although traditional American breakfasts are on the menu, this restaurant's morning specialties are huevos rancheros, carne adovada and burritos served with red or green chile. Portions are generous at this Northeast Heights spot. **Address:** 3913 Louisiana Blvd NE 87110 **Location:** Corner of Louisiana and Montgomery blvds; just s of Montgomery Blvd.

B L

YANNI'S MEDITERRANEAN GRILL & OPA BAR
▼◆▼ ▼◆▼
Mediterranean
$8-$35
Phone: 505/268-9250 (75)

AAA Inspector Notes: Convenient to the University of New Mexico and the Nob Hill area, this popular eatery is known for its interesting variety of healthy Mediterranean dishes. Try the delicious pasta entrées or tempting moussaka. The baklava sundae is a sinful dessert. **Bar:** full bar. **Address:** 3109 Central Ave NE 87106 **Location:** I-25 exit 224B, s to Central Ave, then 1.7 mi e. L D

YEN CHING RESTAURANT
▼◆▼
Chinese
$6-$25
Phone: 505/275-8265 (27)

AAA Inspector Notes: Long the scene of an extensive luncheon buffet, this restaurant offers guests a bit more formal of a dinner experience. All the traditional Asian favorites are served. **Bar:** beer & wine. **Address:** 4410 Wyoming Blvd NE 87111 **Location:** Jct Montgomery and Wyoming blvds; southeast corner. L D

ZEA ROTISSERIE & GRILL
▼◆▼ ▼◆▼
International
$8-$26
Phone: 505/878-9327

AAA Inspector Notes: Stylish, upscale decor and a creative menu that draws from European, American and Asian cuisines are the salient features of this popular restaurant. **Bar:** full bar. **Address:** 4800 Montgomery Blvd NE 87109 **Location:** Jct Montgomery and San Mateo blvds, just w. L D CALL 🖧M

ZINC WINE BAR & BISTRO
▼◆▼ ▼◆▼
American
$8-$28
Phone: 505/254-9462 (76)

AAA Inspector Notes: A stylish place to be seen, this bistro presents a finer-than-casual menu with French rotisserie meats as a highlight. The wine selection is legend. **Bar:** full bar. **Reservations:** suggested. **Address:** 3009 Central Ave NE 87106 **Location:** Jct Central Ave and Monte Vista Blvd, just e. **Parking:** street only.

L D

ALGODONES pop. 814

HACIENDA VARGAS BED AND BREAKFAST INN
▼◆▼ ▼◆▼
Historic Bed
& Breakfast
Rates not provided
Phone: 505/867-9115

Address: 1431 SR 313 (El Camino Real) **Location:** I-25 exit 248, 0.3 mi w, then 0.3 mi s. Located beside train tracks. **Facility:** Set along the Royal Road that once led from Santa Fe to Mexico City, this 18th-century hacienda features adobe-style architecture. 7 units. 1 story, interior corridors. **Terms:** check-in 4 pm. **Activities:** hiking trails, jogging.

ANGEL FIRE (E-4) pop. 1,216, elev. 8,415'

Nestled in the Moreno Valley of the Sangre de Cristo Mountains, Angel Fire is so named for the fiery light that flashes off its alpine peaks. At different points in time American Indians, miners, ranchers, trappers, pioneers and cowboys all called the area home.

Angel Fire was a filming location for the 1989 film "Lonesome Dove," and you can still visit the cabin built for the classic cowboy movie that saw New Mexico standing in for Montana.

Sports enthusiasts seek out the area for its year-round outdoor activities. Boating, fishing, hunting, golfing, hiking, mountain biking and horseback riding lure visitors in the warmer months, while torchlight parades, races and a web of runs (from beginner to advanced) keep boarders, skiers and snowshoers busy during the winter months.

Duffers looking to improve their game will find that golf balls travel 10 percent farther due to the high altitude. Angel Fire Resort Golf Course is one of the area's premier public courses.

Culturally, the Music from Angel Fire festival brings chamber music to the mountain community from late August to early September.

Angel Fire Chamber of Commerce: 3407 SR 434, Centro Plaza, P.O. Box 547, Angel Fire, NM 87710. **Phone:** (575) 377-6661 or (800) 446-8117.

◆GEM **VIETNAM VETERANS MEMORIAL STATE PARK** is at 34 Country Club Rd. This curvilinear structure originally was built as one family's memorial to a young son killed in an enemy ambush in Vietnam. President Ronald Reagan proclaimed it "a memorial of national significance" in November 1987. The chapel is dedicated to Vietnam War casualties. Its hilltop vantage affords views of the Sangre de Cristo Mountains and the broad Moreno Valley. **Hours:** Chapel daily 24 hours. Visitor center daily 9-5. Closed Jan. 1, Thanksgiving and Christmas. **Cost:** Donations. **Phone:** (575) 377-2293 (park office), or (575) 377-6900 (foundation).

ARROYO SECO pop. 1,785
• Hotels & Restaurants map & index p. 481

ADOBE AND STARS B & B
▼◆▼ ▼◆▼
Bed & Breakfast
Rates not provided
Phone: 575/776-2776 (16)

Address: 584 State Hwy 150 87571 **Location:** 1.1 mi ne of Arroyo Seco village, at Valdez Rd. Located in a rural area. **Facility:** The B&B offers a garden with moving sculptures and a location with wonderful Taos mountain views. The host is very relaxed with a casual manner. 8 units. 1-2 stories (no elevator), interior/exterior corridors. **Terms:** check-in 4 pm. **Activities:** whirlpool.

BIZ 🛜 ✕ 🏋 ☎ / SOME UNITS FEE 🐾 🐾 ▤

COTTONWOOD INN BED & BREAKFAST
▼◆▼ ▼◆▼
Bed & Breakfast
$125-$265
Phone: (575)776-5826 (17)

Address: 2 SR 230 87514 **Location:** On SR 150 at SR 230. **Facility:** A private balcony is just one place to relax at this inn characterized by patios, gardens with trickling fountains and gathering areas. 8 units. 2 stories (no elevator), interior/exterior corridors. **Terms:** check-in 4 pm, 2 night minimum stay - weekends, 14 day cancellation notice-fee imposed. **Activities:** hiking trails, jogging. **Fee:** massage.

BIZ 🛜 ✕ 🏋 FEE 🏋 ☎ 🛏 ▤ ▤ / SOME UNITS FEE 🐾 🐾

ARTESIA (I-5) pop. 11,301, elev. 3,379'

Artesia was named for its huge underground water supply, which is pumped to the surface via numerous artesian wells. The water irrigates thousands of acres of area farmland.

Another underground resource—oil—was discovered in 1924. This, coupled with reserves of natural gas, has bolstered Artesia's economy and made it one of New Mexico's most productive oil centers. The city also claims what was once the first underground school in the country, built to shelter about 500 students and 2,000 other citizens in the event of a nuclear attack.

Artesia Chamber of Commerce and Visitors Center: 107 N. First St., Artesia, NM 88210. **Phone:** (575) 746-2744 or (800) 658-6251.

ARTESIA HISTORICAL MUSEUM AND ART CENTER is at 505 W. Richardson Ave. Two preserved houses built at the beginning of the 20th century contain historical and cultural displays. The museum, devoted to local heritage, displays equipment used in industrial development as well as such Western paraphernalia as saddles, barbed wire and clothing. The art center next to the museum offers traveling exhibits and work by area artists. **Time:** Allow 30 minutes minimum. **Hours:** Tues.-Fri. 9-noon and 1-5, Sat. 1-5. Closed major holidays. **Cost:** Free. **Phone:** (575) 748-2390.

ARTESIA INN   Phone: 575/746-9801
Motel
$75-$110
Address: 1820 S 1st St 88210 **Location:** 1.5 mi s on US 285. **Facility:** 34 units. 1 story, exterior corridors. *Bath:* shower only. **Pool(s):** outdoor. **Free Special Amenities:** local telephone calls and high-speed Internet.

BEST WESTERN PECOS INN   Phone: (575)748-3324
Hotel
$109-$129
AAA Benefit: Members save up to 20%, plus 10% bonus points with Best Western Rewards®.
Address: 2209 W Main St 88210 **Location:** 1.5 mi w on US 82. **Facility:** 82 units, some two bedrooms and kitchens. 2 stories (no elevator), interior corridors. **Amenities:** *Some:* high-speed Internet. **Pool(s):** heated indoor. **Activities:** sauna, whirlpool, exercise room. **Guest Services:** valet and coin laundry. **Free Special Amenities:** full breakfast and high-speed Internet.

LEGACY INN & SUITES ARTESIA   Phone: (575)748-3904
Hotel
$80-$110
Address: 2210 W Main St 88210 **Location:** 1.6 mi w of jct US 82 and 285. **Facility:** 40 units. 2 stories (no elevator), interior corridors. **Terms:** cancellation fee imposed. **Amenities:** high-speed Internet. **Pool(s):** heated outdoor. **Activities:** exercise room. **Guest Services:** valet and coin laundry. **Free Special Amenities:** full breakfast and high-speed Internet.

HOTEL ARTESIA   Phone: 575/746-2066
[fyi] Not evaluated. **Address:** 203 N 2nd St 88210 **Location:** Jct US 285 and Main St, just n. Facilities, services, and decor characterize a mid-scale property.

WHERE TO EAT

LA FONDA RESTAURANT   Phone: 575/746-9411
Mexican
$7-$17
AAA Inspector Notes: This family restaurant combines a Southwestern atmosphere with American fare. Also on the menu are regional and Mexican selections, including flautas, chimichangas and tacos. Portions are large. The luncheon buffet is a popular offering. **Address:** 206 W Main St 88210 **Location:** Center. [L] [D]

AZTEC (D-2) pop. 6,763, elev. 5,623'

In 1948 an investigator named Frank Scully gathered information from a variety of sources about a purported alien crash-landing in the area. While there is no evidence a real-life Mulder assisted Scully in the investigations, modern-day X-Files enthusiasts gather to swap alien stories and theories at the annual Aztec UFO Symposium in March. Tours of the nearby crash site are available during the symposium.

Originally founded by pioneers in 1890 along the Animas River and across from ancient pueblo ruins, Aztec today lays claims to those ruins as a popular day trip. Another area attraction is the Aztec Arches, a series of natural rock formations that were considered sacred by the Puebloan Indians.

Aztec Chamber of Commerce and Visitors Center: 110 N. Ash St., Aztec, NM 87410. **Phone:** (505) 334-9551.

Self-guiding tours: Information on walking tours of the city's historic sites is available from the Aztec Museum & Pioneer Village.

AZTEC MUSEUM & PIONEER VILLAGE is 1 mi. s. of Aztec Ruins National Monument at 125 N. Main Ave. The historical museum of northwest New Mexico consists of 14 original and replicated structures dating from the 1880s forward. The outdoor oil and gas exhibit depicts the history of the industry. Farm and ranch equipment used by early settlers also is displayed. **Hours:** Tues.-Sat. 10-4, May-Oct. Closed major holidays. **Cost:** Donations. **Phone:** (505) 334-9829.

STEP BACK INN   Phone: 505/334-1200
Motel
$75-$98
Address: 123 W Aztec Blvd 87410 **Location:** On SR 516, jct US 550. **Facility:** 39 units. 2 stories (no elevator), interior corridors. *Bath:* shower only.

WHERE TO EAT

THE MAIN STREET BISTRO   Phone: 505/334-0109
American
$6-$11
AAA Inspector Notes: This cheerful cafe serves a variety of tasty sandwiches, soups and salads in a relaxed atmosphere. **Address:** 122 N Main St 87410 **Location:** US 550, follow signs to historic downtown; jct Main and Blanco sts. [B] [L] [K]

RUBIO'S

Mexican
$7-$22

[L] [D]

Phone: 505/334-0599
AAA Inspector Notes: This lively restaurant serves generous portions of flavorful Mexican favorites. Save room for the fluffy sopaipilla drizzled with honey. **Bar:** full bar. **Address:** 116 S Main St 87410 **Location:** Center.

AZTEC RUINS NATIONAL MONUMENT (D-2)

In the northwest corner of New Mexico, just north of Aztec on US 516 to Ruins Road, is one of the largest and best preserved Ancestral Pueblo ruins in the Southwest. The misnomer Aztec was applied by early settlers who incorrectly inferred the builders' identity. The largest of these sandstone pueblos, the West Ruin, was built about 1110; it contained more than 500 rooms, some of which remain intact. Several smaller structures adjoin the main ruin.

A large ceremonial building, the Great Kiva, is the only reconstruction of its kind in North America. The visitor center features artifacts found during excavations. A 25-minute videotape presentation introduces visitors to the region's pre-Columbian Ancestral Puebloan history. Daily 8-6, Memorial Day-Labor Day; 8-5, rest of year. Closed Jan. 1, Thanksgiving and Christmas. Admission (valid for 7 days) $5; free (ages 0-15). **Cards:** DS, MC, VI. Phone (505) 334-6174.

BANDELIER NATIONAL MONUMENT (B-3)

Just 50 miles northwest of Santa Fe via US 285 to Pojoaque, then west on SR 502 and south on SR 4, this 50-square-mile monument is on the Pajarito Plateau in the rugged canyon and mesa country of northern New Mexico. Remnants of an Ancestral Puebloan community established 7 or 8 centuries ago include pueblo and cliff dwellings.

The most accessible sites consist of cave rooms hewn out of the soft tuff rock, houses built on the talus slopes and a circular community village. Bandelier also contains 33,000 acres of designated wilderness, including 70 miles of hiking trails. Offering views of archeological sites, the 1.2-mile round-trip paved Main Loop Trail starts at the visitor center and includes ladders that allow visitors to climb into cavates (alcoves). Free permits, required for overnight back-country travel, can be obtained at the visitor center. Pets or bicycles are not permitted on any trails in the monument.

In summer a variety of ranger-led activities are offered including guided walks, interpretive programs and craft demonstrations. The Nightwalk tour of archeological sites is conducted largely in silence so as to appreciate the nighttime solitude.

An introductory slide program and a small museum in the visitor center provide orientation to the area. One- and 2-hour self-guiding walking tours of the principal sites start at the visitor center. Monument open daily dawn-dusk. Visitor center open daily 8-6, Memorial Day-Labor Day; 9-5:30, mid-Mar. to day before Memorial Day and day after Labor Day-early Oct.; 9-4:30, rest of year. Closed Jan. 1 and Christmas. Admission $12 per private vehicle. Visitor center free. Nightwalk tours $6; $3 (ages 6-15); reservations are required. **Cards:** MC, VI. Visitors are advised to phone ahead for current road conditions before visiting the site. Phone (505) 672-3861, ext. 517.

BELÉN (G-3) pop. 7,269, elev. 4,808'

Belén, which in Spanish means "Bethlehem," was founded by Capt. Don Diego Torres and Antonio Salazar in 1740. By the late 19th century, the farming community was a major hub on the Atchison, Topeka and Santa Fe Railroad.

HARVEY HOUSE MUSEUM is at 104 N. First St. The building served as a restaurant for Santa Fe Railroad passengers 1910-39. Exhibits depict railroad and town history. A model train display and changing exhibits are offered. **Time:** Allow 1 hour, 30 minutes minimum. **Hours:** Tues.-Sat. 12:30-3:30, Sun. 1-3. Closed major holidays. **Cost:** Donations. **Phone:** (505) 861-0581.

HOLIDAY INN EXPRESS

Hotel
$97-$98

Phone: (505)861-5000
Address: 2110 Camino del Llano 87002 **Location:** I-25 exit 191, just w. **Facility:** 63 units. 2 stories, interior corridors. **Terms:** 3 day cancellation notice-fee imposed. **Amenities:** high-speed Internet. **Pool(s):** heated outdoor. **Activities:** whirlpool, exercise room. **Guest Services:** valet and coin laundry.

CALL / SOME UNITS

BERNALILLO (F-3) pop. 8,320, elev. 5,052'

Still essentially a Spanish and American Indian farming community and livestock shipping point, Bernalillo (bern-a-LEE-oh) nevertheless is growing as the Albuquerque metropolitan area expands northward along the Rio Grande. The first settlers—descendants of Bernal Díaz del Castillo, chronicler of Hernando Cortés' conquest of Mexico—arrived in 1698.

Remnants of times past remain. Northwest of Bernalillo is the pueblo of Santa Ana and the Spanish-American village of San Ysidro. The Santa Ana Pueblo Mission is one of the oldest missions in the United States. Open to visitors only on its feast day, July 26, it is believed to have been built by Spanish missionary Fray Juan de Rosas, who accompanied Juan de Oñate on his expedition to New Mexico in 1598.

In September Bernalillo hosts the New Mexico Wine Festival, which features wine tastings, food, music and arts and crafts.

Sandoval County Visitor Center: 264 S. Camino del Pueblo, P.O. Box 40, Bernalillo, NM 87004. **Phone:** (505) 867-8687 or (800) 252-0191.

CORONADO STATE MONUMENT is 2 mi. w. on US 550 (old SR 44) to 485 Kuaua Rd. The 98-acre site includes ruins of the Tiwa pueblo of Kuaua. Lured by the Rio Grande's fertile land, an ancient tribe first settled Kuaua around 1300. The area is named for Francisco Vázquez de Coronado, whose army camped here in 1540 while searching for the fabled Cities of Gold. A kiva excavated in the 1930s features many layers of pre-Columbian art, some of which is displayed in the visitor center.

Hours: Wed.-Mon. 8:30-5. Closed major holidays. **Cost:** $3; free (ages 0-16). Combination ticket with Jémez State Monument *(see Jémez Springs p. 419)* $5. **Phone:** (505) 867-5351.

DAYS INN BERNALILLO
Phone: (505)771-7000

Hotel
$58-$165

Address: 107 N Camino del Pueblo 87004 **Location:** I-25 exit 242, just w. **Facility:** 56 units. 3 stories. interior corridors. **Amenities:** high-speed Internet, safes (fee). **Pool(s):** heated indoor. **Activities:** whirlpool, exercise room. **Guest Services:** coin laundry. **Free Special Amenities: expanded continental breakfast and high-speed Internet.**

SAVE | ⛓ | 🛆 | BIZ | 📶 | 🖵 | / SOME UNITS | FEE 🐾 | 🗗 | 📠

HOLIDAY INN EXPRESS-BERNALILLO
Phone: (505)867-1600

Hotel
$70-$190

Address: 119 Bell Ln 87004 **Location:** I-25 exit 242, just w. **Facility:** 70 units. 3 stories, interior corridors. **Terms:** 3 day cancellation notice. **Amenities:** high-speed Internet. **Pool(s):** heated Indoor/outdoor. **Activities:** whirlpool, exercise room. **Guest Services:** valet and coin laundry. **Free Special Amenities: full breakfast and high-speed Internet.**

SAVE | ⛓ | CALL 🛗 | 🛆 | BIZ | 📶 | 🗙 | 🖵 | / SOME UNITS | 🗗 | 📠

HYATT REGENCY TAMAYA RESORT AND SPA
Phone: (505)867-1234

Resort Hotel
$99-$389

HYATT
HOTELS & RESORTS

AAA Benefit: Members save 10% or more everyday.

Address: 1300 Tuyuna Tr 87004 **Location:** I-25 exit 242, 1 mi w on SR 44 to Tamaya Blvd, then 1 mi n, follow signs. **Facility:** Nestled along the Rio Grande in a secluded location, the luxury resort boasts incredible views and well-appointed guest units. 350 units. 4 stories, interior corridors. **Parking:** on-site (fee) and valet. **Terms:** check-in 4 pm, 7 day cancellation notice-fee imposed. **Amenities:** safes. *Fee:* video games, high-speed Internet. **Dining:** 4 restaurants. **Pool(s):** 3 heated outdoor. **Activities:** saunas, whirlpools, steamrooms, 2 tennis courts, recreation programs in season, bicycles, jogging, playground, horseshoes, exercise room, spa. *Fee:* golf-18 holes, horseback riding. **Guest Services:** valet laundry, area transportation-Santa Ana Casino & golf course. **Free Special Amenities: high-speed Internet and children's activities.**

SAVE | ECO | ⛓ | 🍸 | ⛳ | CALL 🛗 | 🛆 | BIZ | 📶 | 🗗 | 🖵 | / SOME UNITS | FEE 🐾

MOTEL 6 BERNALILLO
Phone: 505/771-9500

Hotel
Rates not provided

Address: 210 N Hill Rd 87004 **Location:** I-25 exit 242, just w. **Facility:** 57 units. 3 stories, interior corridors. **Activities:** exercise room. **Guest Services:** coin laundry.

⛓ | BIZ | 📶 | 🗗 | 📠 | / SOME UNITS | FEE 🐾

WHERE TO EAT

ABUELITA'S NEW MEXICAN RESTAURANT
Phone: 505/867-9988

Mexican
$6-$10

AAA Inspector Notes: Abuelita means grandma in Spanish, and this unpretentious cafe uses Grandma's recipes for its traditional New Mexican dishes. Tamales, enchiladas and carne adovada are good enough to eat every day. **Bar:** beer & wine. **Address:** 621 Camino del Pueblo 87004 **Location:** I-25 exit 242, 0.5 mi w on US 550, then 0.7 mi s. B L D

FLYING STAR CAFE
Phone: 505/404-2100

American
$6-$16

AAA Inspector Notes: Fresh-from-scratch cooking techniques employed by the kitchen staff use minimally processed foods, with a focus on organic, local, natural and humanely farmed ingredients. Breakfast is served all day and for lunch and dinner you'll find soups, salads, sandwiches, burgers and a wide variety of entrées. Save room for the luscious house-baked desserts. **Bar:** beer & wine. **Address:** 200 S Camino del Pueblo 87004 **Location:** I-25 exit 242, just s; jct Camino del Pueblo and US 550. B L D

PRAIRIE STAR
Phone: 505/867-3327

American
$19-$32

AAA Inspector Notes: Ideal for special occasions, the restaurant affords guests breathtaking views of the Sandia Mountains and Rio Grande Valley. Imaginative, skillfully prepared cuisine blends nouvelle American and Asian influences, as well as the flavors and spices used in traditional New Mexican cuisine. The result is an exciting and unforgettable fine dining experience. **Bar:** full bar. **Reservations:** suggested. **Address:** 288 Prairie Star Rd 87004 **Location:** I-25 exit 242, 2.2 mi w on US 550 to Tamaya Blvd, then 0.5 mi n. D

THE RANGE CAFE
Phone: 505/867-1700

American
$8-$16

AAA Inspector Notes: This colorful, lively eatery features a Hoosier tenderloin, New Mexican food, pasta preparations and good ol' American favorites, as well as a fine selection of sandwiches. This spot is a good meeting place for coffee and scrumptious made-in-house desserts. **Bar:** full bar. **Address:** 925 Camino del Pueblo 87004 **Location:** I-25 exit 242, 1 mi s; exit 240 to Camino del Pueblo, then 0.5 mi n. **Parking:** street only. B L D

Breakfast/Lunch/Dinner/Bar & Bakery/Wine & Gift Shop

BLOOMFIELD (E-2) pop. 8,112, elev. 5,453'
• Hotels p. 392 • Restaurants p. 392

Bloomfield was settled about 1876 and quickly became a classic Wild West town, complete with a gang of rustlers headed by its own ex-sheriff. The gang operated openly, marketing stolen beef through its own butcher shop. After the gang's decline, outlawry found haven at Blancett's Saloon, which attracted gunmen from throughout the San Juan Basin.

That violent era passed unmourned. By the early 20th century residents were more interested in stimulating agriculture through irrigation, an endeavor that persists. Navajo Reservoir, 25 miles northeast via US 64 and SR 511, is the source of much of the area's irrigation water. Navajo Lake

State Park, surrounding the reservoir in Navajo Dam, offers recreational opportunities *(see Recreation Chart)*.

Nearby oil and gas reserves contribute significantly to the town's economy.

Bloomfield Chamber of Commerce: 224 W. Broadway Ave., Bloomfield, NM 87413. **Phone:** (505) 632-0880.

SALMON RUIN is 2 mi. w. on US 64. The site was built in the late 11th century by people from the Chaco culture *(see Chaco Culture National Historical Park p. 396)*. The E-shaped masonry complex measuring 450 feet along the back wall and 150 feet along the arms features an elevated kiva in the center of the pueblo and an excavated great kiva. Some of the more than 1 million artifacts recovered are displayed in San Juan County Archaeological Research Center and Library, next to the ruin. **Hours:** Mon.-Fri. 8-5, Sat.-Sun. 9-5, May-Oct.; Mon.-Fri. 8-5, Sat. 9-5, Sun. noon-5, rest of year. **Cost:** (Includes Heritage Park) $3; $2 (ages 60+); $1 (ages 6-16). **Phone:** (505) 632-2013. 🎫

Heritage Park is 2 mi. w. on US 64 at 6131 US 64 at Salmon Ruin. Offering a glimpse into the lifestyles and cultures of the San Juan Valley, the park features Navajo log homes, Apache teepees and a Basketmaker pithouse—a semi-underground house that conserved heat in winter and remained cool in summer. Visitors can examine ancient figures etched into stone and view the unusual construction of the Salmon homestead, built about 1900. **Phone:** (505) 632-2013.

BEST WESTERN PLUS TERRITORIAL INN & SUITES
　　　　　　　　　　　　　　Phone: (505)632-9100
▼▼▼▼▼
Hotel
$105-$129

AAA Benefit: Members save up to 20%, plus 10% bonus points with Best Western Rewards®.

Address: 415 S Bloomfield Blvd 87413 **Location:** Just s of jct US 64 and 550. **Facility:** 65 units. 3 stories, interior corridors. **Amenities:** high-speed Internet. **Pool(s):** heated indoor. **Activities:** whirlpool, exercise room. **Guest Services:** coin laundry. **Free Special Amenities:** local telephone calls and high-speed Internet.

[SAVE] [🍴⁺] [🏊] [BIZ] [📶] [❓] [🖨] [🖵]

SUPER 8　　　　　　　　**Phone:** (505)632-8886
▼▼▼ ▼▼▼
Motel
$49-$76

Address: 525 W Broadway Blvd 87413 **Location:** Jct of US 64 and 550. **Facility:** 42 units. 2 stories (no elevator), interior corridors. **Terms:** 10 day cancellation notice-fee imposed.

Guest Services: coin laundry.
[🍴⁺] [📶] [🖵] / SOME UNITS FEE [🐾]

WHERE TO EAT

ROADSIDE RESTAURANT　　　**Phone:** 505/632-9940
◆
American
$7-$15

AAA Inspector Notes: This down-home restaurant is a favorite of locals and travelers alike. An interesting and extensive collection of Coca-Cola collectibles is showcased. **Address:** 319 S Bloomfield Blvd 87413 **Location:** Just s of jct US 64 and 550. [B] [L] [D]

CAPITAN (H-4) pop. 1,489, elev. 6,351'

Capitan began to flourish in 1897 when the El Paso and Northeastern Railway built a line to nearby coal reserves. After the mines were depleted and the railroad abandoned its branch, Capitan became a business center for farmers, ranchers and visitors to the recreation lands of Lincoln National Forest *(see place listing p. 427)*.

SMOKEY BEAR HISTORICAL PARK is on US 380. Exhibits trace the history of Smokey Bear and the government's efforts to combat forest fires; a 10-minute film is shown several times per hour. Having survived a devastating fire in 1950, Smokey was found clinging to a burned tree in Lincoln National Forest and became the national symbol for wildfire prevention. He died in 1976 and is buried in the park. **Hours:** Daily 9-5. Closed Jan. 1, Thanksgiving and Christmas. **Cost:** $2; $1 (ages 7-12). **Phone:** (575) 354-2748. 🎫

CAPULIN VOLCANO NATIONAL MONUMENT (D-5)

Three miles north of US 64/87 and Capulin on SR 325, Capulin Volcano National Monument contains one of the best examples of a volcanic cinder cone in the nation. About 60,000 years ago ash, cinders and lava erupted and formed a classic cinder cone that stands more than 1,000 feet above the surrounding prairie. Today, a 2-mile road winds up the volcano, and five trails lead into the crater and around the rim. The view from the summit includes the Rocky Mountains, volcanic features of the Raton-Clayton Volcanic Field, and the distant horizons of Colorado, Oklahoma and Texas. Ranger-led programs are offered in summer.

The visitor center offers information and a 10-minute videotape program. Pets are not allowed on trails. Road to the crater rim, park and visitor center open daily 8-5:30, Memorial Day weekend-Labor Day; 8-4:30, rest of year. Closed Jan. 1, Thanksgiving and Christmas. Admission (valid for 7 days) $5 per private vehicle. **Cards:** AX, DI, DS, MC, VI. Phone (575) 278-2201.

Are we meeting your travel needs?

TourBook Comments

If your visit to an establishment listed in a AAA TourBook guide doesn't meet your expectations, tell us about it.

Complete an easy online form at **AAA.com/TourBookComments.**

CARLSBAD (I-5) pop. 26,138, elev. 3,111'
• Restaurants p. 394

The fields of cotton, alfalfa and vegetables that surround Carlsbad are made possible by the U.S. Bureau of Reclamation's system of dams and canals, which irrigates 25,000 acres. The city also benefits from the rich neighboring oil and gas fields and potash mines as well as its proximity to Carlsbad Caverns National Park *(see place listing p. 394).* Lake Carlsbad *(see Recreation Chart)* offers fishing, boating and water sports.

Residents along the Pecos River decorate their houses, yards and docks with Christmas lights for ❄ Christmas on the Pecos, an annual celebration lasting from Thanksgiving weekend through New Year's Eve. Nighttime pontoon boat tours make it impossible to *not* get into the holiday spirit.

Carlsbad Chamber of Commerce: 302 S. Canal St., Carlsbad, NM 88220. **Phone:** (575) 887-6516 or (866) 822-9226.

CARLSBAD MUSEUM AND ART CENTER is 1 blk. w. of Canal St. (US 285) at 418 W. Fox St. in Halagueno Arts Park. Established in 1931, this municipal museum houses local and regional history displays, archeological specimens, contemporary and Southwestern art, Peruvian and Pueblo pottery and pioneer ranching artifacts. The McAdoo Room features paintings by the founders of the Taos Society of Articto. Changing exhibits range from works by local artists to 3D photography of local cave explorations and cultural exhibits produced by the Smithsonian Institution. **Time:** Allow 1 hour minimum. **Hours:** Mon.-Sat. 10-5. Closed major holidays. **Cost:** Free. **Phone:** (575) 887-0276.

LIVING DESERT ZOO AND GARDENS STATE PARK stands atop the Ocotillo Hills off US 285. Dedicated to the interpretation of the Chihuahuan Desert, this living museum displays some 40 native animal species and hundreds of succulents from around the world. Endangered Mexican gray wolves are featured as part of a species conservation exhibit. **Hours:** Daily 8-5, Memorial Day weekend-Labor Day; 9-5, rest of year. Last admission 90 minutes before closing. Closed Christmas. **Cost:** $5;

$3 (ages 7-12). **Phone:** (575) 887-5516.

BEST WESTERN STEVENS INN   Phone: (575)887-2851

Hotel
$104-$126

AAA Benefit: Members save up to 20%, plus 10% bonus points with Best Western Rewards®.

Address: 1829 S Canal St 88220 **Location:** 1 mi s on US 62, 180 and 285. **Facility:** 220 units, some kitchens. 1-2 stories (no elevator), exterior corridors. **Dining:** The Flume Restaurant, see separate listing, entertainment. **Pool(s):** outdoor. **Activities:** exercise room. **Guest Services:** valet and coin laundry. **Free Special Amenities: full breakfast and high-speed Internet.**

SAVE ✈ ❌ ❚❙ ▼ 🏊 BIZ 📶 🔌 📺 💻 / SOME UNITS FEE 🐾

HAMPTON INN & SUITES   Phone: (575)725-7500

Hotel
$139-$299

AAA Benefit: Members save up to 10% everyday!

Address: 120 Esperanza Cir 88220 **Location:** Jct US 285. **Facility:** 85 units. 4 stories, interior corridors. **Terms:** 1-7 night minimum stay, cancellation fee imposed. **Amenities:** high-speed Internet. **Pool(s):** heated indoor. **Activities:** whirlpool, exercise room. **Guest Services:** coin laundry.

❚❙➕ CALL 📶 🏊 BIZ 📶 ❌ 🔌 📺 💻

HOLIDAY INN EXPRESS & SUITES

Phone: 575/234-1252

Hotel
Rates not provided

Address: 22101 W Pierce St 88220 **Location:** N on US 285. **Facility:** 80 units. 3 stories, interior corridors. **Amenities:** high-speed Internet. **Pool(s):** heated indoor. **Activities:** sauna, exercise room. **Guest Services:** coin laundry. *(See ad this page.)*

❚❙➕ CALL 📶 🏊 BIZ 📶 ❌ 🔌 📺 💻

U.S. TRAVELERS INN & SUITES   Phone: (575)887-1994

Hotel
$90-$100

Address: 2429 W Pierce St 88220 **Location:** N on US 285. Across from medical center. **Facility:** 54 units. 2 stories (no elevator), interior corridors. **Pool(s):** heated indoor. **Activities:** whirlpool, limited exercise equipment.

CALL 📶 🏊 BIZ 📶 ❌ 🔌 📺 💻

THE TRINITY HOTEL   Phone: 575/234-9891

[fyi] Not evaluated. **Address:** 201 S Canal St 88220 **Location:** Jct Fox St. Facilities, services, and decor characterize a mid-scale property.

▼ *See AAA listing this page* ▼

STAY IMPRESSED.

Holiday Inn Express & Suites®
2210 I W Pierce Street
Carlsbad, NM 88220
575-234-1252
holidayinnexpress.com/carlsbadnm

©2010 InterContinental Hotels Group. All rights reserved. Most hotels are independently owned and/or operated. Stay You.™ is a registered trademark of Six Continents Hotels, Inc.

STAY YOU.™

WHERE TO EAT

BAMBOO GARDEN
▼▼ ▼▼
Chinese
$6-$13

Phone: 575/887-5145
AAA Inspector Notes: Diners can choose from the house specialty duck, volcano shrimp and other Chinese dishes. **Address:** 1511 S Canal St 88220 **Location:** 0.7 mi s on US 62, 180 and 285.

L D

THE FLUME RESTAURANT
▼▼ ▼▼
American
$6-$25

Phone: 575/887-2851
AAA Inspector Notes: Although prime rib is the specialty, this restaurant also offers a choice of seafood, Mexican and pasta dishes. The salad bar is served with each entrée. **Bar:** full bar. **Address:** 1829 S Canal St 88220 **Location:** 1 mi s on US 62, 180 and 285; in Best Western Stevens Inn. B L D CALL &M

THE TRINITY RESTAURANT
▼▼ ▼▼
American
$8-$21

Phone: 575/234-9891
AAA Inspector Notes: The upscale chic atmosphere in this renovated bank building features tall ceilings and sparkling chandeliers. The menu offers a selection of entrées as well as a luscious tiramisu. **Bar:** beer & wine. **Address:** 201 S Canal St 88220 **Location:** Jct Fox; center; in The Trinity Hotel. **Historic**

B L D

CARLSBAD CAVERNS NATIONAL PARK (I-4)

Elevations in the park range from 3,596 ft. in the southeastern corner to 6,368 ft. in the southwestern region. Refer to AAA maps for additional elevation information.

Carlsbad Caverns National Park is 20 miles southwest of Carlsbad off US 62/180. The park covers 46,776 acres in the rugged foothills of the Guadalupe Mountains, with miles of caves cutting through a Permian-age fossil reef. Among more than 117 known caves is Lechuguilla, thought to be the nation's deepest limestone cavern. The park's showpiece is Carlsbad Cavern, a series of enormous rooms that make up one of the world's largest caves.

Unlike most limestone caves that form when surface water flows through cracks in the rock, these passageways in the Guadalupe Mountains are the rare product of sulfuric acid. A hydrogen sulfide gas solution rose from petroleum deposits thousands of feet below the surface and mixed with the water table to create an aggressive chemical that dissolved holes in the subterranean limestone. As the mountains rose over a period of 20 million years, ground water drained from the caves, revealing the wonders of Carlsbad.

A steep, paved trail leads into the cavern's natural entrance, which measures 90 feet wide and 40 feet high. The cavern has more than 30 miles of surveyed subterranean corridors and great chambers. Formations range from small, delicate growths resembling plants to massive stalagmites, stalactites and columns. Many are tinted by iron and other minerals present in the limestone. Highlights include Bat Cave, Devil's Spring, Iceberg Rock, Green Lake Overlook and the Boneyard, a maze of limestone rock reminiscent of Swiss cheese.

The 8-acre Big Room, one of the most impressive chambers, has a 255-foot ceiling. Its clear pools contain limestone masses resembling lily pads. Other formations evoke an atmosphere of snow-banked forests, adding to the tranquil beauty of the cavern.

Every evening from mid-May to mid-October, hundreds of thousands of bats emerge from Carlsbad Cavern's uppermost chamber at dusk to feed on flying insects. Park rangers give a pre-flight talk in an amphitheater at the mouth of the cave. The flight outward lasts a half-hour to 2 hours; the bats return near dawn. Cameras, cellular phones and other electronic devices are prohibited. During the day, bats hang head down from the walls and ceilings of a portion of the cavern not open to visitors. At the ▽ Carlsbad Caverns Bat Flight Breakfast in mid-summer, visitors gather at the park just before dawn to watch the bats' spectacular return flight.

General Information and Activities

The park is open all year, except Christmas. The visitor center is open daily 8-7 (cave tours are offered 8:30-5), Memorial Day weekend-Labor Day; 8-5 (cave tours are offered 8:30-3:30), rest of year. Last cave entry via natural entrance is 1 hour, 30 minutes before closing. Visitors may explore Carlsbad Cavern on two self-guiding routes, the Natural Entrance and the Big Room, and return to the surface by elevator. The Big Room route is recommended for visitors who are short on time or who prefer a less strenuous walk.

A brief orientation is presented prior to tours. Interpretive signs explain cavern features, history and geology, and an audio guide providing descriptive commentary is available to rent. Additional activities include ranger talks, self-guiding nature trails and a desert automobile drive.

Guided cave tours *(see Carlsbad Caverns Guided Tours attraction listing)* are led by park rangers and range from easy walks to difficult crawls and climbs. These tours fill quickly in the summer and are available by reservation only.

The visitor center includes educational exhibits about the area's geology, biology, history and archeology; works of art depicting cave features; and original Ansel Adams photographs. A half-mile self-guiding desert nature trail begins near the cave entrance.

The 9.5-mile Walnut Canyon Desert Drive, a one-way loop drive over a graded gravel road, offers views of Rattlesnake Canyon and upper Walnut Canyon; the loop is not maintained for low-clearance vehicles. A permit is required for overnight back-country trips; inquire at the visitor center for hiking information. *See Recreation Chart.*

The temperature underground is a constant 56 F. A sweater and flat-heeled shoes with rubber soles are recommended. Baby strollers are not permitted inside the caves. Flash and time-exposure photography is allowed, but all photographs must be taken from paved trails. Food is available but is not permitted on cave trails. **Note:** To prevent the spread of fungus that causes a deadly disease to bats, visitors entering park caves may be screened; some clothing and equipment may not be permitted or disinfection may be required.

ADMISSION to the park area and the visitor center without entrance to the caves is free. Cave admission (valid for 3 days) including the Natural Entrance and Big Room self-guiding routes $6; free (ages 0-15). Ranger-led tours $7-$20; $3.50-$10 (ages 3-15); age restrictions may apply. Audio guide rental $4. **Cards:** DS, MC, VI. **PETS** (except Seeing Eye dogs) are not permitted inside caves. The visitor center provides kennels for $6 per pet.

ADDRESS inquiries to the Superintendent, Carlsbad Caverns National Park, 3225 National Parks Hwy., Carlsbad, NM 88220; phone (575) 785-2232.

CARLSBAD CAVERNS GUIDED TOURS depart from various sites in Carlsbad Caverns National Park. Offered in addition to the Natural Entrance and Big Room self-guiding tours of Carlsbad Caverns are six guided tours led by park rangers. Tours range from easy to difficult, and participants must supply their own equipment, batteries and flashlights for some routes. **Note:** Sturdy hiking boots are required. Tours fill quickly in the summer. **Hours:** Departure times and tour lengths vary. **Cost:** Fees, group sizes and age restrictions vary. Reservations are required. **Phone:** (877) 444-6777 for reservations.

Hall of the White Giant Tour departs from the Carlsbad Caverns Visitor Center 7 mi. off US 62/180. This strenuous 4-hour guided tour leads to a remote chamber. Participants must crawl long distances, squeeze through crevices such as the tight Matlock's Pinch and climb a slippery passage. **Note:** Hiking boots or other sturdy shoes, kneepads, gloves and four new AA batteries are required; a long-sleeved shirt and long pants are recommended. Backpacks are not permitted. Headlamps are provided. The tour is limited to eight participants. **Hours:** Tours depart Sat. at 1. **Cost:** (In addition to cavern admission) $20; $10 (ages 12-15). Ages 0-11 are not permitted. Reservations are required. **Phone:** (877) 444-6777.

King's Palace Tour departs from the underground rest area in Carlsbad Cavern. This 1.5-hour tour covers 1 mile and descends to the deepest part of the cave open to the public, 830 feet below the surface. Cave formations include helictites, draperies, columns and soda straws. **Note:** The tour is limited to 55 participants. **Hours:** Tours are given daily at 10, 11, 2 and 3, Memorial Day weekend-Labor Day; at 10 and 2, rest of year. **Cost:** (In addition to cavern

admission) $8; $4 (ages 4-15). Ages 0-3 are not permitted. Reservations are required. **Phone:** (877) 444-6777.

Left Hand Tunnel Tour departs from the Carlsbad Caverns Visitor Center 7 mi. off US 62/180. This 2-hour lantern tour highlights cavern history and geology along a half-mile route. Sights along this easy tour include cave pools and fossils. **Note:** Walking shoes are required. Backpacks are not permitted. Lanterns are provided. The tour is limited to 15 participants. **Hours:** Tours depart daily at 9. **Cost:** (In addition to cavern admission) $7; $3.50 (ages 6-15). Ages 0-5 are not permitted. Reservations are required. **Phone:** (877) 444-6777.

Lower Cave Tour departs from the Carlsbad Caverns Visitor Center 7 mi. off US 62/180. Entered by descending a 10-foot rope and 50 feet of ladders, this area of the cavern contains beautiful formations and evidence of early exploration. The Rookery is a showcase for cave pearls. **Note:** The 3-hour tour involves scrambling and heights and is moderately strenuous. Hiking boots, four new AA batteries and gloves are required; helmets and headlamps are provided. Backpacks are not permitted. The tour is limited to 12 participants. **Hours:** Tours depart Mon.-Fri. at 1. **Cost:** (In addition to cavern admission) $20; $10 (ages 12-15). Ages 0-11 are not permitted. Reservations are required. **Phone:** (877) 444-6777.

Slaughter Canyon Cave Tour departs 23 mi. s.w. of the Carlsbad Caverns Visitor Center on US 62/180 to CR 418, following signs to the cave entrance. Dramatic formations in this undeveloped cave include the 89-foot-high Monarch, the sparkling Christmas Tree column and the delicate Chinese Wall.

   Note: An unpaved, half-mile trail leads from the parking area to the cave, climbing 500 feet; allow 45 minutes to make this steep and strenuous climb. Hiking boots or other sturdy shoes, two C-cell flashlights with new batteries and water are required. The 2-hour tour is limited to 25 participants. **Hours:** Tours depart daily at 10, Memorial Day weekend-Labor Day; Sat.-Sun. at 10, rest of year. Hikers should arrive at the cave entrance 15 minutes prior to tour time. **Cost:** $15; $7.50 (ages 8-15). Ages 0-7 are not permitted. Reservations are required. **Phone:** (877) 444-6777.

Spider Cave Tour departs from the Carlsbad Caverns Visitor Center 7 mi. off US 62/180. This three-dimensional maze includes tight crawlways, canyonlike passages and bizarre formations. Highlights include the Mace and Medusa rooms and Cactus Spring. **Note:** Hiking boots or other sturdy shoes, gloves, kneepads and four new AA batteries are required for this strenuous tour; a long-sleeved shirt, long pants and water are recommended. Backpacks are not permitted. Helmets and headlamps are provided. The 4-hour tour is limited to eight participants. **Hours:** Tours are given Sun. at 1. **Cost:**

Fee $20; $10 (ages 12-15). Ages 0-11 are not permitted. Reservations are required. **Phone:** (877) 444-6777.

CARRIZOZO (H-4) pop. 996, elev. 5,426'

Once a shipping and commercial center for area ranches, Carrizozo now is a busy county seat and tourist center. In addition to its own parks and recreational facilities, it offers easy access to the northern portion of Lincoln National Forest *(see place listing p. 427)*. Established in 1899 as a division point on the El Paso & Northeastern Railroad, the community takes its name from *carrizo,* a regional grass.

Nine miles northeast via US 54 and SR 349 is the ghost town of White Oaks. For 20 years after the original gold strike on nearby Baxter Mountain in 1879, White Oaks was a substantial community with stone buildings, two banks, four churches, four newspapers and more than 50 established businesses. Although White Oaks faded with the gold market in the 20th century, one of the first strikes—the Old Abe Mine—produced $3 million in gold until it closed around 1960.

Carrizozo Chamber of Commerce: P.O. Box 567, Carrizozo, NM 88301. **Phone:** (575) 648-2732.

VALLEY OF FIRES RECREATION AREA is 4 mi. w. on US 380, immediately adjacent to the Malpais (badlands) Lava Flow. About 5,000 years ago, Little Black Peak erupted and flowed 44 miles into the Tularosa Basin, filling the basin with molten rock. The resulting lava flow is 4-6 miles wide, 160 feet thick and covers 125 square miles. This lava flow is considered to be one of the youngest lava flows in the Continental United States. A three-quarter-mile nature trail winds through the park; trail guides are available at the visitor center.

Further information is available from Carrizozo Travel Information Center. **Hours:** Daily 24 hours. Visitor center daily 8-4. **Cost:** $3 per person or $5 per private vehicle. Admission is half-price for Golden Age and Golden Access pass holders. Camping $7-$18. **Phone:** (575) 648-2241. 🏕️ 🍴

CARSON NATIONAL FOREST (D-4)

Elevations in the forest range from 6,000 ft. in the Pinon Juniper Tree region to 13,161 ft. at Wheeler Peak. Refer to AAA maps for additional elevation information.

In north central New Mexico, Carson National Forest encompasses 1,500,000 acres. Its scenic and recreational focus is in the districts that encompass the Sangre de Cristo and the San Juan mountains flanking the upper Rio Grande Valley.

Five wilderness areas—Wheeler Peak, Latir Peak, Cruces Basin, the northern portion of the Pecos and Chama wildernesses and an 8-mile-long section of the Rio Grande Wild River—preserve the region's pristine beauty.

Enchanted Circle Scenic Byway is an 84-mile drive offering panoramic views of the southern Rocky Mountains, including Wheeler Peak. It loops from Taos east to Eagle Nest, then north to Questa via SR 38, and south on SR 522 back to Taos.

The curved cliff side of Echo Amphitheater, 9 miles south of Canjilon on US 84, is a prime spot for photography. Summer and winter recreation is available. Trails for bicycling, hiking, horseback riding, snowmobiling and cross-country skiing traverse the forest.

For further information contact Carson National Forest, 208 Cruz Alta Rd., Taos, NM 87571; phone (575) 758-6200. *See Recreation Chart.*

CHACO CULTURE NATIONAL HISTORICAL PARK (E-2)

Located in northwestern New Mexico, the recommended park access is from the north via the US 550 exit at CR 7900—entry is about 3 miles southeast of Nageezi and approximately 50 miles west of Cuba. Follow signs to the park for 21 miles. This route has 8 miles of paved road (CR 7900) and 13 miles of dirt road (CR 7950). The road is only lightly maintained, and may be impassable during or after inclement weather. Phone the park visitor center at (505) 786-7014, ext. 221 for current road conditions. Unless you are planning to camp in the park, it is not recommended that you drive a motor home on the access roads.

Chaco Culture National Historical Park preserves the remains of 13 major great houses, or monumental public buildings, and several thousand smaller sites that exemplify the culture of the Ancestral Puebloan people A.D. 850-1250.

By about A.D. 500 the Ancestral Puebloan people gradually exchanged their nomadic ways for agriculture and permanent settlements. They began to build Pueblo Bonito at the base of the northern canyon wall, 4 miles west of the headquarters area, during the mid-9th century. By the late 12th century Pueblo Bonito had attained a height of at least 4 stories and contained more than 600 rooms and kivas (ceremonial rooms).

In addition to the large public buildings, numerous smaller village sites in the canyon attest to the settlement's sizable and diverse populations, which were greater than those found in the area today. It is one of the most imposing cultural sites in the Southwest.

Not content with building great public buildings and an elaborate irrigation system of gates and canals that diverted runoff from summer storms into their cornfields, the Chacoans also constructed a vast road network. These straight, 30-foot-wide corridors linked the canyon settlements with more than 150 satellite communities, some as distant as Arizona, Colorado and Utah.

One route, the Great North Road, runs from Pueblo Alto near Pueblo Bonito to a point near

Salmon Ruin *(see Bloomfield p. 392)* and may continue to Aztec Ruins National Monument *(see place listing p. 390).*

Another major achievement of the Chaco is a highly sophisticated solstice marker. High on the isolated Fajada Butte a sliver of noontime sunlight slashes between stone slabs onto two spiral petroglyphs, precisely timing the equinoxes and solstices by which the Chacoans planted their crops and scheduled their ceremonies. The butte is closed to the public due to its fragile condition.

Eventually Chaco's influence waned and new centers emerged at Aztec and Mesa Verde—by 1250 only the wind whispered among the colossal masonry walls of Pueblo Bonito and its sister cities. The people were assimilated into the existing populations in the Zuni, Hopi, Acoma and Rio Grande pueblos. Descendents continue to return to honor these sacred places.

Note: Due to the park's remote location and its extensive ruins and trails, it may be worth planning 2 or 3 days for the visit. A full day is required for travel and to see a portion of the park. A second or third day is necessary to view the entire site. There are no lodgings or food service facilities in the park, but there is a campground (located 1 mile east of the visitor center) with 49 campsites available on a first-come, first-served basis. Due to Gallo Campground's popularity, especially April through October, visitors should arrive early in the day. Trailers and RVs more than 35 feet in length may not be accommodated.

Because Chaco is accessible only over dirt roads that are rough, towing trailers more than 35 feet long is not advised. There are no services or gas in the park. Campers must bring their own wood or charcoal. Drinking water and dump station facilities are available year round.

Self-guiding trails explore seven major sites, including Pueblo Bonito, Chetro Ketl, Pueblo del Arroyo, Casa Rinconada and three village sites. Allow 1 hour minimum per trail. Four other back-country trails for day hiking lead to more distant sites; free permits, available at the visitor center and trailheads, are required.

Tours, hikes and evening programs are offered April through October. The Chaco Night Sky Program features astronomy activities and solar viewing April through October. Picnicking is permitted in designated areas. *See Recreation Chart.*

CHACO CULTURE NATIONAL HISTORICAL PARK VISITOR CENTER is 2.5 mi. from the park entrance. Displays trace the history of the canyon and the cultures that developed there. A short film about the area is shown. **Hours:** Visitor center daily 8-5. Closed Jan. 1, Thanksgiving and Christmas. Trails open daily dawn-dusk year-round. **Cost:** (valid for 7 days) $8 (per private vehicle), $4 (per person arriving by other means). **Phone:** (505) 786-7014, ext. 221.

CHAMA (D-3) pop. 1,022, elev. 7,875'
• Hotels p. 398 • Restaurants p. 398

Like the railroad that is its most popular attraction, Chama grew during the silver mining boom of the 1880s. The old railroad yards, shops, a roundhouse and one of the last coal tipples in the nation are relics of that era. In addition to tourism, lumber and outdoor recreation contribute to the town economy.

Chama Valley Chamber of Commerce: 2732 SR 17, Chama, NM 87566. **Phone:** (575) 756-2306 or (800) 477-0149.

CUMBRES & TOLTEC SCENIC RAILROAD is on SR 17. The 64-mile railroad, built in 1880, is jointly owned by the states of New Mexico

▼ See AAA listing this page ▼

"America's Highest & Longest"

Cumbres & Toltec
SCENIC RAILROAD

1-888-CUMBRES
CUMBRESTOLTEC.COM
SEE LISTING UNDER CHAMA

485

and Colorado, with trips originating from Antonito, Colo., and Chama, New Mexico. All-day trips on the vintage, narrow-gauge, coal-burning trains afford spectacular views of the rugged San Juan and Sangre de Cristo mountain ranges.

Osier, an old stagecoach stop, is the transfer and lunch point for those making the complete trip and returning by bus, as well as the turnaround and lunch point for passengers making the round-trip to their point of origin.

AAA offices in New Mexico and Colorado can make reservations. **Hours:** Trains depart from Chama and Antonito daily at 10, Memorial Day weekend to mid-Oct. **Cost:** Fares (including lunch) $75-$165; $40-$50 (ages 2-11). Reservations are recommended. **Phone:** (575) 756-2151 in N.M., (719) 376-5483 in Colo. or (888) 286-2737. *(See ad p. 397.)* 🍴

VISTA DEL RIO LODGE **Phone:** 575/756-2138

◆◆◆ ◆◆◆
Motel
$65-$150

Address: 2595 US Hwy 84/64 87520 **Location:** 0.5 mi s of SR 17. Located in a quiet area. **Facility:** 19 units. 1 story, exterior corridors. **Parking:** winter plug-ins. **Terms:** 3 day cancellation notice-fee imposed. **Activities:** fishing, basketball, volleyball. **Free Special Amenities: continental breakfast and high-speed Internet.**

WHERE TO EAT

HIGH COUNTRY RESTAURANT **Phone:** 575/756-2384

◆◆ ◆◆
American
$10-$30

AAA Inspector Notes: Near the town center, this eatery features casual service in a turn-of-the-20th-century saloon atmosphere. Among New Mexican favorites are tamales, steak asada, red and green chile and house specialties of garlic shrimp con pequin, seasoned to the diner's taste, and trucha con piñon, mountain trout in butter and piñon sauce. **Bar:** full bar. **Reservations:** required. **Address:** 2299 Hwy 17 87520 **Location:** SR 17, just n of jct US 64 and 84. L D

CHIMAYÓ (A-5) pop. 3,177, elev. 6,075'

The Spanish village of Chimayó is the home of the softly colored Chimayó blankets and rugs woven by Ortega and Trujillo family members. Throughout the village winding dirt roads lead past adobe houses. Vibrant colors decorate the village each autumn as the golden foliage of cottonwood trees provides a backdrop for garlands of red chili peppers drying in the sun.

Chimayó was founded near the end of the 17th century and for the next 100 years was the easternmost outpost of the Province of New Mexico, the frontier place of banishment. The reconquest of the rebellious Pueblo and Apache in 1692 initiated a new settlement in the western foothills of the Sangre de Cristo Mountains, and Spaniards were granted permission to settle along the Santa Cruz River.

In 1740 the Plaza of San Buenaventura de Chimayó—Chimayó of the Good Venture—was built. Now called Plaza del Cerro, it is one of the oldest of Spanish colonial origin surviving in the Southwest; many surrounding structures are homes of the settlers' descendants.

East of Chimayó on SR 76—a route known as the High Road to Taos—are two other well-known craft villages. Cordova maintains a tradition of excellence in woodcarving, in which the Lopez family is most prominent. Beyond Cordova, Truchas is the home of the Cordova family of master weavers. Visitors are welcome to browse during daylight hours in the workshops scattered throughout the villages.

Shopping areas: Galleria Ortega and Rancho Manzana, in the Plaza del Cerro, offer weavings, pottery and furnishings. Centinela Traditional Arts specializes in handwoven wool products.

EL SANTUARIO DE CHIMAYÓ is at the s.e. end of town via SR 76 and CR 98. In 1810 Bernardo Abeyta, a farmer, was praying and claimed to see a light emanating from the soil. Upon investigation he found a cross, which is now kept inside the chapel. Legend maintains that the earth surrounding this cross has healing power. Many pilgrims come to touch the dirt in a pit inside the chapel, where castoff crutches and braces line the walls. **Hours:** Daily 9-5, Oct.-May; 9-6, rest of year. **Cost:** Free. **Phone:** (505) 351-4360.

CASA ESCONDIDA BED & BREAKFAST
Phone: (505)351-4805

◆◆ ◆◆
Bed & Breakfast
$105-$165

Address: 64 CR 100 87522 **Location:** Jct SR 76 and 98, just w on SR 76, then 0.5 mi ne on CR 100, follow signs; 7.5 mi e of Espanola on SR 76. Located in a rural area. **Facility:** 8 units, some efficiencies. 2 stories, interior/exterior corridors. **Terms:** check-in 4 pm, 14 day cancellation notice-fee imposed. **Activities:** whirlpool.

WHERE TO EAT

RANCHO DE CHIMAYO **Phone:** 505/351-4444

◆◆ ◆◆
Regional Mexican
$7-$21

AAA Inspector Notes: A scenic drive off the beaten path leads to this lovely setting. Enjoy a leisurely meal in the historic, renovated farmhouse. Friendly staffers will tempt diners with a wide selection of hearty regional favorites. The spicy chile rellenos topped with green chile sauce is a must and the homemade flan is the perfect palate pleaser. **Bar:** full bar. **Address:** 300 Juan Medina Rd 87522 **Location:** Santa Fe CR 98; on High Road to Taos. L D

CHURCH ROCK (F-1) pop. 1,128, elev. 6,765'

Church Rock, which received its name from a prominent sandstone formation, was called *Kinlitsoh sinili* by the Navajo, or "place of yellow houses." This small settlement was the unlikely site of a nuclear disaster in 1979, when a dam containing uranium waste collapsed, spilling millions of gallons of radioactive water into the Puerco River.

RED ROCK PARK is off I-40 exit 26/33 via SR 566. Red sandstone cliffs provide a striking backdrop for this 640-acre park, which features hiking and nature trails, a rodeo arena, a convention center, campgrounds and a museum. Archeological evidence of ancient Pueblo dwellings dates to the third century. Red Rock Museum traces prehistoric habitation and the modern-day culture of Zuni, Hopi and Navajo tribes through displays of artwork and crafts.

Hours: Park open daily 24 hours. Museum open Mon.-Fri. 8-5. Phone ahead to confirm schedule. **Cost:** Park free. Museum by donation. **Phone:** (505) 722-3839. ⛺

CIBOLA NATIONAL FOREST (G-2)

Elevations in the forest range from 5,000 ft. in the Magdalena district to 11,301 ft. at Mt. Taylor. Refer to AAA maps for additional elevation information.

The forest comprises scattered mountain ranges rising from the desert east and south of Albuquerque and stretching west to Arizona. Cibola National Forest's 1,625,542 acres encompass four wilderness areas: Sandia, Manzano, Apache Kid and The Withington. Recreational opportunities include camping, fishing and hiking. *See Recreation Chart.*

The rugged Canadian River Canyon west of Roy provides another type of beauty within Kiowa National Grassland. The forest also administers Black Kettle National Grassland, in neighboring western Oklahoma and the Texas panhandle. Camping and fishing center on the grassland's five lakes. In some areas, hunting is available in season, and there is skiing at Sandia Peak Ski Area.

A chairlift carries visitors to the northeastern face of Sandia Peak. The lift may be accessed via the Sandia Peak Aerial Tramway *(see attraction listing p. 359)* or by automobile, taking I-40 exit 175 north to SR 536. It operates Sat.-Sun. 10-4, Memorial Day through Labor Day and during the Albuquerque International Balloon Fiesta. It also transports mountain bikes for cyclists who wish to explore the peak's upper trails; phone (505) 856-7325.

SANDIA CREST is 16 mi. e. of Albuquerque on I-40, 6 mi. n. on SR 14, then 14 mi. n.w. on the Sandia Crest National Scenic Byway (SR 536). At the observation deck atop the 10,378-foot crest, the panorama encompasses 15,000 square miles. A self-guiding nature trail begins here and loops for a half-mile. The byway is a 14-mile spur of the Turquoise Trail, the scenic stretch of SR 14 that links Albuquerque and Santa Fe. Volcanic rock formations, ghost towns and old mines are visible.

Snowboarding and downhill and cross-country skiing are available in winter; hiking and mountain biking are popular in summer. Equipment can be rented in both seasons. Food is available at the top of the crest. **Cost:** Free. **Parking:** $1 at the base of the tramway. **Phone:** (505) 281-3304.

◤**SANDIA PEAK AERIAL TRAMWAY—**
see Albuquerque p. 359.

CIMARRON (E-4) pop. 1,021, elev. 6,428'
• Hotels p. 400 • Restaurants p. 400

Meaning "wild" or "untamed," Cimarron was fitting for both the brawling stream and the settlement that developed on its banks. Although Eagle Nest Lake ultimately tamed the river, nothing could contain the activities in town from the late 1860s to about 1880. The Las Vegas *Gazette* once reported, "Things are quiet in Cimarron; nobody has been killed in three days."

Clay Allison, Billy the Kid, Bob Ford and Black Jack Ketchum were among notorious part-time residents. Gunfights killed 26 men, and New Mexico's first printing press was dumped into the Cimarron River before the range wars ended and the town ceased to be a magnet for every outlaw in the Southwest.

Cimarron languished after losing the county seat to Springer in 1880 but revived in the early 1900s with the arrival of two railroads and the lumber industry. The modern-day city serves nearby ranches, some logging operations and a lively tourist trade. St. James Hotel, where Annie Oakley joined Buffalo Bill Cody's Wild West Show, and the old jail are among the buildings that stand as reminders of a boisterous past. Just 4 miles south on SR 21 is Philmont Scout Ranch *(see attraction listing)*, a high-adventure camp for more than 20,000 Boy Scouts each summer.

The 3,700-acre Maxwell National Wildlife Refuge, 30 miles east off I-25, supports sizable populations of eagles, hawks and falcons around its grasslands, lakes and farmland. As part of Carson National Forest, Valle Vidal offers 100,000 acres of rugged back country for backpacking, hunting and fishing. It is 4 miles north on scenic US 64, then 21 miles northwest on Valle Vidal Road, following signs. Cimarron Canyon State Park, 12 miles west on US 64, features brown trout fishing, hiking and camping *(see Recreation Chart).*

Cimarron Chamber of Commerce: 104 N. Lincoln Ave., P.O. Box 604, Cimarron, NM 87714. **Phone:** (575) 376-2417.

Self-guiding tours: A walking tour map available from the chamber of commerce describes 14 historic buildings in the old town of Cimarron.

OLD MILL MUSEUM is s. of US 64 in Old Town on SR 21. An 1864 building houses four floors of artifacts relating to county history. Included are American Indian arts and crafts, furnishings, historic items, vintage clothing and books. Placards explain the mill's original workings, which are partially intact. **Time:** Allow 1 hour minimum. **Hours:** Fri.-Wed. 10-noon and 1-5, June 1-Labor Day. **Cost:** Donations.

PHILMONT SCOUT RANCH is 5 mi. s. off SR 21 at 17 Deer Run Rd. The 137,493-acre national camping center is operated by the National Council of the Boy Scouts of America. More than 20,000 Scouts from around the world visit each summer. Philmont Museum and Seton Memorial Library presents Southwestern art and history. Tours are available of Villa Philmonte, the summer home of Tulsa oilman Waite Philips, benefactor of Philmont Scout Ranch.

Hours: Library and museum daily 8-5, June-Aug.; Mon.-Fri. 8-5, rest of year. Villa tours depart every 30 minutes daily 8-noon and 1-5, June-Aug.; by appointment rest of year. Last tour begins 30 minutes before closing. **Cost:** Donations. **Phone:** (575) 376-2281.

CASA DEL GAVILAN
Phone: 575/376-2246

Historic Bed & Breakfast
$95-$160

Address: 570 Hwy 21 S 87714 **Location:** SR 21, 5.7 mi s of US 64, follow signs. Located in a secluded area. **Facility:** The remote hacienda-style ranch dates from 1905 and is in a serene setting with very fine mountain views. 5 units, some two bedrooms. 1 story, interior corridors. **Terms:** 2 night minimum stay - seasonal, 7 day cancellation notice-fee imposed. **Activities:** hiking trails. **Free Special Amenities:** full breakfast and early check-in/late check-out.

CIMARRON INN & RV PARK
Phone: 575/376-2268

Motel
$49-$65

Address: 212 10th St 87714 **Location:** On US 64. **Facility:** 15 units, some kitchens, cabins and cottages. 1 story, exterior corridors. **Free Special Amenities:** local telephone calls and high-speed Internet.

EXPRESS ST. JAMES HOTEL
Phone: 575/376-2664

[fyi]
Classic Historic Hotel

Did not meet all AAA rating requirements for locking devices in some guest rooms at time of last evaluation on 05/16/2011. **Address:** 617 S Collison Ave 87714 **Location:** Center. Facilities, services, and decor characterize a mid-scale property.

WHERE TO EAT

ST. JAMES RESTAURANT
Phone: 575/376-2664

American
$6-$33

AAA Inspector Notes: This dining room features Western decor and many antiques related to the local ranching community. Patio dining is available in season. **Bar:** full bar. **Address:** 617 S Collison Ave 87714 **Location:** Center; in Express St. James Hotel.

[B] [L] [D]

Check out
our travel blog at
AAATravelViews.com

CLAYTON (E-6) pop. 2,980, elev. 5,053'

So numerous were the herds of cattle driven through this small farming community in the mid-1880s that the Denver & Fort Worth Railroad established the settlement as a division point. As a railhead and trading center, Clayton underwent a Wild West phase. Celebrated train robber Black Jack Ketchum was hanged from a gallows enclosed in a stockade to foil yet another rescue by his gang.

Clayton, at the foot of the Rabbit Ear Mountains, is still a cattle town; some of the largest feedlots in the region are just to the north. It also is one of the world's largest producers of carbon dioxide, which is used for recovering oil in the Permian Basin in New Mexico and Texas.

Livestock studies are conducted at Clayton Livestock Research Center, 5 miles east in the Kiowa and Rita Blanca National Grasslands. The University of New Mexico and the U.S. Forest Service investigate problems related to the health, nutrition and management of cattle. Free 45- to 60-minute tours of the facility are available by appointment; phone (575) 374-2566.

Recreational opportunities abound at Clayton Lake State Park *(see Recreation Chart)*, known for its excellent trout, catfish, walleye and bass fishing. Dinosaur tracks were discovered on the spillway of the dam in 1982; more than 500 such tracks have been plotted.

Clayton-Union County Chamber of Commerce: 1103 S. First St., P.O. Box 476, Clayton, NM 88415. **Phone:** (575) 374-9253 or (800) 390-7858.

THE HERZSTEIN MEMORIAL MUSEUM is at 22 S. Second St. Offering a glimpse into the local area's rich history, the collection is wide-ranging and includes pioneer artifacts, paintings and antique furniture. **Time:** Allow 1 hour minimum. **Hours:** Tues.-Sat. 10-4. Closed major holidays. **Cost:** Donations. **Phone:** (575) 374-2977.

BEST WESTERN KOKOPELLI LODGE
Phone: (575)374-2589

Hotel
$110-$125

AAA Benefit: Members save up to 20%, plus 10% bonus points with Best Western Rewards®.

Address: 702 S 1st St 88415 **Location:** US 87, 0.5 mi se of jct US 56 and 64. **Facility:** 51 units. 2 stories (no elevator), exterior corridors. **Amenities:** *Some:* high-speed Internet. **Pool(s):** heated outdoor. **Activities:** playground, shuffleboard. **Free Special Amenities:** full breakfast and high-speed Internet.

DAYS INN & SUITES
Phone: (575)374-0133

Hotel
$76-$134

Address: 1120 S 1st St 88415 **Location:** US 87, 1 mi s of jct US 56 and 64. **Facility:** 41 units. 2 stories, interior corridors. **Terms:** cancellation fee imposed. **Amenities:** high-speed Internet. **Pool(s):** heated indoor. **Activities:** whirlpool, limited exercise equipment. **Guest Services:** coin laundry. **Free Special Amenities:** expanded continental breakfast and high-speed Internet.

CLOUDCROFT (I-4) pop. 674, elev. 8,663'

A flourishing resort and recreation center at the summit of the Sacramento Mountains, Cloudcroft offers skiing and snow play in winter and varied summer activities such as hiking and camping, especially in Lincoln National Forest *(see place listing p. 427).*

This high, wide country was settled when the Southern Pacific Railroad ran a spur from Alamogordo to tap the timber reserves in the Sacramento Mountains. To lure excursion passengers the railroad built an elaborate resort, The Lodge, in 1901. Though the last freight train arrived in 1947, the resort still operates. Today's visitors enjoy hiking, bicycling and skiing along trails where trains once traveled. Local artisans create a variety of crafts. In downtown, shopping, dining and entertainment are offered along historic Burro Avenue.

Sacramento Mountains Historical Museum on US 82 recalls the town's settlement days. Within the museum complex, the Cloudcroft Pioneer Village, (575) 682-2932, features historic buildings furnished in period, a granary, a barn and antique farm equipment.

Cloudcroft Chamber of Commerce: 1001 James Canyon Hwy., P.O. Box 1290, Cloudcroft, NM 88317. **Phone:** (575) 682-2733 or (866) 874-4447.

Explore the Travel Guides
on AAA.com/Travel or
CAA.ca/Travel

THE LODGE RESORT   **Phone:** (575)682-2566

Historic Hotel
$115-$335

Address: 601 Corona Pl 88317 **Location:** US 82, 0.3 mi s on Curlew Pl/Corona Pl. **Facility:** The historic hotel, constructed in 1899, features a fine-dining restaurant, elegantly appointed guest rooms and lush, hilly surroundings. 59 units. 3 stories (no elevator), interior corridors. **Terms:** check-in 4 pm, 14 day cancellation notice-fee imposed. **Amenities:** high-speed Internet. **Dining:** Rebecca's, see separate listing. **Pool(s):** heated outdoor. **Activities:** sauna, whirlpool, hiking trails, jogging, horseshoes, volleyball, exercise room, spa. *Fee:* golf-9 holes, bicycles. **Guest Services:** valet laundry. **Free Special Amenities: high-speed Internet.**
(See ad this page.)

WHERE TO EAT

BIG DADDY'S DINER   **Phone:** 575/682-1224

American
$7-$60

AAA Inspector Notes: Big Daddy might watch over the dining room but it is Little Mama who oversees the kitchen and turns out generous portions of country favorites. The hand-cut, fresh sweet potato fries are especially tasty. **Address:** 1705 James Canyon Hwy 82 88317 **Location:** Just e. [B] [L] [D] [K]

REBECCA'S *Menu on AAA.com*   **Phone:** 575/682-2566

American
$8-$45

AAA Inspector Notes: In a lovely hotel that dates back to 1899, the restaurant has wonderful stained-glass porch windows that enhance the mountain views. Lunch offerings include sandwiches and pasta, while dinner is more formal, with piano music, steak, seafood and the tasty fruit cobbler for which it's well known. **Bar:** full bar. **Reservations:** suggested. **Address:** 601 Corona Pl 88317 **Location:** US 82, 0.3 mi s on Curlew Pl/Corona Pl; in The Lodge Resort. *(See ad this page.)* [B] [L] [D]

▼ See AAA listing this page ▼

As you drive up the Sacramento Mountains to Cloudcroft...

you discover a place where the air is always crisp, the dining elegant and the golf world-class. You discover The Lodge Resort. The Lodge Resort & Spa is a full-service hotel nestled in the Village of Cloudcroft in the Sacramento Mountains featuring:

🌲 *Award-winning* Rebecca's Restaurant *specializing in Continental and Southwestern cuisine*

🌲 *A breathtaking golf course*

🌲 *The Spirit of the Mountain Spa*

🌲 *Unique shopping*

THE LODGE
RESORT & SPA
CLOUDCROFT, NM
It's Charmed

601 Corona Place   Cloudcroft, NM 88317

(866) 595-6343   (575) 682-2566

www.TheLodgeResort.com

CLOVIS (G-6) pop. 37,775, elev. 4,266'

Clovis is located on the high plains of eastern New Mexico in the heart of cattle country, with ranching, farming, the dairy industry and the railroad comprising important components of the community's economic base. Six miles to the west is Cannon Air Force Base, another important component of the local economy.

In rock 'n' roll circles, Clovis also is known for the Norman Petty Recording Studios where Buddy Holly recorded the 1957 hit, "Peggy Sue." The studios, which no longer operate, have been maintained with their original 1950s appearance and feature music memorabilia and vintage recording equipment. Guided tours are available by appointment only made at least 1 month in advance; phone (575) 763-3435.

Hillcrest Park, at 10th and Sycamore streets, encompasses a sunken garden, picnic areas and Hillcrest Park Zoo; phone (575) 769-7873.

Clovis/Curry County Chamber of Commerce: 105 E. Grand Ave., Clovis, NM 88101. **Phone:** (575) 763-3435 or (800) 261-7656.

BEST WESTERN CLOVIS INN & SUITES
Phone: (575)762-5600

Hotel
$81-$91

AAA Benefit: Members save up to 20%, plus 10% bonus points with Best Western Rewards®.

Address: 2912 Mabry Dr 88101 **Location:** 1.8 mi e on US 60/70/84. **Facility:** 96 units, some efficiencies. 2 stories (no elevator), exterior corridors. **Amenities:** high-speed Internet. **Pool(s):** heated outdoor. **Activities:** whirlpool, exercise room. **Guest Services:** valet and coin laundry. **Free Special Amenities:** local telephone calls and high-speed Internet.

COMFORT INN & SUITES
Phone: (575)762-4536

Hotel
$99-$119

Address: 201 Schepps Blvd 88101 **Location:** Jct US 60/70/84 and Schepps Blvd, just n. **Facility:** 66 units, some two bedrooms. 3 stories, interior corridors. **Terms:** cancellation fee imposed. **Amenities:** high-speed Internet. **Pool(s):** heated indoor. **Activities:** whirlpool, exercise room. **Guest Services:** valet and coin laundry. **Free Special Amenities:** expanded continental breakfast and high-speed Internet.

ECONO LODGE
Phone: (575)763-3439

Motel
$50-$99

Address: 1400 E Mabry Dr 88101 **Location:** 0.5 mi e on US 60/70/84. **Facility:** 46 units. 1 story, exterior corridors. **Terms:** cancellation fee imposed. **Amenities:** high-speed Internet. **Pool(s):** heated indoor. **Guest Services:** coin laundry.

FAIRFIELD INN & SUITES BY MARRIOTT
Phone: (575)762-1411

Hotel
$89-$109

AAA Benefit: AAA hotel discounts of 5% or more.

Address: 4305 N Prince St 88101 **Location:** Jct US 84 and Prince St, 2.5 mi n. **Facility:** 69 units. 3 stories, interior corridors. **Amenities:** high-speed Internet. **Pool(s):** heated outdoor. **Activities:** whirlpool, exercise room. **Guest Services:** valet and coin laundry.

HAMPTON INN
Phone: (575)763-3300

Hotel
$84-$109

AAA Benefit: Members save up to 10% everyday!

Address: 2212 Mabry Dr 88101 **Location:** Jct US 60/70/84, 1.1 mi e. **Facility:** 55 units. 2 stories, interior corridors. **Terms:** 1-7 night minimum stay, cancellation fee imposed. **Pool(s):** heated indoor. **Activities:** whirlpool, exercise room. **Guest Services:** valet and coin laundry.

HOLIDAY INN EXPRESS & SUITES
Phone: (575)935-8777

Hotel
$99-$169

Address: 4728 N Prince St 88101 **Location:** Jct US 60/84 and SR 209, 3 mi n. **Facility:** 80 units. 3 stories, interior corridors. **Amenities:** high-speed Internet. **Pool(s):** heated indoor. **Activities:** whirlpool, exercise room. **Guest Services:** valet and coin laundry.

LA QUINTA INN & SUITES CLOVIS
Phone: (575)763-8777

Hotel
$108-$204

Address: 4521 N Prince St 88101 **Location:** Jct US 60/84 and Prince St, 3 mi n. **Facility:** 66 units. 3 stories, interior corridors. **Amenities:** high-speed Internet. **Pool(s):** heated indoor. **Activities:** whirlpool, exercise room. **Guest Services:** coin laundry.

Don't Let a Traffic Ticket Ruin Your Vacation

AAA.com

Restore your humor – and good driving record – with AAA's online traffic ticket dismissal course* on AAA.com.

*Available through participating AAA clubs in states/jurisdictions where permitted.

WHERE TO EAT

COTTON PATCH CAFE
American
$7-$18
Phone: 575/762-2233
AAA Inspector Notes: This family friendly restaurant features a variety of sandwiches, burgers, salads and comfort food entrées. Save room for the peach cobbler a la mode. **Address:** 2604 N Prince St 88101 **Location:** Jct Parkland Dr; across from mall. L D

RIB CRIB BBQ AND GRILL
Barbecue
$6-$15
Phone: 575/742-0200
AAA Inspector Notes: Most guests need extra napkins to tackle the ribs, brisket, ham, pork and chicken selections. The menu also lists sandwiches and wraps, along with tempting sides and large desserts. The decor is decidedly Western. **Bar:** beer & wine. **Address:** 4020 N Prince St 88101 **Location:** Jct US 84 W and Prince St, 2.6 mi n. L D

TACO BOX
Mexican
$3-$7
Phone: 575/935-8226
AAA Inspector Notes: This popular quick service restaurant features tacos, burritos and burgers for dining in or taking out. This is a favorite stop on the New Mexico Green Chile Cheeseburger Trail. Complimentary Wi-Fi is offered. **Address:** 136 W 21st St 88101 **Location:** Just w of jct Main St; in Hilltop Plaza. B L D

COCHITÍ PUEBLO (C-3) pop. 528, elev. 5,258'

West of the Rio Grande and a few miles southwest of Cochiti Dam, this ancient Keresan pueblo retains few of its old landmarks. The mission church, San Buenaventura de Cochiti, was built in 1628. The tribe leases land to the community of Cochiti Lake, where a recreation area offers boating, camping, fishing, sailing, windsurfing and nature trails *(see Recreation Chart)*. Visitors to the pueblo are welcome dawn to dusk. Drawing, painting, photography or tape recording is not permitted.

KASHA-KATUWE TENT ROCKS NATIONAL MONUMENT is roughly midway between Albuquerque and Santa Fe. From Albuquerque, take I-25 n. to exit 259, then SR 22 w. to Cochiti Pueblo and follow signs to the national monument. From Santa Fe, take I-25 s. to exit 264, then SR 16 w. about 8 mi. to SR 22 and follow signs. Located on north-central New Mexico's Pajarito Plateau, Tent Rocks is a remarkable wonderland of cone-shaped rock formations, the product of volcanic eruptions that occurred millions of years ago. The pumice, ash and tuff deposits left behind were subsequently shaped by wind, water and erosion.

Boulder caps perch precariously atop many of these tapering formations—which range in height from a few to more than 90 feet—protecting the softer rock below. Another fascinating geologic feature are the slot canyons, narrow, twisting passageways carved over time by rushing water. Ponderosa and piñon pines grow along with desert plants like Indian paintbrush and Apache plume.

The area's austere beauty can be explored on two hikes. The 1.2-mile Cave Loop Trail is an easy trek that leads to an above-ground cave. The more strenuous Canyon Trail (3 miles round-trip) ascends a narrow canyon with a steep 630-foot elevation gain. The trail ends atop a mesa that offers breathtaking 360-degree views of the tent rocks below, the Rio Grande Valley and the Sangre de Cristo, Jémez and Sandia mountains looming in the distance.

Note: The trailhead is 5 miles from the monument entrance gate via a bumpy dirt-gravel road. Some hands-free climbing is required on the Canyon Trail; steps built into the trail in a couple of places help facilitate the ascent. Wear hiking boots or nonslip athletic shoes and a hat, and bring water. Stay on the designated trail; climbing on the tent rocks is prohibited. There are parking areas and restrooms at the trailhead. Dogs are not permitted. **Time:** Allow 2 hours, 30 minutes minimum. **Hours:** Daily 7-7, Mar. 11-Oct. 31; 8-5, rest of year. Last admission 1 hour before closing. Closed Thanksgiving, Christmas Eve and Christmas. **Cost:** $5 per private vehicle. **Phone:** (505) 761-8953.

COLUMBUS (J-2) pop. 1,664, elev. 4,064'

Just before dawn on March 9, 1916, the revolutionary activities of Pancho Villa and his 500 guerrillas spilled over the international border into drowsy Columbus and its military outpost—the first attack on U.S. soil since the War of 1812. The raiders seized livestock, burned the town and killed 18 Americans, eliciting immediate retaliation from President Woodrow Wilson.

Within a week Gen. John "Black Jack" Pershing marched his 6,000 troops, accompanied by motorized vehicles and airplanes, into Mexico to mark the first mechanized U.S. military action. Pershing's forces pursued the rebel leader for 11 months but never captured him; Villa was assassinated in 1923.

COLUMBUS HISTORICAL SOCIETY MUSEUM is at jct. SRs 9 and 11. Chronicling local history from the pioneer era to modern times, the museum is housed in a 1902 Southern Pacific Railroad depot that stood witness to Pancho Villa's raid on the city. This attack and the U.S. Army's subsequent retaliation are depicted with photographs, military artifacts and a 20-minute film. Displays include Mexican pottery and beads, pioneer implements and railroad memorabilia. **Time:** Allow 30 minutes minimum. **Hours:** Daily 10-4, Sept.-Apr.; Mon.-Fri. 10-1, Sat.-Sun. 10-4, rest of year. Closed Christmas. **Cost:** Free. **Phone:** (575) 531-2620.

PANCHO VILLA STATE PARK is at jct. SRs 9 and 11. The site of Pancho Villa's raid into American territory is preserved at the park, which commemorates the event with historical exhibits, including pre-World War I vehicles used by Gen. John Pershing's men in their pursuit of Villa. The 61-acre park includes a visitor center, a 7,000-square-foot exhibit hall, buildings from Camp Furlong, nature trails, a playground and an exotic botanical garden with some 30 varieties of cacti. **Hours:** Daily 24 hours. Visitor center daily 8-5. **Cost:** $5 per private vehicle. Camping $8-$14. **Phone:** (575) 531-2711, or (575) 531-2119 for visitor center.

CORRALES (F-3) pop. 8,329, elev. 5,023'
• Hotels & Restaurants map & index p. 362

Corrales, about half an hour north of downtown Albuquerque via I-40 exit 155, is not only a pleasant escape from the city but a step back in time to an earlier New Mexico. For a dozen or so miles after leaving the interstate, Coors Boulevard is solid suburban sprawl—walled-in housing developments, strip centers, car dealerships, Starbucks outlets. But once you bear right onto Corrales Road (SR 448), and especially after crossing the Sandoval County line, the scene abruptly changes.

Suddenly you're in the country. Cottonwood trees line the roadside. (Credit the nearby presence of the Rio Grande for that.) The landscape is greener. The two-lane road winds past adobes and (in fall) produce stands selling fresh apple cider. Sample the bounty from local farmers—everything from arugula to green chiles to tomatillos—at the Corrales Growers' Market. It sets up at the Recreation Center at Jones and Corrales roads (south of the post office) Sundays 9-noon, May through October (also Wednesday afternoons from 3-6, early July through late October). The rest of the year it is open the first Sunday of the month from 11 to 1; phone (505) 898-7927.

Sunday in Corrales, the third Sunday of the month from May through September, offers family-friendly events like Art in the Park, where local painters, potters, metalworkers, jewelers and sculptors exhibit their wares under the shade of cottonwood trees. Kids can engage in activities like making bread and crafting mosaic art out of glass. It all happens at La Entrada Park (corner of Corrales and La Entrada roads).

Poke around the shops and galleries scattered along Corrales Road. Artist-owned Corrales Bosque Gallery (in the Mercado de Maya) displays landscape paintings, sculpture, ceramic pieces and collage art by New Mexico artists working in a variety of media (everything from clay to torn paper). Local artwork adorns The Oasis (in the Village Plaza Center at 4940 Corrales Rd.), where you can relax with a barista-brewed coffee or iced specialty concoction in the cool green surroundings of an indoor garden.

Explore the village's history at Casa San Ysidro on Old Church Road (just off Corrales Road; watch for the sign). This partially reconstructed 19th-century adobe displays Spanish Colonial furnishings, hand-woven floor coverings, iron tools and an authentic 18th-century loom. The house is open for tours February through November; phone (505) 898-3915 for information. Behind it is a country cemetery with interesting statues and headstones and a view framed by the Sandia Mountains. Don't be surprised if a jackrabbit lopes by in this serene rural setting.

Across the street is the Old Church (Iglesia de San Ysidro), which dates from around 1868. Shaped like a cross, it features massive adobe walls nearly 3 feet thick. Twin bell towers were added in the 1930s to help support the weakening facade. Today this historic structure serves as a venue for community activities and music programs.

WINERIES
• **Corrales Winery** is at 6275 Corrales Rd. Tours and tastings are offered. **Hours:** Wed.-Sun. noon-5. **Phone:** (505) 898-5165.

THE CHOCOLATE TURTLE BED & BREAKFAST
          Phone: 505/898-1800   **77**

▼▼▼▼   **Address:** 1098 W Meadowlark Ln
Bed & Breakfast   87048 **Location:** I-25 exit 233
$119-$149   (Alameda Blvd), just w, 4 mi to Corrales Rd, 1 mi n to Meadowlark Ln, then 1 mi w. **Facility:** The B&B features a large, colorful, southwestern-style living room and attractively decorated guest rooms. A patio and garden provide nice views. 4 units. 1 story, interior corridors. **Terms:** 2 night minimum stay - seasonal and/or weekends, age restrictions may apply, 14 day cancellation notice-fee imposed. BIZ 🛜 ✕ ⓦ ⓩ

WHERE TO EAT

HANNAH & NATE'S MARKET CAFE
          Phone: 505/898-2370   (102)

▼▼▼   **AAA Inspector Notes:** In addition to hearty breakfasts, guests can sample
American   from an eclectic selection of
$7-$9   sandwiches and delectable cakes, pies and cookies produced in the in-house bakery of this cafe. **Address:** 4512 Corrales Rd 87048 **Location:** Center. B L

INDIGO CROW CAFE   **Phone:** 505/898-7000   (101)
▼▼▼▼   **AAA Inspector Notes:** A dining room with territorial charm, a patio
American   surrounded by a Mexican-style wall
$7-$30   and an imaginative menu are some of the features of this café in the center of town. The tasty Cobb salad is gigantic. **Bar:** beer & wine. **Reservations:** suggested. **Address:** 4515 Corrales Rd 87048 **Location:** Center. L D

DEMING (I-2) pop. 14,855, elev. 4,337'
• Restaurants p. 407

Fields of chilies flourish in the seemingly riverless valley around Deming, with secondary crops of cotton, onions, pecans, grapes and sorghum. The water that sustains them is the subsurface flow of the Mimbres River, which vanishes into the earth north of the city and reappears in a lake in the Mexican state of Chihuahua. Stock raising and some manufacturing augment the economy of this busy county seat, which also is a growing retirement center. Southeast the Little Florida (flo-REE-da) Mountains yield an abundance of agate, fire opal, jasper and semiprecious stones.

Deming-Luna County Chamber of Commerce and Visitors Center: 800 E. Pine St., P.O. Box 8, Deming, NM 88031. **Phone:** (575) 546-2674 or (800) 848-4955.

Self-guiding tours: A walking-tour brochure listing 16 historic buildings and sites is available from the Deming-Luna County Chamber of Commerce and Visitors Center.

CITY OF ROCKS STATE PARK is 30 mi. n.w. via US 180, then 3 mi. n.e. on SR 61. Millions of years ago wind and water shaped volcanic rock into the curious monolithic formations that give this 680-acre park its name. The Mimbres Indians and Spanish conquistadors left evidence of their visits. A cactus garden, hiking trails, interpretive exhibits and visitor center also are featured. **Hours:** Daily 7 a.m.-9 p.m. Visitor center daily 9:30-noon and 1-4:30 (when staff is available). Phone ahead to confirm visitor center schedule. **Cost:** $5 per private vehicle. Camping $10-$14. **Phone:** (575) 536-2800.

DEMING LUNA MIMBRES MUSEUM is at 301 S. Silver St. The museum depicts Southwest history with an 1853 customs house, pioneer artifacts, military items from early cavalry days through World War II, railroad and cowboy memorabilia, gems and minerals, and a Mimbres Indian pottery exhibit. The transportation annex features street scenes and antique automobiles representing Deming's past. **Hours:** Mon.-Sat. 9-4, Sun. 1:30-4, Sept.-June; Mon.-Sat. 9-4, rest of year. Closed Jan. 1, Easter, Thanksgiving and Christmas. **Cost:** Donations. **Phone:** (575) 546-2382.

ROCKHOUND STATE PARK is 14 mi. s.e. off SR 11. Abundant agate and quartz crystals are found within this park on the western slope of the Florida Mountains. Up to 15 pounds of rock may be collected, making it a favorite spot for "rockhounds." **Hours:** Gate open daily 7:30-dusk. Office daily 10-noon and 1-4. **Cost:** $5 per private vehicle. Camping $8-$18. **Phone:** (575) 546-6182.

BEST WESTERN MIMBRES VALLEY INN
Phone: (575)546-4544

Hotel
$78-$130

AAA Benefit:
Members save up to 20%, plus 10% bonus points with Best Western Rewards®.

Address: 1500 W Pine St 88030 **Location:** I-10 exit 81, just e. **Facility:** 40 units. 1 story, exterior corridors. **Amenities:** *Some:* high-speed Internet. **Pool(s):** outdoor. **Guest Services:** coin laundry. **Free Special Amenities: full breakfast and high-speed Internet.**

SAVE / SOME UNITS FEE

Best Western

All Ground Floor Rooms, Free Breakfast & WiFi, Pets Welcome, Microwave-Fridge in All Rooms

DAYS INN
Phone: (575)546-8813

Motel
$49-$79

Address: 1601 E Pine St 88030 **Location:** I-10 exit 85 westbound, 2 mi w on business loop; exit 81 eastbound, 1 mi e on business loop. **Facility:** 57 units. 2 stories (no elevator), exterior corridors. **Pool(s):** outdoor. **Free Special Amenities: full breakfast and high-speed Internet.**

SAVE / SOME UNITS FEE

Download eTourBook guides for ereaders and smartphones at AAA.com/ebooks

KEEP YOUR CHILDREN SAFE IN THE CAR

Use the right car seat and follow the guidelines at **AAA.com/SafeSeats4Kids.** To learn how to install your car seat properly, call an expert at **866-SEAT-CHECK(732-8243)** or visit **seatcheck.org.** Remember, car seats save lives!

Busytown Mysteries™ and all related and associated trademarks are owned by Cookie Jar Entertainment Inc., and used under license from Cookie Jar Entertainment Inc. ©2011 Cookie Jar Inc. All rights reserved.

GRAND MOTOR INN

Phone: (575)546-2632

Hotel
$50-$65

Address: 1721 E Pine St 88030 **Location:** I-10 exit 85 westbound, 2 mi w on business loop; exit 82 eastbound, 1 mi e on business loop. **Facility:** 58 units. 2 stories (no elevator), interior/exterior corridors. **Pool(s):** outdoor. **Guest Services:** valet and coin laundry, area transportation-bus stop & train station. **Free Special Amenities:** early check-in/late check-out and high-speed Internet.
(See ad this page.)

HAMPTON INN

Phone: (575)546-2022

Hotel
$98-$109

AAA Benefit:
Members save up to 10% everyday!

Address: 3751 E Cedar St 88030 **Location:** I-10 exit 85, just s to Cedar St, then just w. **Facility:** 75 units. 3 stories, interior corridors. **Terms:** 1-7 night minimum stay, cancellation fee imposed. **Amenities:** high-speed Internet. **Pool(s):** heated indoor. **Activities:** whirlpool, exercise room. **Guest Services:** coin laundry.

HOLIDAY INN

Phone: (575)546-2661

Hotel
$70-$90

Address: 4600 E Pine St 88030 **Location:** I-10 exit 85, just w. **Facility:** 116 units. 2 stories (no elevator), exterior corridors. **Amenities:** *Some:* high-speed Internet. **Pool(s):** outdoor. **Activities:** exercise room. **Guest Services:** coin laundry. **Free Special Amenities:** local telephone calls and newspaper.

LA QUINTA INN & SUITES DEMING

Phone: (575)546-0600

Hotel
$75-$144

Address: 4300 E Pine St 88030 **Location:** I-10 exit 85, just w. **Facility:** 58 units, some kitchens. 3 stories, interior corridors. **Amenities:** high-speed Internet. **Pool(s):** outdoor. **Activities:** whirlpool, limited exercise equipment. **Guest Services:** coin laundry. **Free Special Amenities:** expanded continental breakfast and early check-in/late check-out.

Award Winning Customer Service, Pet Friendly Facility with Attached Dog Run, FREE WIFI in all rooms.

SUPER 8 - DEMING

Phone: (575)546-0481

Hotel
$63-$120

Address: 1217 W Pine St 88030 **Location:** I-10 exit 81, just e. **Facility:** 43 units. 2 stories (no elevator), interior/exterior corridors. **Terms:** cancellation fee imposed. **Amenities:** safes. **Pool(s):** heated indoor. **Activities:** whirlpool. **Guest Services:** coin laundry.

Discover mobile travel solutions at AAA.com/mobile and CAA.ca/mobile

▼ See AAA listing this page ▼

GRAND MOTOR INN
DEMING, NEW MEXICO

AAA Discounted Rate
$42 sgl $48 dbl
Thru 12/12

- Restaurant & room service
- Cocktail Lounge • Free HBO/Full Cable
- Free Wi-Fi and Local Calls
- Refrigerators, microwaves & hair dryers
- Pool • Laundry
- *Bed & Breakfast packages available*
- Tour buses, RV's & Truckers Welcome

Get the free mobile app at
http://gettag.mobi

1721 E. Pine St. • Deming, New Mexico • (575) 546-2632
www.grandmotorinndeming.com

WHERE TO EAT

EL MIRADOR　　　　　Phone: 575/544-7340

Mexican
$6-$11

AAA Inspector Notes: This modest cafe is very busy at lunch time. Diners will find Mexican food here which is prepared in the traditional way, including carefully prepared enchiladas, tacos and burritos. **Address:** 510 E Pine St 88030 **Location:** Center.

B　L　D

PALMA'S ITALIAN GRILL　　Phone: 575/544-3100

Italian
$6-$24

AAA Inspector Notes: The menu centers on authentic fare prepared from true Italian recipes. Pasta dishes include traditional spaghetti with meatballs coated in great-tasting marinara, while thin and crispy eggplant parmigiana is done the old-fashioned way. **Bar:** beer & wine. **Address:** 110 S Silver Ave 88030 **Location:** Jct Silver Ave and Pine St; center. **Parking:** street only.

L　D

RANCHER'S GRILL　　　Phone: 575/546-8883

American
$7-$22

AAA Inspector Notes: Great steaks and a well-stocked salad bar are hallmarks of the busy eatery. Lots of Western memorabilia and decor entertain and amuse. The restaurant is equally popular with travelers and locals who visit frequently. **Bar:** beer & wine. **Address:** 316 E Cedar 88030 **Location:** I-10 exit 82B (US 180), just e.

L　D

DULCE (D-3) pop. 2,743, elev. 6,769'

Dulce is the capital and principal town of Jicarilla Apache Indian Reservation. The Jicarillas (hek-a-REH-yas), whose name means "little baskets," are renowned for woven baskets and other ornate craftwork. Visitors may watch artisans at work at the Jicarilla Arts and Crafts Museum on the reservation.

The town, at the northeastern corner of the reservation, is a popular provision point with hunters and anglers. The 14,500-acre Horse Lake Mesa Game Park is one of the country's largest elk enclosures.

Jicarilla Apache Nation, Public Relations Department: P.O. Box 507, Dulce, NM 87528. **Phone:** (575) 759-3242.

BEST WESTERN JICARILLA INN & CASINO
　　　　　　　　　Phone: (505)759-3663

Hotel
$105

AAA Benefit: Members save up to 20%, plus 10% bonus points with Best Western Rewards®.

Address: 13603 US Hwy 64 87528 **Location:** Center. **Facility:** 41 units. 2 stories (no elevator), interior corridors. **Activities:** exercise room. **Free Special Amenities:** local telephone calls and high-speed Internet.

SAVE　♨　🍴　🛎　📶　/SOME UNITS　FEE　🐾　🔲　🖥　🖵

EDGEWOOD (F-3) elev. 6,645'

A relative newcomer in state history, the farming community of Edgewood was settled in the 1930s and incorporated in 1999.

WILDLIFE WEST NATURE PARK is off I-40 exit 187 to 87 N. Frontage Rd. The 122-acre habitat park contains animals and plants native to New Mexico. Trails allow visitors to see elk, black bears, Mexican wolves, mountain lions, pronghorn antelope, foxes, raccoons, raptors and other birds. Hayrides are offered Saturday summer evenings prior to the Chuckwagon Dinner Show, which features barbecue and Western musical entertainment.

Time: Allow 1 hour, 30 minutes minimum. **Hours:** Park daily 10-6, mid-Mar. through Oct. 31; noon-4, rest of year. Dinner show is offered Sat. at 7 p.m., mid-June through Labor Day. **Cost:** $7; $6 (ages 60+); $4 (ages 5-11). Dinner show $20; $19 (ages 60+); $10 (ages 5-11); reservations required by 2 on day of show. **Phone:** (505) 281-7655.

ELEPHANT BUTTE pop. 1,431

ELEPHANT BUTTE INN & SPA　　Phone: (575)744-5431

Hotel
$79-$150

Address: 401 Hwy 195 87935 **Location:** I-25 exit 83, 4 mi e. **Facility:** 45 units. 2 stories (no elevator), exterior corridors. **Terms:** cancellation fee imposed. **Pool(s):** heated outdoor. **Activities:** spa. **Guest Services:** valet laundry. **Free Special Amenities:** newspaper and high-speed Internet.

SAVE　🍴　🍷　CALL　🛗M　🏊　BIZ　📶　✕　🖵
/SOME UNITS　FEE　🐾　🔲　🖥

EL MORRO

CIMARRON ROSE BED & BREAKFAST
　　　　　　　　　Phone: 505/783-4770

fyi　Not evaluated. **Address:** 689 Oso Ridge Rt 87321 **Location:** 12 mi e; between MM 56 and 57, on SR 53. Facilities, services, and decor characterize a mid-scale property.

WHERE TO EAT

ANCIENT WAY CAFE EL MORRO RV PARK & CABINS
　　　　　　　　　Phone: 505/783-4612

American
$5-$15

AAA Inspector Notes: Local folks and tourists alike enjoy the hearty American, New Mexican and vegetarian specials and monthly themed dinners created by the friendly, comfortable country-style cafe. Fresh pies and pastries are to die for. **Reservations:** suggested. **Address:** 4018 Ice Caves Rd (SR 53) 87321 **Location:** SR 53 at MM 46.　B　L

EL MORRO NATIONAL MONUMENT (F-2)

El Morro National Monument is 43 miles southwest of Grants via SR 53. The central features of the 1,278-acre monument are 200-foot-high Inscription Rock and the water hole fed by snowmelt and rainfall pouring off the rock. The Spanish called the sandstone mesa *El Morro*, meaning "the bluff" or "the headland."

Carved into the soft rock are centuries-old petroglyphs. The first known European inscription was left in 1605 by Juan de Oñate, governor and colonizer of New Mexico. Others include those of Gov.

Manuel de Silva Nieto in 1629; a soldier in 1632; Don Diego de Vargas, leader of the 1692 reconquest; and Lt. Edward Beale, who passed by with a camel caravan in 1857. Other soldiers and settlers making their way west added their names and dates.

Two Ancestral Puebloan villages once thrived atop this mesa. Remains of an 875-room dwelling from about the 13th century have been partly excavated.

Self-guiding tours are available. A half-mile trail and a 2-mile trail take about 45 minutes and 1.5 hours, respectively. A 15-minute videotaped presentation in the visitor center offers a glimpse into the cultural and natural history of the area. A small campground is available on a first-come, first-served basis. For further information contact the Superintendent, El Morro National Monument, HC 61, Box 43, Ramah, NM 87321.

Visitor center daily 9-5; phone for extended summer hours. Closed Jan. 1 and Christmas. Last admission to hiking trails 1 hour before closing. Trail fee $3; free (ages 0-15). Phone (505) 783-4226.

ESPAÑOLA (A-4) pop. 10,224, elev. 5,589'

In the northern Rio Grande Valley between the Jémez Mountains and the Truchas Peaks, Española was founded in 1598 by the Spaniards as the first capital of New Mexico.

The town assumed its present role as a trading and distribution center when the Denver and Rio Grande Western Railroad built its Chili Line between Española and Antonito, Colo., in the late 1870s. In late summer garlands of *ristras*—strings of scarlet chilies drying in the sun—decorate houses and fences.

Española is the central point for visiting the eight northern pueblos and Hispanic villages selling arts and crafts, including Nambé, Picurís, Pojoaque, San Ildefonso, Ohkay Owingeh, Santa Clara, Taos and Tesuque *(see place listings)*.

COMFORT INN
Phone: 505/753-2419
Hotel
Rates not provided
Address: 604-B S Riverside Dr 87532 **Location:** US 84 and 285, just s of jct SR 68. **Facility:** 41 units. 2 stories (no elevator), interior corridors. **Pool(s):** heated indoor. **Free Special Amenities: expanded continental breakfast and high-speed Internet.**

INN AT THE DELTA
Phone: 505/753-9466
Bed & Breakfast
Rates not provided
Address: 243 Paseo de Onate 87532 **Location:** US 84 and 285, 1 mi n of jct SR 68; 0.3 mi n of jct SR 30. **Facility:** Hand-carved wooden furniture, original artwork and a kiva fireplace fill each room of this tranquil Inn. 10 units. 1-2 stories (no elevator), exterior corridors. **Terms:** office hours 7:30 am-10 pm. **Activities:** *Fee:* massage.

SANTA CLARAN HOTEL CASINO
Phone: (505)367-4900
Hotel
$89-$149
Address: 464 N Riverside Dr 87532 **Location:** SR 68; center. **Facility:** Adjacent to Big Rock Casino. Guests will enjoy spacious and well-appointed rooms. 124 units. 7 stories, interior corridors. **Parking:** on-site and valet. **Terms:** check-in 4 pm, cancellation fee imposed. **Amenities:** high-speed Internet. **Dining:** 3 restaurants, entertainment. **Activities:** game room, exercise room. *Fee:* golf-18 holes. **Guest Services:** valet and coin laundry. **Free Special Amenities: local telephone calls and high-speed Internet.**

ANGELINA'S RESTAURANT
Phone: 505/753-8543
Southwestern
$6-$18
AAA Inspector Notes: Locals flock to this casual spot for traditional New Mexican food. Popular dishes include chiles rellenos, fajitas, enchiladas and burritos. Local farmers raise lamb especially for this place, and many of its most famous dishes include this specialty item. **Bar:** beer & wine. **Address:** 1226 N Railroad Ave 87532 **Location:** Jct SR 30 and US 84/285, 1.4 mi n, then 4 mi e on Fairview Dr.

EL PARAGUA
Phone: 505/753-3211
Mexican
$8-$32
AAA Inspector Notes: Experience true northern New Mexican culture and cuisine at El Paragua, a local favorite since 1966. Guests will find generous portions of authentic Mexican dishes, mesquite wood-grilled steaks and fish in addition to traditional, homemade desserts. **Bar:** full bar. **Reservations:** suggested. **Address:** 603 Santa Cruz Rd 87532 **Location:** SR 76, just e of SR 68.

LA COCINA RESTAURANT & CANTINA
Phone: 505/753-3016
Mexican
$7-$14
AAA Inspector Notes: Enjoy generous portions of flavorful northern New Mexican cuisine at this lively eatery. A longtime local favorite, the eatery starts each meal with complimentary fresh tortilla chips with salsa then ends the meal with puffy a sopaipilla with honey. **Bar:** full bar. **Address:** 415 Santa Clara Bridge Rd 87532 **Location:** Just e of jct SR 30 and 84.

FARMINGTON (E-2) pop. 45,877, elev. 5,292'
• Restaurants p. 410

Apple orchards replaced saloons and coal miners ousted card sharks as Farmington evolved into the major commerce and industrial center of the Four Corners region in northwestern New Mexico.

Navajo Mine, west of town, is one of the largest coal mining operations in the world. Its output fuels the adjacent Four Corners Power Plant, which in turn heats the waters used by windsurfers on nearby Morgan Lake. Anglers favor the San Juan River and Farmington and Jackson lakes.

West of town the vast Navajo Indian Reservation extends into Arizona. The convention and visitors bureau distributes a list of trading posts.

Forty miles south via SR 371 is the Bisti/De-Na-Zin Wilderness, an area of weirdly eroded hoodoos and slate-topped *mesitas*—geological formations made up of sandstone and shale that have become eroded by wind and rain. Angel Peak

Scenic Area lies 30 miles southeast via SR 550. Once considered by the Navajos as the dwelling place of sacred ones, the colorful sandstone formations crowning the peak were shaped over millions of years.

Changing exhibits by area artists are displayed at San Juan College Fine Arts Center. Outdoor theatrical performances are offered mid-June to mid-August in the Lions Wilderness Park, a natural sandstone amphitheater.

Farmington Convention and Visitors Bureau: 3041 E. Main St., Farmington, NM 87402. **Phone:** (505) 326-7602 or (800) 448-1240. *(See ad this page.)*

FARMINGTON MUSEUM is at 3041 E. Main St. Permanent exhibits depict local history, including the region's oil and gas industry, through such items as clothing, photographs, tools and equipment. The facility hosts year-round lectures, educational programs and art shows highlighting regional heritage and culture. An atrium affords excellent views of the Animas River. **Time:** Allow 30 minutes minimum. **Hours:** Mon.-Sat. 8-5. Closed Jan. 1, Thanksgiving and Christmas. **Cost:** Free. **Phone:** (505) 599-1174.

E³ Children's Museum & Science Center is just n. of jct. Main and Orchard sts. Permanent and changing science exhibits encourage interactive learning for children. Children 0-5 can practice early motor skills in Tot's Turf. **Time:** Allow 30 minutes minimum. **Hours:** Tues.-Sat. 10-5. **Cost:** Free. **Phone:** (505) 599-1425.

CASA BLANCA BED & BREAKFAST INN
Phone: 505/327-6503

Bed & Breakfast
$135-$175

Address: 505 E La Plata St 87401 **Location:** From Main St, just n on Court Ave, then just e. Located in historic Spanish Hacienda Estate; in a quiet residential area. **Facility:** The luxurious 1950s mission-style home is set on a bluff overlooking the community and surrounding cliffs. 8 units, some efficiencies. 1-2 stories (no elevator), exterior corridors. **Terms:** office hours 8 am-6 pm, 14 day cancellation notice-fee imposed. **Amenities:** *Some:* high-speed Internet. **Activities:** exercise room. **Guest Services:** complimentary laundry.

COMFORT INN
Phone: (505)325-2626

Hotel
$70-$120

Address: 555 Scott Ave 87401 **Location:** 1 mi e on SR 516 (Main St), just s. **Facility:** 59 units. 2 stories (no elevator), interior corridors. **Terms:** cancellation fee imposed. **Amenities:** high-speed Internet. **Pool(s):** heated outdoor. **Guest Services:** valet laundry. **Free Special Amenities:** full breakfast and high-speed Internet.

/ SOME UNITS FEE

COURTYARD BY MARRIOTT
Phone: (505)325-5111

Hotel
$77-$118

AAA Benefit:
AAA hotel discounts of 5% or more.

Address: 560 Scott Ave 87401 **Location:** 1 mi e on SR 516 (Main St), just s. **Facility:** 125 units. 4 stories, interior corridors. **Pool(s):** heated indoor. **Activities:** whirlpool, exercise room. **Guest Services:** valet and coin laundry.

/ SOME UNITS

▼ *See AAA listing this page* ▼

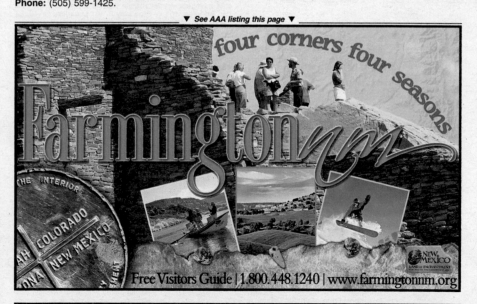

four corners four seasons

Farmington nm

Free Visitors Guide | 1.800.448.1240 | www.farmingtonnm.org

Find valuable AAA/CAA member savings
at AAA.com/discounts

HAMPTON INN & SUITES
Phone: 505/564-3100

Hotel
Rates not provided

AAA Benefit:
Members save up to 10% everyday!

Address: 1500 Bloomfield Blvd 87401 **Location:** 0.3 mi e of jct E Broadway and Scott Ave. **Facility:** 73 units. 4 stories, interior corridors. **Amenities:** high-speed Internet. **Pool(s):** heated indoor. **Activities:** whirlpool, exercise room. **Guest Services:** valet and coin laundry.

HOLIDAY INN EXPRESS
Phone: (505)325-2545

Hotel
$99-$169

Address: 2110 Bloomfield Blvd 87401 **Location:** 1.6 mi e on US 64 (Bloomfield Blvd), just past jct Broadway; on Frontage Rd. **Facility:** 101 units. 3 stories, interior corridors. **Terms:** 2 night minimum stay - seasonal, 3 day cancellation notice-fee imposed. **Pool(s):** heated indoor. **Activities:** whirlpool, exercise room. **Guest Services:** valet and coin laundry.

LA QUINTA INN FARMINGTON
Phone: (505)327-4706

Hotel
$72-$144

Address: 675 Scott Ave 87401 **Location:** 1 mi e on SR 516 (Main St), just s. **Facility:** 107 units, some two bedrooms. 2 stories (no elevator), interior/exterior corridors. **Amenities:** video games (fee). *Some:* high-speed Internet. **Pool(s):** heated outdoor. **Guest Services:** valet laundry.

QUALITY INN
Phone: 505/325-3700

Motel
Rates not provided

Address: 1901 E Broadway 87401 **Location:** On US 64 (Bloomfield Blvd), 1.6 mi e. **Facility:** 62 units. 3 stories, interior corridors. **Activities:** exercise room.

THE REGION INN
Phone: (505)325-1191

Hotel
$82-$125

Address: 601 E Broadway 87401 **Location:** 0.7 mi e on US 64 (Bloomfield Blvd). **Facility:** 75 units. 3 stories, interior corridors. **Terms:** 14 day cancellation notice-fee imposed. **Pool(s):** heated outdoor. **Activities:** whirlpool. **Guest Services:** valet and coin laundry, area transportation-within 5 mi. **Free Special Amenities: continental breakfast and high-speed Internet.**

ROYAL INN
Phone: 505/325-5061

Motel
$45-$85

Address: 701 Airport Dr 87401 **Location:** From Main St, 0.5 mi n. **Facility:** 21 units. 1 story, exterior corridors. **Amenities:** high-speed Internet. **Free Special Amenities: local telephone calls and high-speed Internet.**

TOWNEPLACE SUITES BY MARRIOTT
Phone: (505)327-2442

Extended Stay Hotel
$76-$127

AAA Benefit:
AAA hotel discounts of 5% or more.

Address: 4200 Sierra Vista Dr 87402 **Location:** 5 mi e on SR 516 (E Main St), just s. **Facility:** 116 units, some two bedrooms, efficiencies and kitchens. 5 stories, interior corridors. **Amenities:** high-speed Internet. **Pool(s):** heated indoor. **Activities:** whirlpool, exercise room. **Guest Services:** valet and coin laundry.

WHERE TO EAT

BLUE MOON DINER
Phone: 505/324-0001

American
$8-$13

AAA Inspector Notes: This 1950s theme diner is a true blast from the past. Enjoy all the favorites from burgers, fries and a shake to chicken-fried steak. For dessert, enjoy any one of the twenty flavors of homemade ice cream or a slice of pie. **Address:** 1819 E 20th St 87402 **Location:** Jct Sullivan St, just e; adjacent to movie theater.

KB DILLON'S BAR & GRILLE
Phone: 505/325-0222

American
$7-$33

AAA Inspector Notes: Appealing to those seeking a hearty meal, this downtown restaurant has rustic surroundings on the outside and a warm, boisterous atmosphere inside. Guests can relax in the large bar, which has a large-screen TV, as they wait to be seated or for an after-dinner drink. The menu lists steak, poultry, fish and veal choices, as well as several seafood selections. Attentive staff members in casual attire provide full service. **Bar:** full bar. **Address:** 101 W Broadway 87401 **Location:** On US 64 (Bloomfield Blvd); downtown.

LOS HERMANITOS RESTAURANT
Phone: 505/326-5664

Mexican
$7-$19

AAA Inspector Notes: This family-owned restaurant serves traditional Mexican favorites in a relaxed atmosphere. Hearty portions and quick service have guests fed and on their way in no time. **Address:** 3501 E Main St 87401 **Location:** 3 mi nw of historic town center.

RIVERWALK PATIO & GRILL
Phone: 505/327-5221

American
$8-$26

AAA Inspector Notes: This hotel restaurant's dinner menu lists a variety of steak and seafood entrees, pasta dishes and sandwiches. The salad and soup bar is well stocked. Varied areas are sectioned off with memorabilia tied to themes of fishing, farm and ranch, sports and the '50s and '60s. **Bar:** full bar. **Address:** 700 Scott Ave 87401 **Location:** 1 mi e on SR 516 (Main St), just s; in Red Lion Hotel Farmington.

ST. CLAIR WINERY & BISTRO
Phone: 505/326-1978

American
$8-$19

AAA Inspector Notes: The menu at this bistro features French-country dishes paired with award-winning New Mexico wines served in a charming dining room and seasonal outdoor patio. Enjoy live jazz music Thursday through Sunday nights. **Bar:** full bar. **Address:** 5150 E Main St, #101 87402 **Location:** 5.5 mi e on SR 516.

SI SEÑOR RESTAURANT   Phone: 505/324-9050

New Mexican
$8-$21

AAA Inspector Notes: Attentive uniformed staff at this restaurant serve traditional Mexican fare featuring daily lunch specials seven days a week. Menu items include homemade flour tortillas, delicious posole, red or green chile con carne and Mexican-style steaks. **Bar:** beer & wine. **Address:** 4015 E 30th St 87402 **Location:** 3.8 mi e; jct SR 516 (E Main St) and E 30th St. ⓑ Ⓛ Ⓓ

THREE RIVERS EATERY AND BREW HOUSE
                                   Phone: 505/324-2187

American
$7-$30

AAA Inspector Notes: This popular and lively local eatery features an extensive list of award-winning, hand-crafted beers and a menu that will satisfy any appetite. Located in the renovated Andrews Building in the historic downtown, the decor features antiques salvaged during construction plus the state's largest collection of beer labels and beer coasters. **Bar:** beer & wine. **Address:** 101 E Main St 87401 **Location:** Jct Orchard St; downtown. **Parking:** street only. Ⓛ Ⓓ

FORT SUMNER (G-5) pop. 1,031, elev. 4,049'

The agricultural potential of the Pecos River bottomlands surrounding this quiet farming and ranching center so impressed Maj. James Carleton that in 1852 he recommended the site for an Army post. A decade later, as brigadier general, he realized his dream. He established Fort Sumner and made it the core of a permanent reservation for the Navajos and Apaches, whose resettlement was being supervised by Col. Kit Carson.

In 1864 Carson forced more than 8,000 Navajos to make the 300-mile Long Walk from Fort Defiance, Ariz., to the 1,024,000-acre reservation at Fort Sumner. The fort was abandoned in 1868, and the Navajos returned to their tribal lands.

After he was sentenced to death in Lincoln *(see place listing p. 427)*, the notorious Billy the Kid fatally shot his guards and fled the town's courthouse on April 28, 1881. Nearly 3 months after the escape, a pistol-packing sheriff named Pat Garrett tracked down and killed the outlaw in Fort Sumner. Billy the Kid's grave, flanked by those of cronies Tom O'Folliard and Charlie Bowdre, sticks out like a sore thumb in Old Fort Sumner Cemetery, 3.5 miles south off Billy the Kid Road. All three tombs are surrounded by a big steel cage built after the Kid's footstone was stolen and recovered twice.

Fort Sumner Chamber of Commerce: 707 N. Fourth St., P.O. Box 28, Fort Sumner, NM 88119. **Phone:** (575) 355-7705.

FORT SUMNER STATE MONUMENT is 3 mi. e. on US 60, then 3 mi. s. on Billy the Kid Rd. The site marks the former Bosque Redondo Indian Reservation where some 9,000 Navajo and Mescalero Apache Indians were interned in the 1860s after the U.S. government removed them from tribal lands. Troops led by Kit Carson marched the Navajo some 300 miles to the prison camp, a grueling ordeal that came to be known as the "Long Walk." Exhibits and artifacts at the Bosque Redondo Memorial recount 5 years of starvation, disease and forced labor before the Navajo were allowed to return to their homes.

Hours: Wed.-Mon. 8:30-4:30. Closed Jan. 1, Easter, Thanksgiving and Christmas. Phone ahead to confirm schedule. **Cost:** $3; free (ages 0-16). **Phone:** (575) 355-2573.

FORT UNION NATIONAL MONUMENT (E-4)

Eight miles northwest of Watrous on SR 161 (off I-25 exit 366), ranks of chimneys are stark reminders of the days when Fort Union was one of the largest military posts on the Southwestern frontier. Fort Union was the chief quartermaster depot 1851-91 for all garrisons throughout the region as well as the primary station for troops assigned to protect settlers and Santa Fe Trail travelers.

The site was well chosen, for the two branches of the Santa Fe Trail—the Mountain Branch and the Cimarron—pass through the Fort Union Valley. In addition, the remote location put the soldiers closer to the tribes and farther from towns that might distract them from their duties.

A group of log buildings west of Wolf Creek constituted the first Fort Union. For a decade it served as a way station on the Santa Fe Trail and as a headquarters for battling the Utes, Jicarilla Apaches, Comanches and Kiowas.

The outbreak of the Civil War abruptly turned the Army's attention away from these conflicts. The second Fort Union, an earthwork defense bastion, was built east of the creek in late 1861. It was constructed by local volunteers just before Confederate forces from Texas, eager to control Colorado's mineral resources and Fort Union's supplies, swept up the Rio Grande Valley. After their supply train was destroyed in the Battle of Glorieta, the Confederate troops retreated and headed for home.

The third fort, whose garrison, quartermaster depot and arsenal still stand today, dates from the mid-1860s. For the next 15 years the Indian wars occupied the military, while tons of goods flowed through the depot. Gradually local tribes were subdued. The Santa Fe Railway reached New Mexico in 1879, making travel safer. Fort Union was abandoned in 1891.

Interpretive signs relay the history of the fort and the local area. A self-guiding 1.6-mile interpretive trail explores 100 acres of adobe ruins. A half-mile trail also is an option. A visitor center with a museum relates fort history. Living-history demonstrations and other events are offered during summer. Daily 8-6, Memorial Day-Labor Day; 8-4, rest of year. Closed Jan. 1, Thanksgiving and Christmas. Admission $3, free (ages 0-15). Phone (505) 425-8025.

GALLUP (F-1) pop. 21,678, elev. 6,508'
• Hotels p. 412 • Restaurants p. 414

The Atchison, Topeka & Santa Fe Railway pushed into this red rock mesa region in 1881 to use area coal deposits for its engines. Until then mostly stockmen had lived in the area; Gallup was a stage stop consisting of a saloon/general store called the Blue Goose. Coal mining and the presence of the railroad attracted settlers from other nations, giving the city an especially cosmopolitan heritage.

The city is best known as the main trading center for most Navajos, whose vast reservation extends north and west into Arizona as well as for the residents of the nearby Zuni Pueblo *(see place listing p. 489)*. Gallup has more than 100 trading posts, shops and galleries. At many trading posts handmade articles ranging from rugs and baskets to turquoise jewelry are sold.

Gallup Development Commission: 110 W. Aztec Ave., P.O. Box 1270, Gallup, NM 87301. **Phone:** (505) 726-2040.

GALLUP CULTURAL CENTER is at 201 US 66E. Southwest American Indian history is presented within the setting of a restored Santa Fe Railroad depot. Audio-narrated exhibits include vintage photographs, sand paintings, ancient pottery and a 10-foot bronze statue honoring World War II Navajo code talkers. The Kiva Cinema presents films about American Indian culture. **Tours:** Guided tours are available. **Time:** Allow 30 minutes minimum. **Hours:** Mon.-Fri. 9-5, Sat. 9-4, Memorial Day-Labor Day; Mon.-Fri. 9-5, rest of year. **Cost:** Free. **Phone:** (505) 863-4131.

AMERICAS BEST VALUE INN & SUITES
Phone: 505/722-0757
Motel
Rates not provided
Address: 2003 Hwy 66 W 87301 **Location:** I-40 exit 20, 1 mi w. Across from train tracks. **Facility:** 65 units, some kitchens. 2 stories (no elevator), interior/exterior corridors. **Amenities:** high-speed Internet, safes. **Guest Services:** coin laundry. **Free Special Amenities:** continental breakfast and high-speed Internet. *(See ad this page.)*
/ SOME UNITS FEE

BEST WESTERN RED ROCK INN Phone: 505/722-7600
Hotel
Rates not provided
AAA Benefit: Members save up to 20%, plus 10% bonus points with Best Western Rewards®.
Address: 3010 E US 66 87301 **Location:** I-40 exit 26, 1 mi w. **Facility:** 77 units. 2 stories (no elevator), interior corridors. **Pool(s):** heated indoor. **Activities:** whirlpool. **Guest Services:** coin laundry. **Free Special Amenities:** local telephone calls and high-speed Internet.
/ SOME UNITS FEE

Enjoy great savings on hotel rates at AAA.com or CAA.ca

▼ See AAA listing this page ▼

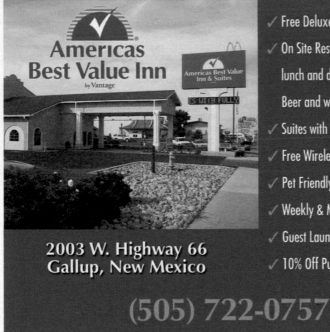

Americas Best Value Inn by Vantage

Americas Best Value Inn & Suites

✓ Free Deluxe Continental Breakfast

✓ On Site Restaurant serving breakfast, lunch and dinner

Beer and wine also available

✓ Suites with Fully Equipped Kitchens

✓ Free Wireless & High Speed Internet

✓ Pet Friendly (with fee)

✓ Weekly & Monthly Rates Available

✓ Guest Laundry

✓ 10% Off Published Rates

2003 W. Highway 66
Gallup, New Mexico

(505) 722-0757

Reservations (888) 315-2378 • www.AmericasBestValueInn.com

COMFORT SUITES

Phone: (505)863-3445

Hotel
S89-S129

Address: 3940 E Hwy 66 87301 **Location:** I-40 exit 26, just e. **Facility:** 66 units. 3 stories, interior corridors. **Amenities:** high-speed Internet. **Pool(s):** heated indoor. **Activities:** whirlpool, exercise room. **Guest Services:** valet and coin laundry. **Free Special Amenities: full breakfast and high-speed Internet.**
(See ad this page.)

HAMPTON INN & SUITES

Phone: 505/726-0900

Hotel
Rates not provided

AAA Benefit:
Members save up to 10% everyday!

Address: 1450 W Maloney Ave 87301 **Location:** I-40 exit 20, 1 mi w. **Facility:** 63 units. 4 stories, interior corridors. **Amenities:** high-speed Internet. **Pool(s):** heated indoor. **Activities:** whirlpool, limited exercise equipment. **Guest Services:** valet and coin laundry.

▼ See AAA listing this page ▼

GALLUP, NEW MEXICO

Comfort Suites®. Relax and Get Recharged.

- 3 Miles from Red Rock State Park, 2 Miles from Fire Rock Casino
- Free hot breakfast
- Free High Speed Wired/Wireless Internet access throughout hotel
- Large Spacious Suites
- 100% smoke free
- Swimming pool, Spa, Fitness Center
- Business Center

choicehotels.com
3940 E Hwy 66
Gallup, NM 87301
800.228.1222
505.863.3445

Get the free mobile app at
http://gettag.mobi

▼ See AAA listing p. 414 ▼

An affordable Stay, everyday!

- Business King Rooms
- Free Continental Breakfast
- High Speed Internet
- USA Today
- Coffee Maker and Refrigerator in all rooms
- Outdoor Pool (Seasonal)
- Fitness Center
- Pets Welcome
- Truck Parking in Rear

Red Roof Inn®

Scan this tag on your smartphone and start saving today!

10% Off Published Rates for AAA

www.redroof.com
3304 W. Hwy 66 Gallup, NM 87301 • 505-722-7765

Get the free mobile app at
http://gettag.mobi

HAMPTON INN WEST
Phone: 505/722-7224

Hotel
Rates not provided

AAA Benefit:
Members save up to 10% everyday!

Address: 111 Twin Buttes Rd 87301 **Location:** I-40 exit 16, just e. **Facility:** 60 units. 3 stories, interior corridors. **Amenities:** high-speed Internet. **Pool(s):** heated indoor. **Activities:** whirlpool, exercise room. **Guest Services:** valet and coin laundry.

LA QUINTA INN & SUITES GALLUP
Phone: (505)722-2233

Hotel
$116-$179

Address: 3880 E Hwy 66 87301 **Location:** I-40 exit 26, just e. **Facility:** 67 units. 3 stories, interior corridors. **Amenities:** high-speed Internet. **Pool(s):** heated indoor. **Activities:** whirlpool, steamroom, exercise room. **Guest Services:** coin laundry.

MICROTEL INN
Phone: (505)722-2600

Motel
$50-$59

Address: 3270 W Hwy 66 87301 **Location:** I-40 exit 16, just e. **Facility:** 53 units. 2 stories (no elevator), interior corridors. **Terms:** 7 day cancellation notice. **Free Special Amenities: continental breakfast and high-speed Internet.**

QUALITY INN & SUITES
Phone: (505)726-1000

Motel
$90-$130

Address: 1500 W Maloney Ave 87301 **Location:** I-40 exit 20, just n on Muñoz Dr, then just w. **Facility:** 71 units. 2 stories (no elevator), interior/exterior corridors. **Terms:** cancellation fee imposed. **Pool(s):** heated indoor. **Activities:** sauna, whirlpool. **Guest Services:** valet and coin laundry. **Free Special Amenities: full breakfast and high-speed Internet.**

RED LION HOTEL GALLUP
Phone: 505/722-2221

Hotel
$62-$109

Address: 3009 W US 66 87301 **Location:** I-40 exit 16, 1 mi e. **Facility:** 126 units. 2 stories (no elevator), interior corridors. **Terms:** cancellation fee imposed. **Pool(s):** heated indoor. **Activities:** whirlpool, exercise room. **Guest Services:** valet and coin laundry, area transportation-casino.

RED ROOF INN
Phone: (505)722-7765

Motel
$44-$59

Address: 3304 W Hwy 66 87301 **Location:** I-40 exit 16, just se. Adjacent to RV/truck parking. **Facility:** 104 units. 2 stories (no elevator), exterior corridors. **Pool(s):** heated outdoor. **Activities:** sauna, exercise room. **Guest Services:** coin laundry. **Free Special Amenities: continental breakfast and high-speed Internet.** *(See ad p. 413.)*

WHERE TO EAT

ANGELA'S CAFE CON LECHE
Phone: 505/722-7526

Sandwiches
$5-$9

AAA Inspector Notes: Nestled in the historic train depot, this comfy café is a local favorite serving excellent homemade soups, salads and sandwiches. **Address:** 201 E Hwy 66 87301 **Location:** I-40 exit 20, s to US 66, then 1.5 mi e; in historic train depot.

BADLANDS GRILL
Phone: 505/722-5157

Steak
$17-$39

AAA Inspector Notes: This restaurant prepares a good selection of steaks, seafood and tempting pastry desserts made in house. **Bar:** beer & wine. **Reservations:** suggested. **Address:** 2201 W Hwy 66 87301 **Location:** I-40 exit 16, 2.7 mi e.

EARL'S FAMILY RESTAURANT
Phone: 505/863-4201

American
$6-$14

AAA Inspector Notes: Since 1947, this landmark family restaurant has served a wide variety of American and Mexican dishes. The favorite steak and enchiladas is a blend of the two cuisines. A long held tradition allows Native American artists to sell jewelry and crafts directly to dining patrons inside and at tables outside the eatery. **Address:** 1400 E Hwy 66 87301 **Location:** I-40 exit 22, just s to US 66, then e. **Classic**

EL SOMBRERO
Phone: 505/863-4554

Mexican
$9-$15

AAA Inspector Notes: Along famous Route 66, this restaurant has a Southwestern feel with informal service and easy-going hospitality. Although American dishes are available, Mexican foods reign supreme. **Bar:** beer & wine. **Address:** 1201 W US 66 87301 **Location:** I-40 exit 20, just w.

KING DRAGON
Phone: 505/863-6300

Chinese
$4-$14

AAA Inspector Notes: Specializing in Mandarin, Szechuan and Hunan dishes, this restaurant also lays out a popular buffet at lunch. In addition to beef, pork and chicken entrees, the menu lists a good choice of soups. Portions are generous. **Bar:** full bar. **Address:** 1212 N Hwy 491 87301 **Location:** I-40 exit 20, 1.5 mi n.

SAMMY C'S ROCK'N SPORTS PUB, GRILLE & COFFEE BAR
Phone: 505/863-2220

American
$9-$20

AAA Inspector Notes: This family-friendly restaurant features many sporting events broadcasted on flat-screen TVs, a cabaret, Wi-Fi and a coffee bar. The varied menu, including a separate and fun child's menu, offers four daily soup choices, Cobb and chef salads, juicy burgers, a variety of pasta dishes, grilled trout and tempting desserts. **Bar:** full bar. **Address:** 107 W Coal Ave 87301 **Location:** I-40 exit 20, between 1st and 2nd sts; downtown.

GILA CLIFF DWELLINGS NATIONAL MONUMENT (H-2)

Gila Cliff Dwellings National Monument is a minimum 2-hour drive 44 miles north of Silver City via SR 15; vehicles pulling trailers 20 feet or longer should use SR 35 north from San Lorenzo. In this rough and desolate country near the west fork of the Gila (HEE-la) River, seven natural cavities indent the face of a cliff some 175 feet above the canyon floor. Five of these hollows contain rooms constructed during the late 13th century by people of the Mogollon culture—these remain the focus of the monument.

A 1-mile hiking trail loops from the contact station to the dwellings. Gila Visitor Center *(see attraction listing below.)* is 2 miles south of the monument entrance. Guided 1-hour tours of the cliff dwellings depart daily at 1 from the dwellings themselves (allow 30 minutes to walk from the trailhead). Pets are not permitted on the monument trails; free kennels are available.

Park open daily 8:30-5, Memorial Day weekend-Labor Day; 9-4, rest of year. Visitor center open daily 8-5, Memorial Day weekend-Labor Day; 8-4:30, rest of year. Admission $3; free (ages 0-15 and Federal Recreational Lands Pass holders); $10 (family). Exact change is required and may be obtained at the visitor center. Self-guiding trail pamphlets and travel guide brochures are available at no cost. Phone (575) 536-9461.

GILA NATIONAL FOREST (H-1)

Elevations in the forest range from 4,000 ft. in the desert to 11,000 ft. at Whitewater Baldy. Refer to AAA maps for additional elevation information.

In southwestern New Mexico, Gila (HEE-la) National Forest occupies 3,321,000 acres of forest and rangeland. The smaller of its two units extends north from Lordsburg along the Big Burro Mountains. The main unit, north of Silver City *(see place listing p. 474),* embraces the Black, Mogollon, Tularosa and Diablo mountains. These wild ranges and remote canyons were the stronghold of such Apache warriors as Geronimo and Mangas Coloradas.

Much of the Mogollon Mountains lies within the Gila Wilderness, the first area in the nation to be so designated. Instrumental in its 1924 establishment was Aldo Leopold, the forester and naturalist whose "Sand County Almanac" and other writings have become classics of environmental literature.

A plaque 9 miles south of Glenwood on US 180 at the Aldo Leopold Overlook marks the Leopold Vista Historical Monument. The Gila, Blue Range and Aldo Leopold wilderness areas as well as Gila Cliff Dwellings National Monument *(see place listing p. 414)* lie north of Silver City.

In the 1870s the region was the center of a mining boom, of which ghost towns and old mine structures are silent reminders. The half-mile-long Catwalk National Recreation Trail passes through the steep walls of Whitewater Canyon. A metal suspension bridge carries hikers across a creek that once provided water to a nearby mill. Now a popular recreation area, it is reached via SR 174 from US 180. A $3 fee is charged per private vehicle.

The 110-mile Trail of the Mountain Spirits Scenic Byway travels from Silver City east to San Lorenzo, through the Mimbres Valley, down Sapillo Creek, past Clinton P. Anderson Vista to Gila Cliff Dwellings National Monument, and returns to Silver City over

the Pinos Altos Range. Overlooks along the byway provide perspective on the magnitude of the cliffs and the surrounding countryside.

There are numerous developed recreation areas in the forest. Stream and lake fishing and big game hunting are available in season. *See Recreation Chart.*

GILA VISITOR CENTER is 2 mi. s. of Gila Cliff Dwellings National Monument, 43 mi. n. of Silver City via SR 15; vehicles pulling trailers 20 feet or longer should use SR 35 north from San Lorenzo. Cultural artifacts and an exhibit about the Apache and Mogollon people and the Gila Wilderness are presented. A 15-minute videotape is shown. **Hours:** Visitor center daily 8-5, Memorial Day weekend-Labor Day; 8-4:30, rest of year. Closed Jan. 1 and Christmas. **Cost:** Free. **Phone:** (575) 536-9461.

GRANTS (F-2) pop. 9,182, elev. 6,450'
• Hotels p. 416 • Restaurants p. 416

Navajo rancher Paddy Martinez's curiosity about the odd yellow rock he found on Haystack Mountain about 10 miles west had far-reaching effects. The rock was uranium, and within months of the day he happened upon it in 1950, Grants was transformed from a farming community to a mining town.

With huge contracts from the Atomic Energy Commission for all the uranium they could produce, mining companies rushed to the area, which soon proved to contain one of the largest uranium reserves in the world. A 1982-83 recession forced the closure of mills and mines, bringing to an end a prosperous era.

Grants/Cibola County Chamber of Commerce: 100 N. Iron Ave., Grants, NM 87020. **Phone:** (505) 287-4802 or (800) 748-2142.

EL MALPAIS NATIONAL MONUMENT AND NATIONAL CONSERVATION AREA is 23 mi. s.w. of I-40 via SRs 53 and 117. The monument preserves 376,000 acres of *mal país*, or badlands, a landscape of lava flows, volcanoes and lava tube caves. Primitive camping, hiking, caving (equipment needed) and mountain biking are permitted. Information is available at the National Park Information Center, 23 mi. south of Grants on SR 53; the Northwest New Mexico Visitor Center, off I-40 exit 85 in Grants; and the Bureau of Land Management Ranger Station, 9 mi. s. of I-40 on SR 117. *See Recreation Chart.*

Note: Use heavy footgear and extreme care when hiking on the sharp lava. **Hours:** Daily 24 hours. Visitor center closed Jan. 1, Thanksgiving and Christmas. **Cost:** Free. **Phone:** (505) 783-4774 for the El Malpais Information Center, (505) 280-2918 for the Bureau of Land Management Ranger Station, or (505) 876-2783 for the Northwest New Mexico Visitor Center.

ICE CAVE AND BANDERA VOLCANO is 25 mi. s.w. of Grants on SR 53, w. of El Malpais National Monument. A partially collapsed lava tube formed the cave, which contains perpetual formations of ice. At an elevation of 8,000 feet, the temperature is a constant 31 F. The dormant Bandera Volcano, which erupted 10,000 years ago with massive lava flows, rises above the mountain valley. Self-guiding tours depart from the trading post located a half mile south of SR 53.

Comfortable shoes are recommended. Gem stone mining also is available. **Time:** Allow 1 hour minimum. **Hours:** Daily 8 a.m.-1 hour before dusk. **Cost:** $10; $9 (ages 65+); $5 (ages 5-12). **Phone:** (505) 783-4303 or (888) 423-2283. 🎫

NEW MEXICO MINING MUSEUM is 2 mi. w. off I-40 exit 85 at 100 N. Iron Ave. Exhibits chronicle the area's 1950 uranium discovery. Beneath the museum, reached by elevator, is a replica of a mine—complete with equipment. **Time:** Allow 30 minutes minimum. **Hours:** Mon.-Sat. 9-4. Closed major holidays. **Cost:** $3; $2 (ages 7-18 and 60+). **Phone:** (505) 287-4802 or (800) 748-2142.

COMFORT INN   **Phone:** (505)287-8700
◆◆ ◆◆   **Address:** 1551 E Santa Fe Ave 87020
Hotel   **Location:** I-40 exit 85, 0.3 mi n.
$90-$109   **Facility:** 52 units. 2 stories (no elevator), interior corridors. **Terms:** cancellation fee imposed. **Amenities:** high-speed Internet. **Pool(s):** heated indoor. **Activities:** whirlpool. **Guest Services:** coin laundry.
🛎️ 🏊 BIZ 🛜 🖥️ / SOME UNITS FEE 🐾 📶 📺

HOLIDAY INN EXPRESS   **Phone:** (505)287-9252
◆◆ ◆◆ ◆   **Address:** 1512 E Santa Fe Ave 87020 **Location:** I-40 exit 85, just n. **Facility:** 76 units. 3 stories, interior corridors. **Amenities:** high-speed Internet. **Pool(s):** heated indoor. **Activities:** whirlpool, limited exercise equipment. **Guest Services:** valet and coin laundry. **Free Special Amenities:** expanded continental breakfast and high-speed Internet.
SAVE 🛎️ CALL 🆎 🏊 BIZ 🛜 ❌ FEE 🐾 🖥️ / SOME UNITS 📶 📺

Contemporary hotel featuring triple sheets, 32″ flat TV, WiFi, microfridge, free hot breakfast, & pool

Safety tip: Keep a current AAA/CAA Road Atlas in every vehicle

QUALITY INN & SUITES   **Phone:** 505/285-4676
◆◆ ◆◆   **Address:** 1496 E Santa Fe Ave 87020 **Location:** I-40 exit 85, 0.3 mi n. **Facility:** 58 units. 2 stories (no elevator), interior corridors. **Pool(s):** heated indoor. **Activities:** whirlpool, limited exercise equipment. **Guest Services:** coin laundry. **Free Special Amenities:** expanded continental breakfast and high-speed Internet.
Hotel
Rates not provided
SAVE 🛎️ 🆎 BIZ 🛜 ❌ 📶 📺 🖥️ / SOME UNITS FEE 🐾

Free hot breakfast, WiFi, microfridge, Indoor pool, fitness ctr. Easy I-40 access. Pet friendly w/fee.

WHERE TO EAT

CANTON CAFE   **Phone:** 505/287-8314
◆
Chinese
$6-$10
   AAA Inspector Notes: Locals keep this eatery busy for lunch and dinner. The buffet lines up a good selection of traditional items along the lines of sweet and sour pork, Szechuan shrimp and kung pao chicken, in addition to salads and desserts. **Address:** 1212 E Santa Fe Ave 87020 **Location:** I-40 exit 85, 0.8 mi w on Business Loop 40 (Santa Fe Ave). L D

EL CAFECITO   **Phone:** 505/285-6229
◆
New Mexican
$5-$10
   AAA Inspector Notes: Convenient to Interstate 40, this friendly and colorful cafe offers drive-through service and is open for breakfast and lunch. Examples of New Mexican cuisine include stuffed sopaipillas, chimichangas and a signature fritta frutta topped with ice cream. **Address:** 820 E Santa Fe Ave 87020 **Location:** I-40 exit 85, 1.5 mi w on Business Loop 40 (Santa Fe Ave). B L D

LA VENTANA RESTAURANT   **Phone:** 505/287-9393
◆◆ ◆◆
American
$9-$42
   AAA Inspector Notes: The city's business community flocks to the relaxed restaurant's comfortable Southwestern setting. A full-service bar complements tempting selections of great steak, salad and tasty desserts. Good choices include the succulent prime rib, fresh seafood and well-seasoned Mexican favorites. **Bar:** full bar. **Reservations:** suggested. **Address:** 110 1/2 Geis St 87020 **Location:** Just n of Santa Fe Ave; center. L D

HOBBS (I-6) pop. 34,122, elev. 3,621'
• Restaurants p. 418

Oil and water mix in the economy of Hobbs, a modern city on the western edge of the flat Llano Estacado. Grasslands first attracted farmers and cattlemen to this streamless region in the early 20th century; one of them, James Hobbs, gave his name to the community. A vast underground reserve of water produced bountiful crops of cotton, alfalfa, vegetables and grain as well as a thriving cattle industry.

In 1928, however, the discovery of another kind of well changed pastoral Hobbs into a boomtown. Within a decade the city was the home of some

10,000 citizens, most associated with tapping the oil field that still produces 90 percent of the state's petroleum. Many oil companies operating in the area have headquarters in Hobbs.

For history buffs, the Thelma A. Webber Southwest Heritage Room in Scarborough Memorial Library at the University of the Southwest, 6610 Lovington Highway, contains a small exhibit of prehistoric American Indian artifacts, art pieces and pioneer collectibles; phone (800) 530-4400.

Hobbs Chamber of Commerce: 400 N. Marland Blvd., Hobbs, NM 88240. **Phone:** (575) 397-3202.

WESTERN HERITAGE MUSEUM AND LEA COUNTY COWBOY HALL OF FAME
is about 4 mi. n. to 5317 Lovington Hwy./SR 18 on the New Mexico Junior College campus. Well-known ranchers and rodeo performers of Lea County are honored. Exhibits depict the cultures—American Indian to pioneer—that shaped the area for 150 years. **Time:** Allow 30 minutes minimum. **Hours:** Tues.-Sat. 10-5, Sun. 1-5. Closed major holidays. **Cost:** $3; $2 (ages 6-18 and 65+). **Phone:** (575) 392-6730.

BEST WESTERN EXECUTIVE INN
Phone: (575)397-7171

Hotel
$90-$120

AAA Benefit: Members save up to 20%, plus 10% bonus points with Best Western Rewards®.

Address: 309 N Marland Blvd 88240 **Location:** US 62, 180 and Snyder St. **Facility:** 62 units. 2 stories (no elevator), exterior corridors. **Amenities:** high-speed Internet. **Pool(s):** outdoor. **Free Special Amenities: full breakfast and high-speed Internet.**

COMFORT SUITES - HOBBS
Phone: (575)492-1000

Hotel
$79-$129

Address: 2708 W Scenic Dr 88240 **Location:** Jct SR 18 N (Lovington Hwy) and W Millen Dr, 0.8 mi s. **Facility:** 75 units, some efficiencies. 4 stories, interior corridors. **Terms:** cancellation fee imposed. **Amenities:** high-speed Internet, safes. **Pool(s):** heated indoor. **Activities:** exercise room. **Guest Services:** valet and coin laundry. **Free Special Amenities: full breakfast and high-speed Internet.**

COUNTRY INN & SUITES HOBBS NEW MEXICO
Phone: (575)391-0282

Hotel
$79-$109

Address: 5220 N Lovington Hwy 88240 **Location:** Jct SR 18 N (Lovington Hwy) and W Millen Dr, 1 mi s. **Facility:** 63 units. 3 stories, interior corridors. **Amenities:** high-speed Internet. **Pool(s):** heated indoor. **Activities:** whirlpool, exercise room. **Guest Services:** valet and coin laundry. **Free Special Amenities: full breakfast and high-speed Internet.**

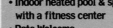

Free Hot Breakfast, High Speed Internet & Indoor Pool/Spa. Just 1 mile North of Zia Park and Casino.

DAYS INN
Phone: (575)397-6541

Motel
$66-$81

Address: 211 N Marland Blvd 88240 **Location:** 2 mi e on US 62 and 180. **Facility:** 58 units. 3 stories (no elevator), exterior corridors. **Amenities:** safes. *Some:* high-speed Internet. **Pool(s):** outdoor. **Guest Services:** coin laundry.

▼ See AAA listing p. 418 ▼

HOBBS, NEW MEXICO

Sleep Inn.® Well rested, every time.

- 1/2 mile from Black Gold Casino & Zia Park Horseracing
- Enjoy a full complimentary hot breakfast
- Free Hi-Speed Internet & Wi-Fi
- In-room fridge, microwave & coffee
- Indoor heated pool & spa along with a fitness center
- Pets Welcome

choicehotels.com
4630 N. Lovington Hwy
Hobbs, NM 88240
575.393.3355

Get the free mobile app at
http://gettag.mobi

ECONO LODGE

Phone: 575/397-3591

Hotel
Rates not provided

Address: 619 N Marland Blvd 88240 **Location:** 2.5 mi e on US 62 and 180. **Facility:** 37 units. 2 stories (no elevator), exterior corridors. **Amenities:** high-speed Internet. **Pool(s):** heated outdoor. **Guest Services:** coin laundry. **Free Special Amenities: continental breakfast and high-speed Internet.**

FAIRFIELD INN & SUITES

Phone: (575)393-0667

Hotel
$107-$123

AAA Benefit:
AAA hotel discounts of 5% or more.

Address: 1350 W Joe Harvey Blvd 88240 **Location:** 0.4 mi n on Grimes St to Joe Harvey Blvd, just w. **Facility:** 94 units. 4 stories, interior corridors. **Amenities:** high-speed Internet. **Pool(s):** heated outdoor. **Activities:** whirlpool, exercise room. **Guest Services:** valet and coin laundry.

HAMPTON INN & SUITES

Phone: 575/492-6000

Hotel
Rates not provided

AAA Benefit:
Members save up to 10% everyday!

Address: 5420 Lovington Hwy 88242 **Location:** Jct SR 18 N (Lovington Hwy) and Millen Dr, 1 mi n. **Facility:** 67 units. 3 stories, interior corridors. **Amenities:** high-speed Internet. **Pool(s):** heated indoor. **Activities:** exercise room. **Guest Services:** valet and coin laundry.

HOLIDAY INN EXPRESS

Phone: (575)392-8777

Hotel
$89-$169

Address: 3610 N Lovington Hwy 88240 **Location:** Jct SR 18 (Lovington Hwy) and Business Rt 19, 1.2 mi n. **Facility:** 65 units. 3 stories, interior corridors. **Amenities:** high-speed Internet. **Pool(s):** heated indoor. **Activities:** whirlpool, exercise room. **Guest Services:** valet and coin laundry.

LA QUINTA INN & SUITES HOBBS

Phone: (575)397-8777

Hotel
$94-$160

Address: 3312 N Lovington Hwy 88240 **Location:** SR 18 (Lovington Hwy), just s of jct Joe Harvey Blvd. **Facility:** 68 units. 3 stories, interior corridors. **Amenities:** high-speed Internet. **Pool(s):** heated indoor. **Activities:** whirlpool, exercise room. **Guest Services:** valet and coin laundry.

SLEEP INN & SUITES

Phone: (575)393-3355

Hotel
$89-$139

Address: 4630 Lovington Hwy 88240 **Location:** Jct SR 18 N (Lovington Hwy) and W Millen Dr, 0.8 mi s. **Facility:** 67 units. 3 stories, interior corridors. **Terms:** cancellation fee imposed. **Amenities:** high-speed Internet. **Pool(s):** heated indoor. **Activities:** whirlpool, exercise room. **Guest Services:** valet and coin laundry. *(See ad p. 417.)*

WHERE TO EAT

CATTLE BARON STEAK & SEAFOOD

Phone: 575/393-2800

American
$8-$22

AAA Inspector Notes: A scrumptious array of menu selections includes steak, seafood, chicken and prime rib as well as desserts such as caramel apple pie. An upscale Western decor includes wood trim and distinctive chandeliers made from deer antlers. **Bar:** full bar. **Address:** 1930 N Grimes St 88240 **Location:** Jct Broadway and Grimes St, 1.3 mi n; downtown.

GRANDY'S RESTAURANT

Phone: 575/397-2219

American
$4-$8

AAA Inspector Notes: Fried chicken and country-fried steak are menu standbys at the restaurant, a regional franchise. They also offer family-style dining menu. The decor is a step up from that of most quick-serve eateries and more resembles that of a conventional restaurant. Some elements of increased service include additional rolls, iced tea refills and tray removal. **Address:** 1917 N Turner St 88240 **Location:** Just se of jct N Turner St and SR 18 N (Lovington Hwy).

PACIFIC RIM

Phone: 575/392-0030

Pacific Rim
$10-$28

AAA Inspector Notes: Enjoy creative Pacific Rim-inspired Asian cuisine in a peaceful setting. A wide variety of seafood, shellfish, beef and chicken entrées are featured as well as custom stir-fry and custom pasta dishes. Vegetarian selections are available. Finish the meal with one of the luscious homemade desserts. **Bar:** beer & wine. **Address:** 1309 Joe Harvey Blvd 88240 **Location:** N on Lovington Hwy to Joe Harvey Blvd, just e.

TIA JUANA'S MEXICAN GRILLE & CANTINA

Phone: 575/392-0500

Mexican
$6-$21

AAA Inspector Notes: Hearty portions of flavorful Mexican favorites is served in a colorful and lively atmosphere. The homemade flour tortillas are a must-try item. **Bar:** full bar. **Address:** 3510 Lovington Hwy 88240 **Location:** SR 18 (Lovington Hwy), just s of jct Joe Harvey Blvd.

ISLETA PUEBLO (G-3) elev. 4,887'

Thirteen miles south of Albuquerque in the Rio Grande Valley, Isleta Pueblo was established in the 14th century. Its name in Spanish means "little island."

SAN AGUSTÍN DE LA ISLETA MISSION is s. of Isleta Blvd., following signs. The heavily buttressed structure was erected in 1613 by Spanish missionary Fray Juan de Salas. During the Pueblo Rebellion the mission was burned partially and then used as a corral. The church, restored after the 1692 reconquest, has been in constant use since. **Hours:** Mon.-Fri. 10-3. **Cost:** Donations. **Phone:** (505) 869-3398.

JÉMEZ PUEBLO (C-2) pop. 1,788, elev. 5,604'

When European explorers arrived in 1541, the Jémez nation was one of the most powerful pueblo cultures in the Southwest. With an estimated population of 30,000, the Towa-speaking people lived in numerous villages spread far across the high mountain mesas. Clashes between the two cultures eventually ensued and the Jémez defended their land for some 80 years. Eventually, their defenses—but not their traditions—were broken by gunfire.

Through perseverance Jémez traditions, religion and language remain alive. Today the tribe numbers about 3,400 members, many of whom live within the pueblo community of Walatowa.

Note: To preserve privacy and culture, the pueblo is closed to the public except for certain feast days throughout the year when colorful ceremonial dances are performed. Photography, tape recording, sketching or painting is prohibited.

The Walatowa Visitor Center, at 7413 SR 4, offers cultural exhibits, photographs, pottery displays, a reconstructed field house and nature walks. Guided 1.5-hour hikes into the canyon are offered; cost is $7 per person; $5 camera permit. On weekends from late August to late October, the Jémez Farmers' Market features traditional foods. Arts and crafts shows and tribal dances are held at various times throughout the year. For further information, including dates the pueblo is open to the public, phone the visitor center at (575) 834-7235.

The Jémez Mountain Trail (SR 44/US 550) is a National Scenic Byway which runs through the Jémez and Zia reserves between Cuba and San Ysidro.

JÉMEZ SPRINGS (B-2) pop. 250, elev. 6,200'

About 13 miles north of Jémez Pueblo, the hot mineral waters at Jémez Springs attracted Spanish explorers, pueblo dwellers, cowboys, miners and pioneers. A bath house built here in the 1870s continues to serve weary travelers. Five miles north are the Soda Dam and Battleship Rock formations; there are picnic facilities at Battleship Rock, and trout fishing is available.

JÉMEZ STATE MONUMENT is 1 mi. n. on SR 4. The site preserves the 500-year-old stone ruins of Giusewa Pueblo, ancestral home of the present-day Jémez people. About 1621 the Spanish built the fortresslike San Jose de los Jémez Mission; its massive walls still stand. A visitor center offers interpretive history exhibits and information about self-guiding tours. Special events are scheduled throughout the year. **Hours:** Wed.-Sun. 8:30-5. Closed major holidays. **Cost:** $3; free (ages 0-16). Combination ticket with the Coronado State Monument $5 (see Bernalillo p. 390). **Phone:** (575) 829-3530.

CAÑON DEL RIO RIVERSIDE INN   Phone: 575/829-4377

Bed & Breakfast
Rates not provided

Address: 16445 Hwy 4 87025 **Location:** 1 mi s of center. **Facility:** Known for great massage treatments and retreat-like luxuries, the inn is situated along the river at the base of dramatic cliffs. 6 units. 1 story, interior/exterior corridors. **Pool(s):** heated outdoor. **Activities:** sauna, whirlpool, cross country skiing, hiking trails, jogging, spa.

WHERE TO EAT

LOS OJOS RESTAURANT & SALOON
Phone: 575/829-3547

American
$8-$15

AAA Inspector Notes: Rustic decor and vintage Western memorabilia sets the stage in this village restaurant, popular for its northern New Mexico cuisine, generous one-third-pound burgers and the weekend prime rib dinner. Vegetarians will find plenty of selections. The fresh-baked fruit of the forest pie is a must for dessert. Live music is presented every Monday, Wednesday and Saturday. **Bar:** full bar. **Address:** 17596 Hwy 4 87025 **Location:** Center. L D

LAGUNA PUEBLO (C-2) elev. 5,807'

Rich in American Indian history, Laguna Pueblo is divided into six villages, with Old Laguna Village having served as the capital since the early 1300s. Casa Blanca is a tourist and commercial center for the reservation, which is known for its traditional crafts, pottery and jewelry.

After the completion of the mission church, the Spanish government recognized the pueblo as one of the largest Keresan pueblos. Completed in 1699, the Mission of the Pueblo of Laguna is a long, narrow stone structure notable for its bright and unusual interior design.

The pueblo can be visited dawn to dusk weekdays, although religious ceremonies are closed to the public on weekends. Photographing, sketching, painting or recording pueblo ceremonies is not permitted.

Governor's Office of Pueblo-Laguna: P.O. Box 194, Laguna Pueblo, NM 87026. **Phone:** (505) 552-6654.

Shopping areas: The Dancing Eagle Supermarket, off I-40, offers a number of stores featuring traditional American Indian crafts and wares.

GAMBLING ESTABLISHMENTS

• **Dancing Eagle Casino** is off I-40 exit 108. **Hours:** Fri.-Sun. 24 hours, Mon.-Thurs. 8 a.m.-4 a.m. **Phone:** (505) 552-7777 or (877) 440-9969.

LA MESA pop. 728

CHOPE'S BAR & CAFE
Phone: 575/233-3420

Mexican
$4-$9

AAA Inspector Notes: This legendary cafe and bar has been serving locals since 1915 and has become a favorite pilgrimage for many fans from across the country. The chile rellenos are a must along with the green chile enchiladas. Be sure to save room for the fluffy sopaipillas with honey. **Bar:** full bar. **Address:** 16165 S Hwy 28 88044 **Location:** Center. L D

LAS CRUCES (I-3) pop. 97,618, elev. 3,908'
• Hotels p. 420 • Restaurants p. 424

A little forest of crosses marking the graves of members of a caravan ambushed by Mescalero Apaches soon came to identify this spot on El Camino Real at the foot of the Organ Mountains. By the mid-19th century Las Cruces—the crosses—was a major supply point for mining operations and forts that protected the trade routes to Santa Fe and points west. The largest of these posts was Fort Selden in nearby Radium Springs *(see place listing p. 434).* In the Mesquite Street Historic District, parts of the original 1849 town still remain. Small adobes painted shades of pink, blue and green are found east of Main Street between Picacho and Lohman avenues.

The town's real foundation, however, is agriculture. Irrigated by the Rio Grande, the surrounding Mesilla Valley is a leading producer of alfalfa, chilies, onions, corn, cotton and pecans. With a growing roster of manufacturers broadening the economic picture, the city is now the largest business center in southern New Mexico.

Las Cruces, home of New Mexico State University, balances agriculture and industry with education and the Space Age. About 25 miles northeast on US 70/82, then 4 miles south, is White Sands Missile Range, where experimental rockets are tested *(see place listing p. 488).*

Las Cruces hosts the 3-day ⟱ Whole Enchilada Festival in late September. Festival-goers can enjoy live music and a carnival, participate in running events and watch as "the world's largest enchilada" is prepared. In early November thousands flock to Young Park for the ⟱ Renaissance Artsfaire, a cultural event featuring the works of local and regional artisans; musical and theatrical performances; sword tournaments and more.

Las Cruces Convention and Visitors Bureau: 211 N. Water St., Las Cruces, NM 88001. **Phone:** (575) 541-2444 or (800) 343-7827.

BRANIGAN CULTURAL CENTER is on the n. end of Downtown Mall at 501 N. Main St. Traveling and permanent exhibits highlight regional history. **Time:** Allow 30 minutes minimum. **Hours:** Tues.-Sat. 9-4:30. Closed major holidays. **Cost:** Free. **Phone:** (575) 541-2154.

Las Cruces Museum of Art is at 491 N. Main St., next to the Branigan Cultural Center. The 3,000-square-foot gallery features changing exhibits of contemporary art, many featuring local artists. **Time:** Allow 30 minutes minimum. **Hours:** Tues.-Sat. 9-4:30. **Cost:** Free. **Phone:** (575) 541-2137.

LAS CRUCES MUSEUM OF NATURAL HISTORY is in Mesilla Valley Mall at 700 S. Telshor Blvd., Suite 1608. Permanent and temporary exhibits relate to the area's natural history, science and environment. More than 50 live animals and hands-on displays are included. **Time:** Allow 30 minutes minimum. **Hours:** Mon.-Sat. 10-5 (also Fri. 5-8), Sun. 1-5. Closed major holidays. **Cost:** Donations. **Phone:** (575) 522-3120.

⟱**GEM NEW MEXICO FARM & RANCH HERITAGE MUSEUM** is off I-25 exit 1, then 1.5 mi. e. to 4100 Dripping Springs Rd. New Mexico's rural life and 3,000-year-old farming history are presented with interactive displays and demonstrations. The 47-acre site includes a working cattle ranch where daily milking and blacksmith techniques are showcased. Other residents include horse, mule, donkey, goat and sheep. Also featured are pecan, pistachio and apple orchards, gardens and a theater.

Hours: Mon.-Sat. 9-5, Sun. noon-5. **Cost:** $5; $3 (ages 60+); $2 (ages 5-17). **Phone:** (575) 522-4100. 🍴 🚼

UNIVERSITY MUSEUM is on the New Mexico State University campus in Kent Hall at Solano Dr. and University Ave. The museum on this 15,500-student campus presents changing exhibits about the archeology, history and culture of southern New Mexico and northern Mexico. **Tours:** Guided tours are available. **Time:** Allow 30 minutes minimum. **Hours:** Tues.-Fri. noon-4, Sat. 9-4. Closed major holidays. **Cost:** Donations. **Phone:** (575) 646-5161.

BEST WESTERN MISSION INN   Phone: (575)524-8591

◈◈◈ Hotel $90-$110

AAA Benefit: Members save up to 20%, plus 10% bonus points with Best Western Rewards®.

Address: 1765 S Main St 88005 **Location:** I-10 exit 142 (University Ave), 1 mi n. **Facility:** 68 units. 2 stories (no elevator), exterior corridors. **Terms:** cancellation fee imposed. **Pool(s):** heated outdoor. **Activities:** horseshoes. **Guest Services:** valet laundry. **Free Special Amenities:** expanded continental breakfast and high-speed Internet. *(See ad p. 421.)*

SAVE 🍴 🍸 📶 ⊕ BIZ 📶 🔲 🖥 🖨 / SOME UNITS FEE 🐾

COMFORT INN & SUITES DE MESILLA
Phone: 575/527-1050

◈◈◈ Hotel Rates not provided

Address: 1300 Avenida de Mesilla 88005 **Location:** I-10 exit 140, just s. **Facility:** 50 units. 2 stories, interior corridors. **Amenities:** high-speed Internet. **Pool(s):** heated indoor. **Activities:** whirlpool, limited exercise equipment. **Guest Services:** coin laundry.

SAVE 🍴➕ CALL 🕭M 📶 BIZ 📶 🔲 🖥 🖨 / SOME UNITS FEE 🐾

COMFORT INN OF LAS CRUCES   Phone: (575)527-2000

◈◈ Hotel $79-$105

Address: 2585 S Valley Dr 88005 **Location:** I-10 exit 142 (University Ave), just n. **Facility:** 38 units. 2 stories (no elevator), interior corridors. **Terms:** cancellation fee imposed. **Amenities:** high-speed Internet. **Pool(s):** outdoor. **Activities:** whirlpool.

SAVE 🍴➕ 📶 BIZ 📶 🔲 🖥 🖨 / SOME UNITS FEE 🐾

COMFORT SUITES BY CHOICE HOTELS
Phone: (575)522-1300

◈◈◈ Hotel $81-$91

Address: 2101 S Triviz Dr 88001 **Location:** I-25 exit 1 (University Ave), just w, then just n. **Facility:** 61 units. 3 stories, interior corridors. **Terms:** cancellation fee imposed. **Amenities:** safes (fee). *Some:* high-speed Internet. **Pool(s):** heated indoor. **Activities:** whirlpool. **Guest Services:** valet and coin laundry.

🍴➕ CALL 🕭M 📶 FEE ⊕ BIZ 📶 ✕ 🔲 🖥 🖨 / SOME UNITS FEE 🐾

DREAMCATCHER INN BED & BREAKFAST DE LAS CRUCES

Phone: 575/522-3035

Bed & Breakfast
$115-$145

Address: 10201 Starfly Rd 88011 **Location:** US 70 E to NASA/Baylor Canyon Rd, 0.5 mi s, then 0.5 mi w. **Facility:** The inn offers a rural setting with magnificent desert and mountain views. Rooms and baths are comfortable and well decorated. 4 units. 1 story, exterior corridors. **Terms:** 7 day cancellation notice-fee imposed. **Amenities:** high-speed Internet.

CALL ⓢⓂ ⊠ / SOME UNITS FEE 🐾

DRURY INN & SUITES LAS CRUCES

Phone: (575)523-4100

Hotel
$100-$144

Address: 1631 Hickory Loop 88005 **Location:** I-10 exit 140, just e. **Facility:** 73 units. 4 stories, interior corridors. **Terms:** cancellation fee imposed. **Amenities:** high-speed Internet. **Pool(s):** heated indoor. **Activities:** whirlpool, exercise room. **Guest Services:** valet and coin laundry.

🍴 CALL ⓢⓂ ⇨ BIZ 🛜 FEE 🎦 ▯ ▭ ▯ / SOME UNITS 🐾

FAIRFIELD INN BY MARRIOTT

Phone: (575)522-6840

Hotel
$89-$109

AAA Benefit: AAA hotel discounts of 5% or more.

Address: 2101 Summit Ct 88011 **Location:** I-25 exit 6 (US 70), 2 blks e to Telshor Blvd, then 0.8 mi s. **Facility:** 77 units. 3 stories, interior corridors. **Amenities:** high-speed Internet. **Pool(s):** heated outdoor. **Activities:** limited exercise equipment. **Guest Services:** valet and coin laundry.

🍴 CALL ⓢⓂ ⇨ BIZ 🛜 ⊠ ▯ / SOME UNITS ▯ ▭

HAMPTON INN

Phone: (575)526-8311

Hotel
$80-$90

Hampton

AAA Benefit: Members save up to 10% everyday!

Address: 755 Avenida de Mesilla 88005 **Location:** I-10 exit 140, just e. **Facility:** 117 units. 2 stories (no elevator), exterior corridors. **Terms:** 1-7 night minimum stay, cancellation fee imposed. **Amenities:** video games (fee). **Pool(s):** outdoor. **Activities:** exercise room. **Guest Services:** valet laundry. **Free Special Amenities:** expanded continental breakfast and newspaper.

SAVE 🍴 ⇨ BIZ 🛜 ▯ ▭ ▯ / SOME UNITS 🐾

▼ See AAA listing p. 420 ▼

Best Western

Mission Inn of Las Cruces

- Free HOT Breakfast
- Free Wireless Internet
- Outdoor Pool
- Pets Welcome (Call Hotel for details)
- Suites Available

1765 S. Main St.
Las Cruces, NM 88005

(575) 524-8591
(800) 390-1440

AAA Members receive a 15% discount off Best Available Rate

Come enjoy a memorable stay at the Mission Inn...where you'll be sure to find great southwestern hospitality, peaceful surroundings and our tastefully decorated hacienda-style guest rooms!

Scan this tag on your smartphone and start saving today!

Get the free mobile app at
http://gettag.mobi

www.bwmissioninn.com

Make Your Next Trip a Journey ... With AAA and Hertz.

For reservations, **visit** your AAA/CAA travel office, **click** on AAA.com/hertz or CAA.ca/hertz, or **call** 800-654-3080 U.S./ 888-333-3120 Canada.

Show Your Card & Save

Hertz.

HAMPTON INN & SUITES
Phone: (575)527-8777

Hotel
$114-$129

AAA Benefit:
Members save up to 10% everyday!

Address: 2350 E Griggs Ave 88001 **Location:** I-25 exit 3 (Lohman Ave), just w, just n on Walton Blvd, then just e. **Facility:** 73 units. 4 stories, interior corridors. **Terms:** 1-7 night minimum stay, cancellation fee imposed. **Amenities:** high-speed Internet. **Pool(s):** heated indoor. **Activities:** whirlpool, exercise room. **Guest Services:** valet and coin laundry.

HILLTOP HACIENDA B & B
Phone: (575)382-3556

Bed & Breakfast
$115-$155

Address: 2600 Westmoreland Ave 88012 **Location:** I-25 exit 6 (US 70), just e to Del Rey Blvd, 3 mi n, then 1 mi e. **Facility:** Perched on a hilltop, the Southwestern adobe B&B affords panoramic views of the valley and mountains from its spacious patios. 3 units. 2 stories (no elevator), interior corridors. **Terms:** age restrictions may apply, 14 day cancellation notice-fee imposed. **Activities:** hiking trails. **Guest Services:** complimentary laundry.

HILTON GARDEN INN LAS CRUCES
Phone: (575)522-0900

Hotel
$95-$112

AAA Benefit:
Unparalleled hospitality at a special Member rate.

Address: 2550 S Don Roser Dr 88011 **Location:** I-25 exit 1 (University Ave), just e. **Facility:** 114 units. 4 stories, interior corridors. **Terms:** 1-7 night minimum stay, cancellation fee imposed. **Amenities:** high-speed Internet. **Pool(s):** heated outdoor. **Activities:** whirlpool, exercise room. **Fee:** massage. **Guest Services:** valet and coin laundry.

HOLIDAY INN EXPRESS & SUITES
Phone: 575/522-0700

[fyi]
Hotel
Rates not provided

Too new to rate, opening scheduled for October 2011. **Address:** 2142 Telsnor Ct 88011 **Location:** I-25 exit 6 (US 70). **Amenities:** 80 units, pets, coffeemakers, microwaves, refrigerators, pool, exercise facility.

HOLIDAY INN EXPRESS HOTEL & SUITES
Phone: (575)527-9947

Hotel
$99-$299

Address: 2635 S Valley Dr 88005 **Location:** I-10 exit 142 (University Ave), just n. **Facility:** 87 units. 4 stories, interior corridors. **Terms:** cancellation fee imposed. **Amenities:** high-speed Internet. **Pool(s):** heated indoor. **Activities:** whirlpool, steamroom, exercise room. **Guest Services:** valet and coin laundry. *(See ad this page.)*

HOTEL ENCANTO DE LAS CRUCES
Phone: (575)522-4300

Hotel
$89-$159

Address: 705 S Telshor Blvd 88011 **Location:** I-25 exit 3 (Lohman Ave), just e, then just s. **Facility:** 205 units, some two bedrooms. 7 stories, interior corridors. **Terms:** cancellation fee imposed. **Dining:** entertainment. **Pool(s):** heated outdoor. **Activities:** whirlpool, exercise room. **Guest Services:** valet laundry, area transportation-within 5 mi. **Free Special Amenities: preferred room (subject to availability with advance reservations) and high-speed Internet.** Affiliated with A Preferred Hotel.

LA QUINTA INN & SUITES LAS CRUCES ORGAN MOUNTAIN
Phone: (575)523-0100

Hotel
$64-$126

Address: 1500 Hickory Dr 88005 **Location:** I-10 exit 140, just se of jct I-25 and Avenida de Mesilla. **Facility:** 87 units. 4 stories, interior corridors. **Amenities:** video games (fee). **Pool(s):** heated outdoor. **Guest Services:** valet and coin laundry.

▼ See AAA listing this page ▼

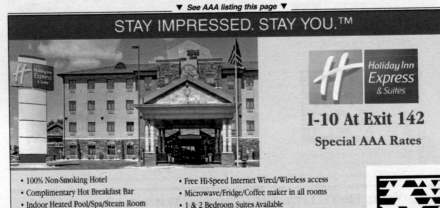

STAY IMPRESSED. STAY YOU.™

Holiday Inn Express & Suites

I-10 At Exit 142
Special AAA Rates

- 100% Non-Smoking Hotel
- Complimentary Hot Breakfast Bar
- Indoor Heated Pool/Spa/Steam Room
- 24 Hrs. Fitness Center
- 32" LCD T.V. with Cable/HBO/ESPN
- Free Hi-Speed Internet Wired/Wireless access
- Microwave/Fridge/Coffee maker in all rooms
- 1 & 2 Bedroom Suites Available
- Large Hot Tub Suites Available

www.hiexpress.com/lascrucesnm
2635 S.Valley Drive, Las Cruces, NM 88005 • (575)527-9947

Get the free mobile app at
http://gettag.mobi

LA QUINTA INN LAS CRUCES MESILLA VALLEY
Phone: (575)524-0331

Hotel
$68-$130

Address: 790 Avenida de Mesilla 88005 **Location:** I-10 exit 140, just e. **Facility:** 139 units. 2 stories (no elevator), interior corridors. **Amenities:** video games (fee). *Some:* high-speed Internet. **Some:** heated outdoor. **Activities:** exercise room. **Guest Services:** coin laundry.

LUNDEEN'S INN OF THE ARTS
Phone: (575)526-3326

Historic Bed & Breakfast
$79-$125

Address: 618 S Alameda Blvd 88005 **Location:** Jct Lohman Ave, just s; center. Located in historic district. **Facility:** The restored century-old territorial inn also incorporates a gallery that displays an interesting collection of art. 7 units, some kitchens. 2 stories (no elevator), interior corridors. **Terms:** 3 day cancellation notice.

QUALITY INN & SUITES
Phone: 575-524-4663

Hotel
Rates not provided

Address: 2200 S Valley Dr 88005 **Location:** I-10 exit 142 (University Ave), 2 blks w. **Facility:** 54 units. 2 stories (no elevator), exterior corridors. **Amenities:** high-speed Internet, safes. **Pool(s):** outdoor. **Activities:** whirlpool, limited exercise equipment. **Guest Services:** coin laundry.

RAMADA PALMS DE LAS CRUCES
Phone: (575)526-4411

Hotel
$69-$109

Address: 201 E University Ave 88005 **Location:** I-10 exit 142 (University Ave), just n. **Facility:** 114 units. 2 stories (no elevator), interior corridors. **Terms:** cancellation fee imposed. **Amenities:** *Some:* high-speed Internet. **Pool(s):** heated indoor. **Activities:** game room, exercise room. **Fee:** massage. **Guest Services:** valet and coin laundry.

SLEEP INN BY CHOICE HOTELS
Phone: (575)522-1700

Hotel
$69-$110

Address: 2121 S Triviz Dr 88001 **Location:** I-25 exit 1 (University Ave), just w, then just n. **Facility:** 63 units. 3 stories, interior corridors. **Terms:** cancellation fee imposed. **Amenities:** safes. **Pool(s):** heated indoor. **Activities:** whirlpool. **Guest Services:** valet laundry.

SPRINGHILL SUITES BY MARRIOTT
Phone: (575)541-8887

Hotel
$89-$159

AAA Benefit: AAA hotel discounts of 5% or more.

Address: 1611 Hickory Loop 88005 **Location:** I-10 exit 140, just ne. **Facility:** 101 units. 3 stories, interior corridors. **Amenities:** high-speed Internet. **Pool(s):** heated outdoor. **Activities:** whirlpool, exercise room. **Guest Services:** valet and coin laundry. **Free Special Amenities:** expanded continental breakfast and high-speed Internet. *(See ad this page.)*

STAYBRIDGE SUITES
Phone: 575-521-7000

Extended Stay Hotel
Rates not provided

Address: 2651 Northrise Dr 88011 **Location:** I-25 exit 6 (US 70), just e. **Facility:** 115 efficiencies, some two bedrooms. 4 stories, interior corridors. **Amenities:** high-speed Internet, safes. **Pool(s):** heated outdoor. **Activities:** whirlpool, putting green, exercise room. **Guest Services:** complimentary laundry.

▼ *See AAA listing this page* ▼

SpringHill Suites by Marriott®

All rooms are suites and include microwaves, refrigerators, and sleeper sofas. We also offer a complimentary full hot breakfast, free wireless Internet, on-site fitness center, outdoor heated pool and business center. Accessible rooms are also available.

Approved

*10% Off Published Rates for AAA Members

To reserve your room, call (800) MARRIOTT or visit springhillsuites.com

SpringHill Suites by Marriott®
1611 Hickory Loop • Las Cruces, NM 88005
t (575) 541- 8887 • f (575) 541- 8837

Space ▪ Light ▪ Inspiration®

*Rates are per room, per night, based on availability; not available for groups of 10 or more rooms.
© 2010 Marriott International, Inc.

TOWNEPLACE SUITES LAS CRUCES

Phone: (575)532-6500

Extended Stay Hotel
$102-$120

AAA Benefit:
AAA hotel discounts of 5% or more.

Address: 2143 Telshor Ct 88011 **Location:** I-25 exit 6 (US 70), just s. **Facility:** 81 kitchen units, some two bedrooms. 3 stories, interior corridors. **Amenities:** high-speed Internet. **Pool(s):** heated outdoor. **Activities:** whirlpool, exercise room. **Guest Services:** valet and coin laundry.

WHERE TO EAT

AQUA REEF EURO ASIAN CUISINE

Phone: 575/522-7333

Asian
$7-$20

AAA Inspector Notes: A distinctive dining experience can be found in this cozy contemporary Asian eatery. Menu highlights showcase dim sum, sushi and creatively presented entrées. The sushi bar features boats floating along a stream of water carrying plates of sushi from the kitchen. **Bar:** beer & wine. **Address:** 900 S B S Telshor Blvd 88011 **Location:** Just s of jct E Lohman Ave.

BOBA CAFE

Phone: 575/647-5900

Sandwiches
$6-$11

AAA Inspector Notes: Offering friendly service, this lively café is popular with nearby university staff and students. The creative soups, sandwiches and salads feature an Asian twist. Arrive hungry as the portions are very generous. **Bar:** beer & wine. **Address:** 1900 S Espina St, Suite 8 88001 **Location:** Just n of jct University Ave.

BREAK AN EGG RESTAURANT

Phone: 575/647-3000

Breakfast
$5-$8

AAA Inspector Notes: This egg-centric restaurant has a fun old movie theme decor along with the menu. Watch old movie classics while enjoying a creative breakfast and lunch menu. **Address:** 201 S Solano Dr 88001 **Location:** I-25 exit 3 (Lohman Ave), 1.4 mi w, then just n.

CATTLE BARON STEAK & SEAFOOD

Phone: 575/522-7533

Steak
$8-$25

AAA Inspector Notes: A scrumptious array of menu selections includes steak, seafood, chicken and prime rib as well as desserts such as caramel apple pie. An upscale Western decor includes wood trim and distinctive chandeliers made from deer antlers. **Bar:** full bar. **Address:** 790 S Telshor Blvd 88011 **Location:** I-25 exit 3 (Lohman Ave), just e, then just s.

CHILITOS

Phone: 575/526-4184

Mexican
$6-$14

AAA Inspector Notes: It is the heaping platters of flavorful, authentic Mexican favorites that keeps the locals coming back to this eatery. Be sure not to fill up on the complimentary homemade salsa and chips--take-out jars are available for purchase. **Bar:** beer & wine. **Address:** 2405 S Valley Dr 88005 **Location:** I-10 exit 142 (University Ave), just n, jct S Valley Dr and S Main St.

DE LA VEGA'S PECAN GRILL & BREWERY

Phone: 575/521-1099

American
$8-$45

AAA Inspector Notes: Enjoy prime beef, chicken and fish cooked over a state-of-the-art pecan wood grill at this eatery. Specialty brewed beers are on tap to accompany the house-smoked ribs. Sandwiches and burgers are served on homemade rolls and a variety of soups and salads round out the menu. The talented baker features a selection of luscious desserts while the bartender can whip up a creative milkshake for an after-dinner treat. **Bar:** full bar. **Address:** 500 S Telshor Blvd 88011 **Location:** I-25 exit 3 (Lohman Ave), just e.

EL SOMBRERO PATIO CAFE

Phone: 575/524-9911

Mexican
$6-$11

AAA Inspector Notes: This bustling local favorite has been serving traditional New Mexico cuisine since 1956. Generous portions of steak, chicken and salads are served up. Many of the dishes come with flavorful sauces. **Bar:** beer & wine. **Address:** 363 S Espina St 88001 **Location:** I-25 exit 3 (Lohman Ave), 2 mi w on Lohman and Amador aves; jct Espina St.

FARLEY'S

Phone: 575/522-0466

American
$7-$15

AAA Inspector Notes: The menu at this laid-back restaurant includes hot dogs, pizza and grilled cheese for the kids, as well as choices for mom and dad, including ribs, sandwiches, steak, fajitas, soups, salads, beer and fantastic margaritas. **Bar:** full bar. **Address:** 3499 Foothills Rd 88011 **Location:** I-25 exit 3 (Lohman Ave), 0.3 mi e to Nacho Dr, then 0.3 mi s.

GRANDY'S RESTAURANT

Phone: 575/526-4803

American
$4-$8

AAA Inspector Notes: Fried chicken and country-fried steak are menu standbys at the restaurant, a regional franchise. They also offer family-style dining menu. The decor is a step up from that of most quick-serve eateries and more resembles that of a conventional restaurant. Some elements of increased service include additional rolls, iced tea refills and tray removal. **Address:** 1345 El Paseo Rd 88001 **Location:** Just se of jct El Paseo Rd and E Idaho Ave.

HIGH DESERT BREWING CO.

Phone: 575/525-6752

American
$6-$11

AAA Inspector Notes: This very popular gathering spot for locals features award-winning, hand-crafted brews and a menu of hearty pub fare. Live music is offered in the evenings on Thursdays and Saturdays. **Bar:** beer only. **Address:** 1201 W Hadley Ave 88005 **Location:** Just e of jct Valley Dr. **Parking:** on-site and street.

INTERNATIONAL DELIGHTS CAFE

Phone: 575/647-5956

Mediterranean
$7-$15

AAA Inspector Notes: This popular local eatery has a variety of Mediterranean dishes from creamy hummus and flavorful soups to delectable desserts. Free Wi-Fi and specialty coffee keeps this a favorite late night hangout for university students. **Address:** 1245 El Paseo Rd 88001 **Location:** Jct Idaho Ave; in Brazito Plaza.

JAPANESE KITCHEN

Phone: 575/521-3555

Japanese
$6-$38

AAA Inspector Notes: Enjoy a wide variety of Japanese favorites from sushi to tempura to teriyaki at this eatery. The sushi bar is the best seat in the house to watch the friendly Japanese chefs create beautiful presentations. **Bar:** beer & wine. **Address:** 141 Roadrunner Pkwy, Suite 115 88011 **Location:** I-25 exit 3 (Lohman Ave), 1 mi e, then just n.

LA IGUANA   Phone: 575/523-8550

♦♦ ♦♦

American
$6-$28

AAA Inspector Notes: This casual café features patio dining, a fun place to sit and people watching during the weekly farmer's market. Weekend brunch features omelets, quiche, breakfast sandwiches plus a very yummy peach brandy French toast. Lunch offers a variety of sandwiches, burgers, salads and soups. A special dinner menu is served Thursday through Saturday evenings. **Bar:** beer & wine. **Address:** 139 N Main St 88001 **Location:** In historic downtown. [B] [L] [D] CALL [M]

LEMONGRASS   Phone: 575/523-8778

♦♦ ♦♦

Thai
$7-$19

AAA Inspector Notes: Flavorful Thai cuisine is served in an upscale setting at this eatery. Spinach basil pot stickers and spicy old fisherman are favorites, while the seasonal mango with sticky rice is a must. **Bar:** beer & wine. **Address:** 2540 El Paseo Rd 88001 **Location:** I-10 exit 142 (University Ave), just e. [L] [D]

LORENZO'S   Phone: 575/521-3505

♦♦ ♦♦

Italian
$7-$21

AAA Inspector Notes: Sicilian dishes are served offering imported pasta, varied sauces and hand-tossed pizza with unusual combinations. Enjoy cannelloni, eggplant parmigiana or calamari appetizers. Finish with tiramisu or cheesecake. They use pure Durum wheat, imported from Italy, to make their pasta. **Bar:** beer & wine. **Address:** 1753 E University Ave 88001 **Location:** I-25 exit 1 (University Ave), just sw. [L] [D]

MIX PACIFIC RIM CUISINE   Phone: 575/532-2042

♦♦ ♦♦

Asian
$9-$24

AAA Inspector Notes: The cozy and contemporary restaurant presents an extensive menu of sushi prepared with a Southwest twist, as well as Asian fusion entrées and bento box specials. Worth a try are tempura green chile and the Mexico roll. Creative sake cocktails are served in fun decanters. **Bar:** beer & wine. **Address:** 1001 University Ave, Suite D4 88001 **Location:** Jct Espina St, just e.

[L] [D]

OLD MESILLA PASTRY CAFE-THE SHED RESTAURANT   Phone: 575/525-2636

♦♦ ♦♦

American
$6-$10

AAA Inspector Notes: This busy café with casual service features breakfast offerings ranging from huevos rancheros and eggs Benedict to pancakes and omelets. The wood-burning oven produces pizza, calzone and house bread. Such vegetarian delights as garden burgers and grilled eggplant sandwiches also are served. **Bar:** beer & wine. **Address:** 810 S Valley Dr 88005 **Location:** I-10 exit 142 (University Ave), just e, then 1 mi nw. [B] [L]

ST. CLAIR WINERY & BISTRO   Phone: 575/524-0390

♦♦ ♦♦

American
$8-$19

AAA Inspector Notes: This lively neighborhood bistro prepares creative comfort food, which guests can enjoy with an excellent selection of New Mexico wines. Wine tastings are popular here, as is the lush dining patio. **Bar:** wine only. **Address:** 1800 Avenida de Mesilla 88005 **Location:** I-10 exit 135, just w. [L] [D] CALL [M]

SI ITALIAN BISTRO   Phone: 575/523-1572

♦♦ ♦♦

Italian
$6-$25

AAA Inspector Notes: This restaurant presents an extensive menu of Italian entrées, as well as pasta, salads, sandwiches and wood-fired pizza, which guests can enjoy with beer or wine. The talented pastry chef creates exceptional eat-in or take-out desserts in an open bakery. **Bar:** beer & wine. **Address:** 523 E Idaho Ave 88001 **Location:** Jct El Paseo Rd, just e. [L] [D]

SI SEÑOR RESTAURANT   Phone: 575/527-0412

♦♦ ♦♦

Mexican
$7-$16

AAA Inspector Notes: Come hungry for generous portions of authentic New Mexican cuisine served in a lively atmosphere. Homemade tortillas and flavorful chile sauce are highlights at this eatery. Try a selection from the extensive margarita menu to go along with the meal. **Bar:** full bar. **Address:** 1551 Amador Ave 88001 **Location:** I-25 exit 3 (Lohman Ave), 1 mi w. [L] [D]

ZEFFIRO PIZZERIA NAPOLETANA   Phone: 575/525-6757

♦♦ ♦♦

Pizza
$7-$12

AAA Inspector Notes: Fresh-baked artisan bread is the specialty at this bustling café and bakery. Friendly servers greet patrons with a basket of warm bread and a dish of olive oil seasoned with herbs. This is a popular lunch spot for delicious hand-tossed pizza, salads, soups and sandwiches. Before leaving, diners can purchase a loaf of bread from the adjacent Popular Artisan Bread Bakery. **Address:** 136 N Water St 88001 **Location:** Downtown; in historic Main Street area. [L] [D]

LAS VEGAS (F-4) pop. 13,753, elev. 6,430'
• Hotels p. 426 • Restaurants p. 426

The faint wagon wheel ruts still visible outside Las Vegas attest to the town's era as a mercantile center on the Santa Fe Trail. Las Vegas also was a military post until Fort Union *(see Fort Union National Monument p. 411)* was built. During the 1880s it was known as one of the roughest towns on the frontier, with such desperados as Billy the Kid and Doc Holliday frequenting the area.

The arrival of the Santa Fe Railroad in 1879 ushered in commercial activity and prosperity. Las Vegas soon became a major retail center. The townspeople embarked on a flurry of building and rebuilding, which utilized previously unavailable materials and established an array of architectural styles. The city boasts some 900 historic buildings, many of which are highlighted on walking and driving tours.

Outdoor recreation is available at Storrie Lake State Park, 4 miles north off SR 518 *(see Recreation Chart)*; at Morphy Lake State Park, 25 miles north off SR 518 *(see Recreation Chart)*; and in the Sangre de Cristo Mountains, which rise to the west *(see Santa Fe National Forest p. 472)*.

Las Vegas-San Miguel Chamber of Commerce: 503 Sixth St., P.O. Box 128, Las Vegas, NM 87701. **Phone:** (505) 425-8631 or (800) 832-5947.

Self-guiding tours: A brochure of walking and driving tours is available from the chamber of commerce.

CITY OF LAS VEGAS MUSEUM AND ROUGH RIDER MEMORIAL COLLECTION is just n. of I-25 exit 345 at 727 Grand Ave. The museum illustrates the cultural heritage of the town through its collection. Exhibits include the Rough Riders, the first U.S. Volunteer Cavalry regiment led by Theodore Roosevelt in the Spanish-American War; the Santa Fe Trail; and railroad history. **Time:** Allow 30 minutes minimum. **Hours:** Tues.-Sat. 10-4. Closed major holidays. **Cost:** Donations. **Phone:** (505) 426-3205.

LAS VEGAS NATIONAL WILDLIFE REFUGE is 6 mi. s.e. via SRs 104 and 281. Covering 8,672 acres of prairie bordered by the timbered canyons of the Gallinas River and Vegosa Creek, the refuge has more than 300 species of wildlife and is noted for its birds of prey. In season, bald eagles, hawks and kestrels are seen. Brochures, an auto loop map and nature-trail permits are available at the refuge office. Allow 1 hour minimum for the driving tour, 2 hours minimum for the nature trail. **Hours:** Auto loop drive open daily 24 hours. Office Mon.-Fri. 8-4. Closed major holidays. **Cost:** Free. **Phone:** (505) 425-3581.

BEST WESTERN PLUS MONTEZUMA INN & SUITES
Phone: (505)426-8000
Hotel
$79-S109

AAA Benefit: Members save up to 20%, plus 10% bonus points with Best Western Rewards®.

Address: 2020 N Grand Ave 87701 **Location:** I-25 exit 347, just sw. **Facility:** 67 units. 3 stories, interior corridors. **Amenities:** high-speed Internet. **Pool(s):** heated indoor. **Activities:** sauna, whirlpool, exercise room. **Guest Services:** coin laundry. **Free Special Amenities:** local telephone calls and high-speed Internet.

Built 2009, Hot Breakfast, Pool, Hot Tub, Sauna, Truck & RV Parking Right off of I-25

COMFORT INN
Phone: (505)425-1100
Hotel
$75-$101
Address: 2500 N Grand Ave 87701 **Location:** I-25 exit 347, just sw; US 85 and I-25 business route. **Facility:** 101 units. 2 stories (no elevator), interior corridors. **Pool(s):** heated indoor. **Activities:** whirlpool, exercise room. **Guest Services:** coin laundry. **Free Special Amenities:** full breakfast and high-speed Internet.

Minutes from New Mexico Highlands Univ., National Monument Fort Union, National Wildlife Refuge.

HOLIDAY INN EXPRESS HOTEL & SUITES
Phone: (505)426-8182
Hotel
$96-$126 5/1-1/31
$91-$120 2/1-4/30
Address: 816 S Grand Ave 87701 **Location:** I-25 exit 343, just n. **Facility:** 68 units. 3 stories, interior corridors. **Terms:** check-in 4 pm. **Amenities:** high-speed Internet. **Pool(s):** heated indoor. **Activities:** whirlpool, exercise room. **Guest Services:** coin laundry.

PLAZA HOTEL
Phone: (505)425-3591
Historic Hotel
$69-$132
Address: 230 Plaza St 87701 **Location:** I-25 exit 343W, just w, follow signs to Old Town Plaza. **Facility:** This 1882 western Victorian hotel on the main town square offers nicely appointed rooms and public areas. 71 units. 3 stories, interior corridors. **Parking:** street only. **Terms:** cancellation fee imposed. **Amenities:** Some: high-speed Internet. **Dining:** Landmark Grill, see separate listing. **Activities:** exercise room. **Guest Services:** coin laundry. **Free Special Amenities:** full breakfast and high-speed Internet.

WHERE TO EAT

DICK'S RESTAURANT
Phone: 505/454-8084
American
$9-$25
AAA Inspector Notes: This hidden gem is a favorite of locals. You'll enjoy a large selection of regional specialties plus some creative entrées. Start with an excellent Margarita and then enjoy the spicy chipotle shrimp on spinach and cool off with the homemade flan, a true burst of flavors. **Bar:** full bar. **Address:** 705 Douglas Ave 87701 **Location:** Jct 7th St; center. [L] [D]

K-BOB'S STEAKHOUSE
Phone: 505/425-6322
Steak
$6-$18
AAA Inspector Notes: The steakhouse prepares a great variety of plump, juicy fillets. A fireplace opens up into both dining rooms, and antique clocks decorate the walls. Rustic wagon-wheel chandeliers illuminate the room. **Address:** 1803 7th St 87701 **Location:** Jct SR 65 and 7th St, 1 mi n. [L] [D]

LANDMARK GRILL
Phone: 505/425-3591
American
$8-$26
AAA Inspector Notes: The menu at this historic grill offers New Mexican specialties, steaks, pasta and desserts served in a comfortable Victorian dining room. Located in the Old Town Historic District on the first floor of the Plaza Hotel, the eatery overlooks the plaza area. **Bar:** full bar. **Reservations:** suggested. **Address:** 230 Plaza St 87701 **Location:** I-25 exit 343W, just w, follow signs to Old Town Plaza; in Plaza Hotel. **Parking:** street only. **Historic** [B] [L] [D]

LITTLE SAIGON
Phone: 505/454-1842
Asian
$8-$12
AAA Inspector Notes: Large portions of flavorful Asian specialties include spicy noodles, stir-fries and sweet rice banana cakes. **Address:** 2001 N Grand Ave 87701 **Location:** I-25 exit 347, 0.8 mi sw; US 85 and I-25 business route. [L] [D]

Visit AAA.com or CAA.ca for one-stop travel planning and reservations

LA UNION (J-3) pop. 1,106, elev. 3,795'

WINERIES

• **La Viña Winery** is off I-10 exit 2, 4 mi. w. to SR 28, then 1 mi. n. Tours and tastings are offered. **Hours:** Thurs.-Tues. noon-5. Tours are given at 11:30 by appointment. Closed major holidays. **Phone:** (575) 882-7632.

LINCOLN (H-4) elev. 5,715'

Lincoln's main street is lined with adobe houses and commercial structures dating from the late 19th century, when stock raising, farming, mining and the status of a frontier county seat sustained the village. But Lincoln's prominence in Billy the Kid lore is by far the town's most well-known aspect.

Billy was tried, convicted and sentenced to hang as retribution for a life of rustling and murder, but instead he killed his guards and escaped from Lincoln County Courthouse. Sheriff Pat Garrett tracked him to Fort Sumner *(see place listing p. 411)*, where two shots from his pistol ended the outlaw's story July 14, 1881.

Fort Stanton Recreation Area, approximately 9 miles west off US 380, comprises 24,000 acres of BLM lands with mountains, streams, mesas and bottomlands for recreation *(see Recreation Chart)*.

FORT STANTON STATE MONUMENT is w. of Lincoln on US 380, then s. on SR 220. Established in 1855 to protect settlers against Apache raids, the fort was later occupied by Confederate soldiers, John J. "Blackjack" Pershing, New Mexico volunteers under "Kit" Carson, and the Buffalo Soldiers. The Army abandoned the fort in 1896. An interpretive center chronicles the fort's history. Living-history events take place the first weekend in August; among the living-history sites are an Apache encampment and the fort bakery and blacksmith. **Time:** Allow 1 hour minimum. **Hours:** Thurs.-Sat. and Mon. 10-4, Sun. noon-4, Apr.-Nov.; Sat. 10-4, Sun. noon-4, rest of year. **Cost:** Free. **Phone:** (575) 354-0341. 🅰 🎫

LINCOLN STATE MONUMENT covers the half-mile stretch of town. Nearly a dozen 19th-century stone and adobe buildings are preserved as they appeared during the violent era of the Lincoln County War 1878-81. The Tunstall Store and the Lincoln County Courthouse Museum contain exhibits. Other buildings include the Montaño Store and the San Juan Mission Church.

Time: Allow 1 hour minimum. **Hours:** Daily 8:30-4:30. Closed major holidays. **Cost:** $5; free (ages 0-16 with adult). **Phone:** (575) 653-4372.

LINCOLN NATIONAL FOREST (H-4)

Elevations in the forest range from 4,440 ft. at Grapevine Canyon to 11,580 ft. at Lookout Mountain. Refer to AAA maps for additional elevation information.

In south central New Mexico, most of the Sacramento, Jicarilla, Guadalupe and Capitan mountains lie within the three districts of Lincoln National Forest. Covering 1,103,441 acres of pine, juniper and fir timber, the forest ranges from desert to subalpine terrain. The Smokey Bear Ranger District includes two wilderness areas offering pristine back country for horseback riding or hiking trips. The district office is located in the mountain community of Ruidoso *(see place listing p. 440)*, which is a popular recreation and resort center.

The Smokey Bear Ranger District also was home to the original Smokey Bear, the living symbol of fire prevention. The Smokey Bear Historical Park in Capitan, north of Ruidoso, displays memorabilia about the tiny cub and information about wildfire prevention along with the town's original train depot. In fire season from April through July, campfires and charcoal grills may be prohibited. Along the Billy the Kid National Scenic Byway are a variety of villages, scenic vistas, events and attractions that make this an area well worth exploring.

The Sacramento Ranger District is located in and around the small village of Cloudcroft *(see place listing p. 401)*. Nestled high in the tall pines, Cloudcroft attracts many who want to escape the heat of the desert below and enjoy fresh, cool air. Recreation activities range from what is purported to be one of the highest 9-hole golf courses in the country, to camping, hiking, fishing, horseback riding, hunting, off-highway-vehicles trails and winter sports. The Sunspot Scenic Highway (SR 6563) offers spectacular views of the Tularosa Basin and the dunes of White Sands National Monument *(see place listing p. 488)*.

The southern Guadalupe Ranger District embraces the relatively less-traveled, semiarid Guadalupe Mountains. A 150-foot waterfall, uncommon to this region, is the focus of an oasis in the desert at Sitting Bull Falls Picnic Area, 49 miles southwest of Carlsbad via US 285, SR 137 and FR 276. The area is open daily 8:30-6, April through September; 8:30-5, rest of year. Closed Christmas. Admission is $5 per vehicle (exact change required); Federal Recreational Lands Pass holders enter free. Phone (575) 885-4181.

Numerous caves throughout the forest can be explored by obtaining permits which are issued on a first-come, first-served basis. For further information contact the Lincoln Forest Supervisor's Office, 3463 Las Palomas Rd., Alamogordo, NM 88310. Visitors are advised to phone ahead for current road conditions before visiting the site; phone ahead for current road conditions before visiting the site; phone (575) 434-7200. *See Recreation Chart.*

LORDSBURG pop. 2,797

BEST WESTERN WESTERN SKIES INN
Phone: (575)542-8807

Hotel
$70-$121

AAA Benefit: Members save up to 20%, plus 10% bonus points with Best Western Rewards®.

Address: 1303 S Main St 88045 **Location:** I-10 exit 22, just s. **Facility:** 40 units. 1 story, exterior corridors. **Amenities:** *Some:* high-speed Internet. **Pool(s):** heated outdoor. **Activities:** horseshoes. **Guest Services:** coin laundry. **Free Special Amenities:** local telephone calls and high-speed Internet.

COMFORT INN & SUITES
Phone: (575)542-3355

Hotel
$70-$120

Address: 400 W Wabash St 88045 **Location:** I-10 exit 22, just n, then w. **Facility:** 64 units. 3 stories, interior corridors. **Terms:** cancellation fee imposed. **Amenities:** high-speed Internet. **Pool(s):** heated indoor. **Activities:** sauna, whirlpool, exercise room. **Guest Services:** coin laundry. **Free Special Amenities:** full breakfast and room upgrade (subject to availability with advance reservations).

DAYS INN & SUITES
Phone: (575)542-3600

Hotel
$45-$80

Address: 1426 W Motel Dr 88045 **Location:** I-10 exit 20, just n. **Facility:** 56 units, some two bedrooms and kitchens. 2 stories (no elevator), interior corridors. **Pool(s):** heated indoor. **Activities:** whirlpool, exercise room.

ECONO LODGE
Phone: 575/542-3666

Hotel
Rates not provided

Address: 1408 S Main St 88045 **Location:** I-10 exit 22, just s. **Facility:** 40 units. 2 stories (no elevator), exterior corridors. **Pool(s):** outdoor. **Guest Services:** coin laundry.

HAMPTON INN
Phone: (575)542-8900

Hotel
$89-$99

AAA Benefit: Members save up to 10% everyday!

Address: 412 W Wabash 88045 **Location:** I-10 exit 22, just w. **Facility:** 64 units. 3 stories, interior corridors. **Terms:** 1-7 night minimum stay, cancellation fee imposed. **Amenities:** high-speed Internet. **Pool(s):** heated outdoor. **Activities:** whirlpool, exercise room. **Guest Services:** coin laundry.

WHERE TO EAT

KRANBERRY'S FAMILY RESTAURANT
Phone: 575/542-9400

American
$7-$15

AAA Inspector Notes: In an atmosphere much like that found at well-known pancake house chains, this restaurant serves generous breakfasts, lunches and dinners. The menu lists a good selection of good old American food, including burgers, sandwiches and cooked-to-order dinners. Just off the interstate, the clean, bright setting appeals to motorists and locals alike. **Address:** 1405 S Main St 88045 **Location:** I-10 exit 22, just s.

LOS ALAMOS (A-3) pop. 12,019, elev. 7,320'

In 1943 the federal government selected Los Alamos Ranch School as the top secret, maximum security site for the Manhattan Project, an atomic bomb research and testing program where Little Boy and Fat Man—the atomic bombs that ended World War II—were built. By 1945, when the first atomic device was detonated at Trinity Site *(see White Sands Missile Range p. 488)*, more than 3,000 civilian and military personnel were working at the laboratory.

Los Alamos National Laboratory continues to apply science to issues of national security, economic strength and energy security. Its staff of nearly 9,000 conducts extensive research about technology associated with nuclear weapons, deterrence and other defense applications, energy production, health, safety and environmental concerns, astrophysics and life sciences.

Explosions of another sort created the rugged setting that was so essential for maintaining the secrecy of the Manhattan Project. About a million years ago the volcanic vents that had built the Jémez Mountains issued 100 cubic miles of ash and pumice, then collapsed. The result is Valle Grande, one of the largest measured calderas on Earth. Covering 148 square miles, the depression has a rim averaging 500 feet above its floor.

SR 4, about 15 miles west of Los Alamos, outlines the crater's southern curve and permits views into its vast, grassy bowl. The erupted ash hardened into a layer of tuff, the Pajarito Plateau, which is characterized by a remoteness protected by the finger canyons serrating its edges. Within the plateau Bandelier National Monument *(see place listing p. 390)* contains extensive Ancestral Puebloan ruins. Guided hiking trips, wagon rides and van tours of Valles Caldera National Preserve *(see Recreation Chart)* offer a glimpse of the region's geology, archeology and wildlife; phone (505) 661-3333 for information and (866) 382-5537 for reservations.

Los Alamos Chamber of Commerce and Visitor Center: 109 Central Park Sq., Los Alamos, NM 87544. **Phone:** (505) 662-8105 or (800) 444-0707.

Self-guiding tours: A guidebook available at the visitor center and Los Alamos County Historical Museum *(see attraction listing)* outlines a walking tour of local history sites.

BRADBURY SCIENCE MUSEUM is at 15th St. and Central Ave. The museum features films and interactive exhibits interpreting Los Alamos National Laboratory's contributions to modern science, research and technology, including its role in the Manhattan Project and current mission in national security. **Hours:** Tues.-Sat. 10-5, Sun.-Mon. 1-5. Closed Jan. 1, Thanksgiving and Christmas. **Cost:** Free. **Phone:** (505) 667-4444.

LOS ALAMOS COUNTY HISTORICAL MUSEUM is next to Fuller Lodge on Central Ave. A restored log and stone cottage once served as the infirmary and guest house for the Los Alamos Ranch School. The museum details area history, including the Manhattan Project. Newspaper articles, military uniforms, photographs of bomb tests and changing exhibits are displayed. A Tewa ruin dating from the 13th century and a relocated homesteader's cabin are other highlights.

Hours: Mon.-Fri. 9:30-4:30, Sat. 11-4, Sun. 1-4, Apr.-Oct.; Mon.-Fri. 10-4, Sat. 11-4, Sun. 1-4, rest of year. Closed Jan. 1, Easter, Thanksgiving and Christmas. **Cost:** Donations. **Phone:** (505) 662-6272 or (505) 662-4493.

HOLIDAY INN EXPRESS & SUITES
Phone: (505)661-2646
Hotel
$95-$179
Address: 60 Entrada Dr 87544 **Location:** Jct Airport Basin Dr and SR 502. **Facility:** 86 units, some efficiencies. 4 stories, interior corridors. **Amenities:** high-speed Internet. **Pool(s):** heated indoor. **Activities:** whirlpool, exercise room. **Guest Services:** valet and coin laundry.

WHERE TO EAT

THE BLUE WINDOW BISTRO
Phone: 505/662-6305
International
$9-$26
AAA Inspector Notes: This vibrant eatery has a pleasant, cheerful atmosphere that appeals to business people, tourists and staffers at the Los Alamos National Laboratory. On the menu is a good selection of popular New Mexican dishes, sandwiches, salads and desserts. **Bar:** beer & wine. **Address:** 813 Central Ave 87544 **Location:** 0.5 mi w of jct SR 502 and Central Ave. ⃞ L ⃞ D

LOS LUNAS pop. 14,835

WESTERN SKIES INN & SUITES   **Phone:** (505)865-0001
Hotel
$65-$95
Address: 2258 Sun Ranch Village Loop 87031 **Location:** I-25 exit 203, just w. **Facility:** 57 units. 3 stories, interior corridors. **Pool(s):** heated outdoor. **Activities:** exercise room. **Guest Services:** coin laundry. **Free Special Amenities:** expanded continental breakfast and high-speed Internet.

WHERE TO EAT

HENRIETTA'S RESTAURANT   **Phone:** 505/865-5284
American
$8-$10
AAA Inspector Notes: Right in the center of town, this restaurant serves breakfast anytime during the day. A good selection of burgers, sandwiches, soups and salads also is offered. Chicken-fried steak satisfies. **Address:** 740 Main St 87031 **Location:** Center.
⃞ B ⃞ L ⃞ D   CALL ⃞

TEOFILOS RESTAURANTE   **Phone:** 505/865-5511
Mexican
$9-$17
AAA Inspector Notes: New Mexican cuisine is served in a renovated adobe house that dates back to the 1800s. Red chile enchiladas are fantastic. **Bar:** beer & wine. **Address:** 144 Main St NW 87031 **Location:** I-25 exit 203.
1.5 mi e. ⃞ L ⃞ D

LOS RANCHOS DE ALBUQUERQUE pop. 6,024

LOS POBLANOS INN
Phone: (505)344-9297
Historic Country Inn
$135-$195
Address: 4803 Rio Grande Blvd NW 87107 **Location:** I-40 exit 157A (Rio Grande Blvd), 3.3 mi n. **Facility:** Mornings are kicked off with a full breakfast prepared using organic ingredients from the on-site garden and from other local growers. 20 units, some kitchens and cottages. 1 story, exterior corridors. **Terms:** office hours 7 am-8 pm, check-in 4 pm, 10 day cancellation notice-fee imposed. **Amenities:** high-speed Internet. **Pool(s):** heated outdoor. **Activities:** bicycles, jogging, horseshoes, exercise room. *Fee:* horseback riding, massage. **Guest Services:** valet laundry.

MADRID (D-4) pop. 204, elev. 6,020'
• Restaurants p. 430

Madrid couldn't be more different from the Spanish capital it shares a name with, starting with its pronunciation (say "MAH-drid"). This spot of a hamlet in the high desert country of central New Mexico has had several incarnations over the course of approximately 2 centuries: coal mining boomtown, home of the Madrid Miners minor league baseball team, all-but-deserted "ghost town," offbeat artists' collective. The last one describes Madrid today and is one reason why it's one of the state's most distinctive small communities.

The nearby, mineral-rich Ortiz Mountains ensured Madrid's early success. By 1892 coal was being extracted from mines with shafts as deep as 2,500 feet. A company town of wood-framed cabins rose up, supplying coal for the Santa Fe Railway and the U.S. Government. Beginning in the early 1920s, Madrid became famous for its big Fourth of July parade and a lavish Christmastime display of lights, powered by electricity provided by coal-fed generators. Baseball games were played in the first lighted ballpark in the West.

But the development of cheaper and cleaner fuels brought about Madrid's decline. By the end of the 1950s the mines had closed and only a handful of people were left. Rebirth began in the early 1970s, when artists and craftspeople who didn't mind roughing it started converting old miners' cabins into funky little galleries and shops.

Today there are reminders of Madrid's past in names like the Mine Shaft Tavern and the Ghost Town Trading Post. There's a definite hippie sensibility—a stone gargoyle here, a whiff of incense there. And more recently a biker contingent has made its presence known. The 2007 hit movie "Wild Hogs," a comedy about a group of suburbanites (led by Will Ferrell and Tim Allen) turned wannabe bikers, was partially filmed in town; Maggie's Diner, built specifically for the film, was left standing.

Another blink-and-you'll-miss-it town is Cerrillos, a couple of miles north of Madrid off SR 14 (watch for the signed turnoff). As early as 1,000 B.C., prehistoric people using stone axes and antler picks worked the surrounding region for turquoise, that beautifully hued mineral long prized as a gem and ornamental stone. Cerrillos turquoise even ended up adorning the crown jewels of Spain. Gold, silver, lead and zinc also were extracted from area mines that reached their peak in the 1880s, when the town boasted four hotels and more than 20 saloons.

Today's Cerrillos is a far cry from its boisterous past, but there's still a rustic Old West look to the cottonwood-shaded dirt streets and adobe houses. While "sleepy" is an accurate description, there are a couple of shops and artist studios for visitors to explore. The Cerrillos Turquoise Mining Museum (17 Waldo St.; watch for the signs) has an interesting collection of rocks, Cerrillos turquoise, bottles, curios, tools, coffee cans, hand grinders and antiques amassed by the owners, plus an adjacent fenced enclosure where you can feed llamas, goats and chickens. The museum is open daily 9-5; phone (505) 438-3008.

The stretch of SR 14 between I-40 exit 175 and I-25 exit 278 is called the Turquoise Trail National Scenic Byway. Tijeras is the gateway to this popular alternate route between Albuquerque and Santa Fe. The natural setting is grand—forests of juniper and piñon pine, sagebrush-speckled hills, rolling prairies, vistas of the Sandia Mountains. The Turquoise Trail scenery is particularly spectacular from the village of Golden north to Madrid. Just north of Cerrillos is the Garden of the Gods, a grouping of vertical sandstone and mudstone rocks. While not as large, impressive or famous as the towering red sandstone formations at Garden of the Gods Park in Colorado Springs, they were shaped by the same geological forces.

Shopping areas

Narrow, winding SR 14, Madrid's main—and only—drag, is lined with an eclectic collection of art galleries and little shops housed in fancifully decorated wooden houses. Parking is a do-it-yourself affair; in other words, grab a spot wherever you can along the road or in one of the few gravel lots. Some establishments are open seasonally or have reduced hours during the winter months.

Galleries like the Chumani Gallery (2839 SR 14), Spirit in Art (just off SR 14 on Firehouse Road), Johnsons of Madrid (2843 SR 14) and Indigo (2854 SR 14) deal in contemporary paintings, Navajo jewelry, Mata Ortiz pottery, Cerrillos turquoise and fiber art. For souvenirs, Madrid T-shirts and Route 66-themed gifts check out Tumbleweeds (just off SR 14 on Firehouse Road). Cowgirl Red (2865 SR 14) has Wild West art, antiques and vintage cowboy boots. Heaven (2853 SR 14) is a Victorian-style boutique selling clothing, jewelry, hats and gifts. Hanuman's (2872 SR 14) calls itself a "world gallery" and carries cool items like tribal and sacred objects, metal sculpture, and Native American and world music CDs.

Madrid's meeting place is the Java Junction (2855 SR 14), where you can mingle with the locals over coffee or a smoothie before checking out the kitschy array of novelty coffee mugs, kitchen magnets and T-shirts, as well as a killer selection of hot

sauces and regional salsas. The best food in town is at Mama Lisa's Ghost Town Kitchen (2859 SR 14). Everything is made from scratch, and desserts like red chile chocolate cake are not to be missed; the chalkboard next to the front door lists daily specials.

OLD COAL MINE MUSEUM is at 2846 SR 14. This once bustling 1890s mining village became a ghost town when digging ceased in 1959. A 1901 Richmond Steam locomotive, mining equipment, vintage vehicles and various buildings, including the mine office and a machinist shop, remain. The Engine House Theatre offers music and many special events on weekends in season.

Tours: Guided tours are available. **Time:** Allow 1 hour minimum. **Hours:** Fri.-Mon. 11-5, Apr. 1 to mid-Oct. Schedule varies rest of year; phone ahead. Closed Christmas. **Cost:** $5; $3 (children and senior citizens). **Phone:** (505) 438-3780. 〔¶〕

MINE SHAFT TAVERN	**Phone:** 505/473-0743
♦♦ American $7-$14	**AAA Inspector Notes:** Originally built for coal miners' entertainment, this rustic watering hole serves a good selection of sandwiches, lunch and dinner specials and spirits to please its jovial clientele. **Bar:** full bar.

Reservations: suggested. **Address:** 2846 SR 14 87010 **Location:** Center. 〔L〕 〔D〕

MESCALERO (H-4) pop. 1,338, elev. 6,600'

Mescalero is the largest town within the Mescalero Apache Reservation and serves as its headquarters. The more than 460,000-acre tract embraces the Sierra Blanca Mountains and their wealth of timber, grazing lands and scenic beauty. Among the last American Indians to lay down arms against the U.S. government, the tribe now operates as a federally chartered corporation.

Capitalizing on their land's recreational potential, the Mescaleros have developed a ski area and a major resort near Ruidoso (see place listing p. 440). Information about ceremonials and recreational facilities is available from the community center; phone (575) 464-4494.

MESILLA (I-3) pop. 2,196, elev. 3,886'

Mesilla had its official beginning around 1848, when some residents of a nearby community that had become part of the United States by the Treaty of Guadalupe Hidalgo elected to move to the town in order to retain Mexican citizenship. They received a Mexican land grant in 1850, but in 1854 the Gadsden Purchase transferred nearly 30,000 square miles west of the Rio Grande to the United States.

The combination of excellent farmland and strategic location spurred Mesilla's growth. By the time the Butterfield Trail Overland mail route established a major stage stop in 1858, Mesilla was the largest town in the southern part of New Mexico Territory, which then included present-day Arizona. By contrast, El Paso, Texas, and neighboring Las Cruces *(see place listing p. 419)* were mere hamlets. Billy the Kid was tried and sentenced in Mesilla, a former territorial capital.

The Mesilla Plaza, designated a state monument in 1957, hosts many local cultural events. Its surrounding buildings, which have been restored to their 19th-century appearance, now house shops and businesses.

The Gadsden Museum, 1875 Boutz Rd., is open by appointment only and includes exhibits relating to Colonel Albert Jennings Fountain and five generations of family and local history; phone (575) 526-6293.

Mesilla (J. Paul Taylor) Visitor Center: 2231 Avenida de Mesilla, P.O. Box 10, Mesilla, NM 88046. **Phone:** (575) 524-3262, ext. 117.

MESON DE MESILLA BOUTIQUE HOTEL
Phone: 575/652-4953

[fyi]   Not evaluated. **Address:** 1803 Avenida de Mesilla 88046 **Location:** Just ne of jct SR 28 and 292. Facilities, services, and decor characterize a mid-scale property.

WHERE TO EAT

ANDELE! RESTAURANTE   **Phone:** 575/526-9631

Mexican
$7-$15

AAA Inspector Notes: Authentic New Mexican cuisine is served at this popular neighborhood cafe. Carne adovada is excellent, as is the salsa. Flan satisfies for dessert. **Bar:** beer & wine. **Address:** 1950 Calle del Norte 88046 **Location:** Jct Calle del Norte and Avenida de Mesilla; in Onate Plaza Shopping Center. [B] [L] [D]

DOUBLE EAGLE RESTAURANT   **Phone:** 575/523-6700

Steak
$9-$66

AAA Inspector Notes: On the National Register of Historic Places, this restaurant is decorated with Baccarat crystal and 19th-century art. A cafe inside the restaurant prepares regional cuisine, including delicious grilled chicken Mesilla and banana enchiladas. The formal dining room allows for more of a fine-dining experience. **Bar:** full bar. **Reservations:** suggested. **Address:** 2355 Calle de Guadalupe 88046 **Location:** In The Plaza; in Old Mesilla. **Historic** [L] [D]

JOSEPHINA'S OLD GATE   **Phone:** 575/525-2620

Sandwiches
$6-$10

AAA Inspector Notes: Enjoy a relaxing lunch or a cup of tea at this quaint little restaurant, just a short stroll from The Plaza. This is a popular subject for local photographers and painters. **Address:** 2261 Calle de Guadalupe 88046 **Location:** N of The Plaza. **Parking:** street only. [B] [L]

LA POSTA DE MESILLA
Menu on AAA.com
Phone: 575/524-3524

Mexican
$7-$16

AAA Inspector Notes: Once a stagecoach stop, the 1840s adobe structure now houses an atrium of shops and Southwestern gourmet foods. On the eastern edge of the Plaza, this busy, popular restaurant serves traditional New Mexican meals, all cooked to order. Enchilada plates-which come with a choice of tasty green chile or thick, rich red chile sauce-are especially tasty. **Bar:** full bar. **Address:** 2410 Calle de San Albino 88046 **Location:** I-10 exit 142; on eastern edge of The Plaza. **Historic** [L] [D]

LORENZO'S DE MESILLA   **Phone:** 575/525-3174

Italian
$7-$22

AAA Inspector Notes: This locally favorite dining spot serves generous portions of southern Italy specialties with a wide variety of pasta entrées and hand-tossed brick oven pizza. The hearty green chile lasagna is a house original, while on the lighter is the Di Lusso salad along with the comforting warmth of minestrone soup. Patio dining is offered in season and live jazz is featured every Friday. **Bar:** beer & wine. **Reservations:** required. **Address:** 1750 Calle de Mercado, #4 88005 **Location:** I-10 exit 140 (La Mesilla), just s; jct Avenida de Mesilla. [L] [D] CALL [M]

MESON DE MESILLA RESTAURANT   **Phone:** 575/652-4953

American
$8-$26

AAA Inspector Notes: Casually elegant atmosphere featuring steak, seafood and pasta. A well-priced wine list can be ordered from in the dining room or at the wine bar. **Bar:** full bar. **Address:** 1803 Avenida de Mesilla 88046 **Location:** Just ne of jct SR 28 and 292; in Meson de Mesilla Boutique Hotel. [L] [D] CALL [M]

PAISANO CAFE   **Phone:** 575/524-0211

Regional American
$5-$25

AAA Inspector Notes: A favorite breakfast and lunch spot, this bustling restaurant serves classics with a creative local flair. Try the green chile Mesilla omelet for breakfast or the pecan-crusted chicken or Southwest cobb salad at lunch. **Bar:** beer & wine. **Address:** 1740 Calle de Mercado 88046 **Location:** I-40 exit 140 (La Mesilla), just s. [B] [L] [D]

MORIARTY pop. 1,910

• Restaurants p. 432

AMERICAS BEST VALUE INN   **Phone:** (505)832-4457

Hotel
$52-$85

Address: 1316 Route 66 W 87035 **Location:** I-40 exit 194, 0.5 mi se on US 66 and I-40 business loop. Located in a commercial area. **Facility:** 29 units. 2 stories (no elevator), interior corridors. **Terms:** cancellation fee imposed. **Free Special Amenities: expanded continental breakfast and high-speed Internet.**

BEST WESTERN MORIARTY HERITAGE INN
Phone: (505)832-5000

Hotel
$89-$110

AAA Benefit: Members save up to 20%, plus 10% bonus points with Best Western Rewards®.

Address: 111 Anaya Blvd 87035 **Location:** I-40 exit 194, 0.4 mi e. **Facility:** 70 units. 2 stories, interior corridors. **Amenities:** high-speed Internet. **Pool(s):** heated indoor. **Activities:** whirlpool, exercise room. **Fee:** game room. **Guest Services:** valet and coin laundry. **Free Special Amenities: full breakfast and high-speed Internet.**

[SAVE] [↑] CALL [M] [≈] [BIZ] [◈] [✕] [⊟] [▱] [▭] / SOME UNITS FEE [⊟]

COMFORT INN   **Phone:** 505/832-6666

Hotel
Rates not provided

Address: 119 Route 66 E 87035 **Location:** I-40 exit 196, just s, then just e. **Facility:** 61 units. 2 stories (no elevator), interior corridors. **Amenities:** safes (fee). **Pool(s):** heated indoor.

[↑] CALL [M] [≈] [BIZ] [◈] [▭] / SOME UNITS [⊟] [⊟] [▱]

SUPER 8
Hotel
$55-$85

Phone: (505)832-6730
Address: 1611 W Old Route 66 87035 **Location:** I-40 exit 194, 0.5 mi e on Central Ave. **Facility:** 68 units. 2 stories (no elevator), interior corridors. **Terms:** cancellation fee imposed.

Guest Services: coin laundry. **Free Special Amenities: expanded continental breakfast and high-speed Internet.**

WHERE TO EAT

THE BUFORD
American
$6-$20

Phone: 505/832-6525
AAA Inspector Notes: Although the town for which it is named is long gone, this busy, inviting steakhouse is for real. Tasty beef cuts, juicy hamburgers and Mexican entrées are the specialty here. The tempting desserts merit a splurge. **Bar:** full bar. **Address:** 5 Carl Cannon Rd 87035 **Location:** I-40 exit 196, just n.

SHORTY'S BAR BE CUE
Barbecue
$4-$15

Phone: 505/832-0400
AAA Inspector Notes: A favorite of both locals and travelers, this modest eatery turns out house specialties like barbecue beef and succulent fried chicken. Ice cream finishes off meals on a sweet note. **Address:** 1202 Main St 87035 **Location:** Center.

NAMBÉ PUEBLO (A-4) elev. 6,058'

This settlement in the foothills of the Sangre de Cristo Mountains was established in the 1300s. Its name in the Tewa language means "people of the round earth."

NAMBÉ PUEBLO is 8 mi. s. of Española on US 84, then 2 mi. e. on SR 503. Fleeing drought, disease and Navajo invasions, the Pojoaque settled in the Rio Grande Valley and prospered until an 1890 smallpox epidemic decimated the population. A few survivors reclaimed the land in 1932, and today about 400 people live there. Above the pueblo, Nambé Falls Recreation Area is popular for camping, fishing, hiking, picnicking and boating.

Note: Still-camera photography is not permitted in the pueblo but is permitted in the recreation area. **Hours:** Pueblo daily 8-noon and 1-5. Recreation area daily 7-7. Phone ahead to confirm schedule. **Cost:** Pueblo free. Recreation area $10. Still-camera photography fee $5. Fishing fee $15. Contact the ranger station for fees for other recreational activities. **Phone:** (505) 455-2304 for the ranger station, or (505) 455-2036 for the tribal office.

OHKAY OWINGEH (A-4) elev. 5,660'

Juan de Oñate established the first Spanish capital of New Mexico here in 1598 at the Tewa settlement of *O'ke*, where villagers offered the explorer a hospitable welcome. Oñate named the pueblo San Juan de los Caballeros in honor of his horsemen. A traditional meeting ground, the pueblo became so powerful that only an *O'ke* native had the authority to declare war for the Pueblo Indians. Today, Ohkay Owingeh is one of the largest Tewa-speaking communities. Before the arrival of Oñate,

the village was named Ohkay Owingeh (O-keh o-WEENG-eh). In September 2005, the pueblo's tribal council restored the traditional name.

OHKAY OWINGEH is 4 mi. n.e. of Española off SR 68. Some 2,000 inhabitants of Ohkay Owingeh—headquarters for the Eight Northern Indian Pueblos Council—maintain farms and produce red pottery, beadwork and embroidery. Ceremonial dances are held throughout the year and most are open to the public. Dance of the Matachines is performed Dec. 25. Inquire about photography restrictions and fees. **Hours:** Daily dawn-dusk. Phone ahead to confirm schedule. **Cost:** Free. **Phone:** (505) 852-4400.

OHKAY CASINO RESORT HOTEL
Hotel
$79-$119

Phone: (505)747-1668
Address: Hwy 68 87566 **Location:** 3.4 mi n of jct US 84 and 285, 1 mi n of Española, then right at light. **Facility:** Guest rooms are spacious and boast custom furnishings, authentic Native American artwork and good storage space. 101 units. 3 stories, interior corridors. **Amenities:** high-speed Internet. **Dining:** entertainment. **Pool(s):** heated outdoor. **Free Special Amenities:** preferred room (subject to availability with advance reservations) and high-speed Internet.

OHKAY
HOTEL•CASINO
YOUR best bet!

101 room non-smoking resort, 3 restaurants, pool, meeting rooms, full-service casino, lounge & bar

OJO CALIENTE (F-1) elev. 6,257'

First enjoyed by American Indians, then by Spaniards, the Ojo Caliente Mineral Springs are still sought for their purported therapeutic properties. Fueled by a volcanic aquifer, five springs each supply a different mineral: iron, sodium sulphate, lithium, soda and arsenic.

Perhaps additional qualities are lent to the springs by virtue of their being sacred. According to Tewa tradition, the spiritual figure Poseyemo returns to the waters each year to visit her grandmother. The springs themselves were considered to be the windows between the outer world and the below world, where the people originated. The Spanish name, *Ojo Caliente*, means "hot eye." Numerous bath facilities and pools are open to the public; phone (505) 583-2233 or (800) 222-9162.

Get pet travel tips and enter the photo contest at AAA.com/PetBook

RANCHO DE SAN JUAN COUNTRY INN & RESTAURANT
Phone: 505/753-6818

Country Inn
$525-$1050

Address: RR 34020, US Hwy 285 87549 **Location:** 3 mi nw of jct US 285 and 84, just n of MM 340. **Facility:** These luxury accommodations are in a serene rural setting, with four casitas remotely located a short distance from the main lodge and additional spacious guest rooms just steps away. Near the Ojo Caliente Mineral Hot Springs and Spa. 7 units. 1 story, exterior corridors. **Terms:** open 3/14-11/25, office hours 7 am-9:30 pm, 30 day cancellation notice-fee imposed. **Activities:** hiking trails. *Fee:* massage. **Guest Services:** valet laundry.

OJO CALIENTE MINERAL SPRINGS RESORT & SPA
Phone: 505/583-2233

[fyi] Not evaluated. **Address:** 50 Los Baños Dr 87549 **Location:** Jct US 285, just w. Facilities, services, and decor characterize a mid-scale property.

WHERE TO EAT

THE ARTESIAN RESTAURANT   **Phone:** 505/583-2233

Southwestern
$10-$30

AAA Inspector Notes: Serving breakfast, lunch and dinner, the restaurant's creative menu features a variety of fresh, healthful, organic selections from granola and pancakes to salads, sandwiches and pasta. **Bar:** beer & wine. **Address:** 50 Los Baños Dr 87549 **Location:** Just w of US 285. [B] [L] [D]

PECOS NATIONAL HISTORICAL PARK (F-4)

Two miles south of Pecos on SR 63, Pecos National Historical Park preserves the ruins of one of the largest ancient pueblos as well as two mission churches built by Franciscans in the 17th and 18th centuries. The American Indian population dwindled over the years because of famine, diseases, emigration and the changing needs of the mission. In 1838 the remaining Pecos people moved to Jémez Pueblo *(see place listing p. 418).*

Visitors can walk through the ruins on a 1.2-mile self-guiding trail and the 2.25-mile Civil War Battle of Glorieta Pass trail; guided 1- to 2-hour tours are available by reservation. Narrated van tours also are available. A visitor center offers a film depicting Pecos' history and displays hand-carved furniture, artifacts from excavations, tin chandeliers and original artwork.

Picnicking is permitted. Allow 1 hour, 30 minutes minimum. Trails open daily 8-6, Memorial Day weekend-Labor Day; 8-5, rest of year. Visitor center open daily 8-6, Memorial Day weekend-Labor Day; 8-4:30, rest of year. Closed Jan. 1, Thanksgiving and Christmas. Admission $3; free (ages 0-15 and

Create complete trip routings and custom maps with the TripTik® Travel Planner on AAA.com or CAA.ca

Federal Recreational Lands pass holders); van tour $2. Phone (505) 757-7241.

PENASCO   pop. 589

SUGAR NYMPHS BISTRO   **Phone:** 575/587-0311

American
$7-$16

AAA Inspector Notes: On the scenic drive between Santa Fe and Taos, this off-the-beaten-path restaurant occupies a charming old adobe mercantile and movie theater in the center of a village that feels as if it is torn from a history book. The menu focuses on fresh salads and sandwiches. **Address:** 15046 Hwy 75 87553 **Location:** On SR 75; center. [L]

PICURÍS PUEBLO (E-4) pop. 68, elev. 7,320'

Once one of the largest Tewa pueblos, Picurís (or *We-Lai*) is now among the smallest. Tribal leaders estimate the number of "people of the hidden valley" at less than 300. Picurís pottery is known for its sparkling bronze finish, which comes from mica in the regional clay.

PICURÍS PUEBLO is about 30 mi. n.e. of Española off SR 75. Believed to have been built in 1150, the pueblo was a site of unrest during the revolts of the late 17th century. Mission of San Lorenzo, erected after the 1692 reconquest, has been in use for more than 2 centuries. **Hours:** Pueblo Mon.-Fri. 8-5. **Cost:** Fees apply for sketching, videotaping and still-camera photography. **Phone:** (575) 587-2519.

PILAR (E-4) elev. 6,082'

The Rio Grande flows through a deep gorge between Pilar and Taos, making this one of the state's prime white-water rafting areas. Hot springs along the river are testament to ongoing seismic activity on the Rio Grande Rift, which stretches from Colorado to Mexico.

RECREATIONAL ACTIVITIES
White-water Rafting

- **Big River Raft Trips** departs from various locations. **Hours:** Daily Mar.-Sept. **Phone:** (575) 758-9711 or (800) 748-3746.
- **Far Flung Adventures** departs from Pilar Café. **Hours:** Daily late Apr.-Sept. 30. **Phone:** (575) 758-2628 or (800) 359-2627.
- **New Wave Rafting Co.** departs from either the Rio Grande Gorge Visitor Center or the County Line Meeting Place on US 68, depending on the trip. **Hours:** Daily mid-Apr. to late Aug. **Phone:** (505) 579-0075 or (800) 984-1444.

PINOS ALTOS   pop. 198
- Restaurants p. 434

BEAR CREEK MOTEL & CABINS   **Phone:** 575/388-4501

Cabin
$109-$189

Address: 88 Main St 88053 **Location:** 1 mi n of town on SR 15. **Facility:** 15 cabins. 2 stories (no elevator), exterior corridors. **Terms:** office hours 9 am-7 pm, 2 night minimum stay - seasonal and/or weekends. **Activities:** whirlpool, hiking trails.

WHERE TO EAT

THE BUCKHORN SALOON   Phone: 575/538-9911

Steak
$9-$22

AAA Inspector Notes: The original 1870s saloon makes diners feel like a real cowboy when they belly-up for a cocktail before dinner, and some nights, live music enhances the bar's atmosphere. Dinner is a little more elegant and romantic in the fireplace-accented dining room, but the service remains casual and attentive. The specialty is cooked-to-order steaks and just plain good food. **Bar:** full bar. **Reservations:** suggested. **Address:** 32 Main St 88053 **Location:** Center. **Historic** [D]

POJOAQUE PUEBLO (A-4) pop. 1,907, elev. 5,852'

At the joining of three rivers, Pojoaque (po-WALK-ee) was named "the water-drinking place" by Tewa travelers. Smallpox wiped out the settlement twice before it was abandoned in 1915. Tribal members returned in the 1930s, and casino gambling now fuels the local economy.

POJOAQUE PUEBLO is 8 mi. s. of Española on US 84 to SR 502 at 96 Cities of Gold Rd. The Pojoaque people's Tewa ancestors migrated to the Four Corners region in the first millennium. The Poeh Cultural Center, 78 Cities of Gold Rd., presents centuries of culture through art, archeological artifacts and history exhibits. Photography is not permitted. **Hours:** Visitor center and gallery Mon.-Sat. 9:30-5:30. **Cost:** Free. **Phone:** (505) 455-3460.

PORTALES (G-6) pop. 12,280, elev. 4,009'

The discovery of shallow groundwater in 1890 ensured the prosperity of Portales. Wells irrigate thousands of acres of peanuts, sorghum, cotton and other crops that surround this commercial center. Dairy production and propagation of drought-resistant crops also are important.

Blackwater Draw Archaeological Site, 7 miles northeast via US 70 on SR 467, has yielded evidence of Paleo-Indian habitation stretching back more than 11,000 years. Exhibits on this dig can be seen at the Blackwater Draw Museum, (575) 562-2202, on US 70. This museum is maintained by the Eastern New Mexico University, a local educational institution with some 5,000 students. On the 550-acre campus off US 70 at the south edge of town is the Roosevelt County Museum, (575) 562-2592, which traces area history focusing on the late 19th and early 20th centuries. If you are looking to generate some energy, drive past the Dalley Windmill Collection, off SR 70 at 1506 S. Kilgore. Featuring some 75 windmills from around the world, it is one of the largest such collections in the country.

Various recreational pursuits are available at Oasis State Park *(see Recreation Chart)*, 6.5 miles north on SR 467, then 2 miles west.

Roosevelt County Chamber of Commerce: 100 S. Ave. A, Portales, NM 88130. **Phone:** (575) 356-8541 or (800) 635-8036.

RADIUM SPRINGS (I-3) pop. 1,699, elev. 3,980'

As its name suggests, Radium Springs first became a travel destination for its hot mineral waters. The Apaches considered the springs sacred, and Chief Geronimo is said to have camped here. Soldiers from Fort Selden enjoyed a bathhouse near the springs' source, a rhyolite dome along the Rio Grande. In the 1930s the Santa Fe Railroad carried weekend travelers from El Paso to the Radium Hot Springs Resort. The temperature of the springs averaged 127 F.

FORT SELDEN STATE MONUMENT is at 1280 Ft. Selden Rd. The Mogollón farmed this site long before Civil War forces arrived. Crumbling adobe walls are all that remain of the 1865 fort, which protected travelers and settlers in the Mesilla Valley from desperados and Apache Indians. After the war, African-American Buffalo Soldiers occupied the fort. As a boy in the 1880s, Gen. Douglas MacArthur also lived here while his father served as post commander. A visitor center displays military artifacts. Frontier Days at Fort Selden is celebrated one weekend in mid-September with period encampments and re-enactments.

Hours: Wed.-Mon. 8:30-5. Living-history demonstrations are offered the second weekend of every month. Cowboy cooking demonstrations are offered on Sat. Closed Jan. 1, Thanksgiving and Christmas. **Cost:** $3; free (ages 0-16). **Phone:** (575) 526-8911.

RANCHOS DE TAOS pop. 2,518
• **Hotels & Restaurants map & index p. 481**

THE STAKEOUT GRILL & BAR   Phone: 575/758-2042

American
$20-$40

AAA Inspector Notes: Overlooking the valley from Outlaw Hill, this restaurant affords views of fabulous desert sunsets and the mountains in the distance. Seating on the seasonal patio offers the best vantage points. Friendly, yet expert, staff members serve attractively presented dishes, such as grilled shrimp scampi, lobster, duck, steaks cooked to order and crab legs. Among palate-tempting desserts are chocolate ganache cake and coconut crème brûlée. **Bar:** full bar. **Address:** 101 Stakeout Dr 87557 **Location:** 4 mi sw on SR 68, 1.3 mi e on gravel road, follow signs. [D]

TRADING POST CAFE & ITALIAN RESTAURANT
    Phone: 575/758-5089   [19]

Italian
$8-$38

AAA Inspector Notes: Italian dishes are prepared with the freshest ingredients and served in the cozy dining room or on the breezy patio at this casual dining spot. The wine list includes many good-value choices. Accomplished servers are prompt and friendly. Homemade desserts are simply a must, so be sure to save room. **Bar:** beer & wine. **Address:** 4179 Hwy 68 87557 **Location:** On SR 68, jct SR 518. [L] [D]

RATON (D-5) pop. 6,885, elev. 6,680'

In 1866 Uncle Dick Wootton, an enterprising man, completed 27 miles of road over Raton Pass, set up a tollgate at his ranch near the summit and charged

$1.50 per wagon to use his improvement. As the Santa Fe Trail was the main route between the East and Southwest, he did well. It is said that his bank deposits consisted of whiskey kegs full of silver dollars.

By 1880 this pleasant watering hole 7 miles south of the summit of Raton Pass evolved into a thriving community. Raton based its economy on the railroad, commerce, cattle ranching and, later, the development of nearby coal reserves. These industries, along with outdoor recreation and the tourism generated by the ease of traveling I-25, continue to sustain Raton. The name, pronounced *ra-TONE*, means "rat" in Spanish.

The Victorian architecture along First Street preserves the atmosphere of Raton's 19th-century mining and railroad heyday. The 1890s Palace Hotel is at First and Cook streets.

Sugarite Canyon State Park *(see Recreation Chart)*, 10 miles northeast via SR 72, provides lakes and picnic sites.

Raton Chamber and Economic Development Council, Inc.: 100 Clayton Rd., Raton, NM 87740. **Phone:** (575) 445-3689.

Self-guiding tours: Brochures detailing tours of the city's historic district are available from the chamber and economic development council.

NRA WHITTINGTON CENTER is 4 mi. w. of I-25 exit 446 on US 64. A variety of gun ranges are available at the National Rifle Association's 33,300-acre shooting facility. An unaltered section of the Santa Fe Trail cuts through the complex. A museum also is on site. **Time:** Allow 1 hour minimum. **Hours:** Ranges open daily dawn-dusk. Museum Mon.-Fri. 8-5, Sat.-Sun. 10-4, Memorial Day-Labor Day; Mon.-Fri. 8-5, rest of year. Closed major holidays. **Cost:** Visitor center free. Gun ranges $20. Other fees may apply. **Phone:** (575) 445-3615 or (800) 494-4853.

RATON MUSEUM is at 108 S. Second St. Photographs, household articles, railroad and coal camp memorabilia and other items depict 19th-century life. **Hours:** Tues.-Sat. 9-5, Memorial Day-Labor Day; Wed.-Sat. 10-4, rest of year. Closed major holidays. **Cost:** Free. **Phone:** (575) 445-8979.

BEST WESTERN PLUS RATON HOTEL
Phone: (575)445-8501

Hotel
$99-$149

AAA Benefit: Members save up to 20%, plus 10% bonus points with Best Western Rewards®.

Address: 473 Clayton Rd 87740 **Location:** I-25 exit 451, just w. **Facility:** 64 units. 2 stories, interior/exterior corridors. **Amenities:** *Some:* high-speed Internet. **Dining:** Mulligan's, see separate listing. **Pool(s):** heated indoor. **Activities:** exercise room. **Guest Services:** coin laundry. **Free Special Amenities:** full breakfast and high-speed Internet.

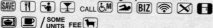

BUDGET HOST RATON
Phone: (575)445-3655

Motel
$69-$84 3/1-9/15
$57-$72 9/16-1/31

Address: 136 Canyon Dr 87740 **Location:** I-25 exit 454, 0.8 mi s on I-25 business loop. **Facility:** 27 units, some two bedrooms. 1 story, exterior corridors. **Terms:** open 3/1-1/31. **Activities:** steamrooms. **Free Special Internet.**
Amenities: continental breakfast and high-speed Internet.

HOLIDAY INN EXPRESS HOTEL & SUITES
Phone: (575)445-1500

Hotel
$129-$179

Address: 101 Card Ave 87740 **Location:** I-25 exit 450, just w. **Facility:** 80 units, some two bedrooms. 2 stories, interior corridors. **Amenities:** high-speed Internet. *Some:* video games. **Pool(s):** heated indoor. **Activities:** whirlpool, putting green, exercise room. **Guest Services:** valet and coin laundry. **Free Special Amenities:** expanded continental breakfast and high-speed Internet.

Holiday Inn Express

Located in the foothills of the Sangre de Cristo Mountains where outdoor adventure awaits!

RATON MICROTEL INN
Phone: (575)445-9100

Hotel
$63-$76

Address: 1640 Cedar St 87740 **Location:** I-25 exit 451, just w. **Facility:** 61 units. 2 stories (no elevator), interior corridors. **Terms:** cancellation fee imposed. **Guest Services:** coin laundry.

RATON PASS INN
Phone: 575/445-3641

Motel
$48-$64

Address: 308 Canyon Dr 87740 **Location:** I-25 exit 454, 0.8 mi s. **Facility:** 14 units. 1 story, exterior corridors. **Terms:** open 4/15-10/15.

WHERE TO EAT

K-BOB'S STEAKHOUSE
Phone: 575/445-2548

Steak
$6-$21

AAA Inspector Notes: The steakhouse prepares a great variety of plump, juicy fillets. A fireplace opens up into both dining rooms, and antique clocks decorate the walls. Rustic wagon-wheel chandeliers illuminate the room. **Bar:** beer & wine. **Address:** 1228 S 2nd St 87740 **Location:** US 87 N and 2nd St, just w.

MULLIGAN'S
Phone: 575/445-8501

American
$7-$26

AAA Inspector Notes: One of Raton's newer restaurants, this casual spot features a contemporary atmosphere with a center bar and an expansive view. The casual menu boasts sandwiches, burgers, barbecue, pizza and pasta. **Bar:** full bar. **Address:** 473 Clayton Rd 87740 **Location:** I-25 exit 451, just w; in Best Western Plus Raton Hotel.

PAPPAS SWEET SHOP RESTAURANT
Phone: 575/445-9811

American
$7-$28

AAA Inspector Notes: This restaurant's well-rounded menu offers spaghetti, steak, seafood and sandwiches. Diners also find displays of antiques, collectibles and items related to the family-owned restaurant and its early years of candy and ice cream making. **Bar:** full bar. **Reservations:** suggested, in season. **Address:** 1201 S 2nd St 87740 **Location:** I-25 exit 451, 0.5 mi w on US 64 and 87, then just s on US 64. L D

THE SANDS RESTAURANT
Phone: 575/445-4024

Mexican
$7-$18

AAA Inspector Notes: Sharing space on the menu are generous portions of Mexican favorites and seafood and steak dishes. **Bar:** beer & wine. **Address:** 350 Clayton Rd 87740 **Location:** I-25 exit 451, just w.

B L D

RED RIVER (E-4) pop. 477, elev. 8,650'

Gold drew early settlers to this former frontier town on the northeastern face of Wheeler Peak. Today's visitors are drawn by the prospect of fun. Skiing and snowmobiling are popular winter pursuits, while hiking, fishing and mountain biking lure summer guests.

Red River Visitor Center: 100 E. Main St., P.O. Box 870, Red River, NM 87558. **Phone:** (575) 754-3030 or (877) 754-1708.

RECREATIONAL ACTIVITIES

Skiing

- **Enchanted Forest Cross Country Ski Area** is 3 mi. e. of downtown. **Hours:** Daily mid-Nov. to late Mar. **Phone:** (575) 754-6112 for ski area.
- **Red River Ski & Snowboard Area** is at 400 Pioneer Rd. **Hours:** Daily 9-4, late Nov.-late Mar. **Phone:** (575) 754-2223.

ALPINE LODGE
Phone: 575/754-2952

Motel
Rates not provided

Address: 417 W Main St 87558 **Location:** Just nw of center on SR 38. **Facility:** 46 units, some two bedrooms, three bedrooms and kitchens. 1-3 stories (no elevator), interior/exterior corridors. **Parking:** winter plug-ins. **Terms:** office hours 8 am-8 pm. **Activities:** whirlpools, fishing, hiking trails, playground, horseshoes. **Fee:** downhill & cross country skiing, snowmobiling. **Guest Services:** coin laundry.

BEST WESTERN RIVERS EDGE
Phone: (575)754-1766

Hotel
$60-$200

AAA Benefit: Members save up to 20%, plus 10% bonus points with Best Western Rewards®.

Address: 301 W River St 87558 **Location:** 1 blk s of W Main St (SR 38); center. **Facility:** 31 units, some kitchens. 2 stories (no elevator), exterior corridors. **Parking:** winter plug-ins. **Terms:** office hours 7 am-9 pm, 2 night minimum stay - seasonal and/or weekends, 7 day cancellation notice. **Activities:** whirlpool, fishing, hiking trails. **Fee:** downhill & cross country skiing, snowmobiling. **Guest Services:** coin laundry. **Free Special Amenities:** local telephone calls and high-speed Internet.

THE RIVERSIDE LODGE & CABINS
Phone: 575/754-2252

Historic Motel
$72-$225

Address: 201 E Main St 87558 **Location:** On SR 38; center. **Facility:** Individual, duplex housekeeping cabins and apartments; some lodge rooms, many fireplaces. On grounds along the Red River. 38 units, some two bedrooms, three bedrooms and kitchens. 1-2 stories (no elevator), exterior corridors. **Parking:** winter plug-ins. **Terms:** office hours 8 am-7 pm, 1-3 night minimum stay - seasonal and/or weekends, cancellation fee imposed. **Activities:** whirlpool, fishing, playground, horseshoes, shuffleboard. **Fee:** downhill & cross country skiing, snowmobiling. **Free Special Amenities:** local telephone calls and high-speed Internet.

WHERE TO EAT

MOUNTAIN TREASURES BISTRO
Phone: 575/754-2700

Sandwiches
$5-$10

AAA Inspector Notes: The fragrance of fresh-baked bread lures patrons in for homemade soups, sandwiches and baked goods. Also on the menu are great smoothies and an excellent selection of gourmet coffee. **Address:** 121 E Main St 87558 **Location:** Center. B L

ROBERTO'S FIESTA MEXICAN RESTAURANT
Phone: 575/754-6270

Mexican
$6-$19

AAA Inspector Notes: Enjoy hearty servings of Mexican favorites for breakfast, lunch and dinner at this eatery. Highlights include excellent spicy salsa and flavorful tortilla soup. **Bar:** beer & wine. **Address:** 201 W Main St 87558 **Location:** Center. B L D

RIO RANCHO (F-3) pop. 87,521, elev. 5,550'

• Hotels & Restaurants map & index p. 362

The housing development of Rio Rancho Estates opened outside Albuquerque in the early 1960s. Lots were marketed to retirees from the Midwest. By the time the community was incorporated in 1981, it numbered 10,000 residents and covered 72 square miles. Intel Corporation opened an office here in the 1980s, bringing younger home buyers. Now the largest private industrial employer in New Mexico, Intel employs some 5,200 people in the manufacturing of microchips and computer processors.

J&R VINTAGE AUTO MUSEUM is off I-25 exit 242, 2.4 mi. w. on US 550, then .5 mi. s. to 3650A SR 528. More than 65 restored vintage cars are displayed, including several that have competed in the Great American Race. Highlights include a 1917 Marmon, a 1928 Model A Ford and a 1932 Packard. **Time:** Allow 30 minutes minimum. **Hours:** Mon.-Sat. 10-5. Closed Jan. 1, Thanksgiving and Christmas. **Cost:** $6; $5 (ages 55+); $3 (ages 6-12). **Phone:** (505) 867-2881.

DAYS INN RIO RANCHO
Phone: (505)892-8800   70

Hotel
$55-$117

Address: 4200 Crestview Dr 87124 **Location:** I-25 exit 233 (Alameda Blvd), 8 mi w on SR 528; I-40 exit 155, 8 mi n on Coors Rd (SR 448). **Facility:** 48 units. 2 stories (no elevator), exterior corridors. **Amenities:** high-speed Internet. **Pool(s):** heated indoor. **Activities:** whirlpool.

(See map & index p. 362.)

EXTENDED STAYAMERICA ALBUQUERQUE-RIO RANCHO
Phone: (505)792-1338   **74**

Extended Stay
Motel

$64-$99

Address: 2608 The American Rd NW 87124 **Location:** Corner of SR 528 and Cottonwood Dr, just n, then just w. **Facility:** 101 efficiencies. 3 stories, interior corridors. **Terms:** office hours 7 am-11 pm. **Guest Services:** coin laundry.

HILTON GARDEN INN ALBUQUERQUE NORTH/RIO RANCHO
Phone: (505)896-1111   **73**

Hotel

$89-$159

AAA Benefit:
Unparalleled hospitality at a special Member rate.

Address: 1771 Rio Rancho Blvd 87124 **Location:** I-25 exit 233 (Alameda Blvd), then n (which becomes SR 528/Rio Rancho Blvd). Across from Intel; convenient to retail area. **Facility:** 129 units. 4 stories, interior corridors. **Terms:** 1-7 night minimum stay, cancellation fee imposed. **Pool(s):** heated indoor. **Activities:** whirlpool, exercise room. **Guest Services:** valet and coin laundry.

INN AT RIO RANCHO HOTEL AND CONFERENCE CENTER
Phone: (505)892-1700   **72**

Hotel

$59-$119

Address: 1465 Rio Rancho Dr SE 87124 **Location:** I-25 exit 233 (Alameda Blvd), 6.5 mi w; I-40 exit 155, 10 mi n on Coors Rd/Coors Bypass to SR 528, then 1 mi n. **Facility:** 118 units, some efficiencies. 1-2 stories (no elevator), exterior corridors. **Amenities:** Some: high-speed Internet. **Pool(s):** heated outdoor. **Activities:** whirlpool, exercise room. **Guest Services:** valet and coin laundry. **Free Special Amenities:** full breakfast and high-speed Internet.

RIO RANCHO SUPER 8
Phone: (505)896-8888   **71**

Hotel

$40-$85

Address: 4100 Barbara Loop SE 87124 **Location:** I-25 exit 233 (Alameda Blvd), 0.5 mi w, 3.8 mi nw on SR 528, then just e. **Facility:** 48 units. 2 stories (no elevator), interior corridors. **Terms:** cancellation fee imposed. **Guest Services:** coin laundry.

WHERE TO EAT

BANANA LEAF ASIAN CUISINE
Phone: 505/892-6119   **94**

Asian

$7-$15

AAA Inspector Notes: Traditional Thai, Vietnamese and Chinese dishes with flavorful sauces are served in generous portions at this casual restaurant. Vietnamese yellow curry and beef vermicelli salad are favorites, along with plenty of vegetarian offerings. Its convenient location makes the eatery a popular lunch spot for the local business community. **Bar:** beer & wine. **Address:** 355 Hwy 528 SE 87124 **Location:** I-25 exit 233 (Alameda Blvd), 8 mi w on SR 528; I-40 exit 155, 8 mi n on Coors Rd.

Learn about
AAA/CAA Diamond Ratings
at AAA.com/Diamonds

FEDERICO'S MEXICAN FOOD
Phone: 505/891-7218   **98**

Mexican

$5-$10

AAA Inspector Notes: This quick-serve restaurant, which offers a great variety of Mexican drinks, dishes up hearty portions of such specialties as the shrimp cocktail-chunks of avocado, cucumbers and tomatoes in a spicy broth. **Address:** 1590 Deborah Rd SE 87124 **Location:** Jct SR 528 and Barbara Loop SE, just e.

HOT TAMALES
Phone: 505/962-0123   **97**

New Mexican

$6-$14

AAA Inspector Notes: Quick service, along with great spicy tamales, burritos, enchiladas and tacos are served here. The chile packs a punch with great New Mexico flavor. **Address:** 1520 Rio Rancho Blvd 87124 **Location:** Jct Barbara Loop and Rio Rancho Blvd.

O'HARE'S GRILLE & PUB
Phone: 505/896-0123   **95**

American

$7-$30

AAA Inspector Notes: Guests can unwind in this busy, cheerful place with a meal complemented by a choice from the large selection of beers and spirits. The friendly pub attracts folks who work in the neighborhood. A short lunchtime wait is typical. **Bar:** full bar. **Address:** 4100 Southern Blvd SE 87124 **Location:** Jct SR 528 and Southern Blvd; in Rio Rancho Shopping Center.

SMOKEHOUSE BBQ
Phone: 505/892-1914   **96**

Barbecue

$5-$12

AAA Inspector Notes: Near the Intel plant, this neighborhood restaurant sells great barbecue brisket by the pound, as well as great meals with side dishes. Breakfast is served daily. **Address:** Hwy 528 & Barbara Loop 87124 **Location:** Jct SR 528 and Barbara Loop, just e.

RODEO (J-1) pop. 101, elev. 4,128'

In a line of ghost towns, Rodeo was one of the few survivors after the passing of the El Paso and Southwestern Railroad. The train line, built in 1902 to connect El Paso, Texas, with copper mines in Bisbee, Ariz., closed in 1952.

CHIRICAHUA GALLERY is at 5 Pine St. Works by local artists and artisans include paintings, photographs, ceramics, basketry, woodwork, quilted items, leather work, silver jewelry and pottery. **Time:** Allow 30 minutes minimum. **Hours:** Tues.-Sat. 10-4; closed Thanksgiving, Dec. 25 and Dec. 31. **Cost:** Free. **Phone:** (575) 557-2225.

ROSWELL (H-5) pop. 48,366, elev. 3,573'
• Hotels p. 439 • Restaurants p. 440

Roswell's economy has long been based on agriculture, manufacturing and oil production, but the tourism industry—mainly fueled by reports of flying saucers and little green men—has grown in importance in recent years. The community's main intergalactic port, the International UFO Museum & Research Center *(see attraction listing p. 438)* showcases a variety of exhibits documenting what has come to be known as the "Roswell Incident"—the military's supposed recovery (and subsequent cover-up) of extraterrestrial debris from a local ranch in 1947. Additionally, each July the Roswell UFO Festival attracts curious earthlings with four days of alien-inspired activities, including a costume contest, a parade, and lectures given by UFO investigators and witnesses.

While it's *possible* you'll have your own "Close Encounter of the Third Kind" in the self-proclaimed "Alien Capital of the World," you're more likely to meet a few undergrads than a bug-eyed space creature. Roswell, with a student population of about 7,000, is home to a branch of Eastern New Mexico University as well as the prestigious New Mexico Military Institute, a 4-year high school and 2-year junior college that originated in 1891. The latter institution boasts such alumni as journalists Sam Donaldson and Chuck Roberts, founder of the Hilton Hotels chain Conrad Hilton and Pulitzer Prize-winning author Paul Horgan. The city's schools as well as its fine museums and the Roswell Symphony Orchestra, (575) 623-5882, make up the bulk of the cultural scene.

More often than not, your eyes will be fixed on the skies while in Roswell, but be sure to take a breather from stargazing to explore some of this destination's alluring Blue Planet landscapes. The city offers a handful of bicycle trails highlighting scenic views, including the 1.5-mile Hondo River Recreation Trail, accessed via its western terminus just east of Hendricks and S. Main streets or its eastern terminus off E. Second Street; the 5-mile Spring River Recreation Trail between Enchanted Lands Park, 306 N. Sycamore Ave., and Spring River Park and Zoo *(see attraction listing)*; and the pretty, tree-lined 1-mile and 2-mile bicycle paths at Cielo Grande Recreational Area off W. College Boulevard.

Established in 1933, Bottomless Lakes State Park *(see Recreation Chart)* is 15 miles southeast via US 380 and SR 409. New Mexico's first state park comprises a series of water-filled sinkholes ranging in depth from 17 to 90 feet and bordered by high red bluffs. The deepest, Lea Lake, welcomes swimmers and scuba divers. It's stocked with rainbow trout in winter, and in summer you can traverse the lake's greenish-blue waters aboard a rented paddleboat. Other recreational pursuits at the park include camping, hiking and wildlife viewing.

Roswell Chamber of Commerce: 131 W. Second St., Roswell, NM 88202. **Phone:** (575) 623-5695.

ANDERSON MUSEUM OF CONTEMPORARY ART is at 409 E. College Blvd. The museum displays the collective work of the Roswell Artist-In-Residence Program, which attracts visual artists from around the world. The permanent collection includes more than 400 paintings, sculptures, photographs and mixed-media pieces. **Time:** Allow 1 hour minimum. **Hours:** Mon.-Fri. 9-4, Sat.-Sun. 1-5. Closed major holidays. **Cost:** Free. **Phone:** (575) 623-5600.

BITTER LAKE NATIONAL WILDLIFE REFUGE is 8 mi. e. via Pine Lodge Rd. The refuge occupies more than 24,000 acres of grassland, ponds and desert shrubs. An 8-mile drive tour offers glimpses of wintering waterfowl, sandhill cranes, roadrunners, quails, pheasants and more than 300 other species of birds. Salt Creek Wilderness can be entered only on foot or horseback; the access point is off US 70 near the Pecos River. The best time for wildlife viewing is October through February.

The refuge also supports one of the most diverse populations of dragonflies in North America, and the Dragonfly Festival is celebrated every year in September. **Hours:** Daily 1 hour before dawn-1 hour after dusk (weather permitting). Visitor center Mon.-Sat. 8-4. **Cost:** Free. **Phone:** (575) 625-4011.

INTERNATIONAL UFO MUSEUM & RESEARCH CENTER is at 114 N. Main St. The center is dedicated to the study of Unidentified Flying Objects (UFOs) thought to be from other planets. Exhibits include paintings, murals and dioramas depicting the purported 1947 crash of a UFO in Roswell along with other alleged sightings of alien beings and their spacecraft. On the premises is a research library with extensive works dealing with UFOs. **Time:** Allow 1 hour, 30 minutes minimum. **Hours:** Daily 9-5. **Cost:** $5; $3 (ages 65+ and military with ID); $2 (ages 5-15). **Phone:** (575) 625-9495.

LT. GEN. DOUGLAS L. McBRIDE MUSEUM is at W. College Blvd. and N. Main St., on the campus of New Mexico Military Institute. Displays examine methods of waging war and preserving peace. Exhibits emphasize the service of New Mexicans and the institute's graduates throughout American history. **Hours:** Mon.-Fri. 7:30-4:30, Oct.-May; 7:30-3:30, rest of year. Closed major holidays. **Cost:** Donations. **Phone:** (575) 624-8380.

ROSWELL MUSEUM AND ART CENTER is in the Civic Center Plaza at 11th and Main sts. Known for its New Mexico modernism collection, the museum showcases Southwestern culture through historical artifacts and fine art. Highlights include works by Andrew Dasburg, Stuart Davis, Marsden Hartley, Victor Higgins and Georgia O'Keeffe. Roswell landscape artist Peter Hurd also is represented as is the Rogers and Mary Ellen Aston Collection of the American West.

The Goddard wing has a re-creation of Dr. Robert Goddard's early laboratory with displays about rocketry and space. The Robert H. Goddard Planetarium presents monthly astronomy programs and multimedia presentations. **Hours:** Mon.-Sat. 9-5, Sun. and holidays 1-5. Closed Jan. 1, Thanksgiving and Christmas. **Cost:** Free. **Phone:** (575) 624-6744.

SPRING RIVER PARK AND ZOO is 1 mi. e. off US 285/Main St. on College Blvd., or 1 mi. n. of US 380/Second St. on Atkinson St. More than 150 animals and birds represent 60 species. Within the 36-acre zoo are a wooden-horse carousel, a miniature train ride and a children's fishing lake. **Time:** Allow 1 hour minimum. **Hours:** Daily 10-dusk. Closed Christmas. **Cost:** Free. Train rides and antique carousel 25c. **Phone:** (575) 624-6760. 🎠

BEST WESTERN EL RANCHO PALACIO
Phone: (575)622-2721

◈◈◈
Hotel
$70-$110

Best Western

AAA Benefit: Members save up to 20%, plus 10% bonus points with Best Western Rewards®.

Address: 2205 N Main St 88201 **Location:** 1.8 mi n on US 70 and 285. **Facility:** 45 units. 2 stories (no elevator), exterior corridors. **Amenities:** high-speed Internet. **Pool(s):** heated outdoor. **Free Special Amenities: local telephone calls and high-speed Internet.**

[SAVE] 🛗 🍽️ 🛎️ [BIZ] 📶 🔌 💻 🖥️ 🍺 / SOME UNITS 🐕

BEST WESTERN PLUS SALLY PORT INN & SUITES
Phone: 575/622-6430

[fyi]
Hotel
Rates not provided

Best Western PLUS

AAA Benefit: Members save up to 20%, plus 10% bonus points with Best Western Rewards®.

Under major renovation, scheduled to be completed September 2011. **Last Rated:** ◈◈◈ **Address:** 2000 N Main St 88201 **Location:** 1.5 mi n on US 70 and 285. **Facility:** 124 units. 2 stories (no elevator), interior corridors. **Amenities:** high-speed Internet. **Pool(s):** heated indoor. **Activities:** saunas, whirlpool, exercise room. **Guest Services:** valet and coin laundry. **Free Special Amenities: local telephone calls and high-speed Internet.**

[SAVE] ✈️ 🍽️ 🍷 🛎️ 📶 🔌 💻 🖥️ / SOME UNITS FEE 🐕

CANDLEWOOD SUITES ROSWELL
Phone: (575)623-4300

◈◈◈
Extended Stay Hotel
$114-$144

Address: 4 Military Heights Dr 88201 **Location:** Jct US 70 and 285, just n of US 385. **Facility:** 87 efficiencies. 4 stories, interior corridors. **Amenities:** high-speed Internet. **Pool(s):** heated outdoor. **Activities:** whirlpool, exercise room. **Guest Services:** valet and coin laundry.

🍽️ CALL 🅼 🛎️ [BIZ] 📶 🗙 🔌 💻 🖥️ / SOME UNITS FEE 🐕

COMFORT INN
Phone: (575)623-4567

◈◈◈
Hotel
$90-$110

Address: 3595 N Main St 88201 **Location:** 3 mi n on US 70 and 285. **Facility:** 55 units. 2 stories (no elevator), interior corridors. **Terms:** cancellation fee imposed. **Amenities:** high-speed Internet, safes (fee). **Pool(s):** heated indoor. **Activities:** whirlpool. **Guest Services:** valet and coin laundry. **Free Special Amenities: full breakfast and high-speed Internet.**

[SAVE] 🍽️ CALL 🅼 🛎️ 🛗 [BIZ] 📶 🔌 💻 🖥️ / SOME UNITS 🐕

COMFORT SUITES ROSWELL
Phone: (575)623-5501

◈◈◈
Hotel
$79-$250

Address: 3610 N Main St 88201 **Location:** Jct US 70 and 285 N, 1 mi s. **Facility:** 68 units. 3 stories, interior corridors. **Terms:** cancellation fee imposed. **Amenities:** high-speed Internet, safes. **Pool(s):** heated indoor. **Activities:** whirlpool, exercise room. **Guest Services:** valet and coin laundry. **Free Special Amenities: full breakfast and high-speed Internet.**

[SAVE] ✈️ 🍽️ CALL 🅼 🛎️ [BIZ] 📶 🗙 🔌 💻 🖥️ / SOME UNITS 🐕

▼ See AAA listing p. 440 ▼

Wake up on the bright side

La Quinta Inn and Suites Roswell

- Free high speed internet access
- Complimentary breakfast
- Microwave/Refrigerator in all suites
- Indoor pool/hot tub & fitness center
- 37" Cable TV with HBO
- Business center

LA**QUINTA** INNS & SUITES

AAA Approved ◈◈◈

10% Off published rates for AAA members

www.lq.com
200 E 19th St • Roswell, NM 88201 • 575-622-8000

Enjoy great savings on hotel rates at AAA.com or CAA.ca

DAYS INN

Phone: (575)623-4021

Hotel

$77-$88

Address: 1310 N Main St 88201 **Location:** 0.8 mi n on US 70 and 285. **Facility:** 62 units. 2 stories (no elevator), exterior corridors. **Amenities:** high-speed Internet. **Pool(s):** outdoor. **Activities:** whirlpool, limited exercise equipment. **Free Special Amenities: expanded continental breakfast and high-speed Internet.**

SAVE ⬛ ⬛ ⬛ BIZ 🛜 ⬛ ⬛ ⬛ / SOME UNITS 🐾

FAIRFIELD INN & SUITES

Phone: (575)624-1300

Hotel

$116-$130

AAA Benefit: AAA hotel discounts of 5% or more.

Address: 1201 N Main St 88201 **Location:** Jct US 380 and 285, 0.7 mi n. **Facility:** 67 units. 3 stories, interior corridors. **Amenities:** high-speed Internet. **Pool(s):** heated outdoor. **Activities:** whirlpool, exercise room. **Guest Services:** valet and coin laundry.

⬛ CALL 🅜 ⬛ BIZ 🛜 ❌ ⬛ ⬛ ⬛

HAMPTON INN & SUITES

Phone: (575)623-5151

Hotel

$119-$139

Hampton

AAA Benefit: Members save up to 10% everyday!

Address: 3607 N Main St 88201 **Location:** Jct US 70 and 285 N, 1 mi s. **Facility:** 70 units. 3 stories, interior corridors. **Terms:** 1-7 night minimum stay, cancellation fee imposed. **Amenities:** video games (fee), high-speed Internet. **Pool(s):** heated indoor. **Activities:** sauna, whirlpool, exercise room. **Guest Services:** valet and coin laundry. **Free Special Amenities: expanded continental breakfast and high-speed Internet.**

SAVE ⬛ CALL 🅜 ⬛ BIZ 🛜 ⬛ ⬛ ⬛

HOLIDAY INN EXPRESS

Phone: (575)627-9900

Hotel

$110-$170

Address: 2300 N Main St 88201 **Location:** 1.8 mi n on US 70 and 285. **Facility:** 80 units, some efficiencies. 3 stories, interior corridors. **Amenities:** *Some:* high-speed Internet. **Pool(s):** heated indoor. **Activities:** sauna, whirlpool, exercise room. **Guest Services:** valet and coin laundry. **Free Special Amenities: full breakfast and high-speed Internet.**

SAVE ➕ ⬛ CALL 🅜 ⬛ BIZ 🛜 ❌ ⬛ ⬛

⬛ / SOME UNITS FEE 🐾

LA QUINTA INN & SUITES ROSWELL

Phone: (575)622-8000

Hotel

$93-$189

Address: 200 E 19th St 88201 **Location:** Jct N Main and 19th sts, 2 blks e. **Facility:** 75 units. 3 stories, interior corridors. **Amenities:** high-speed Internet. **Pool(s):** heated indoor. **Activities:** whirlpool, exercise room. **Guest Services:** valet and coin laundry. **Free Special Amenities: full breakfast and high-speed Internet.** *(See ad p. 439.)*

SAVE CALL 🅜 ⬛ BIZ 🛜

❌ ⬛ ⬛ ⬛ / SOME UNITS 🐾

LEISURE INN

Phone: 575/622-2575

Hotel

Rates not provided

Address: 2700 W 2nd St 88201 **Location:** 2.5 mi w on US 70 and 380. **Facility:** 32 units. 1-2 stories (no elevator), exterior corridors. **Parking:** winter plug-ins. **Pool(s):** heated outdoor. **Guest Services:** coin laundry. **Free Special Amenities: continental breakfast and local telephone calls.** SAVE ➕ ⬛ ⬛ 🛜 / SOME UNITS ⬛

WHERE TO EAT

CATTLE BARON STEAK & SEAFOOD

Phone: 575/622-2465

Steak

$8-$24

AAA Inspector Notes: A scrumptious array of menu selections includes steak, seafood, chicken and prime rib as well as desserts such as caramel apple pie. An upscale Western decor includes wood trim and distinctive chandeliers made from deer antlers. **Bar:** full bar. **Address:** 1113 N Main St 88201 **Location:** US 380 and 285, 0.7 mi n.

L D

KWAN DEN

Phone: 575/622-4192

Chinese

$8-$10

AAA Inspector Notes: Lunch and dinner buffets-which line up traditional preparations of beef, shrimp, chicken and pork-offer the best value at this comfortable restaurant. The menu also lists a limited number of American chicken and seafood dishes. Service is prompt and friendly. **Address:** 1000 W 2nd St 88201 **Location:** 0.8 mi w on US 70 and 285; corner of 2nd St and Union Ave. L D

PASTA CAFE ITALIAN BISTRO

Phone: 575/624-1111

Italian

$6-$35

AAA Inspector Notes: The menu at this bistro comprises tasty classic pasta dishes, pizza selections and hot appetizers, as well as a limited number of steak, veal, seafood and pork entrées. Two types of fresh bread tempt patrons. A small bar area is off the dining room and features an excellent selection of wines by the glass. **Bar:** full bar. **Address:** 1208 N Main St 88201 **Location:** Jct N Main and 12th sts. L D CALL 🅜

PEPPERS GRILL & BAR

Phone: 575/623-1700

American

$7-$25

AAA Inspector Notes: This restaurant prepares a good variety of appetizers, burgers, salads, pasta, sandwiches and traditional Mexican dishes, as well as steak and seafood entrées, for lunch and dinner. Entertainers perform on the patio Friday and Saturday in summer. **Bar:** full bar. **Address:** 500 N Main St 88201 **Location:** US 70 and 285; corner of Main and 6th sts. L D

RIB CRIB BBQ AND GRILL

Phone: 575/625-1200

Barbecue

$7-$22

AAA Inspector Notes: Most guests need extra napkins to tackle the ribs, brisket, ham, pork and chicken selections. The menu also lists sandwiches and wraps, along with tempting sides and large desserts. The decor is decidedly Western. **Bar:** beer & wine. **Address:** 4495 N Main St 88202 **Location:** Just s of SR 48. L D

TIA JUANA'S MEXICAN GRILLE & CANTINA

Phone: 575/627-6113

Mexican

$6-$21

AAA Inspector Notes: Hearty portions of flavorful Mexican favorites are served in a colorful and lively atmosphere. The homemade flour tortillas are a must. **Bar:** full bar. **Address:** 3601 N Main St 88201 **Location:** On US 70 and 285, 3 mi n. L D

RUIDOSO (H-4) pop. 8,029, elev. 6,720'

• Restaurants p. 443

With skiing in winter, golfing, horseback riding, camping, hiking and fishing in spring and summer, and the gilded beauty of the aspen highlighting autumn, Ruidoso is among the state's premier year-round mountain playgrounds. So popular is it during the summer that prospective visitors are advised to make reservations several months in advance for holiday weekends.

The town's setting is the timbered Sacramento Mountains within Lincoln National Forest *(see place listing p. 427)*. The community that now extends 10 miles along the Ruidoso River began in the 1890s as a tin-roofed trading post. The post's old water-wheel still stands on the main street.

Ruidoso Valley Chamber of Commerce and Visitors Center: 720 Sudderth Dr., Ruidoso, NM 88345. **Phone:** (575) 257-7395 or (877) 784-3676.

RECREATIONAL ACTIVITIES

Skiing

- **Ski Apache** is 16 mi. n.w. at the end of SR 532. **Hours:** Daily 9-4, Thanksgiving-early Apr. **Phone:** (575) 464-3600, or (575) 464-1234 for ski conditions.

BEST WESTERN PLUS RUIDOSO INN
Phone: 575/257-3600

Hotel
Rates not provided

AAA Benefit: Members save up to 20%, plus 10% bonus points with Best Western Rewards®.

Address: 97 Camelot Dr 88355 **Location:** US 70, just w of jct Sudderth Dr, then just n. **Facility:** 57 units. 3 stories, interior corridors. **Amenities:** *Some:* high-speed Internet. **Pool(s):** heated indoor. **Activities:** whirlpool, playground, exercise room. **Guest Services:** coin laundry. **Free Special Amenities: local telephone calls and high-speed Internet.**

COMFORT INN-RUIDOSO
Phone: (575)257-2770

Hotel
$69-$169

Address: 2709 Sudderth Dr 88345 **Location:** On SR 48, just w, then s. **Facility:** 54 units. 3 stories, interior corridors. **Terms:** cancellation fee imposed. **Amenities:** high-speed Internet, safes (fee). **Pool(s):** heated indoor. **Activities:** sauna, whirlpool, exercise room. **Guest Services:** coin laundry. **Free Special Amenities: full breakfast and high-speed Internet.**

CROWN POINT CONDOMINIUMS
Phone: (575)257-7641

Condominium
$125-$225

Address: 220 Crown Dr 88355 **Location:** US 70 W; at entrance to Camelot Subdivision. **Facility:** Perched on a high mountain ridge, the attractive vacation condos offer spectacular views of the town below as well as the pine-covered mountains. 60 condominiums. 2 stories, exterior corridors. **Terms:** office hours 7:30 am-9 pm, check-in 4 pm, 2 night minimum stay, 3 day cancellation notice-fee imposed. **Pool(s):** heated indoor/outdoor. **Activities:** whirlpool, 2 lighted tennis courts, sports court, basketball, exercise room. **Guest Services:** coin laundry.

HOLIDAY INN EXPRESS
Phone: (575)257-3736

Hotel
$99-$209

Address: 400 W Hwy 70 88345 **Location:** US 70, just w of jct Sudderth Dr. **Facility:** 104 units. 3 stories, interior corridors. **Pool(s):** heated outdoor. **Activities:** whirlpool. **Guest Services:** coin laundry.

HOTEL RUIDOSO - MIDTOWN
Phone: (575)257-2007

Hotel
$90-$180 5/21-1/31
$80-$170 2/1-5/20

Address: 110 Chase St 88345 **Location:** Just s of jct Sudderth Dr. **Facility:** 55 units. 3 stories, interior corridors. **Terms:** cancellation fee imposed. **Amenities:** high-speed Internet. **Pool(s):** heated indoor. **Activities:** whirlpool, exercise room. **Guest Services:** coin laundry. **Free Special Amenities: full breakfast and high-speed Internet.**

INN OF THE MOUNTAIN GODS RESORT & CASINO
Phone: (575)464-7777

Resort Hotel
$79-$269

Address: 287 Carrizo Canyon Rd (Rt 4) 88345 **Location:** Jct Sudderth Dr, 3.4 mi w, follow signs. **Facility:** Located on the Mescalero Apache Reservation, this resort hotel features a breathtaking view of a nearby lake and pristine natural setting. 273 units. 6 stories, interior corridors. **Parking:** on-site and valet. **Terms:** cancellation fee imposed. **Amenities:** video games (fee), high-speed Internet, safes, honor bars. **Dining:** 3 restaurants, also, Wendell's, see separate listing. **Pool(s):** heated indoor. **Activities:** saunas, whirlpool, steamrooms, hiking trails, jogging, exercise room. *Fee:* boats, canoes, paddleboats, fishing, golf-18 holes, downhill skiing, snowmobiling, horseback riding, game room, massage. **Guest Services:** valet laundry, area transportation (fee). **Free Special Amenities: newspaper and high-speed Internet.** *(See ad p. 442.)*

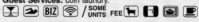

THE LODGE AT SIERRA BLANCA
Phone: (575)258-5500

Hotel
$99-$209

Address: 107 Sierra Blanca Dr 88345 **Location:** Jct Sudderth Dr. **Facility:** 120 units, some two bedrooms and efficiencies. 3 stories, interior corridors. **Terms:** 2-3 night minimum stay - seasonal and/or weekends, cancellation fee imposed. **Amenities:** *Some:* video games (fee). **Pool(s):** heated indoor. **Activities:** whirlpool, lighted tennis court, jogging, playground, exercise room. *Fee:* golf-18 holes, massage. **Guest Services:** coin laundry.

STORY BOOK CABINS
Phone: 575/257-2115

Cabin
Rates not provided

Address: 410 Main Rd 88345 **Location:** 1 mi w on Upper Canyon Rd. **Facility:** Stylishly rustic, comfortable cabins are nestled among tall pine trees in the Upper Canyon area. 26 units, some houses and cabins. 1 story, exterior corridors. **Terms:** office hours 8:30 am-8:30 pm. **Activities:** fishing, hiking trails.

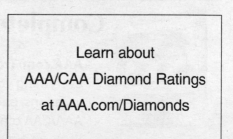

Learn about

AAA/CAA Diamond Ratings

at AAA.com/Diamonds

▼ See AAA listing p. 441 ▼

Brighter { }

INN OF THE MOUNTAIN GODS
RESORT & CASINO

Above. Beyond.

New Mexico's premier mountain resort awaits your arrival with impeccable service, mouthwatering cuisine for every palate, and breathtaking alpine scenery to nurture your soul. Of course, if your idea of a winning view is from a blackjack table, we've got you covered there, too.

Scan this tag with your smart phone to book your stay today!

Get the free mobile app at http://gettag.mobi

InnoftheMountainGods.com f
1-800-545-9011 | Mescalero, NM
FULL CASINO | CHAMPIONSHIP GOLF

The Mescalero Apache Tribe promotes responsible gaming. For assistance, please call 1-800- GAMBLER (1-800-426-2537).

Complete Vacation Planning

AAA.com/Travel and **CAA.ca/Travel** – everything you need to plan and book your vacations, backed by the travel experts at local AAA/CAA offices.

VILLAGE LODGE
Phone: (575)258-5442

◆◆◆
Condominium
$89-$179

Address: 1000 Mechem Dr 88345 **Location:** 2 mi n on SR 48. **Facility:** The facility consists of well-maintained units with living rooms and full kitchens. Guests will have access to the clubhouse. 28 condominiums. 2 stories (no elevator), exterior corridors. **Terms:** office hours 9 am-9 pm, check-in 4 pm, 7 day cancellation notice-fee imposed. **Activities:** whirlpool, exercise room, massage. **Guest Services:** coin laundry. **Free Special Amenities:** local telephone calls and high-speed Internet.

SAVE 📶 ✕ 🛏 📷 💻 /SOME UNITS FEE 🐕

Surrounded by 100 ft pines. Comfortable condos with fireplaces. Near all major attractions.

WHISPERING PINE CABINS
Phone: 575/257-4311

◆◆ ◆◆
Cabin
$99-$450

Address: 422 Main Rd 88345 **Location:** 0.9 mi w of jct SR 48 and Sudderth Dr. **Facility:** 37 units, some kitchens and cabins. 1 story, exterior corridors. **Terms:** office hours 9 am-9 pm, 2-3 night minimum stay - seasonal and/or weekends, 30 day cancellation notice-fee imposed. **Activities:** whirlpool, fishing.

📶 ✕ 🏊 /SOME UNITS FEE 🐕 🎿 🛏 📷 💻

RUIDOSO LODGE CABINS
Phone: 575/257-2510

fyi
Cabin

Did not meet all AAA rating requirements for locking devices in some guest rooms at time of last evaluation on 11/18/2010. **Address:** 300 Main Rd 88345 **Location:** 0.7 mi w on Upper Canyon Rd. Facilities, services, and decor characterize a mid-scale property.

WHERE TO EAT

BLUE GOOSE CAFE
Phone: 575/257-8652

◆◆◆ ◆◆
Sandwiches
$7-$10

AAA Inspector Notes: This bustling café offers hearty sandwiches, made-from-scratch soups and colorful salads. The homemade desserts are worth a visit and the lemon pie is especially luscious. **Address:** 201 Eagle Dr 88345 **Location:** Jct Sudderth Dr, just n. L

CAFE RIO
Phone: 575/257-7746

◆
Italian
$7-$15

AAA Inspector Notes: This main-street cafe serves pizza, salads, jambalaya and a fine selection of sandwiches. There is a great selection of ice cream and desserts, including cakes baked on site. **Address:** 2547 Sudderth Dr 88345 **Location:** Center. **Parking:** street only. L D

CASA BLANCA
Phone: 575/257-2495

◆◆◆ ◆◆
Mexican
$7-$18

AAA Inspector Notes: A local favorite, the restaurant features generous portions of flavorful Mexican specialties. A frosty margarita will definitely cool the taste buds after a mouthful of spicy salsa and warm tortilla chips or the house favorite, green chile chicken enchiladas. Save room for the sopaipilla. **Bar:** full bar. **Address:** 501 Mechem Dr 88345 **Location:** 1 mi n on SR 48 (Mechem Dr). B L D

CATTLE BARON STEAK & SEAFOOD
Phone: 575/257-9355

◆◆ ◆◆
Steak
$7-$24

AAA Inspector Notes: A scrumptious array of menu selections includes steak, seafood, chicken and prime rib as well as desserts such as caramel apple pie. An upscale Western decor includes wood trim and distinctive chandeliers made from deer antlers. **Bar:** full bar. **Address:** 657 Sudderth Dr 88345 **Location:** 1.3 mi s. L D

CORNERSTONE BAKERY CAFE
Phone: 575/257-1842

◆◆◆ ◆◆
Breads/Pastries
$7-$10

AAA Inspector Notes: The bakery and cafe has a bright, clean look. Sandwiches, soups and desserts are perfect for a casual lunch. Bakery items, such as the strawberry-filled croissant, are exceptional. **Address:** 359 Sudderth Dr 88345 **Location:** 1 mi n of jct US 70 and Sudderth Dr. B L

EL CAMINO NUEVO
Phone: 575/258-4312

◆◆ ◆◆
Mexican
$7-$15

AAA Inspector Notes: Adobe-style architecture and terra-cotta tile floors provide the backdrop for a "New Mex" meal at this eatery. Proudly displayed throughout the restaurant, Southwestern prints from local artists add to the festive atmosphere. The wide variety of selections are marked by good presentation, sizable portions and reasonable prices. **Bar:** beer & wine. **Reservations:** suggested. **Address:** 1025 Mechem Dr 88345 **Location:** On SR 48, 1 mi n of jct Sudderth Dr. L D

K-BOB'S STEAKHOUSE
Phone: 575/378-0025

◆◆◆ ◆◆
American
$7-$22

AAA Inspector Notes: The steakhouse prepares a great variety of plump, juicy fillets. A fireplace opens up into both dining rooms, and antique clocks decorate the walls. Rustic wagon-wheel chandeliers illuminate the room. **Bar:** beer & wine. **Address:** 157 Hwy 70 88345 **Location:** Jct US 70 and SR 48, just e. L D

LUCY'S MEXICALI RESTAURANT & CANTINA
Phone: 575/257-8754

◆◆◆ ◆◆
Mexican
$8-$20

AAA Inspector Notes: The house margarita is a good pick among 25 tasty recipes, all of which go well with excellent New Mexican specialties. A mariachi band plays once at week at this spot, which has been in operation for more than 30 years. **Bar:** full bar. **Address:** 2408 Sudderth Dr 88345 **Location:** Center. L D

MICHELENA'S ITALIAN RESTAURANT
Phone: 575/257-5753

◆◆ ◆◆
Italian
$5-$17

AAA Inspector Notes: This bustling family restaurant serves up plentiful helpings of favorite Italian specialties. **Address:** 2703 Sudderth Dr 88345 **Location:** Center. **Parking:** on-site and street. L

SANTINO'S ITALIAN
Phone: 575/257-7540

◆◆ ◆◆
Italian
$10-$28

AAA Inspector Notes: This classy setting displays photographic art from years gone by. Service is efficient and friendly, and such traditional dishes as lasagna are expertly prepared. Clams Santino are extraordinary. **Bar:** full bar. **Address:** 2823 Sudderth Dr 88345 **Location:** Jct SR 48 and Sudderth Dr; center. D

TEXAS CLUB

Phone: 575/258-3325

◆◆◆◆

Steak
$13-$36

AAA Inspector Notes: Guests interested in meeting real Texans and noshing on great steaks will find the lively, fun restaurant just the ticket. On the menu is a good selection of pasta, chicken and fish dishes. **Bar:** full bar. **Address:** 212 Metz Dr 88345 **Location:** Jct SR 48 and Sudderth Dr, 2 mi n, then just e. D

THE VILLAGE BUTTERY

Phone: 575/257-9251

◆◆◆

Sandwiches
$6-$9

AAA Inspector Notes: This cozy neighborhood café is a favorite local lunch spot. The healthy menu features homemade soups, pasta salads, green salads and quiche. Save room for the luscious Granny Guthrie's buttermilk pie, famous throughout the county. **Address:** 2107 Sudderth Dr 88345 **Location:** Center. **Parking:** street only.

L

WENDELL'S

Phone: 575/464-7777

◆◆◆◆

Steak
$8-$66

AAA Inspector Notes: This fine dining restaurant, offering spectacular lake and mountain views, presents locally grown and harvested elk as well as fine beef cuts, fowl and seafood dishes. The professional staff will create a memorable occasion. **Bar:** full bar. **Reservations:** suggested. **Address:** 287 Carrizo Canyon Rd 88345 **Location:** Jct Sudderth Dr, 3.4 mi w, follow signs; in Inn of the Mountain Gods Resort & Casino.

B L D CALL ⚫M

WILLMON'S PRIME GRILLE

Phone: 575/257-2954

◆◆◆◆

Steak
$16-$45

AAA Inspector Notes: USDA certified Prime steaks are the highlight of this cozy restaurant. Other entrée selections range from fresh wild salmon to pan-seared duck with dark cherry sauce. The extensive wine list includes Willmon Vineyard's own labels. **Bar:** beer & wine. **Reservations:** suggested. **Address:** 2523 Sudderth Dr 88345 **Location:** Midtown. **Parking:** street only. D

RUIDOSO DOWNS (H-4) pop. 2,815, elev. 6,420'

From its humble origins in a mountain field in 1947, Ruidoso Downs Race Track, which also is the site of the Racehorse Hall of Fame, has become a premier facility for Quarter Horse and Thoroughbred racing and one of the area's major attractions. The All-American Futurity is held Labor Day, the final day of the racing season. Tagged the world's richest Quarter Horse race—the purse exceeds $2 million—it is the final leg of Quarter Horse racing's Triple Crown. The first two, the Ruidoso Quarter Horse Futurity and the Rainbow Futurity, take place at Ruidoso Downs in June and July, respectively. Phone (575) 378-4431.

Note: Policies concerning admittance of children to pari-mutuel betting facilities vary. Phone for information.

The 84-mile-long Billy the Kid National Scenic Byway offers sweeping mountain views and a glimpse into the desperado's past. Maps and information are available from the scenic byway interpretive center on US 70 next to the Hubbard Museum of the American West *(see attraction listing).*

The 🦄 Lincoln County Cowboy Symposium, held the second full weekend in October, includes cowboy poets, musicians, a chuck wagon cook-off, western arts and crafts and roping demonstrations.

HUBBARD MUSEUM OF THE AMERICAN WEST

is 1 mi. e. of the racetrack off US 70. The museum displays horse-related items from the Anne C. Stradling Collection. Included are life-size models, saddles, wagons and carriages, harnesses and paintings. An interactive area for children also is available. Outdoors is the monumental horse sculpture "Free Spirits at Noisy Water."

Time: Allow 1 hour minimum. **Hours:** Daily 9-4:30. Closed 1 day in July (for annual fund-raiser), Thanksgiving and Dec. 25. **Cost:** $6; $5 (ages 60+ and military with ID); $2 (ages 6-16). **Phone:** (575) 378-4142.

BEST WESTERN PINE SPRINGS INN

Phone: 575/378-8100

◆◆

Hotel

Rates not provided

AAA Benefit: Members save up to 20%, plus 10% bonus points with Best Western Rewards®.

Address: 1420 W Hwy 70 88346 **Location:** Just e of jct US 70 and SR 48. Across from racetrack. **Facility:** 98 units. 2 stories (no elevator), exterior corridors. **Terms:** check-in 4 pm. **Amenities:** Some: high-speed Internet. **Pool(s):** heated outdoor. **Activities:** whirlpool, exercise room. **Guest Services:** coin laundry. **Free Special Amenities:** local telephone calls and high-speed Internet.

SAVE ⊇ BIZ 📶 🖥 🖨 📺 / SOME UNITS 🐾

LA QUINTA INN & SUITES

Phone: (575)378-3333

◆◆◆

Hotel

$85-$215

Address: 2115 W Hwy 70 88346 **Location:** Just e of jct US 70 and SR 48. **Facility:** 63 units. 3 stories, interior corridors. **Amenities:** high-speed Internet. **Pool(s):** heated indoor. **Activities:** whirlpool, exercise room. **Guest Services:** coin laundry.

CALL ⚫M ⊇ BIZ 📶 ✕ 🖥 🖨 📺 / SOME UNITS 🐾

RAMADA INN

Phone: (575)378-1199

◆◆◆

Hotel

$54-$179

Address: 2191 Hwy 70 W 88346 **Location:** Just e of jct US 70 and Sudderth Dr. **Facility:** 61 units. 3 stories, interior corridors. **Pool(s):** heated indoor. **Activities:** whirlpool, exercise room. **Guest Services:** coin laundry.

🍴+ CALL ⚫M ⊇ BIZ 📶 🖥 🖨 📺

SALINAS PUEBLO MISSIONS NATIONAL MONUMENT (C-4)

Near Mountainair, Salinas Pueblo Missions National Monument contains three geographically and historically related pueblos and 17th-century Spanish Franciscan missions. The 1,100-acre park includes the former Gran Quivira National Monument and two former state monuments, Abó and Quarai.

Because there was no further resettlement after the Spaniards and the Tompiro and Tewa Indians abandoned the site in the late 17th century, the masonry ruins are remarkably intact. A visitor center on

US 60 a block west of SR 55 offers a 15-minute orientation film and an exhibit depicting regional history. All three sites and visitor center open daily 9-6, Memorial Day weekend-Labor Day; 9-5, rest of year. Closed Jan. 1, Thanksgiving and Christmas. Free. Phone (505) 847-2585.

ABÓ RUINS is 9 mi. w. of Mountainair on US 60, then .7 mi. n. on SR 513. Once a large pueblo, this Tompiro Indian village was abandoned in the 1670s. Ruins of the 1620 church San Gregorio de Abó, built in medieval style with a 40-foot-tall buttressed curtain wall, rise curiously out of the desert. Brochures, available at the visitor center, as well as interpretive trail markers offer information for self-guiding tours. **Time:** Allow 1 hour minimum. **Hours:** Daily 9-6. Closed Jan. 1, Thanksgiving and Christmas. **Phone:** (505) 847-2400 or (505) 847-2585.

GRAN QUIVIRA RUINS is 26 mi. s. of Mountainair on SR 55. Gran Quivira was one of the most populous pueblos of Salinas Province, with more than 2,000 inhabitants. The 20 limestone house mounds date 1300-1670; 300 rooms and six kivas can be viewed. Also preserved are 17th-century ruins from San Isidro and San Buenaventura. A visitor center displays artifacts and interpretive exhibits. Interpretive trail markers provide information for self-guiding tours. **Time:** Allow 1 hour minimum. **Hours:** Daily 9-6. Closed Jan. 1, Thanksgiving and Christmas. **Phone:** (505) 847-2585.

QUARAI RUINS is 8 mi. n. of Mountainair on SR 55 and 1 mi. w. on a hard-surface road. The site preserves 10 large unexcavated pueblo house mounds and the remains of the 1630 church and convent of Nuestra Señora de La Puríma Concepción de Cuarac. The sandstone church has walls nearly 40 feet high. Another small church may date from 1820 or earlier. A visitor center displays artifacts and interpretive exhibits. Brochures outlining self-guiding tours are available. **Hours:** Daily 9-6. Closed Jan. 1, Thanksgiving and Christmas. **Phone:** (505) 847-2290 or (505) 847-2585.

SAN ANTONIO (H-3) pop. 165, elev. 4,568'

Founded in 1629 as a mission, San Antonio is a trading center for nearby farms and ranches. Corn and alfalfa thrive in the fields along the Rio Grande Valley. To the southeast, beyond the river valley, lies a 35-mile-wide, 90-mile-long stretch of merciless desert. In the days of El Camino Real the desert earned the name Jornada del Muerto—Journey of the Dead.

Some 21 miles south across the Rio Grande from San Marcial is Valverde Battlefield, scene of the first Civil War engagement in New Mexico. Confederate forces led by Gen. H.H. Sibley beat back Union troops from nearby Fort Craig in a daylong battle in February 1862, and went on to occupy Albuquerque. Eroded remnants of the fort survive and are accessible by way of a 5-mile gravel road; however, the battlefield is not.

San Antonio is the birthplace of famed hotelier Conrad Hilton. The ruins of the Hilton family's mercantile boardinghouse and home are 1 mile south of US 380 west of SR 1 at Sixth and Main streets.

BOSQUE DEL APACHE NATIONAL WILDLIFE REFUGE is 8 mi. s. of I-25 exit 139 at US 380 and SR 1. It was established in 1939 to protect critical winter habitat along the Rio Grande for migrating birds. Today the 57,331-acre refuge features a 12-mile wildlife auto tour route with seven observation decks, six hiking trails and two scenic overlooks which provide access to marsh, grasslands and desert upland habitats. A visitor center contains exhibits about the refuge's wildlife resources which include sandhill cranes, snow geese and more than 300 other bird species, as well as coyote, mountain lion, deer, elk, javalina, turkey and rattlesnakes. The Laura Jean Deal Desert Arboretum features one of the most complete collections of cacti, succulents and native trees and plants in the Southwest.

Wildlife viewing is best late November through early February; plants are in bloom April through August. Fishing and hunting are permitted in designated areas. **Time:** Allow 1 hour, 30 minutes minimum. **Hours:** Refuge daily 1 hour before dawn-1 hour after dusk. Visitor center Mon.-Fri. 7:30-4, Sat.-Sun. 8-4:30. **Cost:** Automobile route $5 per private vehicle. **Phone:** (575) 835-1828.

SANDIA PARK (F-3) pop. 237, elev. 7,159'

Sandia Park is about 25 miles east of Albuquerque on the Turquoise Trail National Scenic Byway, a mountain route that passes through the Sandias and Cibola National Forest *(see place listing p. 399)*.

TINKERTOWN MUSEUM is 1 mi. w. on SR 536 to 121 Sandia Crest Rd. The museum displays the life's work of New Mexican folk artist Ross Ward, whose carved and hand-painted miniatures include an animated Western town and a three-ring circus. A wall made of more than 50,000 glass bottles surrounds the museum. **Hours:** Daily 9-6, Apr.-Oct. Last admission 30 minutes before closing. **Cost:** $3; $2.50 (ages 63+); $1 (ages 4-16). **Phone:** (505) 281-5233.

SAN FELIPE PUEBLO (D-3) pop. 2,404, elev. 5,130'

Founded in 1706, San Felipe Pueblo is the most culturally conservative of the Keresan-speaking communities. Villagers are protective of ancient traditions and invite visitors only during the Green Corn Dance in May, when hundreds of men, women and children dance in traditional costumes, and during the Christmas Eve service and the traditional dances that follow. An arts and crafts show is held in October.

GAMBLING ESTABLISHMENTS
• **San Felipe's Casino Hollywood** is at 25 Hagen Rd. **Hours:** Mon.-Thurs. 8 a.m.-4 a.m., Fri.-Sun.

24 hours. **Phone:** (505) 867-6700 or (877) 529-2946.

SAN ILDEFONSO PUEBLO (A-4) pop. 524, elev. 5,550'

Twenty-three miles north of Santa Fe, this settlement sits in the shadow of Black Mesa. This natural mountain stronghold helped the Pueblo people withstand a Spanish attack in 1694.

SAN ILDEFONSO PUEBLO is 13 mi. s. of Española via SR 30/502. For nearly 100 years, this Tewa village has been at the center of a pueblo arts revival. It is best known as the home of Maria Martinez, celebrated potter and creator of the black-on-black pottery prized by collectors. Family members and other potters continue her tradition. A museum depicts pottery-making techniques. Shops on the main plaza display and sell artwork.

Hours: Daily 8-5. Hours may vary. Closed major holidays. Phone ahead to confirm schedule. **Cost:** $10 (per private vehicle). Fees for drawing $25, videotaping $20 and still-camera photography $10. **Phone:** (505) 455-3549.

SAN PATRICIO

HURD- LA RINCONADA GALLERY & GUEST HOMES
Phone: 575/653-4331
[fyi] Not evaluated. **Address:** 105 La Rinconada Ln 88348 **Location:** US 70 at MM 281. Facilities, services, and decor characterize a mid-scale property.

SANTA CLARA PUEBLO (A-4) elev. 5,605'

In the 12th century, the ancestors of today's Santa Clara Pueblo carved their first dwellings into the cliffs above Santa Clara Canyon, where they hunted and farmed. The tribe moved east to the Rio Grande Valley, site of present-day Santa Clara Pueblo around 1600.

The Puye Cliff Dwellings featured a multi-storied complex built around a large central plaza. The south part of the complex contained 173 rooms on the ground floor. The ruins are open daily 8:30-6, mid-April through September 30; 9:30-3, rest of year (weather permitting). The ruins are closed the week before Easter, June 13, August 12 and Christmas. An interpretive center offers exhibits and during the summer local artisans display their works. Cliff Side, Mesa Top and Puye Adventure tours lasting 1 to 2.5 hours are offered on the hour. Tour prices range from $20-$35; $18-$33 (ages 0-14 and 55+). Interpretive center $7; $5 (ages 0-14 and 55+). Phone (888) 320-5008.

SANTA CLARA PUEBLO is 2 mi. s. of Española on SR 30. Established in 1550, this Tewa-speaking pueblo traces its ancestry to the Puye cliff dwellers. Santa Clara artists are noted for their glossy black and red pottery adorned with meticulously incised designs as well as for their paintings and sculpture. **Hours:** Daily 9-4. **Cost:** Free. Photography fee $5. **Phone:** (505) 753-7326.

SANTA FE (F-4) pop. 67,947, elev. 6,989'
• Hotels p. 458 • Restaurants p. 466
• Attractions map p. 450
• Hotels & Restaurants map & index p. 454

Having just celebrated its 400th birthday, you'd think Santa Fe would stop, take a deep breath and rest on that considerable achievement. Not a chance. While this city treats preservation of the past as paramount, there's always something new to discover. You can return to Santa Fe a dozen times and still come away with a different experience.

The high desert country that surrounds New Mexico's capital city, however, is timeless. Undulating hills that stretch to the horizon in all directions are a study in shades of buff, beige and brown. The landscape is speckled with clumps of *Artemisia tridentate*—more commonly known as sagebrush—a hardy shrub with silvery-gray leaves, a pungent fragrance and a tolerance for arid conditions. In the distance, mountains stand like sentinels—the Jemez range to the northwest, the Sangre de Cristos to the northeast. It's an austere but awesome natural setting heightened by remarkably clear air and the intense azure blue of the vast New Mexico sky.

Surely it's a setting that captivated Spanish explorer Juan de Oñate. In 1598 he led the initial effort to colonize the region that was claimed for the Spanish Crown as the province of Santa Fé de Nuevo México. Ten years later the newly appointed Spanish governor, Don Pedro de Peralta, founded a city that was to be the seat of power for all imperial holdings north of the Rio Grande. Peralta lived up to the Spanish penchant for cumbersome titles, naming it La Villa Real de la Santa Fé de San Francisco de Asis—the Royal Town of the Holy Faith of St. Francis of Assisi.

In 1610 Santa Fe became the provincial capital. It's a designation the city has retained ever since, except for a brief period during the Pueblo Revolt of 1680 when Indian villages banded together to expel the colonizers. That same year a mission was established to serve as headquarters for a second power in the region: the church. Franciscan fathers fanned out to usher the Indians into the Christian fold; according to a 1617 report, 14,000 souls had been converted. Four hundred years later the sturdy walls of the San Miguel Mission Church *(see attraction listing p. 452)* are still intact.

Spanish colonists adopted a tried-and-true method of construction for their own churches, government buildings and other structures. The Pueblo Indians used adobe, a mixture of earth, straw and water that was shaped into bricks and dried in the sun. The bricks were stacked and bonded together with more adobe. Pueblo walls were frequently several feet thick, with entry to their dwellings through an opening in the rooftop accessed via ladder. These walls efficiently kept the interiors cool in summer and warm in winter.

(See map & index p. 454.)

Innovations like mud-brick fireplaces and *hornos* (outdoor ovens) were added. A few buildings from this era survive today. The Oldest House on E. De Vargas Street (across from the San Miguel Mission Church) was built around 1646; although the "oldest" title also is claimed by houses in Connecticut, Florida and Massachusetts, this is the only one made of adobe. Another place to see adobe dwellings in their original state (minus doors and windows that were added later) is at Taos Pueblo *(see attraction listing p. 480).*

Question: What's a non-authentic adobe? Answer: Most of the buildings in town. In 1912 a code was passed requiring the use of a style called Spanish Pueblo Revival. It incorporated the defining features of local architecture, which included earthtoned, flat-topped buildings, wood-beamed ceilings *(vigas),* and door and window frames painted white or turquoise. But the majority of houses and commercial structures in the city have stucco surfaces that mimic adobe, referred to amusingly as "Santa Fake" and faux-dobe (foe-dough-bee).

Authentic adobe or not, Santa Fe still looks like no other place in the country. "The City Different" prides itself on the cultivation of "Santa Fe style." It's a term that goes beyond decorative details like clay pots, cow skulls, Southwestern blankets and Native American artifacts (there are plenty of those). Santa Fe style embraces the use of natural materials to enhance the stark natural beauty of the landscape. That's why you'll see, along with the omnipresent adobe, weathered stone walls and picturesque fences made from tree branches lashed together. And everything is suffused with the elusive quality of light that has long attracted painters and photographers, a constant interplay between piercing sun and flickering shadow that's downright mesmerizing.

It's all a nice backdrop for a packed social calendar. One event that has been drawing crowds since 1949 is the annual ☜ Rodeo de Santa Fe in late June, when hundreds of cowboys and cowgirls compete in barrel racing, bull riding, calf roping and steer wrestling. The ☜ Santa Fe International Folk Art Market in July showcases the work of artists from some 35 countries. Both the ☜ Traditional Spanish Market in late July and the ☜ Winter Spanish Market in early December celebrate Hispanic heritage through art, music and dance. The Indian Market in mid-August is Santa Fe's oldest and largest market, celebrating emerging and established artists from some 100 tribes.

By Spanish decree the original town was laid out around a central square, bordered on one side by the seat of government (the Palace of the Governors, which looks much the same now as it did 4 centuries ago), and on the other by a church (the present-day Cathedral Basilica of St. Francis of Assisi). A grid of narrow streets and alleyways radiated out from this central point. Today, of course, these streets are lined with a plethora of shops, restaurants, art galleries and museums, forming a compact downtown core just meant to be strolled.

A magnet for residents and visitors alike, the Plaza is a meeting place morning, noon and evening. It has tree-shaded green lawns and plenty of benches where you can relax and take in the scene. Street musicians contribute a frequent soundtrack. In summer flower baskets hang from the ornamental wrought-iron lampposts, and during the Christmas holidays walkways and rooftops glow with the soft light from *farolitos,* small paper bags holding sand and a single lit candle. The Plaza is Santa Fe's heart, a perfect starting point for exploring a city that's different in the most delightful way.

Guided tours, led by docents from the New Mexico History Museum, depart from the blue gate at the Palace of the Governors mid-April to mid-October; phone (505) 476-5200. Historic Walks of Santa Fe also offer guided walking tours departing from various hotels; phone (505) 986-8388.

Santa Fe Convention and Visitors Bureau: 201 W. Marcy St., Santa Fe, NM 87504. **Phone:** (505) 955-6200 or (800) 777-2489.

Shopping

Shopping is a favorite way to while away the time in Santa Fe, but where you go depends on your agenda. Downtown is shopping central, with stores and boutiques catering to just about every taste (and disposable income level). Serious art collectors for whom money is no object head for Canyon Road, while the Railyard District is an up-and-coming area.

Many downtown shops traffic in the usual T-shirts and Southwestern-themed souvenirs, but you also can find more offbeat and specialized merchandise. The shopping plazas are as good a place as any to start. Plaza Mercado (entrances on San Francisco, Galisteo and Water streets) has more than 30 galleries and boutiques. POP Gallery (133 W. Water St.) offers modern art, photography and sculpture in varied media, while D R Fine Art (123 Galisteo St.) sells contemporary Southwest landscape paintings. Moon Rabbit Toys (112 W. San Francisco St.) stocks toys from all over the world and the latest mustowns for serious gamers.

The Santa Fe Arcade (60 E. San Francisco St. on the south side of the plaza) is a sleek three-level indoor mall filled with trendy retailers specializing in stylish Western wear, custom-made boots, home accessories and gold and silver jewelry. The Shops at La Fonda at the La Fonda Hotel (100 E. San Francisco St.) offer clothing, designer jewelry, handmade textiles, folk art and kitchen accessories. Sample a chocolate piñon nut cluster at Señor Murphy's candy shop. Across the street is the O'Farrell Hat Shop, where you can purchase a customized cowboy hat and peruse the selection of "Santa Fe sticks," locally handcrafted canes and walking sticks made from fine hardwoods.

(See map & index p. 454.)

The buildings surrounding Sena Plaza (125 E. Palace Ave. opposite the plaza) were once part of one big single-family residence, with multiple rooms for family members as well as various tradesmen. Today the spaces are occupied by funky shops selling pottery, ceramics and gifts. The plaza's little courtyard (accessible only through two narrow entryways on Palace Avenue), with its shade trees, benches, fountain and arbor covered with trailing wisteria, is perhaps the most secluded—and delightful—spot in town to relax for a spell.

Few cities in the country have a better selection of Native American art. Packard's on the Plaza (on the plaza's east side) is a feast of treasures: Navajo weavings, Zuni fetishes, Kachina dolls made by Hopi carvers, traditional turquoise jewelry, pottery, silver-studded belts. Ortega's on the Plaza (101 W. San Francisco St.) has a similar selection, along with a beautiful array of beadwork.

For a more personalized shopping experience, wander among the displays of traditional and contemporary jewelry, arts and crafts, pottery, sand paintings and other handmade items sold under the *portal* (porch) of the Palace of the Governors (105 W. Palace Ave.). Vendors spread their wares on blankets on the sidewalk outside this low-slung adobe building. Although the casual setting might imply that haggling is acceptable, prices are usually fixed (though often a bargain compared with many shops). And it's fun to meet the artists and learn about their work.

Within walking distance of downtown, Canyon Road (between East Alameda and Acequia streets) is the upscale center of the Santa Fe art scene. The 10 or so blocks between Paseo de Peralta and Palace Avenue constitute a "gallery row" of festively decorated adobes trading in all manner of fine art, from paintings and sculpture to rugs, jewelry and custom-designed furniture.

Galleries dealing in contemporary works include Adieb Khadoure Fine Art (610 Canyon Rd.), Patricia Carlisle Fine Art (554 Canyon Rd.) and the Waxlander Gallery & Sculpture Garden (622 Canyon Rd.). At the Wiford Gallery (403 Canyon Rd.) there's an outdoor garden with Utah artist Lyman Whitaker's contemporary wind sculptures, delicate-looking copper and stainless steel creations that twirl in the slightest breeze. Western-themed paintings by artists representing the early Taos and Santa Fe schools are displayed at the Nedra Matteucci Galleries (1075 Paseo de Peralta).

The Railyard District (along Guadalupe Street between Paseo de Peralta and Montezuma Avenue) is worth investigating. Casa Nova (530 S. Guadalupe St.) has a little bit of everything—vibrantly colorful furniture, dinnerware, baskets, wall decorations and handicrafts, mostly created by African artists. And for Southwestern products like locally grown white corn, cactus honey and an incredible variety of heirloom tomatoes and dried chiles, check out the Santa Fe Farmers Market (Guadalupe Street at Paseo de Peralta). During the summer months it sets up Tuesdays and Saturdays from 7-noon and Thursdays from 3-7.

Nightlife

Given Santa Fe's close relationship with the fine arts, it's no surprise that highbrow cultural events top the social calendar. First and foremost is the Santa Fe Opera, where classics like "Madame Butterfly," contemporary works and world premieres are performed in a state-of-the-art, open-air venue that has the Sangre de Cristo and Jemez mountains as a backdrop. This may be the only opera company in the world that has to compete with a spectacular sunset for the audience's attention. Nature's show actually begins a couple of hours earlier, when people begin arriving with lavish tailgate picnics in tow. Opera goers also can take advantage of a preview buffet set up on the landscaped rehearsal grounds.

Some 40 performances are offered in July and August. Ticket prices start at $35. A roof covers all seating areas, but evenings can occasionally be cool, rainy or both. The facility is located 7 miles north of Santa Fe on the west side of US 84/285 (exit 168). The box office is open Mon.-Fri. 9-5 (Mon.-Sat. 9-5 during the season); phone (505) 986-5900 or (800) 280-4654.

A variety of events—from the Santa Fe Chamber Music Festival, performances by the Santa Fe Symphony Orchestra and the Paul Taylor Dance Company, and popular music headliners to theater, ballet and classic film festivals—take place at the Lensic Performing Arts Center (211 W. San Francisco St.). The Lensic opened in 1931 as a movie palace and vaudeville theater; a major renovation in 2001 retained the building's distinctive Spanish-style facade and rooftop line of undulating sea serpents. Phone (505) 988-7050 for schedule information, (505) 988-1234 for the box office.

The Pink Adobe (406 Old Santa Fe Tr. across from the San Miguel Mission Church) has been around since 1944, when Rosalea Murphy opened the doors of her restaurant. Locals refer to it as "the Pink," and the restaurant's Dragon Room Lounge is a popular hangout with the artsy crowd. The ambience is classy: dim lighting, walls decorated with carved wood dragons, and a bar with elm trees growing through the roof. Live music runs to jazz, salsa and flamenco, and the specialty margaritas pack a potent punch. Phone (505) 983-7712.

More raucous is Evangelo's (200 W. San Francisco St.), a good ol' dive bar. Local rock and reggae bands keep the joint jumping several nights a week, and the mahogany bar dispenses a variety of imported brews; phone (505) 982-9014. Cowgirl BBQ (319 S. Guadalupe St.) has a big outdoor patio with a lantern-festooned tree, huge portions of barbecued ribs, brisket, chicken and sides, country bands, Cowgirl Karaoke nights and—parents take note—a Kid Corral to keep the young 'uns happy.

Or you could just take a quiet evening stroll around Santa Fe Plaza. Weather permitting

(See map & index p. 454.)

(meaning if it isn't too chilly), the plaza is a pretty, peaceful spot to relax on a bench, enjoy an ice cream cone and people watch. You may even be treated to an impromptu concert by a couple of jamming musicians.

BATAAN MEMORIAL MILITARY MUSEUM & LIBRARY is at 1050 Old Pecos Tr. The museum houses exhibits from early Mexican wars to the present. Artifacts include uniforms, equipment and original artwork relating to the captivity of the 200th Coast Artillery Regiment in the Philippine Islands. **Time:** Allow 30 minutes minimum. **Hours:** Tues.-Sat. 10-4; closed holidays except Bataan Memorial Day and Veterans Day. **Cost:** Free. **Phone:** (505) 474-1670.

CATHEDRAL BASILICA OF ST. FRANCIS OF ASSISI is 1 blk. e. of the Plaza on Cathedral Pl. Built to serve the fledgling settlement's Catholic community, this became the first church in New Mexico to attain the status of cathedral basilica. The parish was founded in 1610; the present church, built in 1869, is one of Santa Fe's most widely recognized landmarks.

Bordered by a lovely tree-shaded park, it's also one of the few downtown buildings that isn't an adobe. The cathedral's sharp, French Romanesque lines provide a striking contrast to the rounded contours of its neighbors, making it a popular subject to photograph.

Archbishop J.B. Lamy, who inspired Willa Cather's novel "Death Comes for the Archbishop," is buried beneath the main altar beside missionary priests Fray Zarate and Fray Gerónimo de la Lama. When services are not being held visitors may view a display of ecclesiastical art in the sanctuary. **Hours:** Mon.-Sat. 6-6, Sun. 7-7. Services are held on Saturday night and throughout the day on Sunday. **Cost:** Free. **Phone:** (505) 982-5619.

THE CENTER FOR CONTEMPORARY ARTS AND CCA CINEMATEQUE is at 1050 Old Pecos Tr. The center is a forum for contemporary art exhibits, independent and foreign films, theater, lectures and workshops. **Time:** Allow 30 minutes minimum. **Hours:** Gallery open Wed.-Thurs. 1-8, Fri.-Sun. 1-10. Movies presented daily; film times vary. Phone ahead to confirm schedule. **Cost:** Donations; fee varies for films. **Phone:** (505) 982-1338.

CRISTO REY CHURCH is at Canyon Rd. and Cristo Rey St. One of the largest adobe structures in the country, the church contains a hand-carved stone *reredos* (altar screen) dating from 1761. **Hours:** Daily 8-4. **Cost:** Donations. **Phone:** (505) 983-8528.

CUSTOM TOURS BY CLARICE departs from corner of Lincoln and West Palace aves. on Santa Fe Plaza. The narrated, open-air tram tour transports guests past such historic sites as the Cathedral Basilica of St. Francis of Assisi and the Loretto

Chapel. An insider's guide to restaurants and recommendations on where to shop also are offered. **Time:** Allow 1 hour, 30 minutes minimum. **Hours:** Tours are given daily at 10, noon, 2 and 4, Apr.-Oct. No tours are offered during inclement weather or when under 50 F. **Cost:** $15. Cash only when boarding tram without reservations; credit cards accepted with 24-hour notice. Reservations are recommended. **Phone:** (505) 438-7116.

EL RANCHO DE LAS GOLONDRINAS is off I-25 exit 276, following signs to 334 Los Pinos Rd. The living-history museum's name means "The Ranch of the Swallows." It was once a stopping place on El Camino Real (The Royal Road) from Mexico City to Old Santa Fe. Exhibits depict Spanish colonial life in New Mexico. Restored buildings include an 18th-century *placita* house with a defensive tower as well as a mill, smithy, schoolhouse and church. A 1.5-mile path leads to the buildings.

Time: Allow 1 hour, 15 minutes minimum. **Hours:** Wed.-Sun. 10-4, June-Sept. Guided tours are offered daily by reservation, Apr.-Oct. **Cost:** $6; $4 (ages 13-18, ages 62+ and military with ID). **Phone:** (505) 471-2261.

GEORGIA O'KEEFFE MUSEUM is at 217 Johnson St. The artist's best-known works include many pieces inspired by New Mexico's stark beauty. More than half of O'Keeffe's lifetime output of paintings, drawings and sculptures comprise the permanent collection, which spans 7 decades. Special exhibits combine O'Keeffe's paintings with other works from the American Modernism Movement.

Tours: Guided tours are available. **Time:** Allow 1 hour minimum. **Hours:** Sun.-Wed. 10-5, Thurs.-Sat. 10-7, Memorial Day-Labor Day; daily 10-5 (also Fri. 5-7), rest of year. Guided tours are given at 10:30. Closed Easter, Thanksgiving, Dec. 25 and between some exhibits. **Cost:** $10; $8 (ages 60+ and students ages 18+ with ID); $5 (New Mexico residents and military and law enforcement with ID); free (ages 0-17 and to all first Fri. of the month 5-7). **Phone:** (505) 946-1000.

LORETTO CHAPEL is at 207 Old Santa Fe Tr. The "Miraculous Staircase" to the chapel's choir loft has two 360-degree turns and no visible means of support. An anonymous carpenter is said to have fashioned the spiral steps in 1878 using only wooden pegs. Legend suggests that St. Joseph, the patron saint of carpenters, inspired the work.

Time: Allow 30 minutes minimum. **Hours:** Mon.-Sat. 9-6, Sun. 10:30-5, June-Oct.; Mon.-Sat. 9-5, Sun. 10:30-5, rest of year. Chapel may close part of a day for weddings and other special events. **Cost:** $3; $2 (ages 7-11). **Phone:** (505) 982-0092.

LORETTO LINE TRAM TOURS departs near Loretto Chapel at 211 Old Santa Fe Tr. Passengers board an open-air tram for a guided 1.25-hour historical tour of Santa Fe. **Hours:** Tours depart daily, Apr.-Oct. **Cost:** Fare $15; $10 (ages 4-11). **Phone:** (505) 982-0092.

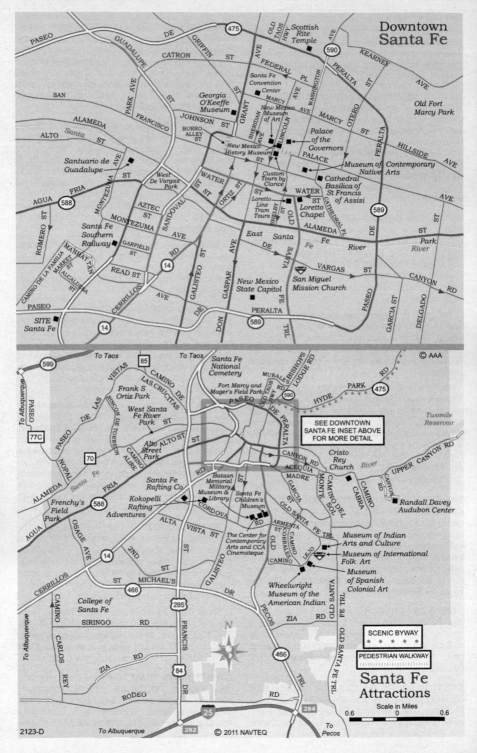

Downtown Santa Fe

© AAA

SEE DOWNTOWN
SANTA FE INSET ABOVE
FOR MORE DETAIL

SCENIC BYWAY

PEDESTRIAN WALKWAY

Santa Fe
Attractions

Scale in Miles

0.6   0   0.6

2123-D

© 2011 NAVTEQ

(See map & index p. 454.)

MUSEUM OF CONTEMPORARY NATIVE ARTS is

at 108 Cathedral Pl. The museum organizes contemporary art exhibitions devoted exclusively to the display of dynamic and diverse arts practices representative of Native North America. **Time:** Allow 1 hour minimum. **Hours:** Wed.-Sat. and Mon. 10-5, Sun. noon-5. Closed Jan. 1, Easter, Thanksgiving and Christmas. **Cost:** $10; $5 (ages 62+ and students with ID); free (ages 0-16, American Indians and veterans with ID). **Phone:** (505) 983-8900.

MUSEUM OF INDIAN ARTS AND CULTURE is on Museum Hill off Old Santa Fe Tr. The museum has an inclusive collection of New Mexican and Southwestern anthropological artifacts. Objects from the museum's collection include pottery, basketry, textiles, jewelry and contemporary arts. One permanent exhibition examines the comprehensive story of the Navajo, Apache and Pueblo peoples in their own words and voices, and the other focuses on 4 centuries of pueblo pottery.

Time: Allow 1 hour minimum. **Hours:** Daily 10-5, Memorial Day-Labor Day; Tues.-Sun. 10-5, rest of year. Closed Jan. 1, Easter, Thanksgiving and Christmas. **Cost:** $9; $8 (students with ID); $6 (New Mexico residents); free (ages 0-16 and for New Mexico residents on Sun. and New Mexico senior citizens on Wed.). Combination tickets are available with Museum of International Folk Art, New Mexico History Museum, New Mexico Museum of Art and Palace of the Governors. **Phone:** (505) 476-1250.

◤**GEM** **MUSEUM OF INTERNATIONAL FOLK ART,** on Museum Hill off Old Santa Fe Tr., houses the world's largest such collection. The Girard Wing features folk art, toys and miniature scenes of marketplaces and villages from 100 countries. Textiles are exhibited in the Neutrogena Wing, which also features a behind-the-scenes look at museum storage and conservation activities. The Bartlett Wing presents changing exhibits.

Time: Allow 1 hour minimum. **Hours:** Daily 10-5 (also Fri. 5-8), Memorial Day-Labor Day; Tues.-Sun. 10-5, rest of year. Closed Jan. 1, Easter, Thanksgiving and Christmas. **Cost:** $9; $8 (students with ID); free (ages 0-16). Combination tickets are available with Museum of Indian Arts and Culture, Museum of Spanish Colonial Art, New Mexico History Museum, New Mexico Museum of Art and Palace of the Governors. **Phone:** (505) 476-1200.

MUSEUM OF SPANISH COLONIAL ART is 2 mi. s.e. of the Plaza at 750 Camino Lejo. Housed in a 1930 Pueblo Revival building designed by architect John Gaw Meem, the museum presents traditional Spanish art produced throughout the world since the start of Spanish colonization. The collection of some 3,500 objects includes painted images of saints, sculpture, textiles, metal work, ceramics, furniture and books. **Time:** Allow 1 hour minimum. **Hours:** Daily 10-5, Memorial Day-Labor Day; Tues.-Sun.

10-5, rest of year. Closed Jan. 1, Easter, Thanksgiving and Christmas. **Cost:** $8; $4 (New Mexico residents); free (ages 0-15 and for New Mexico residents on Sun.). **Phone:** (505) 982-2226.

NEW MEXICO HISTORY MUSEUM, 113 Lincoln Ave. is on the Historic Santa Fe Plaza and combines the state's oldest museum with its newest. Permanent and changing exhibits focus on the history of New Mexico from Native Americans to Spanish colonists, the Mexican Period, the Santa Fe Trail, the railroad era, statehood, World War II and modern-day New Mexico. The museum serves as the anchor for the campus which consists of the Palace of the Governors *(see attraction listing),* the Palace Press, the Portal, the Fray Angelico Chavez History Library and the Photo Archives.

The Palace Press, situated in the rooms adjoining the courtyard, is a working exhibit dedicated to the history of the state's printing techniques. The *portal* (porch) is a gathering place for local Native American artisans to sell authentic jewelry, pottery and weavings. The Fray Angelico Chavez History Library, with some 40,000 book titles, is available Monday through Friday 1 to 5 and Wednesday until 8 p.m. The Photo Archives contain more than 750,000 images dating back to the early 1850s and is open Monday through Friday 1-5. **Tours:** Guided tours are available. **Time:** Allow 3 hours minimum. **Hours:** Daily 10-5 (also Fri. 5-8), Memorial Day-Labor Day.; Tues.-Sun. 10-5 (also Fri. 5-8), rest of year. Closed Jan. 1, Easter, Thanksgiving and Christmas. **Cost:** (Includes Palace of the Governors) $9; $8 (students with ID); $6 (New Mexico residents); free (ages 0-16, New Mexico residents on Sun., New Mexico senior citizens on Wed., and for all Fri. 5-8). Combination tickets are available with Museum of Indian Arts and Culture, Museum of International Folk Art and New Mexico Museum of Art. **Phone:** (505) 476-5200.

Palace of the Governors is on the Historic Santa Fe Plaza at 105 W. Palace Ave. Built in 1610, the Palace is considered one of the oldest public buildings in the United States and is a National Historic Landmark. The long, low adobe structure with 4-foot-thick walls was the seat of government under Spanish, Pueblo Indian, Mexican and U.S. territorial rule until 1909, when it became the state history museum.

Period rooms and exhibitions tell tales of the nearly 400 years of New Mexico History. There are several open-pit excavation sites showing layers of foundations, different types of wall constructions and middens. Artifacts on display include ceramics, glassware, metal utensils, buttons, jewelry and weapons. The chapel room is a replica of a mid-19th century chapel with a simple, brightly-colored altarpiece made in 1830. **Tours:** Guided tours are available. **Time:** Allow 2 hours minimum. **Hours:** Daily 10-5 (also Fri. 5-8), Memorial Day-Labor Day.; Tues.-Sun. 10-5 (also Fri. 5-8), rest of year. Closed Jan. 1, Easter, Thanksgiving and Christmas. **Cost:**

(See map & index p. 454.)

(Includes New Mexico History Museum) $9; $8 (students with ID); $6 (New Mexico residents); free (ages 0-16, New Mexico residents on Sun., New Mexico senior citizens on Wed., and for all Fri. 5-8). Combination tickets are available with Museum of Indian Arts and Culture, Museum of International Folk Art, Museum of Spanish Colonial Art and New Mexico Museum of Art. **Phone:** (505) 476-5100.

NEW MEXICO MUSEUM OF ART is just off the Plaza at 107 W. Palace Ave. The museum, completed in 1917, houses contemporary and traditional American art. Changing exhibits focus on Southwestern artists from the 19th century to the present, including the Santa Fe and Taos masters. **Time:** Allow 1 hour minimum. **Hours:** Daily 10-5 (also Fri. 5-9), Memorial Day-Labor Day; Tues.-Sun. 10-5 (also Fri. 5-9), rest of year. Closed Jan. 1, Easter, Thanksgiving and Christmas. **Cost:** $9; $8 (students with ID); $6 (New Mexico residents); free (ages 0-16, for New Mexico residents on Sun., New Mexico senior citizens on Wed. and to all Fri. 5-9). Combination tickets are available with Museum of Indian Arts and Culture, Museum of International Folk Art, New Mexico History Museum and Palace of the Governors. **Phone:** (505) 476-5072.

NEW MEXICO STATE CAPITOL is at Old Santa Fe Tr. and Paseo de Peralta, 4 blks. s. of the Plaza. The capitol building is designed in the shape of the state's official emblem, the Zia sun symbol, and features a collection of contemporary artwork and furnishings handcrafted by New Mexicans. Galleries on the second floor permit views of the house and senate chambers. **Hours:** Self-guiding tours are available Mon.-Fri. 7-6. Guided tours are offered Mon.-Fri. by appointment. Closed Jan. 1, Easter, Labor Day, Thanksgiving, Christmas Eve and Christmas. **Cost:** Free. **Phone:** (505) 986-4589.

RANDALL DAVEY AUDUBON CENTER is 3 mi. e. of the Plaza at the end of Upper Canyon Rd. This 135-acre preserve in the Santa Fe Canyon hosts more than 130 bird species as well as bears, bobcats, coyotes, deer and foxes. The site includes an education center and nature trails. The Historic Randall Davey House, originally an 1847 sawmill, was converted into a home by the noted painter. It contains his studio, antiques and art work. **Time:** Allow 1 hour minimum. **Hours:** Daily 8-dusk, Apr.-Sept.; 8-5, rest of year. Guided house tours are offered Fri. at 2 and by reservation. Guided bird walks depart Sat. at 8:30. Phone to confirm hours and tour times. **Cost:** Audubon center $2; $1 (ages 0-12). House tours $5; free (ages 0-12). Guided bird walks free. **Phone:** (505) 983-4609.

SAN MIGUEL MISSION CHURCH is 3 blks. s. of the Plaza at 401 Old Santa Fe Tr. (at E. De Vargas St.). A feeling of timelessness emanates from this simple mission church, built by Tlaxcala Indians under the direction of Franciscan *padres* (priests). Constructed around 1610, it is thought to be the nation's oldest active church. Records of its early history were burned during the Pueblo Indian Rebellion of 1680, but the thick, sturdy adobe walls remained unscathed; stone buttresses were subsequently added to strengthen the walls and bell tower.

The sanctuary has wooden pews and massive timber roof beams *(vigas)*. The hand-carved wooden *reredos* (altar screen) dates from 1798. Paintings of saints and Christ the Nazarene surround a gilded and painted wooden statue of St. Michael the Archangel, brought from Mexico in the early 18th century. In the rear of the church is a painting of Our Lady of Guadalupe. The 780-pound San Jose Bell that once hung in the bell tower now is displayed in the gift shop, and visitors are welcome to ring it; according to legend, those who do are destined to return to Santa Fe.

Hours: Mon.-Sat. 9-5, Sun. 10-4. Mass is given on Sun. Closed Christmas. **Cost:** $1; free (ages 0-5). **Phone:** (505) 983-3974.

SANTA FE CHILDREN'S MUSEUM is 1 mi. s. of the Plaza at 1050 Old Pecos Tr. Geared to children ages 0-12, interactive exhibits focus on the arts, sciences and humanities. Among the highlights are an outdoor garden learning environment, bubble exhibits, a rock climbing wall and water works. Artists, scientists and environmental educators conduct hands-on activities; phone ahead for schedule. **Hours:** Tues.-Sat. 10-6, Sun. noon-5. Closed major holidays. **Cost:** Tues.-Sat. $9; $6 (New Mexico residents). Admission Sun. $5; $2 (New Mexico residents). **Phone:** (505) 989-8359.

SANTA FE NATIONAL CEMETERY is 1.5 mi. n. of the Plaza on US 285 at 501 N. Guadalupe St. Originally the military post cemetery, the site contains the graves of soldiers from the Indian Wars as well as those killed in the battles of Pigeon's Ranch and Valverde during the Civil War. It also is the final resting place for nine Congressional Medal of Honor recipients. **Hours:** Gates open daily dawn-dusk; office open Mon.-Fri. 8-4:30. **Cost:** Free. **Phone:** (505) 988-6400.

SANTA FE SOUTHERN RAILWAY departs from Santa Fe Depot at 410 S. Guadalupe St. Sightseeing passengers travel the desert spur built by the Atchison, Topeka & Santa Fe Railway in 1880. Historic Lamy and the scenic Galisteo overlook are among the destinations for 2.5- to 4-hour excursions in vintage coaches or luxury cars. Other excursions are offered.

Food usually is available for purchase in Lamy. **Hours:** Scenic Day Trains depart Fri. at 11, Sat. at noon. Departure times may vary. Phone ahead to confirm schedule. **Cost:** Day train $32-$45; $27-$40 (ages 60+); $18-$32 (ages 3-13). Reservations are recommended. **Phone:** (505) 989-8600.

SANTUARIO DE GUADALUPE is 4 blks. w. of the Plaza at Agua Fria and Guadalupe sts. The 18th-century church is called the nation's oldest shrine

(See map & index p. 454.)

dedicated to Our Lady of Guadalupe. A 1783 oil-on-canvas altar painting by Mexican baroque artist José de Alzibar is considered among the finest oil paintings in the Spanish Southwest. Also included are the meditation chapel with religious woodcarvings, a pictorial history room and the Plants of the Holy Land botanical garden. An 18th-century mission is at the end of El Camino Real. **Hours:** Mon.-Fri. 9-4; call for mass schedule. **Cost:** Donations. **Phone:** (505) 983-8868, ext. 21.

SITE SANTA FE is at 1606 Paseo de Peralta. This contemporary arts organization provides exhibit space for national, international, local and regional artists. Typically, the changing collections are showcased three times a year; visitors should phone ahead to confirm. **Time:** Allow 1 hour minimum. **Hours:** Wed.-Thurs. and Sat. 10-5, Fri. 10-7, Sun. noon-5, mid-June through Aug. 31; Thurs. and Sat. 10-5, Fri. 10-7, Sun. noon-5, rest of year. **Cost:** $10; $5 (ages 60+ and students with ID); free (ages 0-18 and to all Fri. 10-7 and Sat. 10-noon). **Phone:** (505) 989-1199.

SOUTHWEST SAFARIS departs from and returns to the Santa Fe Airport. Full-day air/land combination tours travel to the Grand Canyon, Monument Valley, Canyon de Chelly, Arches/Canyonlands and Mesa Verde. The expeditions include exploration of landmarks, pueblos, cliff dwellings and ruins. Regional geology, archeology and history are explained. Local scenic flights and half-day air/land adventures also are available. **Hours:** Tour lengths range from 30 minutes to 8 hours; some include lunch. **Cost:** Fares $89-$799. Reservations are required. **Phone:** (505) 988-4246 or (800) 842-4246.

TESUQUE PUEBLO—*see place listing p. 485.*

WHEELWRIGHT MUSEUM OF THE AMERICAN INDIAN is 2 mi. s.e. of the plaza at 704 Camino Lejo on Museum Hill. Reminiscent of an eight-sided Navajo hogan, the museum offers exhibits of historic and contemporary American Indian art with emphasis on the Southwest. Among the displays are pottery, jewelry, rugs and baskets. **Tours:** Guided tours are available. **Hours:** Mon.-Sat. 10-5, Sun. 1-5. Closed Jan. 1, Thanksgiving and Christmas. **Cost:** Donations. **Phone:** (505) 982-4636 or (800) 607-4636.

RECREATIONAL ACTIVITIES
White-water Rafting

- **New Mexico River Adventures** departs from 2217 SR 68. Other activities are available. **Hours:** Daily Apr.-Sept. **Phone:** (505) 983-7756 or (800) 983-7756.

- **Kokopelli Rafting Adventures** departs from various locations. **Hours:** Daily Apr.-Oct. **Phone:** (505) 983-3734 or (800) 879-9035.

- **Santa Fe Rafting Co.** is 1.5 mi. s.w. of the Plaza on Cerrillos Rd. **Hours:** Daily Apr.-Sept. **Phone:** (505) 988-4914 or (888) 988-4914.

Fly for Less with AAA Member Fares

Save 5-10% on airfares for participating international airlines when you book at any of 1,000 AAA travel offices across the USA! Contact your local AAA office for details on exclusive member savings.

Member Fares

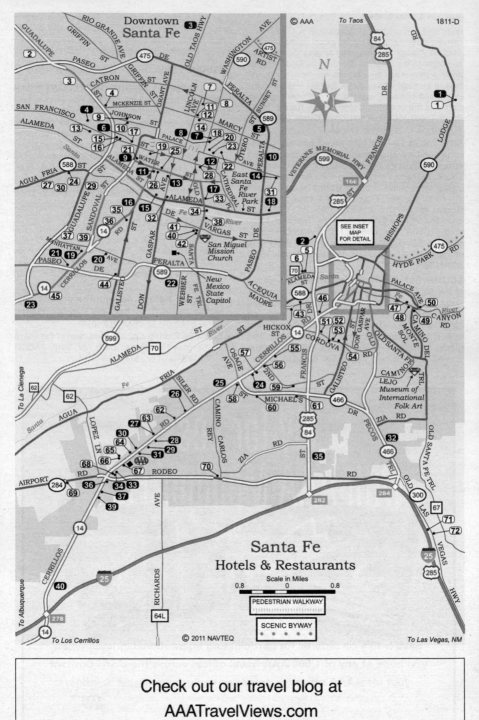

Downtown Santa Fe

© AAA

1811-D

To Taos

N

SEE INSET MAP FOR DETAIL

East Santa Fe River Park

San Miguel Mission Church

New Mexico State Capitol

Museum of International Folk Art

Camino Lejo

HICKOX ST

MICHAEL'S

RODEO

To La Cienega

To Albuquerque

To Los Cerrillos

To Las Vegas, NM

Santa Fe
Hotels & Restaurants

Scale in Miles

0.8   0   0.8

PEDESTRIAN WALKWAY

SCENIC BYWAY

© 2011 NAVTEQ

Check out our travel blog at
AAATravelViews.com

Santa Fe

This index helps you "spot" where approved hotels and restaurants are located on the corresponding detailed maps. Hotel daily rate range is for comparison only and show the property's high season. Restaurant rate range is a combination of lunch and/or dinner. Turn to the listing page for more detailed rate information and consult display ads for special promotions.

SANTA FE

Map Page	Hotels	Diamond Rated	High Season	Page
1 p. 454	**Bishop's Lodge Ranch Resort & Spa**	◆◆◆	$135-$1299 SAVE	458
2 p. 454	The Lodge at Santa Fe	◆◆◆	Rates not provided	464
3 p. 454	**Casa Cuma B & B**	◆◆◆	$169-$219 SAVE	459
4 p. 454	**Las Palomas**	◆◆◆	$99-$498 SAVE	464
5 p. 454	**Inn on the Paseo**	◆◆	$79-$259 SAVE	464
6 p. 454	**Eldorado Hotel & Spa** (See ad p. 460.)	◆◆◆◆	$139-$419 SAVE	461
7 p. 454	Hotel Plaza Real	[fyi]	Rates not provided	463
8 p. 454	**Rosewood Inn of the Anasazi**	◆◆◆◆	Rates not provided SAVE	465
9 p. 454	**Hilton Santa Fe Historic Plaza**	◆◆◆	$159-$239 SAVE	462
10 p. 454	Hacienda Nicholas	◆◆◆	$110-$260	462
11 p. 454	Otra Vez en Santa Fe	◆◆◆	$165-$215	465
12 p. 454	**La Fonda On the Plaza**	◆◆◆	$229-$799 SAVE	464
13 p. 454	Hotel St. Francis	◆◆◆	Rates not provided	463
14 p. 454	**La Posada de Santa Fe Resort & Spa**	◆◆◆◆	$169-$659 SAVE	464
15 p. 454	Inn of the Governors	◆◆◆	$149-$419	464
16 p. 454	**The Old Santa Fe Inn**	◆◆◆	$99-$390 SAVE	464
17 p. 454	**The Inn & Spa at Loretto**	◆◆◆◆	$189-$599 SAVE	463
18 p. 454	**Inn On The Alameda**	◆◆◆	$125-$390 SAVE	464
19 p. 454	**Santa Fe Motel & Inn**	◆◆	$79-$199 SAVE	465
20 p. 454	**El Paradero Bed & Breakfast**	◆◆◆	$100-$200 SAVE	461
21 p. 454	**Hotel Santa Fe, The Hacienda & Spa**	◆◆◆	$119-$500 SAVE	463
22 p. 454	Four Kachinas Inn	◆◆◆	$140-$250	462
23 p. 454	**Santa Fe Sage Inn** (See ad p. 465.)	◆◆	$45-$140 SAVE	465
24 p. 454	**El Rey Inn** (See ad p. 461.)	◆◆◆	$89-$265 SAVE	461
25 p. 454	**Americas Best Value Lamplighter Inn** (See ad p. 458.)	◆◆	$59-$110 SAVE	458
26 p. 454	Motel 6 - 150	◆	$45-$65	464
27 p. 454	**Courtyard by Marriott - Santa Fe** (See ad p. 459.)	◆◆◆	$101-$144 SAVE	459
28 p. 454	**Comfort Suites by Choice Hotels**	◆◆◆	$60-$300 SAVE	459
29 p. 454	Holiday Inn Express-Santa Fe	◆◆◆	$99-$119	462
30 p. 454	**Hampton Inn Santa Fe**	◆◆◆	$99-$149 SAVE	462
31 p. 454	**Best Western Plus Inn of Santa Fe**	◆◆◆	$89-$110 SAVE	458
32 p. 454	**Pecos Trail Inn**	◆◆	$89-$155 SAVE	465
33 p. 454	**Red Roof Inn**	◆◆	$49-$149 SAVE	465
34 p. 454	**DoubleTree by Hilton Santa Fe**	◆◆◆	$99-$209 SAVE	459
35 p. 454	**The Santa Fe Suites**	◆◆	$79-$99 SAVE	465

SANTA FE (cont'd)

Map Page	Hotels (cont'd)	Diamond Rated	High Season	Page
36 p. 454	Fairfield Inn by Marriott	◆◆	$81-$105	462
37 p. 454	La Quinta Inn Santa Fe	◆◆	$54-$152	464
39 p. 454	Hyatt Place Santa Fe (See ad p. 463.)	◆◆◆	$79-$249 [SAVE]	463
40 p. 454	Inn at Santa Fe	◆◆◆	$89-$249 [SAVE]	464

Map Page	Restaurants	Diamond Rated	Cuisine	Meal Range	Page
1 p. 454	Las Fuentes	◆◆◆	Regional American	$12-$42	469
2 p. 454	Jinja Bar & Bistro	◆◆◆	Asian	$9-$19	468
3 p. 454	Clafoutis	◆◆	French	$5-$13	467
4 p. 454	Bumble Bee's Baja Grill	◆	Regional Mexican	$6-$13	466
5 p. 454	Xiclo Vietnamese- Korean Restaurant	◆◆	Asian	$7-$19	472
6 p. 454	Masa Sushi	◆◆	Sushi	$6-$25	469
7 p. 454	Osteria d'Assisi	◆◆◆	Northern Italian	$9-$36	469
8 p. 454	Santacafe	◆◆◆	New American	$9-$33	470
9 p. 454	Shohko Cafe	◆◆	Japanese	$10-$30	471
10 p. 454	Trattoria Nostrani	◆◆◆	Northern Italian	$24-$40	471
11 p. 454	Il Piatto	◆◆	Italian	$9-$28	468
12 p. 454	La Boca	◆◆◆	International	$10-$14	468
13 p. 454	Vanessie	◆◆◆	American	$16-$60	471
14 p. 454	The Bull Ring	◆◆◆	Steak	$10-$48	466
15 p. 454	Thai Cafe	◆◆	Thai	$9-$15	471
16 p. 454	Tokyo Sushi Bar Cafe	◆◆	Sushi	$8-$20	471
17 p. 454	The Old House (See ad p. 460.)	◆◆◆	Regional International	$12-$36	469
18 p. 454	Anasazi Restaurant	◆◆◆	Regional American	$14-$39	466
19 p. 454	Tia Sophia's	◆	Southwestern	$5-$10	471
20 p. 454	The Burrito Company	◆	Regional American	$5-$8	466
21 p. 454	Blue Corn Cafe & Brewery	◆◆	Southwestern	$7-$16	466
22 p. 454	La Casa Sena Restaurant	◆◆◆	Regional American	$12-$40	468
23 p. 454	The Shed	◆◆	Regional Mexican	$8-$20	470
24 p. 454	Azur	◆◆◆	Mediterranean	$19-$23	466
25 p. 454	Cafe Pasqual's	◆◆◆	Regional American	$9-$40	467
26 p. 454	Coyote Cafe	◆◆◆	Southwestern	$27-$56	467
27 p. 454	Ristra	◆◆◆	Regional Continental	$9-$39	470
28 p. 454	La Plazuela Restaurant	◆◆◆	Regional American	$14-$32	469
29 p. 454	Cowgirl Bar and Grill	◆◆	Regional American	$8-$22	467
30 p. 454	Flying Star Cafe	◆◆	Natural/Organic	$8-$16	467
31 p. 454	Fuego	◆◆◆◆	International	$23-$36	468
32 p. 454	India Palace Restaurant	◆◆	Indian	$10-$25	468
33 p. 454	Luminaria Restaurant & Patio	◆◆◆	International	$10-$34	469

Map Page	Restaurants (cont'd)	Diamond Rated	Cuisine	Meal Range	Page
③④ p. 454	315 Restaurant & Wine Bar	▽▽▽	French	$18-$40	466
③⑤ p. 454	Saveur	▽▽	French	$6-$16	470
③⑥ p. 454	Yin Yang	▽▽	Chinese	$2-$25	472
③⑦ p. 454	Tomasita's Restaurant	▽▽	Regional Mexican	$7-$15	471
③⑧ p. 454	**Upper Crust Pizza**	▽	Pizza	$5-$25	471
③⑨ p. 454	Cafe Cafe	▽▽▽	Italian	$7-$24	466
④⓪ p. 454	The Pink Adobe	▽▽▽	American	$8-$34	469
④① p. 454	Rio Chama	▽▽	Steak	$11-$46	470
④② p. 454	Guadalupe Cafe	▽▽	Southwestern	$8-$15	468
④③ p. 454	Tune-Up Cafe	▽	International	$6-$14	471
④④ p. 454	Restaurant Martin	▽▽▽	New American	$9-$29	470
④⑤ p. 454	Vinaigrette	▽▽	Natural/Organic	$10-$19	472
④⑥ p. 454	La Choza	▽▽	Regional Mexican	$9-$16	469
④⑦ p. 454	The Compound Restaurant	▽▽▽	American	$15-$45	467
④⑧ p. 454	**Geronimo**	▽▽▽▽	Regional International	$28-$44	468
④⑨ p. 454	El Farol Restaurant	▽▽▽	Mediterranean	$8-$52	467
⑤⓪ p. 454	The Teahouse	▽▽	Deli	$10-$15	471
⑤① p. 454	Maria's New Mexican Kitchen	▽▽	Mexican	$7-$25	469
⑤② p. 454	Santa Fe Baking Company and Cafe	▽	American	$5-$11	470
⑤③ p. 454	Pyramid Cafe	▽▽	Mediterranean	$8-$24	470
⑤④ p. 454	Body Cafe	▽▽	Natural/Organic	$5-$15	466
⑤⑤ p. 454	Mu Du Noodles	▽▽	Asian	$12-$22	469
⑤⑥ p. 454	Dara Thai Restaurant	▽▽	Thai	$8-$16	467
⑤⑦ p. 454	The Pantry	▽▽	Regional American	$5-$14	469
⑤⑧ p. 454	Jambo Cafe	▽▽	African	$7-$14	468
⑤⑨ p. 454	Chocolate Maven Bakery & Cafe	▽▽	American	$3-$24	467
⑥⓪ p. 454	Pizzeria Espiritu	▽▽	Italian	$8-$19	470
⑥① p. 454	Chow's Asian Bistro	▽▽▽	Asian	$7-$18	467
⑥② p. 454	**Tortilla Flats**	▽▽	Southwestern	$6-$15	471
⑥③ p. 454	**Castle Ranch Steakhouse**	▽▽	American	$9-$30	467
⑥④ p. 454	Bumble Bee's Baja Grill	▽	Regional Mexican	$5-$12	466
⑥⑤ p. 454	Santa Fe Capitol Grill	▽▽▽	International	$8-$27	470
⑥⑥ p. 454	Cleopatra's Cafe	▽	Mediterranean	$6-$16	467
⑥⑦ p. 454	Osaka Bistro Sushi & Sake Bar	▽▽	Japanese	$11-$41	469
⑥⑧ p. 454	Blue Corn Cafe & Brewery	▽▽	Southwestern	$8-$22	466
⑥⑨ p. 454	Puerto Penasco	▽▽	Mexican	$7-$15	470
⑦⓪ p. 454	Joe's Diner and Pizza	▽▽	American	$7-$27	468
⑦① p. 454	Harry's Road House	▽▽	American	$5-$22	468
⑦② p. 454	Steaksmith at El Gancho	▽▽	Steak	$8-$27	471

(See map & index p. 454.)

AMERICAS BEST VALUE LAMPLIGHTER INN
Phone: (505)471-8000 **25**

Hotel
$59-$110

Address: 2405 Cerrillos Rd 87505 **Location:** I-25 exit 278, 7.7 mi n. **Facility:** 80 units, some two bedrooms and kitchens. 2 stories (no elevator), exterior corridors. **Pool(s):** heated indoor. **Activities:** whirlpool, limited exercise equipment. **Guest Services:** valet and coin laundry. **Free Special Amenities: expanded continental breakfast and high-speed Internet.**
(See ad this page.)

SAVE 🍴 ➡️ BIZ 🛜 💾
💻 /SOME UNITS 🖨️

BEST WESTERN PLUS INN OF SANTA FE
Phone: (505)438-3822 **31**

Hotel
$89-$110

Best Western PLUS

AAA Benefit: Members save up to 20%, plus 10% bonus points with Best Western Rewards®.

Address: 3650 Cerrillos Rd 87507 **Location:** I-25 exit 278, 2.8 mi n. **Facility:** 95 units. 3 stories, interior corridors. **Amenities:** safes (fee). **Pool(s):** heated indoor. **Activities:** whirlpool, exercise room. **Guest Services:** valet and coin laundry. **Free Special Amenities: continental breakfast and high-speed Internet.**

SAVE 🍴 ➡️ BIZ 🛜 ❌ 💻
/SOME UNITS 🐾 💾 🖨️

BISHOP'S LODGE RANCH RESORT & SPA
Phone: 505/983-6377 **1**

Resort Hotel
$135-$1299

Address: 1297 N Bishop's Lodge Rd 87501 **Location:** 3.5 mi n of jct Paseo de Peralta. Located in a quiet area. **Facility:** Expansive landscaped grounds surround the 1800's ranch-style resort, situated in the foothills of the Sangre de Cristo Mountains. Summer activities include horseback riding, yoga and trap and skeet shooting. Winter fun includes snowshoeing and sledding. 119 units, some two bedrooms, kitchens and houses. 1-3 stories (no elevator), interior/exterior corridors. **Terms:** check-in 4 pm, 3 day cancellation notice-fee imposed. **Amenities:** high-speed Internet, safes. **Dining:** Las Fuentes, see separate listing. **Pool(s):** heated outdoor. **Activities:** whirlpool, 2 tennis courts, tobogganing, recreation programs, bicycles, hiking trails, playground, sports court, horseshoes, volleyball, exercise room, spa. *Fee:* horseback riding. **Guest Services:** valet laundry, area transportation-shuttle to The Plaza & local area. **Free Special Amenities: high-speed Internet and local transportation.**

SAVE FEE ✈️ 🎿 🧖 🍴 🛝 ➡️ BIZ 🛜 ❌
💾 💻 /SOME UNITS FEE 🐾 🖨️

THE BOBCAT INN
Phone: 505/988-9239

Bed & Breakfast
$99-$149

Address: 442 Old Las Vegas Hwy 87505 **Location:** I-25 exit 284, just n on Old Pecos Tr, then 4.3 mi ne, at Bobcat Tr. Located in a rural area. **Facility:** The property was originally an old hacienda but has been authentically renovated to an inviting inn that's surrounded by piñon and juniper trees in a secluded area. 5 units. 1 story, interior/exterior corridors. **Terms:** check-in 4 pm, 2 night minimum stay - seasonal and/or weekends, age restrictions may apply, 14 day cancellation notice-fee imposed. **Activities:** hiking trails. **Free Special Amenities: full breakfast and high-speed Internet.**

SAVE 🍴 CALL 🖥️ FEE 🧖 🛜 💻 /SOME UNITS 📶 📞

▼ *See AAA listing this page* ▼

Traditional Santa Fe Style at Old-Fashioned Rates

- 80 AC Rooms: Refrigerator, Coffee, Hair dryer, Iron/Board
- 16 AC Kitchenettes: Microwave, Stove & Oven, Fridge, DVD
- Heated Indoor Pool, Hot Tub • 62-Channel Cable, free HBO
- Guest Computer with Hi-Speed Internet • Garden Courtyard
- Rec/Exercise Room • Guest Laundry • Reasonable Rates

— Friendly Personal Service —
Central Location close to the plaza, galleries, museums, dining, shops

Americas Best Value Inn
by Vantage

Lamplighter Inn
AAA Approved

2405 Cerrillos Rd. Santa Fe, NM • 87505 (505) 471-8000
Reservations: 1-800-767-5267
mail@abvilamplighter.com • www.abvilamplighter.com
MC/Visa, AmEx, Discover, Diners Club

GOURMET CONTINENTAL BREAKFAST
with Healthy Choices!

HIGH SPEED & WIRELESS INTERNET

Plan. Map. Go.
TripTik® Travel Planner
Where premier mapping technology meets complete travel information. Only on AAA.com and CAA.ca.

(See map & index p. 454.)

CASA CUMA B & B   Phone: 505/216-7516 **3**

Bed & Breakfast
$169-$219

Address: 105 Paseo de la Cuma 87501 **Location:** Just w off Old Taos Hwy. **Facility:** Near Cross of the Martyrs, this 1950s adobe-style inn offers well-appointed guest rooms, a lush patio with a fire pit and a hot tub with views. 4 units. 1 story, interior/exterior corridors. **Terms:** 2 night minimum stay - weekends, 30 day cancellation notice-fee imposed. **Activities:** whirlpool. *Fee:* ice skating, massage. **Guest Services:** valet laundry. **Free Special Amenities: full breakfast and high-speed Internet.**

SAVE 〔↑→〕 FEE〔✚〕 〔✚〕 〔✕〕
/ SOME UNITS 〔Ⓩ〕 〔▯〕 〔▭〕 〔▭〕

COMFORT SUITES BY CHOICE HOTELS
Phone: (505)473-9004 **28**

Hotel
$60-$300

Address: 3348 Cerrillos Rd 87507 **Location:** I-25 exit 278, 2 mi n; jct Avenida de las Americas. **Facility:** 60 units. 3 stories, interior corridors. **Terms:** cancellation fee imposed. **Pool(s):** heated indoor. **Activities:** whirlpool, exercise room. **Guest Services:** valet laundry. **Free Special Amenities: full breakfast and high-speed Internet.**

SAVE 〔↑→〕 CALL 〔&M〕 〔➡〕 〔BIZ〕 〔✕〕 〔▯〕 〔▭〕 〔▭〕

Simply Reliable

The Diamond Ratings in this TourBook guide are backed by our expert, in-person evaluations, whether the hotel or restaurant is no-frills, moderate or upscale.

Learn more at **AAA.com/Diamonds**

COURTYARD BY MARRIOTT - SANTA FE
Phone: (505)473-2800 **27**

Hotel
$101-$144

AAA Benefit: AAA hotel discounts of 5% or more.

Address: 3347 Cerrillos Rd 87507 **Location:** I-25 exit 278, 3.2 mi n. **Facility:** 209 units. 3 stories, interior/exterior corridors. **Amenities:** high-speed Internet. **Dining:** Castle Ranch Steakhouse, see separate listing. **Pool(s):** heated indoor. **Activities:** whirlpool, exercise room. **Guest Services:** valet and coin laundry, area transportation-The Plaza. **Free Special Amenities: newspaper and high-speed Internet.** *(See ad this page.)*

SAVE 〔✈〕 〔↑↑〕 CALL 〔&M〕 〔➡〕 〔BIZ〕 〔✕〕 〔▯〕 〔▭〕
/ SOME UNITS 〔▭〕

DOUBLETREE BY HILTON SANTA FE
Phone: (505)473-4646 **34**

Hotel
$99-$209

DOUBLETREE
BY HILTON

AAA Benefit: Members save 5% or more everyday!

Address: 4048 Cerrillos Rd 87507 **Location:** I-25 exit 278, 2.3 mi n; just n of Rodeo Dr. **Facility:** 130 units. 4 stories, interior corridors. **Terms:** 1-7 night minimum stay, cancellation fee imposed. **Pool(s):** heated indoor/outdoor. **Activities:** saunas, whirlpool, exercise room. **Guest Services:** valet and coin laundry. **Free Special Amenities: room upgrade (subject to availability with advance reservations) and high-speed Internet.**

SAVE 〔✈〕 〔↑↑〕 CALL 〔&M〕 〔➡〕 〔BIZ〕 〔✕〕 〔▯〕 〔▭〕
〔▭〕 / SOME UNITS FEE〔➡〕

Explore the Travel Guides on AAA.com/Travel or CAA.ca/Travel

▼ *See AAA listing this page* ▼

Santa Fe Courtyard by Marriott

- Complimentary Wireless Internet
- Castle Ranch Steakhouse & Lounge
- Heated Indoor Pool & Spa
- Complimentary Shuttle Service to Plaza, Galleries, Airport
- Complimentary Parking

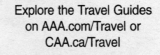

Get the free mobile app at
http://gettag.mobi

15% Off Published Rates
(Mention AAA Advertisement)

COURTYARD®
Marriott

A Familiar Place in "The City Different"

3347 Cerrillos Road . Santa Fe . New Mexico . 87507
P. 505.473.2800   www.marriott.com/safcy

▼ See AAA listing p. 461 ▼

HAVE A RENEWING EXPERIENCE IN THE HEART OF SANTA FE —
Eldorado Hotel & Spa.

Featuring new room upgrades. The new Agave Lounge.
And a renewed tradition of warm hospitality.

AAA members enjoy a 15%
discount off our best available rate.

1.800.955.4455

309 W. San Francisco | Santa Fe, NM
Nidah Spa | The Old House Restaurant
EldoradoHotel.com

Follow us on f *and* t

ELDORADO
HOTEL & SPA

Where Santa Fe begins.

Four Diamond Award

Preferred
HOTELS & RESORTS

TourBook Comments

Are we meeting your travel needs?

If your visit to an establishment listed in a
AAA TourBook guide doesn't meet your
expectations, tell us about it.

Complete an easy online form at
AAA.com/TourBookComments.

(See map & index p. 454.)

ELDORADO HOTEL & SPA
Phone: (505)988-4455 **6**
Hotel
$139-$419
Address: 309 W San Francisco St 87501 **Location:** Just w of The Plaza; at Sandoval St. **Facility:** Custom décor marks the hotel's public facilities. The property is centrally located for an easy day of shopping, museum gazing and gallery hopping. 219 units. 5 stories, interior corridors. **Parking:** on-site (fee) and valet. **Terms:** check-in 4 pm, 3 day cancellation notice-fee imposed. **Amenities:** video games (fee), safes. **Dining:** The Old House, see separate listing. **Pool(s):** heated outdoor. **Activities:** saunas, whirlpool, steamrooms, exercise room, spa. **Guest Services:** valet laundry. **Free Special Amenities:** local telephone calls and high-speed Internet.
(See ad p. 460.)

Download eTourBook guides
for ereaders and smartphones
at AAA.com/ebooks

EL PARADERO BED & BREAKFAST
Phone: (505)988-1177 **20**
Historic Bed & Breakfast
$100-$200
Address: 220 W Manhattan Ave 87501 **Location:** 0.3 mi s on Cerrillos Rd, 1/2 blk e. **Facility:** Within walking distance of Guadalupe Street, guests at this early 1800s farmhouse can enjoy tea under a cherry tree or in the cheerful breakfast room. 15 units, some two bedrooms and efficiencies. 1-2 stories (no elevator), interior/exterior corridors. **Terms:** open 2/7-1/23, office hours 8 am-6 pm, 2 night minimum stay - seasonal and/or weekends, age restrictions may apply, 14 day cancellation notice-fee imposed. **Guest Services:** valet laundry. **Free Special Amenities:** full breakfast and high-speed Internet.

EL REY INN
Phone: (505)982-1931 **24**
Hotel
$89-$265
Address: 1862 Cerrillos Rd 87505 **Location:** I-25 exit 278, 6 mi nw. **Facility:** 86 units, some two bedrooms, efficiencies and kitchens. 1-2 stories (no elevator), exterior corridors. **Terms:** cancellation fee imposed. **Amenities:** safes. **Pool(s):** heated outdoor. **Activities:** sauna, whirlpools, playground, exercise room. **Guest Services:** coin laundry. **Free Special Amenities:** expanded continental breakfast and use of on-premises laundry facilities.
(See ad this page.)

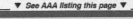
▼ See AAA listing this page ▼

Classic!
Widely Acclaimed El Rey Inn Offers An
Authentic & Affordable Santa Fe Experience

El Rey Inn www.elreyinnsantafe.com
1862 Cerrillos Rd • Santa Fe, NM 87505 • 505/982-1931 • 800/521-1349

(See map & index p. 454.)

ENCANTADO, AN AUBERGE RESORT

Phone: (505)946-5700

Resort Hotel
$275-$675

Address: 198 SR 592 87506 **Location:** US 285/84 N exit 172, 0.5 mi e, then 2 mi n. **Facility:** Guest rooms are spacious, well appointed and have private patios with grand vista views. A fleet of late model Mercedes will drive you into Santa Fe. 65 units. 1-2 stories (no elevator), exterior corridors. **Parking:** valet only. **Terms:** 2 night minimum stay - seasonal and/or weekends, 14 day cancellation notice-fee imposed. **Amenities:** high-speed Internet, safes, honor bars. **Dining:** Terra, see separate listing. **Pool(s):** heated outdoor. **Activities:** saunas, whirlpools, steamrooms, hiking trails, exercise room, spa. **Guest Services:** valet laundry, area transportation-The Plaza. **Free Special Amenities:** newspaper and high-speed Internet.

[SAVE] FEE [icons] / SOME UNITS FEE [icon]

FAIRFIELD INN BY MARRIOTT

Phone: (505)474-4442 **36**

Hotel
$81-$105

AAA Benefit: AAA hotel discounts of 5% or more.

Address: 4150 Cerrillos Rd 87505 **Location:** I-25 exit 278, 2 mi n. **Facility:** 56 units. 2 stories (no elevator), interior corridors. **Amenities:** high-speed Internet. **Pool(s):** heated indoor. **Guest Services:** valet laundry.

[icons]

FOUR KACHINAS INN

Phone: (505)988-1631 **22**

Bed & Breakfast
$140-$250

Address: 512 Webber St 87505 **Location:** Jct Cerrillos Rd and Paseo de Peralta, 4 blks e, then just s. **Facility:** Rooms appointed with Spanish-Colonial reproductions enhance the inn's appeal. Breakfast is served in a room that opens to a sunlit patio. 6 units. 1-2 stories (no elevator), interior/exterior corridors. **Terms:** 2 night minimum stay - weekends, 15 day cancellation notice-fee imposed. **Guest Services:** valet laundry.

[icons] / SOME UNITS [icons]

HACIENDA NICHOLAS

Phone: 505/986-1431 **10**

Bed & Breakfast
$110-$260

Address: 320 E Marcy St 87501 **Location:** Just e of jct Paseo de Peralta; 4 blks e of historic plaza. **Facility:** A southwestern flair--including vigas, high ceilings and thick adobe walls--gives the property a Santa Fe feel. 7 units. 1 story, interior/exterior corridors. **Terms:** office hours 8 am-8 pm, 2-3 night minimum stay - seasonal and/or weekends, 14 day cancellation notice-fee imposed. **Activities:** Fee: massage. **Guest Services:** valet laundry.

[icons] FEE [icons] / SOME UNITS FEE [icon]

HAMPTON INN SANTA FE

Phone: (505)474-3900 **30**

Hotel
$99-$149 5/1-1/31
$89-$129 2/1-4/30

AAA Benefit: Members save up to 10% everyday!

Address: 3625 Cerrillos Rd 87505 **Location:** I-25 exit 278, 2.5 mi n. **Facility:** 81 units. 2 stories, interior corridors. **Terms:** 1-7 night minimum stay, cancellation fee imposed. **Pool(s):** heated indoor. **Activities:** whirlpool, exercise room. **Guest Services:** valet and coin laundry. **Free Special Amenities:** full breakfast and high-speed Internet.

[SAVE] [icons] CALL [icons] / SOME UNITS [icon]

HILTON SANTA FE GOLF RESORT & SPA AT BUFFALO THUNDER

Phone: (505)455-5555

Resort Hotel
$109-$339 2/1-9/30
$99-$319 10/1-1/31

AAA Benefit: Members save 5% or more everyday!

Address: 20 Buffalo Thunder Tr 87506 **Location:** N on US 285 exit Buffalo Thunder Rd, just e. **Facility:** From an award-winning golf course, casino, spa, shops and fine dining to a fully staffed kid's camp, the luxurious resort offers something for everyone. 395 units. 6 stories, interior corridors. **Parking:** valet and street only. **Terms:** 1-7 night minimum stay, cancellation fee imposed. **Amenities:** safes, honor bars. Fee: video games, high-speed Internet. **Dining:** 6 restaurants, also, Red Sage, see separate listing, nightclub, entertainment. **Pool(s):** 2 heated outdoor, heated indoor. **Activities:** saunas, whirlpools, steamrooms, 3 tennis courts, hiking trails, jogging, game room, exercise room, spa. Fee: golf-27 holes, horseback riding. **Guest Services:** valet laundry, area transportation-Santa Fe. **Free Special Amenities: local telephone calls and high-speed Internet.**

[SAVE] [icons] CALL [icons] / SOME UNITS FEE [icons]

[Hilton logo] **Vegas Style Gaming, Golf, Spa, Fine Dining and Art only 15 minutes north of Historic Santa Fe.**

HILTON SANTA FE HISTORIC PLAZA

Phone: (505)988-2811 **9**

Hotel
$159-$239 7/1-1/31
$139-$199 2/1-6/30

[Hilton logo] **AAA Benefit:** Members save 5% or more everyday!

Address: 100 Sandoval St 87501 **Location:** Just sw of The Plaza; between San Francisco and W Alameda sts. **Facility:** 158 units, some two bedrooms. 3 stories, interior/exterior corridors. **Parking:** on-site (fee). **Terms:** check-in 4 pm, 1-7 night minimum stay, cancellation fee imposed. **Amenities:** high-speed Internet (fee). **Dining:** 2 restaurants. **Pool(s):** heated outdoor. **Activities:** whirlpool, exercise room. **Guest Services:** valet laundry, area transportation-within 2 mi. **Free Special Amenities:** local telephone calls and newspaper.

[SAVE] [icons] / SOME UNITS FEE [icons]

HOLIDAY INN EXPRESS-SANTA FE

Phone: (505)474-7570 **29**

Hotel
$99-$119 6/1-1/31
$79-$99 2/1-5/31

Address: 3450 Cerrillos Rd 87507 **Location:** I-25 exit 278, 3 mi n. **Facility:** 76 units. 3 stories, interior corridors. **Pool(s):** heated outdoor. **Activities:** exercise room. **Guest Services:** valet and coin laundry.

[icons] CALL [icons] / SOME UNITS [icon]

Enjoy great savings on hotel rates at AAA.com or CAA.ca

(See map & index p. 454.)

HOTEL PLAZA REAL   Phone: 505/988-4900   **7**

(fyi)
Hotel
Rates not provided

Under major renovation, scheduled to be completed July 2011. **Last Rated:** ▼▼▼ **Address:** 125 Washington Ave 87501 **Location:** Just ne of The Plaza; center. **Facility:** 56 units, some efficiencies and kitchens. 2-3 stories, interior/exterior corridors. **Parking:** on-site (fee). **Guest Services:** valet laundry. Affiliated with A Preferred Hotel.

⊤ 📶 ✕ 🖥 / SOME UNITS FEE 🐕 🛗 🖥

HOTEL ST. FRANCIS   Phone: 505/983-5700   **13**

▼▼▼
Historic Hotel
Rates not provided

Address: 210 Don Gaspar Ave 87501 **Location:** Just s of The Plaza. **Facility:** Recently renovated in the style of a Franciscan monastery, the hotel sits in the heart of Santa Fe. 82 units. 3 stories, interior corridors. **Amenities:** safes. **Activities:** exercise room. **Guest Services:** valet laundry.

🍴 ⊤ BIZ 📶 ✕ 🖥 / SOME UNITS FEE 🐕 🛗

HOTEL SANTA FE, THE HACIENDA & SPA   Phone: (505)982-1200   **21**

▼▼▼
Hotel
$119-$500

Address: 1501 Paseo de Peralta 87501 **Location:** At Cerrillos Rd, 0.6 mi s of The Plaza. **Facility:** 163 units. 3 stories, interior corridors. **Terms:** check-in 4 pm, 3 day cancellation notice-fee imposed. **Amenities:** honor bars. *Some:* safes. **Pool(s):** heated outdoor. **Activities:** whirlpools, exercise room, spa. **Guest Services:** valet and coin laundry, area transportation-within 1 mi.

SAVE 🍴 🍽 ⊤ 🏊 BIZ 📶 ✕ / SOME UNITS FEE 🐕 🖥 🖥

HYATT PLACE SANTA FE   Phone: (505)474-7777   **39**

▼▼▼
Hotel
$79-$249

HYATT PLACE

AAA Benefit: Members save 10% or more everyday.

Address: 4320 Cerrillos Rd 87507 **Location:** I-25 exit 278, 2 mi e. **Facility:** 92 units. 3 stories, interior corridors. **Terms:** cancellation fee imposed. **Amenities:** high-speed Internet. **Pool(s):** heated indoor. **Activities:** whirlpool, exercise room. **Guest Services:** valet and coin laundry, area transportation-within 5 mi. **Free Special Amenities:** expanded continental breakfast and high-speed Internet. (See ad this page.)

SAVE 🔧 🍽 ⊤ CALL 🚹 🏊 BIZ 📶 ✕ FEE 📷 🛗 🖥

THE INN & SPA AT LORETTO   Phone: (505)988-5531   **17**

▼▼▼
Hotel
$189-$599 6/1-1/31
$189-$399 2/1-5/31

Address: 211 Old Santa Fe Tr 87501 **Location:** Just s of The Plaza. Located in the historic district. **Facility:** Upscale bedding and punched tin accessories help define a comfortable ambiance in the guest rooms, some of which include a balcony. 134 units, some kitchens. 5 stories, interior corridors. **Parking:** on-site (fee) and valet. **Terms:** check-in 4 pm, 3 day cancellation notice-fee imposed. **Amenities:** high-speed Internet, honor bars. **Dining:** Luminaria Restaurant & Patio, see separate listing. **Pool(s):** heated outdoor. **Activities:** exercise room, spa. **Guest Services:** valet laundry. **Free Special Amenities:** newspaper and high-speed Internet.

SAVE 🍴 🍽 ⊤ CALL 🚹 🏊 BIZ 📶 ✕ 🖥 / SOME UNITS FEE 🐕 🛗 🖥

▼ See AAA listing this page ▼

Hyatt Place Santa Fe

- Complimentary Continental Breakfast
- Complimentary Shuttle
- 24 Hour Food and Beverage
- Complimentary Parking
- Indoor Pool and Hot Tub

Get the free mobile app at
http://gettag.mobi

4320 Cerrillos Rd • Santa Fe, NM 87507
Tel: 505-474-7777 • FAX: 505-474-7778
www.hyattplacesantafe.com

HYATT PLACE

Find valuable AAA/CAA member savings
at AAA.com/discounts

(See map & index p. 454.)

INN AT SANTA FE

Phone: (505)474-9500 **40**

Hotel
$89-$249

Address: 8376 Cerrillos Rd 87507 **Location:** I-25 exit 278, 0.3 mi n. Adjacent to Santa Fe Premium Outlet stores. **Facility:** 98 units. 3 stories, interior corridors. **Terms:** 3 day cancellation notice-fee imposed. **Amenities:** high-speed Internet, safes (fee). **Pool(s):** heated outdoor. **Activities:** sauna, whirlpool, exercise room. **Guest Services:** coin laundry. **Free Special Amenities:** full breakfast and high-speed Internet.

SAVE ❘❘ ￫ CALL ❘M ≥ BIZ 🛜 ❘ ⊞ ▣ / SOME UNITS FEE 🐾

INN OF THE GOVERNORS

Phone: (505)982-4333 **15**

Hotel
$149-$419

Address: 101 W Alameda St 87501 **Location:** Center. Located in the historic district. **Facility:** 100 units. 2-3 stories, interior/exterior corridors. **Terms:** check-in 4 pm, cancellation fee imposed. **Amenities:** Some: honor bars. **Pool(s):** heated outdoor. **Guest Services:** valet laundry.

❘❘ ￫ CALL ❘M ≥ BIZ 🛜 ✕ ⊞ ▣

INN ON THE ALAMEDA

Phone: (505)984-2121 **18**

Hotel
$125-$390

Address: 303 E Alameda St 87501 **Location:** Just e of The Plaza; jct Paseo de Peralta. **Facility:** 71 units. 1-3 stories (no elevator), interior/exterior corridors. **Terms:** check-in 4 pm, 2 night minimum stay - seasonal, 3 day cancellation notice-fee imposed. **Amenities:** Some: safes. **Activities:** whirlpools, exercise room. **Fee:** massage. **Guest Services:** valet and coin laundry.

SAVE ￫ BIZ 🛜 / SOME UNITS FEE 🐾 ⊞ ▣

INN ON THE PASEO

Phone: (505)984-8200 **5**

Boutique Bed & Breakfast
$79-$259

Address: 630 Paseo de Peralta 87501 **Location:** I-25 exit 282, 2 mi e; jct St. Francis Dr. **Facility:** Near The Plaza, this charming B&B offers true southwestern hospitality and cozy guest rooms. A complimentary afternoon refreshment is served daily. 18 units, some two bedrooms. 2 stories, interior/exterior corridors. **Terms:** check-in 4 pm, cancellation fee imposed. **Guest Services:** valet laundry, area transportation-within 1 mi. SAVE 🛜 ✕

HOTEL SANTA FE
THE HACIENDA and SPA

Inn on the Paseo:
An inviting haven of
Southwestern
hospitality that awaits
you in Santa Fe.

LA FONDA ON THE PLAZA

Phone: (505)982-5511 **12**

Historic Hotel
$229-$799

Address: 100 E San Francisco St 87501 **Location:** On The Plaza. **Facility:** The current building dates to the 1920s but there has been an inn on this site since 1620. Whimsically hand-painted furnishings accent the décor. 172 units. 5 stories, interior corridors. **Parking:** on-site (fee). **Terms:** cancellation fee imposed. **Amenities:** safes. **Dining:** 2 restaurants, also, La Plazuela Restaurant, see separate listing. **Pool(s):** heated outdoor. **Activities:** whirlpools, steamrooms, exercise room, spa. **Guest Services:** valet laundry. **Free Special Amenities:** high-speed Internet.

SAVE ❘❘ ￫ ￫ ❘ CALL ❘M ≥ BIZ 🛜 ✕ ▣ / SOME UNITS 🐾 ⊞ ▣

LA POSADA DE SANTA FE RESORT & SPA

Phone: (505)986-0000 **14**

Hotel
$169-$659

Address: 330 E Palace Ave 87501 **Location:** Jct Paseo de Peralta and E Palace Ave. **Facility:** Guest rooms feature smooth adobe-style walls with rustic, homemade, solid wood furniture and the comforts of luxury linens. 157 units, some two bedrooms. 1-2 stories (no elevator), exterior corridors. **Parking:** valet only. **Terms:** check-in 4 pm, 3 day cancellation notice-fee imposed. **Amenities:** safes, honor bars. **Dining:** 2 restaurants, also, Fuego, see separate listing. **Pool(s):** heated outdoor. **Activities:** whirlpool, steamrooms, exercise room, spa. **Guest Services:** valet laundry. **Free Special Amenities:** newspaper and high-speed Internet.

SAVE ❘❘ ￫ ≥ BIZ 🛜 ✕ ▣ / SOME UNITS FEE 🐾

LA QUINTA INN SANTA FE

Phone: (505)471-1142 **37**

Hotel
$54-$152

Address: 4298 Cerrillos Rd 87507 **Location:** I-25 exit 278, 1.8 mi n. **Facility:** 130 units. 3 stories, interior/exterior corridors. **Amenities:** video games (fee). **Pool(s):** heated outdoor. **Guest Services:** valet and coin laundry.

❘❘￫ ≥ BIZ 🛜 ▣ / SOME UNITS 🐾 ⊞ ≥

LAS PALOMAS

Phone: (505)982-5560 **4**

Hotel
$99-$498

Address: 460 W San Francisco St 87501 **Location:** Just w of jct Guadalupe St. **Facility:** 63 units, some two bedrooms, efficiencies, kitchens and condominiums. 2 stories, exterior corridors. **Terms:** check-in 4 pm, cancellation fee imposed. **Activities:** sauna, exercise room. **Fee:** massage. **Guest Services:** valet and coin laundry.

SAVE ❘❘￫ ❘ BIZ 🛜 ✕ ⊞ ≥ ▣ / SOME UNITS FEE 🐾

THE LODGE AT SANTA FE

Phone: 505/992-5800 **2**

Hotel
Rates not provided

Address: 750 N St. Francis Dr 87501 **Location:** Jct of Cerrillos Rd and St. Francis Dr (US 84/285), 1.1 mi nw to Alamo Dr, just w, then just n. **Facility:** 128 units. 1-3 stories, interior/exterior corridors. **Pool(s):** heated outdoor. **Activities:** whirlpool, exercise room. **Guest Services:** valet and coin laundry, area transportation-The Plaza. Affiliated with A Preferred Hotel.

❘❘ ￫ ≥ BIZ 🛜 ✕ ▣ / SOME UNITS FEE 🐾 ⊞ ≥

MOTEL 6 - 150

Phone: (505)473-1380 **26**

Motel
$45-$65

Address: 3007 Cerrillos Rd 87507 **Location:** I-25 exit 278, 3.8 mi n. **Facility:** 104 units. 2 stories (no elevator), exterior corridors. **Bath:** shower only. **Pool(s):** heated outdoor.

❘❘￫ ≥ 🛜 / SOME UNITS 🐾 FEE ⊞ FEE ≥

THE OLD SANTA FE INN

Phone: (505)995-0800 **16**

Motel
$99-$390

Address: 320 Galisteo St 87501 **Location:** Just sw of The Plaza; center. **Facility:** 43 units. 1-2 stories (no elevator), interior/exterior corridors. **Terms:** check-in 4 pm, 3 day cancellation notice-fee imposed. **Amenities:** high-speed Internet, safes. **Activities:** exercise room. **Guest Services:** valet laundry. **Free Special Amenities:** full breakfast and high-speed Internet.

SAVE ❘❘￫ BIZ 🛜 ✕ ▣ / SOME UNITS FEE 🐾 ⊞ ≥

(See map & index p. 454.)

OTRA VEZ EN SANTA FE   Phone: (505)988-2244 **11**

Condominium
$165-$215

Address: 202 Galisteo St 87501 **Location:** Just s of The Plaza; center. **Facility:** Well-appointed units with Santa Fe-style décor are ideal for extended stays. Some rooms include a fireplace. The Plaza is within walking distance. 18 condominiums. 3 stories, interior/exterior corridors. **Terms:** office hours 8 am-5 pm, 3 night minimum stay - seasonal, 3 day cancellation notice-fee imposed. **Activities:** whirlpool. **Guest Services:** complimentary laundry.

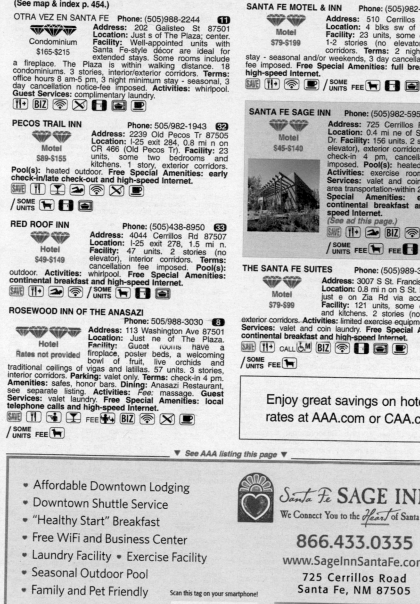

PECOS TRAIL INN   Phone: 505/982-1943 **32**

Motel
$89-$155

Address: 2239 Old Pecos Tr 87505 **Location:** I-25 exit 284, 0.8 mi n on CR 466 (Old Pecos Tr). **Facility:** 23 units, some two bedrooms and kitchens. 1 story, exterior corridors. **Free Special Amenities: early check-in/late check-out and high-speed Internet.**

RED ROOF INN   Phone: (505)438-8950 **33**

Hotel
$49-$149

Address: 4044 Cerrillos Rd 87507 **Location:** I-25 exit 278, 1.5 mi n. **Facility:** 47 units. 2 stories (no elevator), interior corridors. **Terms:** cancellation fee imposed. **Pool(s):** outdoor. **Activities:** whirlpool. **Free Special Amenities: continental breakfast and high-speed Internet.**

ROSEWOOD INN OF THE ANASAZI   Phone: 505/988-3030 **8**

Hotel
Rates not provided

Address: 113 Washington Ave 87501 **Location:** Just ne of The Plaza. **Facility:** Guest rooms have a fireplace, poster beds, a welcoming bowl of fruit, live orchids and traditional ceilings of vigas and latillas. 57 units. 3 stories, interior corridors. **Parking:** valet only. **Terms:** check-in 4 pm. **Amenities:** safes, honor bars. **Dining:** Anasazi Restaurant, see separate listing. **Activities:** Fee: massage. **Guest Services:** valet laundry. **Free Special Amenities: local telephone calls and high-speed Internet.**

SANTA FE MOTEL & INN   Phone: (505)982-1039 **19**

Motel
$79-$199

Address: 510 Cerrillos Rd 87501 **Location:** 4 blks sw of The Plaza. **Facility:** 23 units, some efficiencies. 1-2 stories (no elevator), exterior corridors. **Terms:** 2 night minimum stay - seasonal and/or weekends, 3 day cancellation notice-fee imposed. **Free Special Amenities: full breakfast and high-speed Internet.**

SANTA FE SAGE INN   Phone: (505)982-5952 **23**

Motel
$45-$140

Address: 725 Cerrillos Rd 87505 **Location:** 0.4 mi ne of St. Francis Dr. **Facility:** 156 units. 2 stories (no elevator), exterior corridors. **Terms:** check-in 4 pm, cancellation fee imposed. **Pool(s):** heated outdoor. **Activities:** exercise room. **Guest Services:** valet and coin laundry, area transportation-within 2 mi. **Free Special Amenities: expanded continental breakfast and high-speed Internet.**
(See ad this page.)

THE SANTA FE SUITES   Phone: (505)989-3600 **35**

Motel
$79-$99

Address: 3007 S St. Francis Dr 87505 **Location:** 0.8 mi n on S St. Francis Dr, just e on Zia Rd via access drive. **Facility:** 121 units, some efficiencies and kitchens. 2 stories (no elevator), exterior corridors. **Activities:** limited exercise equipment. **Guest Services:** valet and coin laundry. **Free Special Amenities: continental breakfast and high-speed Internet.**

Enjoy great savings on hotel rates at AAA.com or CAA.ca

▼ See AAA listing this page ▼

- Affordable Downtown Lodging
- Downtown Shuttle Service
- "Healthy Start" Breakfast
- Free WiFi and Business Center
- Laundry Facility • Exercise Facility
- Seasonal Outdoor Pool
- Family and Pet Friendly

Santa Fe SAGE INN
We Connect You to the Heart of Santa Fe

866.433.0335
www.SageInnSantaFe.com
725 Cerrillos Road
Santa Fe, NM 87505

Scan this tag on your smartphone!

Get the free mobile app at
http://gettag.mobi

NOVEMBER 1 – APRIL 30
Rates from $45 to $85

MAY 1 – OCTOBER 31
Rates from $75 to $140

Rates based on availability, dbl. occ., per room, per night

(See map & index p. 454.)

WHERE TO EAT

315 RESTAURANT & WINE BAR
Phone: 505/986-9190 ㉞

French
$18-$40

AAA Inspector Notes: Excellent French and American preparations such as pate, steak and seafood are the focus of the seasonal menu, which also includes splendid desserts such as warm tarte tatin with crème fraiche. Several cozy dining rooms with original art and white table coverings provide an intimate setting; a small patio area at the entrance allows for seasonal dining. A professional, knowledgeable staff provides service. **Bar:** beer & wine. **Reservations:** suggested. **Address:** 315 Old Santa Fe Tr 87501 **Location:** 0.5 mi s of The Plaza; at De Vargas St. **Parking:** street only. D

ANASAZI RESTAURANT **Phone:** 505/988-3236 ⑱

Regional American
$14-$39

AAA Inspector Notes: You'll be treated to superior food preparation and presentation at hand-painted tables in this upscale, casual restaurant near the Plaza's many shops. The chef offers innovative preparation methods of stylish Western cuisine featuring organic produce, free-range meats and fresh fish. The lobster risotto with English peas and spinach is especially flavorful. **Bar:** full bar. **Reservations:** suggested. **Address:** 113 Washington Ave 87501 **Location:** Just ne of The Plaza; in Rosewood Inn of the Anasazi. **Parking:** valet only.
B L D

AZUR **Phone:** 505/992-2897 ㉔

Mediterranean
$19-$23

AAA Inspector Notes: The vibrant atmosphere features a contemporary and sophisticated decor to showcase the creative Mediterranean menu. Start by sharing any number of Spanish-style tapas such as the socco pisaladierre (chickpea galette) and stuffed piquillo peppers with pork belly, both are distinctive and flavorful. I am a great fan of fennel and was happy to see the arugula and fennel salad with feta cheese, which was large enough to share. There also is a selection of exotic spiced entrées and desserts. **Bar:** beer & wine. **Reservations:** suggested. **Address:** 428 Agua Fria St 87501 **Location:** W of Guadalupe St; jct Montezuma Ave. **Parking:** street only.
D

BLUE CORN CAFE & BREWERY
Phone: 505/984-1800 ㉑

Southwestern
$7-$16

AAA Inspector Notes: Just off The Plaza, this upstairs restaurant beckons diners to feast on ample servings of New Mexican cuisine with an American twist. Watch passersby on Water and Galisteo streets as you sip a cool libation-perhaps one of the daily margarita specials or a selection from an extensive list of brewery choices-and indulge your appetite. The staff is friendly and attentive. **Bar:** full bar. **Address:** 133 Water St 87501 **Location:** Jct Galisteo St; center. **Parking:** street only. L D

BLUE CORN CAFE & BREWERY
Phone: 505/438-1800 (68)

Southwestern
$8-$22

AAA Inspector Notes: Across the street from Villa Linda Mall on the southern outskirts of town, this café provides the same menu and tastes as its sister downtown restaurant. Northern New Mexican cuisine, great margaritas and handcrafted microbrews are served. The spicy crab dip with fresh-fried tortilla wedges will serve a crowd. **Bar:** full bar. **Address:** 4056 Cerrillos Rd 87505 **Location:** I-25 exit 278, 2 mi n, jct Rodeo Rd; northwest corner. L D

BODY CAFE **Phone:** 505/986-0362 (54)

Natural/Organic
$5-$15

AAA Inspector Notes: This eatery focuses on organic and healthy food choices. Vegetarian and raw food dishes dominate the menu. Dining room entrées include pasta, grains and in-season wild fish. Turkey and tuna sandwiches are available in the deli. Visitors also can enjoy specialty coffees, fruit smoothies, fresh juices and elixirs. **Bar:** beer & wine. **Address:** 333 W Cordova Rd 87505 **Location:** I-25 exit 282, 2.3 mi n on St. Francis Dr, then just e. B L D

THE BULL RING **Phone:** 505/983-3328 ⑭

Steak
$10-$48

AAA Inspector Notes: Steaks arrive sizzling in hot butter, potatoes are served seven ways and servers are hometown-friendly in this steakhouse offering entrées served a la carte including lamb chops, salmon and Prime beef. The bank's parking garage is made available fee-free for patrons in the evenings. **Bar:** full bar. **Reservations:** suggested. **Address:** 150 Washington Ave 87501 **Location:** Just n of The Plaza; in Wells Fargo Bank building. **Parking:** street only. L D

BUMBLE BEE'S BAJA GRILL
Phone: 505/988-3278 (64)

Regional Mexican
$5-$12

AAA Inspector Notes: When in a hurry, skip the fast food chains and buzz over to this casual quick serve, where guests can dine in or drive through. The salsa and garnish bar is a good stop while waiting inside the cheerful dining area for such dishes as mahi mahi tacos with chunks of avocado, or low-carb naked burritos with homemade pinto or black beans. **Bar:** beer & wine. **Address:** 3777 Cerrillos Rd 87501 **Location:** Jct Cerrillos Rd and Vegas Verdes Dr; downtown. L D

BUMBLE BEE'S BAJA GRILL
Phone: 505/820-2862 ④

Regional Mexican
$6-$13

AAA Inspector Notes: A local favorite for hearty portions of fresh and healthy fast food, this restaurant's flavorful salsa and chips are a treat while waiting inside the cheerful dining area for dishes like grilled mahi mahi tacos with chunks of avocado or low-carb naked burritos without the tortilla. Drive-through is an option for patrons in a hurry. **Bar:** beer & wine. **Address:** 301 Jefferson St 87501 **Location:** Jct Guadalupe St. L D

THE BURRITO COMPANY **Phone:** 505/982-4453 ⑳

Regional American
$5-$8

AAA Inspector Notes: Just off The Plaza, this laid-back restaurant is open for breakfast and lunch. Near shopping, businesses and lodgings, the contemporary spot is especially convenient for those wanting a quick meal. Guests order at the counter and pick up their food when their order number is called. A patio with umbrellas is suited to seasonal dining. **Address:** 111 Washington Ave 87501 **Location:** Between Marcy St and Palace Ave; downtown. **Parking:** street only. B L

CAFE CAFE **Phone:** 505/466-1391 ㊴

Italian
$7-$24

AAA Inspector Notes: This lively bistro offers a creative Italian-inspired menu featuring items prepared with seasonal ingredients. Also of interest is the pizza, pasta dishes, fresh soups and salads. Save room for the homemade gelato. **Bar:** beer & wine. **Address:** 500 Sandoval St 87501 **Location:** Jct Sandoval and Manhattan sts; center. L D

(See map & index p. 454.)

CAFE PASQUAL'S
Phone: 505/983-9340 (25)

Regional American
$9-$40

AAA Inspector Notes: If the line is long at this small and charming spot one block from the downtown plaza, join the community table for good coffee, local chat and such dishes as breakfast quesadillas with applewood smoked bacon or huevos motulenos with grilled bananas. Dinner features a creative changing seasonal menu with a distinctive twist on Latin American favorites. This farm to table restaurant strives to serve only organic food products including produce and chicken plus naturally raised beef and pork. **Bar:** beer & wine. **Reservations:** required, for dinner. **Address:** 121 Don Gaspar Ave 87501 **Location:** Just sw of The Plaza; center. **Parking:** street only.

(B) (L) (D)

CASTLE RANCH STEAKHOUSE
Phone: 505/473-2800 (63)

American
$9-$30

AAA Inspector Notes: The menu features Double D Ranch Northwest beef including steaks and burgers. Bison, pork and some seafood also are offered. This restaurant is near shopping and other lodgings. **Bar:** full bar. **Address:** 3347 Cerrillos Rd 87507 **Location:** I-25 exit 278, 3.2 mi n; in Courtyard by Marriott - Santa Fe.

(B) (D)

Serving tender certified organic beef from Idaho

CHOCOLATE MAVEN BAKERY & CAFE
Phone: 505/984-1980 (59)

American
$3-$24

AAA Inspector Notes: Those looking for an escape from the hustle and bustle of downtown should seek out this cozy and distinctive café. Soups, salads, sandwiches, pizza and baked goods are made from the freshest ingredients. The friendly and attentive staff enhances the dining experience. **Address:** 821 W San Mateo Rd, Suite C 87505 **Location:** Jct St. Michaels Dr and Cerrillos Rd, just n on Cerrillos Rd to 2nd St, then 0.6 mi e; in an industrial building. (B) (L) (D)

CHOW'S ASIAN BISTRO
Phone: 505/471-7120 (61)

Asian
$7-$18

AAA Inspector Notes: A hidden gem for flavorful Asian dishes, attentive service keeps the locals returning. **Bar:** beer & wine. **Address:** 720 St. Michael's Dr 87501 **Location:** Jct St. Francis Dr, just w.

(L) (D)

CLAFOUTIS
Phone: 505/988-1809 (3)

French
$5-$13

AAA Inspector Notes: This small café, featuring typical French bistro fare, is a favorite of local Santa Feans for its strong coffee and delectable homemade pastries. **Address:** 402 Guadalupe St 87501 **Location:** Just s of jct Paseo de Peralta. (B) (L)

CLEOPATRA'S CAFE
Phone: 505/474-5644 (66)

Mediterranean
$6-$16

AAA Inspector Notes: A local favorite, this eatery offers generous portions of flavorful Mediterranean specialties such as organic, New Mexico-raised lamb. Vegetarians will find plenty of offerings. **Address:** 3482 Zafarano Dr 87507 **Location:** I-25 exit 278 (Cerrillos Rd), 2.5 mi n; jct Cerrillos Rd and Zafarano Dr; in San Isidro Plaza.

(L) (D)

THE COMPOUND RESTAURANT
Phone: 505/982-4353 (47)

American
$15-$45

AAA Inspector Notes: In an adobe-style hacienda in the fashionable Canyon Road area, this restaurant prepares a variety of contemporary American cuisine. The menu includes classic sweetbreads and foie gras starters. Entrées include a variety of seafood, steak, lamb and chicken dishes. Grilled beef tenderloin with Italian crepe O'Brien potatoes and foie gras hollandaise is a must for beef lovers. **Bar:** full bar. **Reservations:** suggested. **Address:** 653 Canyon Rd 87501 **Location:** From Paseo de Peralta, 0.4 mi e. (L) (D)

COWGIRL BAR AND GRILL
Phone: 505/982-2565 (29)

Regional American
$8-$22

AAA Inspector Notes: Downhome dining amid the kitschy cowgirl memorabilia at this rustic eatery near The Plaza includes ribs, great salsa and Mexican favorites. It is a prime place for people-watching while sipping on a very good house margarita and listening to eclectic live music on the pleasant patio. **Bar:** full bar. **Reservations:** suggested. **Address:** 319 S Guadalupe St 87501 **Location:** 2 blks s of Alameda St; jct Aztec St. **Parking:** street only. (L) (D) (AC)

COYOTE CAFE
Phone: 505/983-1615 (26)

Southwestern
$27-$56

AAA Inspector Notes: A block from the downtown plaza, the now-iconographic restaurant has a creative seasonal menu and contemporary atmosphere. Diners can enjoy a signature cocktail or fine wine from the extensive wine list. **Bar:** full bar. **Reservations:** suggested. **Address:** 132 W Water St 87501 **Location:** Just sw of The Plaza; between Ortiz and Galisteo sts. **Parking:** street only.

(D)

DARA THAI RESTAURANT
Phone: 505/995-0887 (56)

Thai
$8-$16

AAA Inspector Notes: Patrons walk into another culture in this ethnic restaurant, where brightly painted murals and decor help create an authentically Thai atmosphere. Delicious meat and vegetarian dishes will please the whole family. **Bar:** beer & wine. **Address:** 1710 Cerrillos Rd 87505 **Location:** Jct Cerrillos Rd and 2nd St. (L) (D)

EL FAROL RESTAURANT
Phone: 505/983-9912 (49)

Mediterranean
$8-$52

AAA Inspector Notes: In the fashionable Canyon Road area, this restaurant occupies an old, adobe-style building with a rustic interior. The menu contains a variety of Spanish beef, lamb, veal and seafood preparations. On the wine list is a good variety of Spanish and New World wines, several available by the glass. **Bar:** full bar. **Reservations:** suggested. **Address:** 808 Canyon Rd 87501 **Location:** From Paseo de Peralta, 0.5 mi e. **Parking:** on-site (fee). (L) (D)

FLYING STAR CAFE
Phone: 505/216-3939 (30)

Natural/Organic
$8-$16

AAA Inspector Notes: Enjoy creative comfort food with organic and minimally processed ingredients in a casual and lively atmosphere. Breakfast is served all day and an enticing variety of luscious desserts are hard to pass up. **Bar:** beer & wine. **Address:** 500 Market St 87501 **Location:** Santa Fe Market Station at the Railyard. **Parking:** on-site (fee). (B) (L) (D)

(See map & index p. 454.)

FUEGO

Menu on AAA.com   Phone: 505/954-9670   (31)

International
$23-$36

AAA Inspector Notes: Dinner is served in a traditional Santa Fe dining room, with formal charm and ambiance. Decorative, imaginatively arranged menu selections contain the finest fowl, beef and game available and, of course, a seasonal menu is featured. Service is polished and meal presentation is raised to an art form. **Bar:** full bar. **Reservations:** suggested. **Address:** 330 E Palace Ave 87501 **Location:** Jct Paseo de Peralta and E Palace Ave; in La Posada de Santa Fe Resort & Spa. **Parking:** valet and street only. (D)

GABRIEL'S   Phone: 505/455-7000

Mexican
$6-$24

AAA Inspector Notes: Cold margaritas and guacamole prepared tableside and served with a basket of warm chips make great starters at this roadside restaurant which is a popular place to have lunch on the way to Taos or for dinner before attending a performance at the Santa Fe Opera. **Bar:** full bar. **Reservations:** suggested. **Address:** US 285/84 87501 **Location:** US 84/285 exit 176 (Cuyamungue), just n. (L) (D)

GERONIMO   Phone: 505/982-1500   (48)

Regional
International
$28-$44

AAA Inspector Notes: Whether you choose to dine on the porch to watch the art gallery aficionados and gift shoppers pass by, or inside in the quietly elegant surroundings, the polished and attentive service will smooth your dining experience. The Southwestern-style cuisine highlights fresh seafood dishes, spicy pan-roasted quail and the signature grilled black pepper elk tenderloin. Don't plan to skip dessert--the orange Dreamsicle cake is not to be missed. **Bar:** full bar. **Reservations:** suggested. **Address:** 724 Canyon Rd 87501 **Location:** 0.5 mi e of jct Paseo de Peralta. **Parking:** on-site and valet. (D)

GUADALUPE CAFE   Phone: 505/982-9762   (42)

Southwestern
$8-$15

AAA Inspector Notes: This bustling café serves Mexican-style comfort food. Those who stop in during traditional meal times should be prepared to wait at this local favorite. Diners should take up the waitstaff on their offer to reserve a slice of not-to-be-missed homemade pie. **Bar:** beer & wine. **Address:** 422 Old Santa Fe Tr 87501 **Location:** From Cerrillos Rd, se on E Alameda St, then just n. (B) (L) (D)

HARRY'S ROAD HOUSE   Phone: 505/989-4629   (71)

American
$5-$22

AAA Inspector Notes: The friendly, casual staff give attentive service. You may dine inside, on the porch, or in the garden surrounded by flowers. Next comes menu choices-grilled fish tacos, blue corn turkey enchiladas or grilled pork chops. The homemade desserts are mouthwatering-bread and rice pudding, lemon meringue pie or ice cream sandwiches. **Bar:** full bar. **Address:** 96B Old Las Vegas Hwy 87505 **Location:** I-25 exit 284 (Old Pecos Tr), 0.8 mi se on Frontage Rd (Old Las Vegas Hwy). (B) (L) (D)

IL PIATTO   Phone: 505/984-1091   (11)

Italian
$9-$28

AAA Inspector Notes: In the heart of the downtown historic district a block from The Plaza, the restaurant tempts patrons with specialties such as grilled calamari, pancetta-wrapped trout, roasted chicken pepperonata and roasted garlic- and basil-stuffed duck breast. Pasta is made fresh daily. **Bar:** beer & wine. **Reservations:** suggested, for dinner. **Address:** 95 W Marcy St 87501 **Location:** Between Lincoln Ave and Washington St; just n of The Plaza. **Parking:** street only. (L) (D)

INDIA PALACE RESTAURANT
    Phone: 505/986-5859   (32)

Indian
$10-$25

AAA Inspector Notes: Tourists and locals alike frequent this spot for authentic Northern Indian cuisine. Near the historic plaza, this place sets up a lunch buffet that is perfect for first-time patrons. Patio seating is an option here. **Bar:** beer & wine. **Address:** 227 Don Gaspar Ave 87501 **Location:** At rear of Water St parking lot. (L) (D)

JAMBO CAFE   Phone: 505/473-1269   (58)

African
$7-$14

AAA Inspector Notes: This restaurant, a local favorite, serves flavorful Afro-Caribbean cuisine in a cozy atmosphere with great background music and a friendly staff. The succulent New Mexico lamb with sweet potato fries and curry dipping sauce is a satisfying meal. End the meal with a palate-cooling coconut sorbet. **Bar:** beer & wine. **Address:** 2010 Cerrillos Rd 87505 **Location:** Jct St. Michael's Dr, just sw; downtown. (L) (D)

JINJA BAR & BISTRO   Phone: 505/982-4321   (2)

Asian
$9-$19

AAA Inspector Notes: This cafe appeals to diners who do not want to limit themselves to one style of cuisine. Thai, Japanese, Chinese and Vietnamese dishes are served in an elegant but relaxed atmosphere. **Bar:** full bar. **Address:** 510 N Guadalupe St, Suite P 87501 **Location:** Just nw of Paseo de Peralta; in DeVargas Center Mall. (L) (D)

JOE'S DINER AND PIZZA   Phone: 505/471-3800   (70)

American
$7-$27

AAA Inspector Notes: This diner's classic decor provides a blast to the past with lots of chrome, black-and-white tile floors and booths with red vinyl upholstery. A family friendly neighborhood restaurant, this spot offers fresh and creative specialties using organic and locally-raised produce and meats. Try one of the favorite mesquite grilled burgers made from organic grass-fed beef, lamb or buffalo. The build your own pizza utilizes fresh dough and sauce made daily. The luscious fruit pies are homemade. **Bar:** beer & wine. **Address:** 2801 Rodeo Rd 87507 **Location:** 1.7 mi w of US 84/285. (B) (L) (D)

LA BOCA   Phone: 505/982-3433   (12)

International
$10-$14

AAA Inspector Notes: Creative tapas make this a fun and lively dining experience. A variety of items for sharing includes many vegetarian options. The grilled asparagus with smoked salmon and goat cheese is a must. **Bar:** beer & wine. **Reservations:** suggested. **Address:** 72 W Marcy St 87501 **Location:** Just n of historic central plaza. **Parking:** on-site (fee) and street. (L) (D)

LA CASA SENA RESTAURANT
    Phone: 505/988-9232   (22)

Regional American
$12-$40

AAA Inspector Notes: This restaurant features an extensive wine list and excellent regional preparations of traditional menu selections. Servers are attentive and knowledgeable, and a large outdoor dining area is available. For a fun treat enjoy dessert and after-dinner drinks In the bar area that features waitstaff performing Broadway show tunes. **Bar:** full bar. **Reservations:** suggested. **Address:** 125 E Palace Ave 87501 **Location:** Just e of The Plaza. **Parking:** street only. **Historic** (L) (D)

(See map & index p. 454.)

LA CHOZA

Regional Mexican
$9-$16

Phone: 505/982-0909 (46)

AAA Inspector Notes: The folks who own The Shed, a popular downtown restaurant, also operate this casual eatery in Santa Fe's up-and-coming Railyard District. Offerings feature the same satisfying New Mexican dishes, including the outstanding sopaipilla-puffy fried bread served with warm honey. **Bar:** full bar. **Address:** 905 Alarid St 87501 **Location:** Just e of jct Cerrillos Rd and St Francis Dr; adjacent to Railyard Park. L D

LA PLAZUELA RESTAURANT
Regional American
$14-$32

Phone: 505/982-5511 (28)

AAA Inspector Notes: Bright blue-, orange- and yellow-colored table settings delight the eye and set the stage. The dinner menu includes steak and seafood dishes prepared with a Southwestern accent, as well as several Mexican entrées. **Bar:** full bar. **Address:** 100 E San Francisco St 87501 **Location:** On The Plaza; in La Fonda On the Plaza. **Parking:** on-site (fee). B L D

LAS FUENTES
Regional American
$12-$42

Phone: 505/983-6377 (1)

AAA Inspector Notes: This restaurant features upscale dining in a relaxed Southwestern atmosphere. Specialties include very good New American and Southwestern cuisine selections. The outdoor patio/lounge has a fireplace and overlooks the Sangre de Cristo Mountains. **Bar:** full bar. **Reservations:** suggested. **Address:** 1297 N Bishop's Lodge Rd 87504 **Location:** 3.5 mi n of jct Paseo de Peralta; in Bishop's Lodge Ranch Resort & Spa. B L D

LUMINARIA RESTAURANT & PATIO
International
$10-$34

Phone: 505/984-7915 (33)

AAA Inspector Notes: Modern American cuisine prepared with market-fresh organic vegetables and meats, flavorful sauces and creative desserts plus professional staff make this a memorable dining experience. **Bar:** full bar. **Reservations:** suggested. **Address:** 211 Old Santa Fe Tr 87501 **Location:** Just s of The Plaza; in The Inn & Spa at Loretto. **Parking:** on-site (fee) and valet. B L D CALL M

MARIA'S NEW MEXICAN KITCHEN
Mexican
$7-$25

Phone: 505/983-7929 (51)

AAA Inspector Notes: A local favorite, this kitchen has been cooking and serving New Mexican fare for generations. A casual atmosphere and friendly service make it a great place to kick back with an outstanding margarita and the house specialty carne adovada (roasted pork in a spicy red chile sauce). **Bar:** full bar. **Address:** 555 W Cordova Rd 87505 **Location:** Just e of jct St. Francis Dr. L D

MASA SUSHI
Sushi
$6-$25

Phone: 505/982-3334 (6)

AAA Inspector Notes: Japanese and Korean specialties are served at this neighborhood eatery, including a sushi bar featuring the chef's creations. **Bar:** beer & wine. **Address:** 927 W Alameda St 87501 **Location:** Just w of US 285. L D

MU DU NOODLES
Asian
$12-$22

Phone: 505/983-1411 (55)

AAA Inspector Notes: Do as the locals and hit this spot for flavorful Asian specialties featuring market fresh and organic ingredients. The emerald sautee with seared scallops, green tea noodles and fresh local vegetables shouldn't be missed. Many vegetarian and vegan items are on the menu. **Bar:** beer & wine. **Address:** 1494 Cerrillos Rd 87505 **Location:** 1 mi w of St. Francis Dr; downtown. **Parking:** on-site and street. D

THE OLD HOUSE
Menu on AAA.com
Regional International
$12-$36

Phone: 505/988-4455 (17)

AAA Inspector Notes: Just a short walk from downtown Santa Fe, this gem is a cozy and intimate spot with Southwestern flair. The menu features aged beef plus a selection of seafood. **Bar:** full bar. **Reservations:** suggested. **Address:** 309 W San Francisco St 87501 **Location:** Just w of The Plaza; at Sandoval St; in Eldorado Hotel & Spa. **Parking:** valet only. *(See ad p. 460.)* B L D

OSAKA BISTRO SUSHI & SAKE BAR
Japanese
$11-$41

Phone: 505/471-6698 (67)

AAA Inspector Notes: This trendy bistro is a showcase for very fresh sushi. Distinctive bar lights and custom tables help create a memorable ambience. **Bar:** full bar. **Address:** 3501-A Zafarano Dr 87501 **Location:** Corner of Cerrillos Rd and Zafarano Dr. L D

OSTERIA D'ASSISI
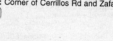
Menu on AAA.com
Northern Italian
$9-$36

Phone: 505/986-5858 (7)

AAA Inspector Notes: Near both the city's business and cultural centers, this convenient, busy restaurant serves delicious Northern Italian cuisine to tourists and business people in comfortable surroundings near the Federal Courthouse. **Bar:** full bar. **Reservations:** suggested. **Address:** 58 S Federal Pl 87501 **Location:** 1 blk n of The Plaza. **Parking:** street only. L D

THE PANTRY
Regional American
$5-$14

Phone: 505/986-0022 (57)

AAA Inspector Notes: Genuine New Mexican cuisine draws locals and tourists to this laid-back restaurant. The menu consists of traditional favorites: enchiladas, burritos, green chile stew and much more. The hearty portions are worth the wait. **Bar:** beer & wine. **Address:** 1820 Cerrillos Rd 87505 **Location:** I-25 exit 278, 6 mi nw, jct 5th St. B L D

THE PINK ADOBE
American
$8-$34

Phone: 505/983-7712 (40)

AAA Inspector Notes: Established in 1944 and known for its pink adobe look, this restaurant is located in what was previously a 350-year-old home just a short walk from The Plaza. The restaurant is popular with locals and visitors alike and frequented by famous actors and politicians. Several intimate dining rooms, each with a fireplace, enhance the dining experience. Patio seating is available in season. **Bar:** full bar. **Reservations:** suggested. **Address:** 406 Old Santa Fe Tr 87501 **Location:** Just s of The Plaza. **Parking:** street only. L D

(See map & index p. 454.)

PIZZERIA ESPIRITU   Phone: 505/424-8000   60

Italian
$8-$19

AAA Inspector Notes: In addition to the pizza, this pizzeria prepares a variety of fresh pasta dishes, sandwiches and soups. Rich Old World decor adds a touch of elegance to an otherwise casual meal. Diners can look up at the ceiling to see a whimsical take on Michelangelo's mural of "The Creation of Adam," in which God and Adam share a slice of pizza. **Bar:** beer & wine. **Address:** 1722-A St Michaels Dr 87505 **Location:** Jct Cerrillos Rd, just se of Llano St; in strip mall. L D

PUERTO PENASCO   Phone: 505/438-6622   69

Mexican
$7-$15

AAA Inspector Notes: A friendly staff is welcoming at this lively, family-run eatery where the essence of true Mexican seaside cuisine is showcased. Start with a typical shrimp cocktail in a cool tomato broth with diced avocados, cilantro and cucumbers. The spicy seafood soup can really warm diners up on a cold day. The Discata Tierra y Mar, served in a mini tabletop disc, allows guests to make their own tacos. Save room for the decadent homemade tres leches cake. **Bar:** beer & wine. **Address:** 4681 Airport Rd 87507 **Location:** SR 14 (Cerrillos Rd), 1.6 mi w. L D

PYRAMID CAFE   Phone: 505/989-1378   53

Mediterranean
$8-$24

AAA Inspector Notes: A Mediterranean restaurant, this café features Tunisian specialties. The menu highlights all-natural foods with no artificial ingredients, preservatives, antibiotics or hormones. Lunch includes menu offerings and a buffet. As a perk, this spot also offers Wi-Fi access. **Bar:** beer & wine. **Address:** 505 Cordova Rd 87505 **Location:** Just e of St. Francis Dr.

L D CALL &M

RED SAGE   Phone: 505/819-2056

Southwestern
$26-$40

AAA Inspector Notes: Reflecting a creative interpretation of American West cuisine, entrées are enhanced by Native American, European and Latin American ingredients. From the vegetarian pueblo garden to poblano lobster relleno and mountain man feast of venison, boar and pheasant, the menu has a selection for every palate. The talented pastry chef will delight you with her beautiful creations. The professional staff will help create a memorable dining experience. **Bar:** full bar. **Reservations:** suggested. **Address:** 30 Buffalo Thunder Tr 87506 **Location:** N on US 285 exit Buffalo Thunder Rd, just e; in Hilton Santa Fe Golf Resort & Spa at Buffalo Thunder. **Parking:** on-site and valet.

B L D CALL &M

RESTAURANT MARTIN   Phone: 505/820-0919   44

New American
$9-$29

AAA Inspector Notes: Well-known chef, Martin Rios presents an innovative menu at this restaurant featuring progressive American cuisine. The menu showcases local, seasonal and organic ingredients from flavorful soups, creative salads and sandwiches in addition to complex entrees. Luscious desserts also are worth a try. **Bar:** beer & wine. **Reservations:** suggested. **Address:** 526 Galisteo St 87501 **Location:** Jct Paseo de Peralta and Galisteo St; center. L D

RIO CHAMA   Phone: 505/955-0765   41

Steak
$11-$46

AAA Inspector Notes: In the heart of the downtown historic district and next door to the state capitol (Roundhouse), this restaurant is a favorite of government officials especially during the annual legislative session. A menu of Prime and Choice dry-aged steaks, prime rib, chops and seafood are presented. The atmosphere is casual, yet dignified, in the intimate dining rooms. **Bar:** full bar. **Reservations:** suggested. **Address:** 414 Old Santa Fe Tr 87501 **Location:** 2 blks s of The Plaza; center.

L D

RISTRA   Phone: 505/982-8608   27

Regional Continental
$9-$39

AAA Inspector Notes: A short distance from the historic Guadalupe Road, this cozy house boasts friendly, accomplished staff members who expertly serve delectable dishes. Appetizers range from black Mediterranean mussels with chipotle and mint to fire-roasted poblano chiles stuffed with brandade of salt cod. Seasonally changing entrées might include such good choices as seared Alaskan halibut, elk tenderloin or duck leg confit. Patio dining under tall evergreens is refreshing. **Bar:** full bar. **Reservations:** suggested. **Address:** 548 Agua Fria St 87501 **Location:** Just w of Guadalupe Rd. L D

SANTACAFE   Phone: 505/984-1788   8

Menu on AAA.com

New American
$9-$33

AAA Inspector Notes: Near The Plaza, the upscale restaurant caters to tourists and locals seeking fine dining with a trendy twist. Crisp linens and fine wines are the order of the day, with American nouvelle cuisine served in a refined atmosphere. Classic Santa Fe architecture characterizes the inside of the grand old circa 1854 hacienda. **Bar:** full bar. **Reservations:** suggested. **Address:** 231 Washington Ave 87501 **Location:** Just ne of The Plaza; between Marcy St and Paseo de Peralta. **Historic** L D

SANTA FE BAKING COMPANY AND CAFE   Phone: 505/988-4292   52

American
$5-$11

AAA Inspector Notes: This coffeehouse is a true community favorite. Gourmet coffee and free Wi-Fi are mainstays, and it is a fun place to people-watch. Breakfast is served all day, the house specialty being a generous breakfast burrito, and live entertainment is offered every Saturday morning. The café menu lists a wide variety of sandwiches, burgers and salads, plus a selection of vegetarian meals. **Address:** 504 W Cordova Rd 87505 **Location:** Just e of US 285. B L D

SANTA FE CAPITOL GRILL   Phone: 505/471-6800   65

International
$8-$27

AAA Inspector Notes: Service at this lively bistro is fun and friendly but efficient. From savory appetizers to creative salads and sandwiches, enjoy a quick meal before the movies or a cocktail and leisurely meal afterward. **Bar:** full bar. **Address:** 3462 Zafarano Dr 87507 **Location:** Northwest of jct Cerrillos Rd; in San Isidro Plaza. L D

SAVEUR   Phone: 505/989-4200   35

French
$6-$16

AAA Inspector Notes: This casual restaurant is set up much like a traditional bistro, but the food is healthier and of considerably higher quality. Diners can choose from an impressive salad buffet, gourmet sandwiches and even fresh French entrées. **Bar:** beer & wine. **Address:** 204 Montezuma Ave 87501 **Location:** Jct Galisteo St, Cerrillos Rd and Montezuma Ave; downtown. B L

THE SHED   Phone: 505/982-9030   23

Regional Mexican
$8-$20

AAA Inspector Notes: Red and green chile enchiladas and mocha cake are the specialties at this restaurant, located in a 17th-century fortified hacienda. Its casual dining features Northern New Mexican dishes. **Bar:** full bar. **Reservations:** suggested. **Address:** 113 1/2 E Palace Ave 87501 **Location:** Just e of The Plaza. **Parking:** street only. **Historic** L D

(See map & index p. 454.)

SHOHKO CAFE

Phone: 505/982-9708   9

Japanese
$10-$30

AAA Inspector Notes: Diners are in for a relaxing meal with friendly service in a quaint adobe-style setting. Established in 1976, this restaurant is known for its fresh sushi, sashimi, bento box specials, rice bowls and noodle dishes. Ingredients such as soft-shell crab, eel, tuna, mackerel, salmon, shrimp, yellowtail and albacore are used to create the various sushi rolls. Sushi specials are skillfully prepared by Chef Shohko. **Bar:** beer & wine. **Reservations:** required. **Address:** 321 Johnson St 87501 **Location:** Just e of jct W San Francisco St.   L   D

STEAKSMITH AT EL GANCHO

Phone: 505/988-3333   72

Steak
$8-$27

AAA Inspector Notes: This eatery lives up to its name, preparing fine beef that has pleased Santa Fe steak lovers for years. Tender, juicy cuts are perfectly grilled and complemented by homemade bread, tasty salads and the traditional sides that mean a real meal. **Bar:** full bar. **Reservations:** suggested. **Address:** 104B Old Las Vegas Hwy 87505 **Location:** I-25 exit 284 (Old Pecos Tr), 1 mi se on Frontage Rd (Old Las Vegas Hwy).

THE TEAHOUSE

Phone: 505/992-0972   50

Deli
$10-$15

AAA Inspector Notes: Patrons delight in sampling exotic teas from around the world. Casual, Asian-themed decor is a welcoming touch in this comfortable dining area. Meals are light and refreshing. **Bar:** beer & wine. **Address:** 821 Canyon Rd 87501 **Location:** Jct Paseo de Peralta, 2 mi e.   B   L   D   AC

TERRA

Phone: 505/946-5800

International
$13-$42

AAA Inspector Notes: The chic contemporary ambiance, outstanding service and creatively prepared Southwest menu make for a truly memorable dining experience. **Bar:** full bar. **Reservations:** required. **Address:** 198 SR 592 87506 **Location:** US 285/84 N exit 172, 0.5 mi e, then 2 mi n; in Encantado, An Auberge Resort. **Parking:** on-site and valet.   B   L   D

THAI CAFE

Phone: 505/982-3886   15

Thai
$9-$15

AAA Inspector Notes: Guests can take a short walk from The Plaza to enter another realm at this café, which uses colorful Asian decor to add a refreshing twist to the traditional Santa Fe adobe building. Flavorful Thai favorites are served in large portions. **Bar:** beer & wine. **Address:** 329 W San Francisco St 87501 **Location:** 3 blks w of The Plaza; jct Guadalupe St.   L   D

TIA SOPHIA'S

Phone: 505/983-9880   19

Southwestern
$5-$10

AAA Inspector Notes: A short walk from The Plaza, this restaurant specializes in traditional New Mexican cuisine. Particularly worth trying are huevos rancheros for breakfast and the flavorful chiles rellenos for lunch. **Address:** 210 W San Francisco St 87501 **Location:** Just w of The Plaza. **Parking:** street only.   B   L

TOKYO SUSHI BAR CAFE

Phone: 505/989-7603   16

Sushi
$8-$20

AAA Inspector Notes: Enjoy Japanese favorites in a cozy dining room or lush garden. The menu focuses on daily sushi specials and tempura and stir-fry dishes. **Bar:** beer & wine. **Address:** 321 W San Francisco St 87501 **Location:** Just e of Guadalupe St.   L   D

TOMASITA'S RESTAURANT

Phone: 505/983-5721   37

Regional Mexican
$7-$15

AAA Inspector Notes: A restored mid-1800s train station is the setting for this bustling restaurant. The menu is lined with generous portions of traditional Northern New Mexican cuisine, including specialty burritos, blue corn enchiladas and rellenos. Locals and visitors alike frequent the place. **Bar:** full bar. **Address:** 500 S Guadalupe St 87501 **Location:** From The Plaza, just w on Alameda St, then just s.   L   D

TORTILLA FLATS

Phone: 505/471-8685   62

Southwestern
$6-$15

AAA Inspector Notes: An inviting Southwestern theme punctuates the interior's adobe-style look. The casual waitstaff provides friendly, welcoming service to patrons who sit down to New Mexican choices such as chiles rellenos, enchiladas, carne adovada and quesadillas. Try the chicken enchiladas served on blue corn shells with mild sauce which sets the taste buds dancing. **Bar:** full bar. **Address:** 3139 Cerrillos Rd 87505 **Location:** I-25 exit 278B, 3.5 mi ne.   B   L   D

TRATTORIA NOSTRANI

Phone: 505/983-3800   10

Northern Italian
$24-$40

AAA Inspector Notes: Organic produce, all grown in the restaurant's own back yard garden, enhance the seasonal, weekly-changing menu offerings. The fresh tomatoes are exquisite and should not be missed. An extensive, award-winning wine list allows for excellent pairings. **Bar:** beer & wine. **Reservations:** suggested. **Address:** 304 Johnson St 87501 **Location:** Jct Guadalupe St, just e.   D

TUNE-UP CAFE

Phone: 505/983-7060   43

International
$6-$14

AAA Inspector Notes: This local café has a true neighborhood feel with counter service, funky decor, shared tables and patio seating. A flavorful menu features many El Salvadoran items such as pupusas and banana leaf tamales. A creative breakfast menu includes pan-fried trout with poached eggs and huevos rancheros. The desserts are excellent. **Bar:** beer & wine. **Address:** 1115 Hickox St 87505 **Location:** 0.5 mi w of St. Francis Dr. **Parking:** on-site and street.   B   L   D

UPPER CRUST PIZZA

Phone: 505/982-0000   38

Pizza
$5-$25

AAA Inspector Notes: Not far from The Plaza, this eatery prepares fresh, made-to-order meals that satisfy patrons with light appetites and lean budgets. Seating can be had on the porch, on the back patio or inside. Among favorites are the build-a-pizza, calzones and sandwiches that come with a choice of bread. **Bar:** beer & wine. **Address:** 329 Old Santa Fe Tr 87501 **Location:** 0.5 mi s of The Plaza at De Vargas St.   L   D

VANESSIE

Phone: 505/982-9966   13

American
$16-$60

AAA Inspector Notes: Serving the best of beef and lamb dishes for many years, this restaurant upholds the tradition of attentive service, pleasing flavors and hearty portions. Enjoy the popular piano bar before or after dinner. **Bar:** full bar. **Reservations:** suggested. **Address:** 434 W San Francisco St 87501 **Location:** Just w of Guadalupe St; parking entrance just w on Water St.   D

(See map & index p. 454.)

VINAIGRETTE   **Phone:** 505/820-9205   ㊺

WWW WWW

Natural/Organic
$10-$19

AAA Inspector Notes: This vibrant, fresh-food restaurant features creative salads, soups and sandwiches with ingredients grown in the chef/owner's 10-acre organic garden. Start with the incredibly flavorful wild mushroom stew with fried olive bread followed by the omega AKA avocado-piñon or nutty pear-fessor salad. A selection of grilled meats or seafood can be added to any salad. Daily fresh-baked desserts plus homemade ice cream are a treat. **Bar:** beer & wine. **Address:** 709 Don Cubero Alley 87505 **Location:** Just e of jct Cerrillos Rd and Guadalupe St, then just w of jct Cerrillos Rd and Paseo de Peralta.

[L] [D] CALL [&M]

XICLO VIETNAMESE- KOREAN RESTAURANT
Phone: 505/820-6777   ⑤

WWW WWW

Asian
$7-$19

AAA Inspector Notes: Flavorful Asian specialties, from traditional Vietnamese salad to Korean bulgogi, share menu space. Vegetarians will find plenty of offerings. **Bar:** beer & wine. **Address:** 919 W Alameda St 87501 **Location:** Just w of St. Francis Dr; in Solana Center.

[L] [D]

YIN YANG   **Phone:** 505/986-9279   ㊱

WWW WWW

Chinese
$2-$25

AAA Inspector Notes: This Chinese restaurant specializes in Hunan- and Peking-style comfort food, including many seafood, beef, chicken and vegetarian options. **Bar:** beer & wine. **Address:** 418 Cerrillos Rd 87501 **Location:** Just sw of The Plaza; near jct Montezuma Ave, Galisteo St and Cerrillos Rd; in Design Center.

[L] [D]

SANTA FE NATIONAL FOREST (A-5)

Elevations in the forest range from 5,300 ft. to 13,103 ft. at Truchas Peak. Refer to AAA maps for additional elevation information.

In the north central part of the state, some 1,600,000 acres of forest and rangeland lie within Santa Fe National Forest. The southern Sangre de Cristo Range, with several 12,000- to 13,000-foot peaks, dominates the eastern half. Within the forest are Pecos Wilderness, the headwaters of the Pecos River and the Santa Fe Basin winter sports area. The 18-mile trip along SR 63 between Cowles and Pecos provides outstanding views of the forest's eastern section.

In the portion west of the Rio Grande are the Jémez Mountains, San Pedro Parks Wilderness, Chama River Canyon Wilderness and Dome Wilderness. Developed recreation sites and day-use picnic areas are near streams, trailheads and other scenic highlights. Recreational opportunities include hiking, fishing, horseback riding and such winter sports as cross-country skiing and snowshoeing. Fees are required for some developed areas.

For information and maps contact the Supervisor, Santa Fe National Forest, 11 Forest Ln., Santa Fe, NM 87508; phone the Public Information Officer at (505) 438-5300. *See Recreation Chart.*

SANTA ROSA (F-5) pop. 2,848, elev. 4,599'

Santa Rosa is surrounded by parcels of land with property lines that were established by Spanish land grants. Many residents are descendents of the men who accompanied Francisco Vázquez de Coronado on his explorations of the area in 1540.

The town is in a semidesert area with artesian springs and lakes. Blue Hole, an artesian spring 81 feet deep and a minimum of 80 feet in diameter, is a half-mile west of Park Lake. Stocked with goldfish, its 64-degree waters attract scuba divers; a diving permit is required. A city park at Perch Lake also offers scuba diving.

Other nearby lakes, such as Park Lake and the lake in Janes-Wallace Memorial Park *(see Recreation Chart)*, yield large catches of trout, crappie and walleye. Channel catfish are taken from the Pecos River. Rock Lake State Fish Hatchery, 2 miles south of town on River Road, propagates rainbow trout and walleye.

Scenic SR 91 follows the Pecos River south for 10 miles to Puerto de Luna, one of several abandoned Spanish settlements in the area. A marker indicates where Coronado encamped to build a bridge across the river. Another pleasant drive leads to Santa Rosa Lake State Park *(see Recreation Chart)*, 7 miles north off SR 91. A .7-mile nature trail and other recreational facilities border the dam and reservoir.

Santa Rosa Visitors Information Center: 244 S. Fourth St., P.O. Box 429, Santa Rosa, NM 88435. **Phone:** (575) 472-3763.

BEST WESTERN ADOBE INN   **Phone:** (575)472-3446

WWW WWW

Hotel
$69-$99

Best Western

AAA Benefit: Members save up to 20%, plus 10% bonus points with Best Western Rewards®.

Address: 2255 Historic Route 66 88435 **Location:** I-40 exit 275. **Facility:** 56 units. 1-2 stories (no elevator), exterior corridors. **Amenities:** high-speed Internet. **Pool(s):** heated outdoor. **Guest Services:** coin laundry. **Free Special Amenities:** continental breakfast and high-speed Internet.

[SAVE] [¶] [≈] [BIZ] [≈] [⊟] [▱] / [SOME UNITS] [🐾]

BEST WESTERN SANTA ROSA INN
Phone: (575)472-5877

WWW WWW

Motel
$72-$120

Best Western

AAA Benefit: Members save up to 20%, plus 10% bonus points with Best Western Rewards®.

Address: 2491 Historic Route 66 88435 **Location:** I-40 exit 277, 0.5 mi w. **Facility:** 44 units. 1 story, exterior corridors. **Amenities:** high-speed Internet. **Pool(s):** heated outdoor. **Guest Services:** coin laundry. **Free Special Amenities:** local telephone calls and high-speed Internet.

[SAVE] [¶] [≈] [BIZ] [≈] [▱] / [SOME UNITS] FEE [🐾] [⊟] [▱]

Safety tip: Keep a current
AAA/CAA Road Atlas
in every vehicle

HAMPTON INN

Phone: 575/472-2300

▼▼▼

Hotel
Rates not provided

AAA Benefit:
Members save up to 10%
everyday!

Address: 2475 Historic Route 66 88435 **Location:** I-40 exit 277, 1 mi w. **Facility:** 64 units. 3 stories, interior corridors. **Amenities:** high-speed Internet. **Pool(s):** heated indoor. **Activities:** whirlpool, game room, exercise room. **Guest Services:** coin laundry.

🛏️ CALL 🅼 🛋️ BIZ 📶 ✕ 🖥️
/ SOME UNITS 🛗 📠

HOLIDAY INN EXPRESS

Phone: (575)472-5411

▼▼▼

Hotel
$80-$199

Address: 2516 Historic Route 66 88435 **Location:** I-40 exit 277, 0.4 mi w. **Facility:** 73 units. 3 stories, interior corridors. **Amenities:** high-speed Internet. **Pool(s):** heated indoor. **Activities:** whirlpool, game room, exercise room. **Guest Services:** coin laundry.

🛏️ CALL 🅼 🛋️ BIZ 📶 🛗 📠 🖥️
/ SOME UNITS FEE 🐕

LA QUINTA INN SANTA ROSA

Phone: (575)472-4800

▼▼▼

Hotel
$85-$150

Address: 2277 Historic Route 66 88435 **Location:** I-40 exit 275, just e. **Facility:** 60 units. 2 stories (no elevator), interior corridors. **Amenities:** high-speed Internet, safes. **Pool(s):** heated indoor. **Activities:** whirlpool, limited exercise equipment. **Guest Services:** coin laundry.

🛏️ 🛋️ BIZ 📶 🛗 📠 🖥️ / SOME UNITS 🐕

QUALITY INN

Phone: (575)472-5570

▼▼▼

Hotel
$59-$89

Address: 3343 E Historic Route 66 88435 **Location:** I-40 exit 277, 0.3 mi w. **Facility:** 45 units. 2 stories (no elevator), exterior corridors. **Terms:** 7 night minimum stay - seasonal, cancellation fee imposed. **Pool(s):** heated indoor. **Activities:** whirlpool. **Guest Services:** coin laundry.

🛏️ 🛋️ BIZ 📶 🛗 📠 🖥️ / SOME UNITS FEE 🐕

SUPER 8-SANTA ROSA

Phone: (575)472-5388

▼▼▼

Motel
$58-$85

Address: 2075 Historic Route 66 88435 **Location:** I-40 exit 275, just w. **Facility:** 88 units. 2 stories (no elevator), interior corridors. **Guest Services:** coin laundry.

🛏️ CALL 🅼 📶 🖥️ / SOME UNITS FEE 🐕 🛗 📠

WHERE TO EAT

SANTA FE GRILLE

Phone: 575/472-5568

▼▼▼

American
$7-$18

AAA Inspector Notes: Traditional, homemade New Mexican cuisine and American specialties are featured at this casual and friendly restaurant. **Bar:** beer & wine. **Address:** 2249 Historic Route 66 88435 **Location:** I-40 exit 275, just e. B L D

SILVER MOON CAFE

Phone: 575/472-3162

▼

American
$6-$16

AAA Inspector Notes: Established in 1959, this casual restaurant fits into the Route 66 nostalgia. The relaxed atmosphere is suitable for families and travelers. The menu blends a nice variety of both American and traditional Mexican fare. Guests can peruse the small gift shop after their meal. **Bar:** beer & wine. **Address:** 2545 Historic Route 66 88435 **Location:** I-40 exit 277, just n. B L D

SANTA TERESA (J-3) pop. 4,258, elev. 4,100'
• Restaurants p. 474

Note: For current information about safety/security issues in Ciudad Juárez, go to the U.S. State Department website (travel.state.gov). The port of entry at Santa Teresa is on the western edge of the El Paso/Juárez metropolitan area; take exit 8 (Artcraft Road) off I-10 and proceed west about 13 miles. Since it bypasses the city, this is the recommended crossing point for tourists and other travelers who are driving to Chihuahua and beyond or otherwise headed for interior Mexico. Banjercito offices at this border crossing and at the 30-kilometer (19-mile) mark on Mex. 45 (the Juárez-Chihuahua Highway) can process the paperwork necessary for vehicle travel into the interior.

Several crossings facilitate border travel for motorists bound for Ciudad Juárez. The Ysleta-Zaragoza Bridge (toll fee $2.50 per vehicle) enters Mexico about 19 kilometers (12 miles) east of the city. There are two separate spans with lanes for commercial and passenger vehicles. The Bridge of the Americas crossing, accessed from I-110/US 54, consists of four bridges—two for northbound and southbound commercial vehicles and two for northbound and southbound passenger vehicles. Once in Mexico the street name changes to Avenida Abraham Lincoln. Motorists returning to the United States via the Bridge of the Americas will often encounter long lines.

The five-lane Stanton Street Bridge, also called the Good Neighbor Bridge (toll fee $2.50 per vehicle), has four lanes for southbound traffic only, plus a fifth northbound "dedicated commuter lane" (open daily 8 a.m.-midnight) for those who cross frequently. This is the major southbound crossing into the city. Once across the border Stanton Street becomes Avenida Lerdo.

Motorists returning to the United States from downtown Juárez use the northbound-only Santa Fe Street Bridge (also called the Paso del Norte Bridge) via Avenida Juárez (toll fee $2.25 per vehicle, 50c for pedestrians). Those visiting for the day who want to park on the U.S. side of the border and walk across from downtown El Paso should use this bridge, since Avenida Juárez is where most of the tourist-oriented businesses are located.

Dollars or pesos are accepted when entering or departing Mexico or the United States. Baggage may be inspected at the customs offices. Both Mexican and U.S. Customs and Border Protection offices are open daily 24 hours at Ciudad Juárez; daily 6 a.m.-midnight at Santa Teresa. AAA/CAA members can obtain Mexico automobile insurance at AAA Texas offices.

WAR EAGLES AIR MUSEUM is off I-10 exit 8, 7.5 mi. w. on Airport Rd. to Santa Teresa Airport. The museum features restored aircraft from the World War II era and jet fighters used in the Korean Conflict. Fighters include the P-51 Mustang, the P-38 Lightning, the P-40 Warhawk, a twin-engine Invader bomber and a Fieseler Storch.

Among the 1950s jets are a T-33 Silver Star and MiG-15. Additional displays feature women aviators, flight equipment and 46 vintage automobiles. **Time:** Allow 1 hour minimum. **Hours:** Tues.-Sun. 10-4. Last admission 30 minutes before closing. Closed major holidays. **Cost:** $5; $4 (ages 65+ and military with ID); free (ages 0-11 and students with ID). **Phone:** (575) 589-2000.

BILLY CREWS   **Phone:** 575/589-2071
♦♦♦ ♦♦♦   **AAA Inspector Notes:** Semi-formal in
                the evenings, the setting is less formal
American   during lunch, which is served in the
$15-$40   lounge at this restaurant. Great,
                generously sized steaks are cooked to
                order. **Bar:** full bar. **Reservations:**
suggested. **Address:** 1200 Country Club Rd 88008
Location: Jct SR 273 (McNutt Rd) and 184 (Country Club
Rd), just e. [L] [D]

SANTO DOMINGO PUEBLO (C-3)
pop. 2,456, elev. 5,185'

Santo Domingo received its name in 1691 when missionaries began renaming New Mexican pueblos for Catholic saints. Keresan people had inhabited the site since the 1200s. The pueblo's actual location has changed over the years with flooding of the Rio Grande. The town of Domingo became a stopover on the way to Pea Blanca during Spanish colonial times; it later served as a stage stop on the road between Albuquerque and Santa Fe. The 1883 Santo Domingo Trading Post is one of the largest in the area.

SANTO DOMINGO PUEBLO is off I-25 exit 259, then 2.5 mi. w. Because of their proximity to the ancient Cerrillos turquoise mines, the Keresan artisans of Santo Domingo earned a reputation for fine jewelry, beadwork and mosaics. Their *heishe* beads are prized today. A community center offers visitors a glimpse into tribal life and traditions. Some 350 artists gather for an arts and crafts festival on Labor Day weekend.

The Church of the Pueblo of Santo Domingo dates from 1886 and replaced a mission that was carried away by Rio Grande floodwaters. Records as well as paintings by American Indian artists can be seen. Photography, sketching and painting are not permitted. **Hours:** Daily 8-5. **Cost:** Donations. **Phone:** (505) 465-2214.

SHIPROCK (E-1) pop. 8,295, elev. 4,900'

The geological formation Shiprock is within the Navajo Indian Reservation, 15 miles southwest via US 491 and Red Rock Road, from which it can be viewed. The basalt core of an old volcano, the rock rises more than 1,700 feet above the desert. At sunset it appears to shimmer and float.

Because the Navajo consider Shiprock to be a sacred place, the tribe does not permit climbers to scale it. Scenic Indian Route 33 runs between Shiprock and Red Rock on the Arizona border.

FOUR CORNERS MONUMENT, 33 mi. n.w. off SR 597, is the only place in the country where four states meet. The juncture of Arizona, Utah, Colorado and New Mexico is marked by a concrete monument bearing each state's seal. The Navajo and Ute sell their wares near the site. **Hours:** Daily 7 a.m.-8 p.m., May-Sept.; 8-5, rest of year. Closed Jan. 1, Thanksgiving and Christmas. **Cost:** $3; free (ages 0-6). **Phone:** (928) 871-6647.

SILVER CITY (I-2) pop. 10,315, elev. 5,938'

Silver City burgeoned with the discovery of silver in the late 1860s. Growth was reinforced by additional discoveries in the area, and the city became the county seat in late 1871. A lumber mill was set up to take advantage of nearby timberland; the mill and other businesses based on supplying the proliferating mines ensured that Silver City's existence would not be the brief, single-minded one of the typical mining town.

Permanence was declared with the establishment of Western New Mexico University in 1893—the same year the bottom dropped out of the silver market. As the mines closed and mining towns faded into history throughout the region, Silver City's economy regrouped around shipping and cattle ranching. The city is remembered as the boyhood home of William Bonney, who later gained notoriety as outlaw Billy the Kid.

Mining processes can be viewed from an open pit copper mine 15 miles east on SR 152. The huge pit, 1.7 miles across and 1,000 feet deep, has produced mountains of ore since the discovery of the deposits in 1800. One of the largest operations of its type in the United States, Chino Mine shows evidence of Spanish and Mexican workings. Chino Mines Co. provides an observation point and a picnic area.

Twelve miles south on SR 90, another vast open-pit mine yields some 50,000 tons of copper ore a day from the original site of Tyrone. Built in 1915 by Phelps-Dodge Corp. to house miners and their families, it was a beautifully designed city until declining markets caused the closure of the mine in 1921. Reactivation in the mid-1960s resulted in a new Tyrone 4.5 miles south of Silver City.

Silver City provides access to the 110-mile Trail of the Mountain Spirits, which leads to Gila Cliff Dwellings National Monument *(see place listing p. 414)* via US 180 and SRs 152, 35 and 15, then crosses the Pinos Altos Range back to Silver City. Contact the visitor center at Gila National Forest *(see place listing p. 415)* at (575) 536-9461.

Silver City/Grant County Chamber of Commerce: 201 N. Hudson St., Silver City, NM 88061. **Phone:** (575) 538-3785 or (800) 548-9378.

Self-guiding tours: Pocket guides for walking tours of the city's three historic neighborhoods Capilla, Gospel Hill and the historic business district—may be purchased for 75c each at the Silver City Museum.

SILVER CITY MUSEUM is at 312 W. Broadway St. Exhibits in the 1881 H.B. Ailman house explore the history of southwest New Mexico. Collections include 19th- and 20th-century regional history objects and photographs, Southwestern American Indian artifacts and objects from an early 20th-century mining camp. The museum also houses a local-history research library. **Time:** Allow 1 hour minimum. **Hours:** Tues.-Fri. 9-4:30, Sat.-Sun. 10-4. Closed Jan. 1, Easter, Thanksgiving, Christmas Eve and Christmas. **Cost:** $3. **Phone:** (575) 538-5921, or (877) 777-7947 out of state.

WESTERN NEW MEXICO UNIVERSITY MUSEUM is on campus .5 mi. s.w. of US 180 at 10th and West sts. in Fleming Hall. Extensive displays depict prehistoric Mimbres culture; artifacts include pottery, stone tools and jewelry. Also featured are Casas Grandes pottery, historical displays, mining items and traveling exhibits. **Hours:** Mon.-Fri. 9-4:30, Sat.-Sun. 10-4; closed university holidays. **Cost:** Donations. **Phone:** (575) 538-6386.

COMFORT INN
Phone: (575)534-1883
Hotel
$95-$155
Address: 1060 E Hwy 180 88061 **Location:** Just e of jct SR 15. **Facility:** 52 units. 2 stories (no elevator), interior corridors. **Terms:** cancellation fee imposed. **Amenities:** safes. **Pool(s):** heated indoor. **Activities:** whirlpool. **Guest Services:** valet and coin laundry. **Free Special Amenities: expanded continental breakfast and high-speed Internet**

ECONO LODGE SILVER CITY
Phone: (575)534-1111
Hotel
$69-$149
Address: 1120 Hwy 180 E 88061 **Location:** 1.5 mi ne on US 180 and SR 90. **Facility:** 61 units. 3 stories, interior corridors. **Terms:** cancellation fee imposed. **Amenities:** *Some:* safes. **Pool(s):** heated indoor. **Activities:** whirlpool, exercise room. **Guest Services:** valet and coin laundry. **Free Special Amenities: full breakfast and high-speed Internet.**

HOLIDAY INN EXPRESS
Phone: (575)538-2525
Hotel
$109-$134
Address: 1103 Superior St 88061 **Location:** 3 mi ne on US 180 and SR 90. **Facility:** 60 units. 3 stories, interior corridors. **Amenities:** high-speed Internet. **Activities:** whirlpool, exercise room. **Guest Services:** valet and coin laundry.

WHERE TO EAT

DIANE'S RESTAURANT
Phone: 575/538-8722
International
$8-$30
AAA Inspector Notes: What looks like an unassuming cafe turns out to be a fine-dining establishment. In the evenings, the eatery presents an upscale menu that lists a good selection of appetizers, such as spanakopita; tasty soups; and fish, poultry and beef entrées. **Bar:** beer & wine. **Address:** 510 N Bullard St 88061 **Location:** Center; in historic downtown. **Parking:** street only.

ISAAC'S GRILL
Phone: 575/388-4090
International
$8-$19
AAA Inspector Notes: A local favorite, this historic downtown eatery features a lively atmosphere. The creative menu has selections from brie quesadillas to free-range New Mexico bison meatloaf as well as salads and sandwiches. **Bar:** beer & wine. **Address:** 200 N Bullard St 88061 **Location:** Jct Bullard St and Broadway; center. **Parking:** street only.

JALISCO CAFE
Phone: 575/388-2060
Mexican
$7-$28
AAA Inspector Notes: Flavorful Mexican favorites are served in hearty portions at this popular eatery. For a tropical treat, try the crab tostadas with mango. A house specialty, the mandarin orange cake is luscious. **Bar:** beer & wine. **Address:** 103 S Bullard St 88061 **Location:** In historic downtown; center. **Parking:** street only.

RED BARN FAMILY STEAK HOUSE
Phone: 575/538-5666
Steak
$8-$24
AAA Inspector Notes: A longtime favorite of the local folks, this traditional steakhouse features a well-stocked salad bar, generous steaks and a good selection of desserts. Also on site is a lively lounge. **Bar:** full bar. **Address:** 708 Silver Heights Blvd 88061 **Location:** Center.

SHEVEK & CO RESTAURANT
Menu on AAA.com
Phone: 575/534-9168
Mediterranean
$7-$30

AAA Inspector Notes: A distinctive dining experience at this restaurant features traditional Mediterranean and Mediterranean-fusion dishes. Every item is available in three sizes: the tapa size gives a diner a taste of a flavor, the mezze size will please the lighter eater, and the entrée portion will satisfy the larger appetite. Also featured is an extensive beer and wine selection (most wines are available by the glass). Diners on the weekend can enjoy an upscale brunch on the informal patio. **Bar:** beer & wine. **Address:** 602 N Bullard St 88061 **Location:** Center. **Parking:** street only.

SOCORRO (G-3) pop. 9,051, elev. 4,605'
• Hotels p. 476 • Restaurants p. 476

Socorro was the biggest—and wildest—city in New Mexico during the 1880s. After the Panic of 1893 sent silver prices plunging, local mines produced zinc and other ores until these reserves became depleted. After most miners left, the remaining townspeople turned their energies to farming and stock raising.

A natural outgrowth of the mining era was the 1889 founding of the New Mexico School of Mines, later renamed New Mexico Institute of Mining and Technology.

Socorro County Chamber of Commerce: 101 Plaza, P.O. Box 743, Socorro, NM 87801. **Phone:** (575) 835-0424.

Self-guiding tours: A brochure outlining a walking tour of historic buildings and places, most within walking distance of the central plaza, is available from the chamber.

EL CAMINO REAL INTERNATIONAL HERITAGE CENTER is off I-25S exit 115, 1.5 mi. s. on SR 1, then 3 mi. e. on CR 1598 (just past marker 24). Used by traders, settlers and American Indian travelers for more than 400 years, El Camino Real served as a thoroughfare for introducing people, products, livestock and ideas to the region. The 120-acre site features such items as hand-hewn carts, tools and leather water jugs. **Time:** Allow 1 hour minimum. **Hours:** Wed.-Sun. 8:30-5. **Cost:** $5; free (ages 0-16). **Phone:** (575) 854-3600.

MINERAL MUSEUM is at Olive Ln. and Canyon Rd. at the New Mexico Institute of Mining and Technology. An extensive mineral collection includes more than 2,000 specimens indigenous to the region and from around the world as well as artifacts and memorabilia related to mining and minerals. Exhibits change periodically. **Hours:** Mon.-Fri. 8-5, Sat.-Sun. 10-3. Closed major holidays. **Cost:** Free. **Phone:** (575) 835-5140.

SAN MIGUEL MISSION is n. of the plaza at 403 El Camino Real. The twin-steeple church, built 1819-21, is still in use. Its predecessor, constructed in the 1620s, was destroyed in the Pueblo Rebellion of 1680. A portion of one wall dates from 1598; hand-carved ceiling beams highlight the interior. Artifacts are displayed in the adjoining church office. **Hours:** Daily 8-7:30, June-Aug.; 8-6:30, rest of year. **Cost:** Free. **Phone:** (575) 835-2891.

VERY LARGE ARRAY (VLA) RADIO TELESCOPE is 50 mi. w. on US 60. One of the world's premier radio telescope observatories, the VLA consists of 27 radio telescopes, each weighing 230 tons. The parabolic dish portion of the antenna measures 82 feet in diameter. For optimum tracking, the antennas are maneuvered along a Y-shaped grid of railroad tracks that stretch for miles across the desert floor. Self-guiding walking tours to a working antenna start at the visitor center, which provides an orientation film and educational exhibits. **Time:** Allow 1 hour minimum. **Hours:** Daily 8:30-dusk. Guided tours are offered on the first Sat. of the month at 11, 1 and 3. **Cost:** Free. **Phone:** (575) 835-7000.

BEST WESTERN SOCORRO HOTEL & SUITES
Phone: (575)838-0556

Hotel
$105

AAA Benefit: Members save up to 20%, plus 10% bonus points with Best Western Rewards®.

Address: 1100 California Ave NE 87801 **Location:** Center. **Facility:** 120 units. 2 stories (no elevator), interior/exterior corridors. **Terms:** 3 day cancellation notice-fee imposed. **Pool(s):** heated indoor. **Activities:** sauna, whirlpools, exercise room. *Fee:* game room. **Guest Services:** coin laundry. **Free Special Amenities: continental breakfast and high-speed Internet.**

COMFORT INN & SUITES **Phone:** 575-838-4400

Hotel
Rates not provided

Address: 1259 Frontage Rd NW 87801 **Location:** I-25 exit 150, just nw. **Facility:** 66 units. 3 stories, interior corridors. **Amenities:** high-speed Internet. **Pool(s):** heated indoor. **Activities:** whirlpool, limited exercise equipment. **Guest Services:** coin laundry.

DAYS INN-SOCORRO **Phone:** (575)835-0230

Hotel
$56-$76

Address: 507 N California St 87801 **Location:** I-25 exit 147, 1.7 mi n; exit 150, just s. **Facility:** 41 units. 2 stories (no elevator), exterior corridors. **Terms:** cancellation fee imposed. **Pool(s):** outdoor. **Free Special Amenities: continental breakfast and high-speed Internet.**

ECONO LODGE **Phone:** (575)835-1500

Motel
$55-$125

Address: 713 N California St NW 87801 **Location:** I-25 exit 150, 1 mi. s. **Facility:** 66 units. 1-2 stories (no elevator), exterior corridors. **Terms:** cancellation fee imposed. **Pool(s):** heated outdoor. **Activities:** sauna, whirlpool, exercise room.

HOLIDAY INN EXPRESS **Phone:** 575-838-4600

[fyi] Not evaluated. **Address:** 1040 N California 87801 **Location:** I-25 exit 150, just s. Facilities, services, and decor characterize a mid-scale property.

WHERE TO EAT

CHINA BEST **Phone:** 575-835-3331

Chinese
$5-$10

AAA Inspector Notes: This reasonably priced buffet lines up well-prepared dishes of familiar Chinese fare, including sweet and sour pork, egg rolls and chicken, fish and beef entrées. **Address:** 900 California Ave 87801 **Location:** I-25 exit 150, 0.5 mi s.

EL CAMINO FAMILY RESTAURANT **Phone:** 575/835-1180

American
$4-$20

AAA Inspector Notes: This family-oriented restaurant caters to hungry diners. New Mexican and American food are served in generous quantities. Breakfast selections such as the egg and chorizo breakfast burrito, with or without a red or green chile topping, are tasty and satisfying. **Bar:** full bar. **Address:** 707 California St 87801 **Location:** I-25 exit 150, 1 mi s.

EL SOMBRERO **Phone:** 575/835-3945

Mexican
$6-$15

AAA Inspector Notes: Diners can order their favorite New Mexican dish-such as carne adovada, flat enchiladas, tamales and sopaipillas stuffed with meat, beans and chicken-at this locally popular café on the edge of town. Chile, in red or green varieties, has authority, and the enchilada plate is a treat. Guests also can taste great pies in the bright, well-decorated dining room. **Bar:** beer & wine. **Address:** 210 Mesquite 87801 **Location:** I-25 exit 150, just e.

K-BOB'S STEAKHOUSE **Phone:** 575/835-2900

Steak
$7-$25

AAA Inspector Notes: The steakhouse prepares a great variety of plump, juicy fillets. A fireplace opens up into both dining rooms, and antique clocks decorate the walls. Rustic wagon-wheel chandeliers illuminate the room. **Address:** 1123 NW Frontage Rd 87801 **Location:** I-25 exit 150, 1.2 mi n.

SOCORRO SPRINGS RESTAURANT AND BREWERY

Phone: 575/838-0650

American
$6-$18

AAA Inspector Notes: Near the central plaza, this brew pub satisfies patrons with well-made suds in several varieties, as well as pizza and sandwiches. Also tempting are a number of good desserts. A Southwestern look complements the location. **Bar:** beer & wine. **Address:** 1012 California St 87801 **Location:** I-25 exit 150, 0.3 mi s. L D

SPRINGER (E-5) pop. 1,047, elev. 5,832'

Springer was named for Frank Springer, who came to New Mexico from Iowa in 1873. Having settled in Cimarron, Springer was a prominent lawyer and paleontologist. His most lasting legacy is the New Mexico Museum of Art *(see attraction listing p. 452)*, of which he was a founder.

The Santa Fe Trail Interpretive Center and Museum, housed in the old county courthouse at 606 Maxwell Ave., displays household items, clothing, period furniture and the only electric chair used in New Mexico; phone (575) 483-5554.

Springer Chamber of Commerce and Visitor Center: 606 Maxwell St., P.O. Box 323, Springer, NM 87747. **Phone:** (575) 483-5554.

SUNSPOT (I-4) elev. 9,200'

NATIONAL SOLAR OBSERVATORY is on Sacramento Peak. At an elevation of 9,200 feet, the research facility makes high-resolution observations of the sun. Exhibits and interactive displays are featured at the Sunspot Astronomy and Visitor Center at the end of the Sunspot Scenic Byway (SR 6563). The observatory also offers views of the Tularosa Basin. A brochure and map are available for self-guiding tours.

Tours: Guided tours are available. **Time:** Allow 1 hour minimum. **Hours:** Daily 9-5, May-Sept.; otherwise varies. Guided tours are given daily at 2, June-Aug. (weather permitting). Phone ahead to confirm schedule. **Cost:** $3; $1 (ages 55+ and students with ID); free (ages 0-9); $7 (family). Guided tours $2; $1 (ages 55+ and students with ID). **Phone:** (575) 434-7190.

TAOS (E-4) pop. 5,716, elev. 6,952'
- Hotels p. 483 • Restaurants p. 484
- Hotels & Restaurants map & index p. 481

Initially dubbed Don Fernando de Taos by the Spanish, this northeastern New Mexico jewel has long been a lure. The natural setting in the shadow of the lofty Sangre de Cristo Mountains is glorious. There's a mystical quality that finds its most evocative expression through art. And how many other towns can you name that have a history embracing the Athabascans, Kit Carson and Dennis Hopper?

The Athabascan people (now referred to as Apaches and Navajos) began settling this area almost a thousand years ago. Adobe dwellings were constructed as early as 1350 A.D. at Taos Pueblo, which has the distinction of being considered the nation's oldest continuously inhabited community as well as being the only UNESCO Living World Heritage Site in the United States. The pueblo's two largest structures appear today much as they did in 1540, when the first Spanish explorers arrived. Searching for the "seven cities of gold" that supposedly contained unlimited riches, the Spaniards unfortunately came face to face with a very early urban legend.

Christopher Houston "Kit" Carson is a major figure in Taos lore. The Missouri-born frontiersman was a fur trapper before gaining renown as the guide for John C. Frémont's successful 1840s exploration of the Continental Divide—a trek that set off a flurry of expeditions charting the American West. He later became a Taos rancher and a U.S. Army general who was instrumental in quelling a Navajo uprising in New Mexico. Carson became a legend thanks to the publication of many dime store novels and pulp magazine stories. You can brush up on the "fighting trapper's" life at the Kit Carson Home and Museum and visit his grave in Kit Carson Park.

Flash back to a more recent time—the 1960s—when hippie communes began springing up in the region's spectacular high desert country. Actor/filmmaker Dennis Hopper came to New Mexico to scout locations for "Easy Rider," a 1969 cult classic that vividly depicts the counterculture vibe of the time, partially filmed in and around Taos. Hopper returned and lived here for the next 12 years. A memorial service for the two-time Oscar nominee, who died in 2010, was held at the historic San Francisco de Asis Church in nearby Ranchos de Taos. Hopper is buried nearby.

What has always attracted people is the sheer beauty of the land. Adventurous sketch and watercolor artists in search of inspiration arrived along with railroad survey teams in the 1870s. The proposed Río del Norte and Santa Fe Railroad never came to fruition, and later efforts to bring rail service to town also failed. This has left Taos somewhat delightfully isolated despite the inevitable presence of modern highways.

It was illustrator Ernest Blumenschein who really got the town's artistic ball rolling. On a covered wagon trip to the Southwest in 1898, he and colleague Bert Phillips were forced to stop in Taos to repair a broken wheel. They became enthralled with the surroundings during their brief stay, and both eventually settled in permanently. In 1915 Blumenschein helped form the Taos Society of Artists, which established the town as an artists' colony with a bent for the eccentric; creative types have gravitated here ever since.

The heart of Taos is Taos Plaza, just off Paseo del Pueblo Norte between Kit Carson Road and Camino de la Placita. It dates back to the late 18th century and has long been a local meeting place. A big cottonwood tree stands in the center of this small plaza; in spring and summer its shiny green leaves flutter

(See map & index p. 481.)

in the slightest breeze and then turn bright yellow in the fall, providing a lovely contrast to the azure blue sky.

The plaza's gazebo was donated by Mabel Dodge, a transplanted New York socialite and art connoisseur who came to town in 1918, married Taos Indian Tony Luhan and championed New Mexico's Indian culture and natural beauty to contemporaries like Georgia O'Keeffe, D.H. Lawrence and Ansel Adams. This is a perfect spot to relax and set your internal clock to a more laid-back rhythm.

Taos also provides plenty of outdoor action for active types who aren't content to sit and contemplate. The nearby Rio Grande makes the area a popular starting point for river rafting excursions. During high-water season, from late April to mid-June, the thrills range from relatively gentle to pulse pounding (the latter courtesy of the infamous Taos Box, 16 miles of wilderness gorge and physically demanding rapids). Outfitters are based in town and in Santa Fe.

Mountain bikers and hikers meet their match on the trails that traverse 13,161-foot Wheeler Peak, and Wheeler Peak Wilderness Area offers summer fishing and camping. Winter sports enthusiasts flock to Taos Ski Valley's world-class downhill facilities; phone (575) 586-0520 for snow conditions and year-round recreational activities.

Town of Taos Visitor Center: 1139 Paseo del Pueblo Sur, Taos, NM 87571. **Phone:** (575) 758-3873 or (800) 732-8267.

Self-guiding tours: A walking tour map of the city's historic district and Taos Plaza is available from the visitor center.

Shopping areas: Many shops at Taos Plaza veer more toward souvenirs, T-shirts and knickknacks than fine art, but it's such a relaxed hangout that you'll want to poke around anyway. Indulge your sweet tooth at the Rocky Mountain Chocolate Factory (next to LaFonda Hotel) before browsing the merchandise at the Taos Trading Co., Taos Cowboy or Mesa's Edge Jewelry.

There's more browsing at the John Dunn House Shops, a tree-shaded, open-air lane of shops between Taos Plaza and Bent Street. Monet's Kitchen has Southwest table and kitchen accessories; Letherwerks sells handmade belts, hats and jackets. Rock hounds should check out the La Tierra Mineral Gallery (fossils, crystals, jewelry). Moby Dickens Bookshop has a good Southwest selection.

Taos Blue (101a Bent St., just off Paseo del Pueblo Norte) offers finely handcrafted Southwestern and northern New Mexico art—pottery, jewelry, beadwork, medicine bags, Kachina dolls and the like. The gallery also sells fetishes, which are small carvings of animals made from turquoise, mother of pearl and other materials. Created by the Zuni for ceremonial purposes, they're prized by collectors of contemporary Native American art.

The town's thriving art scene, in fact, lures collectors from around the country. Ledoux Street, a block southwest of the plaza, is lined with galleries like 203 Fine Art (203 Ledoux St.), the Baumann Gallery (203a Ledoux St.), the Inger Jirby Gallery (207 Ledoux St.) and the R.C. Gorman Navajo Gallery (210 Ledous St.). The Ledoux Art Stroll, held the third Saturday of the month June through August, is a popular way to experience what the local artist community offers. Local merchants usher in the holiday season with Lighting of Ledoux, held the second Saturday in December.

There are more galleries along Kit Carson Road just east of the plaza. Parsons Gallery of the West (122 Kit Carson Rd.) features vintage Western art, while the Timothy O. Sutherland Gallery (140 Kit Carson Rd.) specializes in fine art photography. The Thom Wheeler Studio Gallery (939 Kit Carson Rd.) has paintings and sculptures. Cowboy collectibles and Western-style furnishings are on display at Horse Feathers (109 Kit Carson Rd. next to the Kit Carson Home and Museum).

Take home a bit of Taos history from the El Rincón Trading Post (114 Kit Carson Rd.). Established in 1909, it actually was a trading post back in the day. In addition to selling Indian pottery, baskets and rugs, this is a great place to hunt for old turquoise jewelry pawned more than a century ago. The store also has a museum with a collection of Western and Indian artifacts—everything from buckskin britches to peyote fans (used for powwow ceremonial dances).

Ancient traditions live on at Taos Pueblo. Tourism contributes to the local livelihood, and many of the adobe dwellings contain gift shops that sell items like clay pottery, tanned buckskin moccasins and handcrafted pipes. Family-run Wahleah's Taos Pueblo Gallery has five rooms filled with rugs, deerskin drums, beautiful turquoise jewelry and traditional crafts. Even Wahleah's T-shirts, imprinted with lovely nature scenes and cool-looking Indian symbols, are works of art. And don't leave without trying some Indian fry bread, baked in an outdoor adobe oven.

Nightlife: Taos isn't known for frenetic nightlife; options here are mellow and mostly revolve around live music. The Adobe Bar (125 Paseo del Pueblo Norte in The Historic Taos Inn), fondly known as "the living room of Taos," is *the* place to go if you want to mingle with Taoseños. There's live music every night of the week—everything from jazz, bluegrass and alt-country to flamenco, Celtic and native folk music. Better yet, there's no cover charge. The list of creative margaritas includes the inn's famous "Cowboy Buddha."

The Alley Cantina (just off the plaza at 121 Teresina Ln.) is a lively restaurant and bar where singles congregate at happy hour and diners scarf down the highly regarded fish and chips. This is said to be the oldest building in Taos, although only parts of the walls can make that claim. Legend also has it

(See map & index p. 481.)

that Teresina Bent, daughter of 19th-century territorial governor Charles Bent, haunts the premises. Local bands play several nights a week.

More local talent—from guitarists to oboe players to stand-up comics—takes the stage on open mic nights (Mondays beginning at 6:30 at the Adobe Bar, Wednesdays at 9:30 at the Alley Cantina). Caffe Tazza (122 Kit Carson Rd.) has a Friday open mic night (6-9) that brings young performers and mostly acoustic music to this cozy coffeehouse.

Another popular nightspot is the Anaconda Bar (317 Kit Carson Rd. in the El Monte Sagrado Living Resort and Spa), where the decor includes a snake sculpture slithering across the ceiling and a massive saltwater aquarium. Live entertainment takes place Friday and Saturday evenings beginning at 10.

Or you could just hang out in Taos Plaza. When the weather's warm the plaza becomes a magnet for locals and tourists alike. But it's Taos Plaza Live (every Thursday evening from late May to early September) that brings out the crowds. Two bands perform at each show, and the musical lineup is eclectic: rock, jazz, blues, country, traditional New Mexican and Native American. Performances start at 6; admission is free.

ERNEST L. BLUMENSCHEIN HOME

ERNEST L. BLUMENSCHEIN HOME is 2 blks. w. of historic Taos Plaza on Ledoux St. The artist and co-founder of the original Taos Society of Artists made this his permanent home in 1919. Portions of the adobe house were built in 1797; other sections were added by Blumenschein. The restored 13-room house contains original furnishings and serves as a showcase for works by Ernest and Mary Blumenschein, their daughter, Helen, and other Taos painters. **Hours:** Mon.-Sat. 10-5, Sun. noon-5. Phone ahead to confirm winter hours. **Cost:** $8; $4 (ages 5-16). Combination ticket with Martinez Hacienda $12. Combination ticket with Harwood Museum of Art, Martinez Hacienda, Millicent Rogers Museum and Taos Art Museum $25. **Phone:** (575) 758-0505.

HARWOOD MUSEUM OF ART

HARWOOD MUSEUM OF ART is at 238 Ledoux St. Taos art from the 18th century to the present includes paintings, sculpture and Hispanic religious art. The Agnes Martin Gallery presents seven paintings by this foremost American abstract artist. Changing exhibits focus on Taos artists. **Hours:** Mon.-Sat. 10-5, Sun. noon-5, May-Oct.; Tues.-Sat. 10-5, Sun. noon-5, rest of year. Closed Jan. 1, Thanksgiving and Christmas. **Cost:** $10; $8 (ages 60+); free (ages 0-12). Combination ticket with Ernest L. Blumenschein Home, Martinez Hacienda, Millicent Rogers Museum and Taos Art Museum $25. **Phone:** (575) 758-9826.

HISTORIC TAOS TROLLEY TOURS

HISTORIC TAOS TROLLEY TOURS depart from the Taos County Visitors Center at 1139 Paseo del Pueblo Sur, and from Atira's Southwest at 102 A S. Taos Plaza. Visitors can choose between two narrated tours aboard a trolley-style bus. The Taos

Pueblo Excursion makes a 1-hour visit to the centuries-old pueblo with stops at Historic Taos Plaza and San Francisco de Asis Church. The History and Culture Tour includes Taos Plaza, the Millicent Rogers Museum and the Martinez Hacienda.

Time: Allow 3 hours minimum. **Hours:** Taos Pueblo Excursion departs the visitor center Tues.-Sat. at 10:30 and 2, Sun.-Mon. at 10:30, May-Oct. (15 minutes later from Atira's Southwest). History and Culture Tour departs Sun.-Mon. at 2, May-Oct. (15 minutes later from Atira's Southwest). **Cost:** (Includes admission to attractions) $33; $10 (ages 6-12). A gas surcharge may be added to ticket prices. Tickets may be purchased daily 10:30-6 at Atira's Southwest. **Phone:** (575) 751-0366.

KIT CARSON HOME AND MUSEUM

KIT CARSON HOME AND MUSEUM is at 113 Kit Carson Rd. Housed within a restored building, the museum focuses on the history of the Carson family. Christopher Houston "Kit" Carson was a well-known mountain man, army general and Masonic Lodge member. Exhibits reflect the life of the home's occupants during the mid-1800s. A videotape presentation about Carson also is featured. **Time:** Allow 1 hour minimum. **Hours:** Daily 11-5, early May-Labor Day; daily 11-4, rest of year. Closed Jan. 1, Thanksgiving and Christmas. Phone ahead to confirm schedule. **Cost:** $5; $4 (ages 62+ and military with ID); $3 (ages 13-19). **Phone:** (575) 758-4945.

KIT CARSON PARK

KIT CARSON PARK is 2 blks. n. of Taos Plaza. The park contains the cemetery where Kit Carson, Padre Martinez and other historic figures are buried. **Hours:** Daily 8-8, Apr.-Oct.; 8-5, rest of year. **Cost:** Free. **Phone:** (575) 758-8234.

MARTINEZ HACIENDA

MARTINEZ HACIENDA is 2 mi. w. of Taos Plaza at 708 Hacienda Way. This restored *hacienda* was built in 1804 by Don Antonio Severino Martinez, a merchant and *alcalde* (mayor) of Taos. The fortresslike house has 21 rooms built around two large courtyards. Furnished in period, it contains exhibits of Spanish colonial life and culture. Living-history demonstrations are presented periodically. **Hours:** Mon.-Sat. 10-5, Sun. noon-5. Phone ahead to confirm schedule. **Cost:** $8; $4 (ages 5-16). Combination ticket with Ernest L. Blumenschein Home $12. Combination ticket with Ernest L. Blumenschein Home, Harwood Museum of Art, Millicent Rogers Museum and Taos Art Museum $25. **Phone:** (575) 758-1000.

MILLICENT ROGERS MUSEUM

MILLICENT ROGERS MUSEUM is 4 mi. n. of Taos Plaza near US 64. The adobe house displays the art, history and culture of the Southwest. It focuses on the American Indian, Hispanic and Anglo art of Taos and northern New Mexico. Also presented is one of the largest known pottery collections by Maria Martinez, an early 20th-century Pueblo artist whose career spanned some 85 years. **Time:** Allow 1 hour minimum. **Hours:** Daily 10-5, Apr.-Oct.; Tues.-Sun. 10-5, rest of year. Closed Jan. 1, Easter, Thanksgiving and Christmas. **Cost:** $10; $8 (ages 60+); $6 (students and active and retired military

(See map & index p. 481.)

with ID); $2 (ages 6-16); $18 (family, parents and children 0-16). Combination ticket with Ernest L. Blumenschein Home, Harwood Museum of Art, Martinez Hacienda and Taos Art Museum $25. Prices may vary; phone ahead. **Phone:** (575) 758-2462.

PICURÍS PUEBLO—*see place listing p. 433.*

RIO GRANDE GORGE BRIDGE is 10 mi. w. of Taos on US 64. Built in 1965, this continuous steel deck truss bridge is 1,272 feet long and spans the gorge some 650 feet above the Rio Grande. A raised sidewalk allows daredevils to walk out to the mid-span observation deck for a dizzying look down—the gorge is spectacularly deep at this point—with rugged cliff walls zigzagging to the water far below. If you suffer from acrophobia even hanging on to the guardrail for dear life won't be enough, but the views still are spectacular (and not as vertigo-inducing) from the side.

There are parking areas on both sides of the highway at the east end of the bridge, and vendors set up tables to sell jewelry, T-shirts and other items. The 20-minute drive from Taos is a scenic one, running through a flat, sagebrush-speckled valley framed by the Sangre de Cristo Mountains to the east and the San Juan range to the northwest. **Hours:** Daily 24 hours. **Cost:** Free.

SAN FRANCISCO DE ASIS CHURCH is 4 mi. s. on SR 68 in St. Francis Plaza. Built by Franciscan priests and completed in 1772, this heavily buttressed structure with twin bell towers exemplifies Spanish colonial architecture. Its rounded contours inspired the imaginations of Ansel Adams and Georgia O'Keeffe, among other artists.

You can still see straw glinting in the sunlight on the massive adobe walls. Inside are wood pews, two large, carved *reredos* (altar screens) divided into painted panels, paintings of saints and a ceiling of wood beams *(vigas)*. The church's simple dignity is best appreciated from the arched portal entrance that overlooks a walled courtyard.

Photography is not permitted inside the church. In the parish hall across the plaza is Henri Ault's mysterious—some say miraculous—luminescent painting "The Shadow of the Cross."

Hours: Open to visitors Mon.-Fri. 9-4. Mass given Sun. at 7 a.m. (in Spanish), 9 and 11:30. Weekday Masses Mon.-Wed. and Fri. at 6:45 a.m. **Cost:** Church free. Parish hall admission $3; free (ages 0-9). **Phone:** (575) 758-2754.

TAOS ART MUSEUM is at 227 Paseo del Pueblo Norte. Housed in the historic home of Russian-born artist Nicolai Fechin, the permanent collection includes paintings by the Taos Society of Artists and the Taos Moderns. The Fechin Home, designed and reconstructed in the 1930s, is considered an architectural masterpiece. It is filled with Fechin's hand-carved doors, windows, furniture and art. **Time:** Allow 30 minutes minimum. **Hours:** Wed.-Sun. 10-5,

May-Sept.; Wed.-Sun. 10-4, rest of year. Phone ahead to confirm schedule. **Cost:** $8; $7 (ages 65+); $5 (students with ID); $4 (ages 6-16). Combination ticket with Ernest L. Blumenschein Home, Harwood Museum of Art, Martinez Hacienda and Millicent Rogers Museum $25. **Phone:** (575) 758-2690.

TAOS PUEBLO is 2 mi. n. of the plaza via Paseo del Pueblo Norte, then about half a mile n. on the entrance road to the parking/registration area. Located at the base of Taos Mountain, this is one of the oldest continuously inhabited communities in North America.

Stepping onto pueblo land is like taking a big step backward in time. Buildings are constructed entirely of adobe; roofs are supported by *vigas* (large wood timbers). The only modern additions are simple doors and windows. The two largest structures are composed of individual dwellings with common walls but no connecting doorways. About 150 Taos Indians choose to live in the sacred village as their ancestors did, without conveniences like electricity or plumbing; drinking water comes from Red Willow Creek, which flows through the center of the pueblo.

A cemetery with primitive wood crosses contains a bell tower, all that remains of the original San Geronimo Church, erected in the early 17th century by Spanish priests overseeing Indian labor. The present church dates from 1850 and has a simple dignity; a central altar figure of the Virgin Mary also represents Mother Nature in the blend of Catholic and native religious iconography.

Registration is required to enter the pueblo. Visitors must heed all signs designating restricted access. **Tours:** Guided tours are available. **Time:** Allow 1 hour minimum. **Hours:** Daily 8-4:30; closed during tribal rituals and for approximately 10 weeks from late winter to early spring. Phone ahead to confirm schedule. **Cost:** $10; $5 (students with ID); free (ages 0-10). Video and camera fee $6. **Phone:** (575) 758-1028.

RECREATIONAL ACTIVITIES
Skiing
- **Taos Ski Valley** is in the Sangre de Cristo Mountains in Carson National Forest *(see place listing p. 396).* **Hours:** Daily Thanksgiving-early Apr. **Phone:** (575) 776-2291 or (866) 968-7386.

White-water Rafting
- **Far Flung Adventures** departs from 15 SR 522N. **Hours:** Daily late Apr.-Sept. 30. **Phone:** (575) 758-2628 or (800) 359-2627.
- **Los Rios River Runners** departs from various locations. **Hours:** Daily Mar.-Oct. **Phone:** (575) 776-8854 or (800) 544-1181.
- **Native Sons Adventure Company** departs from 1203 King Dr. or from Pilar, 14 mi. s. on US 68. Other activities are available. **Hours:** Daily Apr.-Oct. **Phone:** (575) 758-9342, or (800) 753-7559 to verify schedule.

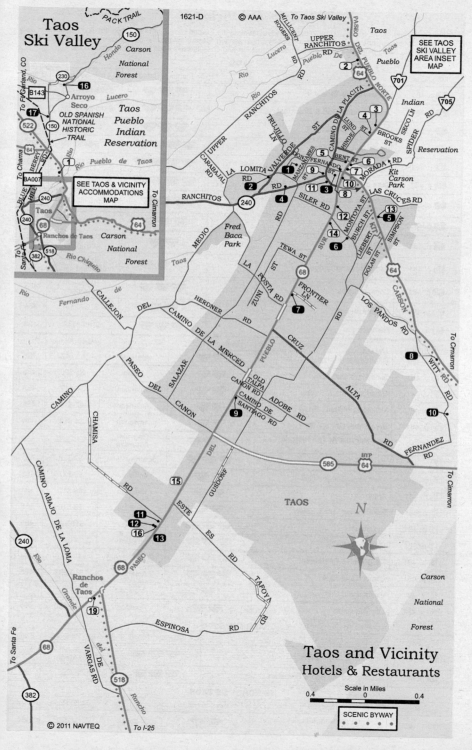

Taos
Ski Valley

PACK TRAIL
1621-D   © AAA

To Taos Ski Valley

Carson
National
Forest

Taos
Pueblo
Indian
Reservation

SEE TAOS
SKI VALLEY
AREA INSET
MAP

Arroyo
Seco

OLD SPANISH
NATIONAL
HISTORIC
TRAIL

Rio Pueblo de Taos

SEE TAOS & VICINITY
ACCOMODATIONS
MAP

Taos

Ranchos de Taos

Carson
National
Forest

Fred
Baca
Park

Kit
Carson
Park

TAOS

N

Ranchos
de
Taos

To Santa Fe

To I-25

© 2011 NAVTEQ

Carson

National

Forest

Taos and Vicinity
Hotels & Restaurants

Scale in Miles
0.4   0   0.4

SCENIC BYWAY

Taos and Vicinity

This index helps you "spot" where approved hotels and restaurants are located on the corresponding detailed maps. Hotel daily rate range is for comparison only and show the property's high season. Restaurant rate range is a combination of lunch and/or dinner. Turn to the listing page for more detailed rate information and consult display ads for special promotions.

TAOS

Map Page	Hotels	Diamond Rated	High Season	Page
❶ p. 481	**La Posada de Taos**	◈◈◈	$129-$239 SAVE	484
❷ p. 481	**Dreamcatcher Bed & Breakfast**	◈◈◈	$115-$180 SAVE	483
❸ p. 481	Hotel La Fonda De Taos	◈◈◈	$99-$699	483
❹ p. 481	**Inn on La Loma Plaza**	◈◈◈◈	$175-$450 SAVE	483
❺ p. 481	**El Monte Sagrado, Autograph Collection**	◈◈◈◈	$169-$309 SAVE	483
❻ p. 481	**Casa de las Chimeneas Inn & Spa**	◈◈◈◈	$195-$325 SAVE	483
❼ p. 481	**American Artists Gallery House Bed & Breakfast**	◈◈◈	$95-$225 SAVE	483
❽ p. 481	**An Inn On The Rio**	◈◈◈	$125-$145 SAVE	483
❾ p. 481	Quality Inn	◈◈	Rates not provided	484
❿ p. 481	**San Geronimo Lodge**	◈◈◈	Rates not provided SAVE	484
⓫ p. 481	Comfort Suites	◈◈◈	Rates not provided	483
⓬ p. 481	Sagebrush Inn	◈◈◈	$79-$219	484
⓭ p. 481	Hampton Inn	◈◈◈	$109-$149	483

Map Page	Restaurants	Diamond Rated	Cuisine	Meal Range	Page
① p. 481	Orlando's New Mexican Cafe	◈◈	Mexican	$8-$12	485
② p. 481	Taos Pizza Outback	◈◈	Italian	$6-$20	485
③ p. 481	Dragonfly Cafe & Bakery	◈◈	American	$6-$17	485
④ p. 481	Michael's Kitchen	◈◈	American	$7-$18	485
⑤ p. 481	Bent Street Deli & Cafe	◈◈	American	$4-$13	484
⑥ p. 481	**Doc Martin's At The Historic Taos Inn**	◈◈◈	Regional American	$11-$26	484
⑦ p. 481	Graham's Grille	◈◈◈	Southwestern	$7-$20	485
⑧ p. 481	The Gorge Bar and Grill	◈◈	American	$9-$27	485
⑨ p. 481	Antonio's	◈◈	Mexican	$5-$17	484
⑩ p. 481	Eske's Brew Pub & Eatery	◈◈	American	$8-$10	485
⑪ p. 481	Byzantium	◈◈◈	American	$11-$26	484
⑫ p. 481	Downtown Bistro	◈◈◈	American	$9-$27	484
⑬ p. 481	**De la Tierra Restaurant**	◈◈◈	Southwestern	$8-$33	484
⑭ p. 481	Lambert's of Taos	◈◈◈	American	$10-$38	485
⑮ p. 481	Guadalajara Grill	◈	Mexican	$7-$16	485
⑯ p. 481	Los Vaqueros	◈◈	American	$13-$29	485

ARROYO SECO

Map Page	Hotels	Diamond Rated	High Season	Page
⓰ p. 481	Adobe and Stars B & B	◈◈◈	Rates not provided	388
⓱ p. 481	Cottonwood Inn Bed & Breakfast	◈◈◈	$125-$265	388

RANCHOS DE TAOS

Map Page	Restaurant	Diamond Rated	Cuisine	Meal Range	Page
⑲ p. 481	Trading Post Cafe & Italian Restaurant	◈◈	Italian	$8-$38	434

AMERICAN ARTISTS GALLERY HOUSE BED & BREAKFAST
Phone: (575)758-4446   **7**

Bed & Breakfast
$95-$225

Address: 132 Frontier Ln 87571 **Location:** 1 mi s of jct US 64 and Taos Plaza, 0.3 mi e. **Facility:** Local artwork that decorate the gallery and walls of every room represents the three diverse cultures that meet in Taos. 10 units, some kitchens. 1 story, interior/exterior corridors. **Terms:** 2-3 night minimum stay - seasonal and/or weekends, 14 day cancellation notice-fee imposed. **Activities:** whirlpool.

/ SOME UNITS FEE

Escape to one of Taos' Most Romantic Inns. Jacuzzi Suites. Wood Burning Fireplaces. Mountain Views.

AN INN ON THE RIO
Phone: 575/758-7199   **8**

Bed & Breakfast
$125-$145 5/16-1/31
$100-$125 2/1-5/15

Address: 910 Kit Carson Rd 87571 **Location:** US 64, 1.5 mi s of jct SR 68 and Taos Plaza. Located in a residential area. **Facility:** The exterior and interior murals and hand-painted furniture were done by two renowned, local folk artists. You'll find the inn just a short drive down Kit Carson Road from the historic Plaza. A patio beside the pool has picnic tables and a barbecue grill, as well as unusual garden "art". 12 units. 1 story, exterior corridors. **Terms:** office hours 8 am-8 pm, 14 day cancellation notice-fee imposed. **Pool(s):** heated outdoor. **Activities:** whirlpool, hiking trails, jogging. **Free Special Amenities: full breakfast and high-speed Internet.**

SAVE FEE / SOME UNITS FEE

CASA DE LAS CHIMENEAS INN & SPA
Phone: (575)758-4777   **6**

Bed & Breakfast
$195-$325 4/1-1/6
$120-$165 2/10-3/31

Address: 405 Cordoba Rd 87571 **Location:** From jct US 64 and SR 68, 0.3 mi s on SR 68, just e on Los Pandos Rd, then just s, follow signs; center. **Facility:** The lovely inn features welcoming fountains, gardens and patios throughout, colorful hand-painted tiles, skylights, well appointed rooms with upscale bed coverings and kiva fireplaces. In addition to a full breakfast, a light snack is offered in the early evening. 8 units. 1 story, exterior corridors. **Terms:** open 2/10-1/6, office hours 24 am-9 pm, 14 day cancellation notice. **Activities:** sauna, whirlpool, exercise room. *Fee:* massage. **Guest Services:** coin laundry. **Free Special Amenities: local telephone calls and high-speed Internet.** SAVE BIZ

COMFORT SUITES
Phone: 575/751-1555   **11**

Hotel
Rates not provided

Address: 1500 Paseo del Pueblo Sur 87571 **Location:** SR 68, 3 mi sw of jct US 64 and Taos Plaza. **Facility:** 60 units. 2 stories (no elevator), interior corridors. **Amenities:** high-speed Internet. **Pool(s):** heated outdoor. **Activities:** whirlpool. **Guest Services:** valet laundry.

CALL FEE BIZ

DREAMCATCHER BED & BREAKFAST
Phone: 575/758-0613   **2**

Bed & Breakfast
$115-$180

Address: 416 La Lomita Rd 87571 **Location:** From Taos Plaza, 0.5 mi sw on Don Fernando St (which becomes La Loma St), just w on San Antonio St. **Facility:** Relaxing is encouraged at this B&B, which offers hammocks in the large garden, a selection of board games and comfortable beds. 7 units, some two bedrooms. 1 story, exterior corridors. **Terms:** office hours 8 am-10 pm, check-in 4 pm, 15 day cancellation notice-fee imposed. **Free Special Amenities: full breakfast and high-speed Internet.**

EL MONTE SAGRADO, AUTOGRAPH COLLECTION
Phone: (575)828-8267   **5**

Hotel
$169-$309

AUTOGRAPH COLLECTION® **AAA Benefit:** Fresh, inventive and positively unique with special member savings.

Address: 317 Kit Carson Rd 87571 **Location:** 0.5 mi e of jct US 64 and SR 68. **Facility:** Select from several adobe-style cottage units, some with mountain views and a fireplace. A large patio area is available. 84 units, some two bedrooms. 2 stories, exterior corridors. **Parking:** valet only. **Terms:** check-in 4 pm, 3 day cancellation notice. **Amenities:** high-speed Internet (fee), safes. **Dining:** De la Tierra Restaurant, see separate listing. **Pool(s):** heated indoor. **Activities:** sauna, whirlpool, steamrooms, game room, exercise room, spa. **Guest Services:** valet laundry, area transportation-downtown. **Free Special Amenities: local telephone calls and newspaper.**

SAVE BIZ / SOME UNITS FEE

HAMPTON INN
Phone: (575)737-5700   **13**

Hotel
$109-$149

AAA Benefit: Members save up to 10% everyday!

Address: 1515 Paseo del Pueblo Sur 87571 **Location:** SR 68, 3 mi s of Taos Plaza. **Facility:** 71 units. 2 stories, interior corridors. **Terms:** 1-7 night minimum stay, cancellation fee imposed. **Amenities:** video games (fee). **Pool(s):** heated indoor. **Activities:** whirlpool, exercise room. **Guest Services:** coin laundry.

CALL BIZ / SOME UNITS FEE FEE

HOTEL LA FONDA DE TAOS
Phone: (575)758-2211   **3**

Historic Hotel
$99-$699

Address: 108 S Taos Plaza 87571 **Location:** Center. **Facility:** Located on Taos Plaza, this updated circa 1820s hotel is home to the scandalous D.H. Lawrence "Forbidden Art" collection banned from England in 1929. 25 units, some kitchens. 3 stories, interior corridors. **Terms:** age restrictions may apply, 7 day cancellation notice-fee imposed. **Amenities:** high-speed Internet. **Activities:** *Fee:* massage.

BIZ / SOME UNITS

INN ON LA LOMA PLAZA
Phone: (575)758-1717   **4**

Historic Bed & Breakfast
$175-$450

Address: 315 Ranchitos Rd 87571 **Location:** 0.3 mi sw on Ranchitos Rd, just w of Taos Plaza; in La Loma Plaza Historic District. **Facility:** This spacious historic fortress offers a variety of individually decorated guest rooms and features a beautiful view of the Sangre de Cristo Mountains. 10 units, some efficiencies. 2 stories (no elevator), interior/exterior corridors. **Terms:** office hours 6 am-10 pm, 2 night minimum stay - weekends, 15 day cancellation notice-fee imposed. **Amenities:** *Some:* high-speed Internet. **Activities:** whirlpool, limited exercise equipment. *Fee:* massage. **Guest Services:** valet laundry. **Free Special Amenities: full breakfast and high-speed Internet.**

SAVE BIZ / SOME UNITS FEE

LA POSADA DE TAOS   Phone: (575)758-8164 **1**

Historic Bed & Breakfast
$129-$239

Address: 309 Juanita Ln 87571 **Location:** From Taos Plaza, just w on Don Fernando St, just s on Manzanares St, then just w. **Facility:** The B&B has a shady courtyard garden, a bright sunroom and many historic architectural elements that enhance the décor. All rooms are on the ground floor. 6 units. 1 story, interior/exterior corridors. **Terms:** check-in 4 pm, 2 night minimum stay - weekends, 3 day cancellation notice. **Activities:** Fee: massage. **Free Special Amenities:** full breakfast and high-speed Internet.

SAVE ⌖ ✕ ☎ / SOME UNITS FEE ⌖ ⌖

QUALITY INN   Phone: 575/758-2200 **9**

Hotel
Rates not provided

Address: 1043 Paseo del Pueblo Sur 87571 **Location:** SR 68, 2 mi sw of jct US 64 and Taos Plaza. **Facility:** 99 units, some kitchens. 2 stories (no elevator), interior/exterior corridors. **Pool(s):** heated outdoor. **Activities:** whirlpool. **Guest Services:** valet laundry.

⌖ ⌖ ⌖ ⌖ FEE ⌖ ⌖ ⌖ ⌖ ⌖ / SOME UNITS FEE ⌖

SAGEBRUSH INN   Phone: (575)758-2254 **12**

Historic Hotel
$79-$219

Address: 1508 Paseo del Pueblo Sur 87571 **Location:** SR 68, 3 mi sw of jct US 64 and Taos Plaza. **Facility:** Originally built in the late 1920s as accommodations for adventurous travelers heading west, the hotel retains its southwest Pueblo-style charm. 100 units. 1-2 stories (no elevator), exterior corridors. **Dining:** Los Vaqueros, see separate listing, entertainment. **Pool(s):** heated outdoor. **Activities:** whirlpools. **Guest Services:** valet laundry.

⌖ ⌖ FEE ⌖ BIZ ⌖ ⌖ ⌖ / SOME UNITS FEE ⌖ ⌖

SAN GERONIMO LODGE   Phone: 575/751-3776 **10**

Historic Bed & Breakfast
Rates not provided

Address: 1101 Witt Rd 87571 **Location:** 1.3 mi e of jct SR 68 and Taos Plaza on US 64, 0.6 mi s. Located in a quiet country area. **Facility:** A meditation garden and labyrinth enhance the setting of this 1925 adobe lodge. Large units are nicely appointed with locally-made furnishings and art. 18 units. 2 stories (no elevator), interior/exterior corridors. **Terms:** office hours 6 am-8 pm. **Pool(s):** heated outdoor. **Activities:** whirlpool. Fee: massage. **Free Special Amenities:** full breakfast and high-speed Internet.

SAVE ⌖ BIZ ⌖ ✕ ⌖ / SOME UNITS FEE ⌖ ⌖

Historic grand lodge B & B, labyrinth, decks, mtn. views, wi-fi, hot tub, serene 3-acre prayer path.

BURCH STREET CASITAS   Phone: 575/737-9038

fyi Not evaluated. **Address:** 310 Burch St 87571 **Location:** US 64, just e of jct SR 68, then just s. Facilities, services, and decor characterize a mid-scale property.

WHERE TO EAT

ANTONIO'S   Phone: 575/751-4800 **9**

Mexican
$5-$17

AAA Inspector Notes: Enjoy patio dining or sit inside to admire the local artwork adorning the walls. Generous portions of flavorful traditional Mexican specialties line the menu. Prepared tableside, the guacamole is a favorite. **Bar:** beer & wine. **Address:** 122 B Doña Luz St 87571 **Location:** Just w of Taos Plaza. L D ⌖

BENT STREET DELI & CAFE   Phone: 575/758-5787 **5**

American
$4-$13

AAA Inspector Notes: A block off Taos Plaza, this eatery's patio seating is a nice good-weather option. **Bar:** beer & wine. **Address:** 120 Bent St 87571 **Location:** Just n of Taos Plaza, just w of US 64. **Parking:** street only.

 B L ⌖

BYZANTIUM   Phone: 575/751-0805 **11**

American
$11-$26

AAA Inspector Notes: A visit to Taos is not complete without a meal at the distinctive restaurant. All of the dishes are creative, attractively presented and wonderful in taste. Friendly staff take good care of patrons. **Bar:** beer & wine. **Reservations:** required. **Address:** 112 La Placita 87571 **Location:** Just s of Taos Plaza; in Courtyard at Ledoux and La Placita. D ⌖

DE LA TIERRA RESTAURANT   Phone: 575/758-3502 **13**

Southwestern
$8-$33

AAA Inspector Notes: The cuisine is primarily Southwestern at this upscale restaurant, with such exotic game offerings as elk and quail as well as halibut, salmon, beef and lamb. Diners will find an extensive selection of wines to complement main courses. **Bar:** full bar. **Reservations:** suggested. **Address:** 317 Kit Carson Rd 87571 **Location:** 0.5 mi e of jct US 64 and SR 68; in El Monte Sagrado, Autograph Collection. **Parking:** on-site and valet. D

DOC MARTIN'S AT THE HISTORIC TAOS INN
Menu on AAA.com   Phone: 575/758-1977 **6**

Regional American
$11-$26

AAA Inspector Notes: Piñon-crusted salmon and Southwestern lacquered duck are among dishes combining New American and New Mexican influences. Tempting desserts too luscious to miss include citrus cheesecake and chocolate mousse with roasted banana sauce. Diners can watch the world go by on the outside patio, a local gathering spot. **Bar:** full bar. **Reservations:** suggested, for dinner and brunch. **Address:** 125 Paseo del Pueblo Norte 87571 **Location:** On US 64, just n of jct SR 68 and Taos Plaza; center; in The Historic Taos Inn. **Historic**

 B L D

DOWNTOWN BISTRO   Phone: 575/737-5060 **12**

American
$9-$27

AAA Inspector Notes: This bistro takes pride in transforming food into art. The menu changes frequently but always lists something to tantalize the taste buds. **Bar:** beer & wine. **Address:** 223 Paseo del Pueblo Sur 87571 **Location:** SR 68, 0.3 mi sw of jct US 64 and Taos Plaza; at Pueblo Alegre Mall. L D

Visit AAA.com or CAA.ca for one-stop travel planning and reservations

DRAGONFLY CAFE & BAKERY
Phone: 575/737-5859 (3)

▼▼▼
American
$6-$17

AAA Inspector Notes: This cheerful, cozy café brings a touch of European bistro to the city. The eclectic menu lines up chef Karen Todd's fresh creations. Dragonflies appear in unexpected places, including one cut from the pastry of the pot pie. Varying daily, baked goods and chocolates also tempt. **Bar:** beer & wine. **Address:** 402 Paseo del Pueblo Norte 87571 **Location:** Just n of Taos Plaza. **Parking:** street only. (L) (D) (AC)

ESKE'S BREW PUB & EATERY
Phone: 575/758-1517 (10)

▼▼
American
$8-$10

AAA Inspector Notes: Bright, cheery and smoke-free, this is a great place to sample beer and root beer brewed on site, or nosh on such pub favorites as the club sandwich: a hearty stack of meat between two slices of beer-battered oat bread. **Bar:** beer & wine. **Address:** 106 Des Georges Ln 87571 **Location:** Just w of Taos Plaza.
(L) (D) (AC)

THE GORGE BAR AND GRILL
Phone: 575/758-8866 (8)

▼▼▼
American
$9-$27

AAA Inspector Notes: The contemporary setting and lively atmosphere of this establishment offers an excellent view for people watching on the plaza below while enjoying a great meal and cocktail from the extensive beverage list. **Bar:** full bar. **Address:** 103-1 E Palace 87571 **Location:** On the Plaza, upstairs in The Shops @103. **Parking:** street only. (L) (D) CALL (&M)

GRAHAM'S GRILLE
Phone: 575/751-1350 (7)

▼▼▼
Southwestern
$7-$20

AAA Inspector Notes: Enjoy Southwest cuisine with international flair in a lively contemporary atmosphere. With taos tamale pie, falafel burger and Tuscan-style grilled veal chops on the menu, patrons can travel from New Mexico to the Middle East to Italy in a matter of minutes. On your return back, sample the luscious mango coconut cake. **Bar:** beer & wine. **Reservations:** suggested. **Address:** 106 Paseo del Pueblo Norte 87571 **Location:** Center of town; just n of Taos Plaza. (B) (L) (D)

GUADALAJARA GRILL
Phone: 575/751-0063 (15)

▼
Mexican
$7-$16

AAA Inspector Notes: This Mexican restaurant packs its menu with all the staples, including tacos, burritos and seafood enchiladas, but the specialty is shrimp and prepared in a variety of traditional ways. Orders are taken at the counter, and cordial servers deliver them to the table. **Bar:** beer & wine. **Address:** 1384 Paseo del Pueblo Sur 87571 **Location:** SR 68, 2.7 mi s of Taos Plaza.
(L) (D)

LAMBERT'S OF TAOS
Phone: 575/758-1009 (14)

▼▼▼
American
$10-$38

AAA Inspector Notes: A short walk from the plaza, this restaurant is surrounded by trees and a small garden. Attentive, friendly servers circulate through the dining room with complimentary aperitifs and dishes such as pepper-crusted lamb loin with red wine demi-glace. Decadent chocolate mousse with raspberry sauce is served in a portion large enough to share. **Bar:** full bar. **Reservations:** suggested. **Address:** 309 Paseo del Pueblo Sur 87571 **Location:** SR 68, 0.4 mi sw of jct US 64 and Taos Plaza. (D)

LOS VAQUEROS
Phone: 575/758-2254 (16)

▼▼
American
$13-$29

AAA Inspector Notes: This restaurant presents a menu of varied steaks, seafood and Mexican offerings. The salad bar is a good meal accompaniment. **Bar:** full bar. **Address:** 1508 Paseo del Pueblo Sur 87571 **Location:** SR 68, 3 mi sw of jct US 64 and Taos Plaza; in Sagebrush Inn. (D)

MICHAEL'S KITCHEN
Phone: 575/758-4178 (4)

▼▼▼
American
$7-$18

AAA Inspector Notes: Just north of Taos Plaza and a short distance from the pueblo, the bustling eatery has a rustic atmosphere and an on-site bakery. All-day breakfast items are served alongside standards such as nachos, tamales, burgers, chicken tacos, salads and enchiladas. **Address:** 304C Paseo del Pueblo Norte 87571 **Location:** US 64, 0.3 mi n of jct SR 68 and Taos Plaza. (B) (L) (D)

ORLANDO'S NEW MEXICAN CAFE
Phone: 575/751-1450 (1)

▼▼
Mexican
$8-$12

AAA Inspector Notes: This lively and colorful spot offers cozy inside seating or popular umbrella tables outdoors. Fresh Mexican eats include burritos, enchiladas, tamales, chiles rellenos, chimichangas, tacos and yummy nacho dishes. **Bar:** beer & wine. **Address:** 1114 Don Juan Valdez Ln 87571 **Location:** 1.8 mi n on US 64.
(L) (D)

TAOS PIZZA OUTBACK
Phone: 575/758-3112 (2)

▼▼
Italian
$6-$20

AAA Inspector Notes: At the heart of the menu at this eatery are freshly made pizza, calzones and pasta dishes. The quaint restaurant proudly serves local and organic produce, which means the salads are mighty tasty. Desserts are displayed near the entrance so diners can plan ahead. **Bar:** beer & wine. **Address:** 712 Paseo de Pueblo Norte 87571 **Location:** Just nw of jct Camino de la Placita. (L) (D)

TESUQUE PUEBLO (B-4) elev. 6,365'

Named by the Tewa-speaking people for the "village at the narrow place of the cottonwood trees," Tesuque (te-SOO-kay) rests in the foothills of the Sangre de Cristo Mountains. The pueblo is just south of Camel Rock, one of many unusual sandstone formations in the area.

TESUQUE PUEBLO is off US 84/285. Tewa-speaking people founded the present settlement in the late 17th century, although habitation dates to 1200 A.D. The 1915 San Diego Mission, designed in the shape of a crucifix, stands on the main plaza. The Pueblos, who have retained their traditional language and culture, hold Three Kings Day festivities in January, a ceremonial Corn Dance the first Saturday in June and the Feast of San Diego on Nov. 12. **Hours:** The pueblo closes to the public on certain days. Phone ahead to confirm schedule. **Cost:** Free. **Phone:** (505) 983-2667.

THREE RIVERS (H-3) elev. 4,568'

Watered by runoff from the surrounding mountains, the grazing lands of the upper Tularosa Valley attracted cattle barons in the 1870s. Three Rivers, once a railroad shipping point, maintains a ranching and farming economy.

THREE RIVERS PETROGLYPH SITE is 5 mi. e. on CR B30 from US 54 following signs. A large group of prehistoric picture writings includes more than 21,000 individual petroglyphs. The Jornada branch of the Mogollon culture is thought to have inscribed them A.D. 900-1400. A trail links many petroglyph sites. **Hours:** Daily 8-7, Apr.-Oct.; 8-5 rest of year. **Cost:** $2 (per private vehicle). **Phone:** (575) 525-4300. 🄰 🄰

TRUTH OR CONSEQUENCES (H-3)
pop. 6,475, elev. 4,242'

Playing host to a live broadcast of the radio program "Truth or Consequences" changed not only Hot Springs' future but also its name. So pleased were residents with the publicity engendered by Ralph Edwards' popular show that they adopted the program's name in 1950.

The fire of the chilies—one of the Rio Grande Valley's major crops—is nearly matched by the 110 F of the thermal springs that bubble to the surface in Truth or Consequences. The mineral springs have been enjoyed for their legendary curative properties since the days when only the Apaches knew of them. Inevitably, popular bathhouses grew up around the springs in the early 20th century.

Elephant Butte Lake State Park in Elephant Butte and Caballo Lake State Park in Caballo offer water activities. *See Recreation Chart.*

Geronimo Trail Interpretive Visitors Center: 211 Main St., Truth or Consequences, NM 87901. **Phone:** (575) 894-1968.

GERONIMO SPRINGS MUSEUM is 211 Main St. The museum houses American Indian artifacts; prehistoric Mimbres pottery; ranching, military and mining items; paleontological and geological finds; a reconstructed log cabin; Southwestern art; and mementos of Ralph Edwards, originator of the "Truth or Consequences" radio show. **Time:** Allow 1 hour, 30 minutes minimum. **Hours:** Mon.-Sat. 9-5, Sun. noon-5. Closed Jan. 1, Easter, July 4, Thanksgiving and Christmas. **Cost:** $6; $5 (ages 55+ and active and retired military with ID); $3 (ages 6-18); $15 (family). **Phone:** (575) 894-6600.

COMFORT INN & SUITES   **Phone:** (575)894-1660
◆◆◆
Hotel
$80-$125
Address: 2250 N Date St 87901 **Location:** I-25 exit 79, just e. **Facility:** 50 units. 2 stories (no elevator), interior corridors. **Terms:** 2 night minimum stay - seasonal and/or weekends, cancellation fee imposed **Pool(s):** heated indoor. **Activities:** whirlpool, exercise room. **Guest Services:** valet and coin laundry.
🄰 🄰 CALL 🄰🄰 🄰 BIZ 🄰 🄰 🄰
/ SOME UNITS 🄰 🄰

SIERRA GRANDE LODGE & SPA   **Phone:** 575/894-6976
◆◆◆
Boutique Hotel
$99-$445
Address: 501 McAdoo St 87901 **Location:** Just w of Foch St; center. **Facility:** Tastefully restored, this neo-rustic downtown hotel features an elegant western flair. The spa offers spring mineral baths and holistic treatments. 18 units, some kitchens and houses. 2 stories (no elevator), interior/exterior corridors. **Activities:** whirlpools, spa. **Guest Services:** valet laundry. 🄰 🄰 🄰 🄰 / SOME UNITS FEE 🄰

WHERE TO EAT

BAR-B-QUE ON BROADWAY   **Phone:** 575/894-7047
◆◆
Barbecue
$7-$13
AAA Inspector Notes: The barbecue brisket tastes great and the portions are generous at this busy café. The combination of fast service, a good selection of sandwiches and daily specials have made this stop a local favorite. **Address:** 308 N Broadway 87901 **Location:** I-25 exit 79, 1.9 mi se. 🄱 🄛

CAFE BELLALUCA   **Phone:** 575/894-9866
◆◆◆
Italian
$6-$20
AAA Inspector Notes: The eatery's casual contemporary atmosphere is inviting and the service welcoming. The menu includes creative hand-tossed pizza and calzones, plus a mouth-watering selection of pasta and Italian entrées. The wild mushroom ravioli or grilled pizza with roasted garlic, goat cheese and onion marmalade are menu favorites. **Bar:** beer & wine. **Address:** 303 Jones St 87901 **Location:** Center. 🄛 🄓

LA COCINA RESTAURANT   **Phone:** 575/894-6499
◆◆◆
Mexican
$6-$30
AAA Inspector Notes: The sign out front says "hot stuff," and sure enough the New Mexican cuisine has real authority in the chile department. Red and green varieties are made from fresh ingredients, making all dishes burst with originality and flavor. Interesting artistic accents-such as tabletops and hand-crafted chairs-are rustic yet elegant. **Bar:** beer & wine. **Address:** 1 Lakeway Dr 87901 **Location:** I-25 exit 79, just e, jct Date St. 🄛 🄓

LOS ARCOS   **Phone:** 575/894-6200
◆◆◆
Steak
$14-$37
AAA Inspector Notes: This local favorite serves a wide variety of steaks and prime rib along with a selection of seafood. One of the steak and seafood combinations is just the ticket for a special occasion. Also good are the salads and desserts. **Bar:** full bar. **Reservations:** suggested. **Address:** 1400 N Date St 87901 **Location:** I-25 exit 83, 0.5 mi e. 🄓

PACIFIC GRILL   **Phone:** 575/894-7687
◆◆◆
Seafood
$7-$15
AAA Inspector Notes: A tropical theme with bamboo and grass sets the mood for a meal of fine Pacific Rim cuisine. Fresh seafood and other ingredients merge in healthful, tasty meals. **Bar:** beer & wine. **Address:** 800 N Date St 87901 **Location:** Center. 🄛 🄓

TUCUMCARI (F-5) pop. 5,363, elev. 4,086'

Established with the Rock Island Railroad in 1901, Tucumcari supposedly takes its name from the 4,999-foot Tucumcari Mountain once used by the Comanches as a lookout point, or *tucumcari*.

A more sentimental theory, however, traces the origin of the name to the legend of an ill-fated romance between the Apache warrior Tocom and Kari, the daughter of an Apache chief. When Tocom died in a fight for Kari's hand, Kari stabbed the victor, then herself. Witness to the tragic scene, her father also ended his life with a dagger, crying out "Tocom-Kari."

In the 1920s Tucumcari became the first stop in New Mexico for westbound travelers on the new federal highway, Route 66. The 2,448-mile road stretching between Chicago and Los Angeles was credited with connecting New Mexico to the rest of the nation. For some 40 years it was one of America's best-known routes for commerce and leisure travel. The interstate highway system eventually supplanted Route 66, which was officially decertified in 1985. Landmarks from the heydays remain. In Tucumcari, neon-lit motor courts and a teepee shaped curios shop are among the more prominent sites.

The two Canadian River reservoirs that irrigate 45,000 acres around the city also provide water sports and other recreation. Conchas Lake is 34 miles northwest via SR 104; Ute Lake is 23 miles northeast via SR 54 at Logan. *See Recreation Chart.*

Tucumcari-Quay County Chamber of Commerce: 404 W. Rte. 66, P.O. Drawer E, Tucumcari, NM 88401. **Phone:** (575) 461-1694.

MESALANDS DINOSAUR MUSEUM is at 222 E. Laughlin St. The 11,000-square-foot exhibit hall showcases original and replicated fossils, skeletons and sculptures from the Mesozoic era. One of the highlights includes a centerpiece display of *Torvosaurus*, a rare carnivorous dinosaur related to *Tyrannosaurus Rex*. **Time:** Allow 1 hour minimum. **Hours:** Tues.-Sat. 10-6, Mar 1-Labor Day; Tues.-Sat. noon-5, rest of year. Closed Jan. 1, Thanksgiving and Christmas. **Cost:** $6.50; $5.50 (ages 65+); $4.50 (students with ID); $4 (ages 5-11). **Phone:** (575) 461-3466.

TUCUMCARI HISTORICAL MUSEUM is at 416 S. Adams St. A 1903 schoolhouse contains three floors of regional artifacts and memorabilia. Thematic exhibits include a pioneer kitchen, general store, bunkhouse, courthouse room, barn, firehouse with a 1926 fire truck and a tribute to the Armed Forces. Native landscaping surrounds the museum and provides the setting for outdoor exhibits including a railroad caboose. **Hours:** Tues.-Sat. 9-3. Closed major holidays. **Cost:** $5; $4 (ages 65+); $1 (ages 6-15). **Phone:** (575) 461-4201.

BEST WESTERN DISCOVERY INN
Phone: (575)461-4884

Hotel
$89-$120

AAA Benefit: Members save up to 20%, plus 10% bonus points with Best Western Rewards®.

Address: 200 E Estrella Ave 88401 **Location:** I-40 exit 332, just n. **Facility:** 80 units. 2 stories (no elevator), exterior corridors. **Pool(s):** heated indoor. **Activities:** exercise room. **Guest Services:** coin laundry. **Free Special Amenities:** local telephone calls and high-speed Internet.

DAYS INN
Phone: (575)461-3158

Hotel
$57-$72

Address: 2623 S 1st St 88401 **Location:** I-40 exit 332, just n. **Facility:** 40 units. 2 stories (no elevator), interior/exterior corridors. **Amenities:** high-speed Internet.

HAMPTON INN
Phone: 575/461-1111

Hotel
Rates not provided

AAA Benefit: Members save up to 10% everyday!

Address: 3409 E Route 66 88401 **Location:** I-40 exit 335, 0.7 mi w. **Facility:** 58 units. 3 stories, interior corridors. **Amenities:** high-speed Internet. **Pool(s):** heated indoor. **Activities:** sauna, whirlpool, exercise room. **Guest Services:** coin laundry.

HOLIDAY INN EXPRESS HOTEL & SUITES
Phone: (575)461-3333

Hotel
$109-$129 6/1-1/31
$99-$119 2/1-5/31

Address: 2624 S Adams St 88401 **Location:** I-40 exit 332, just n. **Facility:** 80 units. 3 stories, interior corridors. **Amenities:** high-speed Internet. **Pool(s):** heated indoor. **Activities:** sauna, whirlpool, basketball, game room, exercise room. **Guest Services:** coin laundry. **Free Special Amenities:** expanded continental breakfast and high-speed Internet.

LA QUINTA INN & SUITES TUCUMCARI
Phone: (575)461-2233

Hotel
$98-$160

Address: 2516 S Adams St 88401 **Location:** I-40 exit 335, just n. **Facility:** 66 units. 3 stories, interior corridors. **Amenities:** high-speed Internet. **Pool(s):** heated indoor. **Activities:** whirlpool, exercise room. **Guest Services:** coin laundry. **Free Special Amenities:** expanded continental breakfast and high-speed Internet.

RODEWAY INN
Phone: (575)461-4094

Hotel
$40-$110

Address: 2800 E Tucumcari Blvd 88401 **Location:** I-40 exit 335, 0.5 mi w. **Facility:** 59 units. 2 stories (no elevator), exterior corridors. **Amenities:** *Some:* high-speed Internet. **Pool(s):** outdoor.

SUPER 8
Phone: (575)461-4444

Motel
$47-$50

Address: 4001 Old Route 66 88401 **Location:** I-40 exit 335, just w. **Facility:** 62 units. 2 stories (no elevator), interior corridors. **Parking:** winter plug-ins. **Terms:** cancellation fee imposed. **Pool(s):** heated indoor.

WHERE TO EAT

BRANDING IRON RESTAURANT
Phone: 575/461-3780

American
$7-$18

AAA Inspector Notes: Pleasing service awaits patrons of this restaurant, which offers a nice cross-section of American fare. Dinner specials are prepared daily. **Bar:** full bar. **Address:** 3716 E Tucumcari Blvd 88401 **Location:** I-40 exit 335, 0.3 mi w on Route 66; in Quality Inn.

DEL'S RESTAURANT　　　Phone: 575/461-1740

♦♦♦ ♦♦♦

American

$7-$17

AAA Inspector Notes: Colorful Southwestern decor punctuates the dining room at this casual, family restaurant located on historic Route 66. Established in 1956, this spot is a local favorite that features American and Mexican dishes. Check out the gift area offering interesting Route 66 and New Mexico souvenirs. **Address:** 1202 E Route 66 88401 **Location:** I-40 exit 333, 1.5 mi n on Mountain Rd, then 0.5 mi w. [L] [D]

K BOB'S STEAKHOUSE　　　Phone: 575/461-0017

♦♦♦ ♦♦♦

American

$5-$24

AAA Inspector Notes: A well-stocked all-you-can-eat salad bar plus a variety of steaks and burgers are offered at this family eatery as well as some fish items. **Address:** 200 W Estrella Ave 88401 **Location:** I-40 exit 332, just n.

[L] [D]

KIX ON 66 COFFEE SHOP & EATERY
　　　Phone: 575/461-1966

♦♦♦ ♦♦♦

American

$5-$9

AAA Inspector Notes: This retro diner serves generous breakfasts and lunch sandwiches and salads. Ice cream sundaes, shakes and floats are a specialty. **Address:** 1102 E Route 66 Blvd 88401 **Location:** I-40 exit 332, 1.5 mi n on Mountain Rd, then just e on Historic Route 66. [B] [L]

POW-WOW RESTAURANT　　　Phone: 575/461-2587

♦♦♦ ♦♦♦

American

$6-$20

AAA Inspector Notes: On historic Route 66, this local favorite offers cocktails plus a wide variety of steaks, chicken, seafood and Mexican food entrées. Save room for luscious homemade pies. **Bar:** full bar. **Address:** 801 W Tucumcari Blvd 88401 **Location:** I-40 exit 332, 1 mi n to Tucumcari Blvd, then 1 mi w.

[B] [L] [D]

ROCKIN' YS' ROADHOUSE　　　Phone: 575/461-9947

♦♦♦ ♦♦♦

American

$6-$15

AAA Inspector Notes: Favored by locals this casual spot serves breakfast all day and offers a variety of American and Mexican specialties. **Bar:** beer & wine. **Address:** 1806 E Route 66 Blvd 88401 **Location:** I-40 exit 333, 0.5 mi n; jct US 54 and Historic Route 66.

[B] [L] [D]

TULAROSA (H-4) pop. 2,842, elev. 4,508'

WINERIES

• **Tularosa Vineyards** is at 23 Coyote Canyon Rd. Tastings offered. Tours are given by appointment; phone ahead. **Hours:** Mon.-Sat. 9-5, Sun. noon-5. **Phone:** (575) 585-2260 or (800) 687-4467.

CASA DE SUEÑOS　　　Phone: 575/585-3494

♦♦♦ ♦♦♦

Mexican

$7-$16

AAA Inspector Notes: Flavorful Mexican dishes and generous portions make this a favorite stop for locals and travelers alike. The dining room features a lively and colorful atmosphere. **Bar:** beer & wine. **Address:** 35 St. Francis Dr 88352 **Location:** Just s on US 54/70. [L] [D]

WHITE ROCK pop. 5,725

LOS ALAMOS HAMPTON INN & SUITES
　　　Phone: (505)672-3838

♦♦♦ ♦♦♦

Hotel

$95-$105

AAA Benefit:
Members save up to 10% everyday!

Address: 124 SR 4 87544 **Location:** Center. **Facility:** 72 units, some kitchens. 3 stories, interior corridors. **Terms:** check-in 4 pm, 1-7 night minimum stay, cancellation fee imposed. **Amenities:** high-speed Internet. **Activities:** sauna, exercise room. **Guest Services:** valet and coin laundry.

[I+] CALL [&M] [BIZ] [📶] [🅿] [▭] [▭]

WHITE SANDS MISSILE RANGE (D-3)
elev. 4,295'

On July 16, 1945, in a remote section of White Sands Missile Range, the first man-made atomic explosion sent a huge multicolored cloud surging to an altitude of 40,000 feet. The resultant sloping crater at Trinity Site is mute evidence of man's transition to the Atomic Age.

With the advent of the Space Age, rocket testing took center stage. In the 1960s the desert proved ideal for testing the lunar module engines that propelled Apollo astronauts off the moon's surface. Today the missile range is known for its world-class test facilities. The U.S. Army as well as private industry and foreign nations conduct laser, radar and flight research here.

Vehicle passes are issued at the main gate; a valid driver's license, registration and proof of insurance are required. Photo ID is required for all car occupants over age 16. Trinity Site is open the first Saturdays in April and in October. Contact the Public Affairs Office, Bldg. 1782, White Sands Missile Range, NM 88002. Phone (575) 678-1134, or the Alamogordo Chamber of Commerce at (575) 437-6120 or (800) 826-0294.

 WHITE SANDS MISSILE RANGE MUSEUM is 19 mi. n.e. of Las Cruces on US 70/80, then 4 mi. e. to just inside main gate. The history of the nation's missile program and the Atomic Age is presented with artifacts, displays and photographs depicting early rocket launches and the first atomic bomb test at Trinity Site. An outdoor park displays some 60 rockets and missiles, including a restored German V-2 rocket exhibited horizontally to reveal its interior.

Exhibits about Paleo-Indian culture as well as 19th-century mining and ranching also are offered. **Time:** Allow 30 minutes minimum. **Hours:** Mon.-Fri. 8-4, Sat. 10-3. Missile park daily dawn-dusk. Closed major holidays. **Cost:** Free. **Phone:** (575) 678-8824. [▭]

WHITE SANDS NATIONAL MONUMENT (I-3)

About 15 miles southwest of Alamogordo on US 70, White Sands National Monument is the source of rare gypsum sands that form snow-white dunes rising up to 60 feet above the Tularosa Basin floor.

Covering 275 square miles, the massive dunes are created when rain and melting snow dissolve gypsum from the surrounding mountains and carry it into the seasonal lake, or *playa*, of Lake Lucero. Desert heat evaporates the *playa*, causing gypsum crystals to form. Dry winds expose the crystals, eroding them into sand-sized particles that are blown into the dune field.

Much of the wide sea of dunes is bare of vegetation. However, a few species of plants exhibit remarkable adaptation to the shifting sands; the soaptree yucca can stretch its stem up to 30 feet to keep from being buried.

Drinking water is available only at the visitor center; covered picnic sites and restrooms are in the heart of the dunes area. A visitor center relates the origin and history of White Sands through interactive exhibits and a videotape presentation that is shown every half hour.

Ranger-guided sunset strolls are offered daily 1 hour before sunset except on Christmas. Several hiking trails are available; brochures describing desert hiking safety can be obtained at the visitor center. On full-moon nights from May through October, the park remains open until 11 p.m. so visitors can witness the celestial light reflecting off the dunes; full-moon ranger-led hikes are available by advance reservation. Music and educational programs pertaining to New Mexico heritage and the monument's geology, plants and animals also are presented on full-moon nights.

The scenic 16-mile round-trip Dunes Drive can be entered daily 7 a.m.-9 p.m., Memorial Day weekend-Labor Day; 7 a.m.-dusk, rest of year; subject to closures of up to 3 hours during missile testing. Visitors must exit the park by 1 hour after dusk, except on full-moon nights May-Oct. Visitor center is open daily 8-5; closed Christmas. Admission (valid for 7 days) $3; free (ages 0-15). Phone (575) 679-2599.

WHITES CITY (I-5) pop. 7, elev. 3,660'

James Larkin White first explored Carlsbad Caverns as a teenager, carving his name into the rock wall in 1898. He spent the rest of his life promoting the cave and succeeded in having it named a national park in 1930. Around that time, Charles White—no relation to James—bought a 120-acre homestead near the entrance to the caves, and Whites City became the base for a series of guano

mining companies, all of which failed. The town today is a stopover for visitors to the national park.

ZIA PUEBLO (B-3) pop. 737, elev. 5,470'

Once one of the largest of the Rio Grande pueblos with some 6,000 residents, Zia now is a community of less than 650 people. Zia potters are renowned for their geometric designs and plant and animal motifs on a white background; thin-walled pottery adorned with the Zia bird symbol is highly prized.

ZIA PUEBLO AND MISSION is off US 550 at 135 Capital Square Dr. Settled in the 13th century, the pueblo stands on a barren mesa where it blends almost invisibly with the natural terrain. New Mexico adopted the pueblo's ancient Zia sun symbol to adorn the state flag. The Zia Cultural Center sells and displays traditional crafts.

Photography, sketching and recording are not allowed. A permit is required for fishing on Zia Lake. **Hours:** Daily dawn-dusk. Cultural center Mon.-Fri. 8-5; hours may vary. Closed during some ceremonial events. Phone ahead to confirm schedule. **Cost:** Free. **Phone:** (505) 867-3304, ext. 239.

ZUNI PUEBLO (F-1) pop. 6,302, elev. 6,282'

About 30 miles south of Gallup *(see place listing p. 411)* via SRs 602 and 53, Zuni is the only surviving settlement of the Seven Cities of Cíbola sought by Francisco Vázquez de Coronado in his quest for gold. It is among the largest of existing inhabited pueblos. Fray Marcos de Niza, bringing the first contact with Europeans in 1539, was followed by Coronado, Juan de Oñate and Franciscan padres, who found the people unresponsive to Christianity.

Long considered master carvers, the Zuni are renowned for their quality inlay jewelry of silver, jet, shell and turquoise, including needlepoint work of finely cut turquoise in silver, and for carved animal fetishes. Ancient rites and traditions are still preserved. Ceremonial dances are held throughout the year.

Photography, videotaping, sketching and hiking are allowed by permit only. Permits must be obtained from the Zuni visitor center; phone (505) 782-7238. More information is available at the Zuni A:shiwi A:wan Museum & Heritage Center; phone (505) 782-4403.

Make Your Next Trip a Journey ... With AAA and Hertz.

For reservations, **visit** your AAA/CAA travel office, **click** on AAA.com/hertz or CAA.ca/hertz, or **call** 800-654-3080 U.S./ 888-333-3120 Canada.

ENJOY A MAGICAL DISNEY VACATION WITH

What's the best way to experience all the enchantment of a vacation to the *Walt Disney World*® Resort in Florida or the *Disneyland*® Resort in California? How do you squeeze the most magic out of the Theme Parks and the whimsically themed *Disney Resort* hotels? And how can you enjoy great savings and exclusive benefits not available anywhere else? By booking a *AAA Vacations*® package from AAA Travel, of course!

DISNEYLAND® RESORT, CALIFORNIA

- Stay just steps away from the magic at a *Disneyland*® Resort Hotel.

- Catch World of Color, a nighttime spectacular at *Disney California Adventure*™ Park.

Disneyland® Resort Hotels

World of Color

LET AAA BE YOUR GUIDE...

With a *AAA Vacations*® package, you can create the Disney vacation that fits your family, your taste and your budget. And not only will your AAA Travel professional help put everything (like accommodations, flights and tickets) together, you'll also get to enjoy great Disney benefits on top of the exclusive AAA benefits and savings once you get there! Then all you need to do is relax and have fun.

ENCHANTING AAA BENEFITS!

WALT DISNEY WORLD RESORT, FLORIDA

- Enjoy amazing theming at a *Walt Disney World®* Resort hotel.

- Experience magical moments in all four Theme Parks.

Disney's BoardWalk Resort

Theme Park magic

READY TO START MAKING MAGIC?
Then contact your **AAA Travel professional** today!

©Disney WDWSALES-10-18431

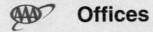 Offices

Cities with main offices are listed in **BOLD TYPE** and toll-free member service numbers in *ITALIC TYPE*.
All are closed Saturdays, Sundays and holidays unless otherwise indicated.
The addresses, phone numbers and hours for any AAA/CAA office are subject to change.
The type of service provided is designated below the name of the city where the office is located:

✛ Auto travel services, including books and maps, and on-demand TripTik® routings.

● Auto travel services, including selected books and maps, and on-demand TripTik® routings.

■ Books/maps only, no marked maps or on-demand TripTik® routings.

▲ Travel Agency Services, cruise, tour, air, car and rail reservations; domestic and international hotel reservations; passport photo services; international and domestic travel guides and maps; travel money products; and International Driving Permits. In addition, assistance with travel related insurance products including trip cancellation, travel accident, lost luggage, trip delay and assistance products.

○ Insurance services provided. If only this icon appears, only insurance services are provided at that office.

✖ Car Care Plus Facility provides car care services.

AAA NATIONAL OFFICE: 1000 AAA DRIVE, HEATHROW, FLORIDA 32746-5063, (407) 444-7000

ARIZONA

CHANDLER—AAA ARIZONA, 4040 W RAY RD STE 2, 85226. WEEKDAYS (M-F) 8:30-5:30. (602) 230-3601 ✛▲○✖

GOODYEAR—AAA ARIZONA, 790 N ESTRELLA PKWY STE C, 85338. WEEKDAYS (M-F) 9:00-5:30. (602) 230-3170 ✛▲○✖

MESA—AAA ARIZONA, 4126 E VALLEY AUTO DR, 85206. WEEKDAYS (M-F) 7:00-6:00, SAT 8:00-4:00. (602) 308-3080 ✖

MESA—AAA ARIZONA, 4126 E VALLEY AUTO DR, 85206. WEEKDAYS (M-F) 9:00-6:00. (602) 241-3901 ✛▲○

PEORIA—AAA ARIZONA, 7422 W THUNDERBIRD RD, 85381. WEEKDAYS (M-F) 7:00-6:00, SAT 8:00-4:00. (602) 308-3080 ✖

PEORIA—AAA ARIZONA, 7422 W THUNDERBIRD RD, 85381. WEEKDAYS (M-F) 9:00-6:00. (602) 230-3101 ✛▲○

PHOENIX—AAA ARIZONA, 1050 E CAMELBACK RD, 85014. WEEKDAYS (M-F) 7:00-6:00, SAT 8:00-4:00. (602) 308-3080 EXT 3 ✖

PHOENIX—AAA ARIZONA, 15439 NORTH 40TH ST, 85032. WEEKDAYS (M-F) 7:00-6:00, SAT 8:00-4:00. (602) 308-3080 ✖

PHOENIX—AAA ARIZONA, 4046 E GREENWAY RD, 85032. WEEKDAYS (M-F) 8:30-5:30. (602) 230-3201 ✛▲○✖

PHOENIX—AAA ARIZONA, 742 E GLENDALE AVE #182, 85020. WEEKDAYS (M-F) 8:30-5:30. (602) 285-6241 ✛▲○✖

PRESCOTT—AAA ARIZONA, 1781 E HWY 69 STE 45, 86301. WEEKDAYS (M-F) 8:30-5:30. (928) 541-8600 ✛▲○✖

SCOTTSDALE—AAA ARIZONA, 14740 N NORTHSIGHT BL 102, 85260. WEEKDAYS (M-F) 8:30-5:30. (602) 248-3701 ✛▲○✖

SUN CITY WEST—AAA ARIZONA, 19802 R H JOHNSON BL #141, 85375. WEEKDAYS (M-F) 8:00-5:00. (602) 230-3301 ✛▲○✖

TUCSON—AAA ARIZONA, 6950 N ORACLE RD, 85704. WEEKDAYS (M-F) 8:30-5:30. (520) 258-0505 ✛▲○✖

TUCSON—AAA ARIZONA, 8204 E BROADWAY, 85710. WEEKDAYS (M-F) 8:30-5:30. (520) 258-0504 ✛▲○✖

NEW MEXICO

ALBUQUERQUE—AAA NEW MEXICO, 10501 MONTGOMERY BLVD NE, 87111. WEEKDAYS (M-F) 9:00-5:30, SAT 10:00-2:00. (505) 291-6611, *(877) 222-1020.* ✛▲○

ALBUQUERQUE—AAA NEW MEXICO, 9231 COORS RD NW STE 5&6, 87114. WEEKDAYS (M-F) 9:00-5:30, SAT 10:00-2:00. (505) 792-1938, *(877) 222-1020.* ✛▲○

LAS CRUCES—AAA NEW MEXICO, 3991 E LOHMAN AVE STE #A, 88011. WEEKDAYS (M-F) 9:00-5:30, SAT 10:00-2:00. (575) 523-5681, *(877) 222-1020.* ✛▲○

SANTA FE—AAA NEW MEXICO, 3517 ZAFARANO DR STE D, 87507. WEEKDAYS (M-F) 9:00-5:30, SAT 10:00-2:00. (505) 471-6620, *(877) 222-1020.* ✛▲○

𝒴our family's travel adventure begins with safe and well-designed roads. Visit www.AAAMakingAmericaStronger.com to learn more about what AAA is doing to ensure the nation's roadway system is there for you to get you on your journey.

MAKING AMERICA STRONGER

Metric Equivalents Chart

TEMPERATURE

To convert Fahrenheit to Celsius, subtract 32 from the Fahrenheit temperature, multiply by 5 and divide by 9.
To convert Celsius to Fahrenheit, multiply by 9, divide by 5 and add 32.

ACRES

1 acre = 0.4 hectare (ha)   1 hectare = 2.47 acres

MILES AND KILOMETERS

Note: A kilometer is approximately 5/8 or 0.6 of a mile.
To convert kilometers to miles multiply by 0.6.

Miles/Kilometers		Kilometers/Miles	
15	24.1	30	18.6
20	32.2	35	21.7
25	40.2	40	24.8
30	48.3	45	27.9
35	56.3	50	31.0
40	64.4	55	34.1
45	72.4	60	37.2
50	80.5	65	40.3
55	88.5	70	43.4
60	96.6	75	46.6
65	104.6	80	49.7
70	112.7	85	52.8
75	120.7	90	55.9
80	128.7	95	59.0
85	136.8	100	62.1
90	144.8	105	65.2
95	152.9	110	68.3
100	160.9	115	71.4

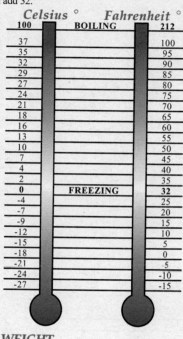

Celsius °		Fahrenheit °
100	BOILING	212
37		100
35		95
32		90
29		85
27		80
24		75
21		70
18		65
16		60
13		55
10		50
7		45
4		40
2		35
0	FREEZING	32
-4		25
-7		20
-9		15
-12		10
-15		5
-18		0
-21		-5
-24		-10
-27		-15

LINEAR MEASURE

Customary	Metric
1 inch = 2.54 centimeters	1 centimeter = 0.4 inches
1 foot = 30 centimeters	1 meter = 3.3 feet
1 yard = 0.91 meters	1 meter = 1.09 yards
1 mile = 1.6 kilometers	1 kilometer = .62 miles

LIQUID MEASURE

Customary	Metric
1 fluid ounce = 30 milliliters	1 milliliter = .03 fluid ounces
1 cup = .24 liters	1 liter = 2.1 pints
1 pint = .47 liters	1 liter = 1.06 quarts
1 quart = .95 liters	1 liter = .26 gallons
1 gallon = 3.8 liters	

WEIGHT

If You Know:	Multiply By:	To Find:
Ounces	28	Grams
Pounds	0.45	Kilograms
Grams	0.035	Ounces
Kilograms	2.2	Pounds

PRESSURE

Air pressure in automobile tires is expressed in kilopascals. Multiply pound-force per square inch (psi) by 6.89 to find kilopascals (kPa).

24 psi = 165 kPa   28 psi = 193 kPa
26 psi = 179 kPa   30 psi = 207 kPa

GALLONS AND LITERS

Gallons/Liters				Liters/Gallons			
5	19.0	12	45.6	10	2.6	40	10.4
6	22.8	14	53.2	15	3.9	50	13.0
7	26.6	16	60.8	20	5.2	60	15.6
8	30.4	18	68.4	25	6.5	70	18.2
9	34.2	20	76.0	30	7.8	80	20.8
10	38.0	25	95.0	35	9.1	90	23.4

494

© AAA

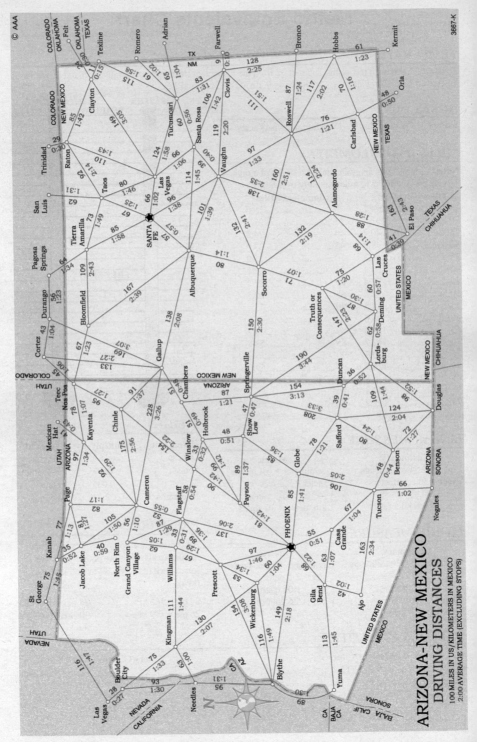

ARIZONA-NEW MEXICO
DRIVING DISTANCES

100 MILES IN US/KILOMETERS IN MEXICO
2:00 AVERAGE TIME (EXCLUDING STOPS)

3667-K

Border Information

Traveling to Mexico

FOR U.S. AND CANADIAN RESIDENTS TRAVELING TO MEXICO

Border Crossing Requirements: Travelers are required to present proper travel documents for travel to Mexico and to return to the United States.

Air travel: U.S. and Canadian citizens traveling between the United States and Mexico by air are required to show a valid passport.

Land or sea travel: A passport or passport card, or other U.S. official ID (not including a state-issued driver's license), is required to enter Mexico by land and sea. U.S. citizens returning to the United States from Mexico by land or sea are required to present proper travel documents according to the Western Hemisphere Travel Initiative. Approved documents include a passport or passport card, Enhanced Driver's License or Trusted Traveler program card; for more information refer to the U.S. Department of State's website travel.state.gov. Canadian citizens should refer to the Canada Border Services Agency website cbsa-asfc.gc.ca for requirements to re-enter Canada.

Children: Minors must be accompanied by parents, or have a notarized letter of consent

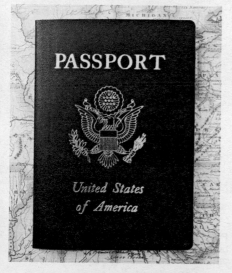

from one or both absent parents giving permission to go on the trip, as well as proof of parent/child relationship, such as a birth certificate or court document.

Automobile insurance: Full coverage from a reliable Mexican insurance company is required, including property damage and public liability. AAA offices in border states (along with offices in Nevada and Utah) can provide Mexican automobile insurance to members. U.S. automobile insurance is not valid in Mexico.

Tourist permits: When traveling to Mexico as a tourist you must obtain an FMM tourist permit. You must show proof of citizenship (valid passport, birth certificate and photo ID, or voter's registration card and photo ID) to obtain a permit.

Permits are issued at Mexican consulates in the United States and Canada, immigration offices at official points of entry and at Mexican tourism offices. You must have a valid tourist permit if you remain within the border zone—the area within 20 to 30 kilometers (12 to 19 miles) of the U.S. border, depending on the Mexican state—for more than 72 hours, or if you travel beyond the border zone.

The permit costs approximately $22 (U.S.), which must be paid at a Mexican bank (see the list of banks on the back of the permit form) or at a bank window at the border. You are required to show the "Fee Paid" stamp on your tourist permit when leaving Mexico. It is recommended that you obtain your tourist permit before leaving the United States and pay the fee at the border.

If traveling by air, the permit is distributed on the flight and the fee is included in the airline ticket price. If arriving by cruise ship, the fee is collected when disembarking or is included in the cruise fare if the stay is longer than 72 hours.

Exemptions:
- Visitors traveling by sea, staying less than 72 hours and remaining in the seaport.
- Visitors traveling by land to destinations within the border zone and staying less than 72 hours.
- Visitors traveling by land beyond the border zone, staying less than 72 hours and limiting their visit to the following

destinations/tourist corridors: Tijuana to Ensenada, B.C.; Sonoyta to Puerto Peñasco, Son.; Ciudad Juárez to Paquime, Chih.; Piedras Negras to Santa Rosa, Coah.; and Reynosa to Presa Cuchillo, N.L.
- Business travelers with a business visa; students (as defined by Mexican immigration laws) with a student visa (contact a Mexican consulate for business/student visa information).

Permit validity:
- The permit is valid for up to 180 days.
- A multiple-entry permit allows unlimited visits into and out of Mexico within the 180-day period.
- In Baja California a tourist permit is good for a maximum of 180 days per year and 30 days per visit.
- Permits must be handed over to Mexican immigration officials at the border prior to the expiration date; failure to do so may result in subsequently being refused entry into Mexico and/or incurring a substantial fine.
- A tourist permit not used within 90 days of issue becomes void.
- Visitors should carry their tourist permit with them at all times while in Mexico.
- If a permit is lost, obtain a duplicate from local immigration officials.
- Visitors not out of the country by the end of the permit validity period are subject to a fine.
- If you choose to remain in Mexico beyond the validity period an extension must be requested from immigration authorities prior to the expiration date.

Vehicle travel beyond the border zone requires a government-issued temporary vehicle importation permit and a promise to return vehicle form. These two documents are not required in Baja California unless the vehicle is put on a ferry bound for the mainland. They also are not required for travel to the following destinations in the state of Sonora: Rocky Point (Puerto Peñasco), Guaymas, San Carlos, Bahía Kino and other locations west of Mex. 15, as well as cities along Mex. 15 (Magdalena, Santa Ana, Hermosillo).

An Only Sonora permit is acceptable if driving is confined within the state east of Mex. 15 as well as south of Empalme (about 350 miles south of the U.S. border). The permit can be obtained at Banjercito offices in Agua Prieta (opposite Douglas, Ariz.), Cananea (on Mex. 2 southwest of Agua Prieta) and Empalme (on Mex. 15 at Km

marker 98, just south of the Guaymas bypass).

To obtain the temporary vehicle importation permit and promise to return vehicle form at an official point of entry (immigration checkpoint), the vehicle owner must have a valid (unexpired) tourist permit, a valid international major credit card and a current vehicle license/registration receipt (the original and two copies). Information on the application for temporary vehicle importation and on the promise to return form must match; the same requirements apply to both.

An administration fee plus tax must be paid with a major international credit card (American Express, Mastercard or Visa) at the official point of entry (mainland border crossing or ferry crossing from Baja California to the mainland) in order to receive a temporary importation permit windshield sticker. The credit card must be in the vehicle owner's name and issued by a U.S. or Canadian bank or lending institution. Vehicle owners who don't have a major credit card must post a bond ($200 to $400 based on vehicle value) with a Mexican bonding firm (Afianzadora) at the point of entry. Cash, checks, money orders or credit cards issued by a Mexican bank are not accepted.

More about temporary importation permits:
- Generally issued for 180 days, the same length as the tourist permit.
- Only one permit will be issued per person, for one motorized vehicle at a time.
- Carry the permit with you; do not leave it in the vehicle.
- Return permit, promise to return vehicle form and windshield sticker to Mexican customs officials at the Banjercito office at the border before or on the expiration date shown on the form, or be subject to a fine.
- If the permit or form is lost or stolen, Mexican customs offices can issue replacement documentation provided you obtain a certified document attesting to the loss from your homeland (U.S. or Canada) embassy or consulate.
- If you remain in Mexico beyond the authorized time period and without the proper documentation, your car will be immediately confiscated.

Pets: U.S. visitors may bring a dog, cat or bird into Mexico with government approval. A pet health certificate signed not more than

15 days before the animal enters Mexico and a pet vaccination certificate showing proof of treatment for rabies, hepatitis and leptospirosis are required at the border for each animal. A pet permit fee is charged at the time of entry.

Leaving Mexico

FOR U.S. AND CANADIAN RESIDENTS LEAVING MEXICO

When leaving the country:
- Temporary vehicle importation permits, promise to return vehicle forms and windshield stickers must be returned to Mexican immigration and customs officials at the border (or at an interior inspection point).
- Those entering Mexico with a motor vehicle must leave the country with the vehicle.
- At highway stations near the U.S. border, Mexican agricultural officials will inspect vehicles traveling north that are carrying any fruits, vegetables, houseplants and other plant matter.
- You must have an export certificate to take cultural artifacts or property items— i.e., pre-Columbian monumental and architectural sculpture or murals, clay figurines, original paintings or other works of art (excluding handicrafts)—out of the country.
- Valuable religious or archeological artifacts may not be taken out of the country.

Returning to the United States:

U.S. citizens returning from Mexico by land or sea are required to present proper travel documents; refer to the U.S. Department of State website for the most current information. Canadian citizens should refer to the Canadian Border Services Agency website cbsa-asfc.gc.ca for requirements to re-enter Canada.

U.S. exemptions:
- You may bring back duty-free articles not exceeding $800 in retail value from a stay abroad of at least 48 hours.
- The exemption is allowed once every 30 days.
- A family (related persons living in the same household) may combine exemptions; i.e., a family of six would be entitled to $1,600 worth of goods duty-free on one declaration, even if the articles claimed by one member exceed that individual's $800 amount.
- Duty must be paid on all items in excess of the exemption amount.
- Payment of duty is required upon arrival.
- Gifts taken across the U.S./Mexico border are considered to be for personal use and are included in the $800 exemption.
- Articles purchased and left behind for alterations or other reasons do not qualify for the $800 exemption when shipped at a later date.
- The $800 exemption may include no more than 1 liter of alcoholic beverages and no more than 200 cigarettes and 100 cigars.

Restricted or prohibited articles: To prevent the introduction of plant and animal pests and diseases into the United States, the agricultural quarantine bans the importation of certain fruits, vegetables, plants, livestock, poultry and meats. All food products brought into the United States must be declared. The U.S. Department of Agriculture also prohibits the importation of any type of pet obtained in Mexico. Visit the Animal and Plant Health Inspection Service at www.aphis.usda.gov/ or U.S. Customs at http://www.cbp.gov/ for more information.

One foreign-made article carrying a protected U.S. trademark (i.e., camera, binoculars, musical instrument, jewelry or watch) may normally be brought into the United States under your personal exemption, provided it is for your private use and not sold within 1 year of importation. Some perfumes are limited to one bottle and others are prohibited. If you intend to purchase perfume, inquire about trademark restrictions beforehand.

Articles considered detrimental to the general welfare of the United States are prohibited entry: narcotics and dangerous drugs, drug paraphernalia, obscene articles and publications, seditious or treasonable matter, lottery tickets, hazardous items (fireworks, dangerous toys, toxic or poisonous substances) and switchblade knives. Any goods originating in embargoed countries, including the following, are prohibited: Western Balkans, Burma, Ivory Coast, Cuba, Democratic Republic of Congo, Iran, Iraq, Liberia, Sierra Leone, Sudan, Syria and Zimbabwe.

If you plan to bring back any purchased articles made of fur or whalebone, any animal skin other than cowhide leather, or any product manufactured wholly or in part from any type of wildlife, contact the U.S. Fish and Wildlife Service's Office of Law Enforcement. The address is 4401 N. Fairfax Dr., MS-LE-3000, Arlington, VA 22203. Phone (703) 358-1949 for regulations, or visit www.fws.gov/le.

Alcoholic beverages: Both federal and state laws govern the importation of alcoholic beverages. When regulations conflict state laws supersede; know the import limits of your state of residence and the state of entry.

U.S. residents 21 years of age or older may bring into the United States 1 liter of alcohol duty-free once every 30 days. However, if you arrive in a state that permits a lesser amount than what you have legally brought into the United States, state law prevails.

Gifts: Gifts in packages with a total retail value not exceeding $100 may be sent to friends or relatives in the United States free of U.S. customs duty or tax, provided no recipient receives more than one gift shipment per day. Gifts may be sent to more than one person in the same package if they are individually wrapped and labeled with each recipient's name. Perfumes valued at more than $5 retail, tobacco products or alcoholic beverages may not be included in gift packages, which should be clearly marked with the designation "Unsolicited Gift," the gift giver's name and the retail value of the contents.

Duties: A flat rate duty of 3 percent is applied to the first $1,000 (fair retail value)

worth of merchandise in excess of the $800 customs exemption. A sales receipt constitutes proof of value. Family members residing in one household and traveling together may group articles for application of the flat-duty rate, which may be taken once every 30 days. Articles must accompany you to the U.S. border.

Canadian exemptions: Citizens who have been outside Canada at least 48 hours may bring back duty- and tax-free goods not exceeding $400 (CAN) in retail value. The exemption can be claimed any number of times a year. Citizens who have been outside Canada 7 days or more may bring back duty- and tax-free goods not exceeding $750 (CAN) in retail value. The $750 exemption can be claimed regardless of any $400 exemption taken on a previous trip and requires a written declaration. The two exemptions may not be combined.

Citizens may claim duty- and tax-free entry for articles (excluding tobacco products or alcoholic beverages) not exceeding $50 (CAN) in retail value when returning from a trip abroad of at least 24 hours. Items brought into Canada under a personal exemption must be for personal or household use, souvenirs or gifts.

Canadian limitations (on either the $400 or $750 exemption): 50 cigars, 200 cigarettes, 200 tobacco sticks, 200 grams (6.4 ounces) of tobacco, 40 ounces (1.1 liters) of liquor, 53 imperial ounces of wine and 300 ounces (8.5 liters) of beer or ale (equivalent to 24 12-ounce bottles/cans). All exemptions are individual and may not be combined with that of another person to cover an article valued at more than the maximum exemption. You may be asked to prove the length of your visit outside Canada. Keep dated sales receipts for goods or services, as they constitute valid proof.

All declared goods associated with the $400 personal exemption must accompany the purchaser to the Canadian border. Declared goods associated with the $750 personal exemption may follow the purchaser by mail.

While AAA makes every effort to provide accurate and complete information, AAA makes no warranty, express or implied, and assumes no legal liability or responsibility for the accuracy or completeness of any information contained herein.

Points of Interest Index

 Attractions appear at the top of each category
and offer a Great Experience for Members®.

Index Legend

HISTORIC SITES & EXHIBITS

OUTDOORS & SCIENCE

SHOPPING

SPORTS & RECREATION

TOURS & SIGHTSEEING

Photo Credits

Page numbers are in bold type. Picture credit abbreviations are as follows:
■ (i) numeric sequence from top to bottom, left to right ■ (AAA) AAA Travel library.

■ (Cover) Antelope Canyon, AZ / © Wolfgang Steiner / iStockphoto

■ **2** (i) © SuperStock / Alamy

■ **2** (ii) © Danita Delimont / Alamy

■ **2** (iii) © SuperStock / Alamy

■ **7** © Monashee Frantz / age fotostock

■ **13** © Adivin / iStockphoto

■ **18** (i) © Norma Jean Gargasz / age fotostock

■ **18** (ii) © Richard Cummins / Lonely Planet Images

■ **19** © MERVYN REES / Alamy

■ **20** (i) Courtesy of Wikimedia Commons

■ **20** (ii) © Everett Collection Inc. / age fotostock

■ **23** (i) © George H.H. Huey / Alamy

■ **23** (ii) © catherine lucas / Alamy

■ **23** (iii) © daniel grill / Alamy

■ **23** (iv) © Art Wolfe / Danita Delimont Stock Photography

■ **23** (v) © Frans Lemmens / SuperStock

■ **24** (i) © Danita Delimont / Alamy

■ **24** (ii) © Emily Riddell / Alamy

■ **24** (iii) © Stock Connection Blue / Alamy

■ **24** (iv) © Kevin Shields / Alamy

■ **133** © Richard Cummins / Lonely Planet Images

■ **136** © Richard Cummins / Lonely Planet Images

■ **137** © Anna Smith / Honey Bear's BBQ

■ **138** © Martin Thomas Photography / Alamy

■ **139** © Richard Cummins / age fotostock

■ **140** © Ron Niebrugge / Alamy

■ **141** © Richard Cummins / SuperStock

■ **267** © MERVYN REES / Alamy

■ **270** © George H.H. Huey / Alamy

■ **271** © Dan Leeth / Alamy

■ **272** © David Wells / Alamy

■ **273** © Gaston Piccinetti / age fotostock

■ **332** (i) © George H.H. Huey / Alamy

■ **332** (ii) © Ray Laskowitz / Lonely Planet Images

■ **333** © Ray Laskowitz / Lonely Planet Images

■ **334** (i) Courtesy of Wikimedia Commons

■ **334** (ii) Courtesy of Wikimedia Commons

■ **337** (i) © Chuck Pefley / age fotostock

■ **337** (ii) © Mark Newman / Lonely Planet Images

■ **337** (iii) © James Shive / Tandem

■ **337** (iv) © SuperStock / Alamy

■ **337** (v) © SuperStock / Alamy

■ **338** (i) © Ernesto Burciaga / Alamy

■ **338** (ii) © Ernesto Burciaga / Alamy

■ **338** (iii) © Peter Adams / age fotostock

■ **338** (iv) © Dennis MacDonald / Alamy

■ **495** © Garry Gay / Alamy

■ **497** © Danita Delimont / Alamy

Vacation with Peace of Mind

Experience an incredible vacation with amazing value on select *AAA Vacations*® tour and cruise departures. Includes our **Best Price Guarantee** and **24/7 Member Care** for a worry-free vacation.

Contact your local AAA Travel Professional or visit **AAA.com/Travel** for full details on these exclusive *AAA Vacations*® benefits.

Terms and conditions apply

514

More choices.
Bigger savings.
Easier booking.

- Hotel discounts up to 35%
- 24/7 access to live support
- AAA Diamond ratings
- Discounts and benefits from Hertz

It all clicks at AAA.com/Travel

For over 100 years members have counted on AAA for their emergency road service, maps, TripTik® routings, travel information and services.

Did you know that AAA offers **Insurance?**

Due to state regulations and local restrictions, insurance is not available through all AAA clubs.

Most AAA clubs provide a variety of insurance products for all phases of your life, at competitive rates from leading companies in their markets. Policies most often available include coverage for your:

- Automobile
- Boat
- Home
- Life and Health
- Home and Vehicle Warranties
- RV
- Trip Cancellation
- Travel Delay/Lost Baggage

Visit us at AAA.com or call your local AAA office today. One of our knowledgeable insurance representatives will be glad to help you with your insurance needs.

Insure With Someone You Trust®

What do these items have in common? AAA members spend less.

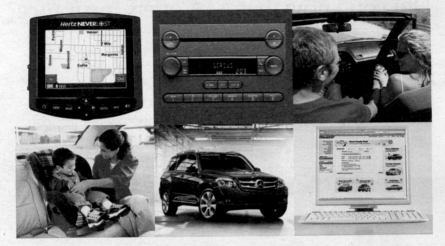

Hertz offers AAA members exclusive discounts and benefits including:

- $6.99 daily fee for Hertz NeverLost® GPS rental
- 50% off SIRIUS XM Radio® rental
- Additional authorized driver at no charge

- Free use of a child seat
- Special Internet pricing
- Member Satisfaction Guarantee
- 10% Off Fuel Purchase Option
- 10% Off U.S. prepaid rates

Show Your Card & Save®

SHOW YOUR AAA CARD AND SAVE

THE ONLY CAR RENTAL COMPANY ENDORSED BY AAA

hertz.com

For restrictions, visit your AAA office or AAA.com/restrictions.

® Reg. U.S. Pat. Off. © 2011 Hertz System, Inc.

| Visit | Over 1,100 AAA Offices | Click | AAA.com/Hertz | Call | 800-654-3080 |

AAA/CAA TRIPTIK MOBILE
Navigation · Gas Prices · Hotels

Free app for your iPhone or Android* device featuring:

· Maps and directions · Updated fuel prices*
· Hotel reservations function · Voice guidance for next maneuver
· AAA inspector notes for lodgings and restaurants
· Location identification for member AAA/CAA roadside assistance

Download it FREE Today
From the iTunes Store or Android Market*

**AAA.com/mobile or
CAA.ca/mobile**

U.S. users: scan this
tag to download the
app to your iPhone
or Android device

Get the free mobile app at
http://gettag.mobi

*Android version and fuel prices/locations available for U.S. users only.

518

Get It To Go

AAA Mobile Solutions for Members On The Go

Free Apps to access Roadside Assistance, Discounts, TripTik® information and Insurance services

GPS with AAA travel information on select Magellan® devices

AAA Mobile Web – compatible with most smartphones for roadside assistance, directions, maps and discount information

Learn more at AAA.com/mobile

Moments that Last a Lifetime.

Save on Theme Park Tickets at AAA.com/Discounts.

Ask your local AAA office about additional savings.

Valid membership card required.

Image compliments of SeaWorld Parks & Entertainment.

AAA Show Your Card & Save

AAA DISCOUNTS

Get the **AAA Discounts app** for iPhone and Android-compatible devices or the **CAA Savings app** for iPhone to find your way to thousands of member discounts. Save on shopping, dining, lodging and more. Get the best route there, plus driving directions and real-time tracking.

The app's Roadside Assistance feature enables members to send their GPS location when calling AAA/CAA for help.

AAA.com/mobile
CAA.ca/mobile

U.S. users: scan this tag to download the app to your iPhone or Android device

Get the free mobile app at
http://gettag.mobi

Get Involved and Keep Teens Safe
TeenDriving.AAA.com

Exploring the countryside or visiting a nearby city can be perfect opportunities for your teen to gain important driving experience. AAA can help you teach good habits and the rules of the road — before and after your teen learns to drive.

Find valuable resources at TeenDriving.AAA.com:

- Information about your state's licensing process
- Tools to help your teen improve driving skills
- Tips for teens to avoid distracted driving
- Downloadable parent-teen driving agreement

Plus, check out the free StartSmart teen driving program, developed by AAA and the National Institutes of Health.

Visit **TeenDriving.AAA.com** today. Get involved. Keep teens safe.

TOUCH, SEND, RELAX

Roadside

Free app for your iPhone and Android:

- Request AAA Roadside assistance without placing a call
- Have the app pinpoint your location and send directly to AAA
- Request a battery quote and replacement, search for AAA Approved Auto Repair facilities and more

AAA.com/roadside

It's how AAA members
turn a drive into a journey.

AAA members get exclusive values on
Hertz rentals in every car class ... ensuring
ideal wheels for every trip!

For offers and complete terms,
visit AAA.com/hertz or Hertz.com.

Visit: Over 1,100 AAA Offices
Click: AAA.com/hertz
Call: 800-654-3080

524

Great Rates!
Great Brands!
Great Guarantee!

*AAA members get best available room rates
with AAA preferred lodging partners.*

Best Western International
Up to 20% Off the Best Rates
Best Western
Best Western Plus
Best Western Premier
The Hilton Family
5% or More Every Day
Conrad Hotels & Resorts,
DoubleTree by Hilton, Embassy Suites,
Hampton Inns & Suites, Hilton,
Hilton Garden Inns,
Hilton Grand Vacations,
Home2 Suites, Homewood Suites,
and Waldorf Astoria Collection
Hyatt Hotels & Resorts
10% Off Best Available Rates
ANdAZ, Grand Hyatt,
Hyatt Place, Hyatt Regency,
Hyatt Summerfield Suites,
and Park Hyatt
Marriott Hotels & Resorts
5% or More Every Day
Autograph Collection by Marriott,
Courtyard, EDITION Hotels by Marriott,
Fairfield Inn, JW Marriott,
Marriott Hotels & Resorts,
Renaissance Hotels, Residence Inn,
Ritz-Carlton Hotels, SpringHill Suites,
and TownePlace Suites
Starwood Hotels & Resorts
5-15% Off Best Available Rates
Aloft, Element, Four Points,
Le Meridien, Sheraton, St. Regis,
The Luxury Collection, Westin,
and W Hotels

Show Your Card & Save
ASSURED STAY
Total Satisfaction Guarantee
Preferred Hotels

Over 1 million rooms to fit your budget
100%
Satisfaction Guarantee
Exclusively for AAA Members!

*Valid AAA Membership required.
Not valid with other discounts or promotions.
Good at participating locations only.
Other restrictions may apply.
Offers subject to change without notice.*

VISIT over 1,100 AAA Offices | **CLICK** AAA.com | **CALL** 1-866-AAA-SAVE (1-866-222-7283)

Your Destination Awaits

From quiet coastal getaways to bustling cities, AAA/CAA online travel information helps you pick the places you want to go.

Online Travel Guides

In-depth destination information with AAA/CAA Approved and Diamond Rated hotel and restaurant listings, AAA editor's top picks for attractions and events, interactive maps and reservations options

TripTik® Travel Planner

Turn-by-turn driving directions with maps showing AAA/CAA Approved and Diamond Rated hotels – complete with AAA Inspector notes and TripAdvisor® reviews – plus restaurants, attractions and more

AAA.com/travel and CAA.ca/travel
For complete trip planning resources

526

Online & On the Go!

Travel smarter with **AAA/CAA Mobile Web** for your smartphone.
Find a AAA/CAA Approved restaurant or hotel and get local event
and attraction information from our trusted TourBook® guides.
AAA/CAA Mobile Web also displays Show Your Card & Save®
discount locations, Approved repair shops and has
one-touch access to AAA/CAA Emergency Road Service.

**Go to AAA.mobi or CAA.mobi on your smartphone or visit
AAA.com/mobile or CAA.ca/mobile for more on-the-go solutions.**

 AAA/CAA Mobile Web

Scan this tag using your
Web-enabled smartphone
to access AAA/CAA
Mobile Web now.

Get the free mobile app at
http://gettag.mobi

We Do Everything But Jump On The Beds

AAA backs the Diamond Ratings in this TourBook® guide with our expert, in-person evaluations – whether the hotel or restaurant is no-frills, moderate or upscale.

▶ AAA/CAA inspections are unannounced to ensure our experience is comparable to yours.

▶ Only hotels and restaurants that meet our published standards are Approved and Diamond Rated.

▶ The Diamond Rating, from One to Five, describes the type of experience you can expect.

 We welcome your feedback at AAA.com/TourBookComments.

Get Your Car Vacation Ready!

Before setting out on vacation, have your car checked out by a dependable AAA Approved Auto Repair **facility.**

AAA
Approved
Auto Repair

Approved
Auto Repair on
AAA.mobi

Get the free mobile app at
http://gettag.mobi